PLEASANTON

10,000
VITAL RECORDS OF
CENTRAL NEW YORK

1813–1850

10,000
VITAL RECORDS OF
CENTRAL NEW YORK

1813–1850

Fred Q. Bowman

GENEALOGICAL PUBLISHING CO., INC.

Baltimore   *1988*

NOTE

This is the second volume in a projected three-volume series of vital records drawn from early New York newspapers. The first volume, *10,000 Vital Records of Western New York, 1809-1850*, covered the region of the state west of Geneva; this second volume covers the segment between Geneva and Utica. The third volume, *10,000 Vital Records of Eastern New York, 1800-1850*, will cover the remainder of the state.

Records in this volume are drawn from the marriage and death columns of central New York newspapers published prior to 1850. Birth announcements were not published in these early papers. Fortunately, many of the marriage and death notices made mention of birth years, birthplaces, and parents' names.

In this book bridegrooms and all those who were subjects of death notices are listed in alphabetical order. Marriage officials are identified in the appendix. All other persons mentioned in the text are listed in the index.

Towns of residence are by no means confined to central New York. Communities in the rest of the state as well as New England and the Mid-West are frequently identified. Occasionally found are references to "East Florida," California, "Burmah," China, and Malta, to name but a few of the more distant places.

The numbers given in parenthesis at the end of each entry are source citations. The first number (see map overleaf) identifies the newspaper; the remaining numbers (following the dash) refer to the month and day of publication, and less frequently the year of publication. Unless given in the citation, the year of issue of the newspaper is that of the vital record itself.

Except for *surv by* (survived by) and *inf s* (infant son) the abbreviations used here are those commonly found in genealogical writings. Unless otherwise noted all cities, towns, villages, and hamlets referred to are in New York. For the locations and histories of these communities and their related counties see J.H. French's *Gazetteer of the State of New York*, 1860.

Fred Q. Bowman

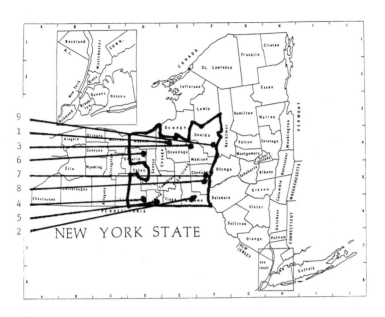

Central New York as outlined above covers an area larger
than that of Massachusetts and Rhode Island combined

Citation code number	Publication town	Newspaper title	Date span of review	Number of vital records secured
1	Baldwinsville	Onondaga Gazette	1846-1850	340
2	Binghamton	Broome County Republican (scattered issues)	1842-1845	83
3	Chittenango	Chittenango Herald	1831-1844	833
4	Corning	Corning Weekly Journal (scattered issues)	1840-1843 1847-1850	222
5	Elmira	Elmira Republican	1847-1850	268
6.	Geneva	Geneva Gazette*	1830-1849	3745
7.	Norwich	Norwich Journal (scattered issues)	1816-1830	103
8.	Oxford	Oxford Gazette Chenango Republican Oxford Republican Oxford Times	1813-1826 1826-1830 1833-1847 1845+	705
9	Utica	Utica Western Recorder Utica Daily Gazette	1824-1834 1842-1850	3722
			Total	10021

* Date span 1809-1829, this newspaper, previously reported in the Western NY volume.

(5124 marriages; 4897 deaths)

1. _____, _____ of Canandaigua m 1/1/32 Jane Hoes of Benton in B (6-1/11)
2. _____, _____ m 5/2/33 Cynthia Tozer in Athen, Bradford Co., PA (6-5/22)
3. _____, _____, an Irishman, d 7/24/49 in Havana, NY - cholera ("well at noon
    but died about 4 o'clock in the afternoon") (5-7/27)
4. _____, Jenny, 90, an African, d 4/9/18 in Coventry (8-4/15)
5. _____, Mary Ann (Mrs.), 22, d 7/14/50 in Elmira (5-7/19)
6. --ck, Frederick M., 1 yr, s of Alvin and Lydia, d 1/29/47 in Utica
    (funeral at home of his father on Spring Street, 3 doors from B'way)
    (9-1/30)
7. ___nson, Hannah, 24, wf of William, d 7/22/46 in Geneva (6-7/31)
8. Abbey, George T. m 10/11/43 Julia Mather, dau of William, in Utica; Rev.
    Charles S. Porter (9-10/13)
9. Abbot, Aaron B. m 1/8/44 Ann Eliza Thurber, both of Oxford, in O; Rev. J. T.
    Goodrich (Oxford Republican, 1/11)
10. Abbott, Albert of the NY, Albany, and Buffalo Telegraph Co. m 12/3/49 Mrs.
    Betsey Dustin, both of Batavia, in B (9-12/5)
11. Abbott, Elizabeth R., 10, only child of Rev. Gorham D. of NYC, d 8/13/50
    at Long Branch (prob. NJ) (9-8/19)
12. Abbott, Henry G., merchant, of Syracuse m 10/9/44 Mary C. Babcock, only dau
    of Dr. Charles of New Hartford, in New H.; Rev. Dr. Lansing of Auburn
    (9-10/9)
13. Abbott, Thomas S., 19, youngest bro of H. G. and W. E. Abbott, merchants,
    d 8/14/46 in Syracuse (Pall bearers were young men from Utica where he
    had lived many years; funeral at Cong'l. Ch., Syracuse) (9-8/20)
14. Abbott, William E., merchant, of firm of H. G. and W. E. Abbott m 8/12/45
    Jane A. Foster in Syracuse; Rev. C. Gold Lee. All of Syracuse (9-8/16)
15. Abeel, David (Rev.), 41, Chinese missionary, d 9/4/46 in Albany, NY (9-9/9)
16. Abeel, Elizabeth, wid of late Garret A., d -- in Catskill (6-7/31/33)
17. Abeel, Mary, relict of late Rev. Dr. Abeel, d -- in NYC (9-6/27/26)
18. Abel, John of Bath m 2/21/33 Eleanor Thomas, dau of Peter R. of Geneva,
    in G; Rev. Phelps (6-2/27)
19. Abel, John V. m 2/28/33 Sally Wheaton in Wheeler (6-3/13)
20. Abel, Martha, 35, wf of Lynden, Esq. of Utica, d 11/12/45 in Rome, NY
    (9-11/19)
21. Aber, Henry m 2/6/36 Mary Jane Tuttle in Bath (6-2/24)
22. Abercrombie, John, late of Picton, Canada West, m 7/18/50 L. Cleora Dustan
    of Utica in U; Rev. William Mygatt (9-7/19)
23. Abercrombie, William T. of Canasaroga m 5/7/33 Mary Lounsbury of Herkimer
    in H; Rev Picher (3-5/14)
24. Abrams (?), Daniel, 65, d 5/19/46 "at the Glass Factory"(in Seneca?)
    (6-5/22)
25. Achorn, Andrew m "Mrs. Kelsey", both of Greene, in G; Robert Monell, Esq.
    (8-5/3/14)
26. Acker, Joel m 4/30/35 Sarah Kuney in Fayette (6-5/13)
27. Ackerman, Maria, 31, dau of Henry M., d 11/15/35 in Fayette (6-11/25)
28. Ackley, Benjamin H. m 9/3/46 Kezia M. Squires, both of Canandaigua, at St.
    John's Ch., Canandaigua; Rev. John W. Clark of Palmyra (6-9/11)
29. Ackley, John D. m 3/21/44 Sally Ann Montgomery in Andover; Rev. Colburn.
    All of Westmoreland (9-4/6)
30. Ackley, Lyman m 2/5/24 Lydia Purple in Greene; Rev. John B. Hoyt (8-2/18)
31. Adams, A. B. m 10/18/43 Charlotte P. Merrell in Cincinnati, OH; Rev.
    Blanchard (9-11/21)
32. Adams, Abigail (Mrs.), 76, d 3/15/44 at the home of her son, Sanford, Adams,
    in Rome, NY (9-3/22)
33. Adams, Ann, 70, relict of late Thomas Boylston Adams (youngest s of John
    Adams, 2nd Pres. of U.S.) and 2nd dau of late Joseph Harvard, Esq. of
    Haverhill, MA, d 9/3/45 in Quincy, MA (9-9/8)
34. Adams, Anna, 34, wf of Albert, d 1/28/48 in Utica (9-1/31)

35. Adams, Benjamin T. of Bloomfield m 1/20/31 Jane E. Gibson in Canandaigua (6-2/2)
36. Adams, Catherine, 20, wf of Aaron, Esq. of Steuben, d 7/23/21 in S (mistakenly took a quantity of dissolved potash - thought it was glauber salts) (8-8/8)
37. Adams, Edward, s of William H., Esq. d 5/26/34 (in Lyons?) (6-6/4)
38. Adams, Eunice, 48, wf of Enos and dau of Joseph Frost, dec'd., d 6/11/49 in Havana, NY (5-6/22)
39. Adams, George m 6/8/42 Mary Ann Forbs in Chittenango; Rev. T. Houston. All of Chittenango (3-6/15)
40. Adams, Gideon, Esq., 84, d 10/1/26 in Pawlet, VT (His was the 8th family to settle in P; he was at the taking of Montreal in 1760 and fought in the Rev. War) (9-10/24)
41. Adams, Grant H., Esq. of NYC m 7/3/49 Mary M. Simmons of Utica at Trinity Ch., Utica; Rev. Dr. Proal (double ceremony - see marr of William White, Esq.) (9-7/4)
42. Adams, Harriet (miss), 16, d 1/20/33 in Bath (6-2/13)
43. Adams, Henry, capt of canal boat "Seneca Chief", d 10/6/26 in Albany (surv by a family in Ithaca where he lived) (9-10/10)
44. Adams, Horace W. m 2/22/44 Caroline S. Peckham in Rome. NY; Rev. G. S. Boardman (9-3/7)
45. Adams, Ira A. (Capt.), 31, of the steamer "Merengo" d 9/3/47 at the home of W. C. Adams on the coast below Plaquemine, LA (yellow fever) (9-9/22)
46. Adams, J. (Dr.), passenger, d -- on board the brig "Concord" on its arrival at Mobile Bay ("informed that his friends lived in Utica") (9-2/14/26)
47. Adams, John Q., 4, youngest s of Jesse, d 8/31/50 at Fly Creek (9-9/9)
48. Adams, John W. (Rev.) of Syracuse m -- Mary Phelps in Lenox (9-5/23/26)
49. Adams, John W. m 12/31/46 Delilah Elliott, both of New Hartford, in New H; Rev. Dr. Paddock (double ceremony - see marr of Thomas Lester) (9-1/27)
50. Adams, John Watson (Rev. Dr.), 53, d 4/4/50 in Syracuse (1-4/4)
51. Adams, Julia, 4, youngest dau of Albert, d 5/29/50 in Utica (9-5/29)
52. Adams, Mary, about 29, 2nd dau of Dr. Elijah, formerly of Geneva, d 12/26/31 in Catlin (6-12/28)
53. Adams, Melos (Mr.), 45, d 4/23/49 in Lowville (9-5/4)
54. Adams, Nancy, 36, consort of Francis, d -- in Utica (9-7/2/45)
55. Adams, Parmenia (Hon.), 56, d 2/23/32 in Attica (was for several years sheriff of Genesee Co. and a member of Congress from that county) (6-3/7)
56. Adams, Reuben Addison, 4 wks., s of Addison D., d 11/21/44 in Greene (Oxford Republican, 11/28)
57. Adams, Samuel H., 28, d 2/27/49 at the home of his father at Painted Post (member Painted Post Lodge 205, Indep. Order of Odd Fellows; surv by parents, a bro, and sisters) (4-3/7)
58. Adams, Sarah, 8, dau of Francis, Esq., d 12/13/50 at the home of her father in Elmira (5-12/13)
59. Adams, Seymour W. of Vernon m 10/10/43 Caroline E. Griggs of Hamilton in H; "Rev. Prof. G. W. Eaton" (9-10/13)
60. Adams, Vespasian m 9/12/41 Sophia Delany at Matthew's Mills; Rev. G. W. Thompson (3-9/22)
61. Adams, William (Dr.), 103, of Schenectady d in "Anapolis (state not given) (6-2/17/30)
62. Adams, William m 2/12/45 Betsey Loomis, both of Smithville, in S; Rev. J. T. Goodrich (Oxford Republican), 2/20)
63. Adgate, C. V. (Rev.), 37, d 2/4/33 in Penn Yan (6-2/6)
64. Adkins, Charles S. of Oxford, formerly of Brattleboro, VT, m 6/21/42 Harriet P. Moore of Rutland, VT in North Granville (Oxford Republican, 7/8)
65. Agan, P. H., editor of the Onondaga Standard, m 10/18/47 Hannah E. Stevens, dau of Hon. J. L. of Cicero, in C; Rev. S. J. May (1-10/20)
66. Agassiz, Louis, Esq., professor of the Lawrence Scientific School of Harvard Col., m 4/25/50 Elizabeth C. Cary, dau of Hon. I. G. of Boston, at the Stone Chapel in Boston; Rev. Dr. Peabody (9-5/3)
67. Aiken, Daniel, 120, d -- in Wexford, Canada (seven marriages - 570 grand-children and great grandchildren - 300 boys; 270 girls) (9-4/27/48)
68. Aiken, Henry Dwight, 20 mo, s of Rev. S. C., d 4/21/25 in Utica (9-4/26)

69. Aiken, James m 3/8/31 Adeline Cook in Palmyra (6-3/23)
70. Albertson, George W. of Elmira m 11/28/48 Hilinda Burt of Chemung in
    Elmira; T. S. Spaulding, Esq. (5-12/1)
71. Alden, Ogden M., Esq. of Springfield, MA m 7/10/44 Maria Weed, dau of
    Thurlow, Esq., editor of the Albany Evening Journal, in Albany (9-7/17)
72 Alden, Spencer B. m 6/5/49 Sarah Ann Flint in Utica; Rev. H. R. Clarke.
    All of Utica (9-6/7)
73. Alden, Timothy (Rev.), 91, d 12/13/28 in Yarmouth, MA (9-12/30)
74. Aldrich, Stephen, 68, formerly of RI and a member of the Society of
    Friends, d 10/15/40 in Cameron, NY (4-10/23)
75. Alexander, Charles H. of Winchester, NH m 10/16/50 Cheoffonette La
    Graschubbuck of Utica; Rev. Wiley, pastor, Dutch Reformed Ch. (9-10/30)
76. Allen, Abigail (Mrs.), 79, d 11/14/50 in Utica (9-11/16)
77. Allen, Adeline, 12, dau of Jefferson, d 10/31/48 in Utica (9-11/4)
78. Allen, Alanson m 9/9/45 Sarah Ann Stilson in Augusta; Rev. Orlo
    Bartholomew. All of Augusta (9-9/20)
79. Allen, Benjamin, 75, --------> d 8/20/48 in Utica (Deceased of Elyria, OH)
    (9-8/22)
80. Allen, Caleb m 6/29/33 Catharine Gunsolus in Wheeler (6-7/10)
81. Allen, Caleb, Esq., about 50, d -- in Millport (5-10/18/50)
82. Allen, Charles, 21, s of Shadrach W. formerly of Geneva, d 8/7/36 in
    St. Louis, MO (6-9/7)
83. Allen, David, 40, d 6/10/48 in Lansingburgh (formerly of Utica and of the
    firm of Stacy, Shipley, and Allen) (9-6/20)
84. Allen, David P., 28, late of Geneva, d 9/24/46 at the home of his bro-in-
    law, John C. Merrell, in Auburn (6-6/26)
85. Allen, Earl, 17, s of R. Allen, d 5/21/44 in Lenox (3-5/29)
86. Allen, Edward (Rev.), 50, Presby minister, d 10/6/46 in Fulton, Rock Co.,
    WI (formerly an attorney in Oneida Co., NY; moved from NY, summer, 1846)
    (9-10/23)
87. Allen, Ethan W., 37, d 12/16/33 in Butler (6-1/1/34)
88. Allen G.(?) E. of Rochester m 6/12/50 Lydia D. Rhodes(?) of Bridgewater
    in B; Rev. C. Graves (9-6/14)
89. Allen, George W., 31, of Ogdensburg d 3/18/50 at sea (9-4/6)
90. Allen, Hannah (Mrs.), 70, d 9/20/33 in Sullivan (3-9/24)
91. Allen, Helen Graves, 13 mo, dau of Elisha and Mary, d 7/13/48 in Utica
    (funeral at home of her father, 12 Washington St.) (9-7/14)
92. Allen, Henry m 4/26/32 Catherine Basset in Ovid; Rev. U. B. Miller
    (6-5/9)
93. Allen, Henry A., inf s of Isaac and Louisa, d 10/11/42 in Oxford
    (Oxford Republican, 10/21)
94. Allen, Ishac S., one of the editors of the Cayuga Patriot of Auburn, m
    8/18/31 Susan Mott of Skaneateles (6-8/31)
95. Allen, John m -- Catharine Larrowe in Wheeler (6-12/22/30)
96. Allen, John m 5/20/31 Cloe Allen, both of Ledyard, in Auburn (6-6/8)
97. Allen, John B. m 12/30/48 Catharine S. Murphy, both of Baldwinsville;
    Rev. Byron Alden (1-1/4/49)
98. Allen, John H. of Utica m 1/16/49 Elizabeth Dungin of Deerfield in Utica;
    Rev. H. R. Clarke (9-1/18)
99. Allen, John K. (Maj.), 27, formerly of Chittenango, d 8/15/38 in Houston,
    TX (moved to Texas in 1832) (3-10/3)
100. Allen, John W., Esq. of Cleveland, OH m 11/26/27 Ann Maria Perkins, dau
     of Gen. Simon of Warren, OH, in W; Rev. Curtis (8-12/28)
101. Allen, Joseph, 74, d 2/28/44 in New Hartford where he had lived many years
     (9-3/20)
102. Allen, Lovina (Mrs.), 54, d 3/5/49 in Baldwinsville (1-4/5)
103. Allen, Mary Elizabeth, 5, dau of Elisha, d 8/10/48 in Utica (funeral at
     12 Washington St.) (9-8/11)
104. Allen, Moses F. m 4/19/32 Sarah Ann Snedecar in Waterloo (6-5/2)
105. Allen, Nathaniel (Maj.), 51, of Richmond, Ont. Co. d 12/22/32 in
     Louisville, KY (had emigrated from KY to New England and had settled
     in Richmond "about thirty years ago") (6-1/23/33)
106. Allen, Solomon, "professor of languages in the college", d -- in
     Middlebury, VT ("fell from the new college ediffice") (8-10/22/17)

107. Allen, William, Esq. of Utica m 9/18/43 Mary P. Hallock, dau of Nicholas
     formerly of Utica, at the home of William Schram in Poughkeepsie (9-9/22)
108. Allen, William H., 33, d 6/12/48 in Utica (consumption - 3 sisters, 2 bros,
     and their mother also died of consumption "within a short time")
     (9-6/13)
109. Allen, William O. m -- Charlotte Saunders in Centerfield (6-10/16/33)
110. Allsworth, Daniel m -- Betsey Perkins in Waterloo (6-11/6/33)
111. Allyn, Henry, Esq., 43, late of Coventry "where he has left a wife and
     8 children", d 4/26/19 in Steubenville, OH (8-6/16)
112. Allyn, Henry Emmet, 1 yr, only s of Henry S. and Elizabeth L., d 11/14/49
     in Whitestown (9-11/17)
113. Almy, William A. (Dr.), 30, d in Mina (6-10/16/33)
114. Alshiemer, John m 8/5/50 Catharine Shaltz, both of Utica, in U; John
     Parsons, Esq. (9-8/10)
115. Alverson, Amy, 62, wf of Stephen, formerly of Seneca, d 4/27/32 in Perry
     (6-5/2)
116. Alverson, William, Esq., 80, d "late" at the home of his son-in-law, T. S.
     Faxton in Utica (funeral at 44 Fayette St.) (9-3/1/49)
117. Alvord, Elisha, Esq. d 7/10/46 in Lansingburgh (a long-time resident there)
     (9-7/11)
118. Alvord, Helen, 37, wf of Elisha, d 9/31/26 in Lansingburgh (surv by
     husband and "young children") (9-10/3)
119. Alvord, Henry J. m -- Henrietta H. Fitch in Le Roy (6-11/27/33)
120. Alvord, William D., 19, d 6/19/33 in Geneseo (6-7/10)
121. Alworth, William of Corning m 1/7/41 Eliza Guernsey of Mill Creek in
     M. C.; Rev. Wells (4-1/8)
122. Amerman, Henry B. of Sodus m 12/20/32 Cassandria Hawks of Phelps in P
     (6-1/2/33)
123. Amsden, Simeon, 69, d 8/18/32 in Phelps (lived there 39 yrs) (6-9/5)
124. Anable, William S. of the firm of Anable & Co. m 9/24/46 Olivia Williams,
     dau of late A. B., Esq., in Utica; Rev. P. A. Proal, D.D. All of Utica
     (9-9/26)
125. Anderson, _____, 2, inf s of William, d 11/26/32 in Geneva (6-11/28)
126. Anderson, _____ (Mrs.) drowned 11/17/33 (by falling in the canal) at
     Seneca Falls (6-11/27)
127. Anderson, _____ m 3/31/35 Margaret Mabie in Geneva; Rev. J. F. McLaren.
     All of Geneva. (6-4/8)
128. Anderson, Albert m 8/23/49 Harriet Eliza Heacox, both of New Hartford, in
     New H.; Rev. John Waugh (9-8/27)
129. Anderson, Andrew, merchant, of Rochester m 5/23/43 Cordelia L. Knox, dau
     of Gen. John of Augusta, in A; Rev. William E. Knox (9-5/24)
130. Anderson, Benjamin S. of Attica m 2/18/44 Elizabeth P. Ford of Fairfield
     in F; Rev. William Baker (9-3/26)
131. Anderson, Charles W., about 25, s of Daniel of Belleville, Jeff. Co.,
     d 2/28/50 in Yuba City, CA (9-5/9)
132. Anderson, Eliza, 72, wid of Dr. William and oldest child of Hon. John
     Sanders, deceased, d 6/21/50 at her home in Schenectady (9-6/26)
133. Anderson, Frances Ann (Miss), 21, d 8/15/36 in Canandaigua (6-8/24)
134. Anderson, James B. of Geneva m -- Jane E. Demming of Phelps; Rev. Strong
     (6-5/1/33)
135. Anderson, James B. m 11/18/47 Harriet S. L. Maines, both of Utica, in U;
     John Parsons, Esq. (9-11/24)
136. Anderson, John (Rev.), D.D., for many years Professor of Theology in the
     "As. Pr. Ch. of the U.S.", d -- in Buffalo, Washington Co., PA
     (6-5/5/30)
137. Anderson, Lydia, 26, wf of William, d 5/7/34 in Geneva (6-5/14)
138. Anderson, Mary, 33, wf of Josiah, d 10/3/31 in Geneva (6-10/5)
139. Anderson, Rossilla Antoinette, 7 wks, dau of James B. and Jane E.,
     d 9/18/46 in Geneva (6-9/25)
140. Anderson, William m 9/24/35 Eliza Newel, both of Geneva; Rev C. B. Coats
     (6-10/7)
141. Andras, Betsey, 48, wf of Giles formerly of Binghamton, d -- in Battle
     Creek, MI (2-2/23/42)
142. Andras, Frederick, M.D., of Plymouth m 9/14/28 Eliza Bunker in Sherburne
     (7-10/8)

4

143. Andrews, J. M. (Dr.) d 11/15/46 in Deerfield (9-11/21)
144. Andrews, John T. (Maj.) m 4/2/32 Eliza Andrews, both of Reading, in R
       (6-4/18)
145. Andrews, Libbeus, 75, d 10/21/47 in Homer (one of first settlers there)
       (1-11/3)
146. Andrews, Mariah, 2, d 12/26/35 (parents' names not posted) in Canandaigua
       (6-1/6/36)
147. Andrews, Mary (Mrs.), 56, d 8/15/31 in Milo (6-8/24)
148. Andrews, Ransom of Oxford m Julia Ann Barnes of East Greene in E. G.;
       Rev. G. W. Mead (Oxford Republican, 12/9/42)
149. Andrews, Rhoda (Mrs.), 84, d 12/20/28 at the home of Major Dickinson in
       Utica (9-12/30)
150. Andrews, Robert of Havana, NY m 7/6/31 Polly Mack, dau of Jonathan of
       Canandaigua, in C; Rev. Nelson Parker (6-7/27)
151. Andrews, Samuel G., Esq., postmaster of Rochester, m 5/19/42 Louise A.
Whitney, dau of late Wareham, in Rochester. All of Rochester. (9-5/23)
152. Androus, John Y. m 3/29/35 Harriet Parker in Seneca Falls (6-4/8)
153. Androus, Samuel m -- Lois Taft in Lyons (6-6/2/30)
154. Andrus, Delia (Mrs.), 24, d -- in Rochester (6-1/26/31)
155. Angeir, Charles T., 20, d 9/1/49 in Van Buren (funeral at Van Buren Center)
       (1-9/1)
156. Angeir, Dwight C. of Van Buren m 8/20/50 Margaret Dygrett of Pompey in P;
       Rev. James Smith (1-8/22)
157. Angel, Benjamin F., Esq. m 5/18/36 Julia Jones in Geneseo (6-6/15)
158. Angel, Joseph m 2/11/31 Cornelia Arnold in Hopewell (6-2/23)
159. Angell, George of Buffalo m 4/20/35 Elizabeth Lowthorp of Geneva in G;
       Rev. Bruce (6-4/22)
160. Anguish, Andrew m 12/22/42 Mary A. Skellenger of Eagle Village in E. V.;
       Rev. Knox (3-12/28)
161. Anguish, Elijah of Sullivan m 3/26/35 Nancy Thompson of Manlius in M;
       A. Nims, Esq. (3-3/31)
162. Angus, Maria, 18, youngest dau of Walter, d 8/14/31 in Benton (6-8/24)
163. Ansley, George m 10/1/35 Sarah W. Emery in Geneva; Elder John Sears.
       All of Seneca (6-10/7)
164. Ansley, Hiram m 9/11/33 Mercy Page in Seneca; Rev. Mandeville (6-9/18)
165. Anson, William m 11/17/33 Emily Rodman in Hopewell (6-11/27)
166. Antes, John J. of Cicero m 6/4/45 Emeline Ann Dana at the home of her
       father, A. Dana, in Kirkland; Bishop William Ottman of Clay (9-6/5)
167. Antes, John W. m 5/12/47 Catharine La Grange in Deerfield; Rev. N. Ferguson.
       All of Deerfield (9-5/15)
168. Anthony, Edward G., 19, late of Brooklyn, d 1/16/50 in San Francisco, CA
       ("remittent fever") (9-4/11)
169. Appleby, Leonard G. m 9/20/48 Charlotte M. Chase, both of Cato, at the
       Empire House, Syracuse; Rev. May (1-9/27)
170. Appleton, Julia, wf of Samuel A. and dau of Hon. Daniel Webster, d 4/29/48
       in Boston, MA (9-5/3)
171. Arden, Daniel D., Esq., about 45, formerly of NYC, d 1/21/32 in Washington
       (6-2/1)
172. Armitage, Erminia, 26, wf of Dr. B. B., d 3/4/31 in Ithaca (6-3/23)
173. Armitage, James, merchant, of Perry m 10/2/34 Eliza Magee, dau of Dr.
       Thomas C., in Tyre; Rev. A. D. Lane (6-10/8)
174. Arms, Ebenezer W., attorney, of Aurora m 11/12/35 Lydia Avery, dau of Hon.
       Daniel of Aurora; Rev. Cook (6-11/18)
175. Armstrong, Elizabeth, 62, wf of James , d -- in Seneca (6-5/14/34)
176. Armstrong, Frederic W., Esq. m 10/1/50 Harriet C. Bedloe, dau of late
       Henry, Esq., at the Ascension Ch. in Utica; Rev. A. N. Littlejohn,
       rector, Christ Ch., Springfield (9-10/4)
177. Armstrong, Henry, 47, d 1/17/50 in Litchfield (9-1/22)
178. Armstrong, Isaac m -- Mrs. Cinthia Willison in Genoa, Tompkins Co.
                                                          (?-1/28/29)
179. Armstrong, James of Vernon m 9/14/42 Elizabeth Sollis of Verona in Verona;
       Rev. D. Robinson (9-10/6)
180. Armstrong, Mary G., 30 or 50 (blurred), wf of William D., d 3/27/50 in
       Albany   eral at the home of Mrs. Patterson, corner Liberty and B'way)
       ("Rochester papers please copy") (9-3/28)

5

181. Army, David, 32, d 10/25/33 in Hopewell (6-11/6)
182. Arnold, Abram of Havana, NY m 8/9/32 Charlotte E. Morris of Seneca Falls (6-8/29)
183. Arnold, Augustus of Fulton m 8/14/48 Sabra A. Fuller of Sauquoit in S; Rev. C. W. Giddings (9-8/16)
184. Arnold, Barnum of Richmond m 10/24/33 Pamela Drowne in Canandaigua (6-11/6)
185. Arnold, John, Esq., 48, d -- in Tyrone (6- 6/25/28)
186. Arnold, Mary, 40, wid of Milo formerly of Utica, d 3/12/47 in Lexington Heights, Greene Co. (9-3/23)
187. Arnold, Oliver, Jr., 8, only s of Oliver, d 1/3/42 in Corning (4-1/5)
188. Arnold, William J. of Corning m 10/26/46 Harriet Kress of Covington, PA in C; Rev. Doane (4-10/27)
189. Arthur, Andrew m 4/24/46 Margaret B. Jemerson, both of New York Mills. in N Y Mills (9-4/30)
190. Arthur, John m 9/14/48 Elizabeth P_____ in state of Michigan; Rev. A. Cornell (9-9/25)
191. Asbury, Daniel (Rev.), 74, of the Meth. Episc. Ch., d -- in Lincoln Co., NC (9-7/19/25)
192. Ashart, Michael m 4/25/50 C. Ladenburger, both of New Bremen, at the parsonage in Lowville; Rev. P. Tyler (9-5/3)
193. Ashbey, John R. m 6/11/37 Sophronia Wood in Sullivan; J. French, Esq. All of Sullivan (3-6/14)
194. Ashcraft, Edward, 60, d 7/19/19 in Preston (8-8/4)
195. Ashley, William F., publisher of the Lyons Argus, m 2/18/36 Eliza Jane Denton in Lyons (6-3/9)
196. Ashman, _____ (Mr.), "agent of the colonization society", d -- in New Haven (6-9/17/28)
197. Ashman, Eli P. (Hon.), 48, late U. S. Senator from Mass., d -- in Northampton, MA (8-6/2/19)
198. Ashmead, William (Rev.), pastor of the 2nd Presy. Ch. in Charleston, SC, d -- in Philadelphia, (PA?) (6-12/23/29)
199. Astor, _____, 70, wf of Henry, d 7/3/33 in NYC (6-7/17)
200. Atcheson, Henry of Canandaigua m 11/4/33 Harriet G. Evarts in East Bloomfield (6-11/20)
201. Atkins, Amos m 6/7/32 Sally Ferrand; Rev. Smith. All of Chittenango (3-6/12)
202. Atkinson, Joseph m -- Eliza McFarland in Canandaigua (6-2/17/30)
203. Attwater, E. M., merchant, of Chittenango m 6/5/34 Elizabeth Budington, dau of A., Esq. of New Haven, CT, in N. H.; Rev. Dr. Croswell (3-6/24)
204. Atwater, Charles (Rev.), 38, (after 16 yrs in the ministry) d 2/21/25 in North Bedford (b New Haven, CT; grad from Yale College in 1805 (9-3/15)
205. Atwell, Peter, Jr. m 10/2/34 Marcia Spencer in Canandaigua (6-10/15)
206. Atwood, Lucius of Barre, MA m 1/30/44 Sementha Merina Atwood of Trenton, NY in T; Elder Thomas Hill (9-2/6)
207. Austin, _____, 70, widow, d 4/23/26 in Utica (9-4/25)
208. Austin, James m 8/26/28 Gitty Seer, both of Fayette, in Geneva; C. Shekell, Esq. (6-9/10)
209. Austin, Orin m -- Mrs. Amy Nye in Genoa, NY (?-1/28/29)
210. Austin, Samuel (Rev.), D. D., 70, late President of Vermont Univ., d 12/4/30 in Glastonbury, CT (9-12/21)
211. Austin, Zebell, 30, dau of William, d 10/25/30 in Newark, NY (6-11/24)
212. Auston, Jeremiah m 10/11/48 Silvia Ann Wing at the Buena Vista Hotel in Big Flats; S. Callender, Esq. (5-10/13)
213. Averell, William J. m 10/25/48 Mary L. Williamson, oldest dau of late Capt. J. D. of the U. S. Navy, at St. John's Ch., NYC; Rev. Dr. Berrian (9-10/28)
214. Averill, Chester, 34, A.M., Prof. of Chemistry and Languages at Union Col., d 8/7/36 at the home of his father in Salisbury, CT (3-8/17)
215. Avery, Benjamin F., Esq. of Aurora m 4/27/44 Susan H. Look of Utica at the Utica Female Academy (9-4/29)
216. Avery, Cyrus m -- Lucinda Jones in Pompey (6-2/23/31)
217. Avery, Daniel (Dr.), 81, d 11/2/48 in Sweden, NY (b Stonington, CT; one of first settlers, Bridgewater, NY; moved to Sweden, NY, 1816; helped form Cong'l. Ch. in Bridgewater; helped form Presby. Ch., Sweden (9-12/21)

218. Avery, Gardiner (Col.) 75, of Paris, NY d 8/17/49 in Saratoga (an early settler in Oneida, NY) (9-8/22)
219. Avery, George A. m 1/25/31 Frances M. Staunton in Rochester (6-2/9)
220. Avery, Humphrey J., 22, s of Col. J. H. of Owego, d 7/27/31 in Petersburgh, VA (had lived in Petersburgh about 5 yrs) (6-8/24)
221. Avery, John S. m 2/22/44 Caroline Hollenbeck, both of Greene, in G; Rev. J. T. Goodrich (Oxford Republican, 2/29)
222. Avery, Oren S., 41, d 8/3/36 in Perryville (surv by wf, 2 sons, and an aged widowed mother) (3-8/10)
223. Avery, T. H., attorney, m 4/14/47 Margaret E. Morris, dau of late Harvey, in Cazenovia; Rev. Daniel Putnam (9-4/16)
224. Avery, William m 12/19/19 Hannah Dixon in Sherburne; Rev. Joshua Knight (7-1/26/20)
225. Avery, William (Deacon) m 10/17/43 Juliett Brown; Rev. Brown (of Sherburne?) (9-10/27)
226. Axon, Robert m 5/9/48 Jane Dutcher, both of Upper New York Mills, in U.N.Y.M.; Rev. Dr. Paddock (9-5/18)
227. Axtell, Daniel C. (Rev.), pastor-elect of 2nd Presby. Ch. in Auburn, m 10/28/30 Maria L. Dey, dau of A. Dey, Esq. of NYC, in NYC (6-11/10)
228. Axtell, Daniel Cook (Rev.), 37, oldest s of Rev. Dr. Axtell of Geneva and formerly pastor of 2nd Presby. Ch. in Auburn, d 7/12/37 in Patterson, NJ (6-7/19)
229. Axtell, Henry (Rev.) of Lawrenceville, NJ m 9/7/30 Juliet Lay, dau of John, Esq. of Clinton, Oneida Co.. NY, in Clinton; Rev. D. C. Axtell (6-9/15)
230. Axtell, Stephen, 28, d 10/21/31 at the home of his father in Sodus (6-11/9)
231. Ayer, James C. (Dr.) m 11/14/50 Josephine M. Southwick, dau of Hon. Royal, in Lowell, MA (9-12/7)
232. Ayer, William B. of Utica m 4/23/48 Cornelia M. Hills of Oneida in Syracuse; Rev. S. J. May (9-5/2)
233. Aylsworth, Mary De Forest (Miss), 22, d 9/28/47 at the home of her father in Utica (funeral at 62 Fayette St.) (9-9/30)
234. Aylsworth, William, formerly of Canaan, Col. Co., d 8/23/26 in Clarence, NY (surv by wife "and a numerous family") (9-10/3)
235. Ayres, Lewis S. (Capt.) of Penn Yan m 9/11/32 Esther McLallen of Ithaca in I (6-9/19)
236. Babbit, Isaac, 76, d 8/8/33 in seneca Falls (6-8/28)
237. Babbit, Joseph F. of Havana, NY m -- Calista Kimball in Jersey, Steuben Co. (6-7/2/34)
238. Babcock, Benedict, 76, d 2/25/43 in Clinton (9-3/1)
239. Babcock, Charles W. m 6/23/41 Cornelia L. Cushman in Sherburne; Rev. Thomas Towell. All of Sherburne (8-6/30)
240. Babcock, Clark of Lawrence, Otsego Co. m -- Lydia Harrison of Vernon in New Hartford; Henry Sherrill, Esq. (9-10/15/45)
241. Babcock, Denison, 66, d 3/31/43 in New Hartford (9-4/5)
242. Babcock, George D. m 10/2/43 Elizabeth Clark in New Hartford; Rev. Moses C. Searle. All of New H (9-10/19)
243. Babcock, Henry of Earlville m 11/17/41 Margaret Becker of Sullivan in Sullivan; J. French, Esq. (3-11/24)
244. Babcock, Hurack(?) of Brookfield m 9/16/45 Sarah M. Desmon of Oxford in O; Rev. Bixby (Oxford Republican, 9/18)
245. Babcock, John H. m 10/4/32 Louisa Brace in Rochester (6-11/7)
246. Babcock, Laning (sic), about 30, d 9/14/31 in Hopewell (6-9/21)
247. Babcock, Oliver W. m 11/10/32 Bethia W. Jones in East Bloomfield (6-11/21)
248. Babcock, Sarah, 63, d 9/20/41 in Caton (4-9/29)
249. Babcock, William m 7/15/45 Mary Marsh in Kirkland; Rev. Dr. Norton 9-7/24)
250. Babwin, George V., U.S. consul at Tangier, formerly of Buffalo, NY, m 5/18/50 Nancy S. Ruggles, dau of Draper Ruggles, Esq. of Worcester, MA, in W (9-5/24)
251. Baby, James (Hon.), Inspector General of the Upper Province of Canada, d 3/19/33 in York, Upper Canada (6-3/27)
252. Bacife, Hartman (Capt.) of U. S. Army m -- Maria del Carmen Meade, dau of late Richard W., in Philadelphia (6-3/18/29)

253. Backus, Albert, 22, merchant, of Rochester and 2nd s of Rev. Dr. Backus, late president of Hamilton Col., d 2/24/19 in Montpellier, France (8-6/9)
254. Backus, Azel (Rev.), President of Hamilton Col., d 12/28/16 in Clinton (typhus) (8-1/1/17)
255. Backus, Charles Enward, 17 mo, s of Charles C. and Harriet N., d 4/19/46 in Utica (funeral from Mrs. Williams' Boarding House on Bleecker St.) (9-4/20)
256. Backus, Clinton L., 25, of Utica d 10/4/49 in NYC (9-10/5)
257. Backus, Elisha, 67, formerly of Utica and for 25 years a resident of Oneida Co., d 8/12/50 at the home of his son-in-law, R. H. Chapman, Esq. in Morristown, St. Law. Co. (buried in Utica) (9-8/15)
258. Backus, J. Trumbullof Schenectady m 4/30/35 Ann Eliza Walworth, dau of Chancellor Walworth, in Saratoga (6-5/13)
259. Backus, John (Capt.), 60, d 3/18/42 in Oxford (Oxford Times, 3/23)
260. Backus, Lucinda, 30, wf of Capt. John formerly of Norwich, CT, d 4/8/20 in Oxford, NY (8-4/12)
261. Backus, Oswald of Bridgeport, CT m 10/8/44 Susan Seymour, dau of Asaph, Esq. of Utica,in U; Rev. Ward (9-10/9)
262. Backus, Rufus, 62, formerly of Hudson, d 1/19/22 in Watertown (funeral sermon by Rev. Pitt(?) Morse) (8-2/6)
263. Backus, Seth A. of Ithaca m 7/5/37 Matilda M. Goodwin, dau of A., Esq. of Ovid, at Kidder's Ferry, Seneca Co. (double ceremony - see m of C. S. Day, Esq.) (6-8/9)
264. Bacon, _____, 9, s of Widow Bacon of West Bloomfield, d 7/4/22 (accidentally run over by the mail stage) (8-7/31)
265. Bacon, Alice, 67, relict of late Rev. David, d 8/2/50 in New Haven, CT (9-8/7)
266. Bacon, Alvin of Avon, OH m 10/14/40 Almeria Northway of Hornby in H; C. K. Miller, Esq. (4-10/23)
267. Bacon, Austin m 7/3/33 Janette Graves in Howard (6-7/3)
268. Bacon, Daniel D. (Rev.) of Wheatland, WI m 9/27/48 Sarah Averille of Chemung, NY in C; Rev. N. N. Beers) (5-9/29)
269. Bacon, Edmund G., printer, m 9/19/33 Catherine E. Bishop of New Haven, CT in Buffalo, NY (6-10/9)
270. Bacon, Eliza Kirkland, 7 mo, dau of William J., d 9/3/45 in Utica (funeral from father's home on Genesee St.) (9-9/4)
271. Bacon, Frederick Augustus, 3, only s of Charles C., d 3/9/44 in Waterville (scarlet fever) (9-3/12)
272. Bacon, Harriet, 25, wf of Charles C., Esq, and dau of late Col. John Williams, d 10/15/43 in Waterville (9-10/19)
273. Bacon, John m -- Hannah Lent in Junius, both of Havana, NY (6-9/24/28)
274. Bacon, John A. m 5/16/37 Harriet Smith; Rev. J. F. McLaren (6-5/17)
275. Bacon, John J. (Dr.), 28, d 6/28/50 in Ogdensburgh (9-6/29)
276. Bacon, Joseph F. of Irelandville m 5/30/33 Matilda Coles of Geneva in G; Rev. Justus W. French (6-6/5)
277. Bacon, Leonard (Rev.) of New Haven, NY m Lucy Johnson of Johnstown, NY in J; Rev. Wisner of Boston, NY (9-8/23/25)
278. Bacon, Mary, 35, wf of James formerly of Oneida Co., d 7/23/48 in Churchville (9-7/27)
279. Bacon, Sophia, 36, consort of Rufus, d 6/18/26 in Hamilton (9-7/18)
280. Badger, A. M. (Dr.) m 9/21/35 Elizabeth North, dau of Theodore, Esq, in Elmira (6-9/30)
281. Badger, Eunice A., 28, consort of H. E., d 8/9/42 in South Corning (4-8/24)
282. Badger, Harvey of Utica m 2/13/26 Sarah Tibbets of Rome, NY in R; Rev. Gillet (9-2/21)
283. Badger, Samuel (Maj.), 72, d 2/31/49 in Elmira (b in Mass.; moved as a child to Broome Co., NY; lived in Elmira 15 yrs until death; his wf d about 1824) (5-3/9)
284. Bagby, Thomas M., Esq. of Houston m 2/23/48 Marianna Baker of Baldwinsville in Houston; Rev. J. W. Miller (1-3/29)
285. Bagg, Abner, Esq., 73, formerly of Trenton, NY, d 12/13/48 in Detroit, MI (9-12/22)
286. Bagg, D. Taylor (Rev.), 33, late pastor of Madison Street Presby. Ch., NYC, d 1/15/48 in West Springfield, MA (9-1/24)

8

287. Bagg, Egbert of Utica m 4/11/49 Cornelia Hunt, dau of late Montgomery, Esq., at the home of Col. John Williams in Salem, Wash. Co.; Rev. George Leeds of Utica (9-4/14)
288. Bagg, G. W., Esq. of Utica m 6/21/48 N. J. Budlong, dau of David, Esq. of Cassville, in C; Rev. I. Lawton (9-6/23)
289. Bagg, Henry (Dr.) of Lowville m 11/4/46 Frances L. Greene of Lanesboro, MA in Albany (9-11/30)
290. Bagg, M. M. (Dr.) m 11/23/47 Marie R. Farwell, oldest dau of Samuel, in Utica; Rev. William H. Spencer (double ceremony - see m of Dr. H. C. Potter) (9-11/24)
291. Bagg, Moses m 12/9/35 Susan Tracy (dau of late William G. of Whitesboro), both of Geneva, in Utica (6-12/23)
292. Bagg, Moses, 65, d 1/9/44 in Utica (9-1/10 & 1/11)
293. Baggerly, Henry, 82, d 1/21/31 in Phelps (6-2/2)
294. Bagley, Albert G. of NYC m11/13/44 Eugenia Adelaide Bernard of Utica at St. Paul's Ch., NYC; Rev. Higbee (9-11/19)
295. Bailey, Adelaide C., inf dau of Rev. Lansing and Louisa M. of Shaftsbury,VT, d 8/31/50 in Utica, NY (9-9/3)
296. Bailey, Ama Louisa, 1 yr, dau of Moses and Frances M., d -- at South Bay, Oneida Lake (9-9/4/50)
297. Bailey, Chancey A. of Pompey m 7/22/49 Mary Lyons of Pompton, NJ; Rev. C. C. Carr (5-7/27)
298. Bailey, Charles S., 18, s of Col. B. P., d 8/27/40 in Corning (4-9/4)
299. Bailey, Edwin, 11, s of Lewis Bailey, merchant, of Whitesboro St., Utica, d 9/30/46 in Utica (9-10/3)
300. Bailey, Esther, 53, wf of Samuel, d 9/2/50 in Whitestown (9-9/4)
301. Bailey, Eunice Janett, 6, only dau of Welsey (sic) Bailey, editor of the Liberty Press, d 2/8/48 in Utica (funeral from father's home, 63 B'way) (9-2/10)
302. Bailey, James F. m 6/11/45 Cornelia Doolittle in Westmoreland (9-6/14)
303. Bailey, Jesse m 1/26/33 Joanna Andrews in Canandaigua (6-2/13)
304. Bailey, Joel Curtis, 4, only s of S. Alonzo and Catherine, d 12/23/44 in Utica (funeral from State St. Bapt. Ch.) (9-12/25)
305. Bailey, John m 6/11/45 Emily Seymour of Kirkland in Westmoreland (9-6/14)
306. Bailey, John m 12/25/50 Mary Swallow in Oriskany; George Graham, Esq. All of Oriskany (9-12/31)
307. Bailey, Lansing of Utica m 6/3/46 Louisa M. Jones, dau of Eli of Schenectady, in S; Rev. William Arthur (9-6/13)
308. Bailey, Lucretia, 2, dau of J. P., d 10/6/36 in Lyons (6-11/2)
309. Bailey (or Dailey?), Robert of Cleveland, OH m 12/7/47 Lucy Case, dau of G. Case of Utica, in U; Rev. H. H. Clarke (9-12/11)
310. Bailey, Sarah E., 24, wf of William H. formerly of Elmira, d 3/31/49 in NYC (5-4/20)
311. Bailey, Stephen, 81, (a Rev. soldier) d 8/15/44 in Whitestown (settled there before 1794 and one remained on one land site continuously (9-8/26)
312. Bailey, Theodorus, 70, postmaster of NYC and formerly member of Congress, d in NYC (6-9/17/28)
313. Bailey, Thomas m 8/20/50 Anna Roth in Utica; Rev. Leeds. All of Utica (9-8/23)
314. Bailey, Wesley m 8/14/33 Eunice Kinne in Manlius (6-9/4)
315. Baily, Azubah (Mrs.), 97, d 9/24/25 in Sangerfield (9-10/11)
316. Bainbridge, Cyrus m Ann Catherine Folwell in Romulus (6-7/7/30)
317. Bainbridge, William, Esq., 24, only s of Com. Bainbridge, d 6/3/31 in Philadelphia (NY or PA not stated) (6-6/15)
318. Baird, E. W. (Capt.) m Amelia M. Thayer in Ithaca (6-1/5/31)
319. Baker, A. B. of Kirkland m 5/16/30 A. T. Loomis of Westmoreland in W; Rev. S. Raymond (9-5/23)
320. Baker, Alexander F., 28, of NYC d 11/30/45 at the home of Samuel Hall in Utica (9-12/2)
321. Baker, Andrew, Jr. (Dr.) of Howard m 9/4/36 Ruth K. Marshall of Geneva in G; Rev. J. Chase (6-9/14)
322. Baker, Arthur, Esq., 26, late of Utica and oldest s of Mrs. Harriet Baker of Utica, d 8/23/46 in Dundee, Kane Co., IL (9-9/5)
323. Baker, Arthur Dickson, 2 mo, s of Hiram and Laura A., d 5/30/50 in West Schuyler (9-6/3)

9

324. Baker, Bazel, "a colored man", formerly of Geneva, d -- in Rochester
     (cholera) (6-9/19/32)
325. Baker, Benjamin R. m 10/27/46 Thirza L. Griffin in Marcellus; Rev. J.
     Tompkins (1-11/9)
326. Baker, Caleb (Hon.), 86, d 6/26/49 in Southport. Emigrated to this area
     about 1790. For many yrs judge of Chemung Co. Served in State
     Legislature and in Congress. (5-6/29)
327. Baker, David of Utica m 12/21/48 Olive Cummings of Frankfort Center
     in Utica; Rev. E, Francis (9-12/23)
328. Baker, Ebenezer C. m -- Marcia B. Stafford in Lansingburgh (?-1/21/29)
329. Baker, Elisha W., 32, printer, formerly of Cazenovia, d 9/19/42 in New
     Orleans (yellow fever) 3-10/19
330. Baker, Irving Dunning, 11 mo, s of Hiram and Laura A., d 11/23/44 in
     Schuyler (9-12/1)
331. Baker, J. C. m 11/1/48 Betsey A. Evans, both of Camillus, in Canton; Rev.
     L. C. Bates (1-11/2)
332. Baker, Jane P., 19, wf of John, d 6/3/50 in Camillus (1-6/6)
333. Baker, Jireh m 8/6/43 Mrs. Mary Warren, both of Syracuse, in Chittenango;
     J. French, Esq. (3-8/9)
334. Baker, John of Camillus m 1/24/30 Jane P. Brown of Baldwinsville in B;
     Rev. Byron Alden (1-1/31)
335. Baker, Joseph m 9/7/34 Rhoda Chase in Galen (6-9/17)
336. Baker, Junius m 10/28/35 Jane Beach (in Waterloo?) (6-11/11)
337. Baker, Mannana, 20, dau of Author, Esq. of Marshall, d 4/9/42 at the home
     of her mother, 61 Charlotte St., Utica (funeral from Grace Ch.) (9-4/12)
338. Baker, Norman C. of Rome, Leneawe Co., Mich. Terr. m -- Harriet Robinson
     of Rome, M.T. (both formerly of Manchester, NY) in Northville, Wayne
     Co., M.T. (6-2/17/36)
339. Baker, Richard (Rev.) m 10/5/35 Mary Baker in Elmira (6-10/14)
340. Baker, Shubel Nelson m -- Catherine Ann Mandeville in Sodus (6-6/26/33)
341. Baker, William of Lima m 9/22/33 Elizabeth Barnard in Canandaigua (6-10/9)
342. Baker, William m 8/31/49 Martha Sixbury, both of Utica, in Clinton; Rev.
     R. G. Vermilyn (9-8/3)
343. Baker, William K., 6, s of Dr. and Sarah Ann and grandson of Dr. William
     Kim____ (blurred), d 7/30/46 in Geneva (6-7/31)
344. Balch, Lewis P. W. (Rev.), rector of St. Bartholomew's Ch., NYC, m 4/10/39
     Anna Jay, oldest dau of Hon. William, in NYC; Rt. Rev. Bishop Onderdonk
     (6-4/17)
345. Balch, Rachel B., 29, wf of V. A. and dau of John Welles of Utica, d
     12/16/30 in Utica (V. A. Balch is of the firm of Balch, Stiles & Co.
     of NYC) (9-1/25/31)
346. Balcom, Ellen Maria, inf dau of H. Balcom, Esq., d 3/23/42 in Oxford
     (Oxford Times, 3/30)
347. Balcom, George of Oxford m 9/6/42 Florinda Keach of Preston in P; Rev.
     Elisha G. Perry (Oxford Times, 9/7)
348. Balcom, Henry m 1/22/22 Mary Honeywell in Oxford; Rev. Bush (8-1/23)
349. Balcom, Hiram, 20, s of Francis of Oxford, d -- (8-9/8/24)
350. Balcom, Keziah (Mrs.), 90, d 9/27/26 in Oxford (8-10/6)
351. Balcom, Samuel, s of Francis of Oxford, NY, d 4/7/23 in Martick, Lancaster
     Co., PA (8-6/11)
352. Balcom, Samuel (Col.), 75, d 8/27/47 in Oxford (9-9/2)
353. Balcom, Uri of Erwin m 9/8/40 Jane A. Besly, dau of Samuel, Esq. of Campbell,
     in C; Rev. Smith (4-9/11)
354. Baldwin, _____, 16 mo, child of Charles, d 7/16/26 in Utica (9-7/18)
355. Baldwin, Abel S. (Dr.) m 6/21/38 Eliza Scott at Trinity Ch. in Geneva;
     Rev. Pierre P. Irving (3-7/11)
356. Baldwin, Alfred (Dr.) of Benton m 10/15 Nancy Whited of Milton in Benton;
     S. G. Gage, Esq. (6-10/26/31)
357. Baldwin, Asa of Fenner m 4/3/38 Louisa C. Button, formerly of Hamilton,
     in Clockville; Rev. Randall (3-4/11)
358. Baldwin, Charles of Kennedyville m 9/19/34 Betsey McClain of Benton in
     Penn Yan (6-10/15)
359. Baldwin, Charles H. of West Boylston, MA m 11/5/46 Harriet H. Aswell
     Grosvenor, only dau of Francis D. of Utica, in U; Rev. Charles Wylie
     (9-11/9)

10

360. Baldwin, David, 74, d 4/30/41 in Fenner (3-5/5)
361. Baldwin, E. W. m 9/21/50 Catharine C. Campbell, both of Erin, NY; Rev. G.
    M. Spratt (5-9/27)
362. Baldwin, Electa (Miss), 17, d 6/9/30 in Macdonough (8-7/7)
363. Baldwin, Elizabeth, 85, wf of Hon. Simeon, d 7/16/50 in New Haven, CT
    (marr 60 yrs; surv by husband) (9-7/22)
364. Baldwin, H. M. (Dr.), 26, d 5/2/42 in Binghamton (2-5/4)
365. Baldwin, Harriet H. G., 22, wf of Charles N. and dau of Francis D.
    Grosvenor of Utica, d -- in West Boyleston, MA (9-7/1/48)
366. Baldwin, Henry of Orange m 7/31/50 Caroline Foster of Worcester; Rev. A.
    G. Lawrie (9-9/12)
367. Baldwin, Isaac, 25, formerly of Bristol, CT, d 2/5/36 in Lyons, NY (6-2/17)
368. Baldwin, Isaac (Maj.), 56, d 2/15/49 at his home in Elmira (formerly in
    state legislature from Chemung Co.) (5-2/16)
369. Baldwin, Isaac, 31, s of Lathrop formerly of Elmira, d 8/30/49 in Chemung
    (at outbreak of Mexican War, a resident then of Michigan, enlisted as
    first sgt. in Capt. Haskin's Co, Col. Williams' Regt.) (5-9/7)
370. Baldwin, Isabella (wf of William and dau of Ex-Consul Buchanan of Niagara
    Falls) d 5/21/50 in Toronto, Canada West (9-5/29)
371. Baldwin, James W., oldest s of Grant B. and lately of Elmira, d 10/24/50
    in Sacramento City, CA (5-12/13)
372. Baldwin, John m 2/17/47 Mary M. Showerman, both of Lyons, in Van Buren;
    Rev. T. Walker (1-2/18)
373. Baldwin, Jonas Sayre, 2, s of G. B. Baldwin, Esq., d 3/15/36 in Elmira
    (6-3/23)
374. Baldwin, Mary, consort of Daniel, d 1/7/29 in Macdonough (8-1/14)
375. Baldwin, Mary (Mrs.) d 9/25/33 in Rochester (6-10/9)
376. Baldwin, S. L. B., Esq., editor of the Newark Monitor, m 10/3/33 Abby
    Eliza Condit, dau of Joseph of Geneva, in G; Rev. Phelps (6-10/9)
377. Baldwin, Samuel (Dr.), 86, (a Rev. soldier) d 9/2/42 in Oxford (b Nov.
    1756 in Egremont, MA; survived attack of small pox in Montreal, Canada;
    in 1800 following wife's death he left W. Stockbridge, MA and moved to
    Wyoming, PA; after living briefly in Ohio came finally to Oxford in 1819)
    (Oxford Times, 9/7)
378. Baldwin, William of Guilford m 2/11/30 Louisa Boothe of Fabius in F;
    Rev. Horace Griswold (7-2/17)
379. Baley, Stephen m 5/12/49 Eunice Webster in Urbana; Rev. Mallory (5-6/1)
380. Balis, Henry G. of Whitestown m 12/10/45 Sarah E. Jones of Albany; Rev.
    D. W. Bristol (9-12/17)
381. Ball, Benjamin m 11/12/35 Eunice Bruce in Wayne (6-12/2)
382. Ball, Calvin S. of Pompey m 10/17/50 Sarah A. Hungerford, 3rd dau of
    Col. Anson of Watertown, in W; Rev. J. Brayton (9-10/24)
383. Ball, Frances S. Chase, 28, wf of Samuel R., d 1/22/50 in Marcellus
    (9-1/30)
384. Ball, Jonathan m 2/8/48 Martha L. Washburn at the Central Hotel, Utica; Rev.
    Samuel Ramsey of Clinton. All of Litchfield (triple ceremony - see m's
    of Joseph Ball and John A. Birdseye) (9-2/10)
385. Ball, Joseph m 2/8/48 Jane A. Howard at the Central Hotel, Utica; Rev.
    Samuel Ramsey of Clinton. All of Litchfield (triple ceremony - see
    m's of Jonathan Ball and John A. Birdseye) (9-2/10)
386. Ball, Samuel R. m 10/19/46 Frances S. Chase in Manlius; Rev. William
    Parsons (9-10/21)
387. Ball, Stephen (Dr.) m 9/27/31 Caroline C. Chase, both of Auburn, in A
    (6-10/12)
388. Ballard, Augustus L., attorney, m 5/24/49 Catharine Reynolds, oldest dau
    of Hon. Joseph of Cortland, in C (9-5/31)
389. Ballard, Elizabeth, 17, d 5/28/28 in Seneca (a sister mentioned but not
    by name) (6-6/4)
390. Ballou, _____ (Col.), 61, d 10/10/33 at his home in Fenner (3-10/22)
391. Ballou, _____ (Mrs.), 42, d -- in Penn Yan (6-5/4)
392. Ballou, Eunice, 86, wid of late Col. Benjamin, d 3/15/44 at the home of
    Charles Brewster (Eagle Tavern) (funeral at Broad St. Bapt. Ch., Utica)
    (9-3/16)
393. Ballou, Obediah, 77, formerly of Utica (an early settler there) d 1/21/47
    in Auburn (9-1/23)

394. Ballou, Q. A. m 11/9/46 M. J. Hill, dau of John, in Perryville (9-12/15)
395. Bally, Sylvester m 11/14/33 Polly Hervey in Hector (6-12/11)
396. Bamker(sic) Isaac m 9/9/30 Hannah Smith in Ovid (6-9/22)
397. Bancker, Abraham, 86, d 12/1/30 in NYC (9-12/7)
398. Bancroft, Anna H. (Mrs.), 28, d 10/21/44 in Rome, NY (consumption)
    9-10/23)
399. Bancroft, De Witt C., attorney, of Rome, NY m 3/31/45 Frances D. Bull, dau
    of Joseph of Westfield, MA, in Meriden, CT (9-4/11)
400. Banks, Benoni, 61, d 6/8/49 in Van Buren (1-6/14)
401. Banks, Horatio m 10/29/48 Martha Ann Adams, both of Veteran, at the Meth.
    Episc. Ch. in Millport; Rev. A. E. Chubbuck (5-11/3)
402. Banks, Tomlin M., of Cincinnati m 4/9/44 Clarissa L. Harrison,
    gr.-dau of late Gen. Harrison, in Sugar Grove, KY; Rev. W. Smith
    (9-4/27)
403. Banks, William, Esq. of Bainbridge m 5/23/19 Sally Mead of Oxford in O;
    Rev. Bush (8-5/26)
404. Bannister, Augustus m 10/20/31 Mary Vandemark, dau of Frederick, Esq., in
    Phelps (6-10/26)
405. Bannister, Charles B. m 4/15/41 Maria W. Lawrence, both of Fayetteville,
    in F; Elder Smitzer (3-4/21)
406. Bannister, Christopher m 11/24/29 Rebecca Simmons, dau of Capt. A., in
    Phelps (6-12/2)
407. Bannister, John m -- Temperance Simmons (dau of Capt. Abraham) both of
    Phelps, in P; Rev. Phelps of Geneva (6-9/15/30)
408. Barber, Gaylord m 12/14/36 Aceneth Hinckley in Lyons (6-12/28)
409. Barber, George, 44, d 5/14/43 in Westmoreland (9-5/20)
410. Barber, Ira U., Esq. of Sacketts Harbor m 9/24/50 Marilla Looker of Utica;
    Rev. William Spencer (9-9/25)
411. Barber, J. of Utica m 3/20/50 Betsey Rowell of Hamilton in H; Rev. Dr.
    Eaton (9-3/25)
412. Barber, John, Esq., 78, d 3/20/49 in Utica (funeral at the McGregor House)
    (9-3/22)
413. Barber, Levrett m 10/4/32 Sophronia Waite in Rochester (6-11/7)
414. Barber, Margaret, 18 wks, dau of A. H. and Margaret, d 11/11/46 in
    Geneva (6-11/20)
415. Barber, Mary Ann, 32, wf of Milo G., d 1/9/50 in Utica (9-1/12)
416. Barber, Milo G. m 11/6/50 Sarah E. Valentine; Rev. D. G. Corey. All of
    Utica (9-11/9)
417. Barber, Nelson m -- Betsey Thompson in Elmira (6-1/19/31)
418. Barber, Rosco m -- Hannah Ellis in Waterloo (6-8/14/33)
419. Barber, Sarah Ann, 1 yr, dau of Milo G. and Mary Ann, d 9/17/48 in Utica
    (9-9/20)
420. Barber, Watts of Homer m 8/18/47 Sarah M. Buell of Waterville in W; Rev.
    William W. Williams (9-8/20)
421. Barber, William, about 32, d 1/12/33 in Bath (6-1/30)
422. Barber, William A., 46, d 7/31/43 at his home in Vernon (b Ireland; for
    several yrs was instructor in English Dept. of the Vernon Academy (surv
    by wf and children) (9-8/7)
423. Barbour, Thomas (Col.), 89, d 5/16/25 in Barboursville, VA (father of
    present Secy. of War. Was an ardent Whig of the Rev. Made the first
    protest against the stamp act as a member of the House of Burgesses of
    VA in 1797) (9-5/31)
424. Barclay, Charles, 66, d -- in Lyons (6-3/17/30)
425. Barclay, John m 10/31/35 Betsey Bennett (in Waterloo?) (6-11/11)
426. Barclay, Thomas (Col.), late British Consul General, d -- in NYC (6-4/28/30)
427. Barclay, Thomas (Capt.), 53, of the Royal Navy d -- in NYC (6-2/14/38)
428. Barden, Henry (Dr.) m 3/24/36 Caroline Purdy of Benton in B; Rev. Champion
    of Penn Yan (6-3/30)
429. Barden, Olive W. (Mrs.), about 37, d 4/26/36 at Flint Creek (member Meth.
    Ch.)(6-5/4)
430. Barden, Otis d "last week" in Benton (6-1/25/32)
431. Bargy, Richard of Frankfort m 1/9/48 Elizabeth Young of Litchfield in L;
    Rev. J. Z. Brown (9-1/15)
432. Barhydt, David Parish of Boston m 8/30/43 Sophia Ellen Hackley of Utica
    in U; Rev. C. W. Hackley (9-8/31/43)

433. Barhydt, Jerome, 85 (a Rev. soldier) d 7/10/49 (in Schenectady?) (9-7/21)
434. Barker, ____, 5 mo, child of Newman Barker, d -- in Utica (9-7/11/26)
435. Barker, Alonzo of Kirkland m 2/26/45 Lucina Billington of Utica in U; Rev. Theodore Spencer (9-3/1)
436. Barker, Dorcas, 33, d 11/19/46 in Salina (1-11/23)
437. Barker, Edward C. m 7/3/46 Adeline Davenport; Rev. Charles H. Ewing. All of Geneva (6-7/10)
438. Barker, James, 73, d 11/3/26 in Madison (9-11/14)
439. Barker, John, merchant, m 10/29/35 Abigail E. Mills, both of Factoryville, (in Southport?) (6-11/4)
440. Barker, Marshal W. of Clinton m 7/10/49 Louisa McLean, dau of late William of Cherry Valley, in Cooperstown; Rev. M. Loomis (9-7/20)
441. Barker, Volsey P. of Camden m 6/18/42 Cornelia H. Bailey of Vienna, NY in V; Rev. George Gerry (9-7/1)
442. Barker, William L. m 4/17/33 Sarah Ann Sleighter in Vienna (6-5/1)
443. Barleson, Benjamin m 11/16/27 Florinda Kelly in Guilford; Rev. Bentley. All of Guilford (8-11/30)
444. Barlow, Harriet (Miss), 22, dau of late Jonathan, d 2/5/47 in Utica (funeral from the home of her bro, corner Water and Division sts.) ("Albany papers please copy") (9-2/17)
445. Barlow, Jonathan, 72, d 7/5/46 in Utica (funeral from his late home, corner Division and Water sts.) (9-7/7)
446. Barlow, Lydia (widow),92, d 3/26/26 in Lee (9-4/11)
447. Barlow, Nathan m -- Sarah Lyman (dau of William, D.D., of China, NY, formerly of East Haddam, CT) in Canandaigua (6-2/10/30)
448. Barlow, Sarah, wf of Rev. William formerly of Canandaigua, d 12/28/32 in Mobile, AL (6-2/13/33)
449. Barnaby, Alonzo E,, printer, of Ithaca, m 5/5/32 Fanny Reins, oldest dau of David H. late of NYC, in Ithaca; Rev. J. D. Carder (6-5/30)
450. Barnard, Charles m 3/27/32 Maria S. Andrews in Bethel (6-4/4)
451. Barnard, Charles O. m 9/11/36 Laney De Marsh in Sullivan; Jairus French, Esq. (3-10/5)
452. Barnard, D. D. (Hon.) of Rochester m -- Catharine Walsh of Albany in A (6-12/5/32)
453. Barnard, Edwin m 9/20/31 Charity Hamilton in Geneseo (6-9/28)
454. Barnard, George m 2/3/30 Laurena Torrance in Geneva; Rev. Martin. All of Geneva (6-2/10)
455. Barnard, George, 57, bro of Harvey of Utica, d 3/24/45 in Hartford, CT (9-3/29)
456. Barnard, Hannah, 102, wid of Moses, d 6/19/48 in Lenox, NY (Moses a Rev. soldier - fought at Bunker Hill) (Hannah b Simsbury, CT and with her husband was settled in Whitestown, NY by 1793; she member of Presby. Ch in Whitesboro; she had 9 children with son Edward of Rochester her lone child alive at her death) (5-11/3)
457. Barnard, Huldah (Miss), 55, d 7/6/50 in Westmoreland (a deaf mute) (9-7/25) (surname possibly spelled Bernard)
458. Barnard, Pardon, Esq., 57, formerly sheriff of Madison Co., d 5/29/41 in Lenox (3-6/16)
459. Barnard, Rufus m 1/6/41 Harriet Waters in Milford; Rev. Martin Marvin. All of Milford (4-1/22)
460. Barnard, Wellington E. of Sullivan m 1/25/41 Louisa Keene, dau of Samuel A. of Lafayette, in L; Rev. McCarthy (3-2/3)
461. Barnard, William, Esq., 85, (a Rev. soldier) d 4/18/50 in Milford (one of first settlers in Otsego Co.) (9-5/9)
462. Barnes, Ann, wid of late Judge Barnes of Philadelphia and mother of David M. Barnes, d 8/16/50 in Philadelphia (9-8/20)
463. Barnes, Anna, 70, wf of Rufus and mother of Rev. Albert of Philadelphia, d 2/25/45 in Rome, NY (9-3/8)
464. Barnes, Caroline (Miss), 15, youngest dau of Joseph, d 8/26/34 in Benton (6-9/10)
465. Barnes, Edmund F. of Rochester m 10/29/46 Caroline Gray, youngest dau of Joshua of Geneva; Rev. Dr. Abeel (6-10/30)
466. Barnes, Eliza (Mrs.), 28, d -- in Auburn (6-1/26/31)
467. Barnes, Enos m 6/21/32 Eliza Kilpatrick at Rockstream (6-6/27)

13

468. Barnes, H. P. (Rev.) of Ithaca m -- Susan Hopkins of Groton in Gorham (6-1/26/31)
469. Barnes, Henry m 4/5/33 Elizabeth Carl in Penn Yan (6-4/17)
470. Barnes, John, 94, d 8/4/39 in Benton (6-8/14)
471. Barnes, Mary, 55, wf of Joseph, d 3/24/37 in Benton (6-4/5)
472. Barnes, Rebecca, 39, wf of Dr. Enos, d 3/7/32 in Starkey (6-3/28)
473. Barnes, Samuel m -- Mary Sleight, both of Perry, in Le Roy (6-2/9/31)
474. Barnes, V. R. L. of Syracuse m 5/14/46 Sarah E. Trask of Marshall; Rev. J. D. Torrey (9-5/23)
475. Barnes, Washington, attorney, of Bath m 10/25/42 Louisa Birdsall of Greene in G (4-11/2)
476. Barnes, William m 5/31/45 Elizabeth Thompson in Syracuse; Rev. E. Bannister. All of Syracuse (9-6/6)
477. Barnes, William, Esq. m 7/10/49 Emily P. Weed, youngest dau of Thurlow, in Albany; Rev. Dr. J. N. Campbell (9-7/12)
478. Barnett, Mills m 3/16/50 Elizabeth A. Gardner, both of Clayville, in Mohawk; Rev. A. Peck (9-4/5)
479. Barnett, Thomas, 59, d 6/7/36 in Lyons (6-6/15)
480. Barney, A. H. of Cleveland, OH m 2/11/47 Susan Tracy, dau of Gardiner, Esq. of Utica, in U; Rev. McIlvaine (9-2/12)
481. Barney (or Harney), A. H. (Capt.), 26, d 10/17/48 in Utica (funeral and burial at his parents' home, Newport, Herk. Co.) (member Indep. Order of Odd Fellows, Utica) (9-10/18)
482. Barney, Nathan m 4/28/35 Ann McWhorter in Avoca (6-5/13 and 5/20)
483. Barns, Maria L., 43, wf of Erastus and dau of Stephen Mather of Utica, d 6/15/44 in Owosso, MI (9-7/16)
484. Barns, Sylvester m 10/7/47 Cornelia E. Parker, both of Westmoreland, in New Hartford; Rev. Oliver Tuttle (9-10/9)
485. Barns, William (Capt.) m 12/28/23 Sarah Squires, both of Harrison, in H (8-12/31)
486. Barnum, _____, wf of Caleb, d -- in Junius (6-3/31/30)
487. Barnum, Caroline Matilda, wf of Egbert W., d 6/21/50 at the home of her father, Lewis Benedict, in Albany (9-6/25)
488. Barnum, Charles R., printer, d 3/26/49 in Brighton (9-3/28)
489. Barnum, George Orrin (or Orris), 1 yr, s of Henry and Johannah, d 9/18/48 in Utica (9-9/20)
490. Barnum, Henry m 5/10/42 Mrs. Johanna Brand in Rome, NY; Rev. C. E ? ester. All of Utica (9-5/16)
491. Barnum, James m 11/7/50 "Miss Rowlandson"; Rev. I. Foster. All of Utica (9-11/9)
492. Barnum, Levi, 70, d 1/26/49 in Utica (funeral at Bleecker St. Meth. Ch.) (9-1/27)
493. Barnum, Richard S. m 4/9/45 Juliet A. Austin, both of Utica, in U (9-4/11)
494. BArnum, Sarah A., oldest dau of E. S., Esq., d 7/18/44 in Utica (funeral at 34 Broad St.) (9-7/20)
495. Barnum, Thomas B., editor of the Syracuse Advertiser, m 9/21/26 Clarissa Atwater of Canandaigua (9-9/26)
496. Barnum, Thomas B., late editor of the Erie Observer and formerly of Rochester, NY, d -- in Farmington, Oakland Co., MI (6-8/22/32)
497. Barrett, Barton T., 30, formerly of Waterville, d 2/19/49 in ___(blurred), Oneida Co. (9-3/1)
498. Barrett, Cornelia C., 28, wf of William, Esq. of Little Falls, d 3/28/49 at the home of her father, Noah Ely, Esq. in New Berlin, Chen. Co. (9-4/7)
499. Barrett, Harris, 30, d 8/24/30 in Lyons (6-9/15)
500. Barrett, Harvey, 45, d 7/18/39 in Chittenango (3-7/24)
501. Barrett, Helen, 14, dau of Widow H. Barrett, d 10/31/42 in Fenner (3-11/2)
502. Barrett, J. S., Esq. m 1/20/48 Charlotte M. Bennett, both of Camillus (9-1/24)
503. Barrett, Lucius, 32, d 6/25/44 in Utica (result of burns)
504. Barrett, S. L. of Cazenovia m 5/7/33 Eliza Shankland of Delphi in D; Elder Smitzer (3-5/14)
505. Barrett, William, Esq. of Little Falls m 10/15/45 Cornelia C. Ely, dau of Hon. N., in New Berlin, Chen. Co. (9-10/24)
506. Barrick, Benjamin m -- Nancy Thompson in Richmond (6-2/17/30)

507. Barrick, David d 6/28/33 in Lyons (6-7/10)
508. Barron, Mary, 39, wf of Fletcher J., Esq., d 7/30/41 in Lisbon, NH (3-8/11)
509. Barrow, Thomas, merchant, of NYC m 3/10/31 Mary W. Brown, dau of Henry C.,
     Esq., in Pittsfield, MA (6-3/23)
510. Barrows, E. S. (Rev.), 57, d 7/28/47 in Utica (9-7/29)
511. Barrows, Sarah M., 14, dau of F. F. of Milwaukee and gr-dau of U. Hollister,
     formerly of Rome, NY, d 5/13/50 in Beloit, WI (9-5/30)
512. Barstow, Samuel of Detroit, MI m Frederica C. Williams of Chicago, IL in
     Chicago (9-2/1/44)
513. Barter, S. S. of Smithville Flats m 10/12/43 Altha Hoadley of Binghamton
     in Greene; Rev. Ira Wilcox (2-10/18)
514. Bartholomew, Oliver (Deacon), 92, d 6/18/50 in Watertown (9-6/29)
515. Bartle, Alanson F. m 10/12/42 Christina Race in Oxford; Rev. E. G. Perry.
     All of Oxford (Oxford Republican, 10/21)
516. Bartle, John H. m 7/4/49 Elmina A. De Forest, both of Norwich, in N;
     Rev. M. Stone (9-7/21)
517. Bartle, Richard R. of Norwich m 7/4/49 Elizabeth U. Rifenbark of Preston
     in Norwich; Rev. M. Stone (9-7/21)
518. Bartle, Warren m 7/23/20 Mary Ingram in Oxford (8-8/20)
519. Bartles, Charles, Esq. of Flemington, NJ m 9/16/46 Eliza E. Randall of
     New Hartford in New H; Rev S. W. Brace (9-9/19)
520. Bartlet, Montgomery R., Esq., 67, formerly of Utica, NY, d 2/9/44 in
     Georgetown, KY (author of Common School Manual and other school books)
     (9-2/29)
521. Bartlett, Clark m 11/27/31 Eliza Closs, both of Lyons, in L (6-12/14)
522. Bartlett, Edward G. (Dr.) m 9/24/50 Jane W. Ball, oldest dau of Dr. A. L.
     of NYC, in NYC; Rev. James P. Thompson (9-9/30)
523. Bartlett, Jacob m 10/28/48 Lana Maria Vincent, both of German Flats, in
     Utica; John Parsons, Esq. (9-10/31)
524. Bartlett, Ruth (Mrs.), 78, d 5/26/45 in Sullivan (3-7/5)
525. Bartletts, Amos m 10/20/33 Nancy Kellogg in Ira (6-11/6)
526. Barto, Henry D., Esq. of Trumansburgh m 2/7/30 Mrs. Frances Montgomery
     of Lodi; Rev. Asa Bennett (6-2/10)
527. Barton, E. H. of the firm of Gregory and Barton m 2/12/33 Angenett Crocker
     in Canastota; Rev. E. A. Frasier. All of Canastota (3-2/12)
528. Barton, Francis N. (Sir) Lt. Gov. of Lower Canada, d -- in Ireland
     (6-4/4/32)
529. Barton, Samuel m 2/15/44 Lydia Rice of Pompey in Chittenango; Rev. James
     Abell (double ceremony - see m of James Nichols) (3-2/21)
530. Barton, William of Brooklyn m 12/19/48 Cornelia M. Churchill, dau of Charles,
     Esq. of Utica, in U; Rev. George Leeds (9-12/20)
531. Bascom, Cornelia C., 25, wf of E. H. of Southampton, MA and dau of Miller
     Babbit of Waterville, NY, d 11/1/43 in Waterville (9-11/11)
532. Bascom, E. H. of Southampton, MA m 7/13/42 Cornelia C. Babbott, dau of
     Miller Babbott of Waterville, NY, in W; Rev. John B. Fish (9-7/15)
533. Bascom, Eliza, wf of Ansel, Esq. and dau of late Isaac Sherwood of Auburn,
     d 6/7/45 at Seneca Falls (9-6/14)
534. Bates, Archibald, 76, d 1/11/38 in Cazenovia (3-1/17)
535. Bates, Asher B., attorney, of Detroit, MI m 10/24/32 Lucilla Beals, dau of
     Thomas, Esq. of Canandaigua, in C (6-11/7)
536. Bates, Asher B. of Jackson, MI m 12/6/43 Elizabeth G. Judd, dau of Dr. E.
     Judd, formerly of Oneida Co., NY, in Troy, MI; Rev. Norman Tucker
     (9-12/20)
537. Bates, Caroline (Miss), 26, d 7/30/45 in Boonville (9-8/13)
538. Bates, Cecilia A., 21, wf of John of Chittenango, d 1/11/38 in Sullivan
     (3-1/17)
539. Bates, David L., Esq., 63, d 11/3/38 in Brighton (6-11/28)
540. Bates, George C., Esq., formerly of Canandaigua, m 5/25/36 Mrs. Ellen Marion
     Wolcott in Detroit, MI (6-6/15)
541. Bates, John of the firm of Sims and Bates, m 11/8/37 Cecilia Hubbell of
     Sullivan in Fayetteville; Rev. Orin Hyde (3-11/15)
542. Bates, John of the firm of Sims and Bates, merchants, m 12/2/38 Charlotte
     Ehle, dau of Col. George, in Chittenango; Rev. James Abell. All of
     Chittenango (3-12/5)
543. Bates, Josiah m 12/19/32 Harriet Hopkins in Benton (6-1/2/33)

544. Bates, Orlando of Ridgeway m -- Irene Spear, dau of Abraham, in Macedon (6-3/3/30)
545. Bates, William, recently a merchant in Cazenovia, d 1/19/37 in Bloomington, IN (3-2/8)
546. Battel, A. T. m 9/24/45 Harriet Storrs, dau of S., Esq; Rev. Theodore Spencer. All of Utica (9-9/25)
547. Battel, Harriet B., 25, wf of A. T., d 9/3/48 in Utica (funeral from her late home, 54 Whitesboro St.) (9-9/5)
548. Battel(?), James, 89, (a Rev. soldier from Roxbury, MA at age 15) d 3/3/48 in Syracuse (9-3/6)
549. Battell, Albert T. of Utica m 9/18/50 Mary M. Fuller of Buffalo at 1st Presby. Ch., Buffalo; Rev. Dr. Thompson (9-9/23)
550. Batterson, Abijah, 71, d 1/24/35 in Chemung where he had lived for more than 40 yrs (6-4/22)
551. Battey, W. P. m 2/7/43 Josephine J. Turner, only dau of Henry W., dec'd., in Utica; Rev. Thomas Martin. All of Utica (9-2/15)
552. Battle, Thomas, 45, d 10/6/26 in Lyons (fell from a canal boat) (9-10/10)
553. Baum, Artemus m 3/4/47 Betsey Snowe(?) in Baldwinsville; Rev. T. Walker. All of Cicero (1-3/10)
554. Baxter, David m 1/22/49 Emeline S. Inman in Little Falls; Rev. Samuel Orvis (9-1/26)
555. Baxter, George Washington, 9 mo, youngest s of John and Sarah, d 8/11/46 in Utica (funeral at 234 Genesee St.) (9-8/12)
556. Baxter, Henry B. of Italy, NY m 10/17/50 Hannah Smith of Newville in N; Rev. A. H. Parmelee (4-10/23)
557. Baxter, Jane (Mrs.), 83, mother of John, d 11/24/48 in Utica (lived in Oneida Co. 52 yrs and in Utica 45 yrs) (funeral at home of John Baxter, 234 Genesee St.) (9-11/25)
558. Baxter, John, Esq. of the firm of Baxter and Hull m 6/29/42 Mrs. Sarah Baxter of Utica in U; Rev. A. B. Grosh (9-6/30)
559. Baxter, William m 11/8/32 Mary White in Benton (6-11/28)
560. Bayard, William, Esq. of firm of Le Roy, Bayard & Co. of NYC, d 9/18/26 at his home in Westchester (9-9/26)
561. Bayard, William M., Esq. m 7/14/35 Rumania Dashiell of Louisville, KY in Seneca Falls, NY; Rev. George Dashiell (6-7/15)
562. Bayeux, Thomas, Esq., 42, d 6/4/44 in Albany (one of the founders and first commanders of the Burgesses Corps of Albany) (9-6/7)
563. Bayles, William m 2/18/35 Jane Hamilton, both of Urbana, in U (6-3/4)
564. Bayley, Clarence S., 41, d 8/17/49 in Baldwinsville (1-8/23)
565. Bayly, Elizabeth (Mrs.), 72, mother of Col. R. M. of Geneva, d 3/26/32 in Washington, D.C. (6-4/4)
566. Bayly, Harriet, 39, wf of Richard M. and dau of Reuben Swift formerly of Waterloo, d 9/15/37 (6-9/20)
567. Bayly, Mountjoy (Gen.), 81, father of Col. R. M. of Geneva, NY and "formerly a resident in this neighborhood", d 3/22/36 in Washington, D.C. (6-3/30)
568. Beach, _____, 1 yr, child of Elias, d 1/14/32 in Geneva (6-1/18)
569. Beach, Alfred B. (Rev.) m 10/13/47 Catharine Russell Nelson, oldest dau of Judge Nelson, at Christ Ch., Cooperstown; Rev. Amos B. Beach (9-10/20)
570. Beach, Charles F. m 9/25/50 Elizabeth T. Ives, dau of William, Esq. of Utica, in U; Rev. D. G. Corey (9-9/28)
571. Beach, Charles Rollin, 38, printer, d 9/12/26 in Buffalo, NY (b in VT; published a newspaper in Bermuda) (9-10/3)
572. Beach, Chauncey, printer, 54, d 6/2/45 in Rochester (9-6/5)
573. Beach, Eliphal, 50, wf of Dr. Thomas, both of Victor, d in Adrian, MI during a visit there (6-11/20/33)
574. Beach, Eliza Skaats, 2, only dau of Elias and Lucinda, d 1/30/35 in Geneva (6-2/11)
575. Beach, Erastus of Seneca Falls m -- Catharine Walters of Waterloo in W 6-3/9/31)
576. Beach, George C. m 8/24/30 Mary Ann Covert, youngest dau of late Col. Rynear, in Ovid; Rev. Abraham Brokaw (6-9/8)
577. Beach, Hervey F., merchant, of firm of H. F. Beach & Co. of Utica d 3/1/25 in Auburn (died one week before his scheduled marriage date)(9-3/8)

16

578. Beach, Huldah A., 66, d 9/13/48 in Utica (funeral from her late home, 95 Fayette St.) (9-9/15)
579. Beach, Jane (Miss), 19, d 6/23/47 in Rochester (third death in this family within three weeks - all from measles) (9-6/26)
580. Beach, John m 3/30/50 Sarah J. Ellis in Baldwinsville; Rev. A. Wells. All of B'ville (1-4/4)
581. Beach, John Henry, Esq. of Saratoga Springs, NY d 5/9/50 in San Francisco, CA (9-6/26)
582. Beach, Mary, 73, relict of late Abner, d 2/5/32 in Hopewell (6-2/15)
583. Beach, Richard, 2, s of Richard, d 3/7/48 in Delhi, NY (1-3/22)
584. Beach, Richard M., 33, d 12/4/49 in Baldwinsville (consumption) (1-12/6)
585. Beal, Arzula, 8, dau of Edward, d 5/15/35 in Jerusalem, NY (6-5/27)
586. Beal, Ezra R. m 1/27/31 Catharine Catner in Wheeler (6-2/16)
587. Beal, Moses, Esq. m 3/20/36 Phebe Maria Moore in Italy, NY (6-3/30)
588. Bealls, Joshua, Esq., 62, a Judge of Jefferson Co. common pleas court, d -- in Ellisburgh (8-10/22/17)
589. Beaman, Dexter m 11/6/33 Corlistia Franklin in Caneadea, Alleg. Co. (6-11/20)
590. Beaman, Horace m 9/21/34 Susan Lewis in Bath (6-10/8)
591. Bear, Launcelot S., 30, d -- in Fayette (6-3/24/30)
592. Beard, James m 9/22/36 Mary Peebles in Painted Post (6-10/12)
593. Beard, Sarah A. Woodbury (Miss), 14, dau of B. F. late of Utica, d 2/18/50 in Utica (funeral at her mother's residence, Orphan's Asylum, Genesee St.) (9-2/20)
594. Beardesley, Peter S. of Honesdale, PA m 12/4/50 Emeline Hammond of Horseheads, NY in H; Rev. C. C. Carr (5-12/6)
595. Beardsley, Arthur M. of Utica m 4/18/50 Louise H. Adams of Norwich, CT in N; Rev. William Morgan (9-4/22)
596. Beardsley, C. C. (Rev.) of Stockton m 10/24/30 Clarissa P. Rust of Sennet in S; Rev. Brace (9-11/2)
597. Beardsley, Morgan I. (Maj.), teller of the Utica Branch Bank, Canandaigua, m -- Sarah M. Williams at Cherry Valley (6-2/24/30)
598. Beardsley, Morgan L., late teller of the Utica Branch Bank in Canandaigua, d -- at Cherry Valley (6-9/28/31)
599. Beary, Henry d 1/8/36 in Fayette (6-1/27)
600. Beattie, Sarah Jane, inf dau of W. D. Beattie, principal of the Oxford Academy, d 6/12/29 in Oxford (8-6/17)
601. Beaumont, Joseph H. m 6/19/30 Ann Maria Brown in Benton (6-7/7)
602. Bebee, William (Capt.) of Sullivan d 10/30/31 (3-11/1)
603. Becker, Caty Maria, 34, 2nd dau of Conrad C. formerly of Montgomery, d 8/26/30 at Natural Bridge, Jeff. Co. (9-10/26)
604. Becker, Henry of Clay m -- Esther Rhodes of Schroepel, Oswego Co. at the home of A. Becker in Schroepel; Rev. H. Warner (groom, 80; bride, 74; and the Rev., 71) (9-12/25/49)
605. Beckwith, A. B. of Bath m 9/29/40 Martha C. Thompson of Painted Post in P. P.; Rev. John Smith (4-10/2)
606. Beckwith, Asahel of Chittenango m 10/22/34 Harriet A. Seymour of New Hartford in New H.; Rev. Coe (3-11/4)
607. Beckwith, Barak (Hon.), about 62, formerly a judge of the Madison Co. court, d 4/11/44 in Cazenovia (3-4/17)
608. Beckwith, Barek (Judge), 64, d 2/12/44 in Cazenovia (9-4/22)
609. Beckwith, Francis J. m 11/27/45 Caroline A. Loomis in Utica; Rev. D. W. Bristol. All of Utica (9-12/2)
610. Beckwith, Francis J., 28, d 8/9/46 in Utica (funeral from his late home, 4 Blandina St.) (9-8/10)
611. Beckwith, Hannah, wf of William, d 3/16/50 in Troy (consumption). Isadorah, their dau, age 1, d 3/4. (9-3/20)
612. Beckwith, Henry, 76, d 3/20/50 in Elmira (one of the first settlers there) (5-3/22)
613. Beckwith, Leva (Miss), 39, sister of Asahel of Chittenango, d 6/18/37 in Chittenango (3-6/21)
614. Beckwith, Matthias W. of Elmira m 10/30/36 Esther P. Howell of Spencer in Elmira (6-11/9)
615. Beckwith, Reed, formerly of Utica, d 7/2/48 in Rome, NY (9-7/7)
616. Beckwith, Richard, 60, d 5/9/36 in Elmira (6-5/18)

17

617. Beckwith, Stephen of Utica m 1/2/50 Anabella Hulser of Herkimer; Rev. William Wyatt (9-1/4)
618. Becraft, William, 100, d 7/10/25 in Schoharie, NY (b in Suffield) (9-8/23)
619. Beddoe, John, Esq., 70, d 11/5/34 in Jerusalem, NY (b in England but lived many years in Ont. Co., NY) (6-11/26)
620. Beddoe, Lynham James of Geneva m 9/6/31 Eleanor Cuyler Cost, dau of Col. Elias of Phelps, in P; Rev. Bruce (6-9/7)
621. Bedell ____ (Mr.), 27, formerly of Geneva, d 9/6/33 in New Orleans (yellow fever) (6-10/9)
622. Bedell, George m 3/4/30 Lucy Barber in Geneva; Rev. Phelps (6-3/10)
623. Bedient, David B. m 1/18/44 Mary L. Pond, both of Smithville, in Oxford; Rev. E. G. Perry (Oxford Republican, 1/25)
624. Bedlow, Henry of NYC m 3/2/50 Josephine De Wolf Horner at the home of Prescott Hall, Esq. in NYC; Rev. Dr. Wainright (9-3/7)
625. Bee, Barlow B. of Deansville m 1/25/43 Mary Jane Snyder of Marshall in M; Rev. Paddock (9-1/27)
    Beebe. See also Bebee.
626. Beebe, David, 32, d 4/27/37 in Sullivan (3-5/3)
627. Beebe, David, 35 or 55(?), formerly of Sullivan, d 3/25/44 in Wayne Co. (3-4/10)
628. Beebe, Eliza, 33, wf of Isaac, d 2/24/34 in Sullivan (consumption) (3-3/4)
629. Beebe, Erastus Ogden, 1 yr, s of E. Beebe, d 4/23/30 in Geneva (6-4/28)
630. Beebe, Franklin m 3/26/35 Ann Lee in East Bloomfield (6-4/8)
631. Beebe, John, about 55, d 7/23/34 in Lenox (3-7/29)
632. Beebe, Joseph L. m 3/5/34 Jane Aurelia Chapin in Tyre (6-3/12)
633. Beebe, L. E. of East Hamilton m 6/6/49 Caroline S. King, dau of Thomas of Springfield, in S (9-6/15)
634. Beebe, Louisa Catharine, wf of A. Beebe and dau of late Francis A. Bloodgood of Ithaca, d 12/10/46 in NYC "whither she had gone for medical aid" (buried in Ithaca) (9-12/19)
635. Beebe, Lydia, 75, consort of David, Esq., d 8/8/39 in Sullivan (3-8/14)
636. Beebe, Lyman C. m 7/26/14 Persis Hacket in Oxford; Ransom Rathbun, Esq. (8-8/2)
637. Beebe, Maryette, 52, wf of Thomas and youngest dau of Capt. Noahdiah Judson of Westmoreland, d 11/3/50 in Jackson, MI (9-11/12)
638. Beebe, Sally (Miss), 27, d 7/6/33 in Canaseraga (3-7/9)
639. Beebe, Sarah L. (Miss), 17, dau of James and Alathea, d 1/27/42 in Sullivan (3-2/2)
640. Beebe, William N. m 6/11/48 Aurelia Carter, both of Vernon, in V; Rev. Isaac P. Stryker (9-6/17)
641. Beebee, Margaret, 45, wf of A. M., Esq., editor of the Baptist Register, d 12/11/30 in Utica (9-12/14)
642. Beecher, Derias, 65, d 12/26/33 in Canaseraga (3-1/7/34)
643. Beecher, Joseph S., 22, only s of Sylvester, Esq. of Lenox, NY, d 4/12/41 in Key West (presumably FL) (consumption) (3-5/5)
644. Beecher, Matilda (Mrs.), 64, d 5/27/39 in Canaseraga (3-5/29)
645. Beecher, Sylvester (Hon.), 68, d 8/19/49 in Canastota (9-8/23)
646. Beeman, James m 4/7/39 Caroline Case in Bolivar; J. French, Esq. All of Sullivan (3-4/24)
647. Beers, Susannah (Mrs.), 84, d 7/8/34 in Elmira (6-7/16)
648. Beers, William H. of Elmira m 10/31/50 Mary E. Gillett of Caton; Rev. Noble Prince (5-11/8)
649. Belcher, William H. of St. Louis, MO m 9/1/47 Mary Hunter, dau of the officiating clergyman, in Boonville; Rev. Dr. Hunter (9-9/2)
650. Belden, George, merchant, m 3/2/31 Mary Putnam of Walworth in Marion (6-3/23)
651. Belden, Josiah, Esq. m 2/1/49 Sarah Margaret Jones, dau of Zachariah, Esq., in the Pueblo de San Joce (not further defined - possibly in CA or NM? - in 1848 New Mexico, by Treaty of Guadalupe-Hidalgo, made a part of U.S.); K. H. Dimmick, 1st Alcalde (9-6/29)
652. Belden, Lavina, 22, dau of Azor, d 1/10/33 in Gorham (member Presby. Ch.) (6-1/30)
653. Beldenbecker, John W. m 2/11/46 Eliza E. Ferguson in Frankfort; Rev. J. H. McIlvaine (9-2/13)
654. Belknap, Royal, 17, m -- Fanny Sprague, 15, in Randolph, VT (8-3/9/27)
    Belknap. See also Bellsknapp

655. Bell, Henry W. (Dr.) of Geneva m 3/15/50 Helen Parmelee Platt, dau of late
    Hon. Jonas Platt, in NYC; Rev. Livingston Willard (9-3/28)
656. Bell, Joseph m -- Rebecca Campbell in Owego (6-10/23/33)
657. Bell, Sarah Ann, 41, wf of Dr. H. W., d 8/23/46 in Geneva (6-8/28)
658. *Bellamy, Alfred of the firm of J. & A. Bellamy of Chittenango m 11/4/35
    Eliza A. Oliphant, dau of R. W., Esq of Granville, in G; Rev. Bellamy
    of Manlius (3-11/17). See also entry 687
659. Bellamy, Edward Henry, 2 yrs, s of A. Bellamy, d 9/16/42 in Chittenango (3/9/21)
660. Bellamy, Julius of the firm of J. & A. Bellamy of Chittenango m 5/23/36
    Sarah J. Barney, dau of Throop Barney, Esq. of Kingsbury, Wash. Co.,
    in K; Rev. N. Fox (3-6/1)
661. Bellamy, Julius, 34, formerly merchant in Chittenango, d 10/4/43 in Clyde
    (typhus) (3-10/11)
662. Bellinger, Margaret, 45, wf of John, d 3/23/48 in Westmoreland ("A few
    weeks since she removed with her family from Whitestown to Westmoreland)
    (9-4/12)
663. Bellinger, Margaret C., 15, dau of John J., d 7/7/47 in Whitestown
    (member Presby. Ch.) (9-9/21)
664. Bellinger, Julia Ann, about 35, wf of John, d 11/16/46 in Baldwinsville
    (1-11/16)
665. Bellsknapp, James of Verona m 4/13/50 Mary Matilda Rockwell of Canastota;
    H. C. Vogell, Esq. (9-5/9)
666. Bellsknapp. See also Belknap
667. Belmont, August m 11/7/49 Caroline Slidell Perry, dau of Commodore M C.
    Perry, U. S. Navy, at the Church of the Ascension, NYC; Rev. Francis
    Vinton, D.D. (9-11/10)
668. Belmore, Joseph m 5/11/44 Sarah Ann Cash in Chittenango; Rev. Abell. All
    of Chittenango (3-5/15)
669. Benchley, David (Capt.) d 11/17/47 in Fairfield, NY (b in RI; a Rev.
    soldier) (9-12/1)
670. Bender, Silas m 2/11/36 Eliza Quackenbush of Julius in J; Elder Paddock
    (3-2/16)
671. Benedict, Amelia C. (Miss), 35, dau of late Amos, Esq., d 2/28/47 in
    Watertown (consumption) (9-3/10)
672. Benedict, Andrew of Bethel, CT m 10/19/35 Margaret Briggs, dau of Elisha
    and Elmira, in Elmira (6-10/28)
673. Benedict, George of Verona m 2/17/47 Sarah Walrath of Chittenango in C;
    Rev. James Abell (9-2/20)
674. Benedict, Gould of the firm of Pomeroy & Benedict m 9/9/50 Helen E.
    Bailey; Rev. Foster. All of Utica (9-9/10)
675. Benedict, Henry M., Esq. of Utica m 11/9/48 Margaret A. Jessup of Rochester
    in R; Rev. Henry W. Lee (9-11/13)
676. Benedict, Isaac, 21, d 8/16/40 in Verona (funeral sermon by Rev. Butler)
    (3-8/26)
677. Benedict, Lewis (Rev.) of Rockton, IL m 7/8/47 Martha D. Tyler, dau of late
    Asa, Esq. of Holland Patent, NY in H. P.; Rev. J. F. Scovill (9-7/12)
678. Benedict, Lewis (Rev.), pastor of 1st Cong'l. Ch., Rockton, IL, m 8/23/50
    Frances H. Wheat in Rome, NY; Rev. W. E. Knox (9-9/5)
679. Benedict, Mary, 63, relict of Deacon Lewis Benedict, late of Verona,
    d 4/3/49 in Binghamton (9-4/7)
680. Benedict, Stephen m 10/24/33 Sarah Truesdell in Canandaigua (6-11/6)
681. Benham Emily, 5, dau of Ebenezer and Betsy, d 11/4/34 in Hopewell (6-11/19)
682. Benham, Frances, 3, dau of Ebenezer and Betsy, d 1/4/35 in Hopewell
    (6-1/21)
683. Benjamin, Anson, Esq. of Chatham m 4/27/32 Lucia Smith of Penn Yan in
    P. Y.; Rev. Todd of Dresden (6-5/2)
684. Benjamin, Moses G. (Col.), postmaster of Bainbridge, d 1/18/33 in B
    (6-2/20)
685. Benjamin, N. (Rev.) of Williamstown, MA, missionary to Greece, m 4/26/36
    Mary G. Wheeler of NYC in NYC (6-5/4)
686. Benjamin, Park m 5/8/48 Mary Brower Western, 2nd dau of Henry M., Esq. of
    Dosoris, at St. Paul's Church, Glen Cove, L.I., NY; Rev. William A.
    Jenks (9-5/12)
687. Benjamin, William C. of Eaton m 9/19/44 Mary B. Mather of Utica in U;
    Rev. William Mather of Concord (9-10/16)
* See entry 688 for a late Bellamy insert (death of Alfred's wife, Eliza A.)

19

688. (a late Bellamy insert - for other Bellamy postings see entries 658-661)
    Bellamy, Eliza A., 27, wf of Alfred and dau of late Robert W.
    Oliphant, Esq. of North Granville d - (date and place lacking)
    (funeral sermon by Rev. T. Houston) (3-7/5/45)
689. Benjamin, Z. F. m -- Jannette Clark in Lockport (6-11/6/33)
690. Bennet, Hannah (Mrs.), 71, of Catlin d 3/1/36 in Willardsburgh, PA
    (6-3/30)   (8-12/1)
691. Bennet, James (Col.), 64, d 11/13/19 in Homer₍surv by wf and many children)
692. Bennet, James A., Esq., editor of the Brooklyn Advocate, m -- Eliza Jane
    Dubois in Catskill (6-11/6/33)
693. Bennet, Lorenzo m 4/5/37 Almira Stone in Homer; Rev. D. Platt (6-4/19)
694. Bennet, Matthew, 85, d 9/18/34 in Geneva (6-10/1)
695. Bennet, Moses P. m 3/10/29 Content Goff in Oxford (7-3/18)
696. Bennett, _____ (Mrs.), 27, d 1/14/32 in Geneva (6-1/18)
697. Bennett, Abraham H., one of the editors of the Penn Yan Herald, m --
    Desdemona Kidder in Penn Yan (8-11/4)
698. Bennett, Albert, 3, s of Hon. Henry, d 3/18/50 in New Berlin (9-4/6)
699. Bennett, Alvin M. m 6/21/49 Eliza C. Butler, 3rd dau of Col. Comfort
    Butler, in Utica; Rev. W. H. Spencer. All of Utica (9-6/22)
700. Bennett, Ambrose, Esq., 41, d 9/15/33 in Geneseo (6-9/18)
701. Bennett, Ann, 10, dau of George and Sally, d 5/10/46 in Seneca (6-5/14)
702. Bennett, Ann (Mrs.), 74, d 8/22/49 at the home of her son, James Stone,
    on West St., Utica (9-8/24)
703. Bennett, Asa (Deacon), 48, d 11/9/25 in Homer (9-11/22)
704. Bennett, Betsey, 32, d 1/14/33 in Milo (6-1/30)
705. Bennett, Dudley m -- Phebe Loper; R. D. Delay, Esq. (8-1/13/19)
706. Bennett, Elisha of Kirkland m 12/9/46 Eliza C. Calder in New York Mills;
    Rev. Z. Paddock (9-12/12)
707. Bennett, Emily (Miss) d -- in Amherst, MA (6-8/21/33)
708. Bennett, Esther (Miss), 37, d 1/10/36 in Starkey (6-1/27)
709. Bennett, Henry L. m 4/15/49 Isabelle A. Marsh, both of Baldwinsville, in B;
    Rev. Ira Dudley (1-4/19)
710. Bennett, James E., 35, d 11/10/44 in Utica (procession from home of Stephen
    Thorn, Fayette St.; service at Grace Ch.) (9-11/12)
711. Bennett, John, s of Nathaniel, late of Clinton, NY, d 3/7/24 in Savannah,
    GA (9-4/13)
712. Bennett, Malcolm of Pompey m 2/16/31 Catherine Beach of Auburn in A
    (6-3/2)
713. Bennett, Newman m 9/24/33 Eliza Randall in Milo (6-10/16)
714. Bennett, Orademona (could this be intended for Desdemona which see in entry
    697?), 45, wid of late Abraham H., d 7/28/46 in Penn Yan (mother of the
    junior proprietor of the Penn Yan Democrat) (6-8/7)
715. Bennett, Ransom m 6/21/49 Mary Jane Baker in Utica; Elder C. P. Grosvenor.
    All of Utica (9-6/22)
716. Benningham, David m 1/22/45 Mary Ann Morey, both of Utica, in U; Rev. D.
    Skinner (9-1/24)
717. Benson, Alfred G., merchant, of Auburn m Philomela Rollo, dau of J. H.,
    in NYC (6-5/12/30)
718. Benson, Egbert, 87, d 8/24/33 in Jamaica, L.I., NY (6-9/4)
719. Benson, Ethan, 35, d 2/5/35 in Sullivan (3-2/10)
720. Benson, Frederick, Esq., sheriff of Onondaga Co., m 6/23/42 Mrs. Caroline
    Morse in Syracuse; Rev. J. B. Storer ((9-6/29)
721. Benson, Gertrude, 53, wf of Levi, d 8/4/49 in Erin, NY (5-8/17)
722. Benson, Harry of Chittenango m 5/5/31 Deborah Manchester of Madison;
    Rev. Pearce (3-5/17)
723. Benson, N. E., Esq., attorney, m Catherine L. Goldthwait of Montgomery,
    Alabama in M (8-3/7)
724. Benthrong(?), James (Col.), 70, d 10/23/50 in Cazenovia (9-10/29)
725. Bentley, William (Capt.), 85, (a Rev. officer) d 5/2/50 at the home of
    his son-in-law, E. Bentley, in Antwerp, NY (b in RI 4/25/1765; enlisted
    in Rev. at age 16; lived in Jeff. Co., NY from 1818 until death)
    (9-5/17)
726. Bentley, William of Verona m 5/13/50 Louisa Gates of New York Mills in
    Whitesboro; Morris Wilcox, Esq. (9-5/23)

727. Bentley, William H. m 1/22/45 Theresa N. Bailey, both of Sauquoit, at Griffin's Hotel in Utica; Rev. D. Skinner (9-1/24)
728. Benton, Beathel, 88, (a Rev. soldier) d 1/27/37 in Seneca (6-2/7)
729. Benton Emeline, 35, wf of Hon. Charles S., d 9/23/50 in Mohawk (9-9/25)
730. Benton, Felitia (Miss), 17, d 12/18/33 in Gaines (6-1/8/34)
731. Benton, Lucy (Miss), 15, d 12/15/33 in Gaines (6-12/25)
732. Berby, John H. of NYC m 9/10/47 Jane Tapecott of Williamsburgh, L.I., NY in Utica; Rev. Dr. Proal (9-9/16)
733. Berdan, Tunis, 62, d 8/26/30 in Phelps (6-9/8)
733a. Berge, Charles Frederick (Rev.), 50, missionary among negroes and Indians in South America, d -- in Bethlehem, PA (arrived in Bethlehem from Barbadoes "about fourteen days before his death") (9-8/9/25)
734. Bernard, Amelia (Mrs.), 50, formerly of Utica, d 7/2/46 in NYC (funeral at home of R. W. Roberts, Charles St., Utica) (9-7/4)
735. Bernard, John C. m 2/8/43 Jane L. Roberts in Utica; Rev. James Griffiths. All of Utica (9-2/10)
736. Berrien, John McPherson (Hon.) m 7/10/33 Eliza Cecil Hunter in Savannah, NY; Rev. Preston (Eliza, oldest dau of Col. James Hunter of Savannah) (6-7/31)
737. Berry, Charles, 18, d 2/10/43 in Preston (Oxford Republican, 2/24)
738. Berry, Charles H., Esq. m 11/14/50 Frances Hubbell; Rev. A. L. Brooks. All of Corning (4-11/20)
739. Berry, Gilbert W. m 8/9/36 Roxy Evarts in East Bloomfield (6-8/24)
740. Berry, Jack (Maj.), an old chief of the Seneca tribe, d 7/3/39 in Jack Berrytown on the Buffalo Creek Reservation (6-7/17)
741. Berry, Lewis, Esq., 84, d 3/24/49 in Whitesboro (9-4/3)
742. Berry, Nehemiah of Lynd, MA m 4/24/33 Maria H. Bassett, dau of late Rev. Mr. Bassett, in Milo; Rev. Crosby (6-5/1)
743. Bessey, Hiram G. m 3/25/49 Hester Ann McKenzie, both of Elmira, at the Meth. Ch., Elmira; Rev. H. N. Seaver (5-3/30)
744. Best, James Albert, 6, oldest s of John and Mary G., d 10/12/47 in Utica (funeral from 48 Jay St.) (9-10/13)
745. Bethune, Divie, Esq. of NYC d -- in NYC (9-9/28/24)
746. Bettiger, P. D. m 2/29/44 S. Jeanette McConnell, both of Russia, NY; Rev. Baker (9-3/7)
747. Bettinger, Anna, 1 yr, dau of Isaac, d 6/26/35 in Sullivan (3-6/30)
748. Bettinger, Nicholas m 2/26/35 Ann Storms in Sullivan; Jairus French, Esq. All of Sullivan (3-3/3)
749. Bettis, Benjamin, 61, d 3/20/50 in Albion (had lived nearly 40 yrs in Westmoreland) (9-3/27)
750. Bettis, Henry W. m 4/12/48 Clara Delano in Clinton; Rev. T. J. Sawyer. All of Westmoreland (9-4/13)
751. Bettis, Josiah, formerly of Mexico, NY, m 5/1/45 Malinda Neville, dau of late John of Westmoreland, in Whitesboro; Rev. Cole (9-5/2)
752. Bettis, Robert J., 34, s of Benjamin, d 11/15/48 in Mexico, NY (9-11/21)
753. Betts, Charles A. H., Esq. of Lysander m 11/12/49 Amelia N. Mather of Mount Morris in M. M.; Rev. C, H, A, Buckley (1-11/22)
754. Betts, D. J., Esq., 26, attorney and clerk of court of equity of Sixth District, d 1/23/26 in Cortland (9-2/28)
755. Betts, Eliza, about 23, consort of N., Esq., d 8/4/28 in Tonawanda, PA (8-8/20)
756. Betts, Hiram of Troy m 1/5/31 Dorcas Gillet of Stuyvesant in Kinderhook (6-2/2)
757. Betts, Nathaniel N. m 7/11/27 Eliza Means, both of Towanda, PA, in T; William Patton, Esq. (8-8/3)
758. Betts, Richard, 90, d 1/24/50 in Holland Patent (9-2/7)
759. Betts, Silas m -- Genett Wheeler in Greene (8-5/26/19)
760. Bidwell, Eli m 8/27/34 Achshah Smallage in Prattsburgh (6-9/3)
761. Biesuyes, Adam m 4/4/39 Catherine Card, both of Lenox, in Perryville (3-4/10)
762. Bigelow, D. T. of Mississippi m 9/11/45 Sarah Brewster, dau of late S. W. of Holland Patent, NY in Rome, NY; Rev. S. Davis (9-9/27)
763. Bigelow, David Munro, 4, oldest s of Faye and Hannah, d 3/19/48 in Baldwinsville (1-3/22)

21

764. Bigelow, Ely m 7/20/37 Mary Long, both of Pompey, in Chittenango; Rev.
E. A. Huntington (3-7/26)
765. Bigelow, Henrietta Maria, 23, wf of J. G. of Syracuse, d 3/9/49 at the
home of her father, Dr. U. G. Bigelow, in Worcester (9-3/29)
766. Bigelow, J. G. of Syracuse m 1/24/49 Henrietta Maria Bigelow, youngest dau
of Dr. U. G. of Worcester, in W; Rev. Hugh Carlisle (9-3/29)
767. Bigelow, John L., Esq. m 5/15/35 Mary T. Davis, both of Seneca Falls, in
Utica (6-5/27)
768. Bigelow, L. B. (Dr.), 83, d 7/6/50 in Auburn (cholera) (9-7/10)
769. Bigelow, Lovice, 36, consort of Abner and dau of Paul and Mary Guilford,
formerly of Conway, MA, d 11/2/24 in Phelps, NY (9-9/12/26)
770. Bigelow, Otis P., 16 mo, youngest and last son of Payn and Hannah,
d 6/7/48 in Baldwinsville (scarlet fever - second child in this family
to die within 3 mos) (1-6/14)
771. Bigelow, Sanford m -- Mary Ann Storms in Seneca (6-6/30/30)
772. Bigelow, Stephen R. m 12/14/48 Rocelia C. Day, dau of Lyman, Esq., in
Sangerfield; Rev. A. Delos Gridley. All of Sangerfield (9-12/18)
773. Bigelow, U. G. (Dr.), 55, father of Dr. U. G. of Albany, d 3/30/50 at his
home in Worcester (9-4/4)
774. Billinghurst, Lucien m 2/3/42 Hannah Fellows (dau of Col. J. Fellows),
both of Corning; Rev. Richard Smith (4-2/9) (married in Corning)
775. Billings, Allen P. of Phelps m 4/26/32 Eliza Burkholder in Hopewell
(6-5/9)
776. Billings, Silas m 3/17/36 Rachel Sloan in Elmira (6-3/23)
777. Billington, George T. m 12/16/50 Elizabeth R. Kingsbury; Rev. H. Dickson.
All of Utica (9-12/18)
778. Billington, Linus W. (Rev.) of Conhocton m Sophia Gardner in Elmira
(6-3/31/30)
779. Bingham, Frederick, about 2, s of Nathaniel, d 5/18/31 in Rochester
(6-6/8)
780. Bingham, Joseph m 10/9/32 Eliza Quackenbush; Rev. William Johnson. All
of Sullivan (3-10/16)
781. Bingham, Samuel, 92, (a Rev. soldier), formerly of Windham, CT, d 9/8/45
in Clinton (9-9/15)
782. Bird, Loring Grant m 6/25/43 Eunice Brownell of Corning in C; Rev. Morgan
Gorton (4-6/28)
783. Bird, Meribeth (Mrs.), 48, d -- in Southport (6-3/13/33)
Birdsall. See also Burtsell.
784. Birdsall, Alfred of Jefferson m 4/30/45 Jenett Kirby, dau of Walter, Esq.
of Winfield, in W; Rev. Woodley (9-5/3)
785. Birdsall, Ann Eliza, 30, wf of Samuel, Esq., d 3/8/31 in Waterloo (6-3/23)
786. Birdsall, Anna, 51, wf of Maurice, Esq., d 6/12/29 in Norwich (member of
Meth. Episc. Ch.; surv by husband "and several children") (7-6/17)
(her death age 54 and deathplace Greene in 8-6/17)
787. Birdsall, Britt, 30, formerly of Clinton, d 3/21/46 in Winfield (9-3/31)
788. Birdsall, E. B. (Lt.) of U.S. Army m 7/4/33 Mary Wilcox, dau of Dr. Wilcox
of East Bloomfield, in E. B.; Rev. Smith, rector of St. James Ch.,
Batavia (6-7/10)
789. Birdsall, Elizabeth, wf of S., Esq. of Waterloo, d -- at Chenango Point
(8-12/8/19)
790. Birdsall, Morris of Greene m 9/2/45 Maria H. Randall, dau of Col. John of
Norwich, in N; Elder Duncan (Oxford Republican, 9/11)
791. Birdsall, Moses, Esq. m 9/29/45 Jane A. Allen at the home of Augustus
Chapman, Esq. in Morristown; Rev. J. A. Brayton (9-10/14)
792. Birdsall, Ransom m 2/4/31 Maria D. Tooker, both of Ovid, in Ithaca (4-2/16)
793. Birdsall, S. (Col.) of Waterloo m 9/26/32 Serene Fosgate of Auburn in A;
Rev. Mason (6-10/10)
794. Birdsall, Sally Ann, 5, dau of Abraham, d 8/30/35 (in Elmira?) (6-9/9)
795. Birdsall, Samuel, Esq. m -- Ann Eliza Kending, dau of Martin, Esq., in
Waterloo. All of W (8-11/29/20)
796. Birdseye, George W. of New Hartford m 11/22/49 Mandane L. King of Paris,
NY; Rev. Merrill "of Litchfield, Norwich Society" (9-11/26)
797. Birdseye, Henry Clay, (age blurred), son of Hon. Victory Birdseye of Pompey,
d 2/18/47 in Albany (1-2/24)
798. Birdseye, James, 50, d 2/22/35 in Hopewell (moved from Huntington, CT before
1800 "to the Genesee Country" of NY)(6-2/25)

22

799. Birdseye, John A. m 2/8/48 Martha S. Ball at Central Hotel, Utica; Rev.
     Samuel Ramsey of Clinton. All of Litchfield (triple ceremony - see
     marriages of Jonathan and Joseph Ball) (9-2/10)
800. Birdseye, Lucien, Esq., attorney, of Albany m 6/16/46 Catharine M. Baker,
     dau of Samuel of Pompey, in P; Rev. Clinton Clark (9-6/18)
801. Birge, Hannah, 60, wf of Seth, d 6/6/47 in New Hartford (9-6/22)
802. Birge, Seth m 8/15/43 Freelove Henderson at Griffith's Hotel in Utica;
     Rev. A. H. Grosh. All of New Hartford (9-8/17)
803. Birkbeck, Morris, Esq. drowned in crossing the Wabash River in Illinois
     (Secretary of State, b in England, founded the town of New Albion -
     state of N.A.'s location not given) (9-7/19/25)
804. Birmingham, Mary Ann, 41, wf of David and sister of John Baxter, d 12/12/48
     in Utica (funeral at her late home, Whitesboro St., West Utica) (9-12/14)
805. Bisdee (sic), Edward, father of Samuel of Baldwinsville, d 2/19/50 in
     Skaneateles (1-2/28)
806. Bisdee, Sidney of Baldwinsville m 1/10/50 Martha Miller of Syracuse in S;
     Rev. H. Gregory (1-1/17)
807. Bishop, Alonzo m 1/29/35 Mrs. Catharine Walrath in Chittenango; Rev. A.
     Yates, D.D. All of Chittenango (3-2/3)
808. Bishop, Dracos of Westmoreland m 6/19/50 E. W. Deland of Utica; Rev. H. S.
     Dickson (9-6/21)
809. Bishop, Edson m 2/13/33 Elizabeth Springsted, both of Montezuma, in
     Waterloo (6-2/27)
810. Bishop, John of Junius m 5/10/32 Jemima Pierce of Vandemark's Corners in
     Seneca at V. C. (6-5/16)
811. Bishop, John (Midshipman) d 6/20/37 in Halifax, PA (6-7/19)
812. Bishop, Joseph A. of Stockbridge m 9/28/42 A. Maria Prentice in Vernon;
     Rev. D. Robinson (9-10/6)
813. Bishop, Lucretia, 29, wid of late Dr. Bishop, d 3/3/41 in Knoxville
     (consumption) (4-2/12)
814. Bishop, William (Dr.) m Lucretia M. McCallock in Painted Post (6-11/7/32)
815. Bishop, William (Dr.), about 36, d 10/22/40 in Corning (4-10/23)
816. Bissel, Gerusha, consort of Roger, d 8/14/20 in Norwich (consumption)
     (surv by husband and children) (7-8/16)
817. Bissel, Julia, 9, youngest dau of Roger and Jersusha, d 5/23/27 in Norwich
     (8-6/1)
818. Bissell, Daniel B. m 3/30/36 Caroline Bartlett in Penn Yan (6-4/13)
819. Bissell, E. G. m 7/21/47 H. C. Pearce, both of Waterville, in W; Rev.
     William W. Williams (9-7/24)
820. Bissell, Epaphras, 61, formerly of East Windsor, CT, d -- in Avon, NY
     (9-12/19/26)
821. Bissell, Josiah, Jr. of Rochester d 4/5/31 in Seneca Falls (6-4/13)
822. Bissell, Lucius of Torringford, CT m 4/1/45 Sarah Patten of Rome, NY in
     R; Rev. Haynes (9-4/11)
823. Bixbe, George E. of NYC m 6/6/49 Anna Cornelia Sayre, oldest dau of James,
     Esq., in Utica; Rev. Dr. Lansing of Brooklyn (9-6/7)
824. Bixby, _____, 6 mo, dau of Green Bixby, d -- in Norwich (7-7/30/18)
825. Black, Emily, consort of Col. James, merchant, of Vandalia, IL and
     formerly of Geneva, NY, d 7/26/34 in Vandalia (6-8/20)
826. Black, Jared of Southfield m 9/26/39 Betsey Daharsh of Chittenango in C;
     Rev. J. Abell (4-10/2)
827. Black, John, a convict from Yates Co., d -- in Auburn Prison (6-5/12/30)
828. Black, John of Geneva m 3/1/32 Jane Welles of Wayne in W (6-3/7)
829. Black, John, 66, d 6/7/48 in Whitesboro (b in Greenock, Scotland - "in
     mercantile pursuits there for 26 years ... crossed the Atlantic
     17 times") (9-6/28)
830. Black, William, about 42, "a stranger but known as the lecturer on Palestine"
     d 12/18/35 in Troy ("supposed to be a native of Ayrshire, Scotland";
     had spent "the past six months in Ontario Co,, NY") (6-12/23)
831. Blackall, William J. of albany m 4/21/45 Hannah Ann Thorn of Utica in U;
     Rev. Leeds (9-4/22)
832. Blackmar, William W. of Buffalo m 1/13/31 Almira Chaffe of Springville in S
     (6-2/2)
833. Blackmarr, Adeline, wf of Ransom, d 6/23/30 in Newark NY (she had been married
     only a few days) (6-7/7)

834. Blackstone, Mary Clark, 67, wf of Stephen F., Esq., d 9/24/45 in Kirkland (9-9/27)

835. Blackwell, Sarah Amelia, 4, dau of Enoch and Sarah, d 12/25/44 in Utica (9-12/28)

836. Blackwell, Titus m -- Elizabeth Stevens in Brutus (6-1/19/31)

837. Blackwood, Joseph, 36, d 7/24/33 in Chittenango (3-7/30)

838. Blackwood, Peter m 6/30/48 Charlotte Castle, both of New Hartford, in Utica; Rev. H. N. Clarke (9-7/4)

839. Blade, Charles of Amsterdam, NY m 5/4/50 Catharine Jane Searban of Utica in U; Rev. Marcus A. Perry (9-5/7)

840. Blair, Abigail, wf of Elinus(?) d 3/2/42 in North Norwich (Oxford Times, 3/16)

841. Blair, Eli, 40, d 10/4/31 in Lyons (also on the same date his wife, Abby, 36, died) (6-10/19)

842. Blake, Edward W., 47, d 6/1/47 in Utica (9-6/3)

843. Blake, John of Peekskill, formerly of England, s of Rev. William, m 12/5/44 Samantha Brown, dau of Rev. William W., at his home in Junius, NY; Rev. William W. Brown (9-12/10)

844. Blake, Joseph (Deacon), 70, formerly of Whitestown, d 1/11/43 at the home of his son in Utica (settled in Whitestown in 1793) (9-1/12)

845. Blake, Sarah, 65, wid of late Joseph, d 1/2/47 in Utica (9-1/7)

846. Blakely, Mark J. m -- Marietta Beman in Canandaigua (6-4/14/30)

847. Blakeslee, D. Franklin of Morrisville m 5/19/47 Elizabeth Mosely, dau of Peabody of Lebanon, in L; Rev. D. Blakeslee (9-5/22)

848. Blanchard, E. of Penn Yan m 10/18/35 Emeline Secor of Geneva in Penn Yan (6-10/28)

849. Blanset, Thomas of Milo m 1/16/33 Sarah Ann Merritt of Jerusalem in J. (6-2/6)

850. Blazier, Ichabod of Western m 2/23/45 Elizabeth Hugernon of New Hartford in New H.; Henry Sherrill, Esq. (9-2/27)

851. Bligh, Amelia, 37, wf of Dr. A. B., d 9/24/50 in Sauquoit (9-9/26)

852. Bliss, Clark W. (Dr.), 25, d -- in Elmira (6-8/4/30)

853. Bliss, Cynthia, 49, wf of Theodore and dau of late Deacon John Punderson of Macdonough, d 1/5/42 in Syracuse (Oxford Times, 1/19)

854. Bliss, Isaac H. of Stratford m 11/23/26 Clarissa Cory, dau of Benjamin of Salisbury in S; Abel Kibbe, Esq. (8-12/1)

855. Bliss, Jason S. of Whitestown m 5/24/48 Marietta Phelps, youngest dau of Jacob of Westmoreland, in W; Rev. P. A. Spencer (9-5/30)

856. Bliss, Johnson m 8/9/32 Eliza Blaksleee in Perryville; Rev. B. Northrop. All of Perryville (3-8/14)

857. Bliss, William T. m 11/26/48 Sarah E. Davenport in Utica; Rev. Joseph Hartwell. All of Utica (9-11/29)

858. Bliss, William Wallace Smith (Brevet Lt. Col.) of U.S. Army m 12/6/48 Mary Elizabeth Taylor, dau of Maj. Gen. Z. Taylor (Pres.-elect of U.S.) at Baton Rouge, LA; Rev. John Burke, rector of St. James Ch. (9-12/20 and 5-12/22)

859. Bloom, Ephraim, 100, d 12/17/28 in Lansing, NY (a soldier in the French and in the Rev. Wars) (9-12/30)

860. Bloom, John C. of NYC m 12/22/47 Mariam H. Roberts, dau of late Warner and Eleanor of Williamsville, at the home of Hon. W. Converse in Westmoreland; Rev. Raymond (9-12/25)

861. Bloom, S. S. of Utica m 7/4/47 Mary T. Lamb of Norwich in N; Rev. C. T. Johnson (9-7/16)

862. Bloomer, Isaac, 37, d 9/9/35 in Ovid (6-9/16)

863. Bloomer, Joshua, 43, d 8/8/35 in Ovid (6-8/12)

864. Bloomer, Maria, 30, wf of Isaac, d 7/31/35 in Ovid (6-8/5)

865. Blossom, Abigail M., 20, niece of Col. William, d 7/5/30 in Canandaigua (6-7/14)

866. Blossom, Magdalin, about 20, wf of William and dau of Abraham A. Post, Esq., d 2/2/33 in Seneca (6-2/6)

867. Blossom, William m 9/22/31 Mandeles(?) Post, dau of Abraham A., Esq., in Seneca (6-9/28)

868. Blossom, William (Col.), 57, for many years proprietor of the Canandaigua Hotel, d 5/29/49 in Canandaigua (9-6/4)

869. Blue, John C. (Capt.) m 9/30/46 Rosetta C. Read, both of Deerfield, in D; Rev. Joseph Rosekrants (9-9/30)
870. Blue, Malcolm A. (Col.) m 9/29/46 Sally M. Hetherington, both of Deerfield, in D; Rev. Joseph Roskrants (9-9/30)
871. Blyth, Elijah K. of Geneva m 9/7/30 Catharine M. Adams, oldest dau of Dr. Elijah of Catlin, in C; Rev. Tooker (6-9/8)
872. Boardman, A. P. of Cazenovia m 10/8/32 S. M. Hawkins of Delphi in D; Elder Smitzen (3-10/16)
873. Boardman, Adrian V., of the firm of Van Alkenburgh and Boardman, merchant tailors, m 9/26/39 Betsey Shaver of Chittenango in C; Elder Paddock of Cazenovia (3-10/2)
874. Boardman, Elizabeth, 21, wf of A. V., d 10/26/40 in Chittenango (3-10/28)
875. Boardman, Adrian V. m 6/3/41 Lavenia Louer in Sullivan; Rev. D. M. D. O'Farrell (3-6/9)
876. Boardman, Alida M., 28, wf of Rev. George S. and dau of Col. Derick Lane of Troy, d 11/20/30 in Watertown (9-11/23) (The father's name is translated to Aaron in 6-12/8)
877. Boardman, Derick L., Esq. m 6/8/48 Mary N. Foster, dau of Hon. Henry A., in Rome, NY (9-6/12)
878. Boardman, Elijah (Maj.), 46, of U.S. Army d 3/22/32 at Fort Niagara (6-4/25)
879. Boardman, L. C. of Geneva m -- Lucinda Stout of Canoga in C; Rev. Hall (6-9/11/33)
880. Boardman, Sarah, wf of Rev. G. S., d 7/18/49 at Cherry Valley (cholera) (9-7/20)
881. Bodes, Caroline, 18, dau of Peter, d 7/11/30 in Geneva (6-7/14)
882. Bogart, M. P. of Utica m 3/6/44 Frances M. Gilbert of Albion in A; Rev. Hawks (9-4/17)
883. Bogert, Augustus Grandin, inf s of Dr. S. V. R. Bogert, d 2/20/39 in Geneva (6-2/27)
884. Bogert, Cornelius I., Esq., 77, of Jamaica, L. I., NY d 2/16/32 in NYC (6-2/29)
885. Bogert, David Ritzema, 76, (a Rev. soldier), postmaster at East Line, d 6/3/39 in Malta, NY (6-6/19)
886. Bogert, Frances, 13 mo, dau of Peter and Frances, d 9/8/46 in Utica (9-9/11)
887. Bogert, Isaac, 55, of the firm of I. Bogert & Co., merchants, and bro of H. H., Esq. of Geneva, d 9/24/32 in Dresden (6-9/26)
888. Bogert, Maria O. d -- in Great Neck, L.I., NY (6-10/9/33)
889. Bogue, Aaron J., 74, d -- in New Lebanon, NY (9-7/25/26)
890. Bogue, Emily S., 16, dau of D. P., Esq. of St. Albans, VT, d 9/12/40 at the home of Rev. J. Abell in Chittenango (she had come to the area one year earlier to attend the Female Seminary in Utica)(3-9/16)
891. Bogue, Franklin R., 5, s of Rev. H. P. Bogue, d 4/18/30 in Norwich (7-4/21)
892. Bogue, Frederick, Esq. of Albany m 6/15/47 Avis Canfield Stirling, dau of Hon. Ansel, at Christ Ch., Sharon, CT; Rev. Moody (9-7/2)
893. Bolles, James A. (Rev.), asistant rector (rest blurred) m 9/3/33 (rest blurred - but perhaps Frances Bolles) in Newark, NY (6-9/18)
894. Bolles, Mary Frances, 37, wf of Rev. James A., D. D., rector of St. James Ch., d 4/29/49 in Batavia (9-5/3)
895. Bond, Ezra m 7/17/34 Charlotte Olcott; Rev. E. Slingerland; All of Chittenango (3-7/22)
896. Bond, Gardiner m 9/17/35 Almira Mower in Sullivan; Rev. J. Bushnel (3-9/29)
897. Bond, S. N., Esq. m 1/21/47 Elizabeth Doxtater in Adams; Rev. F. J. Jackson (1-2/3)
898. Bond, stephen B. m -- Delia Darrow in Lockport (6-2/2/31)
899. Bond, William M. (Col.) of Lockport m 10/3/31 Nancy L. Bond of Keene, NH in Lockport, NY (6-10/5)
900. Bonesteel, Teunis m 11/27/34 Elizabeth Gawtry, both of Geneva, in G; Rev. Dr. Mason (6-12/3)
901. Bonham, D. H. of Campbell m 9/7/42 Sarah G. Reynolds of Big Flats in BF; Rev. Whiting (4-9/14)
902. Bonner, Rudolph, 58, d -- in Oswego (6-8/9/37)
903. Bonney, Harriet F., 30, wf of Col. William F., d 6/5/46 in Eaton (9-6/19)

904. Boone, Damiel (Col.), 89, the first settler of Kentucky, d 9/26/20 in Charette Village, MO (8-11/22)
905. Booth, Alida Lucretia, 25, wf. of William A., d 11/29/32 (typhus) (6-12/5)
906. Booth, Anna, 22, youngest dau of Andrew, d 12/25/38 in Starkey (consumption) (6-1/9/39)
907. Booth, Anson, about 35, d 12/9/21 in Oxford (had lived there several yrs) (8-12/12)
908. Booth, Frances Emmy, 1 yr, dau of Gifford J. and Mary A., d 8/28/49 in Elmira (5-9/7)
909. Booth, Spencer m 4/28/31 Calista S. Kidder in Penn Yan; Rev. A. Chase (6-5/11)
910. Boratt, E. R. of Volney m 1/4/43 Sevilla Isbell of Westmoreland; Rev. C. Budd (9-1/13)
911. Borrows, Sarah, 65, relict of late Dr. Barrows and sister of Mrs. Ann Colt late of Geneva, d 6/4/35 in NYC (6-6/10)
912. Bortles, Francis m 9/1/34 Emily Lilly in Palmyra (6-9/17)
913. Bortles, Jacob H. m 3/5/34 Mary Colt in Palmyra (6-3/12)
914. Bortles, Jacob H., 28, editor of the Wayne Sentinel, d 8/12/36 in Palmyra (6-8/24)
915. "Bostwick, Betsey Maria" is the only legible segment of a mutilated marriage posting in 6-11/21/32. (Betsey Maria is clearly the bride's name)
916. Bostwick, Heman m 2/7/33 Lois Dagget in Geneva; Rev. Alverson (double ceremony - see marr of Henry Smith) (6-2/13)
917. Bostwick, James H. m -- Maria M. Gardner at St. Peter's Ch., Auburn; Rev. Dr. Rudd (6-1/5/31)
918. Bosworth, John m 10/10/50 Emma D. Morse; Rev. C. Wheeler (5-10/18)
919. Bosworth, Joseph H., Esq. of Binghamton m 9/17/33 Frances E. Pumpelly of Owego in O (6-10/9)
920. Bosworth, Joseph S., Esq., attorney, of Binghamton m 9/17/33 Frances E. Pumpelly, dau of Charles, in Owego (6-9/25)
921. Bosworth, Mather, 83, d 5/17/50 in Lowville (b in Sandisfield, MA; as a young man moved to Oneida Co., NY)(surv by an elderly wf and 4 married children; one each in Mich, Penna, as well as Livingston Co., NY and Turin, NY) (9-5/25)
922. Bosworth, Timothy of Pharsalia m Betsey Pabodie of Norwich in N; Rev. Jedidiah Randall (7-5/27/19)
923. Bote, Joseph m 10/27/46 Ann Switzer 10/27/46 in Utica; D. Gillmore, Esq. All of Utica (9-10/28)
924. Botsford, Jonathan, 90, d 1/18/33 in Milo (6-2/6)
925. Botsford, Mary (Miss), 25, dau of John, d 7/8/33 in New York Mills (9-7/16)
926. Boughton, Claudius V. (Maj.), 47, d 11/10/31 near Vienna (Phelps) (4-11/10)
927. Boughton, Henry B., 6 wks, s of Henry D. and Mary A., d 11/28/43 in Utica (9-12/1)
928. Boughton, Mary Jane, 37, wf of Cornelius, d 8/6/48 in Campbelltown (surv by husband and 3 children) (4-8/16)
929. Bourguigen, Francis m 5/31/48 Christine Knoll in Utica; D. Gillmore, Esq. All of Utica (9-6/2)
930. Bourne, Daniel D. T., 33(?), formerly of Utica, d 6/25/50 at the home of Harvey Bradley, Esq. in Whitestown (consumption) (9-6/28)
931. Bours, Edward, 18 mo, youngest s of Peter, d 8/19/30 in Geneva (6-8/25)
932. Bours(?), Thomas Robinson, formerly of Utica, m 2/18/50 Dona Carmen Yberra, dau of Don Juan Antonie of Almos, Mexico, at the home of John A. Robinson, Esq. (U.S. Consul) in Guaymas, Mexico; Rev. Vincente Oviedo (9-5/10)
933. Bovier, Ward m 10/1/35 Rhoda C. Howell in Smithborough (6-10/14)
934. Bow, Titus of Hastings, Oswego Co. m 3/1/48 Sally Scoville of Van Buren in V.B.; Rev. Philips (1-3/8)
935. Bowe, Susan L., 5 mo, dau of O. A. and C. W. Bowe, d 8/19/45 in Little Falls (9-8/23)
936. Bowen, James H. of Little Falls m 9/26/43 Caroline A. Smith, dau of Ira A. of Evans Mills, in E. M.; Rev. Fish (9-10/3)
937. Bowen, T. H., Esq. of Albany m 10/3/47 Jane Brown of Antwerp, NY in A; Rev. Williams (9-10/9)

938. Bowers, Henry J. of Cooperstown m 12/6/48 Philatheta Crain, oldest dau of Hon. William C. of Warren, in W; Rev. Appleton (9-12/11)
939. Bowers, John C. (Col.) m 1/31/42 Emeline B. Peck in Pharsalia; Rev. Peck (Oxford Times, 3/2)
940. Bowers, Walter, 44, d 9/23/47 in Utica (9-9/25)
941. Bowers, John of Otsego m 2/24/49 Mrs. Phebe Patchen in Hornby; C. D. Thomas, Esq. (4-3/7)
942. Bowie, Charles A, m 7/4/36 Mary P. Randolph in Waterloo (6-7/13)
943. Bowman, Adam m 5/27/46 Eve Weaver, both of Deerfield, in D; Rev. McIlvaine (9-5/29)
944. Bowman, Henry m -- Mary Passage in Brutus (6-1/19/31)
945. Bowman, Hiram m 2/14/49 Melinda Earll in Van Buren; Rev. L. Alden (1-2/22)
946. Bowman, James m 10/1/39 Lucia Maria Palmeter in Sullivan; J. French, Esq. (3-10/2)
947. Boyce, _____, 15 mo, s of John, d 10/16/47 in Baldwinsville (1-10/17)
948. Boyce, George C., 2 yrs, s of A. A., Esq., d 8/12/45 in Lockport (9-8/20)
949. Boyce, L. M. of Chicago m 10/9/45 Helen Maria Williams, dau of John, Esq. of Cazenovia, in C; Rev. J. R. Davenport (double ceremony - see marr. of George W. Phillips) (9-10/10)
950. Boyce, Le Roy M. d 7/23/49 in Chicago (cholera) (9-7/26)
951. Boyce, Seymour of Waterloo m 2/8/31 Mary J. Lacey of Seneca Falls in Waterloo (6-2/16)
952. Boyd, David, Jr. of Buffalo m 10/20/50 Jerusha H. Comstock of Cayahoga Falls, OH in C. F.; Rev. L. I. Holden (9-10/29)
953. Boyd, Deborah, 53, d 8/4/34 in Benton (6-8/13)
954. Boyd, Hugh m 1/15/33 Elvira Smith in Phelps; Rev. Bates (6-1/23)
955. Boyd, James R. (Rev.), pastor of 2nd Presby. Ch., Watertown, m 9/26/32 Elizabeth Camp, dau of Col. Elisha, at Sackets Harbor; Rev. G. S. Boardman (9-10/16)
956. Boyd, Margaret (Miss), 22, d 8/2/32 in Penn Yan (6-8/15)
957. Boyd, Tompkins W. m 11/4/35 Rebecca Ann Van Scoy in Jerusalem, NY (6-11/11)
958. Boyd, William F. of Rome, NY m 3/12/50 AnnS. Ashley, adopted dau of late Dr. Ashley of Russell, in R; Rev. Moore (9-3/21)
959. Boyden, Roswell, 27, d 3/30/45 at the American Hotel in Utica (9-3/31)
960. Boyle, Thomas of Ephratah m 2/5/49 Margaret Gibson of Ohio, NY at the Chenango House in Utica; Rev. E. Francis (9-2/6)
961. Brace, Benjamin S. m 12/22/42 Helen M. Miller, both of Slaton's Bush; Rev. B. Hawley (9-12/24)
962. Brackett, Joseph Warren, Esq., 51, attorney and a native of NH, d -- in NYC (9-4/25/26)
963. Bradbury, Thomas U. of Canandaigua m 12/30/35 Harriet A. Smith, dau of George, in Farmington (6-1/13)
964. Bradford, John M. m 5/15/39 Sarah E. Hopkins, dau of late Hon. Samuel M., in Geneva; Rev. Hav (6-5/22)
965. Bradford, Thomas m 9/15/47 Abby Parsons in Skaneateles Rev. C. P. Wyckoff (1-9/29)
966. Bradford, Thomas O. (Rev.) of Gilbertsville m 5/19/46 Eliza Paddock, oldest dau of Rev. Benjamin G. of Clinton, in C; Rev. B. G. Paddock (9-5/23)
967. Bradish, Horace C. of Floyd m 4/21/45 Elizabeth C. Wade, oldest dau of late James of Schuyler, in Trenton, NY; Rev. S. Scoville (9-4/26)
968. Bradish, Irene, 89, relict of late Dr. James, d 4/8/43 at the home of her son in Floyd (9-4/13)
969. Bradish, John C., 18, s of John, Esq. d 7/11/45 in Utica (funeral from his father's home, 179 Genesee St.) (9-7/12)
970. Bradley, Abraham (Capt.), 76, d -- in New Haven, CT ("the oldest merchant in that city") (8-3/19/17)
971. Bradley, Benjamin m 11/3/42 Nancy L. Reymond; Rev. Wayne Gridley. All of Clinton (9-11/5)
972. Bradley, Bernard m 9/1/47 Kate Bryan, dau of D. Bryan of Devereux St, at St. John's Ch. in Utica; Rev. Stokes (9-9/4)
973. Bradley, Elihu, 65, formerly of Litchfield, CT, d 12/27/41 in Binghamton (2-1/5/42)
974. Bradley, Gardner of Utica m 7/28/45 Florinda Simons of Enfield in E; Rev. Robbins (9-8/7)
975. Bradley, Harriet, wf of E. Bloomfield, d -- in Lima (6-6/24/35)

27

976. Bradley, Henry M. m 2/22/44 Esther J. Van Cott in Guilford; Rev. J. L.
     James. All of Guilford (Oxford Republican, 2/29)
977. Bradley, John of Rochester m 2/12/33 Margaret Ward of Auburn in A (6/3/6)
978. Bradley, Margaret (Mrs.), 59, d 10/10/47 in Utica (funeral from her late
     home, 54 Catherine St.) (9-10/11)
979. Bradley, Miles A. m 6/5/32 Delilah White, both of Auburn, in A (6-6/13)
980. Bradley, Nehemiah, 85, father of Harvey and Alvan, formerly of Harwinton,
     CT, d 11/2/46 in Whitesboro, NY (9-11/3)
981. Bradley, Robert, 81, d 12/3/49 at the home of James Benton in New Hartford
     (9-12/13)
982. Bradstreet, Eleanor (Mrs.), about 40, d 2/21/49 in Utica (funeral at the
     home of John G. Webb, 1 Cooper St.) (9-12/22)
983. Bradt, Anthony of Geneva m 10/18/31 Mary Bedell of Phelps in P; Rev.
     Mandeville (6-10/19)
984. Bradt, C. B. of Deerfield m 9/15/46 Eliza E. Jewell of Rochester in R;
     Prof. Dewey (9-9/17)
985. Bradt, Clarence Stuart, 14 mo, s of Samuel, d 12/1/30 in Geneva (6-12/8)
986. Bradt, Emily Caroline, 14, oldest dau of Samuel, d 1/8/31 in Geneva (6-1/12)
987. Bradt, Maria (Mrs.), 29, d -- in Schenectady (6-8/9/37)
988. Brady, James of the firm of J. and P. Brady m 6/17/46 Mary Cary of Utica
     in U; Rev. Cull (9-6/19)
989. Brady, Mary A., 6, dau of William and Catherine, d 3/11/50 in Utica
     (funeral from her father's home, 98 John St.) (9-3/13)
990. Bragg, Braxton (Brevet Lt. Col.), U.S. Army, m 6/7/49 Mary Jane Ellis, dau
     of Mary Jane and late Richard G., at the family home in Terrebone Parish,
     LA; Rev. John Sandel (9-6/21)
991. Brainard, Charles T., 27, d 5/17/50 in Watertown (9-6/1)
992. Brainard, Henry P. W., formerly publisher of the People'sAdvocate in
     Norwich, d 11/9/28 in NYC (7-11/26)
993. Brainard, Mary, 3, dau of H. Brainard, d 5/21/44 in Rome, NY (9-5/23)
994. Brainard, Othniel, 76, (a Rev. soldier) d 5/27/32 in Perryville ("for
     nearly thirty years ... a member of the Episcopal church.") (3-6/5)
995. Brainerd, David, 22, d 4/6/25 at Cornwall of consumption (born in the
     Sandwich Islands and a member of the foreign missions school; after his
     arrival in NY in 1819 went to Boston and later to West Brookfield, MA
     for instruction)(9-5/24)
996. Brainerd, Jeremiah (Capt.), 71, d 1/2/48 in Rome, NY (9-1/8)
997. Braithwaite, Ruth, 33, wf of F. Braithwaite, d 6/7/45 in Sullivan (3-7/5)
998. Brakly, Esther (Mrs.), 72, formerly of New Milford, CT, d 3/10/42 at the
     home of her son-in-law Philo Judson in Oxford (Oxford Times, 3/16)
999. Brand, C. C. (Capt.) m 12/12/47 Delina A. Case, dau of Russel, Esq., in
     Smyrna; Rev. Perry G. White. All of Smyrna (9-12/16)
1000. Brandt, John, Esq., chief of the Mohawk tribe and son of the late chieftain
     in that name, d -- at the Mohawk Village, Upper canada (6-10/3/32)
1001. Brayman, James O., one of the editors of the Buffalo Commercial Advertiser,
     m 4/23/50 Eliza E. Warren, dau of A. Warren of Racine, WI, in Racine;
     Rev. William Rollinson (9-4/26)
1002. Brayman, Mason, Esq., formerly editor of the Buffalo Bulletin, m 9/6/36
     Mary Williams in Buffalo (6-9/14)
1003. Brayton, Benjamin (Maj.), 72, d 12/12/46 at the home of his son in Pulaski
     (9-12/29)
1004. Brayton, Edward S. m 9/28/47 Sarah Miller, dau of late Morris S., in Utica;
     Rev. Wiley. All of Utica (9-9/29)
1005. Brayton, Hervey, Jr., nearly 3, s of Hervey, Esq., d 2/8/45 in Westernville
     (scarlet fever) (9-2/17)
1006. Brayton, Isaac (Rev.) of Watertown m -- Elizabeth S. Boyd, dau of Robert,
     Esq. of Albany, in A; Rev. Dr. J. N. Campbell (9-7/3/45)
1007. Brazie, Henry W. of Utica m 2/17/50 Malvina McPherson of Greenfield; Rev.
     E. Francis (9-2/19)
1008. Breck, Hannah, 71, d 9/17/32 at the home of her son-in-law, Rev. B.
     Northrop (3-9/31)
1009. Brees, Abraham R. m 10/10/33 Lucy Ann Berry (6-10/16)
1010. Brees, Henry, 82, (a Rev. pensioner) d 6/2/35 in Elmira (b in NJ)
     (6-6/24)

28

1011. Breese, Arthur Esq., 53, of Utica, clerk of the Supreme Court, d 8/15/25 in NYC where he had gone for his health (8-8/31)
1012. Breese, Frances Helen, youngest dau of late Arthur, Esq., d 6/4/47 in Utica (funeral from the home of her mother, 35 Broad St.) (9-6/5)
1013. Breese, Mary M. (Mrs.), 33, dau of Joseph and Fanny Conklin, d 12/22/28 near Venetteville, Chemung Co. (joined Presby. Ch. at age 19; surv by widowed mother, husband, and five children) (5-3/2)
1014. Breese, Sylvester W. m 9/24/35 Nancy Stevens in Elmira (6-9/30)
1015. Breese, Thomas M.,purser in the navy, m Lucy Maria Randolph, dau of Richard H.,Esq., in Newport (9-6/7)
1016. Brent, Henry J., Esq. of NYC m 4/3/50 Weltha Backus, dau of Hon. F. F. of Rochester, in R; Rev. J. H. McIlvaine (9-4/15 and 5/30)
1017. Bresser, Cornelius of Devereux m 12/2/47 Emily Cady of New Bedford, MA; Elder W. Tillinghast (9-12/23)
1018. Brewer, Abraham, 97, d -- in Sparta, Liv. Co. (9-6/27/26)
1019. Brewer, John L. m 3/20/36 Sally Lyon in Benton (6-3/30)
1020. Brewer, Laura, 34, wf of Alonzo, Esq., d 6/16/33 in Canandaigua (6-6/26)
1021. Brewer, Margaret (Mrs.), 63, d 8/3/44 in Southport (5-8/8)
1022. Brewster, Charles Wentworth, 14 wks, s of Charles and Mary, d 7/23/47 in Utica (funeral from the American Hotel) (9-7/24)
1023. Brewster, Edwin Augustus, 8, d 11/9/30; Mary Endine, 5, d 11/13; Elizabeth, Maria, 10, d 11/27; and Abby Ann, 3, d 11/28 in Vernon ("canker of the throat"; all are children of Justin and Mary Ann Brewster and all died at home in Vernon) (9-12/7)
1024. Brewster, Frederick W. m 10/2/33 Caroline R. Smith in Catlin (6-10/23)
1025. Brewster, R.(?) W. D. m 9/11/33 Saphrona Burnap in Rochester (6-9/25)
1026. Brewster, Samuel C., Esq. m 2/14/49 Sarah O. Ely, late of Brownville, in Geddes, Onon. Co.; Rev. Dr. Gregory of Syracuse (9-2/20 and 3/19)
1027. Brewster, Sarah G. (Mrs.), 27, d -- in Greece, NY (6-8/21)
1028. Brexton, John m -- Louise Lord in Milo (6-3/2/31)
1029. Bridges, Edmund E. of Prattsburgh m 12/17/35 Sarah A. Gunsolus of Wheeler in W (6-1/6/36)
1030. Bridgman, Jacob F. of Penn Yan m 9/13/46 Lucy A. Sheppard of Jerusalem, NY; Rev. Cranmer (6-9/26)
1031. Bridgman, Marilla, 64, wf of Dr. William, d 4/23/50 in Springfield, MA (9-4/26)
1032. Brigden, Susan Thomson, 4, dau of G. N., d 12/6/48 in Painted Post (4-12/20)
1033. Briggs, J. D. of Virginia m 12/31/44 Eliza Maltby, dau of Seth, Esq., at New York Mills; Rev. Ira Pettibone (9-1/4/45)
1034. Briggs, Jerome J., Esq., district attorney of Onondaga Co., m 1/13/35 Charlotte Strong in Onondaga; Rev. McLaren (6-1/21/35)
1035. Briggs, John W., 14, s of Thomas and Elizabeth of Utica, d 10/2/44 in Utica (scarlet fever) (9-10/7)
1036. Briggs, Nathan (Capt.), 46, d -- in Canandaigua (6-8/11/30)
1037. Briggs, Olive, about 20, d 9/4/30 in Utica (9-9/7)
1038. Briggs, Robert, 40, d 9/20/34 in Benton (6-10/1)
1039. Briggs, Wilber N., 43, d 1/10/44 in Utica (9-1/12)
1040. Brigham, C. D. of Lockport, editor of the Niagara Courier, m 11/16/46 Caroline Rundell of Norwich in N; Rev. Duncan (9-11/20)
1041. Brigham, Mary (Mrs.), 75, d 3/29/28 at the poor house in Hopewell (6-4/16)
1042. Brigham, Origen S., Esq., attorney, m 10/10/43 Frances E. Waterman, both of West Troy, in West Troy; Rev. Dr. Brigham of NYC (9-10/25)
1043. Brigham, Spencer, 12, s of Dr. A. Brigham, superintendent of the State Lunatic Asylum, d 8/16/48 in Utica (funeral at the asylum) (9-8/17)
1044. Brigham, William H., 28, oldest s of Mrs. Lucy Porter of Baldwinsville, d "in December last" in New Orleans (cholera) (1-8/23/49)
1045. Bright, Edward Jr. of Utica m -- Adaline Osborn in Homer (6-2/10/30)
1046. Bright, Lucy (Miss), 20, d 5/16/32 at the home of Israel Huntington in Geneva (6-5/30)
1047. Brightman, Henry, Esq. of Cazenovia m 11/20/50 A. T. Stafford of Utica in U; Rev. B. G. Paddock (9-11/21)
1048. Briglen, Edward, Esq. m 10/26/35 Margaret Perhamus from Ireland (6-11/4)
1049. Brimmer, Harriet, 28, wf of Martin, Esq. of Boston and dau of James Wadsworth, Esq. of Geneseo, d 2/1/33 in Havana, NY (6-2/27)
1050. Brinckerhoff, George, for many years a resident of Utica, d 2/10/46 in Albany (9-2/11)

1051. Brininston, Thaddeus m 11/4/46 Margaret Bogardus, both of Port Byron, in Skaneateles; Rev. J. S. Mitchell (1-11/16)
1052. Brink, Henry W. m -- Hannah French in Arcadia (6-4/7/30)
1053. Brintnall, Sarah (Mrs.), 28, dau of Asahel Carmichael of Western, d 6/5/45 in Western (9-6/12)
1054.* Bristol, Eli, 88, (a Rev. soldier) d 9/28/43 in Clinton (one of the earliest settlers in the town of Kirkland) (9-10/5)
1055. Bristol, Frances P., 13, oldest dau of William, d 12/1/46 in Utica (funeral from the home of her father, 239 Genesee St.) (9-12/3)
1056. Bristol, Harriet E., 19, dau of George, Esq., d 11/7/50 in Clinton (died on her birthday) (9-11/8)
1057. Bristol, John S. of Seneca Falls m -- Elmira Wood of Dryden in D (6-10/9/33)
1058. Bristol, Lucinda, 73, wid of late Eli, d 8/22/45 in Clinton (9-8/26)
1059. Bristol, Margaret (Mrs.), 33 or 38(?) d 7/4/41 inChittenango (3-7/7)
1060. Bristol, Nancy Pratt, dau of George, d 9/8/24 in Clinton (9-9/14)
1061. Bristol, Reuben of Newark, NY m 2/17/31 Polly Watson of Lyons in L (6-3/2)
1062. Bristol, Sarah Cornelia, 10, dau of William d 1/12/46 in Utica (funeral from Trinity Ch.) (9-1/13)
1063. Bristol, William m 11/3/24 Elizabeth Case in Utica; Rev. Brace. All of Utica (9-11/9)
1064. Britain, Nicholas of Auburn m 12/29/35 "Miss Hodgman", youngest dau of William of Seneca Falls, in S. F. (6-1/13/36)
1065. Britell, Eliphalet R., 34, d 12/4/25 in Utica (9-12/6)
1066. Britt, Benjamin m 9/5/31 Catharine Farnham in Perryville; Rev. Northrop (3-9/13)
1067. Britt, Sergeant m 9/27/32 Mabel Judd, both of Perryville, in P; Rev. B. Northrop (3-9/31)
1068. Brittain, Willson J. of Auburn m 9/19/41 Charity Clarke of Centerville in Centerville; Rev. S. S. Howe of Painted Post (4-9/22)
1069. Broadhead, Thomas (Dr.) d -- "at his residence in Clermont"(6-11/24/30)
1070. Brockett, Emma P., 5, d 2/17/50 and Delos, 7, d 3/31 in Westmoreland. Both are children of Timothy and Lucy (scarlet fever) (9-4/4)
1071. Brockway, John C. m 1/31/44 Mary A. Capen at Griffin's Hotel; Rev. A. B. Grosh. All of Frankfort (9-2/2)
1072. Brockway, Reed of Frankfort m 7/4/46 Lydia Carpenter of Bridgewater in Utica; Dexter Gillmore, Esq. (9-7/7)
1073. Brodhead, Thomas (Dr.), 67, d 11/7/30 in Clermont, Columbia Co. (9-11/23)
1074. Brodock, Chauncey of Vienna , NY m 2/27/44 Eliza Perrin of Camden in C; Rev. Kennicott (9-3/7)
1075. Bromley, Augustus, 2, only s of Daniel N. and Angelica, d 6/23/48 in Baldwinsville (1-6/28)
1076. Bronnell, Fannie Maria, 16, youngest dau of Abner and Susan, d 3/30/44 in Sauquoit (9-4/1)
1077. Bronson, Benjamin F., 30, d 12/5/48 in New Hartford (9-12/18)
1078. Bronson, Henry G., Esq. of Utica m 9/8/45 Eliza M. Carpenter of Auburn in A; Rev. S. H. Coxe (9-9/16)
1079. Bronson, Myron H. of Smithfield m 10/24/39 Emeline Fort of Lenox in L; Rev. A. T. Mason of Clockville (3-10/30)
1080. Bronson, Nancy (Miss), 20, d 5/23/39 in Seneca (6-5/29)
1081. Bronson, P., Esq. m 8/19/45 Mrs. Deborah Ann (surname not listed) in Auburn; Rev. Lathrop (9-8/26)
1082. Brook, James, 8 mo, s of John and Margaret, d 4/27/49 in Big Flats (5-5/4)
1083. Brooks, _____ (Mrs.) (notice of her funeral service to be held 11/5/47 at her husband's home, 282 Genesee Street, Utica) (9-11/5)
1084. Brooks, Alanson m 10/1/35 Mary Dean Swift in Phelps (6-10/14)
1085. Brooks, Charles C. of Athens, PA m 10/12/48 Rhoda B. Davidson of Elmira, NY (5-10/13)
1086. Brooks, Emma A. (Miss), 18, dau of Col. Edward of Detroit, d 9/11/43 at Ann Arbor, MI (9-9/26)
1087. Brooks, Fidelia C., 45, of the Mendi Mission, formerly of Bloomfield, ME, d 1/11/50 near Sierra Leone (9-5/23)
1088. Brooks, Horace of Smithville m 2/12/29 Sally Hacket of Preston in P; Rev. Rush (8-2/18)
   * For a late insert for Cyrenus C. Bristol see entry 1224.

1089. Brooks, John m 3/31/34 Polly Phelps (in Penn Yan?) (6-4/9)
1090. Brooks, Lewis Esq. m 12/16/30 Charity McCarty in Phelps (6-12/22)
1091. Brooks, Lorenzo H. m 2/23/32 Harriet E. Toby of East Bloomfield in E. B.;
      Rev. Norton of Richmond (6-3/14)
1092. Brooks, Micah (Gen.) m 9/23/33 Elizabeth Chatten(?) in Salem (6-10/16)
1093. Brooks, Peter, about 35, d 11/20/39 in Chittenango (3-11/20)
1094. Brooks, Philander m 9/1/49 Julian (sic) Whitney, dau of Luke, in
      Springfield, PA; Rev. William Mitchel. All of Springfield, PA
      (5-9/7)
1095. Brooks, Robert B. (Rev.), 22, pastor of Bapt. Ch., Robertsville, SC,
      d 11/29/25 in Robertsville (9-12/6)
1096. Brooks, Stephen, son of Hon. Merritt Brooks of Steuben, m 12/26/48 Frances
      A. Ward, dau of Merrella, Esq. of Middletown, CT, in Middletown, CT;
      Rev. Y. N. Lewis (9-1/13/49)
1097. Brooks, Thomas (Maj.) of Plymouth d 8/30/22 (killed by a falling tree)
      (8-9/4)
1098. Brosseau, Luke m 10/15/43 Jane Hood in Chittenango; Rev. James Abell.
      All of Chittenango (3-10/18)
1099. Brother, Henry, inf s of Henry Sr., d 12/17/32 in Bath (6-1/2/33)
1100. Brother, Valentine, Esq., 47, member of Assembly-elect from Ontario Co.,
      d -- in Seneca (8-1/26/20)
1101. Brotherson, P. R. K. m 6/18/33 Frances B. McReynolds, only dau of M., Esq.,
      in Elmira; Rev. J. D. Carder (6-6/26)
1102. Brouwer, Cornelius (Rev.), 75, d 12/23/45 in Geneva (50 years a minister)
      (9-1/3/46)
1103. Brower, Henry J., 64, formerly of Utica, d 4/11/49 in Lewiston (9-4/28)
1104. Brower, Peter m 5/3/31 Margaret McBride; J. French, Esq. All of Sullivan
      (3-5/17)
1105. Brown, _____, inf child of Jonathan, d -- in Utica (9-8/8/26)
1106. Brown, _____, widow, d -- in Brownville (mother of late Maj. Gen. Jacob
      Brown; first white woman "that set foot on Jefferson County soil")
      (6-2/17/30)
1107. Brown, _____, 49, wf of Jonas, d 9/7/31 (4-9/13)
1108. Brown, _____, 6 mo, dau of Orville C., d 9/18/50 at Williamsburgh, L.I.,
      NY (funeral at the home of Levi Cozzens, 66 Liberty St. [in Utica?])
      (9-9/19)
1109. Brown, Aaron D. m -- Martha W. McCoy in Friendship (6-1/19/31)
1110. Brown, Alonzo m 3/23/28 Harriet Mariah Southworth, both of Bridgewater,
      in B; Rev. W. A. Matson (9-3/30)
1111. Brown, Ann (Mrs.), 57, d 5/8/50 in Utica (funeral "at her sister's,
      Samuel Brown, 69 Fayette street") (9-5/9)
1112. Brown, Charles of Benton m -- Almira Raplee of Milo in M (6-3/9/31)
1113. Brown, Charles m 7/31/32 Julia Belden in Vienna; Rev. Griswold (8/15 and
      8/22)
1114. Brown, Charles m 4/5/35 Mary Wurks, both of Elmira, in E (6-4/22)
1115. Brown, Charles Lyman of Stockbridge m Esther A. Ferry of Sherburne at
      Christ Ch., Sherburne; Rev. Israel Foote, rector of St. Peter's Ch.,
      Bainbridge) (9-10/1)
1116. Brown, Civilian, Esq. m 3/26/50 Harriet R. Norton, both of Elmira, at the
      Methodist Parsonage in Corning; Rev. H. N. Seaver (4-4/3 and 5-4/5)
1117. Brown, Clark m 8/10/42 Mary Elizabeth Dodge, both of Corning, in C; Rev.
      Amos Hard (4-8/17)
1118. Brown, Cornelia, 33, wf of Dr. George and dau of Nathan and Abigail Smith
      of New Haven, VT, d 3/6/25 in Rome, NY (consumption) (9-3/22)
1119. Brown, Daniel E. (Rev.), superintendent of the Green Bay mission,
      m 10/12/34 Harriet Jones Lewis, dau of Ozias, Esq. of Litchfield, at
      St. Michael's Ch., Litchfield, CT; Rev. Samuel Fuller, Jr., rector
      (6-11/5)
1120. Brown, Daniel M. m 3/6/32 Eunice Tiffany in Canandaigua (6-3/21)
1121. Brown, Darius of Benton m 4/6/34 Leah Johnson, dau of Widow Johnson
      of Benton; Rev. Charles P. Wack (6-4/23)
1122. Brown, David of Albany m 6/18/32 Joan Faulkner, dau of William, formerly
      of Geneva, d -- in NYC (6-6/27)
1123. Brown, David (Rev.), formerly of Lockport, m 5/28/35 Miss Morel of Georgia
      in St. Augustine, East florida (6-8/5)

31

1124. Brown, David T. (Dr.) of NYC, formerly first physician at the N. Y. Sate
       Lunatic Asylum,m 12/25/49 Cornelia W. Clapp, dau of H. W., Esq., in
       Greenfield, MA (9-1/5/50)
1125. Brown, E. G. of the firm of Little and Brown in Elmira m 8/14/50 Sarah
       Van Winkle of Lyons in L; Rev. Hull (5-8/16)
1126. Brown, Ebenezer of Macdonough m 9/10/26 Mary Arnold of German in G;
       Job Rockwell, Esq. (8-9/22)
1127. Brown, Eleazer m 12/10/20 Mrs. Hannah Wales (dau of Hascall Ransford,
       Esq.) both of Norwich (7-12/13)
1128. Brown, Elizabeth Fazon, 21, wf of William F. and oldest dau of late
       Robert Fazon, d 11/9/49 in NYC (consumption) (9-11/13)
1129. Brown, Ella, 22 mo, youngest dau of James N. and Eliza A., d 2/5/48 in
       Utica (9-2/7)
1130. Brown, Ezra, Esq. of Bridgewater m 4/13/47 Mrs. Caroline L. Terry of
       Sangerfield in S; Rev. W. A. Matson (9-4/16)
1131. Brown, Frederick H. of Ohio m 5/17/30 Samantha Chandler of Auburn in A
       (6-5/26)
1132. Brown, George Herbert, 23, d 10/23/46 in Geneva (funeral from the home of
       David Field on Castle St.) (6-10/23)
1133. Brown, George S. (of the firm of Dillage and Brown, attorneys, Syracuse),
       late of Rome and son of Dr. George Brown, d 3/4/48 in New Orleans, LA
       (9-3/17)
1134. Brown, George, 76, (a Rev. soldier) d 12/17/33 in Southport (6-1/1/34)
1135. Brown, H. S. of Paris, NY m 7/20/47 C. A. Brainard of Westmoreland
       (9-7/24)
1136. Brown, Harriet, 25, wf of Nathan and dau of John and Polly Woodruff
       formerly of Ithaca, d 3/22/41 in Hector (4-4/2)
1137. Brown, Henry, 3, s of James, d -- in Tioga (6-7/24/33)
1138. Brown, Henry m 2/14/38 Maria Butler in Morrisville; Elder Blakslee
       (3-2/21)
1139. Brown, Henry (Dr.) m 1/16/50 Fanny(?) Smith, both of Floyd; Rev. Walter
       H. Long of Whitesboro (9-1/22)
1140. Brown, Henry K. m 11/3/44 Hannah Story, both of Syracuse, in Utica; Rev.
       D. Skinner (9-12/4)
1141. Brown, Henry V. m 1/31/30 Elizabeth Breed, dau of Elias; Elder J. Randall.
       All of Norwich (7-2/3) (an alternate listing has the bride posted as
       Mary Elizabeth Breed)
1142. Brown, Hiram, merchant, m 6/18/34 Angeline Beach in Sullivan; Rev. E. L.
       North. All of Sullivan (3-6/24)
1143. Brown, Horace of Wellsburgh, NY m 11/28/50 Elizabeth Marsh, dau of Hose(?)
       Marsh, Esq. of Troy, PA, in T; Elam Benuit (5-12/6)
1144. Brown, Israel, 44, d -- in Penn Yan (6-6/4/34 and 6/18/34)
1145. Brown, James Alexander m Charlotte Death in Boston (6-11/10/30)
1146. Brown, James B. m 11/18/30 Eliza Covert in Seneca; Rev. Nisbet (6-12/1)
1147. Brown, James H. m 6/3/49 Lafrance P. Taber at the Meth. Ch. in Elmira;
       Rev. Seaver. All of Elmira (5-6/8)
1148. Brown, James Rodney m 9/1/35 Catharine Jane Hewson in Jerusalem, NY
       (6-9/9)
1149. Brown, Jeanitte F., 22, wf of William H. and dau of William W. Backus of
       Utica, d 7/15/45 in Marshall, MI (9-8/11)
1150. Brown, John, Esq., 72, formerly of Brownville, NY d 4/16/45 in Trenton, NJ
       (went to Jefferson Co., NY from Bucks, PA "at an early day" with his
       bro., late Maj. Gen. Brown) (9-5/8)
1151. Brown, John B. m 1/24/31 Adaline Mooker in Seneca (6-2/9)
1152. Brown, John H. of Brooklyn m 2/20/49 Mahala Jackson of Chemung; Rev. N. N.
       Beers (5-3/2)
1153. Brown, John L., 23, student of medicine, d 4/19/22 in Preston (surv by
       his mother, brothers, and sisters) (7-4/24)
1154. Brown, John P., Esq., 27, d 3/19/47 in Watertown (grad from Union Col;
       studied law and later practiced law with Hon. Joseph Mullin (9-3/26)
1155. Brown, John R., merchant, of PennYan m 10/18/31 Jane Bogert, dau of Isaac,
       Esq. of Dresden, in D; Rev. Todd (6-10/19)
1156. Brown, John R. (possibly H.) ("colored") of Philadelphiam 6/8/50 Mrs.
       Mary Ann Beckler ("white") of Boston; Rev. E. T. Taylor (9-6/14)
1157. Brown, John W. of Phelps m 3/27/33 Bethiah Kelly, dau of Thomas of Phelps,
       in P (6-4/10)

1158. Brown, John W. (Rev.) of Astoria, NY d 4/9/49 on the Island of Malta
(9-5/22) (funeral service conducted by Rt. Rev. Bishop of Gibralter)
1159. Brown, Joseph (Rev.), 45, d 9/16/33 in NYC (6-10/9)
1160. Brown, Joseph of Horseheads m 9/1/36 Louisa Harvey (in Elmira?)
(6-9/7 and 9/14)
1161. Brown, Josephine, 2, dau of Hiram, d 9/16/41 in Canaseraga (3-9/22)
1162. Brown, Josiah P. of Boston, MA m 1/24/49 Amelia E. Lewis, dau of Edwin,
Esq., in Sullivan; Rev. Washington Strickney (5-2/2)
1163. Brown, L. Burdette m 2/10/35 Adaline Whipple of Cazenovia in C; Rev. E. S.
Barrows (3-2/24)
1164. Brown, Lydia Gaven, 80, relict of Elijah T., d -- at the home of her
son in Floyd ("Papers in Taunton, Mass. please copy") (9-6/4/50)
1165. Brown, Martha (Mrs.), 65, formerly of albany, d -- in Utica ("The friends
of Abraham Higham are requested to attend her funeral ... at 64 Columbia
st.") (9-4/2/42)
1166. Brown, Mary, 56, wf of J. P., d 10/2/42 in Utica (funeral at the home of her
husband, 77 Fayette St.) (9-10/8)
1167. Brown, Mary Abby, 1 yr, only dau of Oliver and Almira, d 8/16/48 in Trenton,
NY (9-8/24)
1168. Brown, Mary Frances, 21, consort of William and dau of Myron and Sophia
Jewel, d 1/12/44 in Vernon (9-1/26)
1169. Brown, Nathan of Oxford m 10/15/18 Harriet Ives, dau of Lyman, Esq. of
Guilford, in G; S. A. Smith, Esq. (8-10/28)
1170. Brown, Nehemiah, 56, d 10/23/47 in Utica (funeral at his late home, corner
Mary and Second Sts.) (9-10/25)
1171. Brown, O. R. (Gen.) of Bridgewater m 4/16/44 Fanny Skeel of Lebanon at
Grace Ch., Waterville; Rev. F. C. Brown (9-4/24)
1172. Brown, Oliva (Mrs.) d 5/29/41 in Morrisville (3-6/16)
1173. Brown, Porter T. m 10/20/50 Cynthia A. Allen in Elmira; Rev. Dickinson.
All of Elmira (5-10/25)
1174. Brown, Samuel R., 44, d -- in Cherry Valley (author of The Western
Gazetteer, etc.) (8-10/22/17)
1175. Brown, Simeon (Rev.), 78, d 7/23/26 in Brookfield, NY (9-8/15)
1176. Brown, Stephen E. m 5/11/43 Lydia Rogers, both of Preston, in P; Rev.
J. T. Goodrich (Oxford Republican, 5/19)
1177. Brown, Stephen W., Esq., 49, formerly sheriff of Herkimer Co., d 5/30/46
in Little Falls (9-6/6)
1178. Brown, Thomas m 2/6/33 Nancy McClandish, both of Seneca; Elder Bentley
(6-2/13)
1179. Brown, Thomas m 2/17/33 Mary Miles in Lyons (6-2/27)
1180. Brown, Thomas m -- Sophia Alexander, both of Painted Post, in Elmira
(6-5/21/34)
1181. Brown, Timothy (Capt.), 72, d 8/23/37 at his home in Sullivan (an early
settler in the region) (3-8/30)
1182. Brown, W. H. of Marshall, MI m 10/13/42 Jeanette E. Backus, dau of William
W., in Utica; Rev. John P. Knox (9-10/17)
1183. Brown, Walter m 1/17/21 Elizabeth Smith (in Preston?); Rev. Nathan Noyes
(7-2/14)
1184. Brown, Weltha, 70, relict of Elijah and mother of Edwin Brown of Rochester,
d 5/26/45 at the home of William Rossiter in Little Falls (deceased was
sister-in-law of late Dr. Backus, first president of Hamilton Col.,and
sister of the mother of Dr. F. F. Backus of Rochester (9-6/25)
1185. Brown, William m "in February" Rebecca Wood; Elder N. Noyes. All of
Preston (7-7/20/19)
1186. Brown, William, 19, d 1/9/32 in Utica (nephew of George Stafford who
d 1/15 (Wm. served "past two years" as clerk in the store of Messrs.
Stafford and Beddoe in Geneva)(6-1/18)
1187. Brown, William, about 33, d 7/20/40 in Sullivan (3-7/22)
1188. Brown, William m 3/6/42 Mary Bennett, both of Oxford, in O; Rev. J. T.
Goodrich (Oxford Times, 3/9)
1189. Brown, William m 2/17/48 Matilda Ann Johnson, both of Whitestown, in W;
Elder Thomas Hill (9-3/13)
1190. Brown, William, 9, d 9/2/50; Jonathan, 4, d 9/3; Mary Elizabeth, 2, d
9/4. All died in Jackson Co., MI in the home of their father,
Obediah Zina Brown, formerly of Southport, NY (5-10/25)

1191. Brown, William H. of Waterloo m 11/20/36 Eliza Sherwood of Geneva; Richard Hogarth, Esq. (6-12/7)
1192. Brown, William H. m 2/18/38 Hellen A. Reddish, both of Chittenango; Rev. Tuttle of Fayetteville (3-2/21)
1193. Brown, William W. of Rome, NY m 10/2/50 Emily Wood of New York Mills at the McGregor House in Utica; Rev. William H. Spencer (9-10/3)
1194. Browne, Elizabeth (marr. status not given) d 9/16 in Hopewell at age 70 (6-9/25/46)
1195. Browne, Lydia, 67, widow, of Southeast, Put. Co. d 8/25/34 in Geneva (6-8/27)
1196. Brownell, _____, about 3, child of "Mr. Brownell", d 7/23/33 (4-7/30)
1197. Brownell, Clarissa (Mrs.), 26, d 8/23/36 in Penn Yan (6-9/7)
1198. Brownell, David m -- Matilda Gurnam in Waterloo (6-10/6/30)
1199. Browning, Edwin K. of Utica m -- Harriet P. Pierce of Uxbridge (MA?) in U; Rev. Fish (9-11/19/45)
1200. Browning, John, 47, d 12/11/34 in Manlius (b in Devonshire, England) (3-12/16)
1201. Brownwell, Gilbert of Cayuga Co. m 2/9/31 Charlotte C. Bullard of Seneca in S; Rev. Nisbet (6-2/16)
1202. Brownwell, James, about 50, living near the Susquehannah Factory in Hartwick, d 11/28/16 (suicide by hanging - "left a large family") (7-12/4)
1203. Bruce, Eli (Dr.), formerly sheriff of Niagara Co., d 9/23/32 in Lockport (6-10/3)
1204. Bruce, Hobart, 3, s of Rev. Dr. Bruce, d 5/5/34 in Geneva (6-5/14)
1205. Bruce, Silas, 31, only bro of Mrs. William Greene of Geneva, d -- in Northborough, MA (6-11/2/36)
1206. Bruce, Vandervoort (Rev.), D. D., rector of Trinity Ch., Rockaway and s of late William Bruce, Esq. of NYC, m 11/18/50 Julia Stanton, dau of George W., Esq. of Utica, at St. Peter's Ch., Albany; Rev. Horatio Potter, D. D. (9-11/29)
1207. Bruchhausen, Casper (Dr.) m 3/15 Mary Leonard, both of Oxford; Rev. John B. Hoyt (Oxford Republican, 3/27/45)
1208. Brundage, John m -- Dolly Snow in Hopewell; Esquire Jones (6-12/29/30)
1209. Brundage, Joseph O., 29, d 7/25/39 in Hopewell (6-8/7)
1210. Brundage, Oser m 1/5/31 Sally Knapp in Hopewell; Elder Benham (6-1/12)
1211. Brunn, Alexander H. of Cashong m 11/17/36 Sarah R. Wells, dau of D. D., Esq., formerly of Johnstown, in Geneva; Rev. P. C. Hay (6-11/23)
1212. Brunn, Andrew of Geneva m 10/25/30 Lydia Brown of NYC in NYC; Rev. Phoebus (6-11/1)
1213. Brunn, John, about 30, d 10/9/31 in Cashong (6-10/12)
1214. Brunson, Amos (Deacon), 75, (a Rev. soldier) d 11/8/35 in East Bloomfield (6-11/25)
1215. Brunson, Sherman m -- Lucy A. Thayer in Cameron (6-7/7/30)
1216. Brush, George A., Esq. of Elmira m 11/19/50 Lucinda M. Sly, dau of John, Esq. of Southport, in S; Rev. E. W. Dickinson (5-11/22)
1217. Brush, Mills P. m 11/27/34 Lydia Ray, both of Fenner; Elder Beckwith (3-12/16)
1218. Brush, Sears m 2/16/31 Elizabeth Meeker in Phelps; Rev. Benjamin Farley

(6-3/2)
1219. Brush, William (Col.), 89, (a Rev. officer) d 5/18/30 in Norwich (7-6/2)
1220. Bryan, Daniel P. of Steuben m 10/22/35 Elizabeth B. Hollett of Bethel in B; Rev. J. E. Wagar (6-10/28)
1221. Bryan, John, merchant, m 9/17/44 Catharine O'Neil, dau of Owen, Esq., at St. John's Ch., Utica; Rev. Thomas Martin. All of Utica (9-9/19)
1222. Bryan, Orlando Martin (Dr.) of Sycamore (IL?) m 7/23/49 Jane L. Voorhees at the home of her father, Col. J. L. of Baldwinsville; Rev. T. Walker (1-7/26)
1223. Bryan, Stephen F. m 5/31/46 Sarah A. Pearson, both of Smithville, in S; Rev. L. M. Shepard (9-6/19)
1224. (a late insert: Bristol, Cyrenus C., druggist, of Buffalo m 4/7/35 Martha H. Wells, dau of Dr. Richard, at St. John's Church in Canandaigua; Rev. R. C. Shimeall (6-4/15). For other Bristols see entries 1054 through 1063.)

34

1225. Bryant, John m 10/17/32 Margaret Watson in Rochester (6-11/7)
1226. Bryant, Samuel of the firm of Everson and Bryant d 9/5/25 in Utica (9-9/6)
1227. Bryant, Warren, merchant, of Buffalo m -- J. Stebbins in Clinton (6-4/16/34)
1228. Bryen, A. C. m 10/18/31 Asenith College in Hornby; Rev. Bennet (6-11/2)
1229. Buchanan, Thomas Jr. of Utica m 12/29/46 Eliza A. Crossman of Deerfield
      in D; Rev. D. G. Corey (9-12/31/46)
1230. Bucher, Jacob, Esq. d 8/26/49 "at an advanced age" in Catlin (one of the
      earliest settlers in Chemung Co.) (5-8/31)
1231. Buchman, George of Fayette m 4/14/31 Eliza Straws of Varick (6-4/27)
1232. Buck, Cornelia S. (wf of William J., Esq. and sister of Rev. H. G. O.
      Dwight, missionary of Constantinople, and of Mrs. James Dana of Utica)
      d 6/5/46 in NYC (9-6/8)
1233. Buckbee, Sarah S., 36, d 9/4/36 in Geneva (consumption) (6-9/7)
1234. Buckingham, F. William, Esq. of Boston m 6/30/47 Abbie S. Beecher, dau of
      Mather, Esq. of Remsen, in R (9-7/2)
1235. Buckley, Charles, 2, s of Abel, d 8/19/31 in Dresden (6-8/24)
1236. Buckley, Daniel (Dr.), 85, (a Rev. soldier) formerly of Waterbury, CT,
      d 11/9/43 at the home of his son-in-law, Ely Platt, in Utica (funeral
      at 1st Presby. Ch.) (9-11/11)
1237. Buckley, Hugh m 6/10/32 Mary Ann Todd in Seneca Falls (6-6/27)
1238. Buckley, Philip m 8/27/35 Amelia Taylor in Chittenango; J. French, Esq.
      All of Chittenango (3-9/1)
1239. Bucklin, David N., Esq., 64, formerly of Watertown, d 11/12/48 in NYC
      (9-11/15)
1240. Buckner, Alexander (Hon.), U.S. Senator from Missouri, d 6/10/33 at
      Cape Girardeau, MO (cholera - "his wife died of the same disease at
      about the same time") (9-7/2)
1241. Budd, David, 50, postmaster, d 11/4/48 in Turin (9-11/18)
1242. Budlong, Mary Jane, 4, dau of Samuel and Elizabeth, d 11/15/47 in Schuyler
      (9-11/18)
1243. Budlong, William m 5/14/45 Ruth Morris; Rev. Ferguson. All of Schuyler
      (9-5/17)
1244. Buel, Azel S. m 10/3/33 Maria E. Adams, both of Bloomfield, in Canandaigua
      (6-10/23)
1245. Buel, Theron, 46, d 9/17/33 in East Bloomfield (6-9/25)
1246. Buell, Ezra, 90, (a Rev officer) d 10/28/33 in Stillwater (6-11/13)
1247. Buell, Mariam (Mrs.), 26, d -- in Rochester (6-1/26/31)
1248. Buell, Theron, Esq., 46, d 9/17/33 in West Winfield (6-10/9)
1249. Buhl, C. H. of Detroit, MI m 8/16/43 Caroline Delong, dau of James C., Esq.
      of Utica, in U; Rev. David Plumb (9-8/17)
1250. Bulkley, _____, 3, child of Mr. Bulkley, d 12/14/25 in Utica (9-12/20)
1251. Bulkley, Andrew m 1/26/31 Clara Mills in Havana, NY (6-2/9)
1252. Bull, Edward (Rev.), pastor of the Presby. Ch., Lebanon, CT, m -- Eliza
      Hallman in New London, CT (9-12/6/25)
1253. Bull, Isaac m 9/23/32 Jane E. Bull, both of Sullivan (3-9/25)
1254. Bullard, Ira S. of Alexander m 4/19/32 Jane James of Geneva in G; Rev.
      Bentley (6-4/25)
1255. Bullard, Martin, 54, d 5/21/45 in Utica (9-5/27)
1256. Bullock, Ann Alida, 3, dau of Benjamin F., d 12/17/44 in Utica (whooping
      cough) (9-12/18)
1257. Bullock, Joseph, 27, d 10/20/30 in Gorham (6-11/1)
1258. Bullock, Sarah Elizabeth, 1 yr, dau of Benjamin F. and Eliza, d 12/4/44
      in Utica (funeral at her father's home, corner Elizabeth and Charlotte
      Sts.) (9-12/6)
1259. Bumberger, William, Esq. m 12/28/46 Sarah Matilda Gallup, dau of William,
      formerly of Norwalk, Ohio, in Damascus, Henry Co., Ohio (a double
      ceremony - see the marr of A. H. Plant) (1-1/13/47)
1260. Bump, Joseph, 11 mo, adopted s of Joseph and Sarah Bump, d 1/5/47 in
      Lysander (1-2/18)
1261. Bunday, Francis, 5, s of Warner, d 4/1/35 in Canandaigua (6-4/15)
1262. Bunday, George W., Esq. ("the Canadian Gough") m 1/23/49 Catharine Herkimer,
      a relative of the hero of Oriskany (after whom the county was named) in
      Little Falls, Herkimer Co.; Rev. Samuel Orvis (9-1/31)
1263. Bundy, William, Jr. m 8/12/49 Maria E. Drake; Rev. C. C. Carr (5-8/17)
1264. Bunnel, David of NJ m -- Sarah Conrad in Fayette (6-4/28/30)

35

1265. Bunnell, R. A. m 4/10/50 Eliza Rogers, both of Rochester, in R; Rev. Dr. Judd of Sackett's Harbor (9-4/13)

1266. Bunto, John T. of Chemung m 10/24/50 Julia A. Cooper of Erin in E; Rev. G. Greatsinger (5-11/1)

1267. Burbank, Cynthia W. (Miss), 20, d 5/18/49 in Utica (9-5/21)

1268. Burch, Ephraim J. of Rochester m 6/15/50 Elizabeth Goodman of Utica in New Hartford; Frederick Kellogg, Esq. (9-6/20)

1269. Burch, George R., 8, only s of George, Esq., d 10/7/45 in West Schuyler (9-10/21/)

1270. Burch, I. H. of Chicago, IL m 5/25/48 Mary Weld Turner, dau of late Thomas of Albany, in A; Rev. Dr. Potter (9-5/30)

1271. Burch, Louisa, 37, wf of George, Esq., d 4/14/50 in Schuyler (9-4/17)

1272. Burchard, Gurdon m 1/4/48 Adelaide Phyfe, dau of John,in NYC; Rev. J. W. Alexander. All of NYC (9-1/12)

1273. Burchard, Harriet, 48, wf of Rev. Ely and only child of late Gen. Henry McNiel, d -- (surv by husband and 4 children; was member of Presby. Ch. nearly 35 yrs) (9-6/6/45)

1274. Burdett, Horatio J. of NYC, musical director of Campbell's Minstrels, m 2/13/49 Esther C. Clark, dau of J. M., Esq. of Syracuse, in S; "Worshipful Esquire Judson" (9-3/3)

1275. Burdick, Olive D., 19, youngest dau of Oliver, d 1/20/45 in Fulton (Oxford Republican, 2/13)

1276. Burdick, Perrin of Cassville m 9/12/46 Susan Dutcher of Waterville at Henry C. Burdick's in Brookfield; Rev. Charles Randall (9-10/14)

1277. Burdick, Sandford, formerly of Sullivan, NY, d 8/22/38 in Le Roy, Calhoun Co., MI (3-12/5)

1278. Buren, Catharine (Mrs.), 40, d -- in Kinderhook (6-1/5/31)

1279. Burgess, John m 1/31/32 Janett Simpson, both of Geneva; Rev. Phelps (6-2/8)

1280. Burghart, _____, 10, s of Lambert, d 7/23/42 in Wampsville (3-7/27)

1281. Burgin, William, 70, of Middlefield d 7/6/19 near the house of George Boid, Esq. (in Norwich?) - a suicide (surv by his wf and children) (7-7/13)

1282. Burham, Robert McCoy, about 13, d 7/18/31 in Hopewell (6-7/27)

1283. Burley, Sheldon m 8/10/50 Mary Jane Smith in Corning; B. Pew, Esq. (4-8/14)

1284. Burlingame, Charles, 28, late of Meriden, CT d in Cincinnati, OH (8-10/2/22)

1285. Burlingame, George, 17, d 4/18/30 in Norwich (7-4/21)

1286. Burlinghame, Warren m 10/2/43 Catharine Gale, both of Utica, in U; Rev. Hawley (9-10/3)

1287. Burn, Henry B. m 7/7/37 Mrs. Dorothy Hewit, both of Sullivan, in Chittenango; Rev. E. A. Huntington of Albany (3-7/12)

1288. Burnap, Lucy, 35, wf of Abijah, formerly of Windham, VT, d 3/2/23 in Saratoga, NY (consumption) (8-4/9)

1289. Burnet, Evelina V. (Mrs.), 19, dau of Charles J. Burnet, Esq., d 3/7/33 in Skaneateles (6-3/27)

1290. Burnet, Frederick, 45, d 8/30/30 in Phelps (6-9/8)

1291. Burnet, Polly, wid of late Gen. Burnet, d "last week" in Vienna, NY (6-5/4/31)

1292. Burnett, Alfred of Cincinnati, OH m 4/11/45 Vandalia Blair of Cynthiana, KY in Cincinnati (9-5/2)

1293. Burnett, J. R. D. (1st Lt.), 35, 2nd Regt of Infantry, d 3/15/46 in Detroit, MI (9-3/26)

1294. Burnett, John C., 18, s of Charles J, of Skaneateles, d 8/29/23 in Oxford (8-9/3)

1295. Burnett, John L., about 24, s of Stephen of Skaneateles, d 11/23/35 in Georgetown, KY (6-12/16)

1296. Burnett, William m 2/13/31 Helen Swift in Phelps (6-2/23)

1297. Burnham, Anna, 1 yr, youngest dau of Julius A., d 1/24/45 in Utica (funeral at Grace Ch.) (9-1/25)

1298. Burnham, Anna G., wf of Gordon W. and sister of Mrs. Julius A. Spencer of Utica, d 3/14/47 in NYC (9-3/17)

1299. Burnham, Norman m 9/25/26 Lucena Warner, dau of Richard, in German; Rev. Bradford. All of German (8-10/13)

1300. Burns, Andrew of Geneva m 8/17/31 Mary Clark, formerly of Canandaigua, in Greene (6-8/24)
1301. Burns, Relief (Mrs.), 38, d in Greece, NY (6-9/4/33)
1302. Burnside, Thankful Jane, 19, wf of Amos, d 7/23/50 in Maryland, NY (9-8/12)
1303. Burpee(?), Newton N. of Mohawk m 1/10/50 Mary C. Wadsworth, dau of Maj. John W. of New Hartford, in New H; Rev. S. L. Merrell of Litchfield (9-1/14)
1304. Burr, Aaron (Col.) m Eliza Jumel in Harlem Heights, NY; Rev. Dr. Bogart (6-7/10/33)
1305. Burr, Albert C. (Maj.), 27, d 8/19/32 in Rochester (cholera) (6-8/29)
1306. Burr, Calvin m 10/5/23 Clarissa Gross (in Norwich?); Samuel Pike, Esq. (7-10/8)
1307. Burr, Calvin, 54, d 8/18/40 in New Boston (3-8/26)
1308. Burr, Edson S. of Catharine m 4/2/50 Mary Thompson of Veteran; Rev. G. M. Spratt (5-4/12)
1309. Burr, Sweezy, 16, m -- Hannah Van Northstand, 15, in Tyrone (6-2/10/30)
1310. Burr, Wakeman d -- in Boston (6-2/10/30)
1311. Burrall, _____, consort of Thomas D., Esq. of Geneva, d 4/12/31 in Rochester (funeral in Presby. Ch., Hudson, NY) (6-4/13 and 5/11)
1312. Burrall, Thomas D., Esq. m 3/9/37 Margaret Mott, both of Geneva, in Esperanza (6-3/15)
1313. Burrall, William Davies, 12, oldest s of T. D., d 8/30/34 in Geneva (6-9/3)
1314. Burritt, Elijah, 6, s of Capt. F. J., d in Elmira (6-6/4/34)
1315. Burritt, Frederick J. (Capt.), 38, d 6/6/36 (in Elmira?) (6-6/15)
1316. Burroughs, Alexander J. m 6/6/49 Eliza A. Stebbins, both of Oriskany Falls, in Westmoreland; Rev. F. A. Spencer (9-7/9)
1317. Burroughs, D. J. of Phelps m 6/27/33 Jane Ann Miller in Arcadia (6-7/17)
1318. Burroughs, Jeremiah m 6/3/36 Magdelin Miller in Varick (6-6/15)
1319. Burroughs, John D. m 10/5/34 Sally Vanvoorous, both of Phelps, in Orleans (town of Phelps) (6-10/15)
1320. Burroughs, Stephen m 6/16/50 Malinda Gardner, both of Elmira, at the Bapt. Ch. in E; G. M. Spratt (5-6/21)
1321. Burrows, James m 1/13/36 Rosette E. Tuthill in Seneca Falls (6-1/27)
1322. Burrows, William M. m 8/26/30 Mary Ray, both of Seneca, in Geneva; Rev. Phelps (6-9/1)
1323. Burt, B. B., Esq. of Utica m 6/21/43 Artemisia Noyes, dau of George, Esq. of Oriskany, in O; Rev. Samuel Wells (9-6/24)
1324. Burt, Cyrus R. m 4/26/31 Sarah R. Myers in Rochester (6-5/4)
1325. Burt, Daniel, Esq., merchant, of Buffalo m 9/8/30 Harriet R. Whiting in Utica (double ceremony - see marr of Henry H. Sizer)
1326. Burt, Elizabeth Darling, 8, dau of Erastus, d 3/12/31 in Newark, NY (6-3/23)
1327. Burt, Gideon (Col.), 82, (a Rev. officer) d 6/12/25 in Longmeadow, MA (9-6/28)
1328. Burt, Henry W. m 11/20/33 Eliza U. Yorke in Lima (6-12/11)
1329. Burt, Oliver T. m 1/13/48 Rebecca Johnson; Rev. Samuel J. May. All of Syracuse (3-1/26)
1330. Burtch, Joel m 12/23/32 Clamania Hulbard in Jerusalem, NY (6-1/2/33)
1331. Burtis, Arthur, Esq., 54, late of NYC d 1/9/33 in Phelps (b at Foster's Meadow in town of Hempstead, L. I., NY 12 July 1778; age 21 moved to NYC and became 8th ward alderman and later Supt. of the Alms House and Penitentiary at Bellevue; one of the founders of the House of Refuge there; 1831 moved to Phelps, NY to become a farmer) (6-1/16)
1332. Burtis, Arthur of Phelps m 9/18/33 Grace E. Phillips, step-dau of James E. Morse, Esq., in Cherry Valley; Rev. McAfee (6-10/9)
1333. Burtis, Charles B. m 10/6/46 Catharine D. Heartwell, dau of Benjamin of Phelps, in P; Rev. Arthur Burtis (6-10/9)
1334. Burtis, John W. m 3/31/35 Margaret Graham in Geneva; Rev. Elder Sears (6-4/8)
1335. Burtless, James of Seneca Falls m 12/20/31 Catharine Cell of Fayette; Rev. Lane (6-1/4/32)
1336. Burton, Charles, 66, d 3/11/42 in Nelson (3-3/16)
1337. Burton, Charlotte d at Sag Harbor, L.I., NY (9-6/27/26)

1338. Burton, John (Rev.), 79, d -- in Wilmington, DE (9-7/19/25)
1339. Burton, John G. m 12/6/26 Jane C. Priest, both formerly of Utica, in
       Auburn (9/12/19)
1340. Burton, Sylvester of Sullivan Co. m 3/24/50 Eunice E. Clark of Corning;
       Rev. A. L. Brooks (4-3/27)
1341. Burton, Thomas, merchant, of Elmira m 2/13/31 Anah E. Wild, dau of Levi,
       Esq. of Johnsville, in Hamilton; Prof. Sears (9-2/22)
1342. Burton, William m 12/28/43 Caroline M. Tanner, both of Schuyler, in S;
       Rev. B. Hawley of Utica (9-12/30)
1343. Burtsell, Susan (Mrs.), 45, d 12/29/47 in Utica (funeral from her late
       home, 35 Main St.) (9-12/31)
1344. Burville, Hiram m 8/11/31 Catharine Follet in Phelps (6-8/24)
1345. Busch, A. W. (Dr.), formerly of Utica, d 1/22/46 in Racine, WI Terr.
       (funeral on Mary St., town not stated) (Dr. B. in Racine just 7 mo.)
       (9-2/21)
1346. Busch, ____, 32, consort of William, d 12/20/28 in Oxford (8-12/31)
1347. Bush, B. F. of Lowville, NY m 4/3/50 H. A. Bagg of Sheboygan Falls (Mich.?)
       in S. F.; Rev. Luft (9-5/11)
1348. Bush, David m 4/16/35 Rachel McLaughlin in Benton (6-5/6)
1349. Bush, Edward E., Esq. m 11/4/30 Harriet I. Hawley in Rochester (6-11/17)
1350. Bush, H. B. (Dr.) of Fayetteville m 12/16/32 Marietta Tubbs of Waterloo
       in W; Rev. Dr. Mason (3-1/15/33)
1351. Bush, Isaac, Esq., 32, attorney, d 6/16/43 in Bainbridge (9-6/30)
1352. Bush, John P. "of the Utica Observer" m 11/8/43 Sarah Elizabeth Hart, dau
       of Martin, Esq.; Rev. Dr. Proal. All of Utica (9-11/10)
1353. Bush, Riley (Col.), merchant, of Nineveh m 9/7/45 Abbey Jane Denison of
       Oxford in O; Rev. J. T. Goodrich (Oxford Republican, 9/11)
1354. Bush, Sarah, 63, mother of Mrs. Sarah Blackwell of Utica, d 3/2/48 in
       Milford, CT (9-3/10)
1355. Bush, Timothy, Sr., 84, d 5/4/50 at his home in Rochester (or Utica?)
       (b in CT; his father moved the fam. to Norwich, VT when T. was young;
       in 1810 T. moved to Cayuga Co., NY; in 1833 he settled first in
       Redfield, Oneida Co. and later in Rochester, NY (9-5/9)
1356. Bushnell, Edny, 79, consort of late John, d 11/7/43 (in Utica?) (9-11/13)
1357. Bushnell, George W. of NYC m 5/16/49 Caroline M. Dlossy (sic), dau of
       John J., Esq., at 1st Presby. Ch., Brooklyn; Rev. Dr. Cox (9-5/21)
1358. Bushnell, Harvey m 9/9/30 Emeline Arnold in West Bloomfield (6-9/15)
1359. Bushnell, Jesse (Rev.) of Fort Plain m 5/6/35 Adelia Spalding, dau of
       Levi of Canaseraga, in Sullivan; Rev. S. R. Smith of Clinton (3-5/12)
1360. Bushnell, Margaret, 70, relict of Samuel of Sheffield, MA, d 2/18/35 in
       Victor, NY (6-3/4)
1361. Bushwell (?), William, 70, d 1/14/46 in Victor (6-1/23)
1362. Bussey, Charles H. of Westville m 7/30/49 Louisa Paddock of North Western
       at the home of David Putnam, Esq. in Boonville; Rev. Tuttle (9-8/10)
1363. Bussey, Esick, 76, d 6/8/48 in Lysander (1-6/14)
1364. Butcher, George of Sauquoit m 6/21/49 Eliza Jones of Frankfort at the
       Central Hotel in Utica; Rev. William H. Spencer (9-7/3)
1365. Butler, Arthur Lawrence, 1 yr, only s of James L. and Lydia P., d 7/23/49
       in Brooklyn (9-7/27)
1366. Butler, Charles S. of Kirkland m 7/18/50 Cornelia Nichols of Checkerville
       in C; Rev. E. H. Payson (9-7/20)
1367. Butler, Chauncey S. of Paris, NY m 10/3/44 Julia Sherrill of New Hartford
       in New H.; Rev. Moses C. Searle (9-10/9)
1368. Butler, Chauncy, S. of Paris, NY m 5/16/26 Betsy Mosher of Whitestown in
       W; Rev. Charles Giles (9-5/23)
1369. Butler, Dorastus m 10/4/36 Eliza G. Wood in Canandaigua (6-10/19)
1370. Butler, Hannah Avery, 58, consort of Dr. Benjamin, d 7/31/29 in Oxford
       (8-8/5)
1371. Butler, Hannah Tyler, 5, dau of Benjamin F., d 4/8/33in Albany (6-4/17)
1372. Butler, Jane Eliza (Miss), 19, dau of Chester and Nancy, d -- in Kirkland
       (consumption) (funeral from Presby. Ch., New Hartford (9-8/12/43)
1373. Butler, John m 6/11/50 Kate McWeeney, both of Westmoreland, in Utica; Rev.
       Stokes (9-6/19)
1374. Butler, Laura, nearly 30, wf of William and dau of Jesse Curtis, Esq. of
       Clinton, d 11/10/26 in Perry (9-12/5)
1375. Butler, Nathan m 3/14/47 Almira Dunbar, both of Lee, in Kirkland, James
       Ormsbee, Esq. (9-3/23)

38

1376. Butler, Sarah L., 11 mo., only child of William C. and Emily M., d 8/22/49 in Utica (funeral from her father's home, 103 John St.) (9-8/22)
1377. Butler, William, 68, d 3/9/31 in Northampton, MA (had establisehd the Hampshire Gazette there in 1786 and had run it for 29 yrs) (6-4/6)
1378. Butler, William, 17, d -- in Jerusalem, NY (6-6/19/33)
1379. Butler, William C. of Utica m 11/18/47 Emily M. Lee, dau of Charles of NYC, in NYC; Rev. Dr. Cone (9-11/22)
1380. Butterfield, Catherine, 66, wf of Daniel and mother of J., d 8/16/43 in Utica (funeral at her late home, corner Post and Charlotte Sts.) (9-8/17)
1381. Butterfield, Daniel, Jr., 41, d 3/18/45 in Utica (funeral at the home of his bro., John, 32 Fayette St.) (9-3/19)
1382. Butterfield, Daniel, 73, d 4/18/49 in Utica (funeral at home of his son-in-law, corner 3rd and Lansing Sts.)
1383. Butterfield, Henry, s of Justin, Esq. of Washington, d 9/25/50 in Utica (funeral at the home of John Butterfield, 32 Fayette St.) (9-9/28)
1384. Butterfield, John m 6/8/34 Caroline Ostram, both of Geneva; Rev. Kendicott (6-6/11)
1385. Butterfield, John Lennebacker, inf s of T. F. and C. A., d 8/21/50 in Utica (funeral at home of his father, 68 Broad St.) (9-8/23)
1386. Butterfield, Lewis, 28, attorney, formerly of Watertown, NY, d 11/27/45 in Chicago, IL (9-12/1)
1387. Butterworth. Henry, Esq., 37, d 1/16/31 in Newburgh (6-2/2)
1388. Butterworth, William m 2/28/49 Mrs. Betty Welch, both of New Hartford, at St. Paul's Ch., Utica; Rev. Marcus A. Perry (9-3/2)
1389. <--Buttolph, David, Esq., attorney, m 1/1/28 Mrs. Esther Kelsoe in Norwich; Rev. Rexford (8-1/18)
1390. Buttolph, Edith, 57, wf of John, d 6/3/41 in Sullivan (3-6/16)
1391. Buttolph, Urania, consort of David, Esq., d 4/3/27 in Norwich (8-4/13)
1392. Button, Johial, 16, d 1/13/36 in Sullivan (killed by the fall of a tree) (3-1/19)
1393. Button, Nathaniel m 2/21/44 Eliza Tibbits, dau of Jonathan, in Rome, NY (9-2/29)
1394. Button, William m 11/20/42 Polly Kelly in Sullivan; Rev. J. Abell. All of S (3-11/23)
1395. Butts, Newton of Schroepel m 5/12/50 Lydia Sweeting of Camillus in Baldwinsville; Rev. B. Alden (1-5/16)
1396. Buys, William m 9/6/33 Mary Ann Tuyl in Sodus (6-9/25)
1397. Byington, Patience (Mrs.), 69, d 6/8/44 in Camden (9-6/17)
1398. Cadd, William, 45, d 8/13/47 in Utica (9-8/16)
1399. Cady, Argalus (Maj.), 58, d 7/7/33 in Sullivan (3-7/16)
1400. Cady, Daniel of the firm of N.S. and D. Cady in Clockville m 1/4/41 Fidelia W. Palmer, only dau of A. H., Esq., at the home of her father; Rev. Alanson P. Mason (3-1/20)
1401. Cady, Daniel B., Esq., attorney, m 11/3/31 Mary J. Fay, dau of Dr. Jonas of Utica, in U; Rev. Aiken (3-11/8)
1402. Cady, John W. of Johnstown m 10/13/41 Marianne Hayes of Rome, NY in Sullivan; Rev. A. Handy (3-10/20)
1403. Cady, Stephen, 60, d 12/26/41 in Guilford (Oxford Times, 1/12/42)
1404. Cahill, Daniel, 28, d 10/17/50 in Elmira (member of Indep. Order of Odd Fellows and of the Fire Department) (5-10/25)
1405. Cahoon, Daniel, 112, d in Muskingum, OH (6-4/18/32)
1406. Calhoun, Andrew H., late clerk of the state senate, m 5/20/50 Catharine W. Dickie of Albany in A; Rev. Dr. Wyckoff (9-5/23)
1407. Calder, John m 8/31/48 Margaret Huton in New York Mills; Rev. N. D. Graves. All of N. Y. Mills (9-9/16)
1408. Caldwell, William J., Esq., 45, d 8/23/33 in Metamoras, TX (6-11/6)
1409. Calhoun, A. P., oldest s of Hon. John C., m 1/3/33 E. Chappell in Columbia, SC (6-1/30)
1410. Califf, Thomas m 9/19/48 Caroline Olmstead, both of Bridgeport, CT, in Manchester, NY; Rev. Dr. Brainard (9-9/20)
1411. Calkins, Asa, Jr., merchant, of South New Berlin m 1/23/42 Mary Hovey of Guilford in G; Rev. Bartlett (Oxford Times, 1/26)
1412. Calkins, Joseph, 23, d 4/25/42 in Corning (4-5/4)
1413. Call, Chancy L. m 1/30/36 Catharine C. Bates in Seneca Falls (6-2/10)

1414. Call, Nelson M. of Rushford m 8/22/33 Rosina Bell of Haight in H (6-9/4)
1415. Callaghan, James, 30, late of NYC, d 1/21/50 at McSpedon's ranch on the
       Calavaras River (prob. in Calif.) (9-4/11)
1416. Callahan, Henry m 5/9/43 Mary A. Allis, both of Niagara Falls, in
       Cazenovia; Rev. Henry Bannister (9-5/13)
1417. Callen, Elijah, 22, d 9/1/36 in Canandaigua (6-9/14)
1418. Cambreleng, Churchill C. m 11/17/35 Phebe Glover, dau of late John J.,
       in NYC (6-11/25)
1419. Cameron, Charles, 22, oldest s of late Hon. Dugald of Bath, d 8/8/32
       in Hornellsville (6-8/15)
1420. Cameron, Ewen, father of late Dugald, Esq. of Bath, d 4/22/32 at an
       advanced age in Prattsburgh (6-5/2)
1421. Cameron, Hannah (age blurred), wf of John, d 1/3/33 in Geneva (6-1/9)
1422. Cameron, Hannah, 8 mo, dau of J. Cameron, d 8/22/33 in Geneva (6-8/28)
1423. Cameron, Robert T., 22, s of late Dugald of Bath, d in Charleston, SC
       "while on a journey for the benefit of his health" (a grad of Union
       Col. and late a law student at Oxford, NY) (6-12/4/33 and 12/11/33)
1424. Camnell, Thomas m Eliza Morrison in Rochester (6-2/9/31)
1425. Camp, Abraham, 73, formerly of Whitestown, d 6/30/45 in Springfield, IL
       (9-7/29)
1426. Camp, Charles, 34, d 3/27/34 in Utica (6-4/2)
1427. Camp, George, 60, d 9/22/50 at Sackett's Harbor, NY (b in Glastonbury,
       CT; arrived Utica in his father's family in 1797; moved to Sackett's
       Harbor about 1815) (9-9/27)
1428. Camp, George H. m 10/18/42 Lucretia Merrell in Utica; Rev. Porter. All
       of Utica (9-10/20)
1429. Camp, George H. of Roswell, Cobb Co., GA m -- Jane M. Atwood of Darien,
       CT in Darien; Rev. N. A. Pratt of Roswell (9-4/18/50)
1430. Camp, Henry W. of Oswego m 8/27/37 Lucy A. Marren of Woodstock, VT in W
       (6-9/27)
1431. Camp, John (Rev.) d 7/9/21 at chenango Point (8-7/18)
1432. Camp, John m 1/22/45 Mrs. Abigail P. Doolittle in Utica; Rev. Theodore
       Spencer. All of Utica (9-1/23)
1433. Camp, John, 4 mo, s of John, d 4/11/46 in Utica (9-4/15)
1434. Camp, Lucretia H., 26, late of Utica, d 3/22/45 in Roswell, Cobb Co., GA
       (9-4/2)
1435. Camp, Samuel, 74, late of Whitesboro, NY, d 5/8/49 in Detroit, MI
       (member Presby. Ch., Whitesboro 28 yrs) (9-6/5)
1436. Camp, T. H., Esq. m 6/3/47 AnnElizabeth Sewall, dau of late H. D., Esq.,
       in Watertown; Rev. J. R. Boyd (9-6/11)
1437. Campau, Alexander M., second s of late Barnabe, m 4/14/46 Eliza S. Troop,
       only dau of George B., Esq., in Detroit, MI. All of Detroit (9-4/22)
1438. Campbell, _____, 15 mo, child of Asa, d 7/30/26 in Utica (9-8/1)
1439. Campbell, Desire, 58, wf of James, Esq., d -- in Walpole, NH (9-6/28/25)
1440. Campbell, Duncan of Binghamton, late of Elmira, m 8/9/49 Mrs. Harriet
       B. Haviland of Elmira in E; Rev .Dickinson (5-8/17)
1441. Campbell, George m 9/22/48 Emily Wedge both of Knoxville, in Corning;
       B. Pew, Esq. (4-10/4)
1442. Campbell, George L., Esq., late of Oswego and formerly of Canandaigua,
       d -- in NYC (6-9/30/35)
1443. Campbell, George L., 28, d 9/25/42 in Cleveland (deceased was a resident
       of Chicago, IL and a son of Robert, Esq. of Cooperstown, NY) (9-10/6)
1444. Campbell, Hannah, 67, wid of George, d 6/21/31 in Elmira (6-6/29)
1445. Campbell, Henry d 9/28/49 in Lysander (1-10/11)
1446. Campbell, John m Harriet Green in Naples (6-3/27/33)
1447. Campbell, John of Manlius m 12/17/35 Amy Maria Haight of Sullivan in S;
       J. French, Esq. (3-12/22)
1448. Campbell, John, 59, d 3/15/45 in Utica (9-3/19)
1449. Campbell, John H. m 1/15/50 Laura E. Stockey, both of Elmira; Rev. M.
       Crow (5-1/18)
1450. Campbell, Mary Ann (Miss), 31, dau of Adam I., d 9/12/38 in Chittenango
       (3-9/19)
1451. Campbell, Milton m 1/13/48 R. A. Divine in Camillus; Rev. T. W. Williams
       (9-1/24)
1452. Campbell, Olive, 57, wf of Jeremiah, d 12/19/42 (2-12/21)

1453. Campbell, Phebe (Mrs.), 80, d 8/22/49 at the home of her son, John D. Campbell, in Sauquoit (9-8/25)
1454. Campbell, Robert m 11/5/34 Ann Eliza De Peyster in Catharine (6-11/12)
1455. Campbell, Samuel member of Corngress from Chenango Co., NY m -- Maria Regina Queen of Washington, D.C. in W (8-3/5/23)
1456. Campbell, Wilcox m 1/30/31 Melinda Schuyler, both of Vernon, in V; Rev. A. Garrison (9-2/15)
1457. Campbell, William H. (Rev.), pastor of the Reformed Dutch Ch., Chittenango, m -- Catharine Schoonmaker of Flatbush, L.I., NY in F; Rev. Thomas Strong (3-10/25/31)
1458. Canell, Abial C., one of the editors of the Broome Republican, m 4/21/25 Abigail Parker, dau of late Capt. William of NYC, in NYC; Rev. Stafford (8-5/25)
1459. Canfield, J. M., Esq., 74, d 7/9/49 at Sackett's Harbor (9-7/20)
1460. Canfield, Levi m 1/27/33 Mariam Cox in Canandaigua (6-2/13)
1461. Canfield, Samuel m -- Eliza McDowell (6-3/24/30)
1462. Canning, _____ (Mr.), co-proprietor of the Detroit Currier, d 8/9/34 in Detroit, MI (6-9/3)
1463. Cannon, Esther Bouton, 56, wf of Le Grand Cannon, d 3/23/50 in Troy (9-3/29)
1464. Cannon, Legrand, 63, d 5/7/50 in Troy (9-5/9)
1465. Cantine, G. W. m 1/13/36 Philena Kent in Ithaca (6-1/27)
1466. Cantine, Mary, about 28, consort of John M., d 7/27/29 in Ithaca (8-8/5)
1467. Casper, John S. (Rev.) d -- in Withersville, SC (9-9/20/25)
1468. Carasas, Lucianno m 1/22/35 Delia Ann Orsborn, formerly of Geneva, in St. Patrica, TX (6-6/24)
1469. Card, Jason B. m -- Arminta Goodnoe in Binghamton; Lewis Wright, Esq. All of Vestal (2-10/12/42)
1470. Card, Truman G. m 8/19/47 Ellen R. Williams in Utica; Rev. James Griffiths. All of Utica (9-8/21)
1471. Cardell, J. W., 23, s of William S. of NYC, d -- in Fredonia (9-10/24/26)
1472. Carey, _____, inf ch of David, d 4/1/34 in Geneva (6-4/2)
1473. Carey, Alfred X. m 8/22/33 Sarah Murdock in Newark, NY (6-9/11)
1474. Carey, Jerusha, relict of Capt. Nathaniel "of Windham Scotland Society" and mother of Judge Anson Carey of Oxford, NY, d 11/2/27 in Franklin, Ct ("after her 80th year she spun 2191 run of yarn") (8-12/28)
1475. Carey, John m 12/26/48 Sarah Ann Lloyd in Utica; Elder Thomas Hill. All of Utica (9-12/28)
1476. Carey, John, Jr. m 4/18/50 Alida Astor, dau of William B., Esq., in NYC; Rev. G. T. Bedell (9-4/20)
1477. Carey, Sarah, 21, wf of George and dau of Charles Wattles formerly of Oxford, d 6/18/21 in O (funeral sermon by Rev. Andrews of Norwich) (8-6/20)
1478. Cargill, Nathan, Jr. of Richmond m Polly Woodruff in Canandaigua (6-3/31/30)
1479. Carley, Joseph of Buffalo m 3/16/48 Caroline M. Midlam of Utica in U; Rev. William H. Spencer (9-3/17)
1480. Carlyle, Mary (Mrs.), about 60, d 8/11/45 at German Flats (9-8/16)
1481. Carmon, Charles E. m -- Charlotte Miller, both of Clyde, in Lyons (6-6/13/32)
1482. Carnall, Henry m 11/6/50 Ann Jones, both of Utica, in U; Rev. T. O. Lincoln (9-11/13)
1483. Carnes, Henry S., formerly of Utica, m 2/11/50 Signorita Maria Domitilar Henrigunta Rodejoure Ybaire of Santa Barbara, CA in S. B. (9-5/1U)
1484. Carnes, Richard of Montezuma, NY m 8/23/48 Ann Gaffney of Utica in Rome, NY; A. B. Blair, Esq. (9-9/2)
1485. Carothers, Almira (Miss), 26, d 9/21/37 in Phelps (6-9/27)
1486. Carothers, E. W. m 6/30/39 Phebe A. Burch in Vienna, NY; J. G. Austin, Esq. All of Phelps (6-7/10)
1487. Carothers, Hiram B. of Manchester m Lazy Robinson in Phelps (6-2/10/30)
1488. Carothers, Mary (Mrs.), 33, d 5/26/39 in Geneva (6-5/29)
1489. Carpenter, A. B. (Dr.) of Hopewell m 7/18/30 Jane L. Rowley of Greece, NY in G (6-8/4)
1490. Carpenter, Abby, 42, wf of Amos H. and dau of late Eleazer House, Esq., d 4/2/44 at Houseville, Lewis Co. (9-4/9)
1491. Carpenter, Ammi Ruhannah (Mr.), 40, (formerly of Penfield, NY) d 9/2/46 in Reading, Hillsdale Co., MI (6-10/2)

1492. Carpenter, Calvin, Esq. m 7/14/42 Marietta S. Gridley in Cazenovia; Rev. Francis Hawley. All of Cazenovia (3-8/3)
1493. Carpenter, Catharine, 65, wf of Gen. M. Carpenter, for many years of Elmira and an evangelical member of the Church of Christ, d 10/19/30 in Elmira (6-11/10)
1494. Carpenter, Cyrus of De Witt m 5/11/36 Sophia Williams of Manlius in Chittenango; Rev. John C. F. Hoes (3-5/18)
1495. Carpenter, Edward m 4/7/36 Harriet Strong in Southport (6-4/27)
1496. Carpenter, Edward m 6/7/36 Harriet Carpenter in Southport (6-6/15)
1497. Carpenter, Edward Young, 3, s of C. Tracy and Caroline, late of North(ampton?), MA d 7/21/46 in Geneva, NY (6-7/31)
1498. Carpenter, Elijah, about 50, d 2/25/44 in Western (9-3/7)
1499. Carpenter, Erasmus D. m 11/28/33 Lucy Maria Knapp in Warsaw, NY (6-12/18)
1500. Carpenter, George W., 1, s of Abram and Maria A., d 11/12/49 in Baldwinsville (1-11/15)
1501. Carpenter, Henry T. m 12/13/36 Ann Brown in Elmira (6-12/21)
1502. Carpenter, Isaiah, 84, d 5/14/48 in Augusta (enlisted in Rev. War at age 14 and served also in the War of 1812) (9-7/13)
1503. Carpenter, James, Esq. m 7/17/31 Polly Bigelow, both of Phelps, in Lyons (6-7/27/31)
1504. Carpenter, James S. of Ravenna, OH m 5/1/35 Frances C. Saltenstall of Geneva in G; Rev. N. F. Bruce (6-5/6)
1505. Carpenter, John P. of Utica m 12/12/50 Sarah Knowles, youngest dau of Henry of Smyrna, in S (a Quaker ceremony) (9-12/14)
1506. Carpenter, Margaret, about 24, relict of late Dr. Carpenter and dau of Widow Smith of Hopewell, d 10/17/34 in Hopewell (6-10/22)
1507. Carpenter, Milton B. (Dr.) d 10/11/31 in Hopewell (6-10/19)
1508. Carpenter, Nelson W., druggist, m 10/17/29 Gloriann Guthrie of North Norwich in N. N.; Rev. M. Adams (8-11/4)
1509. Carpenter, Rice P. m 9/14/30 Angeline Pierce in Ovid (6-9/20)
1510. Carpenter, S. W. m 2/23/31 Lucinda Neele in Le Roy (6-3/23)
1511. Carpenter, Samuel of Greene m 1/21/29 Eliza Grant of Smithville in S; Rev. David Leach (8-1/28)
1512. Carpenter, William B., 35, d 10/19/50 at the home of his father in Tioga, PA (5-11/8)
1513. Carpenter, Zeno, 86, d 3/23/49 in Utica (funeral at the Friends Meeting House in New Hartford ("carriages leave from the home of Clark Carpenter, 36 Elizabeth st.") (9-3/24)
1514. Carr, Edward, 25, d 3/15/49 in Utica (funeral at the home of his uncle, Edward Curran, 5 Washington St.) (9-3/17)
1515. Carr, Henry of Junius m 1/12/32 Susan Powell of Galen in Alloway (6-1/25)
1516. Carr, James (Dr.) m 11/16/23 Betsey Garlick, both of Norwich, in N; Rev. Edward Andrews (7-11/19)
1517. Carr, S. T. (Dr.) of Geneva m 6/15/31 Ellen Eliza Wilson, dau of Benjamin of Albany, in A (6-6/22)
1518. Carr, Thomas m 11/12/32 Margaret Anderson in Seneca Falls (6-11/21)
1519. Carr, Thomas, 49, d 1/21/42 in Marcy (consumption) (born in England "but in early life came to this country") (9-2/3)
1520. Carr, William C. m 12/13/46 Ann Stow in Utica; Elder Thomas Hill. All of Utica (9-12/17)
1521. Carrier, Cyrus m 1/31/31 Emma S. Pond in Utica (6-2/9)
1522. Carrier, John of Syracuse m 3/29/32 Saphronia Farwell of Lyons in L (6-4/11)
1523. Carrington, Frederick T. of Peterboro m 9/26/26 Louisa Shute, dau of Maj. William of Hazlewood near Oxford, in H; Rev. Bush (8-10/6)
1524. Carrington, D. of Richmond, VA m 12/13/48 Anna E. Whitall, dau of Benjamin G. formerly of Rome, NY, in White Plains, Henrico Co., VA; Rev. Kepler (9-4/12/49)
1525. Carris, James m 4/9/35 Parmelia Smith, both of Waterloo, in Phelps (6-4/22)
1526. Carrol, Albert B., 4, s of James H and Harriett B., d 5/12/48 in Rome, NY (9-5/23)
1527. Carroll, Alida, wf of Charles H., Esq. and dau of late Jeremiah Van Rensselaer of Canandaigua, d 3/2/32 in Groveland, Liv. Co. (6-3/21)

1528. Carroll, Christopher m 3/16/49 Cynthia Watson, both of Rome, NY, in R; Alfred Martin, Esq. (9-3/22)
1529. Carson, Amirette L., 22, wf of Lafford Carson and dau of Charles Cooley, d 3/20/31 (6-3/30)
1530. Carson, George m 3/12/35 Jane Van Clief, both of Fayette, in Waterloo (6-3/25)
1531. Carson, Robert m 1/2/34 Rebecca Rippey in Seneca; Rev. John F. McLaren (6-1/15)
1532. Carson, Sarah, 63, wf of Robert, d 3/30/38 in Seneca (6-4/4)
1533. Carter, Charles H. A. of Utica m 8/1/44 Elizabeth P. Brooks, dau of Dr. John of Bernardston, MA, in B; Rev. T. Rogers (9-8/5)
1534. Carter, Henry M. m 8/10/50 Salome Gager, both of Clayville, in C; Rev. John Waugh (9-8/13)
1535. Carter, Hiram, Esq., attorney, of Durham m -- Sally Lamb, oldest dau of John, Esq. of Johnstown, in Albany (8-11/4/18)
1536. Carter, Miles m -- Eliza Curtiss in Lima (6-4/14/30)
1537. Carter, Nathaniel H., Esq. of Geneva, NY d 1/2/30 in Marseilles, France (was editor of The Statesman and author of Travels in Europe) (6-3/3)
1538. Carter, Stephen, about 30 or 50?, formerly of Chittenango, d 11/15/41 in Schenecteady (3-11/24)
1539. Carter, Julia (Mrs.), 52, mother of John and Thomas, d 1/8/44 in Utica (b in Ireland; as a widow emigrated with her two sons from Ireland to Utica) (funeral at her late home, 11 Devereux St.) (9-1/9)
1540. Cartright, Garret m -- Electa Pullen in Alloway (6-11/24/30)
1541. Carvenough, Isaac, 2, s of Robert, d 9/25/26 in Utica (9-9/26)
1542. Cary, _____, inf s of Hon. Trumbull Cary, senator, of Batavia, d -- in Albany (6-4/11/32)
1543. Cary, Anson (Hon.), 80, (a Rev. soldier) d 4/3/42 in Oxford (a pioneer settler in this region; formerly justice of the peace; state assemblyman; sheriff of Chenango Co.; and for many years a judge of the court of common pleas) (funeral from the Universalist Ch.) (Oxford Times, 5/1)
1544. Cary, E. of Oxford m 12/29/42 Ann Crider of Whitestown in W; Rev. C. P. Shelden (9-1/11/43)
1545. Cary, George W., 31, d 10/3/50 in Litchfield (9-10/4)
1546. Cary, Hannah, 78, wid of late Hon. Anson, d 7/10/42 in Oxford (Oxford Times, 7/20)
1547. Cary, P.C. of Oxford m 4/17/25 Rowena Osgood of Preston in P; Rev. Bush (8-4/20)
1548. Cary, Sarah (Mrs.), 21, d 6/18/21 in Oxford (surv by husband and an infant child) (7-6/27)
1549. Cary, William m 4/7/31 Celestia Loisa Gridley in Sennett (6-4/20)
1550. Cary, Zalmon S. m Parmela Randall in Oxford; Rev. Ackley (8-12/8/24)
1551. Casada, Gideon of Chemung m 11/5/35 Nancy Brown of Southport in S (6-11/18)
1552. Case, _____, 6 mo, ch of William B., d -- in Utica (9-8/8/26)
1553. Case, Content, 56, wf of Pliny, d 12/17/25 in New Hartford (9-12/22)
1554. Case, Everett m 6/8/47 Eva Wilson, dau of E., in Vernon; Rev. Henry Emmons. All of Vernon (9-6/24)
1555. Case, Henry of New Hartford m 2/24/47 Mary Eliza Birdsall of Paris, NY in P; Rev. John Waight (9-2/27)
1556. Case, Henry R. m 6/30/44 Eliza M. Snell, both of Verona, in Hampton; Rev. F. A. Spencer (9-7/6)
1557. Case, James m 11/19/34 Sophia Eaton, both of Sullivan, in S; Rev. Atwell (3-11/25)
1558. Case, Rodney m 10/3/33 Celistia Joy in Sullivan; Rev. Dr. Yates. All of Sullivan (3-10/8)
1559. Case, William of Gloversville m 11/18/46 Mary Mathews of Liverpool, NY in L; Rev. E. R(?). Sherwood (1-11/30)
1560. Case. William P., Jr. m 1/30/44 AnnB. Bray in Utica; Rev. B. Hawley. All of Utica (9-2/1)
1561. Cashagance(?), Jason of the Mohawk Tribe m 7/5/48 Margaret Louisa Annance(?) of the Atlantic Tribe, St. Francis, Canada East, in Williamstown, NY (9-7/19)
1562. Casler, Asher of New York Mills m 11/4/50 Esther Whiting of Utica; Rev. Isaac Foster (9-11/11)

1563. Casler, Henry and Robert McMaster were smothered to death 11/23/21 near
Herkimer (had kindled a charcoal fire in their cabin on a boat of Capt.
Leavenworth on the Mohawk River)(8-11/28)
1564. Casler, Marcus, 75, d 9/11/41 at his home near Little Falls (3-9/22)
1565. Cass, Elizabeth S., 21, dau of Hon. Lewis Cass, Secretary of War,
d 7/15/32 in Detroit, MI (6-8/1)
1566. Cass, Hezekiah of Sullivan m 11/9/43 Catharine Sayles of Manlius in
Fayetteville; Rev. James Abell (3-11/15)
1567. Cass, Mary, wid of late Maj. Jonathan and mother of the Secretary of War,
d 8/13/34 in Muskingum Co., OH (6-9/17)
1568. Cass, Nason, 48, d 10/6/36 in Sullivan (3-10/12)

1569. Cassada, Enoch W. m 9/28/30 Susan Warn of Southport (6-10/6)
1570. Cassidy, John, 46, d -- in Albany (6-4/28/30)
1571. Cassidy, William J. A., 1 yr, s of Patrick and Harriet, d 5/21/48 in
Utica (funeral from his father's home, 11 Washington St.)(9-5/22)
1572. Casterlin, Squire, 50, d -- in Meretz (6-3/2/31)
1573. Casterline, Alvah, 26, d 2/23/31 in Auburn (6-3/2)
1574. Castine, Jane, 119, "a colored woman", d at the poor house in Erie Co.
(born in 1711 in Nine Partners, Dutchess Co.) (6-6/16/30)
1575. Castle, Charles S. m -- Lydia Downs, both of Oneida Co., in Buffalo;
Selah Barnard, Esq. (9-11/12/47)
1576. Castle, Horatio C. of Cleveland, OH m 12/28/47 Harriet Wilkinson, only
dau of Charles T. of Utica, in U; Rev. William H. Spencer (9-12/30)
1577. Castleton, Maria Louisa, 17, oldest dau of Rev. Thomas late of Syracuse,
NY and now of Richmond, VA, d 3/31/50 in Le Roy, NY (9-4/19)
1578. Caswell, Jane U. (Miss), 17, d 4/2/48 in Herkimer (9-4/7)
1579. Caswell, Lemuel H. of Oxford m 10/30/23 Joanna Cadwell of Onondaga in O
(8-11/5)
1580. Caswell, Warren, Sr., 75, d 11/14/50 in Herkimer (9-11/22)
1581. Catharine, Charles m 11/4/30 Patience Reed in Seneca; Rev. Nesbit
(6-11/10)
1582. Cathcart, John A. of Brownville, Jeff. Co. m 12/28/48 Sarah Lathrop, dau
of Horace, Esq. of Cooperstown; Rev. Charles K. McHarg (9-1/4/49)
1583. Cathcart, William A. of Brownville, Jeff Co., m 4/24/50 Laura Lathrop,
youngest dau of Herman, Esq., in Cooperstown; Rev. C. K. McHarg
(9-5/4)
1584. Catlin, James, editor of the Montrose (PA) Gazette, m 11/3/23 Abigail
Sayre of Cairo, NY in Montrose, PA; Rev. Baldwin (8-11/12)
1585. Catlin, Silas m 4/7/31 Jennet Lathrop inTioga (6-4/20)
1586. Cattell, William d -- in Utica (funeral from "the Bleecker House")
(9-8/28/44)
1587. Cattle, Joseph m -- Elizabeth Peese in Belvidere, NJ (6-6/23/30)
1588. Caudle, Job m -- Jane Prettyman in London (Eng.?); Very Rev. Dr. Punch
(9-2/7/46)
1589. Cauley, William M. of Seneca m 4/9/32 Sarah Bugby of Penn Yan in P. Y.
(6-4/18)
1590. Cawker, Emanuel of Milwaukee, WI m 1/11/36 Lutia Ann Harrison at
Seneca Falls, NY (6-1/27)
1591. Cevana, Catharine, 85, wid of Peter, d 6/22/48 in Marcy (b in Europe;
arrived in the Marcy area [married and with one child] about 1798;
widowed for about 30 yrs) (9-7/6)
1592. Chaffee, William, 77, (a Rev. pensioner) d 10/28/34 in Enfield, CT
(6-12/3)
1593. Chalmers, Grace, relict of late Thomas Chalmers, D. D. and LL. D.,
d 1/16/50 in Edinborough (prob.Scotland) (9-2/19)
1594. Chamberlain, E. of Utica m 6/20/50 Emma L. Green, only dau of Harry W.,
Esq. of New Berlin, in N. B.; Rev. Corwin (9-6/22)
1595. Chamberlain, John, Esq. (Hon.), one of the judges of the court of
common pleas for Seneca Co., d 7/26/31 at his home in So. Waterloo
(6-8/3)
1596. Chamberlain, Joseph, 45, d -- in Bath (6-7/2/34)
1597. Chamberlain, Levi, 56, d 7/29/49 at his home in Honolulu. Hawaii (for
27 years secular superintendent of the Sandwich Islands mission)
(9-11/14)

1598. Chamberlain, Mary (Mrs.) d 11/24/33 in Rochester (6-12/11)
1599. Chamberlain, Theophilus, 88, d 7/20/24 in Preston near Halifax, Nova Scotia
       (born in CT; grad from Yale Col.; 60 yrs a preacher) (9-12/7)
1600. Chamberlain, William, Jr. m 10/4/32 Susan Hyde, both of Canadice, in C
       (6-11/7)
1601. Chamberlin, Henry W.   m 9/30/46 Catharine M. Hinkley in Norwich;
       Rev. E. Barber. All of Norwich (9-9/30)
1602. Chamberlin, John of Fayette m 12/15/30 Mahala Yost of Seneca Falls
       (6-12/29)
1603. Chambers, John S., Esq., formerly of Geneva, d 11/10/34 in Trenton, NJ
       (6-12/17)
1604. Chambers, Susy, 77, d 5/16/42 in Union (2-5/18)
1605. Champion, Pamela, 47, consort of Col. Roswell, d 5/7/43 in Litchfield
       (9-5/13)
1606. Champion, Roswell (Col.) of Litchfield m 3/10/44 Mrs. Vienna Root of
       Phoenix in P (9-3/14)
1607. Champlain,_____, 30, wf of William C., d 4/25/49 in Whitesboro (9-4/27)
1608. Champlin, John T., Esq., 62, president of the Farmer's Fire Insurance Co.,
       d 7/24/30 in NYC (6-8/4)
1609. Champlin, William C., P.M., m 4/17/19 Elizabeth Stevens in Whitestown;
       Rev. Walter R. Long. All of Whitestown (Possibly P.M. translates
       postmaster) (9-4/19)
1610. Champney, Almira, 19, wf of H. C. Champney, d 4/22/49 in Western (9-5/3)
1611. Chandler, John m 4/7/31 Mrs. Mary Branch in Auburn (6-4/20)
1612. Chandler, John, 104, d 3/13/50 in Jacksonville, AL (b in VA; a Rev.
       soldier 7 yrs under Generals Green and Sumter in battles of Eutaw,
       Camden, and Cowpens) (9-4/13)
1613. Chandler, John B. (Deacon) m -- Maria French ("married by themselves to
       themselves - all on the Sabbath day at the breakfast table calling
       upon God and the family to bear witness to the act" - from the
       Concord Statesman)(9-5/9/43)
1614. Chandler, Winthrop m 9/1/30 Elizabeth White in Auburn; Rev. C. P. Wyckoff
       (6-9/15)
1615. Chapel, Joseph m 3/15/21 Phebe Wood, both of Norwich; Rev. Andrews
       (7-3/28)
1616. Chapen, Alonzo of Antwerp m 10/18/50 Cornelia Wiser of South Trenton, NY
       in S. T.; Rev. A. North (9-10/24)
1617. Chapen, Charles C., 21, d 12/22/35 in Canandaigua (6-1/6/36)
1618. Chapin, Asa F., Esq. of Lafayette, IN m 5/13/46 Sarah A. Keeler of Homer
       in H; Rev. C. Darby (9-5/21)
1619. Chapin, David, 21, of Bath d 10/26/33 in Richmond, NY (6-11/20)
1620. Chapin, Henry, 2nd, merchant, m 2/9/32 Cynthia Chapin, dau of Henry, Esq.,
       in Canandaigua (6-2/22)
1621. Chapin, Hosha F., 48, wf of Joel, d 5/18/44 in Oxford (Oxford Republican,
       5/30)
1622. Chapin, Ichabod, 66, d -- in Le Roy (6-2/9/31)
1623. Chapin, Israel, 70, d 8/31/33 in Hopewell (one of the oldest settlers in
       Hopewell) (6-9/11)
1624. Chapin, Joel, Jr. of Oxford m -- Honor Frances Bulkley in Weathersfield,
       CT (8-10/29/23)
1625. Chapin, Mariah, 18, dau of late Spencer Chapin, d 2/5/36 in Canandaigua
       (6-2/17)
1626. Chapin, Ralph, 15, s of Heman, Esq., d -- in Bloomfield (6-5/12/30)
1627. Chapin, Seth, 36, merchant, d 11/12/26 in Buffalo (9-11/28)
1628. Chapin, Spencer, 42, d 3/15/33 in Canandaigua (6-3/27)
1629. Chapin, Sylvia, 35, relict of Seth and dau of Dr. Cyrenus Chapin,
       d 11/30/31 in Buffalo (6-12/14)
1630. Chapin, Thaddeus, 69, d -- in Canandaigua (one of the earliest settlers
       in C) (6-3/17)
1631. Chapin, Thaddeus m 10/8/32 Rebecca Bemis, dau of James D., Esq., in
       Canandaigua; Rev. Eddy (6-10/17)
1632. Chapman, B. F. (Maj.), attorney, m 11/10/41 Huldah Wilcox, dau of Deacon
       A. Wilcox of Lenox, in Clockville; Rev. Lyman Wright (3-11/17)
1633. Chapman, Charles of Auburn, 36, d 2/17/31 in Cooperstown (6-3/2)
1634. Chapman, Chauncey m 1/26/32 Mercey French, both of Phelps, in P (6-2/15)

1635. Chapman, Daniel, one of the editors of the Lyons Argus, m 10/24/32
      Elizabeth A. Gorgas, dau of Joseph , Esq. of Pennsylvania, in Lyons,
      NY (6-11/7)
1636. Chapman, Edward m 1/16/44 Elizabeth Burnett, both of Utica, in U; Rev.
      Fuller (9-1/26)
1637. Chapman, Epaphras (Rev.), missionary to the Osage Indians, d in Union
      (state not given) (b in East Haddam, CT; grad from Theological
      Seminary, Princeton, NJ; missionary first in Brainerd, TN and later
      on the Arkansas River) (9-8/16/25)
1638. Chapman, James H. of Jefferson m 8/3/48 Frances (Fanny) Denton, dau of
      S. B. of Corning, in C; Rev. S. B. Shearer (4-8/9 and 8/16/48)
1639. Chapman, Jane, 13, dau of J., d 5/22/39 in Canaseraga (3-5/29)
1640. Chapman, Jane, wf of Edward, d 4/8/43 in Utica (b in Halifax, Nova Scotia)
      (funeral at her husband's home, 61 Broadway) (9-4/10)
1641. Chapman, John T., formerly of Geneva, d 9/14/32 in NYC (cholera) (6-9/19)
1642. Chapman, Lewis m -- Rebecca Jones, dau of Amos, Esq., in Hopewell; Rev.
      Oliver Ackley (6-4/10/39)
1643. Chapman, Lucy, consort of Capt. John of Canaseraga, d 9/8/43 in C
      (3-9/13)
1644. Chapman, N. R., Esq. m 5/18/41 S. C. Evans in Lenox; Rev. Washington
      Kingsley (3-6/16)
1645. Chapman, Samuel m 11/16/28 Laura Hull in New Berlin; Rev. James B.
      Sherman. All of New Berlin (7-11/19)
1646. Chapman, Samuel F., formerly of Ithaca, NY, d 9/3/30 in Pensacola (FL?)
      (8-10/20)
1647. Chapman, William E., one of the editors of the Oxford Gazette, m --
      Harriet Sellick of Ulysses in U; Rev. Peck (7-9/30/29)
1648. Chapney, Henry C. of Rome, NY m 3/22/49 Almira Reese of Western at the
      Central Hotel, Utica; Rev. E. Francis (9-3/23)
1649. Charley, John W. m 2/12/31 Ardelia Coon in Oswego (6-3/2)
1650. Charlton, Peter d 8/2/30 in Geneva (6-8/4)
1651. Chase, Benjamin, Jr. m -- Lurinda Mix in Clarkson (6-12/25/33)
1652. Chase, Daniel S. m 10/29/33 Emeline S. Brown in Penn Yan (6-11/6)
1653. Chase, Elizabeth, 49, consort of Ira, Esq., d 9/10/42 in Utica (consumption)
      (funeral from the Bapt. Ch.) (9-9/12)
1654. Chase, Elizabeth I. (Miss), 20, d 10/25/44 in Utica (funeral at Broad St.
      Bapt. Ch.) (9-10/26)
1655. Chase, George W. (Capt.) of the Utica Light Guard m 5/10/42 Susan F.
      Vanderheyden, dau of J., Esq.,(all of Utica) in Utica; Rev. D. C.
      Lansing of Syracuse (9-5/11)
1656. Chase, Helen A., 15, dau of Ira, Esq., d 8/11/42 in Utica (funeral from
      her father's home, 40 Main St.) (9-8/13)
1657. Chase, Henry m -- Charlotte Page, both of Phelps, in Palmyra (6-3/2/31)
1658. Chase, Henry M., 20, only s of Jacob, d 4/14/44 in Jamesville (surv by
      his widowed mother and an only sister) (9-4/19)
1659. Chase, Ira m 10/16/45 Alma A. Hyatt of NYC; Rev. Lott Jones (9-10/25)
1660. Chase, Ira, 18, youngest s of Ira, Esq., d 2/4/49 in Utica (funeral at
      his father's home, 24 Main St.) (9-2/5)
1661. Chase, John m -- Caroline Holt in Hudson (6-2/9/31)
1662. Chase, Josephine Ludlow, youngest dau of Hon. S. P. (U.S. Senator from
      Ohio), d 7/27/50 in Morristown, NJ (9-8/16)
1663. Chase, Joshua, Esq., postmaster of Catharine, d 12/15/36 in Havana, NY
      (6-12/28)
1664. Chase, Leslie (Capt.), asistant quartermaster, U.S. Army, and s of Hon.
      Seth of Worcester, NY, d 4/15/49 in Smithville, NC (served in 2nd
      Artillery in battles of 8 and 9 May, 1845 and breveted Captain for
      his gallant conduct there) (9-5/1)
1665. Chase, Stephen of Lysander m 6/21/48 Martha W. White of Van Buren in
      Auburn; Rev. Austin (1-7/26)
1666. Chase, Walter of Phelps m 1/27/33 Cusiah Elsworth of Seneca in S (6-2/6)
1667. Chatfield, Andrew G. m 6/27/36 Eunice E. Beeman, both of Addison, at Big
      Flats (6-7/13)
1668. Chatfield, Charles J. m 8/15/42 Sarah D. Foster, youngest dau of Robert
      W. and adopted dau of Sylvester Smith, Esq. of Painted Post, in
      Lehman, PA; Rev. Hunt (4-8/30)

1669. Chatfield, Frances J., youngest dau of Cyrus formerly of Utica, d 11/23/49
       at Mammoth Cave, KY (9-12/4)
1670. Chatfield, Solomon of Middlesex m 1/31/33 Elizabeth Carr of Canandaigua
       in C (6-2/13)
1671. Chatfield, T. I. of Owego m 11/9/41 Mary P. Buxby of Elmira in Owego;
       Rev. Peck (4-12/1)
1672. Chatfield, William M. m 8/23/35 Hannah S. Sweet in East Bloomfield (6-9/9)
1673. Chatham, William m -- Eliza Pease, both of Seneca Falls (6-9/29/30)
1674. Chatham, William, Jr., 33, d 12/14/35 in Seneca Falls (6-12/30)
1675. Chatterton, Stephen S., one of the publishers of the Oswego Republican,
       m 10/10/32 Mary W. Chipman in Newfield (6-11/7)
1676. Chauso, John of St. Johnsville m 10/2/34 Catharine Moyer of Chittenango
       in C; Rev. Dr. Yates (3-10/7)
1677. Chawgo, Catharine (Mrs.), 21, dau of Capt. Daniel Moyer formerly of
       Chittenango, d 12/21/35 in Johnstown, NY (3-12/29)
1678. Chawgo, George m 9/19/33 Polly Christman in Sullivan; J. French, Esq.
       (3-9/24)
1679. Cheever, George N., 25, formerly of Whitesboro, d 9/22/48 in Buffalo
       (9-9/30)
1680. Cheever, William M., Esq., 69, d 8/8/43 in New Haven, Oswego Co.
       (was among the first settlers of Oneida Co.) (9-8/28)
1681. Cheney, Jonathan m 8/14/50 Mary Price in Willowvale; Rev. John Waugh
       (9-8/22)
1682. Cheney, Wales (Col.), a tutor in the Middlebury Academy, m 3/27/30 Esther
       Stanton, dau of Gen. Phineas, in Middlebury; Rev. Eli S. Hunter
       ("the dress of the bride was entirely of domestic manufacture and
       made by herself") (6-4/14)
1683. Cherry, Henry (Rev.) of Rochester and missionary to India, m --
       Catharine Lathrop of Norwich, CT in Plainfield, NY (6-9/14/36)
1684. Cherry, Samuel (Maj.), 69, d 10/21/25 in New Haven, Oswego Co. ("buried
       in the Masonic order") (remained in the army from time of the Rev.
       War until retirement) (9-11/8)
1685. Cherry, Talmadge m 10/24/33 Caroline Strong of Salisbury, CT in Auburn,
       NY (6-11/6)
1686. Cherry, William, 17, d 12/9/34 in Geneva (6-12/24)
1687. Chester, Jerusha C., 56, wf of Dr. L. L., d 6/4/45 in Rome, Ohio (9-6/16)
1688. Chester, L. L. (Dr.) of Rome, Ohio m 3/4/46 Mrs. Florilla Austin of
       Austinburgh, NY in A (9-4/1)
1689. Chew, Alexander of New Orleans, LA m 1/11/49 Sarah Augusta Prouty, dau
       of Phineas, Esq. of Geneva, NY in G; Rev. Dr. Abel (9-1/17)
1690. Chickering, Joseph, 15 mo, s of Joseph and Emeline, d 10/5/35 in Geneva
       (6-10/7)
1691. Chidsey, Augustus (Col.), 69, d 10/19/33 in Milo (6-11/6)
1692. Chidsey, R. S. of Geneva m 8/14/31 Eliza Woodin of Hillsdale (6-9/7)
1693. Child, Charles T. m 10/7/46 Diantha Cushman, oldest dau of David, Esq.,
       in Exeter, Ots. Co.; Rev. E. Child. All of Exeter (9-10/10)
1694. Child, David W., 44, attorney, d 7/27/26 in Pittsfield, MA (had lived
       in Utica, NY) (9-8/8)
1695. Child, George M., formerly of Waterloo, m -- Jane Eliza Milligan in
       Mounsterberling, IN (6-9/25/33)
1696. Child, Horace m 12/26/30 Sally Ames in Clyde; Frederick Boogher, Esq.
       (6-1/12/31)
1697. Childs, Catherine, 60, wid of late Perry G., Esq., d 11/6/49 in Cazenovia
       (dau of Benjamin Ledyard, one of the earliest settlers in Cayuga
       County, and sister of Gen. Ledyard of Cazenovia) (9-11/13)
1698. Childs, Nancy, 45, wf of Oliver, d 4/31/31 in Seneca (6-5/11)
1699. Childs, Oliver m 7/24/31 Betsey Jane Gilbert, both of Castleton, in C
       (6-8/3)
1700. Childs, Pearly A. m 4/12/34 Helen M. Pratt in Buffalo (6-4/30)
1701. Childs, Perry G., Esq., 55, a former state senator, d 3/27/35 in
       Cazenovia (a native of Pittsfield, MA; lived in NY more than 30 yrs)
       (3-3/31)
1702. Childs, Phoebe A. (Miss), 16, dau of F., Esq., d 10/10/48 in Clay
       (1-10/26/48)

1703. Childs, Stephen m 10/1/45 Harriet Richardson, both of New Hartford; Rev.
       E. H. Payson ("Boston papers please copy") (9-10/2)
1704. Childs, Timothy (Hon.), member of Congress from this state, m --
       Louisa Dickinson in Norfolk (6-1/19/31)
1705. Childs, William m 4/6/49 Eliza McCrae of Corning in C; B. Pew, Esq.
       (4-4/11)
1706. Childsey, Samuel B. (Dr.), 34, d 10/2/33 in Auburn (6-10/16)
1707. Chilton, Leonard of New Hartford m 2/3/50 Adaline Fuller of Sauquoit in
       S; Rev. Rowe (9-2/6)
1708. Chipman, Austin C., attorney, of Nunda Valley m 12/25/38 Adelia C. Pollard
       of Wyoming, NY in Canandaigua; Rev. A. P. Prevost (6-1/9/39)
1709. Chipman, Daniel (Hon.), 95, one of the oldest lawyers in VT, d 4/23/50
       in Ripton, VT (Congressman, 1814-17) (9-5/9)
1710. Chipman, Lemuel, Esq., 76, d 4/27/31 in Sheldon, NY (a native of
       Salisbury, CT; was an early settler in Vermont state; member there of
       legislature and judge of the Rutland Co. Court. In 1795 moved to
       Pittstown (now Richmond, Ont. Co.), NY; more recently moved to Sheldon.
       There was elected member of NY senate; member of Episc. Ch. at time of
       death (6-5/11)
1711. Chipman, Sarah, 18, of Waterville, ME d 3/23/50 in Newburyport, MA
       ("took passage on the ship 'California Packet' and debarked in Boston
       harbor coming to Newburyport in the pilot boat.") (9-4/1)
1712. Chisholm, William, late a member of Parliament from Hattou Co., d 5/4/42
       in Oakville, Canada (9-5/17)
1713. Chittenden, David of Utica m 9/12/48 Elizabeth Jones of Albany in A; Rev.
       Dr. Wyckoff (9-9/16)
1714. Chittenden, John Denniston, 1 yr, s of Harlow, d 10/12/48 in Utica
       (funeral at 68 Main St.) (9-10/13)
1715. Chittenden, Martin, Esq., 28, surrogate of Erie Co., d 9/4/32 in Buffalo
       (cholera) (6-9/19)
1716. Christian, N. M. m 2/19/46 Jennette Mackie in Utica; Rev. McGowen. All
       of Utica (9-2/26)
1717. Christie, De Witt Clinton, about 26, s of Dr. Asa, d 7/20/50 in Manheim
       (typhus) (9-7/26)
1718. Christman, Joseph, 47, d 2/27/34 in Chittenango (3-3/4)
1719. Christmas, Joseph F. (Rev.), pastor of the Bowery Presby. Ch., d --
       in NYC (6-3/24/30)
1720. Christopher, David of Perryville m 7/27/37 Mary Morgan of Chittenango
       in C; Jairus French, Esq. (3-8/2)
1721. Chubb, Joseph m 2/8/21 Hannah Daniels; Rev. Nathan Noyes. All of Preston
       (7-2/14)
1722. Church, Betsey Ann, 34, wf of William, d 5/5/42 in Coventry (Oxford Times,
       5/11)
1723. Church, Elizabeth (Mrs.), 49, dau of Adonijah Skinner of Hopewell, d --
       at Sandy Hill, Wash. Co. (6-1/26/31)
1724. Church, George W. (Col.) m 5/9/43 Marietta E. Bacon, dau of Hon. Reuben,
       in Waterville; Rev. Samuel W. Whelpley. All of Waterville (9-5/11)
1725. Church, George, 6 mo, s of M. B., Esq., d 11/25/49 in Baldwinsville
       (scarlet fever) (1-11/29)
1726. Church, Jesse, 29, formerly of Norwich, d 8/3/29 in Colesville, Broome
       Co. (7-8/12)
1727. Church, John, 63, d 10/23/25 in Oxford (8-10/26)
1728. Church, John B. of Angelica m -- Maria Trumbull, dau of Benjamin, Esq. of
       New Haven, CT, in New Haven; Rev. Dr. Taylor (6-10/19/31)
1729. Church, Josiah, 64, d 7/11/30 in Oxford (8-7/14)
1730. Church, Ralph m -- Almira Allen, both of Buffalo, in B (6-11/14/32)
1731. Church, Russel, 70, d 9/24/47 in Vernon (9-10/7)
1732. Church, Samuel, 19, d 8/26/42 in Towanda, PA (Oxford Times, 9/7)
1733. Church, Thomas, 60, printer, d 12/25/49 in Utica (funeral at his late home
       on the Minden Turnpike) (9-12/28)
1734. Church, Truman K. of Utica m 1/4/47 Julia A. Benedict of Utica, dau of
       Joseph, Esq., in Utica; Rev. Dr. Proal (9-1/5)
1735. Churchill, V. H. of the firm of V. H. Churchill and Co. of Utica m 11/5/46
       Mary A. Masterson of Sherburne in S; Rev. Tuthill (9-11/17)
1736. Claghorn, Cornelia, 22 mo, dau of Charles and Mary, d 10/12/44 in Utica
       (9-10/17)

1737. Claghorn, Fanny, 2 mo, dau of C. Claghorn, d 11/5/44 in Utica (9-11/12)
1738. Claiborne, William C., late gov. of Louisiana and at time of death a
U. S. Senator, d -- in New Orleans, LA (8-12/31/17)
1739. Clapp, Ebenezer L. m 6/25/44 Catharine P. Bull, both of Hartford, CT, at
Westlake's Market Hotel, Utica, NY; Rev. McIlvaine (9-7/2)
1740. Clapp, Mary B. (Miss), 28, dau of James, Esq., d 1/5/45 in Oxford (9-1/14)
1741. Clapp, Wellington m 6/12/44 Cornelia T. Plumb in NYC; Rev. G. T. Bedell.
All of NYC (9-6/17)
1742. Clapper, Cornelia, 22, wf of John, d 10/28/47 in Van Buren (1-11/10)
1743. Clapper, George of South Bainbridge m 5/18/43 Lucy Ann Seymore of Oxford;
Rev. Arthur Burtiss (Oxford Republican, 5/19)
1744. Clark, _____, 6, dau of late Stephen, d 4/12/35 in Phelps (6-4/22)
1745. Clark, A. B. of New Hartford m 2/7/31 Mary Brainerd, dau of Rev. J. of
Verona, in V (9-2/15)
1746. Clark, Alonzo of Jerusalem, NY m 3/21/35 Eliza Bell of Benton in Milo
(6-4/1)
1747. Clark, Alva, merchant, of Penn Yan m 5/5/31 Charlotte E. Whitney of Troy
in Troy; Rev. Tucker (6-5/11)
1748. Clark, Ambrose, Esq., 79, father of A. W., Esq., editor of the Northern
State Journal in Watertown, d 6/27/48 at Fort Plain (b in Lebanon, CT;
settled first in Otsego, NY) (9-6/29)
1749. Clark, Asahel K. m 9/15/42 Betsey M. Peck in Van Buren; Rev. Houghton
(3-9/28)
1750. Clark, C. A. m 11/6/50 Abigal L. Herrington, both of Erin, in E; Rev.
C. Greatsinger (5-11/8)
1751. Clark, Calvin (Rev.) of Westhampton, MA m 10/5/35 Evelina P. Greves, dau
of late Thomas of Skaneateles, in S; Rev. Brace (6-10/14)
1752. Clark, Celina (Miss), 19, dau of Norman, d 10/9/43 (3-10/18)
1753. Clark, Charity P., 33, wf of H. H., d 1/26/49 in Utica (9-1/29)
1754. Clark, Charles m 9/21/34 Prudence Tucker in Bath (6-10/8)
1755. Clark Charles, Esq. of Buffalo m 10/6/36 Mary Ann Huntington of Geneva
in G; Rev. J. F. McLaren (6-10/12)
1756. Clark, Charles V., Esq. m 1/18/42 Avarilla B. Ladd, dau of Joy Ladd of
Utica, in U; Rev. C. Edwards Lester (Oxford Times, 1/26)
1757. Clark, Corey, 91, d -- in Middlesex (6-4/28/30)
1758. Clark, D. L. of Rushville m 4/16/50 Caroline Mundy of Geneva in G; Rev.
Dr. Hale, Pres. of Geneva Col. (9-4/29)
1759. Clark, Daniel S. m 10/1/45 Harriet F. Spinner, dau of Francis E., Esq.,
in Mohawk; Rev. Diefendorf (9-10/4)
1760. Clark, David of Seneca m 4/29/30 Mercy Crawford of Benton in B; Abner
Woodworth, Esq. (6-5/5)
1761. Clark, Deborah, 52, wf of Oliver, d 4/2/32 in Lenox (3-4/3)
1762. Clark, Deodatus (Dr.), 85, d 6/10/47 in Oswego or in Utica (not clear
which) (b in Lebanon, CT, bro of late Erastus of Utica; settled in
Utica by 1807; previously had been a pioneer settler in Oneida and
in Onondaga Counties; was, at first, the only physician in those areas.
His father died age 95; his brother, age 95; his uncle, Col. Clarke
of CT, age 96. One bro and one sister, each older than he, survive him.)
(9-6/18)
1763. Clark, E. m 9/25/50 Julia Davis at the Central Hotel, Utica; Rev. Wyatt.
All of Trenton, NY (9-9/27)
1764. Clark, Edward P. of Rushville m 8/19/35 Jemima Tozer of Gorham in G;
Rev. Gaylord (6-8/26 and 9/2)
1765. Clark, Eleanor, 82, d 2/16/33 in Hudson (6-2/27)
1766. Clark, Elijah (Deacon), 50, d 10/15/33 in Marion (6-10/23)
1767. Clark, Elijah m 5/27/47 Jane A. Wright in Adams; Rev. Charles Clark
(1-6/2)
1768. Clark, Ephraim, about 80, d 1/20/40 (fell downstairs at night in a public
house in Chittenango; had said he was from Windsor, VT "and was on his
way to Waterloo and Clyde to visit his children") (3-1/22)
1769. Clark, Ephraim D., 19, s of Chester D., d 4/4/44 in Utica (funeral from
51 Broad St.) (9-4/6)
1770. Clark, Erastus, Esq, 67, attorney, d 11/6/25 in Utica (an early settler
there) (son of John; b in Lebanon, CT 5/11/1768; grad from Dartmouth
Col; admitted to CT bar at age 22. In 1791 moved to Clinton, NY [then
a part of Whitestown]; in 1797 moved to Fort Schuyler (Utica) (9-11/22)

1771. Clark, Erastus, Esq., 57, d 11/13/25 in Utica (8-11/16)
1772. Clark, Erastus, Esq. m 1/26/46 Frances O. Beardsley, both of Utica, in
      Syracuse; Rev. Dr. Adams (9-2/3)
1773. Clark, Eunice A., 37, wf of Hon. James M., formerly of Baldwinsville,
      d 3/27/50 in Clay (1-4/4)
1774. Clark, Ezekiel m 12/6/35 Gertrude Van Ness; Elder Sears. All of Geneva
      (6-12/9)
1775. Clark, George W. of Naples m -- Mary Wallace of Cohocton in C (6-11/6/33)
1776. Clark, H. R. of Waterville m 6/14/49 Caroline Birdsell of Waterloo in
      Waterville; Rev. T. N. Benedict (9-6/15)
1777. Clark, Harriet M. (Miss), 20, oldest dau of Russel Clark of Ashtabula, OH
      (formerly of Clinton, NY) d 1/27/31 in Ashtabula (9-2/8)
1778. Clark, Harry m 10/3/32 Nancy A. Bruce, dau of Maj. Joseph, in Lenox; Rev
      Edward A. Fraser. All of Lenox (3-10/9)
1779. Clark, Harvey m -- Rhoda Ticein Elmira (6-2/9/31)
1780. Clark, Hiram m 5/7/44 Susan C. Reed in Utica; Rev. Baldwin. All of U
      (9-5/9)
1781. Clark, Hovey K., Esq. of Allegan, MI m 6/27/37 Elizabeth M. Taylor, dau
      of Rev. James of Sunderland, MA, in Canandaigua, NY; Rev. Thompson
      (6-7/26)
1782. Clark, Jerusha, 49, wf of Thomas E., Esq. d 3/10/44 in Utica (funeral from
      the Dutch Reformed Ch.) (9-3/12)
1783. Clark, Jesse, Jr. d 7/12/49 "in the black Hills of the Rocky Mountains"
      while on his way to California in the gold rush (left Corning, NY
      23 March with his last communication from Fort Laramie)(4-12/19)
1784. Clark, Jesse S. m 4/12/49 Eunice Person, both of Corning, in C; Rev.
      H. Pattengill (4-4/18)
1785. Clark, John of Oswego m 4/18/50 Jane F. Palmer of Whitesboro in W; Rev.
      William A. Matson (9-4/20)
1786. Clark, John C. m 12/29/42 Olive Leet, dau of Deacon Nathaniel of
      West Stockbridge; Rev. Sidney Bryant (9-1/1343) Note: Perhaps this
      West Stockbridge is in Massachusetts although not so indicated on
      the press release.
1787. Clark, John R. m 9/10/50 Nancy Sink; Rev. W. K. Knox. All of Rome, NY
      (9-9/12)
1788. Clark, Jonathan, 55, formerly of the firm of R. and J. Clark of Somers,
      CT, d 11/21/48 in Boston (brother of C. D. Clark of Utica, NY)
      (9-12/12)
1789. Clark, Joseph W. of Naples m 9/20/33 Arethmea(?) Lee in East Bloomfield
      (6-10/16)
1790. Clark, Joseph, Esq., 68, d 4/13/36 (in Canandaigua?) (6-4/27)
1791. Clark, Joseph B. of Rochester m 6/30/36 Jane B. Symes of Syracuse in S
      (6-7/20)
1792. Clark, Josephine S., 15, dau of Hon. John C., d 4/6/43 in Washington, D.C.
      (2-4/19)
1793. Clark, Julius H., one of the editors of the Syracuse Argus, m 12/15/31
      Cornelia Morse, both of Syracuse, in S (6-1/4/32)
1794. Clark, Justin, 26 (late editor of the Montrose [PA] Gazette and younger
      bro of the editor of the Albany Register) d 5/6/22 at his father's
      home near Cooperstown, NY (8-6/5)
1795. Clark, L. D. (Dr.) m 11/24/44 Adeline Allen, dau of Rev. E. W. R. Allen;
      Rev. E. W. R. Allen. All of Oriskany (9-12/4)
1796. Clark, Lany (Mrs.), 56, d -- in Canandaigua (6-8/14/33)
1797. Clark, Levi G. m 11/3/31 Nancy S. Smith in Seneca Falls (6-11/30)
1798. Clark, Lovina, 18, dau of Vine H., d 8/10/46 in Utica (consumption)
      (9-8/11)
1799. Clark, Luke, 48, of Brookfield d 9/22/26 in Utica (9-9/26)
1800. Clark, Mareena W. m 6/23/35 Mary Newton in East Bloomfield (6-7/8)
1801. Clark, Matthew of Whitestown m 1/4/48 Anna Maria Nellis of St. Johnsville
      in S. J.; Rev. A. Rumph (9-1/7)
1802. Clark, Nancy (Mrs.), 49, d 3/5/33 in Bath (6-3/13)
1803. Clark, Napoleon B. m 1/2/50 Alva Ann Adsit, both of Lysander, in L; Rev.
      Byron Alden (1-1/3)
1804. Clark, Oliver of Sullivan, NY m 5/20/42 Sarah Green of Pawtucket, RI; Rev.
      Silas Spalding (3-6/8)

1805. Clark, Orasmus B., editor of the Seneca Falls Journal, m 1/20/30 Prudence Darrow at Seneca Falls (8-2/17)
1806. Clark, Oren, 57, d 6/21/44 in Cleveland, OH (9-6/27)
1807. Clark, Orrin m 7/18/48 Gertrude Dorman of Albany Co. at Durhamville; Rev. J. A. Arnold (9-7/21)
1808. Clark, Parsons, formerly of New Haven, CT, d 2/23/25 in Clinton, NY (9-3/8)
1809. Clark, Rhoda (Mrs.), 42, wf of Henry, d 3/11/32 in Canandaigua (6-3/21)
1810. Clark, Richard, 50, d -- in Romulus (6-8/27/28)
1811. Clark, Richard L. of NYC m -- Julia I. Fenton, dau of J. S., Esq., in Palmyra; Rev. Schemway (6-2/11/35)
1812. Clark, Russel, Esq., 64, formerly of Oneida Co., NY d 10/8/48 in Ashtabula, OH (9-10/14)
1813. Clark, Ruth, 64, wf of Thomas, d 4/22/42 in Sullivan (3-4/27)
1814. Clark, Salina (Miss), about 18, d 10/9/43 in Lenox (3-10/11)
1815. Clark, Samuel m 9/21/34 Mary Willson in Jerusalem, NY; Rev. Potter. All of Jerusalem (6-10/1)
1816. Clark, Samuel M. m 12/3/40 Mary Ann Burns in Centerville; Rev. Hopkins (4-12/11)
1817. Clark, Samuel ?. m 1/13/45 Cornelia Crum, both of Edmeston, at the U. S. Hotel in Utica; Otis Whipple, Esq. (9-1/15)
1818. Clark, Sarah Ann, 25, wf of William B. formerly of Utica and dau of Abraham Miner of Lansing, d 1/25/46 in Kalamazoo, MI (9-1/31)
1819. Clark, Silas, merchant, m 11/15/27 Lavina Sherwood, dau of John, in Guilford; Rev. N. Bentley. All of Guilford (8-11/23)
1820. Clark, Silas m 5/15/50 Pamilla Sprague, dau of Judge Asa of Mexico, NY, in Mexico; Rev. L. Whitcomb. All of Mexico, NY (9-5/18)
1821. Clark, Stephen (Hon.), canal commissioner, of Rochester m 7/22/45 Mrs. Sarah Phillips of Waterford in W; Rev. Reuben Smith (9-8/8)
1822. Clark, Stephen, 63, formerly of Rome, NY, d 6/17/48 in Buffalo (9-7/1)
1823. Clark, Stephen V. of Middlesex m 12/5/44 Hannah J. Nettleton of Clinton in C; Rev. H. Whicher (9-12/25)
1824. Clark, Susan R., 31, wf of Rev. O. Clark, rector of Trinity Ch., Geneva, d. 6/30/26 in Geneva (she the dau of Hon. John Nichols) (9-8/8)
1825. Clark, Theodore L., 20, s of John of Lawrence, Ots. Co., d 2/25/42 at the home of N. L. Somers in Corning (4-3/2)
1826. Clark, Theodore Weld, 10, youngest s of Starr Clark, Esq., d 3/30/33 in Mexico, NY (9-4/9)
1827. Clark, Thomas, 69, d 3/14/44 in Chittenango (3-3/20)
1828. Clark, Warren (Capt.) m 2/9/32 Eunice Dorman in Canastota; Rev. Olds. All of Lenox (3-2/21)
1829. Clark, William, bro of Charles of Corning, m 3/9/43 Susan Moore, sister of Hon. Francis Moore, Jr., in Houston, TX; Rev. Atkinson (4-4/5)
1830. Clark, William J. m 12/24/50 (in the Friends' form [Quaker]) Ann Bowman, both of Elmira (5-12/27)
1831. Clark, William S., 30, d 3/6/50 in San francisco, CA (9-5/9)
1832. Clarke, Albert m 11/10/36 Martha Stephens, both of Tyre (6-11/23)
1833. Clarke, Ann L., 66, wid of late George, Esq., d 2/10/50 at her home in Springfield (9-2/19)
1834. Clarke, Charles (Dr.) m March 1814 Anna Gidman ("after a short courtship of 26 years!") at Roadstown, Cumberland Co., NJ (8-5/24)
1835. Clarke, Clarinde B., 17, d -- in Conesus (6-8/14/33)
1836. Clarke, Delia Adelaide, 21. oldest dau of Dr. Thaddeus of Pompey, NY, formerly of Lebanon, CT, d 10/6/26 in Salina, NY (9-10/31)
1837. Clarke, Harlow H., 25, s of Hampton of NYC (formerly of Utica), d 4/2/49 in Loredo, TX, on his way to California (cholera and typhus) (9-5/21)
1838. Clarke, Henry B., formerly of Utica, d 7/22/49 in Chicago, IL (cholera) (9-7/27)
1839. Clarke, John m 2/5/33 Mary Wadsworth, both of Hopewell, in Geneva; Rev. Mandeville (6-2/6)
1840. Clarke, John Shellman, 9, oldest s of William d 2/11/50 in New Orleans, LA (9-3/5)
1841. Clarke, Josiah L. m 3/12/44 Phebe T. Allen; Rev. J. T. Goodrich. All of Oxford (Oxford Republican, 3/21)
1842. Clarke, Sarah Cornelia, 11 mo, only dau of Dr. S. R., d 2/20/42 in Oxford (Oxford Times, 3/2)

1843. Clarke, Satterlee (Maj.), 64, of Michigan (formerly a paymaster in the U.S. Army and for many years a resident of Utica) d 3/1/48 in Washington, D.C. (9-3/7)
1844. Clarke, Silas, merchant, of Watertown m 5/25/26 Joanna Sickles of Utica; Rev. S. C. Aiken (9-5/30)
1845. Clarke, William m 2/26/43 Rosanna McQuade, dau of Thomas, Esq., at St. John's Ch., Utica; Rev. Thomas Martin. All of Utica (9-3/1)
1846. Clarkson, Matthew (Gen.), 66, d -- in NYC (a Rev. officer and later acting vice pres. of the American Bible Soc.) (9-5/3/25 and 6-5/4/25)
1847. Clary, Alida (Mrs.), 48, d 4/27/30 in Geneva (6-4/28)
1848. Clary, Eliza, 14, dau of William formerly of Geneva, d 3/6/30 in Rochester (6-3/17)
1849. Clary, Joseph S. of Chittenango m 3/1/31 Louisa Mallory of Smithfield in S; Rev. Smith (3-3/8)
1850. Clary, Stalham (Rev.), 48, of Benton d 11/25/31 in Hopewell (6-11/30)
1851. Class, Abraham of Galen m 1/29/31 Rhoda Malcolm of Geneva in Galen (6-2/9)
1852. Clawson, _____, 16 mo, ch of Zephaniah, d 7/20/26 in Utica (9-7/25)
1853. Clay, Porter (Rev.), 70, last surviving bro. of Hon. Henry Clay, d 2/16/50 in Camden, AR (9-3/13)
1854. Cleaveland, Emery B., 9, s of Dr. W. P., d 6/23/48 in Waterville (9-7/7)
1855. Cleaveland, D. m 4/15/44 Annis Clarke, dau of Samuel, in Delta; Rev. W. W. Ninde. All of Delta (9-4/27)
1856. Clegg, George m 4/22/50 Elizabeth Adams, both of Sauquoit, in New Hartford; Rev. Oliver Tuttle (9-5/7)
1857. Clemens, James W. of Wheeling, VA m 9/20/48 Caroline Elizabeth Wright of Troy, NY in Utica, NY; Rev. D. G. Corey (9-9/23)
1858. Clement, John of Geneva m 10/24/35 Christiana Life in Geneva; Rev. Abeel (6-10/28)
1859. Clemons, Anson B. m 10/20/35 Anna Mariah Northrup, both of Geneva, in G; Elder Sears (6-10/28)
1860. Clesson, Alice, 43, wf of Dr. Samuel, d 10/27/32 in Sodus (6-11/7)
1861. Clifton, William C. of the Buffalo Theater m -- Maria Clark of Penn Yan in Auburn (6-4/22/35)
1862. Clinton, _____, one of the officers of the Brig "Spark", a son of the Hon. De Witt Clinton, d "lately at sea" (9-7/20/24)
1863. Clinton, Charles m -- Clarissa Crabtree in Gorham (6-1/26/31)
1864. Clinton, De Witt (his Excellency) m 4/21/19 Catharine Jones, dau of late Dr. Thomas of NYC, in NYC; Rev. Arthur J. Stansbury (8-5/5)
1865. Clinton, George W., Esq. of Albany m 5/15/32 Laura Catherine Spencer, dau of Hon. John C., at St. John's Ch. in Canandaigua; Rev. Kenny (6-5/23)
1866. Clinton, James G., 46, formerly a member of Congress from Orange and Rockland Cos., d 5/28/49 in NYC (9-6/1)
1867. Clinton, Maria, wf of Gov. Clinton, d 7/31/18 at Mount Vernon near NYC (8-8/12)
1868. Clizbee, David d -- in Galway, Sara. Co. (3-9/27/31)
1869. Close, Ransom m 7/4/49 Emily Brooks, both of Norwich, in N; Rev. M. Stone (9-7/21)
1870. Closs, Harvey m 10/19/36 Emelina Henderson, both of Rose, in R (6-11/9)
1871. Closs, John, 38, d -- in Rose (6-2/15/32)
1872. Clough, Benjamin of Sanbornton, MA m -- Caroline Bowers of Bridgewater, MA in B ("both deaf and dumb" - ceremony performed in writing) (6-12/4/33)
1873. Clough, Henry, 20, d 8/6/48 in Westmoreland (9-8/9)
1874. Clover, Benjamin F., 22, d 10/2/35 in Lenox (3-10/13)
1875. Clum, S. m 7/11/39 H. P. Marsh in Clyde; Rev. D. Hutchins (6-7/24)
1876. Clute, Gerardus m 5/26/31 Mary Ann Dunham, dau of Samuel, in Pompey, NY; Rev. Stockton. All of Pompey (3-5/31)
1877. Clute, Jellis, Esq., about 52, d 6/14/33 in Moscow, NY (6-6/26)
1878. Clymer, George, 86, late of Philadelphia (PA?) and inventor of the Columbian Printing Press, d 9/27/34 in London, England (6-10/22)
1879. Coakly, Cornelius of Kirkville m 4/3/34 Charlotte Livingston of Chittenango; Rev. L. Myrick (3-4/8)
1880. Coan, Julius of Verona m 1/1/46 Cornelia A. Hills of Kirkland in K; Rev. Kendall (9-1/22)
1881. Cobb, Dexter of Tonawanda m 11/6/47 Celia Deming of Utica in Buffalo; Selah Barnard, Esq. (9-11/12)

1882. Cobb, Ebenezer (Capt.) d 7/13/41 in Stonington, CT (3-7/28)
1883. Cobb, J. C. (Dr.) of Beach Island, SC m 10/16/41 Emma C. Bennett of
       Charleston, SC in Northampton(NY?); Rev. Mitchell (Oxford Times, 10/27)
1884. Cobb, Lucy Ann, 24, d 7/28/49 in Sauquoit (scrofula) (9-8/3)
1885. Cobb, Mary S. (Mrs.), 87, d -- in NYC (6-9/25/33)
1886. Cobb, Samuel, 41, "a business man", d 9/3/32 in Penn Yan (6-4/5 and 9/12/32)
1887. Cobb, Thomas W. (Hon.), a circuit judge for many years and a member of
       Congress, d -- in Georgia (6-2/24/30)
1888. Coburn, Charles m 6/9/45 Mary C. Post, both of Utica, in Syracuse; Rev.
       J. W. Taggart (9-6/12)
1889. Coburn, Charles, 30, d 6/24/48 in Utica (9-6/26)
1890. Coburn, John, s of late Charles, d 3/19/50 in Utica (funeral from the
       Orphan Asylum on Genesee St. (9-3/20)
1891. Coburn, Joseph T. of Caton m 9/4/42 Mary Roberts of Burton, Tioga Co. in
       Caton; Jacob Robbins, Esq. (4-9/7)
1892. Coburn, Paul, 37, formerly of Utica, d 10/2/49 in Buffalo (fell through
       an open coal hatch on the steamer "Atlantic"; funeral at the home of
       his bro-in-law, H. Greenman) (9-10/5)
1893. Coburn, Silas, 74, d 6/6/42 in Utica (9-6/11)
1894. Coby, John, Jr., 19, m Mrs. Houck, 55, in Wayne (6-4/28/30)
1895. Cochran, Samuel of Macdonough m 12/31/42 Mary Louisa Sweet of Norwich;
       Rev. E. G. Perry (Oxford Republican, 1/6/43)
1896. Cochrane, Rupert, Esq. of NYC m 6/4/35 Isabella Clarke of Geneva at
       Trinity Ch., Geneva; Rev. Dr. Mason, pres. of Geneva Col. (6-6/10)
1897. Cochrane, Samuel (Rev.), 63, of the Meth. Episc. Ch., d 5/19/45 in
       Poughkeepsie (9-5/30)
1898. Codd, Matthew, 83, formerly of Utica, d -- in Toronto, Canada (9-6/3/44)
1899. Coe, Albert E. of Peterboro m 5/31/45 Charlotte T. Read in Kirkland
       (9-6/10)
1900. Coe, Calvin (Deacon) m 10/18/43 Polly Hebbard; Rev. Brown. All of
       Sherburne (9-10/27)
1901. Coe, Chauncey H., 40, d 4/25/35 in Canandaigua (6-5/6)
1902. Coe, Ithamar (Deacon), 70, d 8/26/26 in Le Roy (9-9/12)
1903. Coe, Martha (Mrs.), 65, mother of Mrs. A. C. Flagg, d 8/25/33 in
       Plattsburgh (6-9/18)
1904. Coe, Wesley m 9/5/48 Sarah Lovell in Horseheads; Rec. C. C. Carr (5-9/22)
1905. Coffeen, Henry, Esq., formerly of Watertown, d -- in Illinois (8-10/11/20)
1906. Coffin, Alva m 11/24/36 Harriet Allington in Bellona (6-11/30)
1907. Coffin, Daniel D. Tompkins m 11/11/46 Jane Louisa Davis in Deerfield
       (9-11/30)
1908. Coffin, Ralph, 63, father of John A., Esq. of Geneva, d 2/14/34 in Medina
       (formerly clerk of Genesee Co.) (6-2/26)
1909. Coffin, William, 52, d 11/2/50 in Utica (9-11/4)
1910. Coffin, Uriel (Capt.), 64, formerly of Nantucket, MA, d 2/21/31 in
       Chatham, NY (6-3/23)
1911. Colburn, Benjamin N. m 10/6/33 Almira Sargent in Rochester (6-10/23)
1912. Colburn, Warren of Keene, NH m -- Lavina Parmelee at St. Paul's Ch. (Episc.)
       Syracuse; Rev. W. B. Ashley (9-6/22/50)
1913. Cole, A. J. (Mr.), 36, d 7/26/50 in Floyd (9-8/8)
1914. Cole, A. W. of Rome, NY m 4/23/50 Emeline R. Collins of Turin; Rev. A. S.
       Wightman (9-5/3)
1915. Cole, Albert, gospel minister, of CT m 3/30/31 Louisa M. Woodworth of Fenner
       in F; Elder Samuel Gilbert (3-4/5)
1916. Cole, Andrew, 74, d 8/22/49 in Warren (funeral from the home of his son,
       H. S. Cole, 67 Liberty St.) (9-8/24)
1917. Cole, Ann (Mrs.), 67 or 87?, d 7/29/33 in Lyons (6-8/14)
1918. Cole, Anna M., 68, wf of Andrew, d 5/2/49 in Utica (funeral from the home
       of her son, H. S. Cole, 73 Liberty St.) (9-5/4)
1919. Cole, Calvin (Capt.) m 2/24/30 Fayett Balcom in Oxford; Rev. Bush (8-3/3)
1920. Cole, Clarinda, wf of Abel H., d 10/12/45 in Plainfield, NY (9-10/14)
1921. Cole, Cyrus C. m 8/30/32 Charity Boardman in Gorham (6-9/12)
1922. Cole, Eunice, 27, dau of Chauncey and Eunice, d 5/30/50 in Lenox (9-6/1)
1923. Cole, G. S. m 10/16/45 A. M. Lawpaugh in Utica; Rev. William H. Spencer;
       All of Utica (9-10/17)

1924. Cole, Helen I., 16, step-dau of Ward Dudley formerly of Elmira, d 4/5/49 in Wellsborough, Chemung Co. (5-4/13)
1925. Cole, James m 6/25/35 Ann Ehle, dau of Col. George, in Chittenango; Rev. C. G. Sommers of NYC (3-6/30)
1926. Cole, Jerome B., about 14, d 3/23/32 in Penn Yan (6-4/4)
1927. Cole, John m 10/21/47 Melinda Storey at the Central Hotel in Utica; Rev. D. G. Corey. All of Whitestown (9-10/26)
1928. Cole, Lemuel P., Esq. of Sandy Hill m 9/12/48 Susan P. S. Wayland, gr-dau of the officiating clergyman, at Saratoga Springs; Rev. Francis Wayland (9-9/21)
1929. Cole, Miriam, 89, wid of late Thomas, d 12/15/27 in Oxford (8-12/28)
1930. Cole, Myron m 5/4/36 Susan Sheppard, dau of M. F., Esq., in Penn Yan; Rev. F. J. Champion (6-5/18)
1931. Cole, Nathan, 65, father of John B. of Utica, d 5/21/42 at his home in Schenectady (9-5/23)
1932. Cole, Nelson m 9/15/30 Huldah Carpenter in Ovid (6-9/29)
1933. Cole, Sally, consort of Asa, d 3/11/36 in Penn Yan (6-3/30)
1934. Cole, W. G. m 6/25/50 Phebe Ann Dewey in Utica; Rev. J. Stanford Holme. All of Utica (9-6/27)
1935. Cole, Willard m -- Lucy Hurd in Gorham; Rev. Gaylord (6-9/15/30)
1936. Cole, Wolcott m 11/8/35 Eliza Durham (in Jerusalem, NY?) (6-11/11)
1937. Colegrove, Nelson, editor of the Havana Republican, m 7/31/34 Roxey Fulkerson of Catlin in Newfield (6-8/13)
1938. Coleman, Betsey, 36 or 56?, wf of Ezekiel, d 5/31/47 in Van Buren (1-6/2)
1939. Coleman, Daniel m 3/28/33 Esther Ansley, dau of William, in Seneca (6-4/3)
1940. Coleman, James m 1/6/33 Harriet McQueen, both of Tyre, in Seneca Falls (6-2/6)
1941. Coleman, John, 62, d 12/11/32 in Bellone (town of Benton) (6-12/17)
1942. Coleman, John, 64, d 11/10/43 in Whitestown (9-11/14)
1943. Coleman, John of Whitestown m 6/15/46 Mrs. Anna Hollister of Warrensville, OH in Utica, NY; Dexter Gillmore, Esq. (9-6/16)
1944. Coleman, John S., 35, d 3/1/45 in Whitestown (surv by wf and 5 small ch) (9-3/8)
1945. Coleman, Levi m 11/24/30 Sarah Parker in Seneca Falls; Rev. Orton (6-12/1)
1946. Coles, Edward, Esq., late gov. of Illinois, m 11/28/33 Sally Logan Roberts, dau of Hugh, Esq. of Pine Grove, PA, in Philadelphia, PA (6-12/11)
1947. Colgate, Ellen S. (also Sarah Ellen), 27, wf of James B. and dau of David P. Hoyt of Utica, d 9/3/47 in NYC (surv by husband and young son) (9-9/6 and 9-10/28)
1948. Colgate, James B. of the firm of Colgate and Abbey, NYC, m 12/4/44 Ellen S. Hoyt, dau of late David P. of Utica, in U; Rev. Dr. B. T. Welch of Albany (9-12/5)
1949. Collamer, Elizabeth, consort of Samuel and mother of the late Postmaster General, d 7/27/50 in Shelburne, VT (9-8/7)
1950 Collens, John C. m 3/6/32 Frances Godfrey in Middlesex (6-3/21)
1951. Collier, John m 2/15/38 Mary Ann Walrath, both of Chittenango, in Sullivan (3-2/21)
1952. Collier, Lydia Ann, wf of John A. of Chenango Point, d 10/2/29 in Norwich, CT "where she had gone for her health" (8-10/14)
1953. Collier, Thomas, 81, d 3/11/42 in Binghamton (b in Boston, MA; moved to CT in early life and later established a newspaper in Litchfield, CT; lived last 20 years of his life in Binghamton) (2-3/16)
1954. Collingwood, Francis, 69, d 2/2/49 in Elmira (a member of the Masonic Order) (5-2/2)
1955. Collins, Abel Francis of North Stonington, CT m 1/11/44 (in the order of the Soc. of Friends [Quaker]) Electa Jane Collins, dau of Job S. of Utica, in New Hartford, NY (9-1/13)
1956. Collins, Alfred H. of Utica m 3/21/49 Maria Blackett of NYC in NYC; Rev. Henry Anthon (9-3/24)
1957. Collins, Clarkson T. (Dr.) of NYC m 11/6/44 Lydia C. Coffin, dau of Charles G., Esq. of Nantucket Island, on N. I., MA (9-11/18)
1958. Collins, Ela, Esq., 62, d 11/23/48 in Lowville, NY (b in Meriden, CT 2/14/1786; moved at an early age, with his father, Gen. Oliver, to Oneida Co., NY; studied law with Thomas R. Gold of Whitesboro; member of state assembly, 1814; later prosecuting attorney for the district of Lewis, Jeff. and St. Law. Cos.; Congressman, 1822 (9-11/30)

1959. Collins, Henry, 43, d 10/8/35 in Benton (6-10/21)
1960. Collins, Nancy, wf of Henry, d 8/11/32 in Benton (6-8/15)
1961. Collins, Polly M., 63, wf of Selden, Esq. and dau of late Rev. James
       Murdock, d 1/20/48 in West Turin (9-1/29)
1962. Collins, William S. m 7/5/48 Helen Maria Robbins, both of Utica, in
       Holland Patent, NY; Rev. J. F. Scoville (9-7/7)
1963. Collis, William of Cazenovia m 8/28/47 Mahala E. Mortley of Utica in U;
       Rev. H. R. Clark (9-9/1)
1964. Collyer, Lambert of Milwaukee, WI m 11/10/41 Martha Cunningham, dau of
       William of Manlius, in M; Rev. Wadsworth (3-11/17)
1965. Colt, _____ (Mrs.), over 80, relict of Peter, Esq. and mother of Mrs.
       John C. Devereux, d 8/22/44 in Patterson, NJ (this family formerly
       lived in Rome, NY) (9-8/27)
1966. Colt, Jabez, merchant, youngest bro. of Gen. S. of Geneva, d 11/29/32 in
       NYC (6-12/5)
1967. Colt, Joseph, Esq., bro. of Gen. S., d 1/4/31 in Palmyra (age 65 at time
       of death) (6-2/9)
1968. Colt, Joseph (Maj.), 64, d 2/4/31 at his home in Geneva (6-2/16)
1969. Colt, Joseph S., Esq. of Palmyra m 9/30/30 Henrietta L. Peckham of Albany
       in A (6-10/6)
1970. Colt, Judah, Esq., 71, bro. of Gen. Samuel of Geneva, d 10/12/32 in Erie,
       PA (6-10/17)
1971. Colt, Samuel (Gen.), 63, d 8/8/34 in Geneva (settled in Ontario Co., NY
       from Lime, CT in 1795 and stayed a short time in Canandaigua; in 1796
       came to Geneva; in 1833 moved to NYC but served as a merchant in
       Geneva for about 40 yrs.) (6-8/13)
1972. Colter, John m 9/19/33 Clarissa Crane in Buffalo (6-10/9)
1973. Colton, Abby N., 29, wf of Rev. C. Colton, d -- in Batavia (9-2/14/26)
1974. Colton, Chauncey (Rev.) of Washington, D.C., late rector of St. Paul's
       Ch. in Rochester, NY, m 10/15/32 Ann Coxe, dau of late William, in
       Burlington, NJ (6-11/21)
1975. Colton, Melza (Mr.), 55, d 6/9/35 in Manlius (3-6/16)
1976. Colvin, J. H., Esq., 56, d 12/11/49 in Syracuse (9-12/14)
1977. Colwell, John, 25, s of late Deacon Colwell of Trenton, NY, d 2/25/24 in
       Utica (9-3/2)
1978. Colwell, Joseph m 9/9/24 _____ _____ (sheet torn) of Utica; Rev. S. C.
       Aiken (9-9/14)
1979. Coman. B. F. m 1/10/49 Harriet E. White in Eaton; Rev. Hammond. All of E
       (9-1/11)
1980. Coman, L. D. of the firm of Hopkins and Co. of NYC, m 6/29/48 Margaret
       Jeanette Bradt, oldest dau of late John J., Esq., at 1st Presby. Ch.,
       Troy; Rev. Dr. Beman (9-7/7)
1981. Combs, _____, wf of William, d 5/13/37 in Seneca (6-5/17)
1982. Combs, William, 29, d 4/5/26 in Utica (9-4/11)
1983. Comee, Christopher m 9/1/47 Maroah Griswold, both of Adams, in A; Rev. J.
       F. Davan (1-9/8)
1984. Compson, Edward, 65, d 4/1/36 in Seneca Falls (6-4/13)
1985. Comstock, A. Waldo, Esq. of Fort Huron, MI m 11/10/49 W. Ann Brainard of
       Oriskany in O; Rev. E. C. Pritchett (9-12/7)
1986. Comstock, Arnon (sic) (Judge), 70, d 3/7/50 in Western (9-3/15)
1987. Comstock, Clark, 2, s of Col. Samuel, d 7/6/26 in Clinton (9-7/18)
1988. Comstock, John m 2/20/38 Abbey Cossett in Morrisville; Rev. Willis (3-2/28)
1989. Comstock, John Gifford, 11 mo, only ch of Samuel and Eliza, d 1/25/50 in
       Utica (9-1/28)
1990. Comstock, Laura, 28, consort of Moses, d 11/13/25 in Utica (9-11/22)
1991. Comstock, Mary Jane, 23, wf of James, d 11/1/48 in Schenectady (9-11/4)
1992. Comstock, Miles C. of Utica m 9/12/49 Emily M. Roseboom, only dau of
       Gerritt, Esq. of Westford, in W; Rev. Charles Wadsworth (9-9/13)
1993. Comstock, Permelia, 21, dau of Lucian and Margaret, d 3/14/50 in Boonville
       (consumption) (9-3/21)
1994. Comstock, Sarah, 54, consort of Rev. Alkanah, d 2/12/31 in Pontiac
       (6-3/9)
1995. Comstock, Taragah 65, (a Rev. soldier) d 2/23/26 in Williamstown (9-3/21)
1996. Comstock, William H. m 5/14/44 Mary E. Curtis, dau of Salmon, Esq., in
       Westmoreland; Rev. F. A. Spencer. All of Westmoreland (9-5/17)

1997. Comterman, Charles, clerk of the Averill House, Utica, m 6/6/50 Caroline Sherman in New Hartford. (both of Utica; "Albany papers please copy") (9-6/8)
1998. Condit, J. D., Esq. of West Dresden m 10/6/47 Sarah A. Vezie of Utica in U; Rev. D. Skinner (9-10/13)
1999. Congden, Jane, 21, wf of Edwin, d 10/5/42 (2-10/12)
2000. Conkey, Lyman W. m 8/12/47 Lucy M. Barker, both of Syracuse; Rev. Dr. Adams (1-8/18)
2001. Conklin, John, 96, d 3/13/36 in Hopewell (6-3/30)
2002. Conklin, John m 8/14/36 Julia Hill, both of Waterloo, in Geneva; Rev. Hay (6-8/24)
2003. Conklin, Stodard m 4/30/34 Emma Seeley, dau of Judge Seeley, in Romulus; Rev. Barton. All of Romulus (6-5/14)
2004. Conley, Litire(?) of Utica m 10/3/49 Margaret Duffy of New York Mills in Utica; Rev. William Wyatt (9-10/5)
2005. Conley, Philip m 9/24/35 Cynthia Edwards in Seneca Falls (6-10/14)
2006. Conn, David of Newberry, PA m 5/27/34 Ann Burnham, dau of Asahel of Chemung, NY, in C; James Griswold, Esq. (6-6/4)
2007. Connell, Thomas m 2/17/31 Eliza Morrison in Rochester (6-2/16)
2008. Connelly, Matthew d 9/1/48 in Rome, NY (injured by a railroad train 8/17) (9-9/11)
2009. Conover, John R. of Freehold, NJ m 8/12/34 Drusilla T. Simmons, dau of late Capt. A. of Phelps, in P; Rev. Allen (6-8/20)
2010. Conrad, Vincent of Fayette m -- Electa Bradway in Alexandria, NY (6-2/10)
2011. Conradt, Adam, 84, d 5/11/35 in Chittenango (3-5/19)
2012. Convis, Ezra (Hon.), late a member of the Michigan legislature, d 2/27/37 in Detroit, MI (6-3/15)
2013. Cook, _____, 3 yrs, ch of Charles H., d 1/13/36 in Sullivan (3-1/19)
2014. Cook, Albert A. m 9/24/35 Calinda Dart in Seneca Falls (6-10/14)
2015. Cook, Anna Maria, 22, wf of Russel S. and oldest dau of Prof. Henry Mills of the Auburn Theological Seminary, d 7/10/39 in Lenox, MA (6-7/24)
2016. Cook, Caroline, 20, 2nd dau of Abiel, Esq., d 7/19/42 in Norwich (Oxford Times, 7/27)
2017. Cook, Charles Augustus, 7 mo, s of Charles A., d 3/29/36 in Geneva (6-3/30)
2018. Cook, Daniel, 47, merchant, of Geneva, brother of David, Esq., d 11/28/31 in Hartford, CT (6-12/7)
2019. Cook, David, Esq,, 61, d 2/17/35 in Geneva (lived in G 40 yrs; funeral at Presby. Ch.) (6-2/18)
2020. Cook, Elias R. of Sodus m 6/23/30 Caroline M. Barbarin of Geneva in G; Rev. Mason (6-6/30)
2021. Cook, Francis H. and Cook, Solomon, sons of Ambrose, d in Auburn (6-1/26/31)
2022. Cook, Hannah, 16, dau of late Rev. Henry of NJ, d 6/15/31 in Geneva, NY (6-6/22)
2023. Cook, Henry B., 33, merchant, d in Albany (9-6/7/25)
2024. Cook, Hiram, 31, d 9/8/33 in Havana, NY (6-9/25)
2025. Cook, James m 3/2/43 Abigail Bradley in Clinton; Rev. Wayne Gridley. All of Clinton (9-3/9)
2026. Cook, James N. of Hornellsville m 10/14/50 Susan Squeir of Cooperstown in Addison; Rev. A. H. Parmelee (4-10/23)
2027. Cook, Janitjie, about 105, d 6/7/30 in Bethlehem, Alb. Co. (6-6/30)
2028. Cook, John, Esq, 45, formerly District Attorney of Allegany Co., d 9/9/30 in Angelica (6-9/22)
2029. Cook, John m 12/21/30 Jane Pinkney in Fayette (6-12/29)
2030. Cook, John m 9/10/40 Elizabeth M. Somers, both of Lawrence, Tioga Co, PA, in L; Rev. Breck of Wellsborough (4-9/11)
2031. Cook, John O., Esq., about 43, bro. of David, Esq. of Geneva, d 6/4/32 in Starkey (6-6/20)
2032. Cook, Lambert E. m 1/19/32 Louisa L. Norton, only dau ofCapt. Miles Norton, in Westfield, OH (6-2/22)
2033. Cook, Maria (Miss), 57, d 12/21/35 at the home of C. A. Cook in Geneva (6-1/6/36)
2034. Cook, Martha, 64, consort of Nathan, d 7/23/31 in Fayette (6-7/27)
2035. Cook, Mary E., 33, wf of Eli, Esq., d 9/23/49 in Syracuse (9-9/27)
2036. Cook, Moses of Vienna, NY m 7/31/36 Roxanna Curlough of Hopewell in Palmyra (6-8/10)

2037. Cook, Peyton R., attorney, m 10/12/20 Harriet Steere, dau of Mark, in Norwich; Rev. Andrews (8-10/25)
2038. Cook, R. S. (Rev.), pastor of the Presby. Ch. of Lanesboro, MA, m 11/1/36 Ann Maria Mills (oldest dau of Rev, Henry, D.., Prof. of Biblical Criticism at the Auburn Theological Seminary) in Auburn (6-11/16)
2039. Cook, Sarah (Mrs.), 66, d 2/19/46 at the home of C. C. Cook in Clinton (9-2/20)
2040. Cook, W. D. (Dr.) of Seneca Falls m 8/21/34 Caroline M. Ward, formerly of NYC, in Seneca Falls (6-9/3)
2041. Cooke, Benjamin Gorton, merchant, of Gorham m 1/17/33 Rhoda A. Cole of Benton in B; Rev. Gaylord (6-1/23)
2042. Cooke, H. G. P. (Rev.), 29, A.M., d -- in Gloucester, England and a few weeks afterward John F. Cooke, 34, M.D. d -- (place not stated). Both men are younger bros of Dr. Cooke of Albany (6-4/22)
2043. Cooke, Henry D., Esq., s of Hon. E. Cooke of Sandusky, OH and late of San Francisco, CA, m 8/21/49 Laura S. Humphreys, dau of late Dr. E. of Utica, at Trinity Ch., Utica; P. A. Proal, D.D. (9-8/24)
2044. Cooke, Joseph P. m 1/26/31 Sophia Ferris in Walden (6-2/9)
2045. Cooke, Oliver B., bookbinder, late of NYC and formerly of Geneva, d 12/6/34 at the home of P. Ruckle, Esq. in Geneva (6-12/10)
2046. Cooke, Oliver S. of the firm of Meriam and Cooke, book printers, m 4/21/42 Abby E. Barnes in Brookfield, MA; Rev. Moses Chase. All of Brookfield (3-5/18)
2047. Cool(?), James W. m 6/10/34 Lovisa Morrison in Geneva; Rev. McLaren (6-6/18)
2048. Cool, William m 11/19/35 Maria Louisa Warner. both of Phelps (6-12/16)
2049. Cooley, Anna (Mrs.), 61, d in Onondaga (6-3/9/31)
2050. Cooley, Mary (Mrs.), 24, d in Auburn (6-10/12/31)
2051. Cooley, Mary, 30, wf of James, d 6/10/33 in Penn Yan (6-6/19)
2052. Cooley, Oliver B., 35, d 1/25/44 in Utica (funeral from his late home, 3 Seneca St.) (9-1/27)
2053. Cooley, Richard, 51, d 4/25/50 in Cooperstown (9-5/4)
2054. Cooley, Sarah Sophronia, dau of late O. B., d 11/12/46 in Utica (funeral from her mother's residence, the Orphan's Asylum, Broadway) (9-11/3)
2055. Cooley, Warren m 11/5/45 Isabella H. Martin in Utica; Elder T. Hill. All of Utica (9-11/13)
2056. Coolidge, Henry A., editor of the Madison County Whig, m 10/18/49 A. Almene Horton of Stockbridge in S; Rev. Daniel Holmes (1-10/25)
2057. Coombs, Leslie (Gen.) of Lexington, KY m 4/11/49 Mary E. Man of Cumberland, RI in Manville, RI; Rev. Penny (9-4/17)
2058. Coon, John m 2/4/33 Julia Ingraham, both of Bristol, in Canandaigua (6-2/13)
2059. Coons, William m Sally Wheeler in Benton (6-3/17/30)
2060. Cooper, Apollos, Esq. m 2/1/31 Elizabeth Griffin, both of Utica, in U; Rev. Aiken (9-2/22)
2061. Cooper, Charles m 8/16/49 Catharine Knickerbacker, both of Clayville, in C; Rev. John Waugh (9-8/27)
2062. Cooper, Charles D., 61, d 1/30/31 in Albany (6-2/9 and 9-2/8)
2063. Cooper, Francis m 5/23/48 Emeline Hall, dau of Hiram, at the American Hotel in Baldwinsville; Rev. T. Walker. All of Baldwinsville (1-5/24)
2064. Cooper, George m 12/8/36 Eleanor W. Mitchell in Southport (6-12/21)
2065. Cooper, George V., portrait painter, m 9/20/42 Caroline E. Page in NYC; Elder Benedict. All of NYC (9-9/26)
2066. Cooper, Gilbert m 11/14/41 Laura Yale, dau of Zebedee, in Guilford; Rev. Igenburgh, All of Guilford (Oxford Times, 11/17)
2067. Cooper, Isaac S. d in Cooperstown (8-1/14/18)
2068. Cooper, James of Corning m 4/9/49 Margaret Whelan of Utica at St. John's Ch. (in Utica?); Rev. Beecham of Rome, NY (9-4/11)
2069. Cooper, James, 96, d 5/1/49 in Oswego (bro of late Judge William Cooper and uncle to J. Fenimore Cooper; served in the Navy from Pennsylvania ⚹ in the Rev. War) (9-5/5)
2070. Cooper, Margery, 39, dau of Capt. Samuel formerly of Stark, d 10/10/48 in Rochester, WI (9-11/29)
2071. Cooper, Richard, 90, d 2/28/36 in Brooklyn, Cuyahoga Co., OH (6-3/23)
*2069.5 Cooper, Levi m 5/22/34 Jane Harriet Schriver, both of Waterloo (6-5/28)

2072. Cooper, Richard m 12/10/50 Maria Frances Cooper, dau of James Fenimore
       Cooper, at Christ Ch., Cooperstown; Rev. S. H. Battin (9-12/16)
2073. Cooper, William m 6/12/43 Lois Burrell, both of Binghamton, in Conklin;
       Rufus Finch, Esq. (2-8/2)
2074. Cooper, Z. H. of the late firm of Cooper and Ellis of Utica d 1/18/31
       in U (9-1/25)
2075. Cop, Arthur m 2/3/31 Sarah Redner in Geneva; Rev. Mattison (6-2/9)
2076. Corbett, Mary d near Fayetteville, NC (6-11/1/30)
2077. Cordell (or Cornell?), Luke of Hornby m 7/7/41 Martha Cushing of New
       Bedford, MA in Painted Post, NY; Rev. S. S. Howe (4-7/9)
2078. Corell, John N. of NYC m 8/5/32 Angelina Gardner of Boston at Zion Ch.
       in Palmyra (double ceremony - see m of John H. Merrill) (6-8/8)
2079. Corey, Daniel G. (Rev.), pastor of Bleecker St. Bapt. Ch., Utica,
       m 7/3/49 Jane J. Backus, youngest dau of Elisha, Esq. formerly of Utica,
       in Morristown, NY; Rev. Robert R. Raymond (9-7/6)
2080. Corey, Hannah W., 36, wf of Rev. D. G. and dau of Dr. E. Whitmore of
       Georgetown, d 3/4/48 in Utica (funeral from Bleecker St. Bapt. Ch.)
       (9-3/6)
2081. Corey, Mary Ann (Miss), sister of Rev. Daniel G. (pastor of Bleecker St.
       Bapt. Ch.) d 10/1/47 at the home of her father in Utica ("funeral at
       said church") (9-10/2)
2082. Corey, Walter Augustus, 3, s of Rev. Sidney A., d 4/24/50 (in Utica?)
       (9-4/27)
2083. Corlay, Joseph of St. Louis, MO m 11/25/40 Donna Maria Del Refugio
       Antonina Mucia Isadora Johanna Bernarda de Jesu Solares Corras of
       New Mexico in St. Louis (3-12/23)
2084. Corlies, Albert H. (Rev.) of Western m 8/29/48 Susanna Lawson, dau of
       George of Rome, NY, in R; Rev. E. C. Pritchett (9-9/1)
2085. Cornelis, John m 10/29/50 Alishquets Augustine, both descendants of the
       old Indian Chief Shenendoah, at the Oneida Railroad House; Rev. James
       Nichols (9-11/4)
2086. Cornell, Abijah, Jr. of Guilford m 11/16/32 Amanda Cady of Chenango in C
       (6-11/7)
2087. Cornell, John L. of Painted Post m 1/1/49 Sarah Lovell of the Buena Vista
       Plains at the Buena Vista Bridal Saloon; Rev. D. Read (4-1/17)
2088. Cornish, Seneca W. m 6/5/50 Mary Ann Johnson, both of Lee Center, in L.C.;
       Frederick Tracy, Esq. (9-6/13)
2089. Cornish(?), Whiting A. m 4/30/42 Mary Mallory in Coventry; Zenas
       Hutchinson, Esq. (Oxford Times, 5/11)
2090. Cornwall, Samuel m 10/18/43 Sarah N. Hayt, dau of Samuel, Esq., in
       Patterson, Put. Co.; Rev. E. P. Benedict. All of Patterson (9-10/25)
2091. Cornwell, Elihu of Guilford m 2/1/27 Philamela Root of Oxford in O;
       Rev. E. Andrews (8-2/9)
2092. Cornwell, James of Seneca Falls m Lucilla Kirkland of Waterloo in W (6-3/9/31)
2093. Cornwell, Lendell m Clarissa Tracy; R. D. Delay, Esq. (8-1/13/19)
2094. Corson, Harriet A., 25, wf of Jacob, d 4/30/32 in Canandaigua (6-5/9)
2095. Corson, Jacob m 1/15/33 Nancy F. Wilder in Canandaigua (6-1/30)
2096. Corson, Maria Elizabeth, 1 , dau of L. Corson, d 2/18/32 in Canandaigua
       (6-2/29)
2097. Corwin, Eleazer of Geneva m 2/17/30 Margaret Whiteford in Waterloo; Rev.
       Lane (6-2/24)
2098. Coryell, Ann D. (Mrs.), 29, dau of Thomas Lowthorp of Geneva, d 4/21/36
       in Lambertville, NJ (6-5/18)
2099. Coryelle, E. C. of Nichols m 12/27/42 M. E. Thayer of Bainbridge in B;
       Rev. Warner (Oxford Republican, 1/6/43)
2100. Cosgrove, Bernard, 60, d 12/21/46 in Utica (9-12/23)
2101. Cosmon, Hiram, 25, m 3/13/49 Julia Ann Rowley, 50, in Hector (double
       ceremony - see m of John Gottry) (9-4/6)
2102. Costen, Christopher m 8/18/36 Nancy Morgan in Bath (6-8/31)
2103. Cotes, _____ of Manchester m 3/20/36 Ruth Eliza Scott of Benton in B;
       Rev. Chase (6-4/27)
2104. Cotton, Caroline (Mrs.), 25, dau of Capt. Oliver Clark, d 5/6/44 in
       Canastota (3-5/15)
2105. Cotton, Henry G., Esq. m 3/8/31 Maria McBurney, both of Painted Post,
       in Bath (6-3/23)

2106. Cotton, Jeremiah m 2/19/35 Sally Chesebro, both of Farmington, in Canandaigua (6-3/4)
2107. Cotton, Maria, 28, wf of Henry G., Esq. and dau of late Thomas McBurney, d. 1/29/32 in Painted Post (6-2/15)
2108. Cotton, Owen, Esq. m 2/9/31 Laura Adams, dau of Parmenio, in Attica (6-2/23)
2109. Couch, Leonard m 1/20/31 Nancy Batrick in Tioga Village (6-2/2)
2110. Countee, John m 1/17/33 Harriet Riley in Vienna, NY (6-1/30)
2111. Courtenay, Edward Henry, 9, s of E. H., Esq. of Boston,d 1/24/38 in Geneva (funeral at thehome of W. T. Taylor, Esq. in Pulteneyville) (6-1/24)
2112. Courtright, Mary (Mrs.), 66, formerly of Williamsburg, PA, mother of Mrs. H. G. Phelps, d 9/9/41 at the home of H. G. Phelps (member of Meth. Episc. Ch.) (4-9/22)
2113. Covell, Edward of Elmira m 8/23/49 Georgianna D. Parsons of Santa Mohague, CT at the home of Dr. William Lord in S. M., CT; Rev. D. Brainard (5-8/31)
2114. Coventry, Alexander (Dr.) d 12/9/31 in Utica (6-12/21)
2115. Coventry, Mary D., 12, dau of Dr. C. B., d 2/22/48 in Utica (9-2/23)
2116. Covert, Peter H. m Caroline Covert in Ovid (6-1/26/31)
2117. Covey, Lavinia, 17, dau of Deacon Amos, d 11/12/41 in Fenner (3-12/1)
2118. Covey, Silas H. (Capt.) m 10/5/37 Adelia Ann Cornell, both of Fenner, in F; Rev. J. N. T. Tucker (3-10/11)
2119. Cowan, Luther (Dr.), 29, d 9/6/26 in Lyons (9-9/12)
2120. Cowan, William D. of Utica m 2/21/49 Ruth Ann Prescott of New Hartford in New H; Rev. J. E. Davenport (bride the dau of Oliver, Esq., member of state assembly) ((9-2/23)
2121. Cowder, F. (Capt.), 34, "master of form one of the packets between Utica and Rochester", d 4/5/45 in Herkimer (consumption) (9-5/8)
2122. Cowdrey, Christina, 55, consort of Col. John, d 4/26/30 in Junius (6-4/28)
2123. Cowdrey, John (Col.), 76, (a Rev. soldier), an early resident of Geneva and later of Waterloo, d 1/27/35 in NYC (took part in the throwing of the tea overboard in Boston) (6-2/4)
2124. Cowdry, _____, 63, widow, d 7/22/26 in Utica (9-7/25)
2125. Cowen, James m 5/26/41 Miranda Brown in Smithfield; Rev. Stanley (3-6/16)
2126. Cowen, Joseph, 59, formerly of Utica, d 10/ 15/45 at the home of his dau in Ottawa, IL (9-11/5)
2127. Cowen, Marriette, 18, sister of T. C. Cowen of Elmira, d 7/4/49 in Candor (5-7/13)
2128. Cowen, Sidney J., Esq., 29, of Albany, s of late Judge Cowen of Saratoga, d 9/10/44 on board the packet "Ashburton" on a voyage to Liverpool (buried in L) (9-10/24)
2129. Cowing, Fordice m 1/17/43 Betsey Jane Kellogg of Cazenovia in C; Rev. Clarke (3-1/18)
2130. Cowing, John (Capt.) (a Rev. soldier) d in Jamestown (6-10/9/33)
2131. Cowles, Elisha, about 25, d 5/16/26 in Otisco (9-6/6)
2132. Cowles, George m 3/4/30 Almira Barber in Geneva; Rev. Phelps (6-3/10)
2133. Cowles, Hiram m 7/17/23 Susan Towsley of Walton in Smithville; W. Gray, Esq. (8-7/23)
2134. Cowles, Hiram m Juliette Caulkins in Lakeville (6-2/9/31)
2135. Cowles, Myron m 4/18/25 Margaret Townley in Smithville (8-4/20)
2136. Cowles, Oren m 4/1/44 Matilda H. Bilsell in Rome, NY; Rev. G. S. Boardman (9-4/11)
2137. Cox, Diana, 24, d 1/16/33 in Vienna, NY (6-1/23)
2138. Cox, George m 8/29/50 Amanda McHuron in Lysander; Rev. Seward. All of Lysander (double ceremony - see m of Harvey Cox) (1-9/5)
2139. Cox, Harvey m 8/29/50 Susan Stephens in Lysander; Rev. Seward. All of Lysander (double ceremony - see m of George Cox) (1-9/5)
2140. Cox, Mary, 16, dau of Malachi and Olive, d 10/11/49 in Lysander (consumption) (1-10/18)
2141. Cox, Peter m 8/24/34 Hannah Holmes in Chittenango; Rev. James T. Hough (3-8/26)
2142. Cox, Truman m 7/3/49 Maria R. Pell, both of Deerfield, in North Gage; Rev. Pratt (9-7/6)
2143. Cozier, Eliza, 19, oldest dau of Ezra S., Esq., d 8/2/26 in Utica (9-8/8)

2144. Cozzens, Charles, 3, s of Levi, d 11/9/25 in Utica (9-11/22)
2145. Crafts, Albert B., 35, formerly of Cherry Valley, NY, d 5/10/49 in San Francisco, CA (9-7/31)
2146. Crafts, Eelcta, 26, wf of Willard and dau of late Dr. Upham, d 11/21/48 in Mayville, Chaut. Co. (9-12/2)
2147. Crafts, Samuel, Esq., 89, (father of Willard Crafts of Utica) d 12/27/48 in Hartwick (b in Munson, MA in 1759; a Rev. soldier; settled in Springfield, Ots. Co., NY in 1790 or 1791) (9-1/1/49)
2148. Craig, Archibald (Dr.), 71, d 6/25/46 in Schenectady (9-7/27)
2149. Crandall, Ambrose m 8/1/32 Calista Allen in Vienna, NY; Rev. Griswold (6-8/22) also (6-8/15)
2150. Crandall, Charles H., 19, d 7/28/37 in Millport, Chemung Co. (6-8/9)
2151. Crandall, Horace B. m 1/31/49 Maria Snider, both of Corning; Rev. E. W. Dickinson (5-2/2)
2152. Crandall, Peter B. m 5/15/44 Eunice C. Priest, both of Bridgewater, at Griffin's Hotel (prob. in Utica); Rev. A. B. Grosh (9-5/16)
2153. Crandall, R. m 11/3/32 Mary W. Burrell, both of Palmyra, in Canandaigua (6-11/14)
2154. Crandall, Reuben m Cynthia Ellis in Gorham (6-1/26/31)
2155. Crane, _____, 2, child of Lebbeus, d 6/20/26 in Utica (9-6/27)
2156. Crane, Barnabas, Jr. of Miami Co., OH m 6/29/34 Alinda Briggs in East Bloomfield (double ceremony - see m of George W. Crane) (6-7/16)
2157. Crane, Charles m 10/11/40 Mrs. Sarah Nobles in Erwin; C. K. Miller, Esq. All of Erwin (4-10/23)
2158. Crane, Daniel, 85, d 9/12/48 in Jefferson, Schoharie Co. (5-9/22)
2159. Crane, David J. m 7/2/50 Sarah A. Lindsey; Rev. A. Francis. All of Utica (9-7/3)
2160. Crane, George W. m 6/29/34 Louisa Briggs in East Bloomfield (double ceremony - see m of Barnabas Crane) (6-7/16)
2161. Crane, George W., 32, d 6/2/50 at the home of Deacon Wood in Litchfield (9-6/8)
2162. Crane, Hannah E., 47, wf of Rev. Abijah, d 6/12/46 in Clinton (9-6/18)
2163. Crane, Hector H., 46, late keeper of the Eagle Tavern in Rochester, d 11/27/38 in Albany (6-12/5)
2164. Crane, Henry, 69, d 8/12/50 in Sauquoit (9-8/14)
2165. Crane, Hiram of Havana, NY m Emeline Deverest of Catskill in C (6-1/5/31)
2166. Crane, Hiram m 8/25/35 Minerva T. Jones in Elmira (6-9/2)
2167. Crane. Lafayette of Waterville m 4/7/46 Jane McCon, dau of John of Marshall, in M; Rev. Elder Kenyon (9-4/11)
2168. Crane, Minerva, 23, wf of Hiram, d 10/27/36 in Elmira (6-11/2)
2169. Crane, Rufus W., Esq. of Warren m 5/1/50 Antoinette O. Winsor of Utica in U; Rev. William H. Spencer (9-5/3)
2170. Crane, Samuel D. of Lyons m Ann Olmstead of Vienna, NY in V; Elder Bentley (6-5/29/33)
2171. Cranmer, J. M. (Dr.), about 30, homeopathic physician, d 7/22/49 in Millport (cholera) (5-7/27)
2172. Cranson, Aaron of Lenox m 9/8/31 Dianthe Flardino of Fenner in F; Rev. Northrop (3-9/13)
2173. Cranson, Asa, 80, (a Rev. patriot) d 1/5/41 in Lenox (3-1/20)
2174. Cranson, Asa of Lenox Hill m 4/24/42 Olive Ward in Canastota; Rev. Stokes (3-5/18)
2175. Crapsey, Catherine, 46, d 9/29/39 in Sullivan (breast cancer) (3-10/2)
2176. Crapsey, John G. of Sullivan m 2/14/42 Eliza Ann Olin of Skaneateles in S; Rev. S. W. Brace (3-2/23)
2177. Crawe, T. B. (Dr.) of Watertown drowned 6/2/47 in Perch Lake (1-6/16)
2178. Crawford, J. m 6/5/31 Maria Ransier, dau of John, in Canaseraga; J. French, Esq. All of Chittenango (3-6/7)
2179. Crawford, Thomas, 81, d 11/14/46 in Geneva (6-11/20)
2180. Crego, Ira m 4/18/49 Charlotte Bowman, both of Van Buren, in V. B.; Rev. T. Walker (1-4/19)
2181. Crippen, Ephraim P., 62, d 6/30/39 in Phelps (6-7/10)
2182. Crippen, Theodore, 18 mo., only child of Samuel and Minerva, d 3/18/44 in Utica (9-3/26)
2183. Crips(?), _____, s of Adam, d 10/3/34 in Dresden. "Mrs. Crips", wf of Adam, d 10/4 (6-10/15)

2184. Crissey, E. F. m 9/22/42 Sarah S. Powers in NYC; Rev. Dr. P_?_ton.
All of NYC (9-9/26)
2185. Crissey, Sarah S., 21, wf of E. F., d 2/12/45 in Utica (consumption)
(9-2/19)
Crittenden. See also Cruttenden.
2186. Crittenden, _____, inf dau of Fortiscue, d 9/4/30 in Seneca (6-9/15)
2187. Crittenden, Byron H., 10 mo, s of Dr. L. W., d 12/25/35 in Gorham
(6-12/30)
2188. Crittenden, William T. m 12/26/38 Deborah Whitman, dau of Augustus, in
Rushville; Rev. M. Gilliston (6-1/9/39)
2189. Crocker, David H. m 12/27/42 Polly Elvia Shaw, dau of Andrew, in
Binghamton; Rev. William Delong. All of Binghamton (2-1/25/43)
2190. Crocker, Ezekiel (Deacon), 76, m 1/16/14 Marilla Cornish, 17, at
Chenango Point (8-2/8)
2191. Crocker, Hans m Augusta Potter, dau of P. Potter, in Milwaukee, Wisc.
Terr.; Rev. Hutch (9-4/12/44)
2192. Crocker, John Milton, 4, s of Hugh, d 6/11/44 in Utica (funeral at 65 Main
St.) (9-6/12)
2193. Crocker, Mary Elizabeth, 3, dau of Hugh, d 6/10/46 in Utica (funeral from
the home of her father, 65 Main St.) (9-6/12)
2194. Croes, John (Rt. Rev.), D.D., Bishop of the Prot. Episc. Ch. of NJ,
d 7/30/32 in New Brunswick, NJ (6-8/15)
2195. Crolius, William, 78, (a Rev. soldier) d in NYC (6-4/28/30)
2196. Crook, Coonrad of Bainbridge m 3/1/24 Sarah Billings of Guilford in G;
Samuel A. Smith, Esq. (8-3/17)
2197. Crook, Milton Curtis, 1, only s of Elias and Electa H., d 9/29/49 in Paris,
NY (9-10/2)
2198. Crook, Sarah Evaline, 4 mo, dau of Elias and Electa Ann, d 5/12/45 in
Sauquoit (9-5/20)
2199. Crooks, William K. of Lyons m 2/21/33 Phebe L. Fisher of Bristol in
Bloomfield (6-3/6)
2200. Crosby, Arvin of Oswegatchie m 1/26/46 Hannah Maria Hulett of Whitesboro
in New Hartford; T. A. Holt, Esq. (9-1/31)
2201. Crosby, William, Jr., 27, editor of the Auburn Gazette, d in Auburn
(8-1/14/18)
2202. Crosby, William M. m 9/28/46 Mary C. Prescott, both of Geneva, in G;
Rev. J. M. Austin (6-10/2)
2203. Cross, Alfred m 10/6/44 Elizabeth A. Doney, both of Saratoga Springs,
in Cayuga; Rev. Dr. Abul of Geneva (9-10/28)
2204. Cross, Erastus, 57, d 11/28/48 in Utica (funeral from the home of David
Wood, corner of Elizabeth and Charlotte Sts.) (9-11/29)
2205. Cross, Erastus E. of Buffalo m 7/5/47 Harriet A. Bradford of Utica in U;
Rev. D. A. Shepard (9-7/7)
2206. Cross, Oliver M. of Rochester m 6/23/46 Mary Jane Shelt of Aurora in A;
Rev. C. N. Mattoon (6-6/26)
2207. Crossman, Benjamin P. (Dr.), 44, formerly of Oneida Co., NY, d 9/3/46
at New Diggings, Wisc. Terr., 12 mi. from Galena (had divided his time
in Wisc. between mining and medicine; had previously lived in Paris,
France and in England) (9-9/22)
2208. Crossman, George H. m 12/16/45 Jane A. Hicks, both of Deerfield, in D;
Rev. Harvey (9-12/23)
2209. Crossman, John of Paris, NY m 9/2/47 Susan Dexter of Newport in Utica;
Zenas Wright, Esq. (9-9/3)
2210. Crossman, John Andrews m 8/27/33 Gertrude Dayton, only dau of Dr. Daniel,
in Geneva; Rev. Dr. Bruce (6-8/28)
2211. Crossman, Nathaniel, 50, d 9/17/45 in Deerfield (emigrated from Mass.
nearly 50 years ago) (9-9/23)
2212. Crossman, Olivia L., 20, youngest dau of Nathaniel and Betsey, d 6/22/46
in Deerfield (9-7/7)
2213. Crouse, James of the firm of J. Crouse and Co., merchants, of Chittenango
m 8/30/37 Laura Beecher, dau of Sylvester, Esq. of Lenox, in L;
Rev. Barrows (3-9/6)
2214. Crouse, Sarah Catherine, 1, only child of James, Esq., d 7/24/41 in
Chittenango (3-7/28)
2215. Crowell, Seth (Rev.), 46, of the Meth. Episc. Ch. d 7/6/26 in NYC (9-7/11)

61

2216. Crowell, Truman m 9/19/33 Phebe Gustin in Bath (6-10/9)
2217. Crowley, J. M. (Dr.), 43, d 9/13/42 in Utica ("a practical phrenologist") (9-9/15)
2218. Crownhart, William Henry m 10/23/35 Esther Hopkins in Sullivan; J. French, Esq. (3-11/3)
2219. Crowninshield, George (Capt.), 51, d 11/26/17 in Salem, MA("on board the celebrated Cleopatra's barge") (8-12/10)
2220. Crows, James of Clayville m 4/23/45 Fanny Eels in Sauquoit; Rev. Waugh (9-5/8)
2221. Cruger, Daniel (Gen.) of Bath, NY m 7/16/33 Mrs. Lydia Shepherd at the mansion of the late Col. Shepherd near Wheelier, VA; Rev. James Harvey (6-7/31)
2222. Cruger, Hannah, 40, wf of Gen. Donald, d 12/7/31 in Syracuse (6-12/21)
2223. Cruger, Jefferson m 12/17/31 Mary Sherwood in Poughkeepsie (6-1/11/32)
2224. Cruger, Washington m 7/23/31 Jane Ann Brown of Poughkeepsie in P (6-1/11/32)
2225. Crulzer, John (Rev.) d "recently" in Chester, PA ("He was in the pulpit and had just given his text, 'We must all appear before the judgment seat of Christ' when he fell and instantly expired") (9-1/4/25)
2226. Crum, Gardner (Rev.) of Dix, Chemung Co. m 6/9/41 Mrs. Nancy Parker of Addison in A; Rev. C. S. Davis (4-6/18)
2227. Crumb, _____, 45, wf of Abraham, d 12/23/35 in Phelps (6-12/30)
2228. Crumb, Joshua of Plainfield m 2/4/41 Grace Brown of Brookfield in B; Rev. J. Wells ("The groom about six feet in height and the bride a little more than half his stature") (3-2/10)
2229.Crump, Emma H., 21, wf of Josiah H., d 4/21/42 in Utica (consumption) (funeral from 82 Bleecker St.) (9-4/22)
2230. Crump, Joab J. m 5/5/49 Mary Ann Arnott in Utica; Rev. P. A. Proal, D.D. All of Utica (9-5/9)
2231. Crump, Josiah H. m 3/31/42 Emma H. Nash in Utica; Rev. Dr. Proal. All of Utica (9-4/2)
2232. Crump, Josiah Harrison of Utica m 11/6/45 Julia Stuart, dau of Henry Y. of Little Falls, at Emanuel Ch., Little Falls; Rev. Livermore (7-11/11)
2233. Cruttenden, Charles D. m 1/14/36 Melinda Monroe, oldest dau of Jesse, in Perryville; Elder Skinner (3-1/26)
2234. Cuddeback, De Witt m Sarah Peckham in Skaneateles (6-3/9/31)
2235. Cuddeback, Levi, 49, d 6/4/49 in Skaneateles (consumption) (1-6/14)
2236. Cullings, Thomas, 48, d at his home in New Scotland (9-2/21/50)
2237. Culver, Artemus B. m 9/20/48 Maria W. Franklin, both of Phoenix, at the Empire House, Syracuse; Rev. May (1-9/27)
2238. Culver, Matilda, 2, dau of John, d 11/5/26 in Utica (9-11/7)
2239. Culver, Reeves of Palmyra m 8/15/33 Ursula Squires of Newark in Phelps (6-8/28)
2240. Cuming, Francis H. (Rev.), rector of Christ Ch., Reading, PA, m 4/6/31 Charlotte Hart, dau of late Roswell, Esq. of Rochester, NY,at St. Luke's Ch., Rochester; Rev. Dr. Rudd (6-4/20)
2241. Cumming, Alexander (Rev.), formerly of NYC,d in Brooklyn (9-2/14/26)
2242. Cumming, Vanranslaer of Frankfort m 1/26/47 Lydia Wright of Utica in U; N. B. Howard, Esq. (9-1/28)
2243. Cummings, Damaris, 17, d 1/16/31 in Binghamton (6-2/2)
2244. Cummings, David m 8/16/48 Susanna Heanay of Boonville (in New York Mills?); Rev. N. D. Graves (9-8/19)
2245. Cummings, Edward, 4 mo, s of H., Esq., d 7/15/36 in Chittenango (3-7/20)
2246. Cummings, Henry of Yorkville m 9/7/47 Mary Eliza Smith of New Hartford in New H; Rev. Dr. Paddock (9-9/9)
2247. Cummings, James m 4/12/39 Hannah Taylor, both of Jerusalem, NY, in Benton; E. Ganung, Esq. (6-4/24)
2248. Cummins, Mary (Mrs.), formerly of New Hartford, NY, d -- in Sugar Grove, Warren Co., PA (9-6/2/42)
2249. Cumpson, Jonas m 10/1/35 Ruth Ann Cornell (at Seneca Falls?) (6-10/14)
2250. Cumpston, Samuel, 60, d 4/3/50 in Corning (4-4/10)
2251. Cunningham, Elza (Mrs.), 26, d 8/4/50 in Utica (consumption) (funeral from her late home, 57 Jay St.) (9-8/5)
2252. Cunningham, Henry, Esq., 35, d 7/25/26 in Johnstown (9-8/15)

62

2253. Cunningham, John, 16, oldest s of late John of Utica, d 9/27/45 in Nassau, Isle of New Providence (9-11/27)
2254. Currier, William m 11/18/33 Julia Ann Babcock in China, NY (6-12/18)
2255. Curry, Helen Jane, 6, dau of Elijah P. and Mary C., d 11/18/47 in Utica (funeral from her father's home on Cooper St. near Broadway) (9-11/20)
2256. Curry, John, 90, d 2/27/26 in Trenton, NY (9-3/21)
2257. Curtis, _____, wf of Solomon, d 8/11/23 in Oxford (8-8/20)
2258. Curtis, Clarissa Ann, 26, dau of John and Clarissa M., d 8/24/48 in Elmira (5-9/1)
2259. Curtis, E. L. B. of Danby m 11/13/50 Anna K. Mills of Corning; Rev. Lightbourne (4-11/20)
2260. Curtis, Ephraim m 10/31/19 Susan Rogers in Preston (8-11/10)
2261. Curtis, Gold T., Esq., attorney, of Peterboro m 10/8/46 Mary F. Gay, dau of William F. of Canastota, in C; Rev. Washington Stickney (9-10/16)
2262. Curtis, Harriet D., 1, only dau of Ransom and Eunice, d 10/16/47 in Cazenovia (9-10/23)
2263. Curtis, Harvey m Polly Steele in Owego (6-10/23/33)
2264. Curtis, James of Pompey, NY m 7/2/37 Philinda Goodle of Sullivan in S; J. French, Esq. (3-7/5)
2265. Curtis, James J. of Lairdsville, Oneida Co., d 4/16/49 at the home of Col. Warford on Washington St., Utica (buried in Oneida) (9-4/19)
2266. Curtis, Jane M., 16, of Campbell d 9/11/41 in Newtown, CT "while on a visit to her friends") (4-9/29)
2267. Curtis, Joel m 9/13/50 Eliza Goodenow of Vernon in Utica; Rev. William Wyatt (9-9/17)
2268. Curtis, John m 5/17/35 Ann Truax in Sullivan; J. French, Esq. (3-5/19)
2269. Curtis, Judith, 71, relict of Capt. Oliver of Pelham, MA, d 12/31/29 in Preston, NY (8-1/6/30)
2270. Curtis, Lee (Dr.), about 30, d 8/13/34 in Sennett (6-9/3)
2271. Curtis, Lucius (Rev.) of Woodbury, CT m 6/28/48 Emily Chauncey Whittlesey, dau of late Rev. Samuel of NYC; Rev. Charles A. Goodrich (9-7/3)
2272. Curtis, Patrick of Chittenango m 6/28/40 Thirza Browning of Fayetteville in F; Rev. M. Hase (3-7/1)
2273. Curtis, Ransom, 41, d 10/6/43 in Sullivan (3-10/11)
2274. Curtis, Rhoda, 30, wf of William, d 4/12/24 in Oxford (8-5/26)
2275. Curtis, William m B. A. Clark in Caroline (6-10/9)
2276. Curtis, William T. of Groveland, Liv. Co., m 10/17/50 Caroline E. Briggs, dau of Nymrod, Esq. of Floyd, in Rome, NY; Rev. H. C. Vogell (9-10/24)
2277. Curtis, Zachariah m 12/19/27 Emeline Dickerman in Guilford; Rev. Donaldson. All of Guilford (8-1/4/28)
2278. Curtiss, Amelian, 22, wf of Samuel F., d in Penn Yan (6-2/17/30)
2279. Curtiss, Gabriel m Orpah Hart in Elmira (6-2/9/31)
2280. Curtiss, George of Utica m 1/20/47 Elizabeth A. Austin of Frankfort in Utica; Rev. D.A. Shepard (9-1/22)
2281. Curtiss, H. H. of Utica m 11/13/44 Mary A. Child of Exeter in E; Rev. Aaron P. Allen (9-11/15)
2282. Curtiss, H. H. of Utica m 10/16/50 Mary Burt Cooley of Long Meadow, MA in L. M.; Rev. John W. Harding (9-10/17)
2283. Curtiss, Hastings (Hon.), 36, sheriff of Oswego Co., d 7/26/31 at his home in Hastings (6-8/10)
2284. Curtiss, Jesse, Esq. d 2/19/50 at an advanced age at his home in Clinton (b in Plymouth, CT; at age 22 migrated to Clinton, NY; was supervisor of the town of Paris, NY for 28 yrs.) (9-2/23)
2285. Curtiss, Judson, Esq., 57, d 3/22/50 in New Haven, CT (only bro of George, Esq. of Utica; deceased earlier lived several yrs in Westmoreland, NY (9-3/29)
2286. Curtiss, Milton H. of PennYan m 2/14/33 Deborah Mallory of Benton in B (6-2/27)
2287. Curtiss, R. Alonzo of Exeter m 1/19/43 Maria W. Langley of Franklin in F; Elder C. Hartshorn (9-1/25)
2288. Curtiss, Ruth, 64, wf of Joseph, d 6/5/35 in Lyons (6-6/24)
2289. Cushing, Helen M., 33, wf of Pyau___ Cushing of Medford, MA and dau of late Thomas H. Whitemore (formerly of Utica), d 7/6/49 in Rome, NY (consumption) (9-7/12)
2290. Cushing, Lelon of Campbell m 9/3/48 Catharine Mowry of NYC in Corning (4-9/7)

2291. Cushing, Orlando of Sullivan m 6/24/40 Clara Hyatt of Nelson in N; Rev.
      E. L. Wadsworth (3-7/1)
2292. Cushman, Benjamin, 80, d 12/24/32 in Burlington, Ots. Co. ("He was the
      companion of Washington, Wooster, and Huntington for many years during
      the Revolutionary struggle.") (6-1/9/33)
2293. Cushman, Charles T. (Dr.) of Columbus, formerly of Lairdsville, m 7/16/50
      Jane A. W. Shaw, dau of Capt. James of Wynton, GA, in W; Rev George
      F. Cushman (9-8/8)
2294. Cushman, Haldah (Mrs.), dau of late Publius V. Bouge of Clinton, NY,
      d 2/12/43 in Buffalo Grove, Ogle Co., IL (moved to B. G. in 1836)
      (9-3/27)
2295. Cushman, Isaac (Dr.), 60, d 3/25/50 in Sherburne (9-4/19)
2296. Cushman, James F., 22, of Greene, s of U. and L. Greene, d 3/7/50 in St.
      Augustine, FL (9-4/19)
2297. Cushman, Joshua m 11/17/33 Louise Morgan in Canadice (6-12/4)
2298. Cushman, Ralph, late pastor of the Presby. Ch. in Manlius, d 8/27/31 in
      Worcester, OH (6-9/21)
2299. Cushney, John m 7/29/37 Mariet Weeks, both of Syracuse, in Chittenango;
      Judge Warner (3-8/9)
2300. Cutbush, James (Dr.), Prof. of Chemistry at the Military Academy, d at
      West Point (8-12/31/23)
2301. Cuthbert, Emily Rush, wf of Hon. Ross Lanoraie Cuthbert of Canada and dau
      of late Dr. Benjamin Rush of Philadelphia, d 4/27/50 (9-5/9)
2302. Cutter, Andrew J. m 8/26/49 Hannah Blackbourn of Athens, PA at the
      Wellsburgh House (presumably in Wellsburgh, NY) (5-8/31)
2303. Cuyler, Benjamin L., Esq. of Cayuga Co. d in Aurora (9-7/25/26)
2304. Cuyler, George W. (Maj.) of Palmyra m 9/13/31 Caroline Porter, dau of
      Chauncey, Esq. of Pittsford, in P; Rev. B. W. Hickox (6-9/21)
2305. Cuyler, Glen, 58, d 9/1/32 in Aurora (6-9/12)
2306. Cuyler, Marcus m 4/6/48 Charlotte Kill at the Exchange in Baldwinsville;
      E. B. Wigent, Esq. (1-4/12)
2307. Cuyler, Richard G., 33, merchant, d 4/14/32 in Vienna, NY (consumption)
      (buried at the home of his father, Glen, Esq., in Aurora)(6-4/18)
2308. Cuyler, Vernor (Dr.) of Albany m 5/10/32 Caroline Riggs, dau of Isaac, Esq.,
      in Schenectady (3-5/22)
2309. Cuyler, William Howe of Palmyra m 5/22/33 Eliza Akin of Owasco in O (6-6/5)
2310. Daggett, Betsey, 4, dau of Levi, d 3/22/31 in Bath (6-3/30)
2311. Daggett, Charlotte, 18, youngest dau of Seth and Mary, d 12/10/47 in
      Tioga, PA (5-4/12/50)
2312. Daggett, George, 36, d 3/18/50 at his home in Tioga, PA (most of his life
      he resided in Jackson, PA) (5-4/12/50)
2313. Daharsh, Peter m 2/27/39 Mary Ann Bell in Sullivan; J. French, Esq.
      (3-3/6)
2314. Dailey, John, 80, (a Rev. soldier) d 8/24/35 in Veteran (6-9/2)
      Dailey, Robert. See Bailey, Robert
2315. Daily, John m 12/25/27 Widow Patty Church in Oxford; Rev. Bush (8-1/4/28)
2316. Dakin, Eldridge of Geneva m 12/26/32 Mary Ann Brizse, dau of Stephen of
      Lockport, in L (6-1/2/33)
2317. Dakin, Mary Ann, 20, wf of Elbridge d 3/26/35 inGeneva (consumption)
      (6-4/1)
2318. Dakin, Samuel, Esq., 74, d 1/29/44 at his home in New Hartford (9-2/5)
2319. Dale, ____, wf of Charles Augustus and formerly Mrs. Robert Fulton, d
      at Tivolidale, Col. Co. (9-4/4/26)
2320. Dale, William T. of Romulus m 9/4/34 Mrs. Bethiah McClure of Hector; Rev.
      E. Everett (6-9/10)
2321. Dalliba, James E., Esq., attorney, m 9/4/44 Achsah D. Swift, dau of William
      P., in Utica; Rev. Pierre A. Proal, D.D. (9-9/6)
2322. Dalrympal, Mary (Mrs.) d 7/28/34 in Lenox (3-8/5)
2323. Daly, John S. m 6/17/34 Charity H. Mosher (in Waterloo?) (6-7/2)
2324. Dana, James D. of Utica m 6/5/44 Henrietta F. Silliman, dau of Prof.
      Silliman, in New Haven (state not given); Prof. Fitch of Yale Col.
      officiating (9-6/12)
2325. Dana, John W. (Dr.), s of James, Esq, d 8/27/49 in NYC (9-9/4)
2326. Dana, Lorenzo, D. m 10/26/47 Lucy A. Sandford, dau of Robert, in Chittenango;
      Rev. James Abell. All of Chittenango (9-11/6)

2327. Dana, Samuel W, formerly a U.S. senator and for many years mayor of Middletown, CT, d in M (6-8/18/30)
2328. Danels, Elizabeth, 22, dau of late Jonas D., d 1/13/47 in Utica (consumption) (9-1/14 and 1/15)
2329. Danforth, Charles, attorney, m 7/11/31 Charry T. Foster (dau of Daniel, Esq.), both of Le Roy, in L. R.; Rev. Rodgers (6-7/20)
2330. Danforth, George, Esq. of Ovid m 9/3/34 Mary B. Foster, dau of Daniel, Esq. of Le Roy, in L. R.; Rev. Metcalf (6-9/10)
2331. Daniels, John H. m 9/17/45 Frances L. Pomeroy, both of Cayuga, in C; Rev. M. Pomeroy (9-9/27)
2332. Daniels, Jonas D., 53, d 12/26/42 in Utica (9-1/4/43)
2333. Daniels, Margaret, wf of late Jonas D., d 9/11/50 "at the Chittenango Railroad Station" (9-9/18)
2334. Daniels, Peter of Nelson m 2/12/45 M. A. Cummings in Warren; Rev. Boyce (9-2/20)
2335. Daniels, Theodore, 52, d 4/2/42 in Oxford (had supervised construction of the county courthouse) (Oxford Times, 5/1)
2336. Daniels, Warner, Jr., 31, d 1/7/49 in NYC (9-1/10)
2337. Daniels, William of Utica m 12/4/49 Mary C. Griffith of Marcy in Utica; Rev. William Wyatt (9-12/6)
2338. Danielson, Gaylord m Caroline Storms in Sodus (6-1/26/31)
2339. Danks, _____, 3, dau of Widow Jane, d 10/15/50 in Van Buren (1-11/7)
2340. Danks, Benoni R., 21, d 4/7/49 in Van Buren (surv by wf and 1 ch) (1-4/12)
2341. Danks, Elizabeth (Mrs.), 31, d 9/6/47 in Baldwinsville (consumption) (1-9/8)
2342. Danks, Orson m 8/27/48 Elizabeth Lester, both of Van Buren, in V. B.; Rev. I. Dudley (1-8/31)
2343. Danks, Rosseter m 12/10/46 Jane E. Marvin, both of Van Buren, in V. B.; Rev. T. Walker (1-12/14)
2344. Dann, Jonathan m 4/24/50 Sarah M. Jones in Utica; Rev. D. G. Corey. All of Utica (9-4/26)
2345. Danton, William m Phebe Reynolds in Howard (6-3/3/30)
2346. Darby, Joseph of New Hartford m 7/13/50 Catharine Harris of NYC; Rev. Raymond (9-7/16)
2347. Darling, Henry (Rev.) of Vernon m 9/1/45 Julia Strong of Fayetteville in F; Rev. William L. Strong (9-9/3)
2348. Darling, Lorenzo m 10/16/37 Mary Ann Guile, both of De Witt, in Sullivan; J. French, Esq. (3-10/18)
2349. Darling, Nathaniel, 83, d 7/18/47 in Utica (9-7/26)
2350. Darling, Timothy (Capt.) m 2/9/46 Eliza Wetmore, dau of Ezra, Esq., in Yorkville; Rev. Cole (9-2/19)
2351. Darling, William F. m 12/18/50 Harriet O. Langworthy, both of Lysander, in L; Rev. L. D. White (double ceremony - see m of William Thompson) (1-12/26)
2352. Darlington, George d 5/9/45 in Williamsburgh (9-5/16)
2353. Darrow, Ann Eliza, 26, wf of L. R. of Utica, d 5/10/47 at the home of Oliver Benson in Barre (consumption) (9-5/18)
2354. Darrow, O. W. m 10/29/48 Elizabeth T. Ev----, both of Utica, in U; Rev. D. G. Corey (9-11/1)
2355. Darrow, Ruth, 37, wf of John formerly of Oneida Co., d 9/3/47 in Van Buren (1-9/15)
2356. Darrow, Sally (Mrs.), 55, wf of Pliny, d 8/10/45 in Rome, NY (9-8/13)
2357. Dart, Jonathan B. m 9/5/50 Lucy Swatman in Baldwinsville; Rev. White (1-9/12)
2358. Dartt, Cordelia E., 23, d 9/1/50 in Elmira (5-9/6)
2359. Daskane, William H. m 9/15/50 Aseneth Cummings, both of Caton; Rev. A. L. Brooks (4-9/25)
2360. Dauby, _____, inf s of A. G., d 9/4/25 in Utica (9-9/6)
2361. Dauby, Augustus G., editor of the Rochester Gazette, m 1/21/18 Mary E. Parmele in Utica (8-2/25)
2362. Dauby, Mary E., wf of Augustine G., Esq., d 11/9/44 in Utica (funeral at Trinity Ch.)(9-11/11)
2363. Davenport, Henry, about 40, d 10/31/47 at his home, 176 Genesee St., Utica (9-11/1)

Rev. W. F. Purrington (6-7/10)

2364. Davenport, Horace of Geneva m 7/4/46 Emeline -ostedo of Montezuma in M; ∧
2365. Davenport, John, formerly of NYC, d 1/30/50 in Sacramento, CA (9-4/11)
2366. Davenport, Moses, 55, of Geneva d 8/23/33 in Seneca (6-8/28)
        Davenport, Seaman. See Devenport, Seaman
2367. Davids, Charlotte, adopted ch. of R. V. and dau of P. B. Underhill of
        Phelps, d 3/21/32 in Albion (6-4/4)
2368. Davidson, Daniel S. (Maj.), 46, d 11/4/33 in Black Rock (6-11/27)
2369. Davidson, J. T. m 8/22/49 Amanda Beers in Elmira; Rev. H. N. Seaver. All
        of Elmira (5-9/7)
2370. Davidson, John m 11/9/33 Mehitable Benedict, both of Jerusalem, NY, in
        Penn Yan (6-11/20)
2371. Davidson, Oliver (Dr.), 69, d 12/9/47 in Amsterdam, NY (he father of
        Lucretia M. and Margaret M. Davidson) (he buried in Greenridge Cem.,
        Saratoga Springs, beside his wife, dau, and son, Lt. Davidson)
        (9-12/22)
2372. Davies, John, 44, d 11/25/50 in Utica (consumption) (funeral at his late
        home, corner Cooper and Varick Sts.) (9-11/26)
2373. Davies, Laura A., 24, d 10/26/48 in Utica (funeral at State St. Meth. Ch.)
        (9-10/28)
2374. Davies, Thomas, 30, d 6/16/43 in Utica (consumption) (funeral at his
        father's home, 44 Main St.) (9-6/17)
2375. Davies, Thomas, Esq. of Providence, RI m 4/19/49 Pauline Wright, late of
        Philadelphia, in Brooklyn; Rev. F. A. Farley (9-4/25)
2376. Davis, _____, 10, dau of John, d 12/30/49 in Knoxville, NY (fatally shot,
        reportedly, by Barnard Madden of Corning, (4-1/9/50)
2377. Davis, Abigail, 13, dau of Edward and Abigail, d 6/16/38 in Sullivan
        (3-6/20)
2378. Davis, Abigail, 62, wf of Edmund, d 7/14/38 in Sullivan (3-7/18)
2379. Davis, Abram of Fenner m 9/28/36 Mercy Cushing of Sullivan in S; Rev.
        R. H. Barrows of Cazenovia (3-10/5)
2380. Davis, Asahel (Rev.) m Matilda Merrell in Utica; Rev. Baldwin (8-2/25/18)
2381. Davis, Calvin m 9/27/36 Pamelia Keeler in Fenner; Elder H. C. Skinner.
        All of Fenner (3-10/5)
2382. Davis, Catharine, 42, wf of William, d 5/2/31 in Elmira (6-5/18)
2383. Davis, Cornelius, 73, d in NYC (6-5/25/31)
2384. Davis, Edward of Western m 2/13/46 Catharine Davis of Utica; Rev. Griffith
        (9-2/19)
2385. Davis, Edward m 3/16/50 Martha Lloyd, both of Waterford, at the Central
        Hotel, Utica; Rev. E. Francis (9-3/19)
2386. Davis, Elijah, 84 (a Rev. soldier) d 8/27/49 in Paris, NY (9-8/29)
2387. Davis, Elizabeth, 56?, wf of Henry, d 7/10/38 in Chittenango (3-7/18)
2388. Davis, Hiram of the firm of Matrick, Davis and Co. of Oswego, d 4/20/50
        in Watertown (9-4/24)
2389. Davis, Ichabod, 42, d in Butternuts (9-6/27/26)
2390. Davis, James T. of Benton m 10/29/35 Nancy Millspaugh in Milo (6-11/4)
2391. Davis, Jerusha, 61, wf of Elijah, d 3/25/24 in Paris, NY (she among the
        early settlers in Paris) (surv by husband only) (9-3/30)
2392. Davis, John m 4/11/47 Jane R. Chase in Lysander; Rev. Hause of Fulton
        (1-4/14)
2393. Davis, John A., 47, d 5/11/48 in Utica (consumption) (funeral from his
        late home, 2 Hotel St.; Fire Co. #4 was requested to attend the funeral)
        (9-5/12)
2394. Davis, John R. m 3/18/49 Sarah M. Thurstin in Frankfort; John Morgan, Esq.
        All of Frankfort (9-3/21)
2395. Davis, L. B. of Reading m 12/10/50 Julia H. Hudson, dau of Dr. L. of
        Millport; Rev. C. C. Carr (5-12/13)
2396. Davis, Lot m 1/21/49 Maria Byer, both of Utica, in U; Rev. H. R. Clark
        (9-1/24)
2397. Davis, Margaret, 50, wf of Roland, d 3/27/46 in Deerfield (9-3/31)
2398. Davis, Mary (Miss), 25, dau of Edmond, d 2/15/41 in Sullivan (3-2/24)
2399. Davis, Melchior H., 23, s of James C. of Corning, d 5/1/48 (four years
        earlier had left home for the west. Finally, en route back east, he
        was killed by a falling barrel on a steamer near St. Louis) (4-5/31)
2400. Davis, Nathaniel Morton (Hon.), 63, of Plymouth, MA d 7/29/48 in Boston
        (son of Hon. William of East Plymouth and nephew of late Judge Davis;
        eleventh member of Class of 1804, Harvard, to die in 3 yrs)(9-8/4)

2401. Davis, Nancy (Mrs.), 37, d 3/1/34 (in Vienna, NY?) (6-3/12)
2402. Davis, Obadiah, 97, (a Rev. patriot) d in Bradford, VT (9-1/26/30)
2403. Davis, Seth (Rev.), formerly of Geneva and now of Seneca Falls, m Mary
      E. Thayer of Palmyra in P; Rev. Hickox (6-12/12/32)
2404. Davis, William m 10/28/47 Mary Hackett, both of Utica, in U; Rev. George
      Leeds (9-10/29)
2405. Davis, William Henry, Esq. ofCincinnati, OH m 10/29/50 Catharine O.
      Landon, dau of John of Eaton, in E; Rev. S. Norton, rector of St.
      Thomas Ch. in Hamilton (9-11/11)
2406. Davison, Clement M. of NYC m 12/1/46 Mary F. Pomeroy, dau of Dr. Theodore
      of Utica, in U; Rev. E. S. Barrows (9-12/3)
2407. Davy, John of Skaneateles m 10/28/33 Phebe Lee of Marcellus in M
      (6-11/6)
      Day. See also Dey.
2408. Day, Almeron of Sauquoit m 3/28/50 Julia Grace Everett, 2nd dau of Hon. B.
      of Litchfield, in L (9-3/30)
2409. Day, Angelina, 26, wf of Rev. Norris Day, formerly of East Hampton, MA,
      d 12/13/35 in Jamesville, NY (3-12/22)
2410. Day, Benjamin F., 24, one of the editors of the Ontario Messenger,
      d 8/5/31 in Canandaigua (6-8/17)
2411. Day, Betsey (Mrs.), 41, d in Tonawanda (6-3/23/31)
2412. Day, C. S., Esq. of Ithaca m 7/5/37 Hester Ann Goodwin, dau of A. Esq. of
      Ovid, at Kidd's Ferry, Seneca Co. (double ceremony - see m of Seth A.
      Backus) (6-8/9)
2413. Day, Edward Warren, 17 mo, s of Rev. Warren Day, d 5/16/34 in Geneva
      (6-5/21)
2414. Day, Eliza (Mrs.) d in Waterloo (9-8/8/26)
2415. Day, Jeremiah of Appelachicola, FL m 11/10/46 Emily C. Day, dau of Orin,
      Esq. of Catskill, in C (Rev. O. N. Judd (9-11/21)
2416. Day, Levi (Deacon), 84, d 6/11/49 in Lima (formerly of Sangerfield)
      (9-6/21)
2417. Day, Samuel H. m 11/13/36 Sophia Lincoln, both of Canandaigua, in C
      (6-11/23)
2418. Day, Sherwood, Esq. of Catskill m 6/15/42 Cornelia E. Spencer, dau of
      Joshua A., Esq. of Utica, in U; Rev. Duncan Kennedy of Albany (9-6/18)
2419. de Alba, Don Pedro, 74, d 9/24/35 in Pensacola, FL (last survivor of those
      who came to this country with the army of Don Galvez in 1781) (6-11/11)
2420. Dean, Edward of Geneva m Susan Augusta Jones, dau of James, merchant, of
      Greigsville, in G; Rev. Porter (6-10/30/33)
2421. Dean, Elisha, 33, of Rochester d "off the coast of E. Florida on the
      brig "Alpha" (6-4/30/34)
2422. Dean, Emily, 27, wf of Elisha, d 5/29/47 in Van Buren (1-6/2)
2423. Dean, Erastus, Esq. d 9/1/23 in Laurens (8-10/8)
2424. Dean, Ezra (Col.) d 2/9/42 in Utica (9-2/10)
2425. Dean, Freeman m Lydia Blackburn in Covert (6-7/28/30)
2426. Dean, James F., Esq. of Laurens m 9/18/49 Harriet A. Benjamin, dau of
      Orson, Esq. of Canandaigua, in C; Rev. A. B. Beach (9-9/21)
2427. Dean, John m 3/19/48 Adeline E. Town in Baldwinsville; Rev. T. Walker.
      All of Baldwinsville (1-3/22)
2428. Dean, John, 57, d 7/24/49 in Westmoreland (surv by wf and 7 ch) (son of
      late Hon. James, Esq.) (born and always lived in Westmoreland) (9-7/31)
2429. Dean, Joseph of Halifax, England m 10/26/48 Eliza Clark of Utica in U;
      Rev. Turner (9-10/27)
2430. Dean, Lydia Camp, dau of L. C. and gr-dau of late James, d 11/3/46 in
      Westmoreland (9- 11/11)
2431. Dean, S. H. Esq. m Mary Thomas in Dryden (6-8/9/37)
2432. Debar, Elias "and a Mr. Clark" drowned 11/13/21 in Oppenheim, NY when
      "Capt. Myers' boat while descending the Mohawk River fouled one of the
      piers of the bridge ...") (8-11/28)
2433. Deberard, ____, 3 mo, child of C. J. J., d 9/16/26 in Utica (9-9/26)
2434. Debevoise, Covert of Utica m 11/24/46 Jane Armenia Valentine, dau of
      E., Esq. of NYC, in NYC; Rev. Dr. Ferris (9-12/1)
2435. Debnam, Susan, 39, wf of Robert, d 3/31/44 in Utica (funeral from her
      husband's home, 7 Steuben Park) (9-4/2)
2436. Debnam, William B. of Clinton m 8/6/49 Jennette Fletcher Brown of Utica
      at Grace Ch., Utica; Rev. George Leeds (9-8/10)

2437. De Bresson, Charles Joseph, Secretary of the Legation of his most
Christian Majesty to the U.S., m Catharine Livingston Thompson,
oldest dau of Hon. Smith Thompson, Secretary of the Navy, in Washington,
D.C.; Rev. Matthews and Rev. Lowrie (8-3/5/23)

2438. Decatur, John F. (Col.) (one of the settlers of that fort) d "early in
November last" at Fort Gibson (formerly Navy Agent at Portsmouth, NH
and brother of the late Stephen Decatur of the U.S. Navy) (6-1/9/33)

2439. De Cay, Henry m 9/18/42 Amanda Conklin of Binghamton in Conklin; Rev.
Evans (2-9/21)

2440. Decker, Jacob m 6/6/32 Mary Ann Bain, both of Lenox, in Chittenango; Rev.
Dr. Yates (3-6/12)

2441. Decker, Jacob of Geneva m 5/29/34 Mary A. Ringer, formerly of G., in
Junius; Rev. Merrell (6-6/4)

2442. Decker, John S. m 9/15/33 Betsey Hammond in Palmyra (6-9/25)

2443. Decker, Julia (Mrs.), 54, d 10/16/33 in Elmira (6-11/6)

2444. Decker, Sidney S. d 8/26/49 in Havana, NY (was sick only 10 hours -
cholera) (5-8/31)

2445. De Ferriere, Julia Bedlow, 8 mo, dau of Charles J., d 9/27/42 in Utica
(9-9/30)

2446. De Ferusson, _____ (Count) m 8/27/45 Alice Thorn, dau of Col. Thorn of
NYC, in Paris, NY; Rev. Robert Lovett (9-9/27)

2447. De Forest, David C., Esq., 51, late Consul General from the Republic of
Buenos Ayres to this government, d 2/22/25 in New Haven (CT?) (9-3/15)

2448. De Forest, Mary (Mrs.), 73, d in Livonia (6-8/14/33)

2449. Degolier, Anthony m 2/10/42 Mary Jane Seely in Painted Post; Rev. S. S.
Howe. All of P. P. (4-2/16)

2450. De Golyer, Hanmer C. m 8/6/50 Gertrude E. Parker at the home of S. C.
Parker, Esq.; Rev. T. Walker. All of Baldwinsville (1-8/8)

2451. De Graff, Abraham, 55, d 7/1/42 in Delhi (Oxford Republican, 7/8)

2452. De Graff, Harman of the firm of De Graff and Townsend, merchants, of
Geneva m 5/9/33 Mary Vernor, dau of late John of Albany, in A; Rev.
Ferris (6-5/15)

2453. De Graff, Harriet, 17, youngest dau of Abraham, d 6/22/42 in Delhi
(Oxford Republican, 7/8)

2454. De Graw, Andrew m 9/5/50 Clarissa Shappee in Chemung; Rev. C. Wheeler
(5-10/18)

2455. De Keszynski, Albert (Dr.) m 8/1/48 Mary A. Van Ness, dau of John, Jr.,
in Albany; Rev. Martin (9-8/9)

2456. Delabar, Abraham, 73, d 8/25/50 in Elmira (an early settler "in this
neighborhood") (member Presby. Ch.) (5-9/6)

2457. De La Fazleton, John m 3/11/50 "Miss Rathburn" in Lysander; Rev. A. Wells
(1-3/14)

2458. Delamater, Stephen D. m 4/15/48 Minerva Filkins in Corning; Rev. T. B.
Hudson (4-4/19)

2459. Delamather, Elizabeth, 84 (mother of Prof. Delamather of Cleveland, OH
and of Mrs. J. D. and Mrs. Dr. Stuler) d 3/25/50 in Utica (9-4/6)

2460. De La Montange, Robert of Orange Co. m 2/14/43 Polly Ann Foote of New
Milford in N. M.; Rev. Delong (2-3/8)

2461. De Lancey, Edward F. of Albany m 11/16/48 Josephine M. De Zeng, dau of
William S. Esq. of Geneva, at Trinity Ch., Geneva; Rt. Rev. Dr. De
Lancey (9-11/23)

2462. Delano, Douglass C. m 9/2/35 Matilda Dickerson of Geneva in Benton
(6-9/9)

2463. Delano, Harvey of Van Buren m 8/6/47 Huldah Smith of Baldwinsville in
Syracuse; Rev. Delano (1-8/11)

2464. Delano, Mortimer F, Esq. m 1/31/31 Sarah __?__ in Pittsford; E. Guernsey,
Esq. (6-2/16)

2465. Delano, Obadiah, 43, d 2/23/26 in Utica (9-3/7)

2466. De Lap, John m 2/13/31 Caroline Westbrook in Phelps (6-2/23)

2467. Delester, Peter F. m 6/3/48 Frances Costello at St. Francis Ch. in Utica;
Rev. S. Schwininger. All of Utica (9-6/7)

2468. Delavan, Edward C., Esq. m 6/27/49 Margaret M. M. Bryson, youngest dau of
late David, Esq., in NYC; Rev. Dr. De Witt. All of NYC (9-6/30)

2469. Delavan, Edward C. m 8/21/49 Harriet A. Schuyler, dau of Cornelius, in
Ballston; Rev. G. T. Geer. All of Ballston (9-8/24)

2470. Delevan, Abby M., wf of Edward C., d 6/20/48 at Ballston Center (9-6/22)
2471. Delevenne(?), Joseph G. of Hornesdale m 9/10/49 Mary E. Broadwell(?),
       dau of Ara of Utica, in U; Rev. William H. Spencer (9-9/12)
2472. De Line, Abraham, 33, d 4/8/42 in Chittenango (consumption) (3-4/13)
2473. Deline, Benjamin m 9/9/47 Mary Ann Keller in Baldwinsville; Rev. T. Walker
       (1-9/15)
2474. Deline, Eliza, wf of Henry, d 8/6/40 in Sullivan (3-8/12)
2475. De Line, Martin d 9/17/36 in Sullivan (3-9/21)
2476. De Long, Charles, 32, late of Utica, d 1/28/47 in Monroe, MI (9-2/17)
2477. Delong, Henry, Jr. m 10/15/35 Betsey Worden, both of Manlius, in
       Chittenango; J. French, Esq. (double ceremony - see m of James De Long)
       (3-10/20)
2478. Delong, James of De Witt m 10/15/35 Catharine Christman of Lenox in
       Chittenango; J. French, Esq. (double ceremony - see m of Henry Delong,
       Jr.) (3-10/20)
2479. Delvin, Frances M., 38, widow, d 6/25/26 in Utica (9-6/27)
2480. Delvin, James, merchant, d "last week" in Utica (9-12/27/25)
2481. Delvin, John, Esq. m 6/15/46 Mrs. Susan Andrews, both of Utica, in U;
       Dexter Gillmore, Esq. (9-6/17)
2482. Delvin, Mary, 45, widow, d in Utica (9-10/10/26)
2483. Demer, Lodowick m 9/23/47 Mrs. Elizabeth Francis of Staten Island, NY in
       Utica; Rev. D. G. Corey (9-9/25)
2484. Deming, Abby C. d 6/11/46 in Brattleboro, VT (9-6/18)
2485. Deming, B. C. m 12/18/48 Elizabeth Sayles; Rev C. C. Carr (5-12/29)
2486. Deming, Orren of Reading m 8/15/30 Jane Townsend in Catlin (6-9/1)
2487. Demmon, John of Geneva m 10/6/36 Phidelia Nims of West Vienna in
       Vienna, NY (6-10/19)
2488. De Mott, Peter, 44, d 9/3/33 in Burdette, Tompkins Co. (6-9/18)
2489. Dempster, John Haslet, 23, d 9/29/50 at his mother's home on Frankfort
       Hill (consumption) (9-10/4)
2490. Denio, Israel, 83, d 3/17/46 at his home in Rome, NY (b in Greenfield, MA;
       came to Oneida Co., NY in 1795 and settled in Rome, NY in 1797) (9-3/21)
2491. Denison, Daniel (Capt.) (a Rev. officer), formerly of Stonington, CT,
       d 3/17/18 "at an advanced age" in Oxford (funeral sermon by Rev. Lacy)
       (8-3/18)
2492. Denison, Eleanor, 66, wf of Latham Denison, d 5/18/46 in Floyd (9-5/30)
2493. Denison, Louisa (Miss), 15, dau of William, d 3/3/19 in Norwich (7-3/11)
2494. Denison, Samuel, 76, d 12/12/49 in Floyd (lived on same farm in Floyd 50
       yrs.) (9-12/20)
2495. Denison, William, 16, d 5/27/17 in Norwich (7-6/14)
2496. Denison, William, formerly of Oxford, d 5/24/19 in Norwich (8-5/26)
2497. Dennis, Jacob m 11/11/34 Mary Bowen, both of Manlius, in Chittenango; J.
       French, Esq. (3-11/18)
2498. Dennis, John m 6/4/35 R. Hogarth, both of Ovid, in Havana, NY (6-6/24)
2499. Dennis, Simeon m 11/24/36 Julia Ann Capron, both of Manchester, in M
       (6-12/7)
2500. Dennison, Ann R., wf of David and dau of late Rev. Samuel Mills of
       Saybrook, CT, d in NYC (9-6/14/25)
2501. Denniston, George, 21, of Seneca d 8/9/46 in Portland, Iowa Co., MI
       (6-8/28)
2502. Denslow, Jasper, s of Benjamin, m Abigal Pride in Litchfield (8-12/4/22)
2503. Densmore, Zemri, 44, of Hopewell, NY d 10/16/31 in Sunderland, MA
       (6-10/26/31)
2504. Densmore, Zorei m 12/7/34 Elizabeth Page, both of Castleton, in C;
       Rev. Coates (6-1/14/35)
2505. Dent, Ann (Mrs.), 63, d in Bath (6-7/28/30)
2506. Denton, Daniel of Churchville m 2/11/39 Maria Cady of Sullivan in S; Rev.
       James Abell of Chittenango (3-2/13)
2507. Denton, S. M. S. m 4/6/34 Hannah A. Cady, both of Sullivan; Rev. Bort
       (3-4/8)
2508. Denton, Seymour F. m 10/19/48 Lucretia Morse, both of Corning, in C; Rev.
       Gilbert of Painted Post (4-10/25)
2509. Depew, Nancy, 6, dau of Moses, d 10/12/31 (in Hopewell?) (6-10/26)
2510. De Pue, Moses, 45, d 4/25/31 in Hopewell (6-5/4)
2511. Depuy, Cornelius, 38, d 6/3/50 in Baldwinsville (1-6/6)

2512. Derbishire, Fanny (Mrs.), 61, d 8/10/49 in Lysander (1-8/16)
2513. Derbishire, Nathaniel M., 29, d 5/3/48 in Baldwinsville (1-5/5)
2514. De Riemer, Jacob R. of Auburn m 9/22/35 Sarah Margaret Dederer, dau of David of NYC, in NYC (6-9/30)
2515. De Shon, Fanny, 36, d 4/25/29 in Preston, Chen. Co. (wife of Henry) (7-5/13)
2516. Despar, John, 58, d in Buffalo (6-1/26/31)
2517. Deuel, Harvey, formerly of Utica, m 6/7/46 Almira Austin of Junius in J.; Rev. Jacob Fowler (9-6/20)
2518. De Vall, Eleazer of Junius m 3/22/32 Nancy Gomer of Phelps (6-4/4)
2519. De Van Lick, Almira, 22, d 11/18/50 in NYC (9-11/25)
2520. Devenport, Horace of Smithville m 12/17/20 Emelia Bradley of Oxford; William Knowlton, Esq. (8-1/24/21)
2521. Devenport, Jonathan m 11/25/36 Mrs. Sarah Estes, both of Geneva; Richard Hogarth, Esq. (6-12/7)
2522. Devenport, Seaman, 18, d 2/2/35 in Geneva (6-2/4)
2523. Devereaux, Luke, formerly of Utica, NY,d 10/20/17 in Natchez (Mississippi?) (yellow fever) (8-3/18/18)
2524. Devereux, John m 8/6/50 Susan M. Vicker, dau of late Archibald, in NYC; Rev. George H. Houghton (9-8/9)
2525. Devereux, John C., 14, d 12/11/48 in Utica (funeral at the home of Nicholas Devereux, Esq. on Elizabeth St.) (9-12/13)
2526. Devereux, John C., Jr. of Ellicottville m 2/13/49 Ellen M. Jenkins, dau of late Edward, Esq., at St. Mary's Chapel, Baltimore (MD?); Rev. L. R. Deluol (9-2/19)
2527. Devereux, Nicholas, merchant, of Utica m Mary D. Butler, dau of Benjamin, Esq. of NYC, in NYC (8-12/10/17)
2528. Devereux, P. m 4/13/49 Sarah McQuade, dau of Thomas, Esq, at St. Thomas Ch., Utica; Rev. John Stokes. All of Utica (9-4/14)
2529. Dewey, Achsah, 75, relict of John, Esq., dec'd, d 6/28/33 in Leyden, Lewis Co. (9-7/16)
2530. Dewey,Chester, Esq., prof. of math and natural philosophy in Williams Col., m Olivia H. Pomeroy, dau of Lemuel, Esq. in Pittsfield, MA (9-6/7/25)
2531. Dewey, Elias of Deerfield m 2/5/44 Jane Walker of North Gage in Deerfield; Rev. W. Salmon of Trenton, NY (bride is dau of Alexander Dewey of Deerfield) (9-2/7)
2532. Dewey, George of Pompey, NY m "Miss Helmer" at Mr. Balch's Hotel in Chittenango; Rev. Blakslee (3-7/5/45)
2533. Dewey, Hiram (Capt.) m 2/23/36 Mable Osborn in Cohocton (6-3/9)
2534. Dewey, Mary Ann, 19, wf of Henry, d 4/14/36 in Chittenango (3-4/20)
2535. Dewey, Nelson (His Excellency), gov. of Wisconsin, m 12/18/49 Catherine Dunn, dau of Hon. Charles, in Belmont, WI (9-1/11/50)
2536. Dewhurst, Thomas m 11/27/49 Anne Hall, both of Willowvale, in W; Rev. John Waugh (9-11/29)
2537. Dewing, Horatio A., 26, d 12/16/44 in Litchfield (consumption) (9-12/18)
2538. Dewit, Newton Allen, 3 mo, s of W. P. and Betsey E., d 9/3/49 in Elmira (5-9/7)
2539. De Witt, _____, wf of Simeon, surveyor general of Albany, d in Philadelphia (9-6/8/24)
2540. De Witt, _____, widow of John, d 4/26/31 in Sullivan (3-5/10)
2541. De Witt, 3, ch of James of Chittenango, d 4/29/33 (3-5/7)
2542. De Witt, Christopher m 5/22/36 Marien Wentworth in Manlius (3-5/25)
2543. De Witt, Daniel m 10/11/35 Delia Willard in Chemung (6-10/21)
2544. De Witt, Gariot m 6/11/35 Harriet Warren in Canandaigua (6-6/24)
2545. De Witt, John (Rev.), D.D., for many years pastor of the South Dutch Ch. in Albany and at his death Pres. of Rutgers Col., d in New Brunswick, NJ (6-10/19/31)
2546. De Witt, John m 4/19/37 Laney Bellenger, both of Chittenango, in Fayetteville; A. Neely, Esq. (3-4/26)
2547. De Witt, Lydia, wf of Allen and 2nd dau of Philo Wickham, d 5/7/43 in Utica (9-5/10)
2548. De Witt, Nicolaus of Rotterdam, Holland m 11/4/49 Katarina Elizabet Nellius of Arnhem, Holland in NYC; Rev. Nicolaus J. Marselus (This full announcement printed in Dutch in the newspaper) (9-11/8/49)
2549. De Witt, Thomas (Rev.) of Fishkill m 10/11/26 Eliza Ann Waterman of NYC in NYC; Rev. McMurray (9-11/7)

2550. De Witt, Wiliam m 1/28/36 Mary Ann Snell in Sullivan; Jairus French, Esq. All of Sullivan (3-2/2)

2551. De Wolf, Mary Ann, 31, wf of D. O. and sister of William H. Farwell of Utica, d 4/17/49 in Sackett's Harbor (9-4/25)

2552. Dexter, Andrew, Esq. m 6/16/47 Sarah Sill, dau of Theodore S. Gold, in Whitesboro; Rev. Dr. Proal. All of Whitesboro (9-6/17)

2553. Dexter, Laura, 53, wf of Hon. S. Newton Dexter, d 12/9/46 in Whitesboro (for many years member of Episc. Ch.; funeral from Brick Ch., Whitesboro) (9-12/11)

2554. Dexter, Rosanna, 74, wf of Daniel and mother of Chester Dexter, d 3/23/42 in Paris, NY (9-4/8)

2555. Dexter, S. Newton m 2/3/48 Mrs. Martha Gold, both of Whitesboro, in W; Rev. North, Pres. of Hamilton Col. (9-2/7)

2556. Dexter, Zadock of Henderson m 6/2/46 Rebecca A. Cunningham of North Adams in N.A.; Rev. L. M. Shepard (9-6/19)

2557. Dey, Francis, 45, d 3/21/31 in Geneva (6-3/23)

2558. Dey, John m 1/15/33 Margaret T. Sinclair in Romulus (6-1/30)

2559. Dey, John G. m 3/31/39 Sarah Ann Brooks in Seneca Falls; Elder Freeman (6-4/10)

2560. Dey, Peter L. of Varick m 10/1/33 Lydia C. Johnson of Waterloo in W (6-10/16)

2561. Dey, Rebecca, 35, wf of Peter I., d 9/25/32 in Varick (6-10/17)

2562. Diamond, Jonathan d in Covert (6-11/10)

2563. Dibbel, John E. m 9/30/41 Ann Eliza Blood in Guilford; Rev. P. Bartlett (Oxford Times, 10/6)

2564. Dibble, Charles P. of Marshall, MI m 9/14/42 Hetty Johnson, dau of Ben, Esq., in Ithaca; Rev. Montgomery Schuyler of Marshall, MI (9-10/3)

2565. Dibble, Cornish, 70, d 5/16/32 in Arcadia (6-5/30)

2566. Dibble, Ralph m 3/6/31 Mary Osborn of Goshen, CT in Bloomfield, NY (6-3/23)

2567. Dibble, Shelden (Rev.), about 37, missionary, d 1/22/45 in Lahainaluna on the Island of Mani, one of the Sandwich Islands (Hawaii) (9-8/2)

2568. Dick, Elisha C. (Dr.), 71, one of the physicians who attended George Washington in his last moments, d 9/23/25 in Alexandria (VA?) (9-10/11)

2569. Dickerson, Jacob P. m 12/18/31 Sally Ann Garrison in Benton (6-12/28)

2570. Dickerson, Lyman B. m 1/24/31 Sarah Ford in Clyde (6-2/2)

2571. Dickerson, Platt B. of Lyons m 11/19/35 Eliza Harford of Seneca in S (6-11/25)

2572. Dickerson, Thomas, 54, d 11/27/34 in Chittenango (3-12/2)

2573. Dickinson, _____ (Miss), late of Horseheads, d 1/31/35 in Geneva (6-2/4)

2574. Dickinson, Ebenezer (Maj.), 73, formerly of New Hartford, d 5/5/45 at the home of his son, George L. in Utica (funeral at the home of G. L. Dickinson in Steuben Park; funeral sermon at Presby. Ch. in New Hartford which he joined in 1832. Born in Wethersfield, CT 6/11/1771; moved to Whitestown, NY in Feb. 1792) (9-5/6 and 5/26)

2575. Dickinson, Francis H. of Massachusetts m 12/1/47 Elizabeth Vanderheyden, dau of J., in Utica; Rev. William H. Spencer (9-12/3)

2576. Dickinson, Francis H., 25, son-in-law of Jacob Vanderheyden of Utica, d 10/18/50 (funeral at the home of J. Vanderheyden, 36 Charlotte St., Utica) (9-10/19)

2577. Dickinson, L. Theodore, 5, s of G. L. of the firm of Foster and Dickinson of Utica, d 9/6/50 in Smithville, Jeff. Co. (9-9/10)

2578. Dickinson, Manco C., 22, only s of Hon. D. S., d 10/17/50 at his father's home in Binghamton (9-10/22)

2579. Dickinson, Margaret D., 43, wf of Morris G., d 4/2/45 in Utica (funeral from her late home on Whitesboro St., West Utica (9-4/3)

2580. Dickinson, Russell m 1/10/31 Harriet Porter in Hopewell (6-1/19)

2581. Dickinson, Sarah Elizabeth, 25, wf of William P., d 4/23/44 in Utica (funeral from Mrs. Lundegreen's, 11 Hotel St.) (9-4/24)

2582. Dickinson, Thomas m 12/2/24 Charlotte Eliza Thompson, both of Guilford, in G; Rev. Asa Donaldson (8-12/8)

2583. Dickinson, Thomas of Chittenango m 1/22/44 Cynthia Britt, dau of A., Esq. of Perryville in P; Rev. Daniel S. Morey (3-1/24)

2584. Dickinson, William P. of Chicopee, MA m 10/2/50 Mary Tyler Pomeroy of Southampton, MA in S; Rev. M. White (9-10/8)

2585. Dickson, Cornelia, 33, wf of T. B. and oldest dau of J. M. Church,
d 8/6/42 in Utica (also their child, age 1 yr, d at about the same
time) (9-8/13)
2586. Dickson, Delia Elizabeth, 14, only dau of Truman B., d 10/26/45 in Utica
(9-10/29)
2587. Dickson, Truman B., 45, d 6/3/46 in Utica (funeral from his late home on
Varick St.) (9-6/4)
2588. Dikeman, Czar, about 55, d 2/2/41 in Smithfield (3-2/10)
2589. Dikeman, John, Esq., 75, d 2/1/48 in Marcy (9-2/3)
2590. Dill____, 13 mo, dau of Maj. John, d 5/22/31 in Auburn (6-6/8)
2591. Dillon, Electa, 31, wf of Patrick, d 12/10/25 in Utica (9-12/13)
2592. Dillon, Patrick, formerly of Chittenango, d 10/11/31 in Schenectady
(3-10/18)
2593. Dillon, Thomas A., 58, d 11/3/33 in Vienna, NY (6-11/13)
2594. dimick, Moore K. of Talmadge, OH m 11/11/33 Sarah Whiteford of Waterloo
in W (6-12/11)
2595. Dirgan, Joseph m 6/26/44 Mary Davis in Utica; Rev. D. Cory. All of U
(9-6/29)
2596. Disney, Ann, 79, wf of Robert, Esq., d 3/12/48 in Utica (funeral from
her late home, 22 Devereux St.) (9-3/14)
2597. Diven, Alexander H. m 7/8/34 Amanda M. Beers, both of Angelica, in Elmira
(6-7/16)
2598. Divine, Delos m 2/4/47 Sarah Parker in Yorkville; Rev. N. D. Graves
(9-2/15)
2599. Divoll, Freeman m 10/21/32 Lucy Ann Burchard of Rochester in Pittsford
(6-11/7)
2600. Dixon, George C., Esq., attorney, of PennYan m 9/10/33 Henrietta C. C.
Gourgas, step-dau of John A. Coffin, Esq. of Geneva, in G; Rev. Bruce
(6-9/11)
2601. Dixon, John m 5/27/30 Lucinda Baxter, both of Seneca, in S; Rev. Smith
(6-6/9)
2602. Dixon, Patrick, 48, d 4/14/42 at his home on Whitesboro St. in Utica (came
from Ireland about 1822) (9-4/15 and 4/16)
2603. Dixon, William, Esq. of Reading m 9/19/32 Mrs. Clarissa Hibbard of Big
Flats in Jersey, NY; Judge Dow (6-9/26)
2604. Dixson, Archibald m 9/29/45 Mrs. Lydia Millard, both of Butternuts, at
Trinity Church in Utica; Rev. Dr. Proal (9-10/2)
2605. Dixson, John of Richmond m ___? Southwick in Auburn (6-3/24/30)
2606. Dobbin, John, 69, of Geneva d 9/9/34 in Buffalo (deceased and his wife
of nearly 40 years had come to Buffalo to visit their children for a
few months) (6-9/17)
2607. Dobbin, Lodowick (Col.), 42, (an officer in the War of 1812) d 11/2/33
in Waterloo (6-11/20)
2608. Dobell, Benjamin, Jr. m 12/26/49 Phebe Ann Seelye, both of Westmoreland;
Rev. F. A. Spencer (9-1/7/50)
2609. Dobson, Rachael Harriet, 1, youngest dau of C. L. and Margaret, d 9/3/48
in Utica (funeral at her parents' home, 164 Genesee St.) (9-9/4 and
9/5)
2610. Dockstader, Leonard, 63, d at his home in Sullivan (3-9/24/33)
2611. Dodd(?), Charles, Esq. m 3/1/48 Emily Barton, both of Florence, in F;
Rev. P. Gordon (9-3/15)
2612. Dodd, William, Jr. of Lyons m 10/11/32 Hannah Jeffers of Rose in R
(6-11/7)
2613. Dodge, Alfred m 6/14/29 Almira Beeman in Oxford; Amos A. Franklin, Esq.
(8-6/24)
2614. Dodge, Almira, 40, wf of Ira formerly of Oxford, NY, d 8/5/42 in Albany,
Bradford Co., PA (Oxford Times, 8/17)
2615. Dodge, David B. of Canoga m Mrs. Susan Towns in Fayette (6-2/17/30)
2616. Dodge, Frederick m 2/8/49 Sarah Mayhew, both of New Hartford, at Eagle
Tavern in Utica: John Parsons, Esq. (9-2/10)
2617. Dodge, Hiram m 7/13/43 Sabrina L. Phillips, both of Frankfort, in F; Rev.
D. Skinner (9-7/19)
2618. Dodge, Ira of Oxford m 3/11/21 Almyra Betts of Preston; Elder Noyes
(8-3/14)
2619. Dodge, Ira m 4/19/48 Hannah Kellogg in Utica; Rev. D. Skinner. All of
Frankfort Hill (9-4/21)

2620. Dodge, James, 58, formerly of Poughkeepsie, d 4/14/44 in Verona (9-4/27)
2621. Dodge, Jemima (Miss), about 20, d 12/4/19 in Oxford (8-12/8)
2622. Dodge, John (Maj.) m 10/16/42 Amanda C. Sheldon at the Bapt. Meeting House in Oxford; Rev. E. G. Perry (Oxford Republican, 10/21)
2623. Dodge, John C., Esq. of Chicago, IL m 12/14/48 Catherine L. Prentiss of Cooperstown, NY in Milwaukee, WI; Rev. Ackerly (9-12/30)
2624. Dodge, Leicester m 4/30/30 Sarah Elizabeth Benson in Canandaigua (6-5/26)
2625. Dodge, S. H. of Canoga m 7/19/37 Sophrenia C. Henion of West Fayette in W.F. (6-7/26)
2626. Dodge, William m 1/17/31 Philena Griggs in Newburgh (6-2/2)
2627. Dodge, William P. m 1/15/45 Lucy Munsell in Westmoreland; Rev. F. A. Skinner. All of W (9-1/21)
2628. Dolson, Henry W. m 9/1/31 Anna B. Thayer in Newburgh (6-9/14)
2629. Dolton, John of Geneva m 6/11/31 Catherine Cooper of Canandaigua in C (6-6/22)
2630. Donaldson, Alexander m 9/6/43 Maria A. Dickey in Utica; Rev. B. Hawley. All of Utica (9-9/12)
2631. Donaldson, Francis (Rev.) m 10/11/48 Fanny Leek, both of Catlin, in Fairport; Rev. G. M. Spratt (5-10/13)
2632. Donaldson, Mary, 20, wf of Peter F., d 5/23/33 in Ovid (6-6/5)
2633. Donaldson, Peter F. m 10/11/36 Ann Nevius in Ovid (6-10/26)
2634. Donaldson, Ruby Eliza, inf dau of James C., d 3/5/44 in Utica (9-3/7)
2635. Donalson, Alonzo m 9/21/43 Maranda Rice, both of Pompey, NY, in Chittenango; Rev. T. Houston (3-10/11)
2636. Doney, George of Geneva m 8/25/31 Sarah Maria Frisbie, dau of Dr. Frisbie of Vienna, NY, in V (6-9/7)
2637. Doney, James, 60, d 9/14/37 in Geneva (6-9/20)
2638. Donnelly, Augustus, Esq. of Homer m Eliza Dudley of Durham in D; Rev. Seth Williston (8-3/14/21)
2639. Doolittle, Charles H. of Utica m 12/1/47 Julia T. Shearman, dau of late William P., in Rochester; Rev. Dr. Van Ingen (9-12/3)
2640. Doolittle, Clarissa, 32, wf of Dotman Doolittle, d 5/31/42 in Colesville (2-6/7)
2641. Doolittle, F., about 30, d 8/9/39 in Lenox (3-8/14)
2642. Doolittle, Franklin m 3/1/43 Amanda W. Watrous in Colesville; Rev. H. W. Gilbert (See also marr of Franklin Foote this date) (2-3/22)
2643. Doolittle, George (Gen.) d 2/21/25 in Whitesboro (9-2/22)
2644. Doolittle, Jesse W., 61, merchant, d 9/18/45 in Utica (grandson of Amos, the second inhabitant in Whitestown)(lived in Utica more than 40 yrs.) (funeral from his late home on Whitesboro St.) (9-9/19)
2645. Doolittle, John J. m 6/6/49 Kate A. Bogert (oldest dau of Lawrence K. and gr-dau of James Bogart, Esq. of NYC) in Utica; Rev. William H. Spencer (9-6/8)
2646. Doolittle, Joseph m Mary Bronson in Wallingford, CT (8-8/29/21)
2647. Doolittle, Lemuel m Duadama Mattom in Wallingford, CT (8-8/29/21)
2648. Doolittle, Nancy (Mrs.), 44, d 2/25/31 in Henderson (consumption) (6-3/23)
2649. Doolittle, Roswell m Polly Moss in Wallingford, CT (8-8/29/21)
2650. Doram, Philo m 10/26/33 Elizabeth Shaw in Waterloo (6-11/13)
2651. Dorchester, Abigal, 87, mother of Mr. Eliaseph Dorchester, d 11/16/42 in Utica (funeral from her son's home on Lansing St.) (9-11/19)
2652. Dorchester, P. J. of Geneva m 1/14/46 Mary A. Griffin of West Bloomfield in W.; Rev. D. Millard (6-1/23)
2653. Doremas, Jacob, Esq. of Michigan m 12/20/45 Mrs. Phebe Stuart of NYC in NYC; Rev. Dr. Mason (9-12/27)
2654. Doremus, Jacob, 67, d 2/25/47 at Ann Arbor, MI (9-3/16)
2655. Dorman, Jabez of NYC d 6/8/49 ("Tombes Fever") (9-7/4)
2656. Dorman, Joel, 48, d 3/24/36 in Jerusalem, NY (6-4/6)
2657. Dorr, Rittenhouse of Cambridge m Ann L. Carrington of Peterboro; Rev. H. M. Boyd (8-7/27/25)
2658. Dorrance, David (Capt.), 71, (a Rev. officer) d 6/23/22 in Mamakating, Sullivan Co. (born in RI - his father was an emigrant from Ireland to RI and,shortly after, to Voluntown, CT[had a large family]; David, at age 22, enlisted as a sergeant in the Rev, and rose to the rank of Capt.) (7-7/24)

2659. Dorsey, Caleb, 25, youngest s of late Daniel, Esq. of Lyons, NY, d 8/26/30 ∧ in Chilicothe, OH (moved to C "in October last"; surv by widow only)

2660. Dorsey, Eleanor, 73, wid of late Daniel, d 5/22/34 in Lyons (with her husband moved to L. in 1801 from the state of Maryland) (6-6/4)

2661. Doty, Charles D. m Cynthia Haviland in Phelps; Rev. Orton (6-9/28/31)

2662. Doty, William of Norwich m 8/9/42 Alzady Bowers of Oxford in O; Rev. Pearne (Oxford Times, 8/10)

2663. Doubleday, Ammi of Chenango Point m 2/5/14 Susan Pierce of New Lebanon in N. L. (8-3/8)

2664. Doubleday, Eunice, 22, wf of Elisha and dau of Isaac Williams, d in Cooperstown (9-6/27/26)

2665. Doubleday, Harriet, 32, dau of Ammi and Lois, d 8/1/25 in New Hartford (9-8/16)

2666. Doubleday, Hester Elizabeth, 3, dau of U. F., Esq., d in Auburn (6-12/20/30)

2667. Doubleday, John T. m Mary Whiting, both of Binghamton, in B (double ceremony - see m of William Woodruff, Jr.) (8-10/6/19)

2668. Doud, Augustus of Pitcher m 12/5/43 Sarah Haven of Guilford in G; Rev. J. T. Goodrich (Oxford Republican, 12/7)

2669. Doud, C. Sherman, 20, d 10/7/42 in Utica (9-10/15)

2670. Douglas, Charles of Buffalo, formerly of Columbia Co., m 8/15/36 Harriet Rossiter, dau of N., Esq. of Buffalo, at the Presby. Ch. in Geneva; Rev. P. C. Hay) (6-8/17)

2671. Douglass, Arthur P. of Whitestown m 5/25/48 Esther L. Hewitt of Westmoreland in W; Rev. P. A. Spencer (9-5/30)

2672. Douglass, Eliza (Miss), 19, dau of Col. Zebulon, d 2/26/35 in Sullivan (3-3/3)

2673. Douglass, Harvey R. m 10/4/36 Nancy M. Rogers in Bristol (6-10/19)

2674. Douglass, John D., 26, formerly of Utica, d 5/19/47 in Cincinnati, OH (9-5/26)

2675. Douglass, Mary, 66, wf of Benjamin, d 6/9/47 in New Hartford (9-6/15)

2676. Douglass, Polly G., 61, wf of Col. Zebulon, d 8/5/33 in Sullivan (apoplexy) (3-8/6)

2677. Douglass, Silas H. (Dr.) m 5/1/45 Helen Welles, dau of John, Esq., in Ann Arbor, MI; Rev. William Curtis. All of A. A. (9-5/23)

2678. Douw, Catharine (Mrs.), mother of Mrs. William C. Johnson of Utica, d 4/14/48 in Albany (9-4/15)

2679. Dove, Alexander of Philadelphia m 5/15/50 Martha McNall of Utica; Rev. S. W. Brace of Utica (9-5/16)

2680. Dow, Emmet A., 10 mo, youngest s of Edward H., d 7/18/48 in Van Buren (1-7/26)

2681. Dow, John, printer, m 3/8/43 "Miss Marshall" in Bath; Rev. Frazer. All of Bath (4-3/15)

2682. Dow, Uriah m 6/8/48 Maria Marvin in Van Buren; Rev. Wagoner (1-6/14)

2683. Dowe,_____ (Mr.), 23, printer, d in Lyons (6-3/10/30)

2684. Downer, Abner P., Esq. of Chittenango m 10/12/42 Harriet Hamblin of Fenner in F; Rev. T. Houston (3-10/19)

2685. Downer, Don S. m 9/9/46 Mrs. Eleanor Evans in Utica; Elder Thomas Hill. All of Utica (9-9/14)

2686. Downer, Phebe, 63, wf of Norman, Sr., d 3/16/46 in Utica (9-3/18)

2687. Downer, Rachel, 42, wf of Abner P., Esq., d 10/28/41 in Chittenango (consumption) (3-11/3)

2688. Downey, Rachel, 56, wf of Robert, d 12/13/32 in Dresden (6-12/26)

2689. Downey, Robert, 65, d 10/27/32 in Benton (6-11/7)

2690. Downing, James, 29, s of John, d 7/21/31 in Geneva (6-7/27)

2691. Downing, John, 75, d 5/23/39 in Geneva (6-5/29)

2692. Downs, James B. G. m 4/16/33 Emily E. Morgan (6-4/24)

2693. Dows, John of the firm of Dows and Cary of NYC d 2/21/44 in Jersey City (NJ?) (9-2/26)

2694. Dox, George Nicholas (Dr.) m 6/26/46 Susan Lawson Clark, oldest dau of late Rev. Orin Clark, D.D., at Trinity Ch., Geneva; Rev. John Henry Hobart. All of Geneva (6-7/3)

2695. Dox, George Talcott, 2, youngest s of Gerrit L., d in Albany (6-3/24/30)

2696. Dox, Myndert M., Esq., 42, late Collector of the Port of Buffalo and, during the War of 1812, a captain in the U.S. Army, d 9/8/30 in Buffalo (6-9/15)

2697. Dox, Peter m 11/25/30 Elsie McDaniels in Geneva; Rev. McLaren (6-12/1)
2698. Dox, Peter, 90, d at the home of his son, Abraham, in Geneva (Peter b in Albany where he spent most of his life)(6-11/30/31)
2699. Dox, Peter G. of Albany m 6/25/46 Susan Lawson Dox, dau of Abraham, Esq. of Hopeton in H; Rev. John N. Norton (6-6/26)
2700. Dox, Tunis of Geneva m 3/12/33 Clarissa Dimick of Seneca in Waterloo (6-3/27)
2701. Dox, Wyntie (Miss), dau of Peter, Esq. formerly of Albany, d 3/10/26 in Geneva (9-3/11)
     Doxtader. See also Dockstader.
2702. Doxtader, _____ (Mrs.), consort of late Leonard, d 12/17/39 in Sullivan (3-12/18)
2703. Doxtader, Henry, 24, d 11/21/40 in Sullivan (3-11/25)
2704. Doyle, Andrew, 55, d 6/30/36 in Cheshire (6-7/27)
2705. Doyle, James m 7/14/44 Julia Boyle, both of Utica, in U; Rev. T. Martin (9-7/19)
2706. Doyle, Michael of York, Upper Canada m 3/21/31 Rachael Cameron of Brockport in Canandaigua (6-3/30)
2707. Doyle, Michael H., 23, d 11/26/44 in Utica (funeral at his late home, 24 Jay St.) (9-11/29)
2708. Drake, Andrew Jackson m 10/12/48 Mary Buchannon, both of Elmira, in E; Rev. E. W. Dickinson (5-10/13)
2709. Drake, Isaac W. of Dansville m Eliza W. Graham of Elmira in Dansville; Rev. J. Selmer (5-12/29/48)
2710. Drake, Jacob A. m Hannah Shrives at Harpending's Corner (6-4/16/34)
2711. Drake, Joshua, 40, formerly of Geneva, d 8/10/34 in Gorham (6-9/10)
2712. Drake, Lucius of Sauquoit m 2/18/46 Susan Smith of Norway, NY in N; Elder Towner (9-2/27)
2713. Drake, Peter m 5/29/32 Eunice Reed, dau of Josiah, in Seneca; Rev. Phelps (double ceremony - see m of Vincent Reed) (6-5/30)
2714. Drake, Theodore H. m 4/15/33 Caroline C. Deming, both of Vienna, NY, in Canandaigua (6-5/1)
2715. Draper(?), Asa N.,. 37, d 8/24/46 in Brattleboro, VT (formerly, for many years, a merchant in Waterloo, NY; was a member of Indep. Order of Odd Fellows there) (6-8/28)
2716. Draper, Franklin m 11/24/46 Catharine Weber in Herkimer (9-11/28)
2717. Draught, Isaac of Camden m 11/29/48 Harriet Amanda Burpee of Litchfield in L; Rev. John Waugh (9-12/15)
2718. Dresser, Diana M. (Miss), 15, d 11/30/33 in Millville (6-12/25)
2719. Drew, James m 3/26/43 Phebe Sunderland at Reformed Dutch Ch., Chittenango; Rev. James Abell. All of Chittenango (3-7/5)
2720. Drew, Noah m Amy Lyon in Pultney (6-1/27/36)
2721. Driggs, George W., Esq. of Genesee Co. m 5/7/32 Mrs. Mary Streeter of Benton in B; A. Woodworth, Esq. (6-5/23)
2722. Drinkwater, Brooks m Temperance Pond in NYC (6-6/23/30)
2723. Droot (or Dygot?), John W., 23, d 5/8/49 in Frankfort (9-5/10)
2724. Drown, Daniel Gillespie, formerly of Canandaigua, d in New Orleans, LA (yellow fever) (6-1/19/31)
2725. Drummond, Gertrude, 2, dau of David G., d 5/22/45 in Lee (9-5/29)
2726. Drury, Leander M. of Canandaigua m 2/2/48 Emily M. Mervine, dau of Capt. William of the U.S. Navy, at Grace Ch., Utica (9-2/3)
2727. Dryer, A. C. of Addison m 2/15/49 Mrs. Mary Biles of Bath in Painted Post; Rev. B. F. Pratt (4-2/15)
2728. Dryer, Thomas J. m Nancy B. Webber(?) in Angelica (6-1/26/31)
2729. Dudgson, Wemyes (sic) m 11/4/47 Eliza Jane Rose, both of Utica, in U; Rev. D. G. Corey (9-11/6)
2730. Dudley, Abraham of Newfield m 3/31/31 Martha Hulet of Veteran in V (6-4/27)
2731. Dudley, Ambrose (Rev.), 72, d 1/27/25 near Paris, KY (pastor of Bapt. Ch. there; born in Spottsylvania Co., VA) (9-5/31)
2732. Dudley, Elizabeth, 40, wf of John, d in Bath (6-6/19/33)
2733. Dudley, Herbert S., about 23, s of Rev. Ira, d 8/30/49 in Albany (cholera) (deceased formerly of Baldwinsville; studied law in office of M. B. Church, Esq.; at time of death was attending the State Normal School at Albany) (1-9/1)

2734. Dudley, John m Eliza Ann Adams in Bath (6-10/8/34)
2735. Dudley, William Henry, 1 yr, s of Ward, d in Elmira (6-3/9/31)
2736. Duel, Frances (Miss), 21, d 3/28/36 in Waterloo (6-4/6)
2737. Duer, William, youngest s of William of NYC, d 7/25/49 in Georgetown, D.C.
       (9-8/1)
2738. Duffin, James m Irene Canfield in Farmington (6-2/10/30)
2739. Duffin, John, 60, d 10/15/46 in Geneva (6-10/23)
2740. Dufrainoit, Harriet Cornelia, 17 mo, youngest dau of Henry and Jane,
       d 5/3/47 in Utica (funeral at her father's home, 183 Genesee St.)
       (9-5/4)
2741. Dumond, William H., 48, d 2/26/31 in Kingston (6-3/23)
2742. Dumont, Alida, 73, consort of Waldron, Esq., d 8/11/48 in Van Buren
       ("Albany papers please copy") (1-8/16)
2743. Dunbar, Cynthia, 56, wf of Rev. M. Dunbar, d 7/29/47 in Baldwinsville
       (1-8/4)
2744. Dunbar, Miles (Rev.) d 12/12/48 in Oran, Onon. Co. ("Pulaski Currier
       pelase copy") (1-12/28)
2745. Dunbar, Roderic of Marshall m 8/14/50 Caroline M. Marsh of Lee in
       Hampton; Rev. H. F. Row (9-8/19)
2746. Duncan, Charles m 3/28/50 Emma Smith in Marcellus; Rev. Levi Parsons.
       All of Marcellus. (Triple ceremony - see marriages of Sereno C. Smith
       and Sylvester Smith) (all were married at the home of Benjamin Smith,
       father of Sereno and Emma and brother of Sylvester; Charles is brother
       to Lydia and Cothia [brides of Sylvester and Sereno respectively];
       Sylvester is uncle to Sereno and Emma; and all the marriage persons
       except Sylvester are under age 20) (9-4/11)
2747. Duncan, David m 9/10/47 Laura Ripley in Adams; Rev. J. F. Dayan (1-9/22)
2748. Duncan, James, 56, d 12/7/46 in Syracuse (1-12/21)
2749. Duncan, Margaret, 2, dau of Alexander, Esq. of Canandaigua, d 6/23/30
       on board the packet ship "Cambria" from London to NYC (6-7/7)
2750. Dundas, William Alexander, 5 mo, s of William and Olivia, d 9/3/50 in
       Elmira (5-9/6)
2751. Dunham, Albert T., merchant, of the firm of Parmelee and Dunham, m 5/25/31
       Elvira Ann Sage, dau of Col. Hezekiah; Rev. A. Yates. All of Sullivan
       (3-5/31)
2752. Dunham , Darius J. m 2/19/46 Marinda Andrews, both of Sauquoit, in
       Deansville; Rev. A. J. Dana of Clinton (9-2/27)
2753. Dunham, David m Mary Hillman in arcadia (6-7/14/30)
2754. Dunham, William C. m 12/28/48 Cordelia M. Myers. both of Utica, in U; Rev.
       D. G. Corey (double ceremony - see m of Thomas K. Facy) (9-1/1/49)
2755. Dunkle, George m Mary S. Draper (in Vienna, NY?) (6-4/16/34)
2756. Dunks, Sheldon m 1/28/36 Almira E. Sanders, both of Canandaigua, in
       West Bloomfield (6-2/17)
2757. Dunn, _____, 3 mo, child of Robert, d 7/15/26 in Utica (9-7/18)
2758. Dunn, Andrew m 2/13/42 Emeline Spencer in Caton; N. C. Babcock, Esq.
       All of Caton (4-2/16)
2759. Dunn, Henry of Starkey m 1/15/35 Rebecca Jones of Elmira in E (6-1/21)
2760. Dunn, James, 33, d 6/6/43 in Corning (4-6/7)
2761. Dunn, Martin (Dr.) of Dundee m 4/22/39 Lucinda Fairbanks, dau of Rev.
       Ira of Benton, at the Franklin House in Geneva; Rev. W. P. Davis
       (6-4/24)
2762. Dunn, Richard m 11/17/41 Lina Robinson in Sullivan; Rev. Handy (3-11/24)
2763. Dunn, Richard F. m 8/25/33 Elizabeth Ann Taylor in Albany (6-9/4)
2764. Dunn, William m 1/6/48 Harriet Dygart in Utica; Elder Corey. All of
       Utica (9-1/7)
2765. Dunnett, George R., 26, printer, d 7/8/36 in Ovid (6-7/27)
2766. Dunning, Catharine N., 9. dau of Urbane and Eliza, d 8/2/47 in Utica
       (funeral from her father's home on Steuben St.) (9-8/3)
2767. Dunning J. N. m 12/17/43 C. M. A. Cunningham in Utica: Rev. Leeds.
       All of Utica (9-1/20)
2768. Dunning, Jerusha Jane (Miss), 17, d 8/5/33 in Seneca Falls (6-8/21)
2769. Dunning, Julius N. of Rochester, formerly of Utica, d 5/30/49 in Havana,
       Cuba (9-6/20)
2770. Dunning, Nathan of Ithaca m Maria Sprague of Jerusalem, NY in Penn Yan
       (6-3/7/32)

2771. Duralde, Susan H., wf of Martin, Esq. and oldest dau of Hon. Henry Clay, died recently (she is the third dau Mr. Clay has lost within the last two years - one age 17, one 12, and Susan age 22 (9-11/8/25)
2772. Durand, Betsey, 45, d 10/4/34 in Seneca Falls (6-10/15)
2773. Durand, Joseph H. m 10/22/34 Mary Winans of Tyre at Seneca Falls; Rev. A. G. Ortan (6-11/5)
2774. Durfee, Philo m 2/12/33 Mary White in Palmyra (6-2/27)
2775. Durfey, John, 82, d 10/10/43 at his home in Triangle (2-10/18)
2776. Durham, Lorenzo D., 45, d 8/13/49 in Buffalo ("of the prevailing epidemic") (1-8/23)
2777. Durkee, Jireh, 67, d 4/21/48 in Utica (funeral at the Trinity Ch.) (9-4/22)
2778. Durkey, Justus (Capt.) (a member of the Masonic Order) d 2/1/33 in Fulton (funeral at the Episc. Ch. in Perryville) (3-2/5)
2779. Dusenbury, Jane B., 34, wf of John B., d 3/13/50 in Newburgh (5-3/29)
2780. Dusenbury, Lancaster m 1/18/38 Harriet S. Wise, both of Benton, in B (6-1/24)
2781. Dustie(?), Josephene, 5, dau of Peter, d 11/20/49 in Baldwinsville (1-11/22)
2782. Dustin, L. S. m 9/4/49 Elizabeth Coonrad, both of Rome, NY, at the New England House in Utica; Rev. William H. Spencer (9-9/5)
2783. Dutcher, Abraham m 6/19/33 Gitty Ann Van Voorhies in Poughkeepsie (6-7/10)
2784. Dutcher, Salem, Esq., formerly of Albany, d 2/25/44 in NYC (9-2/29)
2785. Dutton, Chauncey m 11/19/35 Elizabeth Rogers in Lockport (6-12/2)
2786. Dutton, Chauncey E., about 35, d 3/19/43 in Utica (funeral at the Bleecker Street Ch.) (9-3/20)
2787. Dutton, Elizabeth B., 18, youngest dau of George, d 6/20/47 in Utica (funeral at her father's home, 35 Whitesboro St.) (9-6/21)
2788. Dutton, Justus R., 36, wf of James, d 6/17/48 in Utica (funeral at her late home, 27 Whitesboro St.) (9-6/19)
2789. Dutton, George, Jr., Esq., formerly of Utica, m Elizabeth Pease in Rochester; Rev. McLaren (9-4/7/46)
2790. Dutton, Sarah, 48, consort of Rev. Nathaniel of Champion, d 1/3/30 (9-1/26)
2791. Dutton, William H. m 12/30/46 Mary H. Daliba (dau of late Maj. James of the U.S. Army), both of Utica, in U (9-12/31)
2792. Duyckinck, Evart, 69, "one of the most extensive publishers and booksellers" of NYC, d 11/20/33 in NYC (6-11/27)
2793. Dwight, Abigail, 80, wf of Theodore, d 4/2/46 in NYC (9-4/4)
2794. Dwight., Almon m 9/28/41 Mary L. Comstock of Auburn in A; Rev. D. A. Shepard (3-10/6)
2795. Dwight. B. W. (Rev.) of Brooklyn m 7/29/46 W. Jane Dewey in Oswego; Rev. Seth Williston, D.D. (9-8/5)
2796. Dwight, Benjamin W. (Dr.), 70, d 5/18/50 at his home in Clinton (funeral from the College Chapel) (9-5/21)
2797. Dwight, Clarissa Smith, 28, wf of Amos T. Dwight of New Orleans, LA and dau of Capt. Walter D. Smith, formerly of Utica, d 9/13/44 in Brooklyn (9-9/23)
2798. Dwight, Edmund m 12/13/49 Harriet Allen Butler, dau of B. F., Esq., in NYC (9-12/21)
2799. Dwight, Francis, Esq., editor of the District School Journal, d 12/15/45 in Albany (9-12/17)
2800. Dwight, Henry, Jr. m 11/25/46 Mary Bushnell, dau of late Campbell, in NYC; Rev. William Adams, D.D. All of NYC (9-12/1)
2801. Dwight, Henry E., 48, d 5/20/25 in Cooperstown (son of Hon. Timothy of Northampton, MA and youngest bro of late Dr. Dwight of Yale Col.) (9-5/31)
2802. Dwight, Henry E., Esq., 42, youngest bro of late Pres. Dwight of Yale Col., d 5/20/25 in Cooperstown, NY (8-6/8)
2803. Dwight, Henry E., Esq., 85, d in New Haven, CT ("well known as an accomplished scholar ...") (6-8/29/32)
2804. Dwight, John W. of New Haven, CT m 6/18/45 Sophia Dwight, oldest dau of Benjamin W., Esq. of New Haven, in Clinton, NY; Rev. Benjamin W. Dwight, Jr. (9-6/21)

2805. Dwight, Joseph Hawley (Capt.), about 60, d 8/6/45 at his home in Oxford ("from a distinguished family" in Berkshire County, MA; "died in the Roman Catholic faith... leaving only distant relatives to inherit his considerable estate") (9-8/8)
2806. Dwight, Margaret S., 23rd dau of Daniel, d in New Hartford, CT (6-1/26/31)
2807. Dwight, Mary Comstock, 22, wf of A., d 7/5/42 in Auburn (member of Meth. Episc. Ch.) (3-7/13)
2808. Dwight, Nathaniel (Rev.), 62, M.D., of Norwich, CT d at Oswego, NY (he was the 10th child and 6th son of Hon. Timothy of Northampton, MA and a bro. of the late Pres. Dwight of Yale Col. (6-7/20/31)
2809. Dwight, Seth, 55, formerly a merchant in Rome, NY, d 4/3/25 in Buffalo (9-4/12)
2810. Dwight, Theodore W. (Prof.) of Hamilton Col. m 8/24/47 Mary B. Olmstead, dau of A. of Clinton, in C; Rev. B. W. Dwight, Jr. of Brooklyn (9-8/27)
2811. Dwight, Timothy E., 24, s of late Josiah, d in Northampton, MA (6-7/10)
2812. Dwight, William C. of Moscow, NY m Laura R. Talbot in Rochester (6-7/3/33)
2813. Dyer, Abigail, 61, relict of late Samuel, Esq., d 11/4/25 in Deerfield (9-11/22)
2814. Dyer, Converse m 11/11/32 Phebe Amanda Bentley in Rochester (6-11/7)
2815. Dyer, Edward G. (Dr.) of Manlius m Ann Eliza Morse of Trenton, NY in T (6-2/16/31)
2816. Dygart, James of Chittenango m 5/25/36 Catherine Lansing of West Troy in W. T. Rev. Wood (3-6/15)
2817. Dygert, William of Frankfort m 8/3/47 Charlotte L. Cutler of Utica; Rev. Wiley (9-8/4)
     Dygot, John W. See Droot, John W.
2818. Dyke, Sylvester of Litchfield m 12/28/42 Priscilla Russel of Utica at Stanwix Hall in Rome, NY; Rev. W. W. Ninde (9-1/6/43)
2819. Dyson, Hester, 38, wf of Robert, d 2/7/50 in Clayville (funeral at St. John's Ch.) (9-2/9)
2820. Eames, ____, 60, wf of Percy B., d 6/14/43 in Milwaukee, WI (6/30)
2821. Eames, Charlotte M., 32, d 8/14/48 (funeral at the home of her mother, Mrs. Sarah Eames, in New Hartford (9-8/16)
2822. Eames, Frances, 20, formerly of New Hartford, d 3/11/50 at Flagg Creek, Cook Co., IL (deceased is dau of late J. Sanger Eames) (9-4/4)
2823. Eames, Lucia Maria, 25, dau of Orlando, d 11/13/48 in New Hartford (9-11/15)
2824. Eames, Orlando d 6/25/49 at his home in New Hartford (funeral at the home of his mother, Mrs. Sarah Eames) (9-6/26)
2825. Eames, Sarah S., dau of O., Esq., d 4/7/49 in New Hartford (9-4/9)
2826. Eames, Sylvia, 50, wid of late Orlando, d 9/28/49 in New Hartford (9-9/29)
2827. Earl, Edgar, 4, s of Edward, d 5/11/39 in Geneva (6-5/15)
2828. Earl, Enoch W. of Canastota m 12/27/32 Dolly Ransier of Chittenango (3-1/1/33)
2829. Earl, Samuel, Esq. m 9/5/48 Isabella Jane Kirk Putnam, dau of Alfred, Esq., in Herkimer; Rev. Dr. Murphy (9-9/18)
2830. Earl, William m 11/3/36 Elana Farlyng in Gorham (6-11/30)
2831. Earll, Caroline, 8, dau of Daniel, d 6/5/49 in Skaneateles (1-6/14)
2832. Earll, Calrissa, 44, wf of Jonas, Esq., d 4/2/35 in Onondaga (6-4/22)
2833. Earll, Daniel, Esq., 82, (a Rev. soldier) d 11/25/33 in Whitehall (6-12/18)
2834. Earll, Edson, 24, d 5/5/33 in Onondaga (6-5/29)
2835. Earll, Helen (Miss), 19, d 2/12/49 in Baldwinsville (consumption) (1-2/15)
2836. Earll, Jonas, Jr., 60, d 10/28/46 at the home of his son in Syracuse (consumption) (1-11/9)
2837. Earls. William of Newfield m 3/9/42 Anna Van Etten of Danby in Knoxville; Rev. S. M. Hopkins (4-3/16)
2838. Earnest, David m Margaret Quigley in Fayette (6-4/14/30)
2839. Easlord, J. G. m 9/3/46 H. A. Salisbury in Waterville; Rev. Davis. All of W (9-9/5)
2840. Easterbrook, James of Manlius m Catherine Casler of Parish in Chittenango; J. French, Esq. (3-2/21/44)

2841. Easterbrook, Martin, 67, d 7/15/50 in Herkimer (9-7/26)
2842. Easterbrook, Nicholas of Manlius m 7/10/41 Susannah Gridley, formerly of
England, in Chittenango Falls; Rev. J. Watson (3-7/14)
2843. Eastlin, Peter m 3/19/35 Harriet Anthony in Canandaigua (6-4/1)
2844. Eastman, Lyman m 7/18/39 Alida Van Epps in Ovid; Rev. McNeil (6-7/24)
2845. Easton, Charity (Miss), 28, dau of Elijah deceased, d 11/16/24 in Columbia
(9-12/7)
2846. Easton, Henry R., 5, only s of James I. and Antoinette D., drowned 5/10/47
in the raceway at Canajoharie (9-5/18)
2847. Easton, W. H. m 4/18/39 Phebe Guiles in Middlesex; Elder Eastman. All of
Middlesex (6-4/24)
2848. Eaton, Amos (Prof.), 65, of Troy d 5/10/42 (3-5/25)
2849. Eaton, Amos B. (Lt.) of the U.S. Army m 4/21/31 Mrs. Elizabeth Spencer in
Rochester (6-5/4)
2850. Eaton, Elizabeth, 65, wid of Gen. William, late consul at ___?___,
d 5/20/31 at the home of her son-in-law, David Hayden, in Auburn (6-6/8)
2851. Eaton, Jefferson m 10/5/42 Jane Brooks, both of New York Mills, in Utica;
Rev. Bostwick Hawley (9-10/6)
2852. Eaton, Theophilus, printer, formerly of Oxford, d 5/6/20 in Bethlehem, NY
(8-5/17)
2853. Eaton, W. H. m 12/31/49 Harriet E. Taylor in Utica; Rev. Dickson. All
of Utica (9-1/4/50)
2854. Eckler, William I., 62, d 2/28/44 in Rome, NY (9-3/7)
2855. Eddington, Vincent R., 24, d 4/10/36 in Seneca (6-4/20)
2856. Eddy, _____, 1, s of John, d 3/29/32 (3-4/3)
2857. Eddy, Adaline, 2, dau of Eli and Betsey, d 1/27/27 in Oxford (8-2/2)
2858. Eddy, Eli of Oxford m 4/27/24 Betsy Davis of Norwich; Rev. Andrews
(8-4/28)
2859. Eddy, Eli, 44, a teacher, d 9/4/32 in Bath (surv by wf in feeble health
and 2 ch) (6-9/12)
2860. Eddy, Isaac (Rev.), 59, pastor of the Cong'l. Ch. in Jamestown, NY,
d 6/26/33 in Jamestown (9-7/16 and 9-7/17)
2861. Eddy, Laban S., 22, d 10/31/33 in Macedon (6-11/20)
2862. Eddy, Mary (Mrs.), 32, d 1/16/32 in Lyons (6-1/25)
2863. Eddy, Mary Ann, 48, wf of late Eli, formerly of Geneva, d 9/26/33 in G
(6-10/2)
2864. Eddy, Nancy (Mrs.), 80, d 3/29/50 in North Norwich (9-4/11)
2865. Eddy, Samuel M. m 11/20/23 Eliza P. Willoughby, dau of B., Esq., in
Oxford; Rev. J. D. Wickham. All of Oxford (8-11/26)
2866. Eddy, William m 6/12/31 Caroline Near in Arcadia; Elder Roe. All of
Arcadia (6-6/15)
2867. Edgebury, Frederick, 66, d 8/28/49 in Utica (funeral from Broad St. Bapt.
Ch.) (9-8/29)
2868. Edgcomb, William m 6/18/43 Maria Orcutt in Utica; Rev. B. Hawley (married
at the pastor's home). All of Utica (9-6/20)
2869. Edgerton, Betsey Ann, 32, wf of Marvin, d 3/24/47 in Van Buren (1-3/24)
2870. Edgerton, Eunice, 79, d 1/12/46 in New Hartford (9-1/19)
2871. Edgerton, Isaac H., 53, d in Bridgeport (consumption) (3-3/9/42)
2872. Edgerton, Jane, 53, wf of Riley, d 1/21/48 in New Hartford (surv by
husband, 2 ch, and her father) (9-1/28)
2873. Edick, Conerod, 86, (a Rev. soldier) d 9/12/46 in Frankfort (9-9/14)
2874. Edmonds, Samuel (Gen.), 66, (a Rev. soldier) d 3/15/26 in Hudson
(paymaster general of State of NY) (9-3/28)
2875. Edson, Alexander of Utica m 9/17/50 Elizabeth Frothingham, dau of George,
at Sand Lake; Rev. Hunford(?) of Sand Lake(?) (9-9/20)
2876. Edson, Cornelia, wf of Thomas H., late of Utica, d 7/18/48 at her father's
home in Utica (consumption). Interred in Richfield (9-7/20)
2877. Edson, Thomas H. m 1/15/47 Cornelia O. Cunningham, both of Utica, in U;
Rev. Dr. Rudd(?) (9-1/16)
2878. Edson, William J., aged 2, d 10/1/48 in Utica (funeral from his late home,
88 Fayette St.) (9-10/3)
2879. Edwards, Charles m 6/13/32 Emily Ryon, both of Seneca Falls, in S.F.
(6-6/27)
2880. Edwards, Daniel S. of Adrian, MI m 10/20/36 Caroline A. Foskett of Gorham
in G (6-11/9)
2881. Edwards, David m Sally Jackson in Elmira (6-3/9/31)

2882. Edwards, Hervey m 12/12/42 Maria Kiteridge in Utica; Zenas Wright, Esq.
All of Utica (9-12/17)
2883. Edwards, John, Jr., 23, d 6/13/49 in Utica (9-6/14)
2884. Edwards, Nartha P., wf of Jacob D. of Utica, d 3/28/45 in Elizabethtown,
NJ (9-4/10)
2885. Edwards, Mary (Mrs.), 41, d 7/28/37 in Skaneateles (6-8/9)
2886. Edwards, Robert m 8/22/46 Julia Dumphrey, both of Utica, in Whitesboro
(9-8/25)
2887. Edwards, Robert H. m 9/14/43 Nancy F. Beckwith in Chenango Forks; Rev.
Woodruff (2-9/20)
2888. Edwards, Thomas A. (Col.), inspector of the Port of St. Joseph, MI m
Henrietta M. Booker of Kalamazoo in K (6-9/21/36)
2889. Edwards, William m "Miss Davis" in Westmoreland; Rev. Holmes (9-10/3/26)
2890. Eggleston, Catharine, 68, relict of late Aaron, d 3/27/42 at the home
of her son in Verona (9-4/1)
2891. Eggleston, Charles Paine, oldest s of Dr. J. S. Eggleston, d 11/6/30 in
Palmyra (6-11/24)
2892. Eggleston, E. D. (Capt.) of the steamer "Lady of the Lake" d 7/5/49 in
Oswego (9-7/9)
2893. Eggleston, Enos m 3/20/41 Mrs. Sally Wattles in Chittenango; Rev.
O'Farrel. All of Chittenango (3-3/24)
2894. Eggleston, Joseph R. m 1/5/32 Maria Buttles in Phelps (6-2/15)
2895. Eggleston, N.A. m 9/10/50 Jane Ann Church, dau of William, Esq. of
Coventry, NY; Rev. A. Eggleston of Windsor (9-9/14)
2896. Eggleston, Sarah (Miss), 22, d 9/31/33 in East Bloomfield (6-10/9)
2897. Eggleston, Wilkerson, 42, d 5/9/34 in Chittenango (3-5/13)
2898. Ehle, Catherine (Mrs.), 92, d 3/16/44 in Sullivan (3-3/20)
2899. Ehle, David m 5/23/32 Caroline Maria Crapsey in Sullivan (3-5/29)
2900. Ehle, David, 20 or 29, s of John P., d 4/28/39 in Woodstock (3-5/1)
2901. Ehle, Hiram m 9/24/34 Almira Blakeslee, youngest dau of Noah, in Perryville;
Rev. B. Northrup (3-10/7)
2902. Ehle, Hiram, about 26, s of Peter P., d 12/14/42 in Sullivan
(consumption) (3-12/21)
2903. Ehle, James C., 4, s of Abram, d 2/22/38 in Chittenango (3-2/28)
2904. Ehle, John P., 85 or 65, d 4/22/40 in Sullivan (funeral from his home in
Sullivan) (3-4/22)
2905. Eickhart, John, 50, d 3/17/31 in Sullivan (3-3/22)
2906. Elderkin, Jonathan, 74, d 3/28/47 in Baldwinsville (1-3/31)
2907. Eldridge, Joseph m Laura Ann Ryon in Farmington (6-2/10/30)
2908. Eldridge, Susan, dau of Clark Eldridge, d 5/27/34 in Canandaigua
(6-6/18)
2909. Eliet, William H., M.D., of NYC m Elizabeth F. Lummis of Maxwell, Wayne
Co. in NYC (6-12/21)
2910. Ellas, Sarah E., 29, wf of F. S., Esq., d 1/26/47 in Buffalo (9-2/1)
2911. Elleson, George G. m 12/17/30 Hannah Drake in Lyons (6-12/29)
2912. Elliot, _____, about 30, wf of David, d 3/18/31 in Canandaigua (6-3/30)
2913. Elliott, Andrew m 9/13/43 Sarah Finkle in New Hartford; Rev. B. Weed
(9-9/20)
2914. Elliott, George W. of Schuyler m 3/6/45 Ann Yeneth Lorraway of Deerfield
in Utica; Elder Thomas Hill (9-3/7)
2915. Elliott, John E. m 5/8/44 Eliza M. Marsh, oldest dau of William N., both
of Clinton, in C; Rev. Samuel H. Gridley (9-5/15)
2916. Elliott, Robert (Col.), for many years a deputy postmaster of Albany,
d 3/10/44 in Albany (9-3/14)
2917. Ellis, _____, wf of Rev. John, d in Jacksonville, IL (also 2 of his ch)
(all of cholera, in the absence of Mr. Ellis) (6-9/4/33)
2918. Ellis, Ann Eliza, wf of Hon. Chesselden Ellis, d 5/25/45 in Waterford
(9-6/6)
2919. Ellis, Asa of Georgetown m 9/16/47 Cynthia Eddy of Utica in U; Rev.
D. G. Corey (9-9/22)
2920. Ellis, E. W. (Dr.) of Westmoreland m 9/23/50 Joanna L. Thompson at the
Central Baptist Ch. of Norwich in N; Rev. E. T. Hiscox (9-9/26)
2921. Ellis, Edward D., editor of the Michigan Sentinel, m Leonora Mary Chapman
(6-3/3/30)

2922. Ellis, Lyman, 87, (a Rev. soldier) d 3/13/47 in Ellisburgh (one of the earliest settlers in the Ellisburgh area, 1797) (9-4/10)
2923. Ellis, M. M. of Utica m 10/6/47 Lucinda A. Fiffield, dau of Dr. Jesse, in Junius; Rev. A. D. Lane (9-10/8)
2924. Ellis, Maria (Miss), 28, d 8/19/33 in Phelps (6-8/28)
2925. Ellis, Mary, wid, 74, d 7/26/26 in Utica (9-8/1)
2926. Ellis, Mary (Miss), d 11/6/44 in Utica ("friends of B. F. Cooper and Edmund A. Graham are invited to her funeral... at the home of Miss Loomis on Broad St. opposite the Dutch Church") (9-11/8)
2927. Ellis, Mary White, wf of John W., Esq. and dau of Philo White, Jr., purser in the U.S. Navy, d 10/18/44 in Salisbury, NC (9-11/8)
2928. Ellison, Christopher m 9/11/33 Esther Maria Fowler of Sempronius in S; Matthias Lane, Esq. (3-10/8)
2929. Ellison, Joseph, 36, d 8/2/31 in Hopewell (6-8/10)
2930. Ellsworth, Wanton m Jane Groesbeck in Gorham; Rev. Gaylord (6-9/15/30)
2931. Elmore, Isaac W. m 11/22/31 Laura Brown, both of Lyons, in L (6-12/7)
2932. Elms, Charlotte, 36, wf of "Mr. Elms" of Fayetteville, d 1/23/41 in Fayetteville (formerly Charlotte Haight of Chittenango (3-2/3)
2933. Ellis, Eli A. m 7/29/35 Myra Mead of Canaseraga in C; J. French, Esq. (3-8/4)
2934. Ellwood, Livingston (Dr.) m Frances Jane Brown in Bridgewater (9-1/31/49)
2935. Elston, William m 2/22/49 Maria Elyea of Erin; Rev. C. C. Carr (5-3/2)
2936. Elsworth, Joseph of Prattsburg m 2/25/50 Julian (sic) Jenkins of Elmira; Rev. C. Greatsinger (5-3/8)
2937. Elsworth, Levi m 2/10/31 Isabella McIntyre in Sodus (6-3/2)
2938. Elton, John m 9/19/46 Annis Chamberlin in Phelps (6-9/25)
2939. Elwell, John m 5/2/32 Charlotte Grant in Ovid (6-5/16)
2940. Elwell, William, Esq. of Towanda, PA m 7/13/33 Clamania Shaw of Factoryville, NY in F (6-8/14)
2941. Elwood, Isaac R., Esq. m 6/19149 Elizabeth F. Gold in Rochester; Rev. J. H. McIlvaine (9-6/22)
2942. Ely, Clara E., 1 yr, dau of Anson C. and Martha M., d 8/29/48 (5-9/1)
2943. Ely, Culick (Capt.), 84, (a Rev. soldier), formerly of CT, d 9/4/46 at the home of his son-in-law, Richard P. Petherick, in Canandaigua (6-9/11)
2944. Ely, David G. m 10/9/33 Ruth S. Marvin (6-10/16)
2945. Ely, Elihu of Binghamton m 10/20/42 Mrs. Caroline Harrison Orcutt of Rochester in R; Rev. Hall (2-10/26)
2946. Ely, Elisha (Hon.), member of Congress, m 2/5/37 Ann Garrison, formerly of Geneva, in Detroit, MI (6-2/22)
2947. Ely, Giles S. of Palmyra m 10/18/32 Caroline Hoe of NYC in NYC (6-11/21)
2948. Ely, William, 82, d 3/2/25 in West Springfield, MA (9-3/15)
2949. Emeric, Elizabeth (Mrs.), 79, mother-in-law of John A. Russ and of Hugh Crocker, d 3/27/50 in Utica (funeral at the home of Mr. Crocker, 65 Main St.) (9-3/28)
2950. Emerick, Thomas, 12, s of Peter, d 11/18/46 in Baldwinsville (1-11/23)
2951. Emerson, Benjamin K. of Tyrone m 10/9/50 Adelia C. Prescott of Elmira; Rev. W. Bement (double ceremony - see m of William H. Prescott) (5-10/18)
2952. Emerson, John E. m 1/27/31 Ruby Blackman in Bath (6-2/9)
2953. Emmons, Simeon S., Esq., attorney, d 5/20/25 in Norwich (8-5/25)
2954. English, David, Sr., 81, d 3/20/50 at the home of his son in Jefferson Co., VA (b in Monmouth Co., NJ but lived in Georgetown, D.C. most of his life; edited for many years The Sentinel of Liberty in Georgetown and the Washington Advertiser; later, 1810-38, was cashier of the Union Bank of Georgetown) (9-4/3)
2955. English, Jacob m 11/23/34 Harriet Elizabeth Curtis in Sullivan; Jairus French, Esq. All of Sullivan (3-11/25)
2956. Ensworth, Dyer of Norwich m 9/12/22 Anna Eldridge of New Berlin; Nathan Taylor, Esq. (7-9/18)
2957. Eodar, Joseph of Lenox, MA m 7/1/47 Ann Kempp of Utica in U; Otis Whipple, Esq. (9-7/3)
2958. Ernst, John F. (Rev.) m 4/3/34 Hannah M. Folger in Geneva; Rev. N. P. Bruce (6-4/9)
2959. Errington, William m 9/10/33 Mary Ann Vance in Rochester (6-10/9)

2960. Erwin, Samuel S., oldest s of Gen. F. E., m 8/7/50 Amelia Shaw in Painted Post; Rev. Youngs. All of Painted Post (4-8/21)
2961. Esma, John P. m 1/20/49 Lucy Carrington in Baldwinsville; Rev. Byron Alden (1-1/25)
Esterbrook. See Easterbrook.
2962. Esterly, Robert m 4/6/31 Amanda Blakely in Sodus (6-4/20)
2963. Estes, Martha Ella, 4, dau of Nathaniel and Sarah Jane, d 11/17/50 inUtica (9-11/19)
2964. Estes, Mary, 53, wf of Stephen, d 8/28/50 in Horseheads (member of Society of Friends) (5-9/6)
2965. Estus, Alexander of Manlius m Elizabeth Burnett in Lyons (6-2/17/30)
2966. Eustis, W. Tracy m 10/3/49 Martha Gilbert Dutton, dau of the senior publisher of the Boston Transcript, in Boston; Rev. Dr. Young (9-10/8)
2967. Evans, _____, inf s of John, d 2/10/34 in Chittenango (3-3/4)
2968. Evans, Ann, 56, wf of Edward, d 1/26/49 in Utica (funeral from Trinity Ch. (9-1/29)
2969. Evans, Arad m 9/29/26 Penelope Shipman, both of Linklaen, in Cincinnatus; Rev. William J. Bradford (8-10/13)
2970. Evans, Civilian E. of Binghamton m 1/27/48 Emma Adele Everts of Utica in U; Rev. George Leeds (9-1/28)
2971. Evans, David H., late of Utica, m 12/20/43 Elizabeth Ackerman Posner, oldest dau of Jacob of NYC, at the Spring Street Presby. Ch. in NYC; Rev. Dr. Patton (9-1/9/44)
2972. Evans, David J. of the NY and B Telegraph Co. m 3/28/50 Jane Edmonds of Utica in U; Rev. Griffiths (9-3/30)
2973. Evans, Evan m 3/14/45 Elizabeth Edwards in Utica; Rev. Phillips (9-4/4)
2974. Evans, Henry F., pulisher of the Livingston Courier, m Harriet Ladd of Haverhill, NH in H (6-12/12/32)
2975. Evans, James of Frankfort m 9/21/48 Mary J. Barrett of Utica; Rev. D. G. Corey (9-9/22)
2976. Evans, Jane, 35, from North Wales, d 3/10/44 in Utica (funeral from the home of John C. Devereux) (9-3/12)
2977. Evans, Jenkin, 90, d 11/27/42 in Utica (b in Cardiganshire, South Wales; emigrated to this country in 1801 and settled at Woodbury, NJ; moved to Utica in 1805 (9-12/2)
2978. Evans, John T. of Remsen m 3/17/47 Elizabeth Roberts of New York Mills in Utica; Rev. William Jones, pastor of the Welsh Independent Ch. (9-3/19)
2979. Evans, O. B. of Troy m 6/21/46 Jane M. Griffing of Little Falls in Utica; Rev. P. A. Proal (9-6/24)
2980. Evans, William B., s of Charles, Esq., d "last week" in Southport leaving a young wife and child (5-10/6/48)
2981. Evans, William S. m 7/23/50 Cornelia Lewis in Remsen; Rev. Buckingham. All of Remsen (9-8/8)
2982. Evarts, William A. m 1/20/47 Jerusha Ames, both of Utica, in U; Rev. D. A. Shepard (9-1/21)
2983. Everest, C. W. (Rev.) of Grace Ch. in Hamden (presumably in NY) m 10/2/45 Catharine Ann Dowdall, dau of late Capt. George R., in Stratford, CT; Rev. J. Morgan (9-10/7)
2984. Everest, Oscar m 8/15/50 Reliance A. Strong in Baldwinsville; Rev. T. Walker. All of Baldwinsville (1-8/15)
2985. Everett, Josiah (Dr.) of the U.S. Army d 7/15/32 at Fort Gratiot (6-8/1)
2986. Everetts, Alfred of Hector m 10/7/34 Emeline Warner of Big Flats in B.F.; Rev. Manly Tooker (6-10/15)
2987. Everingham, John T. m 7/31/30 Jane M. Cowles in Geneva; Elder Martin. All of Geneva (6-8/4)
2988. Everitt, William V. m 4/26/49 Persis M. Cleaveland, both of Jackson, PA, in Elmira, NY; Rev. H. N. Seaver (5-4/27)
2989. Evers, Elizabeth Davidson, 28, wf of John and oldest dau of Thomas Swords, d 2/27/33 in NYC (consumption) (6-3/6)
2990. Everson, John Charles m 11/6/33 Harriet Almida Crapsey, dau of John G., in Sullivan; Rev. Slingerland (3-11/19)
2991. Everton, Samuel, Esq., 52, d 4/26/25 in Broome, Lower Canada (9-6/14)
2992. Eyre, John B. of Cornwall, England m Mary Dent of Westmoreland (England) in Canandaigua, NY (6-3/9/31)

2993. Facy, Thomas K. m 12/28/48 Asenith Buskirk, both of Utica, in U; Rev. D.
       G. Corey (double ceremony - see m of C. Dunham) (9-1/1/49)
2994. Failing, George, 1, s of A. J., d 9/10/50 in Baldwinsville (1-9/19)
2995. Failing, William, 19, d 1/13/34 in Seneca Falls (6-1/22)
2996. Fairchild, Betsey (Miss), 21, d 7/2/33 in Buffalo (6-7/17)
2997. Fairchild, Mary Hulse, 20, wf of B. F., d 10/26/36 in Canandaigua (4-11/9)
2998. Fairchild, R. (Mr.), 25, formerly of Elmira, NY, d 10/21/50 in New Albany,
       IN (5-11/1)
2999. Fairlie, James, Esq. (a Rev. officer), for more than 30 yrs clerk of the
       circuit court, d 10/10/30 at his home in NYC (6-11/1)
3000. Fairman, Hamilton R. m 9/2/33 Celestia Warren; J. French, Esq. (3-9/3)
3001. Faith (or Frith), Christopher C., 38, d 6/18/48 in Utica (9-6/20)
3002. Fake, Sarah, wf of Adam, Esq., d 11/1/36 in Gorham (6-11/30)
3003. Falconer, Archibald, late of Albany NY, d in August, 1849, at the mouth of
       the Sacramento River in California ("knocked overboard by the boom of
       the vessel in a gale") (9-5/10/50)
3004. Falconer, Eliza, 47, wf of Robert, Esq. of Sugar Grove, Chen. Co.
       d 1/20/50 in S.G. (9-2/7)
3005. Fales, Atwood m 1/28/41 Adeline Pierce in South Corning; Rev. C. S. Davis.
       All of South Corning (4-2/5)
3006. Fanning, Priscilla, 88, widow, formerly of Massachusetts and a resident
       of Ontario Co., NY 30 yrs, d 1/14/35 in Gorham (6-2/25)
3007. Fargo, Hiram S., 39, d in Benton (6-4/28/30)
3008. Fargo, John of Geneva m 4/12/32 Amelia Rhodes, dau of Daniel of Lockport,
       in Rochester (6-4/18)
3009. Farlan, John M. m Rebecca Ann Bradt in Schenectady (6-8/9/37)
3010. Farley, Magdalena, 41, relict of John G. formerly of Col. Stevenson's
       1st NY Regt. Volunteers, d 3/22/50 in San Francisco, CA (9-5/9)
3011. Farmer, Grove, printer, m 4/19/48 Hannah L. Stolp in Marcellus; Rev.
       Dean. All of Marcellus (1-4/26)
3012. Farnham, _____, inf dau of Samuel, d 6/15/20 in Oxford (8-6/21)
3013. Farnham, Adeline P. (Mrs.), 26, d 8/31/33 in Rochester (6-9/18)
3014. Farnham, Alexander H. m 1/31/31 Hannah Enos of Norwich in N (6-2/9)
3015. Farnham, Edward m 11/4/33 Elizabeth Edwards in Rochester (6-11/6)
3016. Farnham, George m 8/4/25 Susan Gibson in Oxford; Rev. Bush (8-8/10)
3017. Farnham, John F. (Dr.) of Oxford m 7/25/27 Mary F. Steere(?), dau of
       Mark, Esq. of Norwich, in N; Rev. Edward Andrus (8-7/27)
3018. Farnham, Samuel, 46, d 4/20/22 in Oxford (8-4/24)
3019. Farnham, Susan, 19, wf of Col. George and dau of Thomas Gibson, Esq.
       formerly of Barbadoes (West Indies), d 9/1/26 (had been married 1 yr)
       (8-9/8)
3020. Farnsworth, Henry A. of Boston m 6/6/50 Julia Cushman, dau of late Judge
       Cushman, in Troy; Rev. Dr. Beeman (9-6/11)
3021. Farnsworth, M. L. (Rev.) m 6/22/30 Joanna B. Gosman, dau of Jonathan, Esq.
       (all of Danby) in Danby (6-7/21)
3022. Farnum, Edward Fayette, 3, s of E. J., d 8/21/41 in Bath (4-9/1)
3023. Farr, Joseph M. m 2/1/30 Almira Brown; Elder J. Randall. All of Norwich
       (7-2/3)
3024. Farrar, David, 2 wks, s of David and Mary, d 9/17/50 in Utica (9-9/20)
3025. Farrard, James H. m 10/17/33 Emily Smith in Southport (6-11/6)
3026. Farrell, M. Y. (Dr.) m 8/22/26 Eliza Hunsdon, both of Shoreham, VT, in
       Shoreham; Rev. Prof. Hough (double ceremony - see m of Rev. R. C. Hand)
       (9-10/3)
3027. Farrington, Rufus M, formerly of Baldwinsville, d 8/1/50 in Evansvillw, IN (1-8/15)
3028. Farrington, Thomas T. (Rev.) of Geneva m 10/1/46 Mary M. Wilkins, dau of
       late Thomas D., in Hamptonburgh, Orange Co.; Rev. Joseph Kimball
       (6-10/9)
3029. Farwell, Melissa, 27, consort of William H., d 5/14/47 in Utica (funeral
       from her late home, 21 Mary St.) (9-5/15)
3030. Farwell, Moores, about 55, bro of Samuel, Esq. of Utica, d 12/14/50 in
       Sandusky, OH (9-12/16)
3031. Farwell, Thankful, 89, relict of late Dr. Isaac U. and mother of
       Samuel Farwell, Esq. of Utica, d 7/28/49 at Frankfort Hill (9-7/30)
3032. Farwell, William H. of Utica m 4/11/49 Charlotte E. Wilcox, oldest dau
       of Morris, Esq. of Whitesboro, in W; Rev. William Whitcher (9-4/14)

3033. Fassett, Amos S., s of Amos and formerly of Albany, d 2/12/49 in Vienna,
NY (9-2/14)
3034. Faulkener, John, 78, d 11/23/33 in Urbana (6-12/4)
3035. Faulkner, Joseph M., merchant, m 9/29/34 Eliza P. Willard, dau of A.,
Esq.,, in Perry; Rev. S. H. Gridley. All of Perry (6-10/8)
3036. Faulkner, William, 54, d 11/9/36 in NYC (late keeper of the Western Hotel,
9 Cortland St. and formerly keeper of the Geneva Hotel) (6-11/16)
3037. Faville, Oran, prof. of ancient languages "in the O. C. Seminary",
m 7/24/45 Maria M. Peck, former preceptress of the same institute, in
De Witt, Onon. Co. (9-8/2)
3038. Fay, Almira, 23, consort of Nahum, d 11/8/32 in Canastota (3-11/20)
3039. Fay, Franklin L. m 10/23/43 Hannah Sophia Blackwood, 2nd dau of William,
Esq., in Utica; Rev. Dr. Proal. All of Utica (9-10/24)
3040. Fay, Jonas (Dr.), 59, of Utica d 6/5/35 in Frankfort (3-6/9 and 6-6/17)
3041. Fay, Theodore, Esq., one of the editors of the New York Mirror, m Laura
Gardenier, dau of late Barent, Esq., in NYC (6-4/10/33)
3042. Featherstone, Peter m 10/6/43 Ann Weghorn at Griffin's Hotel in Utica;
Aaron Hackley, Esq. All of Marshall (9-10/9)
3043. Felingham, John m 2/21/44 Susanna Bushmore, both of Frankfort, in Utica;
Elder Thomas Hill (9-2/27)
3044. Fellows, William m 1/26/31 Mary F. Bush, dau of Horace, in Penfield
(6-2/9)
3045. Felt, Emmaline Elizabeth, 2, dau of Norris and Emmaline, d 3/21/38 in
Chittenango (3-4/4)
3046. Fenner, Stephen (Rev.), 64, d in Harpersfield (had been pastor there for
34 yrs) (6-11/6/33)
3047. Fenton, Adonijah, 89, formerly of Oneida Co., d 2/4/44 in "Maysville"
("was among eight patriots who in the Revolutionary War captured a
British armed schooner in the Hudson near Fishkill") (9-2/19)
3048. Fenton, Orrin L., 25, only s of Amariah of Westmoreland, d 6/5/43 in
Westmoreland(accidental discharge of his rifle) (9-6/12)
3049. Fenton, William M. m 4/11/36 Adelaide S. Birdsall in Addison (6-4/27)
3050. Fergison, Hezekiah of Adrian, Mich. Terr. m 10/2/33 Fanny Havens, dau of
Joseph, Esq. of Benton, in B; Rev. Goff (6-10/16)
3051. Ferguson, James G., 51, d 4/4/47 in Frankfort (9-4/6)
3052. Ferguson, John, Esq., 54, naval officer of NYC, d 9/4/32 in NYC (judge
of marine court and former mayor of NYC)
3053. Ferguson, Samuel (Capt.), 81, d 10/11/46 at his home in Frankfort (was
one of the earliest settlers in Whitestown (9-10/13)
3054. Ferguson, Samuel N. of Richmond, VA m 9/3/31 Sarah Swift (6-9/14)
3055. Ferguson, Stephen m 9/4/34 Esther Hall, both of Rose, in Lyons (6-9/17)
3056. Ferguson, Tracy L. of Clayville m 8/23/49 Laura N. Johnson of Cassville
in C; Rev. John Waugh (9-8/27)
3057. Ferguson, William A. of the firm of Vedder and Ferguson m 1/16/49 Malvina
L. Hale, both of Utica, in U; Rev. William H. Spencer (9-1/17)
3058. Ferinbaugh, Charles of Hornby m 2/16/42 Lucy Sweet of Caton in Corning;
Rev. Amos Hard (4-2/23)
3059. Ferre, Emily (Miss), about 18, d 3/21/35 in No. 9, Canandaigua (6-4/1)
3060. Ferris, Alfred m 1/19/35 Susan R. Craven in Phelps; Rev. Bagerly. All
of Phelps (6-2/4)
3061. Ferris, Benjamin G., Esq. m 5/10/30 Cornelia Woodcock in Ithaca (6-5/26)
3062. Ferris, Henry B. m Dolly Ann Townsend, both of Jerusalem, NY, in Milo
(6-2/17/30)
3063. Ferris, John, Jr. m 2/9/31 Pamelia Race in Phelps; Rev. Caleb Rice
(6-2/23)
3064. Ferris, William V., Esq. of New Hartford m 5/31/49 Amelia R. Downes of
Utica in U; Rev. William H. Spencer (9-6/2)
3065. Ferry, Aaron m 11/22/46 Olive Peak in Camillus; Rev. John W. Steves.
All of Camillus (1-12/7)
3066. Ferry, Francis of Elmira m 7/18/49 Margaret M. Stiles of Hume in H;
Rev. Eleazer Thomas (5-7/27)
3067. Field, Alfred B. m 3/7/33 Ann F. Beals, dau of Thomas, Esq., in
Canandaigua (6-3/20)
3068. Field, Experience (Mrs.), 96, d 12/17/34 in Phelps (6-12/31)
3069. Field, Martin m 3/14/27 Ann Williams; Rev. Wells. All of Oxford (8-3/30)

3070. Field, Rufus of Geneva m 4/30/35 Catharine M. Monroe of Bellona in B (6-5/13)
3071. Field, Seth (Deacon), 46, d 10/13/36 in Geneva (6-10/19)
3072. Fiera, Thomas m 3/2/31 Elizabeth Hutchinson in Buffalo (6-3/23)
3073. Fiero, Peter m 4/1/38 Jane Holladay; Rev. Oliver Ackley. All of Seneca (6-4/4)
3074. Finch, Alexander m 2/11/47 Marietta Rollo at New York Mills; Rev. N. D. Graves (9-2/15)
3075. Finch, Alpheus J. of Conklin m 4/14/39 P. Jane Waterman of Binghamton in B; J. Wait, Jr., Esq. (3-5/1)
3076. Finch, Caleb, about 40, d 10/22/30 in Newark (6-11/24)
3077. Finch, Horatio W. of Seneca Falls m 1/13/31 Sally Alida Burger of Newburgh in Seneca Falls (6-2/2)
3078. Finch, Maria (Mrs.), 25, d 10/4/33 in Greenville, Greene Co. (6-10/23)
3079. Finch, Nathaniel m 3/28/31 Clarinda Cornwell, both of Milo, in Penn Yan (6-4/13)
3080. Finch, Thomas of Frankfort m 12/4/50 Mary Ann Copsey of Willowvale in W; Rev. John Waugh (9-12/6)
3081. Finger, John, Jr. (Sgt.) m Elizabeth Rector, both of Benton, in Milo (6-2/17/36)
3082. Fink, Charles of Little Falls m 9/13/43 Nancy Anna Mann, oldest dau of Hon. A. Mann, Jr., in Brooklyn (9-9/18)
3083. Fink, Christian, 35, d 3/10/32 in Manlius (3-3/13)
3084. Fink, Ichabod of Van Buren m 7/9/43 Elizabeth Brown of Sullivan in Lenox; J. French, Esq. (3-7/26)
3085. Fink, John m 10/28/32 Alice Parkhurst in Sullivan; J. French, Esq. All of Sullivan (3-10/30)
3086. Fink, Josiah (Capt.) m 6/14/38 Nancy Norris(?), both of Sullivan, in S; Elder Daggert of Manchester (3-6/20)
3087. Fink, Mary, 45, wf of Alexander H. and oldest dau of late Phineas Rumsey of Goshen, d 2/18/49 near Elmira (5-2/23)
3088. Finkle, Melton, Esq. m 9/13/49 Catherine E. Williams, dau of William, in Utica; Rev. William H. Spencer. All of U (9-9?14?)
3089. Finney, C. G. (Prof.) of Oberlin, OH m 11/13/48 Mrs. Elizabeth Atkinson, formerly of Rochester, in Akron, OH by Pres. Mahan (9-11/22)
3090. Finney, Charles G. (Rev.) of Adams m 10/5/24 Lydia R. Andrews of Whitesboro in W; Rev. Adams W. Platt (9-10/12)
3091. Firman, William m "Miss Benton" of Orlans, NY in Hopewell (6-5/18/31)
3092. Fish, Alexander m 10/24/33 Isabella Dixon, dau of John, in Seneca; Rev. F. McLaren (6-10/30)
3093. Fish, Daniel, about 51, d in Oriskany (9-6/21/50)
3094. Fish, Iam(?) (Mrs.) d 5/10/44 in Taberg ("Herkimer Journal will please copy") (9-5/15)
3095. Fish, James of Oneida m 9/20/48 Harriett O. Nash of Utica in U; Rev. Turner (9-9/21)
3096. Fish, John Henry, 3, s of J. L. and Maria, d 3/28/44 in Rochester (scarlet fever) (Oxford Republican, 4/14)
3097. Fish, Nelson of Covington m 6/27/33 Mary J. Landon in Castile (6-7/10)
3098. Fish, Nicholas (Col.), 74, (a Rev officer) d 6/20/33 in NYC (6-7/2 and 7/10)
3099. Fisher, Ann, 4, dau of George W., d 4/12/34 in Geneva (6-4/16)
3100. Fisher, Catherine, 65, wf of John, d 10/25/26 in Oxford (8-11/17)
3101. Fisher, Chauncey D. m Abigail Hayes in Gorham (6-3/31/30)
3102. Fisher, Eve, 35, wf of Christopher, d in Gorham (6-8/14/33)
3103. Fisher, Ira of Penn Yan m 7/4/33 Lydia Hunt of Milo in Elmira (6-7/17)
3104. Fisher, John, Jr. m 6/12/19 Mary Willson, late of Philadelphia, in Oxford; Rev. Bush (8-6/16)
3105. Fisher, Margaret, 25, wf of John, Jr., d 11/14/27 in Willett (8-11/23)
3106. Fisher, Samuel m 4/2/44 (name blurred) in Chittenango; Rev. T. Houson (3-4/10)
3107. Fisk, Abigail, 51, wf of Bezaleel, d 9/17/24 in Trenton, NY (9-10/12)
3108. Fisk, Ezra (Rev. Dr.), Prof. of Ecclesiastical History and Church Govt. at the West. Theological Seminary, d 12/5/33 in Philadelphia (6-12/25/33)
3109. Fisk, George W. H. of Geneva m 10/8/35 Mary Chadwick of New Hartford in New H. (6-10/21)

3110. Fisk, George W. H., 28, of the firm of Snow and Fisk, formerly of Geneva, d 3/24/38 in Detroit, MI (6-4/11)
3111. Fisk, Harvey, 31, d 3/5/31 in NYC (6-3/23)
3112. Fisk, James, Jr. m 7/4/34 Clamana Harper, both of Junius, in J (6-7/23)
3113. Fisk, Joel (Rev.) of Munkton, VT m Clarinda Chapman of Keene, NH in K (9-10/24/36)
3114. Fitch, Ebenezer (Rev.), D.D., about 78, d 3/21/33 at his home in West Bloomfield (for 24 years was Pres. of Williams Col.) (6-4/10)
3115. Fitch, J. P., Esq., editor of the Roman Citizen, m 12/16/47 Sarah M. Seymour, dau of Ardon, in Rome, NY; Rev. W. F. Williams (9-12/18)
3116. Fitch, John, Jr., 35, d 4/15/21 in Ellicotsville (8-5/9)
3117. Fitch, John (Capt.), 66, d 7/2/23 in Oxford (b in Mass. but many years a resident of Oxford (8-7/9) (a Rev. officer)
3118. Fitch, Morgan L. m 11/6/33 Amanda Roberts in Henrietta (6-12/11)
3119. Fitch, William, Esq. m 3/15/48 Mrs. W. H. Rochester in Buffalo (9-3/18)
3120. Fithian, Clark, 23, s of Morehouse Fithian, a printer and publisher in Philadelphia, d 6/15/50 at the Fullerville(?) Iron Works (9-6/22)
3121. Fitsgerald, William, formerly of Waterford, a member of the Indep. Order of Odd Fellows, d 7/9/50 in Utica (consumption) (funeral from 17 Water St.) (9-7/11)
3122. Fitzburgh, Robert, 29, youngest s of Col. William, d 6/17/36 at his father's home near Geneseo (6-7/13)
3123. Fitzhugh, William, Esq. of Fairfax Co., VA d 5/21/30 in Cambridge, MD (6-6/2)
3124. Fitzsimmons, Jane (Mrs.), 44, d 6/2/36 in Elmira (6-6/15)
3125. Flaget, Benedict Joseph (Rt. Rev.), 86, first Roman Catholic Bishop of Louisville, KY, d 2/11/50 in Louisville (9-2/27)
3126. Flarity, John H. m 5/14/49 Sarah Maria Jarrett in Utica; Rev. Thomas Hills. All of Utica (9-5/15)
3127. Fleming, _____ m Margaret Crawford in Fayette; Rev. McLaren (6-10/12/36)
3128. Fleming, Henry G. m 5/6/46 Arminda Gleason, both of Geneva; Rev. P. C. Hay, D.D. (6-5/14)
3129. Fleming, Ira H. m 5/30/44 Ceriza W. Palmer, both of Morrisville, in Hamilton; Rev. Harvey (9-6/5)
3130. Fleming, John S. of Romulus m Elizabeth Ayres, dau of Nathaniel, in Varick (6-5/5/30)
3131. Fleming, Otis of Elmira m 1/15/50 Betsey A. Cleveland of Southport at the Parsonage in S; Rev. E. Colson (5-1/18)
3132. Fleming, Thomas (Capt.), 88, formerly ofFrederick, MD, d at his home at Big Hill, Butler Co. (state not given) (fought in the Maryland Line in the Rev. War) (6-1/24/38)
3133. Fletcher, Alfred m 6/7/35 Maria Parmoyer (in Canandaigua?) (6-6/17)
3134. Fletcher, Gustavus, 33, d 6/30/42 in Binghamton (2-7/6)
3135. Fletcher, Josiah, Esq., 75, d 2/2/25 in Ludlow, VT (a Rev. soldier and pioneer settler in Ludlow; first meeting house and school-house at Ludlow were built at his expense) (9-9/6)
3136. Fletcher, Zedekiah, 11, d 6/22/19 in Unity Township, PA ("inflammation of the brain occasioned by bathing in cold water while in a state of perspiration") (8-7/21)
3137. Flint, Charles, 47, d 6/25/47 in Utica (9-6/28)
3138. Flint, Davis, 87, (a Rev. pensioner) d 6/18/36 in Gorham (6-7/13)
3139. Flint, Francis "(colored)", 65, d 12/15/37 in Skaneateles (6-12/27)
3140. Flint, Manasseh of Trenton, NY m 9/27/43 Harriet Chapman of New Hartford in New H; Rev. Dana (9-9/29)
3141. Flower, James B. of the firm of T. Burns and Co. m 5/1/39 Mary Pardee, dau of Israel, Esq., in Phelps. All of P (6-5/15)
3142. Floyd, David G. m 7/31/45 Lydia Smith, dau of William, Esq., in Mastic, L.I., NY; Rev. Tomlinson (9-8/8)
3143. Floyd, David J. m 9/18/50 Jane Jones, youngest dau of Griffith O., Esq., in Utica; Rev. H. S. Dickson. All of Utica (9-9/30 and 10/1)
3144. Floyd, Joanna, 79, wid of William, Esq., d 12/2/26 in Western (9-12/5)
3145. Floyd, William Henry, 8 mo, s of W.H. and E. late of Coburg, Canada West, d 5/5/50 inYorkville, NY (9-5/8)
3146. Fluent, Charity, 5, dau of Ezra, d 9/26/33 in Cameron (6-10/9)
3147. Flutcher, George m 12/18/34 Deborah M. Blue in Seneca; Rev. Hannah (6-12/24)

3148. Foat, Samuel m 1/20/38 Jane Becker, bothj of Sullivan (3-1/24)
3149. Follet, George, 36, d 6/16/33 in chittenango (3-6/18)
3150. Follett, Nancy F., 28, wf of Oren, one of the editors of the Buffalo
     Journal, d in Buffalo (6-3/24/30)
3151. Follett, Oren, Esq. of Buffalo m 11/22/32 Eliza G. Ward in Fairport
     (6-12/5)
3152. Folts, Caroline (Mrs.), 91, d 11/4/47 in Frankfort (9-11/17)
3153. Folts, Warner m 9/25/50 Margaret Tanner, dau of Ichabod, Esq.; Rev.
     Marcus A. Perry. All of Frankfort (9-9/27)
3154. Folwell, N. W. (Dr.) of Lodi, NY m 5/7/34 Caroline Reeder of Trenton, NJ
     at Rose Hill near Trenton; Rev. E. F. Cooley (6-6/18)
3155. Fonda, Christopher (Dr.), formerly of Schenectady, m 4/4/33 Mrs. E.
     McKensey of Mobile, AL in M (3-5/14)
3156. Fonda, Harriet (Miss), 19, d 12/2/32 in Watervliet (3-12/11)
3157. Foot, _____, 9 mo, ch of Dennis, d 4/9/40 in Chittenango (3-4/15)
3158. Foot, Charles of Unadilla m 1/20/42 Eliza Clark of Guilford in G; Rev.
     J. C. Ransom of Oxford (Oxford Republican, 2/4)
3159. Foot, Dennis m 2/22/32 Betsey Conrad; J. French, Esq. All of Sullivan
     (3-2/28)
3160. Foot, Lyman and _____ Whaston, surgeons, of the U.S. Army, d 11/4/46 at
     Port Lavacca (9-12/22)
3161. Foot, Marion, 35, consort of Samuel A., Esq. of NYC and oldest dau of
     William Fowler of Albany, d 8/2/32 at the home of her bro-in-law,
     Prof. Webster, in Geneva (6-8/15)
3162. Foote _____ (Judge) of Delhi m 10/2/19 Matilda Rosekrans in NYC; Rev.
     Dr. Kuypers (8-10/13)
3163. Foote, Asa of Sherburne m 1/29/46 Mrs. Almeda A. Gale of New Milford,
     Orange Co. in N. M.; Rev. Timlow (9-2/4)
3164. Foote, Bernice (Mrs.), 64, d 1/23/31 in Burlington, Ots. Co. (9-2/8)
3165. Foote, Ebenezer, Esq., 41, attorney, d in Albany (8-8/2/14)
3166. Foote, Erastus m 2/5/24 Orrilla Gallop, both of Plymouth; Rev. David Moss
     (8-2/18)
3167. Foote, Franklin m 3/1/43 Amanda Watrous in Colesville; Rev. H. M. Gilbert
     (see marr of Frsnklin Doolittle this date) (2-3/8)
3168. Foote, Isaac (Hon.), 96, d 2/27/42 in Smyrna (b in Colchester, CT and
     moved to Stafford, CT where for many years he was a magistrate and
     was a representative in the Gen'l. Assembly of that state; moved to
     area of Smyrna, NY in 1795; was later there first judge of the
     court of common pleas (Oxford Times, 3/16)
3169. Foote, Thomas M. of the Buffalo Commercial Advertiser m 8/10/36 Margaret
     St. John in Buffalo (6-8/24)
3170. Forbes, William, 16, (b in Rutland), MA) d 12/14/33 in Montreal, Canada
     (6-1/1/34)
3171. Forbs, Warren m 4/23/44 Mary Richards, both of Lenox, at H. Judd's Hotel
     in Chittenango; Rev. Houston (3-5/1)
3172. Force, Jonathan of Aiken, IL m 6/3/45 Louisa Way of New Hartford, NY in
     East Hamilton, NY (9-6/14)
3173. Ford, Anastasia, wid of late Col. David, d 11/19/46 in Morrisville
     (9-11/30)
3174. Ford, Dyer m 4/7/31 Sophia Wollage in Dresden (6-4/27)
3175. Ford, Elias of Louisville, Ots. Co. m 1/19/42 Lorinda Thompson of Norwich
     in N; Rev. L. Howard (Oxford Times, 1/26)
3176. Ford, James D. of Newark, NY m 10/2/31 Sarah Wright of Lyons in L (6-10/12)
3177. Ford, Jonathan of Van Buren m 12/13/36 Mrs. Zilphia Henry of Penn Yan
     in P. Y. (6-12/28)
3178. Ford, Lauren, Esq., 85, d 2/21/50 in Perth, NY (9-3/8)
3179. Ford, M. M., Esq., judge of the Onondaga County court of common pleas
     d 8/10/32 in Syracuse (6-8/22)
3180. Ford, Nelson, Jr. m 9/25/33 Wealthy Eastman of Candor in Owego (6-10/9)
3181. Ford, Oliver B. of the firm of Norton, Ford, and Co., m 11/28/38
     Lucretia Shekell in Vienna, NY; Rev. Spaulding. All of Phelps
     (6-12/5)
3182. Ford, William D. (Hon.), 54, d 10/1/33 in Sacket's Harbor (member of
     Congress in 1818) (6-10/9)
3183. Fore, Julian L. m 1/2/Julia Gloutney in Lysander; Rev. T. Walker (1-1/3/50)
3183a. Foreshay, P. m Malvina Graham in Penn Yan (6-3/26/34)

3184. Forrow, Alexander m 8/1/48 Emeline Jenks in New York Mills; Rev. N. D. Graves (9-8/19)
3185. Fosdick, Nancy, 14, d 2/18/38 in Chittenango (3-2/21)
3186. Fosgate, Bela (Mr.), 54, d 1/16/30 in Auburn (9-1/26)
3187. Foster, Alfred, 74, d 3/7/49 at the home of his dau, Mrs. Burgess, in Southport, WI (b in NY state and lived many yrs in Hannibal, Oswego Co. there) (9-4/19)
3188. Foster, Charles G. m 11/22/42 Adah Maria Wilson in Troy; Rev. Charles Wadsworth. All of Troy (9-11/25)
3189. Foster, Edward m 9/4/33 Minerva Gregory (6-9/18)
3190. Foster, Emma, wf of Joab G. and sister of Mrs. Burton Hawley of Utica, d 6/21/49 in Cincinnati, OH (cholera) (9-6/28)
3191. Foster, Henry m 9/5/33 Rebecca Bishop (6-9/18)
3192. Foster, Isaac L. of Lysander m 4/21/50 Betsey Titus of Baldwinsville in B; Rev. A. Wells (1-4/25)
3193. Foster, John m 9/22/33 Isadora Randall in Savannah, NY (6-10/9)
3194. Foster, Mary (Mrs.), 19, d 11/2/33 in Canandaigua (6-12/11)
3195. Foster, Mary (Mrs.), 19, d 12/9/33 in Rochester (6-12/18)
3196. Foster, Mary Jane, 36, wf of Reuben and dau of Ezekiel Curtiss of Utica d 1/30/48 (funeral from her late home on Hamilton Street in West Utica) (9-2/1)
3197. Foster, Milton, 16, s of Joab G. and Emma, d 6/24/49 in Cincinnati, OH (cholera) (Milton formerly of Utica (9-6/28)
3198. Foster, N. C. m 12/12/35 Emeline Cleveland, both of Canandaigua, in Hopewell (6-12/30)
3199. Foster, Nathan, 66, d 4/15/46 in Whitestown (9-4/21)
3200. Foster, Norman C. m 6/22/33 Mary Ann Hubbell in Geneva; Rev. Mandeville (6-7/3)
3201. Foster, Robert m 12/31/45 Elizabeth Armstrong in New Hartford; Henry Sherrill, Esq. All of New Hartford (9-1/5/46)
3202. Foster, Sophia, 32, wf of Jeter, d in Palmyra (6-3/17/30)
3203. Foster, V. (Capt.) of Sherburne d 10/29/29 in S (fatally scalded in his distillery "when the bolier cap flew off"; surv by wf and 2 ch) ("Worcester, Mass. papers are requested to insert this item") (7-11/18)
3204. Foster, William, "a hero of the Revolution" m "Mrs. Hunter" in Middlesex (6-3/2/31)
3205. Foulke, John H. of NYC d 5/20/22 at the Mansion House in Geneva (6-5/22)
3206. Fowle, William K. m 7/14/46 Charlotte Mitchell, both of Geneva, in G; Rev. T. G. Hibbard (6-7/17)
3207. Fowler, Allen of Trnton, NY m 9/12/49 Marriette Potter of Marcy in Holland Patent; Rev. E. Buckingham (9-9/14)
3208. Fowler, Augustus, about 40, d 11/21/48 in Fairhaven (1-11/23)
3209. Fowler, David of Lenox m 1/6/36 Susan Spring of Smithfield; Rev. Cooper of Wampsville (3-1/12)
3210. Fowler, Henry m 7/14/47 Mary W. Perkins, both of Utica, IN U; Rev. Dr. Proal (9-7/16)
3211. Fowler, Miriam, 88, d 1/13/43 in New Hartford (9-1/25)
3212. Fowler, Octavia Louisa, 49, wf of Elisha, Esq. and dau of Levi Carpenter of Bridgewater, d 5/22/46 in Oriskany Falls (9-6/10)
3213. Fowler, Samuel G. of Cohocton m 2/21/47 Susan Cheshbro of Yorkville in Y; Rev. Graves (9-3/30)
3214. Fowler, Stephen m 5/30/32 Catharine Hoyt, both of Geneva, in G; Rev. Mattison (6-6/6)
3215. Fox, Bachus of Penfield, Sara. Co. m Eliza M. Smith of Galway in G (6-10/9/33)
3216. Fox, Hannah, 63, wf of Charles, d 5/11/44 in Warren (9-5/21)
3217. Fox, Henry m 4/6/31 Betsey Norton in East Bloomfield (6-4/20)
3218. Fox, Ira m 12/1/46 Louisa Green in Yorkville; Rev. Dr. Z. Paddock. All of Little Falls (9-12/10)
3219. Fox, Peter, 2, s of late Peter G., d 8/15/47 in Utica (funeral from 47 Charlotte St.) (9-8/17)
3220. Fox, Peter G., 42, d 6/22/47 in Utica (funeral from his late home, 47 Charlotte St.) (9-6/23)
3221. Fox, Royal m 2/22/32 Betsey Baldwin, both of Perryville, in Chittenango; Rev. W. H. Campbell (3-2/28)
3222. Fraer, Peter m Barbara Sharp in Guilderland (6-1/19/31)

3223. Frala, Henry of Utica m 4/20/43 Catharine Foults of Herkimer in H;
Rev. Skinner (9-4/29)

3224. Francis, Albert H., 20, d in Syracuse ("run over by the cars") (funeral
from his mother's home on Water St.) (9-8/31/50)

3225. Francis, Daniel J., 29, d 3/21/44 in Utica (funeral from Trinity Ch.)
(9-3/22 and 3/23)

3226. Francis, James K. m 12/10/35 Catharine Clap in Bath (6-12/23)

3227. Francis, John M., Esq., editor of the Troy Budget, m 12/8/46 Harriet E.
Tucker of Palmyra in P; Rev. D. Harrington (1-12/14)

3228. Francis, Maria O., 28, wf of Richard H., d 4/6/48 in Utica (funeral from
the Broad St. Bapt. Ch.) (9-4/8)

3229. Francis, Martha (Miss), 21, dau of William, d 3/6/44 in Utica (funeral
at the home of her father, 51 Charlotte St.) (9-3/7)

3230. Francis, Richard H. m 4/25/49 Margaret P. Lepper of Utica; Rev. H. R.
Clarke (9-5/3)

3231. Francis, William, 68, bro of Thomas, d 10/8/48 in Utica (funeral at
the Broad St. Bapt. Ch.) (9-10/9)

3232. Francis, William, 33, d 9/5/49 in Utica (funeral at his late home, Cooper
St., rear of Waters Tavern, West Utica (9-9/6)

3233. Francis, William Hampton, 13, only s of Richard H., d 2/25/44 in Brookfield
(funeral from 33 Charlotte St.) (9-2/27)

3234. Francis, William Hampton, 3 mo, only s of Richard H. and Maria P. of Utica,
d 7/4/46 in Stonington, CT (9-7/8)

3235. Francisco, Harriet, 16, dau of J. Francisco, d 1/17/31 in Canandaigua
(6-2/2)

3236. Francisco, Henry, 134 years old (sic) d 10/27/20 near Whitehall, NY
(8-11/22)

3237. Franklin, Benedict W., Esq., late of Kinderhook, m 5/2/31 Mary B. Whiting,
dau of Capt. Augustus of Stuyvesant, Columbia Co., in Stuyvesant
(6-5/18)

3238. Franklin, Richard Benjamin, 18, s of Amos A. of Oxford, d 10/23/43 in
Grand Co., Wisc. Terr. (Oxford Republican, 11/23)

3239. Frary, Delarus W. m 4/17/34 Mrs. Elizabeth Standish (in Waterloo?)
(6-4/30)

3240. Fraser, D. m 3/6/34 Mary D. Lewis in Dresden (6-3/26)

3241. Fraser, Mary D., 23, wf of David, d 8/12/38 in Dundee (6-8/29)

3242. Frasier, Robert (Dr.) m 11/20/44 Theresa McConnell, both of McConnellsville,
in Vienna, NY (9-12/4)

3243. Frazer, Benjamin P., formerly of New Jersey, m 7/18/33 Martha Jane Pinch
of Geneva in G; Rev. Alverson (6-7/24)

3244. Frazer, Horatio N. m 4/15/33 Fanny Danielson in Phelps (6-4/24)

3245. Frazer, Martin m 12/20/35 Mrs. Agnes Logan; Elder Sears. All of Geneva
(6-1/6/36)

3246. Frazier, George m 12/29/48 Jane Story, both of Whitestown, at the Central
Hotel in Utica; Rev. D. G. Corey (9-1/1/49)

3247. Frear, James H. m 2/7/43 Sarah Queal in Utica; Rev. Haynes. All of Utica
(9-2/9)

3248. Frederick, Sarah (Mrs.), 91, d 8/1/43 in Sullivan (3-8/9)

3249. Fredericks, William m 8/17/46 Harriet F. Barnes in Utica; Rev. D. A.
Shepard. All of Utica (9-8/18)

3250. Freeborn, Thomas of Cazenovia m 11/16/37 Lane Mabie of Manlius in M;
C. Hibbert, Esq. (3-11/22)

3251. Freedman, Lewis m 3/8/41 Caty Ann Ostrander at the home of Salmon Wilcox
in Clockville (3-3/17)

3252. Freeman, _____, wid of Charles, d 1/15/35 "at an advanced age" in
Chittenango (3-1/20/35)

3253. Freeman, Charles P. m 7/25/49 Ernestine S. Randall, dau of Col. John of
Norwich, in N; Rev. H. S. Dickson (9-7/27)

3254. Freeman, E. O. of Jefferson Co. m Julia A. Southwick of Lysander in
Baldwinsville; Rev. B. Alden (1-3/15/49)

3255. Freeman, George Edwards, 20, d in Vienna, NY (6-6/30/30)

32'56. Freeman, George Whitfield of Floyd m 8/30/43 Charlotte Ann Dyer of
Shaftsbury, VT in Floyd, NY; Elder Isaiah Matteson (9-9/2)

32'57. Freeman, Henry m 6/23/44 Julia A. Benson, both of Sullivan, at the
Universalist Ch., Canaseraga; Rev. Dolphus Skinner of Utica (3-6/26)

3258. Freeman, Susan R., 28, wf of Charles P. and dau of late Philo Rockwell of Utica, d 1/1/48 in Brooklyn (9-1/4)
3259. Freeman, William, 74, d 9/29/41 in Preston (Oxford Times, 10/6)
3260. Freeman, William, about 26, printer, d 3/19/47 in Clay (1-3/31)
3261. Freer, Alvah m 10/30/33 Phebe Ann Streeter in Geneva; Elder Bentley. All of Seneca (6-11/6)
3262. Freligh, G. W. m 10/10/32 Parthena Kinne in Romulus (6-11/7)
3263. Freeman, Matilda (Mrs.), 99, d 2/6/31 in Orange, NJ (b in the Newark Mountains [now Orange], NJ 17 Nov 1731) (6-2/16)
3264. French, Abel, Esq., 77, a land surveyor, d in Albany (at age 29 had moved to Oneida Co.; served in the county legislature there; moved to Albany late in life) (9-11/21/43)
3265. French, Alpheus, 60, d 1/20/37 in Canaseraga (3-1/25)
3266. French, Andrew J., Esq. m 8/29/48 Mary A. Judd at the Reformed Dutch Ch. in Chittenango; Rev. James Abell (double ceremony - see m of Robert Stewart) (9-8/31)
3267. French, Charlotte, 39, wf of Col. Samuel, d 2/12/38 in Sullivan (3-2/14)
3268. French, Clementina, 43, wf of Thomas, d 6/-/45 in Chittenango (3-7/5)
3269. French, J. Sanger, 18, oldest s of Maynard of Cincinnati, OH, d 5/19/48 at Hamilton College (funeral at the home of Mrs. Sarah Eames of New Hartford (9-4/20)
3270. French, James d 7/29/33 in Bath (age given but blurred) (6-8/14)
3271. French, James of Syracuse m 11/6/43 Harriet Button of Chittenango in C; Rev. James Abell (3-11/8)
3272. French, James C., Esq. m 9/11/49 Elizabeth Arnold(?), 2nd dau of Benjamin of Utica, in U; Rev. Charles Wiley of the Reformed Dutch Ch. (9-9/13)
3273. French, John of Cameron m Mary J. Overhiser of Buena Vista on the Plains of Buena Vista; Elder Carr of Monterey (both communities in Steuben Co.) (5-6/15/49)
3274. French, Mary Olivia, 3, dau of Thomas, d 11/15/41 in Chittenango (funeral from the Dutch Reformed Ch.) (3-11/17)
3275. French, Samuel, 16, s of late Thomas, d 6/15/39 in Canaseraga (3-6/19)
3276. French, Thomas, 56, d 7/25/38 in Canaseraga (3-8/1)
3277. French, Thomas, Esq. m 2/3/43 Olive Ann Lee in Canaseraga; Rev. James Abell. All of Sullivan (3-12/6)
3278. French, William m Calista Bennett in Hornellsville (6-4/14/30)
3279. Fresher, George W. of Hopewell m 9/25/49 Leonora Failing of Baldwinsville in B; Rev. T. Walker (1-10/11)
3280. Frey, Elizabeth, 91, consort of Col. Hendrick, d 12/10/25 in Canajoharie (deceased was sister of Gen. Herkimer who was mortally wounded at the Battle of Oriskany) (9-2/7/26)
3281. Freyer, Benjamin m 12/25/48 Laura A. Ruggles in Chemung; Rev. N. N. Beers. All of Chemung (double ceremony - see m of George W. Palmatier) (5-1/5/49)
3282. Fries, Matthias W. m 10/18/48 Ann E. Fredericks in Utica; Rev. H. R. Clarke. All of Utica (9-10/20)
3283. Frink, Andrew M. of New London, CT m 10/29/32 Julia M. Osborn of Geneva in G; Rev. Dr. Bruce (6-10/31)
3284. Frink, Jesse of Richmond m 11/10/33 Susan Boyd of Canadice in C (6-11/27)
3285. Frisbie, _____, 2, ch of Elihu, d in Utica (9-7/11/26)
3286. Frisbie, Augustus m 11/15/42 Mary E. Sage, dau of Col. H., in Sullivan; Rev. J. Abell (3-11/16)
3287. Frisbie, Irene (Miss), 24, d 8/20/36 in Vienna, NY (6-8/31)
3288. Frisbie, William of Auburn m 5/27/39 Louisa Moore of Lyons in L; S. H. Ashmun, Esq. (6-6/5)
3289. Frisby, Medad, Esq. of Vienna, NY m 10/17/30 Betsy Vancise, youngest dau of Cornelius, Esq. of Lenox (6-11/1)
    Frith, Christopher. See Faith, Christopher.
3290. Frodes, Asa m 3/11/29 Sarah Whitcom (7-3/18)
3291. Frost, Caleb, 86, d on Long Island (cancer) (6-11/10/30)
3292. Frost, Edmund W., 18, printer, d in Geneseo (6-9/18/33)
3293. Frost, Jacob, tailor, of Dundee village in the town of Starkey m 12/28/34 Mary Winter, tailoress, of Barrington in B (6-1/21/35)
3294. Frost, John (Rev.) of Whitesboro d 3/1/42 in Waterville (funeral from the Brick Ch., Waterville) (9-3/3)

3295. Frushour(?), Marcus D. Lafayette, 3, s of Alexander and Laney M.,
      d 10/14/46 in Hopewell (6-10/23)
3296. Fulford, Nathaniel of Marshall m 9/8/42 Mary Cooley of Attica in A; Rev.
      Bunker (9-9/24)
3297. Fuller, _____, 3 mo, ch of Orion, d in Utica (9-8/1/26)
3298. Fuller, Aaron, 73, formerly of Newport,d 6/2/45 in Martinsburgh (9-6/14)
3299. Fuller, Ambroe S. m 2/1/49 Mary Jackson in Big Flats; Nelson Hotchkiss,
      Esq. All of B. F. (5-2/2)
3300. Fuller, Ann Eliza Oakley, 3, dau of __?__ and C. A. Fuller (the mother),
      d 1/9/47 at the home of B. Oakley in Jersey City (presumably in NJ)
      (9-1/16)
3301. Fuller, Clark, 1, s of Dr. S. Fuller, d 11/29/34 in Chittenango (3-12/2)
3302. Fuller, D. K. of Rathboneville m 4/4/50 Lucia E. Arnold of Corning in C;
      Rev. H. N. Seaver (4-4/10)
3304. Fuller, Edward (Dr.) of Chittenango m 10/19/37 Octavia Lee, dau of Col.
      Stephen of Lenox, in L; Rev. Alvah Day (3-10/25)
3305. Fuller, Emma Jane, oldest dau of Carrington A. and Jane, d 1/23/45 in
      NYC (9-1/29)
3306. Fuller, J. Cutler of Buffalo m 12/20/23 Emily H. House of Houseville in
      H; Rev. William H. Spencer (9-12/23)
3307. Fuller, Jacob m 9/7/36 Mary Wilbur(?), both of Geneva, in G; Rev. W. F.
      Walker of NYC (6-9/14)
3308. Fuller, Jeremiah, Esq., about 80, one of the oldest inhabitants of
      Schenectady, d 6/18/39 in Schenectady (3-6/19)
3309. Fuller, L. T. of Corning m 5/30/41 A. Jane Card of Woodstock in W; Rev.
      Putnam (4-6/11)
3310. Fuller, Mary (Mrs.), 95, formerly of Hartland, CT, d 11/26/49 at the home
      of her son-in-law, John Merry, in Frankfort, NY (9-12/1)
3311. Fuller, Morris E. of Little Falls m 10/5/43 Amelia Curtiss of Clinton in
      C; Rev. Norton (9-10/6)
3312. Fuller, Moses N. of Utica m 6/17/46 Ann Jones of Remsen in R; Rev. Welles
      (9-6/20)
3313. Fuller, Reuben, 41, d 10/11/33 in Salem (6-10/23)
3314. Fuller, Richard (Dr.), 32, d 5/15/37 in Schenectady (3-5/24)
3315. Fuller, Willard of Albany m 12/31/48 Julia A. Hall of Utica at the
      Bleecker St. Meth. Episc. Ch. in Utica; Rev. H. R. Clarke (9-1/6/49)
3316. Fuller, William L., 5 mo, s of Dr. E., d 6/4/39 at the home of Col. S.
      Lee in Sullivan (3-6/12)
3317. Fulton, Adeline (Mrs.), 33, d in Bath (6-7/14/30)
3318. Fulton, Caleb P. (Maj.) of Bath m 6/10/31 Eliza Simpson of Cameron in C
      (6-6/15)
3319. Fulton, Joseph m 7/16/35 Clarissa Ackley, both of Seneca, in S; Rev.
      John White (6-7/22)
3320. Fults, John m 8/8/35 Maranda Warner, both of Manlius Center, in
      Chittenango; J. French, Esq. (3-8/11)
3321. Furman, _____, inf ch of George W., d 1/13/29 in Oxford (8-1/21)
3322. Furman, Charles Edwin of Clarkson m 1/19/31 Harriet E. J. Johnson in
      Rochester (6-2/2)
3323. Furman, John T. m 1/13/50 Harriet, Updike, dau of William, Esq. of
      Rutland, Tioga Co., PA, in Rutland; Rev. Samuel Grenell (5-1/18)
3324. Furman, Joshua, 72, d 8/4/49 in Rutherford, NC where he had lived the
      past 21 yrs (formerly first judge of Onondaga Co., NY; founder of
      Syracuse (9-8/21)
3325. Furman, Richard (Rev.) D.D., d 8/25/25 in Charleston, SC (for last
      40 yrs pastor of the Bapt. Ch. in Charleston)(9-9/13)
3326. Furnam, Charles E. m Emiline Johnson in Rochester (6-2/9/31)
3327. Fyler, Byron of Onondaga m 12/25/47 Juliaette Baley of Cicero at the
      Seneca Hotel in Baldwinsville; Rev. T. Walker (1-12/29)
3328. Fyler, Silas, 58, d 4/16/41 in Sullivan (3-4/21)
3329. Gabriel, Louis m 10/12/31 Eliza Dexter in Canandaigua; Rev. Kearny
      (6-11/9)
3330. Gaffney, Owen m 4/25/49 Luisa G. V. Burke at St. John's Ch. in Utica;
      Rev. Joseph Stokes. All of Utica (9-4/26)
3331. Gage, David W. m 3/19/43 Jane Ann Rowley in Binghamton; Rev. Stanton.
      All of Binghamton (2-3/22)

3332. Gage, Delia, 44, consort of Aaron, Esq., d 5/10/32 in Benton (surv by a
       large family) (6-6/6)
3333. Gage,John m 11/3/46 Eleanor Probasco; Rev. Dr. Abeel. All of Waterloo
       (6-11/20)
3334. Gage, Moses B., M.D., m Ann Maria Davis, both of Churchville, in Brockport
       (6-6/8/31)
3335. Gage, William H. of Penn Yan m 1/9/32 Abigail R. Fargo of Benton in B
       (6-2/22)
3336. Gale, WilliamH. m 12/2/41 Elizabeth Marks, dau of Samuel of Chittenango,
       in Syracuse; Rev. Gregory (3-12/8)
3337. Gallagher, Charles, 2, "son of Mrs. Gallagher", d 5/24/35 in Geneva
       (6-5/27)
3338. Gallagher, George, 47, formerly a merchant, of NYC d 5/10/33 in Geneva
       (6-5/15)
3339. Gallagher, James H. of Penn Yan m 1/9/32 Clarissa Dunning of Jerusalem,
       NY, in J (6-1/18)
3340. Gallagher, John Bernard, rector of St. Paul's Ch., Louisville, KY
       (but late of Geneva, NY) d 2/1/49 in Tuscumbia, AL (9-2/12)
3341. Gallagher, Mason (Rev.), missionary of the Protestant Episc. Ch. of
       Cazenovia, m 6/3/45 Lucy Stebbins, oldest dau of Charles, Esq. of
       Cazenovia in C; Rev. Gregory of Syracuse (9-6/11)
3342. Gallagher, Matthew, 65, d 6/10/50 in Deerfield (9-7/22)
3343. Gallagher, Michael of Deerfield m 2/13/47 Mary Cullen, dau of James of
       Schuyler, in S; Rev. John McMemony (9-2/18)
3344. Gallatin, Hannah, 82, wf of Albert and dau of late Commodore James
       Nicholson, d 5/14/49 in NYC (9-5/17)
3345. Gallaudet, Peter W., 87, father of Rev. T. H., d 5/17/43 in Washington,
       D.C. (in Rev. fought at Trenton, NJ and elsewhere) (lived formerly
       in Hartford, CT) (9-6/1)
3346. Gallup, Hiram of Williamson m Abigail Spear in Macedon (6-10/9/33)
3347. Gally, David K. (Rev.), 43, d 8/8/44 in Rochester (consumption) (9-8/15)
3348. Galpin, Joseph m 2/1/31 Susan Wormer in Fleming (6-2/9)
3349. Galusha, Jonas (Hon.), 83, d 10/1/34 in Shaftsbury, VT (for many yrs.
       gov. of VT) (6-10/15)
3350. Galusha, Joseph H. of Lyons m 3/21/49 Catherine S. Morris, dau of late
       Walter H., Esq. of Albany, in Lyons; Rev. Elon Galusha (9-3/31)
3351. Galway, William m 11/30/50 Mrs. Caroline Cool in Mohawk; Rev. O. Adams.
       All of Mohawk (9-12/6)
3352. Gamage, Gilbert Ash, 44, poet, d in NYC (consumption) (6-5/23/32)
3353. Gamber, Henry of Fayette m 1/26/32 Mary Hartranft of Seneca Falls in
       S.F. (6-2/15)
3354. Gamble, William, 78, (a Rev. officer) d 1/15/33 in Washington, D.C.
       (6-2/6)
3355. Ganley, Hugh, 20, formerly of Utica d 1/22/48 in Syracuse (consumption)
       (9-1/26)
3356. Gano, Julius C. m 11/25/42 Lucy Ann Bishop of Binghamton; H. Collier
       (2-11/30)
3357. Ganung, Louisa (Mrs.), 27, d in Benton (6-5/4/31)
3358. Gardinier, Barent, Esq., attorney, d in NYC (8-1/23/22)
3359. Gardner, C. Lewis m 3/13/38 Jane H. Reynolds in Big Flats (6-4/4)
3360. Gardner, Christian m 9/23/48 Cornelia Spaulding, both of Utica, in U;
       Rev. D. G. Corey (9-9/26)
3361. Gardner, George m 9/5/33 Cynthia Talada in Elmira (6-9/11)
3362. Gardner, George W., 35, formerly of Utica, d 5/11/48 at Stanwix Hall in
       Albany(surv by wf and 2 ch) (funeral from 30 Charlotte St., Utica, his
       former home) (had been a clerk at Stanwix Hall) (9-5/13)
3363. Gardner, J. V. P. of the firm of Butterfield and Co. of Utica, m 5/31/42
       Rebecca Williams, dau of Thomas, Esq. of Vernon; Rev. Brisbin of Vernon
       (9-6/3)
3364. Gardner, James V. P. of Utica m 7/29/46 Sophia W. Williams, only dau of
       William formerly of Utica, in Rome, NY; Rev. Haynes (9-7/31)
3365. Gardner, Jesse of Varick m 1/29/34 Elsey Fleming of Romulus in R; Rev.
       Barton (6-2/5)
3366. Gardner, Mary Ann, 35, wf of G. W., d 1/21/44 in Jersey City, NJ (9-2/6)
3367. Gardner, Palmer of Wisconsin m 2/14/44 Margaret Williams of Manlius in M;
       Rev. James Abell (3-2/21)

3368. Gardner, Rebecca S., 24, wf of James V.P. and dau of Thomas Williams of
       Vernon, d 5/21/45 in Utica (interred in V) (9-5/22)
3369. Gardner, S. S., 31, d 11/1/36 in Lyons (6-11/9)
3370. Gardner, Sylvester C. of Eagle Village m 9/25/38 Caroline Coltin, dau of
       David in Fayetteville; Rev. Tuttle (3-10/10)
3371. Gardner, Horatio, oculist, of Utica m 3/8/43 Agnes A. Melville, oldest
       dau of Henry, Esq. of Bond Head, Canada; Rev. Coty (9-3/9)
3372. Gardner, William of PennYan m Amelia C. Bidwell in Prattsburgh (6-4/6/31)
3373. Garland, Richard (Maj.), 65, member of Parliament in the Island of
       Antigua, d 8/8/31 in Albany, NY (6-8/24)
3374. Garlick, Eliphalet d 1/2/34 (in Seneca Falls?) (6-1/22)
3375. Garlinghouse, Nelson of Richmond, Ont. Co. m 5/24/36 Lorinda Short
       (in Geneseo?) (6-6/15)
3376. Garlock, William, 3, s of Isaac and Nancy, d 5/20/42 in Sullivan (3-5/25)
3377. Garrett, _____, a child of "Mr. Garrett", d 7/3/25 and _____ Nichols,
       a child of the late Rev. J. Nichols, d 6/30/25 in Bombay, India (both
       their fathers of the American Mission)(9-12/6)
3378. Garrett, Cheney, 76, formerly of New Haven, CT and for the last fifty
       years a resident of Trenton, NY, d 5/23/45 in South Trenton (9-6/10)
3379. Garrett, Loraney, 65, wf of Cheney, formerly of Branford, CT, d 3/19/33
       in Trenton, NY ("Editors of New Haven papers please copy") (9-4/9)
3380. Garrison, Abraham, formerly of Geneva, d in Matamoros, Mexico (6-6/17/35)
3381. Garrison, George of Cameron m 2/7/36 Lucy Ann Watkins of Bath in B
       (6-2/17)
3382. Garrison, H. D., merchant, of Detroit, MI m E. D. Naglee of Geneva; Rev.
       Abeel (6-9/2/35)
3383. Garvin, Katharine Rowena, 11. oldest dau of S. B. and Julia, d 6/10/48
       in Utica (funeral from 98 John St.) (9-6/12)
3384. Gates, Alanson of Herkimer m 10/19/50 Mary Martha Dygert of Russia, NY in
       Utica; Rev. George Leeds (9-10/22)
3385. Gates, Archelaus (Dr.) d "week before last" in Ovid (6-8/31/31)
3386. Gates, Buel m 9/7/31 Fidelia Hause in Geneva; Rev. Phelps (6-9/14)
3387. Gates, Daniel, Esq., about 90, one of the first settlers at Hopewell,
       d 5/14/32 in Hopewell (6-5/30)
3388. Gates, Daniel m 12/19/36 Lany Ehle, dau of Henry, in Sullivan; Rev. Jesse
       Pound of Manlius (3-1/4/37)
3389. Gates, George B. of Mobile, AL m 8/1/44 Martha Jane Kaph, dau of Col. Bela
       of Otsego Co., in Sauquoit, NY; Rev. Waugh (9-8/12)
3390. Gates, Harvey P. of Bath m 3/28/49 Catharine Chrisley of Pine Valley in
       P. V.; Rev. C. C. Carr (5-3/30)
3391. Gates, Jefferson m Mary Ann Laver in Seneca; Elder Brown (6-7/14/30)
3392. Gates, Jennet, 34, wf of Le Roy, d 12/16/46 in Sauquoit (member of
       Presby. Ch.) (9-12/19)
3393. Gates, Jeremiah, Jr. m 10/13/35 Emeline Doxtader in Chittenango; Rev.
       John C. F. Hoes (3-10/20)
3394. Gates, John C. m 9/1/36 Amanda Scott in Phelps (6-9/7)
3395. Gates, Justin (Dr.) of Rochester m 7/19/48 Sarah L. Bedell, dau of
       Jeremiah of Coxsackie, in C "by a public execution of the marriage
       covenant" (9-7/25)
3396. Gates, Nathan F. B. m Jane N. Robards at Griffin's Hotel in Utica;
       Hon. Aaron Hackley. All of Frankfort (9-3/1/44)
3397. Gates, Sarah (Mrs.), 66, d in Mobile, AL (lived many years in Sauquoit,
       NY (member of Presby. Ch. more than 30 yrs); moved to Mobile in 1837
       where she lived with her son, Dr. H. Gates, druggist (9-2/26/47)
3398. Gates, Thomas m Jane Handley, dau of William formerly of Seneca, in Perry
       (6-11/20/33)
3399. Gates, William m 10/10/32 Achsa Moody, both of Phelps, in Vienna, NY
       (6-11/7)
3400. Gates, William H., 49, d 7/10/45 in New London, Oneida Co. (9-7/17)
3401. Gaton, Nancy, a colored woman, d 1/27/31 in Geneva (6-2/2/31)
3402. Gaul, Julia A. d 9/24/33 in Rochester (6-10/9)
3403. Gavetty, _____, 2, s of John A. and Huldah, d 10/12/48 in Van Buren
       (1-10/14)
3404. Gaw, _____, 10, s of John, d 8/30/33 in Gorham (hydrophobia) (6-9/11)
3405. Gay, Luther m 11/8/32 Almira Williams, both of Bloomfield, in Bristol
       (6-11/21)

93

3406. Gay, Roswell, Jr., 21, d 1/29/33 in Canandaigua (6-2/13)
3407. Gay, Samuel, 74, d 12/23/44 in Utica (funeral at the home of his son-in-law, Henry S. Storm, 6 Broadway) (9-12/24)
3408. Gaylord, Edwin m 10/20/42 Angeline Lake in Utica; Rev. Spencer (9-10/27)
3409. Gaylord, Wells M., 42, formerly of Utica, d 11/4/46 at his home in Rochester (9-11/7)
3410. Gazlay, Ward M., Esq., editor of the Index, m 6/13/22 Elizabeth Carter of Newburgh in N; Rev. John Johnson (8-6/26)
3411. Gear, Charlotte, 35, wf of Capt. Hezekiah and only dau of John Clark of Seneca, NY, d 9/13/33 in Galena, IL (6-10/30)
3412. Gear, Ezekiel G. (Rev.), rector of Zion's Ch., Palmyra, m Mary Y. How in Auburn; Rev. Dr. Rudd (8-6/3/29)
3413. Gear, Hezekiah H. of Gelena, IL m 12/5/34 Deborah Rose of Geneva, NY in G; Rev. Dr. Bruce (6-12/10)
3414. Gear, Miranda, 25, wf of Rev. E. G., rector of St. John's Ch. in Oxford, NY, d 1/25/26 (8-2/1)
3415. Gear, Sarah Elizabeth, 14, dau of Rev. E. G. (chaplain, U.S. Army, Fort Snelling, IA), d 9/20/48 in Utica ("Friends of the parents of the Rev. Dr. Judd and his family are respectfully invited" to the funeral) (9-9/21)
3416. Gedman, John D. (Dr.) d in Philadelphia (PA?) (6-4/28/30)
3417. Gee, Joseph m Eleanor Seaton (6-3/24/30)
3418. Gee, Samuel R. C., 24, d in Elmira (6-6/26/33)
3419. Geer, Caroline L. (Miss), 20, d 12/18/46 in Waterville (consumption) (9-1/1/47)
3420. Geer, Ebenezer, Esq. of Floyd m 3/8/49 Harriet Ann Pardee, late of Earlville, in Binghamton; Rev. Dr. Paddock (9-3/17)
3421. Geer, Margin m Eemline Drake in Alloway (6- 2/17/30)
3422. Genet, Edmund Charles, 70, formerly Minister of the French Republic to the U.S., d 7/14/34 at Prospect Hill near Albany (6-7/23)
3423. Genung, Lewis d in Benton (6-5/5/30)
3424. George, Daniel, 50, d in Catlin (6-3/3/30)
3425. George, Evan, Jr. (Mr.) d 2/7/48 in Utica (consumption) (funeral at the Welsh Cong'l. Ch., corner Washington and Whitesboro Sts.) (9-2/9)
3426. Gere, Eliza L. (Miss), 20, d 9/5/49 in Bellisle (1-9/6)
3427. Gere, Luther, Esq. m 4/25/33 Emily Walker in Ithaca (6-5/22)
3428. German, Andrew m Hannah Force in Tyrone (6-2/3/30)
3429. German, Andrew, Jr. m Olive Bailey in Hector (6-12/11/33)
3430. German, Harriet Isabella, 22, wf of Capt. Walter of Norwich and youngest dau of David Ostrom, Esq. of Utica, d 11/4/19 in Utica (8-11/17)
3431. German, Lewis (Lt.) of the U.S. Navy, s of Gen. German of Norwich, d in Norwich (surv by wf and 2 ch) (7-4/29/19)
3432. German, Obediah (Gen.), 75, d 9/24/42 in Norwich (2-10/12)
3433. Germon, Thomas B., 17, s of Michael and Sarah, d 6/30/50 in West Utica (9-7/2)
3434. Germond, George C. m 6/25/33 Elizabeth Bridgewood (6-7/10)
3435. Gerry, Ann (Mrs.), 85, relict of EldridgeGerry (one of the signers of the Declaration of Independence) d 3/17/49 in New Haven (state not given) (9-3/22)
3436. Gervan, William m 2/5/43 Emily Hill; Rev. Plumb. All of Utica (9-2/7)
3437. Gibb, John B. m 9/16/33 Laura Ann Gibbs in Batavia (6-10/9)
3438. Gibbons, James, 45 ,s of late James, d 7/2/44 in Albany (9-7/8)
3439. Gibbs, Charlotte (Mrs.), 64, d 6/25/34 in Newark, NJ (6-7/9)
3440. Gibbs, George Clinton, Esq. m 11/3/35 Elmina Halsey, dau of Hon. J. H.; Rev. Thomas Lounsbury. All of Ovid (6-11/11/35)
3441. Gibbs, Samuel m 4/27/31 Elizabeth Nose in Ithaca;Rev. Sears (6-5/11)
3442. Gibson, S. J. (Rev.) of Monroeton, PA, formerly of Norwich, NY, m 5/29/42 Sarah Eliza Hancox of Oxford in O; Rev. David Pickering of Louisville, NY (Oxford Times, 6/1)
3443. Giddins, Abigal, 36, wf of Edward, d in Lockport (6-8/15/32)
3444. Gidley, Ann Maria, 28, d 12/13/42 in Chittenango (3-12/21)
3445. Gidley, Nicholas m 12/12/36 Mary Rook, both of Chittenango, in Fayetteville; A. Neely, Esq. (3-12/14)
3446. Giffing, John H., a native of NYC and bro of the Messrs. Giffing of Geneva, d 10/18/32 in New Orleans, LA (yellow fever) (6-11/14)

3447. Giffing, John Sweeney, 2, s of William, d 1/22/34 in Geneva (6-1/29)
3448. Gifford, George Esq. m 5/17/49 Eleanor C. Van Ranst, youngest dau of late
C. W., in NYC; Rev. Dr. Lansing. All of NYC (9-5/24)
3449. Gifford, James T., Esq., about 40, formerly of Oneida Co., d in Elgin,
Kane Co., IL (cholera) (an early settler in northern IL, founder of
Elgin) (9-8/27)
3450. Gilbert, ____, inf ch of "Mr. Gilbert" d 3/31/34 in Geneva (6-4/2)
3451. Gilbert, Baseter of Reading m 8/31/34 Almeda Thompson of Catlin in C
(6-9/10)
3452. Gilbert, Cahrles Henry, 3, d 12/2/49 in Sauquoit (9-12/8)
3453. Gilbert, David, 47, d 8/1/32 in Middlesex (6-8/15)
3454. Gilbert, Eli W. m 11/30/43 Jane Elizabeth Kirkland in Utica; Rev. B.
Hawley. All of Utica (9-12/1)
3455. Gilbert, Hannah, 44, wf of Deacon Joseph T. of Gilbertsville, d 5/5/30
(7-5/19)
3456. Gilbert, Henry, editor of the Western Star, m 9/27/33 Charlotte Case of
Canandaigua in C (6-10/9)
3457. Gilbert, Jasper W. of Rochester m 1/14/47 Catharine Augusta Horn, dau of
James, Esq. of NYC in NYC; Rev. John M. Krebs, D.D. (9-1/19)
3458. Gilbert, Jesse, 51, d 11/9/46 in Carthage (9-11/30)
3459. Gilbert, John F. m 2/17/31 Christiana Wilder in Bristol (6-3/2)
3460. Gilbert, Linus S. of Wayne Co. m Mary Ann Sage of Sandersfield, MA in
Hudson, NY (6-11/7/32)
3461. Gilbert, Lucius M. of Canaseraga m Elizabeth Randall of Augusta in
Canaseraga; J. French, Esq. (3-8/4/35)
3462. Gilbert, Mary P., 32, wf of William D., d 8/18/48 in Corning (4-8/23
3463. Gilbert, Mason H. of Rushville m 2/9/32 Emily W. Bryant of Manchester
in M (6-2/22)
3464. Gilbert, Olive, 13 mo, dau of E. M., d 5/5/46 in Utica (9-5/6)
3465. Gilbert, Theodore, 72, d 7/7/50 in Paris, NY (one of the earliest
settlers there) (9-7/17)
3466. Gilbraith, Samuel m 10/9/50 Mary A. Hammond in Sparta, Liv. Co.; Rev.
Aikens. All of Sparta (5-10/18)
3467. Gilchrist, Caroline (Mrs.), 21, d 8/26/33 in Bath (6-9/4)
3468. Gilchrist, Laura I., 21, wf of Robert, merchant, of Albany and dau of
Hon. Ambrose Spencer, d 3/20/25 (9-3/22)
3469. Gildemeester, ____, consort of Hugo C., Esq., late a resident of
Geneva, d in Cazenovia (6-7/21/30)
3470. Gildersleave, Asa, 76, (a Rev. soldier) d in Elmira (6-4/14/30)
3471. Gildersleeve, J. S. m 1/24/31 Belinda McCarty in Clyde (6-2/2)
3472. Gildersleeve, Romulus (Col.) of Cayuga Co. m 10/26/30 Emiline Peck, dau
of Judge Peck of Benton, in B; Rev. Tooker (6-11/30)
3473. Giles, William B., 69, late gov. of VA, d 12/4/30 in Richmond, VA (6-12/29)
3474. Gill, Horace m 2/10/33 Leandice Hudson in Eaton; Rev. Willis (3-2/19)
3475. Gillam, Henry of Ledyard m 5/20/34 Dulcy Stearns of Gorham; Rev. Gaylord
(6-5/21)
3476. Gillen, Michael, 29, d 7/16/43 in Babylon, L. I., NY (9-8/17)
3477. Gillespie, Albert of Dubuque, IA m 7/12/48 Jane M. B. Wright, dau of
Zenas, Esq. of Utica, in U; Rev. William H. Spencer (9-7/14)
3478. Gillespie, George, 54, a native of Lanarkshire, Scotland, d 9/24/31 in
Geneva (6-9/28)
3479. Gillet, Fidelo B. (Dr.), 32, d in Schenectady (6-10/9/33)
3480. Gillett, Moses (Dr.), 72, d 6/4/48 in Utica (funeral at the Presby. Ch.)
(9-6/6)
3481. Gillett, Truman (Rev.), about 70, d 2/8/50 in Camden (9-3/18)
3482. Gillies, Mary Ann (Mrs.) d in Newburgh (6-1/26/31)
3483. Gilliland, Robert m 11/24/31 Mary Catharine Duryee in Fayette (6-12/7)
3484. Gillman, E. W. (Rev.) of Lockport m 6/5/50 Julia Silliman, youngest dau
of Prof. Benjamin, in New Haven, CT; Rev. Dr. Finch (9-6/13)
3485. Gillman, James m Sarah Andrews in Rochester (6-11/10/30)
3486. Gillmore, Ferdinand B., s of Dexter and Elizabeth, d 2/28/48 in Utica
(funeral at 35 Catharine St.) (9-2/29)
3487. Gillmore, Francis H. m 3/12/50 Frances E. Wilcox of Baldwinsville in B;
Rev. A. Wells (1-3/14)

3488. Gillmore, Maria Louisa, 2, youngest dau of Dexter, Esq., d 8/26/45 in
      Utica (funeral from her father's home, 35 Catharine St.) (9-8/27)
3489. Gilmer, John (Dr.) of Nunda m Ansluida V. Watson in Geneseo (6-5/29/34)
3490. Gilmore, Benjamin m 2/23/42 Mariah Robbins, both of Hornby, in H; Rev.
      Amos Hard (4-3/9)
3491. Gilmore, James, 75, an early settler in Oxford, d 2/18/21 (in Oxford?)
      (8-3/14)
3492. Gilroy, William of Bath m 1/6/49 Sarah Lewis of corning in C; Jesse Clark,
      Esq. (4-1/10)
3493. Gilson, Alonzo m 8/4/50 Adaline G. Mather, both of Boonville, in Turin;
      Rev. Horton (9-8/12)
3494. Giltner, W. of Erie m 8/27/36 Eliza B. Hudenut of Elmira in E (6-9/7)
3495. Glance, Jesse, widower with 14 ch,m Miss Dolly Trace, a widow with 13 ch,
      at Meadville (6-8/22/32)
3496. Glass, Lydia, 53, wf of Erastus, d 5/1/35 in Canadice (6-5/13)
3497. Glassell. James M. (Maj.) of the U.S. Army d at sea on the ship "Seaman"
      off Cape Hatteras (buried in the Episc. burial ground at Hampton, VA
      (6-11/28/38)
3498. Gleason, L. Philanda (Miss), 21, d 3/7/49 in Adams (1-3/15)
3499. Gleason, Thomas M. m 9/212/44 Mary Jane Sibley; Rev. Dr. Proal (9-9/13)
3500. Gleben, Gilbert, Esq. of Vienna (North Bay), NY m 2/2/48 Harriet G. De
      Lano; Rev. L. D. Cole (9-2/4)
3501. Glen George W. m 3/8/35 Ursula Everett in Elmira (6-3/18)
3502. Glenn, Alexander m 9/4/33 Hannah Gregory, both of Hanover, in Buffalo
      (6-9/18)
3503. Glines, Martin m 1/25/31 Hannah Rice in Union Village, Wash. Co. (6-2/2)
3504. Glinnan, Charles M., 18, d 8/3/48 in Utica (funeral from his late home,
      31 Elizabeth St.) (9-8/5)
3505. Glord, Steven V. R. m 10/17/50 Louisa Smith in Newville; Rev. A. H.
      Parmelee (4-10/23)
3506. Glover, Fancis, 56, d in Lyons (6-3/10/30)
3507. Glover, James m 6/29/17 Ann Bradley, both of Oxford; Rev. Lacy (8-7/2)
3508. Glover, Justus S., attorney, m 5/9/39 Achsa A. Cornwell at St. Mark's Ch.,
      Penn Yan; Rev. E. Embury. All of Penn Yan (6-5/22)
3509. Glympse, Moses m 2/23/32 Mary Kenyon, dau of Nathaniel, in Phelps (6-3/7)
3510. Goble, Orrin of Baldwinsville m 11/5/50 Eliza Showerman of Van Buren;
      Rev. L. White (1-11/7)
3511. Goddard, Nathaniel, Esq. of York m Lucinda Peck in Le Roy (6-9/18/33)
3512. Godfrey, Harriet M., 28, wf of John H., d 9/25/50 in Elmira (5-9/27)
3513. Godfrey, Truman of Oneida Co. m 8/21/50 Hannah Dutcher of Troy; Rev.
      G. C. Baldwin (9-9/5)
3514. Goff, Lord Nelson m 8/8/45 Elizabeth E. Dickinson in Rome, NY (9-8/13)
3515. Gold, Ann Louisa, 47, wf of Theodore S. and dau of late James S. Kip of
      Utica, d 8/31/47 in Whitestown (9-9/2 and 9/6)
3516. Gold, Charles R. m 3/16/48 Mrs. Kate T. Atwater in Buffalo (9-3/18)
3517. Gold, Thomas R., 37, of Whitesboro, NY d 10/11/46 at McKendle's Landing
      on the Mississippi (9-11/3)
3518. Golden, Alonzo m 10/3/44 Emily Armstrong in New Hartford; Henry Sherrill.
      All of New H (9-10/9)
3519. Golden, D. V. W. m 8/3/48 Jane Barnum, dau of E. S., Esq., in Utica;
      Rev. D. Skinner. All of Utica (9-8/4)
3520. Golden, Moses of Oswego m 5/9/49 Mary Redmond of Utica at St. John's Ch.
      in Utica; Rev. Stokes (9-5/10)
3521. Goldsmith, Ira m Eliza Smith, dau of Dr. Norman, in Elmira (6-5/5/30)
3522. Goodale, Polly, wf of Rev. S., d 6/18/33 in Bristol (6-7/10)
3523. Goodell, Livingston, Esq., 28, of Port Byron d 3/21/49 in Utica (funeral
      from his father's home, 29 Mary St.) (9-3/22)
3524. Goodell, Moses m 2/10/33 Electa Van Vleet in Angelica (6-3/6)
3525. Goodell, Richard (Maj.), keeper of the state prison at Auburn and late
      speaker of the Assembly of this state, d in Auburn (9-2/7/26)
3526. Goodhue, Clark, 20, s of John, d 11/30/30 in Augusta (9-12/21)
3527. Goodhue, Phineas, 74, (a Rev. pensioner) d 8/1/26 in Andover, MA (fought
      at Bunker hill in the Rev.) (9-10/24)
3528. Goodier, Samuel of Litchfield m 5/16/43 Hester Ann Wadsworth of New
      Hartford; Rev. Hawley (marr. at the pastor's home in Utica) (9-5/17)

3529. Goodland, John m 9/4/50 Caroline M. Clark in Waterville; G. H. Church, Esq. (9-9/7)
3530. Goodman, George W. of Whitestown m 12/20/49 Sarah M. Atwater of Westmoreland in W; Rev. F. A. Spencer (9-1/7/50)
3531. Goodman, John m 6/15/50 Jane Jennison, both of Utica, in New Hartford; Rev. Paddock (9-6/18)
3532. Goodrich, Ansel (Maj. Gen.), about 38, d 7/15/19 in Owego, Broome Co. (8-8/4)
3533. Goodrich, David, 95, (a Rev. pensioner) d 4/13/50 at his home in New Berlin (9-4/20)
3534. Goodrich, Edmund C. m 9/6/49 Harriet E. Curtis, dau of Charles C. of Sauquoit, in Willow Vale; Rev. John Waugh (9-9/8)
3535. Goodrich, Edwin W. of Milwaukee, Wisc m 10/28/46 Mary S. Robinson, dau of James C., Esq. of PennYan in P. Y.; Rev. James Richards (6-11/6)
3536. Goodrich, George m 11/3/36 Ann Larray, both of Geneva; Richard Hogarth, Esq. (6-12/7)
3537. Goodrich, Harman, merchant, of Albion m 5/1/32 Lydia Shepard of Aurora in A; Rev. Hoising (6-5/9) (marr in Aurora)
3538. Goodrich, John, 1, only s of Rev. J. T., d 9/16/42 in Oxford (Oxford Times, 9/21)
3539. Goodrich, Mary Ann (Mrs.) d in Victor (6-12/4/33)
3540. Goodrich, Phebe L. H. (Mrs.), 20, d 10/15/36 in Havana, NY (6-11/2)
3541. Goodsell, Henry, 22, d 1/14/24 in New Berlin (8-1/21)
3542. Goodsell, J. P. of Utica m 12/4/45 L. M. Smith of Durhamville in D; Rev. Theodore Spencer (9-12/6/45)
3543. Goodsell, Thomas of Utica m 11/7/49 Henrietta Lieber of Canajoharie in C; Rev. W. N. Sholl (9-11/13)
3544. Goodwin, Edwin W., 45, late editor of the Albany Patriot, d 9/13/45 in Ithaca (9-9/23)
3545. Goodwin, Ezra S. (Dr.), 33, d 10/9/33 in Lansing (6-10/23)
3546. Goodwin, John, 78, d 10/27/33 in Elmira (6-11/20)
3547. Goodwin, Phebe, 37, wf of Lyman D. formerly of Canaan, CT, d 1/10/48 in Westmoreland (9-1/19)
3548. Goodwin, S. H., Esq. of Havana, NY m 10/11/48 Julia Sweetland of Elmira in E; Rev. H. N. Seaver (5-10/13)
3549. Goodwin, Samuel m 10/8/46 Rebekah Bacon in Waterville; Rev. D. Gridley. All of W (9-10/10)
3550. Goodwin, Stephen A. m 6/9/35 Frances M. Dibble in Auburn (6-6/17)
3551. Goodyear, Joseph (Capt.), 61, d 4/11/33 in Genoa, Cay. Co. (6-4/24)
3552. Gookins, Cyrens Dwight, inf s of Seymour, d (in Penn Yan?) (6-9/2/35)
3553. Goold, Gardner m 12/29/34 Lodemis A. Peck in West Bloomfield; Rev. Goff) (6-2/11/35)
3554. Gorden, Henry, 58, d 11/19/46 in Oxford (9-11/28 and 12/17)
3555. Gordon, Charles, 50, formerly of Geneva and bro of E. H. Gordon, d 4/13/30 in NYC (6-4/21)
3556. Gordon, George W., 22, s of late Charles, d 4/8/32 in NYC (6-4/11)
3557. Gordon, Henry, 49, d 6/21/20 in Oxford (8-6/28)
3558. Gordon, J. Wright, Esq. m 5/6/34 Mary Hudson, dau of Dr. D. Wright, in Geneva; Rev. Dr. Mason. All of G (6-5/7)
3559. Gordon, James H., 22, d 5/14/45 in Oxford (Oxford Republican, 5/22)
3560. Gordon, John H. (Capt.), formerly of Geneva, m 4/9/33 Lydia E. Moore in Opelousas, LA (6-5/22)
3561. Gordon, Peter (Deacon), 87, father of Elijah, d 2/8/35 in Geneva (b in NJ; in NJ early in the Rev. War a capt. of militia but later apptd. Ass't. Quartermaster General ; repeatedly elected to NJ state legislature; was speaker of the Assembly and state treas.; was also postmaster of Trenton, NY)
3562. Gordon, Samuel C., Esq. of Lyons m Mrs. Elizabeth Denny of Sodus in S (6-1/4/32)
3563. Gordon, William W., merchant, of Jacksonville, Morgan Co., IL m 10/7/30 Delia M. Williams of Palmyra in P (6-10/13)
3564. Gorham, Nathaniel, Esq., 63, d 10/22/26 in Canandaigua (son of Nathaniel, Esq. of Charlestown, MA who was a pres. of the Congress under the Articles of Confederation and who with Oliver Phelps, Esq. purchased from Mass. the western portion of NY (Phelps Gorham Tract) (9-10/31) (the deceased had settled near Canandaigua in 1789)

3565. Goslee, Ann Schuyler, 85, relict of late Mathew, Esq., d 4/31/50 in
Coburne, Canada (deceased b Albany, NY) (9-5/15)
3566. Goslin, Pratt F. m Sarah H. Wrily in Waterloo (6-3/10/30)
3567. Goss, Hiram m 12/7/30 Fanny Herrick in Geneva; C. Shekell, Esq. All of
Geneva (6-12/29)
3568. Gottry, John of Lodi m 3/13/49 Widow Colman, 60, in Hector (double
ceremony - see m of Hiram Cosmon) (9-4/6)
3569. Goudelet, Alfred, Esq. of Boston m 1/22/49 Harriet H. Chase, dau of
Col. Paul of Brattleboro, VT, in B; Rev. Mott (9-1/26)
3570. Gould, Augustus G., 28, a student "in the Theological Seminary",
d 11/7/49 in Auburn (9-11/12)
3571. Gould, Edward O. m 1/11/44 Mary Johnson, dau of Col. John H., in
Syracuse; Rev. Gregory. All of S (9-1/20)
3572. Gould, Edwin of Auburn m 4/3/31 Mary Phillips of Skaneateles (6-4/20)
3573. Gould, James F. of St. Simmons, GA m 10/18/36 Charlotte Ann Livingston,
oldest dau of Gen. T., in Clinton, NY (3-10/19)
3574. Gould, Philip N. m Eliza Miller in Tioga (6-6/8/31)
3575. Gould, Sophronia (Miss), 25, d in PennYan (6-10/6/30)
3576. Gould, William, 73, of the firm of Law Booksellers, Gould, Banks, and
Gould d 1/20/46 in Albany (9-1/23)
3577. Goulden, Maria Louisa, 8 mo, dau of George and Emily, d 10/4/50 in Elmira
(5-10/25)
3578. Goulden, Mark m 3/27/50 Harriet Lounsberry; Rev. P. H. Fowler. All of
Elmira (5-3/29)
3579. Goundry, Elizabeth (Mrs.), 77, mother of Gen. George of Geneva, d 7/24/30
in Milo (6-8/4)
3580. Goundry, George (Gen.), 49, d 11/8/35 at his home on Main Street in
Geneva (b in Wicliff, North of England; emigrated to this country
"in early youth"; for many years employed at the Pulteney Estate Land
Office; formerly pres.of the Board of Trustees of Geneva) (6-11/11)
3581. Goundry, Margaret, 33, consort of Gen. George, d 4/16/30 in Geneva
(6-4/21)
3582. Goundry, Thomas, 14, s and only surviving member of the family of the
late Gen. George Goundry, d 9/1/36 in Geneva (6-9/7)
3583. Gowan, James m 7/20/36 Helen Webster in Canandaigua (6-7/20)
3584. Gower, William m Catharine Walters in Schenectady (6-11/17/30)
3585. Graham, George m 1/26/43 Ann Eliza Andrews in Jasper; Rev. T. W. Duncan
(4-2/22)
3586. Graham, J. S. (Dr.) of York, NY m Anne Markel, dau of George of Romulus,
in R; Rev. Barton (6-9/1/30)
3587. Graham, James m 7/19/36 Aurilla Flynn, both of Spring Port, Cay. Co., in
Seneca Falls (6-7/27)
3588. Graham, John, 34, "chief engineer of motive power on the Corning and
Blossburg R.R.", d 9/15/41 in Corning (4-9/22)
3589. Graham, Joseph E. m 3/18/45 Caroline Hecox, dau of Obediah, Esq., in
New Hartford; Rev. J. Waugh (9-3/25)
3590. Graham, Stephen m 10/29/46 Sarah Sixbury; Rev. Shepard (9-10/31)
3591. Graham, William of Oswego m 1/23/31 Angeline Beach of Conquest in C (6-2/9)
3592. Graham, William, 32, d in Oakland (6-3/9/31)
3593. Graham, William, 56, d 9/20/34 in Geneva (6-10/1)
3594. Granger, _____ (Mrs.), over 90, d 5/14/50 in Martinsburgh (9-5/25)
3595. Granger, Cornelia, 29, wf of Frederick, Esq. and dau of Jeremiah V. R. of
Utica (V. R. perhaps Van Rensselaer), d 12/25/23 in Canandaigua
(9-1/6/24)
3596. Granger, Elvira, 27, wf of Otis P., Esq., d 10/14/36 in Morrisville
(3-10/26)
3597. Granger, Franklin, 17, s of Daniel, Esq., d in Woodhull (4-5/24/48)
3598. Granger, Lydia, 87, (wf of a Rev. soldier not named) d 7/28/45 in Steuben
(9-8/13)
3599. Granger, Mary D., 42, wf of Otis P., Esq., d 2/3/49 in Morrisville
(9-2/12)
3600. Granmer, _____ m 1/5/35 Eliza Hill (in W. Bloomfield?) (6-2/11)
3601. Grannis, Annette S., 12, oldest dau of Cephas, d 11/24/26 in Utica
(9-12/5)
3602. Grannis, Cyrus, 55, of Utica d 8/15/42 in Utica (9-8/17)

3603. Grannis, Frances L., 18 mo, dau of Cyrus, d in Utica (9-4/25/26)
3604. Grannis, Frederick Ossias, 5, oldest s of Timothy O. and Julia A.,
    d 11/5/50 in Utica (funeral from his father's home, 304 Genesee St.)
    (9-11/6)
3605. Grant, Caroline, 37, consort of Capt. George of Chittenango, d 8/12/32
    in Chittenango (3-8/14)
3606. Grant, Franklin W. of Auburn m 11/5/46 Sarah Ann Dias of Throopsville
    in T; Rev. J. M. Austin (1-11/30)
3607. Grantt, James, 44, late foreman of the Charlotte Gazette, d 12/12/21
    in Charleston City (SC?) (member of Meth. Ch.) (surv by wf) (8-12/19)
3608. Grason, Henry, Esq., 2nd s of Hon. William J., m 1/16/45 Cornelia
    Brantley, 3rd dau of Rev. Dr. Brantley, in Charleston, SC; Rev.
    William T. Brantley (9-1/29)
3609. Graves, Charles G. of Jordan, NY m 9/11/50 Harriet P. Ormsbee, dau of
    Jacob, formerly of Baldwinsville, in Syracuse; Rev. I. S. Bingham
    (1-9/26)
3610. Graves, Dela m 2/2/31 Mary Ann Howard in Havana, NY (6-2/16)
3611. Graves, Edward H. of Northampton, MA m 2/5/49 Clarissa Ingore, dau of J.
    of Utica, at Warehouse Point, CT; Rev. B. H. Bates (9-2/13)
3612. Graves, George S. of Benton m 1/18/38 Jane Page of Seneca in S (6-1/24)
3613. Graves, James A. m 1/6/36 Jane M. Curtis in Waterloo (6-1/27)
3614. Graves, Jesse of Oxford m 5/8/17 Nancy Fairchild of Hartwick in H; Rev.
    John Smith (8-5/14)
3615. Graves, Lodowick, 20, d 5/26/29 in Oxford (b in Preston but worked as a
    clerk in the store of Ira Willcox in Oxford (8-6/3)
3616. Graves, Mary Jane, 10, dau of Henry and Caroline, d 5/29/47 in Boonville
    (9-6/7)
3617. Graves, N. D. (Rev.) of New York Mills m 9/2/45 Cornelia H. Bradish, 2nd
    dau of Clark, Esq., in Floyd; Rev. Scovill (9-9/4)
3618. Graves, N. F., Esq. of NYC m 11/23/45 Catharine Breese of Sconondoa in S;
    Rev. Nichols (9-12/9)
3619. Graves, Ransford D. m 12/10/33 Mary Ann Stone in Canandaigua (6-12/25)
3620. Graves, Roxa Rena (Mrs.), 87, (consort of a Rev. soldier not named),
    one of the earliest settlers in Rome, NY, d 11/4/48 in Rome
    (possibly the Rev. soldier is Julius of Mass. - BLWT 36748) (9-11/11)
3621. Graves, Sarah, 34, wf of J. O., Esq. and dau of Abner Barlow of Geneva,
    d 1/1/36 in Detroit, MI (6-1/27)
3622. Graves, Sophia (Mrs.), 29, d 12/14/33 in Le Roy (6-1/1/34)
3623. Gray, Alonzo, 37, of Sauquoit d 6/24/49 in New London, Ont. Co. (9-6/28)
3624. Gray, Calvin S. m 1/7/36 Eleanor M. Thomas; Rev. Abeel. All of Geneva
    (6-1/13)
3625. Gray, Cyrus M. of Oxford m 11/23/50 Derinda Lincoln of Elmira; Rev. G. M.
    Spratt (5-11/29)
3626. Gray, Daniel m 11/19/35 Lydia Myrtle in Wheeler (6-12/2)
3627. Gray, David, 69, d 6/15/47 in Deerfield (9-6/16)
3628. Gray, David F. of Buffalo m Louisa Hurd, dau of Gen. J. N. M. of Albany,
    in A; Rev. Kip (9-7/27/46)
3629. Gray, George, 22, d 1/9/48 in Boston (had completed soph. yr. at Harvard
    U. and was on his way to spend the vacation with his relatives and
    friends in Sauquoit, NY)(funeral from the Presby. Ch., (9-1/24)
3630. Gray, Henry, 1, s of Joshua, d 10/2/33 in Geneva (6-10/9)
3631. Gray, John m 1/20/33 Clarissa Coe in Geneva (6-1/30)
3632. Gray, John F. (Hon.) of Ringwood, IL m 7/12/49 Mary White, only dau of
    James, Esq., in Whitesboro, NY; Rev. Shortwell (9-7/13)
3633. Gray, John K., Esq. m 10/18/48 Catherine S. Weaver, both of Deerfield, at
    Deerfield Corners; Rev. William H. Spencer (9-10/23)
3634. Gray, Luther S. m 9/24/48 Elizabeth Winneur, both of New Hartford, in New
    H.; Rev. H. R. Clarke (9-9/29)
3635. Gray, M. M. m 4/23/45 Emily Townsend in Sauquoit; Rev. Dana. All of
    Sauquoit (9-5/8)
3636. Gray, W. B., 61, d 1/6/50 in Utica (funeral from his late home on Charlotte
    St.) (9-1/8)
3637. Gray, William B., Esq.,48, s of late Hon. William, d 7/20/31 in Boston
    (6-8/24)
3638. Gray, William S., 38, d 6/8/49 in Ridgebury, PA (5-6/22)

3639. Greek, Samuel m 8/24/33 Harriet Barrett in Wheeler (6-9/18)
3640. Greeley, Arthur Young, 15, only s of Horace and Mary Y. C., d 7/12/49 in NYC "of the prevailing epidemic" (9-7/17)
3641. Greeley, Zaccheus, 92, father of Horace Greeley, Esq., editor of the New York Tribune, d 6/16/46 in Londonderry, NH (9-7/20)
3642. Green, Alfred (Col.) of Cincinnatus m 10/27/42 Mary S. Hovey of Upper Lisle in U. L.; Rev. Litchfield (2-11/9)
3643. Green, Caleb of Greenville, Greene Co., m 2/17/31 Ann Eliza Winans of Chatham in C (6-3/23)
3644. Green, Celinda, 13; Matilda Ann, 2; La Fayette, 8 mo - children of John of Howard, NY - were all buried within one week (scarlet fever) (6-7/3/33)
3645. Green, Gardiner m 6/27/50 Mary R. Adams, both of Norwich, CT, in NYC; Pres. Nott of Union College (9-6/29)
3646. Green, Garner, about 50, of Constantia, d 9/4/47 at the home of his bro, Henry Green, in Van Buren (1-9/8)
3647. Green, George H., 22, of Rushville, NY (a recent grad of Hamilton Col.) d 4/9/50 in Raymond, Mississippi (consumption) (9-5/18)
3648. Green, H. G., only s of Capt. H., d 5/8/44 in Utica (funeral at the home of Mr. H. Greenman, 14 Seneca St.) (9-5/9)
3649. Green, Helen, 8, only ch of Capt. William H. and Cornelia M., d 5/22/49 at the Bleecker Street House in Utica (9-5/24)
3650. Green, Henry, Esq., secretary of the Utica Insurance Co., m Mary Clark, both of Utica; Rev. Anthon (sic) (9-4/25/26)
3651. Green, John, 30, d in Canandaigua (6-8/4/30)
3652. Green, John, 60, d 9/6/47 in New Hartford (9-9/13)
3653. Green, John R., merchant, m 3/14/31 Elizabeth Simmons, dau of Capt. Abraham, in Phelps; Rev. Strong. All of Phelps (6-3/23)
3654. Green, Lester (Dr.), 53, d 2/6/49 in Utica (25 yrs a physician in Utica) (9-2/21)
3655. Green, Nelson, 20, s of Philip of Troy, d 3/4/26 (9-3/7)
3656. Green, R. M., Esq. of Durhamville m 8/20/50 Hellen L. Barnes of Utica at Trinity Ch., Utica; Rev. P. A. Proal, D.D. (9-8/30)
3657. Green, Robert F. of New Hartford m 11/16/48 Helen M. Wallace, dau of Robert of Yorkville, in Y; Rev. John Fullonton (9-11/21)
3658. Green, Rowland, 81, d 11/13/46 at the home of his son in South Trenton, NY (9-11/17)
3659. Green, Samuel F. m 12/20/33 Harriet McDougall, dau of Peter, in Syracuse; Rev. Adams. All of Syracuse (3-12/24)
3660. Green, Samuel W., Esq. of Albany m 2/14/47 Cornelia S. Wilcox, dau of Reuben, Jr. of Whitesboro, in W; Pres. Green officiating (double ceremony - see marr of J. Delos Underwood) (9-3/20)
3661. Green, Thomas m 2/5/33 Laura Ames in Venice, NY (6-3/6)
3662. Green, Washington A., 9 wks, s of John R., d 4/30/34 in Phelps (6-5/7)
3663. Green, William Wilkinson, Esq., oldest s of William, Esq. of Oriskany, d "in the latter end of October last on his passage from Calcutta to New York" (9-3/8/25)
3664. Green, William Wilkinson, Esq. of Geneva m 4/3/44 Maria Johnson, oldest dau of James, Esq. of Liverpool, NY at the Ascension Ch. in Liverpool; Rev. Samuel Goodale (9-4/17)
3665. Greene, David T., Esq., formerly of NYC, d 9/5/26 in Turin, NY (9-9/12)
3666. Greenleaf, Daniel T. of Calhoun m 11/17/31 Rebecca Peterson of Fayette in seneca Fails; Rev. Lane (6-11/30)
3667. Greenman, William of Hamilton m 8/27/50 Helen Scott of Brookfield in B; Rev. D. Skinner (9-9/7)
3668. Greenwood, George B. m 7/28/42 Roena Crawford in Sullivan (3-8/10)
3669. Greenwood, Henry m 3/25/44 Elizabeth Cornelia Hayward of Lenox in Chittenango; J. French, Esq. (3-3/27)
3670. Greenwood, William (Dr.), 38, d 2/12/31 in Ontario, NY (6-3/23)
3671. Gregg, George C. of Elmira m 1/30/49 Hannah M. Barr of Addison in A; Rev. Dannells (5-2/2)
3672. Gregory, Goodsell m 4/13/36 Maria Taylor in Canandaigua (6-4/27)
3673. Gregory, Henry (Rev.) of Owasco Flats m 9/10/30 Elizabeth Post of Geneva at Trinity Ch., Geneva; Rev. Dr. Mason (6-9/15)
3674. Gregory, Lewis m 6/7/29 Polly Wescott in Norwich; Elder Otis (7-6/17)

3675. Gregory, Matthew (Lt.), 91. d 6/4/48 in Albany (an original member of the Cincinnati) (9-6/7)
3676. Gregory, Odell of Owego m 9/13/48 Hannah A. Hinkley of Norwich in N (9-9/18)
3677. Gregory, Stephen of Cooperstown m 7/5/20 Phebe Fairchild of Oxford in O; Rev. Bush (8-7/12)
3678. Grems, Peter of Westernville m 4/13/48 Amanda A. Gambia of New York Mills in N. Y. M.; Rev. Dr. Paddock (9-4/20)
3679. Grenolds, Stephen M. m 6/10/32 Martha Schuyler, both of Chittenango, in Cazenovia; Elder Peck (3-6/12)
3680. Gresham, George of NYC m 6/25/34 Margaret R. Heslop of Seneca in S; Rev. N. F. Bruce (6-7/2)
3681. Greves, Jane Louisa, inf dau of John, d 9/27/36 in Geneva (6-9/28)
3682. Greves, John, Esq., editor and proprietor of the Skaneateles Columbian, m 7/4/33 Ann Merrell of Utica in U (6-7/17)
3683. Greves, Mary Ann De Mott, 11 mo, dau of Dr. J. P. Greves of Marshall, Mich. Terr., d 8/23/35 at Summer Hill, Cay. Co., NY (6-9/9)
3684. Greves, Thomas, 62, d 6/13/33 in Skaneateles (6-7/3)
3685. Grey, B. W., Esq. of Springfield m 4/9/49 Clarissa P. Dean of Utica in U; Rev. P. A. Proal (9-4/11)
3686. Grey, Edward m 7/30/50 Lucy A. Taggart; Rev. White. All of Baldwinsville (1-8/8)
3687. Grey, Moses, 60, d 10/13/45 in Sauquoit (9-10/24)
3688. Gridley, A. D. (Rev.) m 4/17/44 Ellen M. Bristol, dau of George, Esq., in Clinton; Rev. Dr. North of Hamilton College(9-4/22)
3689. Gridley, Asahel, 76, d 11/10/33 in Vermont (6-12/11)
3690. Gridley, Catharine S., 16, oldest dau of Hon. Philo, d 4/2/44 in Utica (9-4/3)
3691. Gridley, Charles E., 21, (son of Orrin, dec'd), late of Clinton, d 2/6/50 in Paris, France (9-3/2)
3692. Gridley, Cyprian (Rev.) of the Louisiana Conference m 5/18/47 Eliza Janette Morrill of Westmoreland, NY in New Orleans, LA; Rev. John Piper (9-6/1)
3693. Gridley, Eli m 11/15/40 Eliza Roue, both of Caton, in C; Rev. Charles B. Davis (4-11/22)
3694. Gridley, John m 3/12/50 Betsey Parsons at the home of Horace Spaulding in Van Buren; Rev. John W. Coop. All of V. B. (1-3/14)
3695. Gridley, Juliet, 37, relict of late Rev. Wayne Gridley, d 8/30/48 at the home of her father, Dr. S. Hastings in Clinton (9-9/4)
3696. Gridley, Orrin, 60, d 4/3/47 at his home in Clinton (9-4/7)
3697. Gridley, Salina (Mrs.), 63, d 8/8/49 at the home of her son, G. A. Gridley, in Elmira (5-8/17)
3698. Gridley, Wayne (Rev.), 35, formerly pastor of the Cong'l. Ch. in Clinton and recently cashier of the Kirkland Bank, d 11/23/46 in Clinton (9-11/30 and 12/2)
3699. Grieve, Alexander m 10/22/36 Mary Robson, both of Seneca; Richard Hogarth, Esq. (6-12/7)
3700. Grieve, James, merchant, of Genoa, NY m 11/25/34 Harriet McPherson, dau of Capt. William of Seneca; Rev. Phelps (6-11/26)
3701. Grieves, Nancy P. (Miss), 18, dau of widow Minerva P., d 9/20/34 in Skaneateles (6-10/8)
3702. Griffin, Ann, 39, wf of Richard J. and youngest dau of David Buel of Killingworth, CT, d 11/18/25 in Manchester (surv by husband and children) (9-12/6)
3703. Griffin, Charles N. m 1/20/49 Huldah Jane Stone in Kirkland; Rev. Raymond. All of Kirkland (9-1/23)
3704. Griffin, Charles W., 27, "head of a large business establishment"and s of late Joel, Esq. of Sauquoit, d 9/6/46 in NYC (funeral service by Messrs. Comfort and Hartwell) (surv by wife, children, and a widowed mother) (9-9/9)
3705. Griffin, Daniel m 1/20/36 Sophia Haight, both of Fayetteville, in Hamilton; Rev. Knap (3-2/2)
3706. Griffin, George, Jr. m 5/20/45 Mary A. Cooke, dau of late Apollos, Esq., in Catskill; Rev. G. N. Judd (9-6/6)
3707. Griffin, John m Clarissa Slaughter in Potter (6-8/10/36)
3708. Griffin, Kirkland m 3/14/48 Charlotte Nichols in Sauquoit; Rev. Giddings. All of Sauquoit (9-3/23)

3709. Griffing, Edmund D., 25, d 8/31/30 in NYC (9-9/7)
3710. Griffith, Joseph, 30, d 3/5/47 in Van Buren (1-3/10)
3711. Griffith, Thomas R., a clerk in the post office, d 5/23/34 in Lyons
       (6-6/4)
3712. Griffith, Walter S. of Rochester, s of Maj. Griffith P. Griffith, m 8/1/31
       Elizabeth S. Norton, dau of Col. Heman Norton, in NYC; Rev. Erskine
       Mason (6-8/10)
3713. Griffith, William of Collinsville m 6/25/50 Elizabeth Jones of NYC in
       Utica; Rev. J. Stanford Holme (9-6/27)
3714. Griffiths, George, 18, d 12/8/45 in NYC (9-12/20)
3715. Griffiths, Isaac d 7/2/50 in Utica (consumption) (funeral from his late
       home on Varick St. above Fayette St.) (9-7/3)
3716. Griffiths, John of Utica m 8/17/46 Jane Griffin of Vienna, NY in V;
       Rev. Kirk (9-8/21)
3717. Griffiths, John R., 85, d 2/20/44 in Floyd (9-3/2)
3718. Griffiths, Lewis m 11/9/45 Ellen Williams, both of NYC, in NYC (9-11/18)
3719. Griggs, Daniel, 29, d 9/8/26 in Paris, NY (9-10/10)
3720. Griggs, Ichabod, 42, d 11/30/43 in Hamilton (3-12/13)
3721. Grimes, Joseph, 32, of Rome, NY d 7/11/48 at the home of his mother in
       Upper New York Mills (9-7/18)
3722. Grimler, A. (Mr.) d "at an advanced age" in Bloomfield (6-3/9/31)
3723. Grinewood, Robert (Rev.) m 4/21/31 Lydia Handley, formerly of Seneca, in
       Perry (6-4/27)
3724. Grippen, George W. of Lysander m Elizabeth B. Brown of Syracuse at the
       Exchange in Baldwinsville; Rev. B. Phillips (1-4/19/48)
3725. Griswald, Simeon, 66, d 10/1/31 in Galen (6-10/19)
3726. Griswold, Charlotte, 43, wf of Dr. Horace and dau of Andrew Taylor,
       d 11/28/42 in Binghamton (2-12/21)
3727. Griswold, David m 11/20/36 Mary Ann Delano in Canandaigua (6-11/30)
3728. Griswold, Edmund K., 19, d 10/2/43 in New Orleans, LA (son of Samuel B.,
       formerly of the U.S. Army, and grand-son of late Arthur Breese, Esq.,
       one of the earliest settlers in Utica, NY) (deceased left Utica 2 years
       ago to seek his fortune in New Orleans) (9-10/25)
3729. Griswold, Elias, Esq. of St. Mary's m 5/1/45 Elizabeth M. Clark, dau of
       Samuel, Esq., at Glenwood Plantation, Nassau Co., Florida; Rev. J. A.
       Shanklin (9-5/15)
3730. Griswold, H. S. m 12/15/42 Eliza Youmans of Windsor in W; Rev. Gilbert
       (2-12/21)
3731. Griswold, Henry H., 18, s of Chester, d 10/24/26 in Utica (9-11/7)
3732. Griswold, John m Sally Beckwith in Southport (6-8/28 and 9/11/33)
3733. Griswold, Levi (Rev.) of Vienna, NY m 4/16/32 Hannah Thomas of Skaneateles
       in S; Rev. Brace (6-4/25)
3734. Griswold, Mary, 74, widow of late Hon. Gaylord Griswold and mother of Mrs.
       Benjamin F. Brooks of Utica, d 8/2/44 at her home in Herkimer
       (9-8/7 and 8/8/44)
3735. Griswold, Matthew of Peoria, IL m 11/8/49 Charlotte Young, dau of
       Hon. Samuel, in Ballston; Rev. Dr. Geer (9-11/13)
3736. Griswold, Miranda (Mrs.), 48, formerly of Lockport, d in Niles, MI
       (6-1/8/34)
3737. Griswold, S. Collins of Auburn m 7/8/45 Ellen Bacon, dau of late John H.
       of Auburn, in A; Rev. Austin (9-7/12)
3738. Griswold, Walter (Dr.) of Northgage m 4/6/48 Eliza Ann Thomson of
       Newport; Elder William Brown (9-4/11)
3739. Grsiwold, Whiting (Rev.), rector of St. John's Ch., St. Louis, MO,
       m 9/12/43 Ellen Maria Howell, dau of B. B., Esq. of NYC, at St. Luke's
       Ch., NYC; Rev. J. M. Forbes (9-9/16)
3740. Groesbeck, Peter of Chittenango m 2/12/33 Hannah Van Valkenburgh, dau of
       Richard of Sullivan; Rev. A. Yates (3-2/19)
3741. Grogan, Patrick, 45, d 8/16/48 in Utica (funeral from his late home,
       59 Catharine St.) (9-8/17)
3742. Groom, Bradley m 2/21/49 Lucinda Snyder, both of Veteran, in Horseheads;
       Homer Ryant, Esq. (5-3/2)
3743. Grosh, A. B., 49, wf of Rev. A. B. formerly of Utica and mother-in-law
       of John G. Jones of Utica, d 11/10/49 in Reading, PA (9-11/15)

3744. Grosvenor, Charles P. of Rome, NY m 12/5/48 Abby R. Lyon, dau of Samuel, Esq. of New Hartford, in New H.; Rev. Dolphus Skinner (9-12/6)
3745. Grosvenor, Cyrus P. D., 24, s of Rev. C. P. of Utica, d 6/5/49 in Southbridge, MA (9-6/13)
3746. Grosvenor, Francis D. (Col.) of Utica m 2/22/47 Jane M. Allyn, dau of late Henry of Coventry, in Whitesboro; Rev. B. W. Wicker, rector of St. John's Ch. (9-2/26)
3747. Grosvenor, Harriet, 8 mo, youngest dau of Ebenezer O. and Mary Ann, d 3/6/34 in Chittenango (3-3/11)
3748. Grosvenor, Harriet, 59, wid of late Oliver C., d 1/13/50 in Rome, NY (9-1/16)
3749. Grosvenor, Julia, 50, wf of Francis D., d 3/16/46 in Utica (funeral from the Reformed Dutch Ch.) (9-3/17)
3750. Grosvenor, Thomas (Col.), 80, d in Pomfret, CT (fought as a Lieut. at Bunker Hill)(9-8/23/25)
3751. Grove, De Witt C. of Utica m 10/20/45 Caroline L. Pratt of Hamilton in Whitewater, WI; Rev. Kinney (9-11/3)
3752. Grove, John, 59, d 9/3/32 in Sullivan (an early resident there; his funeral in the home of Mr. J. Bellinger (3-9/4)
3753. Grove, Robert m 4/17/37 Isabella McIntyre in Seneca; Rev. Gaylord (6-4/19)
3754. Grover, Anna Maria, 14, dau of Hiram and Keziah, d 5/3/49 in Southport (5-5/11)
3755. Grover, Thankful (Miss), 20, d 4/11/34 in Knowlesville (consumption) (6-4/23)
3756. Grover, William A., Esq. m 4/14/47 Electa E. J. Gurley, dau of late Henry, in Bridgewater; Rev. A. D. Gridley (9-4/16)
3757. Groves, Absalom L., 66, d 6/16/44 in Bridgewater (b in Broomfield, MA but settled in Bridgewater by 1801)(9-6/28)
3758. Groves, Benjamin m 12/27/30 Mary Ann Becker in Geneva; C. Shekell, Esq. (6-12/29)
3759. Groves, Mary (Mrs.), 61, d 6/3/50 in Clay (1-6/13)
3760. Groves, Rebecca, 28, dau of Clinton, d 3/8/44 in Clinton (9-3/26)
3761. Grow, Jacob d 8/15/18 in Norwich (member Bapt. Ch.; surv by wf "and a numerous family") (7-8/27)
3762. Guernsey, Peter B., Jr., Esq., 30, d 4/15/29 at his home in Norwich (was sequentially in the West Indies, southern U. S., and Europe for his health in 1818 and later; surv by wf and 2 inf ch) (funeral sermon at Presby. Ch. by Rev. L. S. Rexford) (7-4/22)
3763. Guest, Joseph m 7/7/36 Lydia Ann Curtis in Lyons (6-7/13)
3764. Guild, Henry A., printer, m 7/27 Harriet A. Conner in Little Falls; H. Thomas, Esq. All of Little Falls (9-7/29)
3765. Guiteau, Francis (Dr.), 59, d 4/18/25 in Whitesboro (9-4/26)
3766. Guiteau, Kenneth M. m 8/20/50 Jane S. Childs; Rev. George Boardman. All of Cazenovia (9-8/24)
3767. Guiteau, Luther (Dr.), 72, d 2/12/50 in Trenton, NY (b in Mass. but arrived in the Trenton area as a young man)(9-2/15)
3768. Guiwits (sic), Betsey E. (Miss), dau of Isaac, d 8/3/49 at the home of her father in Boonville (age 19 at time of her death) ("Herkimer and Little Falls papers please copy") (9-8/8)
3769. Gulick, Margaret, 35, wf of John, d 12/17/34 in Pulteney (6-12/24)
3770. Gunn, Amos B of East Bloomfield m 5/5/31 W. O. Whittlesey, dau of A., Esq., in Ogden (6-6/8)
3771. Gunn, Moses, 73, (a Rev. soldier) d 11/17/30 in Bloomfield (9-12/7)
3772. Gunn, Susan M. (Mrs.), 24, d in Auburn (6-1/26/31)
3773. Gurley, Royal (Dr.) m 7/13/32 Sila A. Draper in Palmyra (6-7/25)
3774. Gurnee, W. S. of Chicago, IL m 6/24/39 Mary M. Coe, dau of Col. M. D., in Romulus; Rev. Barton (6-6/26)
3775. Gurney, Abraham m 10/16/31 Eliza Paddock, both of Sodus, in Williamson (6-11/9)
3776. Gurnsey, Sylvanus (Dr.), 48, formerly principal of the Academy of Onondaga Hollow, d 6/19/33 in Collinsville, IL (cholera) (6-9/25)
3777. Guthrie, Polly, 43, consort of John, d 4/30/21 in Sherburne Village (7-5/2)
3778. Guthrie, Samuel (Dr.) d 10/19/48 near Sacketts Harbor (shared the first procuring of chloroform with Soubeiran of France and Lerbig of Germany) (9-11/18)

3779. Guthrie, William, Esq. of Chemung m 1/17/50 Sarah Ann Rhynders of Caton
       in C; Rev. C. Wheeler (5-1/25)
3780. Haber(?), John (Dr.), 63, d 7/14/43 in Franklin (Oxford Republican, 8/3)
3781. Hackett, Charles of Oxford m 3/3/44 Abigal Ann Hawley of Otego in O;
       Rev. Daniels (Oxford Republican, 3/7)
3782. Hackett, Charles m 5/6/47 Elizabeth Hughes in Utica; Rev. George Leeds.
       All of Utica (9-5/21)
3783. Hackett, Emily, 5 d 9/21/42 and Louisa, 3, d 9/25/42 inUtica (both daus
       of John, late of Leicestershire, England (9-10/6)
3784. Hackett, John of Syracuse m 12/25/46 Sarah Jennison of Utica at Trinity
       Ch. in Utica; Rev. P. A. Proal (9-12/29)
3785. Hackett, John K. m 6/5/45 Laura J. Hall, only dau of late Capt. Edward,
       U.S.M.C., in NYC; Rev. Dr. Higbie (9-6/11)
3786. Hackett, Samuel R. m 11/10/33 Louisa H. Roberson, both of Waterloo, in
       Seneca Falls (6-11/20)
3787. Hackett, William m 3/18/45 Jane Wiley at the Reformed Dutch Ch. in Utica;
       Rev. Charles Wiley. All of Utica (9-3/19)
3788. Hackley, Maria, 57, wid of Abel, d 4/18/49 in Elmira (member of Meth.
       Episc. Ch. about 20 yrs) (5-4/20)
3789. Hackley, Philo M., Esq., formerly and for many years of Herkimer Co.,
       d "recently" at his home in Mich. (9-11/10/49)
3790. Hackley, Roxana, dau of Dr. John of Bridgewater, d 11/18/45 in Albany
       (9-11/21)
3791. Haddock, Hiram m 12/21/48 AnnS. Webb, both of Checkersville, in Utica; Rev.
       D. G. Corey (9-1/1/49)
3792. Hadley, Edward B. of Syracuse m 7/3/39 Mary Lowndsbury of Onondaga Hollow
       in Chittenango; Rev. J. Abell (3-7/10)
3793. Haeger(?), Orrin of Oneida Co. m 10/29/48 Abigal Otile(?) of Rochester
       in R; James Jones, Esq. (9-11/1)
3794. Hahar, Henry m 4/18/44 Adeline Burkard, both of Rome, NY, in R; Rev. M.
       Wetzell (9-4/27)
2795. Hagar, Reuben m 9/17/43 Lefy Ann Kimball in Binghamton; H. Collier, Esq.
       (2-9/20)
3796. Hague, Samuel of Westmoreland m 11/25/50 Mary Hoesin(?) of Utica in U;
       Rev. William Wyatt (9-12/12)
3797. Hahn, J. Jacob, 63, father of John M. Hahn of Utica, d 3/18/47 in
       Bondorf, Kingdom Wurtemberg, Germany (9-9/9)
3798. Hahn. William Alfred, 18 mo, youngest s of John M. and Susan M., d 8/21/47
       in Utica (9-9/9)
3799. Haight, George m 6/19/33 Jane E. Swartout in Seneca Falls (6-7/10)
3800. Haight, Irene, inf dau of Reuben, d 10/15/31 in Chittenango (3-10/18)
3801. Haight, James Thompson, 9 mo, s of John W. and Julia A., d 12/4/41 in
       Auburn (3-12/22)
3802. Haight, John A., merchant, of Benton, NY m "Miss Page" of Salisbury, CT
       in S (6-7/2/34)
3803. Haight, John W. of Auburn m 9/17/38 Julia A. Comstock of Chittenango in
       C; Rev. C. Paddock (3-9/19)
3804. Haight, Sarah, wf of Gen. Samuel, d 11/10/30 in Angelica (6-12/1)
3805. Hailey(?), Theodore(?) A. m 5/9/50 Julia W. Strong, gr-dau of Benjamin,
       Esq.; Rev. A. A. Wood (9-5/15)
3806. Hakes, Jeremiah S., late of Palmyra, m Maria Smith in Prattsburgh
       (6-3/17/30)
3807. Hale, Charles R. of Floyd m 3/14/49 Elizabeth E. Hinman, dau of late
       Livingston Hinman of Stittsville, in S; Rev. Walter R. Long of
       Whitesboro (9-3/17)
3808. Hale, Daniel, 64, d 4/12/44 in Florence (9-4/27)
3809. Hale, Enoch (Dr.), 58, for many years an officer of the Mass. Medical Soc.
       and of the American Academy of Arts and Sciences (a visiting physician
       at the Mass. Hopital) d 11/12/48 in Boston (9-11/17)
3810. Hale, Joseph Orlando, 1, s of Israel of Norwich, d 4/17/23 (7-4/23)
3811. Hall, Adaline, 33, wf of Albro, d 6/10/44 in Sullivan (funeral at
       Bethel Ch.) (3-6/12)
3812. Hall, Albro m 1/25/31 Adaline Blakesley, both of Sullivan, in S; Rev.
       Huntington (9-2/1)
3813. Hall, Amasa, 82, d 10/30 in Marion (grandfather of Mr. S. R. Hall of
       Geneva) (6-11/9)

3814. Hall, Betsey, 15, dau of Asahel and Chloe, d in Fenner (3-8/3/42)
3815. Hall, Caroline, 6 mo, dau of David S., d 8/9/32 in Geneva (6-8/15)
3816. Hall, Edward, Sr., about 90, a native of England, d 2/19/31 at the home
   of his son, Edward, Esq. in Seneca (30 yrs a resident of S) (6-2/23)
3817. Hall, Elisha, about 70 (one of the earliest settlers in the region)
   d 9/24/39 in Sullivan (3-10/2)
3818. Hall, Ephraim (Rev.), 32, d in Cherry Valley (6-3/9/31)
3819. Hall, George m 11/15/49 "Miss Earls", both of Van Buren, in V. B.; Rev.
   Byron Alden (1-11/29)
3820. Hall, George L. of Burdett m 10/23/50 Ellen M. Cleaver, dau of Amos of
   Marcy, in M; Rev. H. Dickinson (9-10/25)
3821. Hall, George S. m Jennette Leonard in Auburn (6-2/23/31)
3822. Hall, Gordon Maitland, 4, s of Rev. G. Hall of the American Mission at
   Bombay, India, d 10/25/25 on passage on the "Ann" with his mother
   and second child of the family en route to America for their health
   (9-12/6)
3823. Hall, Harvey W. m 3/20/42 Lucy J. Miller in Sullivan; J. French, Esq.
   (3-3/23)
3824. Hall, Helen Maria, inf dau of Albro and Adaline, d 8/25/40 in Sullivan
   (3-8/26)
3825. Hall, Heman of Geneva m 9/5/31 Elvira C. Taft OF West Bloomfield in W. B.
   (6-9/14)
3826. Hall, Henry d 10/6/34 in Seneca (b in England) (6-10/8)
3827. Hall, Hiram of Sullivan m 12/14/37 Maria Haight of Fenner in F; Rev.
   Coryell of Cazenovia (3-12/20)
3828. Hall, Hopkins P. m 6/12/44 Maria T. Wilmarth, both of NYC, in NYC; Rev.
   Fisher (9-6/17)
3829. Hall, J. B. of NYC, formerly of Utica, m 6/20/48 Adaline Sackett, dau of
   Adrian, Esq., in Providence, RI; Rev. S. Osgood (9-6/27)
3830. Hall, Janet Scott, 6, dau of D. S.,d 4/25/34 in Geneva (6-4/30)
3831. Hall, John m 9/25/35 Elmira Hall in Painted Post (6-10/14)
3832. Hall, John H., Jr. of Vernon m 6/5/44 Julia A. Gillispie in Clinton; Rev.
   B. Hawley (9-6/12)
3833. Hall, Joseph m Hannah Aldrich in Fayette; Rev. Phelps (6-3/3/30)
3834. Hall, Joseph m Edify Wolcott in Jersey, NY (6-6/9/30)
3835. Hall, Joseph, 84, d 10/9/36 at his home in Fayette (6-10/19)
3836. Hall, Joseph C. of the U.S. Marine Corps d 5/17/33 on board U.S. Ship
   "Franklin" in Brooklyn (6-5/22)
3837. Hall, Lewis of Detroit, MI m 5/9/33 Margaret Edwards, dau of Rev. Thomas,
   in NYC; Rev. Dr. Baldwin (6-5/22)
3838. Hall, Lydia, 42, wf of Isaac, d 7/10/26 in Manlius (in 1816 she was one
   of the eight persons who formed the Trinity Presby. Ch. in Manlius)
   (9-7/18)
3839. Hall, Margaret Ann, formerly of Baldwinsville, wf of R. H., d 7/1/49
   in St. Louis (MO?) (1-7/19)
3840. Hall, Maria, 27, sister of Francis Hall of Elmira, d 10/21/48 in Ellington,
   CT (5-10/27)
3841. Hall, Mary, 54, wf of Moses, d 11/28/35 in Geneva (6-12/9)
3842. Hall, Mary (Mrs.) d 4/15/36 in Wayne (6-4/27)
3843. Hall, Moses (Deacon) m 4/13/37 Phebe Whitaker of Benton in B (6-4/19)
3844. Hall, Pamelia, 46, wf of Amasa and mother of Mr. S. R. Hall of Geneva,
   d 5/4/32 in Marion (consumption) (6-5/16)
3845. Hall, Persis, 20, wf of Amos, d 4/3/19 in Oxford (8-4/14)
3846. Hall, Ralph W., s of Rev. Richard of Castine, m 3/25/49 Harriet A. Buck
   of Lenox, NY at the Oneida Mission (1-4/5)
3847. Hall, Rebecca, 30, wf of Bailey Hall, d in Canandaigua (6-6/2/30)
3848. Hall, Robert (Sir), Naval Commissioner on the Lakes, d in Kingston, Canada
   (8-3/11/18)
3849. Hall, Samuel of Elmira m12/22/42 Eliza D. Dickinson, dau of Hon. A. B.
   of Hornby, in H; Rev Coryell (4-1/4/43)
3850. Hall, Samuel of Utica, about 50, d at the Fox River House in Ottawa, IL
   (had lived there but a short time and was planning to return to Utica)
   (9-3/30/50)
3851. Hall, Sanford R. of Geneva m 2/1/31 Almira R. Higgins, dau of Zadock of
   Marion,in M (6-2/16)

3852. Hall, Sarah, 59, wf of Francis, proprietor of the New York Advertiser, d 9/5/46 at the British American Hotel in Kingston, Canada (she and her husband were on their annual tour proceeding from Montreal to the Falls) (9-9/10 and 6-9/25)

3853. Hall, Sarah, 21, wf of Francis and dau of Miles Covell, Esq., d 8/4/48 in Elmira (her sister, not named, had recently died) (4-8/16)

3854. Hall, Seth F., 30, d 2/2/49 in Baldwinsville (consumption) (1-2/8)

3855. Hall, Thomas m Eliza Curtiss in West Bloomfield (6-8/4/30)

3856. Hall, Warren, 74, d 11/19/46 in Norwich (9-12/17)

3857. Hall, William, 45, d 3/28/50 in Baldwinsville (consumption) (1-3/28)

3858. Hall, William R., 14, of Lenox d 2/12/31 at Hamilton College (6-3/9)

3859. Halladay, Freeman m 11/28/48 Mary McWhorter in Elmira; Rev. G. M. Spratt. All of Elmira (5-12/1)

3860. Halleck, Nancy E., 39, wf of Abraham H., Esq., d 12/10/48 in Sangerfield (9-12/18)

3861. Hallett, William P., Esq., for many years clerk of the Supreme Court, d 10/23/48 in NYC (typhus) (9-10/26)

3862. Halleck, Parker, 76, late of Clinton, d 3/20/48 in North Norwich (9-4/7)

3863. Hallet, Jacob W., Esq., a customs officer, d "recently" in NYC (formerly of Pulteneyville) (6-2/8/37)

3864. Hallock, Amelia A., wf of R. T. late of Utica, d 6/9/48 in Milton (9-6/15)

3865. Hallock, David S. of Utica m 8/21/45 Martha S. Ketcham, dau of John of Jericho, L. I., NY, in J (a Quaker marr.) (9-8/27)

3866. Hallock, David S., 26, of the firm of White and Hallock d 1/28/46 at the home of his bro, N. Hallock, in Utica (9-1/30)

3867. Hallock, Jeremiah (Rev.), 69, d 6/23/26 in Canton, CT (9-7/18)

3868. Hallock,William Edward, inf s of James and Mary, d 10/13 in Utica (funeral from his parents' home, 8 Elizabeth St.) (9-10/15/42)

3869. Halloway, Henry of Ovid m 1/8/33 Lydia Johnson of Benton in B (6-1/30)

3870. Halsey, Edward B. m 10/30/34 Elizabeth Dey, dau of Pierson Dey; Rev. A. W. Platt (bride and groom both of Fayette) (6-11/5)

3871. Halsey, Silas, 89, father of Hon. Jehiel H., d 11/19/32 at his home in Ovid (b in Suffolk Co., L.I., NY where he practiced physic for several years previous to the Rev. War; being a Whig he fled to CT at the outbreak of that war; after the war served as sheriff of Suffolk Co. until 1792 when he moved to Ovid; elected to state assembly and senate as well as to Congress) (6-11/28)

3872. Halsey, William, merchant, m 5/13/39 Mary E. Butler of Ithaca in I; Rev. Hoes (6-5/22)

3873. Halsey, William of Mexico, NY m 9/15/48 Susan J. Halsey, dau of Hezekiah, in Westmoreland; Rev. F. A. Spencer (1-10/4) (marr. dated 9/13 in 9-9/27/48)

3874. Halsted, David m 5/9/31 Lydia Andrews, dau of Chester, Esq., in Bethel; Rev. Witters (6-5/18)

3875. Halsted, Robert (Dr.), 79, d in Elizabethtown, NJ (9-12/6/25)

3876. Ham, John, about 60, d 11/24/46 in Baldwinsville (1-12/7)

3877. Ham, Mary (Mrs.) d 12/3/46 in Van Buren (1-12/7)

3878. Hamblin, L. W. m 5/28/35 Jennette Clemons, both of Geneva; Rev. J. W. French (6-6/3)

3879. Hamilton, _____, 55, wf of E., d 4/6/26 in Utica (9-4/11)

3880. Hamilton, Alexander of Smithville m 12/7/42 Malissa Bartle of Oxford; Rev. Lyman Sperry (Oxford Republican, 12/9)

3881. Hamilton, Alexander of Madison Co. m Chloe C. Hodges of Herkimer Co. aboard the steamer "Great Western" on Lake Huron; Rev. R. Smith of Waterford, NY (9-6/9/45)

2882. Hamilton, Elijah m 12/16/32 Eliza Worden in Sullivan; J. French, Esq. (3-12/25)

3883. Hamilton, Isaac m 3/4/30 Lucy Cline; Rev. Adams. All of Smithville (8-3/10)

3884. Hamilton, John of Rochester m 7/7/47 Ann D. Slocum of Bushnell's Basin; D. Gillmore, Esq. (9-7/9)

3885. Hamilton, Lewis (Rev.) m 2/1/43 Mary E. Balcom, dau of Lyman, in Campbell; Rev. Dr. Graves (bride and groom of Campbell) (4-2/8)

3886. Hamilton, Orville of Hartford, CT m 9/5/44 Elizabeth Lyon of Utica at Grace Ch., Utica; Rev. Leeds (9-9/7)
3887. Hamilton, Samuel of Rochester m 11/14/33 Sarah Carpenter in Lancaster (6-11/27)
3888. Hamilton, Schuyler (Capt.), aide-de-camp of Gen. Scott, m 4/3/50 Cornelia E. Ray, dau of Robert, Esq., at Fitz Ray Place, NYC; Rev. Dr. Taylor (9-4/6)
3889. Hamilton, William of Landgate, VT m 6/27/42 Phebe Whitney of Westmoreland, NY in Manchester; Rev. Charles Simmons (9-6/28)
3890. Hamlet, Benjamin m 1/1/38 Mary Salisbury, both of Nelson, in Clay; Elder Morgan of Salina (3-1/3)
3891. Hamlin, Albert F., 1, youngest s of William D. and Catharine E., d 12/29/50 in Utica (funeral at his father's home on Fayette St.) (9-12/31)
3892. Hemlin, Ebenezer, 52, formerly of West Springfield, MA, d 1/9/31 at his home in West Bloomfield, NY (6-1/19)
3893. Hamlin, Frederick W. of Holland Patent, NY m 2/19/46 Mary Ann White, dau of Broughton White, Esq. of Remsen; Rev. J. F. Scovill (9-2/28)
3894. Hamlin, Harriet M., 13, dau of William D., d 1/7/46 in Utica (funeral from her father's home, 63 Fayette St.)
3895. Hamlin, J. D. of West Bloomfield m 1/26/32 Caroline Bennett of Richmond in R (6-2/8)
3896. Hamlin, Lucy (Miss), 36, d 11/15/33 in Campbell (6-12/4)
3897. Hamlin, W. D. of Utica m 12/19/43 Catharine E. Roberts, dau of Samuel, Esq. of Sharon, CT, in S; Rev. Fitch Reed (9-1/5/44)
3898. Hammond, A. T. G. m 9/6/33 Angeline F. Shelden in Warsaw, NY (6-10/23)
3899. Hammond, Dennis of Junius m 3/18/34 Sarah Opdyke of Fayette in F; Rev. Phelps (6-3/19)
3900. Hammond, Eliza Ann, 19, wf of Dennis, d in Junius (6-5/5/30)
3901. Hammond, James m 7/25/33 Catharine Grady, both of Penn Yan, in Benton; Rev. Goff (6-7/31)
3902. Hammond, John S. m 10/17/32 Emily M. Pratt, both of Manchester, in M (6-11/7)
3903. Hammond, Judah, 75, formerly judge of the Marine Court, d 11/30/49 in NYC (9-12/6)
3904. Hammond, Lazarus, Esq. of Hammondsport m 5/8/32 Mary Prentice of Bath in B; Rev. I. W. Platt (6-5/16)
3905. Hammond, Lebeus, 72, d in Southport (one of the earliest settlers on the Chemung River) (9-8/8/26)
3906. Hammond, Loranda, 65, consort of late Stephen Fairfield, d 4/13/50 at ___?___ Flats (9-4/23)
3907. Hammond, M. D. of Liverpool, NY m 9/24/47 Lydia Ann Fancher of Baldwinsville at the Farmer's Exchange, Syracuse; R. W. Woolworth, Esq. (1-9/29)
3908. Hammond, Mary Jane, 33, wf of Rev. H. L. Hammond, pastor of the Cong'l. Ch. of Morrisville, d 6/25/49 in M (she dau of Dr. N. B. Mead of Smyrna) (9-7/6)
3909. Hammond, Nancy, wid of William R., d 4/16/23 in Norwich (surv by 4 ch) (7-4/23)
3910. Hammond, Oliver of Reading m 12/27/35 Rhoda Thompson of Starkey in S (6-1/6/36)
3911. Hammond, Thomas, 39, worsted manufacturer from Bradford, Yorkshire, England, d 1/28/48 in Utica (9-2/4)
3912. Hammond, Wells S., Esq., 32, s of J. D. of Cherry Valley, d 1/28/49 in Albany (9-1/31/49)
3913. Hammond, William R., 38, s of Samuel, d 12/2/20 in Norwich (surv by wf and 4 ch) (7-12/6)
3914. Hand, Ichabod, 63, d 3/13/46 in Vernon (formerly of Guilford, CT and spent his early life "on the sea"; lived in Verona and Vernon, NY past 30 yrs; was landlord of the Vernon Stage House, (9-3/19)
3915. Hand, Marcus C. of Syracuse m 9/18/50 Malvina S. McHuron in Lysander; Rev. A. Finney (double ceremony - see m of Rufus D. Pettit) (1-9/26)
3916. Hand, R. C. (Rev.) of Gouverneur m 8/22/26 Agnes Hunsdon of Shoreham, VT in S; Rev. Prof. Hough (double ceremony - see m of Dr. M. Y. Farrell) (9-10/3)
3917. Handfield, William, 58, d 8/8/39 in Geneva (6-8/14)
3918. Handley, Jonathan of Perry m Ruth Caward, dau of George, in Seneca; Rev. P. Hollett (6-11/20/33

3919. Handy, Edward P., 28, d 3/21/42 in Utica (funeral from his late home on Fayette St.) (9-3/24)
3920. Handy, Elisha U. of Utica m 5/24/45 Mary Tanner of Annsville in Whitestown (9-6/10)
3921. Handy, Truman P. of Buffalo m 3/7/32 Harriet N. Hall, dau of Col. Abraham B., in Geneva; Rev. E. Phelps (6-3/14)
3922. Handy, Truman Hall, 2, only ch of T. D., Esq., d 9/14/35 in Cleveland, OH (6-9/30)
3923. Hankins, Catharine (Mrs.), 109, d in Braynsville, VA (6-11/13/33)
3924. Hanks, Cyrus D., formerly of NYC, m 7/28/36 Caroline Cobleigh of Waterloo in Geneva; Rev. Abeel (6-8/10)
3925. Hanna, Althai, 42, wf of John, d 3/16/36 in Manchester (6-3/30)
3926. Hanna, Lorentes of Athens, PA m 4/1/50 Mahatable Denman of Factoryville; Rev. E. W. Dickinson (5-4/12)
3927. Hannahs, ____, 41, wf of William, d 1/15/43 in Richfield (9-1/16)
3928. Hannahs, William C. of NYC m 2/14/48 Delia Cushman, dau of David, Esq. of Exeter, in E; Rev. William B. Curtiss (9-2/17)
3929. Hanney, Samuel, esq., secretary of Mutual Life Insurance Co. of NYC and formerly of the firm of Collins and Hanney, publishers, d 8/20/49 in Cumberland, MD (9-8/23)
3930. Hansill(?), William of Junius m 10/23/46 Margaret Jones of Gorham in Junius (6-10/30)
3931. Hanson, Alexander C., a U.S. Senator and formerly editor of the Federal Republican, d 4/23/19 in Baltimore, MD (8-5/19)
3932. Hanson, George C. m 10/7/46 Mary Breese, dau of Hon. Sidney, U.S. Senator, in Carlisle, PA (11/21/46)
3933. Hanson, Henry, 34, d in Black Rock (6-3/2/31)
3934. Hanstis(?), Mary, wf of George C. and dau of Seymour Breese of Illinois, d 7/14/48 in Washington (D.C.?) (9-7/19)
3935. Hara, ____ (Dr.) m 5/31/49 Mrs. Caroline Barnum, wid of late Maj. E. R. Barnum of the U.S. Army, in Oswego (9-6/8)
3936. Hard, Patrick H. (Dr.) of Oswego m 9/28/29 Eliza M. Randall, dau of John, Esq. of Norwich, in N; Rev. Rexford (7-9/30)
3937. Hardin, Thomas m 8/22/35 Elmina McHenry in Southport (6-9/2)
3938. Harding, Leonard of Lowville m 1/24/48 Caroline H. Hale of Newburgh in Utica; Rev. Dr. Proal (9-1/27)
3939. Hare, George Emler (Rev.) m Elizabeth Catherine Hobart, dau of Rt. Rev. Bishop Hobart, at St. John's Chapel in NYC; Rev. Dr. Berrian (6-7/7/30)
3940. Harger, ____, 65, wf of Noah N., Esq., d 5/20/50 in West Martinsburgh (9-5/25)
3941. Harger, George of Jefferson Co., about 20, d 7/30/46 at the American Hotel in Utica (9-8/4)
3942. Hargin, Charles S. R. m Mary C. Ellis in Onondaga (6-2/9/31)
3943. Harington, A. G. of Turin m 11/14/48 L. J. Hutchinson of Deerfield in D; R. Harter, Esq. (9-11/17)
3944. Harkinson, Samuel of Utica m 11/20/50 Jane S. Hayden, dau of Hon. Chester of Ballston, in B; Rev. Steele (9-11/27)
3945. Harkness, Mary Caroline, 22, d 1/8/31 in Springport (6-2/2)
3946. Harmon, Luther m 12/31/35 Jane Van Duzen in Phelps (6-1/13/36)
3947. Harned, Benjamin m 12/24/42 Eliza P. Willard, dau of Rufus of Chittenango, in Niles, MI; Rev. Boughton. All, except Rufus, of Niles (3-1/25/43)
       Harney, A. H. (Capt.). See Barney, A. H.
3948. Haro, John O. m 4/21/47 Elizabeth Spertell in Utica; Rev. Stokes. All of Utica (9-4/23)
3949. Harper, Alonzo of Tyre m Julia Ann Cromwell (6-3/2/31)
3950. Harper, Bobert (sic), Esq., 95, d 4/15/25 in Colesville (8-4/27)
3951. Harper, G. C., Esq. m 11/18/45 Emily Smith, both of Whitestown, at the City Hotel in Utica; Rev. D. W. Bristol (9-11/26)
3952. Harper, James (Hon.) of NYC m 6/18/49 Julia A. Thorne, dau of late Samuel, Jr. of Hempstead, L. I., NY, in Hempstead; Rev. Valentine Buck (9-6/21)
       Harper, Robert. See Harper, Bobert.
3953. Harper, Samuel, 65, d 3/23/41 in Sullivan ("said he had relations near Binghamton") (3-3/24)
       Harrington. See also Herrington.

3954. Harrington, _____)Mr.) m 9/14/43 Sarah J. Marshall in Siloam (town of Smithfield)(3-10/11)

3955. Harrington, Daniel B., 38, formerly of Chittenango, d 7/22/39 at Hanford's Landing, Monroe Co. (3-8/7)

3956. Harrington, J. S. of Utica m 3/2/45 Henrietta Riddle, dau of Robert, Esq. of Chittenango, in C; Rev. James Abell (3-7/5)

3957. Harrington, Martha, 14 mo, youngest ch of Jere S. and H. S., d 9/4/48 in Utica (9-9/5)

3958. Harrington, Perez D. m 11/26/40 Charlotte Riddle, dau of Robert. Esq., in Sullivan; Rev. James Abell (3-12/2) (double ceremony - see m of Benjamin Jenkins)

3959. Harrington, Peter Y. m 8/6/37 Emeline Thompson, both of Geneva; R. Hogarth, Esq. (6-8/9)

3960. Harrington, Phoebe, wf of William, d 3/22/49 in Utica (funeral from his late home on Columbia St., West Utica)(9-3/23)

3961. Harrington, William m 9/10/50 Ann Eliza Beksley(?); Rev. E. Francis (9-9/12)

3962. Harris, Andrus F., 25, d 4/1/36 in East Bloomfield (6-4/13)

3963. Harris, Ann Catharine, 21, wf of S. T., d in Utica (consumption) (9-4/23/46)

3964. Harris, Fayette m 6/9/35 Margery Forbes, both of Clocksville, in Fayetteville; A. Neely, Esq. (3-6/16)

3965. Harris, George (Capt.) m 2/8/49 Lucy Smith, both of Westmoreland, in W; Rev. J. Bicknall (1-2/15)

3966. Harris, George Washington, Esq. m 11/23/30 Mrs. Lucinda Morgan, wf of Capt. William, in Batavia; Hon. Simeon Cumings, a judge of Genesee Co. courts (6-12/8)

3967. Harris, Hamilton, Esq. m 5/20/50 Lucy Rogers, dau of Nathaniel, Esq. of Albany, in Buffalo; Rev. Dr. Chester (9-5/24)

3968. Harris, Ira (Hon.) m 8/1/48 Pauline Hathbone; Rev. Dr. Welch. All of Albany (9-8/3)

3969. Harris, James m 10/30/35 Mrs. Jane Miller, both of Fayette; Rev. J. F. McLaren (6-12/9)

3970. Harris, Jeremiah m 11/20/44 Martha Ann Coonradt in Rome, NY; Rev. Haynes (9-11/30)

3971. Harris, John m 2/8/32 Mary Ann Thomas, both of Ovid (6-2/22)

3972. Harris, Joseph (Rev.), 46, minister of the Free Church, Niagara, d 5/17/50 in Hamilton, Canada (was 5 yrs a Bapt. missionary in Ceylon [Bapt. Mission Soc]; returned to England, 1842, and came to Canada in 1845) (9-6/1)

3973. Harris, Joseph H. m 6/18/50 Mary Walbridge Cooley, dau of Maj. L. J., in Elmira; Rev. A. Hull (5-6/21)

3974. Harris, Lewis B., Esq. m 6/18/46 Jane Wilcox, dau of late Dr. Wilcox of East Bloomfield, NY, at the home of Dr. Birdsall near Houston, TX (6-8/14)

3975. Harris, Martha, 101, wid of David, Esq. formerly of Providence, RI and gr-dau of Hon. Joseph Jenks, formerly Gov. of RI, d in Bridgeport, CT (9-7/25/26)

3976. Harris, Robert Henry, inf s of Thomas and Almira, d 3/16/46 in Utica (9-3/19)

3977. Harrison, Charles R. of Waterloo m 10/15/46 Mary I. Opdyke, dau of Jeremiah, Esq. of Lafayette, in Waterloo; Rev. Gridley (6-10/16)

3978. Harrison, George Washington, 42, machinist, d 8/11/49 in Elmira (5-8/17)

3979. Harrison, Henry m 8/6/33 Catharine Hartman in Dansville (6-8/21)

3980. Harrison, Lucy B., 49, consort of William, d 8/8/38 in Cazenovia (3-8/15)

3981. Harrison, Robert m 5/7/43 Mary A. Button, both of Chittenango, in C; Rev. Blakslee (3-7/5)

3982. Harrower, Levi B., s of B. Harrower, Esq. of Lindley, d 1/20/50 in Jacksonville where he had gone for his health (Jacksonville, Florida) (4-5/1)

3983. Harrower, Mary D. (Mrs.), 22, d 3/19/50 in Big Flats (2 months after the death of her husband, L. B., and two years after her marriage) (4-4/17)

3984. Hart, David, 54, of Hopewell d 8/22/34 in Ypsilanti, MI (6-9/17)

3985. Hart, George W. of NYC m 12/27/42 Julia M. Haight of Rochester at the home of Fletcher M., Esq. in Rochester; Prof. C. Dewey (9-1/6/43)
3986. Hart, Henry R. of Utica m 6/8/48 Mary W. Dodd of Cincinnati in C; Rt. Rev. Bishop McIlvane (9-6/14)   (that is Cincinnati, OH)
3987. Hart, Henry S. m 6/16/50 Mary Eliza Clark at the home of E. T. Throop Martin in Willowbrook; Rev. H. S. Dickson. All of Utica (9-6/21)
3988. Hart, Hiram G. of Clinton m 2/5/45 Adeline Lucy Wilson, dau of William, Esq. of Bloomington, IL, at the home of C. V. Godard, Esq. in Canastota; Rev. W. H. Cooper (9-2/10)
3989. Hart, James S. of Utica m 11/20/47 Harriet K. Gardner, dau of late Richard, Esq. of Salem, in Springfield, MA; Rev. H. W. Lee (9-11/25)
3990. Hart, John P. of Utica m 1/2/48 Frances M. Chipman of Summerville, Cay. Co., in Utica; Rev. D. G. Corey (9-1/6)
3991. Hart, Lyman, about 26, formerly of Geneva, d 8/13/34 in Monroe, Mich. Terr. (6-8/27)
3992. Hart, Roswell, Esq. of Rochester m 6/27/49 Deete E. Phelon, dau of Joseph, Esq. of Cherry Valley, in C. V.; Rev. Ransom (9-7/3)
3993. Hart, Samuel m 1/8/45 Mary Potter in Utica; Rev. Bristol. All of Utica (9-1/10)
3994. Hartehorn(?), Jacob, 74, d 2/30/50 in Lebanon (one of the first settlers in Madison Co.) (9-3/8)
3995. Harter, Moses of Tyrone m 8/17/31 Mary Ann Fowler of Fayette in Waterloo; Rev. A. D. Lane (6-8/31)
3996. Hartness, James, 73, d 4/15/48 at North Gage, town of Deerfield ("Albany papers please copy") (9-4/20)
3997. Hartson, Abel of Ohio m 9/20/33 Roxana Ashley in Caroline (6-10/16)
3998. Hartwell, Sarah Ann, 32, wf of Rev. Joseph, d 7/21/48 in Utica (funeral at the State St. Meth. Episc. Ch.) (9-7/22)
3999. Harvey, _____, inf s of A. Harvey, one of the editors of the Ontario Repository, d 8/9/32 in Canandaigua (6-8/22)
4000. Harvey, Asahel, one of the publishers of the Ontario Repository, m 6/30/31 Eveline Hall, dau of John, formerly of Canandaigua, in Zanesville, OH (6-7/13)
4001. Harvey, Asahel, 36, one of the proprietors of the Ontario Repository, formerly of Surrey, NH, d 7/17/35 in Canandaigua (6-7/22)
4002. Harvey, Benjamin, 111 years old, (a Rev. soldier) d 3/18/47 in Frankfort (9-3/19)
4003. Harvey, Giles, 24, formerly of Elmira, d 4/6/34 in Troy (6-5/14)
4004. Harvey, Robert, 32, wagon-maker, d 1/9/30 at the jail in Geneva (was committed the previous June 23 and was to have had his trial "at the recent circuit in this county"; died of consumption; his parents are "believed to reside in Enfield, Tompkins County, NY") (6-1/20)
4005. Harvey, Robert Williams, 19 mo, s of Uriah, d 9/19/32 in Geneva (6-10/10)
4006. Harvey, Selden, 68, d 6/3/50 at Frankfort Hill ((-6/17)
4007. Harvey, Sylvanus (Dr.) d 8/8/42 in Utica (9-8/9)
4008. Hasbrouck, Lewis, Esq. of Ogdensburg m 6/13/50 Sarah Maria Hasbrouck, dau of Levi of New Paltz; Rev. Slingerland (9-6/22)
4009. Haseham(?), Stephen, 67, d 7/24/50 in Vernon (9-7/26)
4010. Haseltine, William Henry, 3, youngest ch of Ebenezer and Maria, d 6/16/44 in Canaseraga (scarlet fever) (3-6/26)
4011. Haskell, Arnold S. of Junius m 12/29/50 Emily L. Freeman of Oriskany in O; George Graham, Esq. (9-12/31)
4012. Haskell, Minerva S., 26, wf of John H. and dau of late Robert W. Oliphant, Esq. of North Granville, d 10/11/43 in Baltimore, MD (consumption) (3-10/18)
4013. Haskell, Timothy C. m 12/13/33 Fanny Payne in Rochester (6-12/25)
4014. Haslehurst, _____, 47, wf of Richard, d 2/18/48 in Middleville (9-2/22)
4015. Haslehurst, James of NYC m 6/20/50 Irene R. Walcott, dau of Benjamin S., Esq. of New York Mills, in NYM; Rev. R. R. Kirk (9-6/22)
4016. Hasson, Ann, 52, wf of John, d 9/12/49 in Buffalo (9-9/15)
4017. Hastings, _____, 8 mo, s of E. P.. Esq., d 3/4/32 in Dtroit, MI (6-3/28)
4018. Hastings, Catharine Maria, 21, wf of S. A., merchant, of Hammondsport and dau of H. Meech, Esq. of Albany, d 1/21/35 in Hammondsport (6-1/28)
4019. Hastings, Charles m 12/9/48 Lucinda Harrison, both of Corning, in C; Rev. H. Pattengill (4-12/20)

4020. Hastings, Clarissa, 63, wf of Oliver, d 4/5/31 at Bluff Point, Yates Co. (6-4/20)
4021 Hastings, Elizabeth, 48, wf of Horace, d 8/15/37 in Geneva (6-8/16)
4022. Hastings, Frances Amelia, inf dau of Charles, one of the publishers of the Western Recorder, d 9/17/25 in Utica (9-9/20)
4023. Hastings, Francis H. of Chicago, IL m 10/10/48 Amelia H. Gutt, dau of Hon. Daniel of Pompey at Pompey Hill; Rev. S. P. M. Hastings (9-10/14)
4024. Hastings, Frederick W., 21, s of Orlando, Esq. of Rochester, d 10/31/36 at the home of E. P. Hastings in Detroit, MI (6/11/23)
4025. Hastings, George, Esq. of Mount Morris m 9/19/32 Mary H. Seymour, dau of Norman of Rome, NY, in Albany, her residence place (6-10/16 and 11/7)
4026. Hastings, Henry D., 22, only ch of Eurotus P., d 1/25/50 in Detroit, MI (9-2/9)
4027. Hastings, Huldah, wf of Dr. Seth, d 9/21/50 in Clinton (9-9/24)
4028. Hastings, James B., 2, youngest s of Dr. Hastings, d 2/12/46 in Deerfield (9-2/13)
4029. Hastings, Mary, 66, consort of Timothy, d 10/7/32 in Wayne (6-11/7)
4030. Hastings, Mary, 37, wf of Gen. Hastings, Esq. and dau of Norman , formerly of Herkimer, d 3/25/45 at Mount Morris (9-4/11)
4031. Hastings, Mary Ann, 4, dau of Eurotus, Esq., d 7/23/37 in Geneva (6-7/26)
4032. Hastings, Oliver H. H. of Geneva m 10/25/36 Polly W. Inman of Cortland at Horseheads (6-11/2)
4033. Hastings, Samuel (Dr.) of Augusta m 3/2/26 Eliza Rowel of Paris, NY in P; Rev. Zachariah Paddock (9-3/7)
4034. Hastings, Samuel m 4/14/31 Abigail Gannon in Elmira (6-5/4)
4035. Hastings, Samuel A. (Capt.), merchant, of Hammondsport m 5/20/33 Catharine M. Meech, dau of Horace, formerly of Geneva, in Albany (6-5/29)
4036. Hastings, Seth (Dr.), 85, father of E. P., Esq., formerly of Geneva, d in Kirkland (6-5/12/30)
4037. Hastings, Theodore of East Cambridge, MA m 10/12/50 Signora Malinqui Valejio, dau of the founder of Valejio, San Francisco, CA, in San Francisco (9-12/7)
4038. Haswell, N. (Maj.) of Rhode Island m 2/16/46 Mrs. M. Wetmore, widow of Col. J. C.; Rev. Cole. All of Yorkville (9-2/19)
4039. Hatch, Charlotte, 20, wf of James L., d 3/19/42 in Chittenango (3-3/23)
4040. Hatch, Elizabeth (Mrs.), 73, d in Geneseo (6-9/11/33)
4041. Hatch, Elizabeth, 26, wf of Henry A. formerly of Hartford, CT, d 2/29/44 in Utica, NY (9-3/1)
4042. Hatch, H. D. m 6/13/49 Delia Maria Colvin, dau of late Zena H. of Lewiston and adopted dau of Dr. David S. Colvin, in Syracuse; Rev. Dr. Gregory (5-6/22)
4043. Hatch, Harvey, about 35, d 11/5/49 in Van Buren (1-11/15)
4044. Hatch, I. Thompson, Esq. of Buffalo m 3/20/33 Lydia Ann Powers, dau of late Gershom, Esq. of Auburn, in Palmyra (6-4/17)
4045. Hatch, James m 2/10/41 Charlotte Holbrook, both of Chittenango, in Fayetteville; Rev. Smitzer (3-2/17)
4046. Hatch, Thomas, 24, of Oxford d in New Troy, Luzerne Co., PA (8-10/14/29)
4047. Hatfield, Hyatt L. m 4/11/50 Elizabeth M. Knott in Utica; Rev. Charles Wiley. All of Utica (9-4/13)
4048. Hatfield, Richard, Esq., clerk of the court of sessions, d in NYC (6-7/24/33)
4049. Hathaway, Daniel P. m 4/14/35 Catharine McCarty, both of Varick, in Waterloo (6-4/22)
4050. Hathaway, George of Milo m Louisa McMath of Ovid (6-3/10/30)
4051. Hathaway, George A. m 3/13/33 Adaline Chase in Palmyra (6-4/3)
4052. Hathaway, Phebe M., about 25, wf of Asher and dau of Enos Smith formerly of Wallkill, Orange Co., d 11/8/33 in Varick (6-11/13)
4053. Hathaway, Samuel G. (Gen.) of Solon m 11/16/48 Catharine Saxton of Groton in G; Rev. Sacket (5-12/1)
4054. Hathaway, Simeon, 83, d 9/28/26 in Bennington, VT (fought in the Battle of Bennington in the Rev. War) (9-10/24)
4055. Hause, John m 12/30/35 Belinda Burtless (in Waterloo?) (6-1/27/36)
4056. Hausenfraits, Peter of De Witt m 7/4/47 S. A. Newcomb of Baldwinsville; Rev. Phillips (1-8/4)
4057. Haven, Catharine Garrison, 19 mo, dau of Philander B., d 3/20/45 in Sangerfield (9-4/8)

4058. Haven, Charles B. m 5/14/44 Susan Hurd in Poughkeepsie; Rev. A. R. Bartlett. All of Poughkeepsie (9-5/17)
4059. Haven, Henry, 76, d 4/1/44 in Rome, NY (a long-time resident there) (9-4/6)
4060. Haven, William H, Esq. m 3/5/46 Marilla Seymour, dau of late Salmon; Rev. Robert Fox. All of Westmoreland (9-3/9)
4061. Havens, Jesse, 66, d 2/27/37 in West Dresden (6-3/15)
4062. Havens, Obediah m 7/1/32 Prudence Goff in Geneva; Rev. Mandeville (6-7/4)
4063. Havens, Obediah, 31, d 7/13/33 in Geneva (6-7/17)
4064. Havens, William H., 25, d 4/30/29 at his father's home in Guilford (consumption) (funeral sermon by Rev. Bush of Oxford) (8-5/6)
4065. Haverling, _____ (Mr.), teller of the Steuben Co. Bank, d in Bath (6-1/21/35)
4066. Haviland Tertullus A. m 10/1/35 Betsey Rhodes in Galen; Rev. William McKoon (6-10/14)
4067. Hawes, Moses of Richfield m 10/25/27 Mary Cory, dau of Benjamin of Stratford, in S (8-11/2)
4068. Hawkes, Porter m 1/16/33 Sophia Prescott in Geneva; Rev. Phelps. All of Geneva (6-1/23)
4069. Hawkins, James of Boston, MA m 3/21/44 Jane Pratt of Rome, NY in R; Rev. Haynes (9-3/28)
4070. Hawkins, William Frederick, 36, d 5/7/43 at the home of his father, Darius, in Newport (9-5/19)
4071. Hawks, Abigail (Mrs.), 47, formerly of West Cambridge, MA, d 10/6/48 at the home of her sons, F. and A. Frost, in Kirkland (9-10/12)
4072. Hawks, Albert of Newark, NY m Sarah Watkins of Waterloo in W (6-3/28/32)
4073. Hawks, D. K., merchant, m 8/17/31 Deborah Pitts in Richmond (6-9/7)
4074. Hawks, Daniel of Rochester m 6/28/42 Mary Holland, dau of Ivory, Esq. of Richfield, in R; Rev. Hughes (9-6/29)
4075. Hawks, Joel P. m Eliza Norman in Phelps (6-3/10/30)
4076. Hawks, John (Dr.) m Laura Louisa Lathrop, dau of L. E., in Newark, NY (6-7/14/30)
4077. Hawks, Nelson P. of Elmira m 2/22/31 Hannah Crocker of Union, Broome Co., in Union (6-3/23)
4078. Hawley, Amos, 42, formerly of CT, d in NYC (6-2/18/35)
4079. Hawley, Carlos A. of East Bloomfield m 9/3/34 Emeline L. Rose in Canandaigua (6-9/17)
4080. Hawley, Cyrus Madison, merchant, of Penn Yan m 6/30/42 Cornelia Crocker, dau of Amos, Esq. of Hamilton, in H; Rev. Robert Fay (9-7/3)
4081. Hawley, Emily, 17, dau of Abijah, d 8/23/31 in Geneva (6-8/24)
4082. Hawley, Isabella (Mrs.), 64, d 1/14/33 in Canandaigua (6-2/6)
4083. Hawley, James M. m 3/2/42 Eunice Preston in Corning; Rev. S. M. Hopkins. All of Corning (4-3/9)
4084. Hawley, Janna (Mr.), 47, d in Binghamton (6-3/9/31)
4085. Hawley, Malinda, 34, wf of Silas and sister of Joseph Benedict, Esq., d 12/23/48 in Penn Yan (9-1/1/49)
4086. Hawley, Nelson G. of Rochester, formerly of NYC, m 9/7/35 Cornelia Bogart, dau of Cornelius of NYC, in NYC; Rev. William Jackson (6-9/16)
4087. Hawley, Reuben, 45, d 1/13/35 in Chittenango (3-1/20)
4088. Hawley, Richard N. m Prudence Hedges in Cameron (6-7/7/30)
4089. awley, Riggs, 74, d 10/17/48 in Augusta (9-10/24)
4090. Hawley, S. (Mrs.), 47, wf of Abijah, d 9/26/33 in Geneva (6-10/16)
4091. Hawley, William H. m 4/2/45 Elizabeth H. Jones, both of Utica, in U; Rev. H. N. Loring (9-4/5)
4092. Hawly, Elizabeth, 71, wf of Rev. Rufus, d in Farmington (9-8/2/25)
4093. Haws, Emeline C. (Miss) d 3/29/42 in Utica (funeral from her father's home on Bridge St.) (9-3/31)
4094. Haws, Sylvanus S. m 5/22/31 Louisa Hunt, both of Chittenango, in Woodstock (3-5/24)
4095. Hay, George (Hon.), district judge of the U.S. for the district of Virginia, d 9/18/30 in Richmond, VA (6-10/13)
4096. Hay, George D., Esq. of Vincennes, IN m 5/10/46 Harriet H. Axtell, youngest dau of late Rev. Axtell of Geneva, in Indianapols, IN (6-6/26)

112

4097. Hayden, Charles W. of NYC m 9/28/48 Cornelia C. Humphreys, dau of late
      Dr. H. of Utica, at Trinity Ch., Utica; Rev. Dr. Proal (9-9/30)
4098. Hayden, Henry, merchant, of Rome, NY m 4/6/46 Helen M. Humphreys, dau of
      Dr. E., at Trinity Ch., Utica; Rev. Dr. Proal (9-4/9)
4099. Hayden, J. (Lt.), U.S. Army, m 7/19/46 Sarah A. Pardee, dau of L., Esq.,
      in Oswego (9-7/20)
4100. Hayden, Martin F. m 12/15/42 Emily Gambie, both of New York Mills, in
      Utica; Rev. B. Hawley (9-12/19)
4101. Hayden, Moses, Esq., 44, Senator from the 8th District of NY, d 2/13/30
      in Albany (6-2/17)
4102. Hayes, Charles H. m 11/4/46 Harriet N. Van Lew; Rev. B. Parker. All of
      Geneva (6-11/6)
4103. Hayes, Eliza S., 31, wid of late Dr. Pliney Hayes and dau of Dr. Richard
      Wells, d 11/4/31 in Canandaigua (6-11/23)
4104. Hayes, George, 3 mo, only s of David and Elizabeth L., d 9/28/43 in
      Oxford (Oxford Republican, 10/12)
4105. Hayes, James E. of Hopewell m 12/3/33 Mary E. Flagler, dau of Rev. Flagler
      of Chapinville,in C (6-12/18)
4106. Hayes, James E. m 9/7/46 Julia Rogers in Geneva; Rev. T. T. Farrington
      (6-9/11)
4107. Hayes, Lyman, 45, d in Canandaigua (6-4/7/30)
4108. Hayes, Mary, wf of Rev. Joel, d 7/22/25 in South Hadley (9-8/16)
4109. Hayes, Mindwell (Mrs.), 72, d 4/11/24 in Guilford (8-4/14)
4110. Hayes, Pliney, Jr. (Dr.), 42, of Canandaigua d 7/30/31 "at the Medical
      Mansion in New York City" (6-8/10)
4111. Hayes, Pliney, 65, father of Dr. Pliney Hayes, Jr., d 8/2/31 in Bristol
      (6-8/10)
4112. Hayes, Solomon, 64, d 7/16/49 in Albany (messenger for the banks from
      Albany west) (9-7/18)
4113. Hayes, W. Baldwin of Gilboa m 4/22/45 Harriet Louisa Bradish, oldest dau
      of Clark Bradish, Esq. of Floyd, in F; Rev. N. Dwight Graves (9-4/26)
4114. Hayman, S. B. of the U.S. Army m 4/22/50 Mary Seymour Clark, dau of late
      Maj. Satterlee Clark, at Madison Barracks, Sackett's Harbor; Rev.
      Hill (9-4/27)
4115. Haynes, David m 11/15/49 Eliza P. Meigs in Jordan; Rev. Byron Alden
      (double ceremony - see m of Atchison Mellin) (1-11/29)
4116. Haynes, Jacob of Guilford m 6/9/44 Antonett Bennett of Unadilla; Rev. L.
      Sperry (Oxford Republican, 6/13)
4117. Haynes, Nathan, "an old inhabitant of Seneca", d 7/4/31 in S (6-7/6)
4118. Hays, J. Byron m 12/25/32 Sarah Antis in Canandaigua (6-1/2/33)
4119. Hays, William (Sgt.) of Utica d at Camp Jefferson, East Pascagoula,
      Mississippi (yellow fever) (9-11/23/48)
4120. Hayt, George of Ovid, NY m 8/24/36 Mary Ann Torrey of Ludlow, MA
      (6-8/31)
4121. Hayt, Herman, merchant, of the firm of Gaston, Hayt, and Field m 8/28/45
      Caroline V. Woodruff of Lowville; Rev. J. H. McIlvaine (9-8/29)
4122. Hayward, Anna (Mrs.), 83, d 4/21/50 at the home of her son Hartwell
      Hayward (9-5/9)
4123. Hayward, John, 32, d 7/1/33 in Palmyra (6-7/10)
4124. Hayward, Levi m 6/12/32 Minerva Owen of Phelps in Newark, NY (6-6/27)
4125. Hayward, W. P. of Geneva m 9/29/47 Louise Simmons, 2nd dau of John of
      Utica, in U; Rev. Dr. Proal (9-9/30)
4126. Haywood, Mary (Mrs.), 69, d 9/1/33 in Rochester (6-9/11)
4127. Haywood(?), Russell H., Esq. of Buffalo m 5/14/46 Hannah Sophia King,
      dau of late Hon. Cyrus of Saco, ME, at Trinity Ch., Geneva, NY; Rt. Rev.
      Bishop De Lancey (6-5/22)
4128. Hazard, Jason E. m 9/10/43 Catherine Walrath in Chittenango; Rev. T.
      Houson. All of C (3-9/13)
4129. Hazeltine, Ann, 38, wf of John, d 6/5/46 in Geneva (funeral from her late
      home in the Merrill Building on Water St.) (6-6/5)
4130. Hazzard, Brenton W. of Milo m 2/16/31 Harriet Brown of Jerusalem, NY
      in Penn Yan (6-2/23)
4131. Hazzard, Julia Ann (Mrs.), 29, d in Clyde (6-3/17/30)
4132. Head, Andrew m 10/5/48 Maria Adkins, both of Southport, at the Meth.
      Parsonage in Elmira; Rev. H. N. Seaver (5-10/6)

4133. Head, George of Candor m Zenette M. Smiley of Danby in Jacksonville
       (6-10/28/35)
4134. Head, O. S. (Mr.) m 8/30/46 Mary J. Treadwell, both of Southport, WI, in
       Paris, NY; Rev. J. G. Cordell (9-9/1)
4135. Hearsey, James H. of Cazenovia m 6/21/48 Cornelia A. Harris of Waterville
       in W (9-6/22)
4136. Heath, George, 22, d 1/24/50 (b in Casham, England "but lately of Utica,
       NY died the second day on board the steamer 'Canada' bound for England;
       buried in Halifax, Nova Scotia through the U.S. Consul's kindness")
       (9-2/14)
4137. Heath, Horace m 3/3/41 Mary Jane Wesley, both of Sullivan, in Chittenango;
       Rev. J. Abell (3-3/10)
4138. Heath, John m 5/21/43 Catharine Lansing, both of Fenner, in F; Rev. T.
       Houston (3-7/5)
4139. Heath, Orra, 65, wf of Timothy, d 5/11/50 in Adamas Center (weighed
       450 lbs. at time of death) (9-5/24)
4140. Heath, Polly, 54, consort of John, d 8/27/42 in Sullivan (3-8/31)
4141. Heath, Richard K. (Gen.) d in Baltimore (8-1/23/32)
4142. Hecox, Cyrus, 49, d 6/17/31 in Lyons (6-6/29)
4143. Hecox, Emily Louisa, 25, wf of William A., d 8/23/47 at the home of Samuel
       Hecox in Black Rock (deceased was the former Miss Louisa Campbell, for
       many years a member of the Female Seminary in Utica (9-8/31)
4144. Hecox, Franklin, 25, d in Tyre (6-10/6/30)
       Hedges, Almira. See Heggis, Almira.
4145. Hedges, Charles, merchant, of Mansfield, OH m 5/1/49 Jenette Bradley, dau
       of Alvan, Esq. of Whitesboro, NY, in W; Rev. Walter R. Long (9-5/2)
4146. Hedges, Isaac A. m 10/18/35 Hannah Kline in Elmira (6-11/4)
4147. Hedges(?), William T. m 1/1/38 Cornelia A. Coville, formerly of Geneva,
       NY, in Ypsilanti, MI (6-1/24)
4148. Heermans, Cornelius P. (Dr.) m 10/13/31 Charlotte Perkins in Ithaca
       (6-10/26)
4149. Heffron, Daniel S., principal of Whitestown Seminary, m 7/31/45 D. Mandane
       Chapman, only dau of Stephen of Plainfield, NY, in P; Elder John Chaney
       (9-9/8)
4150. Heggis, Almira C., 4, 2nd dau of Archibald, d 10/22/36 in Elmira (6-11/2)
4151. Heidleman, _____ (Mrs.), 83, d 11/28/33 in Chemung (6-12/18)
4152. Heller, David, Jr. m Eleanora Lindsley in Elmira (6-9/11/33)
4153. Hellinger, Frederick, 60, formerly of Herkimer, d 2/7/48 in Mohawk
       (9-2/11)
4154. Helm, Phineas M 1/22/49 Martha J. Brees, both of Southport; Rev. H. N.
       Seaver (5-1/26)
4155. Hemenway, Harvey m 10/18/31 Margaret Rodney at Trinity Ch. in Geneva;
       Rev. Bruce. All of Geneva (6-10/19)
4156. Hemiup, Anthony m 1/28/34 Sarah Davenport in Geneva; Rev. Bruce. All of
       Geneva (6-2/5)
4157. Hemiup, Joseph m 7/3/33 Julia Ann Munger, both of Geneva, in Rochester
       (6-7/17)
4158. Hemiup, Phebe, 34, wf of Anthony of Geneva, d 1/9/33 in Geneva (6-1/16)
4159. Hemstreet, Matilda, 21, dau of Jacob, d 6/27/33 in Martinsburgh (9-7/16)
4160. Hendee, Stephen, merchant, m 9/20/35 Lydia Herrick, both of West Bloomfild,
       in W. B. (6-9/30)
4161. Henderson, A. W. (Rev.) of Utica m 5/11/42 Helen Eddy, dau of Seth Esq.
       of Stillwater, Sara. Co., in S; Rev. V. D. Reed (9-5/14)
4162. Henderson, Eliza, 7 mo, only dau of Rev. A. W., d 2/28/46 in Chicago, IL
       (9-3/18)
4163. Henderson, Mathew H., rector-elect of Trintiy Church, Newark, NJ, m Eliza
       H. McFarlane of the Island of St. Croix in Philadelphia, PA (6-11/17/30)
4164. Henderson, Thomas, 22, d 10/16/50 in Utica (funeral from his mother's
       home, 56 Elizabeth St.) (9-10/17)
4165. Henderson, William B. m 7/4/39 Sophia Hibbard, both of Palmyra, in
       Canandaigua; Rev. L. Runsted (6-7/17)
4166. Hendrick, Solomon U., 29, s of Hendrick Aupaumut and one of the chiefs
       of the Stockbridge Indians, d in New Stockbridge (presumably in
       Massachusetts) (9-8/16/25)
4167. Hendricks, Charles m 6/18/33 Lovina Pulfrey in Waterloo (6-7/3)

4168. Hennington, H., 104, m 7/16/35 E. A. Peck, 83, in Marion Co., Mississippi (6-10/21)
4169. Henry, Amanda, 29, wf of William, d 2/2/36 (in Canandaigua?) (6-2/17)
4170. Henry, Hannah, 31, wf of Dr. John D., d 12/21/21 in Greene (surv by husband and 5 small children including 4 daus) (8-12/26)
4171. Henry, James L., 27, d 10/30/48 in Baldwinsville (1-11/2)
4172. Henry, James, T. of the firm of Frear and Henry, m 6/21/43 Margaret M. Queal in Utica; Rev. A. B. Grosh. All of Utica (9-6/22)
4173. Henry, Jane, 4, oldest dau of James T. and Margaret M., d 5/23/48 in Albany (9-5/25)
4174. Henry, John D. (Dr.) m Elizabeth Case in Rochester (8-1/18/26)
4175. Henry, Josiah m 10/1/35 Polly Logan in Bath (6-10/14)
4176. Henry, Nicholas, Esq., 60, d 10/2/43 in Cazenovia (3-10/18)
4177. Henry, William m 5/19/50 Jane Miller in Whitestown; Rev. William Wyatt. All of Utica (9-5/21)
4178. Henshaw, Emily H., inf dau of J. Sidney and Jane F., d 7/20/48 in Utica (9-7/22)
4179. Henshaw, J. Sidney of the U.S. Navy at Philadelphia, PA m 3/11/46 Jane Handy, dau of late John H., Esq. of Utica, in U; Rev. George Leeds (9-3/13)
4180. Henty, John W., 30, d 12/13/50 in Utica (9-12/16)
4181. Hepworth, James m 8/27/50 Elizabeth Platt, both of Utica, in U; John Parsons, Esq. (9-8/31)
4182. Herendeen, Richard, Esq. of Newport m 12/14/42 Charlotte Scott of Deerfield in D; Rev. B. G. Paddock (9-12/16)
4183. Herkimer, John, 72, nephew of Gen. Nicholas, d 6/18/45 in Danube, Herkimer Co. (Herkimer Co. named after Gen. Herkimer who served many years as Judge and Rep. in Congress) (9-6/21)
4184. Hermon, Ebenezer m 10/18/32 Sally Burgess in Phelps (6-10/24)
4185. Herrick, Eliza H., 22, d 1/28/31 in Utica (6-2/9)
4186. Herrick, Henry m 1/12/43 Fidelia Lee in Sullivan; Rev. James Abell. All of Sullivan (3-1/18)
4187. Herrick, Henry m 9/28/43 Caroline Forbes, both of Clockville, in Morrisville; Rev. Putnam (double ceremony - see m of Royal C. Sayles) (3-10/11)
4188. Herrick, Jonathan Henry, 1, s of Edward, d 8/24/42 in Utica (9-8/26)
4189. Herrick, William P., 33, d 11/11/46 in Utica (9-11/12)
4190. Herrick, William P., 22 mo, s of R. Clarinda, d 7/16/47 in Cincinnati, OH (9-7/27)
4191. Herring, Nichol D. (Dr.) of NYC m 6/20/26 Frances Huntington, 2nd dau of Henry, Esq. of Rome, NY, in R; Rev. Gillett (9-6/27)
4192. Herrington, Caroline, youngest dau of N. M., d 5/11/48 in Corning (4-5/24)
4193. Herrington, Daniel G., inf. s, of Dr. N. M., d 8/23/50 in Corning (4-9/4)
4194. Herrington, Oliver of Middlesex m Lucy Pratt of Rushville in R; Rev. Pickard (6-4/22/35)
4195. Herron, Joseph, Esq. m 6/9/39 Calista Marshall of Seneca Falls in S. F.; Rev. C. G. Acley (6-6/26)
4196. Hertzel, A. R. (Lt.) of the U.S. Army m 11/23/35 Margaretta P. Jack in Rochester (6-12/2)
4197. Hesser, Victor Jupiter Z. K. M., Esq. (Prof.), "citizen of the United States of America", m 10/1/48 Lisette Regina Bail of Zweibrucekan, Europe, at his home, 10 Amity St., NYC (9-10/5)
4198. Hewes, Shubel, 68, d 6/27/50 in Baldwinsville (1-6/27)
4199. Hewet, _____ m Harriet Hall in Seneca Falls (6-2/6/33)
4200. Hewet, Silas m 1/23/33 Elizabeth Matthews, both of Seneca Falls, in Gorham (6-2/6)
4201. Hewett, Clarissa (Miss), 44, d 8/30/46 in Paris, NY (9-9/3)
4202. Hewett, Randall, nearly 90, (a Rev. Soldier) d 5/2/50 in Seneca Falls (b in Old Canaan, CT) (9-5/16)
4203. Hewit, Hannah, 62, d 12/14/46 in Baldwinsville (funeral at Bapt. House; surv by "a number of children, all married") (1-12/14)
4204. Hewitt, Celinda, 22, wf of Gurdon and dau of William Means, Esq., d 7/28/20 in Towanda (8-8/23)
4205. Hews, Moses of Georgetown m 10/11/43 Araminta Holmes of Utica in U; Rev. Corey (9-10/13)

4206. Hibbard, F. G. (Rev.) of the Geneva Conference m 7/8/46 Maria Hyde, dau of A. E.(?) Hyde of Oxford and preceptress of the Oxford Academy; Rev. M. Tooker of Geneva (6-7/17)

4207. Hickcox, Charles Frederick, 10 mo, s of Elisha M. and Margaret, d 8/11/47 in Whitestown (9-8/16)

4208. Hickcox, Lyman of Wisconsin m 7/12/43 Sarah G. Kasson of Deerfield in D; Rev. John P. Knox (9-7/14)

4209. Hickock, Benjamin, Esq., 83, d 9/5/45 at his home in Clinton (one of the earliest settlers in Oneida Co.; had been magistrate and postmaster about 30 yrs) (9-9/19)

4210. Hickock, Harris, Esq., about 41, d 6/11/38 in Sullivan (3-6/13)

4211. Hickock, Mary Ann, wf of Harris, Esq., d 8/3/34 in Bridport (Note: there is a Bridport, VT near Middlebury) (3-8/12)

4212. Hickock, Cornelius Van Ness m 12/12/44 Harriet Newkirk, youngest dau of John P., Esq., in Catskill (all of Catskill); Rev. M. J. Hickock of Utica (9-12/18)

4213. Hickox, Cyrus m Mary W. Gaylord, dau of Flavel, in Havana, NY (6-3/17/30)

4214. Hickox, Hosea B. of Sharon, OH m 7/2/46 Marian Mack, youngest dau of J., Esq. of Canandaigua, NY, in C; Rev. C. Wheeler (6-7/10)

4215. Hickox, Martha M., 26, wf of Walter S. and youngest dau of Matthew Keith, Esq., d 5/6/46 in Winfield (9-6/2)

4216. Hicks, Elias, 81, (an eminent minister of the Society of Friends) d in Jericho, L.I., NY (6-3/10/30)

4217. Hicks, George W. m 10/30/33 Hannah M. Moody in Fayette; Rev. Phelps. All of Fayette (6-11/13)

4218. Hicks, Jacob m 12/3/35 Elner Minnis, both of Phelps (6-12/16)

4219. Hicks, John B. of Lyons m 5/19/39 Catharine Garey of Geneva in G; R. Hogarth, Esq. (6-5/22)

4220. Hicks, John J. m 10/2/25 Sally Crane, both of Paris, NY, in P; Rev. Hollister (9-10/4)

4221. Hicks, Oliver H., Esq., pres. of Farmers Fire Insurance and Loan Co., d in NYC (6-10/3/32) (cholera)

4222. Higby. Henry of Sugar Grove, PA m 11/2/24 Hannah Kellogg of New Hartford, NY in New H. (9-11/9)

4223. Higby, Jared S. m 5/1/50 Sarah Jane Conover, both of West Turin, in W. T.; Elder C. Haven (9-5/10)

4224. Higgins, ____ m 5/6/35 Maria E. Burns in Bath (6-5/20)

4225. Higgins, William Lucius, inf s of William, d 2/1/33 in Bath (6-2/13)

4226. Higgs, Thomas m 5/22/44 Elizabeth Stow in Utica; Elder Thomas Hill. All of Utica (9-5/30)

4227. Higgs, Uriah m 7/24/46 Alice Howarth in Utica; Elder Thomas Hill. All of Utica (9-7/27)

4228. Higley, ____ of PennYan m 11/22/35 Electa Baldwin of Waterloo in W (6-12/2)

4229. Hiland, James m Martha M. Bailey, both of Greensboro, VT, in Irasburgh jail, VT (bridegroom was jailed on perjury charges with the bride the only witness upon which the government relied for conviction; the bride groom "obtained her hand in marriage to checkmate the prosecution") (6-8/20/34)

4230. Hildreth, Rachel, 31, wf of Isaac, d 7/26/46 in Seneca (6-7/31)

4231. Hildreth, William m 11/14/32 Mary Ann Marvin in Vienna, NY (6-11/28)

4232. Hiler, George W. of Penfield m 7/2/46 Amanda M. Parker of Geneva in G; Rev. John Henry Hobart(?) (6-7/3)

4233. Hill, Eli (Dr.), 56, d 11/6/38 in Berrien, MI (had lived many years, and practiced medicine, in Geneseo, NY)(6-12/5)

4234. Hill, Elizabeth (Miss), 20, dau of Nathaniel, d 3/13/41 in Perryville (3-3/17)

4235. Hill, Ezra of Bainbridge m Martha Julliand, dau of Capt. Joseph of Greene, in G; Rev. Lacy (8-1/7/18)

4236. Hill, Fanny, about 30, consort of Ira, Esq., d 11/7/30 in Macedon ("a few moments after the demise of the mother" an 18-month-old dau died also) (6-11/24)

4237. Hill, Francis M., one of the proprietors of the Kingston Chronicle and Gazette, m 7/22/33 Mary Briggs, oldest dau of Thomas, Esq. of Sidney, in Belleville, Upper Canada (9-8/6)

4238. Hill, Henry of the firm of J. and H Hill of Elmira m 6/20/50 Helen M. Paine, dau of David, Esq. of Athens, Bradford Co., PA, in A; Rev. A. Hull (5-6/21)

4239. Hill, Hiland, Esq., 65, cashier of the Catskill Bank, d 10/10/50 in Catskill (9-10/14)

4240. Hill, James, 26, s of Ephraim, d 3/6/31 in Manchester (6-3/9 and 4/20)

4241. Hill (or Hull?), John, 82, d 9/7/47 in Syracuse (funeral from the home of his son, Thomas Hill or Hull, 10 Mary St., Syracuse or Utica?) (9-9/9)

4242. Hill, John F. of Macdonough m 10/19/23 Frances Ann Pinckney, dau of J., Esq. of Catskill, in C; Rev. Prentiss (8-10/29)

4243. Hill, Joseph, 63, d 3/23/33 in Canandaigua (one of the earliest settlers in Ontario Co.) (6-4/10)

4244. Hill, Melancton W. m 12/17/33 Elizabeth Shattuck, both of Alloway, in Geneva; Rev. Bruce (6-12/18)

4245. Hill, Otis m 11/9/35 Isabella McCann in Elmira (6-11/18)

4246. Hill, Phillips, Jr. of Junius m 5/26/31 Barbara Snyder of Lyons in L (6-6/8)

4247. Hill, Thomas, Jr. of NYC m 11/7/49 Mary E. Bullock of Utica ("Will the Baptist Register please copy?") (9-11/8)

4248. Hill, William m Ischabeba Huzza in Glastonbury, NH (6-4/18/32)

4249. Hill, William m 2/18/35 Mary Ann C. Sherman, both of Verona, in Chittenango; Rev. J. T. Hough (3-2/24)

4250. Hill, William W. m Laura Mitchell in Sullivan (3-3/13/39)

4251. Hill, Zacheus of Rome, NY m 9/3/50 Susan L. Whipple, dau of John H., Esq. of Adams, at the Emanuel Ch. in Adams; Rev. H. H. Whipple (9-9/12)

4252. Hillhouse, James (Hon.), 78, d 1/12/33 in New Haven, CT (a member of the Senate) (6-1/16)

4253. Hillhouse, William, Esq., bro of late Hon. James, d 1/23/33 in New Haven, CT (6-2/20)

4254. Hilliard, Daniel B. m 7/4/32 Mary Parker in Seneca Falls; Rev. Kent. All of Seneca Falls (6-7/18)

4255. Hills, Ralph (Dr.) of Delaware, OH m 10/4/49 Emily R. Hunt of Utica in U; Rev. William Hyatt (9-10/5)

4256. Hills, Sylvester of Manlius m 12/27/32 Hannah Sutherland of Sullivan in Chittenango (3-1/1/33)

4257. Hills, Thomas of Jerusalem, NY m 10/15/45 Lydia Ann Davis of Marshall in M; Rev. W. Raymond (9-10/24)

4258. Hilsiker, Henry m 3/26/50 Gamar J. Hayne "at the State Line" (both of Southport); Rev. J. I. Riggs of Wells, PA (5-4/5)

4259. Himrod, Mabel, wf of Gen. Peter, d 2/11/36 in Ovid (6-2/17)

4260. Hine, Russell D., 16, s of Jay S. and Isabella, d 7/9/49 in Southport (5-7/13)

4261. Hines, Lebra m 2/11/49 Elizabeth Howe, both of Elmira; W. P. Kookle, Esq. (5-2/16)

4262. Hinion, Henry, Esq. of Rushville m 1/30/38 Catharine Buer of Seneca Falls in S. F. (6-2/14)

4263. Hinkley, Susan Ann, 21, youngest dau of Amasa and Lucretia, d 9/7/48 in Rome, NY (9-9/11)

4264. Hinman, Abner of Augusta m 1/13/47 Melony Perrin of Camden in Vienna, NY; Rev. A. P. Smith (9-1/20)

4265. Hinman, Elihu m 6/30/31 Calista Inman at the Sulphur Springs House; Rev. B. H. Hickox. All of Palmyra (6-7/13)

4266. Hinman, Ephraim (Gen.), 73, d in Roxbury, CT (a Rev. patriot) (6-2/17/30)

4267. Hinman, H. H. of Sandy Creek m 1/15/46 Amelia M. Hills of Kirkland in K; Rev. Dana (9-1/22)

4268. Hinman, Livingston, 63, d 11/27/47 in Holland Patent, NY (9-12/23)

4269. Hinman, Melony, 29, wf of Abner, d 8/10/48 in Augusta (9-8/22)

4270. Hitchcock, Horace D., 37, d 2/17/38 in Canastota (3-2/21)

4271. Hitchcock, Levi, 88, (a Rev. soldier) d 3/24/44 in Annsville (b in New Haven, CT 5/7/1755; lived 40 yrs in Westerlo, Albany Co. and moved to Oneida Co. in 1832) (9-4/1)

4272. Hitchcock, Luke of Allegany Co. m 4/8/24 Melinda Nickerson of Bainbridge in B; L. Bigelow, Esq. (8-4/14)

4273. Hitchcock, Marcus (Dr.), 68, formerly of Utica, d 2/16/48 in Terre Haute, IN (9-3/3)

4274. Hitchcock, William m 4/15/29 Elsitha Mills in Guilford; Rev. Wells (double ceremony - see marr of Erastus P. Smith) (8-4/22)

4275. Hoag, Ezekiel J. m 1/12/23 Alvira Hooper, both of New Berlin; Rev. D. Burlingame (7-1/15)

Hoag, Margaret. See Hoog, Margaret

4276. Hoag, Philo m 12/24/44 Mary Sexton; Rev. L. Sperry. All of Norwich (Oxford Republican, 1/6/45)

4277. Hobart, Baxter (Col.) m 6/23/30 Esther Clark in Jerusalem, NY (6-7/21)

4278. Hobart, John Henry (Rt. Rev.), 54, D.D., Bishop, Protestant Episcopal Church in New York State, d 9/12/30 in Auburn (8-9/15)

4279. Hobart, Mary G., 72, wid of late Rev. J. H., d 4/4/47 in NYC (9-4/7)

4280. Hobby, Annis Sophia, l. only ch of J. C. A. Hobby, d 8/11/47 in Skaneateles (1-8/25)

4281. Hochstrasser, Julia Louisa, 7, only dau of Ormond and Caroline, d 9/13/43 in Utica (funeral from her parents' home, corner Liberty St. and Broadway (9-9/14)

4282. Hodge, George A. m Nancy McKellup in Canandaigua (6-3/9/31)

4283. Hodges, Lewis (Dr.), 49, d 9/3/34 in West Bloomfield of hydrothorax (6-9/17)

4284. Hodgkin, Silas m 1/20/31 Mercy Sweet in Buffalo (6-2/2)

4285. Hoes, Catharine Anne, 16, dau of Peter I., Esq. of Kinderhook, NY d 9/6/35 at the Seminary for Young Ladies in Pittsfield, MA (3-9/15)

4286. Hoes, John C. (Rev.) of Chittenango m 9/15/36 Lucia Maria Randall, oldest dau of General Roswell, in Cortland; Rev. Jospeh I. Foot (3-9/21)

4287. Hoff, Caroline (Miss), 20, d 9/2/33 in Tioga (6-9/18)

4288. Hoffman, Charles O. m 12/20/31 Susan Ann Benton in Lyons (6-12/28)

4289. Hoffman, Cornelius m 8/7/34 Betsey Jackson in Lenox; Rev. Allen. All of Lenox (3-8/12)

4290. Hoffman, Michael, Esq. m 9/25/49 Jane Usher, both of Herkimer, at the Episc. Ch. in Little Falls; Rev. Livermore (9-9/29)

4291. Hoffman, Ogden, Esq. m 11/14/38 Virginia E. Southard, dau of Hon. Samuel L., in NYC; Rev. Dr. Wainwright (6-11/28)

4292. Hoffman, William m 10/25/48 Ellen Maxwell, dau of H. I., in Elmira; Rev. P. H. Fowler (5-10/27)

4293. Hogan, Garrit (Col.) d 7/16/48 in Albany (consumption) (9-7/18)

4294. Hogan, John, Esq. of Hogansburg m 6/17/43 Ann Margaret Masters of Smith Valley, youngest dau of Hon. Judge Masters, member of Congress from Rensselaer co. (9-6/21)

4295. Hogan, John, Esq., 23, attorney, d 8/24/44 in NYC (9-8/30)

4296. Hogan, John, 47, of Utica d 7/24/50 in Washington, D.C. (9-7/31)

4297. Hogan, Maurice, s of Maurice of New Hartford, d 8/14/47 at his home in Cardenas, Island of Cuba (9-10/5)

4298. Hogarth, Richard, Esq., 61, d 7/9/46 in Geneva (6-7/10)

4299. Hoger, Harriet, 3, dau of Anson, d 12/20/33 in Sullivan (3-12/24)

4300. Hoistram, Peter m Polly Hults in Lyons (6-11/24/30)

4301. Holben, Peter m 6/8/36 Abigail Ettinger (in Varick?) (6-6/15)

4302. Holbrook, John N. of the firm of Holbrook, Bloom and Co, merchants, d 11/13/46 at the Bleecker Street House in Utica (funeral in Presby. Ch. at Whitesboro - sermon by Rev. Long) (9-11/14)

4303. Holbrook, Sarah (Mrs.), 60, wf of Luther, d 11/27/46 in Whitesboro (9-12/1)

4304. Holbrook, Solomon C., about 40, d 10/11/32 in Chittenango (3-10/16)

4305. Holcombe, George (Hon.), a Congressman from NJ, d near Allentown, NJ (8-2/1/28)

4306. Holden, Mary, wf of Horace now residing in San Francisco, d 12/2/49 in Honolulu (9-3/15/50)

4307. Holden, Phineas m 6/11/34 Nancy Bishop in Waterloo (6-7/2)

4308. Holden, William m 12/14/31 Eliza Ann Nichols in Milo (6-12/28)

4309. Holdridge, Gersham of Schuyler m 8/28/21 Abigail Seabert of Smithville in S; Rev. Aaron Baxter (8-9/5)

4310. Holland, Alexander, Esq. of Schenectady m Sophia S. Butterfield of Utica in U; Rev. Dr. Proal (9-12/27/44)

4311. Hollenbeck, Joseph m 6/15/43 Sarah Newton, both of Corning, in C; Rev. Amos Hard (4-6/21)

4312. Hollett, Joseph I. m 2/17/31 Sarah Fairbank, oldest dau of Rev. Ira, in Rushville (6-2/23)

4313. Holliday, Lydia (Mrs.), 38, d 2/1/34 in Burdette (6-2/12)

4314. Holliday, Mary (Mrs.), 33, dau of B. Gildard, d 3/8/36 in Hopewell (6-3/16)
4315. Hollister, Thomas m 7/3/34 Almira Manchester, both of Genoa, NY, in Canandaigua (6-7/16)
4316. Hollister, William, 75, father of Frederick, Esq. of Utica, formerly of Pittsfield, MA, d 1/22/42 in Monroeville, Huron Co., OH (9-2/4)
4317. Holly, Mary Eliza, 9, 4th dau of late John M., d 4/29/50 in Utica (9-5/6)
4318. Holly, Sarah, 76, wid of late Luther, Esq., d 9/21/30 in Salisbury, CT (6-10/6)
4319. Holmes, _____, 4 mo, ch of Milton, d 4/28/37 in Sullivan (3-5/3)
4320. Holmes, David, late gov. of Mississippi and a U.S. senator from that state, d 8/20/32 in Sulphur Springs, VA (6-9/19)
4321. Homes, Harvey H., 33, d 8/9/45 in Waterville (9-8/13)
4322. Holmes, Henry A. of Goshen, MA m 4/20/31 Harriet Butler, dau of Hon. Medad of Stuyvesant, Col. Co., NY, in Stuyvesant (6-5/18)
4323. Holmes, James m Rebecca P. Warring in Milo (6-3/2/31)
4324. Holmes, John, 89, d 5/12/49 in Oxford (enlisted in Rev. War, age 16; settled in Oxford when only one house existed there) (9-5/17)
4325. Holmes, John Hoyt, 14, oldest s of Sylvanus formerly of Utica, d 10/15/43 in Washington, D.C. (9-10/21)
4326. Holmes, John T. 36, d 5/26/49 in Norwich (consumption) (9-5/31)
4327. Holmes, Jonas, 49, a native of Yorkshire, England, d 11/30/32 in Chittenango (3-12/4)
4328. Holmes, Josiah S., 33(?), d 6/10/50 in West Troy (9-6/14)
4329. Holmes, Lewis L. m 10/4/40 Jane M. Barrett, both of Chittenango, in Fenner; Silas Judd, Esq. (3-10/7)
4330. Holmes, Mahala, 57, d 1/13/35 in Chittenango (3-1/20)
4331. Holmes, Miron, merchant, of Sodus m 9/28/30 Eliza Hecox of Lyons in L (6-10/6)
4332. Holmes, Nathaniel, 89, (a Rev. soldier) d at the home of his son in South Richmond (9-4/1/50)
4333. Holmes, Richard, 30, d 1/10/39 in Chittenango (3-1/16)
4334. Holmes, Robert, 30, of the firm of Savage, Moore and Co., paper manufacturers, d 1/17/31 in Sauquoit, Oneida Co. (9-1/25)
4335. Holmes, Ruhan, merchant, of Lenox m 1/18/32 Lucretia Smith of Sullivan in Chittenango; Rev. N. S. Smith (3-1/24)
4336. Holmes, Samuel m 7/28/33 Hannah Fisk in Sackett's Harbor (6-8/21)
4337. Holmes, Seth, 5, d 5/1/41 in Perryville (3-5/5)
4338. Holmes, Simon d 10/26/36 in Chittenango (3-11/2)
4339. Holmes, William, 52, d in Wheeler (6/5/26/30)
4340. Holmes, William m 3/23/34 Hannah Snell in Sullivan; Jairus French, Esq. (3-3/25)
4341. Holst(?), Marias(?), prof. of music, m 6/27/37 Polly Ann Miles; Rev. S. Miles. All of Geneva (6-6/28)
4342. Holstein, H. V. Du Coudray (Gen.) d 5/23/39 in Albany (b in Germany; formerly prof. of French and Spanish languages at Geneva College) (6-5/29)
4343. Holt, Charles, Jr., formerly of Albany, editor of the Gazette, m 2/28/49 Ellen Field, formerly of Durhamville, NY, in Greenfield, Dane Co., WI; Rev. Lord (9-3/22)
4344. Holt, Horatio N., merchant, m "recently" Abby G. Seymour, dau of Henry R., in Buffalo; Rev. Hopkins. All of Buffalo (6-8/7/39)
4345. Holt, John m 7/16/48 Eliza Tryon, both of Rome, NY, in R; George Barnard, Esq. (9-7/22)
4346. Holt, Thomas A. of New Hartford m 8/14/44 Catharine S. Parsons, dau of Samuel, in Utica; Rev. Nichols (9-8/20)
4347. Homan, _____ (Mrs.) d 3/22/31 in Phelps (6-3/30)
4348. Hommidieu, S. S. L., one of the proprietors of the Cincinnati Gazette, m Alma Hammond in Cincinnati, OH (6-6/23/30)
4349. Hood, Benjamin L. of Lenox m 3/10/38 Lucinda M. Toby of Chittenango in Vernon; Rev. H. P. Bogue (3-3/14)
4350. Hood, Henry, 22, d 12/11/35 in Sullivan (3-12/15)
4351. Hood, John G. m 10/12/36 Catharine Yost in Fayette (6-11/2)
4352. Hood, William m 3/30/33 Rhoda Knollin, dau of Richard; Rev. William Johnson. All of Sullivan (3-4/2)

4353. Hood, William m 4/23/42 Catherine Smith; Rev. A. Hard. All of Corning
       (4-4/27)
4354. Hoog, Margaret (Miss), 56, dau of Thomas A., d 1/6/37 in Kinderhook
       (gr-dau of Rev. Johannes Ritzema of the Reformed Dutch Ch, in NYC;
       when the British captured that city in the Rev. War he became pastor
       at Kinderhook) (6-2/8)
4355. Hooker, Fisher M. of Rushville m 6/17/46 Phoebe Ann Oxtoby, dau of Col.
       George of Benton, in B (6-7/3)
4356. Hooker, Henry T. of Rochester m 7/4/38 Mary B. Cobb, dau of Henry S. of
       Sullivan, in S; Rev. James Abell (3-7/11)
4357. Hooker, James H., 46, d 4/5/28 (or 38) in Vienna, NY (6-4/11)
4358. Hooker, Mary Ann (Miss), 15, d 2/25/34 in Vienna, NY (6-3/12)
4359. Hooper, Robert of Seneca m 9/28/30 Sarah Hayes of Hopewell in H (6-10/6)
4360. Hooper, Warren of German, NY m 1/7/20 Charity Andrus of Columbus in C
       (8-1/19)
4361. Hooper, Zeba m 7/9/20 Joanna Drew, both of German, NY, in G (8-7/26)
4362. Hope, David, 60, a native of Scotland but for many years a resident of
       NYC, d 12/3/25 in NYC (9-12/6)
4363. Hopkins, _____, inf ch of Mr. J. D., d in Utica (9-11/7/26)
4364. Hopkins, Almena D., wf of Charles H., d 6/7/49 in Utica (funeral at
       68 Broad St.) (9-6/8)
4365. Hopkins, E. S. of Clinton m 3/6/44 Mary Camp, dau of Willard, Esq. of
       Whitesboro, in W; Rev. D. Og__? (9-3/16)
4366. Hopkins, Elisha W., Esq. m 12/4/49 Amanda S. Parker, dau of I. S., Esq.,
       in Rome, NY; Rev. W. E. Knox (9-12/7)
4367. Hopkins, Hannah (Miss), formerly of Herkimer, d 3/8/25 in Albany (9-3/15)
4368. Hopkins, John F. of Holland Patent, NY m 2/12/49 B. (or H.) Lawrence of
       Marcy at the Central Hotel in Utica; Rev. E. Francis (9-2/13)
4369. Hopkins, R. (Mrs.), relict of late D. Lemuel of Hartford, CT. d 9/20/26
       in NYC (9-10/3)
4370. Hopkins, Samuel of Norwich m 4/3/23 Sally Holmes of Plymouth in P
       (7-4/9)
4371. Hopkins, Samuel M. of Geneva m 5/15/39 Mary Jane Hanson Heacock, dau of
       Reuben B., Esq. of Buffalo, in B; Rev. John C. Lord (6-5/29)
4372. Hopkins, William R. m Mary M. Gallagher at Trinity Ch. in Geneva; Rev.
       P. P. Irving. All of Geneva (6-4/24/39)
4373. Hopper, Alexander M., B.A., (pastor of the 2nd Bapt. Ch., New Haven, CT
       and a late graduate of the Theological Department of Madison University)
       m 8/25/50 Lavantia Lewis, dau of Birdseye Lewis, M.D., of Hamilton,
       in H; Rev. G. W. Eaton (9-8/28)
4374. Horan, Rosanna, 32, wf of Martin, d 4/21/48 in Bellville, Canada West
       (9-6/1)
4375. Horn, Charles E. d 4/28/35 (in Bethany?) (consumption) (6-5/20)
4376. Hornor, Thomas J. of Burford, Upper Canada m Galetsky Turner of Zorra,
       U. C. in Lyons, NY (6-5/5/30)
4377. Horsburgh, _____, inf dau of Alexander, d 8/7/48 in Utica (funeral from
       the corner of Bleecker and 2nd Sts.) (9-8/8)
4378. Horton, Elisha, 81, (a Rev. officer and pensioner) d 12/29/37 in Litchfield,
       CT (was engaged in throwing the tea into Boston Harbor prior to the
       Declaration of Independence) (6-1/24/38)
4379. Horton, Leonard, Jr. m 3/12/29 Jemima Connover, both of Oxford, in O;
       Rev. Parker (8-3/25)
4380. Horton, Lewis A. m Lucy Ann Warden in Pulteney (6-3/2/31)
4381. Hortsen, William (Dr.), 62, d 2/18/32 in NYC (b in Benton, Trent, England
       but for the last 30 yrs a resident of NY state, mostly in Geneva)
       (6-2/29)
4382. Hosack, Nathaniel P. of NYC m 9/21/31 Sophia H. Church, dau of Philip E.,
       Esq., in Angelica; Rev. Thibon (6-10/12)
4383. Hose, John, Esq., 67, d 4/10/32 in NYC (6-4/18)
4384. Hosford, Elisha of the former firm of E. and E. Hosford, printers and
       booksellers of Albany, d 11/15/30 in Hartford, CT (6-12/1 and 12/7)
4385. Hosford, Henry B. (Rev.) of Sunderland, MA m Mary E. Plant, dau of
       Benjamin of New Hartford, NY, in New H; Rev. E. H. Payson (9-9/4/50)
4386. Hoskins, Charles L., Esq. m 4/20/36 Mary E. Woolsey in Seneca Falls
       (6-5/4)

4387. Hoskins, Eliza E., wf of G. L., Esq., d 1/8/35 in Seneca Falls (6-1/21)
4388. Hosmer, Goodell O., 2, oldest ch of William E. and Catharine, d 7/23/49 in New Haven, NY (1-8/30)
4389. Hosmer, Noble S., 26, d 4/27/48 in Mexico, NY (heart attack) (1-5/5)
4390. Hossinger, Frederick, 74, d 1/6/32 in Fayette (6-2/1)
4391. Hotchkin, A. H. m 9/17/33 Sarah Aulls in Wheeler (6-10/9)
4392. Hotchkin, Benjamin F. m 9/20/33 Jane M. Little, both of Watertown, in Waterloo (6-10/9)
4393. Hotchkin, Catharine M., 24, wf of Mark C., d 3/29/45 in Waterville (9-4/8)
4394. Hotchkiss, Calvin S. m 9/10/45 Phebe J. Stillman, both of Smithville, in S; Rev. J. T. Goodrich (Oxford Republican, 9/18)
4395. Hotchkiss, Carver of Windsor, NY m Sally Scott of Prospect in P (6-11/10/30)
4396. Hotchkiss, Eliphalet (Col.), 64?, d 2/10/42 in Vernon (9-2/16)
4397. Hotchkiss, Hiram G. of Vienna, NY m 1/3/33 Mary W. Ashley, dau of Dr. Ashley, in Lyons; Rev. Hubbell (6-1/9)
4398. Hotchkiss, Lyman, 57, d 3/5/25 in Paris, NY (consumption) (ruling elder of the church in Paris, NY, 1817-24; later ruling elder in the Presby. Ch. at Utica until time of his death) (9-3/15)
4399. Hotchkiss, Marshall of Wayne m 5/6/32 Maria French of Bath in B; H. W. Rogers, Esq. (6-5/16)
4400. Hough, Alfred C. of Vienna, NY m 2/26/34 Mary Taylor of Canandaigua in Rochester (6-3/12)
4401. Hough, Susannah, 81, wid of late Col. John (a Rev. soldier) d 11/15/41 at the home of Col. David Hough in Unadilla (Oxford Times, 11/24)
4402. Houghtaling, Jacob m 3/13/38 Lany Conrad in Chittenango; J. French, Esq. (3-3/21)
4403. Houghtaling, Mary B., 3, dau of Thomas, d 12/28/41 in Binghamton (2-1/5/42)
4404. Houghtaling, William, 48, d 2/26/31 in Kingston (6-3/23)
4405. Houghteling, Abraham, Esq., 87, father of Dr. James of Romulus, d 3/5/30 in Kingston (6-3/17)
4406. Houghton, Henry D., 1, youngest s of Henry D. and Mary A., d 3/13/49 in NYC (buried in Utica) (9-3/16)
4407. Houghton, Hiel of Lincklaen m 1/24/28 Eliza Smith, dau of Nehemiah of Preston, in P; Wells Wait, Esq. (8-2/1)
4408. Hounson, Cortland, 2, d 4/13/39 in Geneva (6-4/17)
4409. House, Charles C. of Waterloo, formerly of Houseville, Lewis Co., m 9/13/48 Sarah E. Powers, dau of Erastus of Trenton, NY, in T (9-9/15)
4410. House, Peter A. m 11/12/46 Lydia W. Welch, both of Pamelia, in Whitestown (9-12/4)
4411. Houston, James of Norwich m 2/21/27 Rebecca Morgan, dau of James, Esq. of Guilford, in G; Rev. N. Bentley (8-3/9)
4412. Houston, Sophia (Mrs.), 29, d in Rochester (6-11/10/30)
4413. Houston, Thomas m 5/9/26 Jane Anna Rowan, dau of Rev. Dr. Rowan of NYC, in Schenectady (9-5/30)
4414. Hover, David of Tyrone m 2/22/35 Sarah Emery of Bristol, CT in Tyrone (6-3/4)
4415. Hovey, Albert J. m 9/2/35 Helen Saterlee in Lyons (6-9/9)
4416. Hovey, Ezra, 76, d 3/23/43 in Belville (9-3/29)
4417. Hovey, Horace M. m 4/30/37 Caroline M. Grosvenor, dau of E. O. of Sullivan, in Chittenango; Esq. Huntley (3-5/3)
4418. Hovey(?), J. H. of Alidon, Orleans Co., NY m 10/25/48 Harriett A. Wells, dau of James, Esq. of Kirkland, in K; Rev. E. H. Payson of New Hartford (9-10/27)
4419. Hovey, Jonathan (Rev.), 72, of Piermont, NH d 8/21/25 in Wolcott, NY (b in Mansfield, CT 10/4/1753; married and while practicing the law he moved to a farm in Randolph, VT in 1798; in 1803 became pastor in Waterbury and in 1811 in Piermont; surv by several children in western NY) (9-10/4)
4420. Hovey, Julia R., 32, wf of Alfeed H., Esq., d 4/6/50 in Syracuse (9-4/11)
4421. Hovey, Levi, Esq., formerly of Geneseo, d 10/1/33 in New Orleans, LA (6-11/6)
4422. Hovey, Mary, wid of late Jesse R. and dau of Col. David Norton of Sangerfield, NY, d 11/9/50 in Louisville, KY (consumption) (9-11/29)
4423. Hovey, Otis W. m 6/20/17 C. Smith of Auburn in Owego; Rev. Hezekiah May (8-7/9)

4424. Hovey, Otis W., about 40, d 8/27/22 in Montezuma (8-9/11)
4425. Hovey, Sarah (Mrs.), about 21, d 6/2/33 in Lyons (6-6/12)
4426. Hovey, Sarah Elizabeth, 20, wf of A. J., d in Lyons (6-6/19/33)
4427. How, Caroline, 21, d 7/11/46 in Utica (consumption) (9-7/13)
4428. How, David White m 12/27/38 "Miss Mary Elizabeth Yates", oldest dau of Rev. Charles G. Sommers, at South Bapt. Ch. in NYC. All of NYC (3-1/2/39)
4429. How, E. C., about 30, of Auburn, NY d 2/5/50 in Sacramento, CA (9-5/9)
4430. How, Henry, 13 mo, s of Henry, d in Canandaigua (6-3/24/30)
4431. How, Mary Anna, 1, dau of David White How and gr-dau of Rev. C. G. Sommers, d 3/12/44 in NYC (3-3/20)
4432. How, Thomas Y., Jr. m 6/11/32 Sarah S. Hulbert, dau of late Hon. John W., in Auburn (6-6/20)
4433. Howard, Abel, 22, of Union, a student at the Lyceum in Geneva, d 8/12/32 (6-8/22)
4434. Howard, Christopher of East New York, L.I. m 10/28/47 Mary Eliza Ferguson of Lawrence in Utica; Rev. William H. Spencer ("Cooperstown papers please copy") (9-11/5)
4435. Howard, Eliza Ann, 22, dau of Samuel of Ravenna, OH formerly of Sherburne, NY, d 10/2/26 in Cleveland, OH (8-10/27)
4436. Howard, John L., 27, d 6/2/30 at the Theological Seminary in Auburn (b in Bolton, CT; was to have been ordained on the day he died) (6-6/16)
4437. Howard, Joseph, 83?, d 6/5/49 in Sauquoit (9-6/11)
4438. Howard, Maria Louisa (Miss), 15, d 1/11/32 in Lyons (6-1/25)
4439. Howard, Mary (Mrs.), 78, d 9/3/46 in Utica (b in Seal, County Kent, Eng.; mother-in-law to John Simmons late of the Franklin House in Utica; funeral from the Episc. Ch.) (9-9/4)
4440. Howarth, John of Utica m 9/2/49 Elizabeth Jones of New Hartford in New H.; Elder Thomas Hill (9-9/4)
4441. Howe, Alfred m 2/8/27 Sophia L. Smith in Bettsburg; James H. Humphrey, Esq. All of Baunbridge (8-2/23)
4442. Howe, Amos H., 75, d 9/3/50 in Kirkland ("Connecticut and Pennsylvania papers please copy") (9-9/5)
4443. Howe, Betsy (Mrs.), 74, d 7/4/50 in Marcellus (1-7/11)
4444. Howe, Calvin B. of Brooklyn m 10/9/50 Eliza A. Litchfield, dau of Elisha of Cazenovia, in C; Rev. William Clark (9-10/14)
4445. Howe, Catherine, 28, wf of O. A, of Mohawk, d 7/29/50 in Rhinebeck (9-8/7)
4446. Howe, E. Wilson of Schenectady m 5/1/50 Sarah A. Brown, dau of Ezra, Esq. of Bridgewater, at St. John's Ch. in Clayville; Rev. H. W. Whitaker (9-5/9)
4447. Howe, George H. of Cooperstown m 8/10/48 Harriet H. Perkins of Clinton at the Central Hotel in Utica; Rev. D. G. Corey (9-8/12)
4448. Howe, Henry of New Hartford m 1/2/43 Mary Ann Craske of Utica in U; Rev. Dr. Proal (9-1/6)
4449. Howe, Henry of Canandaigua m 7/9/46 Jane M. Lawrence, dau of Thomas, Esq. formerly of NYC; Rev. Dagett (6-7/10)
4450. Howe, Henry H., 8, oldest s of Amos P. and Sally, d 3/2/45 in Kirkland (scarlet fever) (9-3/19)
4451. Howe, J. B. (Mrs.), 23, dau of John Billings, Esq. of Trenton, NY, d 6/28/47 in Brooklyn where she had gone for her health (9-7/8)
4452. Howe, John S., 24, d 10/12/25 in Oxford (8-10/19)
4453. Howe, Otis B. m 9/12/43 Mary E. Hull, dau of late Dr. C. W. of Eaton, in Hamilton (bride and groom both of Hamilton) (9-9/15)
4454. Howe, Samuel (Rev.) of Hopewell m 8/26/35 Eloisa Lewis Buffet in Stanwich (6-9/9)
4455. Howel, Thomas A., 23, d 9/15/43 in Westfield, MA (9-10/25)
4456. Howell, Alexander H., Esq. m Emily Jackson, dau of late Amasa, Esq., in Canandaigua (6-7/28/30)
4457. Howell, David m 9/5/43 Hannah Ellis, youngest dau of E. Ellis, Esq., in Utica; Rev. James Griffiths (9-9/9)
4458. Howell, Jane (Mrs.), 66, formerly of Mereionoilesshire, Wales d 12/10/43 at the home of her dau in Marcy, NY (46 yrs a member of the Church of Christ) (9-12/20)

4459. Howell, John Greig, 18, s of Hon. N. W. of Canandaigua, d at Yale College, New Haeven, CT (scarlet fever) (6-4/1/35)
4460. Howell, Mary, 4, dau of R. Howell, d 2/10/34 in Chittenango (3-3/4)
4461. Howell, Mary, consort of T. H., d 10/18/42 in Utica (9-10/20)
4462. Howell, Susannah (Mrs.), 83, d 12/18/46 in Utica (funeral from her late home near the corner of Liberty and Charles Sts.) (9-12/19)
4463. Howell, Thomas B. m 2/13/50 Mary E. Latimer, oldest dau of Robert S.; Rev. Edmund Tourney (9-2/15)
4464. Howell, William, Esq. of Bath m 4/29/35 Frances Adelphia Adams of West Avon in W. A. (6-5/20)
4465. Howells, Thomas B. m 8/25/42 Mary Rowlands in Utica; Rev. J. Griffiths (9-8/26)
4466. Howes, Abel W. m 12/23/35 Delia Dodman, both of Hopewell, in Canandaigua (6-1/6/36)
4467. Howes, Anne Eliza,46, wf of Dr. Fitch Howes, d 8/9/50 in Vernon Center (9-8/16)
4468. Howes, Fitch (Dr.) of Hamburgh, Erie Co. m 8/12/27 Eliza Ann Freeman, dau of Moses S. of Warren; Rev. Curtis (8-8/31)
4469. Howes, William of Rochester m 6/4/46 Amanda Couch of Hopewell in H; Rev. E. Harrington (6-6/5)
4470. Howland, Benjamin of Seneca, 77, d 9/18/32 in Macedon (fell from a canal boat while en route to Lockport) (6-10/10)
4471. Howland, Elsey F., about 32, dau of Benjamin, d 10/10/31 in Seneca (6-10/12)
4472. Howland, Frederick m 10/12/33 Jane C. Miller in Batavia (6-10/23)
4473. Howland, G. H. of Rome, NY m 4/9/50 Louisa Savery, dau of Phineas, Esq. of Annsville, in A; Rev. P. P. Brown (9-4/11)
4474. Howlet, Emery d 5/16/30 in Lyons (6-5/26)
4475. Howlett, Myron P. m 8/27/33 Delia M. Cornish in Onondaga (6-9/4)
4476. Hoxsey, Warren m 10/3/36 Aurelia Davenport, both of Catlin, in Elmira (6-10/12 and 10/26)
4477. Hoyt, Alfred m 7/25/33 Sarah Rogers in Seneca Falls (6-8/14)
4478. Hoyt, E.P. of Utica m 7/30/49 Lydia M. Wilmot of Champion in C (9-8/2)
4479. Hoyt, Elizabeth K., 23, dau of late David B., Esq., d in Ravenswood, L.I., NY (9-3/3/49)
4480. Hoyt, Francis B., 36, d 5/18/42 in Brighton (Oxford Times, 5/25)
4481. Hoyt, Joseph D. of Buffalo m 11/10/46 Lucia Caroline Whitcomb, dau of Rev. T. J., in Newport (9-11/30)
4482. Hoyt, Robert H. (Dr.) m Mary Easterbrooks in Painted Post (6-11/7/32)
4483. Hoyt, Sarah Ann Harrison, 23, d 2/28/32 in Painted Post (6-3/14)
4484. Hoyt, Thomas B., 36, d 6/13/42 in Brighton (Oxford Times, 6/15)
4485. Hubbard, Abigail, 26, wf of Solman, merchant, and dau of James Sears formerly of Geneva, d 6/15/33 in Cohocton (funeral service at Presby. Meeting House in Geneva; funeral sermon by Rev. Hubbard of Dansville) (6-6/26)
4486. Hubbard, Bela, Esq. m 3/3/48 Sarah E. Baughman, both of Detroit, MI, in D (9-3/11)
4487. Hubbard, Edward Burr, 18, s of Hon. Thomas H., d 7/14/45 in Utica (spent final two years in NYC studying art; funeral from his father's home on Chancellor Square) (9-7/15)
4488. Hubbard, Elijah H., 28, d in Canandaigua (6-10/13/30)
4489. Hubbard, Henry G., Esq., 33, U.S. consul at St. John's Puerto Rico, d 8/16/46 in St. John's (s of Hon. T. H. of Utica, NY) (9-9/14)
4490. Hubbard, John F., editor of the Norwich Journal, m Almyra Mead, dau of Gen. Mead of Norwich, in N (8-2/16/20)
4491. Hubbard, M. Sanford m 1/21/44 Catherine Packard in Canastota; William E. Fisk, Esq. All of Canastota (3-1/24)
4492. Hubbard, Martin A. of Fenner m 10/9/32 Emily Potter of Paris, NY in P; Rev. Smith (3-10/16)
4493. Hubbard, Morgan, 3, s of "Mr. Hubbard", d 5/16/48 in Baldwinsville (1-5/24)
4494. Hubbard, Smedley, 21, d 11/16/32 in fenner (3-12/4)
4495. Hubbard, Solomon m 11/18/30 Abigail Sears in Benton; Rev. Todd. All of Benton (6-11/24)

4496. Hubbard, William G. (Rev) of Cato Four corners m 10/7/47 Amelia Glezen, dau of Oren of Vienna, NY, in V; Rev. William B. Tompkins of Oneida Castle (9-10/14)

4497. Hubbell, Anna Catharine, 5 mo, dau of Alrick and Laura E., d 8/2/44 in Utica (funeral at 53 Broad St.) (9-8/3)

4498. Hubbell, Eliza, 40, wf of Walter, Esq., d 6/20/39 in Canandaigua (6-7/3)

4499. Hubbell, George of Frankfort m 11/4/46 Sarah M. Smith of New Hartford in New H; Rev. J. Sawyer (9-12/2)

4500. Hubbell, Levi, Esq., State Adjutant General, m Susan De Witt in Ithaca (6-6/15/36)

4501. Hubbell, M. W. of the firm of Wolcott and Hubbell, merchants, m 8/6/33 Lucy Sarsdell(?), both of Pittsburgh, PA, in P (6-8/21)

4502. Hubbell, Maria, 5, dau of Rev. Hubbell, d in Lyons (6-5/12/30)

4503. Hubbell, Ramsey, 18, s of Walter, Esq.,d 6/17/39 in Canandaigua (6-6/26)

4504. Hubbell, Sally, 46, formerly of Utica and sister of Alrick Hubbell, d 11/20/46 at the home of Alfred Hubbell in Rochester (9-11/23)

4505. Hubbell, Susan L., wf of Levi and dau of late Simeon De Witt, d in Milwaukee, WI (9-4/6/49)

4506. Hubbell, William, inf s of William S., d 3/1/33 in Bath (6-3/13)

4507. Hubbs, Rodney m 6/15/17 Laura Barns, both of Columbus, Chenango Co. (8-6/18)

4508. Huber, Charles, 13, d 3/14/30 in Geneva (6/3/17)

4509. Hudnall, Henry W., Esq., 37, formerly of New Hartford, d 9/12/43 in Darien (9-9/26)

4510. Hudon, _____ (Very Rev.), vicar general to the Roman Catholic Bishop of the Diocese of Montreal, Canada d in Montreal "of a disease contracted in attendance upon the sick immigrants" (9-8/20/47)

4511. Hudson, Ann, 59, consort of Francis, d 6/2/46 in Utica

4512. Hudson, Francis, 25, d at the home of his father in Utica (funeral from that home, corner of Mary and John Streets) (9-8/21/43)

4513. Hudson, Francis, 65, d 3/18/49 in Utica (9-3/22)

4514. Hudson, Franklin A. of Utica m 11/1/48 Henrietta B. Webster, youngest dau of Dr. Joshua, in Fort Plain; Rev. Dr. C. G. McLean (9-11/4)

4515. Hudson, George A. m 12/31/38 Helen M. Halstead, both of Buffalo, in Geneva; Rev. McLaren (6-1/9/39)

4516. Hudson, Hannah, 11, 2nd dau of Dr. Daniel, d 11/19/31 (6-11/23)

4517. Hudson, Henry, 23, formerly of Auburn, NY, d 4/6/36 in Washtenaw Co., MI (6-5/4)

4518. Hudson, John H. m 10/7/45 Louesa Clark, both of Auburn, in Utica; Rev. Dr. Proal (9-10/8)

4519. Hudson, John Nicholas Bogert, 7 mo, youngest s of Henry, d 5/10/36 in Geneva (6-5/18)

4520. Hudson, Jonathan of Geneva m 10/17/33 Elizabeth R. Riley, dau of Elder Lawrence Riley of Lyons, in L (6-10/23)

4521. Hudson, Jonathan, 24, local minister of a Meth. Episc. church, d 7/17/34 in Geneva (surv by wf) (6-7/23)

4522. Hudson, Mary Caroline, 7 mo, dau of William, d 8/12/33 in Geneva (6-8/14)

4523. Hudson, Reuben, 50, d 12/30/31 in Jerusalem, NY (6-1/4/32)

4524. Hudson, Schuyler H. m 10/26/46 Margaret McDonald, both of Geneva, in Canandaigua; Rev. Daggett (6-10/30)

4525. Hudson, William S. m 4/21/32 Rebecca Matin in Jerusalem, NY (6-4/25)

4526. Huffman, William B. d 6/5/33 in Phelps (6-7/3)

4527. Huggins, John R. D., hairdresser, of NYC d in Albany at Higham's Tavern (suicide by razor) (7-12/18/16)

4528. Higgins, Stephen, 40, merchant, d 11/20/25 in New Haven (9-12/6)

4529. Huggit, Edward m 10/28/32 Mary Ann Mantle in Geneva; Elder Bentley. All of Geneva (6-11/7)

4530. Hughes, Anna C., 20, wf of William, d 8/24/48 in Utica (funeral from the home of her husband, 49 Seneca St.) (9-8/25)

4531. Hughes, John, 46, formerly of Utica, d 3/2/46 in Remsen (9-3/5)

4532. Hughes, John C., 55, d 1/11/49 in Utica (funeral at the home of William Kemp, 3 Bridge Street (9-1/13)

4533. Hughes, John E. of Little Falls m 12/1/46 Eleanor Quinn of Rome, NY in R; Rev. Davis (9-12/4)

4534. Hughes, Sarah (Miss), 19, d 6/11/43 in Remsen (9-6/15)

4535. Hughes, Stephen W., Esq., 33, sheriff of Cayuga Co., d 7/19/26 in Auburn
      (9-8/1)
4536. Hughes, William m 5/8/48 Anna Haley, both of Utica, in U; Rev. Joseph
      Hartwell (9-5/16)
4537. Hughes, Zebadiah m 12/6/33 Susan Stevens in Ithaca (6-12/25)
4538. Hughston, Mason W. of Sidney m 2/21/22 Ann Hunt, dau of Ransom, Esq. of
      Hamburgh in the town of Unadilla (8-3/6)
4539. Hughston, Nathaniel W. of Norwich m 2/27/22 Damres Morgan of Oxford in
      Guilford (8-3/6)
4540. Hugunin, Hiram of Oswego m 10/27/30 Jane E. Bostwick, dau of late William
      B. of Auburn, in A (6-11/1)
4541. Huie, John (Maj.), 62, (served as a captain in the War of 1812 and was
      wounded in the battle at Fort Erie, 17 Sept 1814) d 2/20/34 in Seneca
      (6-3/19)
4542. Huie, Thomas of Seneca m 10/7/34 Sarah Haines of Maryland (NY?) in
      Penn Yan (6-10/15)
4543. Hulbert, Hannah Castle, 24, wf of Col. John P., d 7/16/30 in Auburn
      (6-7/28)
4544. Hulbert, Jarvis of Wayne m 10/22/35 Abigail Chamberlain of Jersey, NY in
      J (6-11/4)
4545. Hulburt, John W. (Hon.) d 10/19/31 in Auburn (during War of 1812 was
      a member of Congress; moved from Massachusetts to Cayuga Co., NY in
      1816) (6-10/26)
4546. Hull, ____, 64, wf of Ebenezer, d 2/24/44 in Oxford (Oxford Republican,
      3/7)
4547. Hull, A. Dennison (Dr.) m 12/22/42 Mary Alvord, youngest dau of Elisha,
      in Lansingburgh; Rev. Symmes. All of Lansingburgh (9-12/28)
4548. Hull, Andrew (Rev.), rector of St. Andrew's Ch. in New Berlin, m 6/21/43
      Sarah Gold Frost, dau of late Rev. John, in Whitesboro; Rev. J. Jay
      Okill, rector of St. Peter's Ch. in Bainbridge (9-6/27)
4549. Hull, Caroline (Miss), 38, d 3/23/46 in Utica (funeral from the home of
      her sister, Mrs. Lundergreen, 11 Hotel St.) (9-3/24)
4550. Hull, Charles C. of Ellicottville m 5/1/50 Grace M. Kimball of Elmira
      in E; Rev. A. Hull (5-5/10)
4551. Hull, Chester, Jr., editor of the Coxsackie Advertiser, m 2/17/35 Rosa
      M. Hudson of Bainbridge in B (6-3/4)
4552. Hull, H. H., editor of the Steuben Courier of Bath, m 8/15/50 Clara
      Williston, dau of Judge Williston of Athens, PA, in A; Rev. C. Thurston
      (4-8/21)
4553. Hull, Hannah, 65, wf of John, d 1/16/45 in Oxford (Oxford Republican, 2/13)
      Hull, John. See Hill, John, 82, ...
4554. Hull, John G., formerly of the firm of P. Potter and Co. and late publisher
      of the Poughkeepsie Journal, d 2/22/35 at St. Augustine, East Florida
      (6-3/18)
4555. Hull, Nathan (Capt.), 37, formerly master of a packet boat between Rochester,
      Utica, and Buffalo, d 7/6/44 in Newark, NY (9-7/12)
4556. Hull, Peter, 67, "an old resident of New Hartford", d 2/14/43 at the
      home of his son-in-law, Dr. Daniel Thomas, in Whitestown (funeral sermon
      by Rev. Hobart Williams, rector of the Episc. Ch. in New Hartford
      (9-2/22)
4557. Hull, Rachell, about 50, wf of William F., d 12/4/48 in Horseheads
      (5-12/8)
4558. Hull, William (Gen.) d 11/29/25 in Newton (9-12/6)
4559. Hull, William, 65, m 4/23/46 Caroline Woodruff, 83; Rev. F. A. Spencer
      (9-4/28)
4560. Hull, Zerah, 34, formerly of Oxford, d 10/30/41 in Ann Arbor, MI (Oxford
      Times, 11/10)
4561. Humason, James J. m 4/23/50 Jane E. Dewey, both of Turin, in T; Rev. A.
      S. Wightman (9-5/3)
4562. Humaston, J. L. of Vienna, NY m 9/14/43 Catharine T. Griswold, dau of
      Deacon Daniel of Annsville, in A; Rev. T. B. Jervis (9-9/20)
4563. Humphrey, Abner d 9/20/20 in Bainbridge (8-9/27)
4564. Humphrey, Arnold, 31, d 3/29/49 in Skaneateles (1-4/5)
4565. Humphrey, Augustine m 3/9/31 Harriet Augusta Woodbridge in Bloomfield
      (6-3/30)

4566. Humphrey, Eliza, 26, d in East Bloomfield (6-12/20/30)
4567. Humphrey, George, 77, d 8/22/33 in Phelps (one of the oldest settlers there) (6-8/28)
4568. Humphrey, Horace m 4/14/50 Lucinda Howe in Baldwinsville; Rev. B. Alden (1-4/18)
4569. Humphrey, James, 80, (a Rev. soldier) d 9/3/34 in Phelps (6-9/17)
4570. Humphrey, Phidelia, 12, oldest dau of John, d 12/28/47 in Baldwinsville (1-1/5/48)
4571. Humphrey, Sarah (Mrs.), 80, d 2/5/49 at the home of her son in Horseheads (5-2/16)
4572. Humphrey, William m 11/12/33 Rachel S. Harris in Lockport (6-11/27)
4573. Humphreys, David (Gen.) (a Rev. officer) d in New Haven (CT?) (8-3/11/18)
4574. Humphreys, Erastus, 63, d 3/9/48 in Utica (funeral from the home of his son on Fayette St.) (9-3/10)
4575. Humphreys, Felix of Schenectady m 9/30/45 Mary Ann Breakfield of Clinton at Trinity Ch., Utica; Rev. Dr. Proal (9-10/2)
4576. Humphreys, Tryphema, 25, wf of Morris, d 8/1/47 in Van Buren (1-8/4)
4577. Hungerford, Martin L. m 7/11/44 Jane Royce in Sauquoit; Rev. J. Waugh. All of Sauquoit (9-7/12)
4578. Hungerford, S. D., Esq., cashier of the Lewis County Bank, m 5/5/45 Ann E. Huntington, dau of D., Esq., in Watertown; Rev. Isaac Brayton (9-5/26)
4579. Hunt, Benjamin F. of Sullivan m 12/10/35 Mariam Hall of Lenox; Rev. Goodell (3-1/5/36)
4580. Hunt, Charles m 4/12/17 Lucy Preston in Norwich (8-4/16)
4581. Hunt, Charlotte, 45, consort of Alvin, editor of the Jeffersonian, d 4/3/49 in Watertown (9-4/7)
4582. Hunt, Daniel m 9/11/42 Polly L. Thompson, dau of Capt. James, in Norwich; Rev. J. T. Goodrich. All of Norwich (Oxford Times, 9/14)
4583. Hunt, Edwin, formerly of Oxford, m Martha Southmayd in Norwich (8-5/25/25)
4584. Hunt, Frederick (Capt.), formerly a shipmaster and in later years in commerce, d 11/20/25 (in Utica?) (age 75 at time of death) (9-12/6)
4585. Hunt, John of the firm of R. W. and J. Hunt of Utica d 2/1/46 at his home in Ilion (9-2/3)
4586. Hunt, Jonathan (Hon.), a member of Congress from VT, d 5/14/32 in Washington, D.C. (3-5/22)
4587. Hunt, Julia Ann W., inf dau of George of Oxford, d 3/28/25 (8-3/30)
4588. Hunt, Mary, 60, wf of Capt. Walter formerly of Oxford, d 5/31/21 in Candor (7-6/20 and 8-6/20)
4589. Hunt, Matilda, about 33, wf of Richard and oldest dau of Martin Kendig, Esq., d "recently" in Waterloo (6-9/19)
4590. Hunt, Montgomery, Esq., 59, formerly cashier of the Bank of Utica, d "about Jan. 12 on the Island of St. Croix, West Indies" (6-3/15)
4591. Hunt, Montgomery (Lt.) of the U.S. Navy m 9/30/47 Elizabeth Keteltas, dau of late Dr. Philip D., in NYC; Rev. Dr. Anthon (9-10/4)
4592. Hunt, Nancy (Mrs.), 34, d (in Milo?) (6-6/18/34)
4593. Hunt, Rebecca, 60, wf of Luther, d 4/3/23 in Oxford (8-4/9)
4594. Hunt, Rollin B. m 12/23/48 Mary Malinda Gill, both of Harrison, in Elkland; Rev. Potter (4-1/3/49)
4595. Hunt, Sally, 76, wf of Joseph, Esq., d in Smyrna (9-4/11/50)
4596. Hunt, Samuel M. (Dr.) of Lisle m 12/11/23 Mariah Havens of Harrison in H; Rev. Bennet (8-12/17)
4597. Hunt, Samuel Roberts, 15, s of late Elijah, d 6/10/46 in Westmoreland (a student in Clinton Academy) (9-7/4)
4598. Hunt, Sanford, Esq., 72, d 6/7/49 in Portage (father of Hon. Washington Hunt, present comptroller (9-6/13)
4599. Hunt, Simeon, 31, late of Greene, NY but formerly of Greenville, MA, d 9/18/19 in Natchez, Mississippi (8-11/3)
4600. Hunt, William Gibbs, Esq., editor of the National Banner, d 8/13/33 in Nashville, TN (6-9/4)
4601. Hunt, William M. of Enfield, CT m 1/20/46 Orpha Ann Harmond of Westmoreland at the Central Hotel in Utica; Rev. J. H. McIlvaine (9-1/21)
4602. Hunt, Zebuline A. P., wf of John, Esq. and oldest dau of J. C. Symmes Harrison, deceased, d 6/14/49 in Sugar Grove, Boone Co., KY (gr-dau of Generals Pike and Harrison) (9-7/12)

4603. Hunter, Esther, 60, wf of Patrick, d 10/24/36 in Geneva (6-10/26)
4604. Hunter, Ira T. m 8/15/33 Eliza I. Barrett in East Bloomfield (6-9/11)
4605. Hunter, James, 40, formerly editor of the Daily Advertiser, d 7/15/34 in Albany (6-7/23)
4606. Huntington, Anne, 67, d 4/4/42 at her home in Rome, NY (9-4/6)
4607. Huntington, Charles of Rochester m 8/24/46 Amelia Tomlinson, oldest dau of H. of Geneva, in G; Rev. T. T. Farington (6-8/28)
4608. Huntington, E. A. (Rev.) of Albany m 7/30/39 Anna Van Vechten, oldest dau of Rev. Dr. V. V., in Schenectady (double ceremony - see marr of Edward Savage) (3-8/7)
4609. Huntington, Edward of Rome, NY m 9/4/44 Antoinette Randall of Cortland in C; Rev. Hoes of Ithaca (9-9/9)
4610. Huntington, Henry (Hon.), 80, d 10/15/46 in Rome, NY (9-10/16)
4611. Huntington, Henry A. m 3/25/50 Elizabeth Blake, dau of Mrs. E. W., in Utica; Rev. H. W. Spencer. All of Utica (9-3/26)
4612. Huntington, Horace F. of Norwalk (OH?) m 10/1/35 Amelia Webb(?) of Bronson, OH in B; Rev. E. Conger (3-11/3)
4613. Huntington, Jedediah (Gen.), 79, (a Rev. officer), formerly collector of the port of New London, CT, d in New London (8-10/14/18)
4614. Huntington, L. Cheney m 5/10/49 Julia C. Sharp, both of Baldwinsville, in B; Rev. T. Walker (1-5/10)
4615. Huntington, Hannah, 74, wid of late George, Esq., d 9/20/48 in Rome, NY (9-9/26)
4616. Huntington, Mary M. (Miss), 25, dau of George, d 7/31/26 in Rome, NY (9-8/8)
4617. Huntington, Mary P. (Miss), 24, dau of Gurdon, d 3/24/25 in Rome, NY (consumption) (9-4/12)
4618. Huntington, Sarah A. (Miss), 21, dau of Charles of Chittenango, d 12/8/36 in Schenectady (3-12/14)
4619. Huntington, William, 23, oldest s of Israel, d 12/15/30 in Geneva (6-12/29)
4620. Huntley, Adeline Cordelia, inf dau of Elias S., d 3/19/31 in Ithaca (6-3/30)
4621. Huntley, Solomon, 98, (a Rev. soldier) d 3/4/47 in Camillus (1-3/10)
4622. Huntsley, Lewis m 2/17/33 Rebecca Benton, both of Portage, in Angelica (6-3/6)
4623. Hurburt, Kellogg, Esq., 64, d 10/19/47 in Utica (moved to New Hartford in his youth and followed mercantile and manufacturing pursuits there) (9-10/20 and 10/26)
4624. Hurd, Darwin E. (Dr.) of Canastota m 1/25/44 Angeline F. Pratt, dau of Frederick, Esq. of Fayetteville, in F; Rev. Cleveland (3-1/31)
4625. Hurd, Lovell m 1/15/32 Sally Ann Taber of Manchester in Palmyra (6-1/25)
4626. Hurd, Mary Ann, 27, wf of Ward, Esq., d 5/18/46 in Utica (dau of Hon. John Savage) (9-5/20)
4627. Hurd, Rebecca L., 3rd wf of Rev. L. N. and youngest dau of late E. D. Hudson, d 11/17/50 in Big Flats (5-11/22)
4628. Hurlburt, Charles m 6/14/47 Sarah A. Fuller, dau of Robert of Cambridge, MA, in C; Rev. Parker (9-6/15)
4629. Hurlburt, Gilman H. (Dr.), 47, d 6/11/30 in Castleton, Seneca Co. (6-6/16)
4630. Hurlburt, Hiram, Esq., attorney, of Utica m 1/17/43 Marie Antoinette Hungerford of Hadlyme, CT in H; Rev. George Carrington (9-1/23)
4631. Hurlburt, James, 1 , s of Hezekiah, d 9/2/36 in Geneva (6-9/14)
4632. Hurlburt, Jonathan (Dr.), 58, d 8/11/48 in Cornwall, CT (9-8/16)
     Hurlburt, Kellogg. See Hurburt, Kellogg.
4633. Hurlbut, Horace, 38, formerly of Boonville, NY, d 7/23/43 at Planter's House in St. Louis, MO (9-8/18)
4634. Hurst, George W., 35, of Albany d 2/23/31 at the Eagle Tavern in Elmira (6-3/9)
4635. Husted, Henry, Esq. of Penn Yan m 1/28/34 Susan Williams of Potter in P (6-2/12)
4636. Husted, John N., 24, d 5/9/34 in Chittenango (consumption) (3-5/13)
4637. Husted, Willson m 7/16/48 Abigail Pease, dau of Oliver, Esq., both of Troopsburg, in T; Lyman Dodge, Esq. (4-7/26)
4638. Huston, David, 24, bro of James of Geneva and bro-in-law of C. Campbell, d 6/2/30 in Romulus (6-6/23)

4639. Hutchins, Charles, 74, (a Rev. soldier) d in Italy, NY (6-7/28/30)
4640. Hutchins, Charles S. m 8/31/37 Nancy Bitely in Sullivan; Jairus French,
       Esq. All of Sullivan (3-9/6)
4641. Hutchins, Elias of Cortland Co. m 9/20/50 Charlotte Tyler of Painted Post
       in P. P.; B. Pew, Esq. (4-9/25)
4642. Hutchins, Eliza Ann, 19, consort of L. and dau of Jacob Fink, d 6/18/39
       in Sullivan (3-6/19)
4643. Hutchins, Joseph B. m 7/3/25 Martha Dorrance in Vienna, NY; Rev. Stevens
       (9-7/12)
4644. Hutchinson, Charles C. of Lyons m 10/26/47 Mary Gilfillan of Utica in U;
       Rev. Clark (9-10/27)
4645. Hutchinson, Edwin P. m 10/24/50 Mary R. Cutis (sic) in Elmira; Rev. P. H.
       Fowler (5-10/25)
4646. Hutchison, Lucius m 7/4/50 Eliza Ann Widger in Baldwinsville; Rev. A.
       Wells. All of Van Buren (1-7/11)
4647. Hutchison, Seth m 10/6/35 Mary M. Strong, dau of Oliver R., Esq. in
       Onondaga; Rev. J. F. McLaren of Geneva (6-10/14)
4648. Huwey, Sarah, 73, wf of William, Esq., d 6/24/45 in Oswego (9-6/27)
4649. Huyck, William of Herkimer m 8/24/47 Maria Van Dyck of Frankfort in
       Utica; Rev. H. R. Clarke (9-8/25)
4650. Hyatt, George W. of Nelson m 10/2/39 Emily Cushing, dau of Enos, Esq.
       of Sullivan, in S; Rev. E. S. Barrows of Cazenovia (3-10/9)
4651. Hyde, Alvan (Rev.), 30, s of Rev. Dr. Hyde and pastor of the Cong'l. Ch.
       in Madison, OH, d 8/12/24 in Lee, MA (9-9/14)
4652. Hyde, Austin of Oxford m Elizabeth A. Mygatt of New Milford, CT in N. M.;
       Rev. Elliott (8-10/28/18)
4653. Hyde, Austin (Judge), 61, d 2/25/50 in Oxford (consumption) (9-3/7)
4654. Hyde, Edward of Cambridgeport, MA m 12/31/45 Sarah Cutting Gregory of
       Guilford, VT in Utica, NY; Rev. Dr. Proal (9-1/1/46)
4655. Hyde, James, Esq., 53, d 3/31/26 in Richfield (9-4/18)
4656. Hyde, Joseph (Rev.), 24, oldest s of Joseph, Esq. of Greens Farms,
       Fairfield, CT, d at G. F. (9-1/11/25)
4657. Hyde, Lucy, 20, only dau of Rev. Alvan of Lee, MA, d in Sandwich, MA
       (consumption) ("Last August a brother died of the same disease and
       in October a sister") (9-6/28/25)
4658. Hyde, Orrimal J. m 9/6/46 Caroline Park; Rev. D. P. Gorrie. All of
       Camden (9-9/9)
4659. Hyde, William W. m 9/28/50 Lovina Cady at Clayville; Rev. L. Sperry
       (9-10/1)
4660. Hyer, William, 80, d in NYC (6-4/28/30)
4661. Ide, Elizabeth, about 2, dau of John, d 8/29/31 in Geneva (6-8/31)
4662. Ide, Mary H., about 25, wf of John, d 4/1/37 in Geneva (6-4/5)
4663. Imus, Nelson m 7/2/35 Catharine Van Ness in Geneva; Rev. J. Chase. All
       of G (6-7/8)
4664. Ingersoll, ? of Pittsford m Polly Wilbur of Phelps in Vienna, NY
       (6-1/26/31)
4665. Ingersoll, Edward of Philadelphia (state not given) m 6/5/50 Anna C.
       Warren, dau of late Stephen, in Troy; Rev. R. B. Van Kleeck (9-6/11)
4666. Ingersoll, Lamon m 1/12/26 Sally Sherwood in Guilford; Elder Otis (8-1/18)
4667. Ingersoll, Thomas H., 33, d 1/8/44 in Oxford (Oxford Republican, 1/11)
4668. Ingham, Samuel S. (Dr.) d 7/9/47 at the home of his father in Manheim
       Center, Herk. Co. (9-7/12)
4669. Ingleheart, Jacob m 3/21/30 Sophia Kennie; Rev. D. Baker. All of Phelps
       (6-3/24)
4670. Inglesby, Eber d 8/31/50 in Van Buren (1-9/5)
4671. Ingman, George m 10/12/46 Betsy Payne, both of Geneva; Rev. High (6-11/6)
4672. Ingols, Addison m Lucy Batchelder in Canandaigua (6-3/31/30)
4673. Ingols, Harriet S., 44, wf of J., d 4/6/45 in Utica (consumption) (9-4/8)
4674. Ingraham, Mary L., 49, consort of A. formerly of Oneida Co., NY, d 3/12/49
       in Columbus, WI (6-4/19)
4675. Inman, Washington, 8, d 6/15/49 in Yorkville (9-6/19)
4676. Inman, William, 80, d 2/14/43 in West Turin (9-2/22)
4677. Inslee, John m 9/11/32 Julia Miller, both of Gorham, in G (6-9/26)
4678. Ireland, Joanna, relict of late James, d 5/13/33 (in Geneva?) ("Her
       remains were yesterday conveyed to ... Williamson, Wayne co. to be
       interred with those of her husband and child") (6-5/15)

4679. Irvin, James m 3/17/50 Adeline Hutchinson, both of Watertown, at Black River; George W. Hazleton, Esq. (9-4/13)
4680. Irvin, Margaret, widow, d 12/21/32 at the home of her son, Col. William P., in Sodus (6-1/2/33)
4681. Irving, Theodore, Esq. m 8/28/38 Jane B. Sutherland, both of Geneva, in Geneva (6-8/29)
4682. Irwin, John m 6/22/34 Adeline Rue, both of Kennedyville, in Cohocton (6-7/2)
4683. Irwin, Lucretia (Mrs.), 79, d in Utica (funeral at the home of Mrs. Mor_?_ at 5 Washington St.) (9-2/17/47)
4684. Isham, Catharine d in Colchester (by taking a swallow of corrosive sublimate supposing it to be cider) (6-1/26/31)
4685. Isham, Chester (Rev.), 27, of Taunton, MA; d 4/20/25 in Boston (grad from Yale Univ.; studied theology at Andover; ordained at Trinitarian Ch. in Taunton 28 Feb 1824; in Oct. sailed to Cuba for his health; by Feb 1825 was in the home of Rev. Palmer in Charleston, SC; Apr 10 sailed to Boston where he died) (9-5/17)
4686. Ives, Amon m 9/22/25 Alvinah Gridley, both of Clinton, in Westmoreland (9-10/11)
4687. Ives, E. Ruthven m 8/6/33 Minerva Barnes in Ithaca (6-8/14)
4688. Ives, Elizabeth, 69, wf of Jesse, d 3/29/45 in Bridgewater (buried in Whitesboro) (9-4/8)
4689. Jackson, Alfred Edward, 21, d 7/21, d 7/20/47 at Valley View, Fauquier Co., VA (consumption) (grad from Union Col. in Schenectady, NY in 1846; conducted the Academy in Herkimer, NY for one term) (9-8/7)
4690. Jackson, Amasa of NYC m 12/26/31 Jane E. Howell, dau of Nathaniel of Canandaigua, in C (6-1/4/32)
4691. Jackson, Charles, 91, d in China, NY (his wf d 7 days before, age 90; had been married 70 yrs; had fought in 32 battles in the French War) (6-12/21/31)
4692. Jackson, Charles m 12/31/43 Caroline E. Hudson in New Hartford; Rev. B. W. Gorham. All of New Hartford (9-1/20/44)
4693. Jackson, James M., barber, d 11/19/46 in Utica (his shop in the Exchange Bldg., Genesee St.) (surv by wf and 2 young ch) (9-11/20)
4694. Jackson, Lyman m 10/13/50 Leah Teachout; Rev. C. Wheeler (5-10/18)
4695. Jackson, Marcus m 10/14/32 Usebe B. Rosecrants in Bellona (6-11/7)
4696. Jackson, Michael m Betsey Kimble, both of Eldorado, in Geneva; Rev. Mason (6-2/10/30)
4697. Jackson, Samuel m 11/14/46 Jeanette W. Dublin; D. Gillmore, Esq. All of Utica (9-11/25)
4698. Jackson, Samuel Rollin, 2, only s of William, d 9/12/43 in Augusta (9-10/16)
4699. Jackson, William m 4/12/32 Sarah Lacy in Seneca; S. G. Gage, Esq. (6-5/2)
4700. Jackson, William m 5/20/44 Catherine Blow, both of Rome, NY, in R; Rev. S. Haynes (9-5/23)
4701. Jackson, William P. (Rev.) of Bristol m Julia A. Beers in Ithaca (6-4/14/30)
4702. Jacobs, Charles m 9/15/50 Julia Washington; Rev. M. Crow (5-9/27)
4703. Jacobs, David m 11/20/40 Susan Hubbard of Caton in South Corning; Rev. Charles B. Davis (4-11/27)
4704. Jacobs, Elliott m 11/4/47 Catharine Case, both of Salisbury, in Utica; Rev. D. G. Corey (9-11/6)
4705. Jacobs, Philip, Esq., 50, m 2/22/17 Eliza Brown, 18, in NYC (8-3/26)
4706. Jacobs, William m 11/18/27 Phila Gifford, dau of Abner, in Oxford; Rev. Kies(?). All of Oxford (8-11/23)
4707. Jacobus, Jane (Mrs.), 70, d in Binghamton (6-3/9/31)
4708. Jacocks, Daniel m 4/21/33 Ann Starrow; Rev. Mandeville (6-5/1)
4709. Jacops, Nathaniel m 12/14/33 Rachel Jones in Batavia (6-12/25)
4710. James, _____ (Rev.) m 11/24/24 Marcia Ames, both of Albany, in A (9-12/7)
4711. James, Ann (Mrs.), 48, d 8/15/46 in NYC (9-8/18)
4712. James, Daniel (Dr.) of Utica, NY m 9/26/42 Angelica G. Macbeth of Hudson, NY in Warren, ME (9-10/14)
4713. James, Daniel, 59, d 5/3/44 in Utica (funeral from his late home, corner Main and 1st Sts.) (9-5/4)
4714. James, Eliza Frances, 1, dau of Thomas and Mary E., d 5/20/46 in Geneva (funeral from the home of John Morse on Castle St. (6-5/22)

4715. James, John m 3/18/48 Julia Ann Rogers, dau of late Reuben, in Utica; Rev. Marcus A. Perry. All of Utica (9-3/21)

4716. James, John B., s of late William, Esq. of Albany, m 10/9/34 Mary Heen Vanderburgh, late of Geneva, in NYC (6-10/22)

4717. James, Lana, 31, wf of John formerly of Utica, d in Lyonsdale, Lewis Co. (9-12/19/45)

4718. James, Lois, 32, wf of John formerly of Utica, d 2/22/48 in Lyonsdale ("Northern papers please copy") (9-3/9)

4719. James, M. F. m 12/28/46 Margaret A. Miller, both of NYC, in Oswego; Rev. Condit (9-1/1/47)

4720. James, Mary C., 50, wf of Thomas, d 10/18/44 in Utica (funeral from her husband's home on Whitesboro St.) (9-10/19)

4721. James, Mary R. Mellen, dau of late Thomas of Utica, d 5/17/49 in Oswego (funeral at the home of Mr. Wetmore, 81 Whitesboro St., Utica (9-5/18)

4722. James, Morgan m 11/9/42 Mary Louisa White in Utica; Rev. Hawley. All of Utica (3-11/10)

4723. James, Morris m 8/4/48 Charlotte Barker, both of Clinton, in Westmoreland; Rev. F. A. Spencer (9-8/12)

4724. James, Sarah (Miss), 16 d 12/5/31 in Geneva (6-12/7)

4725. James, Thomas, 49, d 10/19/44 in Utica (9-10/21)

4726. James, William, Esq., 63, d 12/19/32 in Albany (6-12/26)

4727. James, William, 32, d 1/13/43 in Utica (funeral at his brother's home, 41 Whitesboro St.) (9-1/14)

4728. Jamison, Jacob (Dr.), 29, surgeon's mate on U.S. Frigate "Java", d 7/30/30 in Algiers (a Seneca Indian, studied his profession, says the Buffalo Journal, with Dr. Chapin in Buffalo; grandson of the white woman Mary Jamison "whose memoirs were published a few years since") (9-1/25/31). For further details concerning this Jamison/Jemison/Jimeson family see Fred Q. Bowman's "Vital Record Postings of an Indian Missionary in Western New York, 1832-1879" (NYGB Record, 117:20-26).

4729. Jane, Silas C. m Mary Benedict in Wheeler (6-4/14/30)

4730. Janek(?), Llewelyn, Esq. of Auburn m 7/29/33 Catharine Hutchinson in Watertown (6-8/14)

4731. Jansen, Henry, Esq. (Hon.), a delegate from Ulster Co. to the state convention, d 9/20/21 in Albany ("belonged to one of the oldest ... families of Ulster ...") (8-9/26)

4732. Jarvis, _____, wf of William, d in Palmyra (6-3/23/31)

4733. Jarvis, Harriet (Mrs.), 45, d in Carbondale, PA (2-7/19/43)

4734. Jarvis, Helen, 3, only dau of A. H., d 2/3/26 in Utica (9-2/7)

4735. Jaycox, Orlin R. of Neenah, WI m 8/28/50 Urania Ann Voorhees at the home of Col. Voorhees in Lysander; Rev. H. Gregory (1-8/29)

4736. Jeaneson, Andrew m 5/12/42 Nancy Haynes, both of Norwich, in N; Rev. W. H. Pearne(?) (Oxford Times, 5/18)

4737. Jeffers, Leverett m1/25/43 Sophronia S. Scofield in Binghamton; Rev. William M. Delong (2-2/1)

4738. Jefferson, Avery m 5/3/50 Elizabeth H. Barker, both of Floyd; H. C. Vogell, Esq. (9-5/9)

4739. Jeffrey, Alexander m 6/20/39 Delia W. Granger, dau of Maj. Gen. John Albert Granger, in Canandaigua; Rev. Thompson (6-7/3)

4740. Jenkins, Aylward, only s of J. Hervey and Angeline Teresa, d 8/30/48 in Utica (funeral from his parents' home, 42 Liberty St.) (9-8/31)

4741. Jenkins, Benjamin m 11/26/40 Frances Riddle, dau of Robert, Esq., in Sullivan; Rev. James Abell. All of Sullivan (double ceremony - see marr of Perez D. Harrington)

4742. Jenkins, J. Whipple, Esq. m 6/24/35 E. Jennette Tuttle in Vernon; Rev. Hough (3-6/30)

4743. Jenkins, James Hervey of Utica m Angeline Therese Reeves of NYC in Utica; Elder C. P. Grosvenor (9-8/11)

4744. Jenkins, John S., Esq., attorney, of Weedsport m 4/18/43 Minerva Porter Fellows, dau of late E. B., Esq. of Sennett, in S; Rev. Swart, missionary of the Episcopal Ch. at Jordan, NY (9-5/9)

4745. Jenkins, Lemuel, Esq., attorney, m Gertrude Huyck, formerly of Kingston, in Bloomingburgh, Sull. Co. (8-6/23/19)

4746. Jenkins, Mary, 37, dau of Jonathan, Esq., d 10/4/50 in Jackson Co., MI (5-10/25)

4747. Jenkins, Robert (Hon.), mayor of Hudson, d 11/10/19 on his way from NYC to Hudson (8-11/24)
4748. Jenkins, William m 3/9/31 Mary Ann Henry, oldest dau of late Dr. John of Geneva, in Utica; Rev. E. Galusha (6-3/30)
4749. Jenks, Sedgwick m 6/26/48 Charlotte Sink, both of Rome, NY, in R; Thomas Dugan, Esq. (9-7/1)
4750. Jenner, James m 2/9/32 Sophia Hathaway in Palmyra (6-2/29)
4751. Jennings, _____ (Mr.) d 12/18/42 in Sullivan (3-12/21)
4752. Jennings, Edmund L. m 10/10/32 Julia McHenry in Southport (6-11/7)
4753. Jennings, Mary, 30, wf of Pliny formerly of Litchfield, CT, d 10/5/31 in Geneva (6-10/12)
4754. Jennings, Moses, 40, d 6/26/43 in Bridgport (sic) (3-7/12)
4755. Jennings, Nancy, 77, relict of Hon. Joseph formerly of Middlesex Settlement, Oneida Co., d 9/10/42 while visiting in Fort Plain (9-9/12)
    Jerman. See also German.
4756. Jerman, Edward m 3/19/45 Mary Ann Seavy, both of Utica, in Sauquoit; Rev. E. Boning (9-3/29)
4757. Jerome, Leonard Walter of Rochester m 4/5/49 Clarissa Hall, youngest dau of late Ambrose of Palmyra, in P; Rev. J. W. French (9-4/7)
4758. Jerome, Milton, Esq. (Dr.) of Madrid, St. Law. Co. m 2/15/49 Louisa A. Chapman of West Martinsburg in W. M.; Rev. C. Graves of Lowville (9-2/23)
4759. Jerome, William P. of Chicago, IL m 12/17/48 Sarah Hatch, dau of Capt. T., at St. Mark's Ch. in Le Roy, NY (1-12/28)
4760. Jerrett, Henry, Esq. m 6/9/47 Mary Stevens, both of Utica, in Hampton; Rev. O. H. Staple (9-6/10)
4761. Jerrety, Louisa, 3, d 1/6/49 in Utica (funeral from her parents' home, corner Bridge and Blandina Sts.) (9-1/8)
4762. Jervis, Susannah, 6, and Asahel, 4, children of James V., d 11/27/25 in Utica (9-12/6)
4763. Jewel, Elisha, 85, (a Rev. soldier) d 3/15/42 in Oxford (Oxford Times, 3/23)
4764. Jewel, Halsey m 8/28/49 Ann Eliza Schermerhorn in Utica; Rev. William Wyatt. All of Rome, NY (9-8/30)
4765. Jewell, Augustus G. m 8/19/32 Maria Colier, dau of Isaac; Rev. William H. Campbell. All of Sullivan (3-8/21)
4766. Jewell, James (Rev.), 47, pastor of the 2nd Cong'l. Ch. in Durham, NY, d 7/10/25 (9-8/9)
4767. Jewell, Joseph H., 18, d 10/6/39 in Wampsville (3-10/9)
4768. Jewell, Nancy, 52, wf of Oliver of Cazenovia, d 2/21/49 at the home of R. M. Dalzell in Rochester (9-2/24)
    Jimeson. See also Jameson.
4769. Jimeson, George m 7/6/31 Sally Tull-Chief (sic) (both of the Seneca Nation of Indians) (6-7/27)
4770. Jimeson, Mary, "the white woman", 91, d 9/19/33 in the Seneca village (taken captive by the Indians in her childhood and chose to remain with them the rest of her life) (6-10/9)
4771. John, Charles C., Esq. of Geneseo m 6/28/43 Sarah M. Wiser, only dau of Jeremiah of South Trenton, NY, in S. T.; Rev. T. C. Hitt (9-7/4)
4772. John, Peter Brant, 24, principal chief of the Mohawk Indians, d 3/3/50 in Brantford, Canada West (grandson of late Capt. Joseph Brant; surv by his mother (9-3/25)
4773. Johnson, _____, inf s of Eli, d in Lyons (6-4/28/30)
4774. Johnson, Abigail Louisa Smith, 37, wf of A. B. and gr-dau of late Pres. John Adams (also niece of ex-Pres. John Q. Adams), d 7/4/36 in Utica (6-7/20)
4775. Johnson, Anson S. m Olive B. Allen in Auburn (6-2/23/31)
4776. Johnson, Asa of Southbury, CT d 11/1/50 in Utica (for many years a merchant and broker in NYC) (9-11/5)
4777. Johnson, Ben, Esq., 64, d 3/19/48 in Ithaca ("a prominent lawyer"; Whig candidate in 1847 for Supreme Court justice) (9-3/24)
4778. Johnson, Benjamin m 5/25/33 Jane Thompson in Lyons; Rev. William Jones (6-6/12)
4779. Johnson, Brian of Sodus m Phebe Perry in Arcadia, NY (6-5/19/30)
4780. Johnson, Bryan, Esq. d 4/12/24 in Utica (9-4/13)

4781. Johnson, Christopher m 8/22/39 Phebe Landers in Chittenango; Jairus French, Esq. (3-8/28)
4782. Johnson, Clinton, 18, s of Nathan of Russia, NY, d 1/24/47 in Utica (9-1/27)
4783. Johnson, Dorcas (Mrs.), 31, d 4/22/32 in Lyons (consumption) (6-5/2)
4784. Johnson, Edward C., Esq. of NYC m 8/31/47 Delia M. Smith, dau of Adam of Hamilton; Rev. William M. Richards (9-9/2)
4785. Johnson, Eli m 11/7/33 Berthana Yates in Bloomfield (6-11/27)
4786. Johnson, Elizabeth, 25, consort of William G., d 2/25/32 in Milo (6-3/14)
4787. Johnson, Eunice, 22, d 1/29/31 in Bath (6-2/9)
4788. Johnson, Francis, about 50, d 4/6/44 in Philadelphia (PA?) ("founder and leader of the celebrated colored band known as 'Frank Johnson's Band'") (9-4/10)
4789. Johnson, G. F. R. m Cecilia Harriet Durand 7/6/33 in NYC (6-7/17)
4790. Johnson, George Field of New Berlin m 5/15/45 Elizabeth Ann Phelps of Utica at Trinity Ch.; Rev. Dr. Proal (9-5/16)
4791. Johnson, Gilbert m 9/16/47 Emily T. Sage, both of Verona, in V; Rev. Stickney (9-9/20)
4792. Johnson, H. W. (Dr.) of Southport, NY m 12/6/42 Adeline Amelia La Tour of Geneva, Walworth Co., Wisc. Terr.; Rev. Jewett (9-12/31)
4793. Johnson, Hiram m 10/2/36 Almira Bundy in Cameron (6-10/12)
4794. Johnson, Ira m 10/2/33 Sally Ann Inslee in Waterloo (6-10/16)
4795. Johnson, James m 10/14/32 Sally Coleman, both of Bellona, in B (6-11/7)
4796. Johnson, James, 68, d 11/1/48 in Liverpool, NY (arrived there as a boy and remained there until death) (1-11/2)
4797. Johnson, James, Jr. m 7/10/49 Abigail Cretsley of Painted Post in Horseheads; Rev. C. C. Carr (5-7/13)
4798. Johnson, John m Jane Cook in Penn Yan (6-7/28/30)
4799. Johnson, John of Otisco m Sarah Palmer in Canandaigua (6-7/10/33)
4800. Johnson, John D. m 1/23/49 Mary E. Hauseleuren at Frankfort Hill; Rev. Howard. All of F. H. (9-1/31)
4801. Johnson, Jonathan F. B. m Sally Bull in Junius (6-3/10/30)
4802. Johnson, Lewis m Prudy Clinton, both of Smithville, in S; William Knowlton, Esq. (8-1/19/25)
4803. Johnson, Lucy E., 35, relict of late Dr. E. of Buffalo and 2nd dau of late Rev. John Lord of Madison Co., d 11/30/50 in Genesee (9-12/6)
4804. Johnson, Maria L., wf of Rev. Evan M. and dau of Rev. John B., d in Newtown, L.I., NY (9-7/26)
4805. Johnson, Mason m 12/2/29 Esther Avery in Preston; Elder Jedediah Randall (7-12/23)
4806. Johnson, Moses of Waterloo m 3/27/33 Mary Dey, dau of Capt. David, in Varick; Rev. Law (6-4/3)
4807. Johnson, Noahdiah (Hon.), member of the state senate from the 3rd district and resident of Delhi, d 4/4/39 in Albany (6-4/10)
4808. Johnson, Philip m 1/1/35 Sarah Blakesly (in Waterloo?) (6-1/14)
4809. Johnson, Samuel, 47, of Binghamton, NY d 1/11/49 in New Orleans, LA (consumption) (9-1/27)
4810. Johnson, Solomon d 3/6/25 in Clinton (9-3/15)
4811. Johnson, Stephen C. m Mary Ann Swift in Delhi (6-1/26/31)
4812. Johnson, Sylvester C., 19, s of E. C. and Melissa of Denmark, Lewis Co., NY, d 6/20/47 in Vera Cruz, Mexico. (in 1846 visited friends in Illinois through the winter and there enlisted in the U.S. Army; died a few days after reaching V. C. (9-12/1)
4813. Johnson, Thomas R. (Dr.), 35, of the U.S. Army d 7/11/37 in Baltimore, MD (6-7/19)
4814. Johnson, Triphena, 13, drowned 9/25/19 in Oxford (8-9/29)
4815. Johnson, Washington m 1/2/49 Elinor Clark in Corning; Elder Balcom (4-1/10)
4816. Johnson, William, 19, "a coloured person", d 3/3/26 in Utica (9-3/7)
4817. Johnson, William C. m 11/1/47 Harriett M. Douw, dau of late John D. P. of Albany, in Millburne, Columbia Co.; Rev. Tucker (9-11/4)
4818. Johnson, William D. m 10/9/31 Melinda Durand in Waterloo (6-10/26)
4819. Johnson, William P. C. of Bristol, PA m 3/22/31 Ann Eliza Washington, oldest dau of Bushrod, Esq. of Virginia (6-4/6)
4820. Johnson, William Samuel, 94, L.L.D., late pres. of Columbia College, d 11/14/19 in Stratford, CT (8-12/1)

4821. Johnston, Hugh (Capt.), 70, d at Sidney Plains, Dela. Co. (6-11/6/33)
4822. Johnston, Margaret, 20, dau of James and Margaret, d 7/19/47 in New York Mills ("New York City papers please copy") (9-7/26)
4823. Jones, Abraham H. m 10/10/47 Amanda Halstead in Van Buren; Rev. J. Smitzer (1-10/20)
4824. Jones, Alvin m 4/11/33 Irene Watkins in Seneca Falls (6-4/24)
4825. Jones, Anna, 81, wid of late Nehemiah, d 10/8/44 in Westmoreland (had lived in W 57 yrs) (9-10/19)
4826. Jones, Anna Louisa, 1, dau of H. E., d 9/19/50 in Utica (9-9/20)
4827. Jones, Antoinette Salina, inf dau of E. B. and P. R., d 12/22/46 in Utica (funeral at 24 Columbia St.) (9-12/23)
4828. Jones, Benjamin of Binghamton m 1/2/43 Lavina Whaley of Fairport, CT in F; Rev. Perry (2-1/25)
4829. Jones, Betsey (Miss), 18, d 3/1/26 in Utica (9-3/7)
4830. Jones, Catharine, 66, wf of Rowland A., d 4/9/46 at Smith's Hill, town of Deerfield (9-4/14)
4831. Jones, Charles (Rev.) of La Fargeville m 4/29/40 Calcina P. Gardner of Fayetteville at the home of John McViccar, Esq.; Rev. Tuttle (3-5/6)
4832. Jones, D. R. F. (Hon.) of Albany m 6/26/45 Mary L. Stanton, dau of G. W. of Albany, in A; Rev. Dr. Seabury of NYC (9-6/28)
4833. Jones, D. S., Esq. m 6/11/33 Mary Clinton, oldest dau of late Gov. Clinton, in NYC (6-6/19)
4834. Jones, David of Albany m 5/6/45 Ann Townsend of Utica in U; Elder Thomas Hill (9-5/15)
4835. Jones, David H. m 11/27/49 Mercy Ann Morris in Troy; Rev. J. C. Warren. All of Troy (9-12/11)
4836. Jones, David H., 23, principal farmer at the N.Y. State Lunatic Asylum, d 9/2/50 in Utica (had been an attendant at the Asylum for more than 2½ yrs) (9-9/7)
4837. Jones, David Lewis of Marshall (state not given) m 12/21/42 Adeline E. Trowbridge, youngest dau of C. of Albion, MI, in A; Rev. E. C. Hodgkin (9-1/2/43)
4838. Jones, David W., 36(?), d 8/29/49 in Utica (funeral at Cong'l. Ch., corner Washington and Whitesboro Sts.) (9-8/30)
4839. Jones, Eben C. m 4/28/31 Lucy Ann Judd, dau of Dr. Judd, in Penn Yan; Rev. C. Eddy (6-5/11)
4840. Jones, Edward m 4/26/40 Rebecca Mills in Chittenango; Rev. Abell. All of Chittenango (3-4/29)
4841. Jones, Edward B. of Utica m 4/9/44 Prudence R. Whitaker of Cherry Valley in C. V.; Rev. Lusk (9-4/22)
4842. Jones, Edward L., 20, formerly of Chittenango, d 6/24/39 at Cohoes Falls (3-6/26)
4843. Jones, Eleanor (Mrs.), 89, d 9/8/45 in Utica (funeral from the home of her son-in-law, William Francis, 50 Charlotte St.) (9-9/10)
4844. Jones, Elleanor, about 60, d 10/29/47 at the home of Mrs Clark in Utica (funeral from Welch Church [sic] on Hotel St.) (9-11/1)
4845. Jones, Elias, 35, d 8/31/33 in Auburn (by taking corrosive sublimate through mistake) (6-9/18)
4846. Jones, Elijah, 2nd, of Elmira m 9/7/48 Mary E. Ross of Oxford in O; Rev. Stone (5-9/22)
4847. Jones, Elizabeth, wf of J. A., formerly of Geneva, d in Philadelphia (state not given) (6-6/26/33)
4848. Jones, Elizabeth (Mrs.), 45, d 5/19/43 in Utica (funeral from her late home on 2nd St.) (9-5/20)
4849. Jones, Elnathan W. of Bristol m 1/28/34 Sarah M. Briggs in Canandaigua (6-2/12)
4850. Jones, Evan of Utica m 5/24/42 Lydia Ward, dau of Nathaniel, Esq. of Floyd, in F; Elder williams (9-5/25)
4851. Jones, Evan m 7/8/44 Eliza Trigg at the home of the Hon. H. Seymour in Utica; Rev. B. Hawley. All of Utica (9-7/10)
4852. Jones, Evans of the firm of Owen and Jones m 3/12/44 Cecilia Jenkins, dau of late Edward of Illinois, at the home of O. J. Owen, Esq. in Remsen; Rev. W. Rowlands (9-3/16)
4853. Jones, H. E. m 7/3/33 Harriet W. Randall, both of Utica; Rev. J. J. Ward of Camillus (9-7/10)

4854. Jones, Humphrey, a native of Wales, d 1/19/31 in Deerfield (surv by wf and several young ch) (9-2/8)
4855. Jones, I. F., Esq. of Syracuse m 7/2/45 Eveline R. Grannis of Utica in U; Rev. Dr. Proal (9-7/4)
4856. Jones, Isaac m 3/11/38 Sally Stone of Chittenango (3-3/14)
4857. Jones, J. G. of Utica m 11/2/47 Emma M. Groah, formerly of Utica, in Reading, PA; Rev. A. B. Groah (9-11/16)
4858. Jones, James Whittaker, 6 wks, only s of Edward B. and Prudence R., d 10/1/48 in Utica (9-10/2)
4859. Jones, Jeremiah m 5/20/49 Frances E. Shares, both of Clay, in Lafayette; Benjamin S. Gregory, Esq. (1-5/31)
4860. Jones, John, 21, printer, s of late Morgan Jones of Utica, d 2/1/44 in Shrewsbury, England (consumption) (had gone to Eng. for his health) (9-2/23)
4861. Jones, John m 2/26/46 Merilla Chapman in New Hartford; Henry Sherill, Esq. (9-3/2)
4862. Jones, John of Columbus, OH m 7/2/50 Maria L. Rees, dau of William of New Hartford, in New H.; Rev. William H. Spencer (9-7/4)
4863. Jones, John B. m 3/14/50 Emily Hill, both of Owego, in Elmira; Rev. M. Crow (5-3/15)
4864. Jones, John C. m 9/9/43 Gwenifred Jones, 2nd dau of David and Marcy, in Utica; Rev. W. Rowlands (9-9/13)
4865. Jones, John J. of Clinton m 4/10/50 Mary Clark of Utica at the home of Mrs. W. F. Potter in Utica; Rev. W. H. Spencer (9-4/11)
4866. Jones, John S. m 12/23/47 Lorinda E. Hill, both of Rome, in Whitesboro; Rev. Jirah D. Cole (double ceremony - see marr of George H. Newman) (9-12/24)
4867. Jones, Jonah of Utica m 6/6/38 Catherine Owen of Sullivan in S; J. French, Esq. (3-6/6)
4868. Jones, Joseph, Jr., about 26, d 8/24/36 in Penn Yan (6-9/7)
4869. Jones, Joshua I., proprietor of the American Hotel in Auburn, d 6/7/39 in Philadelphia (state not given) (6-6/19)
4870. Jones, Julia Mary, 14, oldest dau of John R. and Amantha E., d in Vernon (consumption) (9-8/12/50)
4871. Jones, Leander M. of Baldwinsville m 7/29/49 Harriet Hart of Victor (1-8/9)
4872. Jones, Lot, 30, d 8/18/33 in Phelps (6-8/28)
4873. Jones, Mary Elizabeth, 5, dau of E. Jones, 2nd, d 4/1/50 in Elmira (5-4/5)
4874. Jones. Moreau W. of Elmira m 1/1/50 Lydia M. Allen of Troy, PA in T (5-1/18)
4875. Jones, Morgan, 61, d 7/30/43 at his home (79 Whitesboro St.) in Utica (born in Wales) (9-8/1)
4876. Jones, Olive (Miss), 35, d 11/4/33 in Tioga (6-11/13)
4877. Jones, Orrin B. m 6/22/48 Elizabeth Robinson in Baldwinsville; Rev. T. Walker. All of Baldwinsville (1-6/28)
4878. Jones, Peter, merchant, m 3/9/35 Mary Smith, both of Williamson, in Seneca; Rev. J. F. McLaren (6-3/25)
4879. Jones,Pomeroy (Hon.) of Westmoreland m 5/23/48 Eliza Ann Royce, dau of late Samuel, Esq. of Clinton, in C; Rev. Dr. Norton (9-5/26)
4880. Jones, Prudence Whitaker, 27, wf of Edward B., d 9/10/48 in Utica (funeral from his late home, 46 Fayette St.) (9-9/12)
4881. Jones, Richard, member of Meth. Ch., d 9/17/30 in Lyons (6-9/22)
4882. Jones, Robert H., 23, d 1/7/48 at the home of his father, Robert, at 85 Whitesboro St., Utica (consumption) (9-1/8)
4883. Jones, Robert W., 45, d 9/7/48 in Utica (funeral at 42 Water St.) (b on the Isle of Anylsey, North Wales)(9-9/9)
4884. Jones, Samuel, Esq., 85, formerly state comptroller, d in Queens Co., NY (8-12/8/19)
4885. Jones, Samuel (Hon.), 72, d 2/13/44 in North Adams, Jefferson Co. (was one of the earliest settlers at Bridgewater, Oneida Co. and for several years was one of the judges of Oneida Co.) (9-3/9)
4886. Jones, Sarah, 44, wf of Edward, a native of Wales, d 1/1/35 in Verona, NY (3-1/6)
4887. Jones, Seth, oldest s of Seth C., d 2/24/31 in Rochester (6-3/9)
4888. Jones, Solomon, 67, d 7/23/22 in Lenox, MA (7-8/7)

4889. Jones, Thomas F., 21, s of late William, d 1/5/45 in Utica (funeral from 16 Broad St.) (9-1/6)
4890. Jones, William, 13, oldest s of Robert, d 8/7/26 in Utica (9-8/15)
4891. Jones, William, 24, d 11/24/35 in Elmira (6-12/9)
4892. Jones, William m 12/26/45 Mary Roberts in Utica; Elder Thomas Hill. All of Utica (9-12/29)
4893. Jones, William Baskins, 69, d 9/1/50 in Corning (lived in Canisteo for 40 years) (4-9/11)
4894. Jones, William Till, formerly of Chittenango, d 9/23/39 in Mobile (state not given) (3-10/30)
4895. Josslyn, William B., editor of the Centreville Democrat, m 1/17/43 Eloisa T. Bacon, dau of Dr. William of Jonesville, MI, in J; Rev. Barker (9-2/22)
4896. Joy, Arad Thaddeus, 19, formerly of Geneva, d 9/17/34 at his father's home in Ovid (In July left home on a 4000-mile tour through Mich, Ill, Missouri, Ky., Ind., and Ohio; died fifth day after his return to his father's home) (6-10/1)
4897. Joy, George Nelson m 6/26/50 Caroline Elizabeth Mace (or Mack) in Utica; Rev. William Wyatt (9-6/27)
4898. Joy, Hannah, 73, widow, mother of Mr. Arad Joy of Geneva, d in Clarkson, Monroe Co. (6-5/12)
4899. Joy, Martha Reed, wf of James F., Esq. and dau of Hon. John Reed, lieut. gov. of Massachusetts, d 2/6/50 in Detroit, MI (9-2/19)
4900. Joy, Martin m 8/14/48 Eliza Tisdall (in New York Mills?); Rev. N. D. Graves (9-8/19)
4901. Judd, Benjamin (Rev.), 79, d 7/31/34 in Jerusalem, NY (6-8/20)
4902. Judd, Charles G., Esq. m 2/22/32 Amelia Goodrich in Havana, NY (6-3/14)
4903. Judd, Daniel A., late of Geneva, NY, m 8/12/46 Lucy A. Newton of Westboro, MA in W; Rev. Dey (6-8/28)
4904. Judd, E. (Dr.), father of Dr. G. P. of the Sandwich Islands (Hawaii), d in Troy, Oakland Co., MI (deceased formerly a physician in Paris, NY (9-9/16/45)
4905. Judd, Jarid H. m 11/2/48 Harriet Storey at the Central Hotel in Utica; Rev. E. Francis. All of Whitestown (9-11/4)
4906. Judd. Thomas m 5/2/32 Mary Ann Brewster, dau of William, in Geneva; Rev. Phelps (6-5/9)
4907. Judson, _____, inf ch of Philo of Oxford, d 7/6/23 (8-7/9)
4908. Judson, A. m 5/4/43 Emily S. Nooton in Vernon. All of V (9-5/19)
4909. Judson, A. (Rev. Dr.) of Maulmain, Burmah m 6/2/46 Emily Chubbuck, dau of Charles of Hamilton, NY, in H; Rev. N. Kendrick, D.D., a professor in Hamilton Univ. (9-6/5)
4910. Judson, Ann, 74, d 2/28/48 in Utica (funeral "at Mrs. Brown's, No. 69 Fayette St.") (9-3/2)
4911. Judson, Beda, inf dau of Sherman of Oxford, d 8/10/24 (8-8/11)
4912. Judson, Clarissa, 2, dau of William R. and Elizabeth, d 9/27/48 in Elmira (5-10/6)
4913. Judson, Daniel of Ithaca m 10/9/34 Elizabeth Spencer of Utica, "one of the young ladies belonging to the Geneva Female Academy", in Geneva; Rev. McLaren (6-10/15)
4914. Judson, Elizabeth, 77, relict of Gen. David formerly of Washington, CT, d 6/15/50 in Ogdensburgh, NY (9-6/22)
4915. Judson, Hepshah, 82, d 2/14/43 at the home of her son, David Judson, in Oxford (b 1760 in Huntington, CT; in 1796 with her husband and 7 ch came to Stamford, NY; after her husband's death, 12/27/29, she moved to Chenango Co. (Oxford Times, 3/1)
4916. Judson, John m 9/20/48 Maria Bosworth, both of Utica, in U; Rev. D. G. Corey (9-9/23)
4917. Judson, John Dean, 1, youngest s of Ard Judson, d 9/18/50 in Vernon (9-10/21)
4918. Judson, Philo m 9/29/14 Charity Bradley in Oxford; Rev. Thorp (8-10/1)
4919. Judson, Thomas m 1/15/32 Almira Turner in East Ridge (Sodus) (6-1/25)
4920. Judson, William R. m 8/29/33 Elizabeth Orwin in Elmira (6-9/4)
4921. Juell, _____ (Mrs.), 75, d 2/12/22 in Oxford (8-2/20)
4922. Juliand, Clarissa Paulina, 28, wf of George, d 11/21/41 in Greene (member of Episc. Ch.) (Oxford Times, 11/24)

4923. Juliand, Frederick, Esq. of Greene m 6/13/41 Catharine R. Hayes, dau of
       Isaac, Esq. of Unadilla, at St. Matthew's Ch. in Unadilla; Rev. H.
       Adams (Oxford Times, 6/30)
4924. Juliand, Joseph (Capt.), 73, one of the oldest inhabitants of Oxford,
       d 10/15/21 in Greene (born in France, was marr in CT and in 1791
       moved with his father to Greene, NY) (8-10/17)
4925. Juliand, Joseph of Greene m 10/15/22 Anne Maria Perkins of Oxford in O;
       Rev. Bush (8-10/16)
4926. June, Henry D. of Manlius m 5/9/33 Ann Burlingame of Chittenango in C;
       Rev. H. S. Snyder (3-5/14)
4927. Justice, William H., 17, of Newbern, NC, a student at Geneva College,
       d 8/30/31 in G (6-9/7)
4928. Justin, Emeline C. (Miss), 26, dau of Azariah and Lucinda, d 2/7/47 in
       Marshall (consumption) (funeral sermon by Rev. John Potter) (9-2/15)
4929. Justin, Nelson, 34, s of Azeriah and Lucinda, d 6/11/44 in Marshall
       (9-7/10)
4930. Kane, John Innes m 6/27/48 Mary Kip, youngest dau of late Leonard, Esq.,
       at St. Paul's Ch., Albany (9-7/7)
4931. Kane, Mary A., 23, wf of John A., d 6/3/49 in Elmira ("New York City
       papers please copy") (5-6/8)
4932. Kanouse, Harriet, 16 mo, dau of Rev. Mr. Kanouse, d in Newark, NY
       (6-3/17/30)
4933. Karr, J. Edward m 3/21/49 Margarette Chaney, dau of Elder Chaney, in
       Whitestown; Elder John Chaney (9-3/23)
4934. Karr, Luther m 8/16/49 Lucelia L. Sexton, both of Westmoreland Mills,
       in Whitestown; Rev. J. Fullerton (9-8/17)
4935. Kasson, John Cummings, 2, s of Orange Kasson, d 12/10/49 in Baldwinsville
       (scarlet fever) (1-12/13)
4936. Kasson, William, 23, d 6/20/42 in Lenox Hill (3-7/6)
4937. Kauikeaouli, King of the Sandwich Islands (Hawaii), m 2/2/38 Kalama, dau
       of Maihekukui, in Honolulu; Rev. Bingham (6-2/7)
4938. Kawhise, Peter, 63, a Mohegan Indian, drowned accidentally 6/9/38 in
       Chittenango Creek (3-6/13)
4939. Kear(?), John m 11/16/36 Rebecca Ann Sands in Canandaigua (6-11/30)
4940. Kedzie, John of Attica m 6/4/34 Lemira Morgan of Geneva in G; Rev. J. W.
       French (6-6/11)
4941. Keeler, Rufus m Phebe Vallen in Rochester (6-11/6/33)
4942. Keeley, John d 12/15/36 in Canandaigua (6-12/28)
4943. Keeling, Louisa A., 43, wf of late James H., d 8/9/48 in Utica
       (consumption) (funeral from her late home on Rebecca St.) (9-8/11)
4944. Keeney, J. C., printer, m 10/23/49 Caroline N. Peacock, dau of William R.,
       in Skaneateles; Rev. S. W. Bush (1-10/25)
4945. Keith, George S., 28, d 7/29/32 in Canandaigua (consumption) (6-8/15)
4946. Keith, Henry, Esq. of Clarksville m 10/28/46 Elizabeth Armanda Perkins
       of Utica; Rev. D. G. Corey (9-10/30)
4947. Keith, Myron R. of Cleveland, OH m 10115/44 Mary L. Beebe of Whitesboro, NY
       in W; Rev. D. L. Ogden (9-10/16)
4948. Kelby, John O. m Harriet Shirts in Sodus (6-3/10/30)
4949. Keley, Daniel P. m 4/9/50 Hannah E. Thompson, both of Jefferson, in Elmira;
       Rev. M. Crow (double ceremony - see marr of Dewit C. Seaman)
4950. Keller, Alvin (Maj.) m 6/3/41 Olive Ehle, dau of Henry, Esq., in Sullivan;
       Rev. Breese. All of Sullivan (3-6/9)
4951. Keller, Jacob m Mary Stansell in Lockville (6-7/14/30)
4952. Keller, Solomon m 9/9/47 Emeline Craver in Baldwinsville; Rev. T. Walker
       (1-9/15)
4953. Kellogg, _____, 83, d 11/18/26 in Sangerfield (9-11/28)
4954. Kellogg, _____, 1 yr, child of Samuel, d 1/21/38 in Geneva (6-1/24)
4955. Kellogg, Aaron of Clinton m 2/12/24 Eliza Dodge of Trenton, NY in T; Rev.
       Waters (9-2/17)
4956. Kellogg, Aaron, 78, d 6/27/40 in Chittenango (an early settler in the
       region) (3-7/1)
4957. Kellogg, Beeda, 53, wf of James formerly of Verona, d 3/13/50 in Mottville,
       MI (9-4/5)
4958. Kellogg, Caleb m 1/21/35 Sophia Lamphire (in West Bloomfield?) (6-2/11)
4959. Kellogg, Cyrus m 7/15/47 Rhoda Ann Cooper at the Presby. Ch. in Corning;
       Rev. Dr. Graves (4-7/21)

4960. Kellogg, Daniel, Esq., 56, pres. of the Bank of Auburn, d 5/4/36 in
      Skaneateles (6-5/11)
4961. Kellogg, David Spencer, 3, 2nd s of P. V., Esq,, d 4/27/42 in Utica
      (9-4/28)
4962. Kellogg, Edwin, merchant, of Hampton m 9/12/47 Sarah C. Moulton, dau of
      Hon. David of Floyd, in F; Rev. H. H. Kellogg of Clinton (9-9/14)
4963. Kellogg, Ezra, Esq., 80, d in Great Barrington, MA (fought at Bunker Hill)
4964. Kellogg, Gustavus A. of Utica m 10/4/49 Anna M. Van Eps of Vernon in V;
      Rev. S. Burchard of NYC (9-10/5)
4965. Kellogg, Harriet A., 2, dau of Orchard G. and Frances A., d 9/17/49 in
      Utica (funeral from her father's home, 88 John St.) (9-9/18)
4966. Kellogg, Henry N. m 9/1/42 Miriam M. Moulton, dau of David, Esq.,
      sheriff of Oneida Co., at the home of Mr. N. B. Sleeper; Rev. W. W.
      Ninde (9-9/8)
4967. Kellogg, James, 44, d 4/5/34 in Cazenovia (3-4/8)
4968. Kellogg, Josiah J. (Deacon), 65, d 11/17/33 in Penfield (6-11/23)
4969. Kellogg, Levi, 89, d 1/30/48 at the home of his son, Spencer, in Utica
      (9-1/31)
4970. Kellogg, Romulus, 17, d (in Bath?) (consumption) (6-1/5/31)
4971. Kellogg, T. N. of the firm of Bissell, Leonard, and Co. m 5/23/49
      A. L. Matteson, dau of Jeptha, Esq., in Rome; Rev. Gregory (9-5/31)
4972. Kellogg, U. H. (Dr.), 64, d 2/8/44 in New Hartford (9-3/22)
4973. Kellogg, Urial H. m 12/3/44 M. Elizabeth McElwaine, both of Utica, in U;
      Rev. Bristol (9-12/4 and 12/5)
4974. Kellum, C. B., merchant, of Albany m 1/22/44 C. M. Tibbitts of Cazenovia
      in Chittenango; Rev. T. Houston (3-1/24)
4975. Kelly, _____ m Polly White in Bath (6-7/7/30)
4976. Kelly, Lewis m Sarah Hilton in Wheeler (6-2/24/30)
4977. Kelly, Luther of Seneca m 4/26/42 Jennette E. Sage, dau of Col. H. Sage
      of Sullivan, in S; Rev. James Abell (3-4/27)
4978. Kelly, Mary (Mrs.), 50, d 10/8/47 at the home of William Henry in Utica
      (9-10/9) (funeral from the home of William Henry)
4979. Kelsey, Henry R. of Utica m 10/19/48 Abigail F. Nurse of Paris, NY at
      the home of David Nurse in Paris; Rev. C. W. Giddings (double ceremony
      - see marr of Charles H. Nurse) (9-10/20)
4980. Kelsey, Horace m 3/28/50 Martha Baldwin in Ridgebury, PA; Mark Burt, Esq.
      All of Ridgebury (5-4/12)
4981. Kemp, Clark, 22, formerly of Ulster Township, PA, d 9/1/49 in Wellsburgh,
      NY (5-9/7)
4982. Kemp, John m 4/29/46 Jane T. Arthur, both of Utica, in U; Rev. McIlvaine
      (9-4/30)
4983. Kempton, David m 9/14/43 Mary Henderson at Griffin's Hotel in Utica; Rev;
      C. S. Porter. All of Rome, NY (9-9/16)
4984. Kempton, Sarah E., 30, wf of Rev. George of Philadelphia (state not given)
      and sister of Mrs. Butler, d 8/14/48 at the home of A. T. Butler in
      Syracuse (9-8/23)
4985. Kendal, Wilson, a young man employed in building a Dutch church, d 11/2/30
      in Ithaca (6-11/10)
4986. Kendall, Heman W. m Asenah Smith in Tyrone (6-2/10/30)
4987. Kendall, Marian, 1, dau of S. H. and A., d 6/26/44 in Fonda (9-7/11)
4988. Kendig, S. B. m 9/20/34 Jane Lee in Penn Yan (6-10/1)
4989. Kendrick, Samuel, 91, d 3/13/45 in Hamilton (9-4/11)
4990. Kennedy, Hiero, 40, d 9/21/36 in Kennedyville (6-10/12)
4991. Kennedy, Hiram d 11/1/46 in Skaneateles (typhus) (3-11/9)
4992. Kennedy, John (Capt.), 62, d in Catlin (6-3/2/31)
4993. Kennedy, John (Maj.), 42, d 10/8/32 (6-10/17) (died in Dansville)
4994. Kennedy, Mary (Mrs.) d 9/8/31 (3-9/13)
4995. Kennedy, William W. m 2/15/44 Elmira C. Phillips, oldest dau of Jonathan
      P., in Canastota; Rev. William W. Rand (3-2/21)
4996. Kenney, Alexander, 106, d in Coventry, CT (8-11/12/14)
4997. Kent, Ann (Mrs.), 39, d 1/17/31 in Utica (6-2/9/31)
4998. Kent, Luther M., printer, of Utica m 5/27/46 Helen Lewis of Morrisville
      in M; Rev. E. M. Wooley (9-6/5)
4999. Kent, Phineas of Boonville m 2/20/50 Maria Smith of Lee at the American
      Hotel; H. C. Vogell, Esq. (9-2/28)

137

5000. Kent, Sarah Maria, 5, dau of James of Walworth, d 10/28/38 at the home of her grandfather, A. Hotchkiss, in Sullivan (3-10/31)

5001. Kenyon, Varnum S., Jr. m 6/19/50 Sarah E. Jones of Utica in U; Rev. Pritchett (9-6/20)

5002. Kenyon, B. Franklin m 10/6/50 Mary B. Fox, both of Ilion, in Burlington Flats, Ots. Co.; Rev. Squire S. Cady (9-10/8)

5003. Kenyon, Rhoda Wright, 46, wf of Benjamin and dau of late Ezra Wright of Edmeston, d 2/6/50 in Burlington Flats, Ots. Co. (9-2/15)

5004. Kernan, Francis, Esq. m 5/23/43 Hannah A. Devereux, oldest dau of Nicholas, Esq., at St. John's Ch. in Utica; Rev. Thomas Martin. All of Utica (9-5/25)

5005. Kessler, Joseph, aged above 90, (a Rev. soldier) d 11/18/30 in Oppenheim, Mont. Co., NY (b in Germany) (9-12/7)

5006. Ketcham, Lewis m 1/13/42 Emarilla Bartle in Smithville; Thomas S. Purple (Oxford Times, 1/19)

5007. Ketchman, Gilbert, formerly sheriff of Dutchess Co., d 8/7/33 in Poughkeepsie (Lt. Col. in Hawkins' Regt., U.S. Artillery Volunteers, War of 1812) (6-8/28)

5008. Keyes, Orlando S., 1, s of Stillman and Eliza, d 7/12/49 in Elmira (5-7/20)

5009. Keyes, Perley (Hon.), 60, d 5/13/34 at his home in Watertown (6-6/4)

5010. Keyrns, Michael, 32, d 6/26/45 in Utica (9-6/27)

5011. Keyser, Abraham A., editor of the Schoharie Republican, m 10/1/31 Elizabeth Ann Townsend of Newport, RI at St. Luke's Ch. in Schoharie; Rev. G. A. Lintner (6-10/12)

5012. Kidder, Benjamin E. m 10/2/32 Anne Brown in Penn Yan (6-10/10)

5013. Kidder, James, 4, only s of N. B., Esq., d 9/22/31 in Geneva (6-9/28)

5014. Kilborn, Jesse, Esq. of Cazenovia m 1/31/39 Content Clark of Canandaigua in C (3-2/20)

5015. Kilborn, Jesse, 63, d 5/14/42 in Cazenovia (cancer) (born in Litchfield, CT and settled in Cazenovia before 1807) (3-5/25)

5016. Kilburn Andrew J. m 12/25/48 Sarah Cristman of Floyd at the Central Hotel in Utica; Rev. E. Francis (9-12/27)

5017. Kilburn Delta J., 20, wf of H. C., d 7/29/49 in Rome, NY (9-8/10)

5018. Kimball, Caroline M., 33, wf of James M., d 8/11/46 in Manchester village, town of Kirkland (9-8/12)

5019. Kimball, John m 12/8/31 Lucina Eaton, both of Manlius, in Chittenango (3-12/20)

5020. Kimball, Lovell m Elvira St. John in Geneseo (6-4/16/34)

5021. Kimball, Milo, 43, d 2/15/50 in Utica (9-2/18)

5022. Kimberly, Horace of Augustus m 9/25/50 Esther L. Smith of Herkimer in H; Rev. J. H. Harter of Rockton (double ceremony - see marr of Henry Scranton) (9-9/30)

5023. Kinch, William H. (Capt.) m 1/5/45 Jane R. Marshall in NYC; Rev. Henry Anthon. All of Utica (9-1/14)

5024. King, _____ (Mrs.) d 3/30/34 in Geneva (6-4/2)

5025. King, Aaron m 4/20/39 Catharine Fisher in Gorham; Elder Bateman. All of Middlesex (6-4/24)

5026. King, Amanda, wf of James B. of Binghamton, d 1/4/43 (suicide) (2-1/25)

5027. King, Benjamin m 3/20/32 Mary Conklin in Allen, Alleg. Co. (6-4/4)

5028. King, Charles B. of NYC m 5/30/42 Jane Rockwell, dau of Philo, dec'd., formerly of Utica, in Martinsburgh, Lewis Co. (9-6/2)

5029. King, Charlotte, 22, d 1/20/31 in Milo (6-2/2)

5030. King, Darius m 4/15/46 Sarah A. Waples in New Hartford; Rev. John Waugh (9-4/25)

5031. King, George W m 4/26/29 Melissa Ross in Norwich; Rev. Henry Peck (8-4/29)

5032. King, Janet C., 20, wf of George E. and dau of F. M. Haight, Esq. of Rochester, d 12/21/44 in Lima (9-12/25)

5033. King, Laura, 15, oldest dau of Samuel, d 9/16/25 in Friendship (9-9/27)

5034. King, Robert P. of Lowville m 11/29/49 Cornelia A. West in Rome, NY (9-12/7)

5035. King, Rufus, 72, d 4/30/27 in NYC (late Minister of the U. S. to the Court of St. James) (8-5/11)

5036. King, Rufus m 11/9/43 Susan Elliot, dau of Col. Robert, in Albany; Rev. Dr. Sprague. All of Albany (9-11/11)

5037. King, Seth L. of Brockport m Rachael Proctor of Newark, NY in N; Rev. Parsons (6-5/29/39)
5038. King, Simeon V. m 7/29/46 Sarah W. Sprague, both of Utica; Rev. H. N. Loring (9-10/8)
5039. King, Theodore, 17 mo, s of Simeon V. and Sarah W., d 8/9/49 in Catharine (9-8/16)
5040. Kingman, George C. m 11/27/31 Elizabeth D. Holley, both of Lyons, in L (6-12/14)
5041. Kingsbury, _____, inf ch of J., d 4/21/26 in Utica (9-4/25)
5042. Kingsbury, A. F. of Rochester m 10/11/41 Hennah Mary Calkins of Corning in C; Rev. Hopkins (4-10/13)
5043. Kingsbury, Clarinda, 25, d 2/26/31 in Mentz (6-3/23)
5044. Kingsbury, George H., 29, s of Arden, d 8/15/49 in Aurora, IL (5-9/7)
5045. Kingsbury, William m 9/29/47 Mary Evans, both of Utica, in U; Rev. D. G. Corey (9-9/30)
5046. Kingsland, Edward m 11/7/34 Catharine Lowthorp; Rev. Bruce. All of Geneva (6-11/12)
5047. Kingsley, Anna Julia, 11, only dau of Silas and Julia R., d 3/12/47 in Buffalo (9-3/16)
5048. Kingsley, Henry C., Esq. of Cleveland, OH m 8/26/46 Jane Handy Thomas, dau of B. W., Esq. of Utica, in U; Rev. Samuel H. Hall of Marshall, MI (9-8/28)
5049. Kingsley, Jedediah, 75, d 2/19/43 in Frankfort near Geneva (9-2/22)
5050. Kingsley, Pleides B., 11, dau of Oliver B. and Laura, d 7/28/49 in East Oswego (1-8/16)
5051. Kingwell(?), John N. of Starkey m 8/31/46 Isabella Gates of Geneva in G; Rev. N. Fellows (6-9/4)
5052. Kinne, Elijah (Capt.), 87, d in Ovid (first militia officer commissioned between the Cayuga and Seneca Lakes in 1790-91; "he mustered but 17 men where there are now five regiments") (6-2/17/30)
5053. Kinne, Ephraim (Capt.) d in Ovid (6-11/10/30)
5054. Kinne, James of De Witt m 9/18/42 Almira Hay, youngest dau of Esquire Hay, in Camillus; Rev. Dr. Daggett (3-10/5)
5055. Kinney, Abba, 36, consort of Dr. Stephen J., d 10/7/24 in New Haven, NY (dau of a clergyman in CT) (9-10/26)
5056. Kinney, Amos of Canandaigua m 6/19/34 Mary Ann Hayward of Farmington (6-7/2)
5057. Kinney, Daniel, 24, d 12/28/33 in Canandaigua (6-1/8/34)
5058. Kinney, Joanna (Mrs.), 30, d 8/1/47 in De Witt (1-8/18)
5059. Kinney, Samuel, Jr. m 9/15/42 Sophia Symonds; Rev. Arthur Burtis. All of Oxford (double ceremony - see marr of Derrick Race) (Oxford Times, 9/21)
5060. Kinning, Reuben m 1/2/48 Mary Ann Keough, both of Deerfield, in Schuyler; Rev. H. H. Half (9-1/5)
5061. Kinyon, Allen d 11/14/33 in Hartland (6-12/11)
5062. Kip, James S., Esq., 65, d in Utica (6-9/7/31)
5063. Kip, Mary A., 11. dau of John L., d in Newark, NY (6-7/14/30)
5064. Kipp, Mary Eliza, 16 mo, dau of Jefferson and Mary E., d 11/10/44 in Utica (9-11/19)
5065. Kipp, Nicholas m 2/7/32 Mary Ann Prushour in Geneva; Rev. Phelps. All of Geneva (6-2/15)
5066. Kirby, _____, wf of Maj. R. M. Kirby of the U.S. Army, d in Virginia (6-7/7/30)
5067. Kirby, Barney, Esq., 29, d in Seneca Falls (6-7/31/33)
5068. Kirby, Reuben m 2/15/20 Patience Corbin in Bainbridge (8-3/1)
5069. Kirby, Reuben, 67, d 10/15/27 in Bainbridge (an early settler there) (8-11/9)
5070. Kirk, Helen M., 1, dau of J. S. and N. A., d 9/26/50 in Utica (funeral from 2 Columbia St.) (9-9/26)
5071. Kirk, William m10/15/35 Betsey Austin in Elmira (6-10/28)
5072. Kirkland, Ann, 88, relict of late John, d 1/12/30 in Norwich (she and her husband moved to Norwich in 1769 - he originally from Norwich, CT; Rev. Samuel Kirkland, bro of John, became a missionary and set up residence among the Oneida Indians in 1767) (9-1/26)

5073. Kirkland, Catherine Sedgwick, 22, wf of J. Francis and dau of late Maj.
Douglass W. Sloane of Williamstown, MA, d 8/24/43 in Cleveland, OH
(9-9/2)
5074. Kirkland, Charles m 11/20/50 Elizabeth Julia (surname lacking in record);
Rev. H. S. Dickson. All of Utica (9-11/22)
5075. Kirkland, Charles Pinckney, Esq. m 5/29/33 Mary Walker Kip, dau of late
James S., Esq., in Utica (6-6/12)
5076. Kirkland, Edward, s of Gen. Kirkland of Utica, d 12/4/33 on board the ship
"Niagara" en route from Charleston to NYC (3-12/17)
5077. Kirkland, John, Esq. m 2/10/24 Mary Raymond in Clinton; Rev. Dr. Norton.
All of Clinton (9-2/17)
5078. Kirkland, John Thornton, s of late Gen. Joseph of Utica, NY, d 10/28/50
in Cleveland, OH (9-10/30)
5079. Kirkland, Lydia P., 17 mo, dau of William, d 2/26/33 in Geneva (6-3/13)
5080. Kirkland, Sarah, 70, widow of late Joseph. d 6/14/48 in Utica (funeral at
the home of her son-in-law, William J. Bacon, 245 Genesee St.) (9-6/15)
5081. Kirkland, William , 43, d 9/12/47 in Utica (funeral from his late home on
Varick St. (9-9/14)
5082. Kirkpatrick, William, Esq., for many years superintendent of the Salt
Springs, d 8/24/32 in Salina (cholera) (6-9/19)
5083. Kishlar, Andrew, 3, s of John, d in Canandaigua ("death occasioned by
drinking a quantity of spirituous liquor left in a tumbler on a table")
5084. Kissam, merchant, of NYC m 9/11/22 Sally Betts, dau of Peter, Esq. of
Bainbridge, in B (8-9/18) (Kissam's given name lacking in record)
5085. Kissam, Adrian, inf s of Adrian and Sophia, d 4/8/44 in Utica (9-4/11)
5086. Kissam, Frances, 22 mo, dau of Adrian, Esq., d 7/31/46 at the home of Mrs.
J. Dows in Lyons (9-8/5)
5087. Kissam, Timothy T., merchant, of NYC m 9/10/22 Sally Betts, dau of Hon.
Peter of Bainbridge, in B (7-9/25)
5088. Kittle, David, 72, d 9/3/48 in Schenectady (9-9/12)
5089. Kittle, Nicholas, Esq., 75, formerly of Kinderhook, d in Owego (6-4/27/31)
5090. Kline, Elizabeth (Mrs.), 107, d 2/20/26 in Schoharie (born in Esopus)
(9-3/11)
5091. Kling, Hiram H. of Utica m 9/22/47 Delphia W. Nurse, oldest dau of Elisha,
Esq. of Frankfort, in F; Elder P. C. Grosvenor (9-9/23)
5092. Kling, J. R. of Whitestown m 1/26/43 Emily Bliss of Floyd in F; Rev. R.
Z. Williams (9-2/8)
5093. Kling, Norman of Rome, NY m 10/1/49 Julia A. Mansfield of Westmoreland
in W; Elder D. Olcott (9-10/5)
5094. Kling, William of Troy, WI m 9/19/47 M. Ann Cummings, oldest dau of
John of New York Mills, at the Presby. Ch. in New York Mills; Rev.
N. G. Graves (9-9/21)
5095. Knapp, Andrew H., 33, d 2/4/49 in Westmoreland, NY (formerly of Green Bay,
WI) (9-2/6)
5096. Knapp, Daniel of Farmington m Jane Barton in Lyons (6-3/17/30)
5097. Knapp, George W. of Utica m 1/19/45 Julia A. Bates, formerly of New
Berlin, in Bridgewater; Rev. Wooly (9-1/21)
5098. Knapp, Isaac J. m 5/13/50 Mary E. Saumet of Utica in U; Rev. Eber Francis
(9-5/13)
5099. Knapp, William (Elder) of Corning m 8/6/48 Eunice Rockwell ofMonterey in
M; (4-8/9)
5100. Knickerbacker, Elizabeth, 75, consort of John, Esq., d 11/10/26 in
Schaghticoke (9-11/21)
5101. Knickerbacker, Herman, Esq. of Schaghticoke, a judge of the Rensselaer Co.
courts,m 7/20/26 Mary Buel of Troy, dau of David, Esq., in Troy (9-8/1)
5102. Knickerbocker, Solomon, 46, d in Cameron (6-3/9/31)
5103. Knight, _____, wf of Rev. Joseph and sister of Rev. M. Bardwell, d 4/26/25
at Nellore in Ceylon (Mrs. Knight went to Ceylon as wf of Rev. James
Richards; Rev. Bardwell was formerly American missionary at Bombay)
(9-12/20)
5104. Knight, Eliza, 38, wf of Levi S., d 8/24/42 in Winfield (consumption)
(9-9/7)
5105. Knight, Enos, 71, of Utica d 4/20/49 in Utica (9-4/27)
5106. Knight, F. M., Esq. m 5/7/48 E. T. Wells in Sauquoit; Rev. Giddings.
All of Sauquoit (9-5/9)

5107. Knight, Horatio Q. of Waterloo m 10/27/47 Nancy Hall of Skaneateles in S; Rev. M. W. Bush (3-11/10)
5108. Knight, Louisa (Miss), 18. d 8/29/33 in Gaines (6-9/18)
5109. Knight, Rudolfus E. m 11/13/34 Sally Baltsley, both of Fayetteville, in Chittenango; J. French, Esq. (3-11/18)
5110. Knights, Myndert d in Glenville (6-1/26/31)
5111. Knolan, Thomas m "a short time since" Susan Fulford, both of Canaseraga; H. French, Esq. (3-1/10/32)
5112. Knolls, John B. m 6/30/31 Eliza W. Barnhart at the Sulphur Springs House; Rev. B. H. Hickox (All of Palmyra?) (6-7/13)
5113. Knot, Jesse m 9/11/50 Lydia A. Coultin in Utica; Rev. William Wyatt. All of Utica (9-9/17)
5114. Knott, _____, inf ch of Benjamin, d 6/6/26 in Utica (9-6/13)
5115. Knott, Henry C. m 10/18/48 Mary H. Mackie in Utica; Rev. Spencer. All of Utica (9-10/24)
5116. Knower, Benjamin, 33, son of late Benjamin of Albany, d 5/18/46 in Marseilles, France (9-6/19)
5117. Knower, Sarah, 54, wf of Benjamin, Esq. and mother-in-law of Gov. Marcy, d 2/18/33 in Albany (6-2/27)
5118. Knower, Timothy H. m 9/2/46 Margaret Linacre in Albany (9-9/4)
5119. Knowles, _____, 18 mo, ch of Lyman, d 6/25/26 in Utica (9-6/27)
5120. Knowles, Charles m 7/3/32 Margaretta Dewey; Rev. W. H. Campbell. All of Sullivan (3-7/10)
5121. Knowles, Charles, 26, d 9/11/32 (3-9/18/32)
5122. Knowles, Hezekiah of Varick m 11/12/33 Eliza Freeland of Fayette in Waterloo (6-11/27)
5123. Knowles, Isaac m 9/5/31 Charlotte Dickerson in Chittenango; Rev. Campbell (3-9/13)
5124. Knowles, James m 10/25/31 Eve Bettinger; Rev. William Johnson. All of Chittenango (3-11/1)
5125. Knowles, Porter, 23, s of John, Esq. of Chittenango, drowned 4/28/36 (in passage on the steamboat "United States" en route from Huron to Buffalo)(3-5/4/36)
5126. Knowles, Robert and Hon. Elisha Watson d 7/8/47 in South Kingstown (presumably in RI) (each age 69, born within two hours of each other, lived in the same town, and died within two hours of each other) (9-8/2)
5127. Knowles, Sally, 66, wf of John, Esq., d 5/27/39 in Chittenango (funeral from the home of Judge Knowles; funeral sermon in the Reformed Dutch Ch. by Rev. J. Abell (3-5/29)
5128. Knowlson, Maria (Miss), 58, d 5/27/50 in Utica (funeral from the home of her bro, T. C. B. Knowlson, 27 Catherine St.) (9-5/29)
5129. Knowlton, Dean of Cazenovia m 9/6/36 Merrilla Woods of Pompey Hill in P. H.; Rev. Gridley (3-9/7)
5130. Knowlton, Sarah, 45, wf of Chester, d 10/25/41 in Hornby (4-11/10 and 11/17)
5131. Knowlton, William m 2/14/38 Nancy Cox of Chittenango in Morrisville; Elder Blakslee (3-2/21)
5132. Knox, Alanson R. (Capt.) m 7/4/26 Catharine A. Habermel in Utica; Rev. Zachariah Paddock. All of Utica (9-7/11)
5133. Knox, Almira, 31, d 9/14/47 in Augusta (9-9/23)
5134. Knox, David m 4/15/32 Rhoda Crichet in Waterloo (6-5/2)
5135. Knox, Fanny, 74, wf of Hon. John, d 11/5/48 in Campbell (4-11/8)
5136. Knox, Frederick William, 1, s of Rev. William E., d 10/18/50 in Rome, NY (9-10/24)
5137. Knox, Harman (Col.), about 45, formerly of Knoxville, Mad. Co., NY,d 5/3/41 in Knoxville, IL (3-6/16)
5138. Knox, J. C. of Augusta m 10/2/44 Mary E. Whitely of Utica in U; Rev. J. H. McIlvaine (9-10/3)
5139. Knox, Mary A., 26, wf of Rev. William E. and only dau of Winthrop H. Chandler, Esq. of Avon, d 6/22/45 in Watertown ("married only one year") (9-7/7)
5140. Knox, Orlando D. of Nelson m 5/27/46 Bethiah W. Loring of Sauquoit in S; Rev. Lyman Sperry of Cazenovia (9-6/5)
5141. Knox, Sarah, 60, wf of Hon. John, d 9/27/34 in Painted Post (6-10/8)

5142. Knox, W. E. (Rev.) of Watertown m 6/5/44 Mary A. Chandler, dau of Winthrop
       H., Esq., in Avon; Rev. P. C. Hastings of Clinton (9-6/8)
5143. Kore, Jacob C. m 5/25/35 Charlotte Rodney, dau of William, in Geneva; Rev.
       Dr. Mason (6-6/24)
5144. Kortright, Abram of Venice, NY m Phebe S. Bradley of NYC in Geneva; R.
       Hogarth, Esq. (6-4/24/39)
5145. Kowlson, Maria d 5/27/50 in Utica (9-5/28)
5146. Krauz, Ignatus of Perth, Hungary m 5/18/50 Eliza Smith, dau of Daniel,
       Esq. of Schenectady, NY, in Geddes, NY (9-5/22)
5147. Krum, William m 12/7/19 Phebe Chandler, dau of Stephen of Elizabethtown,
       NJ, in Binghamton, NY; Rev. F. H. Cuming (8-12/15)
5148. Kune(?), Michael m 10/13/46 Margaret Kurby(?) in Seneca; C. J. Folger, Esq.
       (6-10/16)
5149. Kuypers, Gerardus A., 66, D.D., senior pastor of the Reformed Dutch Ch in
       NYC, d 6/28/33 in NYC (6-7/3)
5150. Lacey, Edgar M. (Lt.) of the U.S. Army m Caroline Ann Boardman, dau of
       Maj. E. Boardman of the U.S. Army (6-6/8/31)
5151. Lacey, William B. (Rev.), D.D., m 7/19/32 Elizabeth Hamilton Smith of
       Albany at St. Peter's Ch., Albany; Rev. P. Alexis Proul, rector of
       St. George's Ch., Schenectady (6-7/25)
5152. Lacey, William Spencer, 5, s of Rev. Lacey, rector of St. Peter's Ch.,
       Albany, d 5/21/21 in Albany (8-6/6)
5153. Lacy, Hannah, 37, wf of Rev. Dr. Lacy, d 3/11/31 in Albany (6-3/23)
5154. Ladd, William, long-term member of Fire Company #4 (Utica) d 5/15/47 when
       crushed to death on a canal boat between Syracuse and Montezuma
       (funeral from Meth. Ch.)
5155. La D'Miner, Homer m Amanda Hall in Prattsburgh (6-4/6/31)
5156. Ladieu, William m 7/4/50 Phebe Jane Manwarring in Hornby; Hiram Gardner.
       All of Hornby (4-7/10)
5157. Laidelaw, Alice, 20, dau of Walter and Ann Jane, d 10/17/46 in Geneva
       (6-10/23)
5158. Laidlaw, Robert, 37, d 9/24/34 in Vienna, NY (6-10/8)
5159. Laidlow, ____, inf ch of "Mr. Laidlow", d 3/31/34 in Geneva (6-4/2)
5160. Laird, William O. of Athens, GA, formerly of Oneida Co., NY, m 11/7/44
       Sarah A. Townsend, dau of William, Esq. of Floyd, in F; Rev. Henry
       Emmons (9-11/18)
5161. Lake, Delos of Utica m 1/6/47 Sarah Helen Clark, dau of late Thomas of
       Sullivan, in Manlius; Rev. J. C. Rudd, D.D. (9-1/8)
5162. Lake, Nicholas of Portland m 1/19/33 Mrs. Hannah Barmore of Penn Yan
       in P. Y. (6-1/30)
5163. Lake, Oren D. (Capt.) of Mount Morris m 3/3/31 Sarah P. Gunn in Canandaigua
       (6-3/23)
5164. Lamb, Austin m 1/1/50 Mary Mahala Horton in Lysander; Rev. T. Walker
       (1-1/3)
5165. Lamb, Edward Grant of Utica m 8/1/48 Mary AnnClark ofCincinnati, OH in C
       (9-8/14)
5166. Lamb, Lovicy D., 27, wf of Maj. N. B., d 7/21/42 in Lenox Hill (3-7/27)
5167. Lamb, M. M. of Oneida m 4/10/50 Helen M. Davis, only dau of Dr. E. of
       Schenectady, in S; Rev. Samuel Howe of Waterford (9-4/12)
5168. Lamb, Martin (Capt.), 65, formerly of New Hartford, d 8/25/46 in Lenox
       (9-9/4)
5169. Lamb, N. B. (Col.) of Lenox m 5/8/44 Elmira Roberts of Fenner in F; Rev.
       L. Wright (3-5/15)
5170. Lamb, Nathan m 11/22/32 Lovice Palmer, dau of Elisha, in Lenox; Rev.
       Spaulding (3-12/11)
5171. Lamb, Stephen G. m 11/2/42 Harriet Lewis in Canastota; Rev. Wright. All
       of Lenox (3-11/9)
5172. Lamb, William m 1/8/35 Sarah F. Gates in Benton (6-1/21)
5173. Lambert, George m 8/22/33 Hannah Stotenburgh in Havana, NY (6-9/4)
5174. Lamereaux, John m 3/17/35 Diadama Lee, both of Gorham, in Canandaigua
       (6-4/1)
5175. Lampman, Jacob, 89, (a Rev. soldier) d 7/5/34 in Canandaigua (6-7/16)
5176. Lampman, Sidney S. of Canandaigua m 1/28/35 Nancy S. Sprague, dau of
       William formerly of Canandaigua, in Buffalo; Rev. Shelton (6-2/11)
5177. Lamport, Margaret Sisson, dau of J., d 12/8/33 in Hopewell (6-12/18)

5178. Lamport, William H., merchant, of Barrington m 11/23/31 Mary E. Townsend of Milo in M (6-11/30)
5179. Lamson, John H., about 56, d 6/5/50 in Baldwinsville (1-6/6)
5180. Land, Chauncey B. of Corning m 10/12/42 Harriet E. Bradley of Greene in G; Rev. C. Darby (4-10/19)
5181. Land, Ellen (Miss), 17, oldest dau of Robert, Esq., d 10/14/40 in South Corning (4-10/23)
5182. Landon, Catharine, Almira, 10, only dau of Mills Landon, d 12/9/26 in Sherburne (8-12/15)
5183. Landt, Sylvester of Herkimer Co. m 1/16/50 Lydia Matilda Peake(?) of Sauquoit in S; Rev. John Waugh (9-1/19)
5184. Lane, James of NYC m 7/18/33 Rachael Bush of Hopewell in H (6-7/31)
5185. Lane, Martin T. of Martinsburgh m 2/3/47 Lucy A. Wilcox of Utica in Clinton Rev. Henry Mandeville (9-2/6)
5186. Lane, Samuel S. m 11/26/35 Julia B. McDonald, both of Candor, in C (6-12/23)
5187. Lane, Thomas, Jr. m 7/28/47 Mary Valentine, both of Marcy, in Utica; Rev. H. N. Loring (9-7/31)
5188. Lane, William Walter m 9/17/46 Madeline Karstner, both of Utica; Rev. A. Wetzel (9-9/23)
5189. Lang, Daniel of Erin, NY m 8/24/48 Nancy Stewart of Elmira; Rev. George M. Spratt (5-9/1)
5190. Lang, James, 55, d 8/31/50 in Frankfort (9-9/3)
5191. Langdon, Amos of Masachusetts m 5/27/24 Tirrah Haynes of NH in Greene, NY (8-6/2)
5192. Langmuir, Gabriel m 11/21/33 Julia S. Fitch in Rochester (6-12/11)
5193. Langworthy, _____ (Mrs.) d 8/18/38 in Rochester (6-8/29)
5194. Langworthy, James N., 24, s of L. B., Esq., d 8/21/38 in Rochester (6-8/29)
5195. Lanphear, Amasa J. m 10/19/48 Louise Persons, both of Corning, in C; Rev. H. Pattingall (4-10/25)
5196. Lansing, _____, 3 mo, dau of Harry, d 5/23/44 in Perryville (3-5/29)
5197. Lansing, Arthur Breese (Capt.) of the U.S. Army m 7/2/49 Mrs. Louisa Cochran Lovett, dau of late Thomas, Esq. of NYC (her father's surname not given), in Kalorama near Washington, D.C. (9-7/7)
5198. Lansing, Bleecker Seymour, 2, youngest s of H. and Jane A., d 2/28/50 in Syracuse (funeral from Rush's Hotel) (9-3/2)
5199. Lansing, Cornelius, Esq., 89, of Lansingburgh d 4/23/42 in L (9-4/28)
5200. Lansing, Garret G. (Col.), 71, (a Rev. officer) d in Oriskany (6-6/8/31)
5201. Lansing, Harry of Auburn m 9/6/32 Minerva Bond of Sullivan; "Rev. John Grey, citizen of the world" (3-9/11)
5202. Lansing, Jacob S. m 1/12/32 Nancy P. Douglass, dau of Col. Zebulon of Sullivan, in S; Rev. Willis (3-1/17)
5203. Lansing, Jacob S. m 9/10/43 Amelia Douglass, both of Canaseraga, in C; Jairus French, Esq. (3-9/13)
5204. Lansing, Laura, 37, wf of Rev. D. C., d 3/6/31 in Utica (6-3/23)
5205. Lansing, Nancy P., 33 or 38?, wf of Jacob, d 10/1/40 in Lenox (3-10/7)
5206. Lansing, Peter m 11/29/32 Widow Mabel Blakeslee in Perryville; Rev. B. Northrop (3-12/11)
5207. Lansing, Peter, Esq., about 60, d 5/6/44 in Sullivan (3-5/8)
5208. Lansing, Sanders (Hon.), 84, formerly of Rockton, d 9/26/50 in Manheim (9-9/30)
5209. Lansing, Seymour, Esq. of Albany m 9/24/44 Jane Amelia White, dau of Henry, Esq. of Utica, in U; Rev. Dr. Proal (9-10/1)
5210. Lansing, Spencer S. m 3/2/49 Louisa E. Stafford, dau of Joab, in Waterford; Rev. Edwards. All of Albany (9-4/11)
5211. Lansing, Susan, 50, formerly of Utica, wf of Richard R., d 12/14/43 in Bristol, IN (dau of Hon. Jonas Platt, "nearly related to the late Col. Lansing") (Died "within the same hour and at the same place, of consumption, Mary Lansing, 24, wf of Edward A., son of R. R. Lansing") (9-12/27)
5212. Lansing, Wendell, editor of the Banner, m 5/14/33 Eliza Herrington, dau of John, Esq. of Easton, in Union Village, Wash. Co. (3-5/28)
5213. Lansing, William A., 18, only s of F., Esq., d 9/20/50 in Rockton (9-9/30)
5214. Lansing, Zilpha, 49, wf of Peter, d 8/5/32 in Perryville (3-8/14)

5215. Lapaugh, Henry S., 14, youngest s of Charles N. and Elizabeth, d 8/17/50 in Utica (9-8/22). See entry 5238.
5216. Lapham, E. H. m 12/11/34 Diree A. Brown in Farmington; Rev. Shumway of Palmyra (6-12/17)
5217. Larabee, J. D. m 3/16/45 Helen Clough, dau of late Isaac of Utica, in NYC; Rev. William Patton (9-3/25)
5218. Lard, George m 7/7/36 Eveline Hibbard in Palmyra (6-7/13)
5219. Larkin, Oliver, 92, s of David, d 1/12/45 at the home of his son-in-law, Dr. A. Tyler, in Sauquoit (b in Hopkinton, RI 9 Oct 1752; sargeant major in Rev. War; surv by wf and 3 ch) (9-2/1)
5220. Larned, Asa, formerly of Hopewell, NY, m 10/6/31 Ann M. Mallory of Cleveland, OH in C (6-10/19)
5221. Larzelere, John Y. m Harriet Waldo in Sacketts Harbor (6-8/21/33)
5222. Larzelere, Sally d 2/1/38 (in Seneca Falls?) (6-2/14)
5223. Larzelere, William of Waterloo m 6/15/31 Margaret Maguire of Tyre in Waterloo (6-6/29)
5224. Lasher, George, Esq. m 2/1/27 Adelia D. Frost in Duanesburg; Rev. Rouse. All of Duanesburg (8-2/23)
5225. Lascell, George W. m 3/6/45 Maria S. Odell in Westmoreland; Rev. F. A. Spencer. All of Westmoreland (9-3/7)
5226. Latham, Obadiah, 50, d 10/1/31 in Seneca Falls "leaving a very large family" (6-10/12)
5227. Latham(?), Warren m Sally Young, both of Seneca, in Penn Yan (6-7/31/33)
5228. Lathberry, John m 9/19/33 Betsey S. Jones in Manchester (6-10/9)
5229. Lathrop, _____, Esq. of Oswego m 12/20/43 Dorcas Eliza Beardsley of Richfield in R; Rev. Hughes (9-1/5/44)
5230. Lathrop, Albert W. of Fulton m 8/29/30 Susan Ferguson of Whitesboro in Fulton (6-9/15)
5231. Lathrop, Bostwick Horace, Esq. m 9/10/49 Nancy B. Shankland, both of Cooperstown, at the home of Col. Prentiss in Cooperstown; Rev. Dr. Miller (9-9/12)
5232. Lathrop, George W. m 9/3/50 Mary F. Havery(?) in Sherburne; Rev. A. C. Tuttle (9-9/5)
5233. Lathrop, Henry V. m 1/17/33 Rachel Ransier; J. French, Esq. All of Chittenango (3-1/22)
5234. Lathrop, Nye Adams, 30, d 3/15/45 at the home of his sister, Mrs. Burge, in Utica (9-3/25)
5235. Lathrop, S. G. (Rev.) of the Oneida Conference, m 7/17/43 Cinthia Clary, dau of Aurelius of Warren, in W; Rev. Elias Bowen of Sauquoit (9-8/5)
5236. Laton, Gilbert A. m 12/18/32 Mary Baskin in Starkey (6-1/2/33)
5237. Lattimore, Charles B., 5, youngest s of John and Sarah, d 2/22/49 in Utica (funeral at 13 Washington St.) (9-2/23)
5238. Laupaugh, Charlotte Elizabeth, 13, dau of C. N. and Elizabeth, d 11/20/47 in Utica (9-11/22). See entry 5215.
5239. Laureani, _____ (the learned Dr.), 76, d 10/20/49 in Rome (presumably in Italy) (chief librarian of the Vatican Library)("at the beginning of the late revolution he installed himself in the chambers of the library ... and never removed away till after the restoration of the pontifical authority") (9-12/3)
5240. Lawless, Luke Edward, Esq. of St. Louis, MO m the Baroness Greuhn in Georgetown (state not given); Rev. Cloriviere (9-5/31/25)
5241. Lawrence, Aaron Konkle, 11 mo, s of Richard H. and Lucy of Geneva, d 4/6/49 at the home of A. Konkle, Esq. in Elmira (5-4/13)
5242. Lawrence, Ann, 76, wf of John, d in Milo (6-7/7/30)
5243. Lawrence, Charles, 73, d 1/4/44 in Oxford (Oxford Republican, 1/11)
5244. Lawrence, Christian, wf of J. R., Esq. and sister of Rev. J. F. McLaren of Geneva, d 3/26/35 in Camillus (6-4/8)
5245. Lawrence, John, 80, father of Hon. Samuel, d 5/17/33 in Milo (6-5/29)
5246. Lawrence, John, 38, d 9/15/33 in Milo (6-9/25)
5247. Lawrence, John J. (Rev.) of Geneseo, a missionary destined to Ceylon, Asia, m Mary Hulin, a teacher in Mrs. Willard's Female Seminary in Troy, at a monthly concert in the First Presby. Ch. of Troy; Rev. Beman (6-4/22/35)
5248. Lawrence, John W. of NYC m 6/20/50 Anna Stanton, youngest dau of George W. of Albany, in A; Rev. Dr. Potter (9-6/26)
5249. Lawrence, M. H. of Milo m 12/25/37 Margaret Bogert of Catlin in C (6-1/24/38)

5250. Lawrence, Martha Ann, wf of Augustus S., d 5/18/34 in Elmira (6-5/28)
5251. Lawrence, Robert W. m 10/5/33 Catherine Van Duzen in Elmira (6-10/16)
5252. Lawton, George, 76, formerly of Newport, RI, d 2/2/22 in Oxford (8-2/6)
5253. Lawton, Henry M., Esq. of the firm of Doty and Lawton m 7/2/49 Adelia Ann
       Parker, dau of -. S. Parker, Esq., in Rome, NY; Rev. W. E. Knox (9-7/6)
5254. Lawyer, Alfred G., publisher of the Bainbridge Free Democrat, m 6/10/50
       Sarah J. Parker, dau of Nathan, Jr., in Norwich; Rev. C. D. Burritt
       (9-6/20)
5255. Lay, Damon F., 30, d 3/5/43 in Westmoreland (deceased is only s of late
       Rowland Lay who died in 1842; deceased a member of 2nd Bapt. Ch.,
       Westmoreland) (9-3/27)
5256. Lay, Lucy, wf of Amos, formerly of Albany, d 2/17/24 in Philadelphia
       (state not given) (9-3/16)
5257. Leach, _____, 20, wf of Alva, d 3/29/18 in Greene (8-4/8)
5258. Leach, Ichabod of Millet m 9/1/35 Mary Maria Wheeler of Seneca in S; Rev.
       J. W. French (6-9/9)
5259. Leake, Hannah, relict of Capt. John formerly of New Haven, CT, d (in Savoy,
       NY?) (6-6/4/34)
5260. Leake, Simeon J. m 9/1/46 Hannah Jane Morrow in Albany (9-9/4)
5261. Leal, Robert A., 23, editor and proprietor of the Oxford Republican,
       d 12/25/43 in Oxford (9-2/3/44)
5262. Lean, James F., Esq. of Laurens m 9/18/49 Harriet A. Benjamin, dau of
       Orson, Esq. of Canandaigua, in C; Rev. A. B. Hesch (9-9/19)
5263. Leavenworth, Esther, 87, wid of Amos formerly of Deerfield, d 7/2/42 in
       Truxton (9-12/2)
5264. Leavenworth, Jesse, Esq., 83, d 11/25/26 in Sacketts Harbor (9-12/5)
5265. Lebore, Lucretia (Mrs.), 56(?), d 7/3/33 in Canandaigua (6-7/13)
5266. Le Breton, Edward A., 55, formerly of Geneva, d 9/25/30 in Detroit, MI
       (6-10/13)
5267. Le Breton, John, merchant, m 3/23/26 Eliza Sanford, oldest dau of Hon.
       Nathan, both of Albany, in A; Rev. Proal (9-4/4)
5268. Ledson, Simon m 8/14/49 Elizabeth Clarke; Rev. William Wyatt. All of
       Oriskany (9-8/18)
5269. Ledyard, Sincklaer of Cazenovia m 12/7/43 Helen C. Seymour, dau of late
       Henry of Utica; Rev. Dr. Proal (9-12/9). Correction 12/11: groom's
       given name should read Lincklaen .
5270. Lee, Abram, 60, d 10/28/41 in New Boston (3-11/3)
5271. Lee, Aziel H., merchant, m 5/21/46 Albena O. Jennings, both of Frankfort,
       at the Columbian Hotel in Utica; Otis Whipple, Esq. (9-5/23)
5272. Lee, Charles, s of Joshua of PennYan, m 9/29/35 Mary M. Hall, oldest dau
       of late ambrose, Esq. of Palmyra, in P; Rev. G. R. H. Shumway (6-10/7)
5273. Lee, Daniel S. m Laura S. Gambey (6-7/14/30)
5274. Lee, Elisha, 84, (a Rev. soldier) d 12/17/47 in Clinton Co. (father of
       Charles M., Esq. of Rochester) (9-1/1/48)
5275. Lee, Henry P. of Binghamton m 5/23/50 Julia Rundell, dau of Gen. O. G.
       of Norwich, at Emanuel's Ch. in Norwich; Rev. Cox (9-5/29)
5276. Lee, Mary (Mrs.), 32, d 4/12/32 in Sullivan (3-4/17)
5277. Lee, Nancy (Miss), 53, formerly of Lyme, CT, d 3/31/44 in Utica, NY
       (consumption) (funeral from her late residence in the house of Alfred
       Wells, 63 Broadway) (9-4/1)
5278. Lee, Philomen (Deacon), 76, formerly of Guilford, d in German, NY
       (8-8/20/23)
5279. Lee, Porter m 7/8/36 Catherine Sickles in Chittenango; J. French, Esq.
       (3-7/13)
5280. Lee, Rachel, wid, d 2/25/32 in Milo (6-3/14)
5281. Lee, Sarah Sophia (Miss), 25, d 10/1/48 in Marcellus (1-10/4)
5282. Lee, Seth (Rev.), 49, pastor of the Cong'l. Society in Lyme, CT, d in Lyme
       (9-11/14/26)
5283. Lee, Sherman (Col.), 42, an officer in the War of 1812, d 2/17/30 in Milo
       (6-2/17/30)
5284. Lee, Stephen, 73, of Portland, ME (a Rev. soldier) d 1/29/31 in NYC
       (fought at Bunker hill and Yorktown - the first and last battles for
       independence) (9-2/8)
5285. Lee, Stephen (Col.), 62, d 5/31/42 in Sullivan (3-6/1)
5286. Lee, Waity (Mrs.), 90, d 10/14/33 in Milo (6-11/6)

5287. Lee, William I., Chief Justice, m 3/11/49 Catherine E. ___? of Albany, NY in Honolulu, Sandwich Islands (Hawaii); Rev. C. Damon (9-7/2)
5288. Lefurge, Benjamin m 12/31/35 Sophia Freer, both of Seneca; Elder Sears (6-1/6/36)
5289. Legg, Aaron L., 26, d 8/29/35 in Benton (6-9/2)
5290. Legg, George Mortimer, 2, s of Elijah and Laura Ann, d 8/11/49 in Baldwinsville (1-8/16)
5291. Legg, Mary (Mrs.), 92, mother of John, d 5/28/49 in Skaneateles (1-5/31)
5292. Leggett, William, Esq., 38, d 5/29/39 in NYC (6-6/5)
5293. Leitch, George F., Esq. m 9/16/33 Catharine H. Kellogg in Skaneateles (6-9/25)
5294. Leleomora, a chief of the next rank to the king and son of the late prime minister, d 10/21/48 in Honolulu, Hawaii (9-2/19/49)
5295. Lemmon, William, 38, formerly of Romulus, NY, d 4/4/36 in Washtenaw Co., MI (6-5/4)
5296. Lent, John m 3/13/45 Mary Ann Bellinger (oldest dau of Frederick), both of Whitestown, in W; Rev. E. A. Spencer of Westmoreland (9-3/19)
5297. Leonard, Ann B., 60, d 6/11/50 in Marcellus (1-6/13)
5298. Leonard, B. Noble of NYC m 1/23/50 Margaret H. Snyder, dau of Henry V., Esq. of Utica, in U; Rev. William Wyatt (9-1/24)
5299. Leonard, Frederick B. (Dr.) of Lansingburgh m 5/25/35 Margaret Caroline Nicholas, dau of late Hon. John, at Trinity Ch. in Geneva; Rev. Dr. Mason (6-5/27)
5300. Leonard, H. C. (Col.) of Reading m Catherine Misner in Catlin (6-2/17/30)
5301. Leonard, Joseph (Capt.), 90, d 12/1/42 at his home in Binghamton (b in Plymouth, MA and in his youth "engaged in whale fishery; moved to Wyoming Valley, PA where he lived at the time of the massacre; removed to the Binghamton, NY area in 1787 (2-12/7)
5302. Leonard, Joshua (Rev.), 74, d 12/18/43 in Auburn, NY (b in Raynham, MA; grad from Brown Univ.; first ministry at Ellington, CT; in 1797 or 98 came to the Utica area; was the first pastor who settled west of the present-day Oneida and Otsego counties; in 1799 became first pastor of the Presby. Ch. of Cazenovia) (buried beside his wife in Cazenovia) (9-1/5/44)
5303. Leonard, Marcus, 54, s of late Moses of Herkimer Co. and bro of Mrs. T. E. Jones of Utica, d 8/7/49 in Buffalo (9-8/16)
5304. Leonard, Margaret, 55, wf of Rev. Joshua, d 3/5/24 in German, NY (8-3/24)
5305. Leonard, Oliver E. of Auburn m 10/8/32 Mary Washburn of Utica in U; Rev. Dr. Lansing (double ceremony - see marr of Ruger(?) Swartwout (9-10/16)
5306. Ler, John B. (Gen.) m 10/3/40 Mary Jane Dayton Prentice, dau of Herman V. formerly of Lenox, in Albion, NY; Rev. Gilbert Crawford (3-10/14
5307. Le Roy, Francis L. of Johnstown m 7/4/24 Polly Joslin of Verona in V; Rev. Israel Brainerd (9-7/20)
5308. Lester, James of Duanesburg m 1/6/42 Sarah Whipple of Conklin in C; Rev. J. M. Coley (2-1/12)
5309. Lester, Thomas m 12/31/46 Jerusha Elliott, both of New Hartford, in New H.; Rev. Dr. Paddock (double ceremony - see marr of John W. Adams) (9-1/27/47)
5310. Lewis, ____, four children of William, Jr. of Monroe, NY d 1/19/29 in a house fire at their home at 9 p.m. (3 boys and 1 girl, aged 7 to 16; the parents with the youngest child were at a neighbor's home 1½ miles away at the time) (7-1/21)
5311. Lewis, Catherine H., 24, wf of James M., Esq., d 12/16/42 in Utica (funeral from her late home, 6 Broadway) (9-12/17)
5312. Lewis, Daniel m 3/26/29 Elpha Rodgers in Preston; Rev. Henry Peck. All of Preston (8-4/1)
5313. Lewis, Daniel W., Esq., 70, attorney, d 6/17/37 in Buffalo (6-6/28)
5314. Lewis, Dennis N. of Frankfort m 9/18/50 Mary Ann Wake of Willowvale in W; Rev. John Waugh of Sauquoit (9-9/27)
5315. Lewis, Dwight M., 24, d 1/18/46 in Morrisville (9-1/23)
5316. Lewis, Edwin W. m Relief P. Holden in Starkey (6-7/28/30)
5317. Lewis, Elijah m Hannah Main, both of Norwich, in N; Elder Randall (8-11/29/20)
5318. Lewis, Emanuel m 9/1/31 Mary Clark in Waterloo (6-9/14)
5319. Lewis, Ethan, 48, d 8/15/49 in Elmira (a long-time resident in E) (5-8/17)

5320. Lewis, George W. m Mary Blodgett in Batavia (6-12/2/35)
5321. Lewis, Henry B. m 2/24/48 Nancy B. Haughton of Pratt's Hollow in P. H.;
       Rev. S. G. Lathrop (9-2/29)
5322. Lewis, James G., 24, d 11/9/44 in Utica (9-11/12)
5323. Lewis, John (Dr.), 39, d 7/11/34 in Clyde (6-7/30)
5324. Lewis, John C., 41, speaker of the Conn. "House of Representatives",
       d 11/21/49 in New Haven, CT (9-11/27)
5325. Lewis, Leonard, 65, d 6/23/33 in Poughkeepsie (6-7/10)
5326. Lewis, Lumley of Remsen m 2/12/44 Sophronia Andrews, oldest dau of Aaron
       of Alder Creek, at A. C.; Rev. Kimble (9-2/16)
5327. Lewis, Mariette, 18, wf of Samuel E. and dau of Simon Turner, d 1/9/43 in
       Preston (married 10 months) (Oxford Republican, 1/20)
5328. Lewis, Mary, dau of Stephen, d 10/14/36 in Elmira (6-10/19)
5329. Lewis(?), Mary, wf of Robert(?), d 10/25/46 in Benton (6-10/30)
5330. Lewis, Mary Ann, dau of John G., tailor, of 14 Broad St., d 2/5/44 in
       Utica (9-2/6)
5331. Lewis, Morgan E. m 10/20/47 Sophia Bliss (oldest dau of Nathan), both of
       Whitestown, in W; Rev. F. A. Spencer of Westmoreland (9-10/22)
5332. Lewis, Nathaniel B. of Hopewell m 1/26/32 Wealthy Skinner, dau of Maj. A.
       of Ogden, in O (6-2/1)
5333. Lewis, Richard m 11/6/30 Harriet Smith in Rochester (6-11/17)
5334. Lewis, Samuel B., son of Ethan of Elmira, d at sea 12/21/49 on his
       homeward passage en route from San Francisco to Panama (5-5/10/50)
5335. Lewis, Samuel E. m 3/9/42 Mariette Turner, both of Preston, in P; Rev.
       J. T. Goodrich (Oxford Times, 3/16)
5336. Lewis, Susan 35, d 8/25/33 in New Haven, NY (cancer) (6-9/11)
5337. Lewis, Washington P. m 11/4/47 Maria Johnson in Westmoreland; Rev. Staples.
       All of Utica (9-11/8)
5338. Lewis, Willard P. of Oriskany Falls m 9/2/45 Flora Hurd of Augusta in A;
       Rev. Bartholomew (9-9/10)
5339. Lewis, William, Esq., 38, sheriff of Orleans Co., d 7/25/26 in Clarendon
       (9-8/8)
5340. Lewis, William of Madison m 6/2/46 Mary J. White of Sweden Center, NY in
       Sweden Center; Rev. T. C. Hill (9-6/25)
5341. Lewis, William E. m 2/23/50 Ellea Higbie, both of Remsen; H. G. Vogell,
       Esq. (9-2/28)
5342. Lightbody, Samuel, 48, merchant, d 7/13/46 at his home in Utica (funeral
       from his late home, 53 Elizabeth St.) (b in Berkshire Co., MA and lived
       for a time in Albany, NY prior to his move to Utica in 1824) (9-8/10)
5343. Lille, Edward m 11/20/33 "Mrs. Conger" in Canandaigua (6-12/4)
5344. Lilley, D., editor of the Bradford (PA) Argus, m 8/13/36 Sophia L. Parsons
       of Columbia, Bradford Co., PA in B (6-9/7)
5345. Lillybridge, Freeman of Annsville, late graduate of Madison Univ.,
       m 8/21/46 Mary Bryant of Watertown in Hamilton; Rev. George W. Eaton,
       D.D. (9-8/24)
5346. Lillybridge, Ira, 55, d 4/8/48 in Annsville (9-4/15)
5347. Lincoln, Edward, 17, d 7/29/35 in Sullivan (3-8/4)
5348. Lincoln, Horace m 12/24/43 Nancy Lavintia Campbell in Sullivan; Rev.
       William Morse.   All of Sullivan (3-12/27)
5349. Lincoln, Ira m 9/8/22 Harriet Gibson, both of Norwich, in N; Rev. Spauldng
       (7-9/11)
5350. Lincoln, Nathan C. m 1/30/31 Caroline G. Haviland, both of Vernon, in V;
       Rev. A. Garrison (9-2/15)
5351. Lindeman, N. m Rebecca Whitlock in Ithaca (6-1/19/31)
5352. Lindsay, John m Barbara Morrow in Bath (6-3/31/30)
5353. Lindsay, Merrit m 6/2/41 Emeline Apgar, both of Caton, in C; Rev. C. S.
       Davis (4-6/11)
5354. Lidsley, Ebenezer m 1/17/49 Elizabeth Lovell in Elmira; Rev. H. N. Seaver.
       All of E (5-1/26)
5355. Lindsley, James m Maria Richardson in Bath (6-5/26/30)
5356. Lindsley, Phebe, 27, d 4/16/36 in Seneca Falls (6-4/27)
5357. Lindsley, Rial m 1/26/33 Sarah Wood in Rushville (6-2/6)
5358. Lines, A. G. m 1/1/48 P. A. Scoville in Liverpool; _____ Jaquith, Esq.
       (1-1/5)
5359. Lines, James U., 52, of Utica d 4/23/44 in Utica (consumption) (funeral
       from his late home, 54 Whitesboro St.) (9-4/24)

5360. Lines, Peter W., formerly of Utica, d 1/6/47 in Bridgewater (9-1/8)
5361. Linkletter, Samuel of Howard m 12/29/32 Emily Randal of Milo in M
(6-1/9/33)
5362. Linn, Adam m 9/22/33 Philenda Fisher in Jerusalem, NY (6-10/9)
5363. Linsdee, W. R. m 5/6/49 _?_ Winne, both of Baldwinsville, in B; Rev.
T. Walker (1-5/10)
5364. Linson, John T. m 5/2/50 Sarah Ann Bunyea, both of Elbridge, in
Baldwinsville; Rev. Byron Alden (1-5/2)
5365. Lion, Peter, Esq., 79, a native of North Castle, NY, d 7/6/24 ("Paulding,
Van Wert, and Williams brought Major Andre before this man for
examination and by his orders Andre was sent to Gen. Washington")
(9-8/3)
5366. Lions, William (Col.), a Rev. officer, d in "Opelaucus, Louisiana"
(8-3/11/18)
5367. Lippencott, Joseph m 11/5/34 Mary Jane Williams in Palmyra; F. Smith,
Esq. All of Palmyra (6-11/19)
5368. Litchfield, E. C. m 8/2/38 Mary A. Ten Eyck, dau of Jacob, Esq., in
Cazenovia; Rev. Barrows. All of Cazenovia (3-8/15)
5369. Litchfield, E. Darwin of NYC m 9/20/49 Mary S. Hubbard, only dau of
Thomas H. of Utica, in U; Rev. Dr. Proal (9-9/22)
5370. Little, Amelia L. (Mrs.) d 7/18/48 in Pasumalia, Madura, Southern India
(grad. from Albany [NY] Female Academy, 1845) (dau of Capt. William
Newton of Sherburne, NY and wf of Rev. Charles Little, missionary of
the American Board; sailed 4 Dec 1847 from Boston on the barque "Mary
Adams"; after 133 days arrived in Madras and then travelled 290 miles
overland to Madura) (9/11/7)
5371. Little, Charles (Rev.) of Columbia, CT m 9/29/47 Amelia M. Newton of
Sherburne, NY in S; Rev. A. C. Tuttle (9-10/4)
5372. Little, Jonathan, Esq., 70, d 12/19/26 in NYC (9-12/26)
5373. Little, Susan (Miss), 26, d 7/20/50 in North Chemung (member of Meth. Ch.)
(5-8/16)
5374. Littlejohn, Hetty W., 29, wf of Gilbert H. and only dau of Herbert and
Julia Mann, d 7/4/47 in Whitestown (9-8/2)
5375. Littlewood, Henry m 1/15/43 Eliza Bennett in Oxford. Both of Oxford.
(Oxford Republican, 1/20)
5376. Littlewood, James of Chicago, IL m 9/1/46 Mary E. Butler of Kirkland, NY;
Rev. Brace of Utica (9-9/3)
5377. Livermore, Fidus of Dresden m Caroline S. Lewis of Hopeton in H (6-3/9/31)
5378. Livermore, Samuel, Esq., 56, d 4/5/31 in Independence, NY (6-4/20)
5379. Livesay, Judah m 4/8/31 Caroline Hathorn in Elmira (6-4/20)
5380. Livingston, Ann (Mrs.), 77, d 12/11/40 at the home of Mr. H. Haight in
Kingston (3-12/23)
5381. Livingston, Catherine G., 85, wid of late Gilbert, d in Poughkeepsie
(6-5/26/30)
5382. Livingston, Edward P. of Clermont, lieutenant gov. of NY, m 6/13/32 Mary
C. Broom, dau of late William, Esq. of Hyde Park, NY, in Albany
(6-7/4)
5383. Livingston, Francis A., Esq. of NYC d in Poughkeepsie (6-6/30/30)
5384. Livingston, George R. m 11/27/33 Phebe Van Kleef in Seneca Falls (6-12/4)
5385. Livingston, Henry A. (Col.), 72, d 6/9/49 at his late home near
Poughkeepsie (9-6/13)
5386. Livingston, Henry M., 51, d 3/20/44 in Ephratah (9-4/1)
5387. Livingston, Henry W. m 7/17/49 Lucy Stevens, oldest dau of John, Esq.,
at the Church of the Messiah in NYC; Rev. Dr. Dewey. All of NYC
(9-7/20)
5388. Livingston, Maria, relict of Hon. Robert R. late of Clermont, d 3/22/14
in Washington (D.C.?) (8-4/5)
5389. Lloyd, Ann, 2, dau of John, d 8/9/26 in Utica (9-8/15)
5390. Lloyd, John (Capt.) of Angelica m Mrs. Eliza Coburn in Friendship
(6-12/20/30)
5391. Lloyd, Ransom, Esq. of Angelica m Julia M. Start of Danbury, CT in
Birdsall, NY (6-2/24/30)
5392. Lloyd, Sarah, 14, dau of John, d 2/4/45 in Utica (funeral from the
Broad Street Bapt. Ch. (9-2/6)
5393. Locke, Henry M. m 3/26/35 Eleanor Bassett, both of Geneva (6-4/8)

5394. Locke, Henry M., 36, d 4/20/36 in Penn Yan (6-5/14)
5395. Locke, John D. m 5/17/30 Julia A. Goff at Trinity Ch. in Geneva; Rev. Mason.   All of Geneva (6-5/19)
5396. Locke, Lydia, 42, wf of Alvin, d 8/10/50 in Utica (9-8/16)
5397. Locke, Nathaniel, Esq., 54, formerly a state senator, d 6/16/20 in Oxford (8-6/21)
5398. Lockwood, Albert m 5/14/50 Roxana Francher in Utica; Rev. William Wyatt. All of Utica (9-5/16)
5399. Lockwood, Monson m 8/20/33 Charlotte Whitney in NYC; Rev. Murray (6-9/4)
5400. Loder, Sarah, 80, relict of Samuel, one of the earliest settlers in Lenox, d 3/20/49 in Lenox (9-3/24)
5401. Logan, John m Cordelai Howard, both of Canandaigua, in Palmyra (6-2/17/30)
5402. Lomis, Harry H., 36, of Cazenovia d 6/19/45 in NYC (9-6/27)
5403. Loncust, Susannah (Mrs.), 37, d 4/27/30 in Geneva (6-5/26)
5404. Long, David of Cambridge, NY m 9/6/49 Olivia Russell, only dau of Col. Joseph of Hartford, NY; Rev. Walter R. Long (9-10/3)
5405. Long, E. R. (Lt.) of the U.S. Army d 3/11/46 in Detroit, MI (9-3/23)
5406. Long, Nathan D. of Syracuse m 11/19/44 Cynthia Porter of Windsor, CT at Bagg's Hotel (town not stated); Rev. J. McIlvaine (9-11/21)
5407. Long, Oscar F. m 6/26/48 Caroline Delano of Utica in U; Rev. C. P. Grosvenor (9-7/7)
5408. Longley, Lewis Raymond, 8 mo, inf s of Samuel M. and Lydia A., d 7/8/42 in Binghamton (2-7/27)
5409. Longshore, Richard, about 67, d 5/20/38 in Sullivan (cancer) (3-5/30)
5410. Loomis, _____ m 2/10/29 Mary Cline in Smithville; Elder Kellogg. All of Smithville (8-3/11)
5411. Loomis, Abijah, 76, d 7/16/19 in Greene (8-7/21)
5412. Loomis, Anson C. of Seneca Castle m 11/2/35 Maria Pardy, dau of Stephen of Benton, in B; Rev. Iverson (6-11/18)
5413. Loomis, Benjamin, about 22, s of Nathan, Esq., d 4/13/32 in Middlesex (consumption) (6-4/25)
5414. Loomis, Chauncey m 12/7/45 Sarah E. Finch in Utica; Rev. D. W. Bristol. All of Utica (9-12/9)
5415. Loomis, Daniel A. of Rochester m 10/24/33 Jane E. Bradley of Lanesborough, MA in Lebanon Springs, NY (6-11/27)
5416. Loomis, Edwin D. of Cazenovia m 6/22/48 Mary Jane Root of Mexico, NY in Mexico; Rev. Ezra Scovil (1-6/28)
5417. Loomis, Elisha, 37, d 8/27/36 in Rushville (consumption) (had served a printing apprenticeship "under Mr. Bemis in the office of the Repository"; 1819-24 participated in the mission to the Sandwich Islands (Hawaii) and there established the first printing press; was formerly the proprietor of the Rochester Observer) (6-9/14)
5418. Loomis, Elizabeth, 22, dau of Jerome, d 12/7/31 at the Old Castle near Geneva (6-12/14)
5419. Loomis, Frances Annette, 5 mo, only dau of Dr. Edward, d 9/8/45 in Westmoreland (9-9/9)
5420. Loomis, Gordon G. m 4/30/44 Eliza L. Dean, both of Westmoreland, in W; Rev. Beriah Green of Whitesboro (9-5/4)
5421. Loomis, Henry m 12/31/34 Julia Ann Redfield in Waterloo (6-1/14/35)
5422. Loomis, Hermon H. m 4/25/39 Mary Ann Coleman, both of Jerusalem, NY, in J; Rev. Allen Steele (6-5/8)
5423. Loomis Horatio N., Esq., M.D., of Palmyra m 6/7/33 Mrs. Mary Ann Mott, dau of Col. John Williams of Waterville, in W (6-6/19)
5424. Loomis, Jerome, Jr. (Capt.), late of Geneva, NY, m 3/1/31 Margaret B. Conway in Dexter, Mich. Terr. (6-4/6)
5425. Loomis, Mary, 50, consort of Asa, d 10/1/26 in Utica (9-10/10)
5426. Loomis, Nathaniel S., Esq., 36, of Verona d 4/2/49 in Bath (9-4/26)
5427. Loomis, William, 25, s of Jerome, d 7/25/30 at the Old Castle (Seneca) (6-7/28)
5428. Loomis, William G. m 10/16/44 Dorlesca A. Wood, youngest dau of Gershome, Esq. of Westmoreland, in W; Rev. Rockwell (9-10/23)
5429. Loomis, Winifred S., 33, wf of George A. and oldest dau of Richard and Jane Perry, d 11/22/47 in Utica (funeral from Broad Street Bapt. Ch.) (9-11/14)
5430. Loop, Civilian, 40, d 11/19/33 in Elmira (6-11/27)

5431. Loop, Henry, Esq. m Matilda McKinstry in Hillsdale (6-2/9/31)
5432. Loop, Murray m Mary Ann Arnot, both of Painted Post, in Elmira (6-2/17/30)
5433. Loper, Elijah P., formerly of Seneca Falls, d 8/18/34 in Perrysburgh
       (6-9/17)
5434. Lord, Edward, late of the Seminary in Auburn m 8/2C/46 Mary Jane Sanders
       of Williamstown, MA "on the summit of Petersburgh Mountain in God's
       own temple" (Petersburgh Mt. in the town of Petersburgh, NY. Blue laws
       of Massachusetts precluded their marriage in that state on a Sunday)
       (9-9/3)
5435. Loring, Horatio N. (Rev.), 41, pastor of the Broad Street Bapt. Ch.,
       d 8/15/47 in Utica (9-8/18)
5436. Lossing, Benson J. m 6/10/33 Alice Barrit in Poughkeepsie (6-7/10)
5437. Louke, Charles F. T. m 10/19/17 Addeliza Wood, both of Oxford; _____
       Sherwood, Esq. (8-10/22)
5438. Loucks, Emma A., 10 mo, dau of Walter D. and Mary Ann, d 12/20/48 in Utica
       (funeral at 18 Blandina St.) (9-12/21)
5439. Loucks, Walter, 49, d 1/6/49 in Utica (consumption) (9-1/10)
5440. Loud, Cullen m Lucinda M. Bliss, both of Perington, in Palmyra (6-4/3/33)
5441. Louwer, Anthony m 10/2/43 Alice O'Donnell in Syracuse; Rev. Donohu, pastor
       of the Catholic Ch. (9-10/5)
5442. Love, William, 93, a Rev. soldier, d 11/20/35 in Cazenovia (3-11/24)
5443. Lovejoy, David m 5/7/36 Charity Rector in Benton (6-6/15)
5444. Lovejoy, William C. of Newark, NY m 6/30/31 Emily H. Abbett of East
       Palmyra in E. P.; Rev. Alverson (6-7/13)
5445. Lovel, Anne, dau of Vincent, d 4/15/44 in Whitestown (9-5/6)
5446. Lovel, George m 5/9/50 Sally Ann Quackenbush; Rev. I. N. Hurd. All of
       Big Flats (5-5/10)
5447. Lovel, Margaret, 20, youngest dau of late Vincent, d 5/29/45 in Whitestown
       (9-6/6)
5448. Lovel, Vincent, 57, d 3/3/44 at his home in Whitestown (epilepsy)
       (b in England; emigrated to this country in 1823 and settled
       permanently in Whitestown in 1824; surv by wf and 11 ch.) (9-3/16)
5449. Loveland, George P. m 7/14/42 Marietta Dean of Laurens in L (4-7/27)
5450. Loveless, Louis m 7/2/48 Ursula Earll in Baldwinsville; Rev. I. Dudley
       (1-8/2)
5451. Lovell, C. S. (Lt.), 2nd Reg't., U.S. Army, m 8/12/45 Sarah Ann Tracy,
       dau of Capt. H. N. of the U.S. Revenue Service, at Sacketts Harbor;
       Rev. E. G. Townsend (double ceremony - see marr of Lt. B. P. Tilden)
       ["(These) two officers, with their brides, took passage the same
       evening on the steamer "Rochester" for the Western Frontier... Capt.
       Tingsbury's Company, to which they were attached, having been ordered
       to that section on the 10th inst."] (9-8/23)
5452. Lovell, Henry D. m 7/29/44 Nancy Minier "at the hotel in the village of
       Big Flat"; Rev. Seaman (5-8/8)
5453. Loversy, Sylvester m 5/21/35 Emily Canfield in Canandaigua (6-5/27)
5454. Lovett, John, late of Albany, d 8/15/18 at Fort Meigs (8-9/9)
5455. Lovett, John Erskine, attorney and late secretary of the Albany Insurance
       Co., d 8/19/47 in Albany (9-8/23)
5456. Lovitt, Horatio m 2/2/31 Jane Griswold in Penfield (6-2/16)
5457. Low, Aaron, Jr., editor of the Poughkeepsie Telegraph and Observer,
       m Mary C. Dean (6-6/23/30)
5458. Low, Ezekiel m 9/8/35 Sally Adams, both of Fayette, in Geneva; Richard
       Hogarth, Esq. (6-9/9)
5459. Low, Nicholas, 88, d 11/6/26 in NYC (9-11/21)
5460. Lowell, Alanson m 2/14/33 Malinda Burdick; Rev. H. S. Snyder (3-2/19)
5461. Lowrey, Margaret, 31, wf of George, d in Penn Yan (6-6/9/30)
5462. Lowry, John m 6/13/50 Mary Elizabeth Freeman, both of Oriskany, in Rome,
       NY; Rev. W. E. Knox (9-6/20)
5463. Lowthrop, Walter m 5/16/30 Rebecca Deitz in Geneva; Rev. Phelps (6-5/26)
5464. Lowzee, Isaac m Roxy Torry in Lockville (6-2/23/31)
5465. Lucas, Albert, Esq., 35, d 10/30/35 in Waterloo (6-11/11)
5466. Lucas, Amaziah, 83, (a Rev. soldier), formerly of New Haven, CT, d 2/5/47
       in Augusta (9-2/17)
5467. Lucas, John S. m 9/25/50 Julia H. Coe of Madison in M; Rev. N. Palmer
       (9-9/27)

5468. Luce, G. V., printer, m 8/26/47 Emma Paine at St. Paul's Ch., Syracuse; Rev. H. Gregory (1-9/15)
Luce, Hiram. See, possibly, Luce, Siram.
5469. Luce, Nancy (Miss), 42, d 11/9/47 in Utica (funeral at the home of her sister, Miss Sophia Luce, 47 Broadway) (9-11/11)
5470. Luce, Nicholas, 50, d 5/21/31 in Tioga (6-6/8)
5471. Luce, Siram (sic) A. of Winfield m 11/11/50 Malina A. Walker of New Hartford in Checkerville; Elder J. Mariner (9-11/15)
5472. Luce, Stephen S. m 5/8/36 Fanny Brock in Elmira (6-5/18)
5473. Luce, William J., 14, s of Israel and Matilda, drowned 9/2/48 (5-9/8)
5474. Ludlam, Mary (Miss), 18, dau of John, d 4/9/35 in Varick (6-4/15)
5475. Ludlow, Eunice, 54, wf of Thomas, d 8/31/46 in Seneca (6-9/4)
5476. Ludlow, Henry William, Esq., 38, d 9/7/14 in Norwich (lay in debtors' prison 18 mo; son of _____ Ludlow of NYC "who can boast a fortune of 250,000 dollars with two surviving children only to share it ...") (8-9/17)
5477. Ludlow, John R., 57, d 2/24/43 in Utica (funeral from Universalist Ch. on Devereux St.) (9-2/25)
5478. Ludlow, Mary S., 63, relict of late John R., d 7/20/48 in Utica (funeral from her late home, 43 Washington St.) (9-7/20)
5479. Lum, Charles m 6/5/33 Laura Love in Hartland (6-6/26)
5480. Lum, Charles, Esq., 50, d 11/1/46 at his home in Detroit, MI (consumption) (6-11/13)
5481. Lum, Daniel L. of Geneva m 11/1/32 Sarah P. Tappan, dau of Dr. William, formerly of Geneva, in Hunter; Rev. Duffey (6-11/14)
5482. Lum, Hannah, 28, wf of Daniel L., d 5/9/30 in Seneca (6-5/12)
5483. Lum, Henry, about 44, bro of Daniel L. of Geneva, d 1/14/33 in Ogdensburgh (6-1/23)
5484. Lum, Matthew, 66, d 5/4/30 in Geneva (father of Messrs. Daniel L. and Charles) (6-5/12)
5485. Lumbard, Dan of Lenox m 3/12/44 Mrs. Russigee of Verona in V (9-4/27)
5486. Lumbard, James N. of Cazenovia m 7/5/39 Rebecca M. Lawton of Fenner; Rev. J. Abell (3-7/10)
5487. Lumbard, Nancy, 38, consort of Theophilus, d 4/20/26 in Utica (9-4/25)
5488. Lummis, William N. (Dr.), d 4/16/33 in Sodus (6-4/24)
5489. Lundy, Joel m 1/28/36 Mary Ann Quinby in Waterloo (6-2/10)
5490. Lusk, Charles H. m 4/11/48 Harriet S. Tyler at the home of George W. Robinson, Esq.; Rev. T. Walker. All of Baldwinsville (1-4/26)
5491. Lusk, Jane A., 34, wf of Rev. William and dau of late Capt. Robert Norris of Westmoreland, d 1/5/46 in Cherry Valley (funeral sermon by Rev. Campbell of Cooperstown)(surv by husband and 4 ch) (9-2/3)
5492. Lusk, William (Rev.) of Nunda m 12/2/47 Maria L. Smith of Cooperstown; Rev. Campbell (9-12/7)
5493. Luskins, R. m 10/29/48 Matilda Jane Hill in Elmira; Rev. H. N. Seaver. All of Elmira (5-11/3)
5494. Lutes, Ralsey m 8/15/49 Emeline Breese at the Meth. Parsonage in Elmira; Rev. H. N. Seaver (5-8/17)
5495. Luther, Andrew m 8/12/41 Susan Sickles in Sullivan; Rev. J. abell. All of Sullivan (3-8/25)
5496. Luyport, Jacob m 7/21/47 Deborah Frances Burdick in Newbridge; Rev. Howard. All of Baldwinsville (1-8/11)
5497. Lyell, _____ (Rev. Dr.) m 11/29/25 Elizabeth Bennett at Christ Church in NYC; Bishop Hobart (9-12/6)
5498. Lyle, John (Rev.), 55, d 7/22/25 in Paris, KY (9-8/16)
5499. Lyman, Asa (Rev.), 58, d 1/20/36 in Clinton (6-2/17)
5500. Lyman, Betsey (Mrs.), 30, d 9/16/33 in Penn Yan (6-9/25)
5501. Lyman, Catherine, 20, of Palmyra d 4/12/49 at the home of Mrs. E. A. Blake in Utica (9-4/13)
5502. Lyman, Darius of Ravenna, OH m 6/9/34 Mrs. Lucy Ann Walbridge of Geneva in G; Rev. J. W. French (6-6/11)
5503. Lyman, Henry Munson, 5 mo, s of James and Frances P., d 9/3/43 in St. Louis, MO (9-9/26)
5504. Lyman, Jacob m 2/10/49 Lucretia Snow in Elmira; W. P. Keukle, Esq. (3-2/16)
5505. Lyman, Jonathan H., 42, attorney, d in Northampton (9-11/22/25)
5506. Lyman, William (Rev.), 69, D.D., d 6/5/33 in China, NY (6-6/19)

5507. Lynch, George Harrison, Esq. of NYC m 6/4/48 Louise Frances Foster, youngest dau of Hon. Henry A. of Rome, NY, in Utica (9-6/9)
5508. Lynch, James B. m 4/18/49 Sara Adams Johnson, oldest dau of Alex B., Esq., in Utica; Rev. Pierre A. Proal, D.D. (9-4/19)
5509. Lynch, Jane, 88, relict of Dominick, d 7/2/49 in NYC (9-7/6)
5510. Lynch, Jasper, 58, d 7/3/48 in Rome, NY (9-7/10)
5511. Lynch, Lea, 9 mo, s of Harrison and Louise F., d 2/10/50 in Brooklyn (whooping cough) (9-2/13)
5512. Lyndsey, Robert, 38, d 9/6/31 (3-9/13)
5513. Lyon, Alanson F. m 2/24/23 Harriet Morgan in Oxford; Rev. L. Bush (double ceremony - see marr of Julius Page) (8-2/26)
5514. Lyon, Catharine (Mrs.), 84, d 4/14/39 in Canandaigua (6-4/24)
5515. Lyon, Charity, wf of David of Oxford, d 6/18/25 (8-6/22)
5516. Lyon, David M. ofSalisbury m 9/3/33 Deborah Peek of Schenectady in S; Rev. J. Van Vechten (3-9/17)
5517. Lyon, George of Greene m 12/29/22 Susan Lyon of Oxford; Rev. Bush (8-1/1/23)
5518. Lyon, Hannah P. (Mrs.), 75, dau of Jehu W. Dana, Esq. and gr-dau of Gen. Israel Putnam, d in Pomfret, CT (9-5/20/50)
5519. Lyon, Harvey of Prescott, Upper Canada m 9/5/35 Mrs. Kaura Nesbit of Geneva in Canandaigua; Rev. M. Allen (6-9/16)
5520. Lyon, James m 2/9/35 Sarah Petenger of Canandaigua in Phelps; Rev. Baggerly (6-2/11)
5521. Lyon, James m 1/15/44 Caroline Cook, only dau of Daniel, Esq., in Ogden; Rev. Dunning. All of Ogden (3-2/28)
5522. Lyon, Joseph, 63, d 6/17/49 in Catharine (cancer) (5-6/22)
5523. Lyon, Martin, Esq. of Genoa m 6/22/31 Rachel Haight of Geneva in G; Rev. M. P. Squier (6-6/29)
5524. Lyon, Martin of Genoa m 1/16/49 Harriet Northway of Ithaca in I; Rev. Wisner (9-1/30)
5525. Lyon, Mary E., 3, dau of John N. and Jane, d 4/26/49 in New Hartford (9-5/1)
5526. Lyon, Randall m 2/4/30 Marian Wyckoff in Romulus (6-2/17)
5527. Lyon, Stephen m Rebecca Lamb in South Carolina (8-6/30/19)
5528. Lyon, William, 16, s of David, d 10/17/21 in Oxford (8-10/17)
5529. Lyons, Elizabeth (Mrs.), 75, d 5/26/44 in Utica (funeral at home of her son, David A., corner of Elizabeth and Burnett Sts.) (9-5/27)
5530. Lytton, Emily Elizabeth, only dau of Sir Edward Bulwer, baronet, of Knebworth Park, Herts, England, d 4/20/48 in England (9-6/6)
McAlpin. See also McCalpin.
5531. McAlpin, Thomas H. of Oxford m 1/22/27 Eliza Smith of Winfield in W; Rev. Clay (8-2/2)
5532. McArthur, Sarah J., wf of Joseph, d in Montezuma (6-4/16/34)
5533. McAuley, John m 8/27/48 Rachael Blazies, both of York Mills, at Stanwix Hall, Rome, NY; A. B. Blair, Esq. (9-9/2)
5534. McBride, Calvin Roberts, 18 mo, s of John, d 4/14/43 in Utica (9-4/17)
5535. McBurney, Charles Mills, inf s of Thomas and Jane A., d 8/13/48 in Corning (4-8/23)
5536. McBride, Chloe, 35, wf of John formerly of Utica and dau of Calvin Wood of Schuyler, d 7/17/49 (in St. Louis, MO?) (9-8/1)
5537. McBurney, Lucretia (Mrs.), 50, d 2/8/32 at her home in Hornellsville (6-2/29)
5538. McCain, Sherrod, formerly of Geneva, NY, d 1/20/33 in Detroit, MI (6-2/13)
5539. McCall, Elijah B. m 11/19/29 Mehetabel Smith in Oxford; Rev. Bush. All of Oxford (8-11/25)
5540. McCall, Helen, 2, youngest dau of Wallace and Margaret, d 7/17/46 in Utica (funeral from 90 John St.) (9-7/18)
5541. McCall, James, Esq., 52, attorney, for a short time of Utica and bro of Dr. John McCall, d 2/18/48 in Fort Edward (9-3/1)
5542. McCall, John of Oxford m 8/23/43 Polly R. Carman of Bovina in B; Elder E. Wescott (Oxford Republican, 9/7)
5543. McCall, Wallace, 30, son of "Dr. McCall", d 4/7/47 in Utica (had lived in Utica "since a youth") (9-4/8)
5544. McCalpin, Mary, 23, of Oxford d 3/6/42 (consumption) (Oxford Times, 3/16)
5545. McCann, John m 5/31/32 Susan Van Ness in Lyons (6-6/13)

5546. McCann, Matthew of Albany m Eliza Chrisman of Schuyler at the Central Hotel in Utica; Rev. E. Francis (9-11/11/50)
5547. McCann, Henry m 6/30/50 Ruby Wedge in Corning; Rev. H. N. Seaver. All of Corning (4-7/10)
5548. McCarthy, Dennis, Esq., 57, d 7/29/35 in NYC (6-8/5)
5549. McCarthy, Percy, 46, wf of Hon. Thomas, d 1/11/43 in Salina (surv by husband and children) (9-1/14)
5550. McCartney, Samuel of Canandaigua m Eliza G. Markham in Batavia (6-3/17/30)
5551. McCartney, William, Esq., 60, d 2/10/31 in Sparta (born in Scotland; first settler in Sparta (6-3/2)
5552. McCarty, Abram m 2/2/32 Lydia Westfall, dau of Jacob D., Esq., in Phelps; Elder B. Farley (6-2/8)
5553. McCarty, Horace of Waterloo m 9/24/34 Cornelia Wing of Vienna, NY in V; Rev. Lane (6-10/8)
5554. McCauly, Thomas (Deacon), 54, d 1/23/31 in Seneca (moved from Lancaster, PA to Seneca "about 25 years ago"; member of the Associated Reformed Church at #9) (6-1/26)
5555. McCay, Sarah, dau of William W., d 2/2/33 in Bath (6-2/13)
5556. McChain, Julia W., 23, relict of late James of Ithaca, d 10/7/34 at the home of her father, Rev. William Wisner, in Rochester (this is the 4th child [besides a bro-in-law to the Rev. William and his wife] who died within a two-year period) (9-10/14)
5557. McChesney, Esther, 34, wf of Dr. John H., d 3/28/33 in Potsdam, NY (surv by husband and 5 small children) (9-4/9)
5558. McCleary, David C., 22, former editor of the Litchfield Co. Post and afterwards editor and joint proprietor of the People's Press in Batavia, d 2/11/31 in Rupert, VT (had been incapacitated since September, 1830) (6-3/2)
5559. McCleary, Jane, wf of John late of Seneca, d 6/27/31 in York (6-7/6)
5560. McClelland, David of Syracuse m 10/30/48 Harriet Crump of Utica at Trinity Ch., Utica; Rev. Dr. Proal (9-10/31)
5561. McCloud, Hubbard m Experience Dickinson in Waterloo (6-4/7/30)
5562. McCluer, Joseph (Hon.), 58, first judge of Cattaraugus Co., d 9/11/33 in Wales, NY (6-9/25)
5563. McCluer, Joseph (Gen.), 60, postmaster of Franklinville, Catt. Co., d 9/14/33 (6-10/9)
5564. McClure, _____ (Mr.), 27 or 28, tanner and courier, supposed nephew of Gen. McClure of Steuben Co., d 12/9/36 in Seneca Falls (formerly of the District of Columbia) (6-12/28)
5565. McClure, William m Hannah T. Smith, dau of Archibald, in Elmira (6-5/5/30)
5566. McCollister, Cyrus m 8/21/32 Marion K. Stanton in Penn Yan (6-8/29)
5567. McComber, Joseph C., 3, s of B. McComber, d 6/4/39 in Chittenango (3-6/5)
5568. McCombs, Henry, 6, s of Henry, drowned 3/26/36 in Flint Creek near Bethel (6-4/6)
5569. McCombs, Sarah B., 41, wf of Charles, d 3/5/44 in Utica (9-3/12)
5570. McConnel, Cyrus m Rebecca Amy in Elmira (6-3/31/30)
5571. McConnell, E. H. of Elmira m 9/27/48 Eliza Stowell of Big Flats; Rev. C. C. Carr (5-9/29)
5572. McConnell, James, 40, d 2/21/45 in Leyden (consumption) (9-2/27)
5573. McConnell, James of Cohoes m 9/13/48 Jennette Morton of New York Mills in N. Y. M.; Rev. N. D. Graves (9-9/16)
5574. McConnell, Joseph, 84, d 8/11/50 at his home in Elmira (5-8/16)
5575. McConnell, Phebe, wf of Ziba, d 8/28/49 in Horseheads (5-9/7)
5576. McCormick, Thomas m 5/8/50 Catharine McNamee at St. Patrick's Ch., West Utica; Rev. Carraher (9-5/9)
5577. McCourt, Peter of Buffalo m 5/21/44 Elizabeth Neilis of Utica at St. John's Ch., Utica; Rev. Thomas Martin (9-5/22)
5578. McCracken, Gardner, 59, d 4/30/45 in Rochester (an early resident there) (9-5/8)
5579. McCracken, Joseph (Col.), 89, (a Rev. officer) d in Salem, NY (lost an arm [cannon-ball] at the Battle of Monmouth) (9-5/17/25)
5580. McCulloch, Otis m Zeura Crocker in Auburn (6-11/10/30)
5581. McCulter, Walter of Norwich m 3/26/29 Sarah S. Seabury of Preston in P; Rev. Henry Peck (8-4/1)
5582. McCurdy, Royal m 10/17/33 Rachel Buck in Waterloo (6-11/6)

153

5583. McCurdy, Royal of Waterloo m 2/25/36 Eliza Reed of Canton (6-3/23)
5584. McCuthiel(?), _____ (Mrs.), formerly of Edinburgh, Scotland, d 7/25/33
    in Canandaigua (6-8/14)
5585. McDole, James, Esq. of the Society of Shakers (sic) m 8/22/30 Mrs. Betsey
    George in Clyde (6-9/1)
5586. McDonald, Andrew, 16, s of late Rev. D. McDonald, D.D., d 5/28/30 in Geneva
    (buried in St. Peter's Ch. cem.) ("In 2 yrs 2 mos to a day we have
    attended the funerals of three members of this family interred here
    on Sunday morning in each case") (6-6/9)
5587. McDonald, Daniel, 44, D.D., (Episcopal clergyman), Prof. of Languages in
    Geneva College, d 3/25/30 near Geneva (6-3/31). From Auburn Gospel
    Messenger dated 4/7: deceased former pastor of St. Peter's Ch., Geneva;
    buried in this church's cem.)
5588. McDonald, Dennis of Lyons m 9/1/33 Susannah Pierson of Cayuga Co. in
    Auburn (6-9/25)
5589. McDonald, Donald, 105, d 4/6/50 in Nashwaak, New Brunswick (last survivor
    of those who settled on the Nashwaak belonging to Her Majesty's 42nd
    Reg't.) (9-4/23)
5590. McDonald, Electa (Mrs.), 27, dau of Abraham De Graff, d 6/23/42 in Delhi,
    NY (Oxford Republican, 7/8)
5591. McDonald, Elizabeth, 4 mo, dau of Stephen and Sarah, d 8/12/50 in Elmira
    (5-8/16)
5592. McDonald, James m 8/25/34 Lucy M. Howland in Auburn (6-9/3)
5593. McDonald, Thomas, 70, d 10/13/31 in Geneva (6-10/19)
5594. McDonell, Alexander, Esq. of Greenfield (state or province not stated), member of the
    Provincial Parliament and sheriff of the Ottawa District in Canada,
    d 2/23/35 in Toronto, Upper Canada (3-3/3)
5595. McDonough, Elenor (Mrs.), 67, d 8/6/46 at her home on John St., Utica
    (9-8/7)
5596. McDonough, Lucy Ann (Mrs.), 35, wf of Commodore Thomas McDonough of the
    U.S. Army, d in Middletown (9-8/23/25)
5597. McDonough, P. m 8/23/46 Mary J. Ryan, both of Geneva; Rev. O'Flaherty
    (6-9/11)
5598. McDougall, John of Ava m 2/11/47 Mrs. Jane He_strat of Lee in Augusta;
    Robert J. Morr___, Esq. (9-2/17)
5599. McDowald, S. (Lt.), 106, d at his home on the Isle of Tikes ("left three
    small children under ten years of age") (6-2/16/31)
5600. McDowell, James m Lucretia Hawser in Lockville (6-2/23/31)
5601. McDuffee, Daniel, 88, d 7/6/31 in Athens, PA (b in Ireland; one of the
    first settlers in the Athens area) ("the unfortunate Col. Erwin was shot
    [in McD's house] in ... 1790") (6-7/20)
5602. McDuffee, Mary Ann (Miss), 30, d at Skaneateles ("had taken for a
    toothache, mistakenly for brandy, tincture of colchicum") (6-7/7/30)
5603. McDuffie, Mary R., wf of Hon. George, member of Congress, d in
    Manchester, NC (6-10/6/30)
5604. McElry, James, 43, merchant, of the firm of McElry, McMullen, and McHarg
    of NYC d at his home in New Hartford, NY (funeral from his late home)
    (9-9/16/47)
5605. McElwaine, Martha, 48, wf of John, d 9/27/44 in Utica (funeral at her
    late home, corner of Columbia and State Sts.) (9-9/30)
5606. McEwen, J. H. m 4/25/50 Charlotte A. Knapp in Cooperstown; Rev. Gates
    (9-5/4)
5607. McFarland, _____ (Mrs.), 110, d 1/15/32 in Bovina, NY (b in Ireland)
    (6-2/1)
5608. McFarland, Elizabeth T., 31, wf of Luther W., d 3/10/48 in NYC (9-3/13)
5609. McFarland, L. W. of NYC m 8/17/46 Elizabeth T. Broadway, dau of late
    Thomas of Utica, in U; Rev. D. Skinner (9-8/19)
5610. McFarland, Luther of NYC m 6/25/50 Lucinda M. Hicks, dau of Samuel, Esq.
    of New Hartford, in New H.; Rev. Payson (9-6/29)
5611. McFarrin, John m 1/8/33 Caroline Johnson, both of Benton, in B (6-1/30)
5612. McGarry, _____, inf s of "Mr. McGarry" d 9/12/24 in Utica (9-9/14)
5613. McGee, John, Sr., 53, d 1/29/49 in Utica (funeral at the Catholic Ch.)
    (9-1/30)
5614. McGee, Thomas m 6/29/47 Mary O'Donnell at the Catholic Ch. in Utica;
    Rev. Stokes (9-7/2)
*5584a. *McDermott, Patrick m 10/13/50 Mary A. E. Irvine; Rev. Wm. Wyatt (9-10/17)

5615. McGeorge, _____ (Mrs.), 34,54, or 84 (copy blurred), d in Oxford (8-2/18/18)
5616. McGeorge, _____, 36, wf of H. T., Jr., late of Oxford, d 7/25/23 in Binghamton (8-7/30)
5617. McGilory, Alexander m 4/18/44 Alsina M. Tanner at Griffin's Hotel; Rev. Hawley. All of Schuyler (9-4/19)
5618. McGlashan, James, printer, 30, d in Albany (6-8/28/33)
5619. McGlinnen, Allen, 23, d 2/1/48 in Utica (funeral from the home of his mother, Mrs. Jane McGlinnen, 31 Elizabeth St.) (9-2/2)
5620. McGlinnen, Eliza (Miss), 17, d 6/6/49 in Utica (funeral from her mother's home, 27 Elizabeth St.) (9-6/8)
5621. McGlinnen, James, 21, d 7/6/43 in Utica (funeral from the Catholic Ch.) (9-7/7)
5622. McGlinnen, Mary Ann (Miss), 17, d 12/21/45 in Utica (funeral from her mother's home, 31 Elizabeth St.) (9-12/22)
5623. McGonegal, Harmon m 9/8/48 Lucinda Hall, both of Catharine, in Horseheads; Rev. C. C. Carr (5-9/15)
5624. McGory, John, 21, d 6/30/50 in Utica (consumption) (cigar makers are requested to attend his funeral from his late home on Lansing St.) (9-7/1)
5625. McGown, Hugh, 60, d 4/20/35 in Canandaigua (6-5/20)
5626. McGregor, Flora, 1, dau of James, Esq., d 2/2/42 in Utica (9-2/4)
5627. McGregor, Helen, 4, dau of James, d 7/11/47 in Utica (9-7/13)
5628. McHarg, Charles King m 6/4/49 Harriet Bradford Phinney, oldest dau of Elihu, Esq., in Cooperstown; Rev. C. S. Stewart. All of Cooperstown (9-6/9)
5629. McHenry, Mary M., 30, wf of Daniel, Esq., sheriff of Allegany Co., d 3/25/31 (in Angelica?) (6-4/6)
5630. McIlvaine, J. H. m 1/12/46 Sarah D. Dutton, 2nd dau of George, Esq., in Utica; Rev. A. L. Bloodgood. All of Utica (9-1/13)
5631. McIntosh, _____ (Mrs.) (her funeral service posted: funeral sermon to be at her late home - she a member of the Presby. Ch. - no dates furnished) (her home address: 56 Jay St., Utica) (9-3/14/48)
5632. McIntosh, John W. m Elizabeth Keams in Schenectady (6-2/23/31)
5633. McIntyre, Archibald m 4/3/44 Susan Holmes in North Gage; Rev. W. L. Wilson (9-4/13)
5634. McIntyre, Archibald, 70, d 6/4/49 in Newark, NJ (9-6/9)
5635. McIntyre, Daniel m 9/11/34 Johanna Fowler in Geneva; Rev. J. W. Nevins (6-9/17)
5636. McKane, Robert, 82, d 1/5/38 in Milo (6-1/24)
5637. McKay, David, printer, m Nancy Hulbart in Rochester (6-3/3/30)
5638. McKenzie, William L. m 9/2/46 Sarah Matilda Winne, dau of Giles K., in Albany (9-9/4)
5639. McKie, Peter d 11/26/49 at his home in Johnstown (enlargement of the heart) (9-12/1)
5640. McKinney, Edward, 42, d 5/24/49 in Binghamton (9-6/2)
5641. McKinney, Gabriel m 10/3/50 Roanna Tyrrel; Rev C. Wheeler (5-10/18)
5642. McKinney, James m 2/22/31 Ann E. Haight in Greece, NY (6-3/23). McKinstry, Hiram. See Mikenstry, Hiram.
5643. McKinstry, John m 8/11/31 Mary Ann Colwell, both of Seneca Falls, at the Geneva Hotel; Rev. Nesbit (6-8/17)
5644. McKoon, James Martin, 3, s of Judge Samuel, d 5/29/42 in Oxford (Oxford Times, 6/8)
5645. McKriles, Angeline, 14, adopted dau of H. Rightmyer, Esq., d 7/24/37 in Sullivan (3-8/9)
5646. McLane, John R. of Dresden m 12/31/35 Caroline Hu-- of Starkey in S (6-1/6/36)
5647. McLaren, John F. (Rev.), pastor of the Assoc. Reformed Ch., Geneva, m 1/22/31 Mary B. McCabe, dau of Robert, Esq. of Caledonia, in Geneva (6-1/26)
5648. McLaughlin, Nathan m 1/2/36 Nancy Griswold, both of Penn Yan, in Benton (6-1/6)
5649. McLean, _____, 56, wf of William, printer and editor of the Cherry Valley Gazette, d 10/16/30 in C. V. (9-10/26)
5650. McLean, Jane, 20, dau of John D., d in Benton (6-3/2/31)

155

5651. McLean, John, one of the justices of the U.S. Supreme Court, m 5/11/43
      Mrs. Sarah B. Garrard in Cincinnati, OH; Rev. David S. Burnet (9-5/25)
5652. McLean, William, 73, d 3/12/48 in Cherry Valley (one of the oldest
      printers in NY State; arrived New Hartford, NY in 1794 from Hartford,
      CT; published the Whitestone Gazette, the 2nd paper in Oneida Co.)
      (the lengthy obit. cites his various newspaper editorships) (9-3/14)
5653. McLeod, Alexander (Dr.), 57, pastor of the Reformed Presby. Ch. on
      Chambers St., NYC, d 2/24/33 in NYC (in the 33rd yr of his ministry)
      (6-2/27)
5654. McLeod, Alexander, Esq. m 3/13/42 Helen Norman Morrison, oldest dau of
      Capt. Morrison of Stamford, Upper Canada, in Stamford (described in
      this release is a previous court trial - arson and adultery charged -
      acquitting McLeod of the offenses) (3-4/27)
5655. McLeran, Elijah m 12/31/42 Mary J. Lewis in Utica; Rev. Roberts. All of
      Utica (9-1/7 and 1/9/43 - the latter release spelling her surname
      Lewes and giving a marr. date of 11/13/42)
5656. McMartin, Daniel of Le Roy m 8/15/33 Elizabeth Anderson of Wheatland in
      Rochester (6-9/11 and 9/18)
5657. McMaster, Richard, s of D., d 2/1/33 in Bath (6-2/13)
5658. McMath, Michael m 4/29/35 Elizabeth Akinhead, both of Lyons, in L (6-5/13)
5659. McMonegal, Hugh, 77, d 12/6/31 in Gorham (6-12/14)
5660. McMurray, William (Rev.) m 9/26/33 Charlotte Ogenebugabwa Jouston in
      Sault Ste. Marie, Mich. Terr, (6-10/23)
5661. McMurray, William (Rev.), D.D., 51, pastor of the Market Street Reformed
      Dutch Ch., d 9/24/35 in NYC (6-9/30)
5662. McNair, Robert, 48, d in Sparta (6-3/2/31)
5663. McNaughton, Alexander (Dr.), formerly of Albany, NY, d 12/11/33 in New
      Longuiel, Upper canada (6-1/1/34)
5664. McNaughton, Duncan, 117, d in Moultonborough, NH (6-4/13/31)
5665. McNaughton, Duncan of Amsterdam, NY m 3/14/50 Margaret Eliza Van Alstyne,
      dau of Martin M. of Mohawk, in M; Rev. Douw Van Olinda (9-3/16)
5666. McNeil, David (Hon.), one of the judges of the Ontario Co. courts,
      m 12/7/35 Sarah Young in Phelps (6-12/16)
5667. McNeil, Elizabeth S., 42, consort of Hon. David of Vienna, NY, d 2/22/33
      in Vienna (6-3/6)
5668. McNeil, John H. of the firm of Henry Sheldon and Co., NYC, m 1/4/42
      Helen Reed, dau of Gen. Charles M. of Erie, PA, in Erie; Rev. Tullidge
      (Oxford Times, 1/26)
5669. McNeil, Mary, 72, wid of late John, d 3/15/43 in Oxford, NY (4-4/5)
5670. McNeil, Peter m 1/7/31 Catharine Taylor in Argyle (6-2/2)
5671. McNicholas, Patrick, 40, d 10/29/47 in Utica (9-11/1)
5672. McNichols, Patrick m 5/8/44 Mrs. Ann Hennesy, both of Sullivan, in
      Syracuse; Rev. Hayes (3-5/15)
5673. McNiel, Henry (Gen.), 81 (a Rev. soldier) d 5/16/44 at his home in Clinton
      (an early settler in the region; served from this region in the state
      legislature) (9-6/1)
5674. McNulty, Eveline, 27, wf of John, d 3/3/33 in Big Flat (6-3/20)
5675. McNutley, John m Evelyn, dau of Eleazer (surname not given), in Big
      Flat (6-5/5/30)
5676. McNutty(?), Andrew, 37, d 8/14/34 in Big Flat (6-8/20)
5677. McNutty, John m 1/8/35 Adaline Owens in Big Flat (6-1/21)
5678. McPhail, John m 9/24/47 Elizabeth Beaver at the Central Hotel in Utica;
      Rev. H. R. Clarke. All of Whitestown (9-9/27)
5679. McPherson, Elizabeth, 65, wid of late John, d 6/29/34 in Gorham (6-7/23)
5680. McPherson, Joseph, 41, d 11/16/38 in Gorham (6-11/28)
5681. McPherson, William, 1, only s of Duncan and Elizabeth, d 9/14/49 in Utica
      (9-9/19)
5682. McQuade, Ellen, 17 mo, youngest dau of Michael and Johanna, d 8/11/46 in
      Utica (funeral from 34 Catharine St.) (9-8/12)
5683. McQueen, William, 16, youngest s of George, Esq., d 4/26/48 in Schenectady
      (9-5/6)
5684. McQuhae, John, 33, d 8/20/49 in Danville, PA (consumption) (with Judge
      Donaldson had established in Elmira, NY the firm of Donaldson and
      McQuhae, merchants)(buried beside his mother in Northumberland)
      (5-8/24)

156

5685. McVean, John, 30, editor of the Canajoharie Telegraph, d in Canajoharie (6-5/25/31)
5686. McWilliams, Alexander (Dr.), 75, d 3/31/50 in Washington, D.C. (was the oldest living physician in that city and would have been the oldest surgeon in the U.S. Navy had he remained in that service (9-5/6)
5687. Mabie, Mary Ann, 20, d 9/2/35 in Geneva (6-9/16)
5688. Mabie, William B. of Sullivan, PA m 3/3/50 Candace Dimmick of Corning, NY at the Parsonage in Corning; Rev. H. N. Seaver (4-3/13)
5689. Macdonald, Orrin, 26, d 11/16/49 in Baldwinsville (consumption) (1-11/22)
5690. Macdonnell, Alexander, Esq., 41, of Glengary, Canada (nephew of the Hon. J. B. Yates, dec'd.) d 12/13/41 at the home of Miss Ann Yates in the Glen and Yates allotment on the Sacandaga River, Saratoga Co., NY (3-12/22)
5691. Macdonough, Augustus Rodney, Esq. of St. Louis m 6/10/46 Frances McVickar, dau of Brenton, Esq. of Utica, in U; Rev. George Leeds (9-6/12)
5692. McDonough, Frances, wf of A. R., Esq. and dau of Edward McVicker, Esq. of Utica, d 12/3/46 in St. Louis, MO (had recently gone west from Utica (9-12/19)
5693. Mace, Daniel, 29, editor of the Chenango Republican, d 12/14/30 in Oxford (6-12/29)
5694. Mack, Ebenezer, editor of the American Journal, Ithaca, m 5/9/20 Ellenor Dey, dau of Peter, Esq. of Romulus, in R; Rev. Young (8-6/15)
5695. Mack, Elizabeth (Miss), 19, dau of Warren, d 8/17/45 in Herkimer (9-8/23)
5696. Mack, Zadock of German, NY m 9/14/23 Firzina Emerson of McDonough in M; Gates Willcox, Esq. (8-10/1)
5697. Mackelroy, John m 11/1/46 Emma Atwood, both of Syracuse, in Syracuse; Rev. James Erwin. All of Syracuse (1-11/9)
5698. Mackey, Peter m 2/14/47 Lovina Walt ? , both of New Hartford, in Utica; Rev. William Spencer (9-2/17)
5699. Mackinster, Benair m 2/23/32 Elizabeth Buoyre, both of Varick (6-3/14)
5700. Maclay, Antoinette, 30, wf of William B. late of NYC, d 6/6/49 in Mount Pleasant, IL (cholera) (9-6/22)
5701. Macomb, Alexander, Esq., 82, father of Maj. Gen. Macomb of the U.S. Army, d 1/19/31 in Georgetown, D.C. (had lived many years in NYC and was a member of the state legislature at the time of the adoption of the U.S. Constitution (9-2/1 and 2/2/31)
5702. Macomb, Frances Elizabeth, 7 mo, dau of Capt. John, d 3/11/36 in Seneca (6-3/16)
5703. Macomb, John Navarre (Lt.) of the corps of topographical engineers of the U.S. Army m 4/2/50 Nannie Rodgers, dau of the late Commodore John of the U.S. Navy, in Washington, D.C.; Rev. Pyne (9-4/9)
5704. Macomber, George m 1/27/31 Lydia Barnes in Le Roy (6-2/9)
5705. Macy, Samuel, Esq. m 4/12?/34 Emeline S. Atkins (in Buffalo?) (6-4/30)
5706. Maddock, Adelaide (Miss), 17, sister of Amelia, d 8/31/48 in Rome, NY (9-9/11)
5707. Maddock, Amelia (Miss), 18, sister of Mrs. W. H. Pollard of Rome, NY, d 8/13/48 in Rome (9-9/11)
5708. Maddock, Edward, 58, father of Adelaide and Amelia, d 9/7/48 in Vienna, NY (9-9/11)
5709. Maden, Thomas Joseph, inf s of John, d in Geneva (6-8/4/30)
5710. Madge or Madoe, John D. m 1/1/40 Joanna D. Browning, both of Chittenango, in Fayetteville; Rev. J. Smitzel (3-1/8)
5711. Madison, Eleanor, 98, parent of "our ex-president", d 2/11/29 in Montpelier, VA (the residence of James Madison) (8-3/4)
5712. Madison, Henry of Stratford m 3/22/27 Eliza Ann Cory, dau of Benjamin of Salisbury, in S; Abiel Kibby, Esq. (8-3/30)
5713. Maffet, Robert, 42, d at Jersey Shore, PA (6-12/11/33)
5714. Maffit, William, about 40, d 2/23/48 in Utica (9-2/24)
5715. Magee, Aaron L. of Junius m 9/24/50 Elvia Finley of Liverpool at the home of James Johnson in Baldwinsville; Rev. T. Walker (1-9/26)
5716. Magee, Hugh m 12/3/33 Elizabeth Thomas in Sparta (6-12/18)
5717. Magee, Jane, 43, wf of Thomas J., d 11/25/50 in Hornellsville (4-12/4)
5718. Magee, John (Hon.) of Bath m 3/1/31 Mrs. Arabella Snowden of Washington, D.C. in Albany, NY (6-3/9)
5719. Magee, William of Sodus m Sila Welles of Waterloo in W (6-9/26/32

5720. Maggan, Ephraim, Esq., 70, d "a few days since" in Troy (was "successful as a man of business") (9-10/3/26)
5721. Magoffen, James C. (Dr.), 58, d 5/19/50 in Schenectady (9-5/22)
5722. Main, Alexander, Esq. m 1/6/46 Sarah E. Crandall, formerly of Utica, in Piermont; Rev. C. E. Crispell (9-1/13)
5723. Main, Andrew, 79, formerly of NYC, d 1/31/42 in Binghamton (2-2/2)
5724. Main, Sarah, 5, d 2/5/49; Selima, 2, d 2/6; Morris, 4, d 2/8; Emily, 7, d 2/13; and Ann, 13, d 2/16 (all are children of James and Elizabeth of Skaneateles; all died of scarlet fever; and all arrived recently from England; one child survives) (1-2/22)
5725. Maine, Aaron m 11/19/29 Adelina Maine in Oxford; Elder Otis (8-11/25)
5726. Maine, Cyrus m 8/31/26 Lucy Tracy, dau of D., in Oxford; Elder Otis (8-9/8)
5727. Maine, John W. m 6/2/35 Jane Stevenson, both of Seneca Falls, in Geneva; R. Hogarth, Esq. (6-6/3)
5728. Maine, Z. F. (Dr.), 81, d 1/22/50 in Poughkeepsie (funeral at the home of Mrs. C. S. Wilson of Utica (9-1/26)
5729. Makepeace, George S. m 10/12/43 Elizabeth George in Utica; Rev. Bostwick Hawley. All of Utica (9-10/13)
5730. Makepeace, Mary (Mrs.), 51, d 11/7/48 in Utica (9-11/9)
5731. Malcom, _____, wf of Col. R., d in Utica (8-6/23/19)
5732. Malgan, Henry M. of Albany m 2/25/48 Sarah Eliza White, dau of Henry, Esq. of Utica, in Albany; Rev. Edward Selkirk (9-3/11)
5733. Mallher, Henry, merchant, of NYC m 9/11/37 Sarah Camilla Duflon, youngest dau of John F. L. of Brooklyn, in B; Rev. Evan M. Johnson (6-9/27)
5734. Mallory, John m 11/5/40 Mary Lamb in Knoxville; Rev. S. M. Hopkins of Corning (4-12/18)
5735. Mallory, John S. of Boston, formerly of Utica, m 4/17/49 Mary E. Bentley, dau of Maj. A. of Springville, NY, in S; Rev. H. T. Eddy (9-4/27)
5736. Mallory, Russell, 39, d 1/17/34 (in Lyons?) (6-2/12)
5737. Mallory, William of Belfast, NY m Lucretia Howey in Canandaigua (6-2/13/33)
5738. Maltby, Chandler, Jr., Esq. m 3/29/33 Lydia C. Barker, dau of Dr. J. G., all of Henrietta, in H (6-4/17)
5739. Maltby, Ellsworth P. of NYC m 2/12/49 Sarah A. C. Durkee of Utica at Trinity Ch., Utica; Rev. Dr. Proal (9-2/13)
5740. Maltby, Isaac F. of Buffalo m 9/11/33 Diana I. Opdyke of Fayette in F; Rev. Phelps (6-9/18)
5741. Maltby, Isaac Murray, 2, only child of S. M., d in Waterloo (6-9/30/29)
5742. Maltby, Lucy (Mrs.), 57, d 11/12/44 in Andover (9-12/4)
5743. Maltby, Sarah, 55, wf of Stephen, d 7/2/31 in Hopewell (6-7/27)
5744. Manahan, Francis X. m 10/2/49 Mary H. A. Burke at St. John's Ch., Utica; Rev. Joseph Stokes. All of Utica (9-10/3)
5745. Manchester, George, 50, bro of Otis of Utica, d 8/30/49 in East Boston (state not given) (cholera) (9-9/5)
5746. Manchester, Jeremiah m 11/6/25 Ann Chapman in Robisonville; Rev. A. Tredway. All of Robisonville (9-11/8)
5747. Manchester, Rhoda (Mrs.), 83, d 2/20/44 in New Hartford (9-2/23)
5748. Manchester, T. C. m 1/20/48 Elizabeth Parrish, both of Beloit, WI, in B (9-2/11)
5749. Mandeville, Austin H. m 9/8/36 Eliza Hughs in Elmira (6-9/14)
5750. Mandeville, Austin H., Esq., 34, late of Elmira, d 5/23/49 at Gorgona, New Granada (served as an engineer on the Panama survey) (5-6/29)
5751. Mandeville, John, Esq., 69, an old inhabitant of Coventry, d 6/5/19 in C (8-6/23)
5752. Mandeville, Joshua of Sodus m 10/11/32 Hannah White of Lyons in Newark, NY (6-11/7)
5753. Manges, Jacob m Clarissa Alleman in Fayette (6-4/14/30)
5754. Manley, William J., Esq., 29, d 4/28/46 in Ashtabula, OH (son-in-law of Rev. John Ingersoll, pastor of the 1st Cong'l. Ch., Westmoreland, NY (9-5/26)
5755. Mann, Alexander, senior editor of the Rochester American, m 3/10/49 Caroline Parker in Rochester; Rev. A. G. Hall (9-3/13) also (5-3/16). Name is Rev. J. G. Hall in the latter source.
5756. Mann, Alexander M. (Rev.) of Ithaca m 9/11/33 Susan Walker of Albany in A (6-9/18)

158

5757. Mann, Eliza, 70, relict of late Dr. J. M. Mann of Hudson, d 6/8/39 in Geneva (6-6/12)
5758. Mann, James, 69, keeper of the Franklin House in Geneva, d 9/22/35 in Aurora (6-9/30)
5759. Mann, Jonas, about 60, d 9/6/31 in Syracuse (6-9/21)
5760. Mann, Susan, 19, wf of Alexander M., d 12/6/33 in Ithaca (deceased is dau of Thomas Walker, Esq. of Utica) (6-12/18)
5761. Manning, Jacob m 12/5/33 Sarah Prentiss in Jasper (6-12/18)
5762. Mansfield, Milo B., 28, formerly of Utica, d 1/18/50 in Cascade, Dubuque Co., IA (9-2/21)
5763. Manvill, Charles M. of Towanta (sic), PA m 5/2/39 Mary A. Knowles, dau of John, Esq. of Chittenango, in C; Rev. Clark of Cazenovia (3-5/8)
5764. Mapes, Samuel S. of Westmoreland m 5/26/45 Elizabeth Callen of Utica in U; Elder Rawson (9-6/10)
5765. Marble, Parthenia (Mrs.), 34, d in Benton (6-2/24/30)
5766. Marble, Samuel D. m 5/15/31 Sabina Gaines, both of Bloomfield, in B (6-6/8)
5767. Marchisi, Henry N. of Utica m 5/14/50 Emily Merrill, dau of Elijah E., at the Episc. Ch. in Sherbune; Rev. Dr. Wilson (9-5/17)
5768. Marchisi, John Dominic, 2, s of John B., d 8/24/25 in Utica (9-8/30)
5769. Marchisi, Joseph A., 21, s of J. B. of Utica, d 8/1/50 in Louisville (9-8/10)
5770. Marcy, Randolph B. (Lt.) of the U.S. Army m Mary A. Mann in Syracuse (6-5/29/34)
5771. Markel, Jane Ann, 5, oldest dau of Gen. J. G., d 9/11/37 in West Fayette (6-9/20)
5772. Markham, John B. of Mexico, NY m 8/6/50 Julia M. Betts, dau of C., Esq., at Betts Corners; Rev. E. C. Beach (1-8/15)
5773. Markham, Lewis m Sarah Powell in Palmyra (6-3/2/31)
5774. Markley, Samuel, 56, d in Rochester (6-10
5775. Marriner, John L. of Benton m Elizabeth C. Raywalt in Milo (6-3/31/30)
5776. Marriner, Mellicent (Mrs.), 42, d 8/28/35 in Penn Yan (6-9/2)
5777. Marriott, Martin m 3/10/50 Sophia McDonald, both of Rome, NY, in R; Rev. H. C. Vogell (9-3/15)
5778. Marry, Sarah, 34, d inSennet (consumption) (6-3/2/31)
5779. Marsden, James m 12/24/46 Margaret Jones, both of New Hartford, at Central Hotel in Utica; Dexter Gillmore, Esq. (9-12/29)
5780. Marselle, Peter of Pulteney m Elizabeth Powell in Hammondsport (6-7/31/33)
5781. Marselus, Catharine, about 82, relict of late John N., Esq., d 7/13/45 in Schenectady (9-7/18)
5782. Marsh, ____, wf of Samuel of Rochester, d 6/24/48 at the Franklin House in Utica (died of a seizure - "had been insane since March" and at time of her death, accompanied by her husband, was en route to enter the insane asylum in Utica; interred in Rochester) (9-6/27)
5783. Marsh, Christopher d 4/13/50 in Frankfort (9-5/9)
5784. Marsh, De Witt C., 23, d in Frankfort (9-4/23/44)
5785. Marsh, Elizabeth (Mrs.), 31, d 6/14/45 in Whitesboro (b in Somersetshire England; member of Presby. Ch., Whitesboro past 2 yrs) (9-6/18)
5786. Marsh, George W. of Binghamton m 4/26/42 Harriet Smith of Clinton in C; Rev. Gridley (2-5/4)
5787. Marsh, Hannah, 36, wf of Norman, merchant, d 9/25/25 in Lisle (member of Presby. Ch.) (8-10/5) (death date is 9/29/25 in 9-10/11)
5788. Marsh, Henry W. m 8/23/48 Lucinda M. Shepherd in Baldwinsville; Rev. Alden (double ceremony - see marr. of Harvey Shepherd) (1-8/24)
5789. Marsh, Hiram of Bristol m 1/24/33 Nancy Bush of Canandaigua in C (6-2/13)
5790. Marsh, Ira m 1/27/31 Olive Redfield in Canandaigua (6-2/9)
5791. Marsh, Isaac L., 40, d 4/9/48 in Utica (funeral from his late home on Whitesboro St. "above the Vulcan Works") (9-4/10)
5792. Marsh, Leroy W. of Buffalo m 4/3/50 Amarillus A. Marsh, formerly of Rochester, in Buffalo; Rev. J. P. Fitzpatrick (9-4/11)
5793. Marsh, Luther R., Esq., attorney, m 9/15/45 Jane E. Stewart, dau of Alvin, Esq., all of NYC, in Brooklyn; Rev. Stone (9-9/17)
5794. Marsh, Maria (Mrs.), 39, d 11/26/47 in Utica (9-11/27)
5795. Marsh, Marilla (Mrs.), 25, d 10/12/44 in Utica (9-10/17)
5796. Marsh, Q. of Whitesboro m 11/5/46 H. A. Hall, oldest dau of James, in Utica; Elder D. J. Phillips (9-11/6)

159

5797. Marsh, Thomas m Mrs. Abigail Arnold in Romulus (6-1/13/30)
5798. Marsh, William, 25, s of Silas, Esq. of Schenectady Co. and bro of Silas
       of Oxford, drowned 6/27/18 at Port Deposit, MD - while swimming
       with several other young men who tried unsuccessfully to save him;
       had lived in Maryland 2 yrs) (8-7/15)
5799. Marsh, William C. m 11/8/48 Mary Ann Phileo in Utica; Rev. H. R. Clarke
       (9-11/10)
5800. Marshall, _____ (Mrs.), 45, wf of Cyrenus, formerly of Stockbridge Hill,
       d 9/10/42 in Smithfield (3-9/28)
5801. Marshall, A. G., Esq. m 4/25/33 Jane A. Simmons in Starkey (6-7/24)
5802. Marshall, Charles L. m 1/23/50 Caroline Mould in Sauquoit; Rev. John Waugh.
       All of Sauquoit (9-1/26)
5803. Marshall, J. Thompson of NYC m 10/23/26 Mary Stocking, dau of Samuel of
       Utica, in U; Rev. Aiken (9-11/7)
5804. Marshall, Joseph, 75, bro of Benjamin of Troy, d 9/22/48 in Hudson
       (b in Manchester, England) (9-9/29)
5805. Marshall, Mary (Mrs.), 59, d 3/31/50 in Baldwinsville (1-4/4)
5806. Marshall, Morgan E. m 8/31/50 Elenora E. Dyer, both of Vernon, in V; Rev.
       T. B. Rockwell ("Oswego papers please copy") (9-9/7)
5807. Marshall, Roswell m 10/31/33 Martia Anthony in Waterloo (6-11/13)
5808. Marther, Ebenezer, 36, formerly of Bath d 2/14/31 in Michigan Territory
       (6-4/6)
5809. Martin, Alfred m Catharine Bumgarner at Lincoln Jail "after a courtship
       of half an hour thro' the prison gates." (6-3/9/31)
5810. Martin, Daniel, Esq., 58, Pres. of Mohawk Bank, d in Schenectady
       (6-9/30/35)
5811. Martin, Ebenezer, 29, d 12/15/33 in Genoa, NY (6-1/1/34)
5812. Martin, F. J. of Utica, NY m 9/4/48 Catharine Mooney, dau of D., Esq.,
       in Philadelphia (state not given); Rev. Robert Gerry (9-9/11)
5813. Martin, Harriet Byron, 3, dau of E. T. Throp Martin d 2/6/45 in Utica
       (funeral from her father's home at 31 Broad St.) (9-2/8)
5814. Martin, Lucinda, 30, wf of Delancey and dau of late Samuel Gay of Utica,
       d 4/6/49 in Penn Yan (9-4/14)
5815. Martin, Luther (Hon.), 82, of Baltimore, MD d 7/10/26 in NYC
       ("a distinguished patriot and jurist") (9-7/25)
5816. Martin, Solomon, 55, d 12/27/16 in Unadilla (8-1/1/17)
5817. Martin, V. R. of Martinsburgh m 10/14/45 Charlotte D. Otis of Galway in G;
       Rev. Dr. Ludlow of Poughkeepsie (9-10/18)
5818. Martin, Walter (Hon.), 69, d 12/10/34 "at his mansion in Martinsburgh"
       (6-12/31)
5819. Martin, William C. m 10/2/49 Mary Champlin, both of Lebanon, CT., in
       Whitesboro, NY; Rev. Walter R. Long (9-10/3)
5820. Martindale, Henry C. (Hon.), member of Congress from New York state,
       m Olivia F. Ewell of Washington, D.C. in W (9-12/26/26)
5821. Marvin, Asa, 71, d 12/12/49 in Buffalo (b in Norwalk, CT; lived in Clinton,
       NY 40 yrs) (9-12/14)
5822. Marvin, Daniel W. of Baldwinsville m 9/18/50 Ellen J. Weed of Camillus
       in C; Rev. H. Gregory, D.D. (1-9/19)
5823. Marvin, Henry, 40, m 5/27/27 Abigail Foskitt, 17, in Macdonough; Rev.
       John Lawton. All of Macdonough (8-6/8)
5824. Marvin, Ozias, 85, d 4/9/48 in Clinton (9-4/14)
5825. Marvin, Ralph I. s of Asa of Clinton, d 2/24/25 in NYC (9-3/8)
5826. Marvin, W. H., 22, d 8/22/47 in Phoenix (1-9/1)
5827. Marvin, William, 23, s of Abraham, d 5/12/19 in Cooperstown (8-5/26)
5828. Mason, Alexander E. of New Hartford m 12/24/49 Euphrasia H. Wetmore of
       Paris, NY at the Universalist Ch. in Litchfield; Rev. Francis (9-12/29)
5829. Mason, Dexter, 70, d 9/20/50 in Lowville (9-10/5)
5830. Mason, Edson of Sterling m 2/23/47 Mary Ann Austin of Baldwinsville
       in B; Rev. T. Walker (1-2/24)
5831. Mason, Gardner of Farmington m 1/27/33 Amy A. Cudworth of Bristol in B
       (6-2/13)
5832. Mason, George W., editor of the Elmira Gazette, m 3/25/49 Elizabeth
       Collingwood in Elmira; Rev. A. M. Ball (5-3/30)
5833. Mason, James, Jr., 36, formerly of Lebanon, CT, d 4/3/20 in Preston
       (consumption) (surv by wf and 2 ch) (7-4/12 and 8-4/26)

5834. Mason, James (Gen.), 61, (formerly of Lebanon, CT and "a Rev. War hero") d 9/10/20 in Preston (was for many years a state rep. in the CT legislature) (7-9/13 and 8-9/20)
5835. Mason, James of Palmyra m 2/19/32 Henrietta Hermsley of Sodus in S (6-2/29)
5836. Mason, John W. of Brooklyn m 6/28/49 H. Maria Peckham, oldest dau of John S. of Utica, in U (a Quaker ceremony) (9-6/29)
5837. Mason, Joseph m 3/7/44 Nancy Smith, both of Oxford, in O; Rev. I. Sperry (Oxford Republican, 3/14)
5838. Mason, Levi, 91 (a Rev. soldier) d 8/20/44 at the home of his son, Arnold, in New Hartford. Also his wife, Amy, 93, d 8/26/44 at the same place. They were married 69 yrs and had 11 children with 7 surviving. They were members of the Baptist church, their first pastor having been Elder John Leland of Cheshire, MA. (9-8/31)
5839. Mason, Louisa (Mrs.) d 4/30/42 in Oxford (member of Meth. Episc. Ch.) (surv by husband and an inf s) (Oxford Times, 5/1)
5840. Mason, Louisa A., 8, only dau of Squire M. and Sarah P., d 11/4/44 in New Hartford (9-11/8)
5841. Mason, Luther (Capt.), 86, (a Rev. soldier) d 10/3/42 in Colesville (2-10/12)
5842. Mason, Marenus J. m 2/22/48 Desire R. Eason, both of Truxton, in Cortlandville, Cort. Co.; Rev. Corey of Cortlandville (9-3/3)
5843. Mason, Roswell Arnold of New Hartford m 8/29/48 Aurelia Martha Gillett of Suffield, CT; Rev. Heanon (9-9/5)
5844. Mason, Royal L. m 10/10/42 Betsey Marshal in Smithfield; Rev. S. M. Bainbridge (3-11/30)
5845. Mason, W. N., Esq. of Norwich m 8/30/42 S. M. Cary of Oxford in O; Rev. Dr. Bush (Oxford Times, 8/31)
5846. Massa, Isaiah (Dr.), formerly of Jefferson Co., NY, d in Illinois (8-10/11/20)
5847. Masten, Frederick H. (Lt.) of the U. S. Army m Charlotte Ann Clark, dau of Maj. Saterlee Clark formerly of Utica, NY, at Fort Winnebago, Wisc. Terr.; Rev. Richard casle (9-6/5/43)
5848. Masters, Joseph E., junior proprietor of the Syracuse Daily Star, m 6/5/50 Julia J. Aiken of Hallowell in H; Rev. Jonathan Cole, D.D. (9-6/7)
5849. Masters, Justus, Smith, Esq. of Smith's Valley m 2/1/44 Frances Mary Upton Morris, dau of late Richard, Esq. of Upton Park, Ots. Co. and dau of late Gen. Morris, at Grace Ch., Mount Upton, NY; Rev. Ransom (9-2/3)
5850. Mather, Hiram F. (Hon.), senator from Elbridge, m Mary F. Cole, dau of Dr. Joseph of Auburn, in A (6-12/21)
5851. Mather, Huldah, 68, wf of Asaph, d 3/17/50 in Watertown (9-4/13)
5852. Mather, Mahetabel, 69, wf of Stephen, d 7/18/43 in Utica (cholera) (funeral at her late home, 46 Fayette St.) (9-7/19)
5853. Mather, William H. m 10/30/34 Hannah Jerome, both of Richmond, in R; Rev. Norton (6-11/19)
5854. Mathews, Frederick, Esq. of the firm of A. W. Kinsley, type founders, d 6/4/30 in Albany (6-6/9)
5855. Mathews, George B. m 3/27/36 Hannah Rutraugh in Seneca Falls (6-4/13)
5856. Mathews, Joseph m 11/7/43 Mary Ann Hood in Chittenango; Rev. James Abell. All of Chittenango (3-11/8)
5857. Mathews, Larance (sic) of Hector m 10/22/35 Amanda Bird of Southport in S (6-11/4)
5858. Mathews, Marinus W., Esq., about 40, sheriff of Oswego Co., d 11/26/44 in Pulaski (9-12/12)
5859. Mathews, Robert L., 26, d 8/28/35 in Elmira (6-9/9)
5860. Mathews, Selah (Col.), 72, d 11/9/33 in Elmira (6-11/20)
5861. Mathewson, Ezra m 9/23/39 Fanny Jane Warren, both of Smithfield, in S; Elder Jones (3-10/2)
5862. Mathewson, Russel m 6/28/48 Emma Cornelia Johnson in Corning; Rev. H. Pattengill (4-7/5)
5863. Matson, William E. (Rev.) of Waterville m 7/10/47 Laura Frances Marble, dau of Nathan, Esq. of Port Byron, in P. B.; Rt. Rev. Bishop De Lancey (9-7/15)
5864. Matteson, Abraham (Col.), 50, d 1/30/31 in Pembroke (6-2/9)
5865. Matteson, Elizabeth, 99, wid of late Capt. Hezekiah, d 7/27/50 in Vernon (9-8/8)

5866. Matteson, T. H. of Geneva m 6/2/39 Elizabeth Merrell of Sherburne in S; Rev. L. A. Borrows (6-6/12)
5867. Matthews, Chauncey (Dr.), 36, d 2/27/47 in Maumee, OH (b in Camden, NY) (9-4/10)
5868. Matthews, Edmund, 73, d 9/2/48 in Mexico, NY (father of Henry, of Mrs. R. G. Wellington, and of P. P. Matthews of Utica) (9-9/11)
5869. Matthews, Samuel R. m 4/9/32 Caroline McBurney in Painted Post (6-4/18)
5870. Mattison, Catharine, 44, wf of E. K., d 4/9/35 in Hopewell (6-5/20)
5871. Mattison, Clinton, Esq. of Fond-du-Lac, Wisc. Terr. (formerly of Shaftsbury, VT) m 6/3/47 Caroline E. Potter, dau of William, Esq. of Marcy, in M; Rev. Myron H. Nagus (9-6/8)
5872. Mattison, Henry, 78, d 5/15/43 in Perry (9-5/31)
5873. Mattison, Martha (Miss), 19, dau of Jesse, Esq., d 8/16/43 in Lee (consumption) (9-8/23)
5874. Mattison, Phileon (Mrs.), 27, d 7/3/39 in Geneva (6-7/10)
5875. Maxam, Arthur G., 1, d 2/26/50 and Maxam, Adelbert H., 3, d 3/9/50 in Westmoreland (the only children of John and Laura) (scarlet fever) (see Emma P. Brockett) (9-4/4)
5876. Maxon, Paul m 2/23/29 Jennett Rodgers, both of Preston, in P; Smith Johnson, Esq. (8-3/11)
5877. Maxwell, Anthony (Capt.), 70, d in Hudson (a Rev. soldier) (9-6/7/25)
5878. Maxwell, Charles, 36, d 6/1/36 in Horseheads (6-6/15)
5879. Maxwell, Eunice, 46, wf of Sylvanus, Esq., d 1/28/30 in Heath, MA (6-4/7)
5880. Maxwell, Julia Ellen, 17, dau of Hon. Thomas, d 6/30/32 in Elmira (6-7/11)
5881. May, Desire E. (Mrs.), 24, d 2/19/48 in New Hartford (9-2/21)
5882. May, Ephraim, 108, d in Le Roy (141 descendants) (9-6/7/25)
5883. May, Frederick (Dr.), 74, d 1/23/47 in Washington, D.C. (b in Boston, MA; settled in Washington soon after it was made the Capital; father of Col. May, now in Mexico)(9-2/8)
5884. May, James S. of New Hartford m 6/12/45 Desire E. Babcock, only dau of late Denison of New Hartford, in Syracuse; Rev. Gregory (9-6/20)
5885. May, Samuel F. m Barbara Logan, dau of Robert, in Bath (6-3/3/30)
5886. Maynard, E. A., junior editor of the Oneida Observer, m Wealthy Velona Hart, dau of Ephraim, Esq., in Utica (6-2/10/30)
5887. Maynard, Elisha D. of Arcadia m Delila Ray in Lyons (6-2/24/30)
5888. Maynard, Emerdney (Miss), 30, d 5/12/33 in Hartwick (9-7/2)
5889. Maynard, Ephraim m Ann Maria Bull in Junius (6-3/10/30)
5890. Maynard, Isaac m 8/20/44 Margaret Aitken in Utica; Rev. Plumb. All of Utica (9-8/26)
5891. Maynard, John, 88, d in Junius (6-12/29/30)
5892. Maynard, Polly (Miss), 30, dau of Needham, Esq., d 11/9/26 in Whitesboro (9-11/21)
5893. Maynard, Resin m Mary Andrews in Junius (6-3/10/30)
5894. Maynard, William H. (Hon.) of Utica, "a member of the Senate from the 5th district", d 8/25/32 in NYC (cholera) (3-9/11)
5895. Mayo, A. J. of Chittenango m 8/7/34 Eliza Brown of Durhamville in D; John Otis, Esq. (3-8/12)
5896. Meacham, Ella L., 11 mo, youngest dau of L. D. and E., d 8/19/47 in Deerfield (9-8/21)
5897. Meacham, I. N. (Dr.) of Utica m 10/19/26 Maria M. Tilden of Whitesborough in W (9-10/31)
5898. Meacham, Thomas S., Esq., 53, d 3/20/47 at his home in Sandy Creek, Oswego Co. (had been "proprietor of the Agriculture Hall") (1-3/31)
5899. Meachum, Jacob of Freetown m 12/11/23 Eliza Hunt of Harrison in H; Elder Bennet (8-12/17)
5900. Mead, Abraham A. of Vienna, NY m Rebecca Godley in Ovid (6-1/26/31)
5901. Mead, John m 12/12/32 Mary E. Doney, both of Geneva, in G; Rev. Mandeville (6-12/17)
5902. Mead, John Wallace, 25, late of Greenwich, CT, d 2/21/37 at his home in Canastota, NY (3-2/29)
5903. Mead, Joseph m Clarissa Stewart in Elmira (6-12/25/33)
5904. Mead, Robert of Butler m 3/18/33 Harriet Brown of Penn Yan in P. Y. (6-4/10)

5905. Mead, Warren W. of Lyons m 5/8/39 Susan R. Stearns of Newark, NY in N; Rev. R. Townsend (6-5/15)
5906. Means, Joseph m 9/30/30 Eliza S. Moore in Seneca; Rev. McLaren (6-10/6)
5907. Meeker, Alfred M. m 12/27/42 Mary Leal in Delhi; Rev. S. G. Spock(?). All of Delhi (Oxford Republican, 1/6/43)
5908. Meeker, Ella Louisa, 16 mo, youngest dau of M. T., d 3/8/45 in Utica (9-3/11)
5909. Meeker, Lucien m 1/24/36 Minerva Blodget in Sullivan; Jairus French, Esq. All of Sullivan (3-2/2)
5910. Melcher, John, Esq., 90, the oldest practical printer in New Hampshire and probably in the U.S., d 6/9/50 in Portsmouth, NH (9-6/19)
5911. Melhinch, George, 86, (a Rev. soldier) d 2/12/47 in Lisbon, NY (b in Scotland; arrived before the Rev.; lived in Washington Co., NY, 1783-1828; settled in St. Lawrence Co. in 1828) (9-2/20)
5912. Mellen Julius of Fulton m 4/29/47 Mary E. James, only dau of late Thomas of Utica, in U; Rev. O. Wetmore (9-5/1)
5913. Mellin, Atchison m 11/15/49 Livona B. Meigs, both of Van Buren, in Jordan, NY; Rev. Byron Meigs (double ceremony - see marr. of David Haynes)(1-11/29)
5914. Mentor, Harvey H. m 4/26/36 Lucinda Kishlar in Canandaigua (6-5/11)
5915. Mercereau, John, 41, d 1/3/43 in Vestal (2-1/11)
5916. Merchant, Edward M. of Marcy m 9/18/50 Mary E. Terrill of Sauquoit at the home of Col. Butler in Sauquoit; Rev. C. Graves (9-10/7)
5917. Merchant, Faschel of Guilford m 5/10/43 Susan Smith of Oxford; Rev. E. G. Perry (Oxford Republican, 5/19)
5918. Merchant, George, Esq. d 8/14/30 in Albany (6-8/25)
5919. Merchant, Niram (sic) R. of Lewisville m 12/20/27 Maria Dibble of Fayetteville in Guilford; Rev. Bentley (8-1/4/28)
5920. Merrell, Augusta Matilda, 27, consort of H. H., d 9/28/32 in Geneva (6-10/3)
5921. Merrell, Betsey O., 18, d 9/7/24 in Pompey, NY (9-10/12)
5922. Merrell, Bildad, Jr. m 3/29/26 Julia Mather, both of Utica; Rev. Aiken (9-4/4)
5923. Merrell, Emily P., 18, dau of Isaac, d in Utica (6-5/5/30)
5924. Merrell, Gordon H., druggist, m 9/17/34 Mary Tippetts, dau of Col. William, in Geneva; Rev. Bruce (6-10/1)
5925. Merrell, Harriet (Miss), 23, d 8/18/47 in Utica (funeral from her mother's home, 5 Washington St.) (9-8/19)
5926. Merrell, Harry H., merchant, of Utica m 5/14/26 Agusta Matilda Beebee of Syracuse in S (9-5/30)
5927. Merrell, Helen, 4, d 5/29/45 in Auburn (9-6/6)
5928. Merrell, Hiram, merchant, of Sacketts Harbor m 6/25/21 Maria Brayton of Deerfield in D (8-7/4)
5929. Merrell, Ira, formerly of Utica, one of the publishers of the Geneva Courier, d 4/17/49 in Geneva (an early settler in both Oneida and Chemung Counties; first apprenticed as a printer at the Whitestown Gazette ((9-4/19 and 5-4/27)
5930. Merrell, Jacob S. of Cincinnati, OH m 9/20/48 Catharine G. Kellogg, dau of Deacon Warren of Westmoreland, in W; Rev. F. A. Spencer (9-9/27)
5931. Merrell, John C., printer, m 3/12/34 Jane Ann Allen in Geneva; Rev. Mandeville. All of Geneva (6-3/19)
5932. Merrell, Lewis of Utica m 6/1/48 Rosanna Coventry of Marcy in M; Rev. H. R. Clarke (9-6/5)
5933. Merrell, Louisa, formerly of Geneva and late consort of H. C., d 11/14/38 in Cicinnati, OH (6-12/5)
5934. Merrell, Mason F., one of the publishers of the Fulton Patriot, m 10/26/46 Julia A. Pardee of Waterloo (6-10/30) (see also entry 5939)
5935. Merrell, Nancy, 62, wf of late Ira formerly of Utica, d 6/13/50 in Rochester (9-6/14)
5936. Merrett, George C. m 7/2/45 Catharine Van Valkenburgh, both of Kirkland, at the Central Hotel in Utica; Rev. David Plum (9-7/3)
5937. Merriam, Jonathan (Deacon), 60, d 3/26/26 in Brandon, VT (member of Bapt. Ch. there) (9-4/18)
5938. Merriam, Nathaniel (Hon.), 83, d at the home of his son, Gen. Ela Merriam, in Leyden (had lived in Leyden about 50 yrs) (9-8/26 and 8/28/47)

5939. Merril, Mason F., one of the proprietors of the Fulton Patriot, m 10/19/46
      Julia A. Purdee of South Waterloo in S. W.; Rev. N. Baker
      (1-11/9) (see also entry 5934)
5940. Merrill, Eliza Malfina, 4, dau of John, d 11/20/38 in Palmyra (6-12/5)
5941. Merrill, John H. of NYC m 8/5/32 Eliza Gardner of Boston at the Zion Ch.,
      Palmyra; Rev. B. H. Hickox (double ceremony - see marr. of John N.
      Corell) (6-8/8)
5942. Merrill, Nathaniel, 57, of the firm of Merrill, Milford and Co., merchants,
      d 9/23 in Geneva (an early settler there) (6-9/26)
5943. Merrill, Norton G. of Vernon m 1/15/50 Mary J. Rice, dau of Joseph T. of
      Albany; Rev. Dr. Huntington (9-1/19)
5944. Merrill, Simeon, Jr. m 1/19/34 Polly Sheppard in Butler (6-2/12)
5945. Merriman, E. N., cashier of the Lewis Co. Bank, m 9/6/48 Mary M. Hulbert,
      dau of Hon. R. of Boonville, in B; Rev. E. A. Reneuf (9-9/11)
5946. Merrit, Stephen of Tyre m Deborah Van Dyke in Lyons (6-6/26/33)
5947. Merritt, Adeline E., wf of Arthur and dau of Hon. Nathaniel Garrow,
      d 10/18/30 in Auburn (6-11/1)
5948. Merritt, Ammon m 1/15/20 Tammy Purdy in North Norwich; Elder Gilbert
      (7-1/26)
5949. Merry, Eliphalet R. of Skaneateles m 2/3/48 Lucretia Case, youngest dau
      of Pliny, Esq., in New Hartford; Rev. E. Payson (9-2/9)
5950. Merryfield, John of Middlesex m 10/28/32 Sarah Cronk of Benton in B
      (6-11/14)
5951. Merryweather, _____ (Dr.) of Geneva m 5/25/48 Mary A. Blake of Buffalo
      in Corning; Elder Noble Prince of Caton (4-9/7)
5952. Mersereau, Daniel m 5/26/33 Ann Whiteneck in Horseheads (6-6/12)
5953. Mervin, Charles, 8, d in Havana, NY (6-1/27/30)
5954. Messenger, Charles m 4/10/31 Harriet Whitman in Geneseo (6-4/20)
5955. Messenger, Rosannah Mary Theresa, 20, wf of George, one of the proprietors
      of the Steuben Democrat, d 7/20/48 at the home of her bro-in-law in
      Corning (4-7/26)
5956. Messenger, William H. m 4/19/49 Charlotte Newton, both of Corning, in
      Painted Post; C. F. Platt, Esq. (4-4/25)
5957. Messerole, Peter m 10/18/36 Eliza Swarthout in Benton; Rev. Cornelius
      Brouwer (6-10/19)
5958. Messinger, John A., merchant, m 2/13/34 Elizabeth Ann Van Alstine in
      Lenox; Rev. Cooper. All of Lenox (3-2/25)
5959. Metcalf, Franklin m 9/4/32 Mary Ann Hess in Bath (6-9/19)
5960. Metcalf, John of Chittenango m 8/24/37 Asenath Richards of Virgil in
      Oswego; Rev. Nine (3-8/30)
5961. Metcalf, Lewis, 25, d 8/21/38 in Seneca Falls (6-8/29)
5962. Metcalfe, George, Esq., 64, d in Castleton, Staten Island, NY (9-10/3/26)
5963. Metz, William m 4/3/42 Mary Ann Rhyne, both of Corning, in Big Flat
      (4-4/6)
5964. Middaugh, Jasper, 78, (a Rev. soldier) d 12/15/36 in Phelps (6-12/21)
5965. Middlebrook, George L. m 6/25/33 Eleanor H. K. Trinder in Poughkeepsie
      (6-7/10)
5966. Middleton, Nelson (Dr.) of Norwich, CT m 8/19/47 Jane Barry of Baldwinsville
      in B; Rev. T. Walker (1-9/15)
5967. Miers, John I. m 4/21/33 Harriet Elmira Williams of Cazenovia in
      Canastota (3-4/23)
5968. Mighells, Sally, 34, wf of Eleazer, d in Arcadia (6-3/10/30)
5969. Mikenstry, Hiram m 1/30/34 Lucy Stowell, both of Varick, in Seneca Falls
      (6-2/12)
5970. Miles, Burrage, Jr., 26, youngest s of Maj. B., d 7/23/29 in Coventry
      (less than 4 months previously the only other child of the Major,
      a son, d aged 18 mo) (8-7/29)
5971. Miles, Charles W. m 11/22/46 Laura E. Osterhout in Auburn; Rev. Daniel
      W. Bristol. All of Auburn (1-11/30)
5972. Miles, George m 12/4/36 Mary Mills, both of Seneca Falls; Richard Hogarth,
      Esq. (6-12/7)
5973. Miles, Gilbert, about 42, d 7/24/49 in Milport (cholera) (5-7/29)
5974. Miles, Hollon, 25, d 7/16/36 in Geneva (6-7/20)
5975. Miles, Sarah L., 2, only dau of Ives H. and Sarah, d 7/1/44 in Tecumseh,
      MI (Oxford Republican, 7/18)

5976. Millar, William m 4/2/44 Harriet S. Brayton in Utica; Rev. B. Hawley. All of Utica (9-4/6)
5977. Millard, Edward m 2/18/31 Eliza Laycost, both of Campbelltown, in C (6-3/23)
5978. Millard, Frank Butler, 2, youngest s of Daniel T. and Clarissa, d 11/9/50 in New Hartford (9-11/27)
5979. Millard, J. J., Esq. m 8/19/47 Susan Emeline Brownell, dau of Abner, Esq., in Sauquoit; Rev. J. Waugh. All of S (9-8/21)
5980. Milledge, _____ (Hon.), late gov. of Georgia, d (date not given) (8-3/11/18)
5981. Miller, _____ (Mrs.), 84, mother of Hon. Elijah, d 10/3/35 in Auburn (6-10/14)
5982. Miller, Alice (Mrs.), 58, d 1/18/33 in Gorham (6-2/6 and 2/13)
5983. Miller, Alvin m 11/17/33 Casandra Evans in Canandaigua (6-11/27)
5984. Miller, Amos m 2/1/29 Emily Graves, both of Preston, in P; Rev. Leonard (7-2/4)
5985. Miller, Andrew of Geneva m 1/15/32 Elizabeth Miller of Fayette; Rev. Lane (6-2/1)
5986. Miller, Charles Dudley, cashier of the Madison County Bank, m 10/18/43 Elizabeth Smith, dau of Gerrit, Esq. of Peterboro, in P; Rev. Beriah Greene (9-10/28 and 3-11/1)
5987. Miller, Charles W., 23, formerly editor and proprietor of the Republican Advocate, d 11/21/31 in Batavia (6-12/7)
5988. Miller, Conrad, 23, d in Phelps (6-3/23/31)
5989. Miller, Edmund of Southport m 10/27/35 Parmelia Dubois of Tioga in T (6-11/4)
5990. Miller, Hannibal of Adams, Jeff. Co., m 4/26/47 Eliza Ann Brower of NYC in NYC; Rev. D. Knox (9-5/17)
5991. Miller, Hezekiah, 83, d 5/21/35 in Palmyra (an early settler there) (6-5/27)
5992. Miller, I. A., editor of the Manlius Repository, m Eliza W. Rockwell in Manlius (6-9/25/33)
5993. Miller, J. of Pawtucket, RI m 7/12/43 Eliza Harper of Whitesboro; Rev. B. Hawley of Utica (9-7/14)
5994. Miller, James A. (Dr.) m 4/11/50 Harriet M. Weston in Stittsville; W. Ralph, Esq. All of Trenton, NY (9-4/15)
5995. Miller, John B. of Utica m 12/26/50 Cornelia K. Jones of Schenectady at St. George's Ch., Schenectady; Rev. William Payne (9-12/30)
5996. Miller, John P. m 7/5/50 Nancy Ann Waters in Utica; Rev. William Wyatt. All of Utica (9-7/8)
5997. Miller, Joseph (Capt.), 69, d in Newark, NY (6-1/26/31)
5998. Miller, Joseph, about 50, d 10/13/33 in Chittenango (3-10/15)
5999. Miller, Louisa (Mrs.), 32, d 10/22/36 in Newark, NY (6-11/9)
6000. Miller, Maria Bleecker, 69, relict of Morris, d 3/9/50 in Utica (9-3/11)
6001. Miller, Milton, 6, d 1/23/33 in Canandaigua (6-2/6)
6002. Miller, Morris S. (Hon.), first judge of Oneida Co., d 11/16/24 in Utica (buried in the family vault in Albany) (9-11/23)
6003. Miller, Nathaniel B. m 11/7/33 Lydia A. Tickner in Covington (6-12/11)
6004. Miller, Peter m 2/4/30 Katharine Mans in Geneva; Rev. Brilhartz (6-2/17)
6005. Miller, Polly, 58, wf of Hendrix, d 5/7/34 in Penn Yan (6-5/14)
6006. Miller, Robert m 6/7/35 Roxy Prescott in Canandaigua (6-6/17)
6007. Miller, Samuel P. m 1/24/49 Amy Dayan, dau of Hon. Charles, Esq., in Lowville; Rev. E. A. Renouf. All of Lowville (9-2/17)
6008. Miller, Smith (a Rev. soldier) d 10/17/33 in Centerfield (6-11/6)
6009. Miller, William, 75, d 11/19/42 in Trenton, NY (a pioneer settler there; emigrated from Rensselaer Co. about 1792) (9-11/28)
6010. Miller, William of Orange, Steub. Co.,m 2/22/49 Maranda Bronson of Dix, Chemung Co., in Dix; Lorenzo L. Tracy, Esq. (4-3/7)
6011. Miller, William Otis m 4/19/31 Jane Russell in Newark, NY (6-4/27)
6012. Millington, William of Albany m 9/1/46 Jane Queal of Utica in U; Rev. D. G. Corey (9-9/2)
6013. Mills, _____ (Rev.), pastor of the Presby. Ch., Onondaga Hill, d "very recently" (9-6/8/24)
6014. Mills, _____, wf of David, d in Benton (6-4/28/30)
6015. Mills, Arthur T. of NYC m 8/28/45 Elizabeth L. Spencer of Utica; Rev. Charles Wiley (9-8/29)

6016. Mills, Charles of the firm of S. D. Mills and Co. of Utica d 5/3/49 in
Little Falls ("Hartford papers please copy") (9-5/26)
6017. Mills, Corrill H., 34, d 8/28/37 in Manlius (surv by wf and 4 young ch)
(3-8/30)
6018. Mills, Dan C. m 12/2/30 Jane Campbell in New Hartford; Rev. Coe. All of
New Hartford (9-12/14)
6019. Mills, Daniel, 60(?), formerly of Guilford, d 12/2/41 in New Hamburgh,
Dutchess Co. (Oxford Times, 12/15)
6020. Mills, David m Mrs. Betsey Gregory in Benton (6-6/16/30)
6021. Mills, Ellena Rayner, 21, wf of John W. of NYC, d 9/22/46 in Schwartz
Tyrol, Europe ("This lady was of the original Rayner family) (9-11/21)
6022. Mills, Frederick C., Esq. of the firm of Doolittle, Mills and Co. m 9/7/45
Frederica E. Burckle, oldest dau of C. J., Esq., in Oswego; Rev.
Davenport. All of Oswego (9-9/20)
6023. Mills, G. J., Esq., formerly of Utica, NY, d in Mobile, AL (9-9/13/25)
6024. Mills, George C. of Vienna, NY m 1/3/39 Belinda Edson of Manchester in
M; Elder Roe (6-1/9)
6025. Mills, Israel J. m 4/26/43 Phebe Owens of South Trenton, NY in S. T.; Rev.
Morris Williams (9-5/4)
6026. Mills, James of NYC m 7/24/49 Charlotte Hollum of Orange Co. in Utica;
Rev. E. Francis (9-7/26)
6027. Mills, John of Deerfield m 1/2/43 Susannah Potter of Utica in U; Rev.
Hawley (9-1/12)
6028. Mills, Josiah of Phelps m Lydia Morse in Gorham (6-5/12/30)
6029. Mills, Lucy, 72, consort of Deacon Samuel, d 11/9/26 in Guilford (settled
in G by 1805; in 1812, with nine others, formed the First Cong'l. Ch.
in G) (9-11/28)
6030. Mills, Mary (Mrs.), 77, d 7/9/39 in Geneva (6-7/10)
6031. Mills, Susan (Miss), 60, d 4/26/45 in Fenner (3-7/5)
6032. Mills, Warren m 10/13/32 Lovina Barse, both of Penn Yan, in Starkey
(6-11/7)
6033. Mills, William (Dr.) of England, father of Mrs.Charles Belden and Mrs.
George Belden of NYC, d 5/18/30 in Carmel, Put. Co. (discovered
and used vaccine against small pox prior to Dr. Jenner's publication)
(6-6/9)
6034. Miner, John D. of Preston m 9/22/42 Sarah Maria Bartle of Norwich in N;
Rev. E. C. Perry (Oxford Times, 9/28)
6035. Miner, Lucy, 49, wf of Paul R., d 3/11/42 in Preston (Oxford Times, 3/16)
6036. Miner, Maria, 43, wf of Whitman R., d 4/24/41 in Campbell (4-4/30)
6037. Miner, Mary, 49, wf of Asher, one of the editors of the Village Record,
d 2/6/31 in Westchester, Westchester Co. (surv by husband and
several ch) (6-2/23)
6038. Miner, Paul E. m 9/1/42 Melissa Hewitt, both of Preston, in P; Rev. J. T.
Goodrich (Oxford Times, 9/7)
6039. Minier, Abram m Louisa Knapp, dau of William R., in Wells, PA (6-5/5/30)
6040. Minor, C. S. of Honesdale, PA m 3/30/48 N. P. Brown of Utica in U; P. A.
Proal, D.D. (9-3/31)
6041. Mitchel, Spencer of Perryville m 2/15/40 Matilda L. Dryer of New Woodstock
in N. W. (3-3/11)
6042. Mitchel, Truman m 9/24/48 Ann Taylor, both of Edmeston, (in Utica?);
Rev. D. G. Corey (9-9/26)
6043. Mitchell, _____, 12 mo, child of Dr. David, d 7/26/31 in Chittenango
(3-8/2)
6044. Mitchell, Catharine, 6, dau of Dr. Henry, d 4/18/30 in Norwich (7-4/21)
6045. Mitchell, Frances (Mrs.), 25, d 5/11/34 in Hammondsport (6-5/21)
6046. Mitchell, John of Benton m Merinda Sherwood in Romulus (6-1/13/30)
6047. Mitchell, John m 2/26/35 Mrs. Dorothy Hunt; Rev. Coates. All of Geneva
(6-3/4)
6048. Mitchell, John, 92, (a Rev. soldier) d 2/15/49 at Johnson Settlement,
town of Catharine (4-2/28)
6049. Mitchell, R. of Geneva m 1/1/35 Susanna Anthony, dau of J. of Seneca;
Rev. J. Easter (6-1/7)
6050. Mitchell, Sarah H. (Mrs.), 28, dau of Joseph Tyler of Baldwinsville, NY,
d 7/20/49 in Marshall, MI (1-7/26)
6051. Mitchell, Thaddeus of Lawrence Township, PA m 10/29/50 Margaret M. Warner
of Waverly, NY in W; Elder Kennedy (4-11/20)

6052. Mitchell, Thomas S., 61, d 11/30/43 in Utica (9-12/1)
6053. Mitchell, William, 19, s of Levi, d 6/22/50 in Mexico, NY (1-6/27)
6054. Mitchells, John, inf s of John, d 7/31/37 in Geneva (6-8/9)
6055. Mix, Nancy, 26, wf of Charles d 8/2/26 in Utica (9-8/8)
6056. Moe, John of Genoa m 9/23/33 Sally Ann Conklin of Lansing in L (6-10/9)
6057. Moffat, Benjamin m 3/2/31 Elizabeth Hulse in Blooming Grove (6-3/23)
6058. Moll, Karl Franz m 7/23/48 Myrrou Gertruda Cornelia Helena Van Nahuis
      (both of Holland, Europe) in Albany, NY; Rev. Dr. Wyckoff (9-7/27)
6059. Mollison, Gilbert of the firm of Doolittle and Mollison m 5/26/46
      Harriet W. Condit at the First Presby. Ch. in Oswego; Rev. Condit
      (9-6/4)
6060. Monell, Harvey m "recently" Harriet Fierce in Geneva; Rev. P. C. Hay.
      All of Geneva (6-5/22/39)
6061. Monell, Maria (Mrs.), 49, d 2/24/31 in Hudson (6-3/23)
6062. Monroe, Andrew, Esq., oldest bro of ex-Pres. Monroe, d 12/2/26 in Milton,
      VA (9-12//19)
6063. Monroe, Eliza, 3 mo, dau of William B., d 1/25/44 in Utica (funeral at
      her parents' home, Blandina St., east of 2nd St.) (9-1/26)
6064. Monroe, George I., about 58, d 9/10/42 in New Boston (3-9/21)
6065. Monroe, John m 9/12/42 Selanah Winsor, both of Norwich, in N; Rev. J. T.
      Goodrich (Oxford Times, 9/14)
6066. Monroe, John, 21, d 11/7/45 in Bridgewater (9-11/20)
6067. Monson, Mary (Mrs.), 73, consort of late Rev. Samuel, formerly pastor in
      Lenox, MA, d 9/14/26 in Springfield, NJ, while visiting her dau
      (9-10/3)
6068. Montague, Oreb (Rev.) of Fabius m 10/11/34 Cornelia L. Chamberlin, dau of
      Deacon Henry of Syracuse, in S; Rev. L. Leonard (3-10/14)
6069. Montayne, Benjamin (Rev.), 82, pastor of Deerpark Bapt. Ch. in Sullivan
      Co., d 12/25/25 (9-2/14/26)
6070. Monteath, Thomas L, Stewart, Esq., late Capt. in His Brittanic Majesty's
      Army, of Dunfries, Scotland m 9/7/32 Isabell Maria Tobin, dau of James,
      Esq. from Dublin, Ireland (6-9/26)
6071. Monteith, Anna, wf of Rev. Walter, d 1/20/30 in Watervliet at the home of
      her father, Abraham G. Lansing, Esq. (9-1/26)
6072. Montgomery, Acha m Widow Thorpe in Wheeler (6-12/22/30)
6073. Montgomery, Porter of Adams m 10/27/46 Margaret Hicks of Salina in S;
      Rev. May (1-11/9)
6074. Montgomery, William Rochester m 5/26/45 AmandaMills in Rochester (9-5/29)
6075. Montross, Jacob, 100, d 5/18/43 at the home of his son, John, in Lenox
      ("He spent a handsome fortune in hiring and equipping men for the
      service of his country" in the Rev. War) (9-6/16)
6076. Moody, Augustus of Hammondsport m 9/11/33 Ann Marie Allen, dau of
      Shadrach W. of Geneva, in G; Rev. Phelps (6-9/18)
6077. Moody, Samuel m 8/22/33 Catharine A. Shockey in Elmira (6-8/28)
6078. Mook(?), Jefferson of Russia, NY m 10/16/50 Sarah F. Willoughby of Newport;
      Rev. William Wyatt (9-10/17)
6079. Moon, William m 8/30/35 Cordelia Crooks (in Canandaigua?) (6-9/9)
6080. Moor, Betsey, 25, wf of Franklin, d 12/1/34 in Chittenango (3-12/2)
6081. Moore, Alexander m 1/26/31 Emily Bailey in Catlin (6-2/9)
6082. Moore, David m 7/29/48 Sarah Morris in Corning; Rev. Thomas B. Hudson
      (4-9/7)
6083. Moore, E. W. (Commodore), Commander of the late Texas Navy, m 8/16/49
      Emma Stockton, dau of late William T. of Roxborough, PA, at St. Luke's
      Ch. in Philadelphia, PA; Rev. D. Washburn, A.M. (9-8/24)
6084. Moore, Ebenezer H., "an old ... inhabitant", d in Junius (6-6/9/30)
6085. Moore, Eliza Olive, dau of Francis and Martha, d 9/17/49 in Utica
      (funeral at her father's home on Varick St., West Utica (9-9/18)
6086. Moore, Geroge M. m 2/13/33 Charlotte Warden of Arcadia in A (6-2/27)
6087. Moore, Hugh, Esq., senior editor of the Plattsburgh Republican, m 12/2/33
      Mary Jane Witherell in Hinesburgh, VT (6-12/18)
6088. Moore, John, 55, d in Bath (6-4/7/30)
6089. Moore, Joseph H. m 2/26/23 Esther Pellet in Norwich; Elder Spaulding
      (7-3/5)
6090. Moore, Joshua, Jr., attorney, m Damarius Everest Hungerfield, only dau
      of Joseph B., Esq., in Watertown; Rev. Isaac Brayton. All of Watertown
      (9-6/8/44)

167

6091. Moore, L. C. m 1/23/45 Maria Dempsey in NYC; Rev. E. W. Andrews of Troy
       (9-2/5)
6092. Moore, Madison, 21, d 12/24/30 in Bath (consumption) (6-1/5/31)
6093. Moore, Mary, wf of Maj. Thomas P., late Minister to Colombia, d 7/9/35
       in Harrisburgh, KY (6-8/5)
6094. Moore, Michael m 7/20/43 Julia Ann Carlon, both of Sullivan, in Salina;
       Rev. Hays (3-8/30)
6095. Moore, Nancy A., 25, wf of Dr. Henry B. and dau of Elihu and Polly Ewers
       formerly of Franklin Co., MA, d 1/27/24 in Manlius ("Editors of the
       Boston Recorder, of the Bennington Gazette, and of such Journals as are
       published in the vicinity of Greenfield, Mass. are desired to print the
       above") (9-2/17)
6096. Moot, Daniel B. m 1/25/32 Eliza Nellis, dau of John I. D., in Lenox; Rev.
       Ira M. Olds. All of Lenox (3-1/31)
6097. Morange, _____, 1, child of M., d 12/15/38 in Chittenango (3-12/19)
6098. More, James, about 23, d 7/28/22 in Bainbridge (recently from VT; earlier
       from NH; on one of his arms the letters J M were stamped with India
       Ink; he was decently interred by the citizens of Bainbridge) ("For the
       information of his relatives printers to the north are requested to give
       this an insertion") (7-8/14)
6099. More, Louisa d 10/10/24 ("by the hand of suicide") in Utica ("Her
       friends reside in Adams") (9-10/12)
6100. Morehouse, James A. m 10/22/34 Delaner Barton, both of Seneca; Rev. A. G.
       Ortan (6-11/5)
6101. Morehouse, Richard m 7/9/46 Elizabeth Noyes, dau of George, in Oriskany;
       Rev. Haynes (9-7/11)
6102. Moreland, Benjamin m 6/23/31 Sally Glymps in Phelps; Elder Farley. All
       of Phelps (6-6/29)
6103. Moreland, Caleb m 1/20/31 Caroline Gailey in Auburn (6-2/9)
6104. Moreland, John m 2/3/31 Caroline Westbrook in Phelps (6-2/16)
6105. Moreland, Stephen, Jr. m 11/11/32 Catharine Ann Camp in Auburn; Rev. D.
       C. Axtell (6-11/7)
6106. Morey, _____, wid of late Dr. Morey, d 2/27/30 in Oxford (8-3/3)
6107. Morgan, Alfred B. m 10/9/40 Mary E. Skane in Sullivan; J. French, Esq.
       (3-10/14)
6108. Morgan, Austin S., 30, merchant, d 7/20/46 at Trenton Falls (9-7/29)
6109. Morgan, Christopher, Jr., attorney, of Aurora m 10/24/32 Mary E. Pitney,
       dau of Dr. Joseph T. of Auburn, in Auburn (6-11/7)
6110. Morgan, George m 11/8/32 Elizabeth Minckley, both of Fayette, in Seneca
       Falls (6-11/28)
6111. Morgan, George B., 29, formerly of Seneca, d 4/9/31 in Poughkeepsie
       (6-5/25)
6112. Morgan, George Gilbert, 4 mo, youngest s of Gilbert S., d 2/11/47 in Utica
       (9-2/16)
6113. Morgan, Jedediah (Hon.), late a member of the state senate from the 7th
       district, d 2/9/26 in Aurora (9-12/26)
6114. Morgan, John I. (Hon.) 80, formerly a member of Congress and collector of
       the Port of NY, d 7/29/49 at the home of his son-in-law, Gen. John A.
       Dix of Port Chester, NY (9-8/2)
6115. Morgan, John E. of Deerfield m 11/21/49 Ann Thomas of Frankfort in F;
       Rev. Russel G. Tolles (9-11/26)
6116. Morgan, Lefa Jane, 36, wf of Gilbert S., d 10/10/46 in Utica (surv by
       husband and 3 young ch) (9-10/27)
6117. Morgan, Ruth, 96, d 10/9/48 at the home of Oliver Prescott in New Hartford
       (9-10/10)
6118. Morgan, Sarah Jane, 18 mo, dau of Thomas E. and Mary A., d 8/18/47 in Utica
       (9-8/27)
6119. Morison, Henry B. of Geneva d 9/13/31 in Georgetown, Mercer Co., PA
       (6-9/21)
6120. Morley, Calvin (Maj.) m 3/7/24 Sibley Evans in Bainbridge; Elder Chapin
       (8-3/24)
6121. Morley, Eurutha (Mrs.), 59, d 8/16/47 in Van Buren (1-8/25)
6122. Morley, Samuel, 21, oldest s of Walter and Julia, d 2/24/50 in Wellsburg
       (5-3/8)
6123. Morley, Sarah, 5, gr-dau of Mrs. Eurutha Morley, d 8/19/47 in Van Buren
       (1-8/25)

6124. Morrell, Charles of Lansing m Mary P. Ballard, dau of William, Esq. of
       Prattsburgh, in P (6-2/24/36)
6125. Morrell, L. ___, 60, wf of Stephen, d 12/7/33 (3-12/10)
6126. Morrin, Edward m 11/30/33 Catharine Gardner in Utica (6-12/11)
6127. Morrin, Edward, 32, publisher and proprietor of the Utica Democrat,
       d 2/15/42 in Utica (funeral from St. John's Ch.) (9-2/16)
6128. Morris, Ann, 36, wf of David E., d 4/12/42 in Utica (funeral from the
       home of her husband, corner of Seneca and Whitesboro Sts.) (9-4/13)
6129. Morris, Charles V. of Butternuts m Eliza Mosely of Whitesborough in W
       (6-2/231)
6130. Morris, Gouverneur (Capt.) of the U.S. Infantry m 1/1/44 Anna Maria J.
       De Camp, dau of Surgeon S. G. J. De Camp, at Jefferson Barracks, MO;
       Rev. Hodges, chaplain of the Post (9-2/6)
6131. Morris, Henry, Esq. of Buffalo m 106/31 Mary N. Spencer, dau of Hon. John
       C. of Canandaigua, in C; Rev. Kearney (6-10/12)
6132. Morris, Jacob m 9/7/42 Sarah Tompkins, dau of late Isaac, at Christ Ch.;
       Rev. Andrews (2-9/21)
6133. Morris, Jacob (Gen.), 90, d 1/10/44 in Butternuts (9-1/13)
6134. Morris, John m 9/13/43 Jane Davies, both of Waterville, in Utica; Rev.
       W. Rowland (9-9/16)
6135. Morris, John Cox, Esq., 67, d 2/2/49 in Butternuts (son of late Gen. Lewis
       Morris and uncle of Mrs. Hamilton Fish and Mrs. John S. Collier)
       (9-2/7 and 5-2/9)
6136. Morris, Joseph E., 45, d in Pulteney (6-5/19/30)
6137. Morris, Sophia, oldest dau of Benjamin, d 10/29/18 in Oxford (8-11/4)
6138. Morris, Staats, Esq., 62, d in Lansingburgh (9-10/31)
6139. Morris, William, formerly of Utica, m 7/19/45 Emma Eliza Miller in Mobile,
       AL (9-8/9)
6140. Morrison, _____ (Mrs.), wf of Roderick N., Esq. of Penn Yan, d in
       Whitesboro (6-8/24/31)
6141. Morrison, _____, 5, dau of Alexander, d 5/23/44 on Lenox Hill (scarlet
       fever) (3-5/29)
6142. Morrison, Andrew of Orange Co. m 12/14/33 Jane Belknap of Trumansburgh in
       Ithaca (6-12/25)
6143. Morrison, Betsey (Miss), 22, dau of Dr. G. Morrison, d 10/27/26 in Utica
       (9-11/7)
6144. Morrison, Elizabeth, 11, dau of William, Jr., d 5/7/42 on Lenox Hill
       (3-5/18)
6145. Morrison, Jane, 24, wf of Alexander, d 11/7/48 in Baldwinsville (1-11/9)
6146. Morrison, Jesse of Great Valley, NY m 2/29/36 Amanda Meritt of Asylum,
       Bradford Co., PA in Bath, NY (6-3/9)
6147. Morrison, Lovina (Mrs.) d 10/23/33 in Vienna, NY (6-11/6)
6148. Morrison(?), Mary (Mrs.), 72, d 6/18/46 in Geneva (6-6/19)
6149. Morrison, Sarah Verselia, 4, dau of John B. and Sarah, d 8/27/46 in Geneva
       (6-9/25)
6150. Morrow, Cornelia R., 33, wf of F. W., Esq., d 1/3/49 in Hornby (4-1/17)
6151. Morrow, Joseph of Phelps m 1/17/38 Lucy Ann Bill of Seneca in S; Rev.
       P. C. Hay (6-1/24)
6152. Morse, Abner (Rev.) of Portage, IN m 10/11/36 Hannah Peck of Onondaga, NY
       in Ohio; Rev. Taylor of Salina (3-10/26)
6153. Morse, Charles W. of Poughkeepsie m 6/16/48 Manette A. Lansing, dau of
       B. B. of Utica, in U; Rev. William H. Spencer (9-6/16)
6154. Morse, Daniel W. of Preble m 2/7/42 Harriet N. Hull of Corning in C; Rev.
       Hard (4-2/9)
6155. Morse, Evander, 42, printer, formerly of Onondaga Co., NY, d in
       Cincinnati, OH (6-2/10/30)
6156. Morse, Finley B. (Prof.) of Poughkeepsie m 8/10/48 Sarah Griswold of
       New Orleans, LA at Trinity Ch. in Utica, NY; Rev. Dr. Proal (9-8/11)
6157. Morse, H. H. m 12/31/35 Polly Vanderhoof in Manchester (6-1/13/36)
6158. Morse, Hezekiah, 60, of Oxford d 7/18(?)/27 in Oxford (funeral sermon by
       Rev. Bush) (deceased was a member of Episc. Ch.) (b in Mass. but lived
       in NY from 1802 until death; moved to Oxford from Madison Co., NY)
       (8-7/27)
6159. Morse, James O. of Cherry Valley, NY m 6/16/47 Gargia A. Whitwell, dau
       of Furman A., Esq. of Fairhaven, MA, in F; Rev. J. Roberts (9-6/23)

169

6160. Morse, Lucian m 6/21/35 Emeline Curtiss in Geneva; Rev. Snow (6-6/24)
6161. Morse, Ogden m Hepsta Ann C. Watrus in Lyons (6-3/31/30)
6162. Morse, Samuel m Jane Green in Ithaca (6-1/19/31)
6163. Morse, Stephen, 35, d in Kingston (6-2/2/31)
6164. Morse, William m 10/24/33 Mahala P. Freeman in Walworth (6-11/20)
6165. Morton, Amanda, 34, wf of Elisha, 2nd, d 1/16/44 in Rome, NY (consumption) (9-1/26)
6166. Morton, Clarissa, dau of Benjmain, d 6/27/42 in Annsville (9-7/1)
6167. Morton, Jane, 27, wf of Jay W. and dau of late Burrell Hatch, d 5/2/50 in Rome, NY (9-5/9)
6168. Morton, Samuel W., 61, d 7/30/46 in Rome, NY (father of one of the publishers of the Rome Sentinel) (9-8/1)
6169. Moseley, Elizur (Dr.), 73, late of Whitesboro, d 8/15/33 in Penn Yan (buried in Whitestown) (father-in-law of R, N. Morrison, Esq.) (6-9/4)
6170. Moseley, John,"an aged coloured man", d in Hartford, CT (willed $100 to each of these: Hartford Female Beneficent Soc., Amer. Colonization Soc., Conn. Bible Soc., Amer. Educ. Soc., and the residue to the Domestic Missionary Soc. of Conn.) (9-6/21)
6171. Moses, Marcus of Mount Morris m 1/21/ Jane E. Spees of Macdonough in M; Rev. Hoyt (8-2/1)
6172. Moses, Savel, 63, (a soldier in the War of 1812) d 11/28/50 in Oriskany (9-12/31)
6173. Mosey, Frank Newton of New Hartford m 9/20/48 Adelaide Eugenia Dodge, youngest dau of Alvin, Esq. of Vernon, in V; Rev. William H. Paddock (9-9/22)
6174. Mosher, C. H. m 3/16/48 Nancy Dickinson of Clayville in C; Rev. John Waugh (9-3/23)
6175. Mosher, Chauncey H., 28, d 1/9/50 in Clayville (funeral at St. John's Ch., Clayville)
6176. Mosher(?), Darwin, 21, d 8/4/33 in Lima(?) (6-8/21)
6177. Mosher, Isaac, Esq. m 6/5/36 Harriet Booth in Waterloo (6-6/15)
6178. Mosher, John m 1/14/36 Margaret Utley in Canandaigua (6-1/27)
6179. Mosher, Reuben m 4/1/32 Phoebe Briggs in Waterloo (6-4/11)
6180. Mosher, Warren of Sauquoit m 6/19/45 Hannah Miles Parson, dau of Samuel of Utica, in U; Rev. James Nichols (9-6/25)
6181. Moss Edward m 3/21/28 Sarah Ann Denison, both of Waterville, in W; Rev. W. A. Matson (9-3/30)
6182. Moss, Samuel m Betsey Doolittle in Wallingford, CT (8-8/29/21)
6183. Moss, William of Oriskany Falls m 9/13/47 Gertrude Helmer West of Waterville in W; Rev. William A. Matson (9-9/15)
6184. Mott, James m 1/18/31 Maria Brown in Ogdensburgh (6-2/2)
6185. Mott, Samuel Henry, inf s of Samuel, Esq., d 12/30/34 in Geneva (6-12/31)
6186. Mott, Samuel, Esq., 38, d 7/24/35 in Geneva (6-7/29)
6187. Mott, Thomas S. Esq. of Hamilton m 7/21/47 Sarah W. B. De Wolf, dau of late Jabez, Esq. of Bridgewater, in B; Rev. W. A. Matson (9-7/24)
6188. Moulter, James of Chittenango m 4/25/37 Caroline Thompson of Manlius in M; Esq. Huntley (3-5/3)
6189. Moulter, Mary Ann, wf of Jacob, d 6/10/33 in Sullivan (3-6/11)
6190. Moulthrop, J. K., Esq. of Albion m 4/26/43 Sarah A. Smith of Utica at Phipps Union Seminary, Albion; Rev. William N. McKarg (9-5/2)
6191. Moulton, Adelia F., 15, dau of Dr. F. of Utica, d 2/18/46 in Marcy (9-2/26)
6192. Moulton, Almira, 43, consort of Dr. Franklin, d 6/12/43 in Marcy (9-6/19)
6193. Mount, Sexton, merchant, of Buffalo (formerly of Geneva) m 11/29/30 Lucretia Kendig, dau of Martin, Esq. late of Waterloo, in W (6-12/22)
6194. Mountain, Jacob (Right Rev.), D.D., 75, late Lord Bishop of Quebec, d 6/16/25 in Marchmont near Quebec (9-7/12)
6195. Mowar, Peter A., Esq. d 9/19/31 in Canandaigua (consumption) (6-9/21)
6196. Mowry, E. D. of Cleveland m 1/26/47 Helen H. Peckhem of Volney in V; Rev. Dunning (1-2/3)
6197. Mowry, George (Dr.), 58, d 10/24/23 in Oxford (buried with Masonic honors) (was a long-time resident of Oxford) (8-10/29)
6198. Mowry, George P. of Geneva, formerly of Oxford, m 6/10/41 Mary Rudman, dau of John of Benton, in B; Rev. E. Hebard (8-Oxford Times, 6/30)
6199. Mowry, Harker of Guilford m Betsey Gibson of German, NY in G; G. Willcox, Esq. (8-3/3/24)

6200. Mowry, Joseph m 9/12/22 Armanda Sloan of Butternuts; Nathan Taylor, Esq.
(7-9/18)
6201. Moyer, Elijah m 12/25/42 Mary Bellinger in Chittenango; Rev. James Abell
(3-12/28)
6202. Moyer, J. W. of Utica m 3/7/46 Caroline E. Hill of Oneida Depot in Clinton;
Rev. T. J. Sawyer (9-4/14)
6203. Mudge, Abram, 27, d 6/15/48 in Earlville (9-8/5)
6204. Mudge, I. R. m 9/19/49 Harriet T. Wheeler; Rev. L. Livermore. All of
Earlville (9-9/22)
6205. Mudge, Ransom m 10/17/43 Junia Beckwith, both of Oxford; Rev. L. Sperry
(Oxford Republican, 10/26)
6206. Muir, Alexander M. (Gen.), 39, Commissary Generalof NY, d 7/13/32 in NYC
(6-7/18)
6207. Muir, John m 7/5/47 Roxa I. Fuller, both of Hamilton, in Utica; Rev.
William H. Spencer (9-7/7)
6208. Mullender, Catharine, 58, d 4/27/31 in Seneca (6-5/4)
6209. Mumford, Charles of Italy m 11/10/33 Phebe Shaw in Potter (6-11/20)
6210. Mumford, David, Esq., 64, d in Schenectady (for many yrs a merchant in
NYC) (8-3/12/23)
6211. Mumford, Elihu H. S. of Rochester d 3/17/44 in NYC (9-3/21)
6212. Mumford, Eliza H., wf of S. Jones Mumford and youngest dau of Hon. E. B.
Strong of Rochester, d 6/5/44 in NYC (9-6/10)
6213. Mumford, George H., Esq. of Rochester m 5/24/36 Ann Elizabeth Hart of
Palmyra in P (6-6/15)
6214. Mumford, Gurdon S., Esq., 67, formerly a merchant in Geneva, d 4/30/31
in NYC (a secretary to Dr. Benj. Franklin in Paris, France during the
Rev. and a congressman during Jefferson's administration)(6-5/11)
6215. Mumford, Lavira, 23, consort of Dr. Ores Mumford, d 8/10/42 in Corning
(4-9/14)
6216. Mumford, Silas D., 69, d 2/1/38 (in Seneca Falls?) (6-2/14)
6217. Mumford, Thomas, Esq. (Col.), 62, d 12/13/31 at his home in Cayuga, NY
(one of the earliest settlers in western NY) (6-1/11/32)
6218. Mundy, G. Merchant, Esq. of Geneva m 6/5/44 Maria M. Ford, youngest dau
of late Arthur C. of Dublin, Ireland, at the home of her bro-in-law,
C. H. Green, Esq. of Broad St., Utica (9-6/12)
6219. Mundy, Henrietta, 13, dau of Barron, Esq. of Seneca Co., NY, d 12/7/35
in Ann Arbor, MI (6-12/23)
6220. Munger, Harriet Maria, wf of S., d 4/27/35 in Elmira (6-5/6)
6221. Munn, Aaron B. m 4/22/30 Nancy McFaren in Benton; Rev. Todd (6-5/5)
6222. Munro, Jane (Miss), dau of Squire Munro, d 2/6/48 in Cincinnati, OH
(typhus fever) (1-2/16)
6223. Munroe, Ebenezer (Lt.), 73, (a Rev. soldier), d 5/25/25 in Ashburnham, MA
(he fired the first American shot at Lexington though wounded in the
arm) (9-6/14)
6224. Munroe, Helen Elizabeth, 2, only child of Jonas A. and Elizabeth,
d 11/29/43 in Chittenango (3-12/6)
6225. Munroe, Jonas A. m 9/26/39 Betsey Tibbits, both of Chittenango; Elder
Paddock of Cazenovia (3-10/2)
6226. Munroe, William of New Boston m Elmira Sayles, dau of Silas, Esq. of Lenox,
in L; Rev. A. P. Mason (3-4/1/40)
6227. Munsell, George of Binghamton m 4/20/24 Mary Ketchem, dau of S., Esq. of
Greene, in G; Rev. Hoyt (8-4/21)
6228. Munson, Hiram S. of East Bloomfield m 9/19/43 Emily Smith, dau of Charles,
Esq. of Paris Hill, in P. H.; Rev. Blodgett (9-9/21)
6229. Munson, Lary m 3/1/32 Perline Gillett in Canandaigua (6-3/14)
6230. Munson, Payson J., Esq. of Paris, NY m 3/5/46 Mrs. Mary Russell of New
Hartford in New H.; Rev. E. H. Payson (9-3/18)
6231. Munson, Stephen H. of Wolcott m 11/15/36 Jane Westfall, dau of Samuel D.,
in Lyons (6-11/23)
6232. Murat, Lucien, 2nd s of Jonathan, the late king of Naples, m 8/18/31
Carolina Georgianna Frazer, youngest dau of late Maj. Thomas of
South Carolina, at St. Michael's Ch. in Trenton, NJ; Rev. Dr. Beasley
(6-8/31)
6233. Murdock, George Pratt, 2, s of James and Hope, d 10/14/42 in Utica
(funeral from his father's home, 45 Fayette St.) (9-12/15)
6234. Murdock, Hiram m 6/30/36 Harriet Furman, both of Benton (6-7/13)

6235. Murdock, James, 53 or 58, d 1/27/50 in Utica (funeral from his late home, 45 Fayette St.) (9-1/29)

6236. Murphy, George, 19, s of Hon. Robert W., d 10/31/46 in Rensselaerville (consumption) (6-11/20)

6237. Murphy, George, attorney, of Utica m 9/16/47 Melissa A. Collamer of Sandy Hill, Wash. Co., in S. H.; Rev. Parry (9-9/27)

6238. Murphy, Mary Sophia, 1, dau of George and Melissa A., d 8/12/50 in Utica (funeral at City Hotel on Genesee St.) (9-8/14)

6239. Murray, Albert G. m 6/11/39 Emily A. Morse in Canandaigua; Rev. Prevost (6-6/19)

6240. Murray, Edwin R. m 11/21/50 Frances A. Stocking in Oriskany Falls; Rev. H. S. Hamilton. All of O. F. (9-11/23)

6241. Murray, Harris m Eliza Canfield in Tioga (6-3/9/31)

6242. Murray, James, 40, d in Almond (6-3/3/30)

6243. Murray, John, 50, merchant, of Harrisburg, PA d 11/21/44 in Philadelphia, PA (b in Half-parish of Kilmeena, County Mayo, Ireland) (9-12/12)

6244. Murray, Josiah, 13, s of Eli E. of Fort Wayne, IN, d 10/22/43 in Utica, NY (9-10/24)

6245. Murray, Lewis m 10/30/50 Prudence Howland, both of Troy, PA, in Wellsburgh; Abner Wells, Esq. (5-11/8)

6246. Murray, Romeyn B. m 5/22/34 Mary Ann Chamberlain, both of Fayette (6-5/28)

6247. Murray, William, 41, s of late John Murray of Whitestown, d 9/28/45 in Juliett, IL (moved there shortly before his death; surv by wf and children) (9-11/11 and 11/12)

6248. Myers, Asa of Newport m 9/7/47 Eliza Pettingill of Bridgewater in B; Rev. S. W. Brace of Utica (9-9/15)

6249. Myers, Caleb m 7/4/32 Lois Burnet, dau of Andrew, Esq., in Alloway; J. Vandemark, Esq. (6-7/18)

6250. Myers, Cornelius C., 61, d 11/29/25 (in Utica?) (9-12/6)

6251. Myers, Hepzibah (Mrs.), 76, d 6/4/48 in Utica (funeral from the home of her son-in-law, J. S. Fuller, 31 Columbia St.) (9-6/6)

6252. Myers, John J. m Orella Stalp in Williamson (6-3/17/30)

6253. Myers, Lydia (Mrs.), sister of Messrs John and A. B. Hall of Geneva, d in Brockport (6-1/4/32)

6254. Myers, Nicholas, about 38, d 8/14/49 in Baldwinsville (consumption) (1-8/16)

6255. Myers, Peter, 54, d 8/18/40 in Sullivan (3-8/26)

6256. Myers, W. H. m 10/18/48 Sarah Van Voast in Elmira; Rev. H. N. Seaver. All of Elmira (5-10/20)

6257. Myers, William E. of Georgetown, D.C. m 12/18 Frances Jerome of Fairmount Onon. Co., NY in F; Rev. William W. Williams of Camillus (double ceremony - see marr of Rev. William W. Williams) (9-12/19/49)

6258. Myers, William H. m 7/29/32 Mary Olcott, both of Cazenovia, in Chittenango; J. French, Esq. (3-7/31)

6259. Mygatt, Henry, merchant, of Oxford m 5/6/20 Susan Hosmer, formerly of Hudson, in Oxford (8-5/10)

6260. Mygatt, Henry, 1, s of Henry, d 5/29/42 in Oxford (Oxford Times, 6/8)

6261. Mygatt, Orlando, 14, s of Henry, d 8/15/27 in Oxford (8-8/24)

6262. Mygatt, Sally S., 27, wf of Henry, merchant, of Oxford, d 9/26/18 in Meredith, Dela. Co. (surv by husband and "a number of small children") (8-9/30)

6263. Mygatt, Susan, 10 mo, dau of Henry, d 7/8/23 in Oxford (8-7/9)

6264. Mynderse, Wilhelmus, 70, d 1/30/38 in Seneca Falls (6-2/14)

6265. Myrick, Luther (Rev.), formerly of Cazenovia, d 9/1/43 in Sandstone, Jackson Co., MI (3-9/20)

6266. Myrick, Thomas S., editor of the Madison County Eagle, m 4/28/42 Hannah B. Sprague of Oswego in O; Rev. R. W. Condit (3-5/11/42)

6267. Napier, James of Jamaica, L.I., NY, m 4/5/31 Elizabeth Thomas of Utica in U (6-4/27)

6268. Nash, Betsey, 37, wf of Ira, d 10/14/49 in Baldwinsville (1-10/18)

6269. Nash, Dyer d in Canandaigua (6-5/29/34)

6270. Nash, James, Jr. m 7/16/48 Mary Ann Stephens of Granby in Baldwinsville; Rev. T. Walker (1-7/26)

6271. Nash, Joseph m 5/11/50 Harriet Dimblery(?) in Oriskany; George Graham, Esq. All of Oriskany (9-5/22)

6272. Nash, Levi m Harriet Glass in Bath (6-12/20/30)
6273. Nash, M. (Mr.), 63, "an old teacher" d in NYC (6-8/4/30)
6274. Nash, Rior, Esq. of Bath m 4/20/35 Ann Scott of Benton in B (6-5/6)
6275. Nash, Sadoe m 11/3/33 Phebe Foster in Seneca Falls (6-11/13)
6276. Nash, William W. m 9/1/30 Lucy E. Green, dau of Byram, Esq., in Sodus
       (6-9/15)
6277. Neal, Joseph C. of Philadelphia, PA, editor of Neal's Saturday Gazette,
       m 12/12/46 Emily D. Bradley of Hudson in H; Rev. Leroy Church (9-12/29)
6278. Neele, Thomas m 10/29/35 Laura A. Wolcott in Canandaigua (6-11/11)
6279. Negus, Timothy m Susan H. Watrow of Colesville (2-5/25/42)
6280. Neill, Samuel M., Esq. m Josepha Yates, dau of Hon. Joseph C., in NYC
       (6-11/17/30)
6281. Neill, William, printer, 40, d 10/10/33 in New Orleans, LA (6-11/13)
6282. Nellis, Bernardt, 56, d 8/3/47 in Whitesboro ("He has left a large
       estate to divide among his children ...") (9-8/5)
6283. Nellis, John G., 62, d 5/15/49 in Herkimer (9-5/24)
6284. Nellis, Nelson S. of Fort Plain m 9/21/48 Georgianna Kirkland of Utica
       in U; Rev. H. R. Clarke (9-9/23)
6285. Nelson, Amasan m 7/4/39 Mary Countryman, both of Manchester, in Geneva;
       Rev. Oliver Ackley (6-7/10)
6286. Nelson, Catharine, dau of late Lord Sterling and relict, successively, of
       William Duer and William Nelson, Esq., d in NYC (she mother of Hon.
       William A. Duer and John Duer, Esq.) (9-8/1/26)
6287. Nelson, Ebenezer (Rev.), late pastor of the Bapt. Ch, Malden, MA, d in M
       (9-5/31/25)
6288. Nelson, N. S., Esq. of St. Louis, MO m 9/28/46 Caroline Case of New York
       Mills in N. Y. M.; Rev. Dr. Paddock (9-9/30)
6289. Nelson, Samuel (Hon.) m Catharine Ann Russel in Cooperstown (8-4/13/25)
6290. Nelson, William m 1/6/33 Jane Morrell, both of Chittenango; Rev. H. Snyder
       (3-1/8)
6291. Nettleton, Chauncey m 1/24/43 "Miss Rice", both of Utica, in U; Rev. Corey
       (9-1/28)
6292. Nettleton, J. Munson m 1/1/45 Mary E. Twichel, dau of George, Esq.; Rev.
       William Thompson. All of Clinton (9-1/8)
6293. Neville, Benjamin m 9/24/50 Olive Blanchard, both of Westmoreland, in
       Utica; Rev. Isaac Foster (9-9/25)
6294. Newberry, George, about 40, (from Suffolk, England) d 7/3/39 in Geneva
       (6-7/10)
6295. Newberry, James Clapp, 3, only s of Walter L. and Julia B., d 3/26/50 in
       Oxford (9-3/28)
6296. Newberry, Walter L. of Chicago, IL m Julia Butler Clapp, dau of James, Esq.
       of Oxford, NY, in O; Rev. Leveret Bush, D.D. (Oxford Republican, 11/25/42)
6297. Newbury, _____, inf child of George, d 8/11/34 in Geneva (6-8/13)
6298. Newbury, Walter Butler, 11 mo, s of Walter L. of Chicago, IL, d 8/17/44
       "in Mackinac" (Michigan?) (9-9/6)
6299. Newcomb, _____, 37, wid of late Luther, d 2/23/30 in Oxford (8-3/3)
6300. Newcomb, Harvey, late editor of the Buffalo Patriot, m Alethia Wells late
       of Auburn, NY, in New Albany, IN (6-6/23/30)
6301. Newcomb, Luther, 38, d 1/15/28 in Oxford (8-1/18)
6302. Newel, Edmund m 3/24/42 A. Pennette Cass in New Hartford; Rev. M. C. Searl
       (9-4/2)
6303. Newel, Theron, 73, d 6/13/43 at his home in New Hartford (9-6/27)
6304. Newell, Jesse, Esq., 62, d 4/19/43 at his home in Utica (funeral from his
       late home, corner Broadway and Liberty Sts.) (9-4/21)
6305. Newell, Jesse, 18 mo, only child of William H. and Mary C., d 6/29/49 in
       Wilmington, DE (9-7/10)
6306. Newell, William H. of Syracuse m 1/18/47 Mary C. Harrison of Utica in U
       (9-1/19)
6307. Newhall, Mary Elizabeth, 25, wf of John and dau of P. B. Underhill, Esq.,
       d 5/7/39 in Phelps (6-5/15)
6308. Newhouse, Benjamin, 76, d in Whitestown (9-12/8/47)
6309. Newkirk, Thomas G., merchant, of Oxford m 5/14/26 Elizabeth Hopkins,
       dau of Frederick, Esq., of Oxford; Rev. Bush (8-5/17)
6310. Newkirk, Warden of the firm of T., G., and W. Newkirk m 1/29/29 Adelaide
       E. Redman, dau of late Daniel, Esq. of Albany, in Oxford; Rev. E. D.
       Wells (8-2/4)

6311. Newland, David, Jr. of Albany m 6/7/43 Susanna Lightbody, dau of Andrew, Esq. of Marcy, in M; Rev. Green (9-6/10)
6312. Newland, Hannah, 67, wf of late John, d 12/23/43 in Utica (9-12/28)
6313. Newland, Hannah Maria, 1, youngest dau of T. J. and Betsey Ann, d 6/6/45 in Utica (funeral from the parson's home, 4 Broad St.) (9-6/7)
6314. Newman, Benjamin m 1/30/36 Eliza Hall in Benton (6-2/10)
6315. Newman, George H. m 12/23/47 Ellenor M. Jones, both of Rome, in Whitesboro; Rev. Jirah D. Cole (double ceremony - see marr. of John S. Jones (9-12/24)
6316. Newman, William W., formerly of Baldwinsville, m 4/18/50 Elizabeth E. Williams of Syracuse in S ("married before the Teachers Institute at Public Schoolhouse #7") Rev. Snow (1-4/25)
6317. Newton, Charles E. of Hamilton m 7/28/47 Caroline M. Damon, dau of Rufus, Esq. of Bridgewater, in New Hartford; Rev. S. H. Battin (9-8/7)
6318. Newton, Charles H. of Litchfield m 1/7/47 Alma Ingersol of Frankfort in Utica; Otis Whipple, Esq. (9-1/14)
6319. Newton, Elias m 1/13/31 Delia Benham in Hopewell (6-1/19)
6320. Newton, Freeman m 2/18/27 Eliza Watson, both of Bainbridge, in Coventry; R. Waters, Esq. (8-3/2)
6321. Newton, Phineas m Sally C. Avery in Sidney Plains, Delaware Co. (6-11/6/33)
6322. Nibbs, Alfred m 9/21/46 Elizabeth Bucher at the Central Hotel in Utica; Rev. Shepard. All of Litchfield (9-9/22)
6323. Nicholas, Nancy Ward, 3, dau of Rev. James and Sarah I., d 7/12/50 in Oneida (9-7/15)
6324. Nichols, Benjamin B., merchant, of Windsor m 2/25/30 Mrs. Delia Beardsley of Edmeston in E; Rev. Edward Andrews (7-3/10)
6325. Nichols, Daniel B. of Sauquoit m 7/3/33 Sarah W. Hale of Munson, MA in Clinton, NY; Rev. Kellogg (9-7/16)
6326. Nichols, Eli, 43, d 10/20/48 in Windsor (2-11/1)
6327. Nichols, Enos, Esq., 75, of Southport, WI d 6/27/49 in Buffalo, NY (one of the early settlers in Clinton, NY; was en route from Wisconsin to Clinton, NY to visit relatives when stricken - with cholera) (9-7/9)
6328. Nichols, Erasmus D. m Velona Williams in Middlesex (6-1/23/33)
6329. Nichols, George of the house of Wasson and Nichols in Augusta, GA m 5/1/26 Mary S. Swift, dau of Reuben, Esq. of Waterloo, NY, in W (9-5/30)
6330. Nichols, Horace S. of Detroit, MI m 7/17/46 Sarah A. Rumbill(?), formerly of Utica, in Buffalo (9-7/20)
6331. Nichols, Ishmael, Esq., about 60, d 6/2/21 (8-6/6)
6332. Nichols, Jacob m Abigail Francisco in Farmington (6-3/24/30)
6333. Nichols, James of Lysander m 2/15/44 Susan Rice of Pompey, NY in Chittenango; Rev. James Abell (double ceremony - see marr. of Samuel Barton) (3-2/21)
6334. Nichols, Leonard m Clorinda Webster in Lansing (6-1/26/31)
6335. Nichols, Lucy Shepard, 4, oldest dau of Rev. James and Sarah J., d 2/28/47 at Oneida Depot (9-3/5)
6336. Nichols, Samuel, 91, of Fenner (a Rev. soldier) d 12/18/49 (9-3/7/50)
6337. Nichols, Sylvester, J. m Susan Crane in Milo (6-1/13/30)
6338. Nichols, William, formerly of Oxford, NY, m 1/20/22 Ceryl Miller, dau of Rev. John, in Abington, PA (8-2/6)
6339. Nichols, William of Bath m 4/20/31 Adeline Bennet of Howard in H (6-5/4)
6340. Nichols, William H. (Dr.), 29, formerly of Oxford, NY, d in Abington, Luzerne Co., PA (8-12/1/24)
6341. Nicholson, Allen m 5/25/17 Esther Harvey, both of Preston; Hon. John Noyes, Esq. (7-6/4)
6342. Nicholson, Fanny C., dau of Commodore John., d 7/21/50 in Blenheim (9-8/9)
6343. Nicholson, Nancy, 43, wf of John, d 11/4/35 in Phelps (6-11/11)
6344. Nickels, Charles m 10/17/48 Rosella Girth, both of Elmira, in E; William Foster, Esq. (5-10/20)
6345. Nickerson, Amanda (Mrs.), 19, d 4/12/35 in Sullivan (3-4/14)
6346. Nickerson, James of Cazenovia m 9/11/17 Julia Mead, dau of Thompson Mead, Esq. of Norwich; Elder John Peck (7-9/20)
6347. Nickerson, Julia (Mrs.), dau of Gen. T. Mead of Norwich, d 10/25/18 in Cazenovia (7-10/29)
6348. Nicoll, Luke, formerly of Connecticut, d 7/16/26 in Utica "on his journey home" ("Printers to the east please insert") (9-7/18)
6349. Nicoll, Matthias (Gen.), 61, d 2/10/30 in Stratford, CT (6-3/10)
6350. Nicolson, John B. (Commodore), 62, of the U. S. Navy d 11/9/46 in Washington, D.C. (b in Richmond, VA; entered navy, 1805, as midshipman) (9-11/14)

6351. Niles, Addison (Dr.), physician and surgeon, of Prattsburgh m 12/17/35 Martha Mills of Naples in N (6-1/6/36)
6352. Niles, Hezekiah, Esq., editor of the Weekly Register, m Sally Ann Warner in Baltimore, MD (9-7/25/26)
6353. Niles, Hiram m 11/4/33 Lovina T. Hunt in Bath (6-11/20)
6354. Niles, John of Geneva m 2/25/30 Catharine Gardner of Romulus in R; Rev. Barton (6-3/3)
6355. Niles, William A. (Rev.) m 6/27/50 Mary E. West, only dau of Silas of Binghamton, in B; Rev. John Humphrey (9-7/4)
6356. Nims, Asa, Esq., 51, d 10/2/35 in Manlius (3-10/6)
6357. Ninde, W. W. (Rev.), 35, d 2/27/45 in Delta (9-3/8)
6358. Nisbet, William (Rev.), pastor of the Associated Reformed Church in Seneca, m 9/20/30 Ann Smith, dau of the late Gerardus of NYC, in NYC (6-10/6)
6359. Nisbet, William, 36, d 11/8/34 in Geneva (6-11/12)
6360. Niven, Charles (Col.), late of Newburgh, d 7/9/48 at the home of his bro-in-law, Henry W. Stone, in Honesdale, PA (deceased was formerly sargeant-at-arms in N.Y. State Senate and formerly sheriff of Orange Co. "and subsequently in the P. O. Department, Washington") (9-7/20)
6361. Nixon, ____, inf child of "Mr. and Mrs. Nixon lately arrived in Cincinnati" (Ohio) from Geneva, NY, d 7/3/30 in Cincinnati (6-7/21)
6362. Nixon, Wilson (Capt.), 77, a native of England and recently of Geneva, d 2/1/31 in Cincinnati, OH (deceased "had crossed the Atlantic upward of fifty times") (6-2/23)
6363. Noble, Curtis of the firm of Condit and Noble of NYC m 1/5/48 Charlotte M. Day, dau of late Orrin, Esq. of Catskill, in C; Rev. G. N. Judd (9-1/11)
6364. Noble, George H., merchant, m 10/15/33 Elizabeth Page, dau of Judge Page, in Unadilla; Rev. Adams. All of Utica (6-10/30)
6365. Noble, J. M. m 8/7/45 Caroline Snell, both of Syracuse, in Skaneateles (9-8/26)
6366. Noble, James (Gen.), a senator from Indiana, d in Washington, D.C. (6-3/9/31)
6367. Noble, John G. m 2/4/21 Abigail S. Mygatt in New Milford, CT; Rev. Elliott (8-2/21)
6368. Noble, Louisa, 20, dau of Cyrenus, Esq., d 7/16/29 in New Lisbon (8-7/22)
6369. Noble, Martha, 29, wf of Stilman, d 10/31/46 in Collinsville (9-11/30)
6370. Noble, Silas m 8/25/35 Mary C. Evarts in Canandaigua (6-9/9)
6371. Noble, William H. (Col.), 61, formerly of Cayuga Co., d 2/5/50 in Rochester (several times state assemblyman and a congressman during Pres. Van Buren's admin.) (9-2/7)
6372. Norman, Robert m 2/24/32 Frances Godfrey in Middlebury (6-3/21)
6373. Norris, J. B. m 8/20/35 Roseanna Brizse, both of Geneva; Rev. Abeel (6-8/26)
6374. Norris, James K. of Elizabethtown, formerly of Utica, m 6/14/43 Jane R. Biddlecom of Utica in U; Rev. D. C. Haynes (9-6/16)
6375. Norris, James L. m 9/19/48 Charlotte P. Doolittle; Rev. William Spencer. All of Utica (9-9/20)
6376. Norris, John B. (Col.) of Canandaigua m 5/4/31 Lydia Densmore of Seneca in S (6-5/18)
6377. Norris, Mary Alida, 11 mo, dau of James L. and Charlotte P., d 9/11/50 in Utica (funeral from 49 Broad St.) (9-9/12 and 9/13)
6378. Norris, Oliver (Rev.), pastor of Christ Ch., d 8/18/25 in Alexandria, D. C. (9-9/6)
6379. Norten, Asa A. m 3/26/35 Mary Stoakes in Penn Yan (6-4/8)
6380. North, Alfred of Boonville m 6/8/35 Minerva Bryen of Fairfield in F (both will sail from Boston about June 20 for the Island of Sumatra "where Mr. North will serve as missionary printer") (6-6/17)
6381. North, Cyrus, 31, d 8/23/25 in Walton (consumption) (had become blind in infancy) (8-9/14)
6382. North, John m 5/2/32 Caroline Pattison, dau of William of Seneca Falls, in S. F. (6-5/23)
6383. North, Theodore, Esq. m 11/6/50 Lue Bradley, dau of Jabez, Esq. of Pine Valley, in P. V.; Rev. C. C. Carr (5-11/8)
6384. North, William Vial, 1, s of Norris, d in Elmira (6-5/26/30)

6385. Northrop, _____, inf s of F. W. and M. J., d 5/16/50 in Lowville (9-5/25)
6386. Northrop, Amos B. m 1/17/44 Almira Dodge (dau of Samuel), both of Rome, NY, in R; Rev. C. M. Lewis (9-1/26)
6387. Northrup, Israel H. (Rev.) of Boonville m 9/12/48 Lydia H. Woodbury of Richfield in R; Rev. Jarvis (9-9/16)
6388. Northrup, James D. of Elbridge m 4/24/50 Eveline Augusta Corey of Baldwinsville in B; Rev. T. Walker (1-4/25)
6389. Northrup, Lydia G., 34, d 4/25/47 in Deerfield (9-5/8)
6390. Northway, David of Greenland m 7/4/41 Sally North of Spitzenbergen; Rev. John Amburg of Kentucky: "Take notice ye frozen souls
                              That ice is melting at the poles" (3-7/14)
6391. Northway, Mary E., inf dau of R. Northway, d 12/17/42 in Utica (9-12/19)
6392. Northway, Mary Elizabeth, 25 mo, only dau of Rufus, d 6/27/50 in Utica (funeral from her father's home, corner Bridge and Steuben Sts.) (9-6/28)
6393. Northway, Rufus, printer, m 11/20/26 Elizabeth Schram, both of Utica; Rev. Aikin (9-11/28)
6394. Norton, Addison S. m 9/23/50 Charlotte S. Barnes, both of New Hartford, in New H.; Rev. E. Francis (9-9/26)
6395. Norton, Charles F., 28, d 2/28/32 in Vienna, NY (6-2/29)
6396. Norton, Edward, 10 mo, s of Charles, d in Buffalo (6-1/26/31)
6397. Norton, Edward, one of the publishers of the Madison Observer, m 9/6/43 Almira Westfall of Morrisville in M; Rev. Harrington. All of NY (9-9/11 and 3-9/20)
6398. Norton, Harriet M., 21, dau of Dr. Ariel, d 3/8/46 in Vernon (9-3/19)
6399. Norton, Henry F., Esq. m 6/25/33 Mrs. Charlotte Palmer in Brockport (6-7/10)
6400. Norton, Ichabod (Col.), 89, d 10/1/25 in Granby (b in Farmington, CT; promoted from Lt. to Maj. in Rev. War; justice of peace in Hartford, CT for 33 yrs; for several yrs served in gen'l assembly of CT) (9-10/18)
6401. Norton, Isaac McNeil m Eliza Edmunston in Waterloo (6-4/7/30)
6402. Norton, James, late first judge of Steuben Co. and since a judge of Yates Co. Common Pleas, d 5/23/31 in Starkey, Yates Co. (6-5/25)
6403. Norton, James, 59, d 8/1/49 in Vernon, Center (arrived Vernon area 1806 from CT) (9-8/28)
6404. Norton, Jennette Ann, 7 mo, dau of Albert T. and Ann E., d 7/3/46 in Utica (9-7/4)
6405. Norton, John N. m 11/15/43 Henrietta Quackenbush in Canastota; Rev. Starkey. All of Canastota (3-11/22)
6406. Norton, Lester m 1/20/31 Lydia Light in Hopewell (6-2/2)
6407. Norton, Lewis Hiram, Esq. of Chicago, IL m 3/4/44 Elizabeth Segar, oldest dau of late Edward, Esq. of Manchester, England, at Christ Ch., Mobile, AL; Hon Henry Clay gave the bride away) (9-3/25)
6408. Norton, Nathan (Maj.), 59, d 3/8/32 in Perinton (his death was occasioned by taking opium voluntarily) (6-4/4)
6409. Norton, O. W. of Buffalo m 3/20/34 Hannah Wood of Seneca in S; Rev. McLaren (6-3/26)
6410. Norton, Orwin R. m 2/23/39 Ann Sammon, both of Chittenango, in Fayetteville; Elder Fippen (3-2/27)
6411. Norton, William W., 9 mo, s of Franklin M. and Elizabeth A., d 1/9/47 in Utica (9-1/11)
6412. Nott, Eliphalet, D.D., pres. of Union College, Schenectady, m 8/8/42 Urania E. Sheldon, principal of the Utica Female Academy, in Utica: Rev. Dr. Potter (9-8/9 and 3-8/17)
6413. Nott, Henry C. m 10/19/48 Mary H. Macrae(?) in Utica; Rev. William H. Spencer. All of Utica (9-10/23)
6414. Nott, Howard of Albany m 10/11/31 Margaret M. S. Bowers, dau of John M., Esq. of Cooperstown, in C (6-10/26)
6415. Nott, Joel B. (Prof.) of Union College, Schenectady, m Margaret T. Cooper of Albany in A; Rev. Dr. Nott (9-12/5/26)
6416. Noxon, George W., Esq., 32, d 8/30/48 at his home in Syracuse (9-9/2)
6417. Noxon, Robert (Dr.), 84, d 11/15/33 in Poughkeepsie (6-11/27)
6418. Noyes, Ebenezer m Fanny Hunt in Oxford; Rev. J. D. Wickham (8-12/8/24)
6419. Noyes, Enoch m 10/23/32 Charlotte Church in Rushville (6-11/7)
6420. Noyes, Frances Sheldon, 58, wf of Dr. Josiah, d 5/4/48 in Clinton (9-5/12)

6421. Noyes, George, Jr., 27, s of George of Oriskany and bro of Curtis, Esq. of NYC, d at the home of his bro-in-law, A. S. Johnson, Esq., in Detroit, MI (9-5/18/50)
6422. Noyes, Joseph, Esq. m 11/29/40 Prudence Corey, both of Southport, in S; Rev. Charles S. Davis (4-12/4)
6423. Noyes, William m 10/16/42 Harriet Holmes of Canaseraga in Lenox (3-10/19)
6424. Noyse, Samuel m 3/4/29 Electa Nichols in Preston; Elder Otis (8-3/11)
6425. Nurse, Charles H. of Frankfort m 10/19/48 Mary Eliza Nurse of Paris, NY at the home of David Nurse in Paris; Rev. C. W. Giddings (double ceremony - see marr. of Henry R. Kelsey) (9-10/20)
6426. Nurse, Charles Henry, 24, only s of Thomas H., d 8/10/49 in Frankfort (9-8/14)
6427. Nurse, Hiram E. of Utica m 2/8/49 Elizabeth Kling of Yorkville in Y; Rev. Graves (9-2/12)
6428. Nye, Mary Elizabeth, 20, wf of Grove A., d 1/17/50 in Elmira (5-1/25)
6429. Oades, Jane (Mrs.), 62, d 6/10/47 at the home of Isaac Whiffen in Utica (funeral from the home of "Mr. Whiffen", corner Rutger and 3rd Sts.) (9-6/11)
6430. Oak, Emeline, 18, d in Athens, VT (6-12/20/30)
6431. Oakley, George, Esq., 35, late of Montgomery, NY d 1/25/50 in San Francisco, CA (9-4/11)
6432. Oakley, Gilbert m 1/16/36 Sally Ann Schutt in Milo (6-2/10)
6433. Oatman, Elijah W. of Adams m 8/29/47 Harriet F. Moore of Lorraine, Jeff. Co.; Charles W. Rogers, Esq. (1-9/8)
6434. Obear, Abigail, wf of late Capt. Oliver of Bushwick, L.I. and formerly of Beverly, MA, d 12/4/49 in Utica (funeral at the home of John Camp, 14 Whitesboro St.) (9-12/15)
6435. O'Brien, John, about 65, d 7/4/32 in Penn Yan (6-7/18)
6436. O'Brien, John (Col.) m 8/31/33 Maria Van Valen, both of Rochester, in Brockport (6-9/18)
6437. O''Brien, Margaret, 47, d at the Hotel Dieu in Montreal (presumably in Canada) (lockjaw - splinter in foot) (6-12/22/30)
6438. Odell, William m 3/8/46 Rosanna Whitehead in Paris Furnace, NY; A. E. Pettee, Esq. (double ceremony - see marr. of Lyman Spencer) (9-3/11)
6439. O'Donoughue, John of Rochester m 8/18/33 Rose Ann Clary of Geneva in G (6-8/28)
6440. O'Farrell, H. T. (Dr.) of Philadelphia (NY?) m 3/18/47 Abby Z. Loomis of New Hartford, NY in New H; Rev. Cartwell (9-3/20)
6441. Ogden, _____ (Mr.), merchant, of Seneca Falls m 12/16/34 Caroline A. Langworthy of Rochester in R; Rev. Dr. Whitehouse (6-12/17)
6442. Ogden Aaron (Col.), 83, (a Rev. soldier and President General of the Cincinnati) d 4/19/39 in Jersey City, NJ (6-5/1)
6443. Ogden, Abraham, 53, d 8/10/25 in Walton (8-8/31)
6444. Ogden, Abram, Esq., 78, formerly of Clyde, NY, d 6/6/45 in Berwick, Warren Co., IL (9-6/6/45)
6445. Ogden, Isaac m 10/15/33 Persilla P. Goodman in Owego (6-10/23)
6446. Ogden, Mordecai of Geneva m 4/28/31 Mary Brown of Jerusalem, NY in Penn Yan; A. Wagener, Esq. (6-5/11)
6447. Ogsen, Moses L. m 6/24/18 Hannah Ogden, dau of Isaac, Esq.. All of Walton (8-7/29)
6448. O'Hara, Margaret, wf of Capt. William, d 5/15/30 in Canandaigua (6-5/26)
6449. O'Hara, Mary (Mrs.), 62, d 9/18/46 at her home in Deerfield (9-9/23)
6450. O'Hara, Patrick of Deerfield m 5/27/47 Mary W. Quin of Utica in U; Rev. Stokes (9-5/29)
6451. O'Keefe, James W. d 10/5/33 in Rochester (6-10/16)
6452. O'Keefengeightery, Denis of Ireland m 3/27/50 Rachael Fitzheingirtzpinger of Germany in Louisville, KY (9-4/11)
6453. Olcott, Harriet, 27, wf of Orville and dau of Marvin Hannahs of Albion, MI, d 4/15/46 in Utica (funeral from her late home in West Utica (9-4/16)
6454. Olcott, Orville of Utica m 5/10/49 Ellen E. Hayden of Oswego at the home of S. Doolittle, Esq.; Rev. Condit (9-5/14)
6455. Olcutt, Charles H., merchant, of NYC m 11/20/43 Maria L. Austin of Utica in U; Rev. C. F. Shelden (9-11/24)
6456. Olin, Stephen (Rev.), D.D., pres. of Wesleyan Univ., Middletown, CT, m 10/18/43 Julia M. Lynch, dau of James, Esq. of NYC, at Glenburn in Rhinebeck, NY; Rev. Holdich (9-10/25)

177

6457. Oliphant, John, 60, d 12/8/31 in Auburn (6-12/21)
6458. Oliver, Andrew F. of Penn Yan m 7/27/31 Almira M. Gilbert of Paris, NY
       in P (6-8/24)
6459. Oliver, Eleanor, wf of Judge Oliver, d 12/15/34 in Penn Yan (6-12/31)
6460. Oliver, Richard m 12/29/41 Emaline Bedell of Binghamton in B; Rev. Gregory
       (2-1/12/42)
6461. Olmstead, Denniston, Esq., prof. of natural philosophy in Yale College,
       m 8/24/31 Julia Mason, sister of Rev. C. Mason of NYC, in NYC (6-8/31)
6462. Olmstead, Samuel S. m 10/5/48 Mary N. Brown, both of Elmira; Rev. E. W.
       Dickinson (5-10/6)
6463. Olmstead, William J. (Dr.) of Remsen m 6/21/42 Susan S. Colburn of Utica
       in U; Rev. C. S. Porter (9-6/28)
6464. Olmstead, Nancy, 43, wf of Timothy, d 3/8/44 in Sauquoit (9-3/20)
6465. Olney, W. B. of Marcellus m 1/13/48 Celestine M. Barney of Henderson,
       Jeff. Co. in H; Rev. J. R. Johnson (1-1/26)
6466. Onderdonk, John (Dr.), 69, d 8/23/32 in NYC (two of his sons "in the
       sacred office of the Episcopate") (6-9/19)
6467. O'Neil, James of Albany m 11/20/49 Caroline M. Grinnell, only dau of C.
       B., Esq. of Northampton, Fulton Co.; Rev. Lyon (9-11/24)
6468. O'Neil, Joseph E., 18, oldest s of Owen, Esq., d 2/18/46 in Utica
       (funeral from St. John's Ch.) (9-2/19)
6469. Onion, William m 5/12/42 Eunice Shelly in Fenner; Rev. L. Wright (3-5/18)
6470. Opdyke, Mary A., 22, wf of John S. of Waterloo and dau of John Y. Manning
       of Varick, d 9/16/46 at the home of her father (6-9/25)
6471. Orcutt, Jabez Beardsley, 2, only s of Giles and Delia, d 3/10/42 in
       Binghamton (2-3/23)
6472. Ormsbee, Hannah Maria, 2, dau of Jonathan and Martha, d 3/2/49 in
       Baldwinsville (1-3/8)
6473. Ormsbee, L. J., formerly of Baldwinsville, m 5/13/47 Caroline Combs in
       Jordan; Rev. H. Houghton. All of Jordan (1-5/19)
6474. O'Rourke, John, Esq., publisher of the Milwaukee Sentinel and formerly of
       Watertown, NY, d in Milwaukee, WI (6-1/24/38)
6475. Orregon(?), V. of Mexico (the country?) m 11/15/31 Margaretta Hurry,
       dau of late Samuel of Philadelphia (PA?), in NYC (Rev. Varela at
       Christ Ch. and afterward by Rev. Berrian at St. John's Ch.) (6-11/23)
6476. Orton, Sophronia, 34, wf of J. R. and dau of late Cyrus Hotchkiss of
       Windsor, d in Binghamton (2-4/19/43)
6477. Orwan, Elizabeth Catharine, 99, d in Fayette (6-8/20/34)
       Osborn. See also Usborn.
6478. Osborn, Amos, 83, d 7/3/48 in Waterville (b in Trumbull, CT 30 Nov 1764;
       settled in Waterville, NY by 1801) (surv by wf and 4 children) (9-7/10)
6479. Osborn, Henry d 8/17/33 in Canandaigua (6-8/28)
6480. Osborn, Jane (Mrs.) d in Canandaigua (6-11/6/33)
6481. Osborn, John H., about 35, merchant, d 9/12/31 in the vil. of Jefferson
       at the head of Seneca Lake (6-9/21)
6482. Osborn, Maria, 8, dau of John, d 2/27/26 in Utica (9-3/7)
6483. Osborn, Marilla (Mrs.) d 12/14/36 in Dix, Chemung Co. (6-12/28)
6484. Osborn, Nathan m 12/10/43 Wealthy Bunn in Vestal; H. Collier (2-12/13)
6485. Osborn, Sally, 59, wf of Kinathon, d 12/17/31 in Cooperstown (6-1/4/32)
6486. Osborn, Samuel B., 15 mo, s of Henry B., d in Utica (9-10/10/26)
6487. Osborne, Archabel m 12/31/23 Lucy Mallory, both of German, NY (8-1/8/24)
6488. Osburn, E. R., 56, wf of H. B. formerly of Utica, d 7/28/50 in NYC
       (9-7/31)
6489. Osceola, _____ (Indian Chief) d 1/30/38 at Fort Moultrie, Charleston, SC
       (6-2/14)
6490. Osgood, E. (Rev.), 47, d 9/12/24 at the home of Elder E. F. Willey in
       Utica (9-9/28)
6491. Osgood, Luke B., 72, d 1/9/45 in Brookline, VT (Oxford Republican, 2/13)
6492. Osmus, William m 3/17/30 Sally Ann Ketcham in Geneva; Rev. Tooker (6-3/24)
6493. Osterhout, Sally (Mrs.), about 52, d 4/8/38 in Fenner (3-4/11)
6494. Ostrander, Jacob m 10/22/35 Catharine Smith, both of Wampsville, in W;
       Rev. Cooper (3-10/27)
6495. Ostrander, William m 4/5/32 Mary Turbush in Phelps; Thomas Smith, Esq.
       (6-4/11)
6496. Ostrom, Gilbert, 35, d 12/17/25 in Utica (9-12/20)

6497. Ostrom, H. B. m 10/5/43 Diana Downer in Utica; Rev. D. G. Corey. All of Utica (9-10/6)
6498. Ostrom, John H., Esq., attorney, m 6/17/22 Mary E. Walker, dau of Thomas, Esq., in Utica; Rev. Aikin. All of Utica (8-6/26)
6499. Ostrom, John H., Esq. (Gen.), 51, d 8/10/45 in Poughkeepsie at the home of his bro-in-law, Rev. A. M. Mann (deceased b in Oneida Co.; son of Hon. David who emigrated from Dutchess Co. to Paris, NY being among its first settlers) (9-8/15)
6500. O'Sullivan, John L., late editor of the <u>Morning News and Democratic Review</u>, m 10/21/46 Susan Kearney Rodgers, dau of Dr. Kearney Rodgers, in NYC; Rev. Dr. Taylor (9-10/26)
6501. Otis, D. D., Esq. of Watertown m 4/13/48 Mrs. S. A. Underwood of Thompson, CT in T; Rev. D. D. Dow, D.D. (9-5/12)
6502. Otis, Ephraim (Dr.), 77, d 3/24/50 in De Ruyter (9-4/11)
6503. Otis, George Harrison, 23, d in Boston (6-11/13/33)
6504. Otis, Hannah Elizabeth, 7, only ch of Matteson and Emma, d 8/31/50 in Earlville (9-9/12)
6505. Otis, Joseph, 80, d 3/22/50 in Rome, NY (one of the earliest settlers there) (9-4/6)
6506. Ottaway, Thomas P. of Utica m 6/19/48 Caroline Carter of Trenton, NY at the home of Dr. L. Guiteau in Trenton; Rev. Buckingham (9-6/20)
6507. Ovenshire, Samuel of Barrington m 10/10/32 Sophia Beebe of Junius in Penn Yan (6-11/7)
6508. Overacer, P. J., Esq. of Little Falls m 5/16/44 Margaret A. Delvin of Utica in U; Rev. B. Hawley (9-5/16)
6509. Overfield, Charles, merchant, of Wysox, Bradford Co., PA m Lucinda Tubbs of Elmira in E (6-5/14/34)
6510. Overhizer, _____, 84, wf of Conrad, d 4/13/40 in Wheeler (3-5/20)
6511. Overhizer, Abigail (Mrs.), 65, wf of James and dau of late Conrad formerly of Chittenango, d in Orange, Steuben Co. (3-3/20/44)
6512. Overhizer, Conrad, 36, formerly of Chittenango, d 7/7/40 in Wheeler. Steuben Co. (3-7/22)
6513. Overhizer, J. W. m 2/19/42 Ann Patterson, both of Binghamton, in B; Rev. Stanton (2-3/30)
6514. Overton, Thomas, Esq., 72, d 11/11/35 in Ulster Township, PA (6-12/9)
6515. Oviatt, Ebenezer, 70, (a Rev. pensioner) d in Southport (6-5/9/32)
6516. Oviatt, Lorenzo m 1/24/50 Mary M. Hunt, both of Corning; Rev. A. L. Brooks (4-1/30)
6517. Oviatt, Lucy, 48, wf of David, d 3/29/50 in Norwich (9-4/11)
6518. Oviatt, Urania (Miss), 28, d 9/22/18 in Oxford (8-9/30)
6519. Owen, Daniel (Deacon), 78, d 8/20/31 in Beekmantown, Clinton Co. (served 7 yrs as a soldier in Rev. War) (6-9/21)
6520. Owen, Eli of Veteran m 10/19/48 Caroline E. Parsons of Catharine; Rev. C. C. Carr (5-10/20)
6521. Owen, James, Jr. m Jane Roberts, both of Remsen, in R; Rev. R. Everett (9-3/18/47)
6522. Owens, James, Esq. of Utica m 1/5/48 Jane Fuller, only dau of Samuel, Esq. of Westmoreland, in W; Rev. F. A. Spencer (9-1/8)
6523. Owen, Jesse m 1/1/33 Mary Roys in Lyons (6-1/9)
6524. Owen, Martin Gage m 9/22/33 Ann Briggs in Benton (6-10/9)
6525. Owens, Agnes, 38, consort of Owen Owens, d 6/11/26 in Utica (9-6/13)
6526. Owens, Catherine, wf of David of Sullivan, d 11/13/33 (3-11/19)
6527. Owens, George T., 15, s of David and Mary Ann, d 9/30/50 in Utica (funeral at the home of his father, corner of Mary and Bridge Sts.) (9-10/1)
6528. Owens, Hugh m 1/9/43 Jane Ann Verson, both of Utica, in U; Rev. B. Grosh (9-1/11)
Owens, James, Esq. See entry 6522 unintentionally posted out of alphabetical order.
6529. Owens, Jane (Miss), 23, dau of David, d 12/10/39 in Chittenango (3-12/18)
6530. Owens, Uzziah B. m 10/25/32 Rhoda Pruden in Bellona (6-11/21)
6531. Ownes, James W. m 10/2/34 Mehala Corson, both of Canastota, in Wampsville; Rev. Cooper (3-10/7)
6532. Pabodie, Benjamin F., 2, s of Ephraim, d 9/20/18 in Norwich (7-9/24)

6533. Pabodie, John, 22, formerly of Norwich, d 10/4/21 in Providence, RI
(surv by parents as well as bros and sisters) (7-10/17)
6534. Pack, Caleb m 1/23/37 Mary C. Brower in Sullivan; J. French, Esq. All
of Sullivan (3-1/25)
6535. Packard, Benjamin D., 53, one of the proprietors of the Evening Journal,
d 5/18/33 in Albany (6-5/29)
6536. Packard, John Chester m 9/2/46 Catharine Jane Pearcey, dau of William,
in Albany. All of A (9-9/4)
6537. Packer, Alonzo of Seneca Falls m 4/14/31 Lydia Ann Brink of Waterloo
(6-4/27)
6538. Packer, Caroline, 19, dau of late Dr. Perez, d 5/16/45 (fell from a wagon)
(Oxford Republican, 5/22)
6539. Packer, Jotham of Preston m 1/14/19 Almira Mason of Norwich in N; Rev.
Isaac Allerton (8-1/27)
6540. Pacy, William, 28, d 4/19/35 in Geneva (6-4/22)
6541. Paddock, Frederick of Litchfield m 6/12/50 Emily P. Smith of New Hartford
in Utica; Rev. E. Francis (9-6/13)
6542. Paddock, Henry C. of Litchfield m 3/21/50 Ellen R. Dodge of Frankfort
in Mohawk; Rev. L. Casler (9-3/30)
6543. Paddock, John, 67, d in Vienna, NY (9-3/25/46)
6544. Paddock, Robert B. of Frankfort m 6/25/50 Mariam F. Tanner of Willowvale;
Rev. H. F. Row (9-6/29)
6545. Paddock, Rosanna, 27, wf of Roswell, d 8/19/50 in Vienna, NY (9-8/26)
6546. Paddock, Roswell m 2/11/45 Rosanna Wright; Rev. Chapin. All of Vienna, NY
(9-2/20)
6547. Paddon, Charlotte J., 20, wf of William W., d 8/22/47 in Utica (9-8/23)
6548. Paddon, William W. m 7/20/46 Charlotte J. Burden, both of Utica, in U;
Otis Whipple, Esq. (9-7/22)
6549. Page, Catharine, 3, dau of Charles and Margaret, d 9/15/46 in Seneca
(6-9/25)
6550. Page, Cyrus, 48, d 3/13/33 in West Dresden (6-3/27)
6551. Page, Erastus of Penn Yan m 9/12/32 Addie Goodwin in Canandaigua (6-9/26)
6552. Page, Erastus of Penn Yan m 9/12/32 Adeline Gooding (6-11/7)
6553. Page, Frederick S., 6 mo, s of J. M., d 8/24/37 in Geneva (6-8/30)
6554. Page, George P. m 10/20/46 Mary Ellen Trall or Teall in Geneva; Rev.
Moses Crow (6-10/23)
6555. Page, Gorham m 6/10/37 Eliza Norton in Geneva; Rev. S. Miles. All of
Vienna,NY (6-6/14)
6556. Page, H. L., merchant, m 9/10/43 L. Maria Camp, dau of James, Esq., in
Nunda; Rev. A. Buck (9-9/14)
6557. Page, John J. m 1/27/31 Elizabeth House in Geneseo (6-2/9)
6558. Page, John M. m 8/28/34 Jane Ramsey, both of Geneva, in G; Rev. E. Phelps
(6-9/3)
6559. Page, Julius of Binghamton m 2/24/23 Sophrona Morgan in Oxford; Rev. E. G.
Gear (double ceremony - see marr. of Alanson F. Lyon) (8-2/26)
6560. Page, Mirza Ann (Mrs.), 37, d 6/28/34 in Plainville (in town of Starkey)
(6-7/16/34)
6561. Page, S. R. m 10/11/48 Sarah N. White, only dau of Lona, Esq., in Millport;
Rev. C. C. Carr (5-10/20)
6562. Page, Theodore, 66, d 10/22/46 in Bridgewater (9-10/29)
6563. Pagett, Anna, 38, consort of John, d 8/5/24 in Oxford (8-8/11)
6564. Pagot, Alonzo, Esq., secretary of the French Legation, m Ann Lewis, dau
of William B., Esq., 2nd auditor of the treasury, "at the President's
house" (6-1/2/33)
6565. Paine, Aaron F. of Betts Corners m 7/1/49 Mary C. Wheeleock of
Baldwinsville; Rev. Byron Alden (1-7/12)
6566. Paine, Chester, 58, postmaster at Paine's hollow, d 9/10/50 in German
Flats (9-9/30)
6567. Paine, Mary (Mrs.) d 8/18/33 in Elmira (6-8/28)
6568. Palmatier, George W. m 12/25/48 Jane P. Ruggles in Chemung; Rev. N. N.
Beers (double ceremony - see marr. of Benjamin Freyer)
6569. Palmer, _____ of Auburn m 4/6/37 Abigail Jacobs of Romulus in R; Rev.
Barton of R (6-4/19)
6570. Palmer, Alexander R. m 11/17/31 Nancy Jane Sears in North Cohocton
(6-11/30)

6571. Palmer, Almira, dau of B., d 9/3/25 in New Hartford (9-9/6)
6572. Palmer, Amelia, 2, dau of N. H., d 6/16/41 in Lenox (3-7/7)
6573. Palmer, C. G., senior editor of the Schenectady Whig, m 5/25/31 Clarine Amelia Colvard, dau of Asa of Rensselaerville, in R (3-5/31)
6574. Palmer, C. S., senior editor of the Schenectady Whig, m 5/26/31 Clavine Colvard in Rensselaerville (6-6/8)
6575. Palmer, Charles S., 35, d in Saginaw (MI?) (9-10/16/46)
6576. Palmer, Charlotte (Miss), 15, d 8/21/33 in Bath (6-9/4)
6577. Palmer, Curtis of Utica m 7/1/45 Elizabeth Buchanan, oldest dau of R. G., Esq., in Buffalo; Rev. Dr. J. C. Lord (9-7/3)
6578. Palmer, Daniel J. m 2/6/46 Roxanie Brown in Clarksville, Mad. Co.; Rev. Dye (9-2/10)
6579. Palmer, Edward Wells, inf s of Lucius O. and Mary W. of Utica,d 5/5/50 in NYC (funeral from the home of E. S. Robbins, Steuben St., Utica (9-5/7)
6580. Palmer, G. W. of Elmira m 8/13/49 Rachel A. Jadwin, dau of Joseph of Elmira, in E; Rev. Daniel Chase (5-9/7)
6581. Palmer, George m 3/26/49 Mary Slick at St. Paul's Ch. in Utica; Rev. M. A. Perry. All of Utica (9-3/28)
6582. Palmer, George Munson, 7 mo, s of Peter and Lavonia N., d 9/1/46 in Orleans (6-9/4)
6583. Palmer, Harriet C., 30, wf of Henry D., M.D., and dau of Asa Cody of Sullivan, d 8/7/41 "at Lake Court House, Ind." (3-9/1)
6584. Palmer, Henry, M.D., of Manlius m 2/21/33 Harriet Cady, dau of Capt. Asa of Sullivan, in S (3-3/12)
6585. Palmer, James M. m 6/1/35 Ruth Ann Francisco in Canandaigua (6-6/17)
6586. Palmer, Jane, dau of Benjamin and Clarenda, d 2/11/47 in Granby, Oswego Co. (a teacher of the young for the last 8 yrs) (1-2/24)
6587. Palmer, Joel S., Esq. of Baldwinsville m 10/31/50 Margaret Ferguson of Lysander; Rev. T. Walker (1-11/7)
6588. Palmer, Mary, 61, wf of Bethel, d 6/2/45 in German Flats (9-6/10)
6589. Palmer, Mary Eliza Ann, 2, dau of Lucius O. and Mary W., d 11/20/48 in Utica (9-11/21)
6590. Palmer, Mary M. (Miss), 20, dau of Sandford Palmer, d 9/14/40 in Fayetteville (consumption) (surv by both parents, a sister, and brothers) (3-9/16)
6591. Palmer, Melvin P. of Baldwinsville m 1/2/49 Sarah Wheelock of Mannsville in M; Rev. M. Cook of Oswego (1-1/4)
6592. Palmer, Sarah G. (Mrs.), 23, d 7/20/43 in Corning (4-7/26)
6593. Palmer, Thomas (Deacon) m 2/11/46 Jane Hutelle; Rev. Fox (9-2/19)
6594. Palmer, Uriah G. of Rome, NY m 8/22/48 Ann Bailey of Utica in U; Rev. H. R. Clarke (9-8/24)
6595. Palmer, Westal m 11/19/46 Eliza Stone in Binghamton (9-11/30)
6596. Palmer, William m 6/4/43 Lida Winfield of Binghamton (2-6/7)
6597. Palmer, William H. m 3/3/41 Sarah S. Warner, both of Lenox, in Fayetteville; Rev. A. C. Tuttle (3-3/10)
6598. Paltz, William M m Margaret Paltz in Kinderhook (6-2/9/31)
6599. Pancko, Joseph C. of Utica m 12/24/48 Mrs. Maria Stewart of Otsego Co. in Utica; Rev. H. H. Clark (9-12/27)
6600. Pangburn, John m 12/31/45 Catharine Senior at the Central Hotel; John Parsons, Esq. All of New Hartford (9-1/3/46)
6601. Pankco, Mary, 54, consort of Joseph C., d 7/25/47 in Utica (9-7/27)
6602. Parcel, Franklin B., 2 mo, s of John A. and Caroline, d 8/14/41 in Corning (4-8/18)
6603. Pardee, Charles, merchant, of Skaneateles m 6/8/25 Eliza Kilburn of New Hartford in New H.; Rev. Brace of Utica (9-6/14)
6604. Pardee, W. (Col.) of Little Falls m 5/28/29 Laura E. S. Rodman, dau of late Daniel, Esq. of Albany, in Oxford; Rev. Wells (7-6/3)
6605. Pardee, W. J. (Col.) of Little Falls m 5/26/29 Laura E. S. Redman, dau of late Daniel, Esq. of Albany, in Oxford; Rev. Wells (8-6/3)
6606. Parish, Josiah D. (Rev.) of Pike village, Alleg. Co. m 9/26/33 Elizabeth Winn of Rochester in Palmyra (6-10/9)
6607. Parish, Sheldon of Baldwinsville m 11/21/46 Hannah Dolph of Van Buren in V. B.; Rev. Nichols (1-11/23)
6608. Parish, William, 30, d 9/20/50 at the home of Oliver Parish, Esq. in New Hartford (9-9/23)

6609. Park, Augustus of Bloomfield m 11/4/32 Hannah A. Gooding of Bristol in B (6-11/21)
6610. Park, Emily A., consort of Henri and youngest dau of late George Gardner of Big Flats, d 4/3/49 in Addison (5-4/6 and 4-4/11)
6611. Park, Harriet H., 45, wf of Nathan, Esq. of Geneva, d 9/28/46 "in Ohio City" (6-10/2) (Note: Ohio City is in the town of Ohio, Herk. Co., NY)
6612. Park, Joan Frances, 40, wf of George, d 4/5/43 in Binghamton (2-4/8)
6613. Park, Phineas m 2/13/31 Ann Gragg in Phelps (6-2/23)
6614. Parke, Fielding, 114, d in Winchester, KY ("His wife died 6 years since, aged 106") (6-3/28)
6615. Parker, A. N., dentist, m 5/7/48 M. J. Randall at the Meth. Episc. Ch. in Sauquoit; Rev. Giddings (9-5/9)
6616. Parker, Alonzo D., 26, oldest s of William B. and Asenath, d 6/10/49 in Varysburgh, Wyo. Co., NY (consumption) ("three years ago the deceased left this country where he had lived for the past ten years and went to New Orleans. On Jan 18th, 1849 left for Calif. At Rio De Janeiro, feeling ill, took ship to New York City and his father's home where he died") (this obit contains much gnealogically significant information) (1-8/2)
6617. Parker, Amos, 68, of Oxford d 7/21/17 (8-7/30)
6618. Parker, Calphurnae, 15, dau of Nathan and Edith, d 1/10/29 in Norwich (7-1/21)
6619. Parker, Catherine, 82?, d 4/7/45 in the wreck of the steamboat "Swallow" (wid of late Milton D. and dau of late William G. Tracy of Whitesboro) (funeral at the Reformed Dutch Ch. in Utica (9-4/12)
6620. Parker, Edward, 21, d 8/6/48 in Utica (consumption) (funeral from his late home, 21 Union St.) (9-8/7)
6621. Parker, Eleazer H., 44, d 1/29/14 in Standish, MA (his dau had previously died from the bite of a wild-cat and the physician claimed that the father who came to her rescue had died of the same cause) (8-3/29)
6622. Parker, Hiram of Phoenix m 3/21/50 Sally Prouty of Baldwinsville; Rev. A. Wells (1-3/21)
6623. Parker, James Knox, 2, s of Ira and Elizabeth, d 10/15/46 in Geneva (6-10/16)
6624. Parker, James W. m 11/24/50 Charlotte Rice; Rev. A. L. Brooks. All of Corning (4-11/27)
6625. Parker, Jason, 66, d 9/27/30 at his home in Utica (first mail carrier in this region) (member of Episc. Ch.) (9-10/5)
6626. Parker, Jason, 67, "one of the original proprietors of the old line of stages", d 9/28/30 in Utica (6-10/13)
6627. Parker, Joel, late of Auburn Theological Seminary, m Harriet Phelps, dau of Col. Thomas W. of Lenox (9-5/23/26)
6628. Parker, JohnT. m 7/2/46 Hannah Emery, both of Geneva, in Milo; Rev. S. Adsit (6-7/3)
6629. Parker, Jones T. m 2/21/43 Calista Mosier, both of Norwich; Rev. L. Sperry (Oxford Times, 3/1)
6630. Parker, Joseph J. m Polly Curtis in Canandaigua (6-2/13/33)
6631. Parker, Milton D. m 10/7/34 Catherine Tracy, dau of late William G. of Whitesboro, in Utica; Rev. Aikin (9-10/14)
6632. Parker, Philip S., 54, d 6/29/31 in Albany (6-7/6)
6633. Parker, Ralzemond of Buffalo m 7/23/44 Mary W. Sterling, dau of late Jacob of New Hartford, in Canandaigua; Rev. Maltby Gelston (9-8/12)
6634. Parker, Richard m Hannah Town in Pittsford (6-1/26/31)
6635. Parker, Roxana, 64, wf of Jason, d in Utica (6-4/7/30)
6636. Parker, Samuel (Rev.) m 10/10/34 Lois Winton in Catharine (6-10/22)
6637. Parker, Simeon, Esq., 46, d 2/7/24 (an early settler in Oxford) (8-2/11)
6638. Parker, Solomon, 49, d 8/14/23 in Oxford (8-8/20)
6639. Parker, William H. (Prof.), principal of St. Lawrence Academy, m 11/24/46 Catharine Denton, preceptress of the same school in Potsdam (9-12/19)
6640. Parkhurst, G. H., Esq. m 3/15/49 Hannah Brockway, both of Bridgewater, in B; Rev. S. W. Brace(?) (9-3/22)
6641. Parkhurst, William H. of Canastota, NY d 12/25/49 inHonolulu, Hawaii (9-4/9/50)
6642. Parkill, George m 7/31/42 Electa Herrick, both of Clockville, in Wampsville; Rev. Cooper (3-8/10)

6643. Parks, Augustus S. m 9/4/50 Sarah A. Shields, both of Corning, in Big Flats; Rev. Hurd (4-9/18)
6644. Parks, Charles, "generally known as the common showman", d in Albany (8-10/25/20)
6645. Parks, Thomas of Waterloo m 1/15/43 Charlotte Van Wie of Chittenango in C; Rev. James Abell (3-1/18)
6646. Parkus, Jonathan m 12/20/46 Sarah Gardner, both of Utica, in U; Rev. D. A. Shepard (9-12/22)
6647. Parmele, Lavinia, 46, wf of Horace formerly of Utica, d 1/12/45 in Syracuse (9-1/17)
6648. Parmelee,_____, 3, s of M. of Chittenango, d 10/13/33 in Chittenango (3-10/15)
6649. Parmelee, Alexis of Lyma, Liv. Co. m 10/4/43 Cornelia Hooker of Marshall in Sangerfield; Rev. John B. Fish (9-10/21)
6650. Parmelee, Charles, 85, (a Rev. soldier) d 12/9/38 in Cazenovia (3-12/12)
6651. Parmelee, George R. m 1/5/37 Jane Hearsey, dau of Capt. John, at the Bapt. Ch. in Cazenovia; Rev. O. Mantague (3-1/11)
6652. Parmelee, Homer W., 2, s of Homer W., d 9/5/34 in Chittenango (3-9/9)
6653. Parmelee, Jane, 23, wf of G. R., d 7/21/42 in Cazenovia (3-8/3)
6654. Parmenter, George, about 14, oldest s of John, d 4/18/35 in Elmira (6-5/6)
6655. Parmlee, Sheldon C., 22, s of Horace, d 9/7/48 in Syracuse (9-9/9)
6656. Parris, Frances Henrietta, 4, dau of Edward H. and Catharine, d 3/15/20 in Utica (9-3/18)
6657. Parrish, Jasper, Esq., 69, d 7/13/36 in Canandaigua (b in Windham, CT in March, 1767; emigrated as a child with his parents to Lackawaxen, PA; captured, at age 11, for seven yrs, by Indians at the Wyoming Massacre; was released at Fort Stanwix (now Rome), NY under the Treaty of 1784; settled in Canandaigua in 1792) (6-7/27)
6658. Parshall, Jesse of Chemung m 2/20/50 Prudence Cole of Oceola, Livingston Co., MI; Rev. J. H. Rasco (5-3/29)
6659. Parshall, John A. m 6/4/44 Juliette Thurber in Delhi; Rev. George Waters. All of Delhi (Oxford Republican, 6/13)
6660. Parsons, Calvin H., 53, d 12/10/45 in Westmoreland (9-12/16)
6661. Parsons, Electa, wf of Rev. Justin and mother of late Levi, missionary to Jerusalem, d in Pittsfield, VT (9-3/16/24)
6662. Parsons, Frances, 10, dau of Theodore, d 6/2/35 in Waterloo (6-6/24/35)
6663. Parsons, George M., Esq. of Columbus, OH m 10/19/43 Jane Swan, youngest dau of Hon. Gustavus of Columbus, OH, in Cambridge, MA; Rev. Allbro (double ceremony - see marr. of Augustus Whiting) (9-10/24)
6664. Parsons, George R., 8, s of Theodore, d 5/1/35 in Waterloo (6-5/13)
6665. Parsons, Stephen H. m 10/23/50 Mary E. Wilcox; Rev. T. Walker. All of Baldwinsville (1-10/24)
6666. Parsons, Warren, Esq., sheriff of Cayuga Co., d 3/26/38 in Auburn (6-4/4)
6667. Partick (sic), Amos P. of Ohio m 4/3/31 Jane E. Wells of Sullivan; Rev. A. Yates, D.D. (3-4/5)
6668. Partridge, Lewis J. m Jane Rose in Barrington (6-3/9/31)
6669. Partridge, Truman m 11/20/42 Clarissey Farley in Clockville (3-11/30)
6670. Pascalis, Felix A. O. (Dr.), 71, d 7/21/33 in NYC (9-7/30)
6671. Pascale, Felix Alexander Oviare, 71, M.D., d 7/29/33 in NYC (6-7/31)
6672. Patchin, Edward of Skaneateles m Mary Gaylord of Hartford, CT in Skaneateles (6-11/7/32)
6673. Patrick, Benjamin of Norwalk (state not given, perhaps Ohio) m 6/28/49 Eliza P. Maxwell, dau of Hon. Thomas of Elmira, NY, in Milan, Ohio (5-7/13)
6674. Patrick, George m 6/2/47 Prudence P. Miller, both of Sangerfield in S; Rev. William W. Williams (9-6/5)
6675. Patrick, Thomas, 41, "the Pyrotechnic Artist at Castle Garden", d in NYC (6-2/17/30)
6676. Patridge, Samuel m Sophia Chase in Pittsfield, MA (6-11/17/30)
6677. Patten, Ruth, dau of Rev. William formerly of Halifax, MA and later of Hartford, CT, d 3/8/50 in Hartford, CT (deceased is gr-dau of Rev. Ebenezer Wheelock, founder and first pres. of Dartmouth College and sister of Rev. William Patten, D. D., of Newport, RI) (9-3/8)
Patterson, Abijah. See, possibly, Batterson, Abijah.

6678. Patterson, Amos, Esq., "an aged inhabitant of the county", d in Union, Broome Co. (8-4/2/17)
6679. Patterson, Benjamin, 70, (a Rev. patriot) d in Erwin (6-7/14/30)
6680. Patterson, David m 4/29/35 Harriet Waite, both of Canadice, in C (6-5/13)
6681. Patterson, Enoch T. m Frances McCann in Elmira (6-3/17/30)
6682. Patterson, J. P., printer, of Syracuse m 7/3/34 Ann Cotton of Oswego in O (6-7/16)
6683. Patterson, J. S. m 8/22/36 Mary Jane Benton in Lyons (6-8/31)
6684. Patterson, Philo W., 21, of Oxford d 1/13/29 in Madison (8-1/21)
6685. Patterson, William (Hon.),member of Congress from NY State, d 8/14/38 in Warsaw, NY (6-8/29)
6686. Patterson, William K. m 6/25/48 Sarah A. Dean, both of Oriskany, in Utica; Dr. Proal, rector of Trinity Ch. (9-8/8)
6687. Patterson, William M. m 5/11/26 Hannah Shapley in Oxford; Rev. Bush (8-5/17)
6688. Patton, Ludlow, s of Dr. Patton, m 2/28/49 Abby J. Hutchinson (of the Hutchinson family of Milford, NH) in NYC; Rev. Dr. William Patton (9-3/1 and 3/3)
6689. Patty, Robert, 54, of the firm of R. and J. Patty d 10/19/32 in Auburn (6-11/7)
6690. Paul, Sylvanus of Bloomfield m Jane Babbins in Brutus (6-2/14/38)
6691. Paul, Thomas (Rev.), 55, minister of the First African Bapt. Ch. in Boston, d 4/13/31 in Boston (6-4/27)
6692. Paulding, John (Maj.), one of the captors of Maj. Andre, d in Yorktown, NY (8-3/11/18)
6693. Payn, Frederick m 1/29/49 Adeline Vincent, both of Cold Brook, town of Russia, NY, at the Catharine Street House in Utica; Rev. E. Francis (9-1/30)
6694. Payne, Abram (Rev.) (a Baptist) of Macedon m 2/3//47 Mary Jane Nichols, dau of Rev. Francis R. of Van Buren, in V. B.; Rev. P. S. Bennett (1-2/10)
6695. Payne, Charles T. of Palmyra m 4/5/32 Rebecca M. Pudney, formerly of Waterford, in Lyons (6-4/18)
6696. Payne, Franklin m 7/11/32 Octavia J. Lewis in Palmyra (6-7/25)
6697. Payne, Gideon R. m 12/11?/34 Mary B. Smith, both of Farmington, in F (6-12/17)
6698. Payne, Lewis W., printer, m 4/4/39 Amelia S. Spear in Seneca Falls; Elder Z. Freeman. All of Seneca Falls (6-4/17)
6699. Payne, Lucretia, 22, wf of Joseph W., d in Arcadia (6-7/24/33)
6700. Payne, Worden, 55, bro of George R., Esq. of Albany, d 2/31/49 in Hounsfield (a pioneer settler in the Black River country; arrived in 1803 from Massachusetts) (9-3/24)
6701. Peabody, Ann (Miss), formerly of Chittenango, d 5/22/44 in New Hartford (4-5/29)
6702. Peabody, Caleb K. m 9/19/25 Sally Maria Smith in Oxford; Rev. Bush (8-9/25)
6703. Peacock, George of Troy m 5/6/45 Sarah R. Herrick of York Mills in Utica; Rev. Green (9-5/15)
6704. Pearce, James M. of New Hartford m 5/13/46 Sarah Davison, dau of Peter I., Esq. of Sherburne, in S; Rev. Barrows (9-5/23)
6705. Pearsall, Reuben m 11/17/41 Mary Wheeler in Oxford; Rev. Bartlet. All of Oxford (Oxford Times, 11/24)
6706. Pearsall, William of Greene m 2/22/27 Eliza Balcom, dau of Col. Samuel, in Oxford; Rev. Andrews (8-3/2)
6707. Pearson, _____, child of George, d 2/10/50 in Utica (funeral from his father's home, Washington and Columbia Sts.) (9-2/12)
6708. Pearson, George m 11/30/43 Clarissa A. White, both of Utica, in U; Rev. S. B. Soule (9-12/1)
6709. Pease, _____ (Rev.) m 5/8/42 Ann Pinney of Clockville (3-5/18)
6710. Pease, Ammi of Seneca Falls m Mrs. Elizabeth Starks of Waterloo in W (6-5/5/30)
6711. Pease, Austin, Esq., 37, formerly of Rochester and a proprietor of the Merchants and Millers Transportation Co., d 9/7/50 at his home near Jackson, MI (surv by wf and 6 ch) (9-9/27)

6712. Pease, James Oliver of Philadelphia (state not given) m 10/31/50 Mary
      Rathbone, oldest dau of J. H., Esq.; Rev. Wiley (9-11/1)
6713. Pease, John B., 33, s of J. B., Esq. of Utica, d 8/30/42 in Madison
      Springs, MS (9-9/21)
6714. Pease, Lorenzo W. (Rev.), missionary to Cyprus, m 6/25/34 Lucinda Leonard
      at the First Presby. Ch. in Auburn (both of A) (6-7/9)
6715. Peck,   (Mrs.), 35, wf of James and dau of John Knowles, Esq.,
      d 12/26/34 in Sullivan (3-12/30)
6716. Peck, Anthony, 59, d 4/19/45 in Marshall (9-5/8)
6717. Peck, Asher m 10/10/31 Margaret Howell of Junius in Phelps (6-11/2)
6718. Peck, Benjamin H. (Col.) of Lima m 9/12/33 Emily Reed of Bethany in
      Batavia (6-10/9)
6719. Peck, Burr of Bath m 7/4/33 Elizabeth Kershner in Dansville (6-7/17)
6720. Peck, Calvin of Kirkland, OH m 6/4/46 Lydia Briggs of Utica in U; Rev.
      McIlvaine (9-6/16)
6721. Peck, Chloe, 36, wf of Everard, bookseller, d 12/5/30 in Rochester
      (9-12/21 and 6-12/22)
6722. Peck, David m 4/28/32 Catharine Hughes, both of Benton, in B (6-5/16)
6723. Peck, Elihu of Amboy m 6/7/49 Agnes J. Bryant of Van Buren in V. B.; Rev.
      Sherwood (1-6/14)
6724. Peck, Garry M., 52, d 8/22/50 in Mansfield, PA (4-8/28)
6725. Peck, Hiram m 1/1/32 Elizabeth Westfall, dau of James, in Phelps. All
      of P (6-1/11)
6726. Peck, James, 52, d 2/24/42 in Sullivan (consumption) (an early settler in
      Sullivan) (3-3/9)
6727. Peck, Jedediah (Hon.), 73, (a Rev. soldier) d 8/15/21 in Cooperstown
      (8-8/29)
6728. Peck, John (Rev.), 68, d 12/15/49 in NYC (funeral at Oliver Street Bapt.
      Ch. but burial in Cazenovia in family plot) (b in Stanford, Dutch. Co.
      11 Sept 1781; arrived Norwich, NY in 1796; licensed to preach at age 21;
      moved to Cazenovia soon after marriage in 1804) (9-12/24)
6729. Peck, Juliette, 5, dau of Anthony and Cynthia, d 3/14/45 in Marshall
      (9-5/8)
6730. Peck, Linus M., A.M., of Cazenovia, late grad of the Hamilton Theological
      Seminary, m 9/17/46 Cordelia C. Kendrick of Hamilton, only dau of
      Nathaniel Kendrick, D.D., in Hamilton; Rev. N. Kendrick, D.D. (9-9/23)
6731. Peck, Loring (Col.), 90, (a Rev. patriot) d 7/29/33 in Lake Pleasant,
      Mont. Co. (6-9/18)
6732. Peck, Norman P., 26, s of Everard, Esq. of Rochester, d 6/18/49 in
      Springfield, MA (consumption) (9-6/22)
6733. Peck, O. H. of Athens, PA m 9/4/48 Hester Jane Smith of Elmira in E;
      Rev. A. M. Ball (5-9/8)
6734. Peckham, Frederick, 3, youngest s of Merritt and Adelia M., d 10/15/48
      in Utica (funeral at 46 Broad St.) (9-10/17)
6735. Peckham, Isabella Adaline, wf of Rufus W. and dau of Rev. Dr. William B.
      Lacey, d 4/4/48 in Albany (9-4/6)
6736. Peckham, James d 9/14/40 in Peru, Onon. Co. (he stated that his father
      lived in or near Perryville, Mad. Co.) (3-10/14)
6737. Peckham, John S., 3, s of John S. and Mary W., d 12/2/45 in Utica
      (funeral from his father's home, 48 Broad St.) (9-12/4)
6738. Peckham, Julia, 15 mo, dau of Merrit and Adelia M., d 10/18/42 in Utica
      (funeral from her father's home, 46 Broad St.) (9-10/20)
6739. Peckham, Lydia, 75, wid of Nathan, d 6/20/50 in Westmoreland (9-7/16)
6740. Peckham, Mary, 80, wid of Seth, d 7/13/50 in Utica (9-7/16)
6741. Peckham, Seth, 83, d 7/30/46 at his home in Utica (funeral at Friends
      Meeting House, New Hartford) (9-7/31)
6742. Peckham, William A. m 2/11/36 Lydisettee Chapin in Ontario, NY (6-3/23)
6743. Peckins, Susan (Mrs.), 24, d in Benton (6-6/2/30)
6744. Peebles, C. (Dr.) of Corning m 6/15/42 Catharine M. Winans, dau of Judge
      Steele of Corning, in C; Rev. Whiting (4-6/22)
6745. Peek, Amelia (Mrs.), 33, d in Schenectady (6-1/26/31)
6746. Peek, Ann, 71, wf of Joseph Y. d 5/28/45 in Rotterdam, NY (9-6/10)
6747. Peek, James C., 42, d in Schenectady (6-1/26/31)
6748. Peek, Oscar Augustus, 2, s of John, d 8/28/31 in Geneva (6-8/31)

6749. Peet, William L. of Orange Co. m 6/9/30 Mrs. Susan Ann Buchanan of NYC
in Utica; Rev. Dr. Lansing (9-10/5)
6750. Peets, Franklin of White Creek m 1/13/31 Margaret Black in Union Village,
Wash. Co. (6-2/2)
6751. Pegg, James B., 15, d 4/16/49 in Utica (9-4/17)
6752. Pegs(?), Mary (Mrs.), 67, d 7/31/49 in Utica (9-8/1)
6753. Pellet, Elias P., senior editor of the Anti Masonic Telegraph, m 2/7/30
Edith Ann Pellet, both of Norwich, in N; Elder J. Randall (8-2/17)
6754. Pellet, Polly (Miss), 21, d 7/21/18 in norwich (7-7/23)
6755. Pelton, Benjamin (Capt.), 78, (a Rev. officer) d in Ithaca (was for many
years first judge of Seneca Co. (before Tompkins Co. was formed)
(8-9/15/30)
6756. Pendleton, _____ (Judge) of Hyde Park, Dutch. Co. d near Poughkeepsie
(fell from his chaise "when the breach tackle gave way") (8-10/31/21)
6757. Pendleton, Benjamin F. of Vernon m 12/28/43 Delia A. Jones, oldest dau of
Pomeroy Jones (9-12/30)
6758. Pendleton, William m 2/2/17 Betsey Pellet in Norwich; Jedediah Randall.
All of Norwich (7-2/5)
6759. Pendleton, William, 74, (a Rev. soldier) d in Troy (8-1/23/22)
6760. Penfield, Harriet L., 46, wf of Henry F., Esq., d 9/3/35 in Canandaigua
(6-9/9)
6761. Penfield, Lewis, 28, d 12/28/43 in Utica (consumption) (funeral at the
home of Ira A. Button, 48 Fayette St.) (9-12/30)
6762. Penn, _____ (Mr.) d 3/30/37 "at an advanced age" in Hopewell (6-4/5)
6763. Penniman, Christopher, 72, d 8/15/42 at his home in Williamstown, MA
(2-9/14)
6764. Penniman, Francis Blair, 2, s of F. B. and J. B., d 3/6/42 in Binghamton
(2-3/9)
6765. Pennock, Simeon of Perryville m 9/18/33 Rebecca Dickinson of Chittenango
in C; Rev. B. Paddock (3-9/24)
6766. Penny, Amial, about 70, d 4/16/48 in New York Mills (9-4/20)
6767. Penny, George m 1/17/31 Eliza McGinnis in Newburgh (6-2/2)
6768. Penrith(?), Isaac H. m 2/11/43 Adelia Vanderhule in Oxford; Rev. E. G.
Perry. All of Oxford (Oxford Republican, 2/17)
6769. Pepoon, Jane E., 24, formerly of Oneida Co., NY, d 4/27/43 in Painesville,
OH (consumption) (9-5/13)
6770. Pepper, William (Elder), 50, formerly pastor of the Bapt. Ch. in Vernon,
d 3/12/46 in Vernon (9-3/19)
6771. Peppinger, George O. m 11/19/36 Jane Sherwood, both of Geneva; Richard
Hogarth, Esq. (6-12/7)
6772. Percy, Ann (Mrs.), 87(?), d 1/18/46 in Geneva (6-1/23)
6773. Perdise, John m 2/27/33 Hannah Lawrence in Phelps (6-3/20)
6774. Perine, G. H., surgeon dentist, of Utica m 10/7/47 Mary Ann Turnbull, dau
of A. N., Esq. of NYC, in NYC; Rev. S. A. Corey (9-10/11)
6775. Perine, George Henry, only s of George H., dentist, of Utica, d 8/7/49 in
New London, CT (9-8/10)
6776. Perine, Matthew Larue (Rev.), D. D., a professor at Auburn Seminary,
d 2/12/36 in Auburn (6-2/24)
6777. Perkins, David of Utica m 5/15/48 Alathea Rose(?), dau of Rufus of
Schuyler, in S; Rev. Dr. Proal (9-5/19)
6778. Perkins, Dyer m 8/25/30 Lomira Smith, both of Smithville, in S; Rev.
Wilcox (8-9/1)
6779. Perkins, Elizabeth, 80, relict of late Jenkins Perkins, d 1/12/43 in
Oriskany (born in Newport, RI; gr-dau of former gov. of that state;
settled in Oriskany about 1803) (9-1/18)
6780. Perkins, Erastus m 6/18/22 Agnes Van Wagenen (dau of Gerrit H.), both of
Oxford; Rev. Bush (8-6/19)
6781. Perkins, Erastus S., merchant, of Oxford m Eunice Butler, late of
Wethersfield, CT, in New Hartford, NY; Rev. Adams (8-1/11/28)
6782. Perkins, Erastus William, 18 mo, s of Capt. James, d 6/30/23 in Oxford
(8-7/2)
6783. Perkins, Gilman W. of Painted Post m 6/23/50 Mariah M. Huntley of Corning;
Rev. A. L. Brooks (4-6/26)
6784. Perkins, Gurden m 12/26/42 Frances Adelia Squires, dau of Anthony, at Zion
Ch., Greene; Rev. Van Ingen. All of Greene (Oxford Republican, 1/6/43)

186

6785. Perkins, Joseph, Esq. m 5/13/49 Cornelia Kennedy, oldest dau of S. R., Esq., in Columbus, Chen Co.; Rev. C. L. Shipman. All of Columbus (9-5/18)
6786. Perkins, Joshua Newton, Esq. m 3/10/31 Elizabeth Perkins Bishop, oldest dau of Daniel L., Esq., all of Ithaca, in I (6-3/23)
6787. Perkins, Lucia R. (Miss), 24, dau of D. L., d 6/2/45 in Utica (funeral from Trinity Ch.) (9-6/4)
6788. Perkins, Lucy, 77, wid of late Frederick, d 11/6/47 in Utica (funeral at the home of her son-in-law, William Tracy, 285 Genesee St.) (9-11/8)
6789. Perkins, Mark m 11/25/46 Eliza R. Swann, both of Utica, in Auburn; Rev. D. W. Bristol (9-11/28)
6790. Perkins, Mary, 77, relict of Elisha, late of Sterling, CT, d 4/10/44 in Plainfield, NY (at the home of O. D. Perkins, s of Elisha) ("Cooperstown, NY and Hartford and Brooklyn, CT papers please copy") (9-4/22)
6791. Perkins, Pliny M. of Burlington, Racine Co., Wisc.Terr. m Elen A. Conkey, formerly of Clinton, NY, in Oak Grove, Dodge Co., Wisc. Terr. (9-2/6/47)
6792. Perkins, Silas D. m 5/21/50 Rhoda M. Gray, both of Western, in Whitestown; Rev. W. A. Mason (9-5/23)
6793. Perkins, Thomas G., merchant, of Utica m 12/7/31 Ellen Sophia Clarke, dau of Dr. Peter of Montezuma, in M (6-1/4/32)
6794. Perkins, Ursula, 42, wf of Erastus and relict of late Hon. John Allen of Litchfield, CT, d 12/26/20 in Oxford, NY (8-1/3/21)
6795. Perkins, William (Mrs.), late of Chenango Co., NY,d in Millegeville, GA (8-10/30/22)
6796. Perkins, William S. of the firm of Davenport and Perkins m 5/12/37 Harriet Burton, dau of William, in Cazenovia; Rev. E. M. Woolley. All of Cazenovia (3-5/17)
6797. Permance, Levi (Dr.) of Auburn m 4/18/39 Sarah Ferris of Ithaca in I; Rev. S. S. Parr (6-5/1)
6798. Perry, Abner, 45, d 9/23/36 in Potter (6-10/12)
6799. Perry, Amanda H., 46, wf of George T. of Chittenango, d 3/6/37 (3-3/8)
6800. Perry, Andrew J. m 9/6/48 Margaret Hilts, both of Herkimer, in Frankfort; Rev. J. Penfield (9-9/18)
6801. Perry, Catharine Taylor, 13 mo, dau of Guy M. and Elizabeth A., d 1/29/49 in Elmira (5-2/2)
6802. Perry, Cornelia B., wf of George formerly of Chittenango, d 10/12/40 in Amsterdam, NY (3-10/14)
6803. Perry, Daniel, formerly of Oxford, d "a few days since" in Bainbridge (8-2/4/18)
6804. Perry, Electa, 1, dau of Henry, d 8/9/34 in Chittenango (3-8/12)
6805. Perry, Elizabeth G., 11, dau of Capt. George T. Perry, d 12/29/38 in Chittenango (3-1/2/39)
6806. Perry, George of Skaneateles m 6/29/43 Julia Frances Burrows of Rome, NY in R; Rev. Vogle (9-7/6)
6807. Perry, George T., merchant, of Chittenango m 9/28/37 Cornelia Sage, dau of Col. H., in Sullivan; Rev. Bellamy of Manlius (3-10/4)
6808. Perry, Henry, about 2, s of H. of Chittenango, d 9/24/31 (3-9/27)
6809. Perry, Horace, about 33, d 8/30/36 in Elmira (6-9/7)
6810. Perry, Hugh m 2/1/44 Ellen Roberts in Utica; Rev. Row. All of Utica (9-2/3)
6811. Perry, James H. of Owego m 5/11/42 Parmelia Hall of Union in U; H. H. Collier, Esq. (2-5/25)
6812. Perry, John B. m 11/20/44 Mary Simpson, dau of Alanson, Esq., in Poughkeepsie. All of P. Rev. Lindsey officiating (9-11/26)
6813. Perry, Malinda, about 6, dau of George T., d 3/19/35 in Chittenango (3-3/24)
6814. Perry, Nathaniel H., Esq., purser in U.S. Navy, d 5/8/32 in NYC (6-5/16)
6815. Perry, P. H. m 6/3/33 Jane V. Dill in Auburn; Rev. Dr. Rudd (6-6/12)
6816. Perry, Richard, 62, d 5/6/48 in Utica (9-5/9)
6817. Perry, Robert (Dr.), a native of Wales, d 6/10/26 in Steuben, NY (9-6/13)
6818. Perry, Stephen B. m 12/15/25 Maria Belnap in Greene (8-12/21)
6819. Perry, Upton R. m 4/28/43 Leah Bump, both of Tioga, PA, in Corning; H. H. Hull, Esq. (4-5/3)
6820, Perry, William, 50, d 10/12/42 in Utica (9-10/24)

6821. Peters, Augustus of Detroit, MI m Lucy Pollard of Massachusetts in
       Rochester, NY (6-11/10/30)
6822. Peterson, Amos m 3/22/32 Ellen Vanlew in Lodi (6-4/4)
6823. Petheram(?), Benjamin of Skaneateles, formerly of Utica, m 10/6/42 Rhoda
       E. Colwell of Richfield in R; Elder Hutchins (9-10/8)
6824. Petheram, John, 72, d 9/13/45 at his home in Utica (9-9/19)
6825. Petrie, Glen m 2/21/44 Hannah Wiggins, dau of John, in Rome, NY; Rev.
       H. C. Vogel (9-2/29)
6826. Petten(?), John of Towanda, PA m 1/10/40 Sarah F. Knowles, dau of J., Jr.,
       Esq. of Sullivan, in S (3-1/22)
6827. Pettit, Warren D. of Benton m 4/9/35 Caroline Mary Coun of Conhocton in C;
       Rev. I. J. B. McKinney (6-4/15)
6828. Petty, Oliver C. m 6/7/35 Mary A. Smith, both of Cazenovia, in Georgetown;
       Rev. Corey (3-6/9)
6829. Petteys, David m Barbara Jenkins in Galen (6-5/5/30)
6830. Pettis, Solomon m Eliza Pike in Fort Edward (6-2/2/31)
6831. Pettit, Rufus D. of Syracuse m 9/18/50 Elvira C. McHuron in Lysander;
       Rev. A. Finney (double ceremony - see marr. of Marcus C. Hand) (1-9/26)
6832. Pettys, Stephen m 11/8/41 Rubiette Angelina Conant in Bainbridge; Elder
       Church (Oxford Times, 12/8)
6833. Peyton, Murray, 3, s of Col. Rowzee, d 11/19/32 inSeneca (6-11/21)
6834. Phelan, Thomas (Dr.), 66, of Litchfield d 2/14/49 in Utica (funeral at
       the home of H. H. Fish, 13 Devereux St.) (9-2/15)
6835. Phelps, Abigail, 75, d 12/10/33 in Mentz (6-12/25)
6836. Phelps, Alonzo, principal of New Berlin Academy, m 11/29/43 Elizabeth C.
       Cesebro, only dau of late Henry, Esq. of Brookfield, in B (9-2/3/44)
6837. Phelps, Chauncey, 76, d 12/28/47 at the home of his son-in-law, Morgan
       Gardner, in Utica (9-12/31)
6838. Phelps, Dudley P. m 9/3/45 Lucy B. Putnam, dau of Hiram, Esq., in
       Syracuse; Rev. S. J. May. All of S (9-9/16)
6839. Phelps, Hannah, 68, wid of Joseph D. and mother of late Charles H. Phelps,
       d 11/2/42 in Stonington. (CT?) (typhus) (4-11/23)
6840. Phelps, Hiel m 11/8/32 Malinda Thompson in W. Bloomfield (6-11/21)
6841. Phelps, J. A. m 12/29/33 Sarah Ann Selby in Pulteneyville (6-1/8/34)
6842. Phelps, John B. of the firm of R. Irons and Co. m 6/6/43 Jane M. Wright,
       formerly of Hartford, CT, in Utica; "Rev. P. Knox at the N.Y. State
       Lunatic Asylum" (6-7/13)
6843. Phelps, Leicester (Gen.), 39, d 6/18/36 in Canandaigua (6-7/13)
6844. Phelps, Mary, relict of late Oliver, Esq., one of the first settlers and
       proprietors in Ontario Co., d 9/13/26 in Canandaigua (9-9/26)
6845. Phelps, Seymour L. of Wellington Valley (near Geneseo) m 5/30/31 Mary Ann
       Culver, formerly of Geneva, in Canandaigua; Rev. Eddy (6-6/8)
6846. Phetteplace, B. (Mrs.), 47, consort of David, d 12/14/27 "in Rhode Island
       Settlement" (8-12/28)
6847. Philips, H. R. m Lydia A. Douglass in Livonia (6-1/19/31)
6848. Philleo, Newton of Verona m 8/22/49 Amelia C. Corbett of Utica in U;
       Rev. E. Francis (9-8/24)
6849. Phillips, Abraham, about 40, d 9/20/31 in Seneca (6-9/28)
6850. Phillips, Amanda, 43, wf of Col. Elijah, d 11/1/31 in Syracuse (gr-dau of
       late Gen. Danforth of Ontario Co. and was the first white child born
       in it) (6-11/16)
6851. Phillips, Derrick m 4/13/17 Amy Willcox, both of Oxford (8-4/16)
6852. Phillips, E. (Col.) of Syracuse m 11/6/33 Emily J. Richards of NYC in NYC
       (6-11/2))
6853. Phillips, George W. of Ithaca m 10/9/45 Laura Williams, dau of John, Esq.
       of Cazenovia, in C; Rev. J. R. Davenport (double ceremony - see marr.
       of L. M. Boyce) (9-10/10)
6854. Phillips, Henry m 4/1/32 Abigail Conrad; Jairus French, Esq. All of
       Sullivan (3-4/3)
6855. Phillips, Henry m 7/3/50 Lucy Peet, both of Sauquoit, in S; Rev. John
       Waugh (9-7/11)
6856. Phillips, Jeremiah m 2/19/50 Agnes Bradley, both of Utica, in Whitesboro;
       Rev. W. A. Matson (9-2/21)
6857. Phillips, John m Betsey Madole in howard (6-4/6/31)

188

6858. Phillips, Levi m 9/1/30 Eleanor Wilcox, both of Waterloo, in Geneva; Cephas Shekell, Esq. (6-9/15)
6859. Phillips, Luther m 1/22/24 Mahetable Jewel, both of Guilford, in G; Rev. Danielson (8-1/28)
6860. Phillips, Mary, 59, wf of Henry, d 10/27/46 in Salinas (1-11/9)
6861. Phillips, Michael (Dr.), 52, d 9/21/47 in Syracuse (1-9/29)
6862. Phillips, Otis m 1/5/19 Olive Sheperson in Norwich; R. D. Delay, Esq. (8-1/13)
6863. Phillips, William of Watertown m 11/1/49 Maria J. Wingate of Baldwinsville in B; Rev. Byron Alden (1-11/15)
6864. Phillips, William C., 54, formerly of Utica, d 1/21/49 in Williamsburgh (9-1/30)
6865. Phinney, Marcus, merchant, of Syracuse m 5/24/42 Emma Coburn of Utica in U; Rev. H. A. Proal (9-5/28)
6866. Pickard, John I. of Lysander m 5/22/48 Mary Ann Burr of the Oneida Depot in O. D.; Rev. Nichols (1-5/24)
6867. Picket, Charles m 10/11/32 Eliza Newmans in Gorham (6-11/7)
6868. Picket, John m 1/11/37 Ann Hager, both of Clockville, in Chittenango; J. French, Esq. (3-1/18)
6869. Pier, George, 36, d 7/13/31 in Otsego ("a teacher of Martial Music") (6-7/27)
6870. Pierce, _____ (Capt.) d 9/3/49 "at an advanced age" in Horseheads (5-9/7)
6871. Pierce, Dennis m 1/15/33 Julia Ann Secor in Geneva; Rev. Phelps (6-1/23)
6872. Pierce, George V. of NYC m 11/26/46 Evelina B. Hall of Brooklyn (formerly of Utica); Rev. F. A. Farley (9-12/12)
6873. Pierce, Hiram m Susan Perry in Corning; Oliver Rouse, Esq. All of Corning (4-9/22/41)
6874. Pierce, Hunting S., 34, d 3/14/26 in New Hartford (9-3/28)
6875. Pierce, J. Augustine Humbolt m 7/7/36 Cyntha (sic) Botsford in Galen (6-7/13)
6876. Pierce, Jesse (Capt.), 24, formerly of Utica, d 6/20/25 in Rochester (from the kick of a horse) (9-6/28)
6877. Pierce, John m 1/27/31 Caroline Wilson, both of Clyde, in Marengo (6-2/9)
6878. Pierce, Maris Bryant, Esq. of Buffalo m 11/21/43 Mary Jane Carrol of Utica in U; Rev. Charles S. Porter (9-11/28)
6879. Pierce, Nathan W. of Strafford, VT m 9/1/47 Sophia A. Spalding of Union, NY in Vernon, NY; Rev. H. Emmons (9-11/11)
6880. Pierce, Sally (Mrs.), 40, d 8/3/34 in PennYan (6-8/13)
6881. Pierce, Samuel B., 20, only s of Lewis and Nancy, d 2/27/50 at the home of George Robenson in Clinton (had been a member of the Clinton Grammar School for the last two months) (9-3/7)
6882. Pierce, Samuel W., editor of the Ulster Palladium, m 10/2/31 Laura B. Hallock in New Paltz; Rev. Beach (6-10/12)
6883. Pierce, Walter H. m 8/21/48 Julia A. Haws, both of Utica; Rev. Minor (of Syracuse?) (9-8/24)
6884. Pierce, William m 5/22/43 Clarissa Doty in Greece, MI; Rev. J. B. Olcott (double ceremony - see marr. of Eri Putnam) (9-5/31)
6885. Pierson, Samuel, s of Hon. Job of Troy and a passenger on the ship "Tarolinta" for California, d 1/27/50 (his was the 10th death of a passenger "since her arrival") (9-3/13)
6886. Piersons, Josiah, 21, oldest s of Anson and Clarissa, d 3/20/44 in Canaseraga (funeral at the Universalist Ch with the funeral sermon by Rev. James Abell of Chittenango) (3-4/3)
6887. Pigeon, Alexander G. of Rochester m 8/5/48 Mary A. Callahan of Utica in U; Rev. H. De Luynes (9-8/17)
6888. Pike, Clara H., 55, wid of late Zebulon M. Pike, d 4/18/47 at her home in Boone Co., KY (9-5/3)
6889. Pine, George W. of Amsterdam, NY m 12/13/43 Lucy De Ferier of Wampsville in Utica; Rev. W. H. Cooper (9-12/16)
6890. Pinkney, Deborah, 21, dau of Dr. John, d 6/13/32 in Vienna, NY (6-6/20)
6891. Pinkney, Isaac m 5/31/31 Mary Ann Watkins, both of Waterloo, in W; Rev. Hubbard (6-6/15)
6892. Pitcher, Joseph m 2/10/47 Caroline Tottingham in Baldwinsville; Rev. T. Walker (1-2/16)
6893. Pitkin, Eliza S., 57, wf of Hon. William, d 4/8/47 in Rochester (9-4/10)

189

6894. Pitkin, Timothy, 81, d 12/18/47 in New Haven, CT ("for some time a resident of Utica, N.Y.") (9-12/20)
6895. Pitman, Melvin C., 9, oldest s of Lemuel and Elizabeth D., d 8/28/47 in Utica (9-8/31)
6896. Pittman, Thomas, 30, d 9/17/50 in Utica member, Oneida Lodge, Independent Order of Odd Fellows) (9-9/18 and 9/19)
6897. Pitney, Joseph T. (Dr.) of Auburn m Harriet Trask in Avon (6-1/19/31)
6898. Pixley, Ann, 47, wf of Isaac, formerly of Clinton, d 4/12/50 in Le Roy (9-4/17)
6899. Plant, A. H., formerly of Onondaga Co., m 12/28/46 Mary Gallup, dau of William formerly of Norwalk, OH, in Damascus, Henry Co., OH; Rev. H. P. Stillwell (a double ceremony - see the marr. of William Bumberger) (1-1/13/47)
6900. Plant, Lucinda, 81, wid of Benjamin of Utica, d 12/25/48 in U (funeral from the home of her son, James Plant, on Genesee St.) (9-1/26/48)
6901. Platt, Benjamin S. m 9/6/42 Elizabeth Thomas in Utica; Rev. Hawley. All of Utica (9-9/7)
6902. Platt, C. B. of Utica m 12/14/48 Frances J. Dey of Geneva in G; Rev. Bissell (9-12/19)
6903. Prentiss, Catharine (Mrs.), 23, (consort of John H., editor of Freeman's Journal, Cooperstown) d 6/28/18 in Butternuts (deceased is dau of Gen. Jacob Morris) (8-7/8)
6904. Platt, Cornelia, 20, 2nd dau of Hon. Jonas of Whitestown, d 5/27/21 in Albany (8-6/6)
6905. Platt, Elias L. m 7/3/33 Henrietta Heinz(?) in Bath (6-7/17)
6906. Platt, George Lewis (Rev.) of Charleston, SC m 5/26/48 Sarah Dickman Willard, dau of D., Esq. of Greenfield, MA, in G (9-6/2)
6907. Platt, Henry L., youngest son of late Jonas, d 4/11/44 in Plattsburg (9-4/22)
6908. Platt, Horatio N., 36, d 2/12/44 in Utica (funeral at the Universalist Ch.) (9-2/15)
6909. Platt, Jesse of Long Island, NY m 10/1/34 Catharine Karney of Benton in Bellona; Rev. Charles P. Wack (6-10/15)
6910. Platt, Luke P., 34, of the firm of Bangs, Platt and Co. d 5/8/50 in NYC (9-5/15)
6911. Platt, Richard, 76, d 3/4/30 in NYC (6-3/10)
6912. Platt, Rufus D. (His Honor the Mayor of NYC) m 6/12/45 Frances Jennett Whiton, dau of James, Esq. formerly of Troy, in T (9-6/25)
6913. Platt, Timothy Dwight, 17, member of freshman class, Yale College, and s of Rev. Dennis of Binghamton, NY, d 2/16/49 in New Haven, CT (9-2/21)
6914. Platt, William Floyd, 29, late a partner in the house of John Steward and Co. in NYC, d 4/14/44 in Oswego (consumption) (oldest s of James Platt, Esq. formerly of Ithaca) (was a member of the First Presby. Ch., Oswego) (9-4/22)
6915. Playford, Edward m 2/15/33 Jane Knight in Phelps (6-2/27)
6916. Ploof(?), Gilbert E. m 9/5/48 Mary C. Rorick; Rev. E. W. Dickinson (5-9/15)
6917. Plum, Edmund M. m 8/5/33 Maria S. Reins in Ithaca (6-8/14)
6918. Plumb, Samuel, Jr. (Capt.) d 2/24/26 in Williamstown (surv by wf and 6 ch) (9-3/11)
6919. Plumb, William D., 6, 2nd s of David and Lucy A., d 8/10/47 in Utica (9-8/19)
6920. Plumb, William, 58, d 4/3/50 in Camden ("interred by his Masonic brethren")
6921. Plummer, Joseph B. (Lt.) of U.S. Army m 7/31/43 Frances H. Clark, formerly of Utica, at Fort Winnebago, Wisc. Terr. (9-8/23)
6922. Poe, Virginia Eliza, 25, wf of Edgar A., d 1/30/47 in NYC (9-2/8)
6923. Pohlhemus, James S. of Astoria m 5/20/48 Harriett E. Martin, dau of late Bradley of Avon, in Albany; Rev. Pohlhemus of Fishkill (9-6/23)
6924. Poindexter, George (Hon.), U. S. Senator from Mississippi, m 5/15/32 Ann Hewes, dau of Samuel, Esq. of Boston (state not given); Rev. Dr. Hawley (6-5/30)
6925. Pollard, Walter, 69, d 11/16/26 in Clinton, NY ("The editors of the Boston Recorder and Telegraph are requested to publish the above") (9-12/5)
6926. Pollard, William m 5/20/47 Julia Ann Gates, oldest dau of Ebenezer S., in Utica; Rev. D. A. Shepard. All of Utica (9-5/21)

190

6927. Pollock, William m 7/29/32 Margaret Macintire in Vienna, NY; James Snow, Esq. (6-8/8)
6928. Polly, Charlotte (Miss), 24, d 9/1/47 in Lysander (1-9/8)
6929. Pomeroy, A. W. of Albany m 6/20/48 Elizabeth A. Saulpaugh of Utica in U; Rev. William H. Spencer (9-6/22)
6930. Pomeroy, Allen m 1/25/31 Linda B. Jones in Bristol (6-2/2)
6931. Pomeroy, Dwight of Steuben Co. m Lucinda Clark in Pine Valley (6-6/12/33)
6932. Pomeroy, Dwight A. of Kirkland m 12/16/46 Maria L. Harding of K, dau of John Harding; Rev. Kinyon (9-12/22)
6933. Pomeroy, Francis (Rev.), 70, d 12/18/36 in Lyons (6-12/28)
6934. Pomeroy, G. m Laura Ellis in Onondaga (double ceremony - see marr. of Charles S. R. Hargin) (6-2/9/31)
6935. Pomeroy, George E. m 8/5/33 Helen L. Robinson in Palmyra (6-8/14)
6936. Pomeroy, Jane, wf of Robert, d 4/28/31 in Canandaigua (6-5/11)
6937. Pomeroy, Joseph H. m 11/20/45 Arminda Brayton in Utica; Rev. D. W. Bristol; All of Utica (9-11/26)
6938. Pomeroy, Lemuel of Smyrna m "Thanksgiving Day" Mrs. E. A. Putnam, wid of Rev. S. G. Putnam late of Guilford, at the First Cong'l. Ch. in Guilford; Rev. J. L. James (Oxford Times, 12/15/41)
6939. Pomeroy, Josiah of Westfield m 5/15/50 Mrs. Phebe C. Hannum of Southampton in S (several family relationships resulting from this marriage are delineated in this release) (9-5/25)
6940. Pomeroy, Theodore (Dr.) of Utica, NY m 7/20/26 Cornelia Voorhees of New Brunswick, NJ in N. B.; Rev. Hardenburgh (9-11/7)
6941. Pomeroy, Theodore, Jr. m 6/11/45 Mary R. Dutton, dau of George; Rev. J. H. McIlvaine. All of Utica (9-6/12)
6942. Pomeroy, Theodore, 2, s of Thomas F. and Mary Ann, d 4/15/48 in Cleveland, OH (9-4/24)
6943. Pond, Edmund G. of Utica m 3/4/44 Caroline Yates, dau of Alexander, Esq. of Fultonville, in F; Rev. Dr. Andrew Yates (9-3/11)
6944. Pond, Erastus of Camden m 10/30/32 Serepta M. Stanton of Gorham in G (6-11/14)
6945. Pond, Ira of Camden m 10/28/46 Mrs. Elizabeth Burge of Utica in U; Rev. William H. Spencer (9-10/29)
6946. Pond, Mary Amelia, 1, dau of T. T. and S. M., d 6/3/34(?) in Utica (funeral from her parents' home, 246 Genesee St.) (9-6/4)
6947. Pond, Samuel C., 29, formerly of Utica, NY, d 8/5/45 in Lafayette, IN (9-8/16)
6948. Pond, Thomas Hart of Rome, NY m 7/22/45 Eleanor G. Fenton, dau of Amariah of Vernon, in V; Rev. Wayne Gridley of Clinton (9-7/24)
6949. Pool, James (Capt.), 91, (a Rev. soldier) formerly of Martha's Vineyard, MA, d 10/12/44 at the home of Elisha Pool in Kirkland, NY (9-11/18)
6950. Pool, Merinus m 6/19/44 Sarah Van Valkenburgh of Oriskany at the Franklin House (in Utica?); Rev. B. Hawley (9-6/22)
6951. Poole, Augustus of Beloit, WI m 9/20/47 Maria B. Manchester, dau of Otis of Utica, in U; Rev. W. H. Spencer (9-9/21)
6952. Poorman, Benjamin m 9/5/33 Roxey Hutchins, both of Phelps, in P (6-9/11)
6953. Porter, ____, only ch of Celow(?), d 2/15/47 in Baldwinsville (1-2/18)
6954. Porter, ____, 3 mo, ch of Orlon, d 8/16/48 (in Baldwinsville?)
6955. Porter, Abel, 93, (a Rev. soldier under Gen. Washington) d 1/21/50 in Sauquoit ("New York [City] papers please copy") (9-2/2)
6956. Porter, Augustus, 80, d 6/10/49 in Niagara Falls (one of the earliest settlers and a wealthy citizen of western NY) (9-6/13)
6957. Porter, Caroline Jermaine, 18, dau of Rev. Stephen and Cornelia, d 5/31/46 in Geneva (6-6/5)
6958. Porter, Charles S. (Rev.) of Plymouth, MA m 7/7/47 Louise Adams, only dau of Col. Samuel, in Derby, NH; Rev. Day (9-7/23)
6959. Porter, Charles W. m 1/9/32 Caroline Ward in Phelps (6-1/18)
6960. Porter, Elizabeth, 69, wf of Stephen, d 6/1/50 in Lee (9-6/6)
6961. Porter, Francis D., 49, d 3/3/50 in New Hartford (funeral from the home of his father, Noah Porter) (9-3/6)
6962. Porter, Jane E., wf of Charles S., pastor of First Presby. Ch. in Utica, d 12/7/43 in U (to be interred in Boston) (9-12/8)
6963. Porter, John C. (Rev.), 22, s of Giles M. of Albany, NY, d 10/20/30 in Washington Co., Mississippi (a deacon in Episc. Ch.) (9-12/7)

6964. Porter, Letitia, about 43, wf of Gen. Peter B., d 7/27/31 in Black Rock (6-8/3)
6965. Porter, Leyden of Skaneateles m 5/30/49 Harriet Herrick of Baldwinsville at the Meth. Ch. in B'ville; Rev. Squires (1-5/31)
6966. Porter, Orren, formerly a merchant in Norwich, m 10/15/29 Sarah Ann Steere, dau of Mark of Norwich, in N; Rev. E. S. Rexford (7-10/21 and 8-10/21)
6967. Porter, Orsan of Lysander m 12/8/47 Sabra S. Webster of Van Buren in Baldwinsville; Rev. B. Phillips (1-12/15)
6968. Porter, Peter B. of New York State m 10/16/18 Mrs. Leticia P. Grayson of KY, dau of late Hon. John Breckenridge (formerly Att'y. Gen'l. of U.S.) in Princeton, NJ by Pres. Smith (8-11/11)
6969. Porter, Ronana, 71, d 10/24/35 in Prattsburgh (6-11/11)
6970. Porter, Sarah C., 22, wf of Edwin W., d 1/17/48 in New Hartford (funeral from the Presby. Ch.) (9-1/19)
6971. Porter, Thomas (Hon.), 93, d in Granville (6-8/14/33)
6972. Porter, Thomas (Deacon), 56, son of Hon. Thomas, d in Granville (6-8/14/33)
6973. Porter, William, 52, d 6/21/41 in Stockbridge (3-7/7)
6974. Post, ____, 3 mo, ch of John, d 8/15/48 in Baldwinsville (1-8/16)
6975. Post, Henry W. of Chemung m 10/5/48 Mary Ann Hanna of Athens, PA at Sayer's Hotel in Elmira; Rev. H. Seaver (5-10/6)
6976. Post, Israel, book publisher, of NYC d 8/7/49 in Panama (whether country or town not given) (9-9/17)
6977. Post, Samuel H. m Elizabeth Hathaway in Palmyra (6-5/19/30)
6978. Potter, ____ of Seneca Falls m 3/12/33 Caroline Squier of Geneva in G; Rev. Phelps (6-3/27)
6979. Potter, A. S. m 1/15/48 Catharine Walsh in Utica; Rev. Dr. Proal. All of Utica (9-1/18)
6980. Potter, Alanson m 10/4/31 Nancy Johnson, both of Penn Yan, in Rushville (6-10/19)
6981. Potter, Alonzo, 18 mo, s of John, d 9/1/46 in Geneva (6-9/4)
6982. Potter, Bradford A., 58, d 2/22/50 in Corning (4-2/27)
6983. Potter, E. C. of Utica m 6/20/44 C. A. Clark of Lee at the Franklin House in Utica; Rev. B. Hawley (9-6/22)
6984. Potter, Edwin R., 17, s of John and Martha, d 3/19/48 in Baldwinsville (1-3/22)
6985. Potter, Elisha R. (Hon.) d 9/26/35 in South Kingston, RI (6-10/14)
6986. Potter, Eliza C. (Mrs.), 21, d 6/24/33 in Canandaigua (6-7/10)
6987. Potter, George of Rockport, OH m 10/1/50 Melissa C. Stetson of Waterville in W; Rev. Williams (9-10/4)
6988. Potter, H. C. (Dr.) m 11/23/47 Sarah A. Farwell, dau of Samuel, in Utica; Rev. William H. Spencer (double ceremony - see marr. of Dr. M. M. Bagg) (9-11/24)
6989. Potter, Horatio (Rev.), D.D., rector of St. Peter's Ch., Albany, m 9/26/49 Margaret Atcheson Podick (dau of Rev. John, D.D., minister, of Govan, Scotland) at Trinity Ch., NYC; Rt. Rev. Bishop Potter (9-9/29)
6990. Potter, John, 62, d 3/31/49 in Baldwinsville (1-4/5)
6991. Potter, Mary (Miss), 66, d 5/16/42 in Utica (funeral from the home of her bro, W. F. Potter, on Whitesboro St.) (9-5/16)
6992. Potter, Mary Jane, wf of Rev. Horatio Potter, D.D., (rector of St. Peter's Ch., Albany) d 6/8/47 in Schenectady (9-6/11)
6993. Potter, S. H. m 6/21/35 Amanda Washburn in hopewell (6-7/8)
6994. Potter, Sabra, 24, wf of Orson, d 8/31/50 in Baldwinsville (consumption) (1-9/5)
6995. Potter, Stephen of Fort Ann m 1/12/31 Charity Baker of Sandy Hill in S. H. (6-2/2)
6996. Potter, Tabor of Seneca Falls m 9/12/37 Mary N. Bradbury of Utica in Geneva (6-9/27)
6997. Potter, W. S. m 12/22/47 Cynthia N. Barber, both of Lee, at the Franklin House in Utica; Rev. D. C. Tomlinson of Richfield Springs (9-12/24)
6998. Potter, William m 1/21/41 Mary See in Erwin; Charles K. Miller, Esq. All of Erwin (4-1/29)
6999. Prall, William H. H., grand secretary, Grand Lodge of Northern NY, m 1/24/50 Martha Voganser of NYC in NYC; Rev. Dr. Hutton (9-1/28)
7000. Potter, William P., 64, d 1/25/50 in Utica (funeral from his late home, 120 Whitestown St.) (9-1/26)

7001. Powell, Archibald C. of Geneva m 8/8/37 Phebe Ann Davis, oldest dau of
       Harvey, Esq. of Schenectady, in S; Rev. Smedes (6-8/16)
7002. Powell, Charlotte, 38, wf of Philo, d 7/19/26 in Utica (9-7/25)
7003. Powell, Elizabeth, 84, wf of Jeremiah, d 7/8/43 in Whitestown (9-7/10)
7004. Powell, Emily, 24, consort of John and dau of Jared Patchen, d 7/16/26 in
       PennYan (9-8/8)
7005. Powell, John C., 35, s of late Thomas of Schenectady, d 7/16/35 in Albany
       (6-7/22)
7006. Powell, Thomas, 55, d 2/27/25 in Schenectady (9-3/8)
7007. Powell, Thomas, 23, s of late Thomas of Geneva, d 8/7/31 at sea on board
       the whaling ship "John and Edward" (6-9/7)
7008. Powell, Thomas C., formerly of Geneva, m 1/8/34 Mragaret R. Gallagher of
       Louisville, KY in L (6-1/29)
7009. Powell, William A., 14, only s of Liberty, d 3/17/44 in Whitestown
       (9-3/22)
7010. Power, Moses, Jr. m 8/29/33 Chloe Terrill (6-9/11)
7011. Powers, _____, 2, ch of Noah, d 9/2/36 in Geneva (6-9/7)
7012. Powers, Charles H. m 1/1/43 Caroline A. Preston, both of Corning, at
       Dean's Corners, Veteran, NY; Rev. Bullard (4-1/4)
7013. Powers, Edward m 9/18/48 Nancy A. Pugsley, both of Utica, in Herkimer;
       Rev. J. E. Dering (9-9/21)
7014. Powers, George, 15 mo, s of Ira, d 8/3/39 in Geneva (6-8/7)
7015. Powers, Gershom, Esq., late a member of Congress from Cayuga Co.,
       d 6/25/31 in Auburn (6-7/6)
7016. Powesland, George m 5/8/33 Mary Easterbrook; Rev. A. Yates, D.D. All of
       Chittenango (3-5/14)
7017. Powis, George m 2/27/34 Phebe Bockoven in Seneca Falls (6-3/12)
7018. Powls, Charles of Cayuga m 10/18/43 Jane Louisa Higham, oldest dau of
       Abraham, Esq. of Utica, in Geneva; Rev. Philip C. Hay (9-12/23)
7019. Pratt, _____ (Dr.) m 12/1/30 Julia Smith, both of Hopewell (6-12/8)
7020. Pratt, _____ (Dr.) of Palmyra m 1/10/33 Mary Boynton of Walworth (6-1/23)
7021. Pratt, Alison, 27, youngest s of Matthew, Esq. of Pratt's Hollow, Mad. Co.,
       NY d 3/5/47 in Milford, PA (9-3/13)
7022. Pratt, Alvin, 28, d in Tioga (6-7/31/33)
7023. Pratt, Cerinthia, d 6/27/41 in South Corning (4-7/9)
7024. Pratt, Edward Fitch of NYC m 6/17/50 Irene Lawrence, dau of Judge James R.
       of Syracuse, in S; Rev. James A. H. Cornell, D.D. (9-6/19 and 1-6/20)
7025. Pratt, Ethan (Rev.) of Horseheads m 7/8/34 Margaret Smith (in Elmira?)
       (6-7/16)
7026. Pratt, John W. of Fulton m 3/3/47 Harriet E. Slausen(?), dau of James,
       Esq. of Lysander, in L; Rev. Dunning (1-3/10)
7027. Pratt, Margaret (Mrs.) d in Elmira (6-8/9/37)
7028. Pratt, Milo m 9/24/45 Harriet L. Pond, youngest dau of Lewis, Esq. of
       Utica; Rev. William B. Hammond of Canton, MA (9-9/25)
7029. Pratt, Orsamus (sic) m 11/14/50 Eliza Corlett in Utica; Rev. M. A. Perry.
       All of U (9-11/16)
7030. Pratt, Sarah S., 31, wf of Orsamus (sic), d 4/9/49 in Utica (consumption)
       (9-4/14)
7031. Pratt, William m 10/26/33 Sarah Belemy in Penn Yan (6-11/6)
7032. Pratt, William m 9/25/45 Eliza P. Judson of Utica in U; Rev. D. G. Corey
       (9-9/27)
7033. Pratt, William H. (Brig. Gen.) of Deerfield m 2/4/44 Eliza Moulton, dau
       of David, Esq. of Floyd, in Holland Patent, NY; Rev. Marcus A. Perry
       (9-3/11)
7034. Predmore, Effe, 42, wf of Benjamin of Hector, d 6/29/33 (6-7/3)
7035. Prentice, David, Esq., attorney, of Bainbridge m Miss Willis of Franklin,
       Dela. Co. in F (8-7/8/18)
7036. Prentis, Margaret (Mrs.), 93, formerly of New London, CT, d 1/27/29 in
       Sherburne, NY (7-2/4)
7037. Prentiss, George W., 37, late partner and editor of the Oxford Republican,
       d 3/1/29 in Keene, NH (had been for the past 8 yrs jr. ed. of the New
       York Statesman) (8-3/18)
7038. Prentiss, J. G. m 10/11/35 Frances Rolo in Cortlandville (6-11/11)
7039. Prescott, Abraham, Jr., 37, d 12/19/45 in New Hartford (9-12/24)
7040. Prescott, O. (Deacon), 84, d 12/22/43 in New Hartford (9-12/28)

7041. Prescott, Samuel H. m 3/8/44 Hannah Claflin, both of Deerfield, in Utica; Rev. Quail (9-3/13)
7042. Prescott, William H. m 10/9/50 Frances B. Dolen of Elmira; Rev. W. Bement (double ceremony - see marr of Benjamin K. Emerson) (5-10/18)
7043. Prescott, Wright m 4/12/34 Mary Pantha in Vienna, NY (6-4/30)
7044. Pressley, Jeremiah, 66, d 3/30/34 in Geneva (6-4/2)
7045. Preston, Calvin, 84, (a Rev. pensioner) d 12/1/49 in North Gage (9-1213)
7046. Preston, Cahndler, 72, d 4/21/43 in Oxford (Oxford Republican, 5/4)
7047. Preston, Giles m 8/10/25 Clarinda Bugsbie in Oxford; Rev. Wells (8-8/17)
7048. Preston, Henry H. m 8/14/50 Roxana M. Skinner of Caseville; Rev. Charles (9-8/15)
7049. Preston, John C. m 3/23/48 Flora Blue in North Gage; Elder William Wells (9-4/11)
7050. Price, Abigail (Mrs.) d 8/30/30 in Lyons (8-9/15)
7051. Price, Ann, 66, wf of Ezekiel, d 8/20/32 in Geneva (an early settler in G) (6-8/22)
7052. Price, David m 8/2/33 Eliza Rowland, both of Chittenango; Rev. Davis of Utica (3-8/6)
7053. Price, George V. of NYC m 11/26/46 Evelina H. Hull of Brooklyn, formerly of Utica, in Brooklyn; Rev. F. A. Farley (9-12/10)
7054. Price, Hervey m 12/28/48 Rebecca M. Snyder, both of Chemung, in C; Rev. N. N. Beers (5-1/5/49)
7055. Price, John of New Jersey m Beula Ann Stiles of VT in Arcadia, NY (6-3/31/30)
7056. Price, John, 63, one of the judges of Ontario Co., d 5/10/37 in Hopewell (formerly a member of the State Constitutional Convention and formerly a state assemblyman from Ont. Co.) (6-5/17)
7057. Price, John C. m 6/11/35 Lucretia Vanderhoof in Phelps (6-6/24)
7058. Price, R. m Ruth Ann Crosby in Phelps (6-3/2/31)
7059. Price, Samuel m 1/1/34 Mary Ann Green in Geneva; Rev. John F. McLaren (6-1/15)
7060. Price, Virgil of Utica m 10/17/45 Lydia T. Fitch of Butler in B; Rev. Bragden (9-10/30)
7061. Price, William m 12/5/33 Margaret Haynes in Geneseo (6-12/18)
7062. Price, William G. (Rev. Hon.), 79, d 12/29/47 in Steuben (a minister there "upwards of 40 years") (9-12/30)
7063. Priest, William, about 50, d 6/11/31 (3-6/14)
7064. Prince, Frederick, 76, d 3/25/45 in Bridgewater (an early settler there - lived there nearly 50 yrs) (9-4/11)
7065. Prins(?), Joachim m Joanna Stuvering in NYC; Dr. T. De Witt (above printed in Dutch in the English-language newspaper) (9-6/22/50)
7066. Prindall, Norman m 1/10/31 Eunice Buck in Kingsbury (6-2/2)
7067. Prindle, Catherine d 7/20/37 in Geneva (6-7/26)
7068. Prindle, Lewis (Rev.), 25, d 6/21/34 in Hopewell (6-7/2)
7069. Prindol, Rebecca (Mrs.), 75, d 9/4/47 (in Lysander?) (1-9/8)
7070. Pritchard, Anna, 46, consort of Calvin, d 2/20/42 in Lawrenceville, PA (surv by husband and 9 ch) (4-3/9)
7071. Proal, Maria, wf of Rev. P. A. Proal, rector of Trinity Ch., d 6/13/39 in Utica (6-6/19)
7072. Proal, Samuel Livingston Breese, inf s of Rev. Dr. Proal, d 9/6/42 in Utica (funeral from Trinity Ch.) (9-9/7)
7073. Proal, William H., M.D., of Wappinger's Falls m 9/24/50 Ann Eliza Baldwin of Fishkill at Fishkill Landing; Rev. Dr. Proal, rector of Trinity Ch., Utica (9-9/27)
7074. Proalt, Joseph of Vienna, NY m 12/26/31 Charlotte Cleveland, dau of Moses of Canandaigua, in C (6-1/4/32)
7075. Probasco, Christian of Seneca m Julia Calkins of Phelps in Geneva (6-6/2/30)
7076. Probasco, George of Seneca m 1/2/34 Lucretia Trowbridge of Arcadia in Geneva; Rev. H. Mandeville (6-1/8)
7077. Pron, Joseph m 9/17/50 Rosetta Jaqua (sic); Rev. M. Crow. All of Elmira (5-9/27)
7078. Prosser, Isaac m 7/16/42 Diana Reis, both of Westernville, in Utica; Rev. Corey (9-7/18)

7079. Prouty, Margaret M., 34, consort of Phineas and youngest dau of late Rev. Nicholas Van Vranken of Fishkill, d 9/12/30 in Geneva (6-9/15)
7080. Provost, George W. of Victor m 5/1/31 Rebecca Lambright in Newark, NY (6-5/25)
7081. Pruden, Moses L. of Romulus m 5/12/35 Jane B. Hudson of Geneva; Rev. C. Coats (6-5/13)
7082. Pruyn, Francis H., Esq., 65, d 11/28/50 in Schuyler (9-12/6)
7083. Puffer, M. Lovell H. m 2/2/34 Maria E. Taylor, both of Bethel, in B; Rev. Phelps of Geneva (6-2/5)
7084. Pugh, Eleanor, 26, wf of Humphrey H., d 11/29/48 in Utica (funeral at her late home, Lansing St. near John St.; service at the Welsh Independent Ch., Hotel St.) (9-11/30)
7085. Pullen, Mary, wf of Jedediah, d 12/14/35 in Geneva (6-12/16)
7086. Pumpelly, John Charles, 25, only s of Charles Esq., d in Owego (6-2/24/30)
7087. Punches, Daniel m 11/15/33 Elizabeth Ward, both of Gorham, in Fayette; Joseph Hall, Jr., Esq. (6-11/20)
7088. Punderson, Charles, 24, only s of Deacon Punderson, d 11/23/13 in Oxford. Polly, 23, wf of Charles, d 11/24 in Oxford. Melissant, 18, dau of the Deacon, d 12/4 in Preston "where she was keeping school at time of her death". All died of typhus. Three of the children of Deacon and Polly survived their parents. (8-12/7)
7089. Punderson, John (Deacon), 89, d 1/12/36 in Macdonough (6-2/17)
7090. Punderson, Rhoda, 63, consort of Deacon John, d 5/31/24 in Macdonough (consumption) (8-6/10)
7091. Purcell, Eliza Bignal, 23, dau of William of Utica, d 7/6/48 in Honesdale, PA ("Schenectady papers please copy") (9-7/12)
7092. Purcell, Elizabeth, 44, wf of William and dau of John I. Clute of Schenectady, d 3/17/42 in Utica (funeral from the home of "Mr. Purcell" on Blandina St) (9-3/19)
7093. Purdy, Jennette Elizabeth, 1, only ch of Edward H., d 3/31/42 in Oxford (Oxford Times, 4/6)
7094. Purdy, Jeremiah, 81, (a Rev. soldier) d at his home in Hamilton (b in Westchester, NY in 1761; after Rev. settled in Duanesburgh after which he moved to Sherburne in 1795; member of Meth. Episc. Ch.) (Oxford Times, 8/17/42)
7095. Purse, Robert G. L. m 12/20/45 Martha Woodhouse of Lenox in Augusta; Robert J. Norris, Esq. (9-12/25)
7096. Purse, Sylvester m 9/19/47 Penelope Ward, both of Utica, in U; Rev. D. G. Corey (9-9/22)
7097. Pusey, Elwood T. of Philadelphia (state not given) m 5/25/48 Clara G. Lyman, dau of late Samuel of Springfield, MA, by the Friends (Quaker) ceremony in the presence of Mayor Swift (in Utica?) (9-5/30)
7098. Putnam, Charles Earl, 4, only s of George and Sarah M., d 3/17/47 in Waterville (9-3/19) (See entry 7101)
7099. Putnam, Daniel m 10/13/33 Laura Jolce(?) in Bethany (6-10/23)
7100. Putnam, Eri m 5/22/43 Martha Close in Greene, MI; Rev. J. B. Olcott (double ceremony - see marr of William Pierce) (9-5/31)
7101. Putnam, Mary Elizabeth, 2, dau of George and Sarah M., d 3/23/47 in Waterville ("membranous croup"). The only s of George and Sarah E. d 3/17 "of the same affliction" (See entry 7098)
7102. Putnam, Mary S., 31, wf of Rev. William, d 9/9/48 in Herkimer (9-9/18)
7103. Putnam, Washington, 49, one of the proprietors of Union Hall, d 4/1/49 in Saratoga Springs (9-4/6)
7104. Quackenboss, Isaac Henry, 1, only s of Isaac and Mary A., d 12/20/37 in Cananstota (3-12/27)
7105. Quackenbush, Elizabeth Gibbons, wf of Nicholas and dau of late James Gibbons, d 7/27/44 in Albany (9-8/3)
7106. Quackenbush, John, 22, d 4/13/41 in Sullivan (3-4/21)
7107. Quackenbush, Richard of Cicero m 7/26/40 Betsey Ehle of Sullivan; Rev. Switzer (3-7/29)
7108. Quail, William (Dr.) m 2/14/44 Ellen Lewis in Uniontown, PA; Rev. W. W. Arnett. All of Uniontown (9-2/23)
7109. Quick, J. W. V. m 3/28/39 Aurelia Morey, both of Phelps, in Geneva; Rev. McLaren (6-4/10)
7110. Quick, John m Francina M. Ribble in Athens, PA (6-11/10/30)

7111. Quigby, Thomas m 12/1/50 Sarah M. Smith in Beaver Dam Village; A. Beecher, Esq. (5-12/6)
7112. Quigley, James m Rosannah Reynolds in Fayette (6-3/3/30)
7113. Quimby, Squire M. of Jacksonville, PA m 4/10/48 Jane A. Fenton(?) of Rathboneville at the home of "Mr. Maxwell" in Knoxville, NY; Rev. J. T. Eaton (4-4/12)
7114. Quin, Edward, Esq. m Margaret Mary Kernan in Tyrone (6-1/19/31)
7115. Quin, John, 28, d 12/3/25 in Utica (9-12/6)
7116. Quine, Philip, Jr., 22, d in Rochester (6-1/26/31)
7117. Quinlan, Alfred F., printer, of Binghamton m 11/4/49 Henrietta Amelia Huntington, dau of Joseph, Esq. of Thompson, Sull. Co.; Rev. Bloomer (9-11/15)
7118. Rabee, John m 11/4/49 Persis M. Phettiplace in Lysander; Rev. J. C. Seward. All of Lysander. (1-11/15)
7119. Race, Catharine, 15 mo, d 12/14; Emeline, 5, d 12/16; and Marsden, 4, d 12/17. All are ch of Whiting Race and all died in Seneca Falls (6-12/23)
7120. Race, Derrick m 9/15/42 Harriet M. Symonds, both of Oxford; Rev. Arthur Burtis (double ceremony - see marr of Samuel Kinney, Jr.) (Oxford Times, 9/21)
7121. Rafferty, William (Rev.), D.D., 52, pres. of St. John's College in Annapolis (MD) and formerly pastor of Presby. Ch., Blooming Grove, Orange Co., NY, d 8/8/30 in Blooming Grove (6-8/25)
7122. Ralph, William m 5/15/44 Jane Johnson, both of Utica, in U; Rev. Corey (9-5/17)
7123. Ramsey, _____, 15 mo, ch of William, d 7/22/32 in Chittenango (3-7/31)
7124. Rand, Asa (Rev.) of Boston, MA m Mary Coolidge in Ashburnham, MA; Rev. Perkins (9-7/25/26)
7125. Rand, Clarissa, 33, wf of Rev. Asa, late editor of the Christian Mirror, d in Portland, ME (9-7/26/25)
7126. Randal, Elizabeth, wf of Jirah, Esq., d 4/14 in Sullivan (3-4/26)
7127. Randal, Nathaniel, 87, d 1/28/31 in Bristol (was a soldier in the old French and Rev. wars) (6-2/9)
7128. Randall, Adelaide Rosabel, 1, dau of R., d 5/21/44 in Lenox Hill (scarlet fever) (3-5/29)
7129. Randall, B. F. (Mr.), 27, d 5/9/44 in Lenox Hill (3-5/15)
7130. Randall, Elias H. m 5/30/30 Eunice B. Weaver, dau of Gen. Lodowick Weaver, Jr., in Norwich; H. Crain, Esq. All of Norwich (7-6/9)
7131. Randall, Isaac M., 7, s of Lewis, d 4/515/34 in Milo (6-4/30)
7132. Randall, Jane, 25, wf of Anthony and adopted dau of Alexander and Nancy Stewart, d 5/2/48 in Winfield (9-5/9)
7133. Randall, John (Capt.) d 10/28/18 in Norwich (7-10/29 and 8-11/11)
7134. Randall, Lucy Ann, 25, consort of Samuel S., d 5/15/30 in Norwich (7-5/19)
7135. Randall, Nathan, editor of the Pulaski Banner, m 5/4/31 Catharine Monell, dau of Hon. Robert of Greene, in G (6-5/25)
7136. Randall, Nicholas P., Esq., 57, attorney, d 3/6/36 in Manlius (3-3/16)
7137. Randall, Orman m 2/26/24 Esther Stafford in Oxford; Elder Randall (8-3/3)
7138. Randall, Orson m 9/22/33 Laura Gilbert in Milo (6-10/9)
7139. Randall, Sally (Mrs.), 40, d 7/18/36 in Milo (6-8/10)
7140. Randall, Samuel d 3/9/36 in Penn Yan (6-3/30)
7141. Randall, Samuel S. m 10/29/29 Lucy Ann Breed, both of Norwich, in N; Rev. Jedediah Randall (7-11/4)
7142. Randall, Warren m 1/11/44 Catherine Betsinger, both of Clockville, in Chittenango; Jairus French, Esq. (3-1/24)
7143. Randel, William, merchant, of Hammondsport m 11/22/35 Hannah Reed in Urbana (6-12/2)
7144. Raney, Thomas, 19, d 2/13/34 in Geneva (6-2/19)
7145. Ranney, Abner, 100, d 9/1/47 in Augusta leaving 9 ch, 87 gr-ch., and 80 gr-gr-ch (9-9/23)
7146. Ransford, James L., 2, s of J. L. and Biancy, d 8/10/47 in Utica (funeral at 68 Liberty St.) (9-8/11)
7147. Ransier, John J., 72, d 1/2/38 in Chittenango (3-1/17)
7148. Ransom, Asa (Col.), 74, d 3/11/35 in Ransom's Grove, town of Clarence (6-4/1)
7149. Ransom(?), David, adult, d 12/3/50 in Utica (funeral at ----'s Temperance Hotel (---- is possibly "Madison's") (9-12/4)

7150. Ransom, Jane, 30, wf of John P. formerly of Herkimer County, d 3/23/49 in Montalona, IL (9-4/19)
7151. Ransom, Joel L., 60, d 8/17/30 in Seneca (6-8/25)
7152. Ransom, John of Lawrenceville, PA m 5/29/49 Sarah Andrus of Elmira, NY; Rev. A. M. Ball (5-6/1)
7153. Ransom, Thomas, Jr. m Mehitable Handy in Salisbury (6-3/31/30)
7154. Raplee, Hiram m Ann Headley in Penn Yan (6-5/19/30)
7155. Raplee, John T. m 5/14/33 Caroline Hathaway in Milo (6-5/29)
7156. Rapp, James A. of Taberg m 9/8/50 Martha J. Potter of Floyd; Rev. James Erwin (9-9/12)
7157. Rash, Jeremiah, 33, d 9/14/31 in Seneca (6-9/21)
7158. Rathbone, Elijah (Col.), 56, d 6/21/49 in Greene (9-6/29)
7159. Rathbone, Justus H., attorney, m 5/31/26 Sarah Dwight, both of Utica; Rev. Aiken (9-6/6)
7160. Rathbun, Eunice (Mrs.), 50, d 6/14/33 in Howard (6-7/3)
7161. Rathbun, Israel of Lewiston m Lucy Gansom in Le Roy (8-1/31/21)
7162. Rathburn, Edward m Ann Huffman in Auburn (6-9/29/30)
7163. Rawson, Philo, merchant, of Geneseo m Charlotte I. Dobbin of Canandaigua in C (6-1/4/32)
7164. Ray, Benjamin F., Esq. m 9/10/50 Susan Alida Trowbridge, oldest dau of Artemas, Esq. of Camden,at Trinity Ch., Camden; Rev. Albert P. Smith, rector, St. Peter's Ch., Cazenovia (9-9/12)
7165. Ray, Gershom m 5/11/44 "Mrs. Mowers", both of Lenox Hill, in L. H.; Rev. L. H. Stanley of Perryville (3-5/22)
7166. Ray, Jane R., wf of William H. and dau of late Grove Cunningham, d 10/27/48 in Rushville, IL (9-11/10)
7167. Ray, Polly (Mrs.) d 12/11/35 in Sullivan (3-12/15)
7168. Ray, Samuel m 3/6/32 Caroline Spoor, both of Phelps, in Manchester; J. Schutt, Esq. (6-4/11)
7169. Ray, Theodore S., 22, formerly of Utica, NY, d 11/8/45 in Rushville, IL (9-11/24)
7170. Ray, William (Maj.), 54, d 7/30/26 in Auburn (had been a prisoner in Tripoli) (surv by wf and 3 daus) (9-8/8)
7171. Ray, William m 2/17/35 Polly Daharsh in Sullivan; J. French, Esq. (3-2/24)
7172. Raymond, ____, wf of Ebenezer,d in Penn Yan (6-3/31/30)
7173. Raymond, Cyrus of Penn Yan m 6/20/33 Lorena Dickinson of Cameron in C (6-7/3)
7174. Raymond, Daniel m Maria Woodworth in Le Roy (6-1/26/31)
7175. Raymond, Frances J., wf of Dr. D. W. and dau of Dr. L. L. Chester formerly of Westmoreland, NY, d 12/4/48 in Conneaut, OH (9-12/16)
7176. Raymond, R. H. of Cedarville m 7/4/49 Julia A. Swift, dau of Ichabod of Lockport, in Richfield; Rev. M. Lawton (9-7/9)
7177. Raymond, Sarah (Mrs.), 31, d in Canandaigua (6-2/2/31)
7178. Rea, James m 8/28/50 Melissa Penner in Sauquoit; Rev. John Waugh (9-9/9)
7179. Read, Daniel of Mississippi, late of Deerfield, NY, m 9/1/46 Amida Whaton in Deerfield; Elder A. F. Rockwell (9-9/12)
7180. Read, Edwin m 10/3/44 Nancy Wamp in New Hartford; Henry Sherrill, Esq. (9-10/9)
7181. Record, Peter J. (Dr.), 20, d 7/28/32 in NYC (consumption) (6-8/8)
7182. Redfield, Beriah m 1/26/34 Cornelia Parkenson in Marengo (6-2/12)
7183. Redfield, George of St. Joseph's, MI m Julia Ann Mason in Palmyra (6-6/24/35)
7184. Redfield, Silas, 54, d 7/20/39 in West Vienna, NY (6-7/31)
7185. Redfield, William m 12/11/33 Mary Scott in Avon (6-12/25)
7186. Redman, Mary, 70, relict of Michael, d 9/17/30 in Seneca (6-9/29)
7187. Redman, Michael, 67, a native of Ireland, d 9/5/30 in Geneva (6-9/8)
7188. Redmond, John, 60, a native of County Wexford, Ireland, d 5/10/45 in Utica (9-5/15)
7189. Redner(?), Peter, 52, d 7/20/46 in Hector (6-8/7)
7190. Reed, Alfred, one of the proprietors of the Penn Yan Democrat, m 2/22/36 Mary Ann Briggs of Benton in B (6-2/24)
7191. Reed, Andrew, 73, d 7/2/50 in Skaneateles (1-7/11)
7192. Reed, Arnold D. of Bath m 8/20/34 Martha Germond of Erwin in Bath (6-9/3)
7193. Reed, Charles H. of Sharon, CT m 7/2/34 Tryphena L. Walker of Seneca Falls in Waterloo (6-7/16)
7194. Reed, Daniel, 71, d in Tonowanda (6-3/23/31)

7195. Reed, David, 26, d 4/2/33 in Hopewell (6-4/24)
7196. Reed, Elizabeth, 49, wf of Robert, d 8/2/30 in Phelps (6-8/11)
7197. Reed, Ira L. m 7/17/44 Harriet E. Tower, both of Springfield, at Griffin's Hotel in Utica; Rev. E. S. Barrows (9-7/18)
7198. Reed, John, 91, d 8/22/33 in Seneca (father of Messrs. Nathan and Josiah and one of the oldest settlers in Seneca (6-8/28)
7199. Reed, John S. of Geneva m 5/3/37 Jane Elizabeth Terek of Lancaster in L; Rev. William Shelton of Buffalo (6-5/10)
7200. Reed, Lathrop B. m 8/16/36 Elice Gooden in Victor (6-9/14)
7201. Reed, Margaret, 15, dau of Seneca, d 5/10/32 in Brighton, Monroe Co. (6-5/23)
7202. Reed, Philo m 10/20/46 Cynthia E. Small, adopted dau of G. H. Feeter, Esq., in Little Falls (9-11/30)
7203. Reed, Riley of Farmington m 3/16/36 Caroline Jackson of Walworth (6-3/23)
7204. Reed, Sally (Mrs.), 36, wf of Romeo late of Ithaca and dau of Samuel and Mary Parcel, d 12/14/40 near Corning (4-1/1/41)
7205. Reed, Silas, 75, one of the first settlers in Gorham, d in G (6-11/27/33)
7206. Reed, Susan, 48, wf of Dr. Reed, rector of Christ's Ch., d 8/21/32 in Poughkeepsie (6-9/12)
7207. Reed, Tabitha, 63, d in Manchester (6-7/28/30)
7208. Reed, Thomas J. m 12/23/34 Eliza Chase in Phelps (6-1/14/35)
7209. Reed, Towner m 2/5/33 Hannah Striker, both of Gorham, in Geneva; Rev. Mandeville (6-2/6)
7210. Reed, Vincent m 5/29/32 Bethiah Reed, dau of Capt. Nathan, in Seneca; Rev. Phelps (double ceremony - see marr of Peter Drake) (6-5/30)
7211. Reed, William B. (Dr.), 34, of Amherst, MA d 12/5/46 in Sangerfield (9-12/10)
7212. Reeder, Coe S. m 1/16/33 Perlina Booth in Starkey (6-1/30)
7213. Reeder, Sylvester d 4/29/34 in Starkey (6-5/14)
7214. Reels, James of Manlius m 12/9/38 Maria Truax of Sullivan in S; J. French, Esq. (3-12/12)
7215. Rees, Charles W. m 1/8/32 Catharine Hallett, dau of Hon. Jacob W., at Trinity ch. in Geneva; Rev. Dr. Bruce (double ceremony - see marr of Charles A. Rose) (6-1/11)
7216. Rees, Evin of Clay m 2/1/49 Emily Cornell of Van Buren in V. B.; Rev. Ira Dudley (1-2/1)
7217. Rees, Gillet m 1/8/24 Druzilla O'Brien in Sherburne; Rev. Kendrick (8-1/14)
7218. Rees, John m 11/21/38 Alma Harris in Rochester; Rev. Abel. All of Rochester (6-11/28)
7219. Rees, Mary Grace, 1, dau of Evan J. and Jane C., d 11/21/46 in Utica (9-11/24)
7220. Rees, Thomas Morris, 27, s of James of Geneva, NY, d 3/29/36 in Grand Gulf, Mississippi (6-5/18)
7221. Reeve, James of Waterloo m 4/15/35 Hannah M. Randall of Middle Island, Brookhaven, L.I., NY (6-5/6)
7222. Reeve, Tappan, 79, formerly Chief Justice of CT, d in Litchfield, CT (8-12/31/23)
7223. Reeves, James m 9/24/35 Caroline Sandford, dau of Luther; Rev. Merrit. All of Palmyra (6-10/14)
7224. Reeves, John m 3/24/35 Mary Doolittle, both of Livonia, in L (6-4/8)
7225. Refer, Henry H. m Mary Ann Cable (in Waterloo?) (6-1/14/35)
7226. Reid, George I. of Smithville m 10/11/43 Louisa Tillotsen of Oxford in O; Rev. J. T. Goodrich (Oxford Republican, 10/12)
7227. Reid, Jasper, 41, d in Canandaigua (6-7/7/30)
7228. Reid, John, merchant, of Albany d 8/31/21 in Saratoga Springs (suicide by hanging) (8-9/5)
7229. Reid, John, about 80, (a Rev. soldier) d 1/27/33 in Canandaigua (6-2/6)
7230. Reid, Moses m 4/21/30 Harriet Squire in Seneca; Rev. Nisbet (6-4/28)
7231. Reid, Robert m Sally Culverson in Canandaigua (6-3/24/30)
7232. Reiggles, Catharine, 25, wf of Daniel R. and dau of Henry Freshour, d 8/30/31 in Geneva (6-8/31)
7233. Relick, William of Rochester m 11/15/42 Cornelia Buckland of Hartford, CT in Syracuse, NY; Rev. Adams (9-11/17)
7234. Remer, Abraham V. of Dresden m 2/29/32 Sarah A. Olney of Benton in B (6-3/14)

7235. Remer, Abraham, 39, d 9/22/32 in Benton (6-10/10)
7236. Remer, Arabella, wf of George I., d "last week" in Milo (6-2/24/36)
7237. Remington, David and Henry Whitman d 10/29/25 in Weedsport (both killed
    by the accidental discharge of a 24-punder while they were acting as
    gunners at the Canal celebration - "both have left young families")
                    (Note: Erie Canal was opened full-length 26 Oct 1825)
    (9-11/22)
7238. Remington, Hannah S., 27, wf of John Y. and dau of Leverett Seymour of
    Westmoreland, d 12/8/47 in Oriskany (9-12/18)
7239. Remington, J. L. of NYC m 8/29/47 Agnes Haliburton of Montreal, Canada
    in Yorkville, NY; Rev. J. D. Cole (9-8/31)
7240. Remington, Jonas I., 26, (b in Whitestown) d 6/4/49 in NYC (9-6/8)
7241. Renwick, John, late editor of the Penn Yan Enquirer, d 9/6/32 in
    Beardstown, IL (6-9/19)
7242. Rew, Frederick A., Esq. of Newark, NY m 8/19/33 Sarah Adams Stow, dau of
    Joseph, in Geneva (6-9/25)
7243. Rexford, Hannah H., wf of Levi of Binghamton, d 6/26/47 in B (9-7/3)
7244. Reynear, William, 83, d 7/7/36 in Manchester (6-7/13)
7245. Reynolds, Abram m Desire Burch in Junius (6-2/24/30)
7246. Reynolds, Elisha of Pompey m 9/5/35 Amanda Priest of Sullivan in S; J.
    French, Esq. (3-9/8)
7247. Reynolds, Ephraim R., 24, d 11.26.41 in Lenox (3-12/1)
7248. Reynolds, Hector Seward, 16 mo, s of S. H. and Emily, d 8/14/49 in Elmira
    (5-8/17)
7249. Reynolds, Hiram, merchant, of Sodus m 3/27/33 Laura L. Houghteling, dau
    of Dr. James, in Geneva; Rev. Dr. Mason (6-4/3)
7250. Reynolds, Isaac H. of NYC m 1/30/49 Mary Jane Chapman, dau of Hon. Hiram
    of Reading, in R; Rev. Sheardown (5-2/2)
7251. Reynolds, Isabell, 2 mo, dau of William H. and Rosetta, d 9/19/48 in
    Elmira (5-10/13)
7252. Reynolds, J. (Mr.), 46, d 6/7/36 (in Elmira?) (6-6/15)
7253. Reynolds, James, 68, "for many years a resident of Geneva" d 8/20/31 in
    Pittsburgh, PA (6-8/31)
7254. Reynolds, John, 30, d in Big Flat (6-1/19/31)
7255. Reynolds, Joseph m 2/5/30 Rebecca Thompson in Geneva; Rev. Goff (6-2/17)
7256. Reynolds, Margaret, 50, wf of Richard, d 1/26/34 in Chittenango (3-1/28)
7257. Reynolds, Noah m 1/10/36 Phebe Ostrander, both of Phelps, in P (6-1/13)
7258. Reynolds, Rosetta, 21, wf of William H. and dau of James Mattocks of
    Springfield, PA, d 10/4/48 in Elmira, NY (5-10/13)
7259. Reynolds, W. W., 40, d 10/7/48 in Big Flats (4-10/13 and 10/18)
7260. Reynolds, William H. m 2/15/49 Jane Ann Schuyler in Elmira; Rev. H. N.
    Seaver. All of Elmira (5-2/16)
7261. Rezeau, Andrew M., 29, (b in Utica) d 3/24/50 in New Orleans, LA (9-4/6)
7262. Rhines, Isaac m 3/23/48 Maria Milner at Central Hotel in Utica; Rev. H. R.
    Clarke. All of New Hartford (9-3/25)
7263. Rhoades, Porter m 11/19/46 "Miss Sherman" in Skaneateles; Rev. S. W. Bush.
    All of Skaneateles (1-12/7)
7264. Rhoades, Sumner (Dr.) of Elmira m 2/19/45 Susan Cordelia Prentice, oldest
    dau of Prof. D. Prentice of Geneva College, at Trinity Ch., Geneva; Rev.
    Samuel Cooke (9-2/28)
7265. Rhoads, Daniel (Col.), 65, formerly a member of the state legislature
    from Seneca Co., d 12/27/34 in Lockport, NY (b in Northumberland, PA)
    (6-12/31)
7266. Rhodes, Anthony (a Rev. soldier) d 5/25/45 at the home of his gr-son,
    Anthony R. Randall, in Winfield (emigrated from RI in 1793 to Bridgewater,
    NY; fought in War of 1812) (9-7/16)
7267. Rhodes, Charles, Esq. of Pulaski m 5/21/45 Algenia Knox, dau of Gen. John
    J., in Augusta; Rev. O. Bartholomew (9-5/24)
7268. Rhodes, Isaac, 19, d 2/21/50 in Corning (4-2/27)
7269. Rhodes, William m Trifena White in Ovid (6-2/24/30)
7270. Rice, _____, 10 mo, ch of Cornelius, d 4/5/30 in Geneva (6-4/7)
7271. Rice, Combs D. of Whitesboro m 11/27/26 AnnHiggins of Albany in A (9-12/5)
7272. Rice, Eleazer m 4/17/36 Amanda Hutchinson in Cazenovia; Jairus French, Esq.
    (3-5/18)

7273. Rice, H. M., Esq. of Minnesota Terr. m 3/20/49 Matilda Whitall, dau of
      B. G., in White Plains, Henrico Co., VA; Rev. Kepler (9-4/12)
7274. Rice, Jane, 21, wf of Stephen, d 4/12/35 in Penn Yan (6-4/15)
7275. Rice, John (Capt.), 61, d in Canandaigua (6-11/6/33)
7276. Rice, John m 2/11/36 Jennett McCauley in Seneca (6-2/17)
7277. Rice, John H. (Rev.), D.D., 64, pres. of Union Theological Seminary in
      Virginia, d 9/3/31 in Richmond, VA (6-9/28)
7278. Rice, Luther (Rev.) of Weathersfield, VT m 5/25/45 Mary Skinner of
      Brownville, NY in Watertown, NY (6-9/6)
7279. Rice, Mandrack of Pompey m 5/6/38 Diana Van Wie of Chittenango in C;
      Rev. J. Abell (3-5/9)
7280. Rice, Morris of NYC m 4/6/42 Margaret L. Lundegreen of Utica in U; Rev.
      P. A. Proal (9-4/7)
7281. Rice, Morris, 28, d 10/7/45 in Utica (9-10/10)
7282. Rice Nelson of Port Byron m 2/28/49 Mary H. Potter, dau of Hiram of Elmira,
      in E; Rev. P. H. Fowler (5-3/2)
7283. Rice, Samuel W., s of Jason, 24, s of Jason and Asia, d 6/3/46 in
      Trenton, NY (9-6/10)
7284. Rice, Selina, 36, wid of late Asa, Esq., d 10/21/25 in Lockport (9-10/25)
7285. Rice, Stephen (Maj.) m 1/30/33 Jane Bates in Benton (6-2/13)
7286. *Rice, Thomas of Syracuse m 9/2/46 Mary A. Dorsey, dau of Upton of Geneva*
7287. Rice, Thomas G., Esq. of Boston (state not given) m 7/31/50 Ellen
      Collamer, dau of Hon. J., in Washington, D.C. (9-8/7)
7288. Rice, Tyrus, 78, d 11/18/47 in Salisbury (9-12/1)
7289. Rice, Zalmon, 14, d in Lyons (6-2/14/38)
7290. Rich, David m 10/13/35 Polly Waldron in Hector (6-10/28)
7291. Rich, Nelson m Maria Rich in Waterloo (6-10/6/30)
7292. Rich, Tracy G., merchant, of East Franklin m 7/10/44 Esther Stoddard, dau
      of William of Delhi; Rev. James McEwan (Oxford Republican, 7/18)
7293. Richards, ____, consort of Col. Daniel, d 3/11/26 in Richfield (9-3/21)
7294. Richards, B. m M. Burkite in Waterloo (6-2/17/30)
7295. Richards, Daniel m 6/3/46 Sarah Cornelia Goff of Geneva; Rev. F. G.
      Hibbard (6-6/5)
7296. Richards, Edward m 2/6/50 Sarah Davis; Rev. H. S. Dickson. All of Utica
      (9-2/9)
7297. Richards, Horace M., formerly of Utica, m 1/31/44 Harriet W. Beers, oldest
      dau of A. S., Esq. of Rochester, in R (9-2/9)
7298. Richards, James, Jr. (Rev.) m 8/25/36 Elizabeth Beals, dau of T., Esq.,
      in Canandaigua (6-9/7)
7299. Richards, Jerry of Kelloggsville m Helmenia Rosaline Hopkins, dau of Dr.
      J. B. of Skaneateles in S (6-11/7/32)
7300. Richards, Mary, 50, wf of John, d 4/19/50 in Utica (funeral from her late
      home, 80 Whitesboro St.) (9-4/20)
7301. Richards, Mary Ann, consort of Owen, d 9/28/44 at the home of her husband,
      corner John and Blandina Sts., Utica) (9-9/30)
7302. Richards, Stephen A. m 8/23/46 Charlotte Flint, dau of Charles, Esq., in
      Utica (9-8/24)
7303. Richardson, A. J. m 1/30/48 Floretta A. Abell in New London; Rev. Josiah
      Arnold (9-2/26)
7304. Richardson, A. L. (Lt.) of U.S. Army m 9/20/30 Sylvia R. Porter in
      Pittsford (6-9/2())
7305. Richardson, David of Rochester m 5/11/31 Emeline E. Carter of Buffalo
      6-5/25)
7306. Richardson, George m "Thanksgiving Day" Jennette Cryne in Westmoreland;
      Rev. F. A. Spencer. All of Westmoreland (9-12/2/47)
7307. Richardson, Helen M., 44, wf of Thomas formerly of Utica, d 3/12/47 in
      Almond (9-3/17)
7308. Richardson, Israel B. (Maj.) of U.S. Army, s of Israel B. of Burlington,
      m 8/3/50 Senorita Rita Stevenson of El Paso, TX at the Cathedral in
      El Paso; Curate Orbs(?) (5-12/6)
7309. Richardson, John of Urbana m 2/27/33 Sarah Oxx of Howard in H (6-3/13)
7310. Richardson, John B. (Rev.) of Salem, CT m Martha Bronson "of this
      neighborhood" (Geneva) 5/21/32 in Seneca; Rev. Phelps (6-5/23)
7311. Richardson, Joseph Henry, 8 mo, only s of Joseph P. and Hannah, d 3/21/43
      in New Hartford (9-4/7)
* 7286 addenda - Rev. Williams officiating. (6-9/4)

7312. Richardson, Marcia, 29, wf of J. B. of Pittsford, d 9/4/34 at the home of her father, Philo Bronson, Esq., in Geneva (6-9/10)

7313. Richardson, William P. (Dr.), 44, d 2/23/33 in Macedon (6-3/13)

7314. Richmond, _____, 2, dau of "Mr. N. Richmond", d 5/28/41 in Morrisville (3-6/16)

7315. Richmond, Gardner of Augusta m 2/9/31 Almira M. Foot, dau of Adonijah of Vernon, in V; Rev. A Garrison (9-2/15)

7316. Richmond, James M. m 6/27/50 Harriet A. Blakeman in Utica; Rev. William H. Spencer. All of Utica (9-6/29)

7317. Ricknell, Bennet, Esq, 59, d 9/16/41 at his home in Morrisville (b in Mansfield, CT; moved to Morrisville in 1808; served sequentially as assemblyman and senator in NY and later as county clerk and Congressman) (3-9/29)

7318. Riddle, David, Esq. d in Owego (6-6/26/33)

7319. Riddle, Robert, Esq. m 10/29/33 Phebe Sunderland in New Brunswick, NJ (both formerly of Chittenango, NY)(3-11/5)

7320. Riddle, Sophia, 34 or 54, wf of Thomas, Esq., d 2/3/37 in Sullivan (3-2/8)

7321. Riddle, Thompson of Chittenango m 3/14/38 A. Selene Livermore from Worcester Co., MA in Chittenango; Rev. J. Abel (3-3/21)

7322. Rider, Henry C. of Camillus m 8/15/49 Janett Schuyler of Canton in C; Rev. L. C. Bates (3-8/23)

7323. Riggs, Stephen S., editor of the Schenectady Cabinet, m 11/24/31 Julia Hannin of Schoharie in S (6-12/14)

7324. Rigler, James m 12/29/41 Harriet K. Smith in Binghamton; Rev. Gregory. All of B (2-1/5/42)

7325. Rigley, Charles m 9/25/50 Mary C. Shoemaker in Herkimer; Rev. S. C. Mead. All of Herkimer (9-9/27)

7326. Riley, Eleanor D., 27, oldest dau of Rev. Lawrence Riley, d 4/2/35 in Lyons (consumption) (6-4/8)

7327. Rindge, Isaac of Geneva m 10/23/34 Abigail Dexter of Ithaca in I; Rev. Alexander Mann (6-10/29)

7328. Rindge, Isaac, 46, formerly of Geneva, d 9/24/50 at the State Lunatic Asylum in Utica (funeral from the home of Elisha Wells, Esq., 197 Genesee St.) (9-9/25)

7329. Ring, Elam, 54, d 4/22/26 in Ellisburgh (9-5/9)

7330. Ringer, Elizabeth (Mrs.), 36, d 7/1/46 in Seneca (6-7?17)

7331. Ringer, Jacob, 77, d 4/12/32 in Seneca (b in Maryland but for many years a resident of Seneca) (6-4/8)

7332. Ringgold, Tench, Esq. d 7/31/44 at his home in Washington, D.C. (9-8/7)

7333. Ripley, Fanny (Mrs.), 62, sister of Mrs. L. Morgan, d 6/14/48 in Utica (funeral in the home of Mr. L. Morgan on Columbia St.) (9-6/15)

7334. Ripley, Laura (Miss), 16, d 9/1/36 in Hammondsport (6-9/14)

7335. Rippey, Thomas m 4/18/39 Martha Carson, both of Seneca, in S; Rev. J. F. McLaren (6-4/24)

7336. Rising, Lucinda, 50, wf of John, d 4/3/48 in Reading, Hillsdale Co., MI (formerly a resident for many years of Westmoreland, NY) (9-5/20)

7337. Risley, Cynthia, 76, relict of late David, d 5/26/45 in New Hartford (9-6/11)

7338. Risley, George W. of Utica m 1/5/50 Amanda C. Curtiss of Sauquoit in S. Rev. Rowe (9-2/7)

7339. Risley, Richard, 95, (a Rev. soldier) d 12/29/48 in New Haven, NY (b in East Hartford, CT in 1754; lived in New Haven, NY, 1828-1838) (9-2/16/49)

7340. Ritchie, George, Jr., 28, printer, d 8/5/31 in Schenectady (3-8/16)

7341. Rixford, Augustus B. m 11/20/31 Mary Lawrence, both of Seneca Falls, in S. F. (6-11/30)

7342. Rizer, William N. m 7/1/49 Sally Denmark, both of Elmira; Rev. J. Hall (5-7/6)

7343. Roach, Thomas of Utica m 1/16/43 Nancy Maria Vroman of Middlesex in St. Johnsville; Rev. A. H. Myers (9-1/25)

7344. Robbins, A. D. m 9/20/46 Betsey Olmsted in Phelps (6-9/25)

7345. Robbins, Ephraim L., 34, d 2/25/47 (in UticA?) (9-2/26)

7346. Robbins, Hannah (Mrs.), 78, mother-in-law of John Baxter, d 4/27/46 in Utica (funeral from her husband's home, 234 Genesee St.) (9-4/28)

7347. Robbins, Henry C. m 7/15/30 Jerusha B. Kinney in Penn Yan (6-7/28)
7348. Robbins, Jacob m 7/17/45 Alma A. Gould, both of Little Falls, in L. F.;
       A. Beardslee, Esq. (9-7/29)
7349. Robbins, John, 83, d 7/25/49 in Campbell (lived in Steuben Co. 31 yrs)
       (4-8/8)
7350. Robbins, Martha (Mrs.), 72, d 6/20/50 at her home in New Hartford (9-7/1)
7351. Robbins, Nelson B. m 11/23/45 Mary J. Averill at the Meth. Ch. in Utica:
       Rev. D. W. Bristol. All of Utica (9-11/24/45)
7352. Robbins, Robert Chauncey, a preacher of the gospel and son of the late
       Rev. Robbins of Colchester, CT, d "recently" in Darien, GA (educated at
       Williamstown Col. and Andover Theological Seminary) (9-7/26/25)
7353. Robbins, Russell m 2/3/48 Harriet Merrell in Geneva; Rev. Hogarth. All
       of Geneva (9-2/11/48)
7354. Robbins, William Edward, 5, s of Russell, d 12/20/33 in Geneva (6-1/1/34)
7355. Roberts, Alvah (Mrs.), about 50, d 5/11/44 in Jenner (3-5/15)
7356. Roberts, Daniel m 10/25/36 Hannah Hurd, both of Varick; Richard Hogarth,
       Esq. (6-12/7)
7357. Roberts, Daniel R., 45, (also known as the "Welch Doctor") d 9/14/20 at
       his home in steuben, NY (born in Wales; surv by wf and 3 ch) (8-9/27)
7358. Roberts, Edward, 22, d 1/16/46 in Utica (9-1/19)
7359. Roberts, Eliakim, 63, d 5/16/32 in Cazenovia (3-5/22)
7360. Roberts, Elizabeth, 15 mo, dau of G. G., d 5/31/47 in Utica (funeral from
       her father's home, 69 Bleecker St.) (9-6/1)
7361. Roberts, Euman T. of Westmoreland m 1/5/43 Mary E. Earlet of Rome, NY in
       R; Rev. I. Edgerton (9-1/13)
7362. Roberts, H. H. of Utica m 9/15/47 Almira J. French, dau of John of New
       Hartford, in New H.; Rev. D. G. Corey (9-9/22)
7363. Roberts, Henry m 9/15/42 Sarah Marsh in Colesville (2-9/28)
7364. Roberts, James m 3/7/35 Abigail Hawley (in Elmira?) (6-3/25)
7365. Roberts, John, 50, d in Utica (9-12/5/26)
7366. Roberts, John m Mary Ann Mills of Middletown, Dela. Co. (6-1/26/31)
7367. Roberts, Joseph C. of Utica m 10/21/47 Matilda Carroll of New York Mills
       in N. Y. M.; Rev. Batien (9-11/1)
7368. Roberts, Mahetable (Mrs.), 60, d 12/25/33 in Seneca Falls (6-1/8)
7369. Roberts, Mary, 30, wf of Thomas D., d 8/17/49 in Utica (funeral from her
       late home, west side of Park St.) (9-8/18)
7370. Roberts, Mary, 44, wf of William, d 2/12/50 in Frankfort, NY (9-2/19)
7371. Roberts, Robert E., 13, youngest s of Evan and Ann E., d 5/25/50 in Utica
       (funeral from his father's home, 7 Seneca St.) (9-5/27)
7372. Roberts, Seth B. of Camden m 7/21/50 Harriet E. Rockwell of Prospect in
       Holland Patent; William Ralph, Esq. (9-7/23)
7373. Roberts, Thomas of Waterville m 1/11/48 Sarah Jones, youngest dau of Ellis,
       Esq. of New Hartford, at the home of Morris Richards in Utica; Rev. James
       Griffith (9-1/17)
7374. Roberts, W. W., 4, s of William drowned 6/21/48 in Utica (funeral from the
       home of his father on Fayette St.)
7375. Roberts, Watkin J. m 8/27/44 Elizabeth Brand in Utica; Rev. D. G. Corey.
       All of Utica (9-8/28 and 8/29)
7376. Roberts, William, 1, d 8/30/47 in Utica (9-9/1)
7377. Robertshaw, ____, 4 mo, ch of Thomas, d 8/16/48 (in Baldwinsville?)
       (1-8/16)
7378. Robertson, A. K., 19, of NYC , a student of divinity, d in Philadelphia
       (state not given) (9-4/26/25)
7379. Robertson, George of Oriskany Valley m 6/11/44 Catharine Hill, recently
       from Paisley, Scotland, in Clinton; Rev. Abijah Crane (9-6/14)
7380. Robie, Jonathan, 22, d 11/23/33 in Bath (6-12/4)
7381. Robins, Harrison m 7/4/39 Jane Mild in Fenner. All of F (3-7/10)
7382. Robinson, Asahel m 11/14/33 Nancy Vince in Geneseo (6-12/11)
7383. Robinson, Benedict, Esq., 74, (one of the earliest settlers in Ontario
       Co.) d 2/18/32 in Milo (6-3/7)
7384. Robinson, Charles, merchant, of Newfield m 3/3/31 Catharine White, dau of
       Hiram, Esq., in Cayata (6-3/23)
7385. Robinson, Gain, M.D., about 60, d 6/21/31 in Lyons (a physician for 30 yrs)
       (6-6/29)
7386. Robinson, George A. of Troy m 7/18/50 Huldah Chesebro, dau of M.(?) P.
       of Whitestown, in W; Rev. R. R. Kirk (9-7/10)

7387. Robinson, George W. of Cleveland, Oswego Co., NY m 9/1/36 Electa Schuyler of Cazenovia; Rev. Rounds (3-9/7)
7388. Robinson, Hopkins, comedian, formerly a performer in Albany, d in NYC (8-12/8/19)
7389. Robinson, Jeremiah B. m 3/10/50 Mary J. Murphy in Baldwinsville; Rev. A. Wells (1-3/14)
7390. Robinson, John, 20, d 8/11/34 in Geneva (6-8/13)
7391. Robinson, John m 9/7/42 Mary Newhouse in Utica; Rev. B. Hawley. All of Utica (9-9/8)
7392. Robinson, John, 27, d 3/18/43 in Utica (9-3/30)
7393. Robinson, John C. (Lt.) of U.S. Army, late of Binghamton m 5/15/42 Sarah Maria Pease of Green Bay, WI at Christ Ch., Green Bay; Rev. S. Davis (2-6/1)
7394. Robinson, Nelson, 28, attorney, d 9/21/45 in Newton, NJ (a grad of Union College) (9-9/25)
7395. Robinson, William (Rev.), 70, d 8/15/25 in Southington, CT (b in Lebanon, CT; admitted to Yale College at age 15; served the ministry at Southington, 1780-1821 when his health failed) (9-8/30)
7396. Robison, Alexander m 3/16/36 Elizabeth Wilkinson in Waterloo (6-3/30)
7397. Robson, Benjamin R., Jr. of NYC m 10/10/48 Mary E. Bogert, dau of Thomas L., Esq. of Utica, at Trinity ch., Utica; Rev. Dr. Proal (9-10/12)
7398. Robson, Thomas N. m 10/8/31 Rachel Reynolds in Syracuse; William Griffin, Esq. All of Syracuse (6-10/12)
7399. Robson, William, 88, d 2/2/47 in Westmoreland (arrived from Yorkshire, England in 1829)
7400. Roby, Joseph, 52, formerly a merchant in Albany and Utica and recently a farmer in Boon Co., IL, d 2/10/47 in Brockport, NY (9-2/20)
7401. Rochester, Amanda, 31, wf of Hon. William B., d 1/16/31 in Buffalo (6-1/26 and 9-2/1)
7402. Rochester, Henry E., Esq. m 4/7/33 Jane Hart, dau of Roswell, at St. Mark's Ch. in Le Roy; Rev. F. H. Cuming. All of Rochester (6-5/8)
7403. Rochester, Nathaniel (Col.), the founder of Rochester, d 5/17/31 "at an advanced age" in R (6-5/25)
7404. Rochester, Sophia, 77, relict of late Col. Nathaniel of Rochester from whom the city derives its name, d 12/9/45 in Rochester leaving these living descendants: 7 ch and 41 gr-ch - all but 10 of them in the immediate vicinity of Rochester (9-12/12)
7405. Rochester, William B., pres of the U.S. Branch Bank at Buffalo, m 4/9/32 Eliza Powers, wid of late Gershom, Esq. of Auburn, in A; Rev. Dr. Rudd (6-4/18)
7406. Rochfield, Ivah (Mrs.), 22, d 12/6/33 in Mount Morris (6-12/18)
7407. Rockwell, Abby, 57, relict of late Philo of Utica, d 1/5/48 in Brooklyn (9-1/8)
7408. Rockwell, Ezra m 10/4/48 Phebe M. Pierce; Rev. Carr. All of Elmira (5-10/6)
7409. Rockwell, H. O. m 12/10/50 Julia Rowe in Utica; Rev. William Wyatt. All of Utica (9-12/12)
7410. Rockwell, Horatio, 23, d 7/21/43 in Corning (4-7/26)
7411. Rockwell, John J. of Utica m 6/12/48 Catharine Van Wormer of Albany in A; Rev. William Clapp (9-6/14)
7412. Rockwell, John W., 60, keeper of the mansion-house, d 12/13/26 in Albany (9-12/19) (Note: "mansion-house" perhaps intended for Van Rensselaer's)
7413. Rockwell, Lemuel, prof. of instrumental and vocal music, of Rushford, m 3/4/50 Mary Van Scoter, preceptress of instrumental music, in Hornellsville; Rev. H. Pattengill (4-3/13)
7414. Rockwell, Lydia, 11, d 8/24/25 in Manlius (9-8/30)
7415. Rockwell, Thomas, Esq., cashier of the Ontario Branch Bank, m 6/10/33 Elizabeth Williams in Utica (6-7/3)
7416. Rockwell, Thomas, cashier of the Ontario Branch Bank, d 8/16/49 in Utica (funeral from his late home on Court St.)
7417. Rodgers, Henry m 12/30/35 Leah Wyant, both of Seneca Falls, in S. F. (6-1/13/36)
7418. Rodgers, R. B. (Dr.), 76, d in NYC (6-2/6/33)
7419. Rodman, Thomas Harvey, Esq. m 4/10/45 Mary A. Mann, youngest dau of Hon. Abijah, Jr., in Brooklyn; Rev. Gilbert H. Sayres. All of Brooklyn (9-4/22)

7420. Rodney, Caesar A., Minister Plenipotentiary, d 6/10/24 in "Buenosayres" (8-8/18)
7421. Rodney, Cornelius (Capt.) of Geneva, NY m 1/1/33 Deborah McCauley of Canandaigua in C; Rev. J. Parker (6-1/9)
7422. Rodney, John m 4/17/37 Lemira Spalding at the Michigan Hotel in Monroe, MI; Rev. J. F. Davidson (6-5/10)
7423. Rodney, Martha, 59, wf of William, d 7/5/34 in Geneva (6-7/9)
7424. Roe, George m 7/24/43 Elizabeth Johnson, both of Little Falls, in Utica; Rev. B. Hawley (9-7/26)
7425. Roe, Lansing, 35, d 7/10/48 in Schenectady (9-7/12)
7426. Rogers, _____, inf s of W. C., d 12/25/43 in Utica (9-12/28)
7427. Rogers, Augustus P. m 8/28/43 Charlotte S. Russ, dau of John A. of Utica, at Trinity Ch., Utica; Rev. P. A. Proal (9-8/29)
7428. Rogers, Charles D. of Williamsville m 8/3/48 Deborah F. Bishop, dau of Dr. Bishop of Sauquoit, in S; Rev. John Waugh (9-8/5)
7429. Rogers, Draper m 7/3/36 Martha Birch in Phelps (6-8/10)
7430. Rogers, Eli, 79, d 4/12/49 in Martinsburgh (9-5/4)
7431. Rogers, Emerson m 8/26/36 Clorinda Cuykendoll, both of Wayne, in Bath (6-9/14)
7432. Rogers, F. (Rev.), rector of Zion Ch., Greene, Chen. Co., m 7/21/47 S. Jennette Loomis, dau of Gen. T. of Brownville, Jeff. Co., at St. Paul's Ch., Brownville; Rt. Rev. W. H. De Lancey (9-8/7)
7433. Rogers, Hannah, 72, wf of Elder Davis Rogers, d 1/4/21 in Preston (8-1/10)
7434. Rogers, Henry of Bradford, CT m 5/16/49 Elizabeth Townsend, youngest dau of John of Westmoreland; Rev. F. A. Spencer (9-7/9)
7435. Rogers, Henry R., 25, postmaster of South Bainbridge, d 5/2/29 in S. B. (7-5/20)
7436. Rogers, James of Sullivan m 2/2/38 Lydia A. Wright of De Witt in D. W.; Rev. Taggart (3-2/7)
7437. Rogers, James H. m 11/30/45 Harriet Smith of Warren, PA in Sauquoit; Rev. Stocking (9-12/3)
7438. Rogers, Jemima (Mrs.), 69, d 6/12/42 at the home of her son Clark Rogers in Preston (Oxford Times, 6/15)
7439. Rogers, Jeremiah, Jr., recently of Binghamton, NY, d 11/21/49 in Sacramento, CA (9-3/13/50)
7440. Rogers, John m 10/10/32 Eliza S. Eldred in Rochester (6-11/7)
7441. Rogers, John (Capt.), 70, principal chief of the Western Cherokees, d 7/4/46 in Van Buren, AR (9-7/27)
7442. Rogers, Joseph m 10/20/36 Julia Sheffield in Lyons (6-11/2)
7443. Rogers, Leonard m 2/10/39 Sally Ann Ryon in Sullivan; J. French, Esq. All of S. (3-2/13)
7444. Rogers, Mariah, 41, relict of Silas, Jr., d 9/4/42 in Preston (member Seventh Day Bapt. Ch.) (Oxford Times, 9/14)
7445. Rogers, Medad (Rev.), 74, d 8/25/24 in New Fairfield, CT (had been pastor of Cong'l. Ch. there for 38 yrs) (9-9/14)
7446. Rogers, Nathan, 48, d 12/2/46 in Utica (9-12/4)
7447. Rogers, Nathan B., 25, under-sheriff of Madison Co., d 2/4/49 in Leonardsville, Mad. Co. (9-2/8)
7448. Rogers, Rebecca (Mrs.), 76, d 1/4/41 in Chittenango (3-1/6)
7449. Rogers, Richard m 1/2/31 Lucy Langdon; Frederick Boogher, Esq. All of Galen (6-1/12)
7450. Rogers, Robert C., 22, s of Hon. Gustavus of Bath, d 10/17/50 at the Crescent City Hotel, Sacramento, CA "of Fever"; took part in the "gold rush") (4-12/4)
7451. Rogers, Thomas, 3rd, m 11/10/31 Mary Jane Thompson in Port Gibson; Rev. B. H. Hickox (6-11/23)
7452. Rogers, W. C., editor of the Vermont Tribune at Brandon, m 4/30/50 Harriet L. Ellis, dau of E. of Glens Falls, NY, in G. F.; Rev. Joseph Baker (9-5/3)
7453. Rogers, William B. of Chicago, IL m 10/1/50 Cornelia A. Follensbe of Utica in U; Rev. Corey (9-10/4)
7454. Rolf, Benjamin D. m 2/13/33 Mary B. Pierce in Sodus (6-2/27)
7455. Rollins, William John m 9/3/50 Nancy Davison in New Hartford; Rev. E. H. Payson. All of New Hartford (9-9/5)

7456. Romeyn, John Brodhead, D.D., 46, pastor of the Cedar Street Presby. Ch. in NYC, d 2/22/25 in NYC (9-3/1)
7457. Romeyn, Theodore Frelinghuysen, 31, attorney, of Oswego, NY and oldest s of Rev. Thomas Romeyn of Amsterdam, NY, d in October 1832 in Wilkesboro, NC where he had gone for his health (6-7/3/33)
7458. Rood, Albert of Clayville m 2/5/50 Elizabeth Spencer of New York Mills in N. Y. M.; Rev. Rounds (9-2/9)
7459. Roosevelt, Elizabeth, wf of Nelson, d in Junius (9-8/8/26)
7460. Root, _____ (Mrs.), 80, d 11/14/25 in Oxford ("tripped on some lumber and struck her head")
7461. Root, Eli, 38 d in Orleans (6-2/2/31)
7462. Root, Eliakim m 4/17/44 Caroline A. Hopkins in Vernon; Rev. Hall. All of Vernon (9-4/22)
7463. Root, Elihu, 69, d 7/10/43 at his home in Vernon (9-1/15)
7464. Root, George of Guilford m 9/7/45 Mary Bush of Oxford in O; Rev. J. T. Goodrich (Oxford Republican, 9/11)
7465. Root, George m 2/26/45 Orissa Burch in Schuyler; Rev. A. D. Skinner (9-2/28)
7466. Root, Luther, 56, d 9/9/32 in Vienna, NY (one of the first settlers in Phelps) (6-9/19)
7467. Root, Luther m 8/28/47 Eunice Rebecca Prichard, both of Baldwinsville; Rev. J. A. Ormsbee (1-9/1)
7468. Root, Lyman m 7/7/25 Lucretia Dodge, both of Oxford; Elder Otis (8-7/13)
7469. Root, Rebecca, consort of William, Esq., d 1/28/26 in Utica (9-2/7)
7470. Root, Rollin m 4/30/44 Susan Elliott, youngest dau of Edward, in Clinton; Rev. Norton. All of Clinton (9-5/15)
7471. Root, William, Esq., 78, d 8/15/46 in Vernon (9-8/25)
7472. Rophenbark, Tunis, 103, d in Sidney, N. B. or N. H.(blurred) (fought under the walls of Quebec when Wolfe and Montcalm fell) (6-10/9/33)
7473. Rorison, Mary (Mrs.), 68, d 12/4/33 in Fayette (6-12/18)
7474. Rosco, William H., 31, d 8/25/47 in Frankfort (9-9/2)
7475. Rose, Alexander F. (Capt.), 51, of Hampstead, Stafford Co., VA d 11/17/31 at the home of Robert S. Rose, Esq. in Fayette (formerly a resident of Hopeton in Yates Co, NY but "moved many years ago to Virginia") (6-11/23)
7476. Rose, Charles A. m 1/8/32 Maria Hallett, dau of Hon. Jecob W., at Trinity Ch., Geneva; Rev. Dr. Bruce (double ceremony - see marr of Charles W. Rees) (6-1/11)
7477. Rose, Charles A., Esq. m 4/10/39 Hester R. Hopkins, dau of late S. M., Esq., in Geneva; Rev. Hay. All of Geneva (6-4/17)
7478. Rose, Henry (Dr.) m 9/4/32 Sarah Clark of NYC in Esperanza, Yates Co.; Rev. Bruce (6-9/12)
7479. Rose, Hester M., 1, youngest ch of Charles A., d 1/20/46 at the home of Mrs. Hopkins in Geneva (6-1/23)
7480. Rose, J. De Witt m 2/22/42 Harriet Rood in Syracuse; Rev. J. P. B. Storer. All of Syracuse (9-3/8)
7481. Rose, James R., Esq. of Albany m 6/17/50 Phebe R. Budlong of Utica in Kenosha, WI; Rev. Gridley (formerly clerk of the assembly) (9-7/2)
7482. Rose, Maria M., 22, wf of Charles A., Esq., d 9/17/37 in Savannah, NY (6-9/27)
7483. Rose, Nathan of Wheeler m 3/11/33 Sarah Leach in Bath (6-3/20)
7484. Rose, Norman m 5/27/32 Polly Cable of Geneva in Junius (6-6/6)
7485. Rose, Robert H., 65, d 2/24/42 at his home in Silver Lake, PA (2-3/2)
7486. Rose, Robert S. of Fayette d 11/24/35 in Waterloo (6-11/25)
7487. Rose, Ruth, 50, wf of Nathan, d 2/12/32 in Wheeler (6-3/7)
7488. Rose, Samuel L., attorney, m 8/5/46 Mary E. Norris, dau of Robert J., in Augusta; Rev. O. Bartholomew (9-8/7)
7489. Rosecrants, James m 3/20/34 Mary Burnett in Phelps; Elder Farley (6-4/2)
7490. Rosekrans, Henry, about 35, d 11/14/30 in Benton (6-11/17)
7491. Roseman, George of Livingston m 3/16/31 Joanna Forrest in Barrington, Dutchess Co. (6-3/23)
7492. Rosenkrans, Elijah m 3/16/31 Nancy Dildine in Pulteney (6-4/6)
7493. Ross, _____, 79, (a Rev. soldier) father of Samuel of Oxford, d 11/9/19 in Oxford (8-11/17)
7494. Ross, Alexander, about 120, 6/-/18 in Milton (b in Scotland; served in the army of the Pretenders in 1745; after defeat of this group served in the army of General Wolf and in the Rev. War) (8-9/30)

7495. Ross, Alexander Mackenzie, Esq. of NYC m 11/29/49 Eliza Kirke Wright, dau
of Z., Esq. of Utica, in U; Rev. William H. Spencer (9-12/1)
7496. Ross, James C. m 11/24/36 Mary Deming, both of Geneva; Richard Hogarth,
Esq. (6-12/7)
7497. Ross, John Z. (Hon.), first judge of Genesee Co., d in Batavia (9-11/28/26)
7498. Ross, Sarah, 9, dau of Samuel, d 4/29/30 in Oxford (8-5/5)
7499. Ross, William (Rev.), 33, an itinerant minister of the Meth. Episc. Ch.,
d 2/10/25 in Brooklyn, NY (9-3/8)
7500. Ross, William (Col.), 85, a Rev. soldier, d 1/23/49 in Binghamton (b in
Canaac, CT 11/17/1763 and volunteered as a musician at age 14 in the
state troops; served also as a private in Gen. Poor's brigade) (9-2/6)
7501. Rossman, John, 72, d 3/29/39 in Plamyra (consumption) (6-4/10)
7502. Rostizer, Frederick m 6/22/45 Mrs. Elizabeth Halter, both of Rome, NY, in
R (9-6/26)
7503. Rotchford, (or Hotchford?), Thomas m 9/5/50 Louisa Holland, both of Utica,
in U; John Parsons, Esq. (9-9/7)
7504. Roth, Jane M., 30, wf of Nelson, d 8/26/49 in Utica (funeral from her
late home on Hotel St.) (9-8/27)
7505. Roth, Nelson of Utica m 10/29/50 Eliza Barton of Brooklyn in B; Rev. John
Stearns (9-10/31)
7506. Roth, Solomon m 4/21/29 Mary Jacobus in Franklin, Dela. Co.; Rev.
Waterbury. All of Franklin (8-5/6)
7507. Round, John W. of the Clinton Liberal Institute m 6/12/48 Elizabeth P.
Warren of Perth, NY in P; Rev. Horace Warren (9-6/20)
7508. Rounds, Ella Emelia, 3, only dau of Stephen S. and Catharine, d 8/23/48
in Utica (9-8/28)
7509. Rounds, Martha A., 10 mo, dau of Stephen S. and Catharine, d 6/7/49 in
Utica (9-6/8)
7510. Rounds, William m 9/27/31 Catharine Doxey in Auburn (6-10/12)
7511. Rouse, Austin (Dr.) m 5/12/25 Jane Eliza Perkins in Oxford; Rev. Bush
(8-5/18)
7512. Rouse, Caroline W., 7, only dau of Lorenzo, d 5/23/44 in Marshall
(scarlet fever) (9-6/3)
7513. Rouse, William Wallace, 11, s of James, d 11/10/41 in Chittenango (3-11/17)
7514. Rowell, Daniel R. m 11/17/33 Nancy M. Thompson in Bath (6-11/27)
7515. Rowland, Catharine (Mrs.), 75, d 9/28/47 in Utica (funeral from her late
home, 8 Washington St. (9-9/29)
7516. Rowland, David, 21, d 4/27/39 in Chittenango (3-5/1)
7517. Rowland, Eliza, 38, d 4/25/46 in Rome, NY (9-4/28)
7518. Rowland, John, Jr. m 6/17/35 Jemima Howell in Chittenango; J. French, Esq.
(3-6/23)
7519. Rowley, Abijah, 56, d 8/2/41 at his home near Corning (4-10/13)
7520. Rowley, Alvah m 4/17/49 Caroline Heart of Big Flats in Corning; Rev. H.
Pettingill (4-4/25)
7521. Rowley, Ansel, 54, d 10/6/50 in Oakland, Livingston Co., MO (9-11/30)
7522. Rowley, Jane (Miss), 19, dau of late Abijah, d 2/12/42 (consumption)
(4-3/2)
7523. Rowley, Jonathan, 67 or 61, d in Dansville (6-8/14/33)
7524. Rowley, William, 60, d 9/7/33 in Wheeler (6-9/25)
7525. Roy, C. A. of NYC m 7/2/46 E. M. Stewart of Utica in U; Rev. William H.
Spencer (9-7/3)
7526. Roy, Cool, 21, d 2/6/32 in Phelps (6-2/15)
7527. Roy, Joseph B., 22, d 9/1/49 at the home of his bro-in-law, S. M. White,
in Southport (5-9/7)
7528. Royce, _____ (Mrs.), 38, wf of Alba G., d in Waterloo (8-11/29/20)
7529. Royce, Phineas A. of Batavia m 3/5/35 Sarah M. Merriam, dau of Ebenezer,
Esq. of West Brookfield, MA, in Geneva; Rev. J. W. French (6-3/11)
7530. Rubart, Samuel E. m 1/27/31 Laura Brooks in Phelps (6-2/2)
7531. Rubin, Joachim m 3/4/48 Sophie K. Sunder, both of Utica, in U; John
Parsons, Esq. (9-3/8)
7532. Rudd, Elizabeth (Mrs.), 72, d 8/16/48 at the home of her son-in-law,
Anson S. Miller in Rockford, IL (b in Franklin, CT; wid of Jabez F., Esq.,
one of the early settlers in Oneida Co., NY) (9-9/2)
7533. Rudd, William T. of Schenectady m 11/9/48 Adeline M. Platt of Utica
in U; Rev. George Leeds (9-11/10)
7534. Rude, Orange m 9/3/33 Lovisa Hart in Albion (6-9/18)

7535. Ruger, Daniel H. m 3/13/36 Mary Louisa Lay in Canandaigua (6-3/30)
7536. Ruggles, David (Dr.), 40, proprietor and physician of the Northampton Water Cure, d 12/16/49 in Northampton, MA (9-12/25/49 and 2/27/50)
7537. Ruggles, Lemuel Warner, Esq., about 42, formerly of Waterloo, NY, d "a few weeks since" in Washington, D.C. (6-4/8/35)
7538. Ruggles, William W., 50, d 4/22/50 in Gaines (an early settler there and a long-time member of the Bar of Orleans Co.; formerly Judge of County Court there) (9-4/27)
7539. Rumney, Eliza, about 30, wf of Capt. George, d 6/20/31 in Geneva (6-6/22)
7540. Rumsey, Levi, Esq. d 12/29/33 in Batavia (6-1/8/34)
7541. Rumsey, Martin S., merchant, of Cameron d 9/21/33 in C (6-10/9)
7542. Rundell, John of Watertown, NY and Samuel Craw of Eastport, ME were washed overboard and drowned 12/26/48 from the barque "Dunbarton"'s flying jib boom while at sea (9-7/4/50)
7543. Rundell, Obediah G. m 10/12/23 Miranda Randall in Pharsalia; Elijah Powell, Esq. (8-10/15)
7544. Runkle, George H. of Westmoreland m 3/6/44 Roby Budlong of Schuyler in S; Elder Ferguson (9-3/7)
7545. Runyan, D. H., merchant, m 12/4/34 Amanda Torrey in Bethel; Rev. M. Ferguson (6-12/10)
7546. Runyan, Stephan O., Esq., 48, attorney, d 4/23/20 in Oxford (8-4/26)
7547. Rupert, Benjamin m Lucy Burnette in Vienna, NY (6-4/16/34)
7548. Rureye, Abraham, 5, drowned 9/8/26 in the canal nearFirst Street Bridge in Utica (9-9/12)
7549. Rusk, Robert, about 50, d 7/17/32 in Albany (cholera) (was a clerk in the comptroller's office) (6-7/25)
7550. Russ, William R. of Lysander m 1/8/50 Lorinda G. Ward of Van Buren in V. B.; Rev. Byron Alden (1-1/10)
7551. Russell,James (Rev.) m Margaret Burhans in Roxbury (6-1/26/31)
7552. Russell, James, M., merchant, m 7/14/42 Chloe Knox, both of Windsor, in W; Rev. E. Bronson (2-7/27)
7553. Russell, John m 5/2/39 Sarah Woodford, both of Lenox, in Chittenango (3-5/8)
7554. Russell, Jonathan (Hon.), 60, d 2/16/32 in Milton, MA (one of the American Commissioners at Ghent, afterwards Minister to Sweden and member of Congress) (6-3/21)
7555. Russell, L. B. m Catharine Ege in Waterloo (6-9/25/33)
7556. Russell, Mary, 20, dau of Robert and Agnes, d 5/23/50 in Rockton (9-5/25)
7557. Russell, Orrimble(?) of the firm of Russell and Walrath, tailors, of Chittenango m 10/12/37 Martha A. Parmeleee, dau of Charles of Cazenovia, in C; Rev. L. Myrick (3-10/18)
7558. Russell, Robert R.(?), 56, d 5/17/46 in Seneca (6-5/22)
7559. Russell, Samuel (Hon.), 74, d 7/1/34 in Buffalo (6-7/16)
7560. Russell, Samuel C. m 5/25/43 Julietta Ballou in Utica; Elder Thomas Hall. All of Utica (9-5/28)
7561. Russell, William (Dr.) of Utica m 12/11/50 Agnes Patterson of New Hartford in New H.; Rev. E. Francis (9-12/14)
7562. Rutgers, Henry (Col.), 84, d 2/17/30 in NYC (6-2/24)
7563. Rutherford, James, Sr., 79, d 11/10/46 in Gouverneur (9-12/15)
7564. Rutherford, Walter, Esq. of NYC m 6/4/46 Isabella Brooks, dau of late David of the U.S. Army at the Ch. of the Holy Cross in Troy; Rev. John J. Tucker (9-6/16)
7565. Ryan, Virtue (Mrs.), about 40, wf of Bage, d 10/18/46 in Marcellus (1-10/18)
7566. Ryan, William, Esq., editor of the Columbian Republican of Hudson, m 5/13/45 Jane F. Rogers, dau of B. T., Esq. of Catskill, in C; Rev. G. N. Judd (9-5/26)
7567. Ryland, George m 12/23/34 Deborah M. Fiero in Gorham; Rev. Catlin (6-12/31)
7568. S____, Henry S., 39, d 1/15/47 in Utica (9-1/16)
7569. Sabine, Alfred of Detroit, MI m 4/27/47 Mary Ann Towers of Utica in U; Elder D. G. Corey (9-4/29)
7570. Sabine, Mary Ann, 20, wf of Alfred and oldest dau of late William Towers of Utica, d 7/7/48 in Detroit, MI (9-7/12)
7571. Sacia, David F., Esq. m Angelica M. Marselis in Schenectady (6-11/17/30)
7572. Sackett, Sarah M., 14, d 6/25/36 in Canandaigua (6-7/13/36)
7573. Saden, Joseph m 9/1/34 Ann Parks, both of Canandaigua, in Phelps (6-9/17)
7574. Safford, Mahew (sic), Esq., attorney, d in Buffalo (6-1/26/31)

7575. Sagar(?), William S. of Utica m 6/2/50 Melissa D. Shear of Floyd at the Unitarian Ch. in Holland Patent; Rev. D. Skinner (9-6/10)
7576. Sage, Benjamin H. m 12/31/40 Sarah M. Holister in Burnt Hills, Sara. Co.; Rev. Greene. All of Burnt Hills (double wedding - see marr of Samuel Titus, Jr.) (3-1/6/41)
7577. Sage, Chauncey m 4/17/44 Lucy Lee in Verona; Rev. E. W. Allen (9-4/27)
7578. Sage, George, Jr. m 3/24/49 Orpha Jennings, both of Southport, at the Meth. Parsonage in Elmira; Rev. H. N. Seaver (5-3/30)
7579. Sage, Joseph W, (Maj.), s of Col. H. of Sullivan, d 9/7/41 in Cohoes Falls (3-9/8)
7580. Sage, Phebe, 38, only dau of Deacon Marcus and Rozanna, d 9/25/42 in Windsor (2-10/12)
7581. Sagues, Mary Adelia, 7 mo, dau of William, d 3/18/47 in Baldwinsville (1-3/24)
7582. St. Clair, Arthur (Maj. Gen.) d 8/31/18 in Laurel Hill, Somerset Co., PA (7-9/24)
7583. St. John, David m 12/3/20 Clarissa Hunt, both of Oxford, in O; Rev. Bush (8-12/6)
7584. St. John, David, merchant, of Norwich d 3/16/44 in N (born in Saratoga but lived inChenango Co. 27 yrs) (Oxford Republican, 3/21)
7585. St. John, John of Little Falls m 2/3/47 Margaret Ballard of Utica in U; Rev. William H. Spencer (9-2/6)
7586. St. John, John m 1/4/49 Sophia Amy, both of Veteran; Gilbert Miles, Esq. (5-1/5)
7587. St. John, Maria Ann (Miss), 20, d 7/25/33 in Peterboro, Mad. Co. (9-8/6)
7588. St. John, Rachel (Mrs.), wf of J. T., d in Oneonta (3-7/12/43)
7589. St. John, Solomon, 47, formerly of Geneva, d 1/23/35 in Buffalo (6-2/4)
7590. St. John, William P. of Deerfield m 1/12/48 Nancy A. Bartlett of Worcester, MA in W; Rev. James Porter (9-1/14)
7591. Sales, Duty of Sempronius m 5/20/31 Betsy Almy of Ledyard (6-6/8)
7592. Salisbury, Benjamin F. m 9/25/34 Ekizabeth Vandemark in Phelps (6-10/1)
7593. Salisbury, Guy H., one of the editors of the Buffalo Commercial Advertiser, m 8/1/37 Alta W. Chapman of Sheldon in S (6-8/16)
7594. Salisbury, Nancy, 43, wf of S. H., editor of the Buffalo Republican, d in Buffalo (6-3/3/30)
7595. Salisbury, Smith H., 46, formerly editor of the Black Rock and Buffalo Republican, d 2/7/32 (one of the earliest settlers in Genesee Co.; surv by "a large and helpless family") (6-2/8)
7596. Salisbury, Stephen, Jr. of the firm of Dickson and Salisbury m 1/5/34 Ida P. Stow in Clyde; Rev. L. Morley (6-1/15)
7597. Salkeld, _____ (Mrs.), wf of George, Esq., British Consul, d 10/10/33 in New Orleans, LA (6-11/13)
7598. Salmon, Richard (Rev.) m 5/19/31 Delia A. Smith in Sheldon (6-6/8)
7599. Salsbury, William m 10/31/44 Eliza J. Terwilliger in McHenry Co., OH; Rev. D. Van Alstyne (Oxford Republican 1/6/45)
7600. Sample, James m Sophia Ann Van Nordstrand in Seneca; Rev. Phelps (6-5/23/32)
7601. Sample, Louisa, 23, wf of James and dau of William Barber, d 12/26/30 in Geneva (6-12/29)
7602. Sampson, Ezra, 76, d 12/13/23 in NYC (8-12/31)
7603. Sampson, John m Clarissa Peck in Le Roy (6-11/27/33)
7604. Sanburn, Joseph m 8/11/33 Laney Buskirk in Sparta (6-9/11)
7605. Sandeforth, Lewis R., 46, formerly of Watertown, d 5/14/47 in Utica (funeral from the home of his bro-in-law, J. W. Wright, 91 Fayette St.) (9-5/15)
7606. Sanders, George B. m Asenath Beebe in Pomfret (6-11/10/30)
7607. Sanders, John Heney, 5, oldest ch of Henry and Lucy, d 4/8/49 in Utica (scarlet fever) (9-4/10)
7608. Sanders, Peter, 59, d in Scotia (9-5/15/50)
7609. Sanders, Rebecca, 76, consort of George, d 6/19/26 in Utica (9-6/27)
7610. Sanders, Rebecca Ann, 3, oldest dau of Henry and Lucy, d 4/2/49 in Utica (funeral from 44 Elizabeth St.) (9-4/3)
7611. Sanders, Susan Rebecca, 2, oldest ch of Henry and Lucy, d 5/30/44 in Utica (consumption) (funeral from her parents' home, 76 Fayette St.) (9-6/1)

7612. Sanderson, Edmond, Esq. of Milwaukee, WI m 8/29/49 Rosanna S. Warner, dau of John of Springfield, MA, in Utica, NY; Rev. D. G. Corey (9-8/30)
7613. Sandford, James of Marshall, MI m 9/5/36 Ann Eliza Porter, dau of Dr. Samuel of Skaneateles, in S; Rev. Johnson (6-9/14)
7614. Sands, David, formerly of Utica, m 2/9/43 Caroline Byington of Pittsburgh, PA in P; Rev. Alexander Wright (9-2/25)
7615. Sands, Edward H. (Dr.) of NYC m 7/26/48 Abigail G. Isham of Salisbury in S; Rev. Green (9-8/5)
7616. Sands, Robert C., Esq., "one of the most popular literary writers of the day", d 12/16/32 in Hoboken, NJ (6-1/2/33)
7617. Sanford, _____ (Maj.) of Marion m Emeline Pratt of Williamson in W (6-4/11/32)
7618. Sanford, Benjamin F. m 2/22/42 Carolyn Maxfield, dau of John, Esq., in Vienna, NY; Daniel Paddock, Esq. All of Vienna (9-3/1)
7619. Sanford, Henry (Maj.) of Durhamville m 4/11/50 Eliza Watson, dau of late Hon. Wheeler Watson of Rensselaerville, at St. Luke's Ch., Mechanicville; Rev. R. B. Fairbairn (9-4/13)
7620. Sanford, Joseph, 65, of Clarendon d 5/14/26 en route to relatives in Brutus. At time of death was in the home of Ebenezer Phelps in Brutus (9-6/13)
7621. Sanford, Joseph (Rev.), 33, pastor of 2nd Presby. Ch. in Philadelphia, PA and formerly of Brooklyn, NY, d 12/25/31 in Phila (6-1/11/32)
7622. Sanford, K. m 7/19/47 E. M. Alben(?) in Corning; Rev. H. Pettengill (4-7/21)
7623. Sanford, Linus, Esq., 60, d 6/29/42 in Camden (9-7/1)
7624. Sanford, Luther J. of Elmira m 1/17/49 Mary Atwater of Ithaca in I; Rev. Wisner (5-2/2)
7625. Sanger, _____, 1, ch of Gerry, d in Utica (9-7/11/26)
7626. Sanger, Araminta, wf of Justus H., d 3/11/32 in Canandaigua (6-3/21)
7627. Sanger, Garrit Smith, 7, youngest sof Henry K., Esq., d 6/6/49 in Canandaigua (scarlet fever) (9-6/15)
7628. Sanger, Lucy M. (Miss), 24, oldest dau of Joseph, Esq. of Chittenango, d 4/22/40 in North Easton, MA (consumption) (3-5/13)
7629. Sanger, Richard, Jr., 32, d 6/5/42 at the home of his bro in Utica (funeral from Grace Ch.) (9-6/6)
7630. Sanger, Richard, Sr., 73, d 8/9/43 at the home of his son in Utica (funeral from the home of Mr. G. Sanger, 253 Genesee St.) (9-8/10)
7631. Sanger, Sarah B., 49, wf of Hon. Jedediah of New Hartford and dau of late Daniel Kissam, Esq. of Long Island, NY, d 4/23/25 while visiting friends in Utica (9-4/26)
7632. Sarsnett, Henry m Mary Brooks in Phelps (6-7/24/33)
7633. Saterlee, Timothy S. of Elmira m Mary Ann Seely in Blooming Grove (6-7/3/33)
7634. Satterlee, Anna (Miss), 33, d 2/24/25 at the home of Allen Worden in Auburn (9-3/8)
7635. Satterlee, Benedict (Dr.) of Elmira m 1/24/36 Martha Ann Mather of Fairfield in F (6-2/17)
7636. Satterlee, Rousseau m 4/26/32 Mary Elizabeth Agnew in Auburn; Rev. D. C. Axtell (6-5/9)
7637. Saulpaugh, Charles E. m 11/5/50 Esther Downer, both of Utica, in U; Elder Thomas Hill (9-11/19)
7638. Saunders, John m Nancy Sage in Gorham (6-5/19/30)
7639. Saunders, Lorenzo m Calista Taber(?) in Manchester (6-7/31/33)
7640. Saunders, Lucius m 11/17/41 Eliza Burlison in Guilford; Rev. Bartlet. All of Guilford (Oxford Times, 11/24)
7641. Saunders, Mary Ann (Mrs.), 35, d 7/24/36 in Seneca Falls (6-8/10)
7642. Saunders, Nathan (Capt.), 70, (a Rev. soldier), formerly of Lyme, CT, d 11/8/26 in Canandaigua (9-11/28)
7643. Savage, Edward (Hon.), father of the chief justice of this state, d 10/12/33 in Salem, NY (6-10/23)
7644. Savage. Edward (Prof.) of Union College m 7/30/39 Sarah Van Vechten, 2nd dau of Rev. Dr. V. V., in Schenectady (double ceremony - see marr of Rev. E. A. Huntington) (3-8/7)
7645. Savage, Stephen, 79, d 12/4/48 in Sauquoit (9-12/6)
7646. Sawdet, Miranda (sic) m 12/11/36 Laura Lamphier of Geneva; R. Hogarth, Esq. (6-12/14)

7647. Sawyer, G. W. m 4/6/50 Elvira A. Curtis in West Martinsburgh; Rev. B. J. Wright (9-4/27)
7648. Sawyer, Henry H., 19, 2nd s of Ezra Sawyer, master builder of the N.Y. State Insane Asylum in Utica, d 1/30/42 in Brattleboro, VT (9-2/4)
7649. Sawyer, Hilliard E. m 10/18/43 Caroline Lockrow of Albany in Sangerfield; Rev. John B. Fish (double ceremony - see marr of John Van Slyck) (9-10/21)
7650. Sawyer, Leicester A. (Rev.), pastor-elect of the Presby. Ch. in Martinsburgh, Lewis Co., m 9/26/32 Pamela B. Bosworth, dau of Roswell, in Smithville; Rev. G. S. Boardman (9-10/16)
7651. Sawyer, Oliver W. m Lucia Cowle in Middlesex (6-4/28/30)
7652. Sawyer, T. C. (Mr.), 24, d 1/30/35 in Manchester (consumption) (6-2/11)
7653. Sawyer, Thomas C. of Manchester m 2/12/33 Mary Benham in Hopewell (6-2/27)
7654. Sayles, Gerrit m 9/15/42 Maria Garvey, both of Clockville, in Morrisville (3-9/21)
7655. Sayles, Royal C. m 9/28/43 Margaret Carpenter, both of Clockville, in Morrisville; Rev. Putnam (double ceremony - see Henry Herrick) (3-10/11)
7656. Sayles, Stukeley, 87, (a Rev. soldier) d 1/14/47 in New Hartford (9-2/26)
7657. Sayles, Welcome (Dr.), 74, d 12/8/50 in Vernon (9-12/16)
7658. Sayre, Charles m 11/7/50 Catharine E. Davis; Rev. C. C. Carr (5-11/8)
7659. Sayre, Daniel, Esq. of Cairo, NY m 2/20/21 Mrs. Willis, wid of Dr. A., of Franklin in F; Rev. Caleb Knight (8-3/14)
7660. Sayre, Elizabeth, 68, consort of Ebenezer, d 11/28/34 in Elmira (6-12/17)
7661. Sayre, Martha Ellen, 11 mo., dau of Willis B. and Annis, d 8/17/49 in Elmira (5-8/24)
7662. Sayre, P. (Mrs.) d 6/10/49 in Utica (funeral from the home of her son, James, 53 Fayette St.) (9-6?11)
7663. Sayre, Sarah (Mrs.), 97, formerly of Westfield, NJ, d 9/22/33 in Lyons, NY (6-10/9)
7664. Sayre, Whittington, Esq., 64, of Elmira d at the home of his son in Jefferson, WI (cholera) (surv by wf and 1 ch) (5-8/24/49)
7665. Sayres, Brown of Manlius m 1/4/43 Henrietta Eastwood of Sullivan in Fayetteville; Rev. Hickock (3-1/18)
7666. Schank, Ann, 18, wf of James, d 2/23/48 in Lysander (1-3/8)
7667. Schenck, Abraham A., 57, d in Fishkill (6-6/8/31)
7668. Schenck, Elsey, 35, wf of Rev. J. Thallimer (incongruity in surnames not explained) d in Mendon (6-11/20/33)
7669. Schenck, Peter m 9/29/33 Almira Powers in Groton (6-10/16)
7670. Schermerhorn, Isaac M. (Gen.), 59, d 1/30/49 in Schenectady (formerly mayor there) (9-2/7)
7671. Schermerhorn, John, inf s of John V. R., d 7/9/32 in Geneva (6-7/11)
7672. Schermerhorn, Morgan L., Esq., attorney, of Urbana m 5/6/33 Elizabeth Colt, dau of late Joseph, Esq. of Palmyra, in P; Rev. B. H. Hickcox of St. Paul's Ch., Rochester (6-5/15)
7673. Schermerhorn, Simeon I. (Dr.), 30, d in Schenectady (6-2/17/30)
7674. Schindler, Catharine (Miss), 16, d 6/11/46 at the Glass Factory (in Seneca?) (6-6/12)
7675. Schooley, Mercy, wf of Abraham, d 1/30/36 in Waterloo (6-2/10)
7676. Schoonmaker, Milton C., 40, of NYC d 3/25/50 in Stockton, CA (9-4/11)
7677. Schott, Frederick of Waterloo m 7/4/36 Catharine M. Bellis in Fayette (6-7/20)
7678. Schram, Daniel K. of Utica m 5/6/47 Frances J. Hulbert of Remsen; Rev. Buckingham (9-5/8)
7679. Schram, Valentine, 4, youngest s of William and Sarah of Poughkeepsie, d 8/29/50 in Utica (9-9/3)
7680. Schryver, Joseph G. of Waterloo m 9/18/39 Lucy Knowles, dau of John, Esq. of Chittenango, in C; Rev. J. Abel (3-9/25)
7681. Schuyler, _____, about 80 or 30(?), wid of late Jacob, d 6/12/31 (3-6/14)
7682. Schuyler, Anthony D., Esq., about 45, formerly of NYC, d 4/4/31 at his home in the town of Ovid (fell into a threshing machine) (6-4/6)
7683. Schuyler, Barnet (Capt.) of Chittenango m 12/24/33 Mrs. Margaret Philips in Cazenovia; Rev. Leonard (3-1/28/34)
7684. Schuyler, Benjamin F., 25, formerly of Chittenango, d 4/11/38 in Grand Rapids, MI (3-5/16)

7685. Schuyler, Henry, 24, d 6/4/43 in New Hartford (9-6/10)
7686. Schuyler, Jacob m 2/14/38 Delia Fairborn in Sullivan (3-2/21)
7687. Schuyler, James, about 70, (a Rev. soldier) d 6/12/31 (3-6/14)
7688. Schuyler, Jerome C., 5, s of Jacob and Adelia, d 4/4/44 in Canaseraga (3-4/1))
7689. Schuyler, John, 35, d 8/9/48 in Whitesboro (9-8/15)
7690. Schuyler, Josephus, formerly of Geneva, m 2/9/32 Nancy Rodgers of Perry in P (6-2/29)
7691. Schuyler, Lucas Van Vechten m 9/29/25 Angelica Lansing, dau of Gerrit R. of Watervliet, in Albany (9-10/11)
7692. Schuyler, Marcus, formerly of Seneca, m 4/11/33 Hannah E. Hoyt of Ledyard in L (6-4/17)
7693. Schuyler, Montgomery of Marshall, MI m 9/7/36 Sarah Sandford, dau of late Dr. Sandford of Ovid, in O (6-9/14)
7694. Schuyler, Phillip (Capt.) d 5/14/44 in Boonville (9-5/23)
7695. Schuyler, Philip C. of Ithaca m 1/12/32 Lucy Matilda Dix in Seneca Falls (6-1/25)
7696. Scofield, Abigal Renette, 15 mo, only ch of Liflet and Martha, d 11/5/47 in Utica (funeral at her father's home on Whitesboro St.) (9-11/8)
7697. Scofield, Chester m 1/17/47 Sarah Tripp, both of Utica in U; Rev. William H. Spencer (9-1/19)
7698. Scofield, Cordelia (Mrs.) d 3/5/33 in Penn Yan (6-3/13)
7699. Scofield, Rennet W., wf of Chester, d 5/1/46 in Utica (9-5/1)
7700. Scofield, Sylvanus, 67, d in Jerusalem, NY (6-6/9/30)
7701. Scot, Michael, 51, d in Jersey, NY (6-4/7/30)
7702. Scott, _____, inf ch of "Mrs. Scott", d 4/7/26 in Utica (9-4/11)
7703. Scott, Abraham (Capt.) m Sarah Campbell in Vienna, NY (6-1/26/31)
7704. Scott, Catharine M. (Miss), 24, d 8/23/46 in Geneva (6-8/28)
7705. Scott, Edward, 64, d 4/25/42 in Deerfield (9-5/6)
7706. Scott, George, Jr. m 12/3/49 Hapsky Hatch in Rome, NY (9-12/7)
7707. Scott, H. L. (Maj.) m 11/28/49 Cornelia Scott, dau of Gen. Scott, at the city home of the General on 8th Street, NYC (9-12/3)
7708. Scott, John of Troy m 4/20/50 Sarah Keeler of Durham in U; Rev. William H. Spencer (9-5/3)
7709. Scott, Merrick of Plymouth m 12/31/20 Sally Harvey of Preston in P; Rev. Nathan Noyes (7-2/14/21)
7710. Scott, Thomas (Rev.), 74, rector of Aston, Sanford, Bucks (Eng.?) and chaplain to the Lock Hospital, d 5/16/21 (known both in Europe and America for his Commentaries on the Scriptures) (8-8/1)
7711. Scott, W. T. of Geneva m 6/12/39 Charlotte Wise, dau of Samuel of Benton, in B; Rev. Ovid Miner (6-6/19)
7712. Scott, Welcome of Brookfield m 2/8/44 Martha L. Alexander of Winfield in W; Rev. Woolley (9-2/10)
7713. Scovell, O. P. of NYC m 11/22/46 Elizabeth E. Shepard, only dau of late Leonard, Esq. of Lewiston, in the Presby. Ch. in Lewiston (9-12/1)
7714. Scovil, _____, 81, consort of Lemuel, d 4/16/50 near the High Falls in West Turin (9-4/27)
7715. Scoville, David, Esq. of Rochester m 1/22/46 Sarah T. N. Williams, youngest dau of Stalham Williams, Esq. of Utica, in Rochester; Rev. A. G. Hall (9-1/27)
7716. Scoville, Edward, Esq., 54, youngest s of Darius, d 6/7/45 in Paris Hill (Darius moved to Paris Hill with his family from Watertown, CT in 1803 (9-6/18)
7717. Scoville, Sheldon, Esq. of Vernon m 10/25/48 Anna R. Bradley, wid of Elder Bryant Bradley of Whitesboro, in W; Rev. Walter H. Long (9-10/28)
7718. Scranton, Henry m 9/25/50 Harriet Dailey of Trenton, NY in Herkimer; Rev. J. H. Harter of Rockton (double ceremony - see marrof Horace Kimberly)
7719. Scribner, Edward m 2/5/39 Elizabeth Gertrude Brown, oldest dau of Allen, Esq., in NYC; Rev. C. G. Sommers, Esq. (3-2/13)
7720. Scrimgeour, James (Rev.), a native of Scotland and for many years pastor of the Reformed Presbyterian Congregational of Little Britain, Orange Co., d 2/4/25 in L. B. (9-2/22)
7721. Scudder, Samuel D., 22, s of Rev. Dr. Scudder of India, d 11/14/49 in New Brunswick (NJ?) (9-11/17)

211

7722. Seaman, Dewit C. m 4/9/50 Catharine E. Thompson, both of Jefferson, in Elmira; Rev. M. Crow (double ceremony - see marr of Daniel P. Keley)
7723. Searing, Augustin V. of the firm of Mack and Searing, editors of the American Journal, m Delia Butler, dau of Comfort, Esq., in Ithaca (8-6/23/19)
7724. Searles, Elijah of Utica m 12/14/47 Jane H. Doolittle, dau of Uri, Jr. of Paris Hill, in P. H.; Rev. Baker (9-12/29)
7725. Searles, George, 37, d 10/2/44 in Utica (funeral at the home of his father on the corner of Elizabeth and Charlotte Sts.) (9-10/5)
7726. Searls, Ziriah, 63, wf of J. C., d 2/22/47 in Utica (funeral from the home of her husband, corner Charlotte and Elizabeth Sts.) (9-2/23)
7727. Sears, James C. of Arcadia m 2/10/31 Lydia Almira Howard (6-2/23)
7728. Sears, Robert H. of Conhocton m 8/6/33 Henrietta Shannon of Dansville, in D (6-8/21)
7729. Sears, Rufus of Van Buren m 9/29/47 Jane Smith of Lysander; Rev. T. Walker (1-10/13)
7730. Seaton, Benjamin W. m 12/30/49 Julia E. Bond, both of Utica; Rev. George Leeds (9-1/1/50)
7731. Seaton, David, Jr., 24, d 1/13/50 at the home of his father in Sauquoit (9-1/14)
7732. Seaton, Edward m 4/30/49 Mary B. Whiffen, both of Utica, at the Dutch Reformed Ch., Utica; Rev. Charles Wiley (9-5/1)
7733. Seaton, Joseph, 68, d 11/19/48 at the home of Isaac Whiffen in Utica (funeral from Bleecker Street Bapt. Ch.) (9-11/21)
7734. Sebring, John m 3/29/32 Sally Ann Reynolds, both of Lyons, in L; Hugh Jameson, Esq. (6-4/11)
7735. Sebring, Lewis of Ovid m 2/1/32 Mary Ann Clark of Romulus in Seneca Falls (6-2/15)
7736. Secor, Charles H. of Geddes m 2/20/50 Abigail Ann Mills of Van Buren in V. B. (1-2/28)
7737. Secor, John of Benton m 10/31/33 Laura Ann Wood in Bellona; Rec. C. P. Wack (6-11/6)
7738. Secor, Worhinston of Penn Yan m 7/16/31 L. Sylvia Havens of Benton in B (6-7/27)
7739. Sedgwick, Charles H., printer, of Utica m 9/15/44 Ann Adams of Western; William S. Wetmore, Esq. (9-9/19)
7740. Sedgwick, Ellen, wf of Charles, Esq., d 5/23/46 in Syracuse (9-5/26)
7741. Sedgwick, Jonathan m 9/28/34 Isabel Pharis, both of Waterloo, in W; Rev. Lane (6-10/8)
7742. Sedgwick, Katharine M., 1, dau of Charles B., Esq. of Syracuse, d 7/28/46 in Pompey (9-8/4)
7743. Sedgwick, Lucy, 33, wf of Rev. Averlyn, d in Ogden (6-3/9/31)
7744. Sedgwick, Susan A., 19, wf of Charles H., d 2/22/46 in Rochester (9-2/28)
7745. Seeber, Austin J., Esq., 29, attorney, d 12/30/49 in Clockville (9-1/11/50)
7746. Seebring, James m 10/28/33 Christian Amsburgh in Waterloo (6-11/13)
7747. Seeley, Thadeus, 71, d in Havana, NY (6-4/7/30)
7748. Seely, Abner m 3/7/35 Polly Sly in Southport (6-3/18)
7749. Seely, Benjamin of Elmira m 8/14/34 Tamer Smith of Charleston, Tioga Co., PA in C (6-9/3)
7750. Seely, C. W. m 5/28/35 Elizabeth E. Bascom in Seneca Falls (6-6/17)
7751. Seely, Charles m Sally Brundage in Ovid (6-7/7/30)
7752. Seely(?), Henry of Starkey, 52 or 82, d 8/12/33 in Erie (state not given) (6-8/28)
7753. Seely, Joseph of Wolcott m 4/15/34 Lorinda Clark of Thompson in Waterloo (9-4/30)
7754. Seely, Stephen B., Esq., 29, one of the editors of the Frontier Sentinel, d 8/17/44 in Ogdensburg (consumption) (9-8/27)
7755. Seelye, Clarissa, 61, wf of Seth, Esq., d 11/14/38 in Lansingburgh (6-11/28)
7756. Seelye, G. C. of Auburn m 6/30/36 Ann Eliza Jackson of NYC in NYC (6-7/13)
7757. Seelye, Julia, 67, relict of Isaac, Esq. late of Cherry Valley ("long since deceased"), d 9/20/50 at the home of Judge Oliver in Penn Yan (9-9/27)
7758. Seelye, Lyman m 5/2/37 Rachael Soule, both of Savannah, NY (6-5/17)
7759. Seeney, Jane, 44, wid, d 3/9/32 in Canandaigua (6-3/21)
7760. Segar, J. Wesley of Utica m 11/25/46 Sophia Talbott of Paris, NY in P; Rev. Waugh (9-12/10)

7761. Segar, Mary, 69, wid of John W., d 9/11/48 in Verona (9-9/16)
7762. Segur, Elisha Cook, 4, oldest s of Thomas B., d 2/10/31 in Utica (9-2/15)
7763. Selah, Sterling of Franklin, Dela. Co. m 10/19/23 Clarissa Twitchell of Coventry in C; Rev. Adams (8-10/29)
7764. Selder, Matilda, 82, d 10/6/50 in Rome, NY (9-10/24)
7765. Sellon, John (Rev.) d 3/2/30 in Albany (6-3/10)
7766. Sentell, Charles, Esq., postmaster of Waterloo m 12/17/34 Caroline Merrill in W (6-12/31)
7767. Sentell, Edward W. m 2/11/30 Deborah Harvey, both of Geneva, at Trinity Ch., Geneva; Rev. Mason (6-2/17)
7768. Sergeant, John (Rev.), 73, missionary, d 9/8/24 at his home in Stockbridge (9-9/14)
7769. Severance, Charles m 3/25/30 Martha P. Lamb; Rev. Martin. All of Geneva (6-3/31)
7770. Severance, Charles m 4/-/45 Sarah Wylie in Canaseraga; Rev. Blakslee (3-7/5)
7771. Severance, Jonathan, 95, d 5/15/45 in Truxton (oldest person in the town if not the county) (9-6/10)
7772. Severance, Moses H. (late of Waterloo) of the firm of R. Robbins and Co., booksellers, of Geneva, d 4/2/33 in Geneva (6-4/3)
7773. Severance, Ralph A. (Dr.) of Saxton's River, VT m 6/11/45 Joanna Bailey in Westmoreland (9-6/14)
7774. Severance, Sophia, 55, wf of Jesse, d 1/16/32 in Phelps (6-1/25)
7775. Sewall, Henry D. d 6/8/46 in Watertown (9-9/18)
7776. Seward, Asahel, 53, of the firm of Seward and Williams d 1/30/35 in Utica (6-2/18)
7777. Seward, Benjamin J., 45, oldest bro of the governor, d 2/24/41 at the home of his father in Florida, Orange Co. (4-3/12)
7778. Seward, Harvey of Syracuse m 1/7/50 Mercy M. Fling of Soleville, Mad. Co. in Utica; John Parsons, Esq. (9-1/10)
7779. Seward, J. Dudley, formerly of Oneida Co., NY, m 11/2/48 Lois Clark, dau of William L. of Akron, OH, in A; Rev. Stevens (9-11/11)
7780. Seward, Jedediah, 47, d 8/19/47 in Lysander (1-9/15)
7781. Seward, Julia, 74, relict of late Dr. Daniel D., d 1/14/49 in Goshen, NY (5-1/26)
7782. Sexton, Edwin m 3/28/50 Phebe Staples, both of Lee, in L; Rev. J. S. Kibbe (9-4/4)
7783. Sexton, Edward, Esq. of Sherburne m 5/20/50 Huldah Cooley of Rome, NY in R; Rev. James Erwin (9-5/23)
7784. Sexton, Horace d 11/5/34 in Lee (3-11/18)
7785. Seymor, _____ m 9/12/22 Lucy Anne Perkins in Norwich; Rev. Andrus (8-9/18)
7786. Seymour, Alonzo m 11/16/30 Huldah W. Rose, both of Geneva, in G; Rev. Phelps (6-11/17)
7787. Seymour, Bela m 10/29/29 Mary Ann Thayer; Rev. Hoyt. All of Oxford (8-11/4)
7788. Seymour, Bridget, 26, wf of Joseph, D.D., member of the Mystic Independent Order of Odd Fellows, d 8/22/44 in Utica (consumption) (9-8/28)
7789. Seymour, Edward P., 65, d 7/6/45 at the home of his brother in West Hartford, CT (deceased moved from West Stockbridge, Conn (sic) [perhaps intended for Mass.] in 1815 at which time he became editor of the Herkimer [NY] American; for several yrs justice of the peace and member of the Herkimer Reformed Dutch Ch.) (surv by an only dau) (funeral sermon by Dr. Murphy of the Herkimer Ref. Dutch Ch.) (9-7/12)
7790. Seymour, George, 28 (s of Deacon Jonathan, late of Otsego, deceased) d 6/16/25 in Otsego (consumption) (9-7/26)
7791. Seymour, Henry m 11/8/46 Sarah Jane Lee in Geddes; W. W. Tripp, Esq. All of Geddes (1-11/23)
7792. Seymour, Hezekiah, 75, d 9/5/25 in Guilford (8-9/7)
7793. Seymour, John of NYC m 9/12/22 Lucy Ann Perkins of Norwich; Rev. E. Andrews (7-9/18)
7794. Seymour, Leverett, 73, d 6/9/48 in Westmoreland (9-6/19)
7795. Seymour, M. M. of Skaneateles m 10/7/35 Almira Hill of Fenner in F; Elder Paddock (6-10/14)
7796. Seymour, Moses (Maj.), 84, d 9/17/26 in Litchfield, CT (9-10/3)
7797. Seymour, Orange m 10/25/48 Mary Whitney in Whitney Point; Rev. Lewis (2-11/1)

213

7798. Seymour, Roderick, 67, d in Hartford (9-8/2/25)
7799. Seymour, Sidney S., 21, d in Palmyra (6-3/24/30)
7800. Seymour, Stephen P., merchant, of Erie, PA m 11/6/35 Almira Norton of
       Canandaigua in C (6-11/14?)
7801. Seymour, Tryphena, 66, d 7/14/43 in New Hartford (9-7/21)
7802. Shade, Catharine (Mrs.), 47, of Galt, Upper Canada d in Canandaigua
       (6-12/11/33)
7803. Shadrack, Eliza H. (Mrs.), 31, d 12/3/48 in Utica (funeral at corner of
       Bleecker and 2nd Sts.) (9-12/5)
7804. Shadrack, Sarah (Mrs.), 44, d 1/14/48 in Utica (funeral from her late
       home, corner Bleecker and 2nd Sts.) (9-1/15)
7805. Shaefer, Jacob, Esq. of Mishawaka, IN m 10/5/47 Sarah Jane Miller, dau
       of Abner, Esq. of Westmoreland, in W; Rev. F. A. Spencer (9-10/22)
7806. Shaffer, Chauncey, Esq., attorney, m 10/26/43 Maria R. Warner, dau of
       Isaac, Esq. of Middletown, CT, in M; Rev. E. E. Griswold (3-11/8)
7807. Shaffer, Samuel m 3/16/35 Susan Kinsman in Elmira (6-3/25)
7808. Shaffer, Sanford m 7/15/33 Rowena Kite(?), both of Veteran, in Elmira
       (6-7/31)
7809. Shaft, Jacob V. of Canastota m 10/8/36 Margaret Putnam of Canajoharie
       in Geneva; Richard Hogarth, Esq. (6-12/7)
7810. Shankland, Robert H., Esq., editor of the Cattaraugus Republican, m 8/3/37
       Mary Hooker, dau of J., Esq., in Freedom; Rev. S. Stevens (6-9/27)
7811. Shankland, William, 88, father of Judge Shankland of the state supreme
       court, d 4/17/50 in Cazenovia (9-5/6)
7812. Shannon, Logan m 10/14/32 Sophia Bennett in Starkey (6-11/7)
7813. Shapley, Calvin H. of Nelson m 7/26/31 Louisa Sutherland of Chittenango;
       Rev. William Johnson (3-8/2)
7814. Shapley, H. N., Esq. m 1/4/43 Jane Eliza Berthrong, only dau of Col.
       James, in Cazenovia; Rev. Redfield. All of Cazenovia (3-1/18)
7815. Shapley, John P., Esq., 29, formerly of Oxford, d 3/23/49 at the Eagle
       Hotel in Elmira (5-3/30)
7816. Shapley, Martha, 63, wid of late Thomas, d 3/22/42 in Oxford (Oxford
       Times, 3/23)
7817. Sharp, Thomas m 11/18/45 Ann Lake, both of Deerfield, in Utica; Otis
       Whipple, Esq. (9-11/20)
7818. Sharpe, William of Elmira m 10/7/50 Mary Case of Utica in U; Rev. D. G.
       Corey (9-10/10)
7819. Shaver, ____, 34 or 54?, wf of Nicholas, d 2/24/32 (3-2/28)
7820. Shaver, James m 12/25/38 Julia Ann Worth, both of Fayetteville, in F
       (3-1/9/39)
7821. Shaver, John m 1/27/31 Lucinda Drown in Bath (6-2/9)
7822. Shaver, John W. m 12/11/34 Mrs. Margaret Porter in Sullivan (3-12/16)
7823. Shaver, Joseph m Paulina West, both of Arcadia, in Lyons (6-3/9/31)
7824. Shaver, Mary E., 12, d 8/17/43 in Chittenango (3-8/30)
7825. Shaver, Symphronia, 90, d 4/25/32 (in Sullivan?) ("emigrated from
       Germany 78 years since") (3-5/1)
7826. Shaver, William m 2/21/33 Lucinda Wood, both of Galen, in Lyons (6-3/6)
7827. Shaver, William m 7/5/40 Ann Jones of Chittenango in C; Rev. Z. Barnes
       (3-7/8)
7828. Shaw, James, 30, d in Waterloo (6-2/24/30)
7829. Shaw, James B. (Rev.), pastor of the Brick Ch., Rochester, m 5/14/45
       Laura J. Rumsey in Silver Creek (9-5/30)
7830. Shaw, John, 21, drowned in the Genesee River "at the Falls" in Rochester
       (9-4/11/26)
7831. Shaw, John (Rev.) m 10/30/33 Lucinda Livermore in Hornellsville (6-11/20)
7832. Shaw, Robert James, 1, s of Col. Daniel J. and Sarah Jane, d 3/26/41
       in Corning (4-4/9)
7833. Shaw, Sarah Elizabeth, 10 mo, only ch of Col. D. J., Jr. and Sarah J.,
       d 3/10/43 in Corning (4-3/15)
7834. Shays, Daniel (Gen.), 84, (a Rev. officer) d 9/29/25 in Sparta (was a
       leader in Shay's Rebellion in Mass.) (9-10/25)
7835. Shearman, Abraham of Penn Yan m 2/18/36 Elizabeth Cole of Benton in B
       (6-3/9)
7836. Shearman, Ebenezer B., Esq., 63, merchant, of Utica d 4/23/45 ("at 2:30
       a.m.") (funeral from his late home, 23 Broad St., Utica) (9-4/23 and 4/24)

7837. Shearman, Francis, 36, d 7/5/34 in Milo (6-7/16)
7838. Shearman, Maria, wf of Robert, merchant, of Utica, d 3/9/25 in St. Augustine, FL (member of First Presby. Ch., Utica) (9-3/29)
7839. Shearman, Pitt (who had died in NYC, date not given) was buried 9/13/24 in Utica (9-9/14)
7840. Shearman, Rebecca, 3, youngest ch of Willett H., d 2/26/50 in Verona (9-2/28)
7841. Shearman, Robert, merchant, m 1/8/22 Maria Sherman, dau of late Watts Sherman of NYC, in Utica; Rev. Anthon (8-1/23)
7842. Shearman, Stukely B., 26, of the firm of E. B. Shearman and Co., d in Utica (8-11/22/20)
7843. Shearman, Wardwell, Esq. of Kirkland m 12/24/45 Lucinda Marion Bessee, youngest dau of Heman, Esq. of Westmoreland in W; Rev. Denison Alcott (9-1/6/46)
7844. Sheather(?), _____ (Mrs.) d 11/16/33 in Seneca Falls (6-11/27)
7845. Sheather, John (Capt.) (a Rev. soldier) d 6/19/35 in Geneva (b in
See   Killingworth, CT 14 Dec 1752; a merchant in Litchfield, CT at time of
also   entering the army, 1775-1779; after the Rev. War lived in and near
Shethar   Albany, NY; moved west sequentially to Steuben Co., NY and, after a stay in the Dist. of Columbia, to Geneva, NY where he remained permanently (6-6/24 and 7/1)
7846. Sheekell, Samuel (Capt.), 78, (a Rev. soldier) formerly of Maryland, d 10/14/26 at his home in Phelps, NY (9-10/24)
7847. Sheffey, Daniel, Esq., formerly a member of Congress, d in Virginia (6-12/20/30)
7848. Sheffield, Henry m 3/2/33 Eliza Adams in Canandaigua (6-3/20)
7849. Sheffield, John of Buffalo m 3/30/32 Mary Pratt of Williamson in W (6-4/11)
7850. Sheffield, William m 11/1/18 Mary Carpenter in Oxford; Isaac Sherwood, Esq. (8-11/4)
7851. Shegren, John, 101, (a Rev. soldier) of Wake m Mrs. Elizabeth Lock, 85, in Granville, NC (6-12/11/33)
7852. Shelden, Allen of Clay m 1/28/44 Lydia Brown of Cazenovia in Syracuse; Rev. Storer (9-2/1)
7853. Shelden, Dorothy, 29, consort of Elias, merchant, d at her home in Pompey, NY (9-2/3/24)
7854. Shelden, William Henry of NYC m 9/6/49 Maria A. Maples, dau of Darius, Esq. of Cannonsville, in C; Rev. Dr. Lansing (9-10/2)
7855. Sheldon, Alexander G. of the firm of Sheldon and Wood, Albany, m 5/1/50 Frances Ellen Carpenter at Silvie Hall, the home of her father, Thomas O., in St. Lawrence Co.; Rev. L. W. Norton of Watertown (9-5/9)
7856. Sheldon, Asa (Deacon), 87, d 3/19/48 in Utica (b in Providence, RI 1 Feb 1761) (funeral "at his dwelling house at the Female Academy")(funeral sermon at Bleecker Street Bapt. Ch.) (9-3/25)
7857. Sheldon, Eli m 4/28/36 Sophia H. Smith in Benton (6-5/4)
7858. Sheldon, Frederic A. m 6/16/46 Anna Kellogg Smith, dau of Harvey, Esq. , at the Bapt. Ch. in Troy; Rev. L. Howard. All of Troy (9-6?25)
7859. Sheldon, Henry L. of Salem, MA m 8/9/49 Hannah W. Munn of Honolulu, Hawaii in H; Rev. E. W. Clark (9-11/14)
7860. Sheldon, Isabella, 80, wf of Deacon Asa, d 1/29/47 at the Female Seminary in Utica (marr. 63 yrs) (funeral at the Bleecker Street Bapt. Ch.) (9-1/30)
7861. Sheldon, James. Esq., attorney, of Buffalo m Sylvia Alexander, dau of Rev. C. of Onondaga, in NYC (8-6/2/19)
7862. Sheldon, Josiah, Esq., 67, d 6/15/49 in Rochester (9-6/21)
7863. Sheldon, Luther of Cincinnati, OH m 5/30/44 Cynthia E. Spencer of Jamestown in Utica; Rev. Theodore Spencer (9-5/31)
7864. Sheldon, O. M. m 10/12/43 Lydia A. Burchard in Hamilton; Rev. B. N. Leach. All of Hamilton (9-10/16)
7865. Sheleon, Albert N. of Waterville m 3/13/44 Frances E. Ladd, dau of late John B. of Hamilton, in Waterville; Amos O. Osborne, Esq. (9-3/20)
7866. Shepard, Charles E., merchant, m 3/2/31 Catharine Ann Cuyler, dau of Glen, Esq. of Aurora, in A (6-3/23)
7867. Shepard, Elizabeth, inf dau of Henry, d "last week" in Geneva (6-8/4/30)
7868. Shepard, Erastus of Ithaca, one of the printers of the American Journal, m 12/5/17 Eliza M. Carpenter, dau of Matthew of Elmira, in E (8-12/17)

7869. Shepard, Frances (Mrs.), 60, d 1/17/32 in Canandaigua (6-1/25)
7870. Shepard, George Hastings, 8, oldest s of Robert B., for many years a
      resident of Utica and latterly of New Orleans, LA, d 5/29/47 in Brooklyn
      ("Mr. S. sailed for Europe on the 15th of May leaving his wife and
      children for the summer in Brooklyn ...") (9-6/3)
7871. Shepard, Jesse, Esq., 67, of New Hartford d 7/7/44 in Cleveland, OH
      (9-7/16 and 7/17)
7872. Shepard, Margaret, 88, relict of the late William of Clifton Park,
      d 5/24/50 at the home of her son-in-law, William Peters, in C. P. (9-6/1)
7873. Shepard, Stephen, about 35, d 7/6/34 in Honolulu, Sandwich Islands (Hawaii)
      (consumption) (a missionary under the Board of Foreign missions; left
      Johnstown [NY?], his birthplace, where he had served as a printer's
      apprentice with late Asa Child; in Nov 1827 with his wife sailed from
      Boston for the Sandwich Islands as a missionary printer) (6-4/8/35)
7874. Shepard, William A. of Troy m 10/23/46 Martha M. Vail of Troy, dau of
      George, Esq., in Schenectady; Rev. Dr. Van Vechten (9-11/2)
7875. Shephard, Elias E., about 35, formerly of Utica, NY and recently of
      Cincinnati, OH, d 7/12/45 in NYC (consumption) (9-7/17)
7876. Shephard, Millicent d 12/15/36 in Dix, Chemung Co. (6-12/28)
7877. Shepherd, _____, 56, wf of Thomas, d 7/20/26 in Utica (9-7/25)
7878. Shepherd, Harvey m 8/23/48 Mary A. Elwood, both of Cicero, in Baldwinsville;
      Rev. Alden (double ceremony - see marr of Henry W. Marsh) (1-8/24)
7879. Shepherd, Moses, 30, d in Benton (6-6/16/30)
7880. Shepherd, Noble H. of Benton m 12/11/34 Clarissa J. Amsbury of Jerusalem,
      NY in J (6-12/24)
7881. Sheppard, Morris F. (Hon.), 72, one of the founders of Penn Yan, d 11/18/46
      in P. Y. (9-11/23)
7882. Sheppard, Robert m Frances A. Belknap in Benton (6-6/4/34)
7883. Sherborne, Frances D. W. (Miss), dau of late Col. Samuel of Portsmouth,
      NH, d 8/2/43 in Utica, NY (funeral from Grace Ch.) (9-8/4)
7884. Sherburne, Elizabeth T., youngest dau of late Col. Samuel of Portsmouth,
      NH, d 11/8/49 in Utica, NY (funeral from Grace Church) (9-11/9)
      Sherman. See also Shearman.
7885. Sherman, Humphrey B. of Rochester m Julia A. Edwards in Marcellus (6-2/2/31)
7886. Sherman, John W. m 4/26/31 Jerusha L. Pratt in Williamson; Rev. John
      Parker (6-5/11)
7887. Sherman, Nathaniel m Ada Aldrich, both of Havana, NY in H (6-6/24/35)
7888. Sherman, Rachel, 70, d 1/23/31 in Sangerfield (9-2/8)
7889. Sherman, Richard U. of Utica, editor of the Oneida Morning Herald,
      m 1/13/48 Mary F. Sherman, oldest dau of Capt. R. W. of Vergennes, VT,
      at the home of W. Barron Williams, Esq. in Rochester, NY; Rev. Dr. Dewey
      (9-1/14)
7890. Sherman, Robert m 11/13/35 Sally Ann Doty. All of Greece, NY (6-12/2)
7891. Sherman, Stukely B., 13, s of Willitt H. d 5/6/50 in Vernon (typhus)
      (9-5/8)
7892. Sherman, Warren, 25, d in Palmyra (6-4/28/30)
7893. Sherrill, Lewis, Jr. of Lisbon, IL m 4/25/49 Jeannette Gilfillan of New
      Hartford, NY in New H.; Rev. E. H. Payson (9-4/27)
7894. Sherrill, T. Dana of Lisbon, IL m 9/19/43 Elizabeth Wilcox, dau of Joseph
      of New Hartford, in New H.; Rev. Searle (9-9/25)
7895. Sherrill, Thomas Dana, 32, s of Lewis of New Hartford, d 9/7/49 in Lisbon,
      Kendall Co., IL (9-9/15)
7896. Sherwin, E. (Mr.), 61, d 10/3/41 in Sullivan (3-10/6)
7897. Sherwood, _____, inf s of Levi, Jr., d 7/15/19 in Oxford (8-7/21)
7898. Sherwood, Catherine, 34, wf of Samuel S. and dau of John Beasac, formerly
      of Hudson, d 10/6/21 (member of Episc. Ch.) ("left 5 small children")
      (8-10/10)
7899. Sherwood, Charles, Esq. of Albany m 9/5/49 Mary J. Risley of Utica at
      Trinity Ch., Utica; Rev. Dr. Proal (9-9/6)
7900. Sherwood, Henry Hall (Dr.), 62, formerly of Watertown, d 9/18/48 in NYC
      (9-9/21)
7901. Sherwood, Isaac, Esq. m 1/8/23 Sarah Knight of Chenango Co. (8-1/22)
7902. Sherwood, Jeremiah, 65, formerly of Geneva, d 7/25/30 in Bath (surv by wf
      and several children) (6-8/4)
7903. Sherwood, John H. of Albany m 11/15/49 Mary Ann Johnson of Utica in Buffalo;
      Rev. Kindad (9-11/22)

7904. Sherwood, Joseph, tobacconist, formerly of Utica, d 11/12/50 in Albany
       (9-11/15)
7905. Sherwood, Lorenzo (Hon.) m 6/9/45 Caroline Eldridge, dau of James B.,
       Esq., in Hamilton (9-6/14)
7906. Sherwood, Lydia, 33, wf of Jesse D. and dau of Rev. M. Dyer of West
       Windsor, d 4/7/50 in Corning (4-4/10)
7907. Sherwood, Marcus m 11/18/21 Jane McCalpin in Oxford; Rev. Bush (8-11/21)
7908. Sherwood, Marcus, 33, d 5/14/30 in Oxford (8-5/19)
7909. Shethar, Mary, 56, wid of late James and dau-in-law of Capt. John,
       d 9/29/30 in Geneva (6-10/6)
7910. Shever, William, 20, d 6/28/50 in Cuyahoga Falls, OH (9-7/19)
7911. Shimeall, Sarah D., inf dau of Rev. B. C., d 8/19/35 (in Canandaigua?)
       (6-9/9)
7912. Shippey, Knapp of Horseheads m 8/15/49 Mary Lovell at the Mansion House
       in Elmira; Rev. H. N. Seaver (5-8/17)
7913. Shockey, James, 42, formerly of Elmira, d 12/22/48 in Will Co., IL
       (5-1/19/49)
7914. Shoecraft, Matthew J., Esq. of Oneida Castle m 4/11/49 Mary Jane Nye of
       Lenox "at the church in Oneida Castle"; Rev. James Nichols (9-4/14)
7915. Sholes, John M., 22, d 4/11/36 in Waterloo (6-4/27)
7916. Sholes, Sally (Mrs.) d 8/11/33 in Junius (6-8/21)
7917. Shorwood, Henry E. m Mrs. Maria Bush in Fredonia (6-11/10/30)
7918. Shufeldt, Peter, farmer, of Chatham drowned 4/28/29 near Schodack Landing
       (his horse and wagon drove off the dock [river flooded] into the Hudson
       River in brick-loading there; his father on the dock, helpless,
       witnessed the drowning) (surv by "a family") (7-5/6)
7919. Shumway, Comfort (Mrs.), 98, d 7/29/42 in Oxford (Oxford Republican,
       8/12)
7920. Shumway, G. R. H. (Rev.), pastor of the Presby. Ch., Palmyra, m 2/17/35
       Emily C. Ford, dau of Hon. James of Lawrenceville, PA, in L (6-3/4)
7921. Shurtleff, J. B., editor of the Tioga County (NY) Gazette, m 5/11/31
       Elizabeth C. Taylor in Owego (6-5/25)
7922. Shute, Theodore, Esq. of Oxford, NY m 9/29/27 Rachel Ann Lee of Leesville,
       NJ in L; Rev. Chester (8-10/5)
7923. Sias, Solomon (Rev.) of the Meth. Episc. Ch. and publisher of Zion's
       Herald, m Mrs. Amelia Hawes in Boston; Rev. Merritt (9-8/23/25)
7924. Sibley, Mark H., Esq., attorney, m 11/28/21 Maria G. Clark in Canandaigua
       (8-12/12)
7925. Sibley, Samuel m 1/5/31 Almira Dixon in West Mindon (6-1/19 and 2/2)
7926. Sibley, Samuel H., 21, d 11/1/45 in Utica (9-11/10)
7927. Sickles, John m 4/5/45 Sarah Farnum, both of Sullivan, in S; Rev. Blakslee
       (3-7/5)
7928. Sickles, Zachariah, 92, (a Rev. soldier) d 6/15/39 in Chittenango
       (3-6/19)
7929. Sidebotham, Thomas of Utica m 3/3/25 Mary Davies, oldest dau of E. of Rome,
       NY, in R; Rev. R. Everett (9-3/15)
7930. Sidmore, Isaac m 12/20/34 Locinda Ester in Seneca; Rev. C. S. Coates
       (6-12/24)
7931. Sidway, Jonathan, Esq., 63, d 1/21/47 in Buffalo (9-1/23)
7932. Sigler, Samuel m 11/22/32 Thirza Barber of Geneva in Seneca (6-11/28)
7933. Signer, John m 3/10/24 Rubey Hutchinson in Bainbridge; L. Bigelow, Esq.
       (8-3/17)
7934. Sigourney, Sarah Elizabeth, 10, dau of John, Esq., d 11/10/46 in Whitestown
       (9-12/10)
7935. Sill, Edward (Dr.) of Redwood, Jeff. Co., m 6/3/50 Melissa D. Owen of
       New York Mills in N. Y. M.; Rev. H. R. Kirk (9-6/19)
7936. Sill, Eliza, 58, of Rome, NY, wid of late Gen. Theodore of Whitesboro,
       d 4/29/49 (9-5/3)
7937. Sill, John E., 24, formerly of Whitesboro, NY, d 11/20/43 in Portsmouth,
       NC (9-12/6)
7938. Sill, Samuel H. m 5/15/39 Susan A. Rose, dau of late Hon. Robert S.;
       Rev. Irving (6-5/22)
7939. Sill, Susan A., 25, dau of Henry Dwight of Geneva, d 3/2/35 (funeral from
       Presby. Ch.) (6-3/4)
7940. Sill, William E., Esq. of Geneva m 9/13/31 Juliana Hopkins, dau of Samuel
       M., Esq. of Albany, in A; Rev. Dr. Sprague (6-9/21)

7941. Sill, William N., Esq., 57, one of the associate judges of the Albany Co. courts, d 3/17/44 in albany (9-3/22)
7942. Silliman, Elisha L., 57, of New Haven, CT d 5/6/50 in San Francisco, CA (9-6/26)
7943. Silliman, Harriet, wf of Prof. Silliman of Yale College, d 1/18/50 in New Haven, CT (9-1/23)
7944. Silliman, William C. m 12/12/49 Mary A. Davis in Utica; Rev. William Wyatt. All of Utica (9-12/14)
7945. Silverside, George, 40, a native of England and a late resident of Geneva, d 4/11/31 at Mead's Creek, Steuben Co. (6-4/27)
7946. Simmons, _____, 4 mo, ch of D., d 6/12/48 in Baldwinsville (1-6/14)
7947. Simmons, Abraham (Capt.), 60, d 4/26/34 in Phelps (6-4/30 and 5/7)
7948. Simmons, Andrew (Capt.) m Hannah Wheeler in Benton (6-1/27/36)
7949. Simmons, Calvin, 60, d 11/29/50 in Bath (4-12/4)
7950. Simmons, Charles W. (Col.) of Ohio m 8/9/29 Eliza C. Dewey of New Berlin in New B.; Rev. Edward Andrews (8-8/26)
7951. Simmons, Eliphalet F., 60, d 4/3/44 in Whitestown (9-4/9)
7952. Simmons, George W, (Capt.), merchant, of Starkey m 10/14/32 Deborah Hathaway, dau of Gilbert, Esq.; A. G. Marshall, Esq. (6-10/17)
7953. Simmons, Joseph, 67, d in Westminster (state not given) (at age 16 fought at Bunker hill in Rev. and later at White Plains, Saratoga, and was at Yorktown at surrender of Cornwallis (9-12/5/26)
7954. Simmons, Leonard of Illinois m 1/20/49 Cordelia Bishop of Cato, NY in Cato; Rev. B. Nichols (1-2/1)
7955. Simmons, Ruth, about 16, dau of late Col. Simmons, d 9/28/36 in Phelps (6-10/12)
7956. Simonds, Albert, merchant, m 8/20/46 Caroline Mansfield of East Mendon in Victor; Rev. Charles Merwin (6-9/4)
7957. Simonds, Juliet, 14, dau of Benona and Sally, d 3/3/50 in Gibson (4-3/13)
7958. Simpson, Andrew m Catharine McNabb in Caledonia; Rev. D. C. McLaren (6-1/19/31)
7959. Simpson, Anthony C. of Geneva, NY m 9/22/46 Emily Williams of Toronto, Canada at the British Wesleyan Chapel in T (6-10/2)
7960. Simpson, Anthony C., Esq. of Elmira m Amelia H. Horton, dau of Hon. J. C. of Northumberland, PA; Rev. B. W. Morris (5-10/18/50)
7961. Simpson, Henry, 94, d 3/22/49 in Saco. ME (one of the "Tea Party" men who threw tea cargoes into Boston Bay) (9-4/6)
7962. Simpson, Henry m 5/20/50 Salona Gillett, both of Taberg, in Oriskany; George Graham, Esq. (9-5/22)
7963. Simpson, Ira, 25, d in Bath (6-7/14/30)
7964. Simpson, William T., formerly of Newburgh, NY d 1/21/50 in Stockton, CA (9-4/11)
7965. Sims, Edward, merchant, m 6/29/31 Harriet C. Wells, dau of Job, Esq. of Sullivan, in Chittenango; Rev. Lewis Leonard of Cazenovia (3-7/5)
7966. Sims, John, about 48, formerly of Geneva, d 12/22/31 in Seneca (6-12/28)
7967. Sinclair, Isabella (Mrs.), 97, d 12/30/31 in Number 9 (Seneca) (6-1/4/32)
7968. Sinclair, James of Romulus m 12/29/31 Nancy Scott of Ovid in O (6-1/11/32)
7969. Sinclair, William M. of Ovid of the firm of Sinclair, Van Horne and Co., merchants, m 6/20/33 Eliza Van Horne, dau of Abraham, Esq. of Cooperstown, in C; Rev. Job Potter (6-7/10)
7970. Sinclear, Robert (Hon.), a member of the Territorial Legislature, d 11/14/33 in Little Rock, AR (6-12/25)
7971. Sink, William m 12/10/45 Sarah McKinney in UticA: Rev. Bristol. All of Utica (9-12/11)
7972. Sinks(?), John m 2/16/43 Eliza Fosgett, both of Mcdonough; Rev. L. Sperry (Oxford Times, 3/1)
7973. Sisk, Catharine, 5, dau of Michael, d 5/12/39 in Geneva (6-5/22)
7974. Sisson, Clinton m 9/17/50 Martha Wilcox; Rev. J. M. Austin. All of Auburn (1-9/26)
7975. Sisson, George, 93, d 12/28/31 in Milo (6-1/4/32)
7976. Sisson, M. Jane (Miss), 17, d 3/20/49 in Baldwinsville (1-4/9)
7977. Sisson(?), Reuben, about 27, of Norwich, NY d 11/30/49 at the Mission of San Rafael, California (arrived in Calif. as a non-commissioned officer, Co. K. 1st NY Reg't.) (9-2/12/50)
7978. Sixbury, Elizabeth, 44, d 8/25/48 in Utica (funeral from the home of her son-in-law, 55 Washington St.) (9-8/26)

218

7979. Sizer, Asa B. (Maj.), 29th Reg't, U. S. Infantry in War of 1812, d in Trenton, NY (6-12/23/29)

7980. Sizer, Henry H., cashier of the Bank of Michigan, m 9/8/30 Mary E. Whiting in Utica (double ceremony - see marr of Daniel Burt, Esq.) (6-9/22)

7981. Sizer, Henry H., 45, d 6/28/49 in Buffalo (9-7/2)

7982. Sizer, W. J. of Remsen m 7/4/46 Esther Coleman of Whitesboro in Utica; Rev. W. H. Spencer (9-7/7)

7983. Skaats, ____, inf s of D. S., d 8/24/38 in Geneva (6-8/29)

7984. Skaats, Bartholomew, 76, a resident of NYC and uncle of D. S. Skaats of Geneva, d 4/9/30 in NYC (6-4/21)

7985. Skaden, Jane C., 48, wf of Joseph C. and mother of F. S. Holdredge, d 5/5/42 in NYC (Oxford Times, 5/18)

7986. Skeele, Olive, 42, wf of Samuel A., d 12/24/22 in Greene (8-1/1/23)

7987. Skellinger, Sarah, 55, wf of S., d in Palmyra (6-4/28/30)

7988. Skinner, ____, 4, ch of Daniel, d in Norwich (fell into a well) (7-8/27/18)

7989. Skinner, Adonijah (Maj.), 74, (a Rev. patriot) d 9/24/33 in Ogden (6-10/16)

7990. Skinner, C. A. (Rev.), pastor of the Universalist Soc. at Dexter, m 5/16/50 Cornelia Bartholomew, only dau of Oliver, in Brownville; Rev. L. Rice (9-5/24)

7991. Skinner, Davis m 3/15/48 AnnE. Marvin in Van Buren Center; Rev. Sherwood (1-3/22)

7992. Skinner, Elizabeth, dau of Dr. Levi, d in Ghent (6-3/23/31)

7993. Skinner, Fanny, 64, wf of Thomas, Esq. and youngest dau of Dr. Reuben Smith of Litchfield, CT, d 12/3/44 in Utica (funeral at First Presby. Ch.; sermon by "Pres. Green") (9-12/5)

7994. Skinner, George W. m 7/24/49 Elizabeth A. Brooks in New York Mills; Rev. B. Foster Pratt (9-7/31)

7995. Skinner, Hezekiah of the house of Webster and Skinners, booksellers, of Albaany d 7/2/33 in Hartford (9-7/16)

7996. Skinner, Roger (Hon.), 52, judge of the U.S. District Court for Northern New York, d 8/19/25 in Albany (8-8/31 and 9-9/6)

7997. Skinner, S. E. of Evans Mills m 9/3/50 Mary Nash of Utica in Oneida; Rev. J. D. Torrey (9-9/5)

7998. Skinner, Thomas, Esq., 70, d 6/19/48 in Utica (funeral from Midlam's City Hotel) (9-6/21)

7999. Skinner, Thomas H. (Rev.) of Philadelphia m 10/29/25 Frances Louisa Davenport, dau of Hon. James of Stafford, CT; Rev. Bruen (9-11/22)

8000. Skinner, W. H. m 12/18/49 Jane Cole of Verona in V; Rev. R. A. Avery (9-12/25)

8001. Skuse, Philetus m 7/4/36 Maria Rogers (in Phelps?) (6-8/10)

8002. Slack, John, 50, d in Springwater (6-4/7/30)

8003. Slamm, Levi D., Esq. of NYC m Jane Morsell of Washington, D.C. in W; Rev. Roffe (9-12/23/46)

8004. Slarrow, John, 21, d 11/6/36 in geneva (6-11/9)

8005. Slate, Hellen Josephine, 13 mo, only dau of Classon and Roxana, d 2/20/42 in Oxford (Oxford Times, 2/23)

8006. Slate, Joseph, Jr. m 5/10/42 Alma Bruce, both of Pharsalia, in Oxford; Rev. J. T. Goodrich (Oxford Times, 5/11)

8007. Slater, Giles, Esq. d in Carlton (6-2/2/31)

8008. Slaughter, James F. m 7/7/36 Elizabeth Stiles, both of Potter, in P (6-7/13 and 8/10)

8009. Slauson, Dennis of Little Falls m 6/15/35 Caroline Drummond of Phelps in P (6-6/24)

8010. Slawson, Henry m 2/25/43 Lorinda W. Newton in Utica; Rev.David Plomb (9-3/15)

8011. Slayter, Hezekiah of Chatham m 3/6/31 Phebe Ann Harder in Claverack 6-3/23)

8012. Sleeper, Abraham m 7/10/34 Sarah Ann Taylor in Starkey (6-7/3))

8013. Slingerland, Sophia (Mrs.), wf of Jacob, formerly of Chittenango and a native of Schoharie Co., d 7/22/35 in Ernestown, Upper Canada (3-8/11)

8014. Sloan, Caroline, 18, dau of John, Jr., d 10/3/36 in Penn Yan (6-10/12)

8015. Sloan, George of Elmira m 3/28/43 Harriet Rowley of East Painted Post in E. P. P.; Rev. Z. Grenell (4-4/5)

8016. Sloan, Robert m 2/24/31 Mrs. Rachel Thompson in Marengo; Rev. James Merrill (6-3/2)
8017. Slocomb, Milton, formerly proprietor and publisher of the Mexican Advocate printed at Nacogdoches, d 8/29/33 in New Orleans, LA (also same day, Charles M. Carmichael, 22, printer) (6-9/25)
8018. Slocum, Barnard, formerly of Baldwinsville, m 9/19/50 Mary L. Ostrander of Syracuse in S; Rev. Maltby (1-9/26)
8019. Slocum, Lucy, 27, wf of Leicester, d 8/5/26 in Utica (9-8/8)
8020. Slosson, Malinda Ann, 26, wf of Gabriel and dau of James C. and Lovina Beard, d 2/16/49 at the home of her father in Chemung (5-2/23)
8021. Sly, Charles m Rhoda Wright in Clyde (6-2/17/30)
8022. Sly, Daniel m 11/13/31 Catherine Depuy, both of Hopewell, at the Sulphur Springs (6-11/23)
8023. Sly, Robert m 9/5/35 Fanny Brewer in Southport (6-9/23)
8024. Sly, Susan C., 24, wf of Matthew McR. Sly and dau of Thomas Maxwell, d 10/4/48 in Elmira (5-10/6)
8025. Smart, Thomas C., 82, d 4/5/43 in New Hartford (b in England) (9-4/15)
8026. Smead, Henry D. of the Bath Advocate m 1/18/31 Mary Smith of Utica in U (6-1/26)
8027. Smead, Timothy H., senior proprietor of the Ohio City Argus, m 8/18/36 Mary E. Herrick of Utica in U (6-8/31)
8028. Smith, _____, wf of Enoch, d "a few days since" in Oxford (8-5/4/25)
8029. Smith, _____ of Elbridge m 6/15/48 Emily Woodruff Patterson of Syracuse in Baldwinsville (after 2 wks courtship); Rev. B. Phillips (1-6/21)
8030. Smith, Almira (Mrs.), 47, d 11/10/33 in Batavia (6-11/27)
8031. Smith, Alvin d 6/21/45 at Prospect Village in Trenton, NY ("Papers in Greene County please copy") (9-6/25)
8032. Smith, Amos (Capt.), 81, d 11/14/43 in New York Mills (funeral sermon by Rev. Ira Pettibone, pastor of Presby. Ch., New York Mills) (b in New Marlboro, MA, 1762; in 1788 moved to area of Westmoreland, NY; member Cong'l. Ch. there) (9-12/1)
8033. Smith, Andre m 5/18/42 Elizabeth Clark, both of Geneva, in Corning; Rev. S. M. Hopkins (4-5/25)
8034. Smith, Andrew P. (Dr.) m 12/22/44 Louisa Weeks, dau of Levi, Esq., in Stark; Rev. Robinson (9-1/14/45)
8035. Smith, Azariah, about 63, d 11/13/46 in Manlius (1-11/16)
8036. Smith, Azariah (Rev.), M.D., missionary under the A.B.C.F. to the Armenians in Turkey, m 7/6/48 Corinth S. Elder, 2nd dau of William, Esq., in Cortlandville, NY ("Mr. and Mrs. S. expect to sail within a few days ...") (9-7/15)
8037. Smith, Benjamin, Esq., 62, clerk of Rensselaer Co., d in Troy (9-4/18/26)
8038. Smith, Benjamin m 1/30/31 Eliza Lindsley of Geneseo in Avon (6-2/9)
8039. Smith, Caroline, 23, wf of the editor of the Onondaga Standard and only dau of Jonas Earll, Jr., Esq., d 4/3/35 in Syracuse (6-4/22)
8040. Smith, Charity, 81, wid of late Daniel, Esq., d 5/20/46 at her home in Whitestown (9-5/28)
8041. Smith, Charles, Jr. of Rochester m 6/13/31 Catharine Colt of Palmyra at Zion's Ch. in Palmyra; Rev. Hickox (6-6/22)
8042. Smith, Charles, 4, s of A. Smith, d 8/31/33 in Bath (6-9/11)
8043. Smith, Charles C. (Lt.) of Tazewell, TN (late of the Tennessee Volunteers in Mexico) m 9/28/47 Adelaide Frances Anderson of Hawkins Co., TN at the home of Mrs. Sarah Anderson in Hawkins Co.; Rev. Josiah Rhoton (9-10/30)
8044. Smith, Charles Henry, 2, s of Squire Smith, d 2/4/29 in Norwich (7-2/11)
8045. Smith, Chauncey m 10/23/50 Mary Jane Scudder (oldest dau of the late T. O.), both of Southport, in S; Rev. Hood (5-10/25)
8046. Smith, Clark m 4/20/33 Mary Ann Robson, dau of Mathew, deceased, in Seneca; Rev. Nisbet (6-5/1)
8047. Smith, Daniel, 65, d in Hamilton (9-6/27/26)
8048. Smith, Daniel m Roda Smith in Hamburg, NY (6-2/2/31)
8049. Smith, Daniel, 3, s of William O. and Anna M. M., d 2/17/45 in Utica (funeral from the home of J. B. Marchisi, 60 Genesee St.) (9-2/19)
8050. Smith, David of Nelson m 9/4/42 Widow Sylvia Warren of New Boston in Chittenango; Rev. T. Houston (3-9/7)
8051. Smith, David of Orange Co. m 10/10/50 Amanda Averril of Chemung in C; Rev. Wheeler (5-10/18)

8052.   Smith, E. Willard of Albany m 9/6/47 Charlotte M. Lansing, dau of Richard
        of Detroit, in D; Right Rev. Bishop McCloskey (9-9/13)
8053.   Smith, Ebenezer (Rev.), 90, d in Stockton, NY (9-8/3/24)
8054.   Smith, Edward m 4/3/50 Elizabeth Breeze Vermilye, dau of Dr. V., in NYC;
        Rev. Dr. Vermilye (9-4/11)
8055.   Smith, Edwin of Butternuts m 4/13/29 Phebe Robinson of Quebec, Lower
        Canada in Q; Rev. Dr. James Harkness (7-5/13)
8056.   Smith, Eleazur, 95, (a soldier in the French and Indian and Revolutionary
        Wars) d 12/8/22 in Greene (one of the earliest settlers there) (8-12/11)
8057.   Smith, Eli (Rev.), "missionary at Beyrout", m 10/23/46 "Miss Butler"
        of North Hampton in North H.; Rev. Rogers ("They embark on Nov. 2 at
        New York for Marseilles on their way to Beyrout.") (9-11/2)
8058.   Smith, Elizabeth, consort of Hon. Peter, first judge of Mad. Co.,
        d 8/27/18 at the home of Walter Cochran, Esq. in Utica (8-9/9)
8059.   Smith, Elizabeth, 2, dau of John U. and Susan, d 7/20/49 in Mohawk
        (1-8/16)
8060.   Smith, Ephraim A., merchant, m Jennet D. Autremont in Angelica (6-1/19/31)
8061.   Smith, Erastus m 5/1/14 Sophia McNeil, both of Oxford; Rev. Thorp
        (8-5/3)
8062.   Smith, Erastus P., s of Samuel A., m 4/15/29 Betsy Mills in Guilford;
        Rev. Wells (double ceremony - see marr of William Hitchcock) (8-4/22)
8063.   Smith, Ezekiel, merchant, of Barre Center m 12/1/35 Clarinda Almy of
        Farmersville in F (6-12/16)
8064.   Smith, Frances I. (Miss), 32, dau of John, d 11/24/36 in Chemung (6-12/14)
8065.   Smith, Garrit, Esq. of Peterborough m 1/3/22 Ann C. Fitzburgh, dau of Col.
        F. of Williamsburgh, Liv. Co., in W; Rev. Cummings of Rochester (8-1/23)
8066.   Smith, George m 4/17/34 Juliet Cobleigh (in Waterloo?) (6-4/30)
8067.   Smith, George C. m 9/30/41 Matilda Cook, both of Sweden, Monroe Co., in S;
        Rev. A. Handy of Chittenango (3-10/6)
8068.   Smith, George E. of Geneva m 11/2/46 Ada B. Means, dau of late Col. John,
        at the home of Joseph Means in Seneca; Rev. S. Topping (6-11/6)
8069.   Smith, George W. of Paris, NY m 7/25/33 Sophia E. Hastings of Utica in
        Clinton; Rev. Dr. Norton (9-7/30)
8070.   Smith, Griffin m Elizabeth Fluent in Canisteo (6-2/23/31)
8071.   Smith, Griswould D. of Mayfield m 1/25/45 Ann Durfee of Perth in Utica;
        Rev. Oliver Wetmore (9-1/28)
8072.   Smith, H. m Ann Maria Snider, both of Utica, in U; Dexter Gilmore, Esq.
        (9-9/14/47)
8073.   Smith, H. H., Esq. of Utica m 1/8/50Martha A. Soules, dau of James of
        Westmoreland; Rev. Turney (9-1/10)
8074.   Smith, H. W., attorney, of Lindlow, Madison Co., OH m 6/18/44 Jennette
        Smith, dau of J. O., Esq. of Whitestown, NY, in W; Rev. F. A. Spencer
        (9-6/24)
8075.   Smith, Hamilton (Dr.) of Harrington m Hannah P. Cooper of Urbana in U
        (6-11/6/33)
8076.   Smith, Harry m 10/14/50 Margaret Peel in Utica; Elder Thomas Hill. All
        of Utica (9-10/17)
8077.   Smith, Henry m 2/7/33 Matilda Bostwick, both of Newark, NY, in Geneva;
        Rev. Alverson (double ceremony - see marr. of Heman Bostwick) (6-2/13)
8078.   Smith, Henry m 11/28/48 Helene Knapp in Utica; Rev. Florian Schwenninger.
        All of Utica (9-11/29)
8079.   Smith, Henry C., s of Ebenezer of Masonville, Dela. Co., m 6/12/43 Lydia
        C. Manning, dau of Rev. Samuel of Chenango Forks (2-8/2)
8080.   Smith, Henry H. of the firm of Peck and Smith m 7/30/44 Maria A. Park,
        dau of late Chester, in Winfield; Rev. W. Loomis (9-8/1)
8081.   Smith, Henry H., 38, d 3/1/45 in Utica (9-3/19)
8082.   Smith, Hiram, about 26, formerly of Spencer, MA, d 9/26/31 in Bethel, NY
        (6-10/5)
8083.   Smith, Hiram m 2/8/35 Almeda Sherwood, both of Waterloo (6-2/18)
8084.   Smith, Hophni, 43, d in Chemung (6-6/26/33)
8085.   Smith, Hoton (sic) m 10/19/47 Miriam Stevens, both of New York Mills, in
        N. Y. M.; Rev. Dr. Paddock (9-10/20)
8086.   Smith, J. Adam, 45, d 11/24/46 in Whitestown (9-11/28)
8087.   Smith, J. Hull, 23, member of junior class of Hamilton College, Hamilton,
        d 3/23/42 (consumption) (9-3/25)

8088. Smith, J. Stanley m 7/16/44 Sophia Payn in Albany; Rev. Duncan Kennedy. All of Albany (9-7/25)
8089. Smith, Jacob of Starkey m 1/10/32 Ruth Gillett of Milo in M (6-1/25)
8090. Smith, James m Phebe Brown in Hector (6-10/8/28)
8091. Smith, James m 3/2/31 Betsey Wood in Buffalo (6-3/23)
8092. Smith, James, about 40, d 5/17/31 in Canandaigua (6-5/25)
8093. Smith, James M., Esq. of Buffalo, attorney, m Margaret Louisa Sherwood, youngest dau of John P. of Vernon, in V; Rev. Sabin McKinnes (9-6/9/45)
8094. Smith, Jared M., Esq. of Moravia d 5/23/46 at the home of his father near Kelloggsville (9-5/28)
8095. Smith, John of Seneca m 12/23/32 Loretta Olney of Benton in B (6-1/2/33)
8096. Smith, John, 2, s of William H. of Oxford, d 2/1/42 in O (Oxford Republican, 2/4)
8097. Smith, John of Utica m 10/3/48 Louisa Thompson, dau of Daniel of Waterville, formerly of Utica; Rev. Walter R. Long (9-10/5)
8098. Smith, John of Waterville m 5/2/50 Mary Elizabeth Bates of Hamilton in Nelson; J. Milton Case, Esq. (9-5/11)
8099. Smith, John Finley (Rev.), 27, Dexter Prof. of Languages at Hamilton Col., d 10/4/43 at the home of his father in Urbana (son of Rev. John Smith, for many years pastor of the Presby. Ch., Cooperstown, where Rev. John F. was born; Rev. J. F. grad. from Hamilton Col. in 1834) (9-10/7)
8100. Smith, John H., 2, s of William H., d 2/1/42 in Oxford (Oxford Times, 2/2)
8101. Smith, John J., about 40, d 8/4/32 in Sullivan "while ... binding wheat in the harvest field" (3-8/7)
8102. Smith, John N., 29, d 3/6/50 at the home of his father, Col. Nicholas of Utica (deceased had been a successful merchant in Watertown "for the last 12 or 15 years") (funeral from the First Presby. Ch.) (9-3/8 and 3/9)
8103. Smith, John W. m 10/9/46 Martha Newbury in Syracuse; Rev. James Erwin (1-11/9)
8104. Smith, Jonas, 39, m 2/3/20 Jane Kenneda, 23, both of Norwich, in Smyrna (7-2/9)
8105. Smith, Jonathan, Esq. d in Farmington (while he was raising a building a brace fell on his head)(6-11/10/30)
8106. Smith, Joshua A., 89, (a Rev. Soldier) d 2/7/49 at the home of his son, John, in Oakfield (9-2/16)
8107. Smith, Josiah, Esq. m 11/19/33 Louise Utley in Henrietta (6-12/11)
8108. Smith, Jud m 1/24/49 Rebecca Mathews in Southport; Rev. B. F. Goldsmith. All of Southport (5-2/2)
8109. Smith, Lament, 47, wf of Avery, Esq., d 9/14/35 in Milo (6-9/23)
8110. Smith, Lois A. (Miss), 19, only dau of William Chauncey, d 12/1/44 in Clinton (9-12/18)
8111. Smith, Luke D. m 5/12/50 Mrs. Anna H. Chandler in Mexico, NY; Rev. T. A. Weed. All of Mexico, NY (1-5/16 and 9-5/21)
8112. Smith, Lymon m 8/28/33 Eveline Christman; J. French, Esq. All of Sullivan (3-9/3)
8113. Smith, Margaret, 1, dau of M., d 10/27/46 on Hotel Street, Utica (9-10/30)
8114. Smith, Maria A., 19, wf of Henry H., d 3/24/48 in Westmoreland Hills (9-3/25)
8115. Smith, Martin m Margaret Homer, both of Seneca, in Phelps (6-8/26/35)
8116. Smith, Mary (Mrs.), 30, d 8/23/34 in Varick (6-9/3)
8117. Smith, Mary, 89, consort of James, Esq., d 3/26/49 in Portsmouth, NH (her [or his?] great grandparent was grand-daughter of John Alden of the "Mayflower"; she also related to Henry Adams from England, 1630, "accompanied with 12 sons") (9-4/6)
8118. Smith, Mary A., 62, wid of late Ebenezer, d 4/4/44 in Paris, NY (9-4/13)
8119. Smith, Milla, wf of Job, d in Southport (6-4/28/30)
8120. Smith, Nathaniel S. of Chittenango m 4/10/32 Susan H. Lord (dau of Rev. J. Lord and late instructress in Mr. Whittlesey's Seminary in Utica) in Morrisville; Rev. Lord (3-5/1)
8121. Smith, Nehemiah, Jr. m 7/28/25 Susan Gordon, both of Oxford; Rev. Elder Otis (8-8/3)
8122. Smith, Newell (Dr.), 60, d 1/27/44 in Portland, CT ("Printers in Western New York please copy.") (9-2/17)
8123. Smith, Oliver of Edgerton, MA m 8/21/48 Mary Allis Cottle of Syracuse, NY in S; Rev. Minor (9-8/24)

8124. Smith, Orrin m 10/18/36 Martha Welton, both of Pompey, in Sullivan; J. French, Esq. (3-10/26)
8125. Smith, Osmand m 5/28/36 Catharine McMann in East Bloomfield (6-6/15)
8126. Smith, Peter of Waterloo m 7/30/34 Elizabeth Badgley of Pleasant Valley in Waterloo (6-8/13)
8127. Smith, Peter m 4/5/44 Margaret Smith, dau of Duncan, Esq., in Russia, NY; Rev. Powel. All of R (9-4/13)
8128. Smith, Philip P. of Western m 1/1/50 Clarissa Shaver of Rome, NY in Syracuse; R. Woodworth, Esq. (9-1/5)
8129. Smith, Platt, merchant, of Perry m 4/1/34 Martha C. Lewis, youngest dau of Ezekiel of Geneva, in G; Rev. Henry Mandeville (6-4/2)
8130. Smith, Posken(?) (Gen.) of Oxford m 5/15/26 Anne V. B. Brentiss, dau of Rev. Joseph of St. Luke's Ch., Catskill, in that church (8-5/24)
8131. Smith, Reuben, 56, d 4/14/35 in Bath (6-5/13)
8132. Smith, Reuben C., about 55, d 12/22/31 in East Bloomfield (6-1/4/32)
8133. Smith, Richard, 88, d 2/6/36 in Milo (6-2/24)
8134. Smith, Richard Uwine, 18, late of Alfriston, Sussex, England, d 11/21/38 in Geneva, NY (6-11/28)
8135. Smith, Sarah, 28, consort of Peter C., d 8/2/32 in Seneca Falls (6-8/15)
8136. Smith, Sarah (Mrs.), 75, d 11/25/49 in Utica (funeral from her late home, 64 Whitesboro St.) (9-11/26)
8137. Smith, Sarah Ann, 5, dau of William and Harriet, d 4/30/42 in Oxford (Oxford Times, 5/4)
8138. Smith, Sarah C., 67, widow and youngest sister of Mr. Stalham Williams of Utica, d at the home of her son-in-law, C. Clark, Esq., in Tuscaloosa, AL (9-4/12/45)
8139. Smith, Sarah Vermelia, 8, dau of Trumbull, d 2/22/46 in Utica (9-2/23)
8140. Smith, Sereno O. m 3/28/50 Cothia Duncan in Marcellus; Rev. Levi Parsons (triple ceremony - see Sylvester Smith and Charles Duncan for further details). All of Marcellus. (9-4/11)
8141. Smith, Seth, 49, d 7/7/26 in Paris, NY (9-7/25)
8142. Smith, Sheldon, Esq., 46, attorney and formerly 5th ward alderman, d 6/4/35 in Buffalo (6-6/10)
8143. Smith, Sheldon of Stafford, NY m 10/6/36 Roxana Mauvel of Middlebury, CT in Vienna, NY (6-10/19)
8144. Smith, Sidney D. of Lansingburgh m Mary Van Cleve, dau of Aaron of Batavia, at Trinity Ch. in Lansingburgh (6-3/7/32)
8145. Smith, Simeon P. m 6/27/33 Hetty H. Smith (dau of Walter D.), both of Utica, in NYC; Rev. David Smith, D.D. (9-7/2)
8146. Smith, Solomon m Eliza Emery in Urbana (6-1/19/31)
8147. Smith, Sophia, about 24, d in Hopewell (6-6/30/30)
8148. Smith, Spencer P., 19, printer, formerly of Seneca Falls, d 5/21/37 in Royalton, OH (consumption) (6-6/14)
8149. Smith, Susan Stevens, 69, relict of Truman formerly of Western, d 11/29/49 in Delta (9-12/7)
8150. Smith, Sylvester m 3/28/50 Lydia Duncan in Marcellus; Rev. Levi Parsons (triple ceremony - see marr of Sereno O. Smith and Charles Duncan for further details). All of Marcellus. (9-4/11)
8151. Smith, Thomas, one of the editors of the Philadelphia Union, d in Phila. (8-2/17/19)
8152. Smith, Thorn m 1/11/32 Mary Wait in Phelps (6-1/18)
8153. Smith, V. W., one of the editors of the Onondaga Standard, m Clarissa Caroline Earl (6-3/2/31)
8154. Smith, W. P., Esq., late of Hudson, m 7/2/44 Elizabeth Russell of Utica in Rome, NY; Rev. Beecham (9-7/6)
8155. Smith, Wessel S. m 4/9/50 Elizabeth H. Cornwall, dau of Richardson Cornwall, in NYC. All of North Hempstead (9-4/11)
8156. Smith, William, 69, d 7/5/47 in Baldwinsville (heart disease) (1-8/4)
8157. Smith, William H. m 9/7/30 Harriet Adams in Oxford; Rev. Bush (8-9/15)
8158. Smith, William M. (Dr.) m 2/8/32 Mary A. Gildersleeve in Clyde (6-2/15)
8159. Smith, William R. of Farmington m 9/7/32 Eliza Wright, dau of late John W. of NYC, in Flushing, L.I., NY (6-9/26)
8160. Smith, William T. m 12/25/23 Lovica Lyon in Oxford; Rev. Randall (8-12/31)
8161. Smith, William Trumbull, 11, oldest s of Trumbull and Sara, d 9/22/46 in Utica (funeral from his parents' home, corner Hopper and Union Sts.) (9-9/24)

8162. Smylie, John G. m 2/10/47 Margaret Paddock, both of Manchester, in M; Rev. Carlin (9-2/12)
8163. Snell, Frederick I., 56, d 4/1/34 in Cazenovia (3-4/8)
8164. Snell, James H. of Geneva m 1/31/37 Angeline B. Gaylord, dau of Lucius of Homer, in H; Rev. Dennis Platt (6-2/8)
8165. Snell, Josiah m 10/7/32 Phebe Stearns in Chittenango; Rev. William Johnson (3-10/9)
8166. Snider, Norman of Jerusalem, NY m 11/15/32 Sally Vanscoy of Milo in M (6-11/28)
8167. Snow, A. (Mrs.), 79, d 8/9/47 in Utica (9-8/12)
8168. Snow, Elizabeth (Mrs.), 57, d at the home of her son, Henry, in Norwich (7-9/11/22)
8169. Snow, Hiram m 5/25/23 Sarah Stafford, both of Preston, in P; Elder Nathan Noyes (8-5/28)
8170. Snowden, Susannah H., 79, relict of late Rev. Samuel Finley Snowden, d 6/8/48 at Sacketts Harbor (9-6/27)
8171. Snyder, Henry of Herkimer m 1/27/31 Sophia A. Kennedy of Verona in V; Rev. Myrick (9-2/1)
8172. Snyder, Henry m 11/4/45 Mrs. Guild in Utica; Rev. D. W. Bristol. All of Utica (9-11/6)
8173. Snyder, Margaret, 15 mo, dau of Jacob, d in Utica (9-10/10/26)
8174. Snyder, Margaret, 50, wf of Henry W, d 11/26/43 in Utica (9-11/28)
8175. Snyder, Peter, 44, d 12/31/33 in Penn Yan (4-1/22/34)
8176. Snyder, Rudolph, 9, s of Jacob, d 11/3/26 in Utica (9-11/7)
8177. Snyder, William of Albany (one of the oldest residents of Albany) d 9/21/26 in Schenectady en route home from Utica (died in a fall from a canal boat) (fought in the French and Indian War) (9-10/3)
8178. Soles, George m 10/14/35 "Sally Jayne" in Penn Yan (6-10/28)
8179. Solomon, William m 7/7/36 "Mrs. Emmons", both of Tyre, in Waterloo (6-7/20)
8180. Sommers, Sarah L., 45, wf of Rev. C. G., d 10/3/43 in NYC (3-10/11)
8181. Soper, Emeline (Miss) d 9/15/46 in Darien, Wisc. Terr. (formerly of Oneida Co., NY) (9-12/10)
8182. Soper, George, 17, d 3/15/34 in Sullivan (3-3/18)
8183. Soper, Harriet, wf of Charles, d 9/18/46 in Darien, Wisc. Terr. (formerly of Oneida Co., NY) (9-12/10)
8184. Soper, Horace U. m Sophronia Allen (in Batavia?) (6-12/2/35)
8185. Soper, Sidney N. m 1/20/33 Rosannah Wood, both of New Haven, NY, in New H. (3-1/22)
8186. Soule, Betsey (Miss), 19, dau of Dr. E. L., d 1/21/49 in Euclid (1-1/25)
8187. Soule, Freeman m 7/28/36 Maria Slaughter in Benton (6-8/10)
8188. Soule, Thomas, 61, d 9/9/44 at his home in Floyd (had lived there many years) (9-9/23)
8189. Sours, Elizabeth Robinson, dau of Peter and Mary W., d 7/23/49 in Geneva (9-7/31)
8190. South, David of Sharon, Schoharie Co., "was lately killed by a bank of earth caving in upon him" (9-12/27/25)
8191. Southerland, William m Parmelia Morse in Milo (6-12/20/30)
8192. Southward, Thomas m 5/24/32 Grace Powsland, "both lately from England but now in Sullivan" (NY), in S; Rev. Dr. Yates (3-5/29)
3193. Southwick, Arthur C., 30, d 12/10/45 in Albany (9-12/16)
3194. Southwick, Henry C., printer, bro of Solomon, Esq. of Albany, d 1/29/21 in NYC (8-2/14)
3195. Southwick, John B., Esq., 27, attorney, and s of Solomon, Esq., d 6/23/33 in Albany (6-7/10)
8196. Souverhill, Isaac, 1, s of James M., d 3/15/34 in Geneva (6-3/19)
8197. Soverhill, James M. m 9/1/31 Phebe Crawford in Geneva; Rev. S. Mattison. All of Geneva (6-9/7)
8198. Soverhill, James M. m 4/4/39 Adelina Crawford in Geneva; Rev. Davis (6-4/10)
8199. Space, Susan, only dau of J. C. formerly of Utica, d 11/4/50 in Waterville (9-11/9)
8200. Spalding, Champion (Deacon), 93, (a Rev. soldier) d 9/7/46 in Whitesboro, NY (b in CT; settled in Plainfield, NH where he had a family of 11 ch, with 4 surviving him)(9-9/14)
8201. Spalding, Erastus "an old resident of Rochester", d 7/16/30 on a canal boat near Schenectady en route to his home at Lockport (6-8/4)

8202. Spalding, Erastus, Esq. of Rochester m Laura M. Wooster of Palmyra in
Auburn (6-3/2/31)
8203. Spalding, John D., junior editor of the Newburgh Gazette, m 4/3/32
Elizabeth L. Johnson, dau of Rev. J. Johnson of Newburgh, in N (6-4/18)
8204. Spalding, Levi B., 39, d 11/22/48 in Willowvale, Oneida Co. (9-11/25)
8205. Spalding, Philo B. m 1/27/31 Catharine Metcalfe in Bath (6-2/9)
8206. Sparhawk, Ebenezer, Jr., 24, d 8/21/33 in Rochester, VT (6-9/11)
8207. Spalding, Eleazer, 91, (a Rev. soldier) d "recently" in Dover, ME
(lived many years in Norridgewock) (9-5/9/50)
8208. Spaulding, G. W. of Utica m 10/7/50 Margaret Winston, dau of David and
Marcy; Rev. George Leeds (9-10/14)
8209. Spaulding, Mary (Miss), 22, d 1/29/31 in New Hartford (9-2/8)
8210. Spaven, Ann, 68, wf of Thomas, d 7/28/47 in NYC ("They had completed
their fifth passage across the Atlantic.") (9-11/29)
8211. Spaven, Thomas, 75 (b in Pickering, Yorkshire, England) d 11/13/47 in
Whitestown, NY (9-11/29)
8212. Spear, Allen, 45, d 12/7/31 in Hopewell (6-12/14)
8213. Spear, Isaac, 51, formerly of Boston, MA, d 11/8/33 in Macedon, NY
(6-11/13/33)
8214. Speechly, Charles m 6/21/43 Mary Wolcott in Utica; Rev. B. Hawley. All
of U (9-6/22)
8215. Speers, Thomas, M. D., surgeon, of New York Mills, formerly of County
Down, Ireland, m 9/28/48 Alice Yourt(?) of Utica in U; Rev. William
H. Spencer (9-9/30)
8216. Spees, Frederick T. m 6/28/27 Jane Skillman of NYC inSmithville; Rev.
Hoyt (8-7/13)
8217. Spell, Sarah Elizabeth, 25, wf of Benjamin and oldest dau of William G.
Miller, d 12/12/48 in Utica (funeral from her father's home on Cooper
St.) (9-12/14)
8218. Spencer, _____, inf child of Norman, d 12/9/25 in Utica (9-12/13)
8219. Spencer, Ambrose, 82, Chief Justice of N. Y. State, d 3/13/48 at his home
in Lyons (interment in Albany) (9-3/14)
8220. Spencer, Anson, Jr., publisher of the Ithaca Chronicle, m Sarah Ann
Mitchell in Ithaca (6-9/19/32)
8221. Spencer, Calvin, Esq. of Hartford, CT m 4/12/43 Caroline E. Hungerford,
dau of Dana, Esq. of Whitesboro, in W; Rev. D. L. Ogden (9-4/14)
8222. Spencer, Catherine N., 82, relict of late Thomas who had been one of the
first settlers in Deerfield, d 3/1/46 in Deerfield (member Bapt. Ch.)
(9-3/11)
8223. Spencer, Charles A. of Canastota m 7/10/38 Mary Stillwell, dau of
S., Esq. of Manlius, in M; Rev. Bellamy (3-7/18)
8224. Spencer, Charles S., attorney, of Ithaca m 8/16/49 Celia Adelaide Loomis,
dau of Clark D. of Auburn, in A; Rev. L. E. Lathrop (5-8/24)
8225. Spencer, Clinton, 7, s of John C., d 4/19/36 in Canandaigua (6-4/27)
8226. Spencer, Edward H., 22, d 5/16/42 in Western (9-5/27)
8227. Spencer, Eliza Cornelia, 23, third dau of Rev. E. M., d 7/24/44 at the
home of her uncle, J. A. Spencer, Esq. in Utica. Buried beside her
mother and 2 older sisters in Vernon (9-7/26)
8228. Spencer, Elizabeth Strother, wf of Dr. T. Rush Spencer and dau of late
George Gallagher of NYC, d 6/8/49 in Geneva (9-6/13)
8229. Spencer, Ellen Julia, 4, oldest dau of G. T. and Harriet, d 4/28/49 in
Corning (4-5/2)
8230. Spencer, F. A. (Rev.), pastor of the Cong'l. Ch., m 9/4/50 Elizabeth King,
dau of late F. A. of Sharon, CT, in Hampton, NY; Rev. William H.
Spencer of Utica (9-9/7)
8231. Spencer, George m 8/23/49 Elizabeth Clarke Upson, dau of late Dana J.;
Rev. Charles Wiley. All of Utica (9-8/24)
8232. Spencer, Georgette W., 10 mo, dau of Albert and Sarah Ann, d 12/28/46 in
Utica (9-12/31)
8233. Spencer, H. G. P. (Dr.) of Champion m 3/30/48 E. Antoinette Decker, dau
of James, Esq. of Troy, in Denmark, NY; Rev. T. N. Benedict (9-4/13)
8234. Spencer, Harriet P., 21, dau of Hon. J. A., d 1/26/50 in Utica (9-1/28)
8235. Spencer, Helen M., 18, dau of Hon. Joshua A., d 8/9/48 at her father's
home in Utica (9-8/10 and 8/11)
8236. Spencer, Henry F., 23, d 3/17/34 in Canastota (3-3/25)

225

8237. Spencer, Ira, Esq. of Wisconsin m 5/20/50 Maria Young of Clay, NY in Clay; Rev. William B. Ashley (1-5/23)
8238. Spencer, Israel S., Esq. of Canastota, attorney, m 7/2/39 Mary Jane Roberts, dau of N. S., Esq., civil engineer, at her father's home in Lenox; Rev. Van Santvoord (3-7/10)
8239. Spencer, Laben m Melinda Richmond in Clyde (6-4/7/30)
8240. Spencer, Lois, about 70, consort of Capt. Truman, d 7/7/30 in Boston (6-7/14)
8241. Spencer, Lyman m 3/8/46 Anna Dewey in Paris Furnace, NY; A. E. Pettee, Esq. (double ceremony - see marr of William Odell) (9-3/11)
8242. Spencer, Mary Jane, 19, wf of Israel S., Esq. and dau of Nathan S. Roberts of Lenox, d 4/14/40 in Canastota (3-5/6)
8243. Spencer, Philip, Esq., formerly of Dutchess Co., NY and bro of Hon. Judge Spencer, d 10/15/17in Bayou Boeuff, near Alexandria, on the Red. River, Louisiana (typhus) (surv by wf and several ch) (8-12/31)
8244. Spencer, Reuben of Norwich m 7/4/49 Nancy Jane Bartle of Preston in Norwich; Rev. M. Stone (9-7/21)
8245. Spencer, Timothy m 4/20/50) Mary Briggs of Painted Post in P. P.; B. Pew, Esq. (4-4/24)
8246. Spencer, Truman m 3/30/34 Martha Wheeler in Penn Yan (6-4/9)
8247. Sperry, Albert of Torrington, CT m 3/16/32 Hannah Van Duzen of Phelps in P (6-4/11)
8248. Spertzell, Marian, 6, oldest dau of Justus and Mary formerly of Utica, d 8/7/47 in Buffalo (9-8/11)
8249. Spicer, Peter W. (Gen) of NYC d 9/18/33 in Springfield, IL (6-10/23/33)
8250. Spink, Samuel, 28, s of Samuel of Barrington, d 2/13/30 in Matanzas, Cuba (6-4/14)
8251. Spinner, Christian F., 36, d 7/24/50 (in Herkimer or Utica?) (9-7/26)
8252. Spinner, John P., 80, d 5/27/48 in Herkimer (9-6/1)
8253. Spinner, Joseph, about 23, cabinetmaker, of Allentown, PA, d 5/19/34 at the home of A. S. Coburn in Warren, PA where he had lived about 6 weeks (said he had friends in Waterloo, NY (6-6/4)
8254. Spoon, Adam m 5/22/45 Catharine Levy, both of Little Falls, at the National Hotel in Utica; Rev. D. Skinner (9-5/23)
8255. Spooner, Prince (Deacon), 77, d 6/22/45 in Madison (9-6/27)
8256. Spoor, _____, wf of John S. of Oxford, d 7/3/20 (8-7/5)
8257. Spoor, C. H. E. (Lt.) of U.S. Army, formerly of Coxsackie, NY, d 12/26/37 in Lockport (6-2/7/38)
8258. Sprague, Almira J., 36, wf of E. W. and dau of James Wells of Baldwinsville, d 3/20/48 in London, Monroe Co., MI (1-4/5)
8259. Sprague, Cornelia Martin, youngest dau of Rev. William U. of Albany, d 1/25/49 (9-1/27)
8260. Sprague, Freelove (Miss), 30, dau of Asa, d 4/2/44 in Utica (funeral from her father's home in West Utica (9-4/3)
8261. Sprague, Leonard (Dr.) d 5/4/50 in Schenectady (9-5/10)
8262. Sprague, Michael m 1/28/36 Irene Reed, both of Canandaigua (6-2/17)
8263. Sprague, Morris of Murray m Polly Dorrance of Rochester in R (6-6/8/31)
8264. Sprague, Nathan Norton, 23, d in East Bloomfield (6-3/24/30)
8265. Sprague, Titus (Capt.) m 12/25/31 Mary Spencer, dau of widow Mary Spencer, in Canandaigua (6-1/4/32)
8266. Springer, Francis D., 35, d 7/29/49 in Utica (funeral from the Franklin House ("Philadelphia papers please copy") (9-7/30)
8267. Springer, Jacob L. (Col.), 46, d 6/16/45 in Warren (9-6/27)
8268. Sproull, John (Maj.), 47, formerly of the U. S. Army, d 11/1/32 in NYC (6-11/7)
8269. Sprung, Abram m 11/3/33 Sarah M. Barker in Rochester (6-11/20)
8270. Spyer, William Tracy, 14 mo, only s of William Curtis Spyer, d 1/28/50 in NYC (9-1/30)
8271. Squier, Adin, 21, d 9/19/31 in Seneca (6-9/28)
8272. Squier, Anna (Mrs.) d 7/10/50 at the home of her son-in-law, A. Hubbell, Esq.,in Utica (buried in Berkshire Co., MA) (9-7/11)
8273. Squier, Roswell W. m 10/15/35 Ann Mariah Ackerson in Bellona; Rev. Peter Stryker (6-10/21)
8274. Squire, _____ (Dr.) of Elmira m 12/5/50 Grace A. Smith, dau of Dr. Nathaniel of Spencerville, in S; Rev. Isaac Todd (5-12/13)
8275. Squires, Anthony, merchant, m 9/29/22 Harriet Beech in Greene; Rev. Gear (8-10/16)

8276. Squires, Samuel, s of James, Esq., drowned 7/24/19 in the Chenango River near Binghamton (8-8/4)
8277. Squires, Samuel m 5/14/43 Martha Babcock in Oxford; Judge Samuel McKoon. All of Oxford (Oxford Republican, 5/19)
8278. Squires, Theodore, 22, s of Charles of Greece, NY, d 5/7/49 at Rathbun's Hotel (town not stated) (9-5/10)
8279. Squires, William of Westmoreland m 6/23/45 Mrs. Mary Stockwell of Kirkland in K; Rev. R. Pratt (9-6/30)
8280. Staats, Barent P. (Dr.) m Maria A. Winne, both of Albany, in A; Rev. Dr. Chester (9-12/6/25)
8281. Staats, Marian, about 5, youngest ch of Dr. J., d 8/11/34 in Geneva (whooping cough) (6-8/20)
8282. Stacy, William, 45, d 12/13/47 in Utica (funeral at his late home, corner Whitesboro and Seneca Sts.) (9-12/15)
8283. Stafford, Amelia, 35, wf of Jacob, d 3/3/43 in Utica (to be interred in Albany) (funeral service at Trinity Ch., Utica) (9-3/9)
8284. Stafford, Arthur Gibbons, 18, only s of Joab, d 7/13/49 at the American Hotel in Albany (9-7/17)
8285. Stafford, Catharine, wf of Rufus, supt. of the Utica Cotton Mills, d 12/18/50 in Utica (funeral at her late home on Cornelia St.) (9-12/19)
8286. Stafford, Charlotte H., 26, relict of late George and only dau of John Beddoe, Esq., d 6/28/33 in Geneva (interred in family burial ground at Eldorado (Jerusalem, NY) (6-7/3)
8287. Stafford, D. S. m 6/16/46 Sarah Roberts in Utica; Rev. D. G. Corey. All of Utica (9-6/18)
8288. Stafford, Ezra M., 1, s of John W. and Sophia d11/27/50. in Frankfort (9-12/16)
8289. Stafford, George, 34, of the firm of Stafford and Beddoe, d 1/15/32 in Geneva ("...buried yesterday in the family burying ground on the Beddoe Estate at Esperanza, Yates Co.") (6-1/18)
8290. Stafford, Horatio N., merchant, of Lyons m 5/2/33 Frances Ann Tippetts, dau of Col. William of Geneva, at Trinity Ch., Geneva; Rev. Bruce (6-5/8)
8291. Stafford, James Romeyn, Esq. of Lockport m 6/20/31 Carolina Augusta Cook, dau of late Samuel of Schenectady, in Jersey City, NJ; Rev. B. C. Taylor of Bergen, NJ (6-6/29)
8292. Stafford, John W. m 6/22/42 Laura H. Tower, dau of Henry, Esq., in Waterville; Rev. S. W. ? elpley. All of Waterville (9-6/25)
8293. Stafford, Lothrop P. of NYC, oldest s of Aaron, Esq. of Waterville, d 5/30/50 in Forksville, CA (at the junction of the South Fork and American Rivers) (9-7/29)
8294. Stafford, Peter m 12/15/49 Priscilla Eastham in New Hartford; Rev. John Waugh. All of New Hartford (9-12/25)
8295. Stafford, Spencer, Jr. (of the firm of Spencer, Stafford and Co., merchants, of Oxford) m 6/21/21 Sarah Eames (oldest dau of John and gr-dau of the Hon. Jeremiah Sanger of New Hartford; Rev. Shaw (6-7/4)
8296. Stafford, Spencer, 71, d 2/10/44 in Albany (9-2/15)
8297. Stainton, _____, inf ch of Bryan, d 3/15/33 in Geneva (6-3/27)
8298. Stake, Frederick A. of Madison, WI m 10/25/48 Elizabeth M. Gardiner of Tioga, PA in T; H. Smith, Esq. (5-11/3)
8299. Staley, Solomon, 22, d 3/14/47 in Utica (funeral at the home of his father on Genesee St. "opposite the home of James Plant") (9-3/16)
8300. Stalker, Margaret, 56, consort of Alexander, deceased, d 10/8/41 in New Salem, Albany Co. (3-10/13)
8301. Stanbrough, James (Maj.) m 12/31/33 Uretta Smith, both of Arcadia, in Palmyra (6-1/8/34)
8302. Standish, David P., 25, d 5/4/31 in Waterloo (6-5/11)
8303. Stanford, _____ (Mrs.), 82, d 1/17/20 in Oxford (8-11/22)
8304. Stanford, Lewis m Mary Ann Bruce, both of Auburn, in A; Rev. Axtell (6-3/9/31)
8305. Stanley, C. M. of Elmira m 2/8/49 Mary W. Peck of Smithfield, PA; Rev. C. C. Carr (5-3/2)
8306. Stanley, Charles Edwin, 2, s of Dr. S. Stanley, d 8/13/50 in Corning (4-8/21)
8307. Stanley, M. H., Esq. of Watertown m 8/16/43 Cornelia E. Osgood of Hamilton in H; Rev. J. S. Maginnis (9-8/22)

227

8308. Stanley, Mary Keyes, 70, wid of late Frederick, Esq., d 11/23/45 in Oswego (9-11/27)
8309. Stanley, Sally, 39, wf of Lucius, d 3/9/37 in Seneca (6-3/15)
8310. Stannard, Erastus of Yates, Monroe Co. m 11/6/39 Zevia Knowles, dau of James of Sullivan, in S; Elder Clark of Cazenovia (3-11/13)
8311. Stansbury Cordelia Agnes, 24, youngest dau of Mrs. Elizabeth Stansbury, d 8/29/35 in Sodus Point (6-9/2)
8312. Stantial, Thomas of Troy m 12/10/46 Lucy Bugden in Utica (9-12/11)
8313. Stanton, J. P. of Gorham m 5/18/30 Emiline Wheadon of Seneca in S (6-5/26)
8314. Stanton, Nancy, 9, dau of Warren D. and Nancy D., d 11/14/46 in South Trenton, NY (9-11/17)
8315. Stanton, Nancy, 56, wf of Elias, d 12/18/48 in South Trenton, NY (9-12/27)
8316. Stanton, Russel of Caton m 3/25/41 Lucy C. Northway of Hornby in Hornby; Rev. J. Gardner. All of H (4-4/2)
8317. Stanton, Sidney m 7/24/35 Fanny Perkins, both of Cazenovia, in Manlius; Rev. Hollister (3-8/25)
8318. Stanton, William Franklin of NYC m 6/17/46 Abby Fosdick Billings, oldest dau of John of Trenton, NY, in T; Rev. E. Buckingham (9-6/25)
8319. Staples, Grace (Miss) d 6/5/31 in Waterloo (6-6/15)
8320. Staples, John m 3/27/50 Sylva Lincoln, both of Elmira; Rev. G. M. Spratt (5-4/5)
8321. Staples, Lydia, 103, wid of late John (she a widow pensioner and he, earlier, a Rev. pensioner) d 7/1/42 in Great Bend, PA (both were at Wyoming, PA at time of the "Great Massacre" by the British and Indians) (2-7/13)
8322. Starin, Charles of Syracuse m 9/27/47 Helen A. Wemple of Wampsville in W; Rev. W. H. Cooper (9-9/29)
8323. Stark, Frederick R., Esq. of Montreal, Canada m 11/6/50 Maria Atwood, dau of John M., Esq. of Philadelphia, PA, in P; Rev. Albert Barnes (9-11/12)
8324. Stark, John (Maj. Gen.), 93, (a Rev. officer) d 5/8/22 in Manchester, NH (b in NH and lived near Amoskeag Falls for nearly a century; at age 21 was captured by Indians and taken to Montreal but later redeemed by "Mr. Wheelright of Boston"; fought in French and Indian War (8-5/29)
8325. Starkey, Hiram m 12/13/25 Esther Corbin in Greene (8-12/21)
8326. Starkey, Rebecca, 34, d 7/31/49 in NYC (9-8/3)
8327. Starkness, J. M. of Gorham m 3/21/38 S. Clark of Italy, NY in I; Rev. J. Morgan (6-4/11)
*8328. *Starks, Henry of Canton m 7/29/47 Lydia Fuller of Lysander in Baldwinsville; Rev. E. C. Beach (1-8/4)
8329. Starr, George L. m 11/10/42 Mary Hubby at Christ's Ch. in Sherburne; Rev. L. A. Harrows (3-11/14)
8330. Starr, James, 90, d in Jay (was one of those who destroyed the tea in Boston Harbor before the Rev.) (9-2/1/31)
8331. Starr, Mary, 16, oldest dau of Seth, Esq., d 5/19/41 in Canaseraga (consumption) (3-5/26)
8332. Starr, Vine (Capt.), 74, d 7/9/31 in Seneca ("Amassed a handsome property, part of which he willed to a distant connexion by the name of Elisha Starr, residing it is believed, in Vermont.") (6-7/13)
8333. Starr, William, 50, d 7/11/40 in Sullivan (3-7/15)
8334. Start, Isaiah m 1/12/50 Amanda Palmer in Lysander; Rev. Augustus Wheelock. All of Lysander (1-1/17)
8335. Start, Robert of Marcy m 12/12/50 Elizabeth Miller of Utica in U; Rev. William Wyatt (9-12/14)
8336. Start, Sarah, 48(?), wf of Isaiah d 12/16/48 in Baldwinsville (1-12/21)
8337. Stearns, ____, 4 mo, ch of Willis, d 9/6/26 in Utica (9-9/12)
8338. Stearns, Albert J. m Charity Dunham in Arcadia (6-4/7/30)
8339. Stearns, Calvin, 69, d 11/12/49 in Utica (funeral from his late home on Broad St.) (9-11/13)
8340. Stearns, Joel, Jr. (Col.) m 11/20/33 Chloe Hotchkiss in Vienna, NY (6-12/4)
8341. Stearns, Marma m Angeline Comstock in Southport (6-11/10/30)
8342. Stearns, Nancy, about 37, wf of Joel, Jr., d 5/28/33 in West Vienna, NY (6-6/5)
8343. Stearns, Eugenia L. (Miss), 24, d 10/1/31 in Jerusalem, NY (consumption) (6-10/19)
* 8328a Starks, Stephen m Tryphena Darrow in Schenectady (6-2/23/31)

228

8344. Stebbins, Eugenia L. (Miss), 24, d 10/1/31 in Jerusalem, NY (consumption) (6-10/19)
8345. Stebbins, Joseph m 1/14/46 Martha Ann Alcott, dau of Chatfield Alcott, at Oriskany Falls; Robert J. Norris, Esq. All of Augusta (9-1/17)
8346. Stebbins, Parlina, 32, wf of George, d 5/13/47 in Waterville (9-5/18)
8347. Stedman, S. (Mr.), 103, d "in March" in Sauquoit (6-4/30/34)
8348. Steel, William m 11/4/30 Elmira Rice in Marion (6-11/24)
8349. Steele, George of the firm of Curtis and Steele, merchants, of Chittenango m 7/15/40 Adelia E. Wright of East Avon, Liv. Co.; Rev. C. Coats (3-7/22)
8350. Steele, Horace of Buffalo, editor and one of the proprietors of the Buffalo Bulletin, m 6/20/33 Mrs. Lavinia F. Spencer, youngest dau of late Isaac Flower, Esq. of Vienna, NY, in Hartford, Trumbull Co., OH (6-7/17)
8351. Steele, Jeduthan L., Jr., 24, editor of The Bulletin, d 10/29/33 in Buffalo (6-11/6)
8352. Steele, John F. m 9/2/46 Frances Mary Steele, dau of Oliver, in Albany (9-9/4)
8353. Steele, Martha, youngest dau of H., Esq., d 8/3/33 in Buffalo (6-8/14)
8354. Steele, Oliver of Albany m 5/15/26 Mary Augusta Livingston, dau of M., Esq., in Livingston Manor, Col. Co.; Rev. Kittle (9-5/30)
8355. Steele, Tabitha, wf of Lemuel, Jr. of Albany, d at the home of her bro, Hervey Barnard, 30 Broad St., Utica (9-3/12)
8356. Steele, Theodore J. m 4/7/36 Sophia M. Pratt in Painted Post (6-4/27)
8357. Steele, Theophilus, 64, d 9/3/48 at his home in Clinton (result of an earlier buggy accident [runaway horse] east of Manchester on the bridge over the Oriskany) (b in Egremont, MA where his father, Rev. Eliphalet was pastor of the Congregational Ch and later pastor at Paris, NY; deceased moved to Clinton in 1832) (9-9/5)
8358. Steere, Esek, 62, d 6/6/46 in Hamilton (9-6/19)
8359. Steers, James R. m Eve Saits in Schenectady (6-1/19/31)
8360. Stephens, Ann, wf of T. C. and dau of Owen Owens of Utica (funeral from Broad St. Bapt. Ch.) (9-3/7 and 3/8)
8361. Stephens, Francis F. of Eaton m 6/27/33 Lavina Smith in Castile (6-7/10)
8362. Stephens, Hannah Coe, 14, dau of Abram E., d 12/25/31 in Hopewell (6-1/4/32)
8363. Stephens, John, Esq., attorney, m Catharine Ravel in Bridgeport, CT (6-9/19/32)
8364. Stephens, John m 5/12/33 Clara Ann Myers; J. French, Esq. All of Chittenango (3-5/14)
8365. Stephens, Matilda, dau of John W., d in Elmira (6-5/5/30)
8366. Stephens, Thomas C. m 8/30/49 Sarah H. Ward, both of Utica, in Syracuse; Rev. R. R. Raymond (9-9/3)
8367. Sterling, Alexander F. m 6/16/49 Elizabeth Jordan, dau of Hon. Ambrose I., d at St. Mark's Ch.; Rev. Dr. Anthon. All of NYC (9-6/21)
8368. Sterling, Anna Hopkins, 3 mo, dau of J. C. and Anna S., d 11/27/50 in Watertown (9-12/7)
8369. Sterling, George of Elmira m 12/25/37 Mary Ann Rogers of Sullivan in S; J. French, Esq. (3-12/27)
8370. Sterling, John C. of Watertown m 6/12/44 Anna Brayton, youngest dau of George, in Westernville; Rev. Isaac Brayton of Watertown (9-6/17)
8371. Sterling, Sarah Caroline, 43, wf of Daniel, d 4/15/44 in Rome, NY (9-4/27)
8372. Stern, Sarah Antonett, 2, dau of Elijah of Chittenango, d 7/7/34 in Chittenango (3-7/15)
8373. Sterns, Curtis m 6/8/36 Mary Ann Dewey in Fayetteville; Rev. Smith. All of Fayetteville (3-6/15)
8374. Stevens, Cyprean, attorney, d in Detroit (6-8/4/30)
8375. Stevens, Edwin, 4, d 9/19/33 in Owego (6-10/9)
8376. Stevens, Frederick m 2/19/50 Catherine Hyde, both of Conradt Settlement, in Rome, NY; H. C. Vogell, Esq. (9-2/28)
8377. Stevens, Henry E., 43, d 4/9/45 in Utica (9-4/12)
8378. Stevens, James S. m Hannah Smith in Hudson (6-2/23/31)
8379. Stevens, John A., Esq., editor of the Ontario Messenger, m 9/13/26 Aurelia Ackley of Montreal, Canada in Canandaigua, NY (9-9/26)
8380. Stevens, N. D. (Deacon) of the Chenango Forks Cong'l. Ch. d 6/4/43 (2-6/14)
8381. Stevens, Nancy (Miss), 31, d 3/25/30 in Geneva (6-3/31)
8382. Stevens, Reuben W. of Phelps m 10/7/34 Julia Babcock of Hopewell in H; Rev. Isaac Crabb (6-10/15)

8383. Stevens, Richard (Dr.), 43, d 8/22/35 in Hoboken, NJ (for many years a surgeon in U.S. Navy; his last voyage on the "Franklin, 74" around the world. His brothers made improvements in the steam engine. Deceased, late in life, worked for the North River Line of Steamboats.) (6-8/26)

8384. Stevens, Samuel, 60, attorney, d 11/25/44 in NYC (for several yrs member of common council and first pres. of Board of Aldermen after reorganization) (was a commissioner to direct construction of the Croton Aqueduct) (9-11/30)

8385. Stevens, Thomas of Jordan m Eliza Clark of Skaneateles in S (6-3/9/31)

8386. Stevens, Thomas, 61, d 1/28/33 in Cuba, Alleg. Co. (6-2/20)

8387. Stevens, William m Eliza Ann Quackenbush in Wheeler (6-12/22/30)

8388. Stevens, William H. (Dr.) of Gorham m 11/12/35 Jane M. Morris of Seneca Falls in S. F. (6-11/25)

8389. Stevenson, Andrew (Hon.) of Virginia m 6/28/49 Mary Shaaff, 3rd dau of late Dr. Shaaff of Maryland, in Georgetown, D. C. (9-7/4)

8390. Stevenson, James, Jr. of Waterloo m 1/27/31 Matilda Edington of Fayette in Seneca Falls (6-2/16)

8391. Stevenson, Phebe (Mrs.), 22?, d in Howard (6-7/3/33)

8392. Stevenson, Susan (Mrs.), 62, d 4/9/44 in Utica (funeral at her late home, 40 Charlotte St.) (9-4/10)

8393. Stewart, A. B. of Oriskany Falls m 4/16/46 Elizabeth M. Northrup of Clockville; Rev. A. A. Graly (9-4/25)

8394. Stewart, Alanson W. m 7/24/20 Sally Bartle (in Oxford?) (8-8/20)

8395. Stewart, Alvan, Esq., 58, formerly of Utica, d 5/1/49 in NYC (9-5/5)

8396. Stewart, Augustus G. E. m 10/29/34 Emily T. Smith in Benton; Rev. Crosby. All of Benton (6-11/5)

8397. Stewart, Cynthia (Miss), 14, d 1/12/32 in Waterloo (6-1/18)

8398. Stewart, E. W., Esq., attorney, of Utica m 11/13/45 Marian Jamieson, youngest dau of John, Jr. of Camden, NY, in C; Rev. Douglas (9-11/17)

8399. Stewart, Frederick Gilmore, 4, and Frank Horatio Stewart, 2, sons of Horation and Lucretia, d 6/17/48 in Medina (scarlet fever) (9-6/27)

8400. Stewart, Horatio of Medina m 6/21/42 Sarah Lucetta Fargo of Sherburne at Christ's Ch. in Sherburne; Rev. L. A. Barrows (9-6/22)

8401. Stewart, James of Lockville m Mabel Vanauken of Lyons in Vienna, NY; James Snow, Esq. (6-8/8/32)

8402. Stewart, James (Col.), 47, an officer in the Indian Dept., d 8/21/33 at Carey Mission near Niles (state or territory not given - perhaps Mich.?) 6-9/11)

8403. Stewart, Jemima (Mrs.), 109, d 3/8/33 near St. David's, Upper Canada (6-3/27)

8404. Stewart, John Jay (Dr.), 41, d 8/8/50 in Chicago, IL (cholera) (formerly of Utica, NY; studied medicine with Dr. Theodore Pomeroy) (9-8/15)

8405. Stewart, Robert, Esq. m 8/29/48 Charlotte M. Van Valkenburgh at the Reformed Dutch Ch. in Chittenango; Rev. James abell. All of Chittenango (double ceremony - see marr of Andrew J. French) (9-8/31)

8406. Stewart, Roswell E. m 4/17/49 Sarah M. Martin, both of Western, at the Central Hotel in Utica; Rev. D. G. Corey (9-4/18)

8407. Stewart, Samuel, 19, d 6/17/34 in Elmira (6-7/2)

8408. Stewart, William, Esq., 72, a native of the state of Maryland, d 2/12/31 in Geneva, NY (a Rev. officer - lived after the war in Great Britain and France; read law in NYC; lived in Ontario Co., NY until 1803 when he moved to Binghamton. Was district attorney and judge of the court of common pleas; married the dau of Gen. James Clinton, sister of the late Gov. De Witt Clinton) (6-2/23)

8409. Stewart, William B. m 8/31/47 Perpetua S. Brook of New Hartford in Utica; Rev. H. R. Clark (9-9/1)

8410. Stewart, William James, 1, s of Daniel and Elizabeth G., d 6/30/49 in Utica (funeral at the home of her father, 21 Seneca St.) (9-7/2)

8411. Stiles, Mary, 14, of Amsterdam, NY d in Ovid (6-3/10/30)

8412. Stillman, Samuel N. m 12/18/47 Betsey Ann Mason, both of Plainfield, in P; Rev. W. B. Maxson (9-12/23)

8413. Stillson, David of Rochester m 9/1/33 Sophia Dickinson in Greece, NY (6-9/18)

8414. Stilwell, _____, 5 mo, ch of John G., d in Utica (9-10/10/26)

8415. Stilwell, Smith, Jr. of Ogdensburgh m 8/26/47 Cornelia M. Welton, 2nd dau of Isaac of Paris, NY, in P; Rev. Baker (9-8/27)

8416. Stivers, David, 7 mo, youngest ch of Edward, d 8/27/31 in Geneva (6-8/31)
8417. Stivers, Edward, 40, d 4/7/39 in Geneva (6-4/10)
8418. Stivers, Horace, 1, d 1/2/34 and George Stivers, 4, d 1/4/34 in Geneva.
     Both are sons of Edward of Geneva (scarlet fever) (6-1/8)
8418a Stocker, Le Grand C., 32, d 9/3/49 in Elmira (a newcomer with his family
     from Danbury, CT) (surv by wf and 2 small ch) (5-9/7)
8419. Stocking, Isaac Train of Bath m 1/27/33 Diadema Burley of Cameron near
     Thurston (6-2/13)
8420. Stocking, James M. of Moorestown, St. Law. Co. m 5/4/31 Catharine Metcalf,
     dau of Elijah late of Cooperstown, in C (6-5/18)
8421. Stocking, Timothy W., Jr. of Phelps m 11/15/38 Sarah Jane Adams of
     Manchester in M; Rev. R. Burnet (6-12/5/38)
8422. Stockman, Josiah L. m 1/15/33 Mrs. Harriet Lisk in Seneca Falls (6-2/6)
8423. Stockwell, Henry of Angelica m 10/23/27 Melina Yale of Guilford in G;
     Rev. Bentley (8-11/16)
8424. Stockwell, Reuben, 52, d 11/17/43 in Kirkland (9-11/21)
8425. Stodard, Eleazer and Josiah, 27, twin brothers of Rupert, VT, m 3/9/14
     Emily and Almira Sill, 25, twin sisters of Moreau, NY (a double ceremony)
     (the brothers, farmers, hold their property in common) (8-4/19)
8426. Stoddard, Frances B., wf of William H. of Northampton, MA and dau of
     John Bradish, Esq. of Utica, NY, d 3/24/50 in Northampton, MA (9-4/15)
8427. Stoddard, James of Lisle d 9/20/42 in NYC (formerly sheriff of Broome Co.
     and a member of state assembly) (2-9/28)
8428. Stoddard, James of Lowville m 9/20/46 Catharine Thrusher of New Hartford
     in New H.; H. Sherrill, Esq. (9-9/22)
8429. Stoddard, Thaddeus m 7/23/37 Mrs. Abigail Avery, both of Perryville, in
     P.; Elder Nicholson of Cazenovia (3-8/9)
8430. Stokoe, James m 5/24/30 Mary Perkins in Seneca (6-6/2)
8431. Stone, _____, inf ch of A., d 4/25/31 in Gorham ("drank a quantity of
     dissolved potash which had incautiously been left in its way") (6-5/4)
8432. Stone(?), Daniel, 43, d 8/7/46 in Chicago, IL (late prof. of languages
     in the Western University of Pennsylvania in Pittsburgh; formerly a
     teacherin a select school in Geneva, NY) (6-8/21)
8433. Stone, George W. of Oxford m 10/8/43 Jane Stratton, dau of William H., Esq.
     of Wellsboro, PA, in Oxford; Rev. E. G. Perry (Oxford Republican, 10/12)
8434. Stone, Jesse M. of Oxford m 2/15/27 Mary Ann Orcutt of Rome, NY in R;
     Rev. Gillet (8-2/23)
8435. Stone, John (Rev.), tutor of Geneva College, m 5/2/26 Sophia Adams of
     Rochester in R; Rev. F. H. Cuming (9-5/23)
8436. Stone, John, 64, d 12/27/38 in Romulus (6-1/9/39)
8437. Stone, John m 3/16/45 Martha A. Schuyler in Utica; Rev. D. G. Corey. All
     of Utica (9-3/18)
8438. Stone, John J. m 9/11/33 Mrs. Sophia Murray in Hopewell (6-9/25)
8439. Stone, John P., 33, d 6/20/26 in Utica (9-6/27)
8440. Stone, Lester m 11/20/36 Mary Clark, both of Cazenovia, in Milan; Rev.
     Z. Barnes (3-11/23)
8441. Stone, W. J. m 11/11/48 E. M. Andrews, both of Kirkland, in Utica;
     Elder A. Thompson (9-11/14)
8442. Stone, William P. (Maj.) of Trumansburgh m Sally Ann Kidder in Ovid
     (6-2/10/30)
8443. Stone, William P. m 11/5/35 Cybele Truman in Candor (6-11/11)
8444. Storer, J. P. B. (Rev.), pastor of the Unitarian Ch. and Soc. in Syracuse,
     d 3/17/44 in Syracuse (9-3/21)
8445. Storer, Peyton R. of Milwaukee, WI m 7/26/49 Helen Meigs, dau of Edmond,
     Esq. of Holland Patent, in H. P.; Rev. M. A. Perry (9-7/28)
8446. Storey, Loraney, 40, d in Lockport (6-1/8/34)
8447. Storm, Walter of NYC m 3/5/45 Zilpha Smith, dau of Hon. Azariah in
     Manlius; Rev. D. Platt (9-3/8)
8448. Storms, John, Jr. of Seneca m 8/29/33 Christina Gates of Phelps in P;
     Elder Demic (6-9/4)
8449. Storms, John (Deacon), 67, d 6/16/34 in Seneca (6-6/25)
8450. Storms, Sylvanus m 5/13/37 Lucinda Ehle in Sullivan; Jairus French, Esq.
     All of S (3-5/17)
8451. Storr,Shubael, 69, d 7/17/47 in Utica (funeral from his late home,
     54 Whitehall St.) (9-7/19)

8452. Storrs, Amelia, 15, youngest dau of Shubael, d 3/7/44 in Utica (funeral at the home of her father, 54 Whitesboro St.) (9-3/8)

8453. Storrs, Helen, 21, consort of Peyton R. of Milwaukee, WI, d 3/21/50 in Holland Patent, NY (9-3/29)

8454. Storrs, John, 73, d 4/23/45 in Trenton, NY (born and lived first 16 yrs on Long Island and then moved to Mansfield, CT. After 4 yrs came to Utica [in 1794]. Served as town supervisor, magistrate, judge of common pleas, and state assemblyman) (surv by wf, children, and gr-children) (9-5/20)

8455. Story, Amos L. of Syracuse m 9/23/40 Laura A. Burr of New Boston in N. B.; Rev. James Abell (3-9/30)

8456. Stout, Charles B. m 10/23/32 Laura Chapin in Canandaigua (6-11/7)

8457. Stout, Emily (Miss), 19, of Philadelphia (state not given) d 9/29/33 in Geneseo (6-10/16)

8458. Stout, Jacob of the firm of Stout, Platt and Co. of NYC m 12/23/25 Susan Breese of Utica; Rev. Anthon (9-1/4/25)

8459. Stow, H. J. of Buffalo m Ann J. Powers of Havana, NY in H (6-8/9/37)

8460. Stow, Henry m 2/23/42 Ann W. Tully of Binghamton in B; Rev. Gregory (2-3/30)

8461. Stow, Samuel Fisher, 29, d 8/2/46 in Lima (6-8/14)

8462. Stow, William S., Esq. m 9/12/25 Maria Augusta De Zeng, both of Bainbridge, in Geneva; Rev. Orin Clark (8-9/25)

8463. Stowel, Elijah m 1/17/27 Susanna Shepherd in Bainbridge; Rev. Sayre Gayley. All of Bainbridge (8-2/9)

8464. Stowell, Samuel, 87, (a Rev. pensioner) d 1/27/50 in Orwell (9-4/1)

8465. Stowits, James, 19, d 12/23/35 (in Canandaigua?) (6-1/6/36)

8466. Stradder, William of Fleet (or Fleer?) village, Lincolnshire, England m 12/29/35 Eliza Baldwin, recently of Rochester, in Seneca Falls (6-1/13/36)

8467. Stranahan, Farrand, lately a state senator from Otsego Co., d 10/23/26 in Cooperstown (9-11/7)

8468. Strang, William m 2/13/31 Betsy Lake in Marengo (6-3/2)

8469. Stratton, E. H. (Rev.) m 3/11/33 Minerva Bennet in Auburn (6-3/20)

8470. Stratton, Thomas J. m 9/8/46 Mary Goff, both of Geneva, in G; Rev. G. Abeel, D.D. (6-9/11)

8471. Straw, Liberty N. of Arcadia m 1/20/31 Lucy Phillips in Lyons (6-2/9)

8472. Straw, Sally, wf of L. N., d in Lockville (6-5/19/30)

8473. Straws, Simon m 3/31/31 Catharine Frantz of Fayette in Waterloo (6-4/27)

8474. Streeter, Ansyl of Oxford m C. Palmer in Norwich (8-4/8/18)

8475. Streeter, Russell, 20, formerly of Rushville, d 8/19/32 (cholera) (6-8/29)

8476. Streeter, Thomas S., 14, m 11/17/42 Maria Palmer, 13, dau of Joshua J., on Lenox Hill; Rev. Lyman Wright (3-11/30)

8477. Stikle, Joseph m Eve Pulver in Kinderhook (6-1/5/31)

8478. Strong, Caleb, late governor of Massachusetts, d in Northampton (8-11/17/19)

8479. Strong, Cyrus, Esq. of Binghamton m 9/1/46 Mrs. Mary Martha Bush, dau of Col. John H. Prentiss of Cooperstown, at Christ Ch., Cooperstown (9-9/4)

8480. Strong, Flavilla, 25, wf of Rev. N. D., d in Auburn (9-11/14/26)

8481. Strong, Henry P. (Rev.), pastor of Presby. Ch., Rushville, d 8/28/35 in R (6-9/9)

8482. Strong, Joseph, 59, d 8/12/47 in Rochester (9-8/20)

8483. Strong, Martha, 65, wf of Joseph, d 5/29/39 in Rose Hill (6-6/5)

8484. Strong, Nelson m 3/3/36 Caroline C. Fisher in East Bloomfield (6-3/30)

8485. Strong, Noble D., 45, d 6/8/33 in Auburn (6-6/19)

8486. Strong, Oliver (Gen.) of Rochester d 7/9/32 in Detroit, MI (cholera) (had been appointed, "last winter" to the command of the Division of Riflemen in place of Gen. B. Whiting, resigned) (6-7/25)

8487. Strong, Theron R., attorney and editor of the Wayne Sentinel, m 6/4/33 Abby L. Hart, dau of Hon. Truman, at Zion Ch., Palmyra; Rev. Jesse Pound. All of Palmyra (6-6/12)

8488. Strong, William of Schodack m 10/17/42 Mrs. Catharine Holt of Floyd in Albany; Rev. B. T. Welch (9-10/20)

8489. Strong, William M. m 12/31/37 Ellen M. Comstock, both of Cazenovia, in Chittenango; Jairus French, Esq. (3-1/3/38)

8490. Strong, William N. of Albany m 6/9/47 Sarah Adelaide Knox of Augusta in A; Rev. O. Bartholomew (9-6/11)

8491. Stryker, Isaac P. of Vernon m 6/7/48 Alida Livingston Woolsey, oldest dau of late Commodore Melancthon T. of the U. S. Navy, in Utica; Rev. Dr. Proal (9-6/8)
8492. Stryker, Sarah, wf of Rev. Peter, d 7/12/37 in Geneva (oldest ch of Harmanus Barkerloo of Long Island, NY She was b in 1766 and married Rev. Peter in 1787 (surv by husband, 3 sons, and 2 daus) (6-7/19)
8493. Stuart, Charles E., Esq. m 11/3/35 Sophia Parsons in Waterloo (6-11/11)
8494. Stuart, Elizabeth, relict of William, Esq., deceased, and sister of Gov. De. Witt Clinton, d 8/27/32 in Binghamton (6-9/5)
8495. Stuart, Nancy (Miss), 29, d 5/28/41 in Knoxville (3-6/16)
8496. Stuart, Nathan, 85, d 6/10/44 in Oneida Castle (9-6/17)
8497. Stuart, Samuel m 3/8/43 Annis Moore of Amber, Onon. Co. in Amber; Rev. A. Hamilton (9-3/15)
8498. Stults, John W. m 8/26/30 Fidelia Crittenden in Gorham (6-9/15)
8499. Sturdevant, D. B. of Brookfield, Ct m 10/31/48 Mary Davis of Corning, NY in C; Rev. J. Pierson (4-11/8)
8500. Sturdevant, Horatio N. m 4/12/48 Mary S. Wolcott in Corning; Rev. H. Pattengill (4-4/19)
8501. Sturdevant, Joseph m 4/29/49 Hannah Adams, both of Wells, Bradford Co., PA, in W; Orr Smith, Esq. (5-5/4)
8502. Sturges, W. R. of Albany m 12/31/48 Lavinia A. Holden, dau of Fox Holden of Elmira, at the Presby. Ch. in Elmira; Rev. P. H. Fowler (5-1/5/49)
8503. Sturtevant, Josiah m Elenor C. Peabody in Rushville (6-2/9/31)
8504. Stuyvesant, John R., Esq. of Edgewood, Hyde Park, m 4/9/40 Mary A. Yates of Schenectady in S; Rev. A. Yates, D. D. (3-4/15/40)
8505. Styker, _____ m Lucinda Hyde in Hopewell (6-2/16/31)
8506. Styres, Michael m 9/13/35 Susan Black in Elmira (6-9/23)
8507. Suell (or Snell), Josiah, 30, d 2/9/41 in Sullivan (3-2/17)
8508. Suits, Benjamin m 6/12/31 Betsey Kennedy; Jairus French, Esq. All of Chittenango (3-6/21)
8509. Suits, Christopher m 3/19/44 Barbara Kellogg, both of Verona, in V; Rev. A. Wetzel (9-3/28/44)
8510. Suits, Live (sic) W. m 3/4/47 Lucretia Parmeter at the Seneca Hotel in Baldwinsville; Rev. T. Walker (1-3/10)
8511. Suits, Mary Ann (Mrs.), 26, wf of Benjamin, d 5/6/39 in Chittenango (3-5/8)
8512. Summerfield, John (Rev.), 26, a Methodist preacher, d 6/13/25 in NYC in the 8th yr of his ministry (9-6/21 and 6/22)
8513. Summerfield, William, 54, father of late Rev. John, d 10/3/25 in Bloomingdale (9-10/4)
8514. Summers, John D. (Col.) of Waterloo m 7/10/39 Harriet P. Sanders of Hector in H; Rev. S. H. Inglet (6-7/24)
8515. Summers, John E., assistant surgeon, U.S. Army, m 2/20/50 Caroline J. Stuart of Buffalo, dau of late L., Esq. of Albany, at the quarters of Maj. Heintzelman in San Diego, CA; Rev. Frederick Buel (9-4/16 and 5/9)
8516. Summers, Peter, 20, printer, d 8/31/47 in Oswego (1-9/1)
8517. Sumner, John, 45, d 10/4/26 in Utica (9-10/10)
8518. Sunderlin, David m 7/5/40 Mrs. Sarah Horner, both of Chittenango, in C; Rev. Z. Barnes (3-7/8)
8519. Sunderlin, David, 44, d 5/26/44 in Chittenango (consumption) (3-5/29)
8520. Sunderlin, Mary (Mrs.), 37, d 10/20/39 in Chittenango (3-10/23)
8521. Sunderlin, Sarah Sophia, 10 mo, dau of David and Sarah, d 3/6/44 in Chittenango (3-3/20)
8522. Surle(?), Richard m 10/19/40 Lucena Mann in Tioga, PA; Rev. Breck (4-10/23)
8523. Sutherland, Isaac (Maj.), 65, d 11/18/38 in Batavia (6-11/28)
8524. Sutherland, Jerusha (Mrs.), 79, d 11/5/35 in Chittenango (3-11/10)
8525. Sutherland, Silas, 62, d 2/12/35 in Chittenango (3-2/17)
8526. Sutherland, Silas G., 19, printer, formerly of Chittenango, d 11/26/35 in Haverstraw, NY (3-12/8)
8527. Sutcliffe, John m 4/21/49 Mary Clark in Utica; Rev. M. A. Perry. All of Utica (9-4/24)
8528. Sutlif, Damaris M., 30, wf of Milo, d 7/6/43 in Smyrna (surv by husband and one young ch) (4-7/19)
8529. Suttle, D. P. of Elmira m 3/17/49 Sarah E. Kinyon of Southport in Elmira; Rev. H. N. Seaver (5-3/23)

233

8530. Sutton, John, about 30, d 10/24/31 in Junius (6-11/9)
8531. Suydam, Alfred E., 7 mo, s of _____ Suydam, d 7/28/46 in Geneva (6-7/31/46)
8532. Swain, Edward F. m Jane King in Brighton (6-8/21/33)
8533. Swain, Freeman, 22, d in Southport (6-6/26/33)
8534. Swan, Chauncy, 29, d 5/19/33 in Phelps (6-5/22)
8535. Swan, Elizabeth W., 35, wf of Maj. L. B. and dau of Alfred Wells, Esq.
      of Utica, d 6/19/48 in Rochester (9-6/21)
8536. Swan, Theodore m 11/12/33 Luania Wilder in Vienna, NY (6-11/27)
8537. Swan, Travers, Jr. (Dr.) of Syracuse m 11/5/46 Margaret Jane Stevenson of
      Cicero in C; Rev. Baldwin (1-11/23)
8538. Swart, Peter m Cornelia Smead in Bath (6-5/12/30)
8539. Swarthout, Irene (Miss) d 3/25/36 in Benton (6-4/6)
8540. Swarthout, Josiah C. m 1/1/38 Clarissa Nutt, both of Benton, in B; Rev.
      Bennett (6-1/24)
8541. Swartwout, Charles Milton, 9 mo, s of R., d 7/25/45 in Utica (9-7/29 and
      7/30)
8542. Swartwout, Rugene (sic) m 10/8/32 Claramond Washburn, both of Utica, in U;
      Rev. Dr. Lansing (double ceremony - see marr of Oliver E. Leonard)
      (9-10/16)
8543. Sweatland, W. A. (Dr.) of Newark, IL m 11/6/50 Elizabeth H. Sherrill of
      Lisbon, IL in New Hartford, NY; Rev. E. H. Payson (9-11/7)
8544. Sweeney, James, Esq., 59, d 1/13/50 in Tonawanda (arrived in Buffalo
      in 1813 and entered business with E. D. Efner, Esq.) (with neighbors
      forced to flee briefly during the British attack in the war of 1812)
      (9-1/16)
8545. Sweeney, John (Col.) m 7/3/32 Caroline Dobbin, dau of John, in Geneva;
      Rev. Bruce (6-7/4)
8546. Sweet, Benjamin of Mount Morris m 7/15/46 Elizabeth Pocock of Utica in U;
      Elder Thomas Hill (9-7/16)
8547. Sweet, Charles m 3/10/44 Mary Ann Martindale in Oxford; Rev. I. Sperry.
      All of Oxford (Oxford Republican, 3/14)
8548. Sweet, G. M. of Phoenix m 1/8/50 Mary Ann Milliman, youngest dau of N. N.,
      Esq. of Lysander, in L; Rev. J. C. Seward (1-1/17)
8549. Sweet, John W. m 6/13/41 Maria Race, both of Corning, in Erwin; Plyna Cobb,
      Esq. (4-6/18)
8550. Sweet, Jonathan N. m 6/10/32 Dorliska C. Meacham in South Sheridan (6-6/20)
8551. Sweet, McKnabb (Capt.) of Utica m 2/6/49 Almira M. Ferguson, oldest dau of
      Hon. William, Jr. of Mayfield, at the Caryville Meth. Chapel (9-3/19)
8552. Sweet, Michael of Taunton, MA d 12/21/49 (9-7/4/50)
8553. Sweetland, Joseph of Sandy Creek m 8/18/35 Vashti Doty of Cazenovia in
      Perryville; J. Whipple, Jr., Esq. (3-8/25)
8554. Sweetland, Samuel E. of Salina m 9/28/35 Julia Hall, dau of Jeremiah of
      Elmira, in E (6-10/14)
8555. Sweett, _____ (Mrs.), formerly Mrs. Pocock, d in Utica (funeral at Mrs.
      Cowen's on Blandina St.) (9-3/4/47)
8556. Sweezy, Rufus m 10/17/33 Philena Wait in Marion (6-11/6)
8557. Swift, Albert A., 22, s of late Charles of Waterloo, d 2/12/31 in St.
      Augustine, East FL where he had gone for his health (6-3/30)
8558. Swift, Donald m Julia Swift in Walworth (6-10/16/33)
8559. Swift, Emily (Miss), 18, dau of Elisha of Sullivan, d 2/15/32 (3-2/21)
8560. Swift, Harriet (Miss), dau of Elisha of Sullivan, d 3/28/44 (3-4/3)
8561. Swift, Hiram m Sarah Raplyee in Ovid (6-7/7/30)
8562. Swift, J. W. (Lt.) of the U.S. Navy m 1/10/33 Isabella Fitzhugh in
      Hampton, Liv. Co. (6-1/23)
8563. Swift, James Foster, 24, s of Gen. Joseph G. of Geneva, d 3/19/30 in
      Washington, D. C. (6-3/31 - obit, same paper, dated 4/14)
8564. Swift, Oliver K. of Canaseraga m 4/24/34 Irene Ehle, oldest dau of Col.
      George of Chittenango; Rev. E. Slingerland (3-4/29)
8565. Swift, Ralf m 11/12/35 Charlotte Waterman, both of Waterloo, in W (6-11/25)
8566. Swift, Rowland, 86, (a Rev. soldier) d 1/21/50 at his home in De Ruyter
      (9-2/13)
8567. Swift, William Hortsen, 7, s of John H. formerly of Geneva, d "recently" in
      NYC (6-5/15/39)
8568. Swinch, Jacob m 10/24/33 Mary Pratt in Rushville (6-11/6)
8569. Switzer, Laurence m 2/1/33 Eliza Baveer in Jersey, Steuben Co., NY (6-2/13)

234

8570. Switzer, Peter Muhlenberg, 18, d 2/5/36 in Jersey, NY (6-2/17)
8571. Swords, Edward J., Esq. of NYC m 10/29/33 Jemima Striker of Bloomingdale in NYC (6-11/6)
8572. Sylvester, J. A., Esq. of Denmark, NY d 9/20/50 in New Grefenberg (Lowville), NY (member Adelphia Lodge 308, Independent Order of Odd Fellows (9-9/23)
8573. Sylvester, John R., senior proprietor of the Catskill Recorder, m 12/10/37 Urania C. Knapp, dau of Edwin G. of Catskill, in NYC; Rev. Ferris (6-12/27)
8574. Symonds, Harvey m 6/17/21 Sarah Atwood, both of Oxford, in O; Amos A. Franklin, Esq. (8-6/20)
8575. Tabald, Jacob m 11/11/47 Mara Ann Wofful, both of Ava, Oneida Co., in Westernville; George Riggs, Esq. (9-11/27)
8576. Taber, Gaylord of Manchester m 4/12/31 Louisa Willcox of Canandaigua in C (6-4/20)
8577. Tabor, Benjamin m Mary Ann Luce in Gorham (6-1/26/31)
8578. Tabor, H. S. m Cornelia Allen in Wyoming, NY (6-12/18/33)
8579. Taggart, Ambrose m Rebecca Evarts in Dansville (6-5/29)
8580. Taggart, Hiram m 1/14/49 Charlotte E. Coleman, both of Baldwinsville; Rev. Ira Dudley (1-1/18)
8581. Tague, Mathew m 10/23/35 Mrs. Mary Browning in Chittenango; Rev. Gregg. All of Chittenango (3-10/27)
8582. Talbot, Oney m 11/3/50 Margaret Hess, both of Oneida, at the Elm House in Whitesboro (9-11/5)
8583. Talbot, Ross H. of Burlington, CT m 12/31/33 Cynthia Ann Stimpson in Macedon, NY (6-1/8/34)
8584. Talbott, John Lytle, Esq., 35, attorney, d 6/8/44 in Detroit, MI (b in Alexandria, Dist. of Columbia but lived mostly in Baltimore "where his family still reside") (9-6/17)
8585. Talcott, Clarissa, 38, wf of Daniel, d 5/4/50 in Mohawk (9-5/9)
8586. Talcott, Daniel of Mohawk m 11/7/50 Fanny Williams of Cooperstown in Richfield; Rev. Manley (9-12/6)
8587. Talcott, Enoch B. of Oswego m 7/6/43 Mary G. Doolittle of Herkimer in H; Rev. Murphy (9-7/12)
8588. Talcott, Mary Aliza (Stanley), wid of Samuel A. Talcott, late attorney general of N. Y. State, d 10/31/48 in New Haven, CT (9-11/8)
8589. Talcott, P. W. of Ogdensburgh m 10/17/50 Mary E. Van Patten, dau of Adam, Esq. of Rome, NY, in R; Rev. H. C. Vogell (9-10/24)
8590. Talcott, S. V. of Albany m 11/23/43 Olivia M. Shearman, dau of late Robert, merchant, of Utica, in Albany; Rev. Charles D. Cooper (9-11/28)
8591. Talcott, Thomas of Sauquoit m 5/17/50 Mary Roberts of Frankfort in Utica; John Parsons, Esq. (9-5/20/50)
8592. Tallett, C. W. of Whitestown m 9/1/46 Minerva A. Thomas, dau of Amos, Esq. of Exeter, Ots. Co., in E; Rev. John Chaney (9-9/2)
8593. Tallmadge, John S., 27, first judge of Wayne Co. and bro of present lieut-gov. of NY, d in Lyons (9-11/1/25)
8594. Tallmadge, Lewis m 6/13/50 Emily Kinsley, both of Van Buren, in V. B.; Rev. B. Alden (1-6/20)
8595. Tallmadge, William Davies, 20, 2nd s of Hon. Nathan P., d 6/12/45 in Taycheedah, Wisc. Terr. (deceased grad from Union College "in July last") (9-6/28)
8596. Tallman, Horace m 8/29/50 Rosetta Webb, dau of late James; Rev. Tolle. All of Frankfort (9-8/31)
8597. Talmadge, Solomon of Fondulac, WI m 10/20/50 Hannah Smith of Elmira; Rev. G. M. Spratt (5-10/25)
8598. Tamlyn, Francis Charles, 4, youngest s of Henry and Anna Maria, recently from Hampshire, England, d 11/5/47 in Utica, NY (9-11/11)
8599. Tangetgutteridge, Robert m 3/12/50 Mary Woods in NYC; Justice Green of the first district court (9-3/18)
8600. Tanner, Alvenzo m 1/4/36 Mary Wentworth, both of Palmyra, in Manchester (6-1/13)
8601. Tanner, John of Voluntown, CT m 11/5/48 Mary Carter of Hopkinton, RI "in the public highway at Green Hollow, the rain pouring in torrents ... with high winds from the southeast by Elder Charles S. Weaver while on his way to attend the funeral of Mrs. Amy E. Gallup, 26," (wife of Benjamin, 2nd, of Voluntown) who d 11/3 (9-11/15)

235

8602. Tappen, Andrew, 18(?), s of Col. Gabriel, d 3/6/47 in Van Buren (1-3/10)
8603. Tappen, John W., 65, editor of the Geneva Gazette, d 4/20/31 in Geneva
       (6-4/27)
8604. Tappen, Reuben S., 28, d 9/1/50 in Belgium, NY (1-9/5)
8605. Tapping, Edward Crawley, 14 mo, s of Isaac and Jane, d 5/25/44 in Utica
       (9-5/28)
8606. Tarbel, J. S., merchant, m 10/8/43 Mary E. Ketchum, both of Smithville,
       at the Universalist Ch. in Smithville Flats (Oxford Republican, 10/12)
8607. Tarbell, John S. m 10/8/43 Mary Ketchum, both of Binghamton, at the
       Universalist Ch. in Smithville Flats; Rev. William Delong (2-10/11)
8608. Tayler, Francis m 5/17/35 Elizabeth Williams, both of Chittenango, at the
       Episc. Ch. in Fayetteville; Rev. B. Northrup (3-5/19)
8609. Taylor, _____, 2, ch of Pomeroy, drowned 10/31 in Lyons (fell into a
       spring near the house) (6-11/10)
8610. Taylor, Alfred S. m 7/6/43 Christiana Goodfellow at Griffin's Hotel in
       Utica; Rev. B. Hawley. All of Kirkland (9-7/7)
8611. Taylor, Alvy of Benton m Ardelissa Genung in Jerusalem, NY (6-2/17/30)
8612. Taylor, Benjamin m 11/24/33 Celistia Barnes in Penn Yan (6-12/4)
8613. Taylor, David, "a youth of 40" m Nancy Bartlett, 19, in North Brookfield,
       CT (8-3/19/17)
8614. Taylor, Edward of Hinsdale, MA m 10/6/47 Jane G. Wood, dau of Leddra, Esq.
       of Aurora, NY, in A; Rev. C. N. Mattoon (9-10/8)
8615. Taylor, Elias W. of Mount Morris m 9/3/48 Jeanette Rosekranes of Catlin;
       Rev. G. M. Spratt (5-9/8)
8616. Taylor, Eliphalet, Esq., 63, d in Canandaigua (6-9/15/30)
8617. Taylor, Eliza, 21, wf of John W., Esq., formerly of Chittenango, d 9/11/39
       in Washington, Wisc. Terr. (3-10/2)
8618. Taylor, Elizabeth d "at an advanced age" in Seneca (6-2/8/37)
8619. Taylor, Erastus of Portland m 2/4/19 Betsey Matthewson of Norwich; James
       Thompson, Esq. (7-2/11)
8620. Taylor, Frederick G. of Lee, MA m 6/11/50 Cornelia Colling, dau of
       Thomas, Esq. of Utica, in U; Rev. Dr. Anthon (9-6/19)
8621. Taylor, Harriet (Mrs.), 23, wf of John W. of Eaton, d at the home of her
       father, Richard Van Valkenburgh (funeral at the Dutch Ch. (3-6/30/35)
8622. Taylor, Helen Antoinette, 2, dau of James W., d 5/16/50 in Sandusky, OH
       (her father and C. L. Taylor, editors of The Mirror) (9-5/21)
8623. Taylor, Henry of Canandaigua m Sarah Comstock in Gorham (6-4/28/30)
8624. Taylor, Henry m 2/15/43 Phebe Longwell in Bath; Elder Beebee (4-2/22)
8625. Taylor, Henry W., Esq. of Canandaigua m Martha C. Masters, dau of Thomas,
       Esq. of NYC, in NYC (6-10/17/32)
8626. Taylor, Hiram W. of Smithfield m 1/1/40 Lovicy C. Chapman of Nelson in N;
       Rev. Elder Aaron Parker of Fenner (3-1/8)
8627. Taylor, Isaac of NYC m 8/16/43 Mary Wiley of Utica in U; Rev. C. S. Porter
       (9-8/17)
8628. Taylor, James, 10, only s of Horace, d 10/28/36 in Canandaigua (6-11/9)
8629. Taylor, James H., Esq. of Cincinnati, OH m 10/6/45 Chloe Langford of
       Westmoreland, NY in W; President North of Hamilton College officiated
       (9-10/8)
8630. Taylor, Jeanette, 11, only dau of Job, d 10/16/42 in Utica (funeral at the
       Universalist Ch. on Devereux St.) (9-10/18)
8631. Taylor, Joel A. of Starkey m Amy Stark of Waterloo in W; Rev. Lane
       (6-9/12/32)
8632. Taylor, John m 10/23/34 Sarah Boyd, both of Richmond, in Lima; _____ Brown,
       Esq. (6-11/19)
8633. Taylor, John E., Esq. of Troy m 7/6/47 Helen A. Tracy, youngest dau of
       Gardiner, Esq. of Utica, in U; Rev. William H. Spencer (9-7/7)
8634. Taylor, John J. m 9/13/25 Mary Jenkins, both of Albany; Rev. Albertus
       (9-10/11)
8635. Taylor, John W. of Eaton m 1/3/32 Harriet Van Valkenburgh of Chittenango
       in C; Rev. Campbell (3-1/10)
8636. Taylor, John W., Esq., postmaster, formerly of Chittenango, m 2/11/38 Eliza
       A. Harrison of Syracuse, NY in Washington, Wisc. Terr.; Rev. J. R. Barnes
       (3-3/14)
8637. Taylor, Josiah, 83, (a Rev. soldier) d 2/2/38 in Waterloo (6-2/14)
8638. Taylor, L. M., city surveyor, m 3/1/43 Susan M. Rumkill, youngest dau of
       Luther, in Utica; Rev. A. B. Grosh. All of Utica (9-3/2)

8639. Taylor, Luther C. m 4/28/47 Sophia B. West at the American Hotel in
Baldwinsville (1-5/12)
8640. Taylor, Pamelia Ann, 14, d 1/25/48 in Baldwinsville (1-1/26)
8641. Taylor, Philip, 55, d 8/9/24 at his home in Clinton (9-8/17)
8642. Taylor, Samuel of Jerusalem, NY m 5/12/31 Maria Hill in Geneva; Rev.
McLaren (6-5/25)
8643. Taylor, Samuel, 87, d 5/5/50 in Hartford, NY (b in Concord, MA; enlisted
in Rev. War at age 14 yrs, 7 mo) (9-5/16)
8644. Taylor, Samuel m 10/29/50 Susanna Austin, both of Baldwinsville, in
Syracuse; J. Judson, Esq. (1-11/7)
8645. Taylor, Solomn, 77, d 5/25/50 in Beekman, Dutch. Co. (lived in only one
house throughout his life) (9-6/3)
8646. Taylor, Stewart of Phelps m Harriet Davis in Canandaigua (6-4/28/30)
8647. Taylor, Susan Preston, relict of late Hon. William and sister of Gov.
McDowell and of Mrs. Senator Benton, d 4/17/49 in Lexington, VA
(9-4/27)
8648. Taylor, Sylvester m 5/20/45 Louisa A. Matteson of Rome, NY in R (9-5/29)
8649. Taylor, Thomas B. (Dr.) of Princeton, MA d 3/14/50 in Sacramento, CA (9-5/9)
8650. Taylor, Walter, 68, d 10/2/30 in Seneca Falls (6-10/6)
8651. Teackle, Elizabeth M., 5, (youngest dau of James H., Esq. and gr-dau of
Elisha Williams, Esq., deceased, formerly of Hudson) d 5/28/35 in
Waterloo (scarlet fever) (6-6/10)
8652. Teacle, Jerusha P., wf of late James H. and dau of late Elisha Williams
of Hudson, d 2/28/44 in NYC (9-3/7)
8653. Teall, Horace (Dr.) of Geneva m 6/2/30 Susan Ann Hall, dau of Judge Hall
of Wayne, in W (6-6/23)
8654. Teed, Sophiona, 3, dau of Zapher and Mary S., d 8/29/48 in Elmira (5-9/1)
8655. Teel, Jacob of Horseheads m 8/31/50 Melissa Darrian of Gibson in G; Oliver
Peak, Esq.(5?-9/4) (possibly 9-9/4)
8656. Teel, Mary A., 20, wf of Daniel E., d 7/5/45 in New Hartford (9-7/12)
8657. Teele, Anson B., 26, formerly of New Hartford d 4/26/45 in Baltimore, NY
(9-5/15)
8658. Tefft, Thomas m 5/31/43 Rachael Decolon of Chittenango in C; Rev. T.
Houston (3-7/5)
8659. Teller, Joseph m 7/12/47 Fidelia Allen in Baldwinsville; Rev. T. Walker
(1-8/4)
8660. Temple, Daniel (Rev.), missionary at Malta, m 1/4/30 Martha Ely of
Longmeadow, MA in Hartford, CT (9-1/26)
8661. Ten Eyck, _____, ch of David, d 1/11/36 in Sullivan (3-1/19)
8662. Ten Eyck, Conrad, 39, d 11/16/26 in Auburn (an elder in the Presby. Ch.;
surv by wf and 4 ch) (9-11/28)
8663. Ten Eyck, Conrad A., 60, d 6/10/49 in Albany (formerly sheriff and clerk
of Albany Co.) (9-6/13)
8664. Ten Eyck, Rebecca, about 60, wid of late Judge Egbert Ten Eyck, d 2/26/50
in Watertown (9-3/1/50)
8665. Ten Eyck, Visscher of Albany m 8/14/33 Eliza Ann Youngs of Stratford, CT
in S (6-8/28)
8666. Tennant, John of Scotland m 9/24/33 Agnes Thompson "in Mark Broom"
(6-10/9)
8667. Terbell, Henry Stokes, 2, s of Dr. W. and A. L. Terbell, d 1/25/41 in
Corning (4-1/29)
8668. Terbush, William m 1/3/32 Hannah Devall in Junius (6-1/18)
8669. Terrell, Lysander H., 27, s of Harman and Mahala, d 12/9/44 in Utica
(funeral from his late home, 86 Liberty St.) ("Editors in Conn. are
requested to copy") (9-12/11)
8670. Terrill, I. P. of Penn Yan m 4/10/33 Sophronia Mills of Canton, CT in C
(6-4/24)
8671. Terry, Caroline P., 3, one of the two daus, twins, of Edmund, d 5/21/44
in Marshall (scarlet fever relapse) (9-6/8 with a correction [d 5/31]
dated 6/17)
8672. Terry, Eliphalet, Esq., 72, merchant, of Utica (late pres. of Hartford
Fire Insur. Co.) d 7/8/49 in Hartford, CT (9-7/12)
8673. Terry, Eliza (Mrs.), 26, d 2/14/31 in Ithaca (6-3/2 and 3/23)
8674. Terry, Guy of Onondaga m 12/21/47 Juliaette Averill of Baldwinsville
in B; Rev. T. Walker (1-12/29)

8675. Terry, Horace Nelson m 10/3/43 Harriet Cornelia Day in Sangerfield; Rev. John B. Fish. All of Sangerfield (9-10/21)
8676. Terry, Jacob m Octavia Griswild of Richmond, Ont. Co., in Ithaca (6-6/20/32)
8677. Terry, Roxanna (Miss), 21, d 115/33 in Pittsford (6-11/27)
8678. Terwilliger, Frederick m 1/23/45 Adeline Griswold, youngest dau of Elder N.; Rev. Walter R. Long. All of Whitesboro (9-1/27)
8679. Terwilliger, Frederick of Whitesboro m 1/7/47 H. Griswold, youngest dau of Elder Norris C. Griswold of Manchester; Rev. W. R. Long (9-1/14)
8680. Thacher, Robert I. of Hamilton m 12/16/46 Martha Sophia Southwick of Sangerfield in S; Rev. Thacher (9-12/17)
8681. Thatcher, Israel m Margaret Newman, both of Hopewell (6-4/16/34)
8682. Thatcher, Polly, 45, wf of John, d in Hopewell (6-10/26/31)
8683. Thatcher, Sarah E., wf of Rev. Washington, d "late February", 1849 in Utica (funeral at First Presby. Ch.) (9-3/1)
8684. Thatcher, Washington (Rev.), 56, d 6/19/50 in Utica (funeral at First Presby. Ch.) (9-7/1)
8685. Thayer, Christopher E. m 3/10/36 Prudence Rogers in Palmyra (6-3/23)
8686. Thayer, Elizabeth, 41, wf of Levi(?) of Palmyra, NY d 10/2/33 in Middle Haddam, CT (6-10/23)
8687. Thayer, George (Capt.) d 6/26/47 in Boston, MA (9-7/3)
8688. Thayer, H. J., merchant, m 5/19/47 R. Antoinette Budd, dau of Dr. Budd, in Turin (9-5/31)
8689. Thayer, Hiram P. m 12/24/32 Sarah E. Williams in Palmyra (6-1/4/32)
8690. Thayer, Joseph, merchant, of Geneva m 8/20/37 Caroline Elizabeth Webb, only dau of Col. Samuel of Brooklyn, CT, in B; Rev. Champ (6-8/30)
8691. Thayer, Levi of Palmyra m Elizabeth Selden of Middle Haddam, CT in M. H. (6-11/7/32)
8692. Thayer, Levi m Susan Westcott in Palmyra (6-9/3/34)
8693. Thayer, Lyman T., merchant, of Phelps m 8/2/32 Ann L. Frazer of Floyd, Oneida Co., in F; Rev. S. W. Burritt (6-8/22)
8694. Thayer, Sally (Mrs.), 47, d in Palmyra (6-5/29/33)
8695. Thayer, William S. m 3/17/50 Eliza E. B. Flandeburgh in New Hartford; Rev. John Waugh of Sauquoit (9-3/25)
8696. Thirkell, ____, 41, widow, d 3/16/36 in Sullivan (had travelled to Niagara County trying to find her brother but there learned that he had moved to Michigan; she was taken fatally ill in Sullivan en route to her family: her mother, Susan Austin, and her two children in Herkimer Co.) (3-3/23)
8697. Thomas, Abijah (Deacon), 81, d 9/25/46 in Utica (arrived in Utica from CT in 1804; remained permanently in U) (funeral from his late home, 60 Whitesboro St.) (9-9/26)
8698. Thomas, Ambrose S. of Middlesex m 11/4/30 Jane McPherson of Seneca in S (6-11/17)
8699. Thomas, David P. of Utica m 1/3/50 Isabella Hart of Rochester; Rev. G. W. Montgomery (9-1/9)
8700. Thomas, Emma, Jane, wf of George formerly of Utica and dau of John H. Parmely, Esq. of Stockbridge, d 8/31/48 in Delavan, WI (9-9/19)
8701. Thomas, Eron N. m 10/20/36 Lucy Ann Davis in Butler (6-11/9)
8702. Thomas, Hannah (Mrs.), 56, d in Ledyard (6-11/20/33)
8703. Thomas, Jacob (Rev.), missionary to Assam, m 8/22/36 Sarah Maria Willsey, only dau of Hon. Jacob of Willeysville, Tioga Co. (6-9/7)
8704. Thomas, James, Jr., 25, d in Canandaigua (6-7/28/30)
8705. Thomas, James S. of Whitestown m 5/7/44 Ellen Foote of Vernon Center in V. C.; Rev. David L. Ogden (9-5/8)
8706. Thomas, John, 71, d 5/25/50 in Henderson, Jeff. Co. (9-6/7)
8707. Thomas, John R., Esq. d 6/21/45 in Remsen (18th victim in one school district who died from "black tongue which has been raging particularly in the east part of Remsen for the last four months")(surv by wf and ch) (he was one of the first Welsh settlers in Steuben Co. having moved when a youth from the city of Philadelphia with his parents and numerous brothers and sisters) (9-7/7)
8708. Thomas, Jonathan, Esq., 62, d 2/11/49 in Millport (5-2/16)
8709. Thomas, Levi of Utica m 10/26/30 Elizabeth T. B. Cuyler, dau of late John, Esq. of Albany, in A; Rev. Campbell (9-11/2)
8710. Thomas, Levi, 75, d 6/18/48 in Utica (inflammation of the lungs) (9-6/20)

238

8711. Thomas, Levi, Jr., 46, s of late Levi of Utica, d 8/24/50 at 100 Canal St.,
    NYC (9-8/29)
8712. Thomas, Lorenzo C. m 2/7/36 Hepsabeth Andrews, both of Rose, in R (6-2/17)
8713. Thomas, Margery, 75, wf of Levi, d 6/13/47 in Utica (funeral from her
    husband's home on Breese St. (9-6/14)
8714. Thomas, Mary, 37, wf of Thomas, d 8/22/48 in Utica (cholera) (funeral from
    her late home, 8 Steuben Pk. (9-8/23)
8715. Thomas, Matilda P. of NYC d 12/24/44 in Whitestown (funeral from the home
    of her bro, Richard Jones of Whitestown (9-12/25)
8716. Thomas, Meredith Howell m 3/26/48 Sarah Owens, both of Chittenango, in
    Waterville;Rev. W. A. Matson (9-3/30)
8717. Thomas, Nancy, 37, wf of Thomas, d 8/22/48 in Utica (cholera) (9-8/24)
8718. Thomas, Philip m 2/27/45 Fanny Thomas in Utica; Rev. James Griffiths
    (9-2/28)
8719. Thomas, Robert W. m 10/3/49 Susan A. Morgan, both of Utica, in U; Rev.
    Daniel G. Corey (9-10/5)
8720. Thomas, Shem m 1/1/33 Mary Hayne in Lyons (6-1/9)
8721. Thomas, Thomas, Jr. of NYC m 9/19/42 Matilda P. Jones of Whitestown in W;
    Rev. David Plumb (9-9/22)
8722. Thomas, Thomas of Herkimer m 3/31/50 Margaret Jones of Waterville in
    Deerfield; Richard Harter, Esq. (9-4/3)
8723. Thomas, William m Julia Smith in Bath (6-7/7/30)
8724. Thomos, Eliza, 45, a native of Wales, d 12/19/34 in Chittenango (3-12/23)
8725. Thompson, _____, wf of Joel, Esq., d 8/22/22 in Norwich (8-9/4)
8726. Thompson, Abigail, wf of Asher, d in Milo (6-2/17/30)
8727. Thompson, Alvin H. m 10/28/34 "Miss Stockwell", late of Bainbridge, in
    Horseheads (6-11/12)
8728. Thompson, Catharine, 39, wf of Capt. Sheldon and dau of Maj. Benjamin
    Barton of Lewiston, d 5/8/32 in Buffalo (6-5/16)
8729. Thompson, Charles (Gen.), 44, d 9/2/26 in Ovid (9-9/12)
8730. Thompson, Cirena, about 35, wf of John, d 7/14/48 in Woodhull (4-7/26)
8731. Thompson, Edwin, Esq. of Riga m Sophia E. Hall, formerly of Canandaigua,
    in Rochester (6-5/25/31)
8732. Thompson, Elizabeth R., 5, dau of German and Juliet, d 1/15/50 in
    Baldwinsville (scarlet fever) ("Brooklyn Advertiser and Cortland County
    Whig please copy") (1-3/14)
8733. Thompson, George W. m 4/29/49 Elizabeth Van Vleck, both of Addison, in
    Hornby; C. D. Thomas, Esq. (4-5/2)
8734. Thompson, Henry, 35, d in Canandaigua (6-11/6/33)
8735. Thompson, Hugh m 9/19/33 Fanny Valentine, both of Trumansburgh, in Owego
    (6-10/9)
8736. Thompson, Jeremiah E. of Rochester m 12/31/43 Sarah B. Weaver of Utica;
    Rev. B. Hawley (9-1/5/44)
8737. Thompson, Jesse, 50, d 7/20/21 in Paris, NY (8-8/8)
8738. Thompson, John m Fanny Whitney, both of Cayuga, in Vienna, NY (6-9/11/33)
8739. Thompson, Joseph F., Esq. of the firm of Barber and Thompson of Syracuse
    m 2/6/50 Mary L.(?) Smith of Camillus in C; Rev. Pinney (9-2/13)
8740. Thompson, Lewis, 45, d 7/23/33 at the head of Seneca Lake (6-8/14)
8741. Thompson, Marie, 32, wf of Pardon, d 8/26/39 in Hartsville, Onon. Co.
    (3-8/28)
8742. Thompson, Orren E., 28, d 5/23/45 in Chittenango (3-7/5)
8743. Thompson, Richard m 3/9/43 Phebe Ann Collins, both of Ithaca; Rev. John
    Tappan of Bath (9-3/13)
8744. Thompson, Sarah (Mrs.), 56, d 10/22/33 in Poughkeepsie (6-11/6)
8745. Thompson, Sarah B., 31, wf of Jeremiah E., d 4/7/47 in Utica (funeral from
    her late home, 76 Washington St.)(9-4/8)
8746. Thompson, Thomas m 11/7/33 Mary Jane Blood in Bath (6-11/20)
8747. Thompson, William of Lisbon, St. Law. Co. m 12/18/50 Nancy Langworthy
    of Lysander in L; Rev. L. D. White (double ceremony - see marr of
    William F. Darling) (1-12/26)
8748. Thomson, Andrew Y. of Jordan, NY m 1/22/44 Mrs. Susan Gibson in Syracuse;
    Rev. Storer (9-1/25)
8749. Thomson, Olive (Mrs.) d 7/7/33 in Lima (6-7/17)
8750. Thorn, Eber m Emily Tharp (sic) in Arcadia (6-3/10/30)
8751. Thorn, Jane (Mrs.), 74, d in Varick (6-5/5/30)

239

8752. Thorn, Jesse, Esq., 44, formerly of NYC, d 8/6/33 in Ulysses (6-8/21)
8753. Thorn, John, formerly editor of the People's Press, Batavia, d in New Orleans, LA (yellow fever) (6-10/16/33)
8754. Thorn, Joseph m 2/12/26 Roxey Hale, both of Deerfield, in D; Amasa Rowe, Esq. (9-2/21)
8755. Thorn, Lawrence m 12/20/35 Hannah Van Winkle in Benton (6-1/6/36)
8756. Thorne, Joseph S. m 6/19/33 Mary E. Wooley in Poughkeepsie (6-7/10)
8757. Thornson, Robert m 10/14/50 Juliette Swartout in Addison; Rev. A. H. Parmelee (4-10/23)
8758. Thornton, Simeon G. m Lydia Chapman, both of Marcellus, in M (6-3/9/31)
8759. Thorp, Charles A., Esq. of Norwich m 11/12/29 Susan Avery of Oxford in O; Rev. Rexford (8-11/18)
8760. Thorp, John, 31, m 7/4/49 Susan Gates, both of Elmira; Rev. E. W. Dickinson (5-7/31)
8761. Thrasher, Aaron d 8/9/39 in Sullivan (3-8/14)
8762. Throop, B. H. (Dr.) of Providence, Luzerne Co., PA m 1/19/42 Harriet F. McKinney of Ellington, CT in Schuylkill Haven, PA; Rev. Drake (Oxford Times, 2/9)
8763. Throop, Evelina, wf of Hon. E. T. Throop, d 6/29/34 in NYC (buried in family burying ground at St. Peter's Ch., Auburn (6-7/9)
8764. Throop, George B., Esq. of Auburn m Frances Hunt, oldest dau of Montgomery, Esq.; Rev. Anthon (9-4/25/26)
8765. Throop, Mary, 72, relict of Maj. Dan, d 10/13/43 in Nineveh (b in CT) (Oxford Republican, 10/19)
8766. Throop, S. G., Esq. m 9/4/14 Asenath Burr in Oxford (8-9/24)
8767. Thurber, Julina Adel, 1, dau of I. L. and Lucy Ann, d 10/4/49 in Utica (funeral from her father's home, 18 Broadway) (9-10/5)
8768. Thurbur, Anna Louisa, 6, youngest dau of Isaiah and Cyrena, d 12/2/47 in Utica (9-12/4)
8769. Thurston, Ariel S., Esq. of NYC m 9/8/36 Julia Hart of Elmira in E (6-9/14)
8770. Thurston, J. C. of Byron m Miranda Seymour of Batavia (in B?) (6-12/2/35)
8771. Thurston, Stephen (Deacon), 63, d 9/13/33 in Bedford, NH (spasmodic cholera) (6-10/2)
8772. Thurston, William A. m Una L. Pratt in Penn Yan (6-10/6/30)
8773. Tibbals, Charles M. m 2/10/35 Delia Lyman, dau of Dr. Isaac, in Cazenovia; Rev. E. S. Barrows. All of Cazenovia (3-2/24)
8774. Tibbitts, John Bleecker m 1/9/50 Amelia A. Cannon, dau of Legrand, Esq., in Troy; Rev. Van Kleeck (9-1/11)
8775. Tibbitts, Obediah m 1/23/34 Editha House in Syracuse; Rev. Allen. All of Sullivan (3-2/4)
8776. Tibbitts, Hiram m 11/4/47 Jane Stevens in Utica; D. Stillman, Esq. All of the town of Rome, NY (9-11/5)
8777. Tiffany, Grace, 5, youngest dau of Isaiah and Mary, d 9/2/45 in Utica (funeral from her father's home, 231 Genesee St.) (9-9/4)
8778. Tiffany, James H., Esq., 38, d 12/23/33 in Bath (6-1/1/34)
8779. Tifft, John, Jr. (Dr.) m 5/28/33 Louisa Fitch in Auburn; Rev. M. L. R. Perine. All of Auburn (6-6/12)
8780. Tilden, Albert G. of Warren m 3/25/50 Emeline Getman of Columbia, Herkimer Co. at the Eagle Hotel in Utica; Rev. E. Francis (9-3/28)
8781. Tilden, B. P. (Lt.), 2nd Reg't., U.S. Army, m 8/12/45 Isabelle R. Allen, dau of late Hon. Zena Allen, at Sacketts Harbor (double ceremony - see marr of Lt. C. S. Lovell and see also the note there) (9-8/23)
8782. Tilden, Luke of Rome, NY m 1/20/48 E. A. Gates of Utica in Clinton; Rev. E. D. Maltbee (9-1/22)
8783. Tilletson, John (Gen.), 70, (a Rev. soldier) d 7/12/26 at his home in Genoa, NY (9-8/8)
8784. Tillman, Elizabeth, 32, wf of James W. formerly of Utica, d 1/26/48 in Detroit, MI (deceased was dau of late Rev. Samuel Whittlesey) (9-2/10)
8785. Tillman, William, Esq. d 7/22/33 in Geneva (6-7/24)
8786. Tillotson, Collins F., 33, d 11/26/46 in Lysander (near Plainville) (1-12/14)
8787. Tillotson, Thomas, Esq., 80, d in Rhinebeck (6-5/16/32)
8788. Tims, William m 12/7/32 Mary Whitwell in Geneva; Rev. Mandeville (6-12/12)
8789. Tinley, Robert (Rev.) d 7/30/49 in Liverpool, NY (consumption) (1-8/2)
8790. Tisdale, William H., Esq., attorney, formerly of Batavia, d 6/7/33 in Carrollton, IL (6-9/4)

8791. Titus, Samuel, Jr. m 12/31/40 Mary Holister in Burnt Hills, Sara. Co;
Rev. Greene. All of Burnt Hills (double ceremony - see marr of
Benjamin H. Sage) (3-1/6/41)
8792. Toby, Lyman m Almira Byington, both of Dundee, in Jersey, NY (6-11/4/35)
8793. Toby, Samuel m 9/30/40 Charlotte Spencer in Caton; Rev. Ambrose Abbbot.
All of Caton (4-10/2)
8794. Todd,   (Mrs.), 85, mother of Dr. S. Todd of Salisbury, Herk. Co.,
d. 9/26/26 in Salisbury (9-10/3)
8795. Todd, Eli, M.D., "physician to the Retreat for the Insane", d 11/17/33 in
Hartford, CT (6-11/27)
8796. Todd, Fanny (Mrs.), 71, d 12/9/46 in Marcellus (1-12/21)
8797. Todd, John M., 41, d 11/6/41 in NYC (3-11/10)
8798. Todd, Laura, wf of Rev. William, formerly of Penn Yan and now a missionary
in Ceylon, East Indies, d in Ceylon (6-2/24/36)
8799. Todd, Thomas m 10/24/31 Mary Ann Sweet, both of Chittenango, in Smithfield;
Elder Chapens (3-11/1)
8800. Todd, Wm, formerly of NY, d in Washington (6-5/12/30)
8801. Tolcott, William, merchant, m 9/8/24 Catherine Elizabeth Curtenius, dau
of late Gen. Peter, in Whitesboro; Rev. Frost (9-9/14)
8802. Toll, De Witt C. m 1/14/49 Ann E. Lasher, both of Baldwinsville, at the
home of Milton Goble in Baldwinsville; Rev. Byron Alden (1-1/18)
8803. Tomb, Samuel (Rev.), 65, pastor of the 1st Presby Ch., Salem, NY d 3/28/32
in Salem (6-4/18)
8804. Tomblin, Charles m 11/16/47 Sarah Fowler, both of Utica, in U; Rev.
Hartwell (9-11/20)
8805. Tomlinson, Florence, 2, dau of Mrs. Harriet, d 6/3/49 at the home of Col.
Voorhees in Baldwinsville (1-6/7)
8806. Tomlinson, John G., 10 mo, only s of Harvey and Aliza Ann, d 10/16/35 in
Geneva (6-10/21)
8807. Tomlinson, Theodore E. m 12/11/44 Abby E. Walden, youngest dau of late
Thomas, at the Church of the Ascension in NYC; Rev. Bedell (9-12/24)
8808. Tompkins, Aaron Edington, 13 mo, s of Ira G., d 2/10/33 in Bethel (6-2/20)
8809. Tompkins, Caroline (Miss), 20, dau of John and Louisa, d 8/11/49 in
Elmira (5-8/17)
8810. Tompkins, Nehemiah, 68, d 3/30/36 in Seneca (6-4/6)
8811. Tompkins, T. B. of Elmira m 12/23/50 B. H. Millard of Tioga, PA in T; Rev.
Brown (5-12/29)
8812. Tompson, Laura S., 5, dau of James and Sarah, d 11/28/48 in Utica (funeral
from her father's home on Kemble St.)(9-12/1)
8813. Tongue, Jonathan m 3/12/50 Ann Eliza Wright, both of Catlin; Rev. C. C.
Carr (5-3/15)
8814. Tooker, James H. m 8/25/31 Cornelia A. R. Clark, dau of late Rev. Orin,
in Seneca (6-8/31)
8815. Tooker, T. H. m 11/8/31 Charlotte Philips; Rev. Smith. All of Seneca
(6-11/9)
8816. Topin, Hannah (Mrs.), 77, d in Wheeler (6-6/8/31)
8817. Topping, William J. of Brooklyn, NY (a cooper) d 1/24/50 on board ship,
"Norman", on her passage from Panama to San Francisco, CA (9-4/11)
8818. Torbert, Samuel (Dr.), 61, d 5/20/25 in Williamstown (surv by wf and 6 ch)
(born and educated in PA then moved to NYC first and Williamstown later)
(9-5/31)
8819. Torey, Abigail (Mrs.), 35, d 11/28/34 in Chittenango (3-12/2)
8820. Torrance, Richard L. d 8/24/32 in Lockport (cholera) (6-9/5)
8821. Torrey, Lydia (Mrs.), 63, d 9/3/33 in Boston, NY (6-9/18)
8822. Torrey, Nathan W. m 11/24/36 Sarah Brown in Elmira (6-11/30)
8823. Tosley, George M. of Palermo, NY m 12/24/44 Lois White of Paris, NY in P;
Rev. J. G. Cordell (9-1/14/45)
8824. Tourtellot, S. K. of Hammondsport m 11/22/31 Eleanor McClure, dau of Gen.
George of Bath, in B; Rev. Platt (6-11/30)
8825. Tousaint, Peter A. of Boston m 6/21/42 Jennett Smith of Utica; Rev. Purns
(9-6/24)
8826. Tousley, Nathan m 3/25/29 Ruth Ann Moore in Smithville; Elder Kelsey.
All of Smithville (8-3/25)
8827. Towar, Charles, s of Henry, Esq., d 5/24/34 (in Lyons?) (6-6/4)
8828. Towar, Dudley, 27, s of Henry, Esq., d 8/2/31 in Lyons (6-8/24)

8829. Towell, William Edward, 16 mo, s of Rev. Thomas, d 11/30/43 in Oxford ("scarletina") (Oxford Republican, 12/7)

8830. Tower, Charlemagne of Waterville m 6/14/47 Almelie Malvina Bartle, dau of late Lambert of Orwigsburgh, Schuylkill Co., PA; Rev. John A. Hoffmeier (9-6/22)

8831. Tower, Charles, 18, lately from England, drowned 6/11/26 "while bathing in the river" at Utica (9-6/13)

8832. Tower, Fayette B. of NYC m 7/11/39 Elizabeth H. Phelps, dau of Hon. John of Westchester, PA, at the Troy Female Sminary; Rev. Coe (or Cox) (6-7/17)

8833. Tower, Fayette B. of NYC m 9/5/43 Ann R. Phelps, dau of Hon. John, at Female Institute in Ellicott Mills; Rev. Alfred Holmead, chaplain (9-9/16)

8834. Tower, Horace S., 8 mo, s of Horace W. and Cornelia S., d 8/9/49 in Waterville (9-8/11)

8835. Tower, Horace W. m 10/21/47 Caroline S. Stafford, dau of late Thomas, in Waterville; Rev. A. D. Gridley. All of Waterville (9-10/28)

8836. Tower, James M. m 8/4/47 M. Catharine Osborn, dau of Amos, Esq., in Waterville; Rev. A. D. Gridley. All of Waterville (9-8/6)

8837. Towle, Sarah (Mrs.), 56, d 1/30/33 in Bath (6-2/13)

8838. Town, Abner (Rev.), 29, d 5/19/26 in Litchfield, Herk. Co. (funeral sermon by Rev. Waters of Paris, NY) ("Mr. Town had been pastor at Litchfield only 11 mos.") (9-6/27)

8839. Towner, Joseph m Harriet Herrington in Bath (6-5/26/30)

8840. Townsend, _____, inf s of Dr. William A., d 12/9/32 in Geneva (6-12/12)

8841. Townsend, Abby, wf of John, Esq. and dau of late Chief Justice Spencer, d 8/17/49 in Albany (9-8/21)

8842. Townsend, Ansell m 4/10/49 Eliza Wilder of Catlin; Rev. G. M. Spratt (5-4/27)

8843. Townsend, David m Catharine Dedrich in Seneca; Rev. Nisbet. All of Seneca (6-2/3/30)

8844. Townsend, Emily (Miss), 25, dau of Stephen and Avis, d 8/8/43 in Albany (9-8/11)

8845. Townsend, Henry M. m 10/31/33 Elizabeth Freer in Geneva; Elder Bentley. All of Seneca (6-11/6)

8846. Townsend, Hepzibah, 66, wid of late Deacon Nathaniel, d 12/26/49 at her home in Westmoreland (member of 1st Cong'l. Ch. where her husband was deacon; funeral sermon by Rev. James Eells, former pastor and under whose ministry she joined the church) (9-1/9/50)

8847. Townsend, Homer m 11/13/43 Emily Hill, dau of Elder Thomas Hill, in Utica; Elder Thomas Hill. All of Utica (9-11/16)

8848. Townsend, Ira L. of Prattsburgh m 3/27/32 Catharine De Long of Hammondsport (6-4/11)

8849. Townsend, Jacob, 81, d 5/10/50 at the home of his son-in-law, James C. Evans, (in Buffalo?) (deceased was earlier a merchant in New Haven, CT; in 1810 moved to Lewiston, NY; "was identified with the early commerce and navigation of the western lakes") (9-5/11)

8850, Townsend, Jesse m 11/27/34 Elizabeth Young, both of Seneca; Rev. C. S. Coats (6-12/3)

8851. Townsend, Joseph L., about 25, of the late firm of William Rice and Co. of Albany and formerly of Geneva, d 3/22/35 in Charleston, SC "on his return from St. Augustine where he had gone for his health") (6-4/15)

8852. Townsend, Mary Ann, 3, dau of Dr. W. A. of Geneva, d 5/30/31 in Ellington, CT (small pox) (6-6/8)

8853. Townsend, Robert of the U.S. Navy m 6/19/50 Harriet Monroe of Elbridge at the Reformed Dutch Ch. in Syracuse; Rev. Cornell (9-6/21)

8854. Townsend, Timothy, 89, m 3/3/27 Mary Olmsted, 69, both of Canaan, in C; Rev. Hall (8-3/9)

8855. Townsend, William H., merchant, of Geneva m 6/9/35 Angelina S. Patrick of Windsor, VT at St. Paul's Ch. in Windsor; Rev. Carlton Chase (6-6/17)

8856. Tracey, James G., Esq., 70, "for many years agent of the Syracuse Company", d 11/8/50 in Syracuse (9-11/12)

8857. Tracy, Albert H. (Hon.) m Harriet Norton, dau of E. F., Esq., in Buffalo (9-11/22/25)

8858. Tracy, Bela, Esq. m 1/1/24 Calista Spurr, both of Columbus, in C; Anthony Olney, Esq. (8-1/8)

8859. Tracy, Catharine, 66, wf of Gardiner, Esq., d 9/21/47 in Utica (funeral from her late home, 28 Whitesboro St.) (9-9/22)
8860. Tracy, Cornelius L., Esq. of Lansingburgh m 9/9/45 Mary Olmsted of Cohoes in C; Rev. Gibson (9-9/11)
8861. Tracy, Daniel (Dr.), provincial member of parliament from Lower Canada, d 7/18/32 in Montreal, Canada (cholera) (6-7/25)
8862. Tracy, Gardiner, 72, d 5/25/49 in Utica (9-5/28)
8863. Tracy, Jane, 19, wf of Col. Otis J., d 11/13/21 in Oxford (8-11/21)
8864. Tracy, Joseph W., 72, bro of Gardner of Utica, d in Norwich, CT (9-4/11/45)
8865. Tracy, N. U. of Corning m 12/29/40 J. A. De Pew of Litchfield, CT in Barrington, NY; Rev. Miner (4-1/8/41)
8866. Tracy, Otis (Col.) m 10/5/23 Eliza Cushman in Oxford; Rev. L. Bush (8-10/8)
8867. Tracy, Otis J. m 1/2/20 Jane Hyde, both of Oxford, in O; Rev. Leverett Bush (8-1/5)
8868. Tracy, Samuel D. of Westmoreland m Emily Crocker, dau of Silas, Esq. of Vernon, in V; Rev. R. C. Brisben (9-3/7/44)
8869. Tracy, Susan, 27, wf of Samuel D. d 6/2/43 in Westmoreland (9-6/6)
8870. Tracy, Uri, Jr. m 1/15/26 Perses Packer in Oxford; Rev. Bush (8-1/18)
8871. Tracy, William G., Esq., 60, d in Whitesboro (one of the early settlers in Oneida Co.) (6-4/28/30)
8872. Train, Henry M. of St. Lawrence Co. m 10/22/45 Marilla E. Pierce of Paris, NY in Sauquoit; Rev. Stocking (9-10/24)
8873. Trall, William W. m 5/14/50 Sarah M. Summer, dau of Col. Summer of the U.S. Army, at St. Paul's Ch., Syracuse; Rev. Henry Gregory, D.D. (9-5/17)
8874. Traver, Charles m 12/25/45 Amelia Wilber, both of Utica, in U; Otis Whipple, Esq. (9-12/27)
8875. Traver, Franklin, 18, d 6/18/35 in Elmira (fell from a horse) (6-6/24)
8876. Traver, Robert M. (Dr.) m 10/29/40 Eliza Young in Centerville; Rev. S. M. Hopkins of Corning (4-12/18)
8877. Treadwell, Charles H. of Broome Co. m 10/10/43 Jane Hamilton of Oxford; Rev. L. Sperry (Oxford Republican, 10/26)
8878. Treat, H. H. of Palmyra m Addela Bosworth of Pennsylvania in Palmyra, NY (6-1/27/30)
8879. Trembley, Henry G. of McGrawville m 1/24/50 Jane A. Carothers of Kirkland in K; Rev. Raymond (9-1/26)
8880. Trenam, Octavus F. m 5/28/49 Mary M. Shepard, oldest dau of Noble, Esq., in Rome, NY; Rev. F. H. Stanton (9-5/31)
8881. Trenor, James, about 45, formerly a merchant in Geneva, d 10/19/31 in Albany (6-10/26)
8882. Tripp, Isaac(?) of Utica m 11/11/46 Emilie T. Rudman of Geneva in G; Rev. G. Abeel (6-11/13)
8883. Tripp, Jonathan of De Ruyter m 10/30/4· Rachel Carpenter of Utica (a Quaker marr.) (9-11/6)
8884. Tripp, Joseph m 11/9/33 Catharine Mickell in Seneca Falls (6-11/20)
8885. Trippe, Charles Mortimer, 5, s of Jefferson and Mary E., d 5/16/45 in Utica (9-5/17)
8886. Trofford, Charles m 3/23/42 Caroline Renimole of Binghamton in B; Rev. J. M. Coley (2-3/30)
8887. Trotier, Lewis m 9/16/47 Catharine Sivers, both of Utica, at the American Hotel in Utica; Rev. D. G. Corey (9-9/22)
8888. Trotter, George James, Esq., editor of the Kentucky Gazette, m 12/13/31 Mary Ann Hall, dau of Rev. N. H. Hall, in Fayette Co., KY (6-1/11/32)
8889. Trotter, Matthew d 12/9/30 in Albany (a Rev. officer; held municipal offices in Albany) (6-12/22)
8890. Troup, Charles G., Esq. of NYC d 1/19/34 in Charleston, SC (was en route to St. Augustine for his health) (deceased was son of late Robert, Esq., chief agent of the Pulteney Estate) (6-2/5)
8891. Trowbridge, Glorianna H., wf of Dr. Amasa, d 6/29/49 in Whitestown (9-7/6)
8892. Trowbridge, M. J. m 8/18/45 Clarinda Lucas in Augusta; Rev. O. Bartholomew (9-8/20)
8893. True, Ann Marie, 5, dau of D. E., d 2/24/47 in Baldwinsville (1-3/3)
8894. Truesdell, Martin (Capt.), formerly of the steamboats "Utica" and "North America" and in 1848 state assemblyman from NYC, d 7/30/49 in New Baltimore, NY (9-8/2)
8895. Truman, Israel G. of Birdsall m 12/17/35 Elizabeth Armstrong, dau of Henry of Burns, in B; Rev. Kendrick (6-1/6/36)

8896 . Truman, Thomas m 1/21/21 Catharine Williams (in Preston?); Rev. Nathan
       Noyes (7-2/14)
8897 . Trumane, R. T. m 4/15/46 Susan Inman, both of Clinton, in New Hartford;
       Henry Sherrill, Esq. (9-5/2)
8898 . Trumbull, James m 2/11/36 Maria Pettibone in Seneca (6-2/24)
8899 . Trumbull, Martha, 92, relict of late Rev. Thomas, D.D., d 6/20/25 in North
       Haven (state not given) (9-7/12)
8900 . Tubbs(?), Hosea m 10/27/41 Sarah Gage, both of Coventry, at the home of
       A. Perkins in Oxford; Rev. W. M. P_____ (Oxford Times, 11/3)
8901 . Tubbs, Nathan of Geneva m 7/27/31 Elizabeth Vervalin, formerly of
       Syracuse, (in Geneva?); Rev. Bentley (6-7/27)
8902 . Tubles, Hannah, 48, consort of Lebbeus formerly of Southport, NY,
       d 9/27/50 in Holly, MI (5-10/18)
8903 . Tuck, Daniel, 85, d 9/7/45 in Oxford (one of the earliest settlers in
       Oxford) (Oxford Republican, 9/18)
8904 . Tucker, Charles P., merchant, of Fulton m 1/16/44 Jennet K. Perkins, 2nd
       dau of late Capt. John of Perkins Corners (Conquest), in P. C.; Rev.
       P. Woodin (9-1/30)
8905 . Tucker, Dan, 82, d 9/7/45 in Oxford (an early settler there) (9-9/17)
8906 . Tucker, Ebenezer of Ohio (NY?) m Lois Patchin, dau of Nathan, Esq. of
       Deerfield, in Deerfield ("Northgage"); Rev. Thomas Salmon of Trenton, NY
       (9-10/9/44)
8907 . Tucker, Frances, about 26, wf of Luther, d 4/14/31 in Walworth (surv by
       husband and 1 ch) (6-4/27)
8908 . Tucker, Horace B. of Perrysville m 1/4/38 Abigail Norris of Chittenango;
       Rev. Taggart of Manlius (3-1/24)
8909 . Tucker, Josiah P. P:, 79, (a Rev. soldier) d 11/27/45 in Granby (one of
       the earliest settlers in Oneida Co.) (9-12/2)
8910 . Tucker, Luther, Esq., editor of the Rochester (NY) Daily Advertiser,
       m 10/17/33 Mary E. Sparhawk in Rochester, NY?(6-11/6)
8911 . Tucker, Luther, editor of The Cultivator, Albany, m "Mrs. M. Lucinda
       Burr of Rochester" in Auburn; Rev. Dr. Lathrop (9-6/4/46)
8912 . Tucker, Naomi S., wf of Luther, one of the publishers of the Rochester
       Republican, and dau of Ebenezer Sparhawk of Rochester, d 8/4/32 in R
       (cholera) (6-8/15). Did Luther marry four times? See 8907. 8910, and
       8911
8913. Tully, D. (Rev.) of Princeton (state not given) m 5/22/50 Margaret Kelly
       of Utica; Rev. A. Tulley (9-5/23)
8914. Tupper, Charles m Clarissa Fish in Binghamton; Rev. William Delong
       (2-3/8/43)
8915. Tupper, Virgil m 1/25/49 Juliette Parcel in Corning; Rev. Wiley (4-1/31)
8916. Turck, Abram, 58, d 4/22/30 in Geneva (6-4/28)
8917. Turk, David of Addison m 1/23/50 Henrietta West of Corning in C; Rev. E.
       Colson (4-1/30)
8918. Turnbull, Adam m 1/24/31 Elizabeth M. Andlish in Seneca (6-2/9)
8919. Turner, Abner, 67, d 11/2/33 in Tioga (6-11/13)
8920. Turner, Don Marshall Murat m 6/17/50 Ellen Chestnut in Watertown; Rev.
       I. Brayton (9-6/28)
8921. Turner, Harvey m 12/28/48 Jane Morehouse at the Meth. Ch. in Millport;
       Rev. C. C. Carr (5-12/29)
8922. Turner, John m 6/27/34 Mary Mitchell of Geneva; Rev. Mitchell (6-7/2)
8923. Turner, Lois, 29, dau of Capt. Enoch, d 5/10/31 in Sodus (6-5/25)
8924. Turner, Martin d 2/22/43 in Vernon (9-3/3)
8925. Turner, Myron W. of Verona m 5/15/44 Caroline M. Gates, dau of Ralph I.,
       Esq. of Fenner in F; Rev. L. H. Stanley of Perryville (3-5/22)
8926. Turner, Nathan m 2/20/49 Julia Ann Shoots of Rutland, PA; Rev. C. C. Carr
       (5-3/2)
8927. Turner, Phoebe Jane, 15 mo, dau of Charles and Anne, d 5/28/46 in Geneva
       (6-5/29)
8928. Turner, Victor, 11, s of Henry J. and Caroline, drowned 12/10/44 in Utica
       Funeral from Grace Ch.) (9-12/11)
8929. Turrell, Abel m Mrs. Relief M. Shay in Penn Yan (6-4/28/30)
8930. Turtelot, Edward A. C., 20, ("only son of his mother"), late of Oxford,
       d 1/19/30 in NYC (had studied at Oxford Academy for Hamilton College to
       the sophomore class of which he was admitted in 1824 and was graduated
       in 1827) (8-2/3)

8931. Tuthill, George W. of Blooming Grove m 10/22/35 Rebecca Halsey, dau of Hon. Zephaniah of Fayette,in F; Rev. A. W. Platt (6-10/28)
8932. Tuthill, Green M., Esq., clerk of Tioga Co., m 10/4/31 Elsie Decker of Newburgh in N (6-10/26)
8933. Tuthill, Green M. of Elmira m 9/20/48 Elizabeth Tuttle of Southport in S; Rev. P. H. Fowler (5-9/22)
8934. Tuttle, Alfred, 27, d 3/11/31 in Batavia (6-3/30)
8935. Tuttle, Archibald B. of Andes m Lucinda M. Lyon of Oxford; Rev. Arthur Burtis (Oxford Times, 1/12/42)
8936. Tuttle, Benjamin, 80, father of Col. Joseph W., d 1/8/35 in Seneca (b in CT; moved to Seneca "45 years ago") (6-2/11)
8937. Tuttle, Cyrus K. m 9/3/49 Mary Ann Smith, both of Baldwinsville; Rev. B. Alden (1-9/6)
8938. Tuttle, David m Parna Richmond in Clyde (6-4/7/30)
8939. Tuttle, Ebenezer, 70, d in Jackson, PA (6-9/14/36)
8940. Tuttle, Elizabeth, 69, consort of late Benjamin, one of the first settlers in Seneca, d 9/3/35 at her home near Geneva (6-9/16)
8941. Tuttle, Joseph E. m 7/10/35 Cassandra Hipple of Hopewell in H; Rev. J. F. McLaren (6-7/22)
8942. Tuttle, Manville, formerly of Utica, d 8/4/48 in Rome, NY (9-8/11)
8943. Tuttle, Margaret, 23, dau of John, d 2/5/41 in Perryville (3-2/10)
8944. Tuttle, William, 67, d 11/23/23 in Oxford (8-11/26)
8945. Twichell, Winslow of Cohoes m 3/17/47 Mary A. Jones of Utica (9-3/20)
8946. Twies(?), George W. of Trumansburgh m 11/14/46 Eliza Griswold of Bainbridge in B (9-12/19)
8947. Twining, Nelson m 1/9/42 Ruth A. Ames, both of Binghamton, at the Bapt. Ch.; Rev. J. M. Coley (2-1/12)
8948. Twist, Ira m 2/23/32 Julia Maria Etheridge, both of Seneca Falls (6-3/14)
8949. Twitchell, Amos(?) (Dr.) d "at a great age" in Keene, NH (a surgeon) (9-6/3/50)
8950. Twitchell, George, 53, d 8/4/49 in Kirkland (9-8/10)
8951. Twitchell, Jonas H. m 10/19/23 Melinda Scott, both of Coventry (8-10/29)
8952. Twitchell, Pliny (Rev.) m 4/9/35 Julia Ann Caulkins in Albion (6-4/22)
8953. Tylee, John T. m 8/15/49 Maria Wever, both of Van Buren, in V. B.; Rev. L. C. Bates (1-8/23)
8954. Tyler, Alexander, Esq. of "Jewitt City, Conn." m 7/30/46 Caroline Halsey, youngest dau of John H., Esq. of Lodi, at Trinity Ch. (town not given); Rev. John Henry Hobart (6-8/7)
8955. Tyler, Caroline (Miss), 18, d 10/29/47 in Marcellus (1-11/3)
8956. Tyler, Harvey, 50, d 9/1/42 in Coventry (surv by wf and 9 daus) (Oxford Times, 9/7 and 9/14)
8957. Tyler, James m 5/20/46 Ann Leacock, both of Whitestown, in W; Rev. F. A. Spencer (9-5/26)
8958. Tyler, Josiah of East Windsor, CT m 2/27/49 Susan W. Clarke, dau of Chester, in Northampton, NY ("They are to proceed immediately to the Mission among the Zulus of South Africa") (9-3/6)
8959. Tyler, Silas, Jr. m 8/8/32 Lydia M. Eggleston, both of Sullivan, in S; J. French, Esq. (3-8/14)
8960. Tyrol, Henry m Calista Wright in Hillsdale (after a courtship of 30 minutes "with her former gallant calling to pay his addresses during the ceremony") (8-11/4/29)
8961. Tyrrell, Thomas m 9/4/42 Susan Wells, both of Oxford, in O; Rev. J. T. Goodrich (Oxford Times, 9/14)
8962. Ubbs, Henry m 1/17/31 Deborah Graham in Newburgh (6-2/2)
Underhill, Charlotte. See Davids, Charlotte
8963. Underhill, Porcia Maria Brooks, 43, wf of Charles, d 12/22/50 in Horseheads (5-12/29)
8964. Underhill, R. L. m 8/25/36 Frances Minerva Stout in Bath (6-9/7)
8965. Underwood, Andrew L. of Utica m 3/1/49 Elizabeth M. Ferguson of Frankfort in F; Rev. Dolphus Skinner (9-3/7)
8966. Underwood, George, Esq. of Auburn m 5/31/43 Charlotte Platt, dau of Jonathan recently of Owego, in Tioga; Rev. Wilcox (9-6/16)
8967. Underwood, J. Delos, Esq. of Herkimer m 2/14/47 Marcia Deming Green, dau of "President Green" in Whitesboro (Pres. Green officiating) (double ceremony - see marr of Samuel W. Green) (9-3/20)

8968. Upcraft, Sarah, 42, wf of Henry, d 11/24/46 in Oswego (9-12/4)
8969. Updike, Elizabeth, 82, wf of late Daniel E., Esq. of Milford, RI d 2/19/47 in New Hartford, NY (9-2/26)
8970. Updike, Lewis of Romulus m 12/6/32 Frances Harris of Canandaigua in Geneva (6-12/12)
8971. Upham, Cyrus N. m 1/3/38 Sarah Jane Garlick in Seneca Falls (6-1/24)
8972. Upson, William Clarke, 5, s of Daniel J., d 12/24/30 in Utica (9-12/28)
8973. Usborn (or Osborn?), Edward m 10/24/48 Eliza R. Furgeson at the Central Hotel in Utica; Rev. W. Thacher. All of Oriskany Falls (9-10/26)
8974. Usher, Robert Bloomfield, 5, youngest s of Bloomfield, Esq., d 4/14/50 in Herkimer (9-4/18)
8975. Utley, David, Esq. of Rome, NY m 4/24/50 Catharine Mason of NYC in NYC; Rev. Dr. Price (9-5/9)
8976. Utley, J. W. m 12/28/48 Calista D. Searls in Turin; Rev. Barber. All of Turin (9-1/1/49)
8977. Utter, Thomas m 2/31/33 Laura Davis in Penn Yan (6-3/13)
8978. Valentine, William N. G. of De Kalb Lodge #255 d 12/21/47 in Durhamville (9-12/23)
8979. Van Allen, D. (Mrs.), 55, d 12/21/33 in Blooming Grove (6-1/1/34)
8980. Van Allen, Daniel E. m 1/22/31 Laura Lawrence of Penn Yan in P. Y. (4-2/2)
8981. Van Allen, George W. m 2/15/33 Susan Reeder in Starkey (6-3/6)
8982. Van Allen, Henry of Starkey m 10/15/50 Jenney Banks of Millport, youngest dau of David, deceased; Rev. J. Shaw of Millport (5-10/18)
8983. Van Allen, John, 13, d 8/18/33 and Daniel J., 3 mo, d 8/20/33, both of Rochester and both sons of D. I. whose wife died 8/23 (6-9/11)
8984. Van Allen, Sally (Mrs.), 49, d 8/23/33.in Rochester (wf of D. I. Van Allen (6-9/11)
8985. Van Alstine, Martin m 9/19/35 Mrs. Nancy _____ (paper torn) in Sullivan; J. French, Esq. (3-9/29)
8986. Van Alstyne, Martin G. (Capt.), 75 (a Rev. patriot) d 1/20/31 in Canajoharie (6-1/26 and 9-2/1)
8987. Van Anden, Lewis m 7/11/32 Mary Foot, both of Auburn; Rev. Orton (6-7/18)
8988. Van Antwerp, Almiron S., 23, of Clinton d 10/15/45 in Clinton (was a member of the sophomore class at Hamilton College at time of death; a copy of a resolution of mourning by his classmates was forwarded to the N.Y. Observer, N.Y. Evangelist, Roman Citizen, Utica Gazette, and Madison County Whig) (9-10/21)
8989. Vanarsdall, Thomas of Heming m 2/16/31 Julia Ann Austin of Sempronius in S (6-3/2)
8990. Vanauken, Dudley L. m 1/11/32 Elizabeth Parker in Phelps (6-1/18)
8991. Vanauken, Isaac, about 37, d 1/24/33 in Canandaigua (6-2/6)
8992. Van Auken, Lawson A. m 4/22/30 Sally Ann Fields in Waterloo; Rev. Butler (6-5/5)
8993. Van Bunschoten, Jacob, 77, d in Fishkill (6-5/26/30)
8994. Van Buren, Caroline Augusta, inf dau of E., Esq., d 11/12/33 in Penn Yan (6-11/27)
8995. Van Buren, Elizabeth, wf of John and dau of late James Vanderpool, d 11/18/44 in Albany (9-11/27)
8996. Van Buren, James S. of Watertown m 5/1/49 Harriet A. Stebbins of Pierrepont Manor at Zion Ch. in P. M.; Rev. J. M. Bartlett (9-5/8)
8997. Van Buren, Preston, 15, s of late Henry S., d 6/8/45 in Sangerfield (9-6/27)
8998. Van Buren, William (Dr.), 61, d 7/17/32 in Albany (cholera) (6-7/25)
8999. Van Campen, Polly, dau of Samuel, d in Scio (6-3/3/30)
9000. Vandemark, E. m 1/14/50 Mrs. H. Clark in Ridgebury, PA; James Webb, Esq. All of Ridgebury (5-1/18)
9001. Vandemark, J., Esq. m 3/2/36 Lydia E. Wilder in Phelps; Rev. J. F. McLaren (6-3/9)
9002. Vandemark, Lodowick m 2/17/36 Jane Westfall, dau of Jacob D., in Phelps; Elder Farley (6-2/24)
9003. Vandemark, Orson m 2/28/33 Jane Brooks in Phelps (6-3/6)
9004. Vandenburgh, Matthias m 10/30/33 Charlotte Berry in Owego (6-11/13)
9005. Vandenburgh, Van Schaick m 1/12/31 Catharine Beecher in Easton (6-2/2)
9006. Van Derheof, Hendrickson m 7/24/49 Lydia Erway, both of Painted Post; Rev. C. C. Carr (5-7/27)

9007. Vanderheul, Van Rensselaer, 18, d 8/17/24 in Oxford (8-8/25)
9008. Vanderheyden, Daniel of Verona m 12/14/43 Sarah A. Bailey of Vernon at the Franklin House; Prof. B. Hawley (9-12/16)
9009. Van Der Heyden, David m 2/25/23 Mrs. Elizabeth Hartt in Schenectady; Rev. Proal (8-3/12)
9010. Vanderheyden, John G. m 9/24/44 Jane R. Rowley; Rev. T. Spencer. All of Utica (9-9/26)
9011. Vanderhoff, Nancy, wf of Philander, d 4/7/49 in Campbell (4-4/11)
9012. Vanderhoof, David m 10/24/33 Sarah Jane Shirts, both of Arcadia, in Palmyra (6-11/20)
9013. Vanderhoof, John d 6/22/33 in Phelps (6-7/3)
Van Derhule. See also Vanderheul.
9014. Van Derhule, Samuel of Oxford m 1/7/42 Susan Reynolds of Sherburne in S; Rev. Lyman Rexford
9015. Vanderkier, Helen M. (Mrs.), dau of Thomas Livingston, formerly of Chittenango, d 6/20/42 in Moscow, NY (3-6/29)
9016. Vanderlip, _____, 1, ch of Philip, d 7/21/26 in Utica (9-7/25)
9017. Vanderlip, Eliza, 2, dau of Samuel L., d 5/12/31 in Syracuse (6-6/8)
9018. Vanderlyn, Garardus of Oxford m 6/1/22 Mrs. Jane Van Gaasbeek of Kingston in K; Rev. Cosman (8-6/19)
9019. Vanderpool, Isaac of Albany m 5/14/50 Susan Foster, youngest dau of A. of Boston, MA, in Cohoes, NY; Rev. Adams (9-5/18)
9020. Vanderpool, T. Oakley (Dr.) m 12/10/50 Gertrude Lansing Wendell, dau of late Dr. Peter, in Albany; Rev. Dr. Kennedy. All of A (9-12/14)
9021. Van De Warker, Daniel of Chittenango m 3/24/36 Serena Moulter, dau of David of Manlius, in Fayetteville; Albert Neely, Esq. (3-4/20)
9022. Vandewater, Richard H. m 6/3/48 Catharine H. Vandewater in Albany; Rev. Dr. Wyckoff. All of Albany (9-6/6)
9023. Van Dewater, William H. m 12/7/48 Elizabeth R. Beardsley, dau of Levi, in Oswego; Rev. Dr. Condit. All of Oswego (9-12/14)
9024. Van Dozen, John of Niagara Co. m 5/19/47 Charlotte Edwards of Waterville in W; Rev. William W. Williams (9-5/21)
9025. Van Etten, John m 3/11/49 Mary Louisa Lawrence in Gibson; Rev. H. Pattengill (4-3/14)
9026. Van Etten, Robert H. m 3/10/42 Lavina Baker; Rev. S. M. Hopkins (4-3/16)
9027. Van Gelder, Sarah, 26, wf of Joseph, d 5/3/49 in Urbana (member of Bapt. Ch) (5-5/18)
9028. Van Gelder, Tobias of Havana, NY m 12/23/48 Emeline Brittain of Millport; Rev. G. M. Spratt (5-12/31?)
9029. Van Horn, Giles Henry Fonda of Fonda m 10/7/45 Margaret Elizabeth Smith, only dau of Col. Nicholas of Utica; Rev. A. Bloodgood (9-10/14)
9030. Van Housen, Hermanus (Rev.), 82, d 11/26/33 in New Scotland, NY (6-12/11)
9031. Van Houten, Aaron of Penn Yan m 5/7/35 Emeline Crosby of Vienna in V (6-5/20)
9032. Vanhusen, Caleb of Knowlesville m 2/11/36 Catharine Jackson, dau of R. C., Esq. of Palmyra, in P (6-2/17)
9033. Van Ingen, John V. (Rev.), D.D., rector of St. Paul's Ch,, Rochester, m 11/9/47 Elizabeth A. Clark, dau of Ethan of Oxford, in St. Paul's Ch., Oxford; Rev. Benjamin W. Stone (9-11/19)
9034. Van Keuren, Mary A., 27, wf of Rev. B. of Esopus, d 8/31/33 in Poughkeepsie (6-9/25)
9035. Van Lennep, H. J. of Constantinople m 4/10/50 Emily Ann Bird of Hartford, dau of Rev. I. Bird, late missionary in Syria, in Hartford (state not given) ("Mr. Van Lennep to depart from Boston to his mission station with Rev. Messrs. Bliss and Parsons with their wives") (9-4/24)
9036. Van Lew, Henry m Elizabeth Scott in Ovid (6-2/9/31)
Van Lick, Almira. See De Van Lick, Almira
9037. Van Ness, Elizabeth, 65, wid of late Henry of New Jersey, d 3/10/44 in Utica (funeral from the home of her son-in-law S. M. Perine, 27 Broad St.; burial in New Brunswick, NJ) (9-3/13)
9038. Van Ness, Jacob G., 30 or 50, formerly of Dutchess Co., d 8/19/33 in Canandaigua (6-8/28)
9039. Van Ness, John Henry, 1, s of J. H. and Catherine E., d 10/13/43 in Utica (9-10/19)

247

9040. Van Ness, William P (Hon.), judge of the U.S. District Court, d 9/6/26 at the home of J. O. Hoffman, Esq. in NYC (9-9/12)

9041. Van Oasterhant, Rancer (sic) of Indiana m 6/13/50 Gertrude T. Fredericks of Utica in U; Rev. William Wyatt (9-6/17)

9042. Van Orden, _____ (Mrs.) d 8/31/33 in Canandaigua (6-9/11)

9043. Van Order, John A. m 2/4/31 Margaret Davenport, both of Ithaca, in I (6-2/16)

9044. Van Ostran, John of Seneca m 6/10/46 Lucinda Coller of Hopewell in H; Rev. S. Parker (6-6/26)

9045. Van Ostrander, Sally Ann, 45, wf of Wandal, d 5/19/48 in Corning (4-5/24)

9046. Van Rensselaer, Cornelia, 64, wid of late Stephen of Albany, d 8/6/44 in New Hartford (9-8/12)

9047. Van Rensselaer, James Carnahan, s of late Jeremiah of Canandaigua, d 6/20/47 at the home of his aunt, Mrs. Schuyler, in NYC (9-6/24)

9048. Van Rensselaer, Henry J. m 1/24/32 Mary E. Sacket in Seneca Falls (6-2/15)

9049. Van Rensselaer, J. Rusten, 40, d 3/19/46 in NYC (9-3/24)

9050. Van Rensselaer, James, Esq., 63, formerly of Utica, d 3/14/47 in Rensselaer, Jasper Co., IN (9-4/8)

9051. Van Rensselaer, Rensselaer (Gen.) "of the Patriot Army" m 11/11/40 Mary Euphemia Forman, only dau of Maj. Samuel S. of Syracuse; Rev. J. W. Adams (3-11/25)

9052. Van Rensselaer, Stephen H. of Albany m 1/18/31 Ann M. Bunnell of Rochester in R; Rev. Dr. Comstock (6-4/13)

9053. Van Schaick, John B., (Col.), editor of the Albany Daily Advertiser, d 1/3/39 in Albany (6-1/9)

9054. Van Seket, U. H. m 4/28/42 Emma Barnes, dau of Thomas, in Syracuse; Rev. J. P. B. Storer. All of Syracuse (9-5/6)

9055. Van Sice, John P., 42, printer, formerly of Utica, d 3/1/43 in NYC (consumption) (9-3/10)

9056. Van Slyck, John of Buffalo m 10/18/43 Gertrude Ann Lockrow of Albany in Sangerfield; Rev. John B. Fish (double ceremony - see marr of Hilliard E. Sawyer) (9-10/21)

9057. Van Slyke, Albert m 2/24/42 Elvira Riant, both of De Witt, in Chittenango Rev. Thomas Houston (3-3/2)

9058. Van Tassel, Truman (Rev.) m 10/17/33 Jerusha Busby in Seneca Falls (6-11/6)

9059. Van Tine, Mary (Mrs.), 58, d 4/22/44 in Rome, NY (9-4/27)

9060. Van Tuyl, John m 5/6/31 Gertrude Martin, both of Jerusalem, NY, in J (6-5/25)

9061. Van Valkenburgh, _____, inf dau of P., d 7/11/36 in Chittenango (3-7/11)

9062. Van Valkenburgh, Elizabeth, wf of Daniel, d 8/24/50 in Utica (9-8/26)

9063. Van Valkenburgh, Peter of Chittenango m 4/23/34 Loania J. Barnes of Brookfield, MA; Rev. Yates (3-4/29)

9064. Van Valkenburgh, Philena, 28, wf of P., d 11/7/32 in Sullivan (3-11/13)

9065. Van Valkenburgh, Richard Henry, 3 mo, youngest ch of P., d 8/27/31 in Chittenango (3-8/30)

9066. Van Velzer, Janus m 11/2/50 Mrs. Azobia E. Baker in Baldwinsville; Rev. T. Walker. All of Baldwinsville (1-11/7)

9067. Van Vleck, Andrew m 10/18/31 Jane Evans; Rev. Dr. Yates. All of Chittenango (3-10/25)

9068. Van Vleck, Harmanus, Esq. of Fenner m 3/28/32 "Mrs. Thompson" of Verona; Rev. E. Ransom (3-4/3)

9069. Van Vleck, Harmanus, Esq., about 70, d 2/17/39 in Fenner (3-2/20)

9070. Van Vleck, Mary, 61, wf of Harmanus, Esq., d 9/17/31 in Fenner (3-9/27)

9071. Van Voast, Anna, 2, dau of James of Chittenango, d 5/19/33 (3-5/21)

9072. Van Voast, Gershom, 84, a former sheriff of Schenectady, d 7/15/49 in Schenectady (9-7/21)

9073. Van Voorhis, James C., 40, d 1/26/33 in Lyons (6-2/6)

9074. Van Voorhis, John H., merchant, of the firm of Brooks and Van Voorhis of Utica, m 9/5/43 Mary E. Griswold, only dau of Maj. Hooker Griswold of Herkimer, in Frankfort (9-9/6)

9075. Van Voorst, Hooper C. m 9/14/48 Maria L. Boyd, youngest dau of late Peter; Rev. John N. Campbell. All of Albany (9-9/18)

9076. Van Voort, William of New York Mills m 1/29/44 Matilda Barber of Camden in New York Mills; Rev. Pettibone (9-1/31)

9077. Van Vorst, Fanny De Pew, wf of Peter of Schenectady, d 3/18/50 in Saratoga Springs (9-3/22)
9078. Van Vorst, Helen (Mrs.), 49, d in Schenectady (6-1/19/31)
9079. Van Vrank, Cornelia, 28, dau of Philip, d 3/6/25 in Whitestown (9-3/15)
9080. Van Vranken, William I., 53, d 8/20/38 in Schenectady (6-8/29)
9081. Van Wagoner, Simeon J., 50, d 2/28/26 in Lee (9-3/21)
9082. Van Wait, Henry, 79, (a Rev. soldier) d in Poughkeepsie (6-11/6/33)
9083. Van Wie, Dolly, 53, wf of Henry, d 10/10/39 in Chittenango (3-10/16)
9084. Varick, Abraham, 61, d 3/15/42 in NYC (9-3/17)
9085. Varick, Richard (Col.), 79, of NYC d 7/30/31 at his summer home in Jersey City, NJ (3-8/9 and 6-8/10)
9086. Varney, Asa m 12/12/33 Caroline McCall in Clarkson (6-12/25)
9087. Varney, Edmund, recently a state senator, d 12/2/47 in Russia, NY (9/12/6)
9088. Vaughn, Harman m 9/19/48 Sarah McMillin, both of Erin, NY at the Eagle Tavern in Elmira; William Foster, Esq. (5-9/22)
9089. Vaughn, Robert of Brandford, C. W. (Canada West?) m Loisa Dodge of Frankfort, NY at the Franklin House in Utica, NY; Rev. Shepard (9-2/3/47)
9090. Veader, George m 5/28/33 Ann Rose in Geneva; Rev. Phelps (6-5/29)
9091. Veazeanna, Josephine, 9, dau of "Mr. Veazeanna", d 8/20/48 in Baldwinsville (1-8/24)
9092. Vedder, Isaac of Whitehall, IL (formerly of Baldwinsville, NY) m 1/15/49 Sarah E. Prettyman of Washington, D.C. in W; Rev. Lanahan (1-2/1)
9093. Vedder, Jane Augusta, 15 mo, dau of F. Vedder, d 3/9/47 in Utica (funeral, corner Genesee and Pearl Sts.) (9-3/10)
9094. Vedder, Lafayette, 25, s of Albert A., Esq. of Schenectady, NY, d 2/10/50 in San Francisco, CA (9-4/19)
9095. Vermilye, A. G. (Rev.) of Little Falls m 11/24/47 Helen L. De Witt, dau of late Prof, De Witt of New Brunswick, NJ, in Albany, NY; Rev. Dr. Vermilye (9-11/29)
9096. Vermilye, William of NYC, 68, d 11/14/49 at the home of his son, Rev. R. G. Vermilye, in Clinton (9-11/15)
9097. Vernon, Edward, Jr. of Utica m 4/18/42 Frances Sill, dau of Thomas, Esq. of Lyme, CT, in Lyme; Rev. Davis S. Brainard (9-4/25)
9098. Vernooy, Samuel m 3/11/50 Amelia C. McBride, both of Elmira, at the Meth. Parsonage in Corning; Rev. H. N. Seaver (4-3/13)
9099. Verplanck, Daniel C., 72, father of J. C., d 3/29/34 at his home at Mount Gulian near Fishkill Landing (6-4/9)
9100. Verplanck, William Gordon, Esq. of Ballston m 2/22/26 Mary Elizabeth Hopkins, dau of Samuel, Esq. of Albany, in A; Rev. Dr. Chester (9-2/28)
9101. Vial, William of Elmira m Cynthia Baldwin of Milo in M (6-3/9/31)
9102. Vibbard, Edwin, about 20, d 9/18/39 in Sullivan (3-9/25)
9103. Victery, Samuel m 12/19/46 Susan Pangburn, both of New Hartford, at the Central Hotel in Utica; D. Gillmore, Esq. (9-12/22)
9104. Victory, _____ (Mr.) m 3/27/47 E. Storey at the Central Hotel in Utica; Rev. Shepard. All of New Hartford (9-3/30)
9105. Viele, Louisa Caroline (Mrs.), 26, d 12/30/33 (in Seneca Falls?) (6-1/22/34)
9106. Vielrey, John, 18 m Mrs. Lucy Williams, 41, in Pittsford, VT (6-1/19/31)
9107. Vincent, Ebenezer, 36, d 2/12/49 in Utica (funeral from his late home, 12 Blandina St.) (9-2/14)
9108. Vincent, Gilbert L. m 6/16/50 Esther E. Pool(?) of Clinton in Utica; Rev. E. Francis (9-6/18)
9109. Vinton, Pamela Brown, 34, wf of Capt. D. H. of U.S. Army and dau of late Maj. Gen. Jacob Brown, d 3/2/45 at Madison Barracks, Sacketts Harbor, NY (9-4/10)
9110. Visscher, Tunis S., 30, d in Schenectady (6-1/19/31)
9111. Voorhies, _____, inf ch of William, Esq., d 5/24/34 (in Lyons?) (6-6/4)
9112. Voorhies, Nancy (Mrs.), 37, d 1/15/34 in Lyons (6-2/12)

9113. Vorce, Allen (Hon.), 53, d 12/19/33 in Milo (for many yrs one of the judges in Wayne Co.) (6-1/1/34)
9114. Vorce, Benjamin, 50, d 9/27/33 in Gorham (6-10/9)
9115. Vorce, Lois, 52, wf of Hon. Allen, d 11/11/33 in Milo (6-11/20)
9116. Vorse, John O. m Rosetta Voorhies in Lyons (6-11/7/32)
9117. Vosburgh, _____, inf ch of John, d 3/16/39 in Chittenango (3-3/20)

9118. Vosburgh, Charles of Washington, PA m 10/14/33 Mary E. West of Canandaigua in Elmira (6-11/6)
9119. Vosburgh, Henry J., 52, d 7/23/48 in Baldwinsville (1-7/26)
9120. Vosburgh, J. H. of Utica m 6/25/50 Susan Jeanette Farley, dau of Rev. John of Trenton, NY, in Utica; Rev. J. Stanford Holme (9-6/26 and 6/27)
9121. Vosburgh, John m 9/7/31 Mary Moss, both of Chittenango; Rev. Dr. Yates (3-9/13)
9122. Vosburgh, Peter I. (Gen.), 86, d 1/29/30 at his home in Stuyvesant, Col. Co. (6-2/10)
9123. Vosburgh, Ruth, 48, wf of Col. Nathaniel, d 2/3/45 in Buffalo (9-2/10)
9124. Vredenburgh, Edward R. (Capt.), merchant, of Auburn m 10/3/30 Ann Scot of Geneva in G; Rev. Dr. R. S. Mason (6-10/6)
9125. Vreeland, Michael m 8/25/31 Margaret Van Riper, both of Fayette; Rev. A. D. Lane (6-9/7)
9126. Vreeland, Nicholas of Bergen m 9/27/34 Elizabeth Van Riper of Fayette; Rev. Cornelius Brouwer (6-10/1)
9127. Wadsworth, Alexani S. (Capt.) of the U.S. Navy m Loa(?) J. Denison (Butler), sister of Mrs. Rodgers and of Nito Benjamin Butler, Esq. of Oxford, in Washington, D.C. at the home of Commodore Rodgers (8-11/24/24)
9128. Wadsworth, Charles Henry of New Hartford m 11/21/49 Margaret Elizabeth Gilbert of Utica in U; Rev. William Wyatt (9-11/22)
9129. Wadsworth, Cornelia, 18, 2nd dau of James, Esq., d 3/28/31 in Geneseo (6-4/13)
9130. Wadsworth, Henry Franklin, printer, lately of NYC, d 3/6/50 in Utica (funeral from Grace Ch.)
9131. Wadsworth, Luke of New Hartford m 11/20/49 Fidelia Rowlingson of Utica in U; Rev. William Wyatt (9-11/22)
9132. Wadsworth, Lydia, 72, consort of Thomas, Sr., d 9/19/46 in New Hartford (9-9/21 and 9/22)
9133. Wadsworth, Naomi, 53, wf of James, Esq., d 3/1/31 in Geneseo (6-3/9)
9134. Wadsworth, William (Maj. Gen.) d 3/6/33 - came (with surviving bro, James, Esq.) into the Livingston County area "more than 40 yrs. ago" and was there a justice of the peace and a town supervisor; in the War of 1812 served as Brig. Gen. in command of the Niagara Frontier (6-3/20)
9135. Wager, Henry m 1/7/39 Maria Williams, both of Middlesex; Rev. John Easter (6-2/27)
9136. Wager, Joseph m 2/24/42 Hannah Niffen (3-3/2)
9137. Wager, Maria Letitia, 1, dau of David and Mary A., d 8/18/42 in Utica (9-8/20)
9138. Wager, Philip, Jr. m 2/15/42 Phebe Ann Barnard in Sullivan; Rev. A. Handy. All of S (3-2/16)
9139. Wagon(?), James W. of Little Falls m 9/25/49 Mary E. Rowe of Deerfield at Deerfield Corners; Rev. William Wyatt (9-9/27)
9140. Wagoner, W. W. of Pulteney m 2/2/36 Elizabeth French of Wayne (6-2/17)
9141. Waid (possibly Wald), William, 25, d 11/16/49 in Lee (9-11/22)
9142. Wainworth, Robert H. m 5/30/44 Hannah Shephardson, both of Oriskany, in O; Rev. Stephen McHugh (9-6/22)
9143. Wait, Marvin, 30, d 5/26/47 in Utica (funeral at Bleecker St. Bapt. Ch.) (9-5/27)
9144. Wait, Roy G. of Jerusalem, NY m 9/24/32 Phebe Remer of Benton; Rev. Phelps (6-9/26)
9145. Wait, Wells (Col.) m 8/16/27 Theda Graves, both of Preston, in P; Rev. Edward Andrus (8-8/24)
9146. Waite, _____, D.D., editor of the Batavia Advocate, m 11/9/35 Elma Anderson in Le Roy (6-12/2)
9147. Wakeley, Wezron of New Hartford m 8/9/43 Orrilla M. Whiting in Westmoreland; Rev. F. A. Spencer (9-8/14)
9148. Wakeman, _____, 18, s of Elisha and Maria of Covert, d 9/10/36 in Pratts-burgh (6-9/28)
9149. Wakeman, Thaddeus B., for many years corresponding secretary and superintending agent of the American Institute, d 11/7/48 in NYC (9-11/10)
9150. Walbridge, Amelia, 4, dau of late Hiram, d 7/14/31 in Geneva (6-7/27)
9151. Wakeman, Harvey m 4/4/42 EmilyHale in Bainbridge (2-4/13)
9152. Walbridge, Cornelia, about 4, dau of late Hiram, d 1/22/33 in Geneva (6-1/23)

9153. Walbridge, Hiram, 41, d 2/24/30 in Lockport (6-3/3)
9154. Walbridge, Increase of Hopewell m 12/14/30 Martha McCracken of Gorham in Hopewell (6-12/22)
9155. Walcott, Theodore M., 2, s of W. D. and Hannah C., d 11/17/46 in New York Mills (9-11/18)
9156. Waldo, Joseph T. (Dr.) m Hannah B. Belcher in Berkshire (6-9/25/33)
9157. Waldo, L. B. (Rev.) of Huron m 8/8/47 Mary S. McEutee of Whitestown in W; Rev. Beriah Green (9-8/12?)
9158. Waldron, A. G. of Geneva m 4/11/36 Jennett Remer of Seneca Falls in S. F.; Rev. Campbell (6-4/27)
9159. Waldron, Benjamin, 68, d 12/11/36 in Bristol (6-12/14)
9160. Wales, Elisha (Dr.) d 10/18/19 in Norwich (consumption) (surv by wf and one ch) (7-10/26)
9161. Walker, Albert, Esq., one of the publishers of the Magazine and Advocate of Utica, m 6/30/42 Anna Burnett, dau of J. Burnett of South Hadley, MA in S. H.; Rev. J. D. Fondit (9-7/6)
9162. Walker, Benjamin (Col.), 64, (a Rev. soldier) d 1/15/18 at his home in Utica (8-1/28)
9163. Walker, Edwin m 6/26/33 Sabrina Ludden in Rochester (6-7/10)
9164. Walker, George S., printer, 26, d 3/14/49 in Rochester (9-3/17)
9165. Walker, James, 31, civil engineer and s of Thomas, Esq., d 9/29/43 in Utica (graduate of Union College) (9-10/3)
9166. Walker, James Bogert, 8 mo, s of Rev. William F., d 4/19/39 in Troy (6-4/24)
9167. Walker, Martin H. of Clinton m 1/23/50 Jane E. Dewhurst of Willowvale in W; Rev. John Waugh (9-1/26)
9168. Walker, Mary (Mrs.), 38, d 5/9/45 at the home of her father, James Soules, in Westmoreland (9-5/15)
9169. Walker, Mary, 73, wf of Thomas, Esq., d 11/1/45 in Utica (an early settler with her husband in Utica; member First Presby. Ch. there)
9170. Walker, Perry m 7/13/49 Lucy Jane Slauson, dau of James, Esq. of Baldwinsville; Elder Seward of Durhamville, Oneida Co. (1-7/19)
9171. Walker, Sidney m 4/1/32 Elizabeth Warring in Fayette (6-4/11)
9172. Walker, William F. (Rev.) m 7/2/35 Alida Ritzma Bogert of Geneva at Trinity Ch., Geneva; Rev. Seabury (6-7/8)
9173. Walker, William H. T. (Capt.) of U.S. Army m 5/9/46 Mary Townsend, youngest dau of Isaiah, in Albany; Rev. Dr. Campbell (9-5/13)
9174. Wallace, Andrew (Sgt.), 105, (a Rev. soldier) d in NYC (b in Inverness, Scotland in 1730; arrived in America in 1752) (6-2/11/35)
9175. Wallace, Anne (Mrs.), 63, d 12/17/33 in Rochester (6-11/34)
9176. Wallace, H. A. (Capt.), 34, formerly master of a packet between Utica and Rochester, NY, d 9/28/43 at Fort Defiance, IN (9-10/13)
9177. Wallace, James (Maj.), 74, d 2/22/49 at the home of his son-in-law, Isaac T. Minard, Esq. in Syracuse (9-2/23)
9178. Wallace, John m 12/23/45 Ellen M. Fesh (dau of late Capt. Michael) both of NYC, at St. Stephen's Ch. in NYC; Rev. Joseph H. Price (9-1/3/46)
9179. Wallace, Joseph m 5/7/44 Mrs. Maria Bissell Palmer in Westmoreland; Rev. Denison Alcott. All of Westmoreland (9-5/10)
9180. Wallace, Richard K m 6/5/34 Dorcas Babcock, both of Geneva, in G; Rev. J. W. French (6-6/11)
9181. Wallace, Thomas D. m 3/24/49 Elizabeth S. E. Hammond, dau of Joseph, Esq., in NYC (father of the groom [not named], editor of the Mirror of the Times, officiated) (5-4/6)
9182. Wallcott, Catharine E., 43, wf of William, Esq. of Utica, d 8/22/46 in Utica (funeral at her husband's home, 232 Genesee St.) (9-8/24)
9183. Walling, John, s of Deacon Ebenezer of Maryland, NY, m 10/1/42 Louisa Boynton, dau of Deacon Elisha of Barker, NY, at the home of Ebenezer Boynton in Maryland, NY (2-10/12)
9184. Wallis, John m Annis C. Howland, both of Palmyra, in Canandaigua (6-5/28/34)
9185. Waln, Robert, Jr., Esq. of Philadelphia (state not given) d in Providence, RI (editor of the biography of the signers of the Declaration of Independence) (9-7/26/25)
9186. Walrath, _____, 3 mo, ch of John I., d 9/11/35 in Sullivan (3-9/15)
9187. Walrath, Abraham of Chittenango d 10/9/31 in Trenton, NJ (was superintending the construction of a canal there) (surv by wf and children) (3-10/18)

9188. Walrath, James of the firm of Bellamy and Walrath, merchants, of Chittenango, m 10/5/42 Esther R. Oliphant, dau of R. W., in North Granville; Rev. Leonard Johnson (3-10/19)

9189. Walrath, Marcus C. m 1/17/44 Alvira Frederick in Chittenango; Rev. James Abell. All of Chittenango (3-1/24)

9190. Walsworth, Louisa (Mrs.), 36, d 2/7/45 in Utica (9-2/19)

9191. Walter, Adam, 82, d 3/13/34 in Sullivan (3-3/18)

9192. Walter, Daniel m 3/10/33 Polly Walts in Sullivan; J. French, Esq. All of Sullivan (3-3/12)

9193. Walter, Michael, 59, of Manlius d 3/9/33 in Canaseraga (3-3/12)

9194. Walters, Thomas m Catherine Folmer in Junius (6-3/17/30)

9195. Walthall, Sarah, 70, relict of late Archibald, Esq., d 9/4/25 at her home in Chesterfield Co., VA (9-9/6)

9196. Walton, Alfred m 1/18/33 Sarah Buys in Sodus (6-1/30)

9197. Walton., Jacob, 76, Rear Admiral of the "Red", H. R. M. Navy, d 5/11/43? in NYC (9-4/15/44)

9198. Walworth, Aphia (Mrs.), 79, formerly of Hoosac, NY, d at the home of her son-in-law, D. J. Matteson, Esq., in Fredonia (mother of Hon. R. H. Walworth, Chancellor of New York state) (6-2/22/37)

9199. Walworth, John, Esq., 54, assistant register of the court of chancery and oldest bro of Chancellor Walworth, d 8/6/39 in NYC (6-8/14)

9200. Ward, _____, wf of Col. William H., d 1/9/31 in Rochester (6-2/2)

9201. Ward, Aaron, Esq., district attorney of Westchester Co., m Mary L. Watson in Albany (8-1/26/20)

9202. Ward, Chandler m 1/12/31 Eliza H. Van Buren in Kingston (6-2/2)

9203. Ward, Darius of Madison m 2/9/48 Urana Adams of Marshall at the Eagle Tavern in Utica; Dexter Gillmore, Esq. (9-2/10)

9204. Ward, Elizabeth, 65, wf of Joseph, d 3/20/46 in Marcy (9-4/7)

9205. Ward, Elizabeth (Miss), 25, d 10/28/47 in New London, NY (9-11/1)

9206. Ward, John of Annsville m 7/1/50 Mrs. Artimissa Hinman of Stockbridge in Taberg; I. C. Thorne, Esq. (9-7/25)

9207. Ward, John P., 17, s of Stephen, Esq., d 12/30/49 in Rome, NY (9-1/5/50)

9208. Ward, Josiah, Esq., attorney, m 4/4/32 Eliza C. Sutton in Naples, NY (6-4/18)

9209. Ward, Levi (Dr.), 67, late of Walworth, d 6/23/36 in Cook Co., IL (6-7/20)

9210. Ward, Samuel (Col.), 75, (a Rev. officer) d in NYC (6-8/29/32)

9211. Ward, Sophia N., 26, a teacher in the Utica Female Academy, (wf of Lysander M., Esq. and dau of Hon. Ephraim Hastings) d 3/13/47 in Heath, MA (9-3/20)

9212. Ward, Thomas, 54, d 7/5/50 in Utica (funeral from the State Street Bapt. Ch.) (9-7/6)

9213. Ward, William (Rev.), 53, a missionary at Serampore, d 3/7/23 (b in Derby, England, 1769; joined Bapt. Ch.; became first a printer but began preaching in Calcutta, India in 1798; had nearly completed the 20th version of the New Testament in the language of India at time of death) (9-1/6/24)

9214. Warden, Abigail (Mrs.), 74, d 3/27/32 in Auburn (6-4/11)

9215. Wardwell, Nathan P., 33, surrogate of Jefferson Co., d 2/15/47 in Water-town (1-2/24)

9216. Ware, _____, inf ch of Newman Ware of Chittenango, d 10/5/32 (3-10/9)

9217. Ware, Calvin W. m 2/12/48 Sarah Jane Rathburn, both of Lysander, in Baldwinsville; Rev. T. Walker (1-2/16)

9218. Ware, Sylvester of Chittenango m 10/13/31 Harriet Smith of Pompey in P (3-10/25)

9219. Warfield, John m 1/23/31 Caroline Post in Canandaigua (6-2/2)

9220. Warne, Israel m Elizabeth Hurlbut in Erin (6-11/26/28)

9221. Warne(?), James, 22, d 11/14/21 in Oxford (8-11/21)

9222. Warner, Aaron (Rev.) m 7/4/28 Mary Hardy in Haverhill, MA. Also "Rev. Mr. Bates" of Newton, MA m Emily Atwood. "These ladies are daughters of late Moses Atwood and sisters of Mrs. Harriet Newell, the first martyr to the missionary cause from America." (6-7/9)

9223. Warner, Alathbia Maria, 3, dau of Jared E., Esq. of Utica, d in Utica (9-4/29/44)

9224. Warner, Cornelia R., wf of J. R., Jr. and dau of Dr. Peter Wendell of Albany, d 6/6/48 (in Utica?) (9-6/8)

9225. Warner, Dorothy (Miss), dau of Maj. Solomon of Geneva and sister of Mrs. C. Shekell, d 3/21/39 in Havre, France (6-5/8)
9226. Warner, Edward A., 31, attorney and state senator, d 2/1/44 in Cold Water, MI (son of James Warner, Esq. of Canaan, NY) (9-3/7)
9227. Warner, Eliza C., 32, relict of late Henry and dau of John Whiting of Canaan, NY, d 8/10/31 in Detroit, MI at the home of her bro, Dr. J. L. Whiting (6-8/31)
9228. Warner, George N. m Annis Blackmar in Hamburg (6-2/2/31)
9229. Warner, H. G., Esq. of Chittenango m 5/5/31 Sarah Warner, dau of Maj. Asahel of Lima, in L; Rev. Barnard (3-5/17 and 6-5/25)
9230. Warner, Harriet (Miss), 20, d 4/2/32 in Rochester (6-4/11). Correction in paper dated 4/18: "The Miss Warner whose death we reported last week is not the lady we were led to suppose, and some of whose connexions reside in this place (Geneva) and neighborhood."
9231. Warner, Harvey, Esq. of Boonville m 9/6/48 Hannah A. Phelps of Westmoreland in W; Rev. F. A. Spencer (9-9/27)
9232. Warner, Horatio Gates, 1, s of Judge Warner, d 2/2/38 in Chittenango (3-2/7)
9233. Warner, J. Lyman m 5/21/34 Mary Guest in Ogdensburgh (6-5/29)
9234. Warner, J. R. of Utica m 6/24/46 Cornelia R. Wendell, dau of Dr. Peter of Albany, in A; Rev. Dr. Welch (9-6/26)
9235. Warner, Jared E. of Utica m 10/8/50 Helen Ryley, dau of late Hon. J. V. S. of Schenectady, in Philadelphia, PA; Rev. Dr. Ludlow (9-10/14)
9236. Warner, Julia W., 41, wf of Jared E. and oldest dau of Dr. Daniel James, d 10/1/47 in Utica (funeral at Westminster Ch.) ("friends are requested not to call at the house on account of the severe illness of Mr. Warner") (9-10/2)
9237. Warner, Mary, wf of Rev. Aaron and sister of Harriet Newell, d in St. Augustine, FL (6-7/30/34)
9238. Warner, Matthias of New Berlin m 1/4/21 Lucy Hoeg of Norwich; Rev. D. Burlingame (7-1/17)
9239. Warner, Myron m 4/25/32 Julia Crane in Hopewell (6-5/2)
9240. Warner, Rebecca, 33, wf of J. R., d 1/26/44 in Utica (funeral from her late residence, 30 Broad St.) (9-2/29)
9241. Warner, Samuel E. of NYC m 8/20/50 Helen Potter, oldest dau of late William F. of Utica, in U; Rev. W. H. Spencer (9-8/21)
9242. Warner, Samuel M. m Emeline Chase in Benton (6-7/28/30)
9243. Warner, Sarah, 70, wf of Deacon Jesse formerly of Conway, MA, d 9/13/26 in Phelps, NY (9-10/3)
9244. Warner, Truman of Coventry m 9/5/42 Harriet Wheeler, dau of Col. Wheeler of Oxford, at the Presby. Ch., Coventry;Rev. John B. Hoyt (Oxford Times, 9/7)
9245. Warner, William C. (Dr.) m 9/1/30 Sarah H. Taylor in New Hartford; Rev. Frost (9-9/7)
9246. Warnick, Ellen, 4, dau of Leslie A. and Ellen, d 9/12/49 in Utica (funeral from her father's home, 15 Devereux St.) (9-9/13)
9247. Warren, Abigail, 75, wid of late Elijah, d 6/8/35 in Canandaigua (6-6/17)
9248. Warren, Cornelius (Hon.), 59, a representative to the last Congess of U.S. from Dutchess and Putnam Counties, NY, d in Cold Spring (9-8/2)
9249. Warren, Daniel, 81, (a Rev. soldier) d 6/23/45 in Augusta (9-7/7)
9250. Warren, Edward S., attorney, m 8/6/39 Agnes Thompson, dau of Sheldon, Esq. of Buffalo, at St. Paul's Ch. in Buffalo; Rev. Shelton (6-8/14)
9251. Warren, Ellen Louisa, 16, oldest dau of David A., d 5/21/50 in Verona (9-5/23 and 6/11)
9252. Warren, Eunice (Mrs.), 79, d 10/5/33 in Bristol (9-10/23)
9253. Warren, H. F., merchant, of Detroit, MI m 7/3/50 Marion M. Griffin, oldest dau of Gen. Griffin of Rochester, MI, in R; Rev. Hills of Detroit (9-7/12)
9254. Warren, Hannah, 33 or 53, wf of James, d 11/7/36 in Chittenango (3-11/9)
9255. Warren, Harvey m 2/18/36 Caroline M. Pierce in Lyons (6-3/9)
9256. Warren, James of Sullivan m "in the present month" Ann Mitchell in Perryville; Rev. B. Paddock (3-3/13/39)
Warren, John G. See Woren, John G.
9257. Warren, Jonathan m 10/27/33 Sarah Johnson in Bath (6-11/20)

9258. Warren, Jonathan, 21, d 1/26/50 at the home of his father, David A. of
Verona (deceased was late a clerk in the house of James Sayre and Son
of Utica) (9-1/28)
9259. Warren, Rachel Hartshorn (wf of John, Esq., dau of late Capt. Thomas
Robinson of the U.S. Navy, and sister of Mrs. P. Bours of Geneva)
d 7/27/34 in NYC (6-8/6)
9260. Warren, Rufus of Auburn m 3/21/32 Adelaide Cobb of Skaneateles in S
(6-4/4)
9261. Warren, Sarah (Mrs.), 78, d 8/6/41 in Sullivan (3-8/18)
9262. Washburn, John Y. of Oxford m 9/8/44 Sarah A. Spencer of Coventry at the
Meth. Ch.; Rev. Bigsby (Oxford Republican, 9/12)
9263. Washburn, Polly, 56, wf of Martin, d 2/27/44 in Lee (9-3/7)
9264. Washington, Anna Maria T, 43, wf of Bushrod C., Esq., d 10/1/33 in
Washington, D.C. (6-10/9)
9265. Washington, Bushrod, U. S. Supreme Court Justice, d in Philadelphia, PA
"a short time ago". His wife (not named) died "on her way to attend
his funeral" (7-12/16/29)
9266. Washington, Bushrod, Esq., 46, d 4/16/31 in Mount Royal, VA (6-5/18)
9267. Washington, George m 9/22/48 Julia Hardy in Corning; B. Pew,Esq. (4-10/4)
9268. Washington, George m 5/16/50 Harriet Owens in Utica; Rev. William Wyatt.
All of Utica (9-5/18)
9269. Waterman, Elijah (Rev.), 56, of Bridgeport, CT d 10/11/25 in Springfield,
MA while on a visit (9-11/8)
9270. Waterman, William G. of Little Falls m 11/30/26 Phebe Tyler of Salisbury
in S; Rev. Chassel (9-12/1()
9271. Waters, Chester C. m 1/3/49 Helen Maria Mansfield, youngest dau of David,
Esq. of Westmoreland, in W; Rev. F. A. Spencer (9-1/13)
9272. Waters, John of Vernon m 1/1/49 Ann Polk of Utica in U; Rev. H. R. Clarke
(9-1/6)
9273. Waters, William H. m 3/21/48 Caroline C. Jones, dau of Hon. Pomeroy, in
Lairdsville; Rev. D. Alcott. All of Westmoreland (9-3/23)
9274. Watkins, Anna Alida, 27, wf of John D., Esq and dau of the hon. Joseph C.
Yates of Schenectady, d 1/30/34 in Lexington, GA (3-2/25)
9275. Watkins, D. C. m 4/11/50 Eliza Maddock in Vienna, NY; Elder Beckwith.
All of Vienna (9-4/25)
9276. Watkins, Daniel I. of Mississippi m 10/15/40 Cornelia A. Wynkoop of
Chemung, NY in C; Rev. E. Pratt (double ceremony - see marr of
N. F. Wynkoop) (4-10/23)
9277. Watkins, Harriet (Mrs.), 40, wf of B. I., d 9/13/33 in Shelby, Mich. Terr.
(6-10/9)
9278. Watkins, Robert of Collinsville m 11/25/50 Eleanor Williams of Utica in U;
Rev. Evan Griffith (9-11/28)
9279. Watkins, Simon, 64, "a colored man", d 8/25/50 in Corning (born a slave
in VA; came to Corning, NY with his master, Capt. Helm, "more than 40 years ago";
set free by Hon. John C. Spencer) (4-9/4)
9280. Watkins, Thomas W. m 5/14/20 Mrs. Betsey Martin, dau of Maj. B. Miles, in
Coventry; Rev. Thorp (8-5/24)
9281. Watrous, John of Coleville m 12/7/42 Emma Hoadley of Windsor in W; Rev.
Gilbert (2-12/21/42)
9282. Watson, _____, inf ch of William d 7/3/33 in Geneva (6-8/7)
9283. Watson, Alamanzer(?) of Oxford m 9/9/45 Jennette M. Hall of Sullivan in S;
Rev. James Abell (Oxford Republican, 9/18)
9284. Watson, Andrew, 40, d 2/1/45 in Auburn (9-2/5)
9285. Watson, Benjamin m 3/29/36 Permelia Andrews in Enfield (6-4/13)
9286. Watson, Elias, 21, d 5/19/34 in Lyons (6-5/29)
9287. Watson, George of Auburn m 2/20/31 Eliza Janet Green of Oswego in O (6-3/2)
9288. Watson, James, 2, twin son of Bildad and Julia of Utica, d 4/30/45 in Utica
(run over while crossing the street 4/29) (9-5/1)
9289. Watson, John m 1/1/47 Sarah Morris at the hotel of D. I. Wood in Yorkville;
E. A. Clark, Esq. (9-1/28)
9290. Watson, Joseph m 7/3/37 Susan Ann Pitts, both of Junius, in J (6-7/26)
9291. Watson, Louisa, 5 mo, dau of Charles W. and Susan Elizabeth, d 1/23/50 in
Elmira (5-1/25)
9292. Watson, Reuben, 64, d 3/13/39 in Clockville (3-3/20)
9293. Watson, Robert m 4/21/31 Margaret R. Standart, both of Auburn, in A
(6-5/4)

9294. Watson, Sarah (Mrs.), 38, d 9/14/33 in Wales (6-10/9)
9295. Watson, Seneca m 8/12/50 Lydia Mills in Bath; Rev. B. R. Swick. All of Bath (4-8/21)
9296. Watson, Susan Elizabeth (Mrs.), 18, dau of Jacob Garr, d 3/28/50 in Elmira (5-3/29)
9297. Watson, Sylvanus of Perryville m 1/28/36 Laura Hill of Fenner in F; Elder Paddock (3-2/9)
9298. Watts, Anna, about 22, dau of John and Nancy, d 8/18/50 in Elmira ("Rochester Democrat please copy") (5-8/23)
9299. Watts, Asa, Esq. of Orange Co. m Hannah Cortright of Chemung in C (6-5/14/34)
9300. Watts, John (Dr.) "physician and surgeon" of NYC d 2/5/31 in NYC (was Pres. of the College of Physicians) (9-2/15 and 6-2/16)
9301. Waugh, John m 5/3/42 Charlotte Rogers, dau of O. G., Esq., in New Hartford; Rev. Machim (9-5/5)
9302. Waugh, Peter, 82, d 6/4/39 in Gorham (b in Ireland) (6-7/3)
9303. Wayland, Francis, Jr. (Rev.) m 11/21/25 Lucy Jane Lincoln in Boston; Rev. Sharp (9-12/13)
9304. Wayland, Francis, Sr. (Rev.), 77, d 4/9/49 in Saratoga Springs (9-4/17)
9305. Wayne, William m 8/18/31 Sarah Aldrich of Hopewell in H (6-8/24)
9306. Weatherly, Mary Lawson, 11, only ch of J. L., Esq., d 3/29/50 in Cleveland, OH (9-4/1)
9307. Weaver, Catharine, 80, relict of late George M., d 2/4/46 in Deerfield (funeral from the Bapt. Ch. in Deerfield) (9-2/5)
9308. Weaver, Elias B. m Lydia Chapman; R. D. Delay, Esq. (8-1/13/19)
9309. Weaver, Gordon m Caroline Bennett; R. D. Delay, Esq. (8-1/13/19)
9310. Weaver, Horace, about 26, of Pharsalia d 4/9/24 (struck by a hand spike in rolling logs) (surv by wf and 2 ch) (8-4/21)
9311. Weaver, Joshua B. m 1/14/30 Roxana Miner, dau of Col. Ephraim, in Pharsalia; H. Crain, Esq. All of P (7-2/3)
9312. Weaver, Julia (Miss), 22, dau of Maj. Gen. Weaver, d 2/20/31 in Deerfield (6-3/2)
9313. Weaver, Lewis m Hannah Barrick in Sodus (6-3/26/34)
9314. Weaver, Noel (Dr.), 41, d 3/22/45 in Auburn (9-3/29)
9315. Weaver, P. C. (Mr.), 28, late of Utica, d 11/14/44 in Geddes (9-11/30)
9316. Weaver, Philo C. of Frankfort m 10/4/41 Rosah C. Willard, dau of Rufus of White Springs in the town of Sullivan, in White Springs; Hon. H. G. Walker (3-10/6)
9317. Weaver, Truman m 11/1/47 Jane Filkin at the Exchange in Baldwinsville; E. B. Wigent, Esq. All of Van Buren (1-11/3)
9318. Webb, Charles, a preacher of the Society of Friends, d in Newburgh (6-1/26/31)
9319. Webb, Daniel, about 24, d 8/23/17 in Oxford (8-8/27)
9320. Webb, E. R., one of the editors of the Citizens Press, m 5/23/32 Charlotte Castle of Syracuse in S (6-6/13)
9321. Webb, Helen Le Penard, wf of James Watson Webb and dau of late Alexander L. Stewart, d 7/31/48 at the home of her husband near Tarrytown (9-8/3)
9322. Webb, John P., Esq. d 10/16/43 in Lenox (3-10/25)
9323. Webb, Judson m Betsey Jones in Onondaga (6-11/10/30)
9324. Webb, Lewis m 9/18/50 Emily C. Dudley in Colosse; Rev. Ira Dudley. All of Colosse (1-9/26)
9325. Webb, Lyman m 1/11/42 Lucinda Phillips in Smithville; Thomas S. Purple (Oxford Times, 1/19)
9326. Webb, Merritt of Smithville m 2/15/27 Eliza Baldwin of Macdonough in M; Elijah Barry, Esq. (8-2/23)
9327. Webb, Solomon m 11/8/40 Harriet Gilbert, dau of William, Esq., in Clockville; Rev. Allen Murray. All of Lenox (3-11/11)
9328. Webb, Thomas (Col.), formerly of the house of Spencer and Webb, booksellers, of Boston but for many years past an inhabitant of Providence, RI, d 7/6/19 in Cleveland, OH (author of Mason's Monitor) (8-8/18)
9329. Webb, William S. m 5/10/49 Diana B. Johnson of Smithfield, PA in Southport, NY; Rev. H. N. Seaver (5-5/11)
9330. Webber, Dorcas, 76, wf of Edward, d 5/19/50 in Vernon (9-5/21)
9331. Webster, Abraham, 80, (a Rev. soldier) d 8/4/31 in Sullivan (3-8/9)
9332. Webster, Ashbell W. m 1/31/32 Julia Strong in Phelps; Rev. Strong (6-2/15)

9333. Webster, Charles R., 71, of the firm of Websters and Skinners of Albany d 7/18/34 in Saratoga Springs (one of the original proprietors of the Daily Advertiser of Albany) (6-7/23)

9334. Webster, Charles W., Esq. of Fort Plain m 6/19/50 Julia Pelley of Norwich in N; Rev. S. Hanson Cox of Oxford (9-6/25)

9335. Webster, Ebenezer m 8/15/47 Margaret Burnside, both of Otsego, in New Hartford; Henry Sherrill, Esq. (9-8/18)

9336. Webster, George, 60, bookseller and one of the editors and proprietors of the Albany Gazette and Daily Advertiser, d in Albany (8-3/12/23)

9337. Webster, Grace, wf of Hon. Daniel, member of Congress from Mass., d 1/21/28 in NYC (burial in Boston) (8-2/1)

9338. Webster, Isaac Catlin m 8/25/35 Amenia Burtis, dau of late Arthur, Esq. of Fort Plain, in Phelps; Rev. Arthur Burtis of Fort Plain (6-9/2)

9339. Webster, James C. of Elmira m Elizabeth Park in Erin (6-2/17/30)

9340. Webster, Jerusha (Mrs.), 68, d 1/16/47 in Whitesboro; Rev. D. A. Shepard (oldest dau of Phieas and Martha Camp; mother of 11 ch; her father died age nearly 100 years; she joined United Presby. Ch. of Whitesboro and Utica, 1802) (9-1/22)

9341. Webster, Joshua (Dr.), 78, d 5/2/49 in Fort Plain (50 yrs a physician in Montgomery Co., NY) (9-5/5)

9342. Webster, Marian Foot, 2, dau of Prof. Webster, d 7/19/32 in Geneva (6-7/25)

9343. Webster, Norman m 3/21/30 Sarah Chase in Geneva; Rev. Tooker (6-3/24)

9344. Webster, Peter G. of Fort Plain m 2/20/44 Helen M. McCall of Utica in U; Rev. H. Mandeville (9-2/23)

9345. Webster, Solomon J. m 8/1/47 Lucy R. Higgins in Van Buren Center; Elder E. L. Reynolds (1-8/4)

9346. Webster, William (Col.), 67, m Martha Winslow , 19, in Kingston, NH (He married his sister's grand-dau which makes the bride a wife to her great uncle, sister to her grandfather and grandmother, aunt to her father, and great aunt to her brothers and sisters. She is a step-mother to five ch, 14 gr-ch, and one gr-grandchild.) (1-8/25/47)

9347. Webster, William Fowler, 1, s of Prof. Webster, d 8/25/46 in Geneva (6-8/28)

9348. Weed, Anson M., 24, late editor of the Livingston Register, d 2/2/31 in Avon (6-2/16)

9349. Weed. George L. (Dr.), M.D., of Catskill, NY m 4/4/25 Eliza H. Lathrop of Pittsfield, MA in P ("Both, having been accepted by the A. B. C. F. M., are soon to engage in missionary labors ... among our Aborigines"); Rev. R. W. Bailey (9-5/10)

9350. Weed. George W., 38, d 6/9/47 in Albany (9-6/11)

9351. Weed, Henry, 42, d 6/24/42 in Binghamton (2-7/6)

9352. Weed, Munroe, A.B., principal of Hamilton Academy, m 7/19/48 Mary A. Morse, dau of Zenas, Esq., in Hamilton; Rev. Jesse R____van (9-7/21)

9353. Weed, Rhoda, 72, wid of late Henry formerly of Utica, d 1/8/49 (sister of G. L. Dickinson) (funeral from her late home, 28 Fayette St.) (9-1/10)

9354. Weed, Waring S. of Binghamton m 6/6/42 Mary E. Ayers, dau of Alvah of New Canaan, CT, in New Canaan (2-7/6)

9355. Weed, William H. m 1/19/31 Clarinda Hutchins in Arcadia (6-2/2)

9356. Weeks, _____ (Rev.), about 50, of Stowe's Square, Lowville, d 5/18/50 in Copenhagen, NY (9-5/24)

9357. Weeks, J. S. m 6/19/49 Elizabeth Kittle in Southport; Rev. E. Colson. All of Southport (5-6/22)

9358. Weeks, John of Concord, NH m Lucetta Donaldson of Utica in U; Rev. H. R. Clarke (9-8/23/47)

9359. Weeks, William R. (Rev.), D.D., 66, d 6/26/48 in Oneida (9-6/30)

9360. Weeler, H. C. of PennYan m 4/10/32 Mary Ann Spencer, dau of E., Esq. of Benton, in B; Rev. C. V. Adgate (6-5/23)

9361. Weems, Mason L. (Rev.) of Dumfries, VA, author of Life of Washington, d 5/23/25 in Beaufort, SC ("scholar, physician and divine"; early in life he liberated his patrimonial slaves") (9-7/12)

9362. Welch, Abraham H., 38, d 5/12/32 in Seneca (6-5/16)

9363. Welch, Anna (Mrs.), 43, d in Wheeler (6-7/28/30)

9364. Welch, Bela, 48, m Melissa Nash, 14, both of Wheeler, in Italy, NY (6-7/28/30)

9365. Welch, Henry H. of NYC m 8/1/43 Aseneth J. Hayes of Guilford in G; Rev. J. T. Goodrich (Oxford Republican, 8/3)

9366. Welch, King, 44, d 1/22/47 in Utica (funeral corner of Division and Whitesboro Sts.) (9-1/23)
9367. Weller, Edward, Esq., merchant, m 7/29/49 Mina Suer 9/3/49 at the home of the bridegroom in California; Rev. Dr. Mines (9-11/14)
9368. Weller, Irene F., 25, wf of Chester, d 5/6/48 in Baldwinsville (1-5/10)
9369. Welles, Edward, 2, s of John, d in Utica (9-11/7/26)
9370. Welles, Frederick, 92, (a Rev. soldier) d 2/28/50 in New London, NY (9-3/23)
9371. Welles, John A., Esq. m 11/22/42 Marie Louise Eaton, only dau of late Horatio, Esq. of New Brunswick, NJ, in Detroit, MI; Rev. Samuel McCoskry (9-12/5)
9372. Wellington, Eli, printer, m 5/12/31 Almira McCullen, both of Troy, in Albany; Rev. Dr. Sprague (3-5/24)
9373. Wells, _____, 61, consort of Fineus (perhaps Phineas?), d 9/1/29 in Norwich (8-9/16)
9374. Wells, Albert F., 5, s of Martin and Christina, d 8/10/47 in Utica (7-8/19)
9375. Wells, Amanda M., 16, dau of Job, Esq., d 12/5/33 in Chittenango. Also Polly Wells, her mother, 52, d 12/8. (both were members of the Church of Christ in New Brunswick, NJ) (3-12/10)
9376. Wells, Charles of Cincinnati, OH m 5/8/50 Elizabeth Hoadley, formerly of Utica, at the New Jerusalem Ch. in Cincinnati; Rev. Barrett (9-5/20 & 22)
9377. Wells, Damon m 11/8/37 Sarah Cossett, both of Chittenango, in Fayetteville; Rev. Orin Hyde (3-11/15)
9378. Wells, David M., 22, d 7/20/36 in Mauch Chunk, PA (son of Job of Chittenango) (killed by an explosion while rock-blasting on the Lehigh Canal (3-7/27)
9379. Wells, E. B. (Dr.) m 6/1/45 Sarah A. Wilkins in Watertown (9-6/6)
9380. Wells, E. W. (for 12 yrs secretary of the Gas Company of New Orleans, LA) d 4/5/50 in New Orleans (b in Schenectady, NY) (9-4/19)
9381. Wells, Hannah, 38, wf of Col. Henry C., d 8/29/49 in Wellsburgh (consumption) (5-8/31)
9382. Wells, Henry C. (Capt.) m Hannah Smith, dau of Col. Solomon I., in Southport (6-2/17/30)
9383. Wells, Henry C. (Col.), 41, d 1/16/50 in Wellsburgh (consumption) (5-1/18)
9384. Wells, Henry M. m 10/11/32 Cassandanah Stewart in Elmira (6-11/7)
9385. Wells, Horace, Esq., 33, of Elmira d in NYC (6-3/3/30)
9386. Wells, James of New Hartford m 11/29/26 Amelia Lewis of Augusta in A; Rev. Lane (9-12/5)
9387. Wells, Job, Esq. of Chittenango m Mrs. Abigail Vannorthwick of New Brunswick, NJ in N. B.; Rev. Jones (3-2/3/35)
9388. Wells, John Appollos, Esq., cashier of Mechanics and Farmers Bank, Detroit, MI, m 10/14/36 Henrietta Hayden Hale of Canandaigua in C (6-10/26)
9389. Wells, John H., s of Dr. Noah of NYC, d 1/6/32 in Mobile (presumably in Alabama) (6-2/1/32)
9390. Wells, John I., 63, inventor of the Wells Patent Leather Press, d 4/12/32 in Hartford, CT (a minister of the Society of Friends) (6-5/16)
9391. Wells, John Milton m 9/5/50 Laura Serepta Hubbard in Sauquoit; Rev. John Waugh (9-9/9)
9392. Wells, Jonathan m 1/4/27 Lucy Dickinson, both of Preston, in P; Rev. Edward Andrews of Oxford (8-1/12)
9393. Wells, Joseph V. of Sullivan m 1/27/41 "Miss Forbes" of Lenox in Clockville (3-2/3)
9394. Wells, Landon (Dr.) m 6/10/46 Elizabeth Mercer, oldest dau of William V. I., Esq., at St. Paul's Ch., Waterloo; Rev. E. Wheeler (6-6/12)
9395. Wells, Lee, formerly of Chittenango, NY, m 10/29/33 Jane Van Horn in New Brunswick, NJ (3-11/5)
9396. Wells, Merriam, 50, wf of Dr. Richard, d 7/28/31 in Canandaigua (6-8/10)
9397. Wells, Nelson m 7/11/33 Betsy M. Bradford in Elmira (6-7/24)
9398. Wells, Philip C. m Alvira Nelson in Clyde (6-2/24/30)
9399. Wells, Relzeman, 43, d 5/20/43 in Orwell, Bradford Co., PA (4-6/21)
9400. Wells, Richard Henry, 27, d 10/2/43 in Utica (son of Alfred and member of the house of A. L. and R. H. Wells) (was supt. of the Sabbath School of the First Presby. Ch.) (funeral from his late home, 63 Broadway) (9-10/4)
9401. Wells, Robert H., Esq. m 9/13/43 Catharine M. Storrs, dau of late Dr. H. formerly of Utica, in Little Falls; Rev. McIlvain (9-9/18)

257

9402. Wells, Samuel R., Esq. m 10/13/44 Charlotte Fowler, sister of O. S., Esq., editor of the American Phrenological Journal, inNYC; Rev. Fenwick T. Williams (9-10/26)
9403. Wells, Sarah, 60, wf of Capt. James, d 6/6/50 in Baldwinsville (congestive fever) (funeral at Presby. Ch.) (1-6/6)
9404. Wells, Shepard (Rev.) of Columbia, TN m 8/28/45 Abby J. Graves, dau of Henry, Esq. of Boonville, NY, in B; Rev. Dr. Hunter (9-9/1)
9405. Wells, Theodore, 17, s of Job, Esq. of Chittenango, d 12/1/35 in Jersey City (NJ?) (3-12/8)
9406. Welsh, Margaret M., 30, wf of Henry, one of the editors of the Harrisburg (PA) Reporter, d 10/8/34 in York, PA (6-10/22)
9407. Welton, Titus, about 80, d 6/25/36 in Richmond (6-7/13)
9408. Wendell, John H. (Gen.), 80, (a Rev. officer) d 7/10/32 in Albany (6-7/18)
9409. Wendell, Robert H., 86, d 7/7/48 at his home on College Hill, Schenectady (9-7/12)
9410. Wentworth, _____, 9 mo, ch of "Mrs. Wentworth", d 9/2/26 in Utica (9-9/12)
9411. Wentworth, George (Dr.), 29, (a Chicago alderman), s of Hon. Paul of Concord, NH and bro of Hon. John, a Congressman from Chicago, d 8/14/50 in Chicago, IL (9-8/21)
9412. Wescott, A. B. (Dr.) m 3/1/49 C. Ermina Byington, both of Salisbury; Rev. J. H. Harter of Little Falls (9-3/9)
9413. Wescott, George, merchant, m 8/27/44 Lucretia Benedict, dau of J., Esq., at Trinity Ch. in Utica; Rev. Dr. P. A. Proal. All of Utica (9-8/28 and 8/30)
9414. Wescott, Tirzy (Mrs.), 36, d 7/11/36 in Manchester (6-7/27)
9415. Wessells, Grace, 3, dau of Maj. H. W. of the 2nd Infantry, U.S. Army, d 5/19/49 on board the storeship "Julia" near Benecia, CA (9-7/31)
9416. Wessels, H. W. (Lt.) of the U.S. Army m H. C. Cooper, dau of late Isaac, Esq. of Cooperstown, at Madison Barracks, Sacketts Harbor; Rev. Dr. Judd (9-5/17/44)
9417. West, _____ m 1/5/32 Catharine Ehle; Rev. Campbell. All of Sullivan (3-1/10)
9418. West, Catherine, 31, wf of Bicknell West, d 5/4/45 in Sullivan (3-7/5)
9419. West, Charles E., principal of Rutgers Female Institute, NYC, m 4/24/43 Elizabeth G. Giles of Worcester, MA (formerly preceptress of Oxford [NY] Academy) in Worcester at the home of Hon. E. Washburn (Oxford Republican, 5/19)
9420. West, Hannah, 47, wf of John, d 7/17/23 in Oxford (8-7/23)
9421. West, Harriet, 22, wf of Mathew and dau of Cad. W. Wiggins, d 1/13/31 in Phelps (6-1/26)
9422. West, Horace m 3/3/30 Susan Weiser, both of Geneva, in G; Rev. Phelps (6-3/10)
9423. West, Joel (Rev.), 61, d 10/26/26 in Chatham, CT (in the 35th yr of his ministry) (9-11/14)
9424. West, John, 66, "a colored man", d 12/6/25 in Utica (9-12/13)
9425. West, Matthew of Phelps m 6/5/32 Harriet Weed of Junius in J (6-6/13)
9426. West, Nathaniel m 4/29/38 Emily Sherwin of Sullivan in S; Jairus French, Esq. (3-5/2)
9427. West, Palatiah, 43, d 2/6/36 in Canandaigua (6-2/17)
9428. West, Russel M. (Rev.), 31, d 11/12/46 in Baldwinsville (member of Black River Conference of Meth. Episc. Ch.) (1-11/16)
9429. West, Samuel H. m Ruth Hillman in Arcadia (6-4/7/30)
9430. West, Solomon of Mount Pleasant, PA m 7/11/43 Harriet T. Bicknell of Utica in U; Rev. B. Hawley (9-7/12)
9431. West, Stephen (Rev.), 84, D.D., d in Stockbridge, MA (pastor there more than 50 yrs) (8-6/9/19)
9432. West, Thomas, about 59, d 9/12/38 in Sullivan (3-10/3)
9433. Westbrook, Alvin, 24, d 9/6/30 in Phelps (6-9/15)
9434. Westcott, Watts Lynds, 4, s of Dr. A., d 8/8/47 in Syracuse (1-8/11)
9435. Westerman, Hannah (Mrs.), 55, d 12/8/35 in Sullivan (3-12/15)
9436. Westfall, Ann, 16, d in Phelps (6-2/16/31)
9437. Westfall, Charles W. of Phelps m 8/16/32 Eleanor Sutton of Lyons in L (6-8/22)
9438. Westfall, James, 79, one of the earliest settlers in Phelps, d in P (6-2/10/30)

9439. Westfall, Polley, 57, d 10/3/36 in Elmira (6-10/12)
9440. Westfall, Samuel, 3rd, m 2/16/32 Elizabeth Kip, dau of Battis of Junius,
in J; Elder B. Farley (6-2/29)
9441. Westlake, Benjamin, 79, formerly of Orange Co., d 9/15/35 at his home in
Elmira (6-9/30)
9442. Westlake, Jacob (Col.) m Julia Wood, both of Horseheads, in Starkey
(6-5/22/33)
9443. Westlake, Lanah, 40, consort of Col. Jacob, d 4/10/32 in Horseheads
(6-4/18)
9444. Westlake, Riley, 30, only s of John of Utica, d 8/20/43 in the Parish of
Pointcoupie, Louisiana (9-9/12)
9445. Wetmore, Cornelia Platt, wf of Frederick, formerly of Oneida Co.,
d 11/11/48 in Utica (9-11/14)
9446. Wetmore, Ezra, 67, d 7/1/49 in Whitestown (son of late Amos, one of the
earliest settlers in Oneida Co.; arrived about 1786 from New England
and with Judge White erected the first grist mill west of Palatine, NY)
(9-7/4)
9447. Wetmore, Frederick of Detroit, MI m 8/16/50 Anna M. Curtenius, dau of
John L., Esq. of Buffalo, NY, in Lockport, NY; Rev. Washington Roosevelt
(9-8/19)
9448. Wetmore, Henry, F., Esq. of Yorkville m 9/15/47 Lucinda Story of Verona
in V; Rev. Burnsides (9-10/1)
9449. Wetmore, Jehiel m 7/28/46 Emeline H. Newcomb in Whitestown; Rev. J. D.
Cole. All of Whitestown (9-7/31)
9450. Wetmore, Mary, 10, dau of Thomas M. and Eliza Frances, d 10/18/48 in Utica
(funeral from the Trinity Ch.) (9-10/19)
9451. Wetmore, Samuel m 1/4/48 Sarah Adams, both of Utica, in U; Rev. D. G. Corey
(9-1/6)
9452. Wetmore, William (Hon.), 81, (a Rev. patriot) d 11/18/30 in Boston
(9-12/7)
9453. Wettenhall, Juliet (Miss), 17, d 8/21/23 in Smithville (8-8/27)
9454. Whaley, Caleb J., Esq., 41, d 6/7/30 in Avon (6-6/16)
9455. Whaples, Rhoda (Mrs.), 61, d 1/3/29 in Norwich (7-1/7)
9456. Wheat, Benjamin, 11, s of David and Electa, drowned 6/26/49 in the Chemung
River about 2 mi west of Elmira (5-6/29)
9457. Wheat, James of Lindon(?) m 9/17/50 Brittania Smith of Campbell, NY; Rev.
A. L. Brooks (4-9/25)
9458. Wheat, L. C. m 8/20/40 Mary Warnick in Hornby; Rev. Gray. All of Hornby
(4-8/28)
9459. Wheaton, _____, wf of Augustus, d 9/26/25 in Pompey, NY (9-10/25)
9460. Wheaton, John m Esther Mason in Wheeler (6-7/7/30)
9461. Wheaton, Oliver, 68, d 7/15/21 in Lisle (8-8/1)
9462. Wheaton, Thomas m Lucinda Demun in Seneca Falls (6-2/23/31)
9463. Whedon, Calvin (Maj.), 38, inspector of the 24th Brigade, Infantry,
d 9/18/30 in Seneca (funeral at Associate Reformed Ch. in #9, town of
Seneca) (6-9/22)
9464. Wheeler, _____, inf ch of George D., d 2/26/38 in Chittenango (3-2/28)
9465. Wheeler, Aaron, 30, d in Wheeler (6-3/27/33)
9466. Wheeler, Aaron R. of Waterloo m 8/3/34 Sarah W. Stevenson of Tyre (6-8/13)
9467. Wheeler, Benjamin, 72, d 2/6/36 in East Bloomfield (6-2/17)
9468. Wheeler, Benjamin, 12, s of A., d 5/12/43 in Binghamton (2-5/17)
9469. Wheeler, Chandler (Rev.) m 12/4/33 Catharine McClure in Bath (6-12/18)
9470. Wheeler, George A., Esq., about 60, d 8/6/37 in Bloomfield (6-8/30)
9471. Wheeler, George Henry of Harmony m 10/16/46 Obre(?) Ide of Canajoharie
in Utica; D. Gillmore, Esq. (9-10/28)
9472. Wheeler, Hezekiah, 81, d 1/8/28 (and his wife, Mary, 84, d 1/9) in Oxford
(married for nearly 60 yrs) (8-1/18)
9473. Wheeler, Horatio N. of Bristol, NY m Celistia R. Phelps of Sugar Grove,
Warren Co., PA in S. G. (6-4/22/35)
9474. Wheeler, Jacob D., attorney and "Legal Author", of NYC d 6/20/48 at the
home of a relative, James Wheeler, Esq., in Orange Co. (9-7/1)
9475. Wheeler, James Augustus, 25, s of Samuel, Esq. of Oxford, NY, d 1/2/43 in
Columbus, IL (left for the west 2 yrs ago) (Oxford Republican, 1/27)
9476. Wheeler, Jonas M., Esq., sheriff of Ontario Co., m 6/18/33 Ann Melvina
Kimball in East Bloomfield (6-6/26)

9477[?]. Wheeler, Josiah of Dresden m 9/23/30 Sarah L. Munn of Benton; Rev. Clary (6-10/6)
9478[?]. Wheeler, Levi, 56, d 6/14/33 in Covert (b 8/7/1776, oldest s of late Hon. Nathan of Weston, CT; was settled in covert by 1811; at death had been for more than 14 yrs a judge of the court of general sessions, Seneca Co.) (6-7/3 and 7/10)
9479. Wheeler, Phoebe H., consort of Maj. George A., d 3/24/34 in East Bloomfield (6-3/26)
9480. Wheeler, Phineas, 67, d 8/5/49 in Rome, NY (9-8/10)
9481. Wheeler, Rachel, 38 or 88 (blurred), wf of James M., Esq., d 12/6/31 in Canandaigua (6-12/21)
9482. Wheeler, Robert B. m 2/25/36 Hannah Doolittle, both of Penn Yan, in Branchport (6-3/9)
9483. Wheeler, Russel of the firm of Wheeler and Co. m 8/5/45 Amanda Bailey, dau of Joel C., in Utica; Rev. D. G. Corey. All of Utica (9-8/6)
9484. Wheeler, Samuel, merchant, of Norwich m 11/20/14 Nancy Bennet of Oxford in Homer (8-11/26)
9485. Wheeler, Samuel A. m Ann E. Stanley, dau of Asa of Canandaigua, in Akron, OH (6-8/22/32)
9486. Wheeler, Solomon of Bloomfield m Orpha Spears in Hopewell (6-6/26/33)
9487. Wheeler, Sylvester, 48, d in Bristol (6-11/6/33)
9488. Wheeler, Thomas m 2/27/37 Everil Norman in Dresden; Rev. S. P. Keyes. All of Dresden (6-3/15)
9489. Wheeler, William D. (Dr.) of Chelsea, MA m 5/8/50 Mary C. Williams of Utica at Trinty Ch., Utica; Rev. Dr. Proal (9-5/9)
9490. Wheeler, William Orville, 7, s of Dr. J. L. and Eleanor, d 5/31/46 in Geneva (6-6/5)
9491. Wheelock, A., 65, d 4/19/50 at the home of his son-in-law, Charles McGiven, in Watertown (deceased a long-time resident there) (9-4/27)
9492. Wheelock, George A. m 10/29/50 Amelia Lyon in Corning; Rev. Lightbourne. All of Corning (4-10/30)
9493. Wheelock, John m 11/8/32 Rhoda Plimpton, both of Bloomfield, in West Bloomfield (6-11/21)
9494. Wheelock, M. M. m 4/5/48 Olive rockwell, both of Corning, in C; Rev. Pierson (4-4/12)
9495. Whelan, William (Rev.), pastor of St. Patrick's Ch. in Buffalo, d 4/27/47 in Buffalo (9-4/29)
9496. Whelpley, Philip M., 30, pastor of the First Presby. Ch. in NYC, d 7/19/24 at Schooley's Mountain (9-8/3)
9497. Whiffen, George, 2, youngest s of Isaac and Elizabeth, d 11/29/48 in Utica (9-11/30)
9498. Whiffin, Isabele Adelaide, 7, dau of David and Jane, d 9/27/48 in Utica (funeral from her parents' home on Miller St.) (9-9/28)
9499. Whipple, Benjamin, 64, for many years keeper to the state assembly, d in Albany (8-6/2/19)
9500. Whipple, Esek (Capt.), 74, (a Rev. patriot) d 12/21/33 in De Kalb (6-1/1/34)
9501. Whipple, F. C., Esq. of Michigan m 6/28/42 Caroline A. Bancroft of Oxford, NY in O; Rev. Burtle (Oxford Times, 6/29)
9502. Whipple, Frances R. (Miss), 15, d 4/8/50 at the home of her father, J. H., in Adams, Jeff. Co. (9-4/27)
9503. Whipple, Jeremiah, Esq., 74, d 9/22/40 in Nelson (3-9/23)
9504. Whipple, Susan, 9 mo, adopted dau of John S., d in Geneva (6-9/21)
9505. Whitaker, Jonathan (Rev.), principal of Monroe High School, d 11/19/35 in Henrietta (6-12/2)
9506. Whitaker, Levi H. m 3/18/35 Malinda B. Allen in Geneva; Rev. C. S. Coates. All of Seneca (6-3/25)
9507. Whitbeck, William W. d 12/15/50 in Utica (9-12/17)
9508. Whitcomb, Cyrus m 10/13/41 Harriet E. Whipple in Cazenovia; Rev. Luther Myrick. All of Cazenovia (3-10/20)
9509. Whitcomb, Erastus, Esq. m 9/3/33 Cynthia Fowler, both of Pittsford, in Henrietta (6-9/18)
9510. Whitcomb, Henry H. of Adams m 9/14/47 Maria J. Mooney of Lorraine in Adams; Rev. J. F. Dayan (1-9/22)
9511. Whitcomb, James (Hon.), governor of Indiana, m 3/23/46 Mrs. Martha Ann Hurst, dau of late William Renwick, Esq. of Mulberry Hill, OH, in M. H.; Rev. David Whitcomb (9-4/8)

9512. White, _____, wf of Joseph, d 12/14/20 in Oxford (8-12/20)
9513. White, Alfred C., 23, printer, d 9/13/48 in Watertown (consumption)
   (1-9/27)
9514. White, Alice L., 12, dau of J. L. and Laura F., d 6/15/50 in Southfield,
   Staten Island, NY (9-6/19)
9515. White, Almer (sic) of Springville m 6/13/42 Rebecca Ellinwood, dau of
   Reuben, in Kirkland; Rev. Asahel Norton, D.D. (9-7/6)
9516. White, Andrew m 4/4/50 Susan A. Drake in Elmira; Rev. E. W. Dickinson.
   All of Elmira (5-4/5)
9517. White, Catharine (Mrs.) d 1/27/31 in Oxford (6-2/9)
9518. White, Charles A., 21, d 11/4/46 in Hamilton (9-12/4)
9519. White, David P. m 9/23/45 Maria Roberts; Rev. W. Bailey. All of Utica
   (9-9/25)
9520. White, Delos (Dr.), 46, d 3/18/35 in Cherry Valley (deceased a surgeon)
   (6-4/15)
9521. White, Edwin, a clerk in the Navy Yard at Gasport, NY, d 7/16/37 in
   Norfolk, VA (6-7/19)
9522. White, G. Hibbard of Baldwinsville m 7/4/48 Nancy Towner of Fountainville
   at the Empire House, Syracuse; Rev. M. Adams (1-7/5)
9523. White, George m 3/1/49 Mrs. Ladd in Utica; Rev. H. R. Clarke (9-3/3)
9524. White, George M. m 9/7/49 Submit ___?___ (dau of Nathan, Esq.) both of
   Whitestown, in W; Rev. Spencer (9-9/8)
9525. White, Henry, Esq., district attorney of Erie Co. and a city alderman,
   d 8/25/32 in Buffalo (6-9/5)
9526. White, Henry (Rev.), 50, D.D, (Prof. of Theology, Union Theological
   Seminary, NYC) d 8/25/50 (9-8/28)
9527. White, Ira (Capt.) of Tyrone m 2/15/31 Phidelia Johnson of Columbia, Herk.
   Co., in C (6-3/2)
9528. White, Ira, merchant, of Palmyra m 6/25/32 Esther Bates, dau of Stephen,
   Esq., in Hopewell (6-7/4)
9529. White, James, 76, d 3/20/50 in Sherburne (9-4/11)
9530. White, James, 70, d 8/7/50 in Utica (funeral from the home of George
   McBride, 37 Broadway)
9531, White, Jane, 38, wf of Ira formerly of Geneva, d 3/22/30 inPalmyra
   (6-3/24)
9532. White, Jane, 18, d 3/5/50 in Addison (4-3/13)
9533. White, Jasper, Jr. m Jane Sackett in Amity (6-4/14/30)
9534. White, John C. of NYC m 6/20/43 Lucy A. Lynch, dau of James of Salina,
   at St. John's Ch. in Salina; Rev. Hines (2-6/28)
9535. White, Joseph (Hon.), 68, physician and surgeon, of Cherry Valley d 6/3/32
   at the home of David Cushman, Esq. in Exeter (6-6/13)
9536. White, Julius of Milwaukee, WI m 9/5/49 C. R. Shackleford of Madison, WI
   in Kirkland, NY; Rev. S. W. Raymond of Kirkland (9-9/7)
9537. White, Lavinia, wf of Henry S. recently of Geneva, d "in October" in
   New Orleans, LA (cholera) (6-11/28/32)
9538. White, Lewis of Whitestown m 5/18/48 Ambrosia Lamb, only dau of John, Esq.
   of Columbus, Chen. Co., in C; Rev. Shipman of Columbus Center (9-5/19)
9539. White, Lucinda, 70, wid of late John, d 1/6/50 in Utica (9-1/8)
9540. White, M. M. (Dr.) m 2/28/49 Almira Hills, both of Syracuse, at the City
   Hotel, Utica; Rev. William H. Spencer (9-3/2)
9541. White, Margaret Vanderhorst Ellis, a native of Charleston, SC and relict
   of late Col. Anthony Walton White (a Rev. officer), d 5/23/50 in New
   Brunswick, NJ (9-6/4)
9542. White, Morris of Racine, WI m 2/17/47 Julia A. Jones, only dau of Isaac H.
   of Columbus Center, Chen. Co., NY, in C. C.; Rev. Redfield (9-2/20)
9543. White, N. Curtiss, Esq. of Utica m 7/31/50 Jane C. Stanton, dau of E. of
   Trenton, NY, in Stonington, CT; Rev. Cook (9-8/5)
9544. White, O. E. m 1/31/49 N. Elizabeth Smith, both of Baldwinsville, in Ionia;
   Rev. Reynolds (1-2/8)
9545. White, Philip, 101, (a Rev. soldier) d 5/24/50 at Long-a-Coming, Camden
   Co., NJ (9-6?/13/50)
9546. White, Philo, Sr., 83, d 4/12/49 in Whitestown (one of the earliest
   settlers in Oneida Co.; emigrated from Middletown, CT with his father,
   late Judge White; arrived mouth of Sauquoit Creek 6/25/1784 (9-5/14)
9547. White, Robert of Varick m 5/10/31 Mary Oliver of West Cayuga (6-5/18)

9548. White, Rozen m 10/15/32 Mary Ann Stimpson in Rochester (6-11/7)
9549. White, Samuel (Dr.), 67, one of the proprietors of the insane asylum in Hudson, d 2/10/45 in Hudson (9-2/17)
9550. White, Sophia Louisa, 2, only dau of Henry S. and Levina, d 5/21/32 in Geneva (6-6/6)
9551. White, Stephen, 23, d in Somers, West. Co. (9-6/27/26)
9552. White, Thomas of Hammondsport m 11/4/33 Jane Caywood in Geneva; Rev. McLaren (6-11/13)
9553. White, Warren S. of Van Buren m 7/3/48 Martha H. Frisbie, both of Lysander, in L; Rev. T. Walker (1-7/5)
9554. White, William, Esq. m 7/3/49 Caroline M. Simmons at Trinity Ch., Utica; Rev. Dr. Proal. All of Utica (double ceremony - see marr of Grant H. Adams) (9-7/4)
9555. White, William H., inf s of Oscar E. and Elizabeth, d 4/4/50 in Syracuse (1-4/11)
9556. White, William Pitt, 9, oldest s of Alvin, d 5/10/48 in Utica (funeral at the Central Hotel) (9-5/12)
9557. White, Worthy of Trenton, NY m Beula AnnPierce in Bloomfield (6-3/31/30)
9558. Whitehouse, Henry J. (Rev.) of Rochester m Harriet Bruin, dau of M., Esq., in Perth Amboy, NJ; Bishop Onderdonk (6-11/23/36)
9559. Whitesides, William m 1/27/36 Susan Rose, both of Lyons, (in Seneca Falls?) (6-2/10)
9560. Whitey, Garrett of Deerfield m 1/6/47 Mary Latus of Frankfort in Utica; Zenas Wright, Justice of Peace (9-1/8)
9561. Whitford, Archibald, 55, d 4/13/49 in Watertown (for many years prof. of mathematics at the Jefferson County Institute (9-4/21)
9562. Whiting, Augustus, Esq. of New Orleans, LA m 10/19/43 Sarah Swan, oldest dau of Hon. Gustavus of Columbus, OH, in Cambridge, MA; Rev. Allbro (double ceremony - see marr of George M. Parsons) (9-10/24)
9563. Whiting, Bowen, Esq. of Geneva, formerly of Oxford, m Nancy McKinstry, dau of Gen. McKinstry of Hillsdale, Columbia County, in Hillsdale (8-10/14/18)
9564. Whiting, George S. m 9/2/33 Elsie Kellogg in Vienna, NY (6-9/11)
9565. Whiting, Henry (Capt.) of the U.S. Army, formerly of Oxford, m Nancy Goodwin, dau of Joseph of Hudson, in H; Rev. B. F. Stanton (8-3/18/18)
9566. Whiting, Henry S., Esq., 39, formerly of Danbury, CT, d 8/10/24 in Herkimer, NY (9-8/17)
9567. Whiting, Joanna (Miss), dau of John, Esq., d 1/27/42 at the home of her father in Canaan, Columbia Co. (9-2/8)
9568. Whiting, John m 12/31/37 Caroline Wing in Fredonia (6-1/24/38)
9569. Whiting, John (Deacon), 80, d 9/2/44 in Canaan, NY (9-9/25)
9570. Whiting, John N. m 8/18/45 Sarah Louisa Jay Sutherland, dau of Judge Sutherland, in Geneva (9-8/22)
9571. Whiting, Mason, Esq., 76, d 1/11/49 in Binghamton (9-2/3)
9572. Whiting, Nathan m 3/22/49 Elmira K. Hewit, both of Veteran, at the Eagle Hotel in Elmira; Rev. H. N. Seaver (5-3/23)
9573. Whiting, Ranford m 4/10/32 Alma Crane, both of Benton, in B; Rev. C. V. Adgate (6-5/23)
9574. Whiting, Sarah A., dau of B. Babcock, Esq. and consort of Joel Whiting, principal of New Woodstock Academy, d 7/20/37 in New Woodstock, Madison Co., NY (3-8/2)
9575. Whiting, Thomas J. m 4/25/32 Harriet Baldwin in Perryville; Rev. Northrup. All of Sullivan (3-5/1)
9576. Whiting, Thomas J., 37, d 5/22/42 in Perryville (consumption) (member of Episc. Ch.) (he died in the home of "Mr. and Mrs. Chapman") (his wife pre-deceased him by two years) (3-5/25 and 6/1)
9577. Whitlock, Daniel, 38, d in Lyons (6-6/16/30)
9578. Whitman, Roswell, formerly of Lenox, m 3/10/41 Betsey Porter of Stockbridge in S; Rev. S. M. Bainbridge (3-3/24)
9579. Whitmore, Joel of Lebanon, Madison Co., m 9/9/44Melitta Newton of Sandy Creek in S. C.; Rev. Davis (9-10/4)
9580. Whitmore, O. S. of Rathboneville m 4/18/50 Martha J. Wilson of Binghamton in West Addison; Rev. J. Southwark (4-5/1)
9581. Whitmore, Robert C., 28, publisher of the Binghamton Democrat, d 8/20/47 in Binghamton (9-9/4)
9582. Whitmore, Thomas, 4, s of M. B., d 11/16/36 in Vienna, NY (6-11/30)

9583. Whitmore, Wells, 70, d 11/25/38 in Vienna, NY (6-12/5)
9584. Whitney, Bascum, 70, d 6/21/39 in Hopewell (one of the earliest settlers in Seneca) (6-7/3)
9585. Whitney, David S. m 8/4/34 Hannah Partridge in Canandaigua (6-8/13)
9586. Whitney, George L., publisher of the Detroit Journal, m 1/18/31 Lucinda B. Williams, dau of Dr. William A. of Canandaigua, in C; Rev. A. D. Eddy (6-1/26)
9587. Whitney, H. m 5/25/50 Lucy Fitch in Norwich; Rev. Dr. Bond (9-8/26)
9588. Whitney, Josiah (Rev.), 94, D.D., d in Brooklyn, CT (9-9/28/24)
9589. Whitney, Lyman, 4, s of Jonas, d in Syracuse (6-6/8/31)
9590. Whitney, Mary, 11, dau of David, d 8/5/34 in Chittenango (3-8/12)
9591. Whitney, Virgil of the firm of J. Whitney and Co. m Marcia Doty, late of Norwich, at Chenango Point; Rev. Cumming (8-12/8/19)
9592. Whittemore, Sephrina, 2, dau of Thomas, d 10/2/26 in Utica (9-10/10)
9593. Whittenhall, Henry H., 1, s of Uriah, d 9/13/30 in Oxford (8-9/15)
9594. Whittenhall, Margaret Agnes, 7, dau of Elihu, d 3/6/42 in Oxford (Oxford Times, 3/9)
9595. Whittenhall, Otis, 38, formerly of Oxford, d 9/23/42 in Addison (Oxford Times, 9/28)
9596. Whittmore, Isaac Harrington, formerly of Utica, d 2/13/45 in New Orleans, LA (9-2/27)
9597. Wickam, Chester m 12/3/47 Mary Wiley, both of Utica, in U; Rev. D. G. Corey (9-1/6/48)
9598. Wicker, Cornelia, 36, wf of James C., d 6/7/45 in Utica (funeral from her former home, corner Bridge and Lansing Sts.) (9-6/9)
9599. Wicker, James m 3/6/31 Catharine Freer, both of Ithaca, in I (6-3/23)
9600. Wicker, Roxanna, wf of Joel H., Esq., d 3/11/45 in Chicago, IL (consumption) (9-3/25)
9601. Wickes, Charles C. m 10/7/34 Martha C. Munson, dau of Justus, in Paris, NY; Rev. Hotchkin (9-10/14)
9602. Wickes, Elizabeth, wf of Capt. Silas, d 12/4/30 in Starkey (6-12/20)
9603. Wickes, James C. of Utica m 5/19/47 Maria P. Smith of Hallowell in H; Rev. Thuston (9-5/26)
        Wickham. See also Wickam.
9604. Wickham, Orrin O. of NYC d 6/15/49 at Sag Harbor, L.I., NY (publisher and author of educational books) (9-7/2)
9605. Wickham, Thomas, 49, d 11/5/34 in Geneva (6-11/12)
9606. Wickham, William C., 28, formerly of Utica, d 4/14/49 at the home of his father, Philo, in East Hamilton, Madison Co. (consumption) (surv by wf and 1 ch) (9-4/24)
9607. Wickoff, Edward, about 40, d 8/21/20 in Conhocton (died from a bee sting: the editor of the Steuben Patriot suggests one wine glass full of olive oil taken immediately after the biting or stinging of any reptile or insect "may put an instantaneous stop to the poison - or chew and swallow the juice of the snail plantain") (8-9/20)
9608. Wicks, Ashumera Wandell m 1/27/33 Ann B. Toy in Sodus (6-2/13)
9609. Wicks, James E., Esq. m 11/6/50 Valancia A. Palmer at St. John's Ch. (Episc.) in Clayville (9-11/9)
9610. Widrig, Jacob, 83, (a Rev. soldier) d 4/6/44 in Schuyler (9-4/12)
9611. Wiers, Nancy (Mrs.), 32, d 8/30/34 in Havana, NY (6-9/10)
9612. Wiggins, Charles E., 28, s of Benjamin, d 7/12/50 in Rome, NY (typhus) (9-8/8)
9613. Wiggins, J. of Rome, NY m 8/17/50 Lois Ann Scoville, dau of H. of Camden, in C; Rev. E. G. Townsend (9-8/29)
9614. Wight, _?_, inf s of George, d 8/23/36 in Geneva (6-8/24)
9615. Wight, George m 5/4/35 Almeda Hewes in Junius; Rev. Phelps. All of Geneva (6-5/6)
9616. Wight, Mary B., 3 mo, dau of George, d 9/28/32 in Geneva (6-10/3)
9617. Wight, Paulina L. (Miss), 30, d 5/1/34 in Geneva (6-5/7)
9618. Wight, Susan, 33, wf of George, d 7/6/32 in Geneva (6-7/11)
9619. Wightman, Joseph P. of Utica m 12/24/49 Sarah Turnock of Oriskany in Whitesboro; Rev. W. R. Long (9-1/4/50)
9620. Wigram, Maria Julianna, dau of late John, Esq., d 4/19/31 in Woodstock (consumption) (6-5/11)
9621. Wilber, Olive, about 24, d 7/22/33 in Geneva (6-7/24)

9622. Wilbor, Sarah, about 62, wid of late Simeon G. formerly of New Hartford, d 8/12/50 in Fon du Lac, WI (consumption) (9-8/20)
9623. Wilbor, Thompson m 1/22/14 Clarissa B(?) Manwaring in Plymouth (8-2/8)
9624. Wilbur, inf ch of J. Wilbur, d in Utica (9-4/25/26)
9625. Wiburn Barton, 27, d 8/16/47 in Syracuse (1-8/18)
9626. Wilcocks, William, 75, (a Rev. officer) d 12/26/26 in NYC (9-12/26)
9627. Wilcomb, Charles S. of Chester, NH m 3/26/49 Harriet A. Symonds, oldest dau of F. of Whitesboro, in W; Rev. Walter R. Long (9-4/4)
    Wilcox. See also Willcox.
9628. Wilcox, Calvin m Hannah Sawyer in Bloomfield (6-3/31/30)
9629. Wilcox, Jerome B. m 9/4/49 Susan M. Shepherd, both of New Hartford; Rev. S. W. Raymond of Kirkland (9-9/7)
9630. Wilcox, John B. of Augusta m 2/7/49 Louisa De Land of Kirkland at the Central Hotel in Utica; Rev. D. G. Corey (9-2/8)
9631. Wilcox, John M. of Solon m 9/10/42 Mary Holmes of Oxford; Rev. E. G. Perry (Oxford Times) (9/14)
9632. Wilcox, Marcus, Esq. of Elba m 10/18/32 Julia A. Humphrey in Onondaga (6-11/7)
9633. Wilcox, Orrin B., 34, d 4/14/50 in Baldwinsville (consumption) (1-4/18)
9634. Wilcox, Roland (Dr.), 36, d 1/21/50 in Elmira (5-1/25)
9635. Wilcox, Sally, 69, wid of Ozias "and for the last ten years a resident with Ephraim Palmer in New Hartford" d 7/12/49 at the home of John Green in Deerfield (funeral from the Bapt. Ch. in Whitesboro) (9-7/13)
9636. Wilcox, Sophia, 40, wf of Admiral Wilcox, d 7/5/33 in Whitestown (consumption) (surv by husband and 2 small ch) (9-7/16)
9637. Wilcox, William (Mrs.) d 6/8/41 in Clockville (3-6/16)
9638. Wilcox, William C. m 8/7/45 Harriet Jane Griswold, dau of Elder Marvin, in Whitesboro; Rev. Walter R. Long. All of Whitesboro (9-8/12)
9639. Wilder, Elijah m 1/15/33 Mrs. Lucy Judd in Geneva; Rev. Phelps (6-1/23)
9640. Wilder, Elijah (Deacon), 84, d 7/9/36 near Geneva (drove the first team that came from Oneida Co. to the Geneva area; aided in the organization of the Presby. Ch. in Geneva)(6-7/13)
9641. Wilder, Jonathan, 82, d 3/12/34 in Canandaigua (6-3/26)
9642. Wilder, Lucy (Mrs.), 27, d 6/19/46 in Seneca (former consort of Deacon Levi Judd formerly from South Hadley, MA and the relict of the late Deacon Elijah Wilder of Seneca) (funeral from the home of her son, Levi Judd) (6-6/19)
9643. Wilder, Rastus of Galen m Mrs. Elizabeth Mead in Lyons (6-3/10/30)
9644. Wiles, William, about 70, d 11/24/33 in Perry (lived there many years (6-12/4)
9645. Wiley, Lovell Ingals, 14, d 7/9/49 in Mohawk (1-8/16)
9646. Wiley, Robert Hall, 4, youngest s of Rev. Charles, d 12/25/47 in Utica (9-12/28)
9647. Wiley, Thomas m 10/16/45 Mary F. Sixbury in Utica; Rev. Wesley Bailey. All of Utica (9-10/17)
9648. Wilgers, Thomas m 1/25/48 Mary Beers, oldest dau of Munson H. of Westmore-land, in W; Rev. F. A. Spencer (9-2/3)
9649. Wilhilmi, Ernest, 84, d in the Parish of Lachanaye, Lower Canada (came to America in 1776 - was a lieutenant of the Hessian chasseurs) (6-4/6/36)
9650. Wilkes, Archibald m 10/30/35 Mrs. Margaret Austin in Sullivan; J. French, Esq. (3-11/3)
9651. Wilkes, Charles, Esq., 79, d "last week" in NYC (6-9/4/33)
9652. Wilkes, Eli R., 39, 2nd s of late Samuel, d 4/13/49 in Buffalo (9-4/17)
9653. Wilkeson, Mary P., 51, wf of Hon. Samuel and dau of late Gen. Absalom Peters of CT., d 8/25/47 in Buffalo (9-8/28)
9654. Wilkie, George m 11/17/36 Mary Ann McIntyre in Seneca: Rev. J. F. McLaren (6-11/23)
9655. Wilkins, Richard P. m 12/10/33 Mary M. Hatch in Rochester (6-12/25)
9656. Wilkins, William L. m 2/26/50 Cornelia Lyport; Rev. T. Walker. All of Baldwinsville (1-2/28)
9657. Wilkinson, George (Rev.) m 12/4/48 Mrs. Joanna Lefler; Rev. N. Fellows. All of Troy, PA (5-12/8)
9658. Wilkinson, James m 10/20/33 Laura R. Kinne in Waterloo (6-11/6)
9659. Wilkinson, Jemima, 70, "the universal friend", d in Jerusalem, NY (8-7/28/19)
9660. Wilkinson, William of Buffalo m 10/1/33 Mary B. Swan of Aurora in A(4-10/9)

264

9661. Willaner, Charles m Barbara Broadstone in Fayette (6-4/14/30)
9662. Willard, Gallio K. (Dr.), formerly of Chittenango, NY, m 7/3/34 Eleanor
D. Smith, dau of Rev. John of Granview, IL, in Granview (3-4/14)
9663. Willard, Helena (Mrs.), 20, d 1/16/36 in Sullivan (3-1/19)
9664. Willard, John (Dr.), 65, d in Troy (9-6/7/25)
9665. Willard, John (Rev.), 66, formerly pastor of the Congregational Ch. in
Lunenburgh, VT, d in Lunenburgh (9-8/8/26)
9666. Willard, John S. m 10/3/35 Eleanor Billington in Chittenango; Rev. John
C. F. Hoes (3-10/6)
9667. Willard, John S. m 2/23/37 Mariah Clark; J. Whipple, Esq. All of
Chittenango (3-2/29)
9668. Willard, Louis of Cayuga m 2/15/33 Phila Daniels of Livonia in L; Rev.
Allen (6-2/20)
9669. Willard, Lucy (Mrs.), 43, d 11/22/33 in Elmira (6-11/27)
9670. Willard, Martha (Miss), 19, d 9/14/31 in Van Buren (3-9/27)
9671. Willard, Mercy (Mrs.), 70, d 9/16/32 in Sullivan (3-9/18)
9672. Willard, Oliver P. m 12/7/43 Phebe Ann Herrick in Sullivan; Rev. James
Abell. All of S (3-12/13)
9673. Willard, Rufus, 80, d 8/25/32 in Sullivan (3-8/28)
9674. Willard, Titus B. (age blurred but possibly 58) d 11/7/38 in Niles, MI
(3-11/28)
9675. Willard, W. H. of Boonville m 8/21/45 Sophia Haggerty, adopted dau of
Daniel Eells of New Hartford, in New H.; Rev. Payson (9-9/10)
9676. Willard, William W. m 5/10/31 Sarah Stokes; Rev. Dr. Yates. All of
Chittenango (3-5/17)
9677. Willcox, Edmund m Mary Maria Stocking in Bath (6-3/24/30)
9678. Willcox, Elizabeth, 45, 2nd wf of Gates, Esq., d 4/10/45 in Montoursville,
Lycoming Co., PA (consumption) (Oxford Republican, 4/17)
9679. Willcox, Eunice, 20, wf of Lyman of Preston, d 6/17/20 (8-6/21)
9680. Willcox, Ira, merchant, of Oxford m 2/16/19 Lucy Willcox of Sheffield, MA
in S; Rev. James Bradford (8-3/3)
9681. Willcox, John m Caroline Hill in Smithville (8-11/16/25)
9682. Willcox, Rachel, 24, wf of Ira, merchant, d 7/31/17 in Oxford (8-8/6)
9683. Willcox, Sarah Ann, 18 mo, dau of Gates, Esq., d 8/24/26 in Macdonough
(8-8/25)
9684. Willett, Marinus, 90, d 8/22/30 in NYC (8-9/1)
9685. Willett, Sidney, 33, d 7/19/37 in Chittenango (3-7/26)
9686. Williams, _____, wf of Gurdon, d "a few days since" in Greene (8-1/14/18)
9687. Williams, _____, 15 weeks, ch of John, d in Utica (9-8/15/26)
9688. Williams, A. G. of Utica m 9/20/48 Jane M. Bush of Branford, CT in Utica;
Rev. William H. Spencer (9-9/21)
9689. Williams, Abraham of Bainbridge m 6/18/21 Olive Barnum of Utica in U; Rev.
Willey (8-7/4)
9690. Williams, Abraham B., Esq., 47, s of late Rev. Abraham, d 4/31/44 in Utica
(funeral from Trinity Ch.) (9-5/1)
9691. Williams, Abram of Hector m 12/21/35 Elizabeth Havens of Pulteney in Bath
(6-12/30)
9692. Williams, Addison G. of Syracuse m 8/16/47 Lavinia C. Roberts, dau of
Judge Roberts of Canastota, in C (1-8/25)
9693. Williams, Albert m 1/6/44 Eliza Ann Patterson in West Monroe, Oswego Co.;
Rev. S. W. Leonard. All of West Monroe (9-1/12)
9694. Williams, Alexander B. m 2/19/32 Sarah M. McCarty in Sodus (6-3/7)
9695. Williams, Amariah, father of Mrs. William H. Ferry of Utica, d 1/17/50
in Morrisville (migrated from Mansfield, CT and became an early settler
in Morrisville, NY) (his wife died less than four months prior to his
death) (9-1/26)
9696. Williams, Antrim m 3/9/36 Elizabeth Osborn, both of De Witt, in
Chittenango (3-3/16)
9697. Williams, Arthur G., inf s of Aras G. and Jane M., d 8/4/50 in Utica
(funeral from 14 Hopper St.) (9-8/5)
9698. Williams, Caroline A., 20, wf of Morris M. and third dau of Col. William
Tippetts, d 4/3/37 at the home of her sister, Mrs. H. N. Stafford in
Lyons (funeral from the home of her brother-in-law, G. H. Merrill
(6-4/5)
9699. Williams, Charles, 4 mo, s of Morris M., d 3/4/37 in Geneva (6-5/15)

9700. Williams, Charles of Vernon m 11/23/48 Frances Foland of Wampsville in W; Rev. W. H. Cooper (9-11/25)
9701. Williams, Charles Edward, youngest s of William Barron Williams, d 4/10/44 in Rochester (9-4/13)
9702. Williams, Charles Eugene, 6, youngest ch of Thomas, Jr., d 2/13/47 in Vernon (9-2/15)
9703. Williams, Comfort (Rev.), 43, former pastor of the Presby. Ch. in Rochester d 8/26/25 in Rochester (b in Wethersfield, CT; grad from Yale College in 1808; attended Andover (MA) Theological Seminary; served at Rochester by 1815) (9-9/6)
9704. Williams Cranstant of Sullivan m 3/8/26 Anna Gray, dau of Thomas, Esq. of Lenox; Rev. Roger Adams (9-3/28)
9705. Williams, David E., formerly of Utica, m 7/18/44 Jane A. Campbell of Albany in A; Rev. Dr. Potter (9-7/22)
9706. Williams, E. S. of Lisbon, IL m 10/13/47 Mary Read of Yorkville, NY in Y; Rev. W. F. Williams (9-10/15)
9707. Williams, Edward of New Berlin m 6/12/17 Sally Beardslee of Pittstown, Otsego Co.; Rev. Lacey (8-6/18)
9708. Williams, Elizabeth Leonard, 58, wf of John, Esq., d 11/1/50 in Cazenovia (9-11/5)
9709. Williams, Evan O., 68, d 7/8/43 in Utica (9-7/10)
9710. Williams, Ezekiel, 94, d 8/30/49 in New Hartford (b Roxbury, MA but an early settler in New Hartford, NY) (9-8/31)
9711. Williams, Fanny Hunt, wf of Col. John of Salem, NY and sister of late Montgomery Hunt of Utica, d 5/11/49 in Albany (9-5/15)
9712. Williams, Foster of Prattsburgh m 1/19/32 Mandaville Beeman in Cayuga (6-1/25)
9713. Williams, George, editor of the Hamilton Recorder, m 2/13/27 Mary Bement of Newark, NY in N (8-2/23)
9714. Williams, George m 12/11/33 Sarah Williams; Rev. Powell. All of Chittenango (3-12/17)
9715. Williams, George C. m Abigail Hoffman in Auburn (6-1/26/31)
9716. Williams, Gilbert E. of Hornellsville m 1/7/33 Joan Neally of Burns, Alleg. Co. in Bath (6-2/6)
9717. Williams, Gurdon m 1/30/18 Betsey Wainright, both of Greene; Charles Joslyn, Esq. (8-2/4)
9718. Williams, Harriet Wells, oldest dau of William, editor of the Utica Sentinel, d in Utica (another child from this same family died "a few days previously") (9-10/12/24)
9719. Williams, Harvey E. of Batavia m 11/22/43 Welthy Ann Cropsey of Sullivan in Chittenango; Rev. James Abell (3-11/29)
9720. Williams, Henry H., 47, s of Hon. Nathan, d 4/8/50 at the McGregor House in Utica (was formerly a teller in the Oneida Bank) (9-4/9)
9721. Williams, Horace B. of Van Buren m 8/24/48 Maria Moyer of Clay in C; Rev. T. Walker (1-8/31)
9722. Williams, J. D. of the firm of Williams and Kellogg m 8/9/44 Mary Downer, dau of A. O., all of Utica, in U; Rev. McElvaine (9-8/28)
9723. Williams, James Watson m 9/30/46 Helen E. Munson, dau of Alfred, at Grace Ch. in Utica; Rev. George Leeds (9-10/2)
9724. Williams, Jane (Mrs.), 67, d 11/7/45 in Utica (his son-in-law, Chester Dexter, is mentioned) (funeral from 50 Broadway) (9-11/8)
9725. Williams, John, Sr. (Elder), 58, pastor of the Olive street Bapt. Ch., NYC, d 5/22/25 (9-5/31)
9726. Williams, John (Maj.) of Mich. Terr. m Caroline Whitney in Rochester (6-7/3/33)
9727. Williams, John (Col.), 63, d 4/3/42 in Waterville (one of the earliest settlers in the town of Sangerfield (9-4/9)
9728. Williams, John of Rome, NY m 2/1/44 J. Caroline Hubby, youngest dau of Thomas, Esq. of New Hartford in New H; Rev. J. D. Cole (9-2/3)
9729. Williams, John, 78, d 3/18/45 at his home in Conway, MA (9-3/29)
9730. Williams, John m 5/8/50 Ellen Owens, both of NYC; Rev. S. A. Corey (9-5/13)
9731. Williams, Jonathan of Quincy, MA m Elizabeth Owens, dau of late Rev. Benjamin, at the Columbian Hotel in Utica; Elder Corey (9-3/26/47)
9732. Williams, Joseph (Col.), 65, (a Rev. officer) d in Greenwich, MA (8-6/9/19)

9733. Williams, Leonard of Chittenango m 9/24/40 Sophia Ehle, dau of Col. George of Cazenovia, in C; Rev. Leonard (3-9/3))
9734. Williams, Levi m 12/12/31 Nancy Twenty Canoes of the Christian party of Indians in Buffalo (6-12/21)
9735. Williams, Lucia, 23, wf of Silas and oldest dau of William Garratt, Esq. of Otsego Co., NY, d 4/20/19 in Columbus, OH (Silas a merchant there) (8-5/26)
9736. Williams, Lucy Charlotte, 1, dau of W. Barron Williams, d 6/9/42 in Rochester (9-6/20)
9737. Williams, Lyman m 11/3/36 Catharine Stanley in Vienna, NY (6-11/9)
9738. Williams M. M. m 8/27/35 Caroline Tippetts, both of Geneva; Rev. Dr. Bruce (6-9/2)
9739. Williams, Maria Louisa, 3, dau of Brown H. Williams, d 8/26/50 in Utica (9-8/30)
9740. Williams, Nathan (Hon.), clerk of the Supreme Court in Geneva, d 9/25/35 in Geneva (lived many years in Utica; was late circuit judge of the 5th state judicial district) (6-9/30)
9741. Williams, Nathan T., Esq., cashier of the Madison County Bank, m 5/16/33 Margaret L. Williams, dau of John, in Cazenovia; Rev. Leonard (3-5/21)
9742. Williams, Nathaniel m 6/25/50 Margaret Elizabeth Roberts in Utica; William H. Spencer. All of Utica (9-6/27)
9743. Williams, Othniel S., Esq., attorney, m 9/6/43 Delia Augusta Avery, dau of Prof. Charles, in Clinton; Rev. Dr. North, Pres. of Hamilton College (9-9/25)
9744. Williams, Peter O. of Plessis m 5/18/45 Marva C. Wightman at the home of R. E. Bacon, Esq. in Watertown; Rev. W. E. Knox (9-5/26)
9745. Williams, Richard S. of Palmyra m Olive Ann Porter, dau of Chauncey, Esq., in Pittsford (6-5/12/30)
9746. Williams, S. Ann, 35, wf of Benjamin S. and dau of Edward Webber, D 6/18/44 in Vernon (9-5/28)
9747. Williams, S. Wells of Canton, China m 11/25/47 Sarah S. Walworth, oldest dau of late John of NYC, in Plattsburgh; Rev. D. Dobie (9-12/3)
9748. Williams, Samuel of Seneca m 6/15/35 Louisa Densmore of Hopewell in Waterloo (6-6/24)
9749. Williams, Sanford m Anne Borce in Le Roy (6-2/17/30)
9750. Williams, T. W. m 11/26/38 E. Addison Parrott of Auburn at St. Peter's Ch. in Auburn; Rev. Lucas (6-12/5)
9751. Williams, Thomas, 32, d 2/13/50 in Cazenovia (9-2/14)
9752. Williams, W. F. (Rev.) m 8/10/48 Sarah A. Pond in Rome, NY; Rev. William H. Spencer (9-8/12)
9753. Williams, William, 61, for many years a resident of Elmira, d 3/1/50 in Wells, Bradford Co., PA (5-3/8)
9754. Williams, William, 62, d 6/10/50 in Utica (9-6/11)
9755. Williams, William A. (Dr.), 70, d 9/4/34 in Canandaigua (6-9/17)
9756. Williams, William W. (Rev.) of Camillus m 12/18/49 Anna E. Jerome of Fairmount in F; Rev. Henry Darling of Hudson (double ceremony - see marr of William E. Myers) (9-12/19)
9757. Williams, Winny, 119, d 10/12/26 in Alexandria (9-11/7)
9758. Williams, Zerina m 6/8/39 Louisa Taylor, both of Waterloo, in W; Rev. Townsend (6-6/26)
9759. Williamson, _____, 21, dau of Hugh, d 12/10/44 in Utica (funeral from Grace Church) (9-12/12)
9760. Williamson, Charles of Cohoes m 7/3/50 Elizabeth Kirkland, dau of Thomas of Utica, in U; Rev. H. S. Dickson (9-7/6)
9761. Williamson, J. D., Esq. of the U.S. Navy m 12/15/23 Sally Frances Shute, dau of Maj. William formerly of Elizabethtown, NJ, at Farmers Hall near Oxford, NY; Rev. Bush (8-12/24)
9762. Williamson, John H. of Jefferson Co., m 10/15/45 Fanny Kirkland, dau of Thomas of Elizabeth St., Utica, at the Meth. Ch. in Utica; Rev. McGowan (9-10/16)
9763. Williamson, Samuel, Esq. of Cleveland, OH m 6/15/43 Mary E. Tisdale of Utica; Rev. B. G. Paddock (9-6/17)
9764. Willis, N. P., Esq. of NYC m 10/1/46 Cornelia Grinnell, dau of Hon. Joseph Grinnell, M.C., in New Bedford (state not given); Rev. Ephraim Peabody (9-10/14) (Note: possibly M.C. stands for Member of Congress)

9765. Willis, W. W. m 12/29/47 S. H. Perkins, both of Rome, NY at the Central Hotel in Utica; Rev. D. G. Corey (9-12/31)
9766. Willmarth, Ira of Deerfield m 3/27/44 Lucy L. Carpenter of New Hartford in New H.; Rev. B. W. Gorham (9-3/29)
9767. Willoughby, Alfred of Oxford m 5/28/21 Nancy Parsons of Dryden in Homer; Rev. Bennett (8-6/6)
9768. Willoughby, Bliss, 82, (a Rev. soldier) d 5/21/49 in Oxford (9-5/31)
9769. Willover, Dewey m 2/2/33 Phebe Rodman of Benton in B (6-2/27)
9770. Wills, James C. m 10/22/45 Charlotte J. Bradish, dau of John, Esq., in Utica; Rev. Theodore Spencer. All of Utica (9-10/23)
9771. Willson, Elisha H. m 3/9/37 Frances Curry in Trumansburgh; M. Smith, Esq. (6-3/15)
9772. Willson, George, Esq. of Detroit, MI, formerly of Canandaigua, NY, m 7/29/32 Arabella M. Farrand of Burlington, VT in Concord, NH; Rev. Burton (6-8/8)
9773. Willson, James, 1, s of Capt. David, d 9/19/23 in Oxford (8-9/24)
9774. Willson, Nehemiah m 5/14/26 Ruthana Beverly of Oxford; Elder Otis (8-5/17)
9775. Willson, Robert, 30, b in NYC, d 3/8/45 in Madison, IA (9-4/2)
9776. Wilmot, Octava, 33, consort of William and dau of Capt. Charles Wattles of Norwich, d 9/16/22 in Unadilla (7-9/25 and 8-10/2)
9777. Wilse, Benjamin, 48, d 9/4/30 in Utica (9-9/7)
    Wilson. See also Willson.
9778. Wilson, Charles m 5/11/33 Polly Quackenbush; Rev. E. Doolittle. All of Sullivan (3-5/14)
9779. Wilson, Frederick m 2/1/32 Harriet Price, both of Phelps, in P (6-3/7)
9780. Wilson, George S. (Rev.) m 8/26/35 Julia R. Preston in Rupert, VT (6-9/9)
9781. Wilson, Gowen (Capt.), 40, d in Westbrook (9-3/22/25)
9782. Wilson,Horace of Lysander m 9/29/47 Charlotte J. Shepherd, only dau of R. Shepherd of Cato Four Corners, in C. F. C.; Rev. William G. Hubbard (9-10/14)
9783. Wilson, John, 38, d 3/18/33 in Albany (6-3/27)
9784. Wilson, John m 3/31/36 Jane Burrel, both of Seneca. in S; Rev. John White (6-4/13)
9785. Wilson, John, 98, (a Rev. soldier) d 7/6/43 at his home in Whitestown (b in Middletown, CT, s of Archibald; emigrated to Whitestown in 1786) (9-7/7)
9786. Wilson, Joseph m 2/22/42 Helena Lamb in Syracuse; Rev. J. P. B. Storer. All of Syracuse (9-3/8)
9787. Wilson, Joseph K. m 5/17/48 Maria Hutchinson, both of Bradford, in Corning; Rev. H. Pattengill (4-5/24)
9788. Willoughby, Richard Amos, 21, s of Joseph d 9/4/44 in Tallahassee, FL (funeral sermon by J. T. Goodrich of Oxford, NY) (Oxford Republican, 9/12)
9789. Wilson, Marian, 74, relict of late John, d 7/13/43 in Whitestown (9-7/19)
9790. Wilson, Morgan m 9/9/46 Althea Case, both of Phelps (6-9/25)
9791. Wilson, Peter, L.L.D., late Prof. of Greek and Latin in Columbia College, d 8/1/25 in Hackensack, NJ (9-8/23)
9792. Wilson, Robert of Geneva m 3/13/42 Sarah Jane Coriell of Hornby in H; Rev. S. S. Howe of Painted Post (4-3/16)
9793. Wilson, Stephen of Geneva m 9/27/31 Bathsheba Nicholson, dau of late Daniel, in Phelps; Rev. Phelps of Seneca (6-10/12)
9794. Wilson, T. O. of Baldwinsville m 7/3/48 Sarah A. Anyer of Camillus in C (1-7/12)
9795. Wilson, Thomas, 68, d 6/20/44 in Fenner (9-7/2)
9796. Wilson, William m 10/14/47 Charlotte Babcock, both of New York Upper Mills, in N. Y. U. M.; Rev. Dr. Paddock (9-10/20)
9797. Wilson, Willam, 40, d 10/4/50 in Utica (funeral at the Globe Tavern on Genesee St.) (9-10/5)
9798. Wimple, Jacob H. S. of Princetown m 6/18/42 Sally Ann McGee of Camden in C; Rev. G. C. Woodruff (9-7/1)
9799. Winans, Elizabeth (Mrs.), 74, d in Big Flats (6-3/9/31)
9800. Winchell, Alexander, Prof. of Amenia Seminary, NY, m 12/10/49 Julia P. Lines of Utica in U; Rev. William Wyatt (9-12/11)
9801. Winchell, John m 6/27/44 Laura A. Barnard, both of Sangerfield, at the Temperance House in Utica; Rev. E. S. Barrows (9-6/28)

9802. Winchell, John D. m 10/6/32 Margaret Ackerman in Rose (6-11/7)
9803. Winchester, H. Willis of Madison m 2/14/50 Jeanette C. Johnson of
       Sangerfield in Waterville; Rev. O. H. Gridley (9-3/29)
9804. Windsor, Francis of NYC m 8/20/32 Elizabeth Burtiss of Phelps; Rev. Bruce
       (6-8/22)
9805. Windsor, Joseph, 83, d 6/11/50 at the home of D. Windsor in Portlandville
       (an early settler in Otsego Co.)(9-6/14)
9806. Wing, Joel A. (Dr.) m Mary Gregory, only dau of Matthew, in Albany;
       Rev. Lacey. All of Albany (8-7/29/18)
9807. Winne, John L., merchant, of Albany m 5/13/25 Sophia Walbridge, dau of
       Stebbins of Bennington, VT; Rev. Dr. Blatchford (9-5/17)
9808. Winnegar, T. S. of Auburn m 6/22/49 Hannah Hathorn of Horseheads; Rev.
       C. C. Carr of Horseheads (5-6/29)
9809. Winship, John of New Hartford m 11/7/47 Maria Louisa Rogers of Utica;
       Rev. H. Emmons (9-11/11)
9810. Winslow, Edward T., 40, of the firm of Wells and Co. d 1/13/50 in Geneva
       (9-1/13)
9811. Winslow, Thomas, 93, formerly and for many years of NYC, d 9/26/31 in
       Vienna, NY (member of Episc. Ch.) (6-10/5)
9812. Winsor, Ellen, 15, oldest dau of Nicholas S. and gr-dau of Col. William
       Foster of Elmira, d 9/21/48 in Brooklyn (5-9/29)
9813. Winston, Horatio N. m Minerva Carpenter in Palmyra (6-4/16/34)
9814. Winston, Morgan I. of Greene m 2/2/42 Polly C. Benedict of Smithville in
       S; Rev. J. T. Goodrich (Oxford Times, 2/9)
9815. Winthrop, Robert c. m 11/6/49 Mrs. Laura Derby Welles in Boston, MA; Rev.
       Dr. Peabody (9-11/10)
9816. Winton, Nelson (Dr.) of Havana, NY m Lucy P. Goodrich in Pittsfield, MA
       (6-5/5/30)
9817. Wirt, Robert Gamble, s of the Attorney General of the U.S., d 10/31/24
       in Havre de Grace, France (9-1/18/25
9818. Wirts, Peter R. (Dr.) m 6/29/36 Lydia Wood, both of Waterloo, in W; Rev.
       P. C. Hay (6-7/6)
9819. Wits, S. M. of Lyons m 7/2/33 Mary Cost of Manchester in M (6-7/17)
9820. Wise, Louisa (Mrs.), 43, d 12/13/33 in Benton (6-12/25)
9821. Wisewell, John M. of Rushville m 8/31/36 Arabella Mace in Caledonaia
       (6-9/14)
9822. Wisner, Barnet N. m 5/18/33 Mary M. Sloan, dau of John, Jr. formerly of
       Geneva, in Penn Yan; Rev. Crosby (6-5/29)
9823. Wisner, Benjamin B. (Rev.), D.D., 41, formerly of Geneva, d 2/9/35 in
       Boston, MA (bro of Henry A., Esq. and Dr. B. N. of PennYan)(formerly
       pastor of Old South Ch., Boston, and at time of death Senior Secretary
       of the Board of Foreign Missions) (6-2/18)
9824. Wisner, Eliza, 28, wf of William Henry, d 3/6/35 in Elmira (6-3/11)
9825. Wisner, George W., Esq., late editor of the Detroit Daily Advertiser,
       d 9/10/49 in Detroit, MI (9-9/15)
9826. Wisner, John, Esq. m Ann Butler, both of Elmira, in Big Flats (6-5/21/34)
9827. Wisner, Polydore B., Esq. of Geneva d 7/13/14 at the home of Spencer
       Coleman, Esq. in East Bloomfield (8-8/2)
9828. Wisner, William C. (Rev.) of Rochester m 11/11/33 Jane Eliza Hanford in
       Scottsville, Monroe Co. (6-11/20)
9829. Wolcott, Abel (Mr.) d in Avon ("killed by the falling of a frame which
       he ... with others was raising") (8-8/7/22)
9830. Wolcott, Alexander (Dr.), 39, Indian agent in Chicago, IL, d 11/23/30 in
       Chicago (6-12/22)
9831. Wolcott, Charles of the firm of Wolcott and Hubbell, merchants, m 8/12/33
       Ellen Plummer, both of Pittsburgh, PA, in P (6-8/21)
9832. Wolcott, Mary (Miss), about 24, d 8/7/18 in Baldwinsville (1-8/9)
9833. Wolcott, Oliver P. (Dr.) of Barrington m Sophia Steward of Milo in M
       (6-6/20/32)
9834. Wolcott, Solomon (Dr.), 49, late one of the judges of Common Pleas of
       Oneida Co., d in Utica (8-11/11/18)
9835. Wolf, Mary (Mrs.), consort of Gov. Wolf, d in Harrisburg, PA (6-12/11/33)
9836. Woliver, Joseph m 2/19/36 Rebecca Davis in Sullivan; J. French, Esq. (3-2/24)
9837. Wollage, Elijah (Rev.), 78, d 7/18/47 in Starkey (served the ministry for
       more than 50 yrs) (4-7/21)

9838. Wolven, James m 9/20/35 Mary Baker, both of Aurelius, in Phelps; Ulysses Warner, Esq, (6-10/7)
9839. Wood, A. D. (Dr.) m 5/25/31 Eliza A. Pease, both of Auburn, in A (6-6/8)
9840. Wood, Archibald, 25, d12/4/33 in Rochester (6-12/18)
9841. Wood, Benjamin (Deacon), 87, of Litchfield d 10/4/50 (9-10/8)
9842. Wood, Clara J., 3, dau of George W., d 2/9/46 in Utica (funeral from her father's home on Broad St.) (9-2/10)
9843. Wood, Deborah (Mrs.), wid of late Gerald C. and sister of Joseph Hall of Fayette, d 11/8/36 (6-11/9)
9844. Wood, George C. m 5/8/31 Sarah McNair, both of Dansville, in Middlesex (6-5/18)
9845. Wood, George C. m 10/23/32 Martha Dona in Geneva; Rev. Mandeville. All of Geneva (6-10/24)
9846. Wood, Henry H., formerly of Geneva, m 11/22/32 Ann R. Reynolds of Kanawha, Salines, VA; Rev. C. H. Spencer (6-2/20/33)
9847. Wood, Horace of Schuyler m 1/11/43 Julia E. Whitney, dau of Franklin of Deerfield, in D; Rev. D. Skinner (9-1/14)
9848. Wood, Jeremiah J., 23 mo, s of Girard C., d 2/28/31 in Geneva; also the father, Girard C., 36, d 3/26 in Geneva (consumption) (6-3/30)
9849. Wood, Jethro, 60, d 9/28/34 in Ledyard (inventor of the cast iron plow) (6-10/14 and 10/15)
9850. Wood, Joel m 11/20/36 Eliza Jane Menter in Gorham (6-11/30)
9851. Wood, Jonathan L. m 1/4/46 Ann Elizabeth Lampher, both of McConnellsville; Albert Morse, Esq. (9-1/23)
9852. Wood, Joseph m Hester Ann Kirtland, both of Seneca Falls (in Geneva?) (6-7/24/33)
9853. Wood, Leddra, Esq., 47, d 2/5/48 in Aurora (9-3/11)
9854. Wood, Rebecca (Mrs.), 84, of Rochester d in Butler (6-9/18/33)
9855. Wood, Sarah Maria, wf of Thomas H., d 9/5/50 in Utica (9-9/6 and 9/7)
9856. Wood, Sylvester, 17, s of Daniel, d 8/19/31 in Seneca; also Ann, about 21, dau of Daniel, d 8/21 in Seneca (6-8/24)
9857. Wood, William m 11/20/33 Annis Douglas in Penfield (6-12/11)
9858. Wood, William of Horseheads m 11/1/34 Mrs. Esther Wood of Connecticut (6-11/12)
9859. Woodall, Calvin m 9/12/44 Gertrude M. Watkins; Rev. A. P. Beebe. All of Oriskany (9-9/14)
9860. Woodard, David A. of Phelps m Sarah A. Pennell of Tyre in Seneca Falls (6-8/14/33)
9861. Woodcock, David, 50, d 9/18/35 in Ithaca (6-9/30)
9862. Wooden, Eliza, 28, consort of James, d 3/26/32 in Chili, NY (6-4/11)
9863. Woodford, Jerome B. of Fulton m 3/5/37 Martha Miller of Manlius in Chittenango; J. French, Esq. (3-3/8)
9864. Woodhull, Henry I. m 7/25/48 Mary W. Tyrrell of Utica in U; Rev. D. G. Corey (9-7/27)
9865. Woodhull, Jared H., 44, late of U.S. Army, d 5/14/50 in Chester, NJ (was in the florida War and fought beside Gens. Taylor and Scott) (9-5/23)
9866. Woodhull, John (Rev.), D.D., pastor of the Presby. Ch. in Freehold, Monmouth Co., NJ, d 12/23/24 in Freehold (9-1/4/25)
9867. Woodhull, William S. m 8/10/47 Elizabeth Tyrrel, both ofUtica, in U; Rev. D. G. Corey (9-8/11)
9868. Woodland, George of the firm of Woodland Donaldson, publishers of the Utica Democrat, m 5/10/42 Hannah Stevens in Utica; Rev. Dr. Proal. All of Utica (9-5/11 and Oxford Times, 5/25)
9869. Woodnugh, Monro m 9/26/47 Susan Corey, both of Manchester, in Waterville; Rev. W. A. Matson (9-9/29)
9870. Woodruff, A. L. of Bellsville, Jeff. Co. m 12/26/43 Eliza A. Benedict, oldest dau of Joseph, Esq. of Utica, at Trinity Ch., Utica; Rev. P. A. Proal (9-12/28)
9871. Woodruff, Benjamin of Fayette m 4/13/31 Mary B. Edwards of Romulus in R (6-4/20)
9872. Woodruff, Benjamin, Jr. m 11/10/35 Emily Larzelier of Seneca Falls (in Waterloo?) (6-11/25)
9873. Woodruff, Bushrod Washington, printer, m 7/9/34 Sarah Ann Rose in Bath (6-7/3))

9874. Woodruff, Curtiss, formerly of Catskill, m 3/19/46 Augusta M. Rust, youngest dau of Col. P. N. of the Syracuse House in Syracuse; Rev. H. Gregory. All of Syracuse (9-3/23)
9875. Woodruff, David m Mary Sage of Bloomfield in Canandaigua (6-3/31/30)
9876. Woodruff, Gurdin m 9/30/41 Betsy Cady, both of Lawrenceville, PA, in Painted Post; Rev. S. S. Howe (4-10/13)
9877. Woodruff, Hezekiah N., 71, d 8/11/33 in Oneida Co. (6-9/18)
9878. Woodruff, Jacob M. m 1/9/32 Maria Cushman of Benton in B; S. G. Gage, Esq. (6-1/18)
9879. Woodruff. L. J. of Frankfort m 9/28/47 E. J. Gilbert also of Frankfort at the Central Hotel in Utica; Elder Corey (9-9/29)
9880. Woodruff, Lyman Henry, 1, only s of A., d 4/9/50 (scarlet fever) (5-4/12)
9881. Woodruff, Selah, 84, (a Rev. soldier) d 11/17/44 in Westmoreland (b in West Farmington, CT; surv by widow three yrs younger than he) (9-12/1)
9882. Woodruff, Walter N., merchant, of Watertown, NY m 10/20/45 Emily R. Foulansbee of Chicago, IL in Utica, NY; Rev. D. G. Corey (9-10/21)
9883. Woodruff, William, Jr. m Priscilla Thurstin, both of Binghamton (double ceremony - see marr of John T. Doubleday) (8-10/6/19)
9884. Woods, James H., Esq. of Geneva m 8/28/30 Mary Stilwell Clark, dau of late Samuel R. of NYC, in NYC (6-9/15)
9885. Woods, James L., Esq. of Elmira m 6/19/49 Susan Van Duser of Veteran; Rev. C. C. Carr of Horseheads (5-6/29)
9886. Woods, Mary Le Row, 22, dau of Dr. P., d 5/26/35 in Geneva (6-6/3)
9887. Woods, William, Esq. of Auburn m 5/15/48 Jane Coventry of Utica in U; Rev. George Leeds (9-5/16)
9888. Woodson, Tucker m 9/5/47 Nancy Jane Howe, both of Utica; Rev. Clark (9-9/6)
9889. Woodward, G. H. m 10/9/50 Mary C. Hollister, youngest dau of C., Esq. formerly of Rome, NY, in Beloit, WI (9-10/24)
9890. Woodward, John G. m 8/18/36 Eleanor Bogardus in Bath (6-8/31)
9891. Woodward, Warren of Coventry m 9/9/19 Martha Miles, dau of Simeon of Oxford, in O; Rev. Charles Thorp (8-9/15)
9892 Woodward, Warren m 7/26/43 Nancy M. Biddlecom in Utica; Rev. W. Rowlands (9-7/27)
9893. Woodward, William (Dr.) of Hector m 6/26/39 Harriet King, dau of John, Esq. of Ithaca, in I; Rev. Judd (6-7/10)
9894. Woodworth, _____, 2 mo, s of Joseph, d 9/29/26 in Utica (9-10/10)
9895. Woodworth, _____, consort of Caleb, d 10/1/36 in Tyre (6-10/12)
9896. Woodworth, Abigail, 78, relict of Samuel, Esq., d 7/6/45 in Bridgewater (9-7/10)
9897. Woodworth, Ann, 19, only dau of F. B., Esq. and sister of Dr. J. L., d 11/3/32 at Flint Creek (in the town of Seneca, NY) (6-11/7)
9898. Woodworth, Ann, 40, wf of Isaac, Esq., d 1/12/44 in Bridgewater (9-1/20)
9899. Woodworth, Benjamin, 83, (a Rev. patriot) d 8/5/42 in Fenner (an early settler in that region; had many ch; member of Meth. Episc. Ch.) (3-8/10 and 8/24)
9900. Woodworth, Benjamin F. m 7/13/50 Sarah Sampson, dau of George, in Utica; Rev. M. A. Perry. All of U (9-7/15)
9901. Woodworth, John L. (Dr.), formerly of Ontario Co., NY, d 9/10/32 in Eaton, OH (arrived in Eaton ill and a stranger; family of James W. Maxwell gave him "every possible attention"; he was attended in Eaton by Dr. Samuel Nixon)
9902. Woodworth, Luther G. of Cazenovia m 3/25/36 Harriet L. Downer, both of Fenner, in F; Rev. House of Cazenovia (incongruity of Luther's simultaneously living in Cazenovia and Fenner not explained in newspaper report) (3-4/6)
9903. Woodworth, William m 10/16/42 Mary Janette Chapen, formerly of Hamilton, in La Fayette, IN (9-10/31)
9904. Woolaver, James m 3/17/33 Eliza Ratnier; Rev. Paddock. All of Sullivan (3-3/19)
9905. Woolsey, Alida (Mrs.), 85, wid of Gen. Melancthon Lloyd of Cumberland Head near Plattsburgh, d 7/14/43 in Oswego (mother of late Commodore M. T. Woolsey, U.S.N. and sister of Rev. John H. Livingston, D.D. of New Brunswick, NJ) (9-7/18)
9906. Woolsey, Eunice, 47, wf of Henry L., d 4/2/30 in Geneva (consumption) (surv by husband and at least one child) (6-4/7)

9907. Woolsey, Henry m 10/27/33 Lucinda Dickey in Vienna, NY (6-11/6)
9908. Woolsey, Henry of Seneca Falls and formerly of Geneva d 11/20/38 in NYC
(6-12/5)
9909. Woolsey, Henry L., bro of late Commodore Woolsey, d 3/6/48 at "Presque
Isle, Lake Huron" (presumably in Michigan) (9-4/4)
9910. Woolsey, Lucretia (Mrs.), dau of Dr. Daniel Goodwin formerly of Geneva,NY,
d in Detroit, MI (cholera) (6-8/27/34)
9911. Woolsey, Melancthon B. (Lt.) of the U.S. Navy m 10/8/50 Mary L. Morrison
of Wheeling, VA at Christ Ch., Baltimore, MD; Rev. C. W. Bolton (9-10/12)
9912. Woolsey, Melancton L., 22, late of Canandaigua and son of H. L. of
Geneva, d 1/17/32 in NYC (6-1/25)
9913. Woolsey, Melancthon Lloyd, 67, of Plattsburgh (a Rev. officer) d 6/28/19
in Trenton, NY while on a visit to his son, Commodore Woolsey of
Sacketts Harbor (surv by wf and 7 ch) (8-7/21)
9914. Woolsey, Melancton T. (Commodore) of the U.S. Navy, about 60, d in Utica
(3-5/30/38)
9915. Wooster, Barclay m 7/30/43 Elizabeth Tifft of Pulaski in P (3-8/9)
9916. Worden, Antha, 14 mo, dau of Ira, d 5/26/44 in Chittenango (3-5/29)
9917. Worden, De Witt, M.D., of Clinton m 3/21/42 Sarah Randall, dau of late
N. P., Esq. of Manlius, in Clinton; Rev. W. W. Hickcox, rector of
Trinity ch., Fayetteville (9-3/23)
9918. Worden, Ebenezer m 10/9/36 Susan Osborn in Elmira (6-10/19)
9919. Worden, Margaret, 82, consort of late Ichabod, d 8/6/45 in Brighton,
Monroe Co. (9-8/13)
9920. Worden,Warren T., attorney, of Auburn m 8/16/32 Emily Bennett of
Bloomfield in Canandaigua (6-8/29)
9921. Woren, John G. m 8/7/34 Lois P. Howland, both of Seneca Falls, in S. F.
(6-8/20)
9922. Wormer, D. S., 37, d 5/8/50 in Monroe, MI (consumption) (past 2 yrs agent
of the Ontario and St. Lawrence Steamboat Co. at Niagara Falls) (9-5/21)
9923. Wride, Jennet, 7, dau of "Mr. Wride", d 9/1/32 in Geneva (6-9/5)
9924. Wright, Alanda and Susannah, his wf, d 1/30 and 2/2/25 respectively
(aged 29 and 27 respectively) in Cavendish, VT (married about 4 yrs)
(9-3/8)
9925. Wright, Allen of Rome, NY m 3/22/25 Julia Ann Guernsey, dau of S., Esq.,
in Oxford; Rev. J. D. Wickham (8-3/30)
9926. Wright, Alpha m 9/15/35 Arabelly J. Langley in Newark, NY (6-10/21)
9927. Wright, Angeline Fraser, dau of Oliver K. and Elizabeth A., d 1/9/43 in
Utica (consumption) (9-1/23)
9928. Wright, Chauncey m 11/16/41 Phebe Philena Wattles in Chittenango; Rev.
J. Abell. All of Sullivan (3-11/17)
9929. Wright, Chauncey L. of Albany m Louisa Griswold of Lyons in L (6-3/9/31)
9930. Wright, Clark m 7/8/30 Polly Hammond, both of Palmyra, in Seneca; E.
Hastings, Esq. (6-7/14)
9931. Wright, Daniel O. m 1/10/49 Maria S. Palmer in Baldwinsville; Rev. Byron
Alden (1-1/11)
9932. Wright, Eli R. of Burdett m 11/23/35 Sally S. Wager of Royalton in R
(6-12/9)
9933. Wright, Francis, 38, d 1/2/45 in Philadelphia (had been a merchant in
Utica, NY many years and had sought in Philadelphia, PA a milder
winter climate) (9-1/11)
9934. Wright, George Francis, 1, only s of Hon. George W., d 4/6/50 at the
Irving house in NYC (9-4/13)
9935. Wright, George M. of Covington, PA m 3/20/50 Charlotte E. Evans of
Southport, NY inS; Rev. E. Colson (5-3/29)
9936. Wright, George S. m 12/21/42 Susan M. Pratt, dau of Daniel. all of
Marshall, MI, in Marshall, MI; Rev. J. P. Cleavland (9-1/6/43)
9937. Wright, Hannah, 36, wf of Chauncey, d 8/13/41 in Sullivan (3-9/8)
9938. Wright, Hannah P., wf of Jay W., d 4/30/49 in Utica (funeral from
her late home, 91 Fayette St.) (9-5/1)
9939. Wright, Henry, 27, s of Judge Wright of NYC, d 10/25/26 (in attempting
to lead his horse across a bridge over the Delaware and Chesapeake
Canal he was thrown and his carriage passed over him) (9-11/7)
9940. Wright, Isaac of Smithville m 1/26/31 Sally Williams of Oxford in O
(6-2/9)
9941. Wright, Isaac, 72, merchant, d in NYC (cholera) (6-8/15/32)

9942. Wright, Jacob, 66, m 3/11/32 Clarisa Blackman, 52, in Henrietta (6-4/4)
9943. Wright, James of Kirkville m 10/3/34 Maria Ayres of Cazenovia in C; J. French, Esq. (3-10/7)
9944. Wright, James B. of NYC m 7/3/49 Louise B. Marble, dau of Nathan, Esq. of Port Byron, in P. B.; Rev. W. A. Matson (9-7/9)
9945. Wright, James W. m 5/7/50 Harriet M. Hancker, both of Utica, in U; Rev. John Stanford Holme (9-5/8)
9946. Wright, Jane Elizabeth, 11 mo., dau of Jay W. and Hannah P., d 3/4/46 in Utica (funeral from her father's home, 91 Fayette St.) (9-3/5)
9947. Wright, Jemima (Mrs.), 93, d 7/14/43 in Utica (funeral at the home of S. Rathbone, corner Blandina and John Sts.) (9-7/15)
9948. Wright, John C. (Hon.) of Schoharie m 6/17/47 Sarah W. Bouck at the Dutch Ch. in NYC; Rev. Dr. Hutton (9-6/23)
9949. Wright, Maria (Mrs.), 64, d 12/5/83 in Ithaca (6-12/18)
9950. Wright, R. S., about 30, d 4/17/48 in Corning (attended the Episc. Ch. in Corning; surv by a widow; interred in Mt. Hope Cem. in Rochester) (4-4/19)
9951. Wright, S. of Seneca Falls m 9/5/50 Caroline A. Powers of Corning in C; B. Pew, Esq. (4-9/11)
9952. Wright, Silas, Jr. (Hon.), junior senator in Congress, m Clarissa Moody in Canton, NY (6-9/25/33)
9953. Wright, Silas, Esq., 83, d 5/13/43 in Weybridge, VT (father of Hon. Silas, Jr., U.S. Senator) (9-6/1)
9954. Wright, Silas (Hon.), ex-gov. of NY, d 8/27/47 at his home in Canton, NY (the release mentions a "Mr. Moody", brother-in-law and late private secretary to the deceased) (9-8/28)
9955. Wright, Thadeus m Mary Munson, both of Murray, in Orleans Co. (6-2/23/31)
9956. Wright, Thomas of Utica m 3/8/49 Dian Johnson of New Hartford at the home of William Hicks, Jr. in Marcy; Norton Ward, Esq. (9-3/9)
9957. Wright, Warren, 50, d 4/14/44 in Utica (9-4/17)
9958. Wright, William G. m 12/25/45 Ann Hutchinson in Utica; Rev. D. W. Bristol. All of Utica (9-1/6/46)
9959. Wright, William Henry, 16, s of Lewis, d 4/20/49 in Baldwinsville (1-5/3)
9960. Wylie, Henry H. m 12/22/32 Sarah Peck in Benton (6-1/2/33)
9961. Wyman, Albert C., 1, s of Levi and Maria, d 8/21/50 in Utica (9-8/30)
9962. Wyman, H. H. of Corning m 5/24/41 Ruth S. Skons of Wallkill in Corning; Rev. S. M. Hopkins (4-5/28)
9963. Wyman, Henry C. of Lee m 8/28/50 Jerusha Preston of Ava in Rome, NY; Rev. James Erwin (9-9/12)
9964. Wyman, Rebecca (Mrs.), 71, d 11/11/43 in Utica (funeral from Trinity Ch.) (9-11/13)
9965. Wyndkoop, Jane (Mrs.), 55, d 10/28/50 in Clay (1-11/7)
9966. Wynkoop, Adam, about 7, s of Tobias, d 7/22/31 in Seneca (6-7/27)
9967. Wynkoop, Alonzo I. m 6/8/37 Phebe Heermans, niece of J. Fellows, Esq.; Rev. Irving (6-6/14)
9968. Wynkoop, Benjamin, Esq., 64, father of A. I. of Geneva, d 7/11/33 at his home in Chemung (6-7/17)
9969. Wynkoop, N. F. of Chemung, NY m 10/15/40 Sarah A. Heermance of Providence, Luzerne Co. PA in Chemung, NY; Rev. E. Pratt (double ceremony - see marr of Daniel I. Watkins) (4-10/23)
9970. Wynkoop, Ninolia T., merchant, of Chemung m 2/11/33 Christiana Moore, dau of David of Brookfield, Orange Co. in Brookfield; Rev. Wood (6-2/20)
9971. Yale, Henry Augustus, 21, d 3/11/30 in Oxford (consumption) (8-3/31)
9972. Yale, Joel C. m 10/10/41 Parmelia Davis in Guilford; Rev. Aaron Parker (Oxford Times, 10/13 and 10/20)
9973. Yale, Street, 47, d 4/3/50 in Baldwinsville (1-4/4)
9974. Yates, Andrew J., Esq. m 1/5/32 Matilda H. Bunner, dau of Hon. Rudolph of Oswego, in O; Rev. Dr. Yates (3-1/10)
9975. Yates, Catharine, wf of Hon. Henry and mother of Charles, Esq. of NYC, d 9/28/41 in NYC (3-10/6)
9976. Yates, Edward, Esq., 30, of Schenectady d 9/16/33 in Oppenheim, Mont. Co. (3-9/24)
9977. Yates, Ellen Medora , 4, dau of Peter and Mary of Milwaukee, WI, d 9/19/49 in Utica, NY (9-9/20)

9978. Yates, Henrietta M., 53, wf of Rev. John Austin Yates, D.D., d 3/27/42 at Union College in Schenectady (3-4/6)
9979. Yates, Jane, 54, wf of Giles and oldest dau of late Hon. John Yates, d 7/20/48 in Schenectady (9-7/27)
9980. Yates, John G., 46, formerly of Sullivan, d 3/8/37 in Greenbush, Renss. Co. (3-3/15)
9981. Yates, Richard, 30, youngest bro of John I., Esq. of Schenectady, d 1/22/49 in New Orleans, LA (9-2/7)
9982. Yates, Robert G., s of John V. N. of Albany, m 8/29/33 Jane Amelia Coffin, youngest dau of late Caleb of NYC, in Rio Janeiro (Argentine?) (3-11/5)
9983. Yates, William Austin, 3 mo, s of A. J., Esq. of Oswego, d 10/26/34 at the home of Rev. Andrew Yates, D.D., in Chittenango (3-10/28)
9984. Yaw, Daniel m 11/16/36 Sarah Menter in Gorham (6-11/30)
9985. Yeckley, John (Deacon), 61, formerly of Montgomery, Orange Co., d 9/17/34 in Seneca (6-10/1)
9986. Yeckley, R. D. H., formerly principal of Geneva Academy, m 2/25/30 Calista Harwood of Rushville in R; Rev. Bracket (6-3/3)
9987. Yeo, Thomas B. m 1/14/36 Clarisa Ryon in Seneca Falls (6-1/27)
9988. Yeoman, Anson, 13 mo, s of C., d 4/12/32 in Geneva (6-4/18)
9989. York Catherine, 36, consort of Jerry, d 1/13/26 in Oxford (8-1/18)
9990. York, E. (Dr.) m 8/10/25 L. Stratton in Macdonough; Rev. N. Otis (8-8/17)
9991. York, M. M. (Rev.), pastor of the Presby. Ch. in Wysox, PA, d 1/2/30 at his home in Wysox (had been 26 yrs a minister) (8-2/3)
9992. Yorke, Ann, 55, wid of late John, d 8/15/50 at North Bay in Vienna, NY (9-8/24)
9993. Yost, William m 3/16/31 Belinda Rathsong, both of Fayette, in Waterloo (6-3/30)
9994. Youlen, George H. of Frankfort m 3/24/47 Elizabeth J. McClelland, youngest dau of John of Utica, in U; Rev. P. A. Proal (9-3/26)
9995. Young, _____ (Capt.) of the U.S. Army d 5/25/30 at Fort Niagara (6-6/9)
9996. Young, Abraham m 5/24/45 Mary Jane Rolfe in Herkimer (9-5/30)
9997. Young, Allen D. m 9/20/36 Mary R. Russel in Bristol (6-10/12)
9998. Young, Catherine, 4 mo, dau of William, d 7/27/32 in Geneva (6-8/1)
9999. Young, David m Catherine Onion, both of Fenner, in F (3-3/13/39)
10000. Young, Henry, 10 mo, s of William, Jr., d 11/27/31 in Geneva (6-11/30)
10001. Young, Jacob m Serophina Dunham in Seneca Falls (6-1/8/34)
10002. Young, John, Esq., formerly a judge of Oneida Co., d 4/26/25 in Whitesboro (9-5/3)
10003 Young, John, Jr., 28, d 8/16/25 in Vincennes, IN (born in Springfield, NJ; grad from Union College in 1821 and later from Princeton [NJ] Theological Seminary; received preacher's license in 1824 from the Presbytery of New Brunswick, NJ) (9-11/1)
10004. Young, Joseph m 8/21/34 Sarah Jane Stillwell, both of Orville, in Chittenango; Rev. E. Slingerland (3-8/26)
10005. Young, Joseph m 3/21/49 Roxy Ann Heamingway, both of Elmira; Rev. G. M. Spratt (5-3/23)
10006. Young, Moses, 29, pastor of the Presby. Ch. in Romulus, d 11/15/24 in
* Young, Romulus in the 10th year of his ministry (b in Morris, NJ; moved to
  Nelson Ontario Co., NY in 1811; installed at Romulus in 1815) (surv by wf and 8 ch) (9-12/7)
10007. Young, Nicholas, 85, d 11/28/47 in Utica (funeral at the home of his son-in-law, Charles Dupre, 21 Catharine St.) (9-11/29)
10008. Young, Robert m 2/28/50 Mary E. Rice at the parsonage in Southport; Rev. E. Colson (5-3/8)
10009. Young, William, merchant tailor, m 11/5/34 Lucinda Vanderin, both of Geneva, in G; Rev. E. Phelps (6-11/12)
10010. Younglove, _____, wf of "Hon. Aaron of the Assembly" d 4/30/34 in Gorham (6-5/7)
10011. Younglove, Aaron of Urbana m Evelyn Clizbe, dau of Jonathan, in Bath (6-3/3/30)
10012. Younglove, Cornelius, merchant, of Wheeler m 5/2/32 Caroline G. Eddy, dau of Eli late of Geneva, in Bath (6-5/9)
10013. Younglove, J. Warren m 9/5/48 Meranda J. Stowal in Trenton Falls; Rev. J. W. Davis (9-9/19)
* 10006a. Young, Nelson D. of Marion m 3/8/36 Achsah M. Kingsley of Sodus (6-3/23)

10014. Younglove, Lewis, 9, s of John, d 8/3/44 in Trenton, NY (9-8/13)
(in same newspaper dated 9/6 this name correction is inserted:
deceased's name is Lucas Younglove)
10015. Younglove, Lucas (Deacon), 83, d 1/17/49 in Trenton, NY (9-1/20)
10016. Younglove, P. Dauchy, 6, s of John, d 10/17/48 in Trenton, NY (9-10/23)
10017. Younglove, Truman G., Esq., attorney, of Albany m 11/8/50 Jane McMartin,
dau of late Senator McMartin of Saratoga Co., in Utica; Rev. Dr.
Kennedy of Albany (9-11/9
10018. Youngs, Hannah, 82, relict of late John, d 9/3/30 in Lyons (6-9/22)
10019. Zeeley, H. of Geneva m 12/19/38 Margaret A. Seelye of Tyre in T; Rev.
McLaren (6-1/9/39)
10020. Lielly, Nancy N. (Mrs.), 39, d 3/23/35 in Geneva (6-3/25)
10021. Ziely, _____ H. of Peterborough, C.W. (Canada West?) m 7/6/50 __?__
Tooker of Elmira; Rev. H. N. Seaver (5-7/19)

MARRIAGE OFFICIALS

Name; religious affiliation (if applicable and given); residence town; date span of ceremonies performed; number of ceremonies performed.

(Probably all persons with the title "esquire" are local justices of the peace)

___elpley, S. W. (Rev.); ___; Waterville; 1842; 1
___ester, C. E. (Rev.); ___; Utica; 1842; 1
Abbot, Ambrose (Rev.); ___; Caton; 1840; 1
Abeel, G. (Rev.); ___; Geneva; 1835; 1
Abell, James (Rev.); Reformed Dutch; Chittenango; 1838-48; 45
Ackerly, ___ (Rev.); ___; Milwaukee, WI; 1848; 1
Ackley, ___ (Rev.); ___; Oxford; 1824; 1
Ackley, Oliver (Rev.); ___; Seneca; 1838-39; 3
Acley, C. G. (Rev.); ___; Seneca Falls; 1839; 1
Adams, ___ (Rev.); ___; Cohoes; 1850; 1
Adams, ___ (Rev.); ___; Utica; 1828-33; 2
Adams, H. (Rev.), ___; Unadilla; 1841; 1
Adams, J. W. (Rev.); ___; Syracuse; 1833-42; 3
Adams, M. (Rev.); ___; Smithville; 1823-30; 3
Adams, M. (Rev. Dr.); ___; Syracuse; 1846-48; 3
Adams, O. (Rev.); ___; Mohawk; 1850; 1
Adams, Roger (Rev.); ___; Lenox?; 1826; 1
Adams, William (Rev.); ___; NYC; 1846; 1
Adgate, C. V. (Rev.); ___; Benton; 1832; 2
Adsit, S. (Rev.); ___; Milo?; 1846; 1
Aiken, S. C. (Rev.); ___; Utica; 1822-34; 10
Albertus, ___ (Rev.); ___; Albany; 1825; 1
Alcott, Denison (Rev.); ___; Westmoreland; 1844-48; 3
Alden, Byron (Rev.); ___; Baldwinsville; 1848-50; 20
Allbro, ___ (Rev.); ___; Cambridge, MA; 1843; 2
Allen, ___ (Rev.); ___; Lenox; 1834; 1
Allen, ___ (Rev.); ___; Livonia; 1833; 1
Allen, Aaron P. (Rev.); ___; Exter; 1844; 1
Allen E. W. R. (Rev.); ___; Oriskany; 1844; 2
Allen, M. (Rev.); ___; Sullivan; 1834-35; 3
Allerton, Isaac (Rev.); ___; Norwich; 1819; 1
Alverson, ___ (Rev.); ___; Palmyra and Geneva; 183133; 4
Amburg, John (Rev.); ___; state of Kentucky; 1841; 1
Anderson, ___ (Rev.); ___; Norwich; 1824; 1
Andrews, ___ (Rev.); Christ Church (possibly in Binghamton); 1842; 1
Andrews, ___ (Rev.); ___; Norwich; 1820-21; 3
Andrews, E. W. (Rev.); ___; Troy; 1845; 1
Andrews, Edward (Rev.); ___; Oxford-Norwich area; 1822-30; 8
Anthon, Henry (Rev.); ___; Utica; 1822-50; 5
Anthon, Henry (Rev. Dr.); St. Mark's Ch., NYC; 1825 and 1847-49; 3
Appleton, ___ (Rev.); ___; Warren; 1848; 1
Arnett, W. W. (Rev.); ___; Uniontown; 1844; 1
Arnold, Josiah A. (Rev.); ___; Durhamville and New London; 1848; 2
Arthur, William (Rev.); ___; Schenectady; 1846; 1
Ashley, William B. (Rev.); St. Paul's Ch. (Episc.); Syracuse; 1850; 2
Ashmun, S. H., Esq.; Lyons?; 1839; 1
Atkinson, ___ (Rev.); ___; Houston, TX?; 1843; 1
Atwell, ___ (Rev.); ___; Sullivan; 1834; 1
Austin, J. G., Esq.; Phelps; 1839; 1
Austin, J. M. (Rev.); ___; Geneva-Auburn area; 1846-50; 5
Avery, R. A. (Rev.); ___; Verona; 1849; 1
Axtell, D. C. (Rev.); ___; Clinton and Auburn; 1830-32; 4
Babcock, N. C., Esq.; Caton; 1842; 1

Baggerly, ___ (Rev.); ___; Phelps; 1835; 2
Bailey, R. W. (Rev.); ___; Pittsfield, MA?; 1825; 1
Bailey, Wesley (Rev.); ___; Utica; 1845; 2
Bainbridge, S. M. (Rev.); ___; Smithfield and Stockbridge; 1841-42; 2
Baker, ___ (Rev.); ___; Paris, NY; 1847; 2
Baker, ___ (Rev.); ___; Russia, NY; 1844; 1
Baker, D. (Rev.); ___; Phelps; 1830; 1
Baker, Joseph (Rev.); ___; Glens Falls; 1850; 1
Baker, N. (Rev.); ___; South Waterloo; 1846; 1
Balcom, ___ (Elder); ___; Corning?; 1849; 1
Baldwin, ___ (Rev.); ___; Cicero?; 1846; 1
Baldwin, ___ (Rev.); ___; Montrose, PA?; 1823; 1
Baldwin, ___ (Rev. Dr.); ___; NYC; 1833; 1
Baldwin, ___ (Rev.); ___; Utica; 1818 and 1844; 2
Baldwin, G. C. (Rev.); ___; Troy; 1850; 1
Ball, A. M. (Rev.); ___; Elmira; 1848-9; 2
Bannister, E. (Rev.); ___; Syracuse; 1845; 1
Bannister, Henry (Rev.); ___; Cazenovia?; 1843;1
Barber, ___ (Rev.); ___; Turin; 1848; 1
Barber, E. (Rev.); ___; Norwich; 1846; 1
Barker, J. (Rev.); ___; Jonesville, MI?; 1843; 1
Barnard, ___ (Rev.); ___; Lima; 1831; 1
Barnard, George, Esq.; Rome;1848; 1
Barnard, Selah, Esq.; Buffalo; 1847; 2
Barnes, Albert (Rev.); ___; Philadelphia, PA?; 1850; 1
Barnes, J. R. (Rev.); ___; Washington, Wisc. Terr.; 1838; 1
Barnes, Z. (Rev.); ___; Milan and Chittenango; 1836-40; 3
Barrett, ___ (Rev.); New Jerusalem Ch.; Cincinnati, OH; 1850; 1
Barrows, E. S. (Rev.); ___; Cazenovia and Utica; 1835-44; 7
Barrows, L. A. (Rev.); Christ Church; Sherburne; 1842and 1846; 2
Barrows, R. H. (Rev.); ___; Cazenovia; 1836; 1
Barry, Elijah, Esq.; Macdonough; 1827; 1
Bartholomew, Orlo (Rev.); ___; Augusta; 1845-49; 6
Bartlett, A. R. (Rev.); ___; Poughkeepsie; 1844; 1
Bartlett, J. M. (Rev.); Zion Church; Pierrepont Manor; 1849; 1
Bartlett, P. (Rev.); ___; Guilford; 1841-42; 4
Barton, ___ (Rev.); ___; Romulus; 1830-39; 6
Bateman, ___ (Elder); ___; Middlesex; 1839; 1
Bates, ___ (Rev.); Phelps; 1833; 1
Bates, B. H. (Rev.); ___; Warehouse Point, CT?; 1849; 1
Bates, L.C. (Rev.); ___; Camillus, Van Buren, and Canton?; 1848-49; 3
Batien, ___ (Rev.); ___; New York Mills; 1847; 1
Battin, S. H. (Rev.); ___; Cooperstown and New Hartford; 1847 and 1850; 2
Baxter, Aaron (Rev.); ___; Smithville; 1821; 1
Beach, ___ (Rev.); ___; New Paltz; 1831; 1
Beach, Amos B. (Rev.); ___; Cooperstorn?; 1847; 1
Beach, E. C. (Rev.); ___; Baldwinsville and Betts Corners; 1847 and 1850; 2
Beardslee, A., Esq.; Little Falls; 1845; 1
Beasley, ___ (Rev. Dr.); St. Michael's Church, NYC; 1831; 1
Beckwith, ___ (Elder); ___; Fenner and Vienna; 1834 and 1850; 2
Bedell, G. T. (Rev.); ___; NYC; 1844 and 1850; 2
Beebe, A. P. (Rev.); ___; Oriskany; 1844; 1
Beebee, ___ (Elder); ___; Bath; 1843; 1
Beecham, ___ (Rev.); St. John's Church; Rome; 1844; 2
Beecher, A., Esq.; Baever Dam Village; 1850; 1
Beeman, ___ (Rev. Dr.); ___; Troy; 1850; 1
Beers, N. N. (Rev.); ___; Chemung; 1848-49; 5
Bellamy, ___ (Rev.); ___; Manlius; 1837-38; 3
Beman, ___ (Rev.); First Presby. Church; Troy; 1835 and 1838; 2
Bement, W. (Rev.); ___; Elmira; 1850; 2
Benedict, ___ (Elder); ___; NYC; 1842; 1
Benedict, E. P. (Rev.); ___; Patterson; 1843; 1
Benedict, T. N. (Rev.); ___; Denmark, NY and Waterloo,NY; 1848 and 1849; 2
Benahm, ___ (Elder); ___; Hopewell?; 1831; 1
Bennet, ___ (Elder); ___; Harrison?; 1823; 2
Bennett, ___ (Rev.); ___; Benton?; 1838; 1

Bennett, ___ (Rev.); ___; Homer?; 1821; 1
Bennett, Asa (Rev.); ___; Lodi and Hornby; 1830 and 1831; 2
Bennett, P. S. (Rev.); ___; Van Buren?; 1847; 1
Bentley, ___ (Elder); ___; Geneva; 1831-33; 6
Bentley, ___ (Elder); ___; Vienna, NY; 1833; 1
Bentley, N. (Rev.); ___; Guilford; 1827; 4
Berrian, ___ (Rev.); St. John's Church; NYC?; 1831 and 1848; 2
Bicknall, J. (Rev.); ___; Westmoreland?; 1849; 1
Bigelow, L., Esq.; Bainbridge?; 1824; 2
Bigsby, ___ (Rev.); Methodist Church; Coventry; 1844; 1
Bingham, ___ (Rev.); ___ Honolulu, Hawaii; 1838; 1
Bingham, I. S. (Rev.); ___; Syracuse; 1850; 1
Bishop of the Island of Gibralter; 1849; 1 (not further identified)
Bissell, ___ (Rev.); ___; Geneva?; 1848; 1
Bixby, ___ (Rev.); ___; Oxford?; 1845; 1
Blair, A. B., Esq.; Rome; 1848; 2
Blakslee, ___ (Elder); ___; Morrisville?; 1838; 2
Blakslee, D. L. (Rev.); ___; Chittenango and Lebanon; 1843-47; 5
Blanchard, ___ (Rev.); Cincinnati, OH; 1843; 1
Blatchford, ___ (Rev. Dr.); ___; Bennington, VT?; 1825; 1
Blodgett, ___ (Rev.); ___; Paris Hill?; 1843; 1
Bloodgood, A. L. (Rev.); ___; Utica; 1845 and 1846; 2
Bloomer, ___ (Rev.); ___; Thompson, Sullivan Co.; 1849; 1
Boardman, G.S. (Rev.); ___; Smithville, Sacketts Harbor, Rome, NY; 1832-44; 4
Boardman, George (Rev.); ___; Cazenovia; 1850; 1
Bogart, ___ (Rev. Dr.); Harlem Heights; 1833; 1
Bogue, H. P. (Rev.); ___; Vernon?; 1838; 1
Bolton, C. W. (Rev.); Christ Church; Baltimore, MD; 1850; 1
Bond, ___ (Rev. Dr.); ___; Norwich; 1850; 1
Boning, E. (Rev.); ___; Sauquoit?; 1845; 1
Boogher, Frederick, Esq.; Clyde and Galen; 1830 and 1831; 2
Bort, ___ (Rev.); ___; Sullivan?; 1834; 1
Boughton, ___ (Rev.); ___; Niles, MI; 1842; 1
Bowen, Elias (Rev.); ___; Sauquoit; 1843; 1
Boyce, ___ (Rev.); ___; Warren; 1845; 1
Boyd, H. M. (Rev.); ___; Peterboro?; 1825; 1
Boyd, J. R. (Rev.); ___; Watertown?; 1847; 1
Brace, ___ (Rev.); ___; Sennet?; 1830; 1
Brace, S. W. (Rev.); ___; Skaneateles; 1832-42; 3
Brace, S. W. (Rev.); ___; Utica: 1824-50; 7
Bracket, ___ (Rev.); ___; Rushville?; 1830; 1
Bradford, James (Rev.); ___; Sheffield, MA?; 1819; 1
Bradford, William J. (Rev.); ___; Cincinnatus?; 1826; 1
Bragden, ___ (Rev.); ___; Butler?; 1845; 1
Brainard, D. (Rev.); ___ Santa Mohague, CT?; 1849; 1
Brainard, Davis S. (Rev.); ___; Lyme, CT?; 1842; 1
Brainerd, ___ (Rev. Dr.); ___ Manchester?; 1848; 1
Brainerd, Israel (Rev.); ___; ___; 1824; 1
Brantley, William T. (Rev.); ___; Charleston, SC?; 1841 and 1845; 2
Brayton, Isaac (Rev.); ___; Watertown; 1844-50; 5
Brayton, J. A. (Rev.); ___; Morristown?; 1845; 1
Breck, ___ (Rev.); ___; Tioga, PA; 1840; 1
Breck, ___ (Rev.); ___; Wellsborough; 1840;1
Breese, ___ (Rev.); ___; Sullivan; 1841; 1
Brentiss, Joseph (Rev.); St. Luke's Church; Catskill; 1826; 1
Brigham, ___ (Rev.); ___; NYC; 1843; 1
Brilhartz, ___ (Rev.); ___; Geneva?; 1830; 1
Brisben, R. C. (Rev.); ___; Vernon?; 1842 and 1844; 2
Bristol, Daniel W. (Rev.); Methodist church?; Utica and Auburn?; 1844-46; 13
Brokaw, Abraham (Rev.); ___; Ovid?; 1830; 1
Bronson, E. (Rev.); ___; Windsor?; 1842; 1
Brooks, A. L. (Rev.); ___; Corning; 1850; 7
Brouwer, Cornelius (Rev.); ___; Fayette and Benton; 1834 and 1836; 2
Brown, ___, Esq.; Lima?; 1834; 1
Brown, ___ (Elder); ___; Seneca?; 1830; 1

279

Brown, ___ (Rev.); ___; Sherburne; 1827 and 1843; 2
Brown, ___ (Rev.); ___; Tioga, PA?; 1850; 1
Brown, F. C. (Rev.); ___; Waterville?; 1844; 1
Brown, J. Z. (Rev.); ___; Litchfield?: 1848; 1
Brown, P. P. (Rev.); ___; Annsville; 1850; 1
Brown, William (Elder); ___; Newport?; 1848; 1
Bruce, ___ (Rev.); ___; Phelps?; 1831 and 1832; 2
Bruce, N. F. (Rev.); Trinity Church; Geneva; 1831-35; 19
Bruen, ___ (Rev.); ___; Stafford, CT?; 1825; 1
Bryant, Sidney (Rev.); ___; West Stockbridge (state not specified); 1842; 1
Buck, A. (Rev.); ___; Nunda?; 1843; 1
Buck, Valentine (Rev.); ___; Hempstead?; 1849; 1
Buckingham, E. (Rev.); ___; Remson; 1846-50; 4
Buckley, C.H. (Rev.) ___; Mount Morris?; 1849; 1
Budd, C. (Rev.); ___; Westmoreland?; 1843; 1
Buel, Frederick (Rev.); ___; San Diego, CA; 1850; 1
Bullard, ___ (Rev.); ___; Veteran?; 1843; 1
Bunker, ___ (Rev.); ___; Attica?; 1842; 1
Burchard, S. (Rev.); ___; NYC; 1849; 1
Burckle, C. J., Esq.; Oswego; 1845; 1
Burke, John (Rev.); St. James Church; Baton Rouge, LA; 1848; 1
Burlingame, D. (Rev.); ___; Norwich and New Berlin; 1821 and 1823; 2
Burnet, David S. (Rev.); ___; Cincinnati, OH; 1843; 1
Burnet, R. (Rev.); ___; Manchester?; 1838; 1
Burnsides, ___ (Rev.); ___; Verona?; 1847; 1
Burritt, C. D. (Rev.); ___; Norwich?; 1850; 1
Burritt, S. W. (Rev.); ___; Floyd?; 1832; 1
Burt, Mark, Esq.; Ridgebury; 1850; 1
Burtis, Arthur (Rev.); ___; Fort Plain, Oxford, Phelps; 1835-46; 6
Burtle, ___ (Rev.); ___; Oxford?; 1842; 1
Burton, ___ (Rev.); ___; Concord, NH?; 1832; 1
Bush, Leverett (Rev.); Episcopal Church?; Oxford; 1819-42; 28
Bush, S. W. (Rev.); ___; Skaneateles; 1846-49; 3
Bushnel, J. (Rev.); ___; Sullivan?; 1835; 1
Butler, ___ (Rev.); ___; Waterloo; 1830; 1
Cady, Squire S. (Rev.); ___; Burlington Flats, Otsego Co.; 1850; 1
Callender, S., Esq.; Big Flats?; 1848; 1
Campbell, ___ (Rev.); ___; Cooperstown; 1846 and 1847; 2
Campbell, ___ (Rev.); ___; Seneca Falls?; 1836; 1
Campbell. John N. (Rev.); ___; A;bany; 1830-49; 5
Campbell, William H. (Rev.); ___; Chittenango; 1831-32; 6
Carder, J. D. (Rev.); ___; Ithaca and Elmira; 1832 and 1833; 2
Carlin, ___ (Rev.); ___; Manchester?; 1847; 1
Carlisle, Hugh (Rev.); ___; Worcester?; 1849; 1
Carr, C. C. (Rev.); ___; Horseheads area; 1848-50; 24
Carraher, ___ (Rev.); St. Patrick's church; Utica; 1850; 1
Carrington, George (Rev.); ___; Hadlyme, CT?; 1843; 1
Cartwell, ___ (Rev.); ___; New Hartford?; 1847; 1
Case, J. Milton, Esq.; Nelson?; 1850; 1
Casle, Richard (Rev.); ___; Fort Winnebago, WI; 1843; 1
Casler, L. (Rev.); ___; Mohawk?; 1850; 1
Catlin, ___ (Rev.); ___; Gorham?; 1834; 1
Champ, ___ (Rev.); ___; Brooklyn, CT?; 1837; 1
Champion, F. J. (Rev.); ___; Penn Yan; 1836; 2
Chaney, John (Elder); ___; Whitestown; 1845-49; 3
Chapens, ___ (Elder); ___; Smithfield? 1831; 1
Chapin, ___ (Elder); ___; Bainbridge?; 1824; 1
Chapin, ___ (Rev.); ___; Vienna, NY; 1845; 1
Charles, ___ (Rev.); ___; Caseville?; 1850; 1
Chase, ___ (Rev.); ___; Benton?; 1836; 1
Chase, A. (Rev.); ___; Penn Yan?; 1831; 1
Chase, Carlton (Rev.); St. Paul's Church; Windsor; 1835; 1
Chase, Daniel (Rev.); ___; Elmira?; 1849; 1
Chase, J. (Rev.); ___; Geneva? 1835 and 1836; 2
Chase, Moses (Rev.); ___; Brookfield, MA; 1842; 1

280

Chassel, ___ (Rev.); ___; Salisbury?; 1826; 1
Chester, ___ (Rev. Dr.); ___; Albany; 1825 and 1826; 2
Chester, ___ (Rev. Dr.); ___; Buffalo; 1850; 1
Chester, ___ (Rev.); ___; Leesville, NJ; 1827; 1
Child, E. (Rev.); ___; Exeter; 1846; 1
Chubbock, A. E. (Rev.); ___; Millport?; 1848; 1
Church, ___ (Elder); : Bainbridge; 1841; 1
Church, G. H., Esq.; Waterville?; 1850; 1
Church, Le Roy; ___; Hudson?; 1846; 1
Clapp. William (Rev.); ___; Albany?; 1848; 1
Clark; ___ (Rev.); ___; Cazenovia; 1839-43; 3
Clark, Charles (Rev.); ___; Adams?; 1847; 1
Clark, Clinton (Rev.); ___; Pompey?; 1846; 1
Clark, E. A. (Elder); ___; Yorkville?; 1847; 1
Clark, E. W. (Rev.); ___; Honolulu, Hawaii?; 1849; 1
Clarke, H. R. (Rev.); Bleecker Street Meth. Episc. Church; Utica; 1846-49; 24
Clark, Jesse (Elder); ___; Corning?; 1849; 1
Clark, John W. (Rev.); ___; Palmyra; 1846; 1
Clark, Orin (Rev.); ___; Geneva?; 1825; 1
Clark, William (Rev.); ___; Cazenovia?; 1850; 1
Clary, ___ (Rev.); ___; Benton?: 1830; 1
Clay, ___ (Rev.); ___; Winfield?; 1827; 1
Cleavland, J. P. (Rev.); ___; Marshall, MI?; 1842; 1
Cleveland, ___ (Rev.); ___; Fayetteville; 1844; 1
Cloriviere, ___ (Rev.); ___ Georgetown; 1825; 1
Coates, C. S. (Rev.); ___; Geneva; 1834-40; 8
Cobb, Plyna, Esq.; Erwin?; 1841; 1
Coe, ___ (Rev.); ___; New Hartford?; 1830 and 1834; 2
Coe (or Cox?), ___ (Rev.); ___; Troy?; 1839; 1
Colburn, ___ (Rev.); ___; Westmoreland; 1844; 1
Cole, Jirah D. (Rev.); ___; Whitesboro; 1844-47; 7
Cole, Jonathan (Rev. Dr.); ___; Hallowell?; 1850; 1
Cole, L. D. (Rev.); ___; Vienna, NY?; 1848; 1
Coley, J. M. (Rev.); Baptist Church; Binghamton and Conklin; 1842; 3
Collier, H. H., Esq.; Binghamton; 1842-3; 4
Colson, E. (Rev.); ___; Southport; 1849-50; 5
Comstock, ___ (Rev. Dr.); ___; Rochester?; 1831; 1
Condit, R. W. (Rev.); First Presbyterian Church; Oswego; 1842-49; 5
Cone, ___ (Rev. Dr.; ___; NYC; 1847; 1
Conger, E. (Rev.); ___; Bronson, OH?; 1835; 1
Cook, ___ (Rev.); ___; Aurora?; 1835; 1
Cook, ___ (Rev.); ___; Stonington, CT?; 1850; 1
Cook, M. (Rev.); ___; Oswego; 1849; 1
Cooke, Samuel (Rev.); Trinity Church, Geneva; 1845; 1
Cooley, E. F. (Rev.); ___; Trenton, NJ?; 1834; 1
Coop, John W. (Rev.); ___; Van Buren; 1850; 1
Cooper, ___ (Rev.); ___; Lenox; 1834; 1
Cooper, Charles D. (Rev.); ___; Albany?; 1843; 1
Cooper, W. H. (Rev.); ___; Wampsville; 1834-48; 8
Cordell, J. G. (Rev.); ___; Paris, NY?; 1845 and 1846; 2
Corey, ___ (Rev.); Cortlandville; 1848
Corey, ___ (Rev.); ___; Georgetown?; 1835
Corey, Daniel G. (Rev.); ___; Utica (1842-50; 52
Corey, S. A. (Rev.); ___; NYC; 1847 and 1850; 2
Cornell, A. (Rev.); ___; state of Michigan?; 1848; 1
Cornell, James A. H. (Rev.); Reformed Dutch Church; Syracuse; 1850; 2
Corwin, ___ (Rev.); ___; New Berlin?; 1850; 1
Coryell, ___ (Rev.); ___; Cazenovia; 1837-1
Coryell, ___ (Rev.); ___; Hornby?; 1842; 1
Cosman, ___ (Rev.); ___; Kingston?; 1822; 1
Coty, ___ (Rev.); ___ Utica; 1843; 1
Cox, ___ (Rev. Dr.); ___ Brooklyn; 1849; 1
Cox, ___ (Rev.); ___; Norwich?; 1850; 1
Cox, S. Hanson (Rev.); ___; Auburn and Oxford; 1845 and 1850; 2
Crabb, Isaac (Rev.); ___; Hopewell?; 1834; 1

Crain, H., Esq.; Norwich and Pharsalia; 1830; 2
Crane, Abijah (Rev.); ___; Clinton?; 1844; 1
Cranmer, ___ (Rev.); ___; Jerusalem, NY?; 1846; 1
Crawford, Gilbert (Rev.); ___; ___; 1840; 1
Crispell, C. E. (Rev.); ___; Piermont?; 1846; 1
Crosby, ___ (Rev.); ___; Benton; 1833-34; 3
Croswell, ___ (Rev. Dr.); ___; New Haven, CT; 1834; 1
Crow, Moses (Rev.); ___; Geneva-Elmira area; 1846-50; 7
Cull, ___ (Re.); ___; Utica?; 1846; 1
Cuming, F. H. (Rev.); St. Mark's Ch., Le Roy; Binghamton, Rochester; 1819-33; 3
Cumings, Simeon (Hon.), Judge, Genesee County Court; 1830; 1
Cumming, ___ (Rev.); ___; Chenango Point?; 1819; 1
Cummings, ___ (Rev.); ___; Rochester; 1822; 1
Curtis, ___ (Rev.); ___; Warren, NY?; 1827; 1
Curtis, ___ (Rev.); ___; Warren, OH?; 1827; 1
Curtis, William (Rev.); ___; Ann Arbor, MI; 1845; 1
Curtiss, William B. (Rev.); ___; Exeter?; 1848; 1
Cushman, George F. (Rev.); ___; Wynton, GA?; 1850; 1
Dagett, ___ (Rev.); ___; NYC?; 1846; 1
Daggert, ___ (Elder); ___; Manchester; 1838; 1
Daggett, ___ (Rev. Dr.); ___; Camillus; 1842; 1
Daggett, ___ (Rev.); ___; Canandaigua?; 1846; 1
Damon, C. (Rev.); ___; Honolulu, Hawaii; 1849; 1
Dana, ___ (Rev.); ___; Kirkland?; k846?; 1
Dana, ___ (Rev.); ___; New Hartford?; 1843; 1
Dana, ___ (Rev.); ___; Sauquoit; 1845; 1
Dana, A. J. (Rev.); ___; Deansville; 1846; 1
Daniels, ___ (Rev.); ___; Otego?; 1844; 1
Danielson, ___ (Rev.); ___; Guilford?; 1824; 1
Dannels, ___ (Rev.); ___; addison?; 1849; 1
Darby, C. ___ (Rev.); ___; Greene?; 1842; 1
Darby, C. (Rev.); ___; Homer?; 1846; 1
Darling, Henry (Rev.); ___; Hudson; 1849; 1
Dashiell, George (Rev.); ___; Seneca Falls?; 1835; 1
Davad, J. F. (Rev.); ___; Adams?; 1847; 1
Davenport, J. E. (Rev.); ___; New Hartford?; 1849; 1
Davenport, J. R. (Rev.); ___; Cazenovia; 1845; 2
Davidson, J. F. (Rev.); ___; Monroe, MI; 1837; 1
Davis, ___ (Rev.); ___; Geneva?; 1839; 1
Davis, ___ (Rev.); ___; Rome?; 1846; 1
Davis, ___ (Rev.); ___; Utica; 1833; 1
Davis, ___ (Rev.); ___; Waterville; 1846; 1
Davis, ___ (Rev.); ___; Sandy Creek?; 1844; 1
Davis, Charles B. (Rev.); ___; Caton and South Corning; 1840-41; 3
Davis, Charles S. (Rev.); ___; Southport, Addison, and Caton; 1840-41; 3
Davis, J. W. (Rev.); ___; Trenton Falls?; 1848; 1
Davis, S. (Rev.); Christ Church; Green Bay, WI; 1842; 1
Davis, S. (Rev.); ___; Rome, NY; 1845; 1
Davis, W. P. (Rev.); ___; Geneva?; 1839; 1
Day, ___ (Rev.); ___; Derby, NH?; 1847; 1
Day, Alvah (Rev.); ___; Lenox?; 1837; 1
Dayan, J. F. (Rev.); ___; Adams?; 1847; 2
Dean, ___ (Rev.); ___; Marcellus; 1848; 1
De Lancey, W. H. (Rt. Rev. Bishop); St. Paul's Church, Brownville; Trinity
   Church, Geneva; and Fort Byron; 1847-48; 4
Delano, ___ (Rev.); ___; Syracuse?; 1847; 1
Delay, R. D., Esq.; Oxford-Norwich area; 1819; 4
De Long, ___ (Rev.); ___; New Milford?; 1843; 1
Delong, William M. (Rev.); ___; Binghamton and Smithville Flats; 1842-3; 4
Deluol, L. R. (Rev.); ___; Baltimore, MD; 1849; 1
De Luynes, H. (Rev.); ___; Utica?; 1848; 1
Demic, ___ (Elder); ___; Phelps?; 1833; 1
Dering, J. E. (Rev.); ___; Herkimer?; ___; 1
Dewey, ___ (Rev. Dr.); Church of the Messiah; NYC; ___; 1
Dewey, C. (Prof. and Rev. Dr.); ___; Rochester?; 1842-48; 3

De Witt, T. (Rev. Dr.); ___; NYC; 1849 and 1850; 2
Dey, ___ (Rev.);___; Westboro, MA?; 1846; 1
Dickinson, E. W. (Rev.); ___; Elmira; 1848-50; 10
Dickson, H. S. (Rev.); ___; Marcy and Utica; 1849-50; 9
Diefendorf, ___ (Rev.); ___; Mohawk?; 45
Dimmick, K. H. ("Alcalde"); Pueblo de Sane Joce, CA?; 1849; 1
Doane, ___ (Rev.); ___; Covington, PA?; 1846; 1
Dobie, D. (Rev.); ___; Plattsburgh?; 1847; 1
Dodge, Lyman, Esq.; Troopsburg?; 1848; 1
Donaldson, Asa (Rev.); ___; Guilford?; 1824 and 1827; 2
Donohu, ___ (Rev.); Catholic Church; Syracuse; 1843; 1
Doolittle, E. (Rev.); ___; Sullivan; 1833; 1
Douglas, ___ (Rev.); ___; Camden; 1845; 1
Dow, ___ (Judge); Jersey, NY; 1832; 1
Dow, D. D. (Rev.); ___; Thompson, CT?; 1848-1
Drake, ___ (Rev.); ___; Schuylkill Haven, PA?; 1842; 1
Dudley, Ira (Rev.); ___; Baldwinsville, Van Buren, and Colosse; 1848-50; 5
Duffey, ___ (Rev.); ___; Hunter?; 1832; 1
Dugan, Thomas, Esq.; Rome, NY; 1848; 1
Duncan, ___ (Elder); ___; Norwich?; 1845 and 1846; 2
Duncan, T. W. (Rev.); ___; Jasper?; 1843; 1
Dunning, ___ (Rev.); ___; Lysander?; 1847; 1
Dunning, ___ (Rev.); ___; Ogden; 1844; 1
Dunning, ___ (Rev.); ___; Volney?; 1847; 1
Dwight, Benjamin W., Jr. (Rev.); ___; Brooklyn and Clinton; 1845 and 1847; 2
Dye, ___ (Rev.); ___; Clockville?; 1846; 1
Easter, J. (Rev.); ___; Seneca?; 1835; 1
Easter, John (Rev.); ___; Middlesex?; 1839; 1
Eastman, ___ (Elder); ___; Middlesex; 1839; 1
Eaton, George W. (Prof. and Rev. Dr.); ___; Hamilton; 1843-50; 4
Eaton, J. T. (Rev.); ___; Knoxville; 1848; 1
Eddy, A. D. (Rev.); ___; Canandaigua?; 1831-32; 3
Eddy, C. (Rev.); ___; Penn Yan; 1831; 1
Eddy, H. T. (Rev.); ___; Springville?; 1849; 1
Edgerton, I. (Rev.); ___; Rome; 1843; 1
Edwards, ___ (Rev.); ___; Albany; 1849; 1
Eells, James (Rev.); ___; ___; 1849; 1
Eggleston, A. (Rev.); ___; Windsor; 1850; 1
Elliott, ___ (Rev.); ___; New Milford, CT?; 1818 and 1821; 2
Embury, E. (Rev.); ___; Penn Yan: 1839; 1
Emmons, Henry (Rev.); ___; Vernon; 1844-47; 4
Erwin, James (Rev.); ___; Syracuse and Rome; 1846-50; 5
Evans, ___ (Rev.); ___; Conklin?; 1842; 1
Everett, E. (Rev.); ___; Hector?; 1834; 1
Everett, R. (Rev.); ___; Rome and Remsen; 1825 and 1847; 2
Ewing, Charles H. (Rev.); ___; Geneva; 1846; 1
Fairborn, R. B. (Rev.); St. Luke's Church; Mechanicville; 1850; 1
Farington, T. T. (Rev.); ___; Geneva; 1846; 1
Farley, Benjamin (Elder); ___; Phelps; 1831-36; 6
Farley, F. A. (Rev.); ___; Brooklyn; 1846-49; 3
Farrington, T. T. (Rev.); Geneva; 1846; 1
Fay, Robert (Rev.); ___; Hamilton?; 1842; 1
Fellows, N. (Rev.); ___; Geneva?; 1846; 1
Fellows, N. (Rev.); ___; Troy, PA; 1848; 1
Ferguson, ___, Esq.; Schuyler?; 1844: 1
Ferguson, ___ (Rev.); ___; Schuyler; 1845; 1
Ferguson, M. (Rev.); ___; Bethel?; 1834; 1
Ferguson, N. (Rev.); ___; Deerfield; 1847; 1
Ferris, ___ (Rev.); ___; Albany; 1833; 1
Ferris, ___ (Rev.); ___; NYC?; 1837; 1
Finch, Rufus, Esq.; Conklin?; 1843; 1
Finney, A. (Rev.); ___ ; Lysander?; 1850; 2
Fippen, ___ (Elder); ___ ; Fayetteville?; 1839; 1
Fish, ___ (Rev.); ___; Evans Mills?; 1843; 1
Fish, ___ (Rev.); ___; Uxbridge, MA?; 1845; 1

Fish, John B. (Rev.); ___; Sangerfield; 1842-43; 5
Fisher, ___ (Rev.); ___; NYC; 1844; 1
Fisk, William E., Esq.; Canastota; 1844; 1
Fitch, ___ (Prof.); ___; New Haven, CT; 1844; 1
Fitzpatrick, J. P. (Rev.); ___; Buffalo; 1850; 1
Folger, C. J., Esq.; Seneca?; 1846; 1
Fondit, J. D. (Rev.); ___; South Hadley, MA?; 1842; 1
Foot, Joseph, I. (Rev.); ___ Cortland?; 1836; 1
Foote, Israel (Rev.); rector, St. Peter's Church; Bainbridge; _?_; 1
Forbes, J. M. (Rev.); NYC?; 1843; 1
Foster, Isaac (Rev.); ___; Utica; 1850; 4
Foster, William, Elder; ___; Elmira?; 1848; 2
Fowler, Jacob (Rev.); ___; Junius?; 1846; 1
Fowler, P. H. (Rev.); Presby. Church; Elmira; 1848-50; 6
Fox, N. (Rev.); ___; Kingsbury?; 1836; 1
Fox, Robert (Rev.); ___; Westmoreland; 1846; 1
Francis, ___ (Rev.); Universalist Church; Litchfield; 1849; 1
Francis, E. (Rev.); Greenfield?; 1850; 1
Francis, Eber (Rev.); ___; Utica; 1848-50; 20
Franklin, Amos A. (Rev.); ___; Oxford; 1821 and 1829; 2
Fraser, Edward A. (Rev.); ___; Lenox; 1832 and 1833; 2
Frazer, ___ (Rev.); Bath; 1843; 1
Freeman, Z. (Elder); ___; Seneca Falls; 1839; 2
French, Jairus, Esq.; Chttenango; 1831-44; 67
French, Justus W. (Rev.); ___; Geneva and Palmyra; 1833-49; 5
Frost, ___ (Rev.); ___; Whitesboro; 1824 and 1830; 2
Fuller, ___ (Rev.); ___; Utica?; 1844; 1
Fuller, Samuel, Jr. (Rev.); rector, St. Michael's church; Litchfield, CT; 1834; 1
Fullerton, J. (Rev.); ___; Whitestown; 1849; 1
Fullerton, John (Rev.); ___; Yorkville?; 1848; 1
Gage, S. G. (Elder); ___; Benton; 1832; 3
Galusha, E. (Rev.); ___; Utica?; 1831; 1
Galusha, Elon (Rev.); ___; Lyons?; 1849; 1
Ganung, E., Esq.; Benton?; 1839; 1
Gardner, Hiram (Rev.?); ___; Hornby; 1850; 1
Gardner, J. (Rev.); ___; Hornby; 1841; 1
Garrison, A. (Rev.); ___; Vernon?; 1831; 3
Gates, ___ (Rev.); ___; Cooperstown?; 1850; 1
Gayley, Sayre (Rev.); ___; Bainbridge; 1827; 1
Gaylord, ___ (Rev.); ___; Gorham and Seneca; 1830-37; 5
Gear, E. G. (Rev.); rector, St. John's Church; Oxford; 1823-26; 2 (Chaplain,
   U. S. Army, Fort Snelling, Iowa, 1848)
Geer, G. T. (Rev.); ___; Ballston; 1849; 1
Gelston, Maltby (Rev.); ___; Canandaigua?; 1844; 1
Gerry, George (Rev.); ___; Vienna, NY; 1842; 1
Gerry, Robert (Rev.); ___; Philadelphia (state not given); 1848; 1
Gibson, ___ (Rev.); ___; Cohoes?; 1845; 1
Giddings, C. W. (Rev.); Meth. Episc. Church; Sauquoit; 1848; 6
Gilbert, ___ (Elder); ___; North Norwich?; 1820; 1
Gilbert, ___ (Rev.); ___; Painted Post; 1848; 1
Gilbert, ___ (Rev.); ___; Windsor?; 1842; 2
Gilbert, H. W. (Rev.); Colesville; 1843; 2
Gilbert, Samuel (Elder); ___; Fenner?; 1831; 1
Giles, Charles (Rev.); ___; Whitestown?; 1826; 1
Gillet, ___ (Rev.); ___; Rome?; 1826-27; 3
Gilliston, M. (Rev.); ___; Rushville?; 1838; 1
Gillmore, D., Esq.; Utica; 1846-48; 11
Goff. ___ (R); ___; Geneva, Benton, and West Bloomfield; 183034; 3
Goldsmith, B. F. (Rev.); ___; Southport; 1849; 1
Goodale, Samuel (Rev.); Ascension Church; Liverpool; _?_; _?_
Goodell, ___ (Rev.); ___; Lenox?; 1835; 1
Goodrich, Charles A. (Rev.?); ___; NYC?; 1848; 1
Goodrich, J. T. (Rev.); ___; Oxford and Guilford; 1842-45; 20
Gordon, P. (Rev.); ___; Florence?; 1848; 1
Gorham, B. W. (Rev.); ___; New Hartford; 1843 and 1844; 2

Gorton, Morgan (Rev.); ___; Corning?; 1843; 1
Graham, George, Esq.; Oriskany; 1850; 4
Graly, A. A. (Rev.); ___; Clockville?; 1846; 1
Graves, ___ (Rev. Dr.); ___; Campbell?; 1843; 1
Graves, ___ (Rev. Dr.); ___; Corning?; 1847; 1
Graves, ___ (Rev.); ___; Yorkville?; 1847-49; 2
Graves, C. (Rev.); ___; Lowville and Bridgewater; 1849-50; 3
Graves, N. Dwight (rev.); ___; New York Mills; 1845-48; 8
Gray, ___ (Rev.); ___; Hornby; 1840; 1
Gray, W., Esq.; Smithville?; 1823; 1
Greatsinger, C. (Rev.); Erin and Elmira?; 1850; 3
Green, ___ (Rev.); ___; Salisbury?; 1848; 1
Green, ___ (President and Rev.); First Presby. Church; Utica; 1843-47; 4
Green, ___ (Justice); NYC; 1850; 1
Green, Beriah (Rev.); ---; Whitestown?; 1847; 1
Greene, ___ (Rev.); ___; Burnt Hills; 1840; 2
Greene, Beriah (Rev.); Peterboro and Westmoreland; 1843 and 1844; 2
Gregg, ___ (Rev.); ___; Chittenango; 1835; 1
Gregory, ___ (Rev.); ___; Binghamton; 1841-2; 3
Gregory, ___ (Rev.); ___; Rome?; 1849; 1
Gregory, Benjamin S., Esq.; Lafayette?; 1849; 1
Gregory, Henry (Rev.); St. Paul's Church; Syracuse; 1841-50; 12
Grenell, Samuel; Rutland, PA?; 1850; 1
Grenell, Z. (Rev.); ___; East Painted Post?; 1843; 1
Grey, John (Rev.); ___; Sullivan?; 1832; 1
Gridley, ___ (Rev.); ___; Kenosha, WI?; 1850; 1
Gridley, ___ (Rev.); ___; Pompey Hill?; 1836; 1
Gridley, ___ (Rev.); ___; Waterloo; 1846; 1
Gridley, A. Delos (Rev.); ___; Sangerfield and Waterville; 1846-48; 5
Gridley, O. H. (Rev.); ___; Waterville?; 1850; 1
Gridley, Samuel H. (Rev.); ___; Perry and Clinton; 1834 and 1844; 2
Gridley, Wayne (Rev.); ___; Clinton; 1842-45; 4
Griffin, William, Esq.; Syracuse; 1831; 1
Griffiths, Evan (Rev.); ___; Utica; 1850; 2
Griffiths, James (Rev.); ___; Utica; 1842-48; 7
Griswold, ___ (Rev.); ___; Vienna, NY?; 1832; 2
Griswold, E. E. (Rev.); ___; Middletown, CT?; 1843; 1
Griswold, Horace (Rev.); ___; Fabius?; 1830; 1
Griswold, James, Esq.; Chemung?; 1834; 1
Groah, A. B. (Rev.); ___; Reading, PA?; 1847; 1
Grosh, A. B. (Rev.); ___; Utica; 1842-44; 7
Grosvenor, C. P. (Elder); ___; Utica; 1847-49; 4
Guernsey, E., Esq.; Pittsford?; 1831; 1
Hackley, Aaron, Esq.; Marshall; 1843; 1
Hackley, Aaron (Hon.); Frankfort, 1844; 1
Hackley, C. W. (Rev.); ___; Utica?; 1843; 1
Hale, ___ (Rev. Dr.); ___; Geneva; 1850; 1
Half, H. H. (Rev.); ___; Schuyler?; 1848; 1
Hall, ___ (Rev.); ___; Canaan?; 1827; 1
Hall, ___ (Rev.); ___; Vernon; 1844; 1
Hall, A. G. (Rev.); ___; Rochester?; 1842-49; 4
Hall, J. (Rev.); ___; Elmira?; 1849; 1
Hall, Joseph, Jr., Esq.; Fayette?; 1833; 1
Hall, Samuel H. (Rev.?); ___; Marshall, MI; 1846; 1
Hall, Thomas, Elder; ___; Utica; 1843; 1
Hamilton, A. (Rev.); ___; Amber?; 1843; 1
Hamilton, H. S. (Rev.); ___; Oriskany Falls; 1850; 1
Hammond, ___ (Rev.); ___; Eaton; 1849; 1
Hammond, H. L. (Rev.); Congregational Church; Morrisville; 1849; 1
Hammond, William B. (Rev.); ___; Canton, MA; 1845; 1
Handy, A. (Rev.); ___; Chittenango; 1841-42; 4
Hard, Amos (Rev.); ___; Corning; 1842-43; 6
Hardenburgh, ___ (Rev.); ___; New Brunswick, NJ?; 1826; 1
Harding, John W. (Rev.); ___; Long Meadow, MA?; 1850; 1
Harkness, James (Rev. Dr.); ___; Quebec, Canada; 1829; 1

Harrington, D. (Rev.); ___; Palmyra?; 1846; 1
Harrington, E. (Rev.); ___; Hopewell; 1846; 1
Harrows, L. A. (Rev.); ___; Sherburne; 1842; 1
Harter, J. H. (Rev.); ___; Little Falls; 1849-50; 3
Harter, Richard, Esq.; Deerfield; 1848 and 1850; 2
Hartshorn, C. (Elder); ___: Franklin?: 1843; 1
Hartwell, Joseph (Rev.); ___; Utica; 1847-48; 3
Harvey, ___ (Rev.); ___; Hamilton and Deerfield; 1844 and 1845; 2
Harvey, James (Rev.?); ___; Wheelier, VA?; 1833; 1
Hase, M. (Rev.); ___; Fayetteville?; 1840; 1
Hastings, E., Esq.; Seneca?; 1830; 1
Hastings, P. C. (Rev.); ___; Clinton; 1844; 1
Hastings, S. P.M. (Rev.); ___; Pompey?; 1848; 1
Hause, ___ (Rev.); ___; Fulton; 1847; 1
Haven, C. (Elder); ___; West Turin?; 1850; 1
Hawks, ___ (Rev.); ___; Albion?; 1830; 1
Hawley, ___ (Rev. Dr.); ___; Boston (state not given); 1832; 1
Hawley, Bostwick (Prof. and Rev.); ___; Utica; 1842-44; 49
Hawley, Francis (Rev.); ___; Cazenovia; 1842; 1
Hay, P. C. (Rev.); Presby. Church; Geneva; 1836-46; 9
Hay, Philip C. (Rev.); ___; Utica?; ? ; 1
Hayes, ___ (Rev.); ___; Syracuse?; 1844; 1
Haynes, D. C. (Rev.); ___; Utica; 1843-46; 7
Haynes, S. (Rev.); ___; 1844; 1
Hays, ___ (Rev.); ___; Salina; 1843; 1
Hazleton, George W. (Rev.); ___; Black River?; 1850; 1
Heanon, ___ (Rev.); ___; Suffield, CT?; 1848; 1
Hebard, E. (Rev.); ___; Benton?; 1841; 1
Hentley, ___, Esq.; Chittenango?; 1837; 1
Hesch, A. B. (Rev.); ___; Canandaigua?; 1849; 1
Hibbard, F. G. (or T. G.?) (Rev.); ___; Geneva?; 1846; 2
Hibbert, C., Esq.; Manlius?; 1837; 1
Hickcox, B. H. (Rev.); St. Paul's Church; Rochester; 1833; 1
Hickock, ___ (Rev.); ___; Fayetteville?; 1843; 1
Hickock, M. J. (Rev.); ___; Utica?; 1844; 1
Hickox, B. H. (Rev.); Zion's Church; Palmyra; 1831-32
Hickox, B. W. (Rev.); ___; Pittsford?; 1831; 1
Hickox, W. W. (Rev.); rector, Trinity Church; Fayetteville; 1842; 1
Higbee, ___ (Rev.); ___; Utica; 1844; 1
Higbie, ___ (Rev. Dr.); ___; NYC; 1845; 1
High, ___ (Rev.); ___; Geneva?; 1846; 1
Hill, ___ (Rev.); ___; Sacketts Harbor?; 1850; 1
Hill, T. C. (Rev.); ___; Sweden Center, NY; 1846; 1
Hill, Thomas (Elder); ___;Utica; 1843-50; 18
Hills, ___ (Rev.); ___; Detroit, MI; 1850; 1
Hines, ___ (Rev.); St. John's Church; Salina; 1843; 1
Hiscox, E. T. (Rev.); ___; Norwich; 1850; 1
Hitt, T. C. (Rev.); ___; South Trenton, NY; 1843; 1
Hobart, ___ (Rt. Rev. Bishop); Christ Church, NYC and St. John's Church; NYC;
    1825 and 1830; 2
Hobart, John Henry (Rev.); Trinity Church?; Geneva; 1846; 3
Hodges, ___ (Rev.); Chaplain, Jefferson Barracks, MO; ? ; 1
Hodgkin, E. C. (Rev.); ___; Albion, MI?; 1842; 1
Hoes, ___ (Rev.); ___; Ithaca?; 1839 and 1844; 2
Hoes, John C. F. (Rev.); ___; Chittenango; 1835-36; 3
Hoffmeier, John A. (Rev.); ___; Orwigsburgh, Schuylkill Co., PA; 1847; 1
Hogarth, ___ (Rev.); ___; Geneva; 1848; 1
Hogarth, Richard, Esq.; Geneva; 1835-39; 14)
Hoising, ___ (Rev.); ___; Aurora?; 1832; 1
Holden, L. I. (Rev.); ___; Cayahoga Falls, OH; 1850; 1
Holdich, ___ (Rev.); ___; Rhinebeck?; 1843; 1
Hollett, ___ (Rev.); ___; Seneca?; 1833; 1
Hillister, ___ (Rev.); ___; Manlius?; 1835; 1
Hollister, ___ (Rev.); ___; Paris, NY; 1825; 1
Holme, John Stanford (Rev.); ___; Utica; 1850; 4

Holmead, Alfred (Rev.); Chaplain, Female Institute; Ellicott Mills; 1843; 1
Holmes, ___ (Rev.); ___; Westmoreland?; 1826; 1
Holmes, Daniel (Rev.); ___; Stockbridge?; 1849; 1
Holt, T. A., Esq.; New Hartford; 1846; 1
Hood, ___ (Rev.); Southport?; 1850; 1
Hopkins, ___ (Rev.); ___; Buffalo; 1839; 1
Hopkins, ___ (Rev.) ___; Centerville?; 1840; 1
Hopkins, S. M. (Rev.); ___; Corning; 1840-42; 8
Horton, ___ (Rev.); ___ Boonville?; 1850; 1
Hotchkin, ___ (Rev.); ___; Paris, NY?; 1834; 1
Hotchkiss, Nelsor, Esq.; Big Flats;1849; 1
Hough, ___ (Rev. Prof.); ___; Shoreham, VT; 1826; 2
Hough, James T.; ___; Chittenango?; 1834-5; 3
Houghton, ___ (Rev.); ___; Van Buren?; 1842; 1
Houghton, George H. (Rev.?); ___; NYC?; 1850; 1
Houghton, H. (Rev.); ___; Jordan, NY; 1847; 1
Houston, T. (Rev.); ___; North Granville?; 1845; 1
Houston, Thomas (Rev.); ___; Chittenango?; 1842-44; 11
Howard, ___ (Rev.); ___; Baldwinsville; 1847; 1
Howard, ___ (Rev.); ___; Frankfort Hill; 1849; 1
Howard, L. (Rev.); ___; Norwich; 1842; 1
Howard, L. (Rev.); Baptist Church; Troy; 1846; 1
Howard, N. B., Esq.; Utica?; 1847; 1
Howe, S. S. (Rev.); ___ Painted Post; 1841-42; 5
Howe, Samuel (Rev.); ___; Waterford; 1850; 1
Hoyt, John B; (Rev.); ___; Oxford and Greene; 1824-29; 6
Hoyt, John B. (Rev.); Presby. Church; Coventry; 1842; 1
Hubbard, ___ (Rev.); ___; Dansville; 1833; 1
Hubbard, ___ (Rev.); ___; Waterloo?; 1831; 1
Hubbard, William G. (Rev.); ___; Cato Four Corners; 1847; 1
Hudson, Jonathan (Rev.); Meth. Episc. Church; Geneva; _?_ ; 1
Hudson, Thomas B. (Rev.); ___; Corning?; 1848; 2
Hughes, ___ (Rev.); ___; Richfield; 1842 and 1843; 2
Hull, ___ (Rev.); ___; Lyons; 1850; 1
Hull, A. (Rev.); ___; Athens,Bradford Co., PA; 1850; 1
Hull, A. (Rev.); ___; Elmira; 1850; 2
Hull, Andrew (Rev.); rector, St. Andrew's Church, New Berlin; 1843; 1
Hull, H. H., Esq.; Corning?; 1843; 1
Humphrey, James H., Esq.; Bainbridge; 1827; 1
Humphrey, John (Rev.); ___; Binghamton?; 1850; 1
Hunford, ___ (Rev.); ___; Sand Lske; 1850; 1
Hunt, ___ (Rev.); ___; Lehman, PA; 1842; 1
Hunter, ___ (Rev. Dr.); Boonville; 1845 and 1847; 2
Hunter, Eli S. (Rev.); ___; Middlebury; 1830; 1
Huntington, E. A. (Rev.); ___; Chittenango?; 1831 and 1837; 2
Huntington, E. A. (Rev.); ___; Albany; 1837 and 1850; 2
Huntley, ___, Esq.; Manlius?; 1837; 1
Hurd, I. N. (Rev.); ___; Big Flats; 1850; 2
Hutch, ___ (Rev.); ___; Milwaukee, Wisc. Terr.; 1844; 1
Hutchins, ___ (Elder); ___; Richfield; 1842; 1
Hutchins, D. (Rev.); ___; Clyde?; 1839; 1
Hutchinson, Zenas, Esq.; Coventry?; 1842; 1
Hutton, ___ (Rev. Dr.); Dutch Church, NYC; 1847 and 1850; 2
Hyde, ___ (Rev. Dr.); Congregational Church; Madison, OH; 1824; 1
Hyde, Orin (Rev.); ___; Fayetteville?; 1837; 2
Igenburgh, ___ (Rev.); ___; Guilford; 1841; 1
Ingersoll, John (Rev.); First Congregational Church; Westmoreland; 1846; 1
Inglet, S. H. (Rev.); ___; Hector?; 1839; 1
Irving, Pierre P. (Rev.); Trinity Church; Geneva; 1837-39; 4
Iverson, ___ (Rev.); ___; Benton?; 1835; 1
Jackson, F. J. (Rev.); ___; Adams?; 1847; 1
Jackson, William (Rev.); ___; NYC?; 1835; 1
James, T. L. (Rev.); ___; First Congregational Church; Guilford; 1841; 1
James, J. L. (Rev.); ___; Guilford?; 1844; 1
Jameson, Hugh, Esq.; Lyons?; 1832; 1

Jaquith, ___, Esq.; Liverpool; 1848; 1
Jarvis, ___ (Rev.); ___; Richfield?; 1848; 1
Jenks, William A. (Rev.); ___; Glen Cove, L. I., NY; 1848; 1
Jervis, T. B. (Rev.); ___; Annsville?; 1843; 1
Jewett, ___ (Rev.); ___; Geneva, Walworth Co., WI; 1842; 1
Johnson, ___ (Rev.); ___; Skaneateles?; 1836; 1
Johnson, C. T. (Rev.); ___; Norwich?; 1847; 1
Johnson, Evan M. (Rev.); ___; Brooklyn; 1837; 1
Johnson, J. R. (Rev.); ___; Henderson, Jefferson Co.; 1848; 1
Johnson, John (Rev.); ___; Newburgh?; 1822; 1
Johnson, Leonard (Rev.); ___; North Granville?; 1842; 1
Johnson, Samuel J. (Rev.); ___; Syracuse; 1848; 1
Johnson, Smith, Esq.; Preston?; 1829; 1
Johnson, William (Rev.); ___; Chittenango; 1831-33; 5
Jones, ___, Esq.; Hopewell?; 1830; 1
Jones, ___ (Rev.); ___; New Brunswick, NJ?; 1835; 1
Jones, ___ (Elder); ___; Smithfield?; 1839; 1
Jones, James, Esq.; Rochester?; 1848; 1
Jones, Lott (Rev.); ___; NYC?; 1845; 1
Jones, William (Rev.); ___; Lyons?; 1833; 1
Jones, William (Rev.); Welsh Independent Church; Utica; 1847; 1
Joslyn, Charles, Esq.; Greene?; 1818; 1
Judd, G. N. (Rev.); ___; Catskill; 1845-50; 3
Judd, ___ (Rev.); ___; Ithaca?; 1839; 1
Judd, ___ (Rev. Dr.); ___; Sacketts Harbor; 1844 and 1850; 2
Judd, Silas, Esq.; Fenner?; 1840; 1
Judson, J., Esq.; Syracuse; 1849 and 1850; 2
Kearny, ___ (Rev.); ___; Canandaigua; 1831; 2
Kellogg, ___ (Elder); ___; Smithville; 1829; 1
Kellogg, ___ (Rev.); ___; Clinton?; 1833; 1
Kellogg, Frederick, Esq.; New Hartford?; 1850; 1
Kellogg, H. H. (Rev.); ___; Clinton; 1847; 1
Kelsey, ___ (Elder); ___; Smithville; 1829; 1
Kendall, ___ (Rev.); ___; Kirkland?; 1846; 1
Kendicott, ___ (Rev.); ___; Geneva?; 1834; 1
Kendrick, ___ (Rev.); ___; Burns?; 1835; 1
Kendrick, ___ (Rev.); ___; Sherburne?; 1824; 1
Kendrick, N. (Rev.); ___; Hamilton; 1846; 2
Kennedy, ___ (Elder); ___; Waverly?; 1850; 1
Kennedy, Duncan (Rev. Dr.); ___; Albany; 1844-50; 3
Kennicott, ___ (Rev.); ___; Camden?; 1844; 1
Kenny, ___ (Rev.); St. John's Church; Canandaigua; 1832; 1
Kent, ___ (Rev.); ___; Seneca Falls; 1832; 1
Kenyon, ___ (Elder); ___; Marshall?; 1846; 2
Kepler, ___ (Rev.); ___; White Plains, Henrico Co., VA; 1848 and 1849; 2
Keukle, W. P., Esq.; Elmira?; 1849; 1
Keyes, S. P. (Rev.); ___; Dresden; 1837; 1
Kibbe, Abel, Esq.; Salisbury?; 1826; 1
Kibbe, J. S. (Rev.); ___; Lee?; 1850; 1
Kibby, Abiel, Esq.; Salisbury?; 1827; 1
Kies, ___ (Rev.); ___; Oxford; 1827; 1
Kimball, Joseph (Rev.); ___; Hamptonburgh?; 1846; 1
Kimble, ___ (Rev.); ___; Alder creek?; 1844; 1
Kindad, ___ (Rev.); ___; Buffalo?; 1849; 1
Kingsley, Washington (Rev.); ___; Lenox?; 1841; 1
Kinney, ___ (Rev.); ___; Hamilton?; 1845; 1
Kip, ___ (Rev.); ___; Albany?; 1846; 1
Kirk, R. R. (Rev.); ___; New York Mills?; 1846-50; 4
Kittle, ___ (Rev.); ___; Livingston Manor, Columbia County; 1826; 1
Knap, ___ (Rev.); ___; Hamilton?; 1836; 1
Knight, Caleb (Rev.); ___; Franklin?; 1821; 1
Knight, Joshua (Rev.); ___; Sherburne?; 1819; 1
Knowlton, William, Esq.; Oxford?; 1820 and 1825; 2
Knox, ___ (Rev.); ___; Eagle Village?; 1842; 1
Knox, D. (Rev.); ___; NYC?; 1835; 1

Knox, John P. (Rev.); ___; Utica?; 1842 and 1843; 2
Knox, P. (Rev.); ___; "at the N. Y. State Lunatic Asylum in Utica; 1843; 1
Knox, W. E. (Rev.); ___; Watertown and Rome; 1845-50; 6
Kookle, W. P., Esq.; Elmira?; 1849; 1
Kuypers, ___ (Rev. Dr.); ___; NYC?; 1819; 1
Lacey, ___ (Rev.); ___; Albany; 1818; 1
Lacey, ___ (Rev.); ___; Pittstown, Otsego County; 1817; 1
Lacy, ___ (Rev.); ___; Oxford?; 1817-18; 3
Lanahan, ___ (Rev.); ___; Washington, D.C.; 1849; 1
Lane, ___ (Rev.); ___; Augusta?; 1826; 1
Lane, ___ (Rev.); ___; Fayette?; 1832; 1
Lane, ___ (Rev.); ___; Vienna, NY; 1834; 1
Lane, ___ (Rev.); ___; Waterloo?; 1830-34; 5
Lane, A. D. (Rev.); ___; Fayette and Tyre; 1831-47; 4
Lane, Matthias, Esq.; Sempronius?; 1833; 1
Lansing, ___ (Rev. Dr.); ___; Auburn; 1844; 1
Lansing, ___ (Rev.); ___; Brooklyn; 1849; 1
Lansing, ___ (Rev. Dr.); ___; Cannonsville; 1849; 1
Lansing, ___ (Rev. Dr.); ___; Utica?; 1830-32; 3
Lansing, D. C. (Rev.); ___; Syracuse; 1842; 1
Lathrop, L. E. (Rev. Dr.); ___; Auburn; 1845-49; 3
Lathrop, S. G. (Rev.); ___; Pratt's Hollow?; 1848; 1
Law, ___ (Rev.); ___; Varick?; 1833; 1
Lawrie, A. G. (Rev.); ___; Worcester?; 1850; 1
Lawton, I. (Rev.); ___; Cassville?; 1848; 1
Lawton, John (Rev.); ___; Macdonough; _?_; 1
Lawton, M. (Rev.); ___; Richfield; 1849; 1
Leach, B. N. (Rev.); ___; Hamilton; 1843; 1
Leach, David (Rev.); ___; Smithville?; 1829; 1
Lee; C. Gold (Rev.); ___; Syracuse; 1845; 1
Lee, H. W. (Rev.); ___; Springfield, MA; 1847; 1
Lee, Henry W. (Rev.); ___; Rochester?; 1848; 1
Leeds, ___ (Rev.); ___; Utica; 1843-50; 15
Leland, John (Elder); Baptist church; Cheshire, MA; 1775 (an indirect reference)
Leonard, ___ (Rev.); ___; Preston?; 1829; 1
Leonard, Lewis (Rev.); ___; Cazenovia; 1831-40; 5
Leonard, S. W. (Rev.); ___; West Monroe; 1844; 1
Lester, C. Edwards (Rev.); ___; Utica?; 1842; 1
Lewis, ___ (Rev.); ___; Whitney Point?; 1848; 1
Lewis, C. M. (Rev.); ___; Rome?; 1844; 1
Lewis, Y. N. (Rev.); ___; Middletown, CT?; 1848; 1
Lightbourne, ___ (Rev.); ___; Corning?; 1850; 2
Lincoln, T. O. (Rev.); ___; Utica?; 1850; 1
Lindsey, ___ (Rev.); ___; Poughkeepsie?; 1844; 1
Lintner, G. A. (Rev.); St. Luke's Church; Schoharie; 1831; 1
Litchfield, ___ (Rev.); ___; Lisle?; 1842; 1
Littlejohn, A. N. (Rev.?); ___; Springfield; 1850; 1
Livermore, ___ (Rev.); Emanuel Church; Little Falls; 1845 and 1849; 2
Livermore, L. (Rev.); ___; Earlville; 1849; 1
Long, Walter R. (Rev.); ___; Whitestown; 1819; 1
Long, Walter R. (Rev.); Presby. Church; Whitesboro; 1845-49; 13
Loomis, M. (Rev.); ___; Cooperstown?; 1849; 1
Loomis, W. (Rev.); ___; Winfield?; 1844; 1
Lord, ___ (Rev.); ___; Greenfield, Dane Co., WI; 1849; 1
Lord, J. (Rev.); ___; Morrisville?; 1832; 1
Lord, John C. (Rev.); ___; Buffalo?; 1839 and 1845; 2
Loring, H. N. (Rev.); ___; Utica?; 1845-47; 3
Lounsbury, Thomas (Rev.); ___; Ovid; 1835; 1
Lovett, Robert (Rev.); ___; Paris, NY; 1845; 1
Lowrie, ___ (Rev.); ___; Washington, D.C.; 1823; 1
Lucas, ___ (Rev.); St. Peter's Church; Auburn; 1838; 1
Ludlow, ___ (Rev. Dr.); ___; Philadelphia, PA?; 1850; 1
Ludlow, ___ (Rev. Dr.); ___; Poughkeepsie; 1845; 1
Luft, ___ (Rev.); ___; Sheboygan Falls, MI?; 1850; 1
Lusk, ___ (Rev.); ___; Cherry Valley; 1844; 1

Lyon, ___ (Rev.); ___; Northampton; 1849; 1
McAfee, ___ (Rev.); ___; Cherry Valley?; 1833; 1
McCarthy, ___ (Rev.); ___; Lafayette; 1841; 1
McCloskey, ___ (Rt. Rev. Bishop); ___; Detroit, MI; 1847; 1
McDonald, Daniel; Episcopal clergyman; Geneva College; 1830; 1
McEwan, James (Rev.); ___; Delhi?; 1844; 1
McGowan, ___ (Rev.); Methodist Church; Utica; 1845 and 1846; 2
McHarg, Charles K. (Rev.); ___; Cooperstown?; 1848 and 1850; 2
McHarg, William N. (Rev.); ___; Albion?; 1843; 1
McHugh, Stephen (Rev.); ___; Oriskany?; 1844; 1
McIlvaine, J. H. (Rev.); ___; Utica?; 1844-50; 15
McIlvane, ___ (Rt. Rev. Bishop); ___; Cincinnati, OH; 1848; 1
McKinnes, Sabin (Rev.); ___; Vernon?; 1845; 1
McKinney, I. J. B. (Rev.); ___; Conhocton?; 1835; 1
McKoon, Samuel (Judge); Oxford; 1843; 1
McKoon, William (Rev.?); ___; Galen?; 1835; 1
McLaren, ___ (Rev.); ___; Rochester; 1846; 1
McLaren, D. C. (Rev.); ___; Caledonia?; 1850; 1
McLaren, John F. (Rev.); ___; Geneva?; 1830-38; 26
McLean, C. G. (Rev. Dr.); ___; Fort Plain; 1848; 1
McMemory, John (Rev.); ___; Schuyler?; 1847; 1
McMurray, ___ (Rev.); ___; NYC?; 1826; 1
McNeil, ___ (Rev.); ___; Ovid?; 1839; 1
Machim, ___ (Rev.); ___; New Hartford?; 1842; 1
Maginnis, J. S. (Rev.); ___; Hamilton?; 1843; 1
Mahan, ___ (President and Rev.); ___; Akron, OH?; 1848; 1
Maltbee, E. D. (Rev.); ___; Clinton?; 1848; 1
Maltby, ___ (Rev.); ___; Syracuse?; 1850; 1
Mandeville, Henry (Rev.); ___; Geneva; 1831-47; 15
Manley, ___ (Rev.); ___; Richfield?; 1850; 1
Mann, Alexander (Rev.); ___; Ithaca?; 1834; 1
Mantague, O. (Rev.); ___; Cazenovia?; 1837; 1
Mariner, J. (Elder); ___; Checkerville?; 1850; 1
Marselus, Nicolaus J. (Rev.); ___; NYC?; 1849; 1
Marshall, A. G., Esq.; Geneva?; 1832; 1
Martin, ___ (Rev.); ___; Albany?; 1848; 1
Martin, ___ (Rev.); ___; Geneva; 1830; 3
Martin, Alfred, Esq.; Rome, NY?; 1849; 1
Martin, Thomas (Rev.); St. John's Church; Utica; 1843-44; 8
Marvin, Martin (Rev.); ___; Milford; 1841; 1
Mason, ___ (Rev.); Trinity Church; Geneva; 1830-35; 13
Mason, ___ (Rev. Dr.); ___; NYC; 1845
Mason, A. P. (Rev.); ___; Lenox?; 1840;1
Mason, A. T. (Rev.); ___; Clockville; 1839; 1
Mason, Alanson P. (Rev.); ___; Clockville; 1841; 1
Mason, Erskine (Rev.); ___; NYC?; 1831; 1
Mason, R. S. (Rev. Dr.); ___; Geneva?; 1830; 1
Mason, W. A. (Rev.); ___; Port Byron and Whitestown; 1849-50; 2
Mather, William (Rev.); ___; Concord; 1844; 1
Matson, Wm. A. (Rev.); ___; Bridgewater and Waterville; 1828-50; 9
Matthews, ___ (Rev.); ___; Washington, D.C.; 1823; 1
Matteson, Isaiah (Elder); ___; Floyd?; 1843; 1
Mattison, S. (Rev.); ___; Geneva; 1831-32; 3
Mattoon, C. N. (Rev.); ___; Auroroa?; 1847; 1
Maxson, W. B. (Rev.); ___; Plainfield?; 1847; 1
May, Hezekiah (Rev.); ___; Owego; 1817; 1
May, S. J. (Rev.); ___; Syracuse; 1845-48; 6
Mead, G. W. (Rev.); ___; ? ; 1842; 1
Mead, S. C. (Rev.); ___; Herkimer; ? ; 1
Meigs, Byron (Rev.); ___; Jordan?; 1849; 1
Merrell, ___ (Rev.); ___; Junius?; 1834; 1
Merrell, S. L. (Rev.); ___; Litchfield; 1850; 1
Merrill, ___ (Rev.); ___; Litchfield; 1849; 1
Merrill, James (Rev.); ___; Marengo?; 1831; 1
Merrit, ___ (Rev.); ___; Palmyra; 1835; 1

Merritt, ___ (Rev.); ___; Boston, MA?; 1825; 1
Merwin, Charles (Rev.); ___; Victor?; 1846; 1
Metcalf, ___ (Rev.); ___; Le Roy?; 1834; 1
Miles, Gilbert, Esq.; Veteran?; 1849; 1
Miles, S. (Rev.); ___; Geneva and Vienna; 1837; 2
Millard, D. (Rev.); ___; West Bloomfield; 1846; 1
Miller, ___ (Rev. Dr.); ___; Cooperstown?; 1849; 1
Miller, Charles K., Esq.; Erwin; 1840-41; 3
Miller, J. W. (Rev.); ___; Baldwinsville?; 1832; 1
Miller, U. B. (Rev.); ___; Ovid?; 1832; 1
Miner, ___ (Rev.); ___; Barrington?; 1840; 1
Miner, Ovid (Rev.); ___; Benton?; 1839; 1
Mines, ___ (Rev. Dr.; ___; California?; 1849; 1
Minor, ___ (Rev.); ___; Syracuse?; 1848; 2
Mitchel, William (Rev.); ___; Springfield, PA; 1849; 1
Mitchell, ___ (Rev.); ___; Geneva?; 1834; 1
Mitchell, ___ (Rev.); ___; Northampton?; 1841; 1
Mitchell, J. S. (Rev.); ___; Skaneateles?; 1846; 1
Monell, Robert, Esq.; Greene?; 1814; 1
Montgomery, G. W. (Rev.); ___; Rochester?; 1850; 1
Moody, ___; (Rev.); ___; Sharon, CT; 1847; 1
Moore, ___ (Rev.); ___; Russell?; 1850; 1
Morey, Daniel S. (Rev.?); ___; Perryville?; 1844; 1
Morgan, ___ (Elder); ___; Salina; 1838; 1
Morgan, J. (Rev.); ___; Italy, NY; 1838; 1
Morgan, J. (Rev.); ___; Stratford, CT?; 1845; 1
Morgan, John, Esq.; Frankfort; 1849; 1
Morgan, William (Rev.); ___; Norwich, CT?; 1850; 1
Morley, L. (Rev.); ___; Clyde; 1834; 1
Morr, Robert J., Esq.; Augusta?; 1847; 1
Morris, B. W. (Rev.); ___; Northumberland, PA?; 1850; 1
Morse, Albert, Esq.; McConnellsville?; 1846; 1
Morse, Pitt (Rev.); ___; Watertown?; 1822; 1
Morse, William (Rev.); ___; Sullivan; 1843; 1
Moss, David (Rev.); ___; Plymouth; 1824; 1
Mott, ___ (Rev.); ___; Brattleboro, VT; 1849; 1
Murphy, ___ (Rev. Dr.); Reformed Dutch Church; Herkimer; 1843-48; 3
Murray, ___ (Rev.); ___; NYC?; 1833; 1
Murray, Allen (Rev.); ___; Lenox; 1840; 1
Myers, A. H. (Rev.); ___; St. Johnsville?; 1843; 1
Mygatt. William (Rev.); ___; Utica?; 1850; 1
Myrick, ___ (Rev.); ___; Verona?; 1831; 1
Myrick, Luther (Rev.); ___; Cazenovia; 1834-41; 3
Nagus, Myron H. (Rev.); ___; ? ; 1847; 1
Neely, Albert, Esq.; Fayetteville; 1835-37; 4
Nesbit, ___ (Rev.); ___; Geneva; 1830 and 1831; 2
Nevins, J. W. (Rev.); ___; ? ; 1834; 1
Nichols, ___ (Rev.); ___; Sconondoa (in town of Verona); 1845; 1
Nichols, ___ (Rev.); ___; Van Buren?; 1846; 1
Nichols, B. (Rev.); ___; Cato?; 1849; 1
Nichols, James (Rev.); "Church in Oneida Castle"; 1848 and 1849; 2
Nichols, James (Rev.); ___; Utica?; 1844-50; 3
Nicholson, ___ (Elder); ___; Cazenovia; 1837; 1
Nims, A., Esq.; Manlius?; 1835; 1
Ninde, W. W. (Rev.); Utica-Rome-Delta area; 1842-44; 3
Nine, ___ (Rev.); ___; Oswego?; 1837; 1
Nisbet, ___ (Rev.); ___; Seneca?; 1830-33; 5
Norris, Robert J., Esq.; Augusta; 1845 and 1846; 2
North, ___ (Pres. of Hamilton College and Rev.); Cliton; 1843-48; several
North, A. (Rev.); South Trenton?; 1850; 1
North, E. L. (Rev.); ___; Sullivan; 1834; 1
Northrop, ___ (Rev.); ___; Fenner?; 1831; 1
Northrop, B. (Rev.); ___; Perryville; 1831-34; 5
Northrup, B. (Rev.); Episcopal Church; Fayetteville; 1835; 1
Norton, ___ (Rev.); ___; Richmond; 1832 and 1834; 2

291

Norton, Asahel (Rev. Dr.); ___; Clinton; 1833-45; 7
Norton, John N. (Rev.); ___; Hopeton?; 1846; 1
Norton, L. W. (Rev.); ___; Watertown; 1850; 1
Nott, ___ (Rev.Dr.); Prof., Union College, Schenectady; 1826; 1
Noyes, John, Esq.; Preston?; 1817; 1
Noyes, Nathan (Rev.); ___; Preston; 1819-23; 7
O'Farrell, D. M. D. (Rev.); ___; Chittenango; 1840 and 1841; 2
O'Flaherty, ___ (Rev.); ___; Geneva; 1846; 1
Ogden, David L. (Rev.); Whitesboro?; 1843-44; 4
Okill, J. Jay (Rev.); rector, St. Peter's Church; Bainbridge; 1843; 1
Olcott, D. (Elder); ___; Westmoreland?; 1849; 1
Olcott, J. B. (Rev.); ___; ? ; 1843; 1
Olcott, J. B. (Rev.); ___; Greece MI; 1843; 1
Olds, Ira M. (Rev.); ___; Lenox; 1832; 2
Olney, Anthony, Esq.; Columbus; 1824; 1
Onderdonk, ___ (Bishop); ___; Perth Amboy, NJ; 1836; 1
Onderdonk, ___ (Bishop); ___; NYC; 1839; 1
Orbs, ___ (Curate); ___; El Paso, TX; 1850; 1
Ormsbee, J. A. (Rev.); ___; Baldwinsville; 1847; 1
Ormsbee, James, Esq.; Kirkland?; 1847; 1
Ortan, A. G. (Rev.); ___; Seneca Falls; 1834; 2
Orton, ___ (Rev.); ___; Auburn, Seneca Falls, Phelps; 183032; 3
Orvis, Samuel (Rev.); ___; Little Falls?; 1849; 2
Osborne, Amos O., Esq.; Waterville?; 1844; 1
Osgood, S. (Rev.); ___; Providence, RI?; 1848; 1
Otis, N. (Rev.); ___; Oxford-Macdonough area; 1825-29; 9
Ottman, William (Bishop); ___; Clay; ? ; 1
Oviedo, Vincente (Rev.); ___; Guaymas, Mexico; 1850; 1
P ? , W. M. (Rev.); ___; Oxford; 1841; 1
P ton, ___ (Rev. Dr.); ___; NYC; 1842; 1
Paddock, ___ (Rev.); ___; Binghamton?; 1849; 1
Paddock, ___ (Elder); ___; Cazenovia; 1835-39; 4
Paddock, ___ (Elder); ___; Julius?; 1836; 1
Paddock, ___ (Rev.); ___; Marshall?; 1843; 1
Paddock, B. (Rev.); ___; Chittenango?; 1833-39; 3
Paddock, B. G. (Rev.); ___; Utica area; 1842-50; 4
Paddock, C. (Rev.); ___; Chittenango?; 1838; 1
Paddock, Daniel, Esq.; Vienna; 1822; 1
Paddock, William H. (Rev.); ___; Vernon?; 1848; 1
Paddock, ___ (Rev. Dr.); New Hartford?; 1846-50; 4
Paddock, Z. (Rev.); ___; Little Falls; 1846; 1
Paddock, Z. (Rev.) Dr.); ___; New York Mills; 1846-48; 6
Paddock, Zachariah (Rev.); ___; Utica area; 1826; 2
Palmer, N. (Rev.); ___; Madison?; 1850; 1
Parker, ___ (Rev.); ___; Cambridge, MA?; 1847; 1
Parker, Aaron (Rev.); ___; Oxford-Guilford area; 1829 and 1830; 2
Parker, Aaron (Elder); ___; Fenner; 1840; 1
Parker, B. (Rev.); ___; Geneva; 1846; 1
Parker, J. (Rev.); ___; Canandaigua?; 1833; 1
Parker, John (Rev.); ___; Williamson?; 1831; 1
Parker, Nelson (Rev.); ___; ? ; 1831; 1
Parker, S. (Rev.); ___; Hopewell?; 1846; 1
Parmelee, A. H. (Rev.); ___; Addison-Newville area; 1850; 4
Parr, S. S. (Rev.); ___; Ithaca?; 1839; 1
Parry, ___ (Rev.); ___; Sandy Hill, Washington Co.?; 1847; 1
Parsons, ___ (Rev.); ___; Newark, NY?; 1839; 1
Parsons, John, Esq.; Utica; 1848-50; 9
Parsons, Levi (Rev.); ___; Marcellus?; 1846-50; 4
Pattengill, H. (Rev.); ___; Corning; 1847-50; 10
Patton, William, Esq.; Towanda?; 1827; 1
Patton, William (Rev. Dr.); Spring Street Presby. Church; NYC; 1843-49; 3
Payne, William (Rev.); ___; Schenectady?; 1850; 1
Payson, E. H. (Rev.); ___; New Hartford; 1845-50; 10
Peabody, ___ (Rev. Dr.); ___; Boston, MA?; 1849 and 1850; 2
Peabody, Ephraim (Rev.); ___; New Bedford (state not given); ? ; 1

Peak, Oliver, Esq.; Gibson?; 1850; 1
Pearce, ___ (Rev.); ___; Madison?; 1831; 1
Pearne, W. H. (Rev.); ___; Oxford-Norwich area; 1842; 2
Peck, ___ (Elder); ___; Cazenovia; 1832; 1
Peck, ___ (Rev.); ___; Owego?; 1841; 1
Peck, ___ (Rev.); ___; Pharsalia?; 1842; 1
Peck, ___ (Rev.); ___; Ulysses?; 1829; 1
Peck, A. (Rev.); ___; Mohawk?; 1850; 1
Peck, Henry (Rev.); ___; Norwich-Preston area; 1829; 3
Peck, John (Elder); ___; Norwich?; 1817; 1
Penfield, J. (Rev.); ___; Frankfort?; 1848; 1
Penny, ___ (Rev.); ___; Manville, RI?; 1849; 1
Perine, L. M. R. (Rev.); ___; Auburn; 1833; 1
Perkins, ___ (Rev.); ___; Ashburnham, MA?; 1826; 1
Perry, ___ (Rev.); ___; Fairport, CT?; 1843; 1
Perry, Elisha G. (Rev.); ___; Oxford; 1842-44; 9
Perry, Marcus A. (Rev.); St. Paul's Church; Utica; 1844-50; 10
Pettee, A. E., Esq.; Paris FurnaCE, NY; 1846; 2
Pettengill. See Pattengill.
Pettibone, Ira (Rev.); Presby. Church; New York Mills; 1843-44; 3
Pew, B., Esq.; Corning-Painted Post area; 1848-50; 6
Phelps, E. (Rev.); ___; Geneva; 1830-35; 34
Phillips, ___ (Rev.); ___; Utica?; 1845; 1
Phillips, B. (Rev.); ___; Baldwinsville; 1847-48; 5
Phillips, D. J. (Elder); ___; Utica?; 1846; 1
Phoebus, ___ (Rev.); ___; NYC?; 1830; 1
Pickard, ___ (Rev.); ___; Rushville?; 1835; 1
Pickering, David (Rev.); ___; Lowville; 1842; 1
Pierson, J. (Rev.); ___; Corning?; 1848; 2
Pike, Samuel, Esq.; Norwich?; 1823; 1
Pinney, ___ (Rev.); ___; Camillus?; 1850; 1
Piper, John (Rev.); ___; New Orleans, LA; 1847; 1
Pitcher, ___ (Rev.); ___; Herkimer?; 1833; 1
Platt, A. W. (Rev.); ___; Fayette; 1834 and 1835; 2
Platt, Adams W. (Rev.); ___; Whitesboro; 1824; 1
Platt, C. F., Esq.; Painted Post?; 1849; 1
Platt, Dennis (Rev.); ___; Homer-Manlius area; 1837-45; 3
Platt, I. W. (Rev.); ___; Bath; 1831 and 1832; 2
Plumb, David (Rev.); ___; Utica; 1835-45; 6
Polhemus, ___ (Rev.); ___; Fishkill; 1848; 1
Pomeroy, ___ (Rev.); ___; Cayuga?; 1845; 1
Porter, Charles S. (Rev.); First Presby. Church; Utica; 1842-43; 6
Porter, James (Rev.); ___; Worcester, MA?; 1848; 1
Potter, ___ (Rev.); ___; Elkland?; 1848; 1
Potter, ___ (Rev.); ___; Jerusalem; 1834; 1
Potter, ___ (Rt. Rev. Bishop); Trinity Church; NYC; 1849; 1
Potter, ___ (Rev. Dr.); ___; Utica?; 1842; 1
Potter, Horatio (Rev.); rector, St. Peter's Church (Episc.); Albany; 1847-50; 5
Potter, Job (Rev.); ___; Cooperstown?; 1833; 1
Potter, John (Rev.); ___; Marshall?; 1844; 1
Pound, Jesse (Rev.); ___; Manlius; 1836; 1
Pound, Jesse (Rev.); Zion Church; Plamyra; 1833; 1
Powel, ___ (Rev.); ___; Russia, NY; 1844; 1
Powell, ___ (Rev.); ___; Chittenango; 1833; 1
Powell, Elijah, Esq.; Pharsalia; 1823; 1
Pratt, ___ (Rev.); ___; North Gage?; 1849; 1
Pratt, B. F. (Rev.); ___; Painted Post?; 1849; 1
Pratt, B. Foster (Rev.); ___; New York Mills?; 1849; 1
Pratt, E. (Rev.); ___; Chemung; 1840; 2
Pratt, N. A. (Rev.); ___; Roswell, GA; 1850; 1
Pratt, R. (Rev.); ___; Kirkland?; 1845; 1
Prentiss, ___ (Rev.); ___; Catskill?; 1823; 1
Preston, ___ (Rev.); ___; Savannah, NY?; 1833; 1
Prevost, A. P. (Rev.); ___; Canandaigua?; 1838 and 1839; 2
Price, Joseph H. (Rev.); St. Stephen's Church; NYC; 1845 and 1850; 2
Prince, Noble (Elder); ___; Caton; 1848 and 1850; 2

Pritchett, ___ (Rev.); ___; Utica?; 1850; 1
Pritchett, E. C. (Rev.); ___; Rome-Oriskany area; 1848 and 1849; 2
Proal, ___ (Rev. Dr.); ___; Schuyler?; 1848; 1
Proal, H. A. (Rev.); ___; Utica; 1842; 1
Proal, P. Alexis (Rev.); rector, St. George's Church; Schenectady; 1823-32; 3
Proal, Pierre A. (Rev.); rector, Trinity Church, Utica; 1839-50; 51
Punch, ___ (Rev.); London, England?; 1846; 1
Purns, ___ (Rev.); ___; Utica?; 1842; 1
Purple, Thomas S. (Rev.?); ___; Smithville; 1842; 2
Purrington, W. F. (Rev.); ___; Montezuma?; 1846; 1
Putnam, ___ (Rev.); ___; Cazenovia-Morrisville area; 1843-47; 3
Pyne, ___ (Rev.); ___; Washington, D.C.; 1850; 1
Quail, ___ (Rev.); ___; Utica?; 1844; 1
R___van, Jesse R. (Rev.); ___; Hamilton?; 1848; 1
Ralph, William (Rev.); ___; Trenton; 1850; 2
Ramsey, Samuel (Rev.); ___; Clinton; 1848; 3
Rand, William W; (Rev.); ___; Canastota?; 1844; 1
Randall, Charles (Rev.); ___; Clockville and Brookfield; 1838 and 1846; 2
Randall, Jedediah (Elder); ___; Norwich; 1819-30; 9
Ransom, ___ (Rev.); ___; Cherry Valley?; 1849; 1
Ransom, E. (Rev.); ___; Verona?; 1832; 1
Ransom, J. C. (Rev.); Grace Church; Oxford and Mount Upton; 1842 and 1844; 2
Rasco, J. H. (Rev.); ___; Oceola, Livingston Co., MI; 1850; 1
Rathbun, Ransom, Esq.; Oxford?; 1814; 1
Rawson, ___ (Elder); ___; Utica?; 1845; 1
Raymond, ___ (Rev.); ___; NYC; 1850; 1
Raymond, R. R. (Rev.); ___; Syracuse?; 1849; 1
Raymond, Robert R. (Rev.); Morristown; 1849; 1
Raymond, S. (Rev.); ___; Westmoreland?; 1830 and 1847; 2
Raymond, S. W. (Rev.); ___; Kirkland; 1849-50; 4
Raymond, W. (Rev.); ___; Marshall?; 1845; 1
Read, D. (Rev.); ___; _?_; 1849; 1
Redfield, ___ (Rev.); ___; Cazenovia; 1843; 1
Redfield, ___ (Rev.); ___; Columbus, Chenango Co.; 1847; 1
Reed, Fitch (Rev.); ___; Sharon, CT?; 1843; 1
Reed, V. D. (Rev.); ___; Stillwater?; 1842; 1
Renouf, E. A. (Rev.); ___; Lowville; 1848 and 1849; 2
Rexford, E. S. (Rev.); ___; Norwich; 1828-29; 4
Rexford, Lyman (Rev.); ___; Sherburne?; 1842; 1
Reynolds, E. L. (Elder); ___; Ionia and Van Buren; 1847; 2
Rhoton, Josiah (Rev.); ___; Hawkins County, TN; 1847; 1
Rice, Caleb (Rev.); ___; Phelps; 1831; 1
Rice, L. (Rev.); ___; Brownville?; 1850; 1
Richards, James (Rev.); ___; Penn Yan?; 1846; 1
Richards, William (Rev.); ___; Hamilton?; 1847; 1
Riggs, George, Esq.; Westernville; 1847; 1
Riggs, J. I. (Rev.); ___; Wells, PA; 1850; 1
Robbins, ___ (Rev.); ___; Enfield?; 1845; 1
Robbins, Jacob, Esq.; Caton?; 1842; 1
Roberts, ___ (Rev.); ___; Utica; 1842; 1
Roberts, J. (Rev.); ___; Fairhaven, MA?; 1847; 1
Robinson, ___ (Rev.); ___; Stark?; 1844; 1
Robinson, D. (Rev.); ___; Vernon-Verona area; 1842; 2
Rockwell, A. F. (Elder); ___; Deerfield and Westmoreland; 1844; 2
Rockwell, Job, Esq.; ___; German, NY; 1826; 1
Rockwell, T. B. (Rev.); ___; Vernon?; 1850; 1
Rodgers, ___ (Rev.); ___; Le Roy?; 1831; 1
Roe, ___, Esq.; Arcadia; 1831; 1
Roe, ___ (Elder); ___; Manchester?; 1839; 1
Roffe, ___ (Rev.); ___; Washington, D.C.?; 1846; 1
Rogers, ___ (Rev.); ___; North Hampton?; 1846; 1
Rogers, Charles W., Esq.; Lorraine, Jefferson County; 1847; 1
Rogers, H. W., Esq.; Bath?; 1832; 1
Rogers, T. (Rev.); ___; Bernardston, MA; 1844; 1
Rollinson, William (Rev.); ___; Racine, WI?; 1850; 1

Roosevelt, Washington (Rev.); ___; Lockport; 1850; 1
Rose, Amasa, Esq.; Deerfield?; 1826; 1
Rosekrants, Joseph (Rev.); ___; Deerfield; 1846; 2
Rounds, ___ (Rev.); ___; Cazenovia; 1836; 1
Rounds, ___ (Rev.); ___; New York Mills; 1850; 1
Rouse, ___ (Rev.); ___; Duanesburg; 1827; 1
Rouse, Oliver, Esq.; Corning; 1841; 1
Row, H. F. (Rev.); ___; Utica-Lee area; 1844-50; 5
Rowlands, W. (Rev.); ___; Utica area; 1843-44; 4
Rudd, ___ (Rev. Dr.); ___; Auburn; 1829-33; 4
Rudd, ___ (Rev. Dr.); ___; Rochester; 1831; 1
Rudd, ___ (Rev.); ___; Utica?; 1847; 1
Rudd, J. C. (Rev.); ___; Manlius?; 1847; 1
Rumph, A. (Rev.); ___; St. Johnsville?; 1848; 1
Runsted, L. (Rev.); ___; Canandaigua?; 1839; 1
Ryant, Homer, Esq.; Horseheads; 1849; 1
Sacket, ___ (Rev.); ___; Groton; 1848; 1
Salmon, Thomas (Rev.); ___; Trenton; 1844; 1
Salmon, W. (Rev.); ___; Trenton; 1844; 1
Sandel, John (Rev.)?; ___; Terrebone Parish, LA; 1849; 1
Sawyer, J. (Rev.); ___; New Hartford?; 1846; 1
Sawyer, T. J. (Rev.); ___; Clinton and Westmoreland; 1846 and 1848; 2
Sayres, Gilbert H. (Rev.); ___; Brooklyn; 1845; 1
Schutt, J., Esq.; Phelps; 1832; 1
Schwenninger, Florian (Rev.)?; ___; Utica; 1848; 1
Schwininger, S. (Rev.); ___; Utica; 1848; 1
Scovil, Ezra (Rev.); ___; Mexico, NY?; 1848; 1
Scoville, J. F. (Rev.); ___; Holland Patent?; 1846-48; 3
Scoville, S. (Rev.); ___; Floyd-Trenton area; 1845; 2
Seabury, ___ (Rev.); Trinity Church; Geneva; 1835; 1
Seabury, ___ (Rev.Dr.); ___; NYC; 1845; 1
Seaman, ___ (Rev.); ___; Big Flats?; 1844; 1
Searle, Moses C. (Rev.); ___; New Hartford?; 1842-44; 4
Sear, ___ (Prof. and Rev.); ___; Hamilton; 1831; 1
Sears, ___ (Rev.); ___; Ithaca; 1831; 1
Sears, John (Elder); ___; Geneva; 1835; 5
Seaver, H. N. (Rev.); Methodist church, Elmira and Methodist Church, Corning;
    1848-50; 25
Selkirk, Edward (Rev.); ___; Albany; 1848; 1
Selmer, J. (Rev.); ___; Dansville?; 1848; 1
Seward, ___ (Elder); ___: Durhamville; 1849; 1
Seward, J. C. (Rev.); ___; Lysander; 1849-50; 3
Shanklin, J. A. (Rev.); ___; Nassau County, FL?; 1845; 1
Sharp, ___ (Rev.); ___; Boston (state not given); 1825; 1
Shaw, ___ (Rev.); ___; New Hartford?; 1821; 1
Shaw, J. (Rev.); ___; Millport; 1850; 1
Sheardown, ___ (Rev.); ___; Reading; 1849; 1
Shearer, S. B. (Rev.); ___; Corning; 1848; 1
Shekell, Cephas, Esq.; GenevA?; 1828-30; 4
Shelden, C. F. (Rev.); ___; Utica; 1843; 1
Shelden, C. P. (Rev.); ___; Whitestown?; 1842; 1
Shelton, William (Rev.); St. Paul's Church; Buffalo; 1835-39; 3
Shepard, D. A. (Rev.); ___; Auburn and Utica; 1841-47; 12
Shepard, L. M. (Rev.); ___; North Adams (state not given); 1846; 1
Shepard, L. M. (Rev.); ___; Smithville?; 1846; 1
Sherman, James B. (Rev.); ___; New Berlin; 1828; 1
Sherrill, Henry E., Esq.; New Hartford; 1844-47; 9
Sherwood, E. R. (Rev.); ___; Liverpool-Van Buren area; 1846-49; 3
Sherwood, Isaac, Esq.; Oxford; 1817 and 1818; 2
Shimeall, R. C. (Rev.); St. John's Church; Canandaigua; 1835; 1
Shipman, C. L. (Rev.); ___; Columbus Center, Chenango Co.; 1848 and 1849; 2
Sholl, W. N. (Rev.); ___; Canajoharie; 1849; 1
Shortwell, ___ (Rev.); ___; Whitesboro?; 1849; 1
Shumway, G. R. H. (Rev.); ___; Palmyra; 1834-35; 3
Simmons, Charles (Rev.); ___; Manchester?; 1842; 1

295

Skinner, ___ (Rev.); ___; Herkimer: 1843; 1
Skinner, ___ (Elder); ___; Perryville?; 1836; 1
Skinner, A. D. (Rev.); ___ ; Schuyler; 1845; 1
Skinner, Dolphus; ___; Utica area and Unitarian Church, Holland Patent; 1843-50; 15
Skinner, F. A. (Rev.); ___; Westmoreland; 1845; 1
Skinner, H. C. (Elder); ___; Fenner; 1836; 1
Slingerland, ___ (Rev.); ___; New Paltz; 1850; 1
Slingerland, E. (Rev.); ___; Chittenango; 1833-34; 4
Smedes, ___ (Rev.); ___; Schenectady?; 1837; 1
Smith, ___ (Rev.); St. James Church; Batavia; 1833; 1
Smith, ___ (Rev.); ___; Campbell?; 1840; 1
Smith, ___ (Rev.); ___; Chittenango; 1832; 1
Smith, ___ (Rev.); ___; Fayetteville, 1836; 1
Smith, ___ (Rev.); ___; Paris, NY?; 1832; 1
Smith, ___ (President of Princeton College, Princeton, NJ and Rev.); ___ ; 1818; 1
Smith, ___ (Rev.); ___; Seneca; 1830 and 1831; 2
Smith, ___ (Rev.); ___; Smithfield?; 1831; 1
Smith, A. P. (Rev.); ___; Vienna?; 1847; 1
Smith, Albert P. (Rev.); St. Luke's Church; Cazenovia; _?_; 1
Smith, David (Rev. Dr.); ___; NYC; 1833; 1
Smith, F., Esq.; Palmyra; 1834; 1
Smith, H., Esq.; ___; Tioga, PA?; 1848; 1
Smith, James (Rev.); ___; _?_; 1850; 1
Smith, John (Rev.); ___; Hartwick?; 1817; 1
Smith, John (Rev.); ___; Painted Post?; 1840; 1
Smith, M., Esq.; Trumansburgh?; 1837; 1
Smith, N. S. (Rev.); ___; Chittenango?; 1832; 1
Smith, Orr, Esq.; Wells, Bradford County, PA; 1849; 1
Smith, Reuben (Rev.); ___ ; Waterford?; 1845; 2
Smith, Richard (Rev.); ___; Corning?; 1842; 1
Smith, S. R. (Rev.); ___; Clinton; 1835; 1
Smith, Samuel A. (Elder); ___; Guilford?; 1818 and 1824; 2
Smith, Thomas, Esq.; Phelps?; 1832; 1
Smith, W. (Rev.); ___; Sugar Grove, KY; 1844; 1
Smitzer, ___ (Elder); ___; Delphi; 1832 and 1833; 2
Smitzer, J. (Elder); ___; Fayetteville?; 1840-41; 3
Smitzer, J. (Rev.); ___; Van Buren; 1847; 1
Snow, ___ (Rev.); ___; Geneva?; 1835; 1
Snow, ___ (Rev.); ___; Syracuse?; 1850; 1
Snow, James, Esq.; Vienna, NY; 1832; 2
Snyder, H. S. (Rev.); ___; Chittenango; 1833; 3
Sommers, C. G. (Rev.); ___; NYC; 1835 and 1839; 2
Soule, S. B. (Rev.); ___; Utica?; 1843; 1
Southwark, J. R. (Rev.); ___; West Addison; 1850; 1
Spalding, Silas (Rev.); ___; Pawtucket, RI?; 1842; 1
Spaulding, ___ (Rev.); ___; Lenox?; 1832; 1
Spaulding, ___ (Rev.); ___; Norwich?; 1822 and 1823; 2
Spaulding, ___ (Rev.); ___; Phelps; 1838; 1
Spaulding, T. S., Esq.; Elmira?; 1848; 1
Spencer, C. H. (Rev.); ___; Kanawha, Salines, VA; 1832; 1
Spencer, F. A. (Rev.); ___; Westmoreland; 1843-49; 23
Spencer, Theodore (Rev.); ___; Utica; 1842-45; 8
Spencer, William H. (Rev.); ___; Houseville; 1823; 1
Spencer, William H. (Rev.); ___; Utica; 1846-50; 47
Sperry, Lyman (Rev.); ___; Oxford, Norwich, Cazenovia, Unadilla; 1842-50; 11
Spock, S. G. (Rev.); ___; Delhi; 1842; 1
Sprague, ___ (Rev. Dr.); ___; Albany?; 1831-43; 3
Spratt, George M. (Rev.); ___; Elmira area; 1848-50; 13
Squier, M. P. (Rev.); ___; Geneva?; 1831; 1
Squires, ___ (Rev.); Methodist Church; Baldwinsville; 1849; 1
Stafford, ___ (Rev.); ___; NYC?; 1825; 1
Stanley, ___ (Rev.); ___; Smithfield: 1841: 1
Stanley, L. H. (Rev.); ___; Perryville; 1844; 2
Stansbury, Arthur J. (Rev.); ___; NYC?; 1819; 1

Stanton, ___ (Rev.); ___; Binghamton?; 1842 and 1843; 2
Stanton, B. F. (Rev.); ___; Hudson?; 1818; 1
Stanton, F. H. (Rev.); ___; Rome, NY; 1849; 1
Staple, O. H. (Rev.); ___; Hampton?; 1847; 1
Staples, ___ (Rev.); ___; Utica; 1847; 1
Starkey, ___ (Rev.); ___; Canastota; 1843; 1
Stearns, John (Rev.); ___; Brooklyn?; 1850; 1
Steele, ___ (Rev.); ___; Ballston?; 1850; 1
Steele, Allen (Rev.); ___; Jerusalem?; 1839; 1
Stevens, ___ (Rev.); ___; Akron, OH?; 1848; 1
Stevens, ___ (Rev.); ___; Vienna, NY; 1825; 1
Steves, John W. (Rev.); ___; Camillus; 1846; 1
Stewart, C. S. (Rev.); ___; Cooperstown; 1849; 1
Stickney, ___ (Rev.); ___; Verona?; 1847; 1
Stickney, Washington (Rev.); ___; Canastota; 1846; 1
Stillman, D., Esq.; Rome, NY; 1847; 1
Stillwell, H. P. (Rev.); ___; Damascus, Henry Co., OH; 1846; 1
Stocking, ___ (Rev.); ___; Sauquoit?; 1845; 2
Stockton, ___ (Rev.); ___; Pompey; 1831; 1
Stokes, ___ (Rev.); ___; Canastota; 1842; 1
Stokes, Joseph (Rev.); St. John's (Catholic?) Church, Utica and St. Thomas Church,
    Utica; 1847-50; 9
Stone, ___ (Rev.); ___; Brooklyn; 1845; 1
Stone, Benjamin W. (Rev.); St. Paul's Church; Oxford; 1847 and 1848; 2
Stone. M. (Rev.); ___; Norwich; 1849; 4
Storer, J. P. B. (Rev.); ___; Syracuse; 1842-44; 6
Strickney, Washington (Rev.); ___; Sullivan; 1849; 1
Strong, ___ (Rev.); ___; Phelps; 1831-33; 3
Strong, Thomas (Rev.); ___; Flatbush, L. I., NY; 1831; 1
Strong, William (Rev.); ___; Fayetteville; 1845; 1
Stryker, Isaac P. (Rev.); ___; Vernon?; 1848; 1
Stryker, Peter (Rev.); ___; Bellona?; 1835; 1
Swart, ___ (Rev.); Missionary of the Episc. Church; Jordan, NY; 1843; 1
Swick, B. R. (Rev.); ___; Bath; 1850; 1
Switzer, ___ (Rev.); ___; Sullivan?; 1840; 1
Symmes, ___ (Rev.); ___; Lansingburgh; 1842; 1
Taggart, J. W. (Rev.); ___; De Witt, Manlius, Syracuse area; 1838-45; 3
Tappan, John (Rev.); ___; Bath; 1843; 1
Taylor, ___ (Rev. Dr.); ___; New Haven, CT?; 1831; 1
Taylor, ___ (Rev. Dr.); ___; NYC; 1846 and 1850; 2
Taylor, ___ (Rev.); ___; Salina; 1836; 1
Taylor, B. C. (Rev.); ___; Bergen, NJ; 1831; 1
Taylor, E. T. (Rev.); ___; Boston, MA?; 1850; 1
Taylor, Nathan, Esq.; Butternuts and New Berlin; 1822; 2
Thacher, ___ (Rev.); ___; Sangerfield?; 1846; 1
Thacher, W. (Rev.); ___; Oriskany Falls; 1848; 1
Thibon, ___ (Rev.); ___; Angelica?; 1831; 1
Thomas, C. D., Esq.; Hornby; 1849; 2
Thomas, Eleazer (Rev.); ___; Hume?; 1849; 1
Thomas, H. (Elder); ___; Little Falls; ? ; 1
Thompson, ___ (Rev. Dr.); ___; Buffalo; 1850; 1
Thompson, ___ (Rev.); ___; Canandaigua; 1837 and 1839; 2
Thompson, A. (Elder); ___; Utica?; 1848; 1
Thompson, G. W. (Rev.); ___; ? ; 1841; 1
Thompson, James, Esq.; Norwich?; 1819; 1
Thompson, James P. (Rev.); ___; NYC; 1850; 1
Thompson, William (Rev.); ___; Clinton; 1845; 1
Thorne, I. C., Esq.; Taberg?; 1850; 1
Thorp, Charles (Rev.); ___; Oxford-Coventry area; 1814-20; 4
Thurston, C. (Rev.); ___; Athens, PA; 1850; 1
Thuston, ___ (Rev.); ___; Hallowell?; 1847; 1
Tillinghast, W. (Elder); ___; New Bedford, MA?; 1847; 1
Timlow, ___ (Rev.); ___; New Milford; 1846; 1
Todd. ___ (Rev.); ___; Benton; 1830; 2
Todd, ___ (Rev.); ___; Dresden; 1831 and 1832; 2

297

Todd, Isaac (Rev.); ___; Spencerville?; 1850; 1
Tolles, Russel G. (Rev.?); ___; Frankfort; 1849 and 1850; 2
Tomlinson, ___ (Rev.); ___; Mystic, L. I., NY; 1845; 1
Tomlinson, D. C. (Rev.); ___; Richfield Springs; 1847; 1
Tompkins, J. (Rev.); ___; Marcellus?; 1846; 1
Tompkins, William E. (Rev.); ___; Oneida Castle; _?_; 1
Tooker, ___ (Rev.); ___; Catlin?; 1830; 1
Tooker, Manly (Rev.); ___; Big Flats and Geneva; 1834-46; 4
Topping, S. (Rev.); ___; Seneca?; 1846; 1
Torrey, J. D. (Rev.); ___; Marshall and Oneida; 1846 and 1850; 2
Tourney, Edmund (Rev.); ___; _?_; 1850; 1
Towell, Thomas (Rev.); ___; Sherburne; 1841; 1
Towner, ___ (Elder); ___; Norway, NY; 1846; 1
Townsend, ___ (Rev.); ___; Waterloo?; 1839; 1
Townsend, E. G. (Rev.); ___; Camden?; 1845 and 1850; 2
Townsend, R. (Rev.); Newark, NY; 1839; 1
Tracy, Frederick, Esq.; Lee Center; 1850; 1
Tracy. Lorenzo L., Esq.; Dix?; 1849; 1
Tredway, A. (Rev.); ___; Robisonville; 1825; 1
Tripp, W. W., Esq.; Geddes; 1846; 1
Tucker, J. N. T. (Rev.); ___; Fenner?; 1837; 1
Tucker, ___ (Rev.); ___; Millburne, Columbia County; 1847; 1
Tucker, John J. (Rev.); Church of the Holy Cross; Troy; 1831 and 1846; 2
Tucker, Norman (Rev.); ___; Troy?; 1843; 1
Tulley, A. (Rev.); ___; Utica?; 1850; 1
Tullidge, ___ (Rev.); ___; Erie, PA; 1842; 1
Turner, ___ (Rev.); ___; Utica; 1848; 1
Turney, ___ (Rev.); ___; Westmoreland?; 1850; 1
Tuthill, ___ (Rev.); ___; Sherburne?; 1846; 1
Tuttle, ___ (Rev.); ___; Boonville?; 1849; 1
Tuttle, A. C. (Rev.); ___; FaYETTEVILLE AND Sherburne; 1838-50; 6
Tuttle, Oliver (Rev.); ___; New Hartford; 1847 and 1850; 2
Tyler, P. (Rev.); ___; Lowville; 1850; 1
Van Alstyne, D. (Rev.); ___; McHenry Co., OH; 1844; 1
Vandemark J., Esq.; Alloway?; 1832; 1
Van Ingen, ___ (Rev.); ___; Greene; 1842; 1
Van Ingen, ___ (Rev. Dr.); ___; Rochester?; 1847; 1
Van Kleeck, ___ (Rev.); ___; Troy; 1850; 1
Van Kleeck, R. B. (Rev.); ___; _?_; 1850; 1
Van Olinda, Douw (Rev.); ___; Mohawk?; 1850; 1
Van Santvoord, ___ (Rev.); ___; Lenox?; 1839; 1
Van Vechten, J. (Rev.); ___; Schenectady; 1833 and 1846; 2
Van Vranken, Nicholas (Rev.); ___; Fishkill; 1830; 1
Varela, ___ (Rev.); Christ church; town not given; 1831; 1
Vermilye, ___ (Rev. Dr.); ___; Albany?; 1847; 1
Vermilye, ___ (Rev. Dr.); ___; NYC; 1850; 1
Vermilyn, R. G. (Rev.); ___; Clinton?; 1849; 1
Vinton, Francis (Rev.); ___; NYC; 1849; 1
Vogell, H. C., Esq.; Utica-Floyd area; 1850; 4
Vogell, H. C. (Rev.); ___; Rome, NY; 1850; 6
Wack, Charles P. (Rev.); ___; Bellona; 1833-34; 3
Wadsworth, ___ (Rev.); ___; Manlius?; 1841; 1
Wadsworth, Charles (Rev.); ___; Westford?; 1849; 1
Wadsworth, E. L. (Rev.); ___; Nelson?; 1840; 1
Wagar, J. E. (Rev.); ___; Bethel?; 1835; 1
Wagener, A. (Elder); ___; Penn Yan?; 1831; 1
Wagoner, ___ (Rev.); ___; Van Buren; 1848; 1
Waight, John (Rev.); ___; Paris, NY; 1847; 1
Wainright, ___ (Rev. Dr.); ___; NYC; 1838 and 1850; 2
Wait, J., Jr.; Esq.; Binghamton?; 1839; 1
Wait, Wells, Esq.; Preston?; 1828; 1
Walker, H. G. (Hon.); White Springs; 1841; 1
Walker, T. (Rev.); ___; Baldwinsville; 1832-50; 35
Ward, ___ (Rev.); ___; Utica?; 1844; 1
Ward, J. J. (Rev.); ___; Camillus; 1833; 1

Ward, Norton, Esq.; Marcy?; 1849; 1
Warner, ___; Rev.; ___; Bainbridge?; 1842; 1
Warner, ___ (Judge); Syracuse?; 1837; 1
Warner, H. (Rev.); ___; Schroepel?; 1849; 1
Warner, Ulysses, Esq.; Phelps?; 1835; 1
Warren, Horace (Rev.); ___; Perth; 1848; 1
Warren J. C. (Rev.); ___; Troy; 1849; 1
Washburn, D. (Rev.); St. Luke's Church; Philadelphia, PA; 1849; 1
Waterbury, ___ (Rev.); ___; Franklin; 1829; 1
Waters, ___ (Rev.); ___; Paris, NY; 1826; 1
Waters, ___ (Rev.); ___; Trenton; 1824; 1
Waters, George (Rev.); ___; Delhi; 1844; 1
Waters, R., Esq.; Coventry?; 1827; 1
Watson, J. (Rev.); ___; Chittenango Falls?; 1841' 1
Waugh, John (Rev.); ___; Sauquoit; 1844-50; 27
Wayland, Francis (Rev.); ___; Saratoga Springs; 1848; 1
Webb, James, Esq.; Ridgebury, PA; 1850; 1
Weed, B. (Rev.); ___; New Hartford?; 1843; 1
Weed, T. A. (Rev.); ___; Mexico, NY; 1850; 1
Welch, B. T. (Rev. Dr.); ___; Albany; 1842-48; 4
Welles, ___ (Rev.); ___; Remsen; 1846; 1
Wells, ___ (Rev.); ___; Guilford?; 1829; 1
Wells, A.)Rev.); ___; Baldwinsville; 1850; 6
Wells, Abner, Esq.; Wellsburgh?; 1850; 1
Wells, E. D. (Rev.); ___; Oxford; 1825-29; 4
Wells, J. (Rev.); ___; Brookfield; 1841; 2
Wells, Samuel (Rev.); ___; Oriskany; 1843; 1
Wells, William (Elder); ___; North Gage; 1848; 1
Wescott, E. (Rev.); ___; Bovina?; 1843; 1
Wetmore, Oliver (Rev.); ___; Utica; 1845; 1
Wetmore, William S., Esq.; Western?; 1844; 1
Wetzel, A. (Rev.); ___; Verona and Utica; 1844 and 1846; 2
Wetzell, M. (Rev.); ___; Rome, NY?; 1844; 1
Wheeler, C. (Rev.); ___; ? ; 1850; 3
Wheeler, C (Rev.); ___; Canandaigua; 1846; 1
Wheeler, C. (Rev.); ___; Caton?; 1850; 1
Wheeler, C. (Rev.); ___; Chemung; 1850; 2
Wheeler, Charles S. (Elder); ___; Voluntown, CT?; 1848; 1
Wheeler, E. (Rev.); St. Paul's Church; Waterloo; 1846; 1
Wheelock, Augustus (Rev.); ___; Lysander; 1850; 1
Whelpley, Samuel W. (Rev.); ___; Waterville; 1843; 1
Whicher, H. (Rev.); ___; Clinton; 1844; 1
Whipple, H. H. (Rev.); ___; Adams?; 1850; 1
Whipple, J., Esq.; Chittenango; 1837; 1
Whipple, J., Jr., Esq.; Perryville?; 1835; 1
Whipple, Otis, Esq.; Utica; 1845-47; 6
Whitaker, H. W. (Rev.); St. John's Church; Clayville; 1850; 1
Whitcher, William (Rev.); ___; Whitesboro; 1849; 1
Whitcomb, David (Rev.); ___; Mulberry Hill; OH; 1846; 1
Whitcomb, L. (Rev.); ___; Mexico, NY; 1850; 1
White, ___ (Rev.); ___; Baldwinsville; 1850; 2
White, John (Rev.); ___; Seneca; 1835 and 1836; 2
White, L. D. (Rev.); ___; Lysander; 1850; 3
White, M. (Rev.); ___; Southampton, MA?; 1850; 1
White, Perry G. (Rev.); ___; Smyrna?; 1847; 1
Whitehouse, ___; Rev. Dr.; ___; Rochester; 1834; 1
Whiting, ___ (Rev.); ___; Corning and Big Flats; 1842; 2
Wicker, B. W. (Rev.); rector, St. John's Church; Whitesboro; 1847; 1
Wickham, J. D. (Rev.); ___; Oxford; 1823-25; 3
Wigent, E. B., Esq.; Van Buren; 1847 and 1848; 2
Wightman, A. S. (Rev.);___; Turin; 1850; 2
Wilcox, ___ (Rev.); ___; Smithville?; 1830; 1
Wilcox, ___ (Rev.); ___; Tioga?; 1843; 1
Wilcox, Ira (Rev.); ___; Greene?; 1843; 1
Wilcox, Morris, Esq.; Whitesboro?; 1850; 1

Wiley, ___ (Rev.); ___; Corning?; 1849; 1
Wiley, Charles (Rev.); Reformed Dutch Church; Utica; 1845-50; 11
Willard, Livingston (Rev.); ___; NYC?; 1850; 1
Willcox, Gates, Esq.; German and Macdonough, NY; 1823 and 1824; 2
Willey, ___ (Rev.); ___; Utica?; 1821; 1
Williams, ___ (Rev.); ___; Antwerp, NY?; 1847; 1
Williams, ___ (Elder); ___; Floyd?; 1842; 1
Williams, ___ (Rev.); ___; Geneva?; 1846; 1
Williams, ___ (Rev.); ___; Waterville; 1850; 1
Williams, Fenwick T. (Rev.?); ___; Utica?; 1844; 1
Williams, Hobart (Rev.); rector, Episcopal Church; New Hartford; 1843; 1
Williams, Morris (Rev.); ___; South Trenton; 1843; 1
Williams, R. Z. (Rev.); ___; ? ; 1843; 1
Williams, T. W. (Rev.?); ___; Camillus; 1848; 1
Williams, W. F. (Rev.); ___; Rome and Yorkville; 1847; 2
Williams, William W. (Rev.); ___; Waterville; 1847-49; 5
Willis, ___ (Rev.); ___; Morrisville?; 1838; 1
Willis, ___ (Rev.); ___; Sullivan?; 1832; 1
Williston, Seth (Rev.); ___; Durham?; 1821; 1
Williston, Seth (Rev.); ___; Oswego?; 1846; 1
Wilson, ___ (Rev. Dr.); Episcopal Church; Sherburne; 1850; 1
Wilson, W. L. (Rev.); ___; North Gage; 1844; 1
Wisner, ___ (Rev.); ___; Boston, NY; 1825; 1
Wisner, ___ (Rev.); ___; Ithaca?; 1849; 2
Witters, ___ (Rev.); ___; Bethel?; 1831; 1
Wood, ___ (Rev.); ___; Brookfield?; 1833; 1
Wood, ___ (Rev.); ___; West Troy?; 1836; 1
Wood, A. A. (Rev.); ___; ? ; 1850; 1
Woodin, P. (Rev.); ___; Conquest?; 1844; 1
Woodley, ___ (Rev.); ___; Winfield?; 1845; 1
Woodruff, ___ (Rev.); ___; Chenango Forks?; 1843; 1
Woodruff, G. C. (Rev.); ___; ? ; 1842; 1
Woodworth, A., Esq.; Benton?; 1832; 1
Woodworth, Abner, Esq.; Benton?; 1830; 1
Woodworth, R., Esq.; Syracuse?; 1850; 1
Wooley, ___ (Rev.); ___; Winfield?; 1844; 1
Wooley, E. M. (Rev.); ___; Cazenovia; 1837-46; 3
Woolworth, R. W., Esq.; Syracuse?; 1847; 1
Wright, Alexander (Rev.); ___; Pittsburgh, PA?; 1843; 1
Wright, B. T. (Rev.); ___; West Martinsburgh?; 1850; 1
Wright, L. (Rev.); ___; Fenner?; 1842 and 1844; 2
Wright, Lewis, Esq.; Vestal; 1842; 1
Wright, Lyman (Rev.); ___; Lenox-Clockville area; 1841-43; 3
Wright, Zenas, Esq.; Utica; 1842-47; 3
Wyatt, William (Rev.); ___; Utica; 1849-50; 26
Wyckoff, ___ (Rev. Dr.); ___; Albany; 1848-50; 4
Wyckoff, C. P. (Rev.); ___; Auburn and Skaneateles; 1830 and 1847; 2
Yates, ___ (Rev.); ___; Brookfield, MA?; 1834; 1
Yates, ___ (Rev. Dr.); ___; Oswego?; 1832; 1
Yates, A. (Rev.); ___; Chittenango; 1831-34; 12
Yates, A. (Rev. Dr.); ___; Schenectady?; 1840; 1
Yates, Andrew (Rev. Dr.); ___; Fultonville?; 1844; 1
Young, ___ (Rev.); ___; Boston, MA; 1849; 1
Young, ___ (Rev.); ___; Romulus?; 1820; 1
Youngs, ___ (Rev.); ___; Painted Post; 1850; 1

(Keyed to entry numbers)

Austin, Julia Ann 8989
Austin, Juliet A. 493
Austin, Margaret (Mrs.) 9650
Austin, Maria L. 6455
Austin, Mary Ann 5830
Austin, Susan 8696
Austin, Susanna 8644
Austin, William 211
Autremont, Jennet D. 8060
Averil, Amanda 8051
Averill, Juliaette 8674
Averill, Mary J. 7351
Averille, Sarah 268
Avery, Abigail (Mrs.) 8429
Avery, Charles 9743
Avery, Daniel 174
Avery, Delia Augusta 9743
Avery, Esther 4805
Avery, J. H. (Col.) 220
Avery, Lydia 174
Avery, Sally C. 6321
Avery, Susan 8759
Axtell, ___ (Rev.) 4096
Axtell, ___ (Rev. Dr.) 228
Axtell, Harriet H. 4096
Ayers, Alvah 9354
Ayers, Mary E. 9354
Ayres, Elizabeth 3130
Ayres, Maria 9934
Ayres, Nathaniel 3130
Babbins, Jane 6690
Babbit, Miller 531
Babbott, Cornelia C. 532
Babbott, Miller 532
Babcock, B. 9574
Babcock, Charles 12
Babcock, Charlotte 9796
Babcock, Denison 5884
Babcock, Desire E. 5884
Babcock, Dorcas 9180
Babcock, Julia 8382
Babcock, Julia Ann 2254
Babcock, Martha 8277
Babcock, Mary C. 12
Backus, ___ (Dr.) 1184
Backus, ___ (Rev. Dr.) 253
Backus, Charles C. 255
Backus, Elisha 2079
Backus, F. F. (Mr.) 1016
Backus, F. F. (Dr.) 1184
Backus, Harriet N. 255
Backus, Jane J. 2079
Backus, Jeanette E. 1182
Backus, John 260
Backus, Weltha 1016
Backus, William 1182
Backus, William W. 1149
Bacon, ___ (Wid.) 264
Bacon, Charles C. 271, 272
Bacon, Ellen 3737
Bacon, Eloisa T. 4895
Bacon, James 278
Bacon, John H. 3737
Bacon, Marietta E. 1724
Bacon, R. E. (Mr.) 9744
Bacon, Rebekah 3549
Bacon, Reuben 1724
Bacon, Rufus 279
Bacon, William 4895
Bacon, William J. 5080
Badger, H. E. 281
Badgley, Elizabeth 8126
Bagg, ___ (Mr.) 5406
Bagg, H. A. (Miss) 1347
Bail, Lisette Regina 4197
Bailey, Amanda 9483
Bailey, Ann 6594
Bailey, B. P. (Mr.)298

Bsiley, Cornelia H. 441
Bailey, Emily 6081
Bailey, Frances M. 296
Bailey, Helen E. 674
Bailey, J. P. 308
Bailey, Joanna 7773
Bailey, Joel C. 9483
Bailey, Louis 299
Bailey, Martha M. 4229
Bailey, Moses 296
Bailey, Olive 3429
Bailey, Samuel 300
Bailey, Sarah A. 9008
Bailey, Theresa N. 727
Bailey, Welsey 301
Bailey, William H. 310
Bain, Mary Ann 2440
Bainbridge, ___ (Commodore) 317
Baker, Author 337
Baker, Azobia E. 9066
Baker, Catharine M. 800
Baker, Charity 6995
Baker, Harriet (Mrs.) 322
Baker, Hiram 323, 330
Baker, John 332
Baker, Laura A. 323, 330
Baker, Lavina 9026
Baker, Marianna 284
Baker, Mary 9838
Baker, Mary Jane 715
Baker, Samuel 800
Baker, Sarah Jane 343
Balch, ___ (Mr.) 2532
Balch, V. A. (Mr.) 345
Balcom, Eliza 6706
Balcom, Fayett 1919
Balcom, Francis 349, 351
Balcom, H. (Mr.) 346
Balcom, Lyman 3885
Balcom, Mary E. 3885
Balcom, Samuel 6706
Baldwin, Ann Eliza 7073
Baldwin, Betsey 3221
Baldwin, Charles 354
Baldwin, Charles N. 365
Baldwin, Cynthia 9101
Baldwin, Daniel 374
Baldwin, Electa 4228
Baldwin, Eliza 8466, 9326
Baldwin, G. B. (Mr.) 373
Baldwin, Grant B. 371
Baldwin, Harriet 9575
Baldwin, Martha 4980
Baldwin, Simeon 363
Baldwin, William 370
Baley, Juliaette 3327
Ball, A. L. (Dr.) 522
Ball, Jane W. 522
Ball, Martha S. 799
Ball, Samuel R. 383
Ballard, Margaret7585
Ballard, Mary P. 6124
Ballard, William 6124
Ballou, Benjamin 392
Ballou, Julietta 7560
Baltsley, Sally 5109
Bancroft, Caroline A. 9501
Baneer, Eliza 8569
Bangs, ___ (Mr.) 6910
Banks, ___ (Mr.) 3576
Banks, David 8982
Banks, Jenney 8982
Barbarin, Caroline M. 2020
Barber, ___ (Mr.) 8739
Barber, A. H. (Mr.) 414
Barber, Almira 2132
Barber, Cynthia N. 6997
Barber, Lucy 622

Barber, Margaret 414
Barber, Mary Ann 419
Barber, Matilda 9076
Barber, Milo G. 415, 419
Barber, Thirza 7932
Barber, William 7601
Bardwell, M. (Rev.) 5103
Barker, Charlotte 4723
Barker, Elizabeth H. 4738
Barker, J. G. (Dr.) 5738
Barker, Lucy M. 2000
Barker, Lydia C. 5738
Barker, Newman 433
Barker, Sarah M. 8269
Barkerloo, Harmanus 8492
Barlow, Abner 3621
Barlow, Jonathan 444
Barlow, William 448
Barmore, Hannah (Mrs.) 5162
Barnard, Edward 456
Barnard, Elizabeth 341
Barnard, Eugenia Adelaide 294
Barnard, Harvey 455
Barnard, Hervey 8355
Barnard, Laura A. 9801
Barnard, Moses 456
Barnard, Phebe A. 9138
Barnes, ___ (Judge) 462
Barnes, Abby E. 2046
Barnes, Albert 463
Barnes, Celistia 8612
Barnes, Charlotte S. 6394
Barnes, David M.
Barnes, Emma 9054
Barnes, Enos 472
Barnes, Harriet F. 3249
Barnes, Hellen L. 3656
Barnes, Joseph 464, 471
Barnes, Julia Ann 148
Barnes, Loania J. 9063
Barnes, Lydia 5704
Barnes, Minerva 4687
Barnes, Rufus 463
Barnes, Thomas 9054
Barney, Celestine M. 6465
Barney, Sarah J. 660
Barney, Throop 660
Barnhart, Eliza W. 5112
Barns, Erastus 483
Barns, Laura 4507
Barnum, Caleb 486
Barnum, Caroline (Mrs.) 3935
Barnum, E. R. (Col.) 3935
Barnum, E. S. (Mr.) 494, 3519
Barnum, Egbert W. 487
Barnum, Henry 489
Barnum, Jane 3519
Barnum, Johannah 489
Barnum, Olive 9689
Barr, Hannah M. 3671
Barrett, Eliza I. 4604
Barrett, H. (widow) 501
Barrett, Harriet 3639
Barrett, Jane M. 4329
Barrett, Mary J. 2975
Barrett, William 498
Barrick, Hannah 9313
Barrit, Alice 5436
Barron, Fletcher J. 508
Barrows, ___ (Dr.) 911
Barrows, F. F. (Mr.) 511
Barry, Jane 5966
Barse, Lovina 6032
Bartholomew, Cornelia 7990
Bartholomew. Oliver 7990
Bartle, Amelia Malvina 8830
Bartle, Emarilla 5006
Bartle, Lambert 8829

302

Bartle, Melissa 3880
Bartle, Nancy Jane 8244
Bartle, Sally 8394
Bartle, Sarah Maria 6034
Bartlett, Caroline 818
Bartlett, Nancy 8613
Bartlett, Nancy A. 7590
Barton, Benjamin 8728
Barton, Delaner 6100
Barton, Eliza 7505
Barton, Wmily 2611
Barton, Jane 5096
Bascom, Ansel 533
Bascom, E. H. (Mr.) 531
Bascom, Elizabeth E. 7750
Baskin, Mary 5236
Basset, Catherine 92
Bassett, ___ (Rev.) 742
Bassett, Eleanor 5393
Bassett, Maria H. 742
Batchelder, Lucy 4672
Bates, ___ (Rev.) 9222
Bates, Catherine C. 1413
Bates, Esther 9528
Bates, Jane 7285
Bates, John 538
Bates, Julia A. 5097
Bates, Mary Elizabeth 8098
Bates, Stephen 9528
Batrick, Nancy 2109
Baughman, Sarah E. 4486
Baxter, John 555, 557, 804, 7346
Baxter, Lucinda 2601
Baxter, Sarah (Mrs.) 555, 557
Bayly, R. M. (Col.) 565, 567
Bayly, Richard M. 566
Beach, Abner 582
Beach, Angeline 1142, 3591
Beach, Catherine 712
Beach, Elias 568, 574
Beach, Jane 336
Beach, Lucinda 574
Beach, Thomas 573
Beal, Edward 585
Beals, Ann F. 3067
Beals, Elizabeth 7298
Beals, Lucilla 535
Beals, ___ (Mr.) 7298
Beals, Thomas 535, 3067
Beard, B. F. 593
Beard, James C. 8020
Beard, Lovina 8020
Beardslee, Sally 9707
Beardsley, Delia (Mrs.) 6324
Beardsley, Dorcas Eliza 5229
Beardsley, Elizabeth R. 9023
Beardsley, Frances O. 1772
Beardsley, Levi 9023
Beasac, John 7898
Beattie, W. D. 600
Beaver, Elizabeth 5678
Becker, A. (Mr.) 604
Becker, Conrad C. 603
Becker, Jane 3148
Becker, Margaret 243
Becker, Mary Ann 3758
Beckler, Mary Ann (Mrs.) 1156
Beckwith, Asahel
Beckwith, Isadorah 611
Beckwith, Junia 6205
Beckwith, Nancy F. 2887
Beckwith, Sally 3732
Beckwith, William 611
Beddoe, ___ (Mr.) 1186, 8289
Beddoe, John 8286
Bedell, Emaline 6460
Bedell, Jeremiah 3395
Bedell, Mary 983

Bedell, Sarah L. 3395
Bedloe, Harriet C. 176
Bedloe, Henry 176
Beebe, A. (Mr.) 634
Beebe, Alathea 639
Beebe, Asenath 7606
Beebe, David 635
Beebe, E. (Mr.) 629
Beebe, Isaac 628
Beebe, James 639
Beebe, Mary L. 4947
Beebe, Sophia 6507
Beebe, Thomas 637
Beebee, A. M. (Mr.) 641
Beech, Harriet 8275
Beecher, Abbie S. 1234
Beecher, Catharine 9005
Beecher, Laura 2213
Beecher, Mather 1234
Beecher, Sylvester 643, 2213
Beeman, Eunice E. 1667
Beeman, Mandaville 9712
Beers, A. S. (Mr.) 7297
Beers, Amanda 2369
Beers, Amanda M. 2597
Beers, Harriet W. 7297
Beers, Julia A. 4701
Beers, Mary 9648
Beers, Munson H. 9648
Beksley, Ann Eliza 3961
Belcher, Hannah B. 9156
Belden, Azor 652
Belden, Charles (Mrs.) 6033
Belden, George (Mrs.) 6033
Belden, Julia 1113
Belemy, Sarah 7031
Belknap,Frances A. 7882
Belknap, Jane 6142
Bell, Eliza 1746
Bell, H. W. (Dr.) 657
Bell, Mary Ann 2313
Bell, Rosina 1415
Bellamy ___ (Mr.) 9188
Bellamy A. (Mr.) 659, 660
Bellamy, Alfred 688
Bellamy, J. (Mr.) 658
Bellenger, Laney 2546
Bellinger, Frederick 5296
Bellinger J. (Mr.) 3752
Bellinger, John 664
Bellinger, John J. 663
Bellinger, Mary 6201
Bellinger, Mary Ann 5296
Bellis, Catharine M. 7677
Belnap, Maria 6818
Beman, Marietta 846
Bement, Mary 9713
Bemis, ___ (Mr.) 5417
Bemis, James D. 1631
Bemis, Rebecca 1631
Benedict, Amos 671
Benedict, Eliza A. 9870
Benedict, J. (Mr.) 9413
Benedict, Joseph 1734, 4085, 9870
Benedict, Julia A. 1734
Benedict, Lewis 487, 679
Benedict, Lucretia 9413
Benedict, Mary 4729
Benedict, Mehitable 2370
Benedict, Polly C. 9814
Benham, Betsy 681, 682
Benham, Delia 6319
Benham, Ebenezer 681, 682
Benham, Mary 7653
Benjamin, Harriet A. 5262
Benjamin, Orson 5262
Bennet, Adeline 6339
Bennet, Minerva 8469

Bennet, Nancy 9484
Bennett, Abraham H. 714
Bennett, Antonett 4116
Bennett, Etsey 425
Bennett, Calista 3278
Bennett, Caroline 3895, 9309
Bennett, Charlotte M. 502
Bennett, Desdemona 714
Bennett, Eliza 5375
Bennett, Elizabeth 5497
Bennett, Emily 9920
Bennett, Emma C. 1883
Bennett, George 701
Bennett, Henry 698
Bennett, Mary 1188
Bennett, Nathaniel 711
Bennett, Sally 701
Bennett, Sophia 7812
Benson, Julia A. 3257
Benson, Levi 721
Benson, Sarah Elizabeth 2624
Bentley, A. (Maj.) 5735
Bentley, E. (Mr.) 725
Bentley, Mary E. 5735
Bentley, Phebe Amanda 2814
Benton, ___ (Miss) 3091
Benton, Charles S. 729
Benton, James 981
Benton, Mary Jane 6683
Benton, Rebecca 4622
Benton, Senator (Mrs.) 8647
Benton, Susan Ann 4288
Bernard, Huldah 457
Berry, Charlotte 9004
Berry, Lucy Ann 1009
Berthrong, James 7814
Berthrong, Jane Eliza 7814
Besley, Samuel 353
Besly, Jane A. 353
Bessee, Heman 7843
Bessee, Lucinda Marion 7843
Best, John 744
Best, Mary G. 744
Betsinger, Catherine 7142
Bettinger, Eve 5124
Bettinger, Isaac 747
Bettis, Benjamin 752
Betts, Almyra 2618
Betts, C. (Mr.) 5772
Betts, Julia M. 5772
Betts, N. (Mr.) 755
Betts, Peter 5084, 5087
Betts, Sally 5084, 5087
Beverly, Ruthana 9774
Bicknell, Harriet T. 9430
Biddlecom, Jane R. 6374
Biddlecom, Nancy M. 9892
Bidwell, Amelia 3372
Bigelow, Abner 769
Bigelow, Faye 763
Bigelow, Hannah 763, 770
Bigelow, Henrietta Maria 766
Bigelow, J. G. (Mr.) 765
Bigelow, Payn 770
Bigelow, Polly 1503
Bigelow, U. G. (Mr.) 765, 766, 773
Biles, Mary (Mrs.) 2727
Bill, Lucy Ann 6151
Billings, Abby Fosdick 8318
Billings, John 4451, 8318
Billings, Sarah 2196
Billington, Eleanor 9666
Billington, Lucina 435
Bilsell, Matilda H. 2136
Bingham, Nathaniel 779
Birch, Martha 7429
Bird, Amanda 5857
Bird, Emily Ann 9035
Bird, I. (Rev.) 9035

303

Brewster, Mary Endine, 1023
Brewster, S. W. (Mr.) 762
Brewster, Sarah 762
Brewster, William 4906
Bridgewood, Elizabeth 3434
Bridgman, William 1031
Brigden, G. N. (Mr.) 1032
Briggs, Alinda 2156
Briggs, Ann 6524
Briggs, Caroline E. 2276
Briggs, Elisha 672
Briggs, Elizabeth 1035
Briggs, Louisa 2160
Briggs, Lydia 6720
Briggs, Margaret 672
Briggs, Mary 4237, 8245
Briggs, Mary ann 7190
Briggs, Nymrod (Mr.) 2276
Briggs, Phoebe 6179
Briggs, Sarah M. 4849
Briggs, Thomas 1035, 4237
Brigham, A. (Dr.) 1043
Brimmer, Martin 1049
Brink, Lydia Ann 6537
Bristol, Eli 1058
Bristol, Ellen M. 3688
Bristol, George 1056, 1060,
  3688
Bristol, William 1055, 1062
Britt, A. (Mr.) 2583
Britt, Cynthia 2583
Brittain, Emeline 9028
Brizse, Mary Ann 2316
Brizse, Roseanna 6373
Brizse, Stephen 2316
Broadstone, Barbara 9661
Broadway, Elizabeth T. 5609
Broadway, Thomas 5609
Broadwell, Ara 2471
Broadwell, Mary E. 2471
Brock, Fanny 5472
Brockett, Delos 1070
Brockett, Lucy 1070
Brockett, Timothy 1070
Brockway, Hannah 6640
Bromley, Angelica 1075
Bromley, Daniel N. 1075
Bronnell, Abner 1076
Bronnell, susan 1076
Bronson, Maranda 6010
Bronson, Martha 7310
Bronson, Mary 2646
Bronson, Philo 7312
Brook, John 1082
Brook, Margaret 1082
Brook, Perpetua S. 8409
Brooks, ___ (Mr.) 9074
Brooks, Benjamin F. (Mrs.)
  3734
Brooks, David 7564
Brooks, Edward 1086
Brooks, Elizabeth A. 7994
Brooks, Elizabeth P. 1533
Brooks, Emily 1869
Brooks, Isabella 7564
Brooks, Jane 2851, 9003
Brooks, John (Dr.) 1533
Brooks, Laura 7530
Brooks, Mary 7632
Brooks, Merritt 1096
Brooks, Sarah Ann 2559
Broom, Mary C. 5382
Broom, William 5382
Brother, Henry 1099
Brower, Eliza Ann 5990
Brower, Mary C. 6534
Brown, ___ (Maj. Gen.) 1150
Brown, ___ (Mrs.) 4910
Brown, Allen 7719

Brown, Almira 1167
Brown, Ann 1501
Brown, Ann Maria 601
Brown, Anne 5012
Brown, Diree A. 5216
Brown, Edwin 1184
Brown, Elijah 1184
Brown, Elijah T. 1164
Brown, Eliza 4705, 5895
Brown, Eliza A. 1129
Brown, Elizabeth 3084
Brown, Elizabeth B. 3724
Brown, Elizabeth Gertrude 7719
Brown, Emeline S. 1652
Brown, Ezra 4446
Brown, Floyd 1164
Brown, Frances Jane 2934
Brown, George 1118, 1133
Brown, Grace 2228
Brown, Harriet 4130, 5904
Brown, Henry C. 509
Brown, Hiram 1161
Brown, J. P. (Mr.) 1166
Brown, Jacob 1106, 9109
Brown, James 1137
Brown, James N. 1129
Brown, Jane 937
Brown, Jane Ann 2224
Brown, Jane P. 334
Brown, Jonas 1107
Brown, Jonathan 1105, 1190
Brown, Juliett 225
Brown, Laura 2931
Brown, Lydia 1212, 7852
Brown, Maria 6184
Brown, Mary 6446
Brown, Mary Elizabeth 1190
Brown, Mary N. 6462
Brown, Mary W. 509
Brown, Miranda 2125
Brown, N. P. (Miss) 6040
Brown, Nancy 1551
Brown, Nathan 1136
Brown, Obediah Zina 1190
Brown, Oliver 1167
Brown, Orville C. 1108
Brown, Phebe 8090
Brown, Roxanie 6578
Brown, Samantha 843
Brown, Samuel 1111
Brown, Sarah 8822
Brown, Sarah A. 4446
Brown, William 1168
Brown, William F. 1128
Brown, William H. 1149
Brown, William W. 843
Brownell, ___ (Mr.) 1196
Brownell, Abner 5979
Brownell, Eunice 782
Brownell, Susan Emeline 5979
Browning, Joanna D. 5710
Browning, Mary (Mrs.) 8581
Browning, Thirza 2272
Bruce, ___ (Rev.) 1204
Bruce, Alma 8006
Bruce, Eunice 381
Bruce, Joseph (Maj.) 1778
Bruce, Mary Ann 8304
Bruce, Nancy A. 1778
Bruce, William 1206
Bruin, Harriet 9558
Bruin, M. (Mr.) 9558
Brundage, Sally 7751
Bryan D. (Mr.) 972
Bryan, Kate 972
Bryant, Agnes J. 6723
Bryant, Mary 5345
Bryen, Minerva 6380
Bryson, David 2468

Bryson, Margaret M. M. 2468
Buchanan, ___ (Mr.) 370
Buchanan, Elizabeth 6577
Buchanan, R. G. (Mr.) 6577
Buchanan, Susan Ann (Mrs.) 6749
Buchannon, Mary 2708
Bucher, Elizabeth 6322
Buck, Eunice 7066
Buck, Harriet A. 3846
Buck, Rachel 5582
Buck, William J. 1232
Buckland, Cornelia 7233
Budd, ___ (Dr.) 8688
Budd, Antoinette 8688
Budington, A. (Mr.) 203
Budington, Elizabeth, 203
Budlong, David 288
Budlong, Elizabeth 1242
Budlong, N. J. (Miss) 288
Budlong, Phebe R. 7481
Budlong, Roby 7544
Budlong, Samuel 1242
Buel, David 3702, 5101
Buel, Mary 5101
Buell, Sarah M. 420
Buer, Catharine 4262
Buffet, Eloisa Lewis 4454
Bugby, Sarah 1589
Bugden, Lucy 8312
Bugsbie, Clarinda 7047
Bulkley, ___ (Mr.) 1250
Bulkley, Honor Frances 1624
Bull, Ann Maria 5889
Bull, Catharine P. 1739
Bull, Frances D. 399
Bull, Jane E. 1253
Bull, Joseph 399
Bull, Sally 4801
Bullard, Charlotte C. 1201
Bullock, Benjamin F. 1256, 1258
Bullock, Eliza 1258
Bullock, Mary E. 4247
Bulwer, Edward (Sir) 5530
Bumgarner, Catherine 5809
Bump, Joseph 1260
Bump, Leah 6819
Bump, Sarah 1260
Bunday, Warner 1261
Bundy, Almira 4793
Bunker, Eliza 142
Bunn, Wealthy 6484
Bunnell, Ann M. 9052
Bunner, Matilda H. 9974
Bunner, Rudolph 9974
Bunyea, Sarah 5364
Buoyre, Elizabeth 5699
Burch, Desire 7245
Burch, George 1269, 1271
Burch, Orissa 7465
Burch, Phebe A. 1486
Burchard, Ely 1273
Burchard, Lucy Ann 2599
Burchard, Lydia A. 7864
Burckle, Frederica E. 6022
Burden, Charlotte J. 6548
Burdick, Deborah Frances 5496
Burdick, Henry C. 1276
Burdick, Malinda 5460
Burdick, Oliver 1275
Burge, ___ (Mrs.) 5234
Burge, Elizabeth (Mrs.) 6945
Burger, Sally Alida 3077
Burgess, ___ (Mrs.) 3187
Burgess, Sally 4184
Burghart, Lambert 1280
Burhans, Margaret 7551
Burkard, Adeline 3794
Burke, Luisa G. V. 3330
Burke, Mary H. A. 5744

305

Burkholder, Eliza 775
Burkite, M. (Miss) 7294
Burley, Diadema 8419
Burlingame, Ann 4926
Burlison, Eliza 7640
Burnap, Abijah 1288
Burnap, Saphrona 1025
Burnet, ___ (Gen.) 1291
Burnet, Andrew 6249
Burnet, Charles J. 1289
Burnet, Lois 6249
Burnett, Anna 9161
Burnett, Charles J. 1294
Burnett, Elizabeth 1636, 2965
Burnett, J. (Mr.) 9161
Burnett, Mary 7489
Burnett, Stephen 1295
Burnette, Lucy 7547
Burnham, Ann 2006
Burnham, Asahel 2006
Burnham, Gordon W. 1298
Burnham, Julius A. 1297
Burns, Maria E. 4224
Burns, Mary Ann 1816
Burns, T. (Mr.) 3141
Burnside, Amos 1302
Burnside, Margaret 9335
Burpee, Harriet Amanda 2717
Burr, Asenath 8766
Burr, Catharine 1308
Burr, Laura A. 8455
Burr, M. Lucinda (Mrs.) 8911
Burr, Mary Ann 6866
Burrall, T. D. (Mr.) 1313
Burrall, Thomas D. 1311
Burrel, Jane 9784
Burrell, Lois 2073
Burrell, Mary W. 2153
Burritt, F. J. (Mr.) 1314
Burrows, Julia Frances 6806
Burt, Erastus 1323
Burt, Hilinda 70
Burtis, Amenia 9338
Burtis, Arthur 9338
Burtiss, Elizabeth 9804
Burtless, Belinda 4055
Burton, Harriet 6796
Burton, William 6796
Busby, Jerusha 9058
Busch, William 1346
Bush, Horace 3044
Bush, Jane M. 9688
Bush, Maria (Mrs.) 7917
Bush, Mary 7464
Bush, Mary F. 3044
Bush, Mary Martha (Mrs.) 8479
Bush, Nancy 5789
Bush, Rachael 5184
Bushmore, Susanna 3043
Bushnell, Campbell 2800
Bushnell, John 1356
Bushnell, Mary 2800
Bushnell, Samuel 1360
Buskirk, Asenith 2993
Buskirk, Laney 7604
Butler, ___ (Col.) 5916
Butler, ___ (Miss) 8057
Butler, ___ (Mrs.) 4984
Butler, A. T. (Mr.) 4984
Butler, Ann 9826
Butler, B. F. (Mr.) 2798
Butler, Benjamin 2527
Butler, Benjamin (Dr.) 1370
Butler, Benjamin F. 1371
Butler, Chester 1372
Butler, Comfort 699, 7723
Butler, Delia 7723
Butler, Eliza C. 699
Butler, Emily M. 1376

Butler, Eunice 6781
Butler, Harriet 4322
Butler, Harriet Allen 2798
Butler, James L. 1365
Butler, Lydia P. 1365
Butler, Maria 1138
Butler, Mary D. 2527
Butler, Mary E. 3872, 5376
Butler, Medad 4322
Butler, Nancy 1372
Butler, Nito Benjamin 9127
Butler, William 1374
Butler, William C. 1376
Butterfield, C. A. (Mrs.) 1385
Butterfield, Daniel 1380
Butterfield, J. (Mr.) 1380
Butterfield, John 1381, 1383
Butterfield, Justin 1383
Butterfield, Sophia S. 4310
Butterfield, T. F. (Mr.) 1385
Buttles, Maria 2894
Buttolph, David 1391
Buttolph, John 1390
Button, Harriet 3271
Button, Ira A. 6761
Button, Louisa C. 357
Button, Mary A. 3981
Buxby, Mary P. 1671
Buys, Sarah 9196
Byer, Maria 2396
Byington, Almira 8792
Byington, Caroline 7614
Byington, Ermina 9412
Cable, Mary Ann 7225
Cable, Polly 7484
Cadwell, Joanna 1579
Cady, Amanda 2086
Cady, Asa 6584
Cady, Betsy 9876
Cady, Emily 1017
Cady, Hannah A. 2507
Cady, Harriet 6584
Cady, Lovina 4659
Cady, Maria 2506
Cady, N. S. (Mr.) 1400
Calder, Eliza C. 706
Calhoun, John C. 1409
Calkins, Hannah Mary 5042
Calkins, Julia 7075
Callahan, Mary 6887
Callen, Elizabeth 5764
Cameron, Dugald 1419, 1420, 1423
Cameron, J. (Mr.) 1422
Cameron, John 1421
Cameron, Rachael 2706
Camp, Catharine Ann 6105
Camp, Elisha 955
Camp, Elizabeth 955
Camp, James 6556
Camp, John 1433
Camp, L. Maria 6556
Camp, Martha 9340
Camp, Mary 4365
Camp, Phieas 9340
Camp, Willard 4365
Campau, Barnabe 1437
Campbell, Adam I. 1450
Campbell, Asa 1438
Campbell, C. (Mr.) 4638
Campbell, Catherine 361
Campbell, George 1444
Campbell, James 1439
Campbell, Jane 6018
Campbell, Jane A. 9705
Campbell, Jeremiah 1452
Campbell, John D. 1453
Campbell, Louisa 4143
Campbell, Nancy Lavintia 5348

Campbell, Rebecca 656
Campbell, Robert 1443
Campbell, Sarah 7703
Canfield, Eliza 6241
Canfield, Emily 5453
Canfield, Irene 2738
Cannon, Amelia A. 8774
Cannon, Le Grand 1463, 8774
Cantine, John M. 1466
Capen, Mary A. 1071
Capron, Julia Ann 2499
Card, Catherine 761
Card, Jane 3309
Cardell, William S. 1471
Carey, ___ (Mr.) 8402
Carey, Anson 1474
Carey, David 1472
Carey, George 1477
carey, Nathaniel 1474
Carl, Elizabeth 469
Carlon, Julia Ann 6094
Carman, Polly R. 5542
Carmichael, Asahel 1053
Carmichael, Charles M. 8017
Carothers, Jane A. 8879
Carpenter, ___ (Dr.) 1506
Carpenter, Abram 1500
Carpenter, Amos H. 1490
Carpenter, C. Tracy 1497
Carpenter, Caroline 1497
Carpenter, Clark 1513
Carpenter, Eliza M. 1078, 7868
Carpenter, Frances, Ellen 7855
Carpenter, Harriet 1496
Carpenter, Huldah 1932
Carpenter, Levi 3212
Carpenter, Lucy L. 9766
Carpenter, Lydia 1072
Carpenter, M. (Gen.) 1493
Carpenter, Margaret 7655
Carpenter, Maria A. 1500
Carpenter, Mary 7850
Carpenter, Matthew 7868
Carpenter, Minerva 9813
Carpenter, Rachel 8883
Carpenter, Sarah 3887
Carpenter, Yhomas O. 7855
Carr, Elizabeth 1670
Carrington, Ann L. 2657
Carrington, Lucy 2961
Carrol, Harriet B. 1526
Carrol, James H. 1526
Carrol, Mary Jane 6878
Carroll, Charles H. 1527
Carroll, Matilda 7367
Carson, Lafford 1529
Carson, Sarah 7335
Carson, Robert 1532
Carter, Aurelia 640
Carter, Caroline 6506
Carter, Elizabeth 3410
Carter, Emeline E. 7305
Carter, John 1539
Carter, Mary 8601
Carter, Thomas 1539
Carvenough, Robert 1541
Cary, ___ (Mr.) 2693
Cary, Anson 1546
Cary, Elizabeth C. 66
Cary, I. G. (Hon.) 66
Cary, Mary 988
Cary, S. M. (Miss) 5845
Cary, Trumbull 1542
Case, Althea 9790
Case, Caroline 646, 6288
Case, Catherine 4704
Case, Delina A. 999
Case, Elizabeth 1063, 4174
Case, G. (Mr.) 309

Case, Lucretia 5949
Case, Lucy 309
Case, Mary 7818
Case, Pliny 1553, 5949
Case, Russel 999
Case, William B. 1552
Cash, Sarah Ann 668
Casler, Catherine 2840
Cass, Jonathan 1567
Cass, Lewis 1565
Cass, Pennette 6302
Cassidy, Harriet 1571
Cassidy, Patrick 1571
Castine, Richard 3846
Castle, Charlotte 838, 9320
Castleton, Thomas 1577
Catner, Catharine 586
Caulkins, Jula Ann 8952
Caulkins, Juliette 2134
Caward, George 3918
Caward, Ruth 3918
Caywood, Jane 9552
Cell, Catharine 1335
Cesebro. See also Chesebro.
Cesebro, Elizabeth C. 6836
Cesebro, Henry 6836
Cevana, Peter 1591
Chadwick, Mary 3109
Chaffe, Almira 832
Chalmers, Thomas 1593
Chamberlain, Abigail 4544
Chamberlain, Mary Ann 6246
Chamberlin, Annis 2938
Chamberlin, Cornelia L. 6068
Chamberlin, Henry 6068
Champion, Roswell 1605
Champlain, William C. 1607
Champlin, Mary 5819
Champney, H. C. (Mr.) 1610
Chandler, Anna H. (Mrs.) 8111
Chandler, Mary A. 5142
Chandler, Phebe 5147
Chandler, Samantha 1131
Chandler, Stephen 5147
Chandler, Winthrop H. 5139,
  5142
Chaney, ___ (Elder) 4933
Chaney, Margarette 4933
Chapen, Mary Janette 9903
Chapin, ___ (Dr.) 4728
Chapin, Cynthia 1620
Chapin, Cyrenus 1629
Chapin, Heman 1626
Chapin, Henry 1620
Chapin, Jane aurelia 632
Chapin, Joel
Chapin, Laura
Chapin Lydisettee 6742
Chapin, Seth 1629
Chapin, Spencer 1625
Chapman, ___ (Mr.) 9576
Chapman, ___ (Mrs.) 9576
Chapman, Alta W. 7593
Chapman, Ann 5746
Chapman, Augustus 791
Chapman, Clarinda 3113
Chapman, Edward 1640
Chapman, Harriet 3140
Chapman, Hiram 7250
Chapman, J. 1639
Chapman, John 1643
Chapman, Leonora Mary 2921
Chapman, Louisa A. 4758
Chapman, Lovicy C. 8626
Chapman, Lydia 8758, 9308
Chapman, Mandane 4149
Chapman, Mary Jane 7250
Chapman, Merilla 4861
Chapman, R. H. (Mr.) 257

Chapman, Stephen 4149
Chappell, E. (Miss) 1409
Chase, Adaline 4051
Chase, Caroline C. 387
Chase, Charlotte M. 169
Chase, Eliza 7208
Chase, Emeline 9242
Chase, Frances H. 386
Chase, Harriet H. 3569
Chase, Ira 1653, 1656, 1660
Chase, Jacob 1658
Chase, Jane R. 2392
Chase, Paul 3569
Chase, Rhoda 335
Chase, S. P. (Hon.) 1662
Chase, Sarah 9343
Chase, Seth 1664
Chase, Sophia 6676
Chatfield, Cyrus 1669
Chatten, Elizabeth 1092
Chauncey, William 8110
Chesebro. See also Cesebro.
Chesebro, Huldah 7386
Chesebro, M. P. (Mr.) 7386
Chesebro, Sally 2106
Cheshbro, Susan 3213
Chester, L. L. (Dr.) 1687, 7175
Chestnut, Ellen 8920
Chickering, Emeline 1690
Chickering, Joseph 1690
Child, Asa 7873
Child, Mary A. 2281
Childs, F. (Mr.) 1702
Childs, Jane S. 3766
Childs, Oliver 1698
Childs, Perry G. 1697
Chipman, Frances M. 3990
Chipman, Mary W. 1675
Chittenden, Harlow 1714
Chrisley, Catharine 3390
Chrisman, Eliza 5546
Christie, Asa 1717
Christman, Catharine 2478
Christman, Eveline 8112
Christman, Polly 1678
Chubbuck, Charles 4909
Chubbuck, Emily 4909
Church, Charlotte 6419
Church, J. M. (Mr.) 2585
Church, Jane Ann 2895
Church, M. B. (Mr.) 1725, 2733
Church, Patty (Wid.) 2315
Church, Philip E. 4382
Church, Sophia H. 4382
Church, William 1722, 2895
Churchill, Charles 530
Churchill, Cornelia M. 530
Claflin, Hannah 7041
Claghorn, C. (Mr.) 1737
Claghorn, Charles 1736
Claghorn, Mary 1736
Clap, Catharine 3226
Clapp, Cornelia 1124
Clapp, H. W. (Mr.) 1124
Clapp, James 1740, 6296
Clapp, Julia Butler 6296
Clapper, John 1742
Clark, ___ (Mrs.) 4844
Clark, A. W.(Mr.) 1748
Clark, B. A. (Miss) 2275
Clark, C. (Mr.)8138
Clark, C. A. (Miss) 6983
Clark, C. D. (Mr.) 1788
Clark, Caroline M. 3529
Clark, Charles 1829
Clark, Charlotte Ann 5847
Clark, Chester 1769
Clark, Content 5014
Clark, Cornelia A. R. 8814

Clark, Elinor 4815
Clark, Eliza 3158, 8385
Clark, Elizabeth 242, 8033
Clark, Elizabeth A. 9933
Clark, Elizabeth M. 3729
Clark, Erastus 1762
Clark, Esther 4277
Clark, Esther C. 1274
Clark, Ethan 9033
Clark, Eunice E. 1340
Clark, Frances H. 6921
Clark, H. (Mrs.) 9000
Clark, H. H. (Mr.) 1753
Clark, Henry 1809
Clark, J. M. (Mr.) 1274
Clark, James M. 1773
Clark, Jannette 689
Clark, John 1770, 1825, 3411
Clark, John C. 1792
Clark, Lois 7779
Clark, Lorinda 7753
Clark, Louisa 4518
Clark, Lucinda 6931
Clark, Maria 1861
Clark, Maria G. 7924
Clark, Mariah 9667
Clark, Mary 1300, 3650, 4865,
  5318, 8440, 8527
Clark, Mary Ann 5165, 7735
Clark, Mary Eliza 3987
Clark, Mary Seymour 4114
Clark, Mary Stilwell 9884
Clark, Norman 1752
Clark, O. (Rev.) 1824
Clark, Oliver 1761, 2104
Clark, Orin 2694, 8814
Clark, R. (Mr.) 1788
Clark, Russel 1777
Clark, S. (Miss) 8327
Clark, Samuel 3729
Clark, Samuel R. 9884
Clark, Sarah 7478
Clark, Sarah Helen 5161
Clark, Satterlee 4114, 5847
Clark, Starr 1826
Clark, Stephen 1744
Clark, Susan Lawson 2694
Clark, Thomas 1813, 5161
Clark, Thomas E. 1782
Clark, Vine H. 1798
Clark, William B. 1818
Clark, William L. 7779
Clarke, Annis 1855
Clarke, Charity 1068
Clarke, Chester 8958
Clarke, Elizabeth 5268
Clarke. Ellen Sophia 6793
Clarke, George 1833
Clarke, Hampton 1837
Clarke, Isabella 1896
Clarke, Peter 6793
Clarke, S. R. (Dr.) 1842
Clarke, Samuel 1855
Clarke, Susan W. 8958
Clarke, Thaddeus 1836
Clarke, William 1840
Clary, Aurelius 5235
Clary, Cinthia 5235
Clary, Rose Ann 6439
Clary, William 1848
Clawson, Zephaniah 1852
Clay, Henry 1853, 2771, 6407
Clay, Susan 2771
Cleaveland, Persis M. 2988
Cleaveland, W. P. (Dr.) 1854
Cleaver, Amos 3820
Cleaver, Ellen M. 3820
Clemons, Jennette 3878
Clesson, Samuel 1860

Cleveland, Betsey A. 3131
Cleveland, Charlotte 7074
Cleveland, Emeline 3198
Cleveland, Moses 7074
Cline, Lucy 3883
Cline, Mary 5410
Clinton, ___ (Gov.) 4833
Clinton, De Witt 1862, 8408, 8494
Clinton, James 8408
Clinton, Mary 4833
Clinton, Prudy 4802
Clizbe, Evelyn 10011
Clizbe, Jonathan 10011
Close, Martha 7100
Closs, Eliza 521
Clough, Helen 5217
Clough, Isaac 5217
Clute, John I. 7092
Cobb, Adelaide 9260
Cobb, Henry S. 4356
Cobb, Mary B. 4356
Cobleigh, Caroline 3924
Coburn, A. S. (Mr.) 8253
Coburn, Charles 1890
Coburn, Eliza (Mrs.) 5390
Coburn, Emma 6865
Cochran?, Thomas 5197
Cochran, Walter 8058
Cody, Asa 3631
Coe, Clarissa 3631
Coe, Julia H. 5467
Coe, M. D. (Col.) 3774
Coe, Mary M. 3774
Coffin, Caleb 9982
Coffin, Charles 1957
Coffin, Jane Amelia 9982
Coffin, John A. 1908, 2600
Coffin, Lydia C. 1957
Colburn, Susan S. 6463
Cole, Abel H. 1920
Cole, Andrew 1918
Cole, Asa 1933
Cole, Chauncey 1922
Cole, Elizabeth 7835
Cole, Eunice 1922
Cole, H. S. 1916, 1918
Cole, Jane 8000
Cole, John B. 1931
Cole, Joseph 5850
Cole, Mary F. 5850
Cole, Prudence 6658
Cole, Rhoda A. 2041
Cole, Thomas 1929
Coleman, Charlotte E. 8580
Coleman, Esther 7982
Coleman, Ezekiel 1938
Coleman, Mary Ann 5422
Coleman, Sally 4795
Coleman, Spencer 9827
Coles, Matilda 276
Colgate, James B. 1947
Colgate, Sarah Ellen 1947
Colier, Isaac 4765
Colier, Maria 4765
Collamer, Ellen 7287
Collamer, J. (Hon.) 7287
Collamer, Melissa A. 6237
Collamer, Samuel 1949
Coller, Lucinda 9044
Collier, John A. 1952
Collier, John S. (Mrs.) 6135
Colling, Cornelia 8620
Colling, Thomas 8620
Collingwood, Elizabeth 5832
Collins, ___ (Mr.) 3929
Collins, Electa Jane 1955
Collins, Emeline R. 1914
Collins, Henry 1960

Collins, Job S. 1955
Collins, Oliver (Gen.) 1958
Collins, Phebe Ann 8743
Collins, Selden 1961
Colman, ___ (Wid.) 3568
Colt, Ann (Mrs.) 911
Colt, Catharine 8041
Colt, Elizabeth 7672
Colt, Joseph 7672
Colt, Mary 913
Colt, Peter 1965
Colt, S. (Gen.) 1966, 1967
Colt, Samuel (Gen.) 1970
Coltin, Caroline 3370
Coltin, David 3370
Colton, C. (Rev.) 1973
Colvard, Asa 6573, 6574
Colvard, Clarine Amelia 6573, 6574
Colvin, Delia Maria 4042
Colwell, ___ (Deavon) 1977
Colwell, Mary ann 5643
Colwell, Rhoda E. 6823
Combs, Caroline 6473
Combs, William 1981
Comfort, ___ (Mr.) 3704
Comstock, Alkanah 1994
Comstock, Angeline 8341
Comstock, Eliza 1989
Comstock, Ellen M. 8489
Comstock, James 1991
Comstock, Jerusha H. 952
Comstock, Julia A. 3803
Comstock, Lucian 1993
Comstock, Margaret 1993
Comstock, Mary L. 2794
Comstock, Moses 1990
Comstock, Samuel 1987, 1989
Comstock, Sarah 8623
Conant, Rubiette Angelina 6832
Condit, ___ (Mr.) 6363
Condit, Abby Eliza 376
Condit, Harriet W. 6059
Condit, Joseph 376
Congden, Edwin 1999
Conger, ___ (Mrs.) 5343
Conkey, Ellen A. 6791
Conklin, Amanda 2439
Conklin, Fanny 1013
Conklin, Joseph 1013
Conklin, Mary 5027
Conklin, Sally Ann 6056
Conlege, Asenith 1228
Conner, Harriet A. 3764
Connover, Jemima 4379
Conover, Sarah Jane 4223
Conrad, Abigail 6854
Conrad, Betsey 3159
Conrad, Lany 4402
Conrad, Sarah 1264
Converse, W. (Hon.) 860
Conway, Margaret B. 5424
Cook, Abiel 2016
Cook, Adeline 69
Cook, Ambrose 2021
Cook, C. A. (Mr.) 2033
Cook, C. C. (Mr.) 2039
Cook, Carolina Augusta 8291
Cook, Caroline 5521
Cook, Charles A. 2017
Cook, Charles H. 2013
Cook, Daniel 5521
Cook, David 2018, 2031
Cook, Eli 2035
Cook, Henry 2022
Cook, Jane 4798
Cook, Matilda 8067
Cook, Nathan 2034
Cook, Russel S. 2015

Cook, Samuel 8291
Cook, Solomon 2021
Cooke, ___ (Dr.) 2042
Cook, Apollos 3706
Cooke, E. (Hon.) 2043
Cooke, John F. 2042
Cooke, Mary A. 3706
Cool, Caroline 3351
Cooley, Charles 1529
Cooley, Huldah 7783
Cooley, James 2051
Cooley, L. J. (Maj.) 3973
Cooley, Mary 3296
Cooley, Mary Burt 2282
Cooley, Mary Walbridge 3973
Cooley, O. B. (Mr.) 2054
Coolidge, Mary 7124
Coon, Ardelia 1649
Coonrad, Elizabeth 2782
Coonradt, Martha Ann 3970
Cooper, B. F. (Mr.) 2926
Cooper, Catherine 2629
Cooper, H. C. (Mrs.) 9416
Cooper, Hannah P. 8075
Cooper, Isaac 9416
Cooper, James Fenimore 2072
Cooper, Julia A. 1266
Cooper, Margaret T. 6415
Cooper, Maria Frances 2072
Cooper, Rhoda Ann 4959
Cooper, Samuel (Capt.) 2070
Cooper, William 2069
Copsey, Mary Ann 3080
Corbett, Amelia C. 6848
Corbin, Esther 8325
Corbin, Patience 5068
Corey, D. G. (Rev.) 2080
Corey, Daniel G. (Rev.) 2081
Corey, Eveline Augusta 6388
Corey, Prudence 6422
Corey, Sidney A. 2082
Corey, Susan 9869
Coriell, Sarah Jane 9792
Corlett, Eliza 7029
Cornell, Adelia Ann 2118
Cornell, Emily 7216
Cornell, Ruth Ann 2249
Cornish, Delia M. 4475
Cornish, Marilla 2190
Cornwall, Elizabeth H. 8155
Cornwall, Richardson 8155
Cornwell, Achsa A. 3508
Cornwell, Clarinda 3079
Corras, Donna Maria 2083
Corson, Jacob 2094
Corson, L. (Mr.) 2096
Corson, Mehala 6531
Cortright, Hannah 9299
Cory, Benjamin 854, 4067, 5712
Cory, Clarissa 854
Cory, Eliza Ann 5712
Cory, Mary 4067
Cossett, Abbey 1988
Cossett, Sarah 9377
Cost, Eleanor Cuyler 620
Cost, Elias 620
Cost, Mary 9819
Costello, Frances 2467
Cttle, Mary Allis 8123
Cotton, Ann 6682
Cotton, Henry G. 2107
Couch, Amanda 4469
Coulton, Lydia A. 5113
Coun, Caroline Mary 6827
Countryman, Mary 6285
Courtenay, E. H. (Mr.) 2111
Covell, Miles 3853
Coventry, C. B. (Dr.) 2115
Coventry, Jane 9887

Coventry, Rosanna 5932
Covert, Caroline 2116
Covert, Eliza 1146
Covert, Mary Ann 576
Covey, Amos 2117
Coville, Cornelia A. 4147
Cowdrey, John 2122
Cowen, ___ (Judge) 2128
Cowen, T. C. (Mr.) 2127
Cowle, Lucia 7651
Cowles, Jane M. 2987
Cox, Malachi 2140
Cox, Mariam 1460
Cox, Nancy 5131
Cox, Olive 2140
Coxe, Ann 1974
Coxe, William 1974
Cozier, Ezra S. 2143
Cozzens, Levi 1108, 2144
Crabtree, Clarissa 1863
Crafts, Willard 2146, 2147
Crain, Philatheta 938
Crain, William C. 938
Crandall, Sarah E. 5722
Crane, Abijah 2162
Crane, Alma 9573
Crane, Clarissa 1972
Crane, Hiram 2168
Crane, Julia 9239
Crane, Lebbeus 2155
Crane, Sally 4220
Crane, Ssuan 6337
Crapsey, Caroline Maria 2899
Crapsey, Harriet Almida 2990
Crapsey, John G. 2990
Craske, Mary Ann 4448
Craven, Susan R. 3060
Craver, Emeline 4952
Craw, Samuel 7542
Crawford, Adelina 8198
Crawford, Margaret 3127
Crawford, Mercy 1760
Crawford, Phebe 8197
Crawford, Roena 3668
Cretsley, Abigail 4797
Crichet, Rhoda 5134
Crider, Ann (Miss) 1544
Crippen, Minerva 2182
Crippen, Samuel 2182
Crips, ___ (Mrs.) 2183
Crips, Adam 2183
Crissey, E. F. (Mr.) 2185
Cristman, Sarah 5016
Crittenden, Fidelia 8498
Crittenden, Fortiscue 2186
Crittenden, L. W. (Dr.) 2187
Crocker, Amos 4080
Crocker, Angenett 527
Crocker, Cornelia 4080
Crocker, Emily 8868
Crocker, Hannah 4077
Crocker, Hugh 2192, 2193, 2949
Crocker, Silas 8868
Crocker, Zeura 5580
Cromwell, Julia Ann 3949
Cronk, Sarah 5950
Crook Electa Ann 2197, 2198
Crook, Elias 2197, 2198
Crooks, Cordelia 6079
Cropsey, Welthy Ann 9719
Crosby, Emeline 9031
Crosby, Ruth Ann 7058
Crossman, Betsey 2212
Crossman, Eliza A. 1229
Crossman, Nathaniel 2212
Crouse, James 2214
Cruger, Donald 2222
Crum, Cornelia 1817
Crumb, Abraham 2227

Crump, Harriet 5560
Crump, Josiah H. 2229
Cryne, Jeanette 7306
Cudworth, Amy A. 5831
Cullen, James 3343
Cullen, Mary 3343
Culver, John 2238
Culver, Mary Ann 6845
Culverson, Sally 7231
Cummings, Aseneth 2359
Cummings, H. (Mr.) 2245
Cummings, John 5094
Cummings, M. A. (Miss) 2334
Cummings, M. Ann 5094
Cummings, Olive 327
Cunningham, C. M. A. 2767
Cunningham, Cornelia O. 2877
Cunningham, Grove 7166
Cunningham, John 2253
Cunningham, Martha 1964
Cunningham, Rebecca A. 2556
Cunningham, William 1964
Curlough, Roxanna 2036
Curran, Edward 1514
Curry, Elijah P. 2255
Curry, Frances 9771
Curry, Mary C. 2255
Curtenius, Anna M. 9447
Curtenius, Catherine Elizabeth 8801
Curtenius, John L. 9447
Curtenius, Peter 8801
Curtis, ___ (Mr.) 8349
Curtis, Charles C. 3534
Curtis, Clarissa M. 2258
Curtis, Elvira 7647
Curtis, Eunice 2262
Curtis, Harriet E. 3534
Curtis, Harriet Elizabeth 2955
Curtis, Jane M. 3613
Curtis, Jesse 1374
Curtis, John 2258
Curtis, Lydia Ann 3763
Curtis, Mary E. 1996
Curtis, Oliver 2269
Curtis, Polly 6630
Curtis, Ransom 2262
Curtis, Salmon 1996
Curtis, Solomon 2257
Curtiss, Amanda C. 7338
Curtiss, Amelia 3311
Curtiss, Eliza 1536, 3855
Curtiss, Emeline 6160
Curtiss, Ezekiel 3196
Curtiss, George 2285
Curtiss, Joseph 2285
Curtiss, Samuel F. 2278
Cushing, Emily 4650
Cushing, Enos 4650
Cushing, Martha 2077
Cushing, Mercy 2289
Cushing, Pyau ? 2289
Cushing, Thomas 2289
Cushman, ___ (Judge) 3020
Cushman, Cornelia L. 239
Cushman, David 1693, 3928, 9535
Cushman, Delia 3928
Cushman, Diantha 1693
Cushman, Eliza 8866
Cushman, Julia 3020
Cushman, Maria 9878
Cuthburt, Lanoraie 2301
Cutis, Mary R. 4645
Cutler, Charlotte L. 2817
Cuykendoll, Clorinda 7431
Cuyler, Catharine Ann 7866
Cuyler, Elizabeth T. B. 8709

Cuyler, Glen 2307, 7866
Cuyler, John 8709
Dagget, Lois 916
Daggett, Levi 2310
Daggett, Mary 2311
Daggett, Seth 2311
Daharsh, Betsey 826
Daharsh, Polly 7171
Dailey, Harriet 7718
Dailey, Robert 309
Dakin, Elbridge 2317
Dale, Charles Augustus 2319
Daliba, James 2791
Daliba, Mary H. 2791
Dalzell, R. M. (Mr.) 4768
Damon, Caroline M. 6317
Damon, Rufus 6317
Dana, A. (Mr.) 166
Dana, Emeline Ann 166
Dana, James 2325
Dana, James (Mrs.) 1232
Dana, Jehu W. 5518
Danels, Jonas D. 2328
Danforth, ___ (Gen.) 6850
Daniels, Hannah 1721
Daniels, Jonas D. 2333
Daniels, Phila 9668
Danielson, Fanny 3244
Danks, Jane (Wid.) 2339
Darrian, Melissa 8655
Darrow, Delia 898
Darrow, John 2355
Darrow, L. R. (Mr.) 2353
Darrow, Pliny 2356
Darrow, Prudence 1805
Darrow, Tryphena 8328a
Dart, Calinda 2014
Dashiell, Rumania 561
Dauby, A. G. (Mr.) 2360
Dauby, Augustine G. 2362
Davenport, ___ (Mr.) 6796
Davenport, Adeline 437
Davenport, Aurelia 4476
Davenport, Frances Louisa 7999
Davenport, James 7999
Davenport, Margaret 9043
Davenport, Sarah 4156
Davenport, Sarah E. 857
Davids, R. V. (Mr.) 2367
Davidson, ___ (Lt.) 2371
Davidson, Lucretia M. 2371
Davidson, Margaret M. 2371
Davidson, Rhoda B. 1085
Davies, E. (Mr.) 7929
Davies, Jane 6134
Davies, Mary 7929
Davis, ___ (Judge) 2400
Davis, ___ (Miss) 2889
Davis, Abigail 2377
Davis, Ann Maria 3334
Davis, Betsey 2858
Davis, Catharine 2384
Davis, Catharine E. 7658
Davis, E. (Dr.) 5167
Davis, Edmond 2398
Davis, Edmund 2378
Davis, Edward 2377
Davis, Elijah 1391
Davis, Harriet 8646
Davis, Harvey 7001
Davis, Helen M. 5167
Davis, Henry 2387
Davis, James C. 2399
Davis, Jane Louisa 1907
Davis, John 2376
Davis, Julia 1763
Davis, Laura 8977
Davis, Lucy Ann 8701
Davis, Lydia Ann 4257

Davis, Mary 2595, 8499
Davis, Mary A. 7944
Davis, Mary T. 767
Davis, Parmelia 9972
Davis, Phebe Ann 7001
Davis, Rebecca 9836
Davis, Roland 2397
Davis, Sarah 7296
Davis, William 2382, 2400
Davison, Nancy 7455
Davison, Peter I. 6704
Davison, Sarah 6704
Day, Charlotte M. 6363
Day, Harriet Cornelia 8675
Day, Lyman 772
Day, Orrin 6363
Day, Rocelia 772
Dayan, Amy 6007
Dayan, Charles 6007
Dayton, Daniel 2210
Dayton, Gertrude 2210
Dean, Clarissa P. 3685
Dean, Eliza L. 5420
Dean, Marietta 5449
Dean, Mary C. 5457
Dean, Sarah A.6686
Death, Charlotte 1145
De Camp, Anna Maria J. 6130
De Camp, S. G. J. (surgeon) 6130
Decatur, Stephen 2438
Decker, E. Antoinette 8233
Decker, Elsie 8932
Decker, James 8233
Decolon, Rachael 8658
Dederer, DAvid 2514
Dederer, Sarah Margaret 2514
Dedrich, Catharine 8843
De Ferier, Lucy 6889
De Ferriere, Charles J. 2445
De Forest, Almina A. 516
De Graff, Abraham 2453, 5590
Deits, Rebecca 5463
Delamarther, J. D. (Mrs.) 2459
Delamather, ___ (Prof.) 2459
Deland, E. W. (Miss) 808
De Land, Louisa 9630
Delano, Ann 3727
Delano, Caroline 5407
Delano, Clara 750
De Lano, Harriet G. 3500
Delany, Sophia 60
Deline, Hanry 2474
Delong, Caroline 1249
De Long, Catharine 8848
Delong, James C. 1249
Delevan, Edward C. 2470
Delvin, Margaret A. 6508
De Marsh, Laney 450
Deming, Caroline C. 2714
Deming, Celia 1881
Deming, Mary 7496
Demming, Jane E. 134
Dempsey, Maria 6091
Demun, Lucinda 9462
Denison, Abbey Jane 1353
Denison, Latham 2492
Denison, Loa J. 9127
Denison, Sarah Ann 6181
Denison, William 2493
Denmark, Sally 7342
Dennison, David 2500
Denny, Elizabeth (Mrs.) 3562
Denslow, Benjamin 2502
Densmore, Louisa 9748
Densmore, Lydia 6376
Dent, Mary 2992
Denton, Catharine 6639
Denton, Eliza Jane 195

Denton, Fanny 1638
Denton, Frances 1638
Denton, S. B. 1638
De Pew, J. A. (Miss) 8865
Depew, Moses 2509
De Peyster, Ann Eliza 1454
De Puy, Catherine 8022
De Shon, Henry 2515
Desmon, Sarah M. 244
Devall, Hannah 8668
Deverest, Emeline 2165
Devereux, Hannah A. 5004
Devereux, John C. 2976
Devereux, John C. (Mrs.) 1965
Devereux, Nicholas 2525, 5004
Dewey, Alexander 2531
Dewey, Anna 8241
Dewey, Eliza C. 7950
Dewey, Henry 2534
Dewey, Jane E. 4561
Dewey, John 2529
Dewey, Margaretta 5120
Dewey, Mary Ann 8373
Dewey, Phebe Ann 1934
Dewey, W. Jane 2795
Dewhurst, Jane E. 9167
Dewit, Betsey E. 2538
Dewit, W. P. (Mr.) 2538
De Witt, ___ (Prof.) 9095
De Witt, Allen 2531
De Witt, Helen L. 9095
De Witt, James 2541
De Witt, John 2540
De Witt, Simeon 2539, 4505
De Witt, Susan 4500
De Wolf D. O. (Mr.) 2551
De Wolf, Jabez 6187
De Wolf, Sarah W. B. 6187
Dexter, Abigail 7327
Dexter, Chester 2554, 9724
Dexter, Daniel 2554
Dexter, Eliza 3329
Dexter, S. Newton 2553
Dexter, Susan 2209
Dey, A. (Mr.) 227
Dey, David 4806
Dey, Elizabeth 3870
Dey, Ellenor 5694
Dey, Frances J. 6902
Dey, Maria L. 227
Dey, Mary 4806
Dey, Peter 5694
Dey, Peter I. 2561
Dey, Pierson 3870
De Zeng, Josephine M. 2461
De Zeng, Maria augusta 8462
De Zeng, William S. 2461
Dias, Sarah Ann 3606
Dibble, Maria 5919
Dibble, Frances M. 3550
Dickerman, Emeline 2277
Dickerson, Charlotte 5123
Dickerson, Matilda 2462
Dickey, Lucinda 9907
Dickey, Maria A. 2630
Dickie, Catharine W. 1406
Dickinson, ___ (Maj.) 149
Dickinson, A. B. (Mr.) 3849
Dickinson, D. S. (Mr.) 2578
Dickinson, Eliza D. 3849
Dickinson, Elizabeth E. 3514
Dickinson, Experience 5561
Dickinson, G. L. (Mr.) 2577, 9353
Dickinson, George L. 2574
Dickinson, lorena 7173
Dickinson, Lucy 9392
Dickinson, Morris G. 2579
Dickinson, Nancy 6174

Dickinson, Rebecca 6765
Dickinson, Sophia 8413
Dickinson, William P. 2581
Dickson, ___ (Mr.) 7596
Dickson, T. B. (Mr.) 2585
Dickson, Truman B. 2586
Dildine, Nancy 7492
Dill, Jane V. 6815
Dill, John 2590
Dillage, ___ (Mr.) 1133
Dillon, Patrick 2591
Dimblery, Harriet 6271
Dimmick, Candace 5688
Disney, Robert 2596
Divine, R. A. (Miss) 1451
Dix, John A. 6114
Dix, Lucy Matilda 7695
Dixon, Almira 7925
Dixon, Hannah 224
Dixon, Isabella 3092
Dixon, John 3092
Dlossy, Caroline M. 1357
Dlossy, John J. 1357
Dobbin, Caroline 8545
Dobbin, Charlotte I. 7163
Dobbin, John 8545
Dobson, C. L. (Mr.) 2609
Dobson, Margaret 2609
Dodd, Mary W. 3986
Dodge, Adelaide Eugenia 6173
Dodge, Almira 6386
Dodge, Alvin 6173
Dodge, Eliza 4955
Dodge, Ellen R. 6542
Dodge, Ira 2614
Dodge, Loisa 9089
Dodge, Lucretia 7468
Dodge, Mary Elizabeth 1117
Dodge, Samuel 6386
Dodman, Delia 4466
Dolen, Frances B. 7042
Dolph, Hannah 6607
Dona, Martha 9845
Donaldson, ___ (Judge) 5684
Donaldson, ___ (Mr.) 9868
Domaldson, James C. 2634
Donaldson, Lucetta 9358
Donaldson, Peter F. 2632
Doney, Elizabeth 2203
Doney, Mary E. 5901
Doolittle, ___ (Mr.) 6022, 6059
Doolittle, Abigail P. 1432
Doolittle, Amos 2644
Doolittle, Betsey 6182
Doolittle, Charlotte P. 6375
Doolittle, Cornelia 302
Doolittle, Dotman 2640
Doolittle, Hannah 9482
Doolittle, Jane H. 7724
Doolittle, Mary 7224
Doolittle, Mary G. 8587
Doolittle, S. (Mr.) 6454
Doolittle, Uri, Jr. 7724
Dorchester, Eliaseph 2651
Dorman, Eunice 1828
Dorman, Gertrude 1807
Dorrance, Martha 4643
Dorrance, Polly 8263
Dorsey, Daniel 2659, 2660
Dorsey, Mary A. 7286
Dorsey, Upton 7286
Doty, ___ (Mr.) 5253
Doty, Clarissa 6884
Doty, Marcia 9591
Doty, Sally Ann 7890
Doty, Vashti 8553
Doubleday, Ammi 2665
Doubleday, Elisha 2664
Doubleday, Lois 2665

Doubleday, U. F. (Mr.) 2666
Douglas, Annis 9857
Douglass, Amelia 5203
Douglass, Benjamin 2675
Douglass, Lydia A. 6847
Douglass, Nancy P. 5202
Douglass, Zebulon 2672, 2676, 5202
Douw, Harriet M. 4817
Douw, John D. P. 4817
Dow, Edward H. 2680
Dowdall, Catharine Ann 2983
Dowdall, George R. 2983
Downer, A. O. (Mr.) 9722
Downer, Abner P. 2687
Downer, Diana 6497
Downer, Esther 7637
Downer, Harriet L. 9902
Downer, Mary 9722
Downer, Norman, Sr. 2686
Downes, Amelia R. 3064
Downey, Robert 2688
Downing, John 2690
Downs, Lydia 1575
Dows, J. (Mrs.) 5086
Dox, Abraham 2698, 2699
Dox, Gerrit L. 2695
Dox, Peter 2701
Dox, Susan Lawson 2698
Doxey, Catharine 7510
Doxtader, Emeline 3393
Doxtader, Leonard 2702
Doxtater, Elizabeth 897
Drake, Eemline 3421
Drake, Hannah 2911
Drake, Maria E. 1263
Drake, Susan A. 9516
Draper, Mary S. 2755
Draper, Sila A. 3773
Drew, Joanna 4361
Drown, Lucinda 7821
Drowne, Pamela 184
Drummond, Caroline 8009
Drummond, David G. 2725
Dryer, Matilda L. 6041
Dublin, Jeanette W. 4697
Dubois, Eliza Jane 692
Dubois, Parmelia 5989
Dudley, Eliza 2638
Dudley, Emily C. 9324
Dudley, Ira 2733
Dudley, John 2732
Dudley, Ward 1924, 2735
Duer, John 6286
Duer, William 2737, 6286
Duer, William A. 6286
Duffy, Margaret 2004
Duflon, John F. L. 5733
Duflon, Sarah Camilla 5733
Dufrainoit, Henry 2740
Dufrainoit, Jane 2740
Dumont, Waldron 2742
Dumphrey, Julia 2886
Dunbar, Elmira 1375
Dunbar, M. (Rev.) 2743
Duncan, Alexander 2749
Duncan, Cothia 8140
Duncan, Lydia 8150
Dundas, Olivia 2750
Dundas, William 2750
Dungin, Elizabeth 98
Dunham, Charity 8338
Dunham, Mary Ann 1876
Dunham, Samuel 1876
Dunham, Serophina 10001
Dunn, Catherine 2535
Dunn, Charles 2535
Dunn, Robert 2757

Dunning, Clarissa 3339
Dunning, Eliza 2766
Dunning, Urbane 2766
Dupre, Charles 10007
Duralde, Martin 2771
Durand, Cecilia Harriet 4789
Durand, Melinda 4818
Durfee, Ann 8071
Durham, Eliza 1936
Durkee, Sarah A. C. 5739
Dusenbury, John B. 2779
Dustan, L. Cleora 22
Dustie, Peter 2781
Dustin, Betsey (Mrs.) 10
Dutcher, Hannah 3513
Dutcher, Jane 226
Dutcher, Susan 1276
Dutton, George 2787, 5630, 6941
Dutton, James 2788
Dutton, Martha Gilbert 2966
Dutton, Mary R. 6941
Dutton, Nathaniel 2790
Dutton, Sarah D. 5630
Dwight, ___ (Dr.) 2801
Dwight, ___ (President) 2802, 2808
Dwight, Amos T. 2797
Dwight, Daniel 2806
Dwight, H. G. O. 1232
Dwight, Henry 7939
Dwight, Josiah 2811
Dwight, Sarah 7159
Dwight, Sophia 2804
Dwight, Theodore 2793
Dwight, Timothy 2801, 2808
Dyer, Charlotte Ann 3256
Dyer, Elenora E. 5806
Dyer, M. (Rev.) 7906
Dyer, Samuel 2813
Dygart, Harriet 2764
Dygert, Mary Martha 3384
Dygrett, Margaret 156
Dyson, Robert 2819
Eames, J. Sanger (Mr.) 2822
Eames, John 8295
Eames, O. (Mr.) 2825
Eames, Orlando 2823, 2826
Eames, Percy B. 2820
Eames, Sarah 8295
Eames, Sarah (Mrs.) 2821, 2824, 3269
Earl, Clarissa Caroline 8153
Earl, Edward 2827
Earlet, Mary E. 7361
Earll, Daniel 2831
Earll, Jonas 2832
Earll, Jonas, Jr. 8039
Earll, Melinda 945
Earll, Ursula 5450
Earls, ___ (Miss) 3819
Eason, Desire R. 5842
Easterbrook, Mary 7016
Easterbrooks, Mary 4482
Eastham, Priscilla 8294
Easton, Antoinette D. 2846
Easton, Elijah 2845
Easton, James I. 2846
Eastwood, Henrietta 7665
Eaton, Horatio 9371
Eaton, Lucina 5019
Eaton, Marie Louise 9371
Eaton, Sophia 1557
Eaton, William (Gen.) 2850
Eddy, Betsey 2857
Eddy, Caroline G. 10012
Eddy, Cynthia 2919
Eddy, Eli 2857, 2863, 10012

Eddy, Helen 4161
Eddy, Seth 4161
Edgerton, Marvin 2869
Edgerton, Riley 2872
Edington, Matilda 8390
Edmonds, Jane 2972
Edmunston, Eliza 6401
Edson, Belinda 6024
Edson, Thomas H. 2876
Edwards, Charlotte 9024
Edwards, Cynthia 2005
Edwards, Elizabeth 2973, 3015
Edwards, Jacob D. 2884
Edwards, Julia A. 7885
Edwards, Margaret 3837
Edwards, Mary B. 9871
Edwards, Thomas 3837
Eells, Daniel 9675
Eels, Fanny 2220
Efner, E. D. (Mr.) 8544
Ege, Catharine 7555
Eggleston, Aaron 2890
Eggleston, J. S. (Dr.) 2891
Eggleston, Lydia M. 8959
Ehle, Abram 2903
Ehle, Ann 1925
Ehle, Betsey 7107
Ehle, Catharine 9417
Ehle, Charlotte 542
Ehle, George 542, 1925, 8564, 9733
Ehle, Henry 3388, 4950
Ehle, Irene 8564
Ehle, John P. 2900
Ehle, Lany 3388
Ehle, Lucinda 8450
Ehle, Olive 4950
Ehle, Peter P. 2902
Ehle, Sophia 9733
Elder, Corinth S. 8036
Elder, William 8036
Eldred, Eliza S. 7440
Eldridge, Anna 2956
Eldridge, Caroline 7905
Eldridge, Clark 2908
Eldridge, James B. 7905
Ellas, F. S. (Mr.) 2910
Ellinwood, Rebecca 9515
Ellinwood, Reuben 9515
Elliot, David 2912
Elliot, Robert 5036
Elliot, Susan 5036
Elliott, Delilah 49
Elliott, Edward 7470
Elliott, Jerusha 5309
Elliott, Susan 7470
Ellis, ___ (Mr.) 2074
Ellis, Chesselden (Mr.) 2918
Ellis, Cynthia 2154
Ellis, E. (Mr.) 4457, 7452
Ellis, Hannah 418, 4457
Ellis, Harriet L. 7452
Ellis, John 2917
Ellis, John W. 2927
Ellis, Laura 6934
Ellis, Mary C. 3942
Ellis, Mary Jane 990
Ellis, Richard G. 990
Ellis, Sarah J. 580
Elms, ___ (Mr.) 2932
Elsworth, Cusiah 1666
Elwood, Mary A. 7878
Ely, Anson C. 2942
Ely, Cornelia C. 505
Ely, Martha 8660
Ely, Martha M. 2942
Ely, N. (Hon.) 505
Ely, Noah 498

Ely, Sarah O. 1026
Elyea, Maria 2935
Emerick, Peter 2950
Emerson, Firzina 5696
Emery, Eliza 8146
Emery, Hannah 6628
Emery, Sarah 4414
Emery, Sarah W. 163
Emmons, ___ (Mrs.) 8179
Enos, Hannah 3014
Erway, Lydia 9006
Erwin, ___ (Col.) 5601
Erwin, F. E. (Gen.) 2960
Ester, Locinda 7930
Estes, Nathaniel 2963
Estes, Sarah (Mrs.) 2521
Estes, Sarah Jane 2963
Estes, Stephen 2964
Etheridge, Julia Maria 8948
Ettinger, Abigail 4301
Ev__?__, Elizabeth T. 2354
Evans, Betsey A. 331
Evans, Casandra 5983
Evans, Charles E. 2980
Evans, Charlotte E. 9935
Evans, Eleanor (Mrs.) 2685
Evans, James C. 8849
Evans, Jane 9067
Evans, John 2967
Evans, Mary 5045
Evans, S. C. (Miss) 1644
Evans, Sibley 6120
Evarts, Harriet G. 200
Evarts, Mary C. 6370
Evarts, Rebecca 8579
Everett, Ursula 3501
Evers, John 2989
Everson, ___ (Mr.) 1226
Everts, Emma Adele 2970
Ewell, Olivia F. 5820
Ewers, Elihu 6095
Ewers, Polly 6095
Failing, A. J. 2994
Failing, Leonora 3279
Fairbank, Ira 4312
Fairbank, Sarah 4312
Fairbanks, Ira 2761
Fairbanks, Lucinda 2761
Fairborn, Delia 7686
Fairchild, B. F. (Mr.) 2997
Fairchild, Nancy 3614
Fairchild, Phebe 3677
Fairfield, Stephen 3906
Fake, Adam 3002
Falconer, Robert 3004
Fancher, Lydia Ann 3907
Fargo, Abigail 3335
Fargo, Sarah Lucetta 8400
Farley, Clarissye 6669
Farley, John 9120
Farley, John G. 3010
Farley, Susan Jeanette 9120
Farlyng, Elana 2830
Farnham, Catharine 1066
Farnham, George 3019
Farnham, Samuel 3012
Farnum, E. J. (Mr.) 3022
Farnum, Sarah 7927
Farrand, Arabella M. 9772
Farrar, David 3024
Farrar, Mary 3024
Farwell, Isaac U. 3031
Farwell, Marie R. 290
Farwell, Samuel 290, 3030, 3031, 6988
Farwell, Saphronia 1522
Farwell, Sarah A. 6988
Farwell, William H. 2551, 3029

Fassett, Amos 3033
Faulkner, Joan 1122
Faulkner, William 1122
Faxton, T. S. (Mr.) 116
Fay, Jonas (Dr.) 1401
Fay, Mary J. 1401
Fay, Nahum 3038
Fazon, Robert 1128
Feeter, G. H. (Mr.) 7202
Fwllows, E. B. (Mr.) 4744
Fellows, Hannah 774
Fellows, J. (Col.) 774
Fellows, J. (Mr.) 9967
Fellows, Minerva Porter 4744
Felt, Emmaline 3045
Felt, Norris 3045
Fenton, Amariah 3048, 6948
Fenton, Eleanor G. 6948
Fenton, J. S. (Mr.) 1811
Fenton, Jane A. 7113
Fenton, Julia I. 1811
Ferguson, Almira M. 8551
Ferguson, Eliza E. 653
Ferguson, Margaret 6587
Ferguson, Mary Eliza 4434
Ferguson, Susan 5230
Ferguson, William, Jr. 8551
Ferrand, Sally 201
Ferris, Sarah 6797
Ferris, Sophia 2044
Ferry, Esther A. 1115
Ferry, William H. (Mrs.) 9695
Fesh, Ellen M. 9178
Fesh, Michael 9178
Field, ___ (Mr.) 4121
Field, David 1132
Field, Ellen 4343
Fields, Sally Ann 8992
Firce, Harriet 6060
Fiero, Deborah M. 7567
Fiffield, Jesse 2923
Fiffield, Lucinda A. 2923
Filkin, Jane 9317
Filkins, Minerva 2458
Finch, Sarah E. 5414
Fink, Alexander H. 3087
Fink, Jacob 4642
Finkle, Sarah 2913
Finley, Elvia 5715
Fish, Clarissa 8914
Fish, H. H. (Mr.) 6834
Fish, Hamilton (Mrs.) 6135
Fish, J. L. (Mr.) 3096
Fish, Maria 3096
Fisher, Caroline C. 8484
Fisher, Catharine 5025
Fisher, Christopher 3102
Fisher, George W. 3099
Fisher, John 3100
Fisher, John, Jr. 3105
Fisher, Phebe L. 2199
Fisher, Philenda 5362
Fisk, Bezaleel 3107
Fisk, Hannah 4336
Fitch, Henrietta H. 119
Fitch, Julia S. 5192
Fitch, Louisa 8779
Fitch, Lucy 9587
Fitch, Lydia T. 7060
Fithian, Morehouse 3120
Fitzburgh, ___ (Col.) 8065
Fitzburgh, Ann C. 8065
Fitzburgh, William (Col.) 3122
Fitzheingirtzpinger, Rachael 6452
Fitzhugh, Isabella 8562
Flagg, A. C. (Mrs.) 1903
Flagler, ___ (Rev.) 4105

Flagler, Mary E. 4105
Flandeburgh, Eliza E. B. 8695
Flardino, Dianthe 2172
Fleming, Elsey 3365
Fling, Mercy M. 7778
Flint, Charles 7302
Flint, Charlotte 7302
Flint, Sarah Ann 72
Flower, Isaac 8350
Floyd, E. (Mrs.) 3145
Floyd, W. H. (Mr.) 3145
Floyd, William 3144
Fluent, Elizabeth 8070
Fluent, Ezra 3146
Flutcher, Deborah M. 3147
Flynn, Aurilla 3587
Foland, Frances 9700
Folger, Hannah M. 2958
Follensbe, Cornelia A. 7453
Follett, Catharine 1344
Follett, Oren 3150
Folmer, Catherine 9194
Folwell, Ann Catherine 316
Foot, Adonijah 7315
Foot, Almira M. 7315
Foot, Dennis 3157
Foot, Mary 8987
Foot, Samuel a. 361
Foote, Ellen 8705
Foote, Polly Ann 2460
Forbes, ___ (Miss) 9393
Forbes, Caroline 4187
Forbes, Margery 3964
Forbs, Mary Ann 39
Force, Hannah 3428
Ford, Arthur C. 6218
Ford, David 3173
Ford, Elizabeth P. 130
Ford, Emily C. 7920
Ford, James 7920
Ford, Maria M. 6218
Ford, Sarah 2570
Forman, Mary Euphemia 9051
Forrest, Joanna 7491
Fort, Emeline 1079
Fosgate, Serene 793
Fosgett, Eliza 7972
Foskett, Caroline A. 2880
Foskitt, Abigail 5823
Foster, ___ (Mr.) 2577
Foster, A. (Mr.) 9019
Foster, Caroline 366
Foster, Charry T. 2329
Foster, Daniel 2329, 2330
Foster, Emma 3197
Foster, Hanry A. 877, 5507
Foster, Jane A. 14
Foster, Jeter 3203
Foster, Joab G. 3190, 3197
Foster, Louise Frances 5507
Foster, Mary B. 2330
Foster, Mary N. 877
Foster, Phebe 6275
Foster, Reuben 3196
Foster, Robert W. 1668
Foster, Sarah D. 1668
Foster, Susan 9019
Foster, William 9812
Foulansbee, Emily R. 9882
Foults, Catharine 3223
Fowler, Charlotte 9402
Fowler, Cynthia 9509
Fowler, Elisha 3212
Fowler, Esther Maria 2928
Fowler, Johanna 5635
Fowler, Mary Ann 3995
Fowler, O. S. (Mr.) 9402
Fowler, Sarah 8804

Fowler, William 3161
Fox, Charles 3216
Fox, Mary B. 5002
Fox, Peter G. 3219
Francher, Roxana 5398
Francis, Elizabeth (Mrs.) 2483
Francis, Maria P. 3234
Francis, Richard H. 3228, 3233, 3234
Francis, Thomas 3231
Francis, William 3229, 4843
Francisco, Abigail 6332
Francisco, J. (Mr.) 3235
Francisco, Ruth Ann 6585
Franklin, ___ (Dr.) 6192
Franklin, Amos A. 3238
Franklin, Benjamin 6214
Franklin, Corlista 589
Franklin, Maria W. 2237
Frantz, Catharine 8473
Fraser, David 3241
Frazer, Ann L. 8693
Frazer, Carolina Georgianna 6232
Frazer, Thomas 6232
Frear, ___ (Mr.) 4172
Frederick, Alvira 9189
Fredericks, Ann E. 3282
Fredericks, Gertrude T. 9041
Freeland, Eliza 5122
Freeman, Charles 3252
Freeman, Charles P. 3258
Freeman, Eliza Ann 4468
Freeman, Emily L. 4011
Freeman, Mahala P. 6164
Freeman, Mary Elizabeth 5462
Freeman, Moses S. 4468
Freer, Catherine 9599
Freer, Elizabeth 8845
French, Almira J. 7362
French, Elizabeth 9140
French, Hannah 1052
French, John 7362
French, Maria 1613, 4399
French, Maynard 3269
French, Mercy 1634
French, Samuel 3267
French, Thomas 3268, 3274, 3275
Freshour, Henry 7232
Frey, Hendrick 3280
Frisbie, ___ (Dr.) 2636
Frisbie, Elihu 3285
Frisbie, Martha H. 9553
Frisbie, Sarah Maria 2636
Frost, A. (Mr.) 4071
Frost, Adelia D. 5224
Frost, F. (Mr.) 4071
Frost, John 4548
Frost, Joseph 38
Frost, Sarah Gold 4548
Frothingham, Elizabeth 2875
Frothingham, George 2875
Frushour, Alexander 3295
Frushour, Laney M. 3295
Fulford, Susan 5111
Fulkerson, Roxey 1937
Fuller, ___ (Mr.) 3300
Fuller, Adaline 1707
Fuller, C. A. (Mrs.) 3300
Fuller, Carrington A. 3305
Fuller, E. (Dr.) 3316
Fuller, J. S. (Mr.) 6251
Fuller, Jane 3305, 6522
Fuller, Lydia 8328
Fuller, Mary M. 549
Fuller, Orion 3297
Fuller, Robert 4628
Fuller, Roxa I. 6207

Fuller, S.(Dr.) 3301
Fuller, Sabra A. 183
Fuller, Samuel 6522
Fuller, Sarah A. 4628
Fulton, Robert (Mrs.) 2319
Furgeson, Eliza R. 8973
Furman, George W. 3321
Furman, Harriet 6234
Gaffney, Ann 1484
Gage, Aaron 3332
Gage, Sarah 8900
Gager, Salome 1534
Gailey, Caroline 6103
Gaines, Sabina 5766
Gale, Almeda A. (Mrs.) 3163
Gale, Catharine 1286
Gallagher, ___ (Mrs.) 3337
Gallagher, George 8228
Gallagher, Margaret R. 7008
Gallagher, Mary M. 4372
Gallatin, Albert 3344
Gallaudet, T. H. (Rev.) 3345
Gallop, Orrilla 3166
Gallup, Amy E. 8601
Gallup, Benjamin 8601
Gallup, Mary 6899
Gallup, Sarah Matilda 1259
Gallup, William 5273
Gambey, Laura S. 5273
Gambia, Amanda A. 3678
Gambie, Emily 4100
Gannon, Abigail 4034
Gansom, Lucy 7161
Gardenier, Barent 3041
Gardenier, Laura 3041
Gardiner, Elizabeth M. 8298
Gardner, Angelina 2078
Gardner, Calcina P. 4831
Gardner, Catharine 6126, 6354
Gardner, Eliza 5941
Gardner, Elizabeth A. 478
Gardner, George 6610
Gardner, Harriet K. 3989
Gardner, James V. P. 3368
Gardner, Malinda 1320
Gardner, Maria M. 917
Gardner, Morgan 6837
Gardner, Richard 3989
Gardner, Sarah 6646
Gardner, Sophia 778
Garey, Catharine 4219
Garlick, Betsey 1516
Garlick, Sarah Jane 8971
Garlock, Isaac 3376
Garlock, Nancy 3376
Garr, Jacob 9296
Garrard, Sarah B. (Mrs.) 5651
Garratt, William 9735
Garrett, ___ (Mr.) 3377
Garrett, Cheney 3379
Garrison, Ann 2946
Garrison, Sally Ann 2569
Garrow, Nathaniel 5947
Garvey, Maria 7654
Garvin, Julia 3383
Garvin, S. B. (Mr.) 3383
Gaston, ___ (Mr.) 4121
Gates, Caroline M. 8925
Gates, Christina 8448
Gates, E. A, (Miss) 8782
Gates, Ebenezer S. 6926
Gates, H. (Mr.) 3397
Gates, Isabella 5051
Gates, Julia Ann 6926
Gates, Le Roy 3392
Gates, Louisa 726
Gates, Ralph I. 8925
Gates, Sarah F. 5172
Gates, Susan 8760

Gavetty, Huldah 3403
Gavetty, John A. 3403
Gaw, John 3404
Gawtry, Elizabeth 900
Gay, Mary F. 2261
Gay, Samuel 5814
Gay, William F. 2261
Gaylord, Angeline B. 8164
Gaylord, Flavel 4213
Gaylord, Lucius 8164
Gaylord, Mary 6672
Gaylord, Mary W. 4213
Gear, E. G. (Rev.) 3414, 3415
Gear, Hezekiah 3411
Genung, Ardelissa 8611
George, Betsey (Mrs.)5585
George, Elizabeth 5729
German, ___ (Gen.) 3431
German, Walter 3430
Germon, Michael 3433
Germon, Sarah 3433
Germond, Martha 7192
Gerry, Eldridge 3435
Getman, Emeline 8780
Gibbons, James 3438, 7105
Gibbs, Ann 3437
Gibson, Betsey 6199
Gibson, Harriet 5349
Gibson, Jane E. 35
Gibson, Margaret 960
Gibson, Susan 3016
Gibson, Susan (Mrs.) 8748
Gibson, Thomas 3019
Giddins, Edward 3443
Gidman, Anna 1834
Giffing, ___ (Mr.) 3446
Gifford, Abner 4706
Gifford, Phila 4706
Gilbert, Almira M. 6457
Gilbert, Betsey Jane 1699
Gilbert, E. J. (Miss) 9879
Gilbert, Frances M. 882
Gilbert, Harriet 9327
Gilbert, Laura 7138
Gilbert, Margaret Elizabeth 9128
Gilbert, William 9327
Gildard, B. (Mr.) 4314
Gildersleeve, Mary A. 8158
Giles, Elizabeth G. 9419
Gilfillan, Jeannette 7893
Gilfillin, Mary 4644
Gill, Mary Malinda 4594
Gillet, Dorcas 756
Gillett, Aurelia Martha 5843
Gillett, Mary E. 648
Gillett, Perline 6229
Gillett, Ruth 8089
Gillett, Salona 7962
Gillispie, Julia A. 3832
Gillmore, Dexter 3488
Girth, Rosella 6344
Glass, Harriet 6272
Gleason, Arminda 3128
Glen, ___ (Mr.) 5690
Glezen. Amelia 4496
Glezen, Oren 4496
Gloutney, Julia 3183
Glover, John J. 1418
Glover, Phebe 1418
Glymps, Sally 6102
Goble,Milton 8802
Godard, C. V. (Mr.) 3988
Godfrey, Frances 1950, 6372
Godfrey, John H. 3512
Godley, Rebecca 5900
Goff, Content 695
Goff, Julia A. 5395
Goff, Mary 8470

Goff, Prudence 4062
Goff, Sarah Cornelia 7295
Gold, Elizabeth F. 2941
Gold, Martha (Mrs.) 2555
Gold, Theodore S. 2552, 3515
Gold, Thomas R. 1958
Goldthwait, Catherine L. 723
Gomer, Nancy 2518
Goodale, S. (Rev.) 3522
Gooden, Elice 7200
Goodenow, Eliza 2267
Goodfellow, Christiana 8610
Goodhue, John 3526
Gooding, Adeline 6552
Gooding, Hannah A. 6609
Goodle, Philinda 2264
Goodman, Elizabeth 1268
Goodman, Persilla P. 6445
Goodnoe, Arminta 1469
Goodrich, Amelia 4902
Goodrich, J. T. (Rev.) 3538
Goodrich, Lucy P. 9816
Goodwin, A. (Mr.) 263
Goodwin, Addia 6551
Goodwin, Daniel 9910
Goodwin, Joseph 9565
Goodwin, Lyman D. 3547
Goodwin, Matilda M. 263
Goodwin, Nancy 9565
Gookins, Seymour 3552
Gordon, Charles 3556
Gordon, E. H. (Mr.) 3555
Gordon, Elijah 356
Gordon, Susan 8121
Gorgas, Elizabeth A. 1635
Gorgas, Joseph 1635
Gorham, Nathaniel 3564
Goslee, Mathew 3565
Gosman, Joanna B. 3021
Gosman, Jonathan 3021
Gould, Alma A. 7348
Goulden, Emily 3577
Goulden, George 3577
Goundry, George 3579, 3581, 3582
Gourgas, Henrietta C. C. 2600
Grady, Catharine 3901
Gragg, Ann 6613
Graham, Deborah 8962
Graham, Edmund A. 2926
Graham, Eliza W. 2709
Graham, Malvina 3183a
Graham, Margaret 1334
Granger, Daniel 3597
Granger, Delia W. 4739
Granger, Frederick 3595
Granger, JohnAlbert 4739
Granger, Otis P. 3596, 3599
Grannis, Cephas 3601
Grannis, Cyrus 3603
Grannis, Eveline R. 4855
Grannis, Julia A. 3604
Grannis, Timothy O. 3604
Grant,Charlotte 2939
Grant, Eliza 1511
Grant, George 3605
Grason, William J. 3608
Graves, Abby J. 9404
Graves, Caroline 3616
Graves, Emily 5984
Graves, Henry 3616, 9404
Graves, J. O, (Mr.) 3621
Graves, Julius 3620
Graves, Theda 9145
Gray, Anna 9704
Gray, Caroline 465
Gray, Joshua 465, 3630
Gray, Rhoda M. 6792

Gray, Thomas 9704
Gray, William 3637
Grayson, Leticia P. (Mrs.) 6968
Greeley, Horace 3640, 3641
Greeley, Mary Y. C. 3640
Green, ___ (Gen.) 1612
Green, ___ (President) 8967
Green, Byram 6276
Green, C. H. (Mr.) 6218
Green, Cornelia M. 3649
Green, Eliza Janet 9287
Green, Emma L. 1594
Green, H. (Mr.) 3648
Green, Harriet 1446
Green, Harry W. 1594
Green, Henry 3646
Green, Jane 6162
Green, John 3644, 9635
Green, John R. 3662
Green, Lafayette 3644
Green, Louisa 3218
Green, Lucy E. 6276
Green, Marcia Deming 8967
Green, Mary Ann 7059
Green, Matilda Ann 3644
Green, Philip 3655
Green, Sarah 1804
Green, William 3663
Green, William H. 3649
Greene, Frances L. 289
Greene, L. (Mrs.) 2296
Greene, U. (Mr.) 2296
Greene, William (Mrs.) 1205
Greenman, H. (Mr.) 1892
Gregory, ___ (Mr.) 527
Gregory, Betsey (Mrs.) 6020
Gregory, Hannah 3502
Gregory, Mary 9806
Gregory, Matthew 9806
Gregory, Minerva 3189
Gregory, Sarah Cutting 4654
Greuhn, ___ (Baroness) 5240
Greves, Evelina P. 1751
Greves, J. P. (Dr.) 3683
Greves, John 3681
Greves, Thomas 1751
Gridley, Alvinah 4686
Gridley, Celestia Loisa 1549
Gridley, G. A. (Mr.) 3697
Gridley, Marietta S. 1492
Gridley, Orrin 3691
Gridley, Philo 3690
Gridley, Susannah 2842
Gridley, Wayne 3695
Grieves, Minerva (Wid.) 3701
Griffin, ___ (Gen.) 9253
Griffin, ___ (Mr.) 2152
Griffin, Elizabeth 2060
Griffin, Jane 3716
Griffin, Joel 3704
Griffin, Marion M. 9253
Griffin, Mary A. 2652
Griffin, Richard J. 3702
Griffin, Thirza L. 325
Griffing, Jane M. 2979
Griffith, Griffith P. 3712
Griffith, Mary C. 2337
Griggs, Caroline E. 59
Griggs, Philena 2626
Grinnell, C. B. (Mr.) 6467
Grinnell, Caroline M. 6467
Grinnell, Cornelia 9764
Griswold, Adeline 8678
Griswold, Catharine T. 4562
Griswold, Daniel 4562
Griswold, Eliza 8946
Griswold, Gaylord 3734
Griswold, H. (Miss) 8679

Griswold, Harriet Jane 9638
Griswold, Hooker 9074
Griswold, Horace 3726
Griswold, Jane 5456
Griswold, Louisa 9929
Griswold, Maroah 1983
Griswold, Marvin 9638
Griswold, Mary E. 9074
Griswold, N. (Elder) 8678
Griswold, Nancy 5648
Griswold, Norris C. 8679
Griswold, Octavia 8676
Griswold, Samuel B. 3728
Griswold, Sarah 6156
Groah, Emma M. 4857
Groesbeck, Jane 2930
Grosh, A. B. (Rev.) 3743
Gross, Clarissa 1306
Grosvenor, C. P. (Rev.) 3745
Grosvenor, Caroline M. 4417
Grosvenor, E. O. (Mr.) 4417
Grosvenor, Ebenezer O. 3747
Grosvenor, Francis D. 359, 365, 3749
Grosvenor, Harriet H. A. 359
Grosvenor, Mary Ann 3747
Grosvenor, Oliver C. 3748
Grover, Hiram 3754
Grover, Keziah 3754
Groves, Clinton 3760
Guernsey, Eliza 121
Guernsey, Julia Ann 9925
Guernsey, S. (Mr.) 9925
Guest, Mary 9233
Guild, ___ (Mrs.) 8172
Guile, Mary Ann 2348
Guiles, Phebe 2847
Guilford, Mary 769
Guilford, Paul 769
Guiteau, L. (Dr.) 6506
Guiwits, ___ (Mr.) 3768
Guiwits, Isaac 3768
Gulick, John 3769
Gunn, Sarah P. 5163
Gunsolus, Catharine 80
Gunsolus, Sarah A. 1029
Gurley, Electa E. J. 3756
Gurley, Henry 3756
Gurnam, Matilda 1198
Gustin, Phebe 2216
Guthrie, Gloriann 1508
Guthrie, John 3777
Gutt, Amelia H. 4023
Gutt, Daniel 4023
Habermel, Catharine A. 5132
Hacket, Persis 636
Hacket, Sally 1088
Hackett, John 3783
Hackett, Louisa 3783
Hackley, Abel 3788
Hackley, John 3790
Hackley, Sophia Ellen 432
Hager, Ann 6868
Haggerty, Sophia 9675
Hahn, John M. 3797, 3798
Hahn, Susan M. 3798
Haight, Amy Maria 1447
Haight, Ann E. 5642
Haight, Charlotte 2932
Haight, F. M. (Mr.) 5032
Haight, Fletcher M. 3985
Haight, H. (Mr.) 5380
Haight, John W. 3801
Haight, Julia A. 3801
Haight, Julia M. 3985
Haight, Maria 3827
Haight, Rachel 5523
Haight, Reuben 3800

Haight, Samuel 3804
Haight, Sophia 3705
Haines, Sarah 4542
Hale, Caroline H. 3938
Hale, Emily 9151
Hale, Henrietta Hayden 9388
Hale, Israel 3810
Hale, Malvina L. 3057
Hale, Roxey 8754
Hale, Sarah W. 6325
Haley, Ann 4536
Haliburton, Agnes 7239
Hall, ___ (Judge) 8653
Hall, A. B. (Mr.) 6253
Hall, Abraham B. 3921
Hall, Adaline 3824
Hall, Albro 3811, 3824
Hall, Amanda 5155
Hall, Amasa 3844
Hall, Ambrose 4757, 5272
Hall, Amos 3845
Hall, Anne 2536
Hall, Asahel 3814
Hall, Bailey 3847
Hall, Chloe 3814
Hall, Clarissa 4757
Hall, D. S. (Mr.) 3830
Hall, David S. 3815
Hall, Edward 3785, 3816
Hall, Eliza 6314
Hall, Elmira 3831
Hall, Emeline 2063
Hall, Esther 3055
Hall, Evelina B. 6872
Hall, Eveline 4000
Hall, Francis 3840, 3852, 3853
Hall, G. (Rev.) 3822
Hall, H. A. (Miss) 5796
Hall, Harriet 4199
Hall, Harriet N. 3921
Hall, Hiram 2063
Hall, Isaac 3838
Hall, James 5796
Hall, Jennette M. 9283
Hall, Jeremiah 8554
Hall, John 4000
Hall, Joseph 9843
Hall, Julia 8554
Hall, Julia A. 3315
Hall, Laura J. 3785
Hall, Lucinda 5623
Hall, Mariam 4579
Hall, Mary Ann 8888
Hall, Mary M. 5272
Hall, Moses 3841
Hall, N. H. (Rev.) 8888
Hall, Nancy 5107
Hall, Parmelia 6811
Hall, Prescott 624
Hall, R. H. 3839
Hall, S. R. (Mr.) 3813, 3844
Hall, Samuel 320
Hall, Sophia E. 8731
Hall, Susan Ann 8653
Halleck, Abraham H. 3860
Hallett, Catharine 7215
Hallett, Jacob W. 7215, 7476
Hallett, Maria 7476
Hallman, Eliza 1252
Hallock, James 3868
Hallock, Laura B. 6882
Hallock, Mary 3868
Hallock, Mary P. 107
Hallock, N. (Mr.) 3866
Hallock, Nicholas 107
Hallock, R. T. (Mr.) 3864
Halsey, Caroline 8954
Halsey, Elmina 3440
Halsey, Hezekiah 3873

Halsey, J. H. (Mr.) 3440
Halsey, Jehiel H. 3871
Halsey, John H. 8954
Halsey, Rebecca 8931
Halsey, Susan J. 3873
Halsey, Zephaniah 8931
Halstead, Amanda 4823
Halstead, Helen M. 4515
Halter, Elizabeth (Mrs.) 7502
Hamblin, Harriet 2684
Hamilton, Charity 453
Hamilton, E. (Mr.) 3879
Hamilton, Jane 563, 8877
Hamlin, Catharine E. 3891, 3894
Hamlin, William D. 3891, 3894
Hammond, Alma 4348
Hammond, Dennis 3900
Hammond, Elizabeth S. E. 9181
Hammond, Emeline 594
Hammond, H. L. (Rev.) 3908
Hammond, J. D. (Mr.) 3912
Hammond, Joseph 9181
Hammond, Orpha Ann 4601
Hammond, Polly 9930
Hammond, Samuel 3913
Hammond, William R. 3909
Hancker, Harriet M. 9945
Hancox, Sarah Eliza 3442
Handley, Jane 3398
Handley, Lydia 3723
Handley, William 3398
Handy, Jane 4179
Handy, John H. 4179
Handy, T. D. (Mr.) 3922
Hanford, Jane Eliza 9828
Hanna, John 3925
Hanna, Mary Ann 6975
Hannahs, William 3927
Hannin, Julia ⟨³²³
Hannum, Phebe C. 6939
Hanstis, George C. 3934
Harder, Phebe Ann 8011
Harding, John 6932
Harding, Maria L. 6932
Hardy, Julia 9267
Hardy, Mary 9222
Harford, Eliza 2571
Harger, Noah N. 3940
Harper, Clamana 3112
Harper, Eliza 5993
Harrington, H. S. (Mrs.) 3957
Harrington, Jere S. (Mr.) 3957
Harrington, William 3960
Harris, Alma 7218
Harris, Almira 3976
Harris, Catharine 2346
Harris, Cornelia A. 4135
Harris, David 3975
Harris, Frances 8970
Harris, Rachel S. 4572
Harris, S. T. (Mr.) 3963
Harris, Thomas 3976
Harrison, ___ (Gen.) 402, 4602
Harrison, Clarissa L. 402
Harrison, Eliza A. 8636
Harrison, J. C. Symmes 4602
Harrison, Lucinda 4019
Harrison, Lutia Ann 1590
Harrison, Lydia 240
Harrison, Mary C. 6306
Harrison, William 3980
Harrower, B. (Mr.) 3982
Harrower, L. B. (Mr.) 3983
Hart, Abby L. 8487
Hart, Ann Elizabeth 6213
Hart, Charlotte 2240
Hart, Ephraim 5886
Hart, Harriet 4871
Hart, Isabella 8699

Hart, Jane 7402
Hart, Julia 8769
Hart, Lovisa 7534
Hart, Martin 1352
Hart, Orpah 2279
Hart, Roswell 2240, 7402
Hart, Sarah Elizabeth 1352
Hart, Truman 8487
Hart, Wealthy Velona 5886
Hartman, Catharine 3979
Hartranft, Mary 3353
Hartt, Elizabeth (Mrs.) 9009
Hartwell, ___ (Mr.) 3704
Hartwell, Joseph 3998
Harvard, Joseph, 33
Harvey, A. (Mr.) 3999
Harvey, Deborah 7767
Harvey, Esther 6341
Harvey, Louisa 1160
Harvey, Sally 7709
Harvey, Uriah 4005
Harwood, Calista 9986
Hasbrouck, Levi 4008
Hasbrouck, Sarah Maria 4008
Haseltine, Ebenezer 4010
Haseltine, Maria 4010
Haskell, John H. 4012
Haslehurst, Richard 4014
Hasson, John 4016
Hastings, ___ (Dr.) 4028
Hastings, ___ (Gen.) 4030
Hastings, Charles 4022
Hastings, E. P. (Mr.) 4017,
   4024, 4036
Hastings, Ephraim 9211
Hastings, Eurotus 4031
Hastings, Eurotus P. 4026
Hastings, Horace 4021
Hastings, Norman 4030
Hastings, Oliver 4020
Hastings, Orlando 4024
Hastings, S. (Dr.) 3695
Hastings, S. A. (Mr.) 4018
Hastings, Seth 4027
Hastings, Sophia E. 8069
Hastings, Timothy 4029
Hastings, Burrell 6167
Hatch, Hapsky 7706
Hatch, Henry A. 4041
Hatch, James L. 4039
Hatch, Mary M. 9655
Hatch, Sarah 4759
Hatch, T. (Capt.) 4759
Hathaway, Asher 4052
Hathaway, Caroline 7155
Hathaway, Deborah 7952
Hathaway, Elizabeth 6977
Hathaway, Gilbert 7952
Hathaway, Sophia 4750
Hathbone, Pauline 3968
Hathorn, Caroline 5379
Hathorn, Hannah 9808
Haughton, Nancy B. 5321
Hause, Fidelia 3386
Hauseleuren, Mary E. 4800
Haven, Philander B. 4057
Haven, Sarah 2668
Havens, Elizabeth 9691
Havens, Fanny 3050
Havens, Joseph 3050
Havens, Mariah 4596
Havens, Sylvia 7738
Havery, Mary 5232
Haviland, Caroline G. 5350
Haviland, Cynthia 2661
Haviland, Harriet B. (Mrs.)
   1440
Hawes, Amelia (Mrs.) 7923
Hawkins, ___ (Col.) 5007

Hawkins, Darius 4070
Hawkins, S. M. (Miss) 872
Hawks, Cassandria 122
Hawley, Abigail 7364
Hawley, Abigal Ann 3781
Hawley, Abijah 4081, 4090
Hawley, Burton (Mrs.) 3190
Hawley, Harriet I. 1349
Hawley, Silas 4085
Hawley, Rufus 4092
Haws, Julia A. 6883
Hawser, Lucretia 5600
Hay, Almira 5054
Hay, Esquire 5054
Hayden, Chester 3944
Hayden, David 2850
Hayden, Ellen E. 6454
Hayden, Jane S. 3944
Hayes, Abigail 3101
Hayes, Aseneth 9365
Hayes, Catherine E. 4923
Hayes, David 4104
Hayes, Elizabeth L. 4104
Hayes, Isaac 4923
Hayes, Joel 4108
Hayes, Marianne 1402
Hayes, Pliny 4103
Hayes, Pliny, Jr. 4111
Hayes, Sarah 4359
Hayne, Gamar J. 4258
Hayne, Mary 8720
Haynes, Margaret 7061
Haynes, Nancy 4736
Haynes, Tirrah 5191
Hayt, Samuel 2090
Hayt, Sarah N. 2090
Hayward, Elizabeth Cornelia
    3669
Hayward, Hartwell 4122
Hayward, Mary ann 5056
Hazetine, John 4129
Heacock, Jane Hanson 4371
Heacock, Reuben B. 4371
Heacox, Harriet Eliza 125
Headley, Ann 7154
Heamingway, Roxy Ann 10005
Heanay, Susanna 2244
Hearsey, John 6651
Heart, Caroline 7520
Heartwell, Benjamin 1333
Heartwell, Catharine 1333
Heath, John 4140
Heath, Timothy 4139
Hebbard, Polly 1900
Hecox, Caroline 3589
Hecox, Eliza 4331
Hecox, Obediah 3589
Hecox, Samuel 4143
Hecox, William A. 4143
Hedges, Prudence 4088
Heermance, Sarah A. 9969
Heermans, Phebe 9967
Heggis, Archibald 4150
Heintzelman ___ (Maj.) 8515
Heinz, Henrietta 6905
Helm, ___ (Capt.) 9279
Helmer, ___ (Miss) 2532
Hemiup, Anthony 4158
Hemstreet, Jacob 4159
Henderson, A. W. (Rev.) 4162
Henderson, Emelina 1870
Henderson, Freelove 802
Henderson, Mary 4983
Hendrick, Hendrick Aupaumut
    4166
Henion, Sophrenia C. 2625
Hennesy, Ann 5672
Henry, James T. 4173

Henry, John 4748
Henry, John D. 4170
Henry, Margaret M. 4173
Henry, Mary Ann 4748
Henry, William 4169, 4978
Henry, Zilphia (Mrs.) 3177
Henshaw, J. Sidney 4178
Henshaw, Jane F. 4178
Herkimer, ___ (Gen.) 3280
Herkimer, Catharine 1262
Herkimer, Nicholas (Gen.) 4183
Hermsley, Henrietta 5834
Herrick, Edward 4188
Herrick, Electa 6642
Herrick, Fanny 3567
Herrick, Harriet 6965
Herrick, Lydia 4160
Herrick, Mary E. 8027
Herrick, Phebe Ann 9672
Herrick, R. Clarinda 4190
Herrick, Sarah R. 6703
Herrington, Abigal L. 1750
Herrington, Eliza 5212
Herrington, Harriet 8839
Herrington, John 5212
Herrington, N. M. 4192, 4193
Hervey, Polly 395
Heslop, Margaret R. 3680
Hess, Margaret 8582
Hess, Mary Ann 5959
He_? strat, Jane 5598
Hetherington, Sally M. 870
Hewes, Almeda 9615
Hewes, Ann 6924
Hewes, Samuel 6924
Hewit, Dorothy (Mrs.) 1287
Hewit, Elmira K. 9572
Hewitt, Esther L. 2671
Hewitt, Gurdon 4204
Hewitt, Melissa 6038
Hewson, Catherine Jane 1148
Hibbard, Clara (Mrs.) 2603
Hibbard, Eveline 5218
Hibbard, Sophia 4165
Hickcox, Elisha M. 4207
Hickcox, Margaret 4207
Hickock, Harris 4211
Hickox, Walter S. 4215
Hicks, Jane A.
Hicks, Lucinda M. 5610
Hicks, Margaret 6073
Hicks, Samuel 5610
Hicks, William, Jr. 9956
Higbie, Ellea 5341
Higgins, Almira R. 3851
Higgins, Ann 7271
Higgins, Lucy R. 9345
Higgins, William 4225
Higgins, Zadock 3851
Higham, Abraham 1165, 7018
Higham, Jane Louisa 7018
Hildreth, Isaac 4230
Hill, Almira 7795
Hill, Caroline 9681
Hill, Caroline E. 6202
Hill, Catherine 7379
Hill, Eliza 3600
Hill, Emily 3436, 4863, 8847
Hill, Ephraim 4240
Hill, Ira 4236
Hill, J. (Mr.) 4238
Hill, John 394
Hill, Julia 2002
Hill, Laura 9297
Hill, Lorinda E. 4866
Hill, M. J. (Miss) 394
Hill, Maria 8642
Hill, Matilda Jane 5493

Hill, Nathaniel 4234
Hill, Thomas 4241, 8847
Hillhouse, James 4253
Hillman, Mary 2753
Hillman, Ruth 9429
Hills, Almira 9540
Hills, Amelia M. 4267
Hills, Cornelia A. 1880
Hills, Cornelia M. 232
Hilton, Sarah 4976
Hilts, Margaret 6800
Himrod, Peter 4259
Hinckley, Aceneth 408
Hine, Isabella 4260
Hine, Jay, S. 4260
Hinkley, Amasa 4263
Hinkley, Catharine M. 1601
Hinkley, Hsnnah A. 3676
Hinkley, Lucretia 4263
Hinman, Abner 4269
Hinman, Artemissa 9206
Hinman, Elizabeth E. 3807
Hinman, Livingston 3807
Hipple, Cassandra 8941
Hoadley, Altha 513
Hoadley, Elizabeth 9376
Hoadley, Emma 9281
Hobart, ___ (Rt. Rev.) 3939
Hobart, Elizabeth Catherine
    3939
Hobart, J. H. (Rev.) 4279
Hobby, J. C. A. (Mr.) 4280
Hochstrasser, Ormond 4281
Hodges, Chloe C. 3881
Hodgman, ___ (Miss) 1064
Hodgman, William 1064
Hoe, Caroline 2947
Hoeg, Lucy 9238
Hoes, Peter I. 4285
Hoesin, Mary 3796
Hoffman, Abigail 9715
Hoffman, J. O. (Mr.) 9040
Hogan, Maurice 4297
Hogarth, R. (Miss) 2498
Hoger, Anson 4299
Holbrook, Charlotte 4045
Holbrook, Luther 4303
Holden, Fox 8502
Holden, Horace 4306
Holden, Lavinia A. 8502
Holden, Relief P. 5316
Holdredge, F. S. (Mr.) 7985
Holister, Mary 8791
Holister, Sarah M. 7576
Holladay, Jane 3073
Holland, Ivory 4074
Holland, Louisa 7503
Holland, Mary 4074
Hollenbeck, Caroline 221
Hollett, Elizabeth B. 1220
Holley, Elizabeth D. 5040
Hollister, Anna (Mrs.) 1943
Hollister, C. (Mr.) 9889
Hollister, Frederick 4316
Hollister, Mary C. 9889
Hollister, U. (Mr.) 511
Hollum, Charlotte 6026
Holly, John M. 4317
Holly, Luther 4318
Hlmes, Araminta 4205
Holmes, Hannah 2141
Holmes, Harriet 6423
Holmes, Mary 9631
Holmes, Milton 4319
Holmes, Sally 4370
Holmes, susan 5633
Holmes, Sylvanus 4325
Holt, Caroline 1661

Holt, Catharine (Mrs.) 8488
Homer, Margaret 8115
Honeywell, Mary 348
Hood, Jane 1098
Hood, Mary ann 5856
Hoog, Thomas A. 4354
Hooker, Cornelia 6649
Hooker, J. (Mr.) 7810
Hooker, Mary 7810
Hooper, Alvira 4275
Hopkins, ___ (Mrs.) 7479
Hopkins, Carolyn A. 7462
Hopkins, Charles H. 4364
Hopkins, D. Lemuel 4369
Hopkins, Elizabeth 6309
Hopkins, Esther 2218
Hopkins, Frederick 6309
Hopkins, Harriet 543
Hopkins, Helmenia Rosaline 7299
Hopkins, Hester R. 7477
Hopkins, J. B. (Dr.) 7299
Hopkins, J. D. 4363
Hopkins, Juliana 7940
Hopkins, Mary elizabeth 9100
Hopkins, S. M. (Mr.) 7477
Hopkins, Samuel 9100
Hopkins, Samuel M. 4960, 7940
Hopkins, Sarah E.964
Hopkins, Susan 468
Horan, Martin 4374
Hroner, Josephine De Wolf 624
Horner, Sarah (Mrs.) 8518
Horsburgh, Alexander 4377
Horton, Almene 2056
Horton, Amelia H. 7960
Horton, J. C. (Hon.) 7960
Horton, Mary Mahala 5164
Hosford, E. (Mr.) 4384
Hoskins, D. L. (Mr.) 4387
Hosmer, Catharine 4388
Hosmer, Susan 6259
Hosmer, William E. 4388
Hotchkin, Mark C. 4393
Hotchkiss, A. (Mr.) 5000
Hotchkiss, Chloe 8340
Hotchkiss, Cyrus 6476
Houck, ___ (Mrs.) 1894
Hough, David 4401
Hough, John 4401
Houghtaling, Thomas 4403
Houghteling, James 4405, 7249
Houghteling, Laura L. 7249
Houghton, Henry D. 4406
Houghton, Mary A. 4406
House, Editha 8775
House, Eleazer 1490
House, Elizabeth 6557
House, Emily H. 3306
Hovey, A. J. (Mr.) 4426
Hovey, Alfeed H. 4420
Hovey, Jesse R. 4422
Hovey, Mary 1411
Hovey, Mary S. 3642
How, David White 4431
How, Henry 4430
How, Mary Y. 3412
Howard, Cordelai 5401
Howard, Jane A. 385
Howard, Lydia Almira 7727
Howard, Mary ann 3610
Howard, Samuel 4435
Howarth, Alice 4227
Howe, Amos P. 4450
Howe, Elizabeth 4261
Howe, Lucinda 4568
Howe, Nancy Jane 9888
Howe, O. A. (Mr.) 4445

Howe, Sally 4450
Howell,B. B. (Mr.) 3739
Howell, Ellen Maria 3739
Howell, Esther P. 614
Howell, Jane E. 4690
Howell, Jemima 7518
Howell, Margaret 6717
Howell, Nathaniel 4690
Howell R. (Mr.) 4460
Howell, Rhoda C. 933
Howell, T. H. (Mr.) 4461
Howes, Fitch 4467
Howey, Lucretia 5737
Howland, Annis C. 9184
Howland, Benjamin 4471
Howland, Lois P. 9921
Howland, Lucy M. 5592
Howland, Prudence 6245
Hoyt, Catharine 3214
Hoyt, David B. 4479
Hoyt, David P. 1947, 1948
Hoyt, Ellen S. 1948
Hoyt, Hannah E. 7692
Hu ? , Caroline 5646
Hubbard, ___ (Mr.) 4493
Hubbard, Laura Serepta 9391
Hubbard, Mary S. 5369
Hubbard, Soloman 4485
Hubbard, Susan 4703
Hubbard, T. H. (Mr.) 4489
Hubbard, Thomas H. 4487, 5369
Hubbell, ___ (Mr.) 9831
Hubbell, ___ (Rev.) 4502
Hubbell, A. (Mr.) 8272
Hubbell, Alrick 4497, 4504
Hubbell, Cecilia 541
Hubbell, Frances 738
Hubbell, Mary Ann 3200
Hubbell, Walter 4498, 4503
Hubbell, William S. 4506
Hubby, Caroline 9728
Hubby, Mary 8329
Hubby, Thomas 9728
Hudenut, Eliza B. 3494
Hudson, Caroline E. 4692
Hudson, Daniel 4516
Hudson, E. D. (Mr.) 4627
Hudson, Francis 4511
Hudson, Henry 4519
Hudson, Jane B. 7081
Hudson, Julia H. 2395
Hudson, L. (Dr.) 2395
Hudson, Rosa M. 4551
Hudson, William 4522
Huffman, Ann 7162
Hugerman, Elizabeth 850
Hughes, Catharine 6722
Hugehs, Elizabeth 3782
Hughes, William 4530
Hughs, Eliza 5749
Hulbard, Clamania 1330
Hulbart, Nancy 5637
Hulbert, Frances J. 7678
Hulbert, John P. 4543
Hulbert, John W. 4432
Hulbert, Mary M. 5945
Hulbert, R. (Mr.) 5945
Hulbert, Sarah S. 4432
Hulet, Martha 2730
Hulett, Hannah Maria 2200
Hulin, Mary 5247
Hull, ___ (Mr.) 558
Hull, C. W. (Mr.) 4453
Hull, Ebenezer 4546
Hull, Evelina H. 7053
Hull, Harriet N. 6154
Hull, John 4553
Hull, Laura 1645

Hull, Mary E. 4453
Hull, Thomas 4241
Hull, William 4557
Hulse. Elizabeth 6057
Hulser, Anabella 617
Hults, Polly 4300
Humphrey, John 4570
Humphrey, Julia A. 9632
Humphreys, Cornelia C. 4097
Humphreys, E. (Dr.) 2043, 4098
Humphreys, H. (Dr.) 4097
Humphreys, Helen H. 4098
Humphreys, Laura S. 2043
Humphreys, Morris 4576
Hungerfield, Damarius Everest 6090
Hungerfield, Joseph B. 6090
Hungerford, Caroline E. 8221
Hungerford, Dana 8221
Hungerford, Marie Antoinette 4630
Hungerford, Sarah A. 382
Hunsdon, Agnes 3916
Hunsdon, Eliza 3026
Hunt. Alvin 4581
Hunt, Ann 4538
Hunt, Clarissa 7583
Hunt, Cornelia 287
Hunt, Dorothy (Mrs.) 6047
Hunt, Elijah 4597
Hunt, Eliza 5899
Hunt, Emily R. 4255
Hunt, Fanny 6418
Hunt, Frances 8764
Hunt, George 4587
Hunt, John 4602
Hunt, Joseph 4595
Hunt, Louisa 4094
Hunt, Lovina T. 6353
Hunt, Luther 4593
Hunt, Lydia 3103
Hunt, Mary M. 6516
Hunt, Mnotgomery 287, 8764, 9711
Hunt, R. W. (Mr.) 4585
Hunt, Ransom 4538
Hunt, Richard 4589
Hunt, Walter 4588
Hunt, Washington 4598
Hunter, ___ (Mrs.) 3204
Hunter, ___ (Rev. Dr.) 649
Hunter, Eliza Cecil 736
Hunter, James 736
Hunter, Mary 649
Hunter, Patrick 4603
Huntington, ___ (Mr.) 2292
Huntington, Ann E. 4578
Huntington, D. (Mr.) 4578
Huntington, Frances 4191
Huntington, George 4615, 4616
Huntington, Gurdon 4617
Huntington, Charles 4618
Huntington, Henrietta Amelia 7117
Huntington, Henry 4191
Huntington, Israel 1046, 4619
Huntington, Joseph 7117
Huntington, Mary Ann 1755
Huntley, Elias S. 4620
Huntley, Mariah M. 6783
Hurd, Flora 5338
Hurd, Hannah 7356
Hurd, J. N. M. (Gen.) 3628
Hurd, L. H. (Rev.) 4627
Hurd, Louisa 3628
Hurd, Lucy 1935
Hurd, Susan 4058
Hurd, Ward 4626

317

Hurlburt, Hezekiah 4631
Hurlbut, Elizabeth 9220
Hurry, Samuel 6475
Hurst, Martha Ann 9511
Huston, James 4638
Hutchins, Clarinda 9355
Hutchins, L. (Mr.) 4642
Hutchins, Roxey 6952
Hutchinson family 6688
Hutchinson, Abby J. 6688
Hutchinson, Adeline 4679
Hutchinson, Amanda 7272
Hutchinson, Ann 9958
Hutchinson, Catharine 4730
Hutchinson, Ellizabeth 3072
Hutchinson, L. J. 3943
Hutchinson,Maria 9787
Hutchinson, Rubey 7933
Hutelle, Jane 6593
Huton, Margaret 1407
Huwey, William 4648
Huyck, Gertrude 4745
Huzza, Ischabeba 4248
Hyatt, Alma A. 1659
Hyatt, Clara 2291
Hyde, ___ (Rev.) 4651
Hyde, A. E. (Mr.) 4206
Hyde, Alvan 4657
Hyde, Catherine 8376
Hyde, Jane 8867
Hyde, Joseph 4656
Hyde, Lucinda 8505
Hyde, Maria 4206
Hyde, susan 1600
Ide, John 4661, 4662
Ide, Obre 9471
Ingersol, Alma 6318
Ingersoll, John 5754
Ingleheart,Sophia Kennie 4669
Ingols, J. (Mr.) 4673
Ingore, Clarissa 3611
Ingore, J. (Mr.) 3611
Ingraham, A. (Mr.) 4674
Ingraham, Julia 2058
Ingram, Mary 518
Inman, Calista 4265
Inman, Emeline S. 554
Inman, Polly W. 4032
Inman, Susan 8897
Inslee, Sally Ann 4794
Ireland, James 4678
Irvin, William P. 4680
Irvine, Mary A. E. 5584a
Isbell, Sevilla 910
Isham, Abigail G. 7615
Ives, Elizabeth T. 570
Ives, Harriet 1169
Ives, Jesse 4688
Ives, Lyman 1169
Ives, William 570
Jack, Margaretta P. 4196
Jackson, Amasa 4456
Jackson, Ann Eliza 7756
Jackson, Betsey 4289
Jackson, Caroline 7203
Jackson, Catharine 9032
Jackson, Emily 4456
Jackson, Mahala 1152
Jackson, Mary 3299
Jackson, R. C. (Mr.) 9032
Jackson, Sally 2881
Jackson, William 4698
Jacobs, Abigail 6569
Jacobus, Mary 7506
Jadwin, Joseph 6580
Jadwin, Rachel A. 6580
James, Daniel 9236
James, Jane 1254

James, John 4717, 4718
James, Mary E. 4714, 5912
James, Thomas 4714, 4720, 4721, 5912
James, William 4716
Jamieson, John, Jr. 8398
Jamieson, Marian 8398
Jamison/Jemison/Jimeson family 4728
Jamison, Mary 4728
Jaqua, Rosetta 7077
Jarrett, Sarah Maria 3126
Jarvis, A. H. (Mr.) 4734
Jarvis, William 4732
Jay, Anna 344
Jay, William 344
Jayne, Sally 8178
Jeffers, Hannah 2612
Jemerson, Margaret B. 189
Jenkins, Angeline Teresa 4740
Jenkins, Barbara 6829
Jenkins, Cecilia 4852
Jenkins, Edward 2526, 4852
Jenkins, Ellen M. 2526
Jenkins, J. Hervey 4740
Jenkins, Jonathan 4746
Jenkins, Julian (Miss) 2936
Jenkins, Mary 8634
Jenks, Emeline 3184
Jenks, Joseph 3975
Jennings, Albena O. 5271
Jennings, Joseph 4755
Jennings, Orpha 7578
Jennings, Pliny 4753
Jennison, Jane 3531
Jennison, Sarah 3784
Jerome, Anna E. 9756
Jerome, Frances 6257
Jerome, Hannah 5853
Jervis, Asahel 4762
Jervis, James V. 4762
Jessup, Margaret A. 675
Jewel, Mahetable 6859
Jewel, Myron 1168
Jewel, Sophia 1168
Jewell, Eliza E. 984
Jewell, Oliver 4768
Johnson, A. B. (Mr.) 4774
Johnson, A. S. (Mr.) 6421
Johnson, Alexander B. 5508
Johnson, Ann 1189
Johnson, Ard 4917
Johnson, Caroline 5611
Johnson, Dian 9956
Johnson, Diana B. 9329
Johnson, E. (Dr.) 4803
Johnson, E. C. (Mr.) 4812
Johnson, Eli 4773
Johnson, Elizabeth 7424
Johnson, Elizabeth L. 8203
Johnson, Emiline 3326
Johnson, Emma Cornelia 5862
Johnson, Evan M. 4804
Johnson, Frank 4788
Johnson, Harriet E. J. 3322
Johnson, Hetty 2564
Johnson, J. (Rev.) 8203
Johnson, James 3664, 5715
Johnson, Jane 7122
Johnson, Jeanette C. 9803
Johnson, John B. 4804
Johnson, John H. 3571
Johnson, Laura N. 3056
Johnson, Leah 1121
Johnson, Lucy 277
Johnson, Lydia 3869
Johnson, Lydia C. 2560
Johnson, Maria 3664, 5337

Johnson, Mary 3571
Johnson, Mary Ann 2088, 7903
Johnson, Melissa 4812
Johnson, Nancy 6980
Johnson, Nathan 4782
Johnson, Phidelia 9527
Johnson, Rebecca 1329
Johnson, Sara Adams 5508
Johnson, Sarah 9257
Johnson, William C. (Mrs.) 2678
Johnson, William G. 4786
Johnston, James 4822
Johnston, Margaret 4822
Jolce, Laura 7099
Jones, Amantha E. 4870
Jones, Amos 1642
Jones, Ann 1482, 3312, 7827
Jnoes, Bethia W. 247
Jones, Betsey 9323
Jones, Betsey S. 5228
Jones, Caroline C. 9273
Jones, Catharine 1864
Jones, Cornelia K. 5995
Jones, David 4864
Jones, Delia A. 6757
Jones, E., 2nd (Mr.) 4873
Jones, E. B. (Mr.) 4827
Jones, Edward 4886
Jones, Edward B. 4858, 4880
Jones, Eli 307
Jones, Eliza 1364
Jones, Elizabeth 1713, 3713, 4440
Jones, Elizabeth H. 4091
Jones, Ellenor M. 6315
Jones, Ellis (Mr.) 7373
Jones, Griffith O. 3143
Jones, Gwenifred 4864
Jones, H. E. (Mr.) 4826
Jones, Isaac H. 9542
Jones, J. A. 4847
Jones, Jane 3143
Jones, John G. 3743
Jones, John R. 4870
Jones, Julia 157
Jones, Julia A. 9542
Jones, Linda B. 6930
Jones, Louisa M. 307
Jones, Lucinda 216
Jones, Marcy 4864
Jones, Margaret 3930, 5779, 8722
Jones, Mary A. 8945
Jones, Matilda P. 8721
Jones, Minerva T. 2167
Jones, Morgan 4860
Jones, Nehemiah 4825
Jones, P. R. (Mrs.) 4827
Jones, Pomeroy 6757, 9273
Jones, Prudence R. 4858
Jones, Rachel 4709
Jones, Rebecca 1642, 2759
Jones, Richard 8715
Jones, Robert 4882, 4890
Jones, Rowland A. 4830
Jones, Sarah 7373
Jones, Sarah E. 380, 5001
Jones, Sarah M. 2344
Jones, Sarah Margaret 651
Jones, Seth C. 4887
Jones, T. E. (Mr.) 5303
Jones, Thomas 1864
Jones, William 4889
Jones, Zachariah 651
Jordan, Ambrose I. 8367
Jordan, Elizabeth 8367
Joslin, Polly 5307
Jouston, Charlotte Ogenebugabwa 5660

Joy, Arad 4898
Joy, Celista 1558
Joy, James F. 4899
Judd, ___ (Dr.) 4839
Judd, ___ (Rev.) 3415
Judd, Elizabeth G. 536
Judd, F. (Dr.) 536
Judd, G. P. (Dr.) 4904
Judd, H. (Mr.) 3171
Judd, Levi 9642
Judd, Lucy (Mrs.) 9639
Judd, Lucy Ann 4839
Judd, Mabel 1067
Judd, Mary A. 3266
Judson, David 4914, 4915
Judson, Eliza P. 7032
Judson, Elizabeth 4912
Judson, Noahdiah 637
Judson, Philo 998, 4907
Judson, Sherman 4911
Judson, William R. 4912
Juliand, George 4922
Julliand, Joseph 4235
Julliand, Martha 4235
Jumel, Eliza 1304
Justin, ___ (Rev.) 6661
Justin, Azariah 4928
Justin, Lucinda 4928
Kalama, Maehekukui, 4937
Kane, John A. 4931
Kanouse, ___ (Rev.) 4932
Kaph, Bela 3389
Kaph, Martha Jane 3389
Karney, Catharine 8909
Karstner, Madeline 5188
* Kasson, Sarah G. 4208
Keach, Florinda 347
Keams, Elizabeth 5632
Keeler, Sarah 7708
Keeler, Sarah A. 1618
Keeling, James H. 4943
Keene, Louisa 460
Keene, Samuel A. 460
Keith, Matthew 4215
Keeler, Pamelia 2381
Keller, Mary Ann 2473
Kellogg, ___ (Mr.) 9722
Kellogg, Barbara 8509
Kellogg, Betsey Jane 2129
Kellogg, Catharine G.5930
Kellogg, Catharine H. 5293
Kellogg, Elsie 9564
Kellogg, Frances A. 4965
Kellogg, Hannah 2619, 4222
Kellogg, James 4957
Kellogg, Nancy 525
Kellogg, Orchard G. 4965
Kellogg, P. V. (Mr.) 4961
Kellogg, Samuel 4954
Kellogg, Spencer 4969
Kellogg, Warren 5930
Kelly, Bethiah 1157
Kelly, Florinda 443
Kelly, Margaret 8913
Kelly, Polly 1394
Kelly, Thomas 1157
Kelsey, ___ (Mrs.) 25
Kelsoe, Esther 1389
Kemp, William 4532
Kempp, Ann 2957
Kempton, George 4984
Kendall, A. (Mrs.) 4987
Kendall, S. H. (Mr.) 4987
Kendig, Lucretia 6193
Kendig, Martin
Kending, Ann Eliza 795
Kending, Martin 795
Kendrick Cordelia C. 6730
* Kasson, Orange 4935

Kendrick, Nathaniel 6730
Kenneda, Jane 8104
Kennedy, Betsey 8508
Kennedy, Cornelia 6785
Kennedy, S. R. (Mr.) 6785
Kennedy, Sophia A. 8171
Kent, James 5000
Kent, Philena 1465
Kenyon, Benjamin 5003
Kenyon, Mary 3509
Kenyon, Nathaniel 3509
Keough, Mary Ann 5060
Kernan, Margaret Mary 7114
Kershner, Elizabeth 6719
Ketcham, Jahn 3865
Ketcham, Martha S. 3865
Ketcham, Sally Ann 6492
Ketchem, Mary 6227
Ketchem, S. (Mr.) 6227
Ketchum, Mary 8607
Ketchum, Mary E. 8606
Keteltas, Elizabeth 4591
Keteltas, Philip D. 4591
Keyes, Eliza 5008
Keyes, Stillman 5008
Kidder, Calista S. 909
Kidder, Desdemona 697
Kidder, N. B. (Mr.) 5013
Kidder, Sally Ann 8442
Kilburn, H. C. (Mr.) 5017
Kill, Charlotte 2306
Killburn, Eliza 6603
Kilpatrick, Eliza 467
Kim, William 343
Kimball, Ann Melvina 9476
Kimball, Calista 237
Kimball, Grace M. 4550
Kimball, James M. 5018
Kimball, Lefy Ann 2795
Kimble, Betsey 4696
King, Caroline S. 633
King, Cyrus 4127
King, Elizabeth 8230
King, F. A. (Mr.) 8230
King, George E. 5032
King, Hannah Sophia 4127
King, Harriet 9893
King, James B.
King, Jane 8532
King, John 9893
King, Mandane L. 796
King, Samuel 5033
King, Sarah W. 5039
King, Simeon V. 5039
King, Thomas 633
Kinsbury, Arden 5044
Kingsbury, Elizabeth R. 777
Kingsbury, J. (Mr.) 5041
Kingsley, Achsah M. 10006a
Kingsley, Julia R. 5047
Kingsley, Laura 5050
Kingsley, Oliver B. 5050
Kingsley, Silas 5047
Kinne, Eunice 314
Kinne, Laura R. 9658
Kinne, Parthena 3262
Kinney, Jerusha B. 7347
Kinney, Stephen J. 5055
Kinsley, A. W. (Mr.) 5854
Kinsley, Emily 8594
Kinsman, Susan 7807
Kinyon, Sarᴀɪ E. 8529
Kip, Battis 9440
Kip, Elizabeth 9440
Kip, James S. 3515, 5063, 5075
Kip, Leonard 4930
Kip, Mary 4930
Kip, Mary Walker 5075

Kipp, Jefferson 5064
Kipp, Mary E. 5064
Kirby, Jenett 784
Kirby, R. M. (Maj.) 5066
Kirby, Walter 784
Kirk, J. S. (Mr.) 5070
Kirk, N. A. (Mrs.) 5070
Kirkland, ___ (Gen.) 5076
Kirkland, Elizabeth 9760
Kirkland, Elizabeth Julia (Mrs. 5074
Kirkland, Fanny 9762
Kirkland, Georgianna 6284
Kirkland, J. Francis 5073
Kirkland, John 5072
Kirkland, Joseph 5080
Kirkland, Joseph (Gen.) 5078
Kirkland, Lucilla 2092
Kirkland, Samuel 5072
Kirkland, Thomas 9760, 9762
Kirkland, William 5079
Kirkland, William J. 270
Kirtland, Hester Ann 9852
Kishlar, John 5083
Kishlar, Lucinda 5914
Kissam, Adrian 5085, 5086
Kissam, Daniel 7631
Kissam, Sophia 5085
Kite, Rowena 7808
Kiteridge, Maria 2882
Kittle, Elizabeth 9357
Kline, Hannah 4146
Kling, Elizabeth 6427
Knapp, Charlotte A. 5606
Knapp, Edwin G. 8573
Knapp, Helene 8078
Knapp, Lucy Maria 1499
Knapp, Sally 1210
Knapp, Urania C. 8573
Knapp, William R. 6039
Knickerbacker, Catharine 2061
Knickerbacker, John 5100
Knight, Jane 6915
Knight, Joseph 5103
Knight, Levi S. 5104
Knight, Sarah 7901
Knoll, Christine 929
Knollin, Rhoda 4352
Knollin, Richard 4352
Knott, Benjamin 5114
Knott, Elizabeth M. 4047
Knower, Benjamin 5116, 5117
Knowles, ___ (Judge) 5127
Knowles, Henry 1505
Knowles, J., Jr. 6826
Knowles, James 8310
Knowles, John 5125, 5763, 6715, 7680
Knowles, Lucy 7680
Knowles, Lyman 5119
Knowles, Mary A. 5763
Knowles, Sarah 1505
Knowles, Sarah F. 6826
Knowles, Zevia 8310
Knowlson, T. C. B. (Mr.) 5128
Knowlton, Chester 5130
Knox, Algenia 7267
Knox, Chloe 7552
Knox, Cordelia L. 129
Knox, John 5135, 5141
Knox, John J. 7267
Knox, Nelson 5140
Knox, Sarah Adelaide 8490
Knox, William E. 5136, 5139
Konkle, A. (Mr.) 5241
Kress, Harriet 188
Kuney, Sarah 26
Kurby, Margaret 5148

319

Lacey, ___ (Rev.) 5152, 5153
Lacey, Mary J. 951
Lacey, William B. 6735
Lacy, Sarah 4699
Ladd, ___ (Mrs.) 9523
Ladd, Avarilla B. 1756
Ladd, Frances E. 7865
Ladd, Harriet 2974
Ladd, John B. 7865
Ladd, Joy 1756
Ladenburger, C. (Miss) 192
La Grange, Catharine 167
La Graschubbuck, Cheoffonette 75
Laidelaw, Ann Jane 5157
Laidelaw, Walter 5157
Laidlow, ___ (Mr.) 5159
Lake, Angeline 3408
Lake, Ann 7817
Lake, Betsy 8468
Lamb, Ambrosia 9538
Lamb, Helena 9786
Lamb, John 1535
Lamb, Martha P. 7769
Lamb, Mary 5734
Lamb, Mary T. 861
Lamb, N. B. (Maj.) 5166
Lamb, Rebecca 5527
Lamb, Sally 1535
Lambright, Rebecca 7080
Lampher, Ann Elizabeth 9851
Lamphier, Laura 7646
Lamphire, Sophia 4958
Lamport, J. (Mr.) 5177
Land, Robert 5181
Landers, Phebe 4781
Landon, Mary J. 3097
Landon, Mills 5182
Lane, Aaron 876
Lane, Derick 876
Langdon, Lucy 7449
Langford, Chloe 8629
Langley, Arabelly J. 9926
Langley, Maria W. 2287
Langworthy, Caroline A. 6441
Langworthy, Harriet O. 2351
Langworthy, L. B. (Mr.) 5194
Langworthy, Nancy 8747
Lansing, ___ (Col.) 5211
Lansing, ___ (Rev.) 295
Lansing, Abraham A. 6071
Lansing, Angelica 7691
Lansing, B. B. (Mr.) 6153
Lansing, Catherine 2816, 4138
Lansing, Charlotte M. 8052
Lansing, D. C. (Rev.) 5204
Lansing, Edward A. 5211
Lansing, F. (Mr.) 5213
Lansing, Gerrit R. 7691
Lansing, H. (Mr.) 5198
Lansing, Harry 5196
Lansing, Jacob 5205
Lansing, Jane A. 5198
Lansing, Louisa M. 295
Lansing, Manette A. 6153
Lansing, Mary 5211
Lansing, Peter 5214
Lansing, R. R. (Mr.) 5211
Lansing, Richard 8052
Lansing, Richard R. 5211
Lapaugh, Charles N. 5215
Lapaugh, Elizabeth 5215
Larkin, David 5219
Larray, Ann 3536
Larrowe, Catherine 95
Larzelier, Emily 9872
Lasher, Ann E. 8802
Lathrop, Catharine 1683
Lathrop, Eliza H. 9349

Lathrop, Herman 1583
Lathrop, Horace 1582
Lathrop, Jennet 1585
Lathrop, L. E. (Mr.) 4076
Lathrop, Laura 1583
Lathrop, Laura Louisa 4076
Lathrop, Sarah 1582
Latimer, Mary E. 4463
Latimer, Robert S. 4463
La Tour, Adelina Amelia 4792
Lattimore, John 5237
Lattimore, Sarah 5237
Latus, Mary 9560
Laupaugh, C. N. (Mr.) 5238
Laupaugh, Elizabeth 5238
Laver, Mary Ann 3391
Lawpaugh, A. M. (Miss) 1923
Lawrence, Augustus S. 5250
Lawrence, B. (Miss) 4368
Lawrence, H. (Miss) 4368
Lawrence, Hannah 6773
Lawrence, Irene 7024
Lawrence, J. R. (Mr.) 5244
Lawrence, James R. 7024
Lawrence, Jane M. 4449
Lawrence, John 5242
Lawrence, Laura 8980
Lawrence, Lucy 5241
Lawrence, Maria W. 405
Lawrence, Mary 7341
Lawrence, Mary Louisa 9025
Lawrence, Richard H. 5241
Lawrence, Samuel 5245
Lawrence, Thomas 4449
Lawson, George 2084
Lawson, Susanna 2084
Lawton, Rebecca M. 5486
Lay, Amos 5256
Lay, John 229
Lay, Juliet 229
Lay, Mary Louisa 7535
Lay, Rowland 5255
Laycost, Eliza 5977
Leach, Alva 5257
Leach, Sarah 7483
Leacock, Ann 8957
Leake, John 5259
Leal, Mary 5907
Leavenworth, ___ (Capt.) 1563
Leavenworth, Amos 5263
Ledyard, ___ (Gen.) 1697
Ledyard, Benjamin 1697
Ledyard, Lincklaen 5269
Lee, Ann 630
Lee Arethmea 1789
Lee, Charles 1379
Lee, Cjarles M. 5274
Lee, Diadama 5174
Lee, Emily M. 1379
Lee, Fidelia 4186
Lee, Jane 4988
Lee, Joshua 5272
Lee, Lucy 7577
Lee, Octavia 3304
Lee, Olive Ann 3277
Lee, S. (Col.) 3316
Lee, Sarah Jane 7791
Lee, Stephen 3304
Leek, Fanny 2631
Leet, Nathaniel 1786
Leet, Olive 1786
Lefler, Joanna (Mrs.) 9657
Legg, Elijah 5290
Legg, John 5291
Legg, Laura Ann 5290
Lent, Hannah 273
Leonard, ___ (Mr.) 4971
Leonard, Jennette 3821
Leonard, Joshua 5304

Leonard, Lucinda 6714
Leonard, Mary 1207
Leonard, Moses 5303
Lepper, Margaret P. 3230
Lerbig, ___ (Dr.) 3778
Le Roy, ___ (Mr.) 560
Lester, Elizabeth 2342
Levy, Catharine 8254
Lewes, Mary J. 5655
Lewis, Amelia 9386
Lewis, Amelia E. 1162
Lewis, Ann 6564
Lewis, Birdseye 4373
Lewis, Caroline S. 5377
Lewis, Cornelia 2981
Lewis, Edwin 1162
Lewis, Ellen 7108
Lewis, Ethan 5334
Lewis, Ezekiel 8129
Lewis, Harriet 5171
Lewis, Harriet Jones 1119
Lewis, Helen 4998
Lewis, James M. 5311
Lewis, John G. 5330
Lewis, Lavantia 4373
Lewis, Martha C. 8129
Lewis, Mary D. 3240
Lewis, Mary J. 5655
Lewis, Octavia J. 6696
Lewis, Ozias 1119
Lewis, Samuel E. 5327
Lewis, Sarah 3492
Lewis, Susan 590
Lewis, William, Jr. 5310
Lewis, William B. 6564
Lieber, Henrietta 3543
Life, Christina 1858
Light, Lydia 6406
Ligthbody, Andrew 6311
Lightbody, Susanna 6311
Lilly, Emily 912
Linacre, Margaret 5118
Lincoln, Derinda 3625
Lincoln, Lucy Jane 9303
Lincoln, Sylva 8320
Lindsey, Sarah A. 2159
Lindsley, Eleanora 4152
Lindsley, Eliza 8038
Lines, Julia P. 9800
Lisk, Harriet (Mrs.) 8422
Litchfield, Eliza 4444
Litchfield, Eliza A. 4444
Little, ___ (Mr.) 1125
Little, Charles 5370
Little, Jane M. 4392
Littlejohn, Gilbert H. 5374
Livermore, Lucinda 7831
Livermore, Selene 7321
Livingston, Charlotte 1879
Livingston, Charlotte Ann 3573
Livingston, Gilbert 5381
Livingston, John H. 9905
Livingston, M. (Mr.) 8354
Livingston, Mary Augusta 8354
Livingston, Robert R. 5388
Livingston, T. (Gen.) 3573
Livingston, Thomas 9015
Lloyd, Angelica 5390
Lloyd, John 5389, 5392
Lloyd, Martha 2385
Lloyd, Sarah Ann 1475
Lock, Elizabeth (Mrs.) 7851
Locke, Alvin 5396
Lockrow, Caroline 7649
Lockrow, Gertrude Ann 9056
Loder, Samuel 5400
Logan, Agnes (Mrs.) 3245
Logan, Barbara 5885
Logan, Polly 4175

Logan, Robert 5885
Long, Mary 764
Longley, Lydia A. 5408
Longley, Samuel M. 5408
Longwell, Phebe 8624
Look, Susan H. 215
Looker, Marilla 410
Loomis, ___ (Miss) 2926
Loomis, A. T. (Miss) 319
Loomis, Abby Z. 6440
Loomis, Betsey 62
Loomis, Caroline 609
Loomis, Celia Adelaide 8224
Loomis, Clark D. 8224
Loomis, Edward 5419
Loomis, George A. 5429
Loomis, Jerome 5427
Loomis, Nathan 5413
Loomis, S. Jennette 7432
Loomis, T. (Gen.) 7432
Loper, Phebe 705
Lord, J. (Rev.) 8120
Lord, John 4803
Lord, Louise 1028
Lord, Susan H. 8120
Lord, William (Dr.) 2113
Loring, Bethiah W. 5140
Lorraway, Ann Yeneth 2914
Loucks, Mary Ann 5438
Loucks, Walter D. 5438
Louer, Lavinia 875
Lounsberry, Harriet 3578
Lounsbury, Mary 23
Love, Laura 5479
Lovel, Vincent 5445, 5447
Lovell, Elizabeth 5354
Lovell, Mary 7912
Lovell, Sarah 1904, 2087
Lovett, Louisa Cochran (Mrs.) 5197
Lowndsbury, Mary 3792
Lowrey, George 5461
Lowthorp, Catharine 5046
Lowthorp, Elizabeth 159
Lowthorp, Thomas 2098
Lucas, Clarinda 8892
Luce, Israel 5473
Luce, Mary Ann 8577
Luce, Matilda 5473
Luce, Sophia 5469
Ludam, John 5474
Ludden, Sabrina 9163
Ludlow, John R. 5478
Ludlow, Thomas 5475
Lum, Chalres 5484
Lum, Daniel L. 5482, 5483, 5484
Lumbard, Theophilus 5487
Lummis, Elizabeth F. 2909
Lundegreen, Margaret L. 7280
Lundergreen, ___ (Mrs.) 4549
Lundgreen, ___ (Mrs.) 2581
Lusk , William 5491
Lyman, Clara G. 7097
Lyman, Delia 8773
Lyman, Frances P. 5503
Lyman, Isaac 8773
Lyman, James 5503
Lyman, Samuel 7097
Lyman, Sarah 447
Lyman, William 447
Lynch, Dominick 5509
Lynch, Harrison 5511
Lynch, James 6456, 9534
Lynch, Julia M. 6456
Lynch, Louise F. 5511
Lynch, Lucy A. 9534
Lyon, Abby R. 3744

Lyon, Amelia 9492
Lyon, Amy 2720
Lyon, David 5515, 5528
Lyon, Elizabeth 3886
Lyon, Jane 5525
Lyon, John N. 5525
Lyon, Lovica 8160
Lyon, Lucinda M. 8935
Lyon, Sally 1019
Lyon, Samuel 3744
Lyon, Ssuan 5517
Lyons, David A. 5529
Lyons, Mary 297
Lyport, Cornelia 9656
McArthur, Joseph 5532
McBride, Amelia C. 9098
McBride, George 1530
McBride, John 5534, 5536
McBride, Margaret 1104
McBurney, Caroline 5869
McBurney, Jane A. 5535
McBurney, Maria 2105
McBurney, Thomas 2107, 5535
McCabe, Mary B. 5647
McCabe, Robert 5647
McCall, ___ (Dr.) 5543
McCall, Caroline 9086
McCall, Helen M. 9344
McCall,John 5541
McCall, Margaret 5540
McCall, Wallace 5540
McCallock, Lucretia M. 814
McCalpin, Jane 7907
McCann, Frances 6681
McCann, Isabella 4245
McCArthy, Thomas 5549
McCarty, Catharine 4049
McCarty, Charity 1090
McCarty, Sarah M. 9694
McCauley, Deborah 7421
McCauley, Jennett 7276
McCay, William W. 5555
McChain, James 5556
McChesney, John H. 5557
McClaim, Betsey 358
McClandish, Nancy 1178
McCleary, John 5559
McClelland, Elizabeth J. 9994
McClelland, John 9994
McClure, ___ (Gen.) 5564
McClure, Bethiah 2320
McClure, Catharine 9469
McClure, Eleanor 8824
McClure, George 8824
McComber, B. (Mr.) 5567
McCombs, Chalres 5569
McCombs, Henry 5568
McCon, Jane 2167
McCon, John 2167
McConnell, S. Jeanette 746
McConnell, Theresa 3242
McConnell, Ziba 5575
McCoy, Martha W. 1109
McCracken, Martha 9154
McCullom, Almira 9372
McDaniels, Elsie 2697
McDonald, D. (Rev.) 5586
McDonald, Julia B. 5186
McDonald, Margaret 4524
McDonald, Sarah 5591
McDonald, Sophia 5777
McDonald, Stephen 5591
McDonough, A. R. (Mr.) 5692
McDonough, Thomas 5596
McDougall, Harriet 3659
McDougall, Peter 3659
McDowell, ___ (Gov.) 8647
McDowell, Eliza 1461

McDuffie, George 5603
McElwaine, John 5605
McElwaine, M. Elizabeth 4973
McEutee, Mary S. 9157
McFaren, Nancy 6221
McFarland, Eliza 202
McFarland, Luther W. 5608
McFarlane, Eliza H. 4163
McGarry, ___ (Mr.) 5612
McGee, Sally Ann 9798
McGeorge, H. T., Jr. 5616
McGinnis, Eliza 6767
McGlinnen, Jane (Mrs.) 5619
McGregor, James 5626, 5627
McHarg, ___ (Mr.) 5604
McHenry, Daniel 5629
McHenry, Julia 4752
McHuron, amanda 2138
McHuron, Elvira C. 6831
McHuron, Malvina S. 3915
McIntyre, Isabella 2937, 3753
McIntyre, Mary Ann 9654
McKellup, Nancy 4282
McKensey, E. (Mrs.) 3155
McKenzie, Hester Ann 743
McKinney, Harriet F. 8762
McKinney, Sarah 7971
McKinstry, ___ (Gen.) 9563
McKinstry, Matilda 5431
McKinstry, Nancy 9563
McKoon, Samuel 5644
McLallen, Esther 235
McLaren, J. F. (Rev.) 5244
McLaughlin, Rachel 1348
McLean, John D. 5650
McLean, Louisa 440
McLean, William 440, 5649
McMann, Catharine 8125
McMartin, ___ (Senator) 10017
McMartin, Jane 10017
McMaster, D. (Mr.) 5657
McMaster, Robert 1563
McMath, Louisa 4050
McMillin, Sarah 9088
McMullen, ___ (Mr.) 5604
McNabb, Catharine 7958
McNair, Sarah 9844
McNall, Martha 2679
McNamee, catharine 5576
McNeil, David 5667
McNeil, John 5669
McNeil, Sophia 8061
McNiel, Henry (Gen.) 1273
McNulty, John 5674
McPherson, Duncan 5681
McPherson, Elizabeth 5681
McPherson, Harriet 3700
McPherson, Jane 8698
McPherson, John 5679
McPherson, Malvina 1007
McPherson, William 3700
McQuade, Johanna 5682
McQuade, Michael 5682
McQuade, Rosanna 1845
McQuade, Sarah 2528
McQuade, Thomas 1845, 2528
McQueen, George 5683
McQueen, Harriet 1940
McReynolds, Frances B. 1101
McReynolds, M. (Mr.) 1101
McViccar, John 4831
McVickar, Brenton 5691
McVickar, Frances 5691
McVicker, Edward 5692
McWeeney, Kate 1373
McWhorter, Ann 482
McWhorter, Mary 3859
Mabie, Lane 3250

Mabie, Margaret 127
Macbeth, Angelica G. 4712
Mace, Arabella 9821
Mace, Caroline Elizabeth 4897
Macintire, Margaret 6927
Mack, ___ (Mr.) 7723
Mack, Caroline Elizabeth 4897
Mack, J. (Mr.) 4214
Mack, Marian 4214
Mack, Polly 150
Mack, Warren 5695
Mackie, Jennette 1716
Mackie, Mary H. 5115
Maclay, William B. 5700
Macomb, ___ (Maj. Gen.) 5701
Macomb, John 5702
Macrae, Mary H. 6413
Madden, Barnard 2376
Madock, Adelaide 5708
Maddock, Amelia 5706, 5708
Maddock, Eliza 9275
Maden, John 5709
Madison, ___ (Ex-President) 5711
Madison, ___ (Mr.) 7149
Madison, James 5711
Madole, Betsey 6857
Magee, Eliza 173
Magee, Thomas C. 173
Magee, Thomas J. 5717
Maguire, Harriet 5223
Maihekukui, ___ 4937
Main, Emily 5724
Main, Hannah 5317
Main, James 5724
Main, Morris 5724
Main, Selima 5724
Maine, Adelina 5725
Malcolm, Rhoda 1851
Mallory, AnnM. 5220
Mallory, Deborah 2286
Mallory, Louisa 1849
Mallory, Lucy 6487
Mallory, Mary 2089
Maltby, Eliza 1033
Maltby, S. M. (Mr.) 5741
Maltby, Seth 1033
Maltby, Stephen 5743
Man, Mary E. 2057
Manchester, Almira 4315
Manchester, Deborah 722
Manchester, Maria B. 6951
Manchester, Otis 5745, 6951
Mandeville, Catherine Ann 340
Mann, A. (Mr.) 3082
Mann, A. M. (Rev.) 6499
Mann, Abijah 7419
Mann, alexander M. 5760
Mann, Herbert 5374
Mann, J. M. (Dr.) 5757
Mann, Julia 5374
Mann, Lucena 8522
Mann, Martha A. 5770, 7419
Mann, Nancy Anna 3082
Manning, John Y. 6470
Manning, Lydia C. 8079
Manning, Samuel 8079
Mans, Catharine 6004
Mansfield, Caroline 7956
Mansfield, David 9271
Mansfield, Helen Maria 9271
Mansfield, Julia A. 5093
Mantle, Mary Ann 4529
Manwaring, Clarissa B. 9623
Manwarring, Phebe Jane 5156
Maples, Darius 7854
Maples, Maria A. 7854
Marble, Laura Frances 5863

Marble, Louise B. 9944
Marble, Nathan 5863, 9944
Marchisi, A. B. (Mr.) 8049
Marchisi, J. B. (Mr.) 5769
Marchisi, John B. 5768
Marcy, ___ (Gov.) 5117
Markel, Anne 3586
Markel, George 3586
Markel, J. G. 5771
Markham, Eliza G. 5550
Marks, Elizabeth 3336
Marselis, Angelica M. 7571
Marselus, John N. 5781
Marsh, Amarillus, A. 5792
Marsh, Caroline M. 2745
Marsh, Eliza M. 2915
Marsh, Elizabeth 1143
Marsh, H. P. (Miss) 1875
Marsh, Hose (Mr.) 1143
Marsh, Isabelle A. 709
Marsh, Mary 249
Marsh, Samuel 5782
Marsh, Sarah 7363
Marsh, Silas 5798
Marsh, William N. 2915
Marshal, ___ (Miss) 2681
Marshall, Benjamin 5804
Marshall, Calista 4195
Marshall, Cyrenus 5800
Marshall, Jane R. 5023
Marshall, Ruth K. 321
Marshall, Sarah J. 3954
Martin, Betsey (Mrs.) 9280
Martin, Bradley 6923
Martin, Delancey 5814
Martin, E. T. Rhroop (Mr.) 3987, 5813
Martin, Gertrude 9060
Martin, Harriett E. 6923
Martin, Isabella H. 2055
Martin, Sarah M. 8406
Martindale, Mary ann 8547
Marvin, Abraham 5828
Marvin, Ann E. 7991
Marvin, Asa 5825
Marvin, Jane E. 2343
Marvin, Maria 2682
Marvin, Mary Ann 4231
Marvin, Ruth S. 2944
Mason, Almira 6539
Mason, Amy (Mrs.) 5838
Mason, Arnold 5838
Mason, Betsey Ann 8412
Mason, C. (Mr.) 6461
Mason, Catharine 8975
Mason, Esther 9460
Mason, Julia 6461
Mason, Julia Ann 7183
Mason, Sarah P. 5840
Mason, Squire M. 5840
Masters, ___ (Judge) 4294
Masters, Ann Margaret 4294
Masters, Martha C. 8625
Masters, Thomas 8625
Masterson, Mary A. 1735
Mather, Adaline G. 3493
Mather, Amelia N. 753
Mather, Asaph 5851
Mather, Julia 8, 5922
Mather, Martha Ann 7635
Mather, Mary B. 687
Mather, Stephen 483, 5852
Mather, William 8
Mathews, Mary 1559
Mathews, Rebecca 8108
Matin, Rebecca 4525
Matrick, ___ (Mr.) 2388
Matteson, A. L. (Miss) 4971

Matteson, D. J. (Mr.) 9198
Matteson, Hezekiah 5865
Matteson, Jeptha 4971
Matteson, Louisa A. 8648
Matthews, Elizabeth 4200
Matthews, Henry 5868
Matthews, P. P. (Mr.) 5868
Matthewson, Betsey 8619
Mattison, E. K. (Mr.) 5870
Mattison, Jesse 5873
Mattocks, James 7258
Mattom, Duadama 2647
Mauvel, Roxana 8143
Maxam, Adelbert H. 5875
Maxam, John 5875
MAXAM, Laura 5875
Maxfield, Carolyn 7618
Maxfield, John 7618
Maxwell, ___ (Mr.) 7113
Maxwell, Eliza P. 6673
Maxwell, Ellen 4292
Maxwell, H. I. (Mr.) 4292
Maxwell, JamesW. 9901
Maxwell, Sylvanus 5879
Maxwell, Thomas 5880, 6673, 8024
May, ___ (Col.) 5883
Mayhew, Sarah 2616
Maynard, Needham 5892
Meacham, Dorlisha C. 8550
Meacham, E. (Mrs.) 5896
Meacham, L. D. (Mr.) 5896
Mead, ___ (Gen.) 4490
Mead, Almira 4490
Mead, Elizabeth 9643
Mead, Julia 6346
Mead, M. B. (Dr.) 3908
Mead, Myra 2933
Mead, Sally 403
Mead, T. (Gen.) 6347
Mead, Thompson 6346
Meade, Maria del Carmen 252
Meade, Richard W. 252
Means, Ada B. 8068
Means, Eliza 757
Means, John 8068
Means, Joseph 8068
Means, William 4204
Meech, Catharine M. 4035
Meech, H. (Mr.) 4018
Meech, Horace 4035
Meeker, Elizabeth 1218
Meeker, M. T. (Mrs.) 5908
Meigs, Edmund 8445
Meigs, Eliza P. 4115
Meigs, Helen 8445
Meigs, Livona B. 5913
Melville, Agnes A. 3371
Melville, Henry 3371
Menter, Eliza Jane 9850
Menter, Sarah 9984
Mercer, Elizabeth 9394
Mercer, William V. 9394
Meriam, ___ (Mr.) 2046
Merrell, Ann 3682
Merrell, Charlotte P. 31
Merrell, Elizabeth 5866
Merrell, H. C. 5933
Merrell, H. H. (Mr.) 5920
Merrell, Harriet 7353
Merell, Ira 5935
Merrell, Isaac 5923
Merrell, John C. 84
Merrell, Lucretia 1428
Merrell, Matilda 2380
Merriam, Ebenezer 7529
Merriam, Ela (Mr.) 5938
Merriam, Sarah M. 7529

Merrill, Caroline 7766
Merrill, Elijah E. 5767
Merrill, Emily 5767
Merill, G. H. 9698
Merrill, John 5940
Meritt, Amanda 6146
Meritt, Arthur 5947
Meritt, Sarah Ann 849
Mery, Abraham 3310
Mervine, Emily M. 2726
Mervine, William 2726
Messenger, George 5955
Messenger, Rosannah Mary
   Theresa 5955
Metcalf, Catharine 8420
Metcalf, Elijah 8420
Metcalfe, Catharine 8205
Mickell, Catharine 8884
Midlam, Caroline M. 1479
Mighells, Eleazer 5968
Mild, Jane 7381
Miles, B. (Maj.) 5970, 9280
Miles, Ives H. 5975
Miles, Martha 9891
Miles, Mary 1179
Miles, Polly Ann 4341
Miles, Sarah 5975
Miles, Simeon 9891
Milford,___ (Mr.) 5942
Millard, B. H. (Miss) 8811
Millard, Clarissa 5978
Millard, Daniel T. 5978
Millard, Lydia 2604
Miller, Abner 7805
Miller, Anson S. 7532
Miller, Ceryl 6338
Miller, Charlotte 1481
Miller, Elijah 5981
Miller, Eliza 3574
Miller, Elizabeth 5985, 8335
Miller, Emma Eliza 6139
Miller, Helen M. 961
Miller, Hendrix 6005
Miller, Jane 4177
Miller, Jane (Mrs.) 3969
Miller, Jane Ann 1317
Miller, Jane C. 4472
Miller, John 6338
Miller, Julia 4677
Miller, Lucy J. 3823
Miller, Magdelin 1318
Miller, Margaret A. 4719
Miller, Martha 806, 9863
Miller, Morris 6000
Miller, Morris S. P. 1004
Miller, Prudence P. 6674
Miller, Sarah 1004
Miller, Sarah Jane 7805
Miller, William C. 8215
Milligan, Jane Eliza 1695
Milliman, Mary Ann 8548
Milliman, N. N. (Mr.) 8548
Mills, Abigail Ann 7736
Mills, Abigail E. 439
Mills, Amanda 6074
Mills, Ann Maria 2038
Mills, Anna K. 2259
Mills, Betsy 8062
Mills, Clara 1251
Mills, David 6014
Mills, Elsitha 4274
Mills, Henry 2015
Mills, Henry D. 2038
Mills, Lydia 9295
Mills, Martha 6351
Mills, Mary 5972
Mills, Mary Ann 7366
Mills, Rebecca 4840

Mills, S. D. (Mr.) 6016
Mills, Samuel 6029
Mills, Samuel (Rev.) 2500
Mills, Sophronia 8670
Millspaugh, Nancy 2390
Milner, Maria 7262
Minard, Isaac T. 9177
Minckley, Elizabeth 6110
Miner, Abraham 1818
Miner, Asher 6037
Miner, Ephraim 9311
Miner, Nancy 5452
Miner, Paul R. 6035
Miner, Roxana 9311
Miner, Whitman R. 6036
Minnis, Elmer 4218
Misner, Catherine 5300
Mitchell, Ann 9256
Mitchell, Charlotte 3206
Mitchell, David 6043
Mitchell, Eleanor W. 2064
Mitchell, Henry 6044
Mitchell, Laura 4250
Mitchell, Levi 6053
Mitchell, Mary 8922
Mitchell, Sarah Ann 8220
Mitchells, John 6054
Mix, Charles 6055
Mix, Lurinda 1651
Monell, Catharine 7135
Monell, Robert 7135
Monroe,___ (Ex-President)
   6062
Monroe, Catharine M. 3070
Monroe, Harriet 8853
Monroe, Jesse 2233
Monroe, Melinda 2233
Monroe, William B. 6063
Monson, Samuel 6067
Monteith, Walter 6071
Montgomery, Frances (Mrs.) 526
Montgomery, Sally Ann 29
Montross, John 6075
Moody,___ (Mr.) 9954
Moody, Achsa 3399
Moody, Clarissa 9952
Moody, Hannah M. 4217
Mooker, Adeline 1151
Mooney, Catharine 5812
Mooney, D. (Mr.) 5812
Mooney, Maria J. 9510
Moor, Franklin 6080
Moore,___ (Mr.) 4334
Moore, Annis 8497
Moore, Christiana 9970
Moore, David 9970
Moore, Eliza $ 5906
Moore, Francis 6085
Moore, Francis, Jr. 1829
Moore, Harriet F. 6433
Moore, Harriet P. 64
Moore, Henry B. 6095
Moore, Louisa 3288
Moore, Lydia E. 3560
Moore, Martha 6085
Moore, Phebe Maria 587
Moore, Ruth Ann 8826
Moore, Susan 1829
Moore, Thomas P. 6093
Moot, John I. D. 6096
Mor ? ,___ (Mrs.) 4683
Morango, M. (Mr.) 6097
Morehouse, Jane 8921
Morel,___ (Miss) 1123
Morey,___ (Dr.) 6106
Morey, Aurelia 7109
Morey, Mary Ann 716
Morgan, Damres 4539

Morgan,Emily E. 2692
Morgan, Gilbert S. 6112, 6116
Morgan, Harriet 5513
Morgan, James 4411
Morgan, L. (Mr.) 7333
Morgan, L. (Mrs.) 7333
Morgsn, Lemira 4940
Morgan, Louise 2297
Morgan, Lucinda (Mrs.) 3966
Morgan, Mary 1720
Morgan, Mary A. 6118
Morgan, Nancy 2102
Morgan, Rebecca 4411
Morgan, Sophrona 6559
Morgan, Susan A. 8719
Morgan, Thomas E. 6118
Morgan, William 3966
Morley, Julia 6122
Morley, Urutha 6123
Morley, Walter 6122
Morrell, Jane 6290
Morrell, Stephen 6125
Morrill, Eliza Janette 3692
Morris,___ (Gen.) 5849
Morris, Benjamin 6137
Morris, Catherine S. 3350
Morris, Charlotte E. 182
Morris, David E. 6128
Morris, Frances Mary Upton
   5849
Morris, Harvey, 223
Morris, Jacob 6903
Morris, Jane M. 8388
Morris, Lewis 6135
Morris, Margaret E. 223
Morris, Mercy Ann 4835
Morris, Richard 5849
Morris, Ruth 1243
Morris, Sarah 6082, 9289
Morris, Walter H. 3350
Morrison,___ (Capt.) 5654
Morrison, Alexander 6141, 6145
Morrison, Eliza 1424, 2007
Morrison, F. W. (Mr.) 6150
Morrison, G. (Dr.) 6143
Morrison, Helen Norman 5654
Morrison, John B. 6149
Morrison, Lovisa 2047
Morrison, Mary L. 9911
Morrison, R. N. (Mr.) 6169
Morrison, Roderick N. 6140
Morrison, Sarah 6149
Morrison, William, Jr. 6144
Morrow, Barbara 5352
Morrow, Hannah Jane 5260
Morse, Ann Eliza 2815
Morse, Caroline 720
Morse, Cornelia 1793
Morse, Emily A. 6239
Morse, Emma D. 918
Morse, James E. 1332
Morse, John 4714
Morse, Lucretia 2508
Morse, Lydia 6028
Morse, Mary A. 9352 ᐟ
Morse, Parmelia 8191
Morse, Zenas 9352
Morsell, Jane 8003
Mortley, Mahala E. 1963
Morton, Benjamin 6166
Morton, Elisha 6165
Morton, Jay W. 6167
Morton, Jennette 5573
Mosely, Eliza 6129
Mosely, Elizabeth 847
Mosely, Peabody 847
Mosher, Betsy 1368
Mosher, Charity H. 2323

Mosier, Calista 6629
Moss, Mary 9121
Moss, Polly 2649
Mott, Margaret 1312
Mott, Mary Ann (Mrs.) 5423
Mott, Samuel 6185
Mott, Susan 94
Mould, Caroline 5802
Moulter, David 9021
Moulter, Jacob 6189
Moulter, Serena 9021
Moulton, David 4962, 4966, 7033
Moulton, Eliza 7033
Moulton, F. (Dr.) 6191
Moulton, Miriam M. 4966
Moulton, Sarah C. 4962
Mower, Almira 896
Mowers, ___ (Mrs.) 7165
Mowry, Catharine 2290
Moyer, Catharine 1676
Moyer, Daniel 1677
Moyer, Maria 9721
Mullin, Joseph 1154
Mumford, Jones 6212
Mumford, Ores 6215
Mundy, Barron 6219
Mundy, Caroline 1758
Munger, Junlia Ann 4157
Munger, S. (Mr.) 6220
Munn, Hannah W. 7859
Munn, Sarah L. 9477
Munro, Squire 6222
Munroe, Elizabeth 6224
Munroe, Jonas A. 6224
Munsell, Lucy 2627
Munson, Alfred 9723
Munson, Helen E. 9723
Munson, Martha C. 9601
Munson, Mary 9955
Murat, Jonathan 6232
Murdock, Hope 6233
Murdock, James 6233
Murdock, James (Rev.) 1961
Murdock, Sarah 1473
Murphy, Catharine S. 97
Murphy, George 6238
Murphy, Mary J. 7389
Murphy, Melissa A. 6238
Murphy, Robert W. 6236
Murray, Eli E. 6244
Murray, John 6247
Murray, Sophia 8438
Myers, Clara Ann 8364
Myers, Cordelia M. 2754
Myers, John 6253
Myers, Sarah R. 1324
Mygatt, Abigail S. 6367
Mygatt, Elizabeth 4652
Mygatt, Henry 6260, 6261, 6262, 6263
Myrtle, Lydia 3626
Naglee, E. D. (Mr.) 3382
Nash, Emma H. 2231
Nash, Harriett O. 3095
Nash, Ira 6268
Nash, Mary 7997
Nash, Melissa 9364
Neally, Joan 9716
Near, Caroline 2866
Neele, Lucinda 1510
Neilis, Elizabeth 5577
Nellis, Anna Maria 1801
Nellius, Katarina Elizabet 2548
Nelson, ___ (Judge) 569
Nelson, Alvira 9398
Nelson, Catharine Russell 569

Nelson, William 6286
Nesbit, Kaura 5519
Nettleton, Hannah J. 1823
Neville, John 751
Neville, Malinda 751
Nevius, Ann 2633
Newberry, Julia B. 6295
Newberry, Walter L. 6295
Newbury, George 6297
Newbury, Martha 8103
Newbury, Walter L. 6298
Newcomb, Emeline H. 9449
Newcomb, Luther 6299
Newcomb, S. A. (Miss) 4056
Newel, Elizabeth 140
Newell, Harriet 9237
Newell, Harriet (Mrs.) 9222
Newell, Mary C. 6305
Newell, William H. 6305
Newhall, John 6307
Newhouse, Mary 7391
Newkirk, Harriet 4212
Newkirk, John P. 4212
Newkirk, T. G. 6310
Newland, Betsey Ann 6313
Newland, John 6312
Newland, T. J. 6313
Newman, Margaret 8681
Newmans, Eliza 6867
Newton, Amelia M. 5371
Newton, Charlotte 5956
Newton, Lorinda W. 8010
Newton, Lucy A. 4903
Newton, Mary 1800
Newton, Melitta 9579
Newton, Sarah 4311
Newton, William 5370
Nicholas, James 6323
Nicholas, John 5299
Nicholas, Margaret Caroline 5299
Nicholas, Sarah I. 6323
Nichols, Charlotte 3708
Nichols, Cornelia 1366
Nichols, Electa 6424
Nichols, Eliza Ann 4308
Nichols, Francis R. 6694
Nichols, J. (Rev.) 3377
Nichols, James 6335
Nichols, John (Hon.) 1824
Nichols, Mary Jane 6694
Nichols, Sarah J. 6335
Nicholson, Bathsheba 9793
Nicholson, Daniel 9793
Nicholson, James 3344
Nicholson, John 6342
Niffen, Hannah 9136
Nims, Phidelia 2487
Nixon, ___ (Mr.) 6361
Nixon, ___ (Mrs.) 6361
Nixon, Samuel 9901
Noble, Cyrenus 6368
Noble, Stilman 6369
Nobles, Sarah (Mrs.) 2157
Nooton, Emily S. 4908
Norman, Eliza 4075
Norman. Everil 9488
Norris, Abigail 8908
Norris, Charlotte P. 6377
Norris, James L. 6377
Norris, Mary E. 7488
Norris, Nancy 3086
Norris, Robert 5491
Norris, Robert J. 7488
North, Elizabeth 280
North, Norris 6384
North, Sally 6390
North, Theodore 280

Northrop, B. (Rev.) 1008
Northrop, F. W. (Mr.) 6385
Northrop, M. J. (Mrs.) 6385
Northrup, Anna Mariah 1859
Northrup, Elizabeth M. 8393
Northway, Almeria 266
Northway, Harriet 5524
Northway, Lucy C. 8316
Northway, R. (Mr.) 6391
Northway, Rufus 6392
Norton, ___ (Mr.) 3181
Norton, Albert T. 6404
Norton, Almira 7800
Norton, Ann E. 6404
Norton, Ariel 6398
Norton, Betsey 3217
Norton, Charles 6396
Norton, David 4422
Norton, Eliza 6555
Norton, Elizabeth A. 6411
Norton, Elizabeth S. 3712
Norton, Franklin M. 6411
Norton, Harriet 8857
Norton, Harriet, R. 1116
Norton, Heman 3712
Norton, Louisa L. 2032
Norton, Miles 2032
Nose, Elizabeth 3441
Nott, ___ (President) 3645
Noyes, Artemisia 1323
Noyes, Curtis 6421
Noyes, Elizabeth 6101
Noyes, George 1323, 6101, 6421
Noyes, Josiah 6420
Nurse, Abigail F. 4979
Nurse, David 4979, 6425
Nurse, Delphia W. 5091
Nurse, Elisha 5091
Nurse, Mary Eliza 6425
Nurse, Thomas H. 6426
Nutt, Clarissa 8540
Nye, Amy (Mrs.) 209
Nye, Grove A. 6428
Nye, Mary Jane 7914
Oakley, B. (Mr.) 3300
Obear, Oliver 6434
O'Brien, Druzilla 7217
Odell, Maria S. 5225
O'Donnell, Alice 5441
O'Donnell, Mary 5614
Ogden, Hannah 6447
Ogden, Isaac 6447
O'Hara, William 6448
Olcott, Charlotte 895
Olcott, Mary 6258
Olcott, Orville 6453
Olin, Eliza Ann 2176
Oliphant, Eliza A. 658
Oliphant, Esther R. 9188
Oliphant, R. W. (Mr.) 658, 9188
Oliphant, Robert W. 688, 4012
Oliver, ___ (Judge) 6459, 7757
Oliver, Mary 9547
Olmstead, A. (Mr.) 2810
Olmstead, Ann 2170
Olmstead, Caroline 1410
Olmstead, Mary B. 2810
Olmstead, Timothy 6464
Olmsted, Betsey 7344
Olmsted, Mary 8854, 8860
Olney, Loretta 8095
Olney, Sarah A. 7234
O'Neil, Catharine 1221
O'Neil, Owen 1221, 6468
Onion, Catherine 9999
Opdike, Diana I. 5740
Opdyke, Jeremiah 3977
Opdyke, John S. 8470

Opdyke, Mary I. 3977
Opdyke, Sarah 3899
Orcutt, Caroline Harrison
   (Mrs.) 2945
Orcutt, Delia 6471
Orcutt, Giles 6471
Orcutt, Maria 2868
Orcutt, Mary Ann 8434
Ormsbee, Harriet P. 3609
Ormsbee, Jacob 3609
Ormsbee, Jonathan 6472
Ormsbee, Martha 6472
Orton, J. R. (Mr.) 6476
Orwin, Elizabeth 4920
Osborn, Adaline 1045
Osborn, Amos 8836
Osborn, Catharine 8836
Osborn, Delia Ann 1468
Osborn, Elizabeth 9696
Osborn, Henry B. 6486
Osborn, John 6482
Osborn, Julia M. 3283
Osborn, Kinathon 6485
Osborn, Mable 2533
Osborn, Mary 2566
Osborn, Susan 9918
Osburn, H. B. (Mr.) 6488
Osgood, Cornelia E. 8307
Osgood, Rowena 1547
Osterhout, Laura E. 5971
Ostram, Caroline 1384
Ostrander, Caty Ann 3251
Ostrander, Mary L. 8018
Ostrander, Phebe 7257
Ostrom, David 3430, 6499
Otile, Abigal 3793
Otis, Charlotte D. 5817
Otis, Emma 6504
Otis, Matteson 6504
Overhizer, Conrad 6510, 6511
Overhizer, James 6511
Overhizer, Mary J. 3273
Oviatt, David 6517
Owen, ___ (Mr.) 4852
Owen, Catherine 4867
Owen, Melissa D. 7935
Owen, Minerva 4124
Owen, O. J. (Mr.) 4852
Owens, Adaline 5677
Owens, Benjamin 9731
Owens, David 6526, 6529
Owens, Elizabeth 9731
Owens, Ellen 9730
Owens, Harriet 9268
Owens, Mary Ann 6527
Owens, Owen 6525, 8360
Owens, Phebe 6025
Owens, Sarah 8716
Oxtoby, George 4355
Oxtoby, Phebe Ann 4355
Oxx, Sarah 7309
P___, Elizabeth P. 190
Pabodie, Betsey 922
Pabodie, Ephraim 6532
Packard, Catherine 4491
Packer, Perez 6538
Packer, Perses 8870
Paddock, Benjamin G. (Rev.)
   966
Paddock, Eliza 966, 3775
Paddock, Louisa 1362
Paddock, Margaret 8162
Paddock, Roswell 6545
Paddon, William W. 6547
Page, ___ (Judge) 6364
Page, ___ (Miss) 3802
Page, Caroline E. 2065
Page, Charles 6549

Page, Charlotte 1657
Page, Elizabeth 2504, 6364
Page, J. M. 6553
Page, Jane 3612
Page, Margaret 6549
Page, Mercy 164
Pagett, John 6563
Paine, David 4238
Paine, Emma 5468
Paine, Helen M. 4238
Palmer, ___ (Rev.) 4685
Palmer, A. H. (Mr.) 1400
Palmer, Amanda 8334
Palmer, B. (Mr.) 6571
Palmer, Benjamin 6586
Palmer, Bethel 6588
Palmer, C. (Miss) 8474
Palmer, Ceriza W. 3129
Palmer, Charlotte 6399
Palmer, Clarinda 6586
Palmer, Elisha 5170
Palmer, Fidelia W. 1400
Palmer, Henry D. 6583
Palmer, Jane F. 1785
Palmer, Joshua J. 8476
Palmer, Lavonia N. 6582
Palmer, Lovice 5170
Palmer, Lucius O. 6579, 6589
Palmer, Maria 8476
Palmer, Maria Bissell 9179
Palmer, Maria S. 9931
Palmer, Mary W. 6579, 6589
Palmer, N. H. (Mr.) 6572
Palmer, Peter 6582
Palmer, Sandford 6590
Palmer, Sarah 4799
Palmer, Valancia 9609
Palmeter, Lucia Maria 946
Paltz, MaRGARET •°(>
Pangburn, Susan 9103
Pankco, Joseph C. 6601
Pantha, Mary 7043
Parcel, Caroline 6602
Parcel, John A. 6602
Parcel, Juliette 8915
Parcel, Mary 7204
Parcel, Samuel 7204
Pardee, Harriet Ann 3420
Pardee, Israel 3141
Pardee, Julia A. 5934
Paree, L. (Mr.) 4099
Pardee, Mary 3141
Pardee, Sarah A. 4099
Pardy, Maria 5412
Pardy, Stephen 5412
Park, Caroline 4658
Park Chester 8080
Park, Elizabeth 9339
Park, George 6612
Park, Henri 6610
Park, Maria A. 8080
Park, Nathan 6611
Parkenson, Cornelia 7182
Parker, Abigail 1458
Parker, Adelia Ann 5253
Parker, Amanda M. 4232
Parker, Amanda S. 4366
Parker, Asenath 6616
Parker, Caroline 5755
Parker, Cornelia 484
Parker, Edith 6619
Parker, Elizabeth 6623, 8990
Parker, Gertrude E. 2450
Parker, Harriet 152
Parker, I. S. (Mr.) 4366
Parker, Ira 6623
Parker, Jason 6635
Parker, Mary 4254

Parker, Milton D. 6619
Parker, Nancy (Mrs.) 2226
Parker, Nathan 6618
Parker, Nathan, Jr. 5254
Parker, S. (Mr.) 5253
Parker, S. C. (Mr.) 2450
Parker, Sarah 1945, 2598
Parker, Sarah J. 5254
Parker, William (Capt.) 1458
Parker, William B. 6616
Parkhurst, Alice 3085
Parks, Ann 7573
Parmele, Horace 6647
Parmele, Mary E. 2361
Parmelee ___ (Mr.) 2751
Parmeleee, Charles 7557
Parmelee, G. R. (Mr.) 6653
Parmelee, Honor W. 6652
Parmelee, Lavina 1912
Parmelee, M. (Mr.) 6648
Parmelee, Martha A. 7557
Parmely, John H. 8700
Parmenter, John 6654
Parmeter,Lucretia 8510
Parmlee, Horace 6655
Parmoyer, Maria 3133
Parris, Catharine 6656
Parris, Edward H. 6656
Parrish, Elizabeth 5748
Parrish, Oliver 6608
Parrott, E. Addison 9750
Parson, Hannah Miles 6180
Parson, Samuel 4346, 6180
Parsons, ___ (Mr.) 9035
Parsons, Abby 965
Parsons, Betsey 3694
Parsons, Caroline E. 6520
Parsons, Catharine S. 4346
Parsons, Georgianna D. 2113
Parsons, Levi 6661
Parsons, Nancy 9767
Parsons, Sophia 8493
Parsons, Sophia L. 5344
Parsons, Theodore 6662, 6664
Partridge, Hannah 9585
Passage, Mary 944
Patchen, Jared 7004
Patchen, Phebe 941
Patchin, Lois 8906
Patchin, Nathan 8906
Patrick, Angelina S. 8855
Patten, Sarah 822
Patten, William 6677
Patten, William, Jr. 6677
Patterson, ___ (Mrs.) 180
Patterson, Agnes 7561
Patterson, Ann 6513
Patterson, Eliza Ann 9693
Patterson, Emily Woodruff 8029
Pattison, Caroline 6382
Pattison, William 6382
Patton, ___ (Dr.) 6688
Patty, J. (Mr.) 6689
Paulding, ___ (Mr.) 5365
Payn, Sophia 8088
Payne, Betsy 4671
Payne, Fanny 4013
Payne, George R. 6700
Payne, Joseph W. 6699
Peabody, Elenor C. 8503
Peacock, Caroline N. 4944
Peacock, William R. 4944
Peak, Olive 3065
Peake, Lydia Matilda 5183
Pearce, H. C. (Miss) 819
Pearcey, Catharine Jane 6536
Pearcey, William 6536
Pearson, George 6707

Pearson, Sarah A. 1223
Pease, Abigail 4637
Pease, Eliza 1673
Pease, Eliza A. 9839
Pease, Elizabeth 2789
Pease, J. B. (Mr.) 6713
Pease, Oliver 4637
Pease, Sarah Maria 7393
Peck, ___ (Mr.) 8080
Peck, Anthony 6729
Peck, Betsey M. 1749
Peck, Clarissa 7603
Peck, Cynthia 6729
Peck, E. A. (Miss) 4168
Peck, Emeline B. 939
Peck, Everard 6721, 6732
Peck, Hannah 6152
Peck, James 6715
Peck, Lodemis A. 3553
Peck, Lucinda 3511
Peck, Maria M. 3037
Peck, Mary W. 3210, 8305
Peck, Sarah 9960
Peckham, Adelia M. 6734, 6738
Peckham, Caroline S. 44
Peckham, Henrietta L. 1969
Peckham, John 5836
Peckham, John S. 6737
Peckham, Maria 5836
Peckham, Mary W. 6737
Peckham, Merritt 6734, 6738
Peckham, Nathan 6739
Peckham, Rufus W. 6735
Peckham, Sarah 2234
Peckham, Seth 6740
Peckhem, Helen H. 6196
Peebles, Mary 592
Peek, Deborah 5516
Peek, John 6748
Peek, Joseph Y. 6746
Peel, Margaret 8076
Peese, Elizabeth 1587
Peet, Lucy 6855
Pell, Maria R. 2142
Pellet, Betsey 6758
Pellet, Edith Ann 6753
Pellet, Esther 6089
Pelley, Julia 9334
Penfield, Henry F. 6760
Pennell, Sarah A. 9860
Penner, Melissa 7178
Penniman,F. B. (Mr.) 6764
Penniman, J. B. Mrs.) 6764
Perhames, Margaret 1048
Perine, George S. 6775
Perine, S. M. (Mr.) 9037
Perkins, A. (Mr.) 8900
Perkins, Ann Maria 100, 4925
Perkins, Betsey 110
Perkins, Charlotte 4148
Perkins, D. L. (Mr.) 6787
Perkins, Elisha 6790
Perkins, Elizabeth Armanda
  4946
Perkins, Erastus 6794
Perkins, Fanny 8317
Perkins, Frederick 6788
Perkins, Harriet H. 4447
Perkins, James 6782
Perkins, Jane Eliza 7511
Perkins, Jenkins 6779
Perkins, Jennet K. 8904
Perkins, John 8904
Perkins, Lucy Ann 7785, 7793
Perkins, Mary 8430
Perkins, O. D. 6790
Perkins, S. H. (Miss) 9765
Perkins, Simon (Gen.) 100

Perrin, Eliza 1074
Perrin, Melony 4264
Perry, Caroline Slidell 667
Perry, Elizabeth A. 6801
Perry, George 6802
Perry, George T. 6799, 6805,
  6813
Perry, Guy M. 6801
Perry, H. (Mr.) 6808
Perry, Henry 6804
Perry, Jane 5429
Perry, M. C. (Commodore) 667
Perry, Phebe 4779
Perry, Richard 5429
Perry, Susan 6873
Person, Eunice 1784
Persons, Louise 5195
Petenger, Sarah 5520
Peters, Absolom 9653
Peters, William 7872
Peterson, Rebecca 3666
Petherick, Richard P. 2943
Pettibone, Ira 8032
Pettibone, Maria 8898
Pettingill, Eliza 6248
Peyton, Rowzee 6833
Pharis, Isabel 7741
Phelon, Deete E. 3992
phelon, Joseph 3992
Phelps, Ann R. 8833
Phelps, Celistia R. 9473
Phelps, Ebenezer 7620
Phelps, Elizabeth H. 8832
Phelps, H. G. 2112
Phelps, H. G. (Mrs.) 2112
Phelps, Hannah A. 9231
Phelps, Harriet 6627
Phelps, Jacob 855
Phelps, John 8832, 8833
Phelps, Joseph D. 6839
Phelps, Marietta 855
Phelps, Mary 48
Phelps, Oliver 3564, 6844
Phelps, Polly 1089
Phelps, Thomas W. 6627
Phetteplace, David 6846
Phettiplace, Persis M. 7118
Phileo, Mary ann 5799
Philips, Charlotte 8815
Philips. Margaret 7683
Phillips, Elijah 6850
Phillips, Elmira C. 4995
Phillips, Grace E. 1332
Phillips, Henry 6860
Phillips, Jonathan 4995
Phillips, Lucinda 9325
Phillips, Lucy 8471
Phillips, Mary 3572
Phillips, Sabrina L. 2617
Phillips, Sarah (Mrs.) 1821
Phinney, Elihu 5628
Phinney, Harriet Bradford 5628
Phyfe, Adelaide 1272
Phyfe, John 1272
Pierce, Adeline 3005
Pierce, Angeline 1509
Pierce, Beula Ann 9557
Pierce, Caroline M. 9255
Pierce, Harriet P. 1199
Pierce, Jemima 810
Pierce, Lewis 6881
Pierce, Marilla E. 8872
Pierce, Mary B. 7454
Pierce, Nancy 6881
Pierce, Phebe M. 7408
Pierce, Susan 2663
Pierson, Job 6885
Pierson, Susannah 5588
*Phelps, Elizabeth Ann 4790

Piersons, Anson 6886
Piersons, Clarissa 6886
Pike, ___ (Gen.) 4602
Pike, Eliza 6830
Pike, Zebulon M. 6888
Pinch, Martha Jane 3243
Pinckney, Frances Ann 4242
Pinckney, J. (Mr.) 4242
Pinckney, Jane 2029
Pinkney, John 6890
Pinney, Ann 6709
Pitkin, William 6893
Pitman, Elizabeth D. 6895
Pitman, Lemuel 6895
Pitney, Joseph T. 6109
Pitney, Mary E. 6109
Pitts, Deborah 4073
Pitts, Susan Ann 9290
Pixley, Isaac 6898
Plant, Benjamin 4385, 6900
Plant, James 6900, 8299
Plant, Mary E. 4385
Platt, ___ (Mr.) 8458
Platt, Adeline M. 7533
Platt, Charlotte 8966
Platt, Dennis 6913
Platt, Elizabeth 4181
Platt, Ely 1236
Platt, Helen Parmelee 655
Platt, James 6914
Platt, Jonas 655, 5211, 6904,
  6907
Platt, Jonathan 8966
Plimpton, Rhoda 9493
Plumb, Cornelia T. 1741
Plumb, David 6919
Plumb, Lucy A. 6919
Plummer, Ellen 9831
Pocock, ___ (Mrs.) 8555
Pocock, Elizabeth 8546
Podick, John 6989
Podick, Margaret Atcheson 6989
Poe, Edgar A. 6922
Polk, Ann 9272
Pollard, Adelia C. 1708
Pollard, Lucy 6821
Pollard, W. H. (Mrs.) 5707
Pomeroy, ___ (Mr.) 674
Pomeroy, Frances L. 2331
Pomeroy, Lemuel 2530
Pomeroy, Mary Ann 6942
Pomeroy, Mary Tyler 2584
Pomeroy, Olivia H. 2530
Pomeroy, Robert 6936
Pomeroy, Theodore 8404
Pomeroy, Thomas F. 6942
Pond, EmmA S. 1521
Pond, Harriet L. 7028
Pond, Lewis 7028
Pond, Mary L. 623
Pond, S. M. (Mrs.) 6946
Pond, Sarah A. 9752
Pond, T. T. (Mr.) 6946
Pond, Temperance 2722
Pool, Elisha 6949
Pool, Esther E. 9108
Porter, Ann Eliza 7613
Porter, Betsey 9578
Porter, Caroline 2304
Porter, Celow 6953
Porter, Charles S. 6962
Porter, Chauncey 2304, 9745
Porter, Cornelia 6957
Porter, Cynthia 5406
Porter, Edwin W. 6970
Porter, Giles M. 6963
Porter, Harriet 2580
Porter, Lucy (Mrs.) 1044

Porter, Margaret (Mrs.) 7822
Porter, Noah 6961
Porter, Olive Ann 9745
Porter, Orlon 6954
Porter, Peter B. 6964
Porter, Samuel 7613
Porter, Stephen 6957, 6960
Porter, Sylvia R. 7304
Porter, Thomas 6972
Posner, Elizabeth Ackerman 2971
Posner, Jacob 2971
Post, Abraham A. 866, 867
Post, Caroline 9283
Post, Elizabeth 3673
Post, John 6974
Post, Mandeles 867
Post, Mary C. 1888
Potter, Augusta 2191
Potter, Caroline E. 5871
Potter, Emily 4492
Potter, Helen 9241
Potter, Hiram 7282
Potter, Horatio 6992
Potter, John 6981, 6984
Potter, Mariette 3207
Potter, Martha 6984
Potter, Martha J. 7156
Potter, Mary 3993
Potter, Mary H. 7282
Potter, Orson 6994
Potter, P. (Mr.) 2191, 4554
Potter, Susannah 6027
Potter, W. F. 6991
Potter, W. F. (Mrs.) 4865
Potter, William 5871
Potter, William F. 9241
Powell, Elizabeth 5780
Powell, Jeremiah 7003
Powell, John 7004
Powell, Liberty 7009
Powell, Philo 7002
Powell, Sarah 5773
Powell, Susan 1515
Powell, Thomas 7005, 7007
Powers, Almira 7669
Powers, Ann J. 8459
Powers, Caroline A. 9951
Powers, Eliza 7405
Powers, Erastus 4409
Powers, Gershom 4044, 7405
Powers, Ira 7014
Powers, Lydia Ann 4044
Powers, Noah 7011
Powers, Sarah E. 4409
Pwers, Sarah S. 2184
Powsland, Grace 8192
Pratt, Angeline 4624
Pratt, Caroline L. 3751
Pratt, Daniel 9936
Pratt, Eemline 7617
Pratt, Emily M. 3902
Pratt, Frederick 4624
Pratt, Helen M. 1700
Pratt, Jane 4069
Pratt, Jerusha L. 7886
Pratt, Lucy 4194
Pratt, Matthew 7021
Pratt, Mary 7849, 8568
Pratt, Orsamus 7030
Pratt, Sophia M. 8356
Pratt, Susan M. 9936
Pratt, Una L. 8772
Predmore, Benjamin 7034
Prentice, D.7264
Prentice, Herman V. 5306
Prentice, Maria 812
Prentice, Mary 3904

Prentice, Mary Jane Dayton 5306
Prentice, Susan Cordelia 7264
Prentiss, ___ (Col.) 5231
Prentiss, Catherine L. 2623
Prentiss, John H. 6903, 8479
Prentiss, Sarah 5761
Prescott, Adelia C. 2951
Prescott, Mary C. 2202
Prescott, Oliver 2120, 6117
Prescott, Roxy 6006
Prescott, Ruth Ann 2120
Prescott, Sophia 4068
Preston, Caroline A. 7012
Preston, Eunice 4083
Preston, Jerusha 9963
Preston, Julia R. 9780
Preston, Lucy 4580
Prettyman, Jane 1588
Prettyman, Sarah E. 9092
Price, Ezekiel 7051
Price, Harriet 9779
Price, Mary 1681
Prichard, Eunice Rebecca 7467
Pride, AbigaL (@%)@
Priest, Amanda 7246
Priest, Eunice C. 2152
Priest, Jane C. 1339
Pritchard, Calvin 7070
Proal, ___ (Rev. Dr.) 7072
Probasco, Eleanore 3333
Proctor, Rachael 5037
Prouty, Phineas 1689, 7079
Prouty, Sally 6622
Prouty, Sarah Augusta 1689
Pruden, Rhoda 6530
Prushour, Mary Ann 5065
Pudney, Rebecca M. 6695
Pugh, Humphrey H. 7084
Pugsley, Nancy A. 7013
Pulfrey, Lovina 4167
Pullen, Electa 1540
Pullen, Jedediah 7085
Pulver, Eve 8477
Pumpelly, Charles 7086
Pumpelly, Frances E. 919, 920
Punderson, ___ (Deacon) 7088
Punderson, John 853, 7090
Punderson, Mellissant 7088
Punderson, Polly (Mrs.) 7088
Purcell, ___ (Mr.) 7092
Purcell, William 7091, 7092
Purdee, Julia A. 5939
Purdy, Caroline 428
Purdy, Edward H. 7093
Purdy, Tammy 5948
Purple, Lydia 30
Putnam, Alfred 2829
Putnam, David 1362
Putnam, E. A. (Mrs.) 6938
Putnam, George 7098, 7101
Putnam, Hiram 6838
Putnam, Isabella Jane Kirk 2829
Putnam, Israel 5518
Putnam, Lucy B. 6838
Putnam, Margaret 7809
Putnam, Mary 650
Putnam, S. G. (Rev.) 6938
Putnam, Sarah M. 7098, 7101
Putnam, William 7102
Quackenboss, Isaac 7104
Quackenboss, Mary A. 7104
Quackenbush, Eliza 670, 780
Quackenbush, Eliza Ann 8387
Quackenbush, Henrietta 6405
Quackenbush, Nicholas 7105
Quackenbush, Polly 9778
Quackenbush, Sally Ann 5446

Queal, Jane 6012
Queal, Margaret M. 4172
Queal, Sarah 3247
Queen, Maria Regina 1455
Quigley, Margaret 2838
Quin, Mary W. 6450
Quinby, Mary Ann 5489
Quinn, Eleanor 4533
Race, Christina 515
Race, Emeline 7119
Race, Maria 8549
Race, Marsden 7119
Race, Pamelia 3063
Race, Whiting 7119
Rachester, Nathaniel 7404
Ramsey, Jane 6558
Ramsey, William 7123
Rand, Asa 7125
Randal, Emily 5361
Randal, Jirah 7126
Randall, Anthony 7132
Randall, Anthony R. 7266
Randall, Antoinette 4609
Randall, Eliza 713, 3963
Randall, Eliza 519
Randall, Ernestine S. 3253
Randall, Hannah M. 7221
Randall, Harriet W. 4853
Randall, Isadora 3193
Randall, John 790, 3253, 3963
Randall, Lewis 7131
Randall, Lucia Maria 4286
Randall, M. J. (Miss) 6615
Randall, Maria H. 790
Randall, Miranda 7543
Randall, N. P. (Mr.) 9917
Randall, Parmela 1550
Randall, R. C. (Mr.) 7128
Randall, Rowell 4286
Randall, Samuel S. 7134
Randall, Sarah 9917
Randolph, Lucy Maria 1015
Randolph, Mary P. 942
Randolph, Richard H. 1015
Ransford, Biancy 7146
Ransford, Hannah 1127
Ransford, Hascall 1127
Ransford, J. L. (Mr.) 7146
Ransier,Dolly 2828
Ransier, John 2178
Ransier, Maria 2178
Ransier, Rachel 5233
Ransom, John P. 7150
Raplee, Almira 1112
Raplyee, Sarah 8561
Rathbone, J. H. (Mr.) 6712
Rathbone, Mary 6712
Rathbone, S. (Mr.) 9947
Rathbun, ___ (Mr.) 8278
Rathburn,___ (Miss) 2457
Rathburn, Sarah Jane 9217
Rathsong, Belinda 9993
Ratnier, Eliza 9904
Ravel, Catharine 8363
Ray, Cornelia E. 3888
Ray, Delila 5887
Ray, Lydia 1217
Ray, Mary 1322
Ray, Robert 3888
Ray, William H. 7166
Raymond, D. W. (Dr.) 7175
Raymond, Ebenezer 7172
Raymond, Mary 5077
Rayner family, 6021
Raywalt, Elizabeth C. 5775
Read, Charlotte T. 1899
Read, Mary 9706
Read, Rosetta C. 869

Rector, Charity 5443
Rector, Elizabeth 3081
Reddish, Hellen A. 1192
Redfield, Julia Ann 5421
Redfield, Olive 5790
Redman, Adelaide E. 6310
Redman, Daniel 6310, 6605
Redman, Laura E. 6605
Redman, Michael 7186
Redmond, Mary 3520
Redner, Sarah 2075
Reed, ___ (Rev.) 7206
Reed, Bethiah 7210
reed, Charles M. 5668
Reed, Eliza 5583
Reed, Emily 6718
Reed, Eunice 2713
Reed, Hannah 7143
Reed, Helen 5668
Reed, Irene 8262
Reed, John 4899
Reed, Josiah 2713, 7198
Reed, Nathan 7198, 7210
Reed, Patience 1581
reed, Robert 7196
reed, Romeo 7204
Reed, Seneca 7201
Reed, Susan C. 1780
Reeder, Caroline 3154
Reeder, Susan 8981
Rees, Evan J. 7219
Rees, James 7220
Rees, Jane C. 7219
Rees, Maria L. 4862
Rees, William 4862
Reese, Almira 1648
Reeves, Angeline Therese 4743
Reiggles, Daniel R. 7232
Reins, David H. 449
Reins, Fanny 449
Reins, Maria S. 6917
Reis, Diana 7078
Remer, George I. 7236
Remer, Jennett 9158
Remer, Phebe 9144
Remington, John Y. 7238
Renimole, Caroline 8886
Renwick, William 9511
Rexford, L. S. (Rev.) 3762
Rexford, Levi 7243
Reymond, Nancy L. 971
Reynolds, Ann R. 9846
Reynolds, Catherine 388
Reynolds, Emily 7248
Reynolds, Jane H. 3359
Reynolds, Joseph 388
Reynolds, Phebe 2345
Reynolds, Rachel 7398
Reynolds, Richard 7256
Reynolds, Rosannah 7112
Reynolds, Rosetta 7251
Reynolds, S. H. (Mr.) 7248
Reynolds, Sally Ann 7734
Reynolds, Sarah G. 901
Reynolds, Susan 9014
Reynolds, William H. 7251,
 7258
Rhodes, Amelia 3008
Rhodes, Betsey 4066
Rhodes, Daniel 3008
Rhodes, Esther 604
Rhodes, Lydia D. 88
Rhynders, Sarah Ann 3779
Rhyne, Mary Ann 5963
Riant, Elvira 9057
Ribble, Francina M. 7110
Rice, ___ (Miss) 6291
Rice, Asa 7284
Rice, Asia 7283

Rice, Charlotte 6624
Rice, Cornelius 7270
Rice, Elmira 8348
Rice, Hannah 3503
Rice, Jason 7283
Rice, Joseph T. 5943
Rice, Lydia 529
Rice, Maranda 2635
Rice, Mary E. 10008
Rice, Mary J. 5943
Rice, Stephen 7274
Rice, Ssuqn 6333
Rice, William 8851
Rich, Maria 7291
Richards, Asenath 5960
Richards, Daniel 7293
Richards, Emily J. 6852
Richards, James 5103
Richards, John 7300
Richards, Mary 3171
Richards, Morris 7373
Richards, Owen 7301
Richardson, Hannah 7311
Richardson, Israel B. 7308
Richardson, J. B. (Mr.) 7312
Richardson, Joseph P. 7311
Richardson, Maria 5355
Richardson, Thomas 7307
Richmond, Melinda 8239
Richmond, N. (Mr.) 7314
Richmond, Parna 8938
Riddle, Charlotte 3958
Riddle, Frances 4741
Riddle, Henrietta 3956
Riddle, Robert 3956, 3958, 4741
Riddle, Thomas 7320
Rifenbark, Elizabeth 517
Riggs, Caroline 2308
Riggs, Isaac 2308
Rightmyer, H. (Mr.) 5645
Riley, Elizabeth R. 4520
Riley, Harriet 2110
Riley, Lawrence 7326
Ringer, Mary A. 2441
Ripley, Laura 2747
Rippey, Rebecca 1531
Rising, John 7336
Risley, David 7337
Risley, Mary J. 7899
Ritzema, Johannes 4354
Robards, Jane N. 3396
Robbins, ___ (Rev.) 7352
Robbins, E. S. (Mr.) 6579
Robbins, Helen Maria 1962
Robbins, Mariah 3490
Robbins, R. (Mr.) 7772
Robbins, Russell 7354
Robenson, George 6881
Roberson, Louisa H. 3786
Roberts, ___ (Judge) 9692
Roberts, Amanda 3118
Roberts, Ann E. 7371
Roberts, Catharine E. 3897
Roberts, Eleanor 860
Roberts, Elizabeth 2978
Roberts, Ellen 6810
Roberts, Elmira 5169
Roberts, Evans 7371
Roberts, G. G. (Mr.) 7360
Roberts, Hugh 1946
Roberts, Jane 6521
Roberts, Jane L. 735
Roberts, Lavinia C. 9692
Roberts, Margaret Elizabeth
 9742
Roberts, Maria 9519
Roberts, Mariam H. 860
Roberts, Mary 1891, 4892, 8591
Roberts, Mary Jane 8238

Roberts, N. S. (Mr.) 8238
Roberts, Nathan S. 8242
Roberts, R. W. (Mr.) 734
Roberts, Sally Logan 1946
Roberts, Samuel 3897
Roberts, Sarah 8287
Roberts, Thomas D. 7369
Roberts, Warner 860
Roberts, William 7370, 7374
Robertshaw, Thomas 7377
Robinson, Elizabeth 4877
Robinson, George W. 5490
Robinson, Harriet 338
Robinson, Helen L. 6935
Robinson, James C. 3535
Robinson, John A. 932
Robinson, Lazy 1487
Robinson, Lina 2762
Robinson, Mary S. 3535
Robinson, Phebe 8055
Robinson, Thomas 9259
Robson, Mary 3699
Robson, Mathew 8046
Robson, Mary Ann 8046
Rochester. See also Rochester.
Rochester, W. H. (Mrs.) 3119
Rochester, William B. 7401
Rockwell, Eliza W. 5992
Rockwell, Eunice 5099
Rockwell, Harriet E. 7372
Rockwell, Jane 5028
Rockwell, Mary Matilda 665
Rockwell, Olive 9494
Rockwell, Philo 3258, 5028,
 7407
Rodgers, ___ (Commodore) 9127
Rodgers, ___ (Mrs.) 9127
Rodgers, Elpha 5312
Rodgers, Jennett 5876
Rodgers, John 5703
Rodgers, Kearney 6500
Rodgers, Nancy 7690
Rodgers, Nannie 5703
Rodgers, Susan Kearney 6500
Rodman, Daniel 6604
Rodman, Emily 165
Rodman, Laura E. S. 6604
Rodman, Phebe 9769
Rodney, Charlotte 5143
Rodney, Margaret 4155
Rodney, William 514, 7423
Rogers, B. T. (Mr.) 7566
Rogers, Charlotte 9301
Rogers, Clark 7438
Rogers, Davis 7433
Rogers, Eliza 1265
Rogers, Elizabeth 2785
Rogers, Gustavus 7450
Rogers, Jane F. 7566
Rogers, Julia 4106
Rogers, Julia Ann 4715
Rogers, Lucy 3967
Rogers, Lydia 1176
Rogers, Maria 8001
Rogers, Maria Louisa 9809
Rogers, Mary Ann 8369
Rogers, Nancy M. 2673
Rogers, Nathaniel 3967
Rogers, O. G. (Mr.) 9301
Rogers, Prudence 8685
Rogers, Reuben 4715
Rogers, Sarah 4477
Rogers, Silas, Jr. 7444
Rogers, Susan 2260
Rogers, W. C. (Mr.) 7426
Rolfe, Jane 9996
Rollo, J. H. 717
Rollo, Marietta 3074
Rollo, Philomela 717

Rolo, Frances 7038
Romeyn, Thomas 7457
Rood, Harriet 7480
Rook, Mary 3445
Roosevelt, Nelson 7459
Root, Mary Jane 5416
Root, Philamela 2091
Root, Vienna (Mrs.) 1606
Root, William 7469
Rorick,Mary C. 6916
Rose, Alathea 6777
Rose, Ann 9090
Rose, Charles A. 7479, 7482
Rose, Deborah 3413
Rose, Eliza Jane 2729
Rose, Emeline L. 4079
Rose, Huldah W. 7786
Rose, Jane 6668
Rose, Nathan 7487
Rose, Robert S. 7475, 7938
Rose, Rufus 6777
Rose, Sarah Ann 9873
Rose, Susan 9559
Rose, Susan A. 7938
Roseboom, Emily M. 1992
Roseboom, Gerritt 1992
Rosecrants, Usebe B. 4695
Rosekranes, Jeanette 8615
Rosekrans, Matilda 3162
Ross, Mary E. 4846
Ross, Melissa 5031
Ross, Samuel 7493, 7498
Rossiter, Harriet 2670
Rossiter, N. (Mr.) 2670
Rossiter, William 1184
Roth, Anna 313
Roth, Nelson 7504
Roue, Eliza 3693
Rounds, Catharine 7508, 7509
Rounds, Stephen S. 7508, 7509
Rouse, James 7513
Rouse, Lorenzo 7512
Rowan, ___ (Rev.) 4413
Rowan, Jane Anna 4413
Rowe, Julia 7409
Rowe, Mary E. 9139
Rowel, Eliza 4033
Rowell, Betsey 411
Rowland, Eliza 7052
Rowlands, Mary 4465
Rowlandson, ___ (Miss) 491
Rowley, Abijah 7522
Rowley, Harriet 8015
Rowley, Jane Ann 3331
Rowley, Jane L. 1489
Rowley, Jane R. 9010
Rowley, Julia Ann 2101
Rowlingson, Fidelia 9131
Royce, Alba G. 7528
Royce, Eliza Ann 4879
Royce, Jane 4577
Royce, Samuel 4879
Roys, Mary 6523
Ruckle, P. (Mr.) 2045
Rudd, Jabez F. 7532
Rudman, Emilie T. 8882
Rudman, John 6198
Rudman, Mary 6198
Rue, Adeline 4682
Ruggles, Draper 250
Ruggles, Jane P. 6568
Ruggles, Laura A. 3281
Ruggles, Nancy S. 250
Rumbill, Sarah A. 6330
Rumkill, Luther 8638
Rumkill, Susan M. 8638
Rumney, George 7539
Rumsey, Laura J. 7829
Rumsey, Phineas 3087

Rundell, Caroline 1040
Rundell, Julia 5275
Rundell, O. G. (Gen.) 5275
Rush, Benjsmin 2301
Russ, charlotte S. 7427
Russ, John A. 2949, 7427
Russel, Catharine Ann 6289
Russel, Priscilla 2818
Russel, Mary R. 9997
Russell, Agnes 7556
Russell, Elizabeth 8154
Russell, Jane 6011
Russell, Joseph 5404
Russell Mary (Mrs.) 6230
Russell, Olivia 5404
Russell, Robert 7556
Russigee, ___ (Mrs.) 5485
Rust, Augusta M. 9874
Rust, Clarissa P. 596
Rust, P. N. (Col.) 9874
Rutraugh, Hannah 5855
Ryan, Bage 7565
Ryan, Mary J. 5597
Ryley, Helen 9235
Ryley, J. V. S. (Mr.) 9235
Rynear, ___ (Col.) 576
Ryon, Emily 2879
Ryon, Laura Ann 2907
Ryon, Sally Ann 7443
Sabine, Alfred 7570
Sacket, Mary E. 9048
Sackett, Adaline 3829
Sackett, Adrain 3829
Sackett, Jane 9533
Sage, Cornelia 6807
Sage, Elvira Ann 2751
Sage, Emily T. 4791
Sage, H. (Col.) 4977, 6807, 7579
Sage, Hezekiah 2751
Sage, Jennette 4977
Sage, Marcus 7580
Sage, Mary 3286, 9875
Sage, Nancy 7638
Sage, Rozanna 7580
Sagues, William 7581
St. John, Elvira 5020
St. John, J. T. (Mr.) 7588
St. John, Margaret 3169
Saits, Eve 8359
Salisbury, H. A. (Mrs.) 2839
Salisbury, Mary 389
Salisbury, S. H. (Mr.) 7594
Salkeld, George 7597
Saltenstall, Frances C. 1504
Sammon, Ann 6410
Sample, James 7601
Sampson, George 9900
Sampson, Sarah 9900
Sanders, Almira E. 2756
Sanders, George 7609
Sanders, Harriet P. 8514
Sanders, Henry 7607, 7610,7611
Sanders, John 132
Sanders, Lucy 7607, 7610, 7611
Sanders, Mary Jane 5434
Sandford, ___ (Dr.) 7693
Sandford, Carol 7223
Sandford, Lucy A. 2326
Sandford, Luther 7223
Sandford, Robert 2326
Sandford, Sarah 7693
Sands, Rebecca Ann 4939
Sanford, Eliza 5267
Sanford, Nathan 5267
Sanger, G. (Mr.) 7630
Sanger, Gerry 7625
Sanger, Henry K. 7627
Sanger, Jedediah 7631

Sanger, Jeremiah 8295
Sanger, Joseph 7628
Sanger, Justus H. 7626
Sargent, Almira 1911
Sarsdell, Lucy 4501
Saterlee, Helen 4415
Saulpaugh, Elizabeth A. 6929
Saumet, Mary E. 5098
Saunders, Charlotte 109
Savage, ___ (Mr.) 4334
Savage, John 4626
Savery, Louisa 4473
Savery, Phineas 4473
Sawyer, Ezra 7648
Sawyer, Hannah 9628
Saxton, Catharine 4053
Sayels, Catharine 1566
Sayles, Elizabeth 2485
Sayles, Elmira 6226
Sayre, Abigail 1584
Sayre, Anna Cornelia 823
Sayre, Annis 7661
Sayre, Ebenezer 7661
Sayre, James 823, 7662, 9258
Sayre, Willis B. 7661
Sayres, Silas 6226
Schank, James 7666
Schermerhorn, Ann Eliza 4764
Schermerhorn, John V. R. 7671
Schooley, Abraham 7675
Schoonmaker, Catharine 1457
Schram, Elizabeth 6393
Schram, Sarah 7679
Schram, William 107, 7679
Schriver, Jane Harriet 2069.5
Schutt, Sally Ann 6432
Schuyler, ___ (Mrs.) 9047
Schuyler, Adelia 7688
Schuyler, Cornelius 2469
Schuyler, Electa 7387
Schuyler, Harriet A. 2469
Schuyler, Jacob 7681, 7688
Schuyler, Jane Ann 7260
Schuyler, Janett 7322
Schuyler, Martha 3679
Schuyler, Martha A. 8437
Schuyler, Melinda 1456
Scofield, Chester 7699
Scofield, Liflet 7696
Scofield, Martha 7696
Scofield, Sophronia S. 4737
Scot, Ann 9124
Scott, ___ (Gen.) 3888, 7707, 9865
Scott, ___ (Mrs.) 7702
Scott, Amanda 3394
Scott, Ann 6274
Scott, Charlotte 4182
Scott, Cornelia 7707
Scott, Eliza 355
Scott, Elizabeth 9036
Scott, Helen 3667
Scott, Mary 7185
Scott, Melinda 8951
Scott, Nancy 7968
Scott, Ruth Eliza 2103
Scott, Sally 4395
Scovil, Lemuel 7714
Scoville, Darius 7716
Scoville, H. (Mr.) 9613
Scoville, Lois Ann 9613
Scoville, P. A. (Miss) 5358
Scoville, Sally 934
Scudder, ___ (Rev. Dr.) 7721
Scudder, Mary Jane 8045
Scudder, T. O. (Mr.) 8045
Seabert, Abigail 4309
Seabury, Sarah S. 5581
Searban, Catharine Jane 839

Slausen, Harriet E. 7026
Slausen, James 7026
Slauson, James 9170
Slauson, Lucy Ann 9170
Sleeper, N. B. (Mr.) 4966
Sleight, Mary 473
Sleighter, Sarah Ann 442
Slick, Mary 6581
Slingerland, Jacob 8013
Sloan, Amanda 6200
Sloan, John, Jr. 8014, 9822
Sloan, Mary M. 9822
Sloan, Rachel 776
Sloane, Douglass W. 5073
Slocum, Ann D. 3884
Slocum, Leicester 8019
Slosson, Gabriel 8020
Sly, John 1216
Sly, Lucinda M. 1216
Sly, Matthew McR. 8024
*Sly, Polly 7748
*Smead, Cornelia 8538
Smiley, Zennette N. 4133
Smith, ___ (Widow) 1506
Smith, A. (Mr.) 8042
Smith, Abigail 1118
Smith, Adam 4784
Smith, Ann 6358
Smith, Anna Kellogg 7858
Smith, Anna M. M. 8049
Smith, Archibald 5565
Smith, Asenath 4986
Smith, Avery 8109
Smith, Azariah 8447
Smith, Benjamin 2746
Smith, Brittania 9457
Smith, C. (Miss) 4423
Smith, Caroline A. 936
Smith, Caroline R. 1024
Smith, Catharine 4353, 6494
Smith, Charles 6228
Smith, Daniel 5146, 8040
Smith, Delia A. 7598
Smith, Delia M. 4784
Smith, Duncan 8127
Smith, Duncan 8079, 8118
Smith, Eleanor D. 9662
Smith, Eliza 4407, 5146, 5531
Smith, Eliza M. 3215
Smith, Elizabeth 1183, 5986
Smith, Elizabeth Hamilton 5151
Smith, Elvira 954
Smith, Emily 3025, 3951, 6228
Smith, Emily P. 6541
Smith, Emily T. 8396
Smith, Emma 2746
Smith, Enoch 8028
Smith, Enos 4052
Smith, Esther L. 5022
Smith, Fanny 1139
Smith, George 963
Smith, Gerardus 6358
Smith, Gerrit 5986
Smith, Grace A. 8274
Smith, Hannah 396, 556, 8378, 8597
Smit, Hannah T. 5565
Smith, Harriet 274, 5333, 5786, 7437, 8137, 9218
Smith, Harriet A. 963
Smith, Harriet K. 7324
Smith, Harvey 7858
Smith, Henry H. 8114
Smith, Hester Jane 6733
Smith, Hetty H. 8145
Smith, Huldah 2463
Smith, Ira A. 936
Smith, J. O. (Mr.) 8074
*Small, Cynthia E. 7202

Smith, James 8117
Smith, Jane 7729
Smith, Jennett 8825
Smith, Jennette 8074
Smith, Job 8119
Smith, John 8064, 8099, 8106, 9662
Smith, John U. 8059
Smith, Julia 7019, 8723
Smith, L. M. (Miss) 3542
Smith, Lavina 8361
Smith, Lomira 6778
Smith, Louisa 3505
Smith, Lucia 683
Smith, Lucretia 4335
Smith, Lucy 3965
Smith, Lydia 3142
Smith, M. (Mr.) 8113
Smith, Margaret 7025, 8127
Smith, Margaret Elizabeth 9029
Smith, Maria 3806, 4999
Smith, Maria L. 5492
Smith, Maria P. 9603
Smith, Mary 4878, 6828, 8026
Smith, Mary Ann 8937
Smith, Mary B. 6697
Smith, Mary Eliza 2246
Smith, Mary Jane 1283
Smith, Mary L. 8739
Smith, Mehetabel 5539
Smith, N. Elizabeth 9544
Smith, Nancy 5837
Smith, Nancy S. 1797
Smith, Nathan 1118
Smith, Nathaniel 8274
Smith, Nehemiah 4407
Smith, Nicholas 8102, 9029
Smith, Norman 3521
Smith, Parmelia 1525
Smith, Peter 8058
Smith, Peter C. 8135
Smith, Reuben 7993
Smith, Roda 8048
Smith, Sally, Maria 6702
Smith, Samuel A. 8062
Smith, Sara 8161
Smith, Sarah 4499
Smith, Sarah A. 6190
Smith, Sarah M. 7111
Smith, Solomon I. 9382
Smith, Sophia H. 7857
Smith, Sophia L. 4441
Smith, Squire 8044
Smith, Susan 2712, 5917, 8059
Smith, Sylvester 1668
Smith, Tamer 7749
Smith, Truman 8149
Smith, Trumbull 8139, 8161
Smith, Uretta 8301
Smith, Walter D. 2797, 8145
Smith, William 3142, 8137
Smith, William H. 8096, 8100
Smith, William O. 8049
Smith, Zilpha 8447
Snedekar, Sarah Ann 104
Snell, Caroline 6365
Snell, Eliza M. 1556
Snell, Hannah 4340
Snell, Mary Ann 2550
Snider, Ann Maria 8072
Snider, Maria 2151
Snow, ___ (Mr.) 3110
Snow, Dolly 1208
Snow, Henry 8168
Snow, Lucretia 5504
Snowden, Arabella (Mrs.) 5718
Snowden, Samuel Finley 8170

Snowe, Betsey 553
Snyder, Barbara 4246
Snyder, Henry V. 5298
Snyder, Henry W. 8174
Snyder, Jacob 8173, 8176
Snyder, Lucinda 3742
Snyder, Margaret H. 5298
Snyder, Mary Jane 625
Snyder, Rebecca M. 7054
Sollis, Elizabeth 179
Somers, Elizabeth M. 2030
Sommers, C. G. (Rev.) 4431, 8180
Sommers, Mary Elizabeth Y. 4428
Soper, Charles 8183
Soubeiran, ___ (Dr.)
Soule, E. L. (Dr.) 8186
Soule, Rachael 7758
Soules, James 8073, 9168
Soules, Martha A. 8073
Sours, Mary W. 8189
Sours, Peter 8189
Southard, Samuel L. 4291
Southard, Virginia E. 4291
Southmayd, Martha 4583
Southwick, ___ (Miss) 2605
Southwick, Josephine M. 231
Southwick, Julia A. 3254
Southwick, Martha Sophia 8680
Southwick, Royal 231
Southwick, Solomon 8194, 8193
Southworth, Harriet Mariah 1110
Souverhill, James M. 8196
Space, J. C. (Mr.) 8199
Spalding, Adelia 1359
Spalding, Lemira 7422
Spalding, Levi 1359
Spalding, Sophia A. 6879
Sparhawk, Ebenezer 8912
Sparhawk, Mary E. 8910
Spaulding, Cornelia 3360
Spaulding, Horace 3694
Spaven, Thomas 8210
Spear, Abigail 3346
Spear, Abraham 544
Spear, Amelia S. 6698
Spear, Irene 544
Spears, Orpha 9486
Spees, Jane E. 6171
Spell, Benjamin 8217
Spencer, ___ (Chief Justice) 8841
Spencer, ___ (Judge) 8243
Spencer, ___ (Mr.) 8295, 9328
Spencer, Albert 8232
Spencer, Charlotte 8793
Spencer, Cynthia E. 7863
Spencer, E. (Mr.) 9360
Spencer, E. M. (Rev.) 8227
Spencer, Elizabeth 4913, 7458
Spencer, Elizabeth (Mrs.) 2849
Spencer, Elizabeth L. 6015
Spencer, Emeline 2758
Spencer, G. T. (Mr.) 8229
Spencer, Harriet 8229
Spencer, Israel S. 8242
Spencer, J. A. (Mr.) 8227, 8234
Spencer, John C. 1865, 6131, 8225, 9279
Spencer, Joshua A. 8235
Spencer, Julius A. (Mrs.) 1298
Spencer, Laura Catherine 1865
Spencer, Lavinia F. 8350
Spencer, Marcia 205
Spencer, Mary 8265
Spencer, Mary (Wid.) 8265
Spencer, Mary Ann 9360
Spencer, Mary N. 6131

Spencer, Norman 8218
Spencer, Sarah A. 9262
Spencer, Sarah Ann 8232
Spencer, T. Rush (Dr.) 8228
Spencer, Thomas 8222
Spencer, Truman 8240
Spertel, Elizabeth 3948
Spertzell, Justus 8248
Spertzell, Mary 8248
Spink, Samuel 8250
Spinner, Francis E. 1759
Spinner, Harriet F. 1759
Spoor, Caroline 7168
Spoor, John 8256
Sprague, Asa 1820, 8260
Sprague, E. W. (Mr.) 8258
Sprague, Fanny 654
Sprague, Hannah B. 6266
Sprague, Maria 2770
Sprague, Nancy S. 5176
Sprague, Pamilla 1820
Sprague, Sarah W. 5038
Sprague, William 5176
Sprague, William U. 8259
Spring, Susan 3209
Springsted, Elizabeth 809
Spurr, Calista 8858
Spyer, William Curtis 8270
Squeir, Susan 2026
Squier, Caroline 6978
Sqire, Harriet 7230
Squires, Anthony 6784
Squires, Charles 8278
Squires, Frances Adelia 6784
Squires, James 8276
Squires, Kezia M. 28
Squires, Sarah 485
Squires, Ursula 2239
Staats, J. (Dr.) 8281
Stacy, ___ (Mr.) 83
Stafford, A. T. (Miss 1047
Stafford, Aaron 8293
Stafford, Caroline S. 8835
Stafford, Esther 7137
Stafford, George 1186, 8286
Stafford, H. N. (Mrs.) 9698
Stafford, Jacob 8283
Stafford, Joab 5210, 8284
Stafford, John W. 8288
Stafford, Louise E. 5210
Stafford, Marcia B. 328
Stafford, Rufus 8285
Stafford, Sarah 8169
Stafford, Sophia 8288
Stafford, Thomas 8835
Stainton, Bryan 8297
Stalker, Alexander 8300
Stalp, Orella 6252
Standart, Margaret R. 9293
Standish, Elizabeth 3239
Stanley, Ann E. 9485
Stanley, Asa 9485
Stanley, Catharine 9737
Stanley, Frederick 8308
Stanley, Lucius 8309
Stanley, S. (Dr.) 8306
Stansbury, Elizabeth (Mrs.) 8311
Stansell, Mary 4951
Stanton, Anna 5248
Stanton, E. (Mr.) 9543
Stanton, Elias 8315
Stanton, Esther 1682
Stanton, G. W. (Mr.) 4832
Stanton, George W. 1206, 5248
Stanton, Jane C. 9543
Stanton, Julia 1206
Stanton, Marion K. 5566
Stanton, Mary L. 4832

Stanton, Nancy D. 8314
Stanton, Phuneas 1682
Stanton, Serepta M. 6944
Stanton, Warren D. 8314
Staples, John 8321
Staples, Phebe 7782
Stark, Amy 8631
Starks, Elizabeth 6710
Starr, Elisha 8332
Starr, Seth 8331
Starrow, Ann 4708
* Start, Isaiah 8336
Staunton, Frances M. 219
Stearns, Joel, Jr. 8342
Stearns, Phebe 8165
Stearns, Susan R. 5905
Stearns, Willis 8337
Stebbins, Charles 3341
Stebbins, Eliza A. 1316
Stebbins, George 8346
Stebbins, Harriet A. 8996
Stebbins, J. (Miss) 1227
Stebbins, Lucy 3341
Steele, ___ (Judge) 6744
Steele, Eliphalet (Rev.) 8357
Steele, Frances Mary 8352
Steele, H. (Mr.) 8353
Steele, Lemuel, Jr. 8355
Steele, Oliver 8352
Steele, Polly 2263
Steere, Harriet 2037
Steere, Mark 2037,. 3017, 6966
Steere, Mary F. 3017
Steere, Sarah Ann 6966
Stephens, Abram E. 8362
Stephens, John W. 8365
Stephens, Martha 1832
Stephens, Mary Ann 6270
Stephens, Susan 2139
Stephens, T. C. 8360
Sterling, Anna S. 8368
Sterling, Daniel 8371
Sterling, J. C. (Mr.) 8368
Sterling, Jacob 6633
Sterling, Lord 6286
Sterling, Mary W. 6633
Stern, Elijah 8372
Stetson, Melissa C. 6987
Stevens, Elizabeth 836, 1609
Stevens, Hannah 9868
Stevens, Hannah E. 65
Stevens, J. L. 65
Stevens, Jane 8776
Stevens, John 5387
Stevens, Lucy 5387
Stevens, Mary 4760
Stevens, Miriam 8085
Stevens, Nancy 1014
Stevens, Susan 4537
Stevenson, ___ (Col.) 3010
Stevenson, Jane 5727
Stevenson, Margaret Jane 8537
Stevenson, Rita 7308
Stevenson, Sarah W. 9466
Steward, John 6914
Steward, Sophia 9833
Stewart, Alexander 7132
Stewart, Alexander L. 9321
Stewart, Alvin 5793
Stewart, Cassandanah 9384
Stewart, Clarissa 5903
Stewart, Daniel 8410
Stewart, E. M. (Miss) 7525
Stewart, Elizabeth G. 8410
Stewart, Frank Horatio 8399
Stewart, Horation 8399
Stewart, Jane E. 5793
Stewart, Lucretia 8399
Stewart, Maria (Mrs.) 6599
* Start, Julia M. 5391

Stewart, Nancy 5189, 7132
Stiles, ___ (Mr.) 345
Stiles, Beula Ann 7055
Stiles, Elizabeth 8008
Stiles, Margaret M. 3066
Stillma, Phebe J. 4394
Stillwell, Mary 8223
Stillwell, S. (Mr.) 8223
Stillwell, Sarah Jane 10004
Stilson, Sarah Ann 78
Stilwell, John G. 8414
Stimpson, Cynthia Ann 8583
Stimpson, Mary Ann 9548
Stirling, Ansel 892
Stirling, Avis Canfield 892
Stivers, Edward 8416, 8418
Stivers, George 8418
Stoakes, Mary 6379
Stockey, Laura E. 1449
STocking, Frances A. 6240
Stocking, Mary 5803
Stocking, Mary Maria 9677
Stocking, Samuel 5803
Stockton, Emma 6083
Stockton, William T. 6083
Stockwell, ___ (Miss) 8727
Stockwell, Mary (Mrs.) 8279
Stodard, Josiah 8425
Stoddard, Esther 7292
Stoddard, William 7292
Stoddard, William H. 8426
Stokes, Sarah 9676
Stolp, Hannah L. 3011
Stone, A. (Mr.) 8431
Stone, Almira 693
Stone, Eliza 6595
Stone, Henry W. 6360
Stone, Huldah Jane 3703
Stone, James 702
Stone, Mary Ann 3619
Stone, Sally 4856
Storey, ___ (Miss) 9104
Storey, Harriet 4905
Storey, Melinda 1927
Storm, Henry S. 3407
Storms, Ann 748
Storms, Caroline 2338
Storms, Mary Ann 771
Storrs, H. (Dr.) 9401
Storrs, Harriet 546
Storrs, Peyton R. 8453
Storrs, S. (Mr.) 546
Storrs, Shubael 8452
Story, Hannah 1140
Story, Jane 3246
Story, Lucinda 9448
Stotenburgh, Hannah 5173
Stout, Frances Minerva 8964
Stout, Lucinda 879
Stow, Ann 1520
Stow, Elizabeth 4226
Stow, Ida P. 7596
Stow, Joseph 7242
Stow, Sarah Adams 7242
Stowal, Meranda J. 10013
Stowell, Eliza 5571
Stowell, Lucy 5969
Stratton, Jane 8433
Stratton, L. (Miss) 9990
Stratton, William H. 8433
Straw, Eliza 1231
Streeter, Mary (Mrs.) 2721
Streeter, Phebe Ann 3261
Striker, Hannah 7209
Striker, Jemima 8571
Strong, Benjamin 3805
Strong, Caroline 1685
Strong, Charlotte 1034
Strong, E. B. (Hon.) 6212

Tibbits, Eliza 1393
Tibbitts, C. M. (Miss) 4974
Tice, Rhoda 1779
Tickner, Lydia A. 6003
Tiffany, Eunice 1120
Tiffany, Isaiah 8777
Tiffany, Mary 8777
Tifft, Elizabeth 9915
Tilden, Maria M. 5897
Tillman, James W. 8784
Tillotson, Louisa 7226
Tingsbury, ___ (Capt.) 5451
Tippetts, Caroline 9738
Tippetts, Frances Ann 8290
Tippets, Mary 5924
Tippetts, William 5924, 8290, 9698
Tisdale, Mary E. 9763
Tisdall, Eliza 4900
Titus, Betsey 3192
Tobin, Isabell Maria 6070
Tobin, James 6070
Toby, Harriet E. 1091
Toby, Lucinda M. 4349
Todd, Mary Ann 1237
Todd, S. (Dr.) 8794
Tomlinson, Aliza Ann 8806
Tomlinson, Amelia 4607
Tomlinson, H. (Mr.) 4607
Tomlinson, Harriet (Mrs.) 8805
Tomlinson, Harvey 8806
Tompkins, Ira G. 8808
Tompkins, Isaac 6132
Tompkins, john 8809
Tompkins, Louise 8809
Tompkins, Sarah 6132
Tompson, James 8812
Tompson, Sarah 8812
Tooker, ___ (Miss) 10021
Tooker, Maria D. 792
Torrance, Lawrena 454
Torrey, Amanda 7545
Torrey, Mary Ann 4120
Torry, Roxy 5464
Tottingham, Caroline 6892
Towar, Henry 8827, 8828
Towell, Thomas 8829
Tower, Cornelia S. 8834
Tower, Harriet E. 7197
Tower, Henry 8292
Tower, Horace W. 8834
Tower, Laura H. 8292
Towers, Mary Ann 7569
Towers, William 7570
Town, Hannah 6634
Towner, Nancy 9522
Townley, Margaret 2135
Towns, Ssuan (Mrs.) 2615
Townsend, ___ (Mr.) 2452
Townsend, Ann 4834
Townsend, Avis 8844
Townsend, Dolly Ann 3062
Townsend, Elizabeth 7434
Townsend, Elizabeth Ann 5011
Townsend, Emily 3635
Townsend, Isaiah 9173
Townsend, Jane 2486
Townsend, John 7434, 8841
Townsend, Mary 9173
Townsend, Mary E. 5178
Townsend, Nathaniel 8846
Townsend, Sarah A. 5160
Townsend, Stephen 8844
Townsend, W. A. (Dr.) 8852
Townsend, William 5160
Townsend, William A. 8840
Towsley, Susan 2133
Toy, Ann B. 9608

Tozer, Jemima 1764
Tozier, Cynthia 2
Trace, Dolly (Wid.) 3495
Tracey, Catherine 6631
Tracy, Clarissa 2093
Tracy, D. 5726
Tracy, Gardiner 480, 8633, 8859
Tracy, Gardner 8864
Tracy, H. N. (Capt.) 5451
Tracy, Helen A. 8633
Tracy, Lucy 5726
Tracy, Otis J. 8863
Tracy, Samuel D. 8869
Tracy, Sarah Ann 5451
Tracy, Susan 291, 480
Tracy, William 6788
Tracy, William G. 291, 6619, 6631
Trall, Mary Ellen 6554
Trask, Harriet 6897
Trask, Sarah E. 474
Treadwell, Mary J. 4134
Trigg, Eliza 4851
Trinder, Eleanor H. K. 5965
Tripp, Sarah 7697
Trippe, Jefferson 8885
Trippe, Mary E. 8885
Troop, Eliza S. 1437
Troop, George B. 1437
Troup, Robert 8890
Trowbridge, Adeline E. 4837
Trowbridge, Amasa 8891
Trowbridge, Artemas 7164
Trowbridge, C. (Mr.) 4837
Trowbridge, Glorianna H. 8891
Trowbridge, Lucretia 7076
Trowbridge, Susan Alida 7164
Truax, Ann 2268
Truax, Maria 7214
True, D. E. 8893
Truesdell, sarah 680
Truman, Cybele 8443
Trumbull, Benjamin 1728
Trumbull, Maria 1728
Trumbull, Thomas 8899
Tryon, Eliza 4345
Tubbs, Lucinda 6509
Tubbs, Marietta 1350
Tubles, Lebbeus 8902
Tucker, Harriet E. 3227
Tucker, Luther 8907, 8912
Tucker, Prudence 1754
Tull-Chief, Sally 4769
Tully, Ann W. 8460
Turbush, Mary 6495
Turnbull, A. N. (Mr.) 6774
Turnbull, Mary Ann 6774
Turner, Almira 4919
Turner, Anne 8927
Turner, Caroline 8928
Turner, Charles 8927
Turner, Enoch 8923
Turner, Galetsky 4376
Turner, Henry J. 8928
Turner, Henry W. 551
Turner, Josephine J. 551
Turner, Mariette 5335
Turner, Mary Weld 1270
Turner, Simon 5327
Turner, Thomas 1270
Turnock, Sarah 9619
Tuthill, rosette E. 1321
Tuttle, Benjamin 8940
Tuttle, E. Jeanette 4742
Tuttle, Elizabeth 8933
Tuttle, Joseph W. 8936
Tuttle, Mary Jane 21

Tuyl, Mary Ann 1396
Twenty Canoes, Nancy 9734
Twichel, George 6292
Twichel, Mary E. 6292
Twitchell, Clarissa 7763
Tyler, A. (Dr.) 5219
Tyler, Asa 677
Tyler, Charlotte 4641
Tyler, Harriet S. 5490
Tyler, Joseph 6050
Tyler, Martha D. 677
Tyler, Phebe 9270
Tyrrel, Elizabeth 9867
Tyrrell, Mary W. 9864
Tyrrell, Roanna 5641
Underhill, Charles 8963
Underhill, P. B. (Mr.) 2367, 6307
Underwood, S. A. (Mrs.) 6501
Upcraft, Henry 8968
Updike, Daniel E. 8969
Updike, Harriet 3323
Updike, William 3323
Upham, ___ (Dr.) 2146
Upson, Dana J. 8231
Upson, Daniel 8972
Upson, Elizabeth Clark 8231
Usher, Bloomfield 8974
Usher, Jane 4290
Utley, Louise 8107
Utley, Margaret 6178
Vail, George 7874
Vail, Martha M. 7874
Valejio, ___ (Mr.) 4037
Valejio, Malinqui (Signora) 4037
Valentine, Fanny 8735
Valentine, Mary 5187
Valentine, Sarah E. 416
Vallen, Phebe 4941
Vance, Mary Ann 2959
Van Alkenburgh, ___ (Mr.) 873
Van Allen, D. I. (Mr.) 8983, 8984
Van Allen, Daniel J. 8983
Van Alstyne, Elizabeth Ann 5958
Van Alstyne, Margaret Eliza 5665
Van Alstyne, Martin M. 5665
Vanauken, Mabel 8401
Van Buren, E. (Mr.) 8994
Van Buren, Eliza H. 9202
Van Buren, Henry S. 8997
Van Buren, John 8995
Van Campen, Samuel 8999
Vancise, Betsy 3289
Vancise, Cornelius 3289
Van Cleve, Aaron 8144
Van Cleve, Mary 8144
Van Clief, Jane 1530
Van Cott, Esther J. 976
Vandemark, Elizabeth 7592
Vandemark, Frederick 404
Vandemark, Mary 404
Vanderburgh, Mary Heen 4716
Vanderheyden, Elizabeth 2575
Vanderheyden, J. (Mr.) 1655
Vanderheyden, Jacob 2576
Vanderheyden, Susan F. 1655
Vanderhoff, Philander 9011
Vanderhoof, Lucretia <)°<
Vanderhoof, Polly 6156
Vanderhule, Adelia 6768
Vanderin, Lucinda 10009
Vanderlip, Philip 9016
Vanderlip, Samuel L. 9017
Vanderpool, James 8995
Vandewater, Catharine H. 9022
Van Duser, Susan 9885

334

Van Duzen, Catherine 5251
Van Duzen, Hannah 8247
Van Duzen, Jane 3946
Van Dyck, Maria 4649
Van Dyke, Deborah 5946
Van Epps, Alida 2844
Van Eps, Anna M. 4964
Van Etten, Anna 2837
Van Gaasbeek, Jane (Mrs.) 9018
Van Gelder, Joseph 9027
Van Horn, Jane 9395
Van Horne, ___ (Mr.) 7969
Van Horne, Abraham 7969
Van Horne, Eliza 7969
Van Keuren, B. (Rev.) 9034
Van Kleef, Phebe 5384
Vanlew, Ellen 6822
Van Lew, Harriet N. 4102
Van Nahuis, Myrrou Gertruda
   Cornelia Helena 6058
Van Ness, Catharine 4663
Van Ness, Catherine E. 9039
Van Ness, Gertrude 1774
Van Ness, Henry 9037
Van Ness, J. H. (Mr.) 9039
Van Ness, John, Jr. 2455
Van Ness, Mary A. 2455
Van Ness, Susan 5545
Van Nordstrand, Sophia Ann
   7600
Van Norstand, Hannah 1309
Vannorthwick, Abigail (Mrs.)
   9387
Van Ostrander, Wandal 9045
Van Patten, Adam 8589
Van Patten, Mary E. 8589
Van Rensselaer, Jeremiah
   1527, 3595, 9047
Van Rensselaer, Stephen 9046
Van Riper, Elizabeth 9126
Van Riper, Margaret 9125
Van Scoter, Mary 7413
Van Scoy, Rebecca Ann 957
Vanscoy, Sally 8166
Van Valen, Maria 6436
Van Valkenburgh, Catharine
   5936
Van Valkenburgh, Charlotte M.
   8405
Van Valkenburgh, Daniel 9062
Van Valkenburgh, Hannah 3740
Van Valkenburgh, Harriet 8635
Van Valkenburgh, P. (Mr.)
   9061, 9064, 9065
Van Valkenburgh, Richard 3740,
   8621
Van Valkenburgh, Sarah 6950
Van Vechten, ___ (Rev. Dr.)
   4608, 7644
Van Vechten, Anna 4608
Van Vechten, Sarah 7644
Van Vleck, Elizabeth 8733
Van Vleck, Harmanus 9070
Van Vleet, Electa 3524
Van Voast, James 9071
Van Voast, Sarah 6256
Vanvoorhous, Sally 1319
Van Vorhies, Gitty Ann 2783
Van Vorst, Peter 9077
Van Vrank, Philip 9079
Van Wagenen, Agnes 6780
Van Wagenen, Gerrit H. 6780
Van Wert, ___ (Mr.) 5365
Van Wie, Charlotte 6645
Van Wie, Diana 7279
Van Wie, Henry 9083
Van Winkle, Hannah 8755
Van Winkle, Sarah 1125

Van Wormer, Catharine 7411
Veazeanna, ___ (Mr.) 9091
Vedder, ___ (Mr.) 3057
Vedder, Albert A. 9094
Vedder, F. (Mr.) 9093
Vermilye, ___ (Dr.) 8054
Vermilye, Elizabeth Brieze
   8054
Vermilye, R. G. (Rev.) 9096
Vernor, John 2452
Vernor, Mary 2452
Verplanck, J. C. (Mr.) 9099
Verson, Jane Ann 6528
Vervalin, Elizabeth 8901
Vezie, Sarah A. 1998
Vicker, Archibald 2524
Vicker, Susan M. 2524
Vince, Nancy 7382
Vincent, Adeline 6693
Vincent, Lana Maria 523
Vinton, D. H. (Capt.) 9109
Voganser, Martha 6999
Voorhees, ___ (Col.) 4735,
   8805
Voorhees, Cornelia 6940
Voorhees, J. L. (Col.) 1222
Voorhees, Jane L. 1222
Voorhees, Urania Ann 4735
Voorhies, Rosetta 9116
Voorhies, William 9111
Vorce, Allen 9115
Vosburgh, John 9117
Vosburgh, Nathaniel 9123
Vroman, Nancy Maria 7343
Wade, Elizabeth C. 967
Wade, James 967
Wadsworth, Hester Ann 3528
Wadsworth, James 1049, 9129,
   9133, 9134
Wadsworth, John W. 1303
Wadsworth, Mary 1839   ✓
Wadsworth, Mary C. 1303
Wadsworth, Thomas, Sr. 9132
Wager, David 9137
Wager, Mary A. 9137
Wager, Sally S. 9932
Wainright, Barsey 9717
Wait, Mary 8152
Wait, Philena 8556
Waite, Harriet 6680
Waite, Saphronia 413
Wake, Mary Ann 5314
Wakeman, Elisha 9148
Wakeman, Maria 9148
Walbridge, Hiram 9150, 9152
Walbridge, Lucy Ann (Mrs.)
   5502
Walbridge, Sophia 9807
Walbridge, Stebbins 9807
Walcott, Benjamin S. 4015
Walcott, Hannah C. 9155
Walcott, Irene R. 4015
Walcott, W. D. (Mr.) 9155
Walden, Abby E. 8807
Walden, Thomas 8807
Waldo, Harriet 5221
Waldron, Polly 7290
Wales, Hannah (Mrs.) 1127
Walker, Emily 3427
Walker, Jane 2531
Walker, Malina A. 5471
Walker, Mary A. 6498
Walker, Susan 5756
Walker, Thomas 5760, 6498,
   9165, 9169
Walker, Tryphena L. 7193
Walker, William F. 9166
Wallace, Helen M. 3657

Wallace, Mary 1775
Wallace, Robert 3657
Wallcott, William 9182
Walling, Ebenezer 9183
Walrath, ___ (Mr.) 7557
Walrath, Catharine (Mrs.) 807
Walrath, Catherine 4128
Walrath, John I. 9186
Walrath, Mary Ann 1951
Walrath, Sarah 673
Walsh, Catharine 452, 6979
Walt ?, Lovina 5698
Walters, Catharine 575, 3584
Walthall, Archibald 9195
Walts, Polly 9192
Walworth, ___ (Chancellor) 258
Walworth, Eliza 258
Walworth, John 9747
Walworth, R. H. (Chancellor)
   9198, 9199
Walworth, Sarah S. 9747
Wamp, Nancy 7180
Waples, Sarah 5030
Ward, ___ 261
Ward, Caroline 6959
Ward, Caroline M. 2040
Ward, Eliza G. 3151
Ward, Elizabeth 7087
Ward, Frances A. 1096
Ward, Joseph 9204
Wrd, Lorinda G. 7550
Ward, Lydia 4850
Ward, Lysander M. 9211
Ward, Margaret 977
Ward, Merrella (Mr.) 1096
Ward, Nathaniel 4850
Ward, Olive 2174
Ward, Penelope 7096
Ward, Sarah H. 8366
Ward, Stephen 9207
Ward, William H. 9200
Warden, Charlotte 6086
Warden, Lucy Ann 4380
Ware, Newman 9216
Warford, ___ (Col.) 2265
Warn, Susan 1569
Warner, ___ (Judge) 9232
Warner, ___ (Mr.) 9236
Warner, Aaron 9237
Warner, Asahel 9229
Warner, Emeline 2986
Warner, Henry 9227
Warner, Isaac 7806
Warner, J. R. (Mr.) 9240
Warner, J. R., Jr. 9224
Warner, James 9226
Warner, Jared E. 9223, 9236
Warner, Jesse 9243
Warner, John 7612
Warner, Lucina 1299
Warner, Maranda 3320
Warner, Margaret M. 6051
Warner, Maria Louisa 2048
Warner, Maria R. 7806
Warner, Rosanna S. 7612
Warner, Sally Ann 6352
Warner, Sarah 9229
Warner, Sarah S. 6597
Warner, Solomon 9225
Warnick, Ellen 9246
Warnick, Leslie A. 9246
Warnick, Mary 9458
Warren, A. (Mr.) 1001
Warren, Anna C. 4665
Warren, Celestia 3000
Warren, David A. 9251, 9258
Warren, Elijah 9247
Warren, Eliza E. 1001

335

Warren, Elizabeth P. 7507
Warren, Fanny Jane 5861
Warren, Harriet 2544
Warren, James 9254
Warren, John 9259
Warren, Lucy A. 1430
Warren, Mary (Mrs.) 333
Warren, Stephen 4665
Warren, Sylvia (Wid.) 8050
Warring, Elizabeth 9171
Warring, Rebecca P. 4323
Washburn, Amanda 6993
Washburn, Claramond 8542
Washburn, E. (Hon.) 9419
Washburn, Martha L. 384
Washburn, Martin 9263
Washburn, Mary 5305
Washington, ___ (Gen) 5365, 6955
Washington, ___ (Mr.) 2292
Washington, Ann Eliza 4819
Washington, Bushrod 4819, 9264
Washington, Julia 4702
Wasson, ___ (Mr.) 6329
Waterman, Charlotte 8565
Waterman, Eliza Ann 2549
Waterman, Frances E. 1042
Waterman, P. Jane 3075
Waters, Harriet 459
Waters, Nancy Ann 5996
Watkins, B. I. 9277
Watkins, Gertrude M. 9859
Watkins, Irene 4824
Watkins, John D. 9274
Watkins, Lucy Ann 3381
Watkins, Mary Ann 6891
Watkins, Sarah 4072
Watrous, Amanda 3167
Watrous, Amanda W. 2642
Watrow, Susan H. 6279
Watrus, Hepsta Ann C. 6161
Watson, Ansluida 3489
Watson, Bildad 9288
Watson, Charles W. 9291
Watson, Cynthia 1528
Watson, Elisha 5126
Watson, Eliza 6320, 7619
Watson, Julia 9288
Watson, Margaret 1225
Watson, Mary L. 9201
Watson, Polly 1061
Watson, Susan Elizabeth 9291
Watson, Wheeler 7619
Watson, William 9282
Wattles, Charles 1477, 9776
Wattles, Phebe Philena 9928
Wattles, Sally (Mrs.) 2893
Watts, John 9298
Watts, Nancy 9298
Way, Louisa 3172
Wayland, Susan P. S. 1928
Weatherly, J. L. (Mr.) 9306
Weaver, ___ (Maj. Gen.) 9312
Weaver, Catherine S. 3633
Weaver, Eunice B. 7130
Weaver, Eve 943
Weaver, George M. 9307
Weaver, Lodowick, Jr. 7130
Weaver, Sarah B. 8736
Webb, Amelia 4612
Webb, AnnS. 3791
Webb, Caroline Elizabeth 8690
Webb, James 8596
Webb, James Watson 9321
Webb, John G. 982
Webb, Rosetta 8596
Webb, Samuel 8690
Webber, Edward 9330, 9746
Webber, Nancy B. 2728

Weber, Catharine 2716
Webster, ___ (Mr.) 7995
Webster, ___ (Prof.) 3161, 9342, 9347
Webster, Clarinda 6334
Webster, Daniel 170, 9337
Webster, Eunice 379
Webster, Helen 3583
Webster, Henrietta B. 4514
Webster, Joshua 4514
Webster, Sabra S. 6967
Wedge, Emily 1441
Wedge, Ruby 5547
Weed, Ellen J. 5822
Weed, Emily P. 477
Weed, Harriet 9425
Weed, Henry 9353
Weed, Maria 71
Weed, Thurlow 71, 477
Weeks, Levi 8034
Weeks, Louisa 8034
Weeks, Harriet 2299
Weghorn, Ann 3042
Weiser, Susan 9422
Welch, Betty (Mrs.) 1388
Welch, Lydia W, 4410
Weller, Chester
Welles, Helen 2677
Welles, Jane 828
Welles, John 2677, 9369
Welles, Laura Derby 9815
Welles, Sila 5719
Welles, Silas 5719
Wellington, R. G. (Mrs.) 5868
Wells, ___ (Mr.) 9810
Wells, A. L. (Mr.) 9400
Wells, Alethia 6300
Wells, Alfred 5277, 8535, 9400
Wells, Christina 9374
Wells, D. D. (Mr.) 1211
Wells, E. T. (Miss) 5106
Wells, Elisha 7328
Wells, Fineus 9373
Wells, Harriet C. 7965
Wells, Harriett A. 4418
Wells, Henry C. 9381
Wells, James 4418, 8258, 9403
Wells, Jane E. 6667
Wells, Job 7965, 9375, 9378, 9405
Wells, Martha H. 1224
Wells, Martin 9374
Wells, Noah 9389
Wells, Phineas 9373 (See Wells, Fineus)
Wells, Polly 9375
Wells, Richard 1224, 4103, 9396
Wells, Sarah R. 1211
Wells, Susan 8961
Welsh, Henry 9406
Welton, Cornelia M. 8415
Welton, Isaac 8415
Welton, Martha 8124
Wemple, Helen A. 8322
Wendell, Cornelia R. 9234
Wendell, Gertrude Lansing 9020
Wendell, Peter 9020, 9224, 9234
Wentworth, ___ (Mrs.) 9410
Wentworth, John 9411
Wentworth, Marien 2542
Wentworth, Mary 8600
Wentworth, Paul 9411
Wescott, Polly 3674
Wesley, Mary Jane 4137
West, Bicknell 9418
West, Cornelia A. 5034
West, Gertrude Helmer 6183

West, Henrietta 8917
West, John 9420
West, Mary E. 6355, 9118
West, Mathew 9421
West, Paulina 7823
West, Silas 6355
West, Sophia B. 8639
Westbrook, Caroline 2466, 6104
Westcott, A. (Dr.) 9434
Westcott, Susan 8692
Western, Henry M. 686
Western, Mary Brower 686
Westfall, Almira 6397
Westfall, Elizabeth 6725
Westfall, Jacob D. 5552, 9002
Westfall, Jane 6231, 9002
Westfall, Lydia 5552
Westfall, Samuel D. 6231
Westlake, Jacob 9443
Westlake, John 9444
Weston, Harriet M. 5994
Wetmore, ___ (Mr.) 4721
Wetmore, Amos 9446
Wetmore, Eliza 2350
Wetmore, Eliza Frances 9450
Wetmore, Euphrasia H. 5828
Wetmore, Ezra 2350
Wetmore, Frederick 9445
Wetmore, J. C. (Col.) 4038
Wetmore, M. (Mrs.) 4038
Wetmore, Thomas M. 9450
Wever, Maria 8953
Whaley, Lavina 4828
Whaston, ___ (Dr.) 3160
Wheadon, Emiline 8313
Wheat, David 9456
Wheat, Electa 9456
Wheat, Frances H. 678
Wheaton, Augustus 9459
Wheaton, Sally 19
Wheeler, A. (Mr.) 9468
Wheeler, Eleanor 9490
Wheeler, Gennet 759
Wheeler, George A. 9479
Wheeler, George D. 9464
Wheeler, Hannah 7948
Wheeler, Harriet 9244
Wheeler, Harriet T. 6204
Wheeler, J. L. 9490
Wheeler, James 9474
Wheeler, James M. 9481
Wheeler, Martha 8246
Wheeler, Mary 6705, 9472
Wheeler, Mary G. 685
Wheeler, Mary Maria 5258
Wheeler, Nathan 9478
Wheeler, Sally 2059
Wheeler, Samuel 9475
Wheelock, Ebenezer 6677
Wheelock, Mary C. 6565
Wheelock, Sarah 6591
Wheelwright, ___ (Mr.) 8324
Whelan, Margaret 2068
Whiffen, Elizabeth 9497
Whiffen, Isaac 6429, 7733, 9497
Whiffen, Jane 9498
Whiffen, Mary B. 7732
Whiffin, David 9498
Whipple, Adaline 1163
Whipple, Harriet E. 9508
Whipple, J. H. (Mr.) 9502
Whipple, John H. 4251
Whipple, John S. 9504
Whipple, Sarah 5308
Whipple, Susan L. 4251
Whitaker, Phebe 3843
Whitaker, Prudence R. 4841
Whitall, Anna E. 1524

336

Whitall, Banjamin G. 1524
Whitall, Matilda 7273
Whitcom, Sarah 3290
Whitcomb, Lucia Caroline 4481
Whitcomb, T. J. (Mr.) 4481
White, ___ (Judge) 9546
White, ___ (Mr.) 3866
White, Alvin 9556
White, Anthony Walton 9541
White, Broughton 3893
White, Catharine 7384
White, Clarissa A. 6708
White, Delilah 979
Whote, Elizabeth 1614, 9555
White, Hannah 5752
White, Harriet E. 1979
White, Henry 5209, 5732
White, Henry S. 9537, 9550
White, Hiram 7384
White, Ira 9531
White, J. L. (Mr.) 9514
White, James 3632
White, Jane Amelia 5209
White, John 9539
White, Laura F. 9514
White, Levina 9550
White, Lois 8823
White, Lona 6561
White, Martha W. 1665
White, Mary 559, 2774, 3632
White, Mary Ann 3893
White, Mary J. 5340
White, Mary Louisa 4722
White, Oscar E. 9555
White, Philo, Jr. 2927
White, Polly 4975
White, S. M. (Mr.) 7527
White, Sarah Eliza 5732
White, Sarah N. 6561
White, Trifena 7269
Whited, Nancy 356
Whireford, Margaret 2097
Whiteford, Sarah 2594
Whitehead, Rosanna 6438
Whitely, Mary E. 5138
Whiteneck, Ann 5952
Whiting, Augustus 3237
Whiting, B. (Gen.) 8486
Whiting, Esther 1562
Whiting, Harriet R. 1325
Whiting, J. L. (Dr.) 9227
Whiting, Joel 9574
Whiting, John 9227, 9567
Whiting, Mary 2667
Whiting, Mary B. 3237
Whiting, Mary E. 7980
Whiting, Orrilla M. 9147
Whitlock, Rebecca 5351
Whitman, Augustus 2188
Whitman, Deborah 2188
Whitman, Harriet 5954
Whitman, Henry 7237
Whitmore, E. (Dr.) 2080
Whitmore, M. B. (Mr.) 9582
Whitney, Caroline 9726
Whitney, Charlotte 5399
Whitney, Charlotte E. 1747
Whitney, David 9590
Whitney, Fanny 8738
Whitney, Franklin 9847
Whitney, J. (Mr.) 9590
Whitney, Jonas 9589
Whitney, Julia E. 9847
Whitney, Julian 1094
Whitney, Louise A. 151
Whitney, Luke 1094
Whitney, Mary 7797
Whitney, Phebe 3889

Whitney, Wareham 151
Whiton, Frances Jennett 6912
Whiton, James 6912
Whittemore, Thomas 9592
Whittenhall, Elihu 9594
Whittenhall, Uriah 9593
Whittlesey,))) (Mr.) 8120
Whittlesey, A. (Mr.) 3770
Whittlesey, Emily Chauncey 2271
Whittlesey, Samuel 2271, 8784
Whittlesey, W. O. (Miss) 3770
Whitwell, Furman A. 6159
Whitwell, Gargia A. 6159
Whitwell, Mary 8788
Wicker, James C. 9598
Wicker, Joel H. 9600
Wickes, Silas 9602
Wickham, Philo 1547, 9606
Widger, Eliza Ann 4646
Wiggins, Cad. W. (Mr.) 9421
Wiggins, Hannah 6825
Wiggins, John 6825
Wight, George 9614, 9616, 9618
Wightman, Marva C. 9744
Wigram, John 9620
Wilber, Amelia >><£
Wilbor, Simeon G. 9622
Wilbur, J. (Mr.) 9624
Wilbur, Mary 3307
Wilbur, Polly 4664
Wilcox, ___ (Admiral) 9636
Wilcox, ___ (Dr.) 788, 3974
Wilcox, A. (Deacon) 1632
Wilcox, Charlotte E. 3032
Wilcox, Cornelia S. 3660
Wilcox, Eleanor 6858
Wilcox, Elizabeth 7894
Wilcox, Huldah 1632
Wilcox, Jane 3974
Wilcox, Joseph 7894
Wilcox, Lucy A. 5185
Wilcox, Martha 7974
Wilcox, Mary 788
Wilcox, Mary E. 6665
Wilcox, Morris 3032
Wilcox, Ozias 9635
Wilcox, Reuben 3660
Wilcox, Salmon 3251
Wild, Anah E. 1341
Wild, Levi 1341
Wilder, Elijah 9642
Wilder, Eliza 8842
Wilder, Luania 8536
Wilder, Lydia E. 9001
Wilder, Nancy F. 2095
Wiley, Charles 9646
Wiley, Jane 3787
Wiley, Mary 8627, 9597
Wilkes, Samuel 9652
Wilkeson, Samuel 9653
Wilkins, Mary M. 3028
Wilkins, Sarah A. 9379
Wilkins, Thomas D. 3028
Wilkinson, Charles T. 1576
Wilkinson, Elizabeth 7396
Wilkinson, Harriet 1576
Willard, A. (Mr.) 3035
Willard, D. (Mr.) 6906
Willard, Delia 2543
Willard, Eliza P. 3035, 3947
Willard, Rosah C. 9316
Willard, Rufus 3947, 9316
Willard, Sarah Dickman 6906
Wilcox, Amy 6851
Willcox, Gates 9678, 9683
Willcox, Ira 3615, 9682
Willcox, Louisa 8576
Willcox, Lucy 9680

Willcox, Lyman 9679
Willey, E. F. (Elder) 6490
Williams, ___ (Mr.) 5365, 7776
Williams, ___ (Mrs.) 255
Williams, A. B. 124
Williams, Abraham 9690
Williams, Almira 3405
Williams, Ann 3069
Williams, Aras G. 9697
Williams, Benjamin S. 9746
Williams, Brown H. 9739
Williams, Catharine 8896
Williams, Catherine E. 3088
Williams, Delia M. 3563
Williams, Eleanor 9278
Williams, Elisha 8651, 8652
Williams, Elizabeth 7415, 8608
Williams, Elizabeth E. 6316
Williams, Ellen 3718
Williams, Ellen R. 1470
Williams, Emily 7959
Williams, Fanny 8586
Williams, Frederica C. 512
Williams, Gurdon 9686
Williams, Harriet Elmira 5967
Williams, Helen Maria 949
Williams, Isaac 2664
Williams, Jane M. 9697
Williams, John 272, 287, 949,
    5423, 6853, 9687, 9711, 9741
Williams, Laura 6853
Williams, Lucinda B. 9586
Williams, Lucy (Mrs.) 9106
Williams, Margaret 3367
Williams, Margaret L. 9741
Williams, Maria 9135
Williams, Mary 1002
Williams, Mary C. 9489
Williams, Mary Jane 5367
Williams, Morris M. 9698, 9699
Williams, Nathan 9720
Williams, Olivia 124
Williams, Rebecca 3363
Williams, Sally 9940
Williams, Sarah 9714
Williams, Sarah E. 8689
Williams, Sarah M. 597
Williams, Sarah T. N. 7715
Williams, Silas 9735
Williams, Sophia 1494
Williams, Sophia W. 3364
Williams, Stalham 7715, 8138
Williams, Susan 4635
Williams, Thomas 3363, 3368
Williams, Thomas, Jr. 9702
Williams, Velona 6328
Williams, W. Barron 7889, 9736
Williams, William 3088, 3364,
    9718
Williams, William Barron 9701
Williamson, Hugh 9759
Williamson, J. D. (Capt.) 213
Williamson, Mary L. 213
Willis, ___ (Miss) 7035
Willis, ___ (Mrs.) 7659
Willis, A. (Dr.) 7659
Willison, Cinthia (Mrs.) 178
Williston, ___ (Judge) 4552
Williston, Clara 4552
Willoughby, B. (Mr.) 2865
Willoughby, Eliza P. 2865
Willoughby, Joseph 9788
Willoughby, Sarah F. 6078
Wills, John W. 6021
Willsey, Jacob 8703
Willsey, Sarah Maria 8703
Willson, David 9773
Willson, Mary 1815, 3104

337

Wilmarth, Maria T. 3828
Wilmot, Lydia M. 4478
Wilmot, William 9776
Wilson, Adah Maria 3188
Wilson, Adeline Lucy 3988
Wilson, Archibald 9785
Wilson, Benjamin 1517
Wilson, C. S. (Mrs.) 5728
Wilson, Caroline 6877
Wilson, E. (Mr.) 1554
Wilson, Ellen Eliza 1517
Wilson, Eva 1554
Wilson, John 9789
Wilson, Martha J. 9580
Wilson, William 3988
Winans, Ann Eliza 3643
Winans, Catharine M. (Mrs.) 6744
Winans, Mary 2773
Windsor, D. (Mr.) 9805
Winfield, Lida 6596
Wing, Caroline 9568
Wing, Cornelia 5553
Wing, Sylvia Ann 212
Wingate, Maria J. 6863
Winn, Elizabeth 6606
Winne, ___ (Miss) 5363
Winne, Giles K. 5638
Winne, Maria A. 8280
Winne, Sarah Matilda 5638
Winneur, Elizabeth 3634
Winslow, Martha 9346
Winsor, Antoinette O. 2169
Winsor, Nicholas S. 9812
Winsor, Selanah 6065
Winston, David 8208
Winston, Marcy 8204
Winston, Margaret 8208
Winter, Mary 3293
Winton, Lois 6636
Wirt, ___ (Mr.) 9817
Wise, Charlotte 7711
Wise, Harriet S. 2780
Wise, Samuel 7711
Wiser, Cornelia 1616
Wiser, Jeremiah 4771
Wiser, Sarah M. 4771
Wisner, B. N. (Mr.) 9823
Wisner, Henry A. 9823
Wisner, William 5556
Wisner, William Henry 9824
Witherell, Mary Jane 6087
Wofful, Mara Ann 8575
Wolcott, ___ (Mr.) 4501
Wolcott, Edify 3834
Wolcott, Ellen Marion (Mrs.) 540
Wolcott, Laura A. 6278
Wolcott, Mary 8214
Wolcott, Mary S. 8500
Wolf, ___ (Gov.) 9835
Wollage, Sophia 3174
Wood, ___ (Deacon) 2161
Wood, ___ (Mr.) 7855
Wood, Addeliza 5437
Wood, Betsey 8091
Wood, Calvin 5536
Wood, D. I. (Mr.) 9289
Wood, Daniel 9856
Wood, David 2204
Wood, Dorlesca A. 5428
Wood, Eliza G. 1369
Wood, Elmira 1057
Wood, Emily 1193
Wood, Esther (Mrs.) 9858
Wood, George W. 9842
Wood, Gerald C. 9843
Wood, Gershome 5428

Wood, Girard C. 9848
Wood, Hannah 6409
Wood, Jane G. 8614
Wood, Julia 9442
Wood, Laura Ann 7737
Wood, Leddra 8614
Wood, Lucinda 7826
Wood, Lydia 9818
Wood, Phebe 1615
Wood, Rebecca 1185
Wood, Rosannah 8185
Wood, Sarah 5357
Wood, Sophronia 193
Wood, Thomas H. 9855
Woodcock, Cornelia 3061
Wooden, James 9862
Woodford, Sarah 7553
Woodhouse, Martha 7095
Woodin, Eliza 1692
Woodruff, A. (Mr.) 9880
Woodruff, Caroline 4559
Woodruff, Caroline V. 4121
Woodruff, Polly 1136, 1478
Woods, Mary 8599
Woods, Merrilla 5129
Woods, P. (Dr.) 9886
Woodworth, Caleb 9895
Woodworth, F. B. 9897
Woodworth, Isaac 9898
Woodworth, J. L. (Dr.) 9897
Woodworth, Joseph 9894
Woodworth, Louisa M. 1915
Woodworth, Maria 7174
Woodworth, Samuel 9896
Wooley, Mary E. 8756
Woolsey, ___ (Commodore) 9913
Woolsey, Alida Livingston 8491
Woolsey, H. L. (Mr.) 9912
Woolsey, Henry L. 9906
Woolsey, M. T. (Commodore) 9905
Woolsey, Mary E. 4386
Woolsey, Melancthon Lloyd 9905
Woolsey, Melancthon T. 8491
Wooster, ___ (Mr.) 2292
Wooster, Laura M. 8202
Worden, Allen 7634
Worden, Betsey 2477
Worden, Eliza 2882
Worden, Ichabod 9919
Worden, Ira 9916
Wormer, Susan 3348
Worth, Julia Ann 7820
Wride, ___ (Mr.) 9923
Wright, ___ (Judge) 9939
Wright, Adelia E. 8349
Wright, Ann Eliza 8813
Wright, Calista 8960
Wright, Caroline Elizabeth 1857
Wright, Chauncey 9937
Wright, D. (Dr.) 3558
Wright, Eliza 8159
Wright, Eliza Kirke 7495
Wright, Elizabeth A. 9927
Wright, Ezra 5003
Wright, George W. 9934
Wright, Hannah P. 9946
Wright, J. W. (Mr.) 7605
Wright, Jane A. 1767
Wright, Jane M. 6842
Wright, Jay W. 9938, 9946
Eright, John W. 8159
Wright, Lewis 9959
Wright, Lydia 2242
Wright, Lydia A. 7436
Wright, Mary Hudson 3558
Wright, Oliver K. 9927
Wright, Pauline 2375

Wright, Rhoda 8021
Wright, Rosanna 6546
Wright, Sarah 3176
Wright, Silas, Jr. 9953
Wright, Susannnah 9924
Wright, Z. (Mr.) 7495
Wriley, Sarah H. 3566
Wurks, Mary 1114
Wyant, Leah 7417
Wyckoff, Marian 5526
Wylie, Sarah 7770
Wyman, Levi 9961
Wyman, Maria 9961
Wynkoop, A. I. (Mr.) 9968
Wynkoop, Cornelia A. 9276
Wynkoop, Tobias 9966
Yale, Laura 2066
Yale, Melina 8423
Yale, Zebedee 2066
Yates, A. J. (Mr.) 9983
Yates, Alexander 6943
Yates, Andrew 9983
Yates, Ann 5690
Yates, Berthana 4785
Yates, Charles 9975
Yates, Caroline 6943
Yates, Giles 9979
Yates, Henry 9975
Yates, J. B. (Mr.) 5690
Yates, John 9979
Yates, John Austin 9978
Yates, John I. 9981
Yates, John V. N. 9982
Yates, Joseph C. 9274
Yates, Josepha 6280
Yates, Mary 9977
Yates, Mary A. 8504
Yates, Mary Elizabeth 4428
Yates, Peter 9977
Ybaire, Maria D. (Miss) 1483
Yberra, Juan A. (Don) 932
Yberra, Carmen (Dona) 932
Yeoman, C. (Mr.) 9988
York, Jerry 9989
Yorke, Eliza U. 1328
Yorke, John 9992
Yost, Catharine 4351
Yost, Mahala 1602
Youmans, Eliza 3730
Young, Charlotte 3735
Young, Eliza 8876
Young, Elizabeth 431, 8850
Young, Maria 8237
Yuong, Sarah 5666
Young, Sally 5227
Young, Samuel 3735
Young, William 9998
Yuong, William, Jr. 10000
Yuonglove, Aaron 10010
Younglove, John 10014, 10016
Younglove, Lucas 10014
Yuongs, Eliza Ann 8665
Youngs, John 10018
Yourt, Alice 8215

338